Fifth Edition

The ELUSIVE EDEN
A New History of California

Richard B. Rice
Professor Emeritus, California State University, East Bay

William A. Bullough
Professor Emeritus, California State University, East Bay

Richard J. Orsi
Professor Emeritus, California State University, East Bay

Mary Ann Irwin
Independent Scholar/Adjunct Faculty,
California State University, East Bay, and
Diablo Valley Community College

Michael F. Magliari
Professor of History, California State University, Chico

Cecilia M. Tsu
Associate Professor of History, University of California, Davis

WAVELAND

PRESS, INC.

Long Grove, Illinois

D0222872

For information about this book, contact:
Waveland Press, Inc.
4180 IL Route 83, Suite 101
Long Grove, IL 60047-9580
(847) 634-0081
info@waveland.com
www.waveland.com

Cover art [*Redlands Foothill Groves* (2000)] courtesy of Joan Sullivan, Los Osos, California. Original watercolor inspired by an early twentieth-century orange crate label.

10-digit ISBN 1-4786-3754-4
13-digit ISBN 978-1-4786-3754-7

Printed in the United States of America

7   6   5   4   3

With deep affection and admiration, we dedicate this fifth edition of
The Elusive Eden: A New History of California to its three original authors:

Dick Rice, Bill Bullough, and Dick Orsi.

Mary Ann Irwin
Michael F. Magliari
Cecilia M. Tsu

Contents

PART THREE   83

The Pastoral Era

PART FOUR   125

Gold and the Americanization of California

PART FIVE   175

The Railroad Era

PART EIGHT   339

World War II and Postwar Expansion

Maps

Preface

Our changes to this edition of *The Elusive Eden* were guided by the same principles that shaped previous revisions. Our collective 150-plus years of teaching the state's history has convinced us of two verities: the first, that Californians—natives and newcomers alike—study their state's past out of a genuine, sometimes avid interest; and second, that Californians like a good story. Consequently, we have retained the book's original organization of ten parts, three chapters each, for a total of thirty chapters. Each chapter has been updated to reflect recent scholarship; the last chapter brings the California story into 2019.

After an introductory prologue of three chapters (Part One), the book is arranged in a series of generally chronological parts, each consisting of three chapters and dealing with a recognized era. Each Part begins with a Feature Chapter about a specific person or event that relates directly to the period under study. Feature Chapters are designed to give the reader a feel for the "texture" of California history, suggesting how groups and individuals grappled with and shaped historical change. Occasionally Feature Chapters include passages from primary sources and direct quotes from those who were there. Our goal in pursuing this design has always been to bring California's history to life, hopefully capturing the interest of readers and provoking thought and debate. The Feature Chapters focus on all sections of the state: north and south, central valleys and coast, urban and rural settings. Two treat individual women (Chapters 10 and 19); one considers early conflicts between Natives and newcomers (Chapter 4), a theme revisited as Mexicans and Natives adjusted to the arrival of Europeans and Anglo Americans (Chapter 7). One chapter examines Asian immigrants in rural California (Chapter 16), one reflects upon the tragedy of Japanese internment in the second World War (Chapter 22), another looks at the black experience (Chapters 25), and the last concentrates on the environment (Chapter 28). The remaining chapters follow a traditional, more or less chronological course through that period's history. Throughout these chronological chapters we have sprinkled Boxed Essays, brief vignettes about individuals, some famous, others not.

Given the book's structure, the Feature Chapters will not appear to follow strict chronological order. They may highlight events that occurred in the beginning, middle, or even at the end of the period under discussion. The authors believe, however, that these stories evoke the main themes of the chronological chapters that follow. We hope that any disadvantages that result from historical discontinuity are outweighed by gains in readability and in the opportunities for deeper thought and discussion.

As in earlier editions, we strive to deal sensitively with questions of race, ethnicity, and gender. We believe that respect for history mandates that we weave Californians of every stripe into the historical narrative, because each group is integral to our understanding of human affairs. Accordingly, we reflect on the status of women, locally and nationally, and on the efforts of groups and individuals of different racial, ethnic, economic, and sexual orientations to prosper and thrive, often against great odds. We endeavor to include the contributions of all sorts of people, rich or poor, famous or infamous, and to tell, for better or worse, the impact each has on our California story.

Dealing with the scope, diversity, and fascinating nuances of California history continues to confront us with painful decisions. In this edition, it was more difficult than ever to fold in new scholarship and to bring the story current without doubling the length—and the cost—of the book. We can only empathize with those who find their favorite episodes in California history neglected. Some of our own favorites fell to the editorial axe this time too. To compensate, we have expanded our lists of suggested readings at the end of the book. There interested readers will find the books, articles, newspapers, and archival materials that informed our efforts.

In this edition of the book, like the first four, each of us undertook responsibility for specific chapters. Professor Orsi is again primarily responsible for chapters 1–6, 13–15, and 28. Professor Magliari updated chapters 7–12 and 17–18. Professor Tsu added her insights to chapters 16, 19–24, and 26. Professor Irwin took charge of Chapters 25, 27, and 29–30. Initials of specific authors appear at the end of the 20 boxed essays. Although collaboration continues to inform our efforts, each of us assumes sole responsibility for the content of his or her chapters.

Acknowledgements

So many people helped us to complete this book that it is impossible to mention each by name. We extend our heartfelt gratitude to all, particularly colleagues in the Department of History, CSU East Bay; the staffs at the Huntington Library; Bancroft Library; Newberry Library; California State Library; Stanford University Library; California Historical Society; California State Railroad Museum; Tulare County Library; Kings County Library; Trinity County Historical Society; California Department of Water Resources; California Department of Transportation; California Air Pollution Control Board; United States Geological Survey; San Francisco Bay National Wildlife Refuge; Save San Francisco Bay Association; CSU Los Angeles Chicano Studies Research Center; California Public Policy Institute; and Women in California Politics 100 (http://www.wicp100.org/).

Several individuals deserve special acknowledgement, but none more than Richard B. Rice (1924–2012) and William A. Bullough (1933–2013) who, along with Richard J. Orsi, co-authored the first three editions of *The Elusive Eden*. Thank you. Our sincerest thanks go as well to Patricia Bullough for her contribution to the boxed essay on John Steinbeck, and to the late Eve Rice, who first suggested the book's title.

Richard J. Orsi
Mary Ann Irwin
Michael F. Magliari
Cecilia M. Tsu

Teaching *The Elusive Eden: A New History of California*, Fifth Edition

The publisher and authors of *The Elusive Eden* recognize the challenges facing California educators. *The Elusive Eden* makes life a little easier for part-time instructors and full-time faculty with a wealth of online resources. On the publisher's website, www.waveland.com, educators will find a detailed guide to changes in this edition; an extensive chapter-by-chapter test bank with multiple choice, short-answer, and essay questions; and other useful resources; brief chapter outlines in Word and PowerPoint formats; links to online resources, including maps and primary sources; and suggestions for field trips and other student activities.

About the Authors

The late RICHARD B. RICE was Professor Emeritus of History at California State University, Hayward. He received the B.A., M.A., and Ph.D. in history from the University of California, Berkeley. He was a staff assistant to the president and assistant to the vice president of the University of California before going to CSU Hayward, where he also served as a department chairman, division head, and dean. He taught United States and California history at CSU Hayward from 1960 to 1995.

The late WILLIAM A. BULLOUGH was Professor Emeritus of History at CSU East Bay. He received his Ph.D. degree from UC Santa Barbara in 1970 after teaching for ten years in the state public schools. He is the author of *Cities and Schools in the Gilded Age: The Evolution of an Urban Institution* (1974), *The Blind Boss and His City: Christopher Augustine Buckley and Nineteenth-Century San Francisco* (1979), and articles in *The San Francisco Irish, 1850–1976*, James P. Walsh, ed., (1978), *The Historian, Pacific Historical Review, California History, The Journal of Ventura County History,* and *Darkroom Photography.* Professor Bullough was an accomplished photographer who wrote and spoke often on the subject, and exhibited and published his prints.

RICHARD J. ORSI is Professor Emeritus of History at CSU East Bay. A graduate of Occidental College in Los Angeles, he received his Ph.D. from the University of Wisconsin, Madison. He has published articles and book reviews in *California History, Pacific Historian, Agricultural History, Journal of American History, American Historical Review, Pacific Historical Review, Western Historical Quarterly, Pacific Northwest Quarterly,* and *Oregon Historical Quarterly.* He is the author of *A List of References for the History of Agriculture in California* (1974) and *Sunset Limited: The Southern Pacific Railroad and the Development of the American West, 1850–1930* (2005). He is editor emeritus of *California History,* originally the quarterly of the California Historical Society and, since 2014, published by University of California Press. He edited (with Alfred A. Runte and Marlene Smith-Baranzini) *Yosemite and Sequoia: A Century of California National Parks* (1993), other anthologies of essays on historical themes of California, and the California History Sesquicentennial Series, four volumes of essays authored by leading scholars interpreting early California history, co-published by the University of California Press and the California Historical Society, 1998–2003.

California-born MARY ANN IRWIN attended Mesa Community College in San Diego, received her B.A. from UC Berkeley, and her M.A. from San Francisco State University. She is an adjunct faculty member teaching the history of women, California, the United States, and the American West at Diablo Valley Community College and at CSU East Bay. Her published works include two anthologies: Robert W. Cherny, Mary Ann Irwin, and Ann Marie Wilson, eds., *Women and Politics: California from the Gold Rush to the Great Depression* (University of Nebraska Press, 2011); and James F. Brooks and Mary Ann Irwin, eds., *Women and Gender in the American West: Jensen-Miller Essays from the Coalition for Western Women's History* (University of New Mexico Press, 2004), and several articles, including "Sex, War, and Community Service: The Battle for San Francisco's Jewish Community Center," *Frontiers: A Journal of Women Studies* (May 2011); "'The Air is Becoming Full of War:' Jewish San Francisco and World War I," *Pacific Historical Review* (August 2005); and "'Going About and Doing Good': The Politics of Benevolence, Welfare, and Gender in San Francisco, 1850–1880," *Pacific Historical Review* (August 1999) (Winner, 1999 Joan Jensen–Darlis Miller Prize, Best Article on the history of women in the American West). She is editor of *California History,* published quarterly by University of California Press (2020–2022), and completing a history of San Francisco's Emanu-El Sisterhood for Personal Service.

A lifelong Californian, MICHAEL F. MAGLIARI is Professor of History at CSU Chico, and received his B.A., M.A.T., and Ph.D. in History from UC Davis. Before arriving at Chico in 1990, he taught at four California community colleges: American River College (in Sacramento), Sierra College (Rocklin), College of the Sequoias (Visalia), and Mount San Antonio College (Walnut). With his late friend and colleague Michael J. Gillis, Magliari co-authored *John Bidwell and California: The Life and Writings of a Pioneer, 1841–1900* (2003). He has published articles and book reviews in numerous professional journals, including *Agricultural History, Journal of American History, California History, Ethnohistory, Pacific Historical Review,* and *Western Historical Quarterly.* A former National Endowment for the Humanities Fellow, Magliari received the Ray Allen Billington Award from the Western History Association (2005) and the Louis Knott Koontz Memorial Award from the Pacific Coast Branch of the American Historical Association (2013) for his articles on Indian slavery in California between 1850 and 1870. He has also held research fellowships at the Hubert Howe Bancroft Library at UC Berkeley, and the Henry E. Huntington Library in San Marino, California.

CECILIA M. TSU is Associate Professor of History at UC Davis, where she teaches courses in U.S. history, Asian American/immigration history, and the history of California. She received her B.A. in History from Swarthmore College, M.A. in American Civilization from Brown University, and M.A. and Ph.D. in History from Stanford University. Professor Tsu is the author of *Garden of the World: Asian Immigrants and the Making of Agriculture in California's Santa Clara Valley* (2013). Her articles have appeared in the *Journal of American Ethnic History, Pacific Historical Review,* and *Western Historical Quarterly.* She has been the recipient an American Council of Learned Societies fellowship and the University of California President's Research Fellowship in the Humanities. Her current book project, *Starting Over: Refugee Resettlement in the Reagan Era,* examines the evolution of Southeast Asian refugee resettlement policy and its intersection with the rise of American conservatism in the 1970s–'80s.

Fifth Edition

The
ELUSIVE EDEN

California, The Land of Promise

California's promotional literature has long portrayed the state as an Eden. This booster pamphlet was published by the California State Board of Trade in 1897. *The Huntington Library, San Marino, California.*

PART ONE

Prologue

Californians
and Their History
Myths and Realities

1

Californians have long identified with their state's past. In the 1870s, historians started producing local and state histories, and in the 1890s efforts began to restore the old Spanish missions and other crumbling historic structures. Since then, authors have penned thousands of books and articles about California's past. Local and state historical journals abound, many with electronic versions and some with wide circulation. Bookshelves groan under the growing burden of Californiana, and specialized libraries, bookstores, and museums have sprouted to gather, preserve, and propagate historical knowledge. Students in high schools, colleges, and extended education programs flock to courses in state and local history. Local historical societies and other entities preserve sites, buildings, and artifacts. To the delight of residents and visitors alike, entire neighborhoods of historic buildings have been restored. San Francisco, Sacramento, Alameda, San José, Monterey, Eureka, Ferndale, Santa Barbara, San Diego, Pasadena, and Los Angeles, along with dozens of gold-rush and other communities, now sport adobe "old towns," streets of pioneer cottages, or graceful Victorian homes.

By the twenty-first century, the state has become one of the most history-conscious states and a national leader in "heritage resources," including history-oriented groups, museums, officially designated national and state historic sites and buildings, national and state historic parks, important Native American archeological sites, and local governments with heritage preservation boards. The lure of tourist dollars accounts for at least some of this enthusiasm. According to the Travel Industry Association of America, California leads the nation in tourist spending, more than $100 billion per year, much of it at history-specific places.

The New Eden

Despite their fixation on history, Californians' understanding of the state's past is largely distorted. Many view history as a romantic tale of swashbuckling heroes engaged in epic adventures: Cabrillo's voyage of discovery in 1542, the Serra-Portolá expedition in 1769, the gold rush of 1849, Leland Stanford's hammering the "golden spike" in 1869 on the first transcontinental railroad, the Progressives triumphing over big business in 1910, and so on. These events, not the complicated social processes associated with them, are often mistaken for the totality of history. Many Californians, for example, are familiar with Father Junípero Serra and his founding of the first Spanish mission at San Diego in 1769. But few know much about how the missions functioned as colonial agencies, or how they shaped relationships between Hispanic colonists and Indians, in what was the region's most important human dynamic in the decades before the American conquest. While many know that the Central Pacific Railroad eventually conquered the Sierra Nevada and completed the western connection to the first transcontinental railway, few appreciate the complexity of the railroad's role in creating—and resisting—social, economic, cultural, and political change, and playing a key part in creating modern California.

In the popular tradition of California history, the story revolves around the exploits of the famous (or infamous) and powerful: Father Serra, John C. Frémont, David Broderick, Denis Kearney, Hiram Johnson, Richard Nixon, Ronald Reagan, Howard Jarvis, and Jerry Brown, among others. In this view, California was built by great individuals, usually politicians, often "old stock," usually white and male. The non-famous— a group that includes everybody else, and especially the poor, workers, women, Indians, Hispanics, blacks, Asians, and more-recent European immigrants— appear in traditional histories only as supporting characters, if they appear at all. Until recently, state and local histories, museum exhibits, and public history sites seldom depicted them.

Popular histories often also emphasize California's uniqueness. The state appears as a land apart from the rest of the world, with a distinctive population, settlement history, climate, and geography combining to create a singular civilization. The region has been variously described as "the great exception," "an experimental society," and "the cutting edge of American civilization," the ultimate frontier where new values, behaviors, and pioneering institutions were born.

The California of popular history is also a "Garden of Eden," a benevolent land where innovative and enterprising people fulfill their individual and national aspirations, buoyed along on a relentless current of untarnished success, especially in the economic realm. Society in frontier California has been portrayed as democratic and classless, built on accessible and abundant resources which, when coupled with the pioneer's egalitarian instincts, shattered the rigid class structures of older societies. Californians succeeded through diligence and intelligence, not by inherited wealth or influence, and if they failed it was because of their own personal fault. Starting out equally most thrived, producing a homogeneous, middle-class society. If popular histories mentioned racial and ethnic minorities at all, it was to emphasize California's role as a great American "melting pot." In the tolerant atmosphere of a new frontier, where there was land and opportunity for all, all were welcome, and different ethnic groups lived in harmony. "California history," as a State Department of Parks pamphlet once concluded, "is a romantic tale of a land blessed by nature and inhabited by men of greatness." That brief, unabashedly chauvinistic statement captures the essence of popular mythology about the state.

The Traditional View of California History

Californians' romantic view of history reflects the normal tendency of each generation to glorify its own past. But it also reflects the fact that, until quite recently, history has been written by and for affluent white men, who predictably overlooked the experiences and contributions of those who were neither white nor male. Just as problematic, California's historical tradition was born of boosterism. John H. Hittell and other early state historians were boosters, and their writings were in part intended to encourage immigration and economic development. The inevitable emphasis on California's growth, progress, success, social equality, and romantic frontier heritage has thus permeated not only popular culture, but also the work of many professional historians. In a region where most residents have been newcomers or their children, personal and family memories are generally too short to offset the boosters' claims.

Californians are also victims of their own success as preservationists. Typically, museums, state parks, libraries, and historical societies focus on preserving the homes, artifacts, and records of powerful elites, individuals who constituted a small minority of the population.

Restorers clean and paint their crumbling mansions, rebuild and replace missing fixtures and ornaments, and often surrounding the whole with lush gardens that never existed originally. Restorations most often return homes and objects to a higher level of elegance than they ever enjoyed in the past. In contrast, preservationists tend to ignore the shanties and personal effects of the poor and middling sorts. Even though they represent the majority of the people by far, their modest worldly goods—common, unadorned, and cheaply constructed—are readily dismantled, discarded, and forgotten.

Although the results of traditional historic preservation can be beautiful, leaving visitors with vivid experiences, they are not genuinely historical. Indeed, many restored sites suggest a false history, a sanitized past of affluence and stability, unmarked by the failure, poverty, inequality, and conflict that mark the California experience. Thus restorers have erected beautiful Spanish missions with lush courtyards and peaceful, bubbling fountains, but without any Indians—the ill-treated, frequently rebellious inhabitants for whom missions were originally created. Likewise, restorers have produced eighteenth-century communities without dirt, flies, disease, noxious odors, or outhouses; mines without poor and disabled miners; farms without strikes or stoop labor; lovely Victorian neighborhoods without their adjacent slums; and entire worlds with few or no women or ethnic and racial minorities.

Until recently, professional historians bore part of the blame for the state's skewed history. Sometimes sharing

Casa del Oro and Carson Mansion

Modern restorations throughout California convey a romanticized impression of the state's past. Casa del Oro in Monterey (*left*) was a simple store in the 1840s; along with other buildings from the Hispanic eras, it has been upgraded, sterilized, and surrounded with lavish landscaping and courtyards, creating an illusion of a vanished aristocratic community. In Eureka, the Carson Mansion (*right*) suggests an affluence uncharacteristic of early years in the American period. *Photographs by William A. Bullough.*

the boosters' patriotic vision of their home state, some authors of traditional California histories perpetuated old myths and stereotypes. Those who advanced beyond boosterism were sometimes limited by parochialism. Working in state and local history—notoriously myopic fields to begin with—some California historians were slow to adopt the interests, theories, and methodologies common to modern scholarship. Many celebrated California's successes uncritically, treating the state as though it existed in a vacuum, without reference to the outside world.

For 70 years, for example, most California historians placed the complex period from 1860 to 1920 within a traditional "Populist-Progressive" framework. As they described it, the unifying theme of that period was the struggle of the common people against the emerging corporate monopolies, which in California's case meant particularly the Southern Pacific Railroad. In many state histories, democratic reformers and corporate bosses continue to stalk another doggedly across the decades. Most national historians, however, have abandoned that rubric as simplistic. They instead propose alternative unifying themes, such as industrialization, modernization, and ethnocultural and gender diversity, conflict, and adjustment. Nevertheless, through textbooks, reference works, and more specialized and popular writings, the traditional view has furnished the factual and interpretive foundations for most historical restorations, has influenced how state history is taught in colleges and public schools, and thus continues to reinforce popular misconceptions about California's past.

Reconsidering California History

In recent decades, modern scholars have begun to question the popular mythologies. Changes within the historical profession have prompted much of this reevaluation of the state's past. Influenced by other social sciences such as anthropology, sociology, economics, and political science, historians have developed more sophisticated systems for measuring and interpreting social change. Contemporary historians have reframed their questions, more systematically gathered and evaluated new evidence, and raised their line of vision to place California in its broader western, national, or even global perspective. Social structure, economics, and culture have replaced politics as a principal focus of research. At the same time, attention to previously overlooked sources that better disclose the history of ordinary people, such as diaries, court files, census records, photographs, archeological evidence, and the written correspondence left by ordinary folk, has resulted in a flood of new information about the past. Armed with fresh materials, broader professional interests, and sharper tools of analysis, state historians are reevaluating old assumptions.

Ideas about race, ethnicity, and gender roles have also changed dramatically since the 1960s, requiring reevaluation of traditional topics in California history, from the missions, to the Gold Rush, to progressivism, to World Wars I and II, and beyond. Emergent ethnic and feminist groups have demanded correction of historical stereotypes and acknowledgement of the struggles and achievements of women and minorities. These efforts have resulted in new publications, reorganization of museum exhibits, and rethinking of public-school programs. Although such work occasionally degenerates into its own kind of boosterism, the surge in ethnic and women's studies has enlivened and strengthened both popular and scholarly history.

Late twentieth and early twenty-first century conflicts over water, energy, wilderness preservation, and climate change have likewise sparked a new environmental history, just as debates over agricultural policy have renewed interest in the study of land, labor, irrigation, mechanization, and the crucial role of government in economic development. Much rethinking remains to be done, and it will always be so. Nevertheless, a new generation of historians has produced a vision of the past that is at once more subtle, complex, and challenging—thus more realistic and fully representative of the rich diversity that is California.

This volume reexamines California history in light of these scholarship trends. While traditional subjects, such as politics, will still be covered, this book's authors emphasize the state's social, economic, and cultural evolution. They will focus not only on the rich and famous, but also seek to reveal the masses of ordinary Californians—their labors, recreations, families, failures, and achievements. Bringing the common people to the fore—reading "history from the bottom up"—exposes a California that is not the model of frontier democracy celebrated in popular mythology. California is not now, nor has it ever been, a harmonious, ethnically homogeneous, middle-class society. The hallmark of the state has always been its diversity, rooted in its contrasting natural environments and in the varied backgrounds and experiences of its settlers. Some succeeded economically, some failed. Some acquired power, others did not. Some were oppressors, some were oppressed, some were both, and many were neither. Society in California has always been hierarchical, with the chasm of wealth and power between the poor and the rich as great as in any other region, on this or any other continent.

Since the first human settlement, ethnic and cultural diversity have characterized California, but the region has never been the proverbial "melting pot." Usually, those in power insisted that minorities relinquish their cultures, adopt those of the dominant group, and accept social, economic, and political inferiority. Although ethnic minorities rarely accepted this fate without resistance, economic exchange and the succession of generations has always brought about a certain amount of long-term adaptation to the dominant culture. Conflict, interaction, and assimilation have always shaped California history, just as persistent inequality, attempts by some groups to subordinate others, and intergroup tensions have always been major themes. But conflict has not been a simple matter of rich versus poor, whites versus ethnics, native-born versus immigrants, men versus women, workers versus employers, reformers versus conservatives, or even north versus south. Instead, conflict among and within groups has been bewilderingly complex and shifting. In California, progress and democracy have been the children, not of homogeneity and agreement, but of diversity and competition.

Success or failure in California has been a function of group cooperation, in addition to personal effort. Instead of celebrating the achievements of rugged individualism, this volume emphasizes the importance of human interaction and organization. Settlers in recent centuries seldom experienced California as a paradise on earth, but rather as a rugged, harsh land that only reluctantly yielded its treasures. California did rise as an enormously successful civilization on the shoulders of great individuals, but it did so also through the energies of countless people who banded together into flexible and often ingenious organizations to overcome obstacles, though not always in fairness to others. California history records the works of farm organizations, squatters' clubs, labor unions, business associations, professional groups, ethnic and women's groups, political parties, racist and anti-immigrant groups, community organizations, water agencies, churches, schools, universities, and a succession of other voluntary and official agencies. The great difficulties of settlement in California also made diverse, flexible, and strong local, state, and federal governments particularly essential to foster and regulate economic

growth, modify natural conditions, and dominate or mediate among contending factions. Those who could organize effectively often succeeded; those who could not typically failed. California today stands as a testament to the power of cooperation and collective action.

All human societies have interacted with nature in distinctive ways that have influenced regional history. Human/nature interaction is a central theme of California history. Nature endowed California with enviable location, topography, climate, and resources. Indians, Hispanic colonists, American pioneers, and modern residents have all developed their own approaches to the natural environment, approaches that have both reflected and shaped their cultures. Gradually, residents acquired greater power to manipulate their environment—particularly water—in order to extract wealth, build more complex economies, and support ever larger populations. Yet, the imposition of control on nature has exposed nature's sensitivity and unpredictability, as well as the human capacity for dangerous, perhaps catastrophic error. To the rest of the world, California has contributed examples of both ruthless environmental destruction and effective conservation and preservation.

For all of California's distinctiveness, however, nature's sway over history and the region's uniqueness and inventiveness must not be exaggerated. Following the lead of the great frontier historian Frederick Jackson Turner, past observers have assumed that pioneers, in confronting raw nature in the wilderness, shed previous ways as impractical and invented new cultures better attuned to never-before-encountered natural conditions. Since California was the ultimate frontier, in the most singular of environments, then it seemed to follow that California must also be the most experimental of American regions.

But comparisons of California with other developed and frontier areas show that continuity of cultures, not deviation, has dominated the western experience. Settlers did not discard their ancestral lifeways, but clung to them even more fiercely as a defense against the disorganizing wilderness. Culture proved resilient to environmental pressures, and Californians eventually imposed their cultures on nature. The region's civilization thus came to resemble the outside world of which it was a part. No single force, not even nature, determined California history. The people found the land and made of it what they willed.

The *Natural Setting*

2

California, an "Island" World

At first, Europeans conceived of California as an island. Even before the Spaniards encountered the region, the name appeared in an early sixteenth-century novel, Garcí Ordoñez de Montalvo's *Las Sergas de Esplandián*. "Know ye," wrote Montalvo, "that at the right hand of the Indies there is an island named California, very close to that part of the Terrestrial Paradise. . . . The island itself is one of the wildest in the world on account of the bold and craggy rocks. . . . The island everywhere abounds with gold and precious stones, and upon it no other metal was found." A few decades later, perhaps in jest, early Spanish mariners gave the name "California" to the first land they sailed to north and west of Mexico, which they scorned as a bleak island. Later explorers eventually discovered that California was actually part of the North American mainland. Ironically, naive original impressions, though geographically false, turned out to be ecologically true.

Although physically attached to North America, California can still accurately be described as an ecological island, its natural history distinct from that of the rest of the continent. Winds, currents, mountains, and deserts isolate the region biologically, almost as effectively as if it were girthed by an ocean moat, and its unique climates and landscapes create a potential for diverse and distinctive life forms unmatched elsewhere on the continent. As many have observed, California is home to the extreme, the unusual, and the spectacular, a veritable "island upon the land." Throughout its human occupation, California's exceptional landscapes, climates, and life forms have nurtured distinctive economies and cultures. Only against such a powerful and dynamic natural setting can we understand the drama of the region's human history.

9

The Dynamic Landscape

Nature is often popularly assumed to be static and eternal, a stable benchmark against which to measure the ups and downs of human affairs. Actually, nature is dynamic. Oceans rise and fall. Whole continents meander around the globe. Mountain chains burst from the earth's surface, then sink below it again. Plants and animals evolve, some becoming new species, others dying out altogether. Climates change from frigid to torrid, humid to arid, and back again. Radically different ecological communities follow one another on the same landscape. Thus has it been for billions of years. Although they usually developed slower than a creeping glacier, these changes have been no less revolutionary.

No locale better illustrates nature's dynamism than California. For hundreds of millions of years, the region's landscape has been evolving. The present coast generally coincides with the borders between the North American and Pacific plates in the earth's crust. These plates continually interact, grinding together, pushing apart, and slipping sideways against each other. This gnashing of plates has made the Pacific Coast a particularly active geological region, with dramatic earthquakes, volcanic eruptions, and frequent shifts in elevation. Over the last hundred million years, mountains have been pushed upward by subterranean pressure or by lava from volcanic eruptions, only to be whittled back down by water and wind erosion, and then their rock and soil to be reformed into other landscapes elsewhere. As the earth heaved and sank, seas roamed back and forth across the landscape. At times, nearly all of California was under water; at others, the coastline was many miles west of its present location. Marshes and forests flourished in turn, and then were buried under hundreds of feet of sediment.

The present landscape began to emerge about thirty million years ago. The Pacific Plate began to drift northward along the San Andreas Fault, where it borders the North American Plate. Over millions of years, it carried part of the Baja California peninsula north, forming the present coastline from San Francisco Bay south to the Imperial Valley. Between ten and 20 million years ago, the Sierra Nevada mountain range loomed up and tilted west (it is still rising). As the younger Coast Range took shape, the great Central Valley—then a vast inland arm of the sea—gradually filled with sediment eroding from surrounding mountains. About two million years ago, the world's climate turned cold, inaugurating a series of ice ages. Although great glaciers moved southward from the poles over much of North America, they missed California. Smaller glaciers did, however, grind down the slopes of the Sierra, sculpting out Yosemite and other valleys.

When the ice finally began to melt, only about fifteen to twenty thousand years ago, the coastline was some twenty miles west of its current location. The present-day Channel Islands in the south were still attached to the mainland, and current San Francisco Bay was an inland river valley. Herds of mammoths shared the cool, moist terrain with camels, giant ground sloths, and saber-toothed cats. Marshes and redwood forests blanketed the land. Oceans rose as the glaciers melted, and salt water again flooded coastal land. The climate grew warmer and drier, and deserts emerged in California's southern reaches. Many animals and plants became extinct or, like the redwoods, retreated to tiny ranges. The Pacific engulfed the Channel Islands, their flora and fauna beginning their evolution into species and varieties distinct from the mainland's. About 10,000 years ago, the sea approached its present shore, where it penetrated the Golden Gate and flooded the north-south valley in the Coast Range. San Francisco Bay waited another several thousand years to approach its present extent. When Native Americans first settled in that area, the bay did not exist. Their ancient villages are now buried under its waters and mud. California as we know it, with its sea cliffs, harbors, forests, grasslands, and deserts, is comparatively young—only a few thousand years old—and still forming. It is a fragile, and by no means immutable, land.

A Mosaic of Climates

As California's present landscape emerged a few thousand years ago, so did its modern climate. The climate results from the interaction of ocean currents and temperatures, air-pressure systems, westerly wind and storm patterns, and the orientation of its mountains and valleys. Most of the densely populated, low-lying areas along the coast and in interior valleys have a Mediterranean climate: moderate, subtropical, with rainy winters and dry summers. Although this climate type is rare, a few other regions are similar, including the Mediterranean region, North Africa, the Near East, and parts of Chile, Australia, and South Africa.

Geographic position, landscape, and a dominant marine influence explain the differences between California's climate and that of its neighbors. The wide California Current carries a stream of relatively cool water from the northwestern Pacific Ocean southeast along the coast. Prevailing westerly winds sweep air masses from the ocean, whose temperature

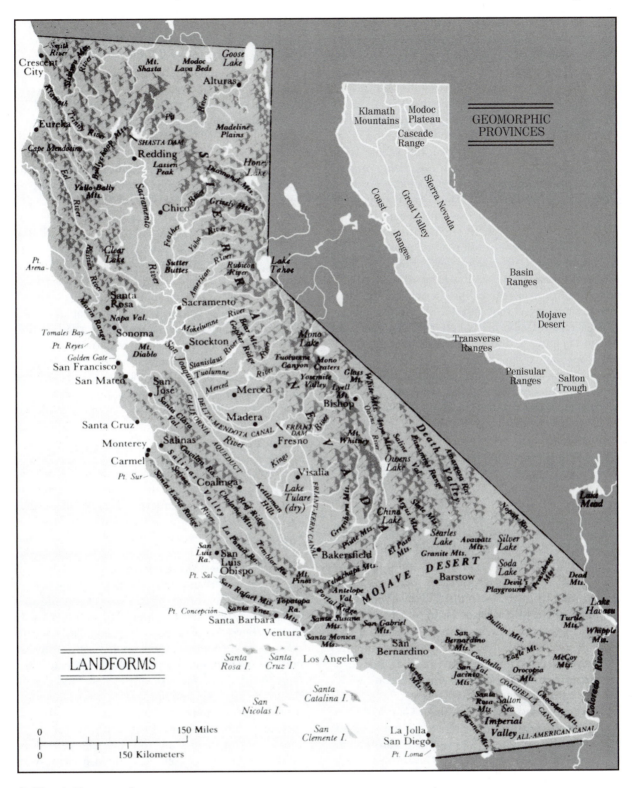

California Topography

Adapted from David Hornbeck, *California Patterns: A Geographical and Historical Atlas* (Mountain View, CA: Mayfield Publishing Co., 1983).

is relatively stable, and then over the land, cooling it in summer and warming it in winter, especially west of the Sierra Nevada.

A large high air-pressure zone called the Pacific High usually hovers about one thousand miles west of the coast. It intensifies the moderating ocean winds and regulates the flow of weather systems, as well as precipitation. In the late spring and early summer, as air and water temperatures increase, the Pacific High moves northward, forcing storms originating in the Gulf of Alaska to track across the Pacific Northwest and into the northern Great Plains. Thus from April through September most of the state is rain free. In autumn, however, the Pacific High drifts southward, opening the door to a succession of winter storms and delivering most of California's precipitation. Mountain chains, particularly the Coast Range, northwestern Siskiyou, and most significantly the Sierra Nevada, slow the storms and extract their moisture before they move east. As a result, California is better watered than its arid inland neighbors, dramatically enriching the state's water supply and other resources, as well as its plant and animal, including human, populations. Almost all of the region's precipitation falls in the winter, however. Water that does not run off quickly is stored in forest watersheds, underground basins, deep mountain snows, and, in modern times, reservoirs.

Moreover, because of its immense size and diverse topography, California encompasses a mosaic of local climates that duplicate many weather patterns elsewhere, from temperate rain forests in the northwestern part of the state, to arctic and alpine climates atop its highest mountains, to the arid steppe and desert climates of the south and southeast. The many distinct local climates vary according to four criteria: distance south from the northern border; distance east from the coast; position relative to mountain ranges; and elevation. Generally, the north is cooler in summer and wetter in winter than the south; the same equation holds between the coast and inland areas, between higher and lower elevations, and between areas west, as opposed to east, of mountain ranges. At the same time, however, low-elevation gaps in the Coast Range allow ocean air to reach some interior zones, such as inland from the Golden Gate and Carquinez Strait. In the far south, another gap in the Coast Range south of Point Conception allows ocean-moderated climates to penetrate farther east. Elsewhere, high coastal peaks inhibit the flow of marine air, casting rain shadows that reduce the land to searing deserts, as in the southern San Joaquin Valley and the southeastern Mojave and Colorado deserts.

California's climatic contrasts can be enormous, even locally. The northwest coast has one of the coolest average summer high temperatures (rarely more than 70 degrees Fahrenheit) and one of the highest average annual rainfalls (more than 100 inches) in the contiguous United States. Yet the southeast's Imperial Valley is one of the hottest and driest places in the Western Hemisphere, with summer temperatures sometimes in excess of 120 degrees and an annual rainfall of less than three inches. Some of the coldest temperatures ever measured in the United States were recorded near Donner Pass in the High Sierra (below –60 degrees), while the nation's highest temperatures (more than 130 degrees) were recorded at Death Valley, only 250 miles to the southeast. Local variations can be nearly as great. Average annual rainfall at San José is about 13 inches; at Boulder Creek in the redwood forest, 20 miles west and over the Santa Cruz Mountains, the average is 60 inches. On a hot summer day within the Los Angeles city limits, the temperature can be 75 degrees at the beaches, 85 degrees in Westwood, 95 degrees downtown, and 105 degrees in the San Fernando Valley. California's local climates—and hence its resources, plant and animal communities, and human settlement patterns—vary more than in any other land of similar size in the world.

Distinctive Plant Life

Because of its geographical location, heterogeneous landscape, and disparate climates, California enjoys unique resources. Microenvironments of distinctive location, elevation, soil, and climate nurture a more varied wildlife than elsewhere in North America. California, for example, has three times as many native plant species as the entire northeastern United States.

As befits an "island upon the land," many plants are endemic, or found only in this state. Endemic species are particularly common along the central coast, from the northern San Francisco Bay south to Point Conception; in this unique zone, cool, moist northwestern climates overlap hot, dry southwestern climates. Mountains in the north and east of the state, and deserts in the southeast, keep endemic plants from spreading and insulate them against invasion by outsiders. Indicative of California's hospitality to diverse, specialized environments and species are the state's coniferous trees. Of the 73 varieties of conifers in the American West, 54 are native to California, including about one-quarter of the world's pine species. Of the state's conifers, 21 are endemic, including the coast redwood (*Sequoia sempervirens*), giant sequoia (*Sequoiadendron giganteum*),

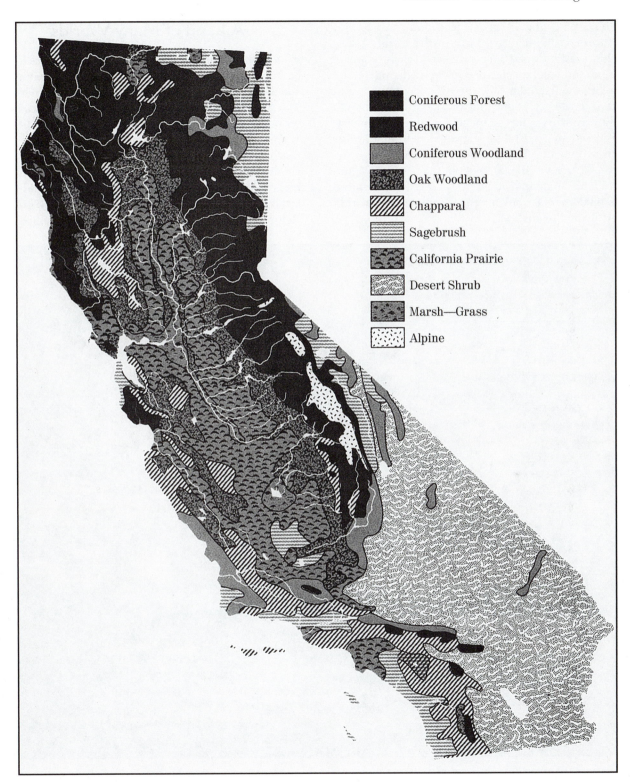

California Vegetation Zones

Adapted from *Historical Atlas of California*, by Warren A. Beck and Ynez D. Haase. Copyright © 1974 University of Oklahoma Press.

Monterey pine, gray ("digger") pine, and many species of cypress. California gave birth to the world's tallest species (coast redwood) and its bulkiest (giant sequoia).

Some endemic species are ancient, dating to the age of dinosaurs; today they survive only in small, specialized locales. The graceful coast redwood, though hardy within its range, depends on the cool, moist, foggy low-lying coastal belt stretching from Big Sur north to Oregon. The gnarled bristlecone pine survives only above 10,000 feet in the eastern White Mountains. Some individual trees have lived for more than 6,000 years, ranking them among the world's oldest living organisms.

A Land of Many Worlds

California is an assemblage of small worlds, each one unique, with a combined capacity for production and self-sufficiency greater than that of most nations. The sub-regions offer an unrivaled mix of resources and economic potentials.

The state has 1,200 miles of seacoast—gentle and warm with wide beaches in the south, rugged, cold, and windswept in the north. Abundant fisheries lie in the rocky tide pools, in shoreline bays and salt marshes, and just off the coast in the nutrient-rich California Current. Before Europeans arrived, these fisheries supported

Sierra Snowpack

Melting Sierra snows feed the Yuba River, near Cisco Grove. Like many Sierra streams, the Yuba's water eventually descends through reservoirs and the Sacramento River to the Delta and San Francisco Bay, slaking the thirst of farms, cities, and industries along the way. *California Department of Water Resources.*

immense populations of birds, sea mammals, and Native peoples. In the last century, salmon, cod, halibut, tuna, crab, shellfish, and, until recently, the whale supported one of the nation's largest fishing industries.

Stretching inland is a coastal plain composed of the valleys of rivers and creeks that flow into the Pacific. The coastal plain has fertile soil, moderate temperatures, and generally higher rainfall than the interior. Wide and warm in the south, the plain becomes increasingly narrow, intermittent, and forbidding until it mostly disappears in the precipitous cliffs and fog banks above Morro Bay. Natural harbors break up the plain at several points. Two, the San Francisco and San Diego bays, are among the largest and best sheltered in the world. Since the early days of European exploration, California's bays have been focal points of Pacific maritime commerce and inland transportation.

Several coastal points open to the interior. Especially important is the path through San Francisco Bay, the Carquinez Strait, and the Sacramento–San Joaquin river system, which offers the only navigable sea-level route through the Coast Range between Mexico and the Columbia River. In the days of sailing ships, this water route led to quick settlement and urban development there in the early period of American settlement. In the south, a relatively low-elevation corridor runs east from Los Angeles across southern Arizona, New Mexico, and Texas to the Mississippi Valley. Its easy grades made Los Angeles the major southwestern terminus for several nineteenth-century transcontinental railroads and twentieth-century highways. For thousands of years, the coastal valleys have supported large human populations. In modern times, they offer great potential for intensive agriculture and urbanization, particularly at San Francisco, San Diego, and Los Angeles.

California's mountains constitute another important resource. Varying from low hills to medium peaks, the Coast Range flanks the Pacific. In the north, California is separated from Oregon by the Siskiyous, Klamaths, and the southern extension of the inland Cascade volcanic range through Mount Shasta and Lassen Peak. California's most monumental chain, the Sierra Nevada, stretches southward from the Cascades in a belt 40 to 80 miles wide and 400 miles long on the state's eastern border. With many peaks over 10,000 feet, it insulates the state from the Great Basin to the east. The Tehachapis, San Gabriels, and San Bernardinos—rare east-west mountain chains collectively called the "Transverse Ranges"—slice through the state about 150 miles north of the Mexican border, dividing southern and northern California into distinct geological, biological, climatic,

Sierra Nevada Forest, Yosemite National Park
Photograph by William A. Bullough.

and cultural regions. Its mountain chains isolate California from the rest of North America, inhibiting the migration of plants and animals to, from, and within the state. Until the modern advent of railroad, automobile, and airplane travel, these ranges deterred human immigration as well as interaction between Californians and their inland neighbors.

California's mountain ranges influence its water supply and flora and fauna, unique among the southwestern states. The north-south ranges, particularly the Sierra Nevada, directly block prevailing westerly Pacific storms, causing their air masses to rise, cool, and drop most of their abundant precipitation primarily on the western slopes, retaining most water in California and preventing it from continuing eastward. The chains themselves also serve as watersheds, storing the storm

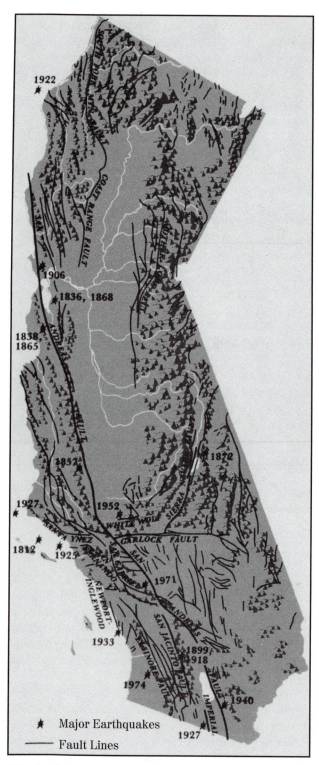

Principal Earthquake Faults

Adapted from Robert Durrenberger, *California: Patterns on the Land* (Mountain View, CA: Mayfield Publishing Company, 1976), p. 11.

water in rocks, soils, and snows as deep as 50 to 75 feet. Then, in spring and summer thaws, water seeps and flows gradually into rivers that deliver it, as well as fertile silt, westward into the lowland valleys, sometimes directly into the ocean. In recent years, the western slopes also furnished reservoir sites for additional water storage, as well as hydroelectric power generation.

The state's mountains also house mineral treasures. More than 100 million years ago, while subterranean rocks were heating and cooling, molten gold collected in their faults and fractures. After the Sierra Nevada rose up, the lodes yielded their yellow metal, depositing it as placer gold along riverbeds in the western foothills. Great fanfare accompanied the discovery of this gold in the 1840s and '50s, triggering the first of many population booms, as well as the state's first great industry.

In moist mountain coolness, large forests thrive—redwood along the northern coast, oak on the central and southern coast and Sierra foothills, pine and fir elsewhere. The trees shelter rodents, birds, grazers, and predators, as well as preserve the mountain watershed. The trees shade and preserve snow into the summer, and their roots solidify soils, increase water-storage capacity, slow runoff, and reduce erosion. Interspersed with rugged peaks, glacial valleys, waterfalls, and sparkling alpine lakes, the forests have attracted artists, sightseers, campers, skiers, and defenders of wilderness. Until the mid-nineteenth century, when heavy logging began, forests blanketed more than half the state. Lumbering, however, has since become a major industry in northern and Sierra counties, and forests have been stripped from the land faster than nature can regenerate them. The divergent needs of lumbering, mining, irrigation, hydroelectric generation, water export to other regions, tourism, and wilderness preservation often conflict, and California's mountains and forests have become the focus of bitter political, economic, sectional, and ideological struggles.

Dramatic as the mountains are, the great Central Valley, particularly its Delta, is in many ways California's most remarkable geographical feature. This low-elevation drainage basin of the Sacramento and San Joaquin rivers lies between the Coast Range and the Sierra Nevada. Filled deep with fertile alluvial soil washed down from surrounding mountains, the valley stretches 500 miles north to south, and from 30 to 70 miles wide. The largest expanse of flat land west of the Great Plains, the Central Valley is about the size of the states of Vermont, New Hampshire, Massachusetts, Connecticut, and Rhode Island combined. Annual rainfall varies enormously north to south, from more than 30 inches at

Delta Channel and Reclaimed Farmland

Aerial photographs from the 1960s reveal the extent to which geometric, man-made patterns dominate Delta farms behind their protective levees. Remnants of original channels and marshes are still evident in some artificial waterways. *California Department of Water Resources.*

Redding to less than seven inches at Bakersfield. Standing in the rain shadow of the Coast Range, the west side of the valley is also far more arid than the east.

Nonetheless, the Central Valley enjoys abundant water resources. Large, perennial rivers originate in the Sierra to the east, snaking slowly back and forth across the gentle country, and recharging underground water basins. Before the dams and flood-control and drainage projects of the last century, marshes covered much of the land. In especially rainy years, chains of lakes dotted the valley floor, and groundwater nearly reached the land surface. With its rich soils, flat terrain, abundant water, and hot climate, in the twentieth century, the Central Valley became the world's largest irrigated plain and the

nation's most productive farm region. In modern times, however, upriver reservoirs diverting water to other regions have greatly reduced downstream flows and groundwater levels have sunk deeper.

An important topographical feature of the valley is the Delta formed by the confluence of the Sacramento and San Joaquin river systems before they flow into San Francisco Bay and the Pacific. Serving as a natural reservoir, the Delta's channels and marshes collect and disperse about one-half of the state's water runoff. At or below sea level, the Delta is also the point at which the salt water from the bay surges on alternating daily tides, eastward, then westward, and mixes with the fresh water flowing downstream from the interior. The back and forth cleansing action of Delta marshes and sloughs maintains the purity of the bay and much of the state's water supply. Along with the state's climate and north-south mountain ranges, the Sacramento-San Joaquin Delta is one of California's most significant natural features.

Despite its importance, the Delta's freshwater supply has become unreliable. The natural extremes of saltwater intrusion into the Delta vary enormously from day to day, season to season, and year to year. Each day the freshwater-saltwater boundary fluctuates naturally, advancing eastward on high tide, then retreating westward on the low ebb. Freshwater supplies are abundant in most rainy winters, but in seasonal summer drought, saltwater penetrates farther into the heart of the Delta. In winter, the salt-fresh water line retreats west, occasionally as far as San Francisco Bay. Annual rainfall levels also affect the Delta's freshwater/saltwater balance. During the wet year of 1974, 40 million acre-feet of freshwater flowed through the Delta. In 1977, one of the driest years on record, the flow dropped to only two million.

In the last century, enormous demands have been placed on the Delta for navigable waterways, sewer drainage, and farmland reclamation behind high levees, as well as water for nearby farms, industries, cities, and more recently for transfer to the water-starved south. Despite development, enough original marshland remains to shelter migratory water birds on the Pacific Flyway, and nearly half the state's anadromous trout, salmon, and striped bass still swim up Delta streams to reach freshwater spawning grounds. Boating, fishing, hunting, and camping are also mainstays of the local economy. Like much of California, the Delta has become a land of multiple uses.

Yet the Delta is a fragile land. All the Delta's functions require a constant outpouring of fresh water from the interior to meet the irrigation, industrial, and municipal needs of local and distant people, to scour channels and prevent siltation, to cleanse waterways and maintain their oxygen levels, but most of all to keep the salty ocean from invading from the west. Fresh water flowing from the Delta also maintains the purity of Suisun Bay, the Carquinez Strait, and San Francisco Bay. Unfortunately, diversions for upstream irrigation and freshwater exports in the last century have upset the Delta's delicate balance between salt- and freshwater. The Delta and the contradictory pressures exerted upon it have become a microcosm of twentieth century and twenty-first century California water management issues.

In stark contrast to the well-watered Delta are the fierce deserts east of the Sierra Nevada and in the southeastern corner of the state. The deserts are generally flat terrain, broken occasionally by alkali sinks, seasonally dry rivers and creeks, and ranges of rocky hills and mountains. Though the deserts support only limited natural plant and animal life, at or beneath the surface lay deposits of gold, silver, copper, borax, lime, salt, and other minerals. Once supporting valuable mining industries, these resources have since been largely depleted. In a few areas, such as the Mojave and Colorado river valleys, fertile soil is deposited by modern streams; ancient rivers also carried productive soils to the Salton Sink, or Imperial Valley. Where outside water can be acquired, the desert's hot climate is ideal for growing winter fruits and vegetables, and such rare crops as dates and melons. When irrigation began in the early twentieth century, the Imperial Valley and the Coachella Valley just to the north housed richly productive croplands, as well as the only below-sea-level agricultural areas in North America.

Water, Flood, and Drought

In its capacity for influencing human settlement, the uneven distribution of water is the most significant feature of California's natural environment. Overall, water has usually been abundant in much of the state, compared to most of the Far West. From pre-contact days to the present, the generous water supply made resources rich and large human populations possible. Yet, California is still fundamentally a semi-arid region. It receives less than half the average annual rainfall of the South Atlantic and Gulf Coast states, and its mean water runoff per acre is a small fraction of that in states east of the Mississippi.

Complex drought patterns have always shaped California's human history. First, extreme seasonal rainfall variations are inherent in the state's Mediterranean climate and west-coast location. Thus, almost 80 percent of the state's rain falls between November and March. The period from May through September—the normal agricultural growing season—is virtually rainless. As a result, without human-engineered water developments, large-scale agriculture and urbanization are difficult or impossible, especially in some areas.

Extreme regional variations in rainfall also distort access to water. Northern and Southern California are fundamentally different water regions. In the north, the air is generally more humid, the storms more frequent and moisture-laden, and the mountains higher and better-positioned to capture and store water. Nearly 90 percent of California's moisture falls north of an imaginary east-west line just south of Monterey. Most often, northwesterly storms expend their moisture before they reach the southern districts, making them, climatically speaking, largely desert. Where northern California more closely resembles the rain-soaked Northwest, the southern counties are more a part of the arid Southwest. Yet, because of other resources—primarily petroleum and natural gas, generally wider coastal valleys, fertile soil, gentle winter climate, and proximity to strategic pathways to the interior—the coastal strip from Santa Barbara to San Diego proved a magnet for settlers after the 1880s. Today it houses more than half the state's population, producing a thirst for water that drastically exceeds local supplies.

Ironically, regionally and sometimes statewide, water can sometimes be too abundant. During particularly fierce winter storms, and occasionally entire years of abnormally high precipitation, far more rain falls than can be naturally absorbed, evaporated, stored, or drained. Much of California is flood-prone, particularly the Central Valley and the low-lying areas along northwestern coastal rivers and southern coastal plains. Great floods sometimes overwhelm towns, farms, mines, irrigation works, transportation lines, and humans. The epic flood of winter 1861–62, for example, turned the Central Valley into a giant lake, cutting state property values in half and touching off lethal epidemics. Sacramento, the state capitol, was hit particularly hard, its riverfront downtown inundated by more than 40 inches of rain just in late December and early January. To preserve its future, the city had to raise its levees 20 feet and its downtown land and buildings 12 to 20 feet. A 1938 Los Angeles area flood inundated 300,000 acres, destroyed $78 million in property, and killed 87 people. Heavy rains in many winters there and elsewhere, particularly 1838, 1968–1969, 1982, 1983, 1986, 1995, 1996–97, and 2016–17, unleashed massive earth slides, wiped out entire neighborhoods, killed scores of people, and made isolated islands of entire communities. In fact, Los Angeles has suffered three dozen such winter flood years over the last two centuries. Ironically, Los Angeles, though located in a semi-arid desert, is one of the most flood-endangered of major United States cities.

Nevertheless, California's prolonged, cyclical water shortages—one- to ten-year periods when northwesterly storms stay in northern latitudes and insufficient winter rain falls over part or all of the state—complicate water problems even more. Such acute, multi-year drought periods have occurred every decade or two for at least the last two centuries, often with catastrophic damage to property, crops, livestock, and human welfare, sometimes with profound historical consequences.

Strangely, for example, the great flood winter of 1861–62 was followed by nearly five years of drought, especially in southern California, bankrupting Mexican-era rancheros, speeding up their loss of livestock, land, social position, and political influence, and solidifying the state's Americanization. Even modest droughts, such as occurred recently in the mid-1970s, early-1990s, and from 2012 to 2016, have intensified squabbles over water and heightened pressures to improve water-storage and transfer facilities.

"Mega-Drought"

Many prehistoric droughts over millennia testify that California is vulnerable to even longer and more severe disruptions of its water supply. Scientific analysis of buried layers of ancient pollens and growth rings from live and dead trees, as well as relict stumps drowned under high lakes, has recorded that, for at least the last several thousand years, California and often the Southwest and beyond have experienced numerous droughts lasting many decades and as long as several centuries. One epic multi-century event in California and southwest North America began in the 800s, CE, ran for 250 years, and after a hiatus of 50 years, resumed for at least another 180 years. Over that nearly 500 year period, only one-half of the previous average precipitation fell.

Such "mega-droughts," as they are sometimes called, have been characterized by temperature increases and major dislocations to plants and animals, as well as to human societies that relied on the unstable resource base. Water courses diminished or dried up altogether, grasses withered away, plants and trees produced fewer seeds, and plant and animal communities died off or migrated to higher, cooler, better-watered, often more northerly refuges. The changing environment forced Indigenous peoples to shift to lower-quality foods or to relocate closer to more stable ecosystems, particularly toward the coast, whose tidal and deep waters sheltered more reliable food supplies. Entire cultures declined in population and splintered into smaller family-oriented groups, now forced to fend for themselves and wander in search of new, livable homelands. Increased violence erupted between hitherto isolated settled groups now competing for the same shrinking resource base.

Drastic natural and human changes driven by mega-droughts are recorded in the archeological record, pictorial writing, legends, oral traditions, and the historical spread of language dialects. Some scholars of Aztec history, for example, have theorized that long-term drought in the 1200s, CE, forced many in the culture to abandon a drying lake in southeastern California (perhaps an ancient lake formed by the Colorado River's terminating in the Salton Sink), and to wander across the Southwest for decades before settling on another giant lake in central Mexico. Other scholars maintain that the same mega-drought dispersed the urbanized Anasazi cliff-dwellers in the Southwest, as well as the far-away Maya of Central America.

Conversely, from the fifteenth century to about 1850, California and much of North America experienced another period of cool, moist weather known as the "Little Ice Age." Thus, in the centuries since the 1500s, while human population and water developments have been growing ever larger, California has received significantly more precipitation than had been true for thousands of years before, with the last century among the wettest in the last 7,000 years. Clearly, over the historical millennia, California cannot be said to have any dependable "average" rainfall, thus any long-term, reliable water supply, even though ever-larger numbers of people have come to depend on it.

Water Development

Since the population spurts of the 1880s, agricultural, industrial, and urban development have necessitated construction of ever-more elaborate facilities for water impoundment, storage, control, and transfer. Indeed, in recent years, questions of California water redistribution have shaped regional, state, and even national politics. During the last hundred years, California farmers, who consume about 80 percent of the state's water supplies, sank wells, built dams and canals, and transferred water—sometimes over hundreds of miles—to irrigate their crops. Cities, too, have reached far: in the early twentieth century, the burgeoning communities of the San Francisco Bay Area reached out 100 miles east to grasp the watersheds of the central Sierra Nevada (including Hetch Hetchy Valley in Yosemite National Park), damming its rivers, and re-routing water supplies via canal and conduit. Simultaneously, booming Los Angeles looked 200 miles north to the eastern Sierra's Owens River Valley, acquired its water rights and, despite opposition by the valley's farmers and townspeople, imported virtually its entire river, tributaries, and groundwater by aqueduct. When severe drought returned in the 1920s, southern cities again looked outward, this time challenging six states to import the silty waters of the Colorado River. Development in post-1940s southern California consumed even these supplies, prompting southerners to turn to state and federal agencies for help in tapping northern watersheds in the Delta, through the southern San Joaquin Valley and over the Tehachapis. South-state water visionaries have hatched yet more ambitious future contingency plans to import water from as far away as the Mississippi Valley, Great Lakes, and Canada's Yukon River.

By the 1980s, the California water-distribution system had evolved into a maze of dams, canals, reservoirs, pipelines, pumping plants, underground storage basins, and flood-control systems. Except for a handful of "wild" north-coast rivers, virtually every major stream from Mexico to Oregon was reduced to an artificial, human-managed waterway, broken by reservoirs, pumping stations, and hydroelectric generation facilities, or forced into earthen, rock, or concrete channels. In some cases, the flow of rivers has actually been forced underground or reversed, moving water in directions nature never intended. The California water system ranks among the greatest accomplishments of human intelligence, organization, and technology, but the achievement is fraught with collateral environmental damage and potential for human dislocation and controversy.

Complex water development shapes California's history and future in countless ways. In the process of encouraging economic and population growth in some areas, large-scale water transfers have also made economic development expensive, limited the growth of areas losing water, aggravated environmental problems at points of origin as well as delivery, and provoked disagreements between urban and rural areas, as well as among the state's regions, other states, and the federal government. Water development has shaped even the state's institutional structure: building and managing such massive systems has produced a seemingly impenetrable labyrinth of contradictory water laws and overlapping water agencies, and has increased the power of state and federal government to regulate vital local interests. The great expense of irrigation and land reclamation has tended to favor larger over smaller farms, wealthier growers above poorer ones, and commercial and specialized interests over those preferring localized, diversified production. In the last century, water has become California's major political, economic, and ideological battleground. Historian Donald Worster has described California as a classic "hydraulic" civilization, like ancient Mesopotamia and Egypt—centralized, hierarchical, dependent on its water facilities, and vulnerable to severe disorder should they collapse. In light of the western region's history of severe mega-drought, that dependence on artificial water systems has become even more tenuous. "We continue to run California as if the longest drought we are ever going to encounter is about seven years," has warned pioneering historical climate scientist and California State University East Bay geographer Scott Stine. "We are living in a dream world."

Environment and History

California's natural environment so dramatically differs from that of the rest of North America that observers often rely on it to explain the state's distinctive history. But several widely shared fallacies about the interaction of environment and history have clouded even scholarly perceptions. Popular and professional writers commonly celebrate the legacy of California's environment as if it were uniformly positive. Like Garcí Ordoñez de Montalvo, many describe California as "very close to . . . the Terrestrial Paradise," or as the State Department of Parks put it, a "land blessed by nature." Topography, climate, and location are frequently offered as the most powerful forces shaping the state's development, responsible for everything from moral values and religious beliefs to land-tenure patterns, from politics and literature to architecture and clothing styles.

This distinctive natural environment influenced pliable human cultures, some have asserted, and caused California to develop values and ways of life as unique as its plant forms. "The regional consciousness of California," wrote geographer James Parsons decades ago, "has had its origins in the common problems and interests imposed by geography." Isolation and climate, he maintained, "strongly influenced the settlement history of the state and the character of its economy and culture." Geography, Parsons concluded, "has had obvious and far-reaching importance for agriculture, industry, and the entire mode of life within the state . . . [and] helps account for whatever quality of regional identity, of uniqueness, that here exists."

Such theories contain kernels of truth. Certainly environment has influenced the state's history. Nature provided a general framework, creating potentials and limitations and opening directions for human activities. Because the area's resources are abundant and diverse, California has nurtured populous, complex, and successful civilizations for thousands of years. Without modifying their environments to any extreme degree, early peoples hunted and gathered abundant natural resources, living more affluently than many Native groups elsewhere. In the past 200 years, later waves of immigrants imported or created technologies and organizations to harvest these and other resources—land, harbors, grass, animals, minerals, timber, water,

The San Andreas Fault at the Edge of the Carrizo Plain
In this view looking south along the San Andreas Fault in the Carrizo Plain area, between Bakersfield and San Luis Obispo, offset streambeds illustrate the northward drift of the western (Pacific) plate. At this point along California's major fault line, single earthquakes have been known to cause the ground to leap as much as 30 feet laterally in only a few seconds, sending out destructive shock waves for hundreds of miles. *Robert Wallace/ U.S. Geological Survey.*

petroleum and natural gas—even more efficiently and profitably. Each resource has given birth to thriving industries and settlements. On the basis of a prolific and distinctive natural endowment, by the twenty-first century, Californians have built their state into the most populous, diverse, productive, and wealthiest region in the Americas. Many would agree that California's history is largely a success story, a testimonial to the capacity of human intelligence to exploit nature's benevolence.

But the geographical-determinist interpretation of California's past and present, however tempting, is problematic. It encourages subscribers to believe that social and economic conditions in California are basically "natural," and therefore inevitable and immutable, blinding them to the existence of real problems, and paralyzing the development of alternative public policies.

Although it is remarkable, California is not a paradise on earth. Nature places severe limits on the aspirations of Californians, generates many of their thorniest problems, and periodically undoes much of their handiwork. In an earlier era, nature furnished bountiful foods for Indians in their island world, willing as they were to spread their populations thin, adapt to conditions as they found them, and to be content with a subsistence economy. For those who would follow, however, the land raised substantial obstacles. Geographical isolation imposed by mountains, deserts, winds, and ocean currents complicated exploration, delayed settlement and development of resources, undermined administration, and retarded the establishment of outside markets for the region's products. Diverse climates and resources, in tandem with internal natural barriers, bred local economies and communities with divergent interests, interrupted communication, and wracked the state with interregional conflicts. Internal secessionist movements, for example, have plagued California more than any other state.

Although usually present in sufficient quantity, the region's resources have proven difficult to exploit. This is especially true of water. Invariably, modern people have wanted to live and work in places where water is in short supply. Imbalances between water supply and human demands have made both agriculture and industry riskier. Like the state's minerals, forests, and soils, water could be used only with technologies that inflicted great environmental damage. Massive relocation of water has destroyed some thriving natural communities, polluted others, poisoned soils, overwhelmed drainage systems, and caused land to sink permanently. These and many other problems caused by environmental manipulation are complex and difficult to resolve, and they jeopardize present and future prosperity.

California's environmental balances are fragile and easily upset, but even the land itself is threatening. It is still under construction and ever-changing, wielding natural forces that remain potent, unpredictable, and perhaps less reliable in the future. The region is more prone than others to natural calamity—earthquakes, droughts, floods, volcanic eruptions, wild-lands fires, and tidal waves. If Californians have been blessed by nature, they have also been cursed.

Nature alone, moreover, cannot sufficiently explain California's human history. Lines of cultural development were not predetermined by natural conditions. Nature offered many alternatives. In all periods, there was wide latitude for Californians to shape their own destinies, through individual and social choices based on values, institutions, technologies, and economic preferences. In fact, successive groups of Californians, for good or ill, have drawn on their cultures to modify the environment according to their needs, a phenomenon that has grown apace with technological development. If there were to be a single interpretation of the state's long and contradictory history, it would not be the power of nature to mold a distinctive, indigenous culture, but rather the expanding ability of humans, for good or ill, to impose their culture on the environment.

By overplaying the supremacy of nature and underplaying the resilience of culture, geographical determinists consistently exaggerate California's separateness. Often asserted but rarely proven, "uniqueness" has become an assumed California attribute. Although the region may be legitimately considered "a land apart," California's peoples at most times and in most important ways have resembled and reproduced the larger cultures to which they belonged. The state's first peoples, whose societies evolved here over thousands of years and who came closest to living the geographic determinist model, closely resembled other hunter-gatherer societies, especially other western groups. Yet, as agriculturalists and controlled burners, even they exerted a measure of control and modified their environments. After 1769, Hispanic California was but one segment of a long colonial frontier stretching across northern Mexico, sharing in broader Spanish colonial goals regarding culture, economy, and institutions. Similarly, following American conquest in the 1840s, California's rapid development and modernization is best understood in terms of that nation's culture, not as a radical departure from it.

California Before Europeans Came

The California of today little resembles the pre-European natural world. The plants, the animals, the climate, the people, and even the shape of the land have all radically changed. California now is the farm, the strip mine, the clear-cut forest, the reservoir, the suburb, the business park, the freeway, the parking lot, the information infrastructure. But before Spaniards began colonizing in 1769, a scant four or five human lifetimes ago, California's rivers ran freely to the ocean. Valleys and hills were studded with oak groves and carpeted with chest-high bunch grasses that, for the most part, no longer survive. Millions of acres of fresh- and salt-water marshes bordered rivers and bays, particularly in the Delta. Large bodies of water such as Tulare Lake, then second in size only to Lake Tahoe, dotted the San

Joaquin and other valleys. Their bottoms now pumped dry by water diversions, old lakebeds raise alfalfa and cotton. Redwood forests covered the western slopes of the Coast Range north of Big Sur, including many of the hills ringing San Francisco Bay. More than 90 percent of these virgin groves have since been cut down. Whales, seals, and otters shared the sites of present-day seaports with hundreds of millions of gulls, egrets, herons, pelicans, and migratory waterfowl. Condors and eagles ruled the sky.

Grizzlies, not humans, sat at the top of the food chain. Ten thousand of the aggressive, powerful bears roamed California in packs. They ate meat from beached whales, salmon from the rivers, and acorns from the oak trees. Fearing no other beasts, they intimidated mountain lions and humans into surrendering their kills. Webs of grizzly trails crisscrossed the state, intersecting human pathways, but Indians wisely avoided them. The world was different then, as was the place of humans in it.

3

The *Native Peoples*

The "Digger" Stereotype

F ew modern Californians know much about the state's original residents. What is commonly known is often tainted by racial bias and misconception. When Anglo-Americans first encountered Great Basin and California Native Americans in the mid-nineteenth century, they derisively called them "Diggers," a reflection of the animosity Americans felt toward all Indians. The "Digger" label and the unfavorable stereotypes associated with it became ingrained in pioneer culture. William Halley, a nineteenth-century historian, spoke for most of his generation when he condemned the California Indian as "one of the most degraded of God's creatures . . . , [who] was without knowledge, religion or morals . . . lived without labor, and enjoyed all the ease and pleasure he could. . . . In so genial a climate as ours, nature easily provided for all his wants." Such negative stereotypes salved the consciences of nineteenth-century pioneers as they murdered California's Indigenous peoples, stole their land, destroyed their cultures, enslaved their children, and confined the survivors to barren reservations.

Unfortunately, pioneers' misperceptions regarding California's original peoples have continued to influence popular attitudes, as well as those of some later historians. Many observers persist in seeing them as the most primitive of North American Indians, devoid of culture, and less evolved than the agriculturalists of the Southwest or the mounted warriors of the Great Plains. This lack of respect explains why Native cemeteries have been desecrated and converted into parking lots, ancient village shell mounds excavated and used to pave streets, priceless archaeological sites plundered and vandalized, and unique rock carvings and paintings defaced with graffiti. Until recently, many historical restorations and published popular works, including public school textbooks, ignored

25

or trivialized California's early peoples, depicting them with such loaded adjectives as "prehistoric," "primitive," "savage," and "Stone Age." More importantly, these treatments dismiss Indians as quaint oddities irrelevant to the flow of California history.

In recent decades, however, anthropologists have developed more sophisticated theories and methods for understanding Indigenous peoples. They have amassed new archeological evidence with new methods, analyzed oral traditions among surviving individuals, and read historical documents objectively. California's Indians are now among the best studied and discussed Native Americans in the world. Alfred L. Kroeber, Robert F. Heizer, Lowell J. Bean, Michael J. Moratto, and others have demonstrated that the early people's cultures were complex and dynamic. Before and since the invasions of Spaniards, Mexicans, and Americans, California's first residents and their descendants have shaped California's land and history.

Native Origins, Languages, and Populations

California's Indians have been popularly viewed as static remnants of ancient Stone-Age peoples. Nothing could be further from the truth. Although the pace of change was relatively slow, local cultures changed and adapted to shifting social and ecological conditions, both before and after strangers arrived in their lands.

Sometime between 50,000 and 15,000 BCE, human groups began to migrate eastward across the Bering Strait between Asia and North America, where the Ice Age had opened a dry land route. Migrating quickly southward in pursuit of large, now-extinct game animals such as the bison, mammoth, and giant sloth, the newcomers had penetrated most of North and South America by 12,000 BCE. By the beginning of the Holocene, or "Human" era, roughly 10,000 BCE, offshoots of these original peoples had made their way to California. Living in small nomadic groups, they hunted large game with spears, sharing a common nomadic lifestyle and a limited material culture.

Between 15,000 and 10,000 BCE, the Ice Age ended. Temperatures rose, rainfall decreased, lush vegetation receded, and huge game animals died out. Humans adapted successfully to the changing California environment, and over the centuries their economies expanded to include hunting small and large animals, fishing, and harvesting wild plants. With more diverse and stable food supplies, Native populations grew. They settled in villages, adapted to their varying ecosystems,

Tattooed Yuki Indian

The first systematic attempt to gather information about the California Indians was made by Stephen Powers in *Tribes of California* (1877). This is one of the volume's many vivid illustrations of Native life at a time when it was rapidly disappearing. From Stephen Powers, *Tribes of California*, Washington, D.C. Government Printing Office, 1877.

and developed more elaborate arts, religions, and social systems. By 1000 BCE, complex cultures similar to those that European explorers encountered after 1542 were firmly established. Over thousands of years, California's original settlers had transformed themselves from nomadic hunters into one of the most complex hunter-gatherer civilizations in human history.

California was originally settled by fragments of many North American cultural groups. Each adjusted to sharply different climates and resources and thus developed distinctive local and regional cultures. Natural barriers, the difficulty of travel, and limited contact with outside cultures reinforced these local differences. By the onset of European colonization, California Indians had divided and subdivided into many small, independent groups. More than 100 different tribes had emerged, each with distinctive economies, technology, arts, religion, and social systems. They spoke between 64 and 80 different languages deriving from most of the major North American language families. Hundreds of local dialects made them virtually unintelligible to others, even those speaking the same basic language. For its diversity of language and culture, California was unmatched in all of North America.

Also unmatched was California's population. Demographers estimate that, on the eve of European contact, between 300,000 and one million individuals inhabited California. Population was sparse and scattered in most desert and mountain environments, but dense among valley and coastal tribes. Yokuts of San Joaquin Valley and Santa Barbara's Chumash lived in communities in excess of 1,000 individuals, with densities of ten to 20 persons per square mile.

The size and density of California populations refutes early European claims of bringing civilization to a vast, unused wilderness. With an average of one-half person per square mile, California was one of the most densely populated regions north of Mexico. At a fundamental level, the European colonization of California was less a conquest of land than it was of peoples.

Economy: Foods

California's flourishing population was made possible by a relatively reliable resource base. Most of the small groups practiced a subsistence economy based on hunting and gathering. Blinded by cultural biases, early Europeans saw the absence of agriculture as a sign of racial inferiority. Early Californians, outsiders assumed, were so primitive and unintelligent that they could not grow their own food, as their neighbors to the southeast did. Instead, the Californians were lazy, just wandering about aimlessly, picking up whatever food nature happened to provide.

In reality, local weather patterns would have made agriculture difficult. The hunting-and-gathering economies that flourished in the drought-prone region were entirely rational. For many groups, hunting and gathering yielded a greater, more dependable standard of living than would have been possible with farming. Native peoples harvested hundreds of varieties of plants, animals, and minerals, their staple foods varying from group to group according to local resources and shifting water supply. Most groups lived where they had access to water, fuel, and several different ecosystems, which usually ensured variety as well as abundance, and they moved when resources failed to support them.

A region with such varied resources as California naturally gave birth to very different cultures. There were numerous "ecological types" of Indian cultures, which are classified according to the ways they exploited California's local climates, topographies, and flora and

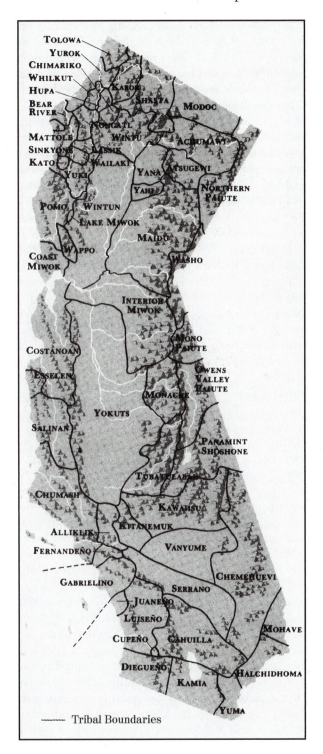

California Indian Tribal Boundaries

Tribes of California drawn by A. L. Kroeber. Reprinted in Robert F. Heizer and Albert B. Elsasser, *The Natural World of the California Indians* (Berkeley: University of California Press, 1980), p. 5.

fauna: coastal tideland collectors; sea hunters and fishers; riverine fishers; lakeshore fishers, hunters, and gatherers; valley and plains gatherers; foothill hunters and gatherers; desert hunters and collectors; and desert agriculturists. Some language groups included several of these ecological types.

Even Indians who organized their lifeways around a specific resource—water, for example—developed cultures that distinguished them from other water-dependent groups. With buoyant tule canoes, the Costanoan, or Ohlone, gathered shellfish and other salt-marsh foods in tidelands along Monterey and San Francisco bays. The Chumash invented long ocean-going plank canoes, and harvested fish, seals, sea otter, and beached whales along the coast, offshore islands, and in the kelp beds of the Santa Barbara Channel. The affluent Chumash built large, well-ordered towns, and made sophisticated baskets, jewelry, stone sculptures, and pictographs. Locating their villages along the rivers of the northern coast, the Yurok and Karok preyed on the salmon as it swam to and from its upstream spawning grounds. On elevated riverbanks in the northern San Joaquin Valley, the Yokuts enjoyed river salmon and fine oak groves, an abundant source of acorns and other foods. They established large villages and a social order that nearly rivaled that of the prosperous Chumash.

Different cultures arose from still other resource bases. In the Sierra Nevada, the Miwok relied on pine nuts; in southern deserts, the Cahuilla harvested the mesquite and screw bean. In especially harsh environments, groups such as the Yuma and Mohave of the Colorado River, the Cahuilla of the Palm Springs area, and the Paiute of the Owens Valley developed agriculture.

California offered a broad array of vegetable staples, including seeds, nuts, roots, stems, and leaves from a multitude of grasses, shrubs, and trees. Like acorns, these products often required special processing. With ingenious snares, weapons, decoys, and trickery, Indigenous peoples also hunted rodents, reptiles, birds, deer and elk, and insects. Only the powerful grizzly, the Indians' major foraging competitor, and some sacred animals such as the coyote, managed to avoid cooking baskets.

But California was not the earthly paradise early experts once assumed. Alfred Kroeber and others attributed early Californians' apparent lack of agriculture, monumental architecture, or complex sociopolitical organization to the region's mild climate and rich plant and animal resources. Abundance, they theorized, made life "too easy" for early peoples, resulting in only rudimentary levels of cultural development. In the late twentieth century, a new generation of anthropologists

rejected Kroeber's environmental determinism. Responding to the growing field of ecology, R. L. Kelly and others argued instead that hunter-gatherers were more intimately connected to the natural world than the residents of modern urban-industrial societies, attaining relative abundance by understanding and living harmoniously with nature, while also modifying it when needing to.

New archaeological tools, including radio-carbon dating, have helped to reframe the debate yet further, by calling two long-standing assumptions about California Native Americans into question. First, California's famously benign climate failed periodically, especially during the great mega-drought, roughly 800 to 1350 CE. Rising temperatures and prolonged drought produced an environmental disaster for many foraging and farming California groups. Archaeological evidence demonstrates that temperature and rainfall fluctuations undercut food sources in many areas, forcing people to abandon once-productive regions, which in turn disrupted long-standing trade and cultural relationships and increased inter-personal and inter-group violence.

Second, California Indians may have been somewhat less eco-friendly than previously imagined. In the San Francisco Bay Area, for example, hunters appear to have over-hunted large, hoofed grazers such as deer, elk, and bighorn sheep, whose numbers dropped over time compared to smaller game. Studies of sea-mammal remains along the Oregon and California coasts similarly reveal that large, land-breeding species also diminished slowly, leading hunters to shift to smaller, more elusive aquatic-breeding varieties, and as well as to move elsewhere. In many areas, after generations in one place, growing villages had to move because they had exhausted easily gathered resources, including local wood for fuel and construction, and middens (trash mounds) were clogging their sites.

Oral traditions among Indigenous Californians confirm that periods of extreme drought and poor hunting brought about social disruption. For example, Maria Oscarpia (Salinan) told an ethnographer in 1918 that her people recalled a great famine, when

> there was no rain and no food. They ate bleached bones pounded in the mortar, and acorn mush made of manzanitas. There were no deer and no meat. . . . One old woman killed and roasted and ate her son. . . . Then her brother came and killed her with three arrows because she had eaten her child. . . . But the people who lived on the shore did not die because they ate abalones. But even they were thin. . . .

Indians Hunting Near San Francisco Bay
Visiting artist Louis Choris depicted hunters belonging to San Francisco Bay or San Joaquin Valley tribes in 1816. Strong and flexible, Indian bows were constructed especially for hunting small game at short or medium distances. Bowmen took great pride in their skills. *The Huntington Library, San Marino, California.*

One truth remains clear: the human landscape of Native California was anything but static and placid.

Switching to the acorn as a more reliable food staple was but one of many examples of human adaptability in overcoming resource shortages. Prolific over many local climatic regions, California's 15 native species of oak offered an abundant supply of fall acorns. Households or kin groups usually cooperated to harvest acorns in oak groves near or distant from their camps, knocking nuts from the trees or collecting those already fallen. One tree might provide 55 pounds of acorns for one day's labor. In nine to ten days, an individual could gather a year's supply of acorns, roughly 500 pounds per person. Relatively non-perishable, dry acorns could be stored for up to two years, providing some insurance against scant rain and other calamities.

When the acorns were needed, women husked and ground them in mortars to produce a fine meal. Grinding was time-consuming, perhaps as much as three hours for six pounds of finished meal. The meal was spread out in lined earthen pits, or layered in finely sewn baskets, then washed with both warm and cold water to leach out toxins. The water had to be heated by placing hot stones in baskets of water, adding to the already-difficult task. When finished, the meal could be consumed as mush, baked into cakes, or added to other foods.

Scholars have long assumed that acorn consumption was widespread and longstanding in some regions, beginning perhaps as early as 5000 BCE. But more recent analysis and dating of grinding tools excavated in ancient middens, suggests that intensive acorn use for some groups was more recent cultural adaptation,

Women Processing Acorns in the Sacramento Valley, ca. 1840

Acorn processing was a constant task for tribeswomen with oak groves in their territories. Along with other strenuous female responsibilities, this practice led early American observers to jump to the false conclusion that Indian women were oppressed by their men. "On the women, all the drudgery seems to be thrown," observed Charles Wilkes, the American military officer in charge of the expedition that produced this illustration. Actually, all tribal members worked hard for the welfare of the group, and responsibility for acorn processing and plant gathering, vital to tribal survival, earned women respect and status within Indian communities. Illustration from Charles Wilkes, *Narrative of the United States Exploring Expedition during the Years 1838, 1839, 1840, 1841, and 1842* (1845). *Courtesy of the California History Room, California State Library, Sacramento, California.*

rather than traditional over thousands of years. Moreover, these acorn economies appeared at different times in different regions—around 4000 BCE in the San Francisco Bay area, 2800 BCE in the Central Valley and Delta, and 1000 BCE in the central and southern Sierra Nevada. The slow adoption of acorn processing technologies suggests that Californians originally preferred other foods, presumably those requiring less effort. A combination of factors, including environmental changes, a shrinking resource base, population growth, migration, and spreading culture might explain the later adoption of the acorn as a food staple.

Economy: Industry and Trade

California's regions offered varied local surpluses and shortages of foods and raw materials. As groups grew in population and complexity, some individuals began to specialize in harvesting and processing surplus items and trading for other necessities among themselves and with outsiders. Some mined for rare minerals such as volcanic black obsidian, a valuable trade commodity ideal for arrow and spear points, cutting edges, and scraping tools. Others quarried granite for mortars and the softer steatite to be carved into bowls and sculpted figures. Salt was another valuable commodity, harvested for seasoning and preserving, as was tar for caulking and gluing, and shells for jewelry or currency. The Costanoan cinnabar mine near New Almaden was one of the region's largest and most organized Indian mining operations, producing a brilliant red pigment prized and exchanged throughout western North America. Other artisans—sometimes entire tribes—specialized in manufacturing goods, everything from redwood dugout canoes and arrows, to tools, shell money, and baskets. Emerging thousands of years ago, these forms of industry and commerce expanded in production and geographic outreach with each passing century.

Elaborate systems developed to organize and regulate the specialized economies, complete with fairs, treaties, merchant classes, regional marketing centers, trade organizations, and fixed-value currencies. Trade linked tribes of various environments, languages, and cultures in networks that stretched inland from the coast, sometimes far beyond California's current borders. Expanding industry and commerce broadened each tribe's resource base, produced a higher and more secure standard of living, and promoted cultural change and diversity within tribes. By spreading resources (especially in times of shortage) trade networks served to increase security, to encourage coexistence among groups of different cultures, and thereby to reduce intertribal conflict.

Plentiful and varied foods, temperate climate, and trade made the early Californians prosperous compared to many hunter-gatherer societies elsewhere. Contrary to perceptions of white pioneers who did not understand their economies, Native peoples had a well-developed work ethic. While labor was rarely grueling, it was constant and carefully planned. Drudgery was lightened because men, women, and children often worked in groups, with plenty of lively music and gossip. Except in times of extreme environmental collapse, their diets were relatively dependable, varied, and high in protein and vitamins. It was probably nutritionally superior to that of the average European at the time of colonization, and certainly superior to the diet of Indians living in the Spanish missions of the eighteenth and nineteenth centuries.

Science, Ecology, and Agriculture

The hunter-gatherer cultures that Europeans first encountered in sixteenth-century California flourished through human skill and resourcefulness. Over many centuries, early peoples experimented with animals, plants, and minerals, developing tools that allowed their efficient use. Lacking written languages and books, they collected the ancestral knowledge of their families and tribes, built on it, and transmitted it orally to succeeding generations. Eventually, Indians evolved an understanding of their immediate world that was as sophisticated as that of most Europeans in the era of colonization, if not more so.

Native Californians classified plants and animals into categories similar to those of modern botany and zoology. They learned the habits of creatures, discovered food chains and other relationships among living beings, and perceived the environmental factors that caused organisms to thrive or decline. Methodically,

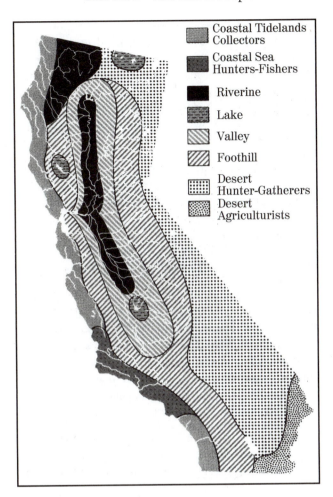

Indian Ecological Zones

From Robert F. Heizer and Albert B. Elsasser, *The Natural World of the California Indians* (Berkeley: University of California Press, 1980), p. 60.

they also followed the celestial movements of the planets and stars as part of their religious rites. The Chumash and others built observatories and marked and predicted the summer solstice, allowing them to keep track of the seasons.

Like other North American groups, early Californians detected and exploited the chemical properties of certain plants, extracting medicines from seeds, roots, bark, and leaves that relieved pain, battled infection, and promoted healing. In the process, early residents discovered many of the chemical agents that are now the basis of modern medicines. Natives also set broken bones, performed surgeries, and practiced basic psychotherapy. Throughout the region, shamans served as religious specialists who used medicines and magic to heal sickness and deflect evil spirits. Given the superstition, brutality, and quackery that dominated contemporary European medicine, the medical practices of early Californians were at least as effective as those of their conquerors. Indeed, Spanish and later Mexican settlers often sought cures for their illnesses and injuries from Native American healers.

Early Californians did not simply react passively to their environment. They applied their acquired knowledge to reshape nature and increase its harvest. To ease the intense labor of gathering, they sowed wild seeds and transplanted wild plants closer to their villages for ready access to materials used for food, rituals, healing, or basket making. To increase the productivity of oak, mesquite, and other trees and shrubs, they pruned away dead and nonbearing branches, thinning for optimum exposure to water, sunlight, and nutrients.

The major environmental manipulation was controlled burning. After observing that natural fires reduced underbrush, attracted game, and made valuable seed grasses lusher the following year, Indians began systematically burning valleys, foothills, and mountain meadows in the autumn or spring. Over the centuries, regular human-set fires dramatically reshaped the flora and fauna of heavily settled regions, maximizing grasslands and the growth of pines, acorn-bearing oaks, and other large trees, increasing the population of grazers, driving back chaparral, and investing the landscape with the tended, park-like quality that amazed early explorers. Over wide stretches of more populated areas, Native burning established the distribution, populations, and relationships of plants, and some animals, that early European settlers mistook for "natural." Modern experts have only recently rediscovered Indigenous methods of controlled burning for forest and grasslands management.

Where naturally occurring foods were deficient, some desert groups devised forms of agriculture suited to their particular environments. Southeastern Yuma, Mohave, and Halchidhoma desert-dwellers practiced floodplain farming, a system they adapted from the irrigation methods of agriculturalists farther east. In the fertile mud left by the annual spring flooding of the Colorado River, they planted maize, beans, pumpkins, and calabashes. In later centuries, they added a few European imports such as watermelon, oats, and wheat, whose seeds they received in trade from post-contact Mexican Native peoples. The Cahuilla of the Salton Sink cultivated the damp soils found along streambeds, in the marshy areas surrounding natural oases, and wherever the underground water table came close to the surface. They sometimes dug wells or carried water

by hand to their thirsty crops. Preserved by the desert's desiccating heat, farm produce furnished nearly half of the food resources required by desert peoples.

The Owens Valley Paiute built the largest true irrigation works in the region. They dammed the streams flowing down the steep eastern face of the Sierra Nevada, dug grids of large canals, and irrigated wild grasses and tubers in fields that were sometimes several square miles in size. The Tipai and Ipai east of San Diego and a few other groups likely farmed as well. Most of Native California was probably familiar with agriculture through trade, observation, or communication with outsiders, but saw no need to adopt the practice. For most, hunting and gathering produced equally reliable lifeways.

Religion

Religion combined with economic necessity to reinforce ecological values. To early Californians, the close interaction of humans and environment was the scientific and spiritual theme. Appreciating their dependence on the natural world, Indians saw themselves as an integral part of it. Respect for nature permeated lifeways, economy, philosophy, and religion.

Like practically everything else, beliefs and rites differed greatly from group to group. Some tribes were monotheistic, believing in a single great deity that presided over all creation. Most groups, however, believed in spirits embodied in animals, places, and natural processes. Spirits, in turn, controlled the resources on which humans depended. To survive in such an animistic universe, early Californians took pains to appease the spirits, especially those thought to resent the misuse of plants, animals, and other valuable resources. All important human events—birth, puberty, marriage, sex, childbearing, hunting, gathering, sickness, and death—required certain rituals, offerings to the spirits by shamans and others to regulate the natural and supernatural world. Specific observances varied, of course, from the unadorned individual and family rituals of the semi-nomadic tribes to the complex, well-attended ceremonies of more settled groups.

Rituals, and even entire religious complexes, were based on environmental imperatives. Early Californians avoided overtaxing the carrying capacity of their territories by limiting population through marriage customs, sexual taboos, continence, abortion, and chemical contraceptives derived from plants to control conception. Yurok and Karok rites and inter-group treaties discouraged overfishing of the salmon and contamination of the rivers on which they depended. The World Renewal ceremony of the northwestern salmon-fishing groups, the major annual religious gathering of riverside villages, redistributed resources to poorer tribal members. In the process, these ceremonies appeased supernatural forces in order to avert floods, earthquakes, and failure of the salmon run. Similar in intent was the elaborate yearly dance of the Kuksu Cult among the Pomo, Patwin, and Maidu. By countless simpler tribal and personal rituals, across California people expressed kinship with plants and animals, thanked spirits for past favors, and taught the respectful and orderly behavior deemed necessary for successful hunting, fishing, and gathering.

Earlier Californians had established the values and practices of environmental management long before Europeans began their conquest. As a result, dense populations had inhabited the region for millennia without substantially polluting soil and water, or annihilating entire plant and animal species. When the invaders arrived, California Native Americans were forced to relinquish a modified, but largely unspoiled land.

Politics and Society

For ecological, linguistic, and historical reasons, California Indians generally organized themselves into small political units. Many small offshoots of distinct language groups originally had settled the region and specialized further as different groups adapted to their local ecosystems. Geographical barriers isolated tribelets, and local food resources were usually insufficient to sustain large population concentrations. Oceans, mountains, and deserts insulated Californians from outside invaders who might have forced them to unite in their own defense.

Over much of the region, the word "tribe" itself must be applied with caution. Large groups of people with a related language and culture did inhabit a general area, but with little overall social or political organization, or even consciousness of a common identity. Across most of these broader cultural groupings, land ownership, sovereignty, and cohesive action resided in small, independent groups that have come to be called "tribelets." Tribelets numbered from as few as 100 to as many as several thousand related persons, living in small groups of one or two camps or a dozen or more villages. Tribelet territories ranged from 50 square miles in relatively rich environments, to upwards of 6,000 square miles in barren ones. The Yokuts, for example, numbered at

least 25,000 persons and occupied 22,000 square miles of the San Joaquin Valley, but they were divided into more than 60 autonomous tribelets. Tribelets developed local economies, dialects, and religious practices that were variants of their larger tribal cultures.

A formal authority structure bound the people of a tribelet together. Usually inheriting their position within elite families, chiefs presided—assisted by family and ritual leaders—over the harvesting, storage, and exchange of resources. Their considerable power derived from their wealth, prestige, and ability to persuade, as well as the tradition of community consensus. Usually second in power to the chiefs, shamans served as the principal religious and medical authorities, and advised chiefs and family heads. Occasionally, women served as shamans, especially among the northwest and north-central tribes. More rarely, as among the Pomo, Chumash, and Miwok, women could be property owners and co-chiefs.

Most groups were relatively affluent, avoiding violent conflict through frequent trade, intermarriage, and mediation. Nevertheless, all tribes maintained military organization to defend against encroachment. Armed conflict did sometimes erupt when outsiders stole property, attacked villages and travelers, murdered or practiced witchcraft against family members, or trespassed on prized hunting and gathering grounds. If peaceful resolution of grievances failed, warfare was the only means of compensation or revenge. Actual fighting, while sometimes vicious, was usually spontaneous and limited in scale. In the absence of large-scale military cooperation, conflicts rarely spread beyond a few villages. Occasionally, one group conquered another or subjected it to imperial tribute. The Mohave and the Yuma of the Colorado River, large and highly organized tribes, had the strongest tradition of militarism. These groups supported a class of professional warriors, boys reared from an early age in the skills of combat. Wars were typically waged to acquire and defend rich agricultural land, or simply for pleasure and glory. Influenced by the Colorado cultures, the Ipai and Tipai of the San Diego area were also particularly aggressive in protecting their borders against intruders, as early Spanish explorers and missionaries would discover.

Although few pioneer Europeans and Americans recognized its diversity, Native California was culturally complex and highly differentiated. The basic unit of southern and south central tribes, which delimited personal behavior and located the individual in the larger society, was the *lineage*, a large extended family of persons related to one another, usually, though not always, through the male line. Several related lineages constituted a *clan*. Clans and lineages were structured and exerted great influence over members. In contrast, throughout most of northern and central California, membership in the community derived from simple residence, not lineage.

Families differed sharply in status and wealth, and individuals' places in the tribelet were usually marked from birth by their family. Generally, California families were divided into four classes: elites, commoners, vagabonds, and slaves. A small minority of elite families controlled property, trade, the observance of ritual, as well as the means of production, such as the best oak groves, fishing spots, and, in the case of the Chumash, the oceangoing boats that were essential to

a marine economy. Elites also furnished the important figures of the tribe: chiefs, diplomats, shamans, merchants, and craftsmen.

Most commoners were less affluent, traveled less, and spent most of their time in subsistence activities. Commoners supported elites through labor, taxes, fees, and gifts. In some areas, a small number of vagabonds lived on the fringes of legitimate society. Vagabonds were sometimes absorbed into tribes, where they started lower-status families. A few tribes also kept slaves, often war captives who were held for ransom or eventually assimilated into the victorious tribe.

California Indian societies were not democratic or egalitarian by modern standards. Individuals inherited

Indian Village Scenes

Differences in local climate and building materials contributed to variations in Indian architecture: (*upper left*) tule-thatch Yokuts houses protected from the hot San Joaquin Valley sun by a shade; (*upper right*) earth-covered Maidu lodges in the equally hot Sacramento Valley; (*lower left*) Miwok bark-slab lodge, Yosemite Valley; (*lower right*) Sierra Nevada bark-slab community house. From Stephen Powers, *Tribes of California*, Washington, D.C. Government Printing Office, 1877.

unequal status, duties, and privileges from their ancestors. Most enjoyed only a slight opportunity for upward mobility, either through hard work or by acquired skills. Nevertheless, since most members sanctioned the class system, and since tribes often alleviated poverty by redistributing resources, there appears to have been little internal dissent. Force was not usually needed to maintain social order.

Sex roles were clearly drawn, though not inflexible. More flexible, the male sphere extended to politics, religion, and harvesting and processing of animal, rock, and wood products, as well as dealing with outside groups in trade, diplomacy, and warfare. Yet the burden of labor was distributed fairly evenly between men and women. Although gathering plant foods and preparation of food was mostly a female pursuit, there were exceptions. A study of 46 ethno-linguistic groups, for example, found that men and women, as well as older children and able older adults, cooperated to gather and store major staples such as pine nuts and acorns. Among the acorn- and agave-dependent Cahuilla, men and boys traveled in groups to harvest agave leaves, stalks, and flowers. Just as women were judged for their acorn-preparing skills, so men were judged for their skill in preparing and roasting the all-important agave plant.

Nor were men solely responsible for procuring essential animal foods. Shellfish, which could be conducted most times of the year along the coast, were gathered by those with limited mobility, including disabled persons, mothers, children, and the elderly. Women's shellfish collecting was especially essential to the group, just as was the hunting done by men. Among coastal tribelets, like those in other environments, women and men both harvested near and distant food supplies to create an optimal diet.

Nevertheless, tradition did allow men greater role flexibility than women. With clearly lower status in families and tribelets, women were usually expected to move to the village of their husbands upon marriage. Although Indigenous peoples expected women to defer to fathers and husbands, and to male family and tribelet leaders, women were accorded great respect and, within their sphere, independence and autonomy. The work of women was central in an economy based largely on plant gathering. Thus, women were central to some of the most revolutionary cultural innovations derived from plants. It is likely, for example, that women first discovered new methods of exploiting and manipulating nature, including controlled burning, acorn processing, and using plant materials in medicine, the arts, and basket-making.

Gender roles were strongly sanctioned by group religious practices and were taught to children at an early age. Although gender roles in some ways resembled those of their European counterparts, there were also striking differences. Deeply ingrained ideas about proper sexual practices and gender roles complicated life for Natives at later Spanish missions. Especially troubling was the European insistence that men perform agricultural tasks: planting, tending, and harvesting crops. Many men resisted doing what they considered women's work. Such gender-based ideological differences intensified the conflict between colonizers and Indians.

The Arts

Native arts were an extension of Indian economic and religious life. Men dominated wood, bone, and stone carving and painting, music, and oral literature, all of which were closely associated with religion. While the fashioning of bone and stone effigies was nearly universal in California, rock carvings (petroglyphs) and rock paintings (pictographs) reached their highest development among southern tribes, particularly the Chumash. In order to honor the gods, bring success in hunting, and establish boundaries, artists engraved and pecked designs, often with recognizable animal and geometrical shapes, into the sides of boulders and the walls of caves. Chumash and southern Yokuts artists painted abstract pictographs—brilliant multi-colored arrangements of human, animal, celestial, and symbolic shapes—usually in remote caves. Pictographs evolved from the introduction of new religious cults, as well as rituals that included the use of hallucinogenic drugs.

Often passed on by elders in male sweathouses, the oral tradition was rich in symbolism, imagery, and poetic expression. Learned by rote and passed from generation to generation, this literature included myths, stories, prayers, songs, and epic poems that incorporated the accumulated philosophy, ethics, history, science, and folk traditions of the people. Common themes were the unity of the natural and the supernatural realms, the power of animal spirits, and the interdependence of human beings and nature.

Women dominated a highly creative form of California art—basketry. Woven from dozens of materials of various textures and colors, these light, portable baskets served an essential purpose for gathering economies. Women produced baskets in many shapes and sizes for all manner of uses, from gathering and processing to storage and cooking. Baskets were needed for ritual; the ceremonial baskets of the Pomo, for example, were inlaid with feathers and mother-of-pearl. Baskets were also valuable trade items. Over thousands of years, tribes developed distinctive methods of basket construction and decorative styles, which skilled craftswomen further refined. The best baskets were beautifully decorated with woven geometrical, animal, and symbolic designs, and so finely stitched that they could hold water. California women developed the art of basketry to an extraordinarily high level.

On the Eve of European Colonization

The last thousand years before European invasion were especially dynamic for early Californians. Cultures were becoming more elaborate, societies more organized. Often driven by ecological stress, some groups migrated to new territories, sometimes driving out or absorbing earlier occupants. The cultures that the Europeans found were still taking shape.

Although, in most areas, the autonomous tribelet remained the primary unit of organization, broadening relationships knit these small groups together in ever more intricate patterns. Alliances transcending the tribelets developed, often linking groups of different languages and cultures. Increasing commerce gave rise to formalized inter-tribelet trade relationships and organizations. At the same time, new prophets began to preach novel religious ideas. With the expanded inter-tribal contacts fostered by commerce, these religious practices spread from group to group. Eventually, people from many tribelets shared allegiance to the new forms and began to gather for large, regional ceremonies.

Since kinship rules forced clans to seek partners outside of their lineage and tribelet, family alliances also evolved beyond the borders of tribelets. By European contact, lineages and clans in some regions had expanded to encompass numerous tribelets and even entire cultures. Some individuals traveled wider circuits,

"A Sweat and a Cold Plunge"

Male sweathouses were common among many California Native Americans. In these large buildings, adult men slept, socialized, and performed various rituals. For example, purification rites were performed before hunts to appease the animal spirits and to remove bodily scents that might alert game to the men's presence. After sweating before fires in the sealed buildings, the men plunged into cool water. The ritual was repeated until body and soul were cleansed. From Stephen Powers, *Tribes of California*, Washington, D.C. Government Printing Office, 1877.

many residing in several locales over the course of their lives. In this way, many individuals became both multilingual and multicultural, and thus less insular and more aware of the world beyond their borders.

As they became more organized, early Californians harvested, processed, and distributed resources more efficiently. Populations and settlement densities increased, particularly in the most favored environments. Urbanization occurred, as smaller villages waned in significance and people clustered around the most important ceremonial and trade centers. Greater productivity and population concentration encouraged specialization. More individuals focused their energies on particular tasks and obtained the necessities of life through purchase or barter.

Prosperity did not breed equality, however. Property-owning and merchant classes expanded, increased in power, and removed themselves further from commoners. Cemeteries used in the last centuries before the Spanish arrived testify to an increase in the wealth of some families, but also to growing segregation between the burials of rich and poor persons. Indian societies were becoming more hierarchical and interdependent in the centuries before European invasion. Although these changes came slowly, these traditions of adaptation provided alternatives in adjusting to the European presence.

Native California was thriving but fragile. The people were generally healthy, humane, and peaceful. They had achieved a remarkably productive relationship with nature, exploiting and manipulating its resources without damaging its delicate balances.

Yet, compared to Europeans, they were technologically and organizationally simple. They had no written languages, wheels, metal tools, or domesticated work animals. Their wood, sinew, and stone weapons were no match for European steel and firearms. More importantly, like their contemporaries throughout the western hemisphere, early Californians lacked immunities to Old World diseases. More complex organizational systems were beginning to emerge but, by and large, groups remained locally autonomous, with strong traditions of isolation and few mechanisms for broader cooperation in government and warfare. They were vulnerable to concerted challenge from aggressive outsiders, particularly those with sophisticated military technologies and even more deadly germs, as well as alien plant and animal species that undermined delicate ecological relationships on which the Native way of life depended. Not only would Spaniards and later-comers assault the people physically, they would also upset their equilibrium with nature, throwing whole cultures into disarray.

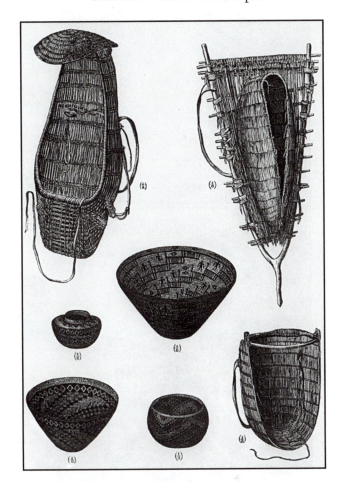

Sampler of Indian Baskets

The two baskets at the top of the illustration were used by women to carry infants. The others served diverse purposes. Although Indigenous peoples preferred baskets because they were portable and of greater use in a mobile, gathering way of life, some southern California tribes also made and used pottery or, like the Chumash, carved steatite bowls. From Stephen Powers, *Tribes of California* (1877). *Courtesy of The Bancroft Library, University of California, Berkeley.*

Old Mission Santa Barbara

Damaged by earthquake in 1925, the beautifully restored Mission Church at Santa Barbara recalls Spain's eighteenth-century attempt to transplant European civilization to the Pacific coast. *Photograph by Richard Orsi.*

PART TWO

Europeans and Indians

The California Experience

Few eras of American history have been as romanticized as the period of Spanish and Mexican rule in California. Many popular writers and restored historic sites testify that a peaceful, harmonious, even glamorous lifestyle prevailed in California from the Serra-Portolá expedition of 1769 to the outbreak of war between Mexico and the United States in 1846. Central to the plot in this mythic story is the triumphant march of European civilization, conquering and colonizing a vast wilderness. The story's essential characters are heroic explorers, soldiers, missionaries, and ranchers, who came with sword, cross, and branding iron to transplant a Mediterranean world to the Pacific Coast frontier. The drama unfolds variously in a gold-lit setting of ornate Spanish missions, adorned with tall bell towers, red-tiled roofs, and gracefully arched verandas, or in tranquil feudal *ranchos* with *casas grandes* of whitewashed adobe and colorful gardens, serenaded by bubbling fountains, beautiful *señoritas*, and guitar-strumming *caballeros*. The land was benevolent and productive, the people graceful and honorable. Hispanic California, as popular legend would have it, was a languid Eden of simple ease and pleasure.

The elaborately restored missions today stand as colorful monuments to Spain's attempt to Christianize Native California, bringing the blessings of progress to its supposedly primitive, culture-deprived peoples. In a famous 1917 essay, the noted historian Herbert E. Bolton captures prevailing popular sentiment when he calls the missions "a force which made for the preservation of the Indians, as opposed to their destruction, so characteristic of the Anglo-American frontier." Unlike the English colonies, where "the only good Indians were dead Indians," he claims, in the Spanish colonies "it was thought worthwhile to improve the natives for this life as well as for the next." When the popular narrative focuses any attention on the Indians themselves, they often appear as peaceful, docile children of nature, backward remnants of the Stone Age, notable for sensibly accepting and thriving under the superior culture carried to them by kindly Franciscan missionaries. This pleasant idyll ended when racist Americans rudely pushed both Indians and Hispanics aside in the 1840s.

But as the following account of Estanislao's rebellion illustrates, the true story clashes starkly with the romantic legend. Far more complicated and influential in shaping the later state's future, the meeting of New and Old World peoples in California, as elsewhere, was dominated by confusion, misery, and conflict. The realities of settling a remote, thinly populated, semi-arid region repeatedly undermined the official colonization policies advanced by Spain and, later, by Mexico after it gained its independence. For the handful of Hispanic settlers clinging to the seacoast, California offered a frustrating mix of geographic, economic, administrative, and biological problems, both within and outside the colony. As late as the 1840s, after nearly a century of effort, the region's economy remained colonial, its institutions fragmented, its military power negligible, and its settlements small and scattered. The good life was indeed elusive in Hispanic California.

Native peoples were themselves a major hindrance to Spanish and Mexican success. Despite the calamities imposed by colonization, the region's diverse peoples proved remarkably resistant to efforts to assimilate and control them. Contact with the intruders greatly changed and threatened Indigenous cultures, but after the first shock of colonization, Indians adapted, reorganized, and reasserted their power of numbers and understanding of the land. Their resistance quickly undermined the colonial ambitions of outsiders. Far from being the bit parts allowed them in the romantic narrative, California's first peoples were lead actors. Their story, the titanic clash between the region's early peoples and the invaders who followed, is the central dramatic theme of Hispanic California.

Estanislao's *Rebellion*

4

When Spain began to colonize California in 1769, Catholic missions were to be the principal instruments for conquering the land and its peoples. Missions were socio-religious settlements in which the Indigenous peoples were to be gathered, controlled, Christianized, and culturally assimilated, with their labor expropriated by their would-be conquerors to develop and pay for the colony. After Mexico gained its independence in 1821, many in the new nation criticized the missions that stretched along its far northern frontier from Texas to California. These and other internal disputes added to Mexico's financial, military, and governmental instability, delaying closure of California's missions until the 1830s and 1840s. Though it came late in the colonial period, Estanislao's rebellion illustrates the many weaknesses of Hispanic rule in California, the limits of the mission's influence on Native cultures, and the central role that Native peoples played in California's history.

One day in February 1829, two Indian *vaqueros* (cowboys) from Mission San José rode their horses along the lonely trail eastward from San Francisco Bay into the San Joaquin River valley. Weary of tending the mission's cattle, Macario and Benigno joined two old Indian fishermen at the marshy riverbank. There the men settled down to fish and perhaps to reminisce about old friends and old ways. Preoccupied, they failed to notice the stealthy approach of seven riders. Quickly surrounded and captured, the *vaqueros* recognized one of the men as the renowned Estanislao, a former *neophyte* (Indian converted to Christianity) at Mission San José. Now the commander of a large renegade band of Christian defectors and gentiles (unconverted Indians), Estanislao and his followers were engaged in a war against colonial authority.

Estanislao had the prisoners stripped of their horses, gear, and clothing. Benigno quickly joined the rebel cause, but Estanislao ordered Macario to return to Mission San José to warn Father Narciso Durán that the rebels intended to storm the ranchos, towns, and missions. Boasting of his firearms, Estanislao taunted the colonists, daring them to resist. With that, Estanislao's party crossed the river and vanished into the wilderness. Shaken and naked, Macario trudged back to the settlements bearing Estanislao's challenge.

Estanislao had been born around 1800 in the San Joaquin Valley. Before the first Spanish explorers arrived, the valley was a vast, fertile land. Melting snows in the Sierra Nevada to the east fed streams that tumbled onto the valley floor, nourishing abundant plant, animal, and human life. With underground waters nearly reaching the surface, the valley was, in the words of Pedro Fages, who first explored it in 1772, "a labyrinth of lagoons and Tulares [marshes]." Along the rivers stood thick forests of oak, poplar, and willow, interlaced with wild berry and grape vines. As missionary at Mission San José, Father Durán made numerous trips into the valley in search of converts and runaways; he marveled at the landscape, so "like a park because of the verdure and luxuriousness of its groves and trees." Salmon and trout freely swam the rivers, waterfowl nested the sloughs, and deer, elk, pronghorn, and grizzly bears roamed the plains and marshes. Indeed, as Fages observed, the San Joaquin Valley teemed with "every kind of animal, terrestrial and aerial."

Fages and Durán also found the valley thickly settled with people. Occupying most of the valley floor, Yokuts tribelets had located their villages on mounds or on the highest riverbanks to escape the annual floods. Their salmon-fishing and hunter-gatherer economy, supplemented by trade with interior and coastal peoples, provided an abundant lifestyle for the Northern Valley Yokuts, who included Estanislao's people, the Lakisamni. Along the major rivers, where most valley people lived, the population density of ten persons per square mile equaled that of any part of California. The confident Yokuts welcomed Fages when he arrived in 1772, and he described them as "good looking, excellently formed, frank and liberal."

For several decades after the first Spanish colonists arrived in California, the Yokuts remained largely untouched by the European presence. From beachheads at San Diego and Monterey, the Spaniards established a string of *presidios* (forts), *pueblos* (towns), missions, and ranches along 500 miles of coastal valleys. Leading the early colonial thrust were the missions, where the Spaniards hoped to assemble the Indians peacefully, convert them to Spanish culture and religion, and transform them into a working citizenry, whose labors would create a prosperous colonial economy. To control northern California, the Spaniards founded communities on San Francisco Bay, just over the Coast Range from Yokuts territory: a presidio at San Francisco (1776), missions at San Francisco (1776) and Santa Clara (1777), and a pueblo at San José (1777). Mission San José was established in 1797 about 15 miles northeast of the pueblo, completing Spain's early Bay Area settlements.

Although many coastal tribes were soon pulled into the Spaniards' orbit, colonial contact with interior groups such as the Yokuts was at first limited. Except for occasional visits by explorers, missionaries, or outlaws, the Yokuts' world went on much as before. After 1800, however, the European influence penetrated deeper into California's heart, and revolutionary change swept the Yokuts and other inland groups.

Relations between Spaniards and the Yokuts had already begun to deteriorate. As early as the 1770s, deserters from the colonial army attacked villages and assaulted Native women. The Yokuts retaliated by capturing and executing some offenders. But soon runaway mission neophytes were fleeing into the interior, bringing deadly diseases and grim news of conditions in the missions.

By the early 1800s, when colonists decided to missionize the interior, Indigenous peoples already mistrusted Spaniards. When Father Juan Martín arrived in 1804, scouting for sites for a new mission, he found mission runaways roaming the valley on horseback, warning gentiles that "the fathers do nothing but kill Indians." European venereal disease was devastating Native populations, and wherever Martín went, the villagers hid their women. More distressing still, they refused to allow Martín to take their children to the mission.

Mission San José itself mirrored the contradictory colonial policy that transformed the Yokuts' way of life and produced Estanislao's rebellion. Perched on the shoulder of the coastal hills overlooking southern San Francisco Bay, San José appeared on the surface to flourish amid sun-drenched valleys, ever-flowing streams, and a large local population of Costanoans. Although founded relatively late in the Spanish mission period, by 1820 Mission San José had become one of the most productive missions, its population exceeded only by San

Mission San José in 1853

The great California photographer Carleton E. Watkins made one of the first photographic images, a daguerreotype, of Mission San José in 1853. By this time, the imposing buildings that had impressed foreign visitors had fallen into disrepair. The large church to the right was demolished in the great 1868 earthquake, one of the state's most violent, along the Hayward Fault. Not until 1985 did a combined church and civic effort succeed in restoring the historic building. *Courtesy of The Bancroft Library, University of California, Berkeley.*

Luis Rey, far to the south and in an area originally more populated by Indians. Clad in coarse wool shirts, pants, and blankets, its 1,700 neophytes tended expansive fields of grain, gardens, and orchards. Thousands of sheep, cattle, and horses were pastured in a swath of land that stretched up to 40 miles inland. The mission compound resembled a medium-size town with flour mill, tannery, soap factory, winery, and weaving, blacksmith, tailor, harness, pottery, and candle-making shops.

Fathers Narciso Durán and Buenaventura Fortuny, who shared management of Mission San José after 1806, oversaw an impressive building program that produced a large church and a rectory, as well as shops, tannery, warehouses, schoolrooms, guesthouses, and several blocks of Indian barracks. Mission sailboats plied the bay, carrying valuable mission goods to merchant ships anchored off San Francisco, 30 miles to the north. In good years, in addition to meeting its own needs, the mission exported cattle hides, tallow, beaver pelts, olive oil, wheat, barley, beans, honey, figs, wool, cotton, and tobacco.

The Natives in and around Mission San José were beginning to assimilate. In the three decades after the mission's founding, thousands had consented to baptism. They attended Catholic liturgies, spoke some Spanish, and adopted the behavior—particularly the craft trades—appropriate to their status as laborers. The mission was a school of European civilization and the neophytes represented varying degrees of assimilation.

San José was particularly famous for Father Durán's music program. Described by one biographer as "the padre musician par excellence of the mission period," Durán developed a simplified notation system and taught neophytes to sing and read music. They also learned to construct and play instruments, and to direct choirs and orchestras. Accomplished Native American musicians from San José toured the northern settlements, testifying to the Indians' potential for assimilation as they taught other neophytes and delighted audiences at church festivals, civil holidays, and *fêtes* for visiting dignitaries.

San José, however, had more than its share of problems. Assimilation was far from complete; many neophytes remained indifferent to Spanish culture and refused to give up their Native language or religious beliefs. This reluctance Fortuny and Durán attributed to the Indians' "extreme and notorious stupidity." Some had to be forced to participate in worship services. Drought and labor shortages also undermined the mission's economy, particularly after Mexico won its independence in 1821. Against the strenuous objections of Durán and other missionaries, the impoverished new government began to commandeer the missions' supplies. These requisitions periodically forced Fortuny and Durán to put mission residents on food rations, while they diverted as much as three-quarters of the mission's crops to feed colonial civilians and soldiers. The decade before Estanislao's rebellion was a lean time for neophytes at Mission San José.

For his part, Narciso Durán demonstrates the ambivalence of missionaries and colonists toward Indigenous Californians. Considered one of the most capable of the padres, Durán dedicated himself to bringing them the blessings of Christianity and European civilization. He took great satisfaction in spreading the faith, building the mission, developing the economy, and educating the neophytes, particularly in music. Reporting to superiors on the state of the mission in 1812, for example, Durán

rejoiced that "in this mission they play 15 violins and 3 violoncellos, and the feasts of the Church are celebrated with a decency and a majesty superior to anything which the land seemed to promise." Deeply pained by Indian suffering or their rejection of the gospel, he was quick to forgive repentant neophytes. While pastor at San José and after 1830, when he became one of Junípero Serra's successors as father-president of all the California missions, Durán was an adamant defender of Indian interests. He often opposed townspeople, ranchers, soldiers, and the Mexican government itself to protect his charges.

But Durán operated within the racist mindset typical of Europeans in his day. Less vituperative than fellow Franciscan Geronimo Boscana, who likened the Indians to "a species of monkey," Durán still looked down on his charges. His report of 1812, for example, denigrated the aboriginal culture, mental capacity, and trustworthiness of Native Americans. "One must consider them," he wrote, "the poorest, most backward, and most stupid of

Father Narciso Durán and an Indian Child

Published in a travel account by a foreign visitor to the California missions, this likeness of Narciso Durán suggests the paternalistic relationship of missionary to Indian. From Eugene Duflot de Mofras, *Exploration du Territoire de l'Oregon* (1844). *The Huntington Library, San Marino, California.*

the peoples of America." To his superior in 1830, Durán blamed the slow progress of conversions on the "invincible repugnance of the natives for civilization and the abandonment of their heathen notions." They were, he complained, "almost without exception and during their whole life like school children" who could not be left to themselves. It is fitting that the best surviving portrait of Durán shows the seated padre giving a piece of fruit to a timid child. He was fond of amusing himself at dinner by tossing corn pancakes to Indian boys, who to his delight scrambled like dogs to catch them in their teeth.

Durán's conviction that such inferior beings could not manage their own affairs caused him to oppose the growing clamor of the 1820s and 1830s to disband the missions and free the Indians. Like many of his peers, he believed that such infantile people would not voluntarily accept the superior religion and culture offered them. They must be brought, forcibly if necessary, to the missions and, once baptized, compelled to remain there. A stern taskmaster, Durán freely used shackles, stocks, pillory, and the lash on recalcitrant neophytes. Single women and girls over age eleven, especially those captured and delivered to the mission, had to be locked up each night in a secured building (*monjerio*) because, as one Franciscan put it, they were so "obstinate in their evil intercourse." José María Amador, an overseer under Durán, recalled the mission's climate of compulsion:

> The treatment accorded the Indians was stern. Their shortcomings were pardoned but rarely or through very special consideration. A very minor dereliction was punished with 15 lashes, a more serious one with 25. A person who was absent from work over two weeks without permission or through laziness or anything else not thoroughly justified suffered 50 lashes. Other serious infractions, such as quarrels at the *rancherias*, fights or the use of arrows brought 100 lashes and a set of shackles in the guard house for one or two weeks during hours off from work, while at the same time working at a loom, gathering wood or performing other tasks during the daily hours of labor.

Since Indians did not sanction corporal punishment, such treatment was more likely to breed further resistance, rather than acceptance, of missionization.

Neophytes fell ill and died at staggering rates. Poor nutrition, concentrated population, and casual sanitation at the missions compounded residents' lack of immunity to European diseases. Venereal disease, cholera, dysentery, tuberculosis, influenza, and measles swept away the weakened people. During frequent ferocious epidemic outbreaks, as many as one-third of the mission residents

might die, often a dozen or more in a single day. Even in non-epidemic years, about 10 percent of San José Indians perished, including 20 percent of the children. So often did death visit the mission that Father Durán assigned five boys the full-time task of informing him of impending deaths so that he might comfort families and administer last sacraments. The boys could not keep pace with the high rates of infection, sometimes failing to warn Durán in time. After one such occurrence, Durán revealed his sadness and disillusionment. "I am weary of so many sick and dying Indians, who are *more fragile than glass*," he added in the margins of the mission's Register of Deaths. A low birth rate (principally because some Indian women deliberately aborted their fetuses rather than having them born to mission life) further depleted the mission's population. By the 1820s, the local Costanoans were virtually extinct.

Beneath its prosperous facade, Mission San José was an unstable community with extraordinarily high turnover, allowing for only minimal acculturation for most neophytes. Mission life was a short-term experience for most neophytes. Although the fathers had baptized almost 5,600 persons in the first 30 years, they could count only 1,700 residents in 1826. Most neophytes had entered the mission then vanished quickly, most by dying, others by defecting. As early as 1806, José Argüello, commander of the San Francisco presidio, complained that San José's neophytes were prone to "agitation and sedition." By the 1820s, the mission had become a hotbed of fugitivism: in that one decade, more than 1,000 neophytes fled the mission to seek sanctuary with interior tribes. The escapes were often coordinated. On May 25 and 26, 1827, 400 neophytes, a full quarter of mission residents, disappeared into San Joaquin's *tulares*.

As was true at other missions, only the soldiers kept San José's population drain in check. Padres dispatched soldiers to catch fugitives and to recruit new converts, willing or not. Unsurprisingly, interior Indians resisted, expanding the vicious circle of violence. Battle survivors were often captured and delivered to the missions, where they were absorbed, often unwillingly, into the neophyte community. Missionaries also journeyed among the interior tribes, sometimes "converting" whole villages and returning with them to the missions. By the early 1800s, so much disease and introduced ecological resource disruption had invaded the interior that some Indigenous groups were driven to accept any relief and shelter the missionaries offered. In that way, some Yokuts, including Estanislao, found themselves at Mission San José. Homesick and unaccustomed to the climate of the coast, valley neophytes were most likely to defect. Distance, difficulty of travel, and Indian hostility added to soldiers' frustrations in attempting to recapture valley Indians, further intensifying the violence of San Joaquin Valley encounters.

Complicating the situation, the migration of wild Spanish horses and cattle by 1800 began revolutionizing the culture of interior groups, making them more mobile and powerful. Mounted Indians took to raiding ranches and missions for more horses and slaughtering domestic and wild cattle, which, from the Native American perspective, were grazing and trampling Indian lands. The explosion in Native horse raiding threatened Spain's fragile colonial economy. Expeditions from San José to punish horse raiders, capture runaway neophytes, and seek new converts embroiled the mission in growing strife with the Yokuts and other interior groups.

In 1805, valley Indians attacked a party led by Father Pedro de la Cueva near the Stanislaus River. Retaliatory colonial expeditions followed, along with increased Indian raiding and attacks on missionaries and soldiers. Major skirmishes occurred in 1813, 1816, 1819, 1823, and 1826. When Estanislao launched his rebellion in 1828, he was reenacting a long, tragic, and violent tradition.

Surprisingly, the fragmented records of colonial California disclose little personal information about Estanislao. It is not clear when or how he was brought to Mission San José, probably as a child. He appears to have adapted more readily than most to the new culture. Trained as a cowboy, Estanislao rose to the position of *alcalde*, the highest Native office in the mission neophyte hierarchy, giving him a measure of authority over fellow neophytes. The specific circumstances that

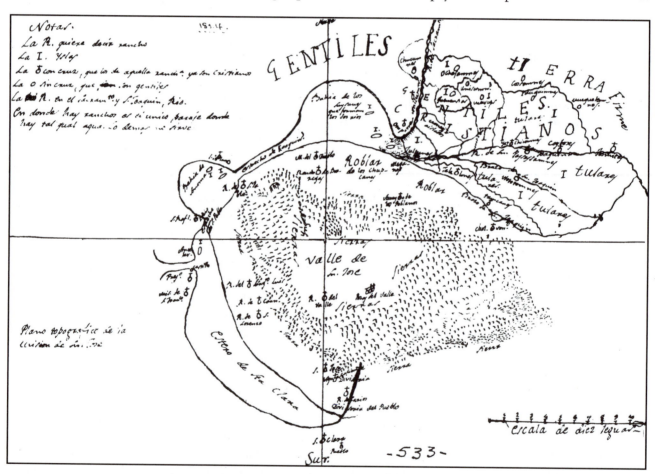

Narciso Durán's Map of Mission San José, 1824

Narciso Durán's topographical map of Mission San José's territory shows San Francisco Bay at the lower left and the complex of rivers in the San Joaquin Valley, beyond the Coast Range, at the upper right. This was the home of the Yokuts. Christianized Native villages are marked with a +, gentile villages with a O. The mission appears along the vertical center line in the lower part of the map. *Courtesy of The Bancroft Library, University of California, Berkeley.*

pushed him to rebel are uncertain. His position required him to dispense punishments and to take part in soldiers' expeditions to the interior; perhaps he was enraged and radicalized by these experiences. Estanislao may have heard the rumors—rampant by the 1820s—about mission secularization, or the end of missionary control over Indian lands and labor. Although Estanislao's objectives and motives are obscure, the circumstances that led to rebellion are clear—widespread Indian hostility toward missions and colonial authority, the instability of civil and military control over Native California, the introduction of horses and growing power of interior tribes, and a long history of violence between the region's earlier residents and European newcomers.

After the Mexican revolution, growing animosity between colonial civilian and religious authorities added fuel to the fire. In 1826, José María Echeandía, a new governor sent from Mexico to disband California's missions, over vigorous protests by the missionaries, proclaimed that married Christian neophytes could leave the missions under certain circumstances. Mission discipline quickly collapsed, as rumors of impending freedom spread among the neophytes. Many neophytes, even those unmarried, abandoned the missions at once, while those who stayed behind grew increasingly disobedient. Although some returned to old homelands, many legally freed ex-neophytes congregated in the colonial towns, ranches, and forts, where their labor was exploited or they were forced to beg or steal to support themselves. Many were flogged, jailed, or returned to the missions. Faced with these problems, Echeandía modified the 1826 order, but not before the Franciscans had instituted even harsher controls on mission Indians, thus increasing neophyte resistance. Antonio María Osio, a soldier who fought against Estanislao, attributed the rebellion to Echeandía's secularization orders.

Thus the Natives in and around Mission San José were ripe for revolution when Estanislao emerged as a leader in 1828. That fall, Estanislao and other mission Indians, as was the mission's custom, were allowed to visit Lakisamni relatives at their villages, located about 60 miles east of Mission San José, near the junction of San Joaquin and Stanislaus rivers. When the time came for them to return to the mission, Estanislao and several hundred others refused. Suggesting a broader conspiracy, several hundred runaways also joined Estanislao from missions Santa Clara, San Juan Bautista, and Santa Cruz, under the command of the Santa Clara Indian *alcalde*, Cipriano. Estanislao boastfully sent word to the mission that he did not fear their soldiers because, in Father Durán's words, they "are few in number,

are very young, and do not shoot well." As the rainy season approached, Durán wrote to Ygnacio Martinez, commandant of the San Francisco presidio, urging an immediate expedition "to take the two ring-leaders, dead or alive, and to punish with a good cudgeling as many as deserved it."

Late in 1828, Martinez responded, sending a company of soldiers under Sergeant Antonio Soto, a seasoned Indian fighter. Another soldier, Antonio María Osio, described the campaign 50 years later in his *Historia de California*. According to Osio, Soto left San Francisco with 15 or 20 men and arrived several days later at the Lakisamni villages. The soldiers were surprised by what they found. To neutralize the effect of cannon, muskets, and horses, the rebels had moved from the open riverbank into a willow thicket, surrounded by marshes and interlaced "by a great quantity of runners and stems of grapevines," making the stronghold impenetrable even to sunlight.

In the tradition of Yokuts warfare, the Indians bombarded the approaching soldiers with insults calculated to lure them into the thicket. Enraged, Soto and six men dismounted and entered the wood. Once they had reached its center, the Indians suddenly attacked. The invisible warriors avoided the soldiers' tough leather jackets and instead shot arrows at the intruders' heads. Leaving two dead soldiers behind, the survivors fled with arrows protruding from their faces, including Soto, who had been shot in the eye. Traveling "with much effort because of the great pain which the wounded suffered," Soto's party retreated to San José, where he died a few days later. According to Osio, the jubilant Indians "solemnized" their triumph "with great celebrations and dances, putting on exhibit the corpses of the soldiers who had been killed so that the neighboring tribes, who had been invited, might admire their great valor and bravery."

Winter rains soon flooded the valley's rivers and marshes, preventing colonial authorities from retaliating immediately, but Estanislao moved quickly to consolidate his forces. News of Soto's crushing defeat spread across the valley, bringing additional support from Yokuts and perhaps the more distant Miwok of the Sierra foothills. By spring, Estanislao had forged a broad inter-tribal alliance. His stronghold boasted an army of 500 to 1,000 neophyte and gentile warriors, one of the largest California Native American forces ever amassed against the intruders. A dozen tribelets moved into the stronghold and more Christian runaways continued to filter in. Runners from outlying villages supplied the willow fortress and Estanislao launched livestock raids on Bay Area missions and ranches. By the time Estanislao captured Macario and Benigno in late February 1829, he felt confident enough to again taunt colonial authorities. Macario's story of his encounter with Estanislao prompted Father Durán to again write to Martinez requesting action against the rebels.

Estanislao had put colonial officials in a difficult position. They realized his rebellion constituted a serious challenge that, if left unpunished, could lead to even broader resistance. But by now, Mexican authorities were struggling with the same military problems that had plagued their Spanish predecessors. In theory, they had the superior strength that came with steel blades, firearms, cannon, and horses. When the Indians acquired horses, however, their skill as mounted warriors blunted the Spaniards' edge. What was worse, an impoverished Mexico could support only a few professional soldiers, several dozen at each presidio and a half-dozen in each mission guard. To sustain the larger Indian campaigns, authorities were compelled to augment these meager forces with unreliable civilians, including neophyte and colonial conscripts. Nor were the few professional soldiers contented. Rarely paid, they wore ragged uniforms, fought with insufficient and dilapidated equipment, and often had to forage for food. Indeed, the troops were prone to mutiny and often fought amongst themselves. Observing a Mission San José expedition against valley tribes in 1826, a British naval officer dismissed California's military organization as "ludicrous."

Nonetheless, officials moved to crush Estanislao's rebellion when good weather returned, dispatching Ensign José Antonio Sanchez of the San Francisco presidio, veteran of more than 20 Indian campaigns. Sanchez left San Francisco on May 1, 1829, with eleven soldiers and one cannon. Guards from missions Santa Clara and Santa Cruz joined the column at Mission San José. Only seven militiamen and five civilians turned out from San José pueblo, but all the civilians and one militiaman went home because Sanchez lacked horses and equipment to outfit them. Sanchez set out on May 4 with a less-than-imposing force of 28 soldiers, six militiamen, and 70 Indian auxiliaries. As they had on earlier campaigns, the auxiliaries proved useful as guides and fighters. Calling on their Native and missionary training, the auxiliaries also rounded up cattle for food and built the tule rafts that ferried troops over the swollen valley rivers.

After slogging through the wet valley for several days, the army arrived at Estanislao's camp early on May 7. Sanchez found mounted warriors already gathered and waiting, well-fortified within a thick forest, and nearly surrounded by a bend of the Stanislaus River. The undergrowth thinned to grassy parkland near the opening to Estanislao's stronghold, while a dense tangle of shrubbery blocked access along the riverbanks, making attack from any other direction virtually impossible.

After trying unsuccessfully to set fire to the damp brush along the river's edge, Sanchez divided his troops into three squads. One guarded the horses, while another forded the river and flanked the village. Sanchez led the third group in a frontal assault through the grassy opening, advancing without resistance until he found his way blocked by the river and three thick log palisades ringing the Indian camp. Stymied, Sanchez retreated and ordered the cannon to be brought forward. At the first shot, a wheel broke; two more shots rendered the piece useless. Reduced only to their carbines, the Mexicans continued to fire on the camp. Moving quickly through the thick underbrush, the warriors returned both arrows and gunfire, although Sanchez later reported that the Indians had no bullets. Finally, after a long battle under a scorching sun, Sanchez withdrew, "perceiving that little if any damage was being done to the enemy."

At daylight on May 8, Sanchez again launched a frontal attack on Estanislao's fortress, leaving half his troops along the perimeter to prevent the Indians' escape. When he reached the palisades, Sanchez used an interpreter to warn the runaways to return to their missions or be killed. Estanislao answered "that he had to defend himself and he would not hesitate to die in the underbrush." Sanchez then offered safe passage to gentiles who wished to return to their villages. Twelve men came forward to confer, but Sanchez could not convince them to abandon the renegade neophytes.

The fighting resumed. For three hours, they battled fiercely, with the Mexican soldiers making little headway. While they failed to penetrate the stockade, and few Indian casualties could be counted, eleven auxiliaries and eight soldiers were wounded, three seriously. They soon ran out of ammunition. "The weapons," Sanchez later reported, "were almost entirely useless." Discipline collapsed, and when he ordered a counterattack to rescue four soldiers surrounded and fighting for their lives, the men refused to budge.

Convinced that his exhausted army could not or would not mount another charge, Sanchez ordered a retreat to Mission San José. Leaving two dead behind, the soldiers collected 20 or more wounded and rode off in defeat. In his memoirs, Juan Bojorges, who had fought in the battle, reported that as the soldiers fled the thicket, Estanislao came out behind them, fired one parting gunshot, threw his hat in the air, and shouted insults in Spanish. "When we reached San José," Bojorges recalled, "news of our defeat had already reached there. The bells were tolled and there were many demonstrations of great sorrow."

The defeat of Soto and Sanchez exposed the colonial government's military weakness as well as the power of united Indian resistance. This latest debacle convinced authorities to mobilize all available resources. Martinez chose Ensign Mariano Guadalupe Vallejo of the Monterey presidio to command a combined force from the northern presidios plus all mission guards who could be spared. In writing to Vallejo on May 16, Martinez emphasized the crisis facing the colony. Estanislao's renegades, he warned, were "extremely insolent, committing murders and stealing horses, stripping bare the unwary, seducing the other Christians to accompany them in their evil and diabolical schemes, openly insulting our troops and ridiculing them and their weapons." Martinez ordered Vallejo "to administer a total defeat to the Christian rebels and to the wild Indians who are aiding them, leaving them totally crushed"—an open-ended command that Martinez may have later regretted.

Despite this new colonial determination, the assault force assembled at Mission San José under much uncertainty. Although he would later become a power in California, the 21-year-old Vallejo had little command experience and had participated in only two Indian campaigns. The Monterey soldiers had not been fully paid and rationed in nearly two years, and they had mutinied only six months earlier. Rumors warned that yet another rebellion was about to break out (the revolt did come later that year.) Also, Vallejo and Sanchez were rivals; the latter was understandably rankled by his defeat and replacement by the young stripling from Monterey. Just returned from a successful campaign against tribes in the southern San Joaquin Valley, Vallejo's troops probably taunted Sanchez's men. Fights between the two garrisons later marred the expedition. Finally, the recent campaigns had strained supplies of firearms, powder, and bullets. Just as they were about to depart, Vallejo discovered that his only cannon had a rotten bed and two broken wheels. Although he repaired it, the cannon broke down repeatedly in the campaign ahead.

Finally, on May 26, Vallejo rode out with 107 soldiers and 50 auxiliaries, armed with the cannon, its ammunition, and 3,500 musket cartridges, one of the strongest forces yet raised against Native Californians. When he arrived at Estanislao's fortress on May 29, Vallejo discovered that the rebels had improved their fortifications yet again, this time with trenches throughout the thicket floor. But the odds now favored Vallejo, who had more regular soldiers and increased firepower. The summer heat also had dried the ground, improving mobility for the invading forces, particularly their artillery. Nevertheless, the Mexicans faced a formidable task.

Vallejo ordered his troops to surround the stronghold, set fire to the woods, and launch an infantry assault against the fort from several directions. Cannonballs pulverized the stockade, weakening the log walls and raining showers of jagged splinters on the defenders. For several hours the Mexicans exchanged musket balls for arrows at close quarters, finally reaching the first wall, where the advance stalled. With their own brush fire now closing in, and an Indian counterattack against the rear threatening their horses and supplies, the Mexicans were forced to retreat.

Vallejo returned the next morning, only to discover that the Indians, no longer confident of their fortifications, had escaped during the night. The Mexicans found only a few corpses, but the blood left behind indicated many Indian casualties. Vallejo trailed the fleeing Indians and caught them the next morning ten miles south along the Tuolumne River. They had taken cover behind another fortified log stockade with, in Vallejo's words, "a system of pits and trenches constructed even better than the first." New gentile allies had joined Estanislao's forces.

After surrounding and again setting fire to the woods, Vallejo attacked with the bulk of his forces. Under heavy fire from the rebels, 25 neophyte auxiliaries penetrated the underbrush "with much labor," using axes to create a trail wide enough for the cannon and infantry. When his gun was ten yards from the wall, Vallejo used an interpreter to urge Estanislao's warriors to surrender. One Indian defected to the Mexican side, a neophyte named Matias, who begged for mercy. Joaquin Piña, a cannoneer from Monterey, recorded in his diary that "the prisoner was consequently immediately shot."

Vallejo's troops now advanced toward the trenches from several directions. The battle raged for four hours, with only brief respites. The Mexicans ran out of cannonballs, and began to blast the stockade with grapeshot and musket fire. Still the Indians held their ground. At that point, the assault stalled. Their ammunition exhausted, some soldiers jumped into the trenches with daggers and fought hand-to-hand. According to Piña, the Indian auxiliaries "became frightened both because of the fury of the attack by arrows . . . and because of the thunder of the cannon," and "as a result, we could not make them move any further." Once again, the fires set by Vallejo completely surrounded his men; to save them, Vallejo ordered a quick retreat through the fire.

The men, recalled Piña, emerged "nearly roasted in the tremendous blaze of the underbrush." The escaping soldiers heard a yell from the burning forest and returned one last shot. Complete silence followed. "One would not have believed," marveled Piña, "so many Indians could still be inside the woods."

That night the soldiers killed a few Indians trying to escape through the river. Early the next morning, the Mexicans captured three women; one reported that many Indians had died in the battle. Vallejo's men reconnoitered the trenches and fort, but they found few bodies or survivors. Most of the defenders, including Estanislao, had escaped under cover of water and darkness, taking their horses and most of their dead with them.

Although Vallejo and his defenders later denied it, the soldiers committed atrocities that day as they prepared to return home. One chronicler of the campaign, Antonio María Osio, emphasized the guilt of the auxiliaries, "ancient enemies of Estanislao's villages," who "burst out like starving hounds and instantly began an atrocious massacre." Other, fuller accounts, show widespread participation, including auxiliaries, soldiers, civilians, and Vallejo himself. Piña's diary is probably the most reliable, because he wrote it just after the event, and because he reported in great detail, despite his clear loyalty to Vallejo.

A number of surviving Indians, mostly women and aged or infirm men, were tortured and killed. As the soldiers swept through the forest, according to Piña, "three old women" found hiding in some grapevines "were immediately pulled out of the bushes and shot on the spot." Auxiliaries captured a Santa Clara neophyte whom they accused of having tortured two of Sanchez's soldiers a month earlier. With Vallejo's permission, the auxiliaries formed a circle around the captive and fired 73 arrows into him. When the rebel still refused to die, a soldier shot him. The Indians then hanged the body. Auxiliaries and soldiers also killed and hanged Matias, to whom Vallejo had promised safety, and four other men and women. Although the vengeful soldiers clamored for the lives of three women they had captured that morning, Vallejo refused. He placed them under guard for return to the missions.

That afternoon, their food and ammunition depleted, the men set off for Mission San José, driving before them a handful of female captives and 18 recaptured horses—small gains when considering the numbers of lives lost. Amazingly, no Mexican soldiers perished in this campaign. Only 13, including two auxiliaries, were wounded. Native losses, although unknown, must have been great. Dozens, perhaps hundreds, of Indians fell in three days of fighting. As Vallejo's party rode away from Estanislao's wrecked fortress, a half-dozen bodies swung from the tops of valley oak trees, grim warnings to other would-be rebels.

By any standard, the Mexican triumph over Estanislao was an inglorious victory. The colonial army did finally succeed in demolishing two Indian fortress-towns, dissipating a large resistance force, and driving a formidable Indian leader into hiding. But if colonial authorities thought that by defeating Estanislao they had quenched the flames of rebellion, they were sadly mistaken. Most of the rebels had escaped and even the colonials realized that their victory had been less than total. Responding to Vallejo's report, which was much more favorable than the facts warranted, Commandant Martinez rejoiced "that this scum has been chastised," but regretted "that due to lack of munitions and supplies you did not inflict a complete rout upon those rebellious and insolent Christians."

Persistent reports of atrocities also embarrassed the government. Father Durán and other leaders demanded that Governor Echeandía punish Vallejo and his cohorts for violation of the laws governing treatment of Indian prisoners. Although an investigation concluded that "those in the party hanged and killed two old, defenseless Indian men and three women" and shot another captive, only one low-ranking solider was singled out for a mild chastisement. The affair remains a stain on the record of Vallejo, one of California's most revered heroes.

Most importantly, the broader problem of Indian resistance remained unresolved. The economic, political, cultural, and ecological forces that precipitated the rebellion persisted. Neophytes continued to die of disease or flee the missions, more converted and neophyte leaders emerged, Indian mounted culture expanded wider, and horse stealing increased. In the 1830s and '40s, resistance disrupted colonial authority more seriously. In 1832, Father Durán exaggerated only a bit when he warned that the Spaniards "were almost on foot because of the incessant horse thefts committed by apostate Christian Indians in league with the pagans. . . . Their insolence causes some to prophesy that in a very few years we shall find ourselves in a sad necessity of abandoning our outposts and uniting at one point for our common defense." By fomenting disorder and delaying exploration, settlement, and colonial control of the interior, resurgent Indian power made the weakened colony even more vulnerable to conquest by the United States a few years later, thus shaping the subsequent history of California.

When his rebellion collapsed, Estanislao nearly vanished from the pages of written history. Shortly after Vallejo's return to the settlements, Estanislao and some followers reappeared at Mission San José seeking mercy and protection. Father Durán helped secure pardons for them from Governor Echeandía. Remarkably, Estanislao returned to the *tulares* a year later, again with Durán's permission. That the authorities punished no repentant neophytes, not even their notorious leader, may seem incredible. Such sporadic flares of compassion, however, testify to the paternalistic dimension of colonial treatment of Indigenous peoples, as well as the contradictions inherent in the mission system.

Estanislao lived in obscurity at Mission San José until he died in the late 1830s during one of the epidemics that decimated the Yokuts. Although a river and a county (Stanislaus) were named after him, generations of Californians remained ignorant of his history. In the 1950s, the state created a new recreation area, Caswell Memorial Park, near the site of the rebels' Stanislaus River fortifications. A small monument added later commemorated Estanislao and his people. A sad testament to persistent misunderstanding of the original Californians, the plaque pictures Estanislao in the dress of a Great Plains warrior.

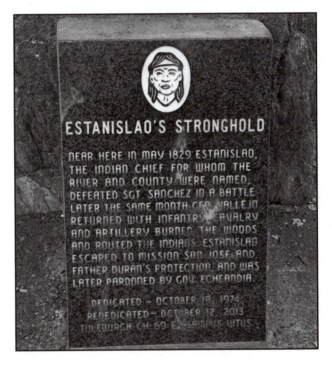

Estanislao as a Great Plains Warrior

In October 1974, the history-conscious fraternal order E Clampus Vitus placed the plaque on the left at Caswell Memorial State Park on the Stanislaus River to commemorate Estanislao's Rebellion. The image incorrectly depicted Estanislao as a Great Plains warrior, complete with eagle feathers, pigtails, and choke collar, reflecting contemporary Americans' fascination with the Plains Indians wars of the late nineteenth century, as popularized in film and television. Indeed, some early state histories described California Indians as roaming the landscape on horseback, hunting buffalo, and living in tepees. In October 2013, almost 40 years later, the "Clampers" returned with a new commemorative plaque (on the right). The new plaque more accurately depicts Estanislao as a Yokuts warrior. However, the new memorial repeats the original text, inaccurately referring to Estanislao as an "Indian chief." *Photograph (left) by Richard J. Orsi; (right) courtesy of California Historical Landmarks.*

Explorers and Native Peoples

5

First Meetings

Early histories of California focused on the daring European mariners who battled the elements to discover and chart this remote coast in the 1500s and 1600s. Neglected was the interaction between these early explorers and Native Californians. Europeans confronted strange peoples, as well as strange lands. Charged with learning more about both, pioneer explorers produced valuable insights into Native American cultures and recorded early Indian/European relations.

As was true when Caribbean peoples had met Christopher Columbus, or when the Aztecs (Mexica) first beheld Hernán Cortés, California's first peoples probably did not recognize the arrival of Spanish ships as a cataclysmic event. Only time would reveal the extent of that disaster. In the meantime, first responses to the newcomers were mixed. As could be expected from such diverse peoples, their cultural values, prior information regarding the newcomers, and the explorers' behavior shaped early Native California's reactions to the interlopers. The variety of first contacts foreshadowed the complexity of future Indian-European relations that was demonstrated centuries later in Estanislao's rebellion.

Discovery and Naming

Remote and self-contained, California's peoples had been sheltered from the cross-currents of Eurasian history for thousands of years. This isolation ended in the mid-sixteenth century, when events thousands of miles away began to reshape the world they knew. In this age of imperialism, European nations competed with one another to subjugate and extract the wealth of Africa, Asia, and North and South America. On the

53

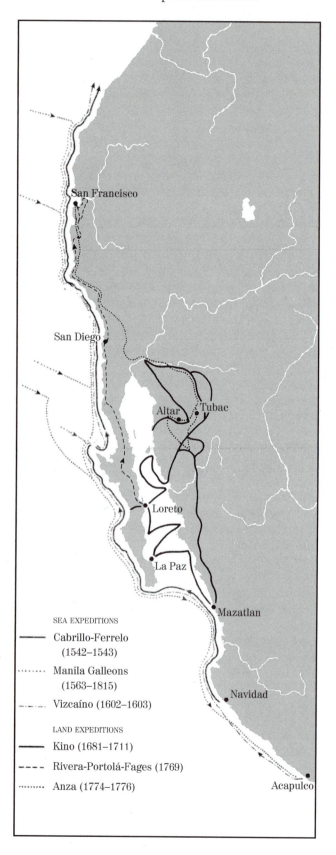

SEA EXPEDITIONS

—— Cabrillo-Ferrelo
(1542–1543)

.... Manila Galleons
(1563–1815)

—··—··— Vizcaíno (1602–1603)

LAND EXPEDITIONS

—— Kino (1681–1711)

- - - - Rivera-Portolá-Fages (1769)

.... Anza (1774–1776)

strength of Columbus's world-changing voyages in the 1490s and early 1500s, Spain was first to control parts of North America, particularly in the Caribbean. By 1515, Spain had established a colonial system on the islands of Hispaniola and Cuba based on military conquest and the religious conversion, cultural assimilation, and economic exploitation of Indigenous peoples.

In 1519, an expedition under the ambitious adventurer Hernán Cortés crossed the Caribbean Sea to the east coast of what would become Mexico, bent on conquering the Aztecs, a wealthy, powerful interior Indian civilization. Cortés marched inland with a small army of few hundred *conquistadores* (soldiers), overpowering resistance and forging alliances with enemies of the Aztecs. With logistical support and many thousands of fighters supplied by allied tribes, Cortés in 1521 defeated the Aztecs and captured their capital, Tenochtitlán. Populous and rich in resources, the former Native empire became the center of Spanish conquest in the western hemisphere. Having subdued the Aztecs, the Spaniards carved out a vast ocean-to-ocean domain in North America that eventually stretched from Central America and the West Indies northward to Florida and westward through Mexico and much of what is now the American Southwest. To control its new possessions, Spain built the capital of New Spain at Mexico City on the ruins of Tenochtitlán and governed by viceroys sent from Spain.

From the 1520s to the 1540s, Spaniards continued to exploit dissension among Mexican tribes, first allying, then subduing and exploiting, one group after another. Lured by false rumors of still more wealthy nations farther north, explorers set sail from Acapulco and other Pacific ports through the late 1520s and early 1530s, reconnoitering Mexico's northwest coast while also searching for the Strait of Anián, the legendary Northwest Passage from Europe through North America to the riches of the Far East. Plagued by mutiny, hostile Natives, and the great hardships of sailing uncharted seas, these early expeditions accomplished little. In 1533, a group of mutineers did cross the Gulf of California and reached Bahía de la Paz, near the tip of the *Baja* (lower) California peninsula. Indians killed all but two of those who tried to land. Somehow managing to return to Mexico, the survivors spread tales of a fabulous island surrounded by rich pearl beds. Two

Explorers of California

Adapted from *Historical Atlas of California*, by Warren A. Beck and Ynez D. Haase. Copyright © 1974 by the University of Oklahoma Press.

years later, Cortés himself accompanied three ships north, taking formal possession of the supposed island in 1535.

Colonial explorers dubbed the new land "California," after the fictitious pearl-rich island of Calafia, Garcí Ordoñez de Montalvo's Amazon queen in his popular romantic adventure, *Las Sergas de Esplandián*. During subsequent voyages in 1539 and 1540, mariners were able to circumnavigate the Gulf of California and discover the mouth of the Colorado River. Although they realized their island was actually a peninsula, the name stuck. Eventually, "California" came to mean all of the coastal territory from the tip of Baja northward to the still undiscovered Strait of Anián.

Cabrillo's Voyage

Encouraged by these discoveries, in 1542 Viceroy Antonio de Mendoza dispatched an expedition of three ships—the San Salvador, the Victoria, and a vessel of unknown name—under the command of Juan Rodríguez Cabrillo, an able shipbuilder, navigator, and veteran of the conquest of Mexico.

Cabrillo's ships sailed from the Mexican port of Navidad on June 27, 1542, rounded the Baja peninsula and cruised northward. At first, summertime seas and winds made navigating easy. Cabrillo leisurely charted islands and bays, landing occasionally to formally announce Spanish possession. Along what Cabrillo termed a "bare and arid" coast, the expedition encountered only a few Native fishermen. Some fled at the sight of the strangers, but others were eager to board the Spanish ships. Using sounds and gestures, they exchanged goods and information with the mariners. Cabrillo learned that other white men had elsewhere landed earlier, most likely members of Francisco de Ulloa's expedition around the Gulf of California to the east. Explorers heard similar stories all along the California coast, evidence that the Indigenous peoples had wide networks into the interior for trade and information.

On September 28, Cabrillo anchored in "a very good closed port" that he christened San Miguel (later renamed San Diego). Then, for the first time, Spaniards set foot in what is now California, territory that was home to Iipay and Tipay, branches of the Kumeyaay people. First contacts between hosts and guests boded ill for the future. Most Natives ran when the explorers approached. Those that remained "displayed much fear" and had to be won over with gifts. That night, when a party of Spaniards landed to fish, Indians attacked them with bows and arrows, wounding three sailors.

Juan Rodríguez Cabrillo

Courtesy of the California History Room, California State Library, Sacramento, California.

A few days later, the Spaniards learned why their arrival had caused such alarm. Native American informants advised that white men dressed like Cabrillo had been wreaking havoc further east, perhaps a reference to the Coronado expedition through the Southwest. A chronicler of the Cabrillo expedition reported that the Indians "showed by signs that these carried crossbows and swords; they made gestures with the right arm as if using lances, and went running about as if they were going on horseback, and further showed that these were killing many of the Native Indians, and for this reason they were afraid."

On October 3, their stores of food and water replenished, the explorers resumed their voyage northward. Cabrillo encountered many more villagers as he toured the coast and nearby islands. He and his men felt the charm of Santa Barbara's Channel Islands. The expedition's chronicler described them as rich in marine life, with "very beautiful and well-populated valleys," and "fine plains and many trees and savannas." Cabrillo's men marveled at the region's Chumash, their well-constructed canoes and nautical skills, their apparent affluence. The spacious plazas of their large towns were surrounded by "round houses, well covered down to the ground," their chronicler reported. "They wear skins of many different animals, eat acorns and a white seed the size of maize, which is used to make tamales. They live well."

Certainly aware of pillaging conquistadores elsewhere, the Chumash nevertheless seemed unafraid of the newcomers. Confident in their numbers, they followed the ships in canoes, accompanying the Spaniards for long distances as they explored the coast. Many came aboard to trade and confer. One night the Europeans entertained a delegation of chiefs, who "danced to the sound of a tambourine and a Castilian bagpipe" and stayed aboard overnight. The friendliness and apparent sophistication of the Chumash did not stop the mariners on their return trip from kidnapping half a dozen children to be taken to Mexico for training as interpreters on future voyages.

On October 18, now too close to winter, the Spaniards attempted to resume sailing north. After rounding Point Conception and leaving the shelter of the Channel Islands, Cabrillo's ships were immediately blasted by "a great storm." Driven out to sea and back south, the Spaniards took refuge for a week at a small harbor on the lee side of San Miguel Island. Here they were again attacked by Indians, and Cabrillo was badly injured. Trying again to head north, the Spaniards embarked on a long ordeal of deprivation and suffering, as would plague all early navigators along the California coast. "Contrary winds" out of the northwest threatened to drive the ships aground, repeatedly forcing them far out to sea, making it difficult to chart the coast accurately. They made scant headway against the constant storms, which also prevented going ashore to collect badly needed water and supplies. Cabrillo's ships fought their way northward for nearly a month until they reached a point somewhere between Monterey Bay and the Oregon border. Unable to continue battling the strong winds, his men were exhausted, racked by hunger, thirst, dissension, and illness, particularly scurvy, and discouraged by their failure to find the mythical Strait of Anián.

Turning around, the Spaniards were blown back to San Miguel Island only a few days later. Here, on January 3, 1543, Cabrillo died from his earlier injuries. Now under the command of first mate Bartolomé Ferrelo, the Spaniards again set sail. From February to March, the Spaniards were buffeted from one hazardous anchorage to another, as they tried to re-provision their ships and again head north to complete their mission. They returned to the northern California coast, but strong winds again prevented landing. Battered by fierce storms, their stores whittled down to "some damaged biscuit," the seamen finally abandoned the cause. On April 14, 1543, Cabrillo's surviving crew staggered

into Navidad, convinced they owed their survival to divine intervention.

These results undoubtedly disappointed officials in New Spain. The costly expedition had unearthed no precious metals, discovered no Strait of Anián, and encountered no opulent civilizations. Cabrillo had made only sketchy coastline charts of the coastline, especially north of Point Conception. Furthermore, the mariners described California as remote and inaccessible, its rugged coast guarded by treacherous winds and currents. California seemed more a desolate wilderness than a fabled paradise.

Still, Spain based its claim to *Alta* (upper) California, the area stretching from Baja to Oregon, on the voyage of Cabrillo. Later mariners relied on his preliminary charts of Baja California and the shoreline as far as the Channel Islands. Moreover, Cabrillo's reports provide invaluable views of Native food, dress, architecture, technology, and early Native-European interactions. Yet for more than a generation, Spain showed little interest in California. Instead, leaders concentrated on quelling Indigenous resistance in Mexico and Central America and developing profitable industries in New Spain.

Francis Drake in California

Englishmen made the second known European landing in Alta California. Encouraged by their government, English privateers began preying on Spanish shipping in the Americas in the 1570s. The most famous of these "sea dogs," Francis Drake, sailed the *Golden Hind* through the Straits of Magellan in 1579, raiding Spanish treasure ships and pillaging colonial seaports along the western coasts of South and Central America. His ship bulging with booty, Drake then sailed north into the Pacific, intent on finding the Northwest Passage for a speedy return east to England. He made landfall near the coast of Oregon and drifted southward, looking for a secluded port in which to repair his leaky ship. On June 17, 1579, at around 38 degrees north latitude, near present-day San Francisco Bay, Drake cast anchor in "a convenient and fit harbor." He named it Nova Albion (New England) because its "white bancks and cliffes, which lie toward the sea" reminded him of home.

Having been attacked by Indians in Latin America, the Englishmen built a fort on the beach for protection. There they stayed for more than a month while they careened, repaired, and re-provisioned their ship. Like other early explorers, Drake's men detested the region's harsh climate and rugged landscape. Much like

Francis Drake Being Welcomed by the California Indians

This fanciful view from a later English illustration depicts an actual ceremony of welcome and crowning described in the narratives of Drake's voyage. The architecture of Indian buildings shown here is totally unlike the domed tule dwellings of the Coast Miwok. *Courtesy of The Bancroft Library, University of California, Berkeley.*

summer-time coastal tourists today, the shivering Englishmen grumbled constantly about the "nipping colds" and "those thicke mists and most stinking fogges." Francis Fletcher, a chronicler of the voyage, thought the "insufferable sharpeness" of the wind caused "the general squalidnesse and barrenesse of the countrie."

The Englishmen spoke highly, however, of the Coast Miwok. Unlike the Spaniards, Drake's crew did not intend to settle permanently or subjugate the Indians, thus their approach was cautious but friendly. Drake's was the most intense contact yet between Europeans and Native Californians. Chroniclers described the culture shock experienced by both groups, as well as their generally positive interactions. Word of the visitors spread quickly among local villages, and throngs of armed warriors fell on the English encampment, ready to make "war in defense of their countrie." When the

English made signs of friendship, the attackers dropped their weapons. To Fletcher they seemed awestruck, "as men ravished in their minds, with the sight of things they had never seene or heard of before that time."

The behavior of the local people puzzled the English. After the ritual exchange of gifts, the women began "crying and shrieking piteously, tearing their flesh with their nailes from their cheekes in a monstrous manner, the blood streaming downe along their brests, . . . [and] with furie cast themselves upon the ground . . . on hard stones, nobby hillocks, stocks of wood, and pricking bushes." This description, reminiscent of a Miwok mourning ceremony, suggests they believed the pale strangers to be ghosts of ancestors. Whatever the performance meant to the Indians, it thoroughly unnerved the Englishmen. Interpreting it as the work of Satan, Drake and his crew immediately fell to their knees.

They prayed and sang psalms, "lifting up our eyes and hands to heaven . . . beseeching God, if it were his good pleasure, to open by some means their blinded eyes." The Miwok, apparently just as baffled by English customs, quieted at once. They sat on the ground and watched the strangers attentively. When the prayers ended, Natives applauded enthusiastically. From then on, whenever the Miwok visited, they asked the English to sing.

Hosts and guests adjusted to one another remarkably well. Within a few days, hundreds of local people converged on Drake's camp, as well as some from far away, arriving in columns, singing, dancing, and bringing gifts. Throughout Drake's sojourn, many remained in camp, working, trading, eating, and worshiping with the Englishmen. Drake's crew also soon discarded its fears, opened up the fortress, and socialized freely with their hosts, and they toured the inland villages to learn more about the people. Although the English never lost their contempt for "heathen" customs, particularly nudity and the self-torture of the women, which recurred often, they soon grew to like their friendly hosts. The English admired the ease and freedom of their demeanor, marveled at their skill with fishing line, bow and arrow, as well as their strength and endurance. The men were so strong, wrote Fletcher, that burdens "2 or 3 of our men could hardly beare, one of them would take upon his back, and without grudging carrie it easily away up hill and downe hill an English mile. . . . They are also exceedingly swift in running, and of long continuance." The English "took pitty" on afflicted visitors and shared what medicines they had, "beseeching God, if it made for his glory, to give cure to their diseases by these means." Drake's men probably also had sexual relations with local women. Overall, concluded Fletcher, he found the people to be "of a tractable, free and loving nature, without guile or treachery."

Drake set sail on July 23, 1579, his ship and crew refreshed. He left behind a brass plate nailed to a post, both to record his visit and to claim Nova Albion for his Queen Elizabeth I. The anguished Miwok wept "bitter teares" at their departure, climbing to the highest hills and lighting beacon fires. Drake stopped briefly at the Farallon Islands to take on a store of seals and sea birds, then, discouraged by fierce northerly winds from further seeking the Northwest Passage, he resumed his voyage westward across the Pacific. More than a year later, the *Golden Hind* returned full of treasure to a jubilant queen and nation, the second vessel to sail around the world.

Drake's placid visit to California produced a legacy of historical controversy. Long sought by historians, a crudely fashioned brass plate bearing Drake's inscription finally surfaced in Marin County in 1937. Put on display at the University of California's Bancroft Library, the plate quickly became one of California's most celebrated historical artifacts. But because of its anachronistic phrasing and lettering, skeptics questioned the plate's authenticity. Hoping to resolve decades of debate, in the 1970s the library subjected the plate to analysis by independent laboratories. Based on its chemical composition and the methods used to flatten and cut the brass, the laboratories reported that "Drake's Plate" was likely a modern forgery.

Another controversy surrounding Drake's visit is the precise location of Nova Albion. Was it San Francisco Bay, or the more commonly accepted Drake's Bay in western Marin County? Most evidence, particularly the white cliffs and blustery climate described in the narratives, favors the latter general location. Yet accounts of the voyage are vague enough as to encourage endless quibbling among local boosters, popular writers, anthropologists, and historians. Writing in the *Western Historical Quarterly* in 1990, historian Harry Kelsey demonstrated that there is even room for doubt that Drake reached California at all, suggesting the entire story was a fabrication. Barring a dramatic discovery of lost manuscripts or other evidence, such as the true brass plate, these controversies may never be settled.

But for all the scholarly sound and fury, Drake's sojourn in California actually signified little. Drake's around-the-world voyage was indeed one of the grand events of European exploration, and it bolstered Great Britain's claims to the Oregon country two centuries later. The voyage's narratives are invaluable sources of information about Native American life along California's blustery North Coast and the dynamics of early Indian-European contact. But ultimately, Drake's influence on the course of California history was negligible. The sea dog came and went, leaving little in his wake except antiquarian controversy. The first published account of the landing, Richard Hakluyt's *Principall Navigations* (1589), may have rekindled European interest in the region. But a new Spanish movement to explore and settle California was already underway by 1589, and there is no direct evidence that Drake's claim of possession influenced Spanish policy. Spain continued to claim authority over California as it would have even without Drake's visit to Nova Albion.

"Drake's Plate"

The inscription on "Drake's Plate" at the Bancroft Library in Berkeley reads: "Bee it knowne vnto all men by these presents, ivne.17.1579. By the grace of God and in the name of Herr Maiesty Qveen Elizabeth of England and her svccessors forever. I take possession of this kingdome whose king and people freely resigne their right and title in the whole land vnto Herr Maiesties keepeing. Now named by me an to bee knowne v(n)to all men as Nova Albion. G. Francis Drake." Ironically, after the library announced that the plate is probably a hoax, the number of sightseers coming to view it increased. *Courtesy of The Bancroft Library, University of California, Berkeley.*

The Manila Galleon and Revived Exploration

In the late sixteenth century, Spain once again looked toward California. Fernando Magellan's first round-the-world voyage in 1521 had established Spain's claim to the Philippines and, by mid-century, it had established a colony there and a lucrative trade in bullion and rare Asian products. Fearful of English and Dutch pirates that preyed on shipping between its mainland and island colonies, Spain eventually concentrated the trade in a single ship that sailed annually between Acapulco and Manila. Seeking advantageous winds and currents, the famed "Manila galleons" eventually charted a new return route, heading north from the Philippines, then east across the northern Pacific to a point somewhere off the upper coast of California, then rapidly south towards Acapulco.

The new route proved long and hazardous for both people and cargo. After sailing for half a year or more over open seas without touching land, the galleons reached California waters in bad repair and short of supplies, often with crew and passengers too ill or weak to go ashore. The battered ships were easy pickings for pirates lurking off the Baja peninsula, who picked off several treasure-laden galleons. These losses, as well as rumors of Drake's "convenient and fit harbor," revived Spanish interest in California as a supply station for its treasure ships.

Spain's search for a safe harbor in California began in earnest in the 1580s. Manila galleon captains initially explored the coastline en route to Mexico. In 1587, for example, officials directed Manila Galleon commander Pedro de Unamuno to make a thorough examination. Arriving off central California in early October, Unamuno finally found a safe anchorage, probably in Morro Bay. Unamuno led a party of twelve heavily armed soldiers and a priest ashore to make contact with the inhabitants, but the skittish people fled. During several days of hide-and-seek, the landing party traveled many miles inland and inspected abandoned villages of large dugout houses. As they returned to the ship, the voyagers were ambushed by a large force of warriors. Pelted by arrows and javelins, five of the explorers were wounded, two mortally. Finally, under cover of darkness, they managed to escape to the ship on a makeshift raft.

Frightened, badly outnumbered, and short on ammunition, Unamuno set sail before dawn. He abandoned his explorations a week later and made haste for Acapulco, thwarted by heavy fog and fierce tides that made exploring the coastline treacherous. Convinced California Native people would be hostile, officials in Mexico prohibited later Manila galleon sailors from leaving their ships and venturing inland, thereby endangering their precious cargoes.

Despite the disappointment of Unamuno's voyage, continued pirate attacks on Manila galleons kept alive Spanish interest in founding a way station in its remote and troublesome province. In 1595, Sebastián Rodríguez Cermeño, a Portuguese-born navigator, sailed from the Philippines in the heavily loaded *San Agustín* with orders to search California's shoreline for a suitable haven. Arriving north of present-day Eureka, the *San Agustín* sailed south, hugging the land. In an incident unfortunately typical of early explorations, an approaching storm forced Cermeño to make anchor on November 6 in present-day Drake's Bay.

Boatloads of Natives soon surrounded the *San Agustín*. After receiving gifts of cloth, the people welcomed the strangers ashore. Landing with 22 men armed with harquebus, sword, and shield, Cermeño claimed the land for Spain and, with Unamuno's experience in mind, built a fortress on the beach and began assembling a small sailing launch, the *San Buenaventura*. They spent nearly a month exploring the shoreline, touring the interior (violating Cermeño's orders), trading and conferring with the Coast Miwok. During one of the longest encounters between Spanish explorers and Indigenous Californians, Cermeño's scribe, Pedro de Lugo, compiled detailed reports of their interactions, as well as notes on local dress, foods, and customs. Lugo observed that the Indians went about "naked without covering and with their private parts exposed." They

were "a well-made people, robust and more corpulent than the Spaniards in general." As Drake had found, most local people were friendly, but some were defiant, requiring proof of the visitors' peaceful intentions. In this, Spanish presents and trade worked miracles, transforming bristling warriors into gracious hosts.

On November 30, 1595, disaster struck. A fierce storm demolished the galleon *San Agustín*, sank its cargo and provisions, and drowned a dozen or more sailors. Completely out of food, Cermeño ordered a sweep through the countryside to gather acorns, wild nuts, and whatever could be salvaged from the shipwreck. Most Indians relinquished these goods peacefully, but when the Spaniards attempted to retrieve ship planks from one village, the enraged people attacked, wounding one sailor. Driving the Indians off with gunfire, the Spaniards stripped the village of its food as well as the salvaged wood. Eighty survivors and their meager supplies crammed into the tiny *San Buenaventura* on December 8 and set sail for Mexico.

The return of the *San Buenaventura* was one of the era's epic adventures. Now in the winter storm season, gales thrashed the tiny open vessel. The shore obscured by heavy fogs, Cermeño's party, like all the previous explorers, failed to see the mist-enshrouded Golden Gate, and the vast, sheltered San Francisco Bay behind it, though they passed only a few miles away. Huddled in the open launch, the survivors suffered thirst, hunger, and exposure, surviving by catching fish, gathering plants on offshore islands, and trading with Natives for food. Bitter acorns and roots made some Spaniards violently ill. Deaf to the pleas of his crew, in clear weather Cermeño doggedly stopped to take soundings, make observations, and annotate his charts. Upon reaching the well-documented coast of Baja, Cermeño finally ordered a speedy passage to Acapulco. Its crew gaunt, nearly naked, but miraculously still alive, the *San Buenaventura* arrived in Mexico at the end of January 1596.

Cermeño received an icy welcome. Enraged by the loss of a cargo worth one million pesos, Mexican officials charged the luckless captain with wandering too far from the ship, exposing the expedition to unnecessary danger, and failing to find a sheltered port as ordered. An investigation cleared Cermeño professionally but pronounced the expedition a failure. As a result, the charts for which Cermeño and his crew had paid dearly were suppressed, although they were the most accurate and detailed to date. Authorities abandoned any further attempt to use the Manila Galleon to explore the California coast. With their exhausted crews and valuable cargoes, the galleons were ordered to avoid the treacherous coast. Any future exploratory missions would venture north from Mexico in light, maneuverable, specially equipped ships, carrying only supplies and trade goods for Indians.

Vizcaíno's Expedition

The viceroy of New Spain at the time of Cermeño's voyage, Gaspar de Zúñiga y Acevedo, still favored the exploration of California. On orders from the Spanish government, he organized a special expedition to chart the California coast and find a port suitable for settlement and resupplying Manila Galleons. Sebastián Vizcaíno, a veteran explorer and developer of pearl fisheries on the Baja Peninsula, headed the venture. To avoid the problems that had thwarted earlier efforts, Zúñiga and Vizcaíno painstakingly prepared the expedition and its vessels. They assembled expert cartographers and officers, along with seasoned sailors and soldiers who "knew how to handle arms well." Zúñiga detailed instructions cautioned Vizcaíno against arousing the Indians. After a year in planning, the captain loaded his large force of more than 130 men aboard three small ships, the *San Diego*, the *Santo Tomás*, and the *Tres Reyes*, and sailed north from Acapulco on May 5, 1602, early enough, they thought, to beat the northerly winter storms.

Despite all precautions, Vizcaíno's voyage still proved difficult. Unseasonably strong northwest winds forced the ships to tack back and forth, "an insufferable labor," according to expedition chaplain Father Antonio de la Ascensión. Vizcaíno's thorough coastal surveys, along with frequent stops to replenish the large crew's supplies, also impeded progress. It took the expedition a month to round the southern tip of Baja. It reached San Diego November 10, a full six months after setting sail. Too late to challenge California's tempestuous waters, Vizcaíno logged a tortured course up the coast, fighting gales and storms all the way. True to his instructions, Vizcaíno charted bays, islands, and landmarks north from San Diego. The place names he chose, all drawn from Catholic saints' days, remain to the present day.

Vizcaíno's relations with southern California Indians resembled those of Cabrillo 60 years earlier. He found the coast and offshore islands densely populated from San Diego to Point Conception. As in Baja, some groups offered resistance. When Vizcaíno's men came ashore at San Diego, they were charged by enraged Natives. The attack ended when Father Ascensión advanced alone with gifts of bead necklaces. During the Spaniards' ten-day sojourn, Ascensión recalled, "contented and happy" local people came often to trade animal skins for European goods. They learned some Spanish words and, like the Baja Indians, reported news of white men in the interior. Vizcaíno recognized these as accounts of Juan de Oñate's reconquest of New Mexico a few years earlier.

The people of the Santa Barbara Channel particularly impressed Vizcaíno's party. At Santa Catalina Island, the explorers stayed a week among the Gabrielino (Tongva), who, according to Ascensión, received them with such familiarity that it appeared "they had seen Spaniards before." (Cabrillo had stopped there briefly 60 years earlier.) Vizcaíno erected a tent and altar, and the chaplains said mass before "a great number of young Indians." Ascensión admired the islanders' swift plank canoes, their "pleasing and easy" methods of taking large fish and seals, and the thriving system of trade and communication that linked mainland and island peoples. The local people also stole skillfully from the Spaniards. Ascensión complained that they were "very light-fingered and clever" and "beat the gypsies in cunning and dexterity." Soldiers triggered one serious incident when they desecrated a shrine by casually shooting two sacred crows guarding it, causing the Indians "to weep and show great emotion."

Word of the Spanish travelers preceded them to the Santa Barbara Channel's Chumash. Boatmen who met the ships whenever they neared land insisted the Spaniards accept their hospitality on shore. One especially outgoing leader came aboard and, seeing no females on the ships, offered the strangers ten women apiece if they would visit the villages. Father Ascensión reported that, when "all of us laughed very much," the chief, thinking that they doubted his sincerity, offered to remain on board as a hostage if the Spaniards would go ashore. Vizcaíno presented him with gifts and sent him home to prepare for the visit, but then seized a rare southeast wind that suddenly came up. Determined to accept the chief's offer on their return voyage, the explorers sailed north on December 3. Within a day, however, they lost their fortuitous wind, and were once again left to combat the elements. Adverse weather prevented them from contacting many people north of Point Conception.

On December 16, the explorers rounded a rocky promontory flanked by pine forests (Point Piños) and anchored in a tiny, north-facing inlet. The expedition was in crisis, with scurvy ravishing the crew. Almost all suffered severe body pains, swollen gums, and loose teeth. Most were too weak to rise from their beds, including some officers and priests. Father Ascensión recalled that "no one was found who could even manage the sails of the ships." Sixteen had perished so far, "while others were dying each day without any remedy." Ignorant of the dietary causes of scurvy (lack of the vitamins found in fresh fruit and vegetables) Ascensión blamed the pestilence on California's sharp, northwesterly winds.

What was worse, Vizcaíno still had not found a suitable site for a port and settlement. Fearing the career-ending consequences of failure, he concocted a report transforming this rocky, inhospitable anchorage into the long-sought California harbor. Shrewdly naming it for the viceroy, Gaspar de Zúñiga y Acevedo, Conde de Monterrey, the explorer wrote descriptions of his "discovery" in a letter to the king. Monterey Bay, Vizcaíno boasted, was "the best port that could be desired, for besides being sheltered from all the winds, it has many pines for masts and yards, and live oaks and white oaks, and water in great quantity, all near the shore." Vizcaíno also reported that the region teemed with gentle people eager to accept both Christianity and Spanish rule. The climate was so benevolent and the soil so fertile that "any seed sown there will give fruit." In truth, the largely open bay offered little protection from pirates or weather, and dangerous tides guarded its approaches. The local Costanoan population was sparse, and the climate was foggy and windy. Vizcaíno's reports and charts so misrepresented the site that, a century and a half later, a frustrated Gaspar de Portolá arrived there by land looking for Monterey, but seeing nothing that matched Vizcaíno's description, he was forced to trudge on.

Vizcaíno and his men spent several weeks at Monterey. After an emergency council on December 29, he sent the disabled seamen back to Mexico on the *Santo Tomás*, with a request for supplies and a relief crew. Five days later, he departed, hoping to push as far as Cape Mendocino.

Another fierce storm struck the *San Diego* and the *Tres Reyes* on January 5. Then, for more than two weeks an unusual southerly wind blew them northward. The ships now separated, Vizcaíno in the *San Diego* was beaten about by swiftly reversing winds. His sails furled, he could neither turn back nor take shelter. Scurvy and exposure continued to take their toll. Only six men could rise from their beds and only two could still climb the mast. During a particularly violent blast, a crate broke loose and injured Vizcaíno. They reached Drake's Bay, where the *San Agustín* had gone down, but the violent weather prevented any attempt to salvage the cargo. When the storms slackened, Vizcaíno found himself off the coast of southern Oregon near an uncharted white promontory he named Cape San Sebastián.

Facing destruction, on January 19 the entire crew, including the sick, made a supreme effort, lifting the sails, turning about, and heading south for Mexico. On March 21, 1603, the *San Diego* struggled into port at Acapulco. The *Santo Tomás* and *Tres Reyes* had already returned. Altogether a third of the men, 40-plus mariners, died.

California Forsaken

Vizcaíno's voyage crowned early Spanish efforts to explore California. The most accurate survey yet north of Baja, Vizcaíno's detailed charts and logs shaped mapmaking for nearly two centuries. The first group of settlers relied on his reports in the 1760s. Vizcaíno called attention to the future site for the town of Monterey, which, after the settlers figured out what he meant, became the new focus of Spanish colonizing efforts. His fanciful embellishment of Monterey's bay, however, along with his failure to discover San Francisco Bay, greatly complicated the already difficult task of settling Alta California.

Although Vizcaíno, Ascensión, and Zúñiga all sang Monterey's praises, the voyage did not produce immediate efforts at colonization. Never more than lukewarm, official Spanish interest in California evaporated soon after Vizcaíno's return. Zúñiga departed, and the new viceroy scoffed at his predecessor's colonial ambitions. By then, officials had come to believe that California was too close to Mexico, thus of little assistance to the Manila galleons, and hence not worth the effort to explore and settle. Moreover, 60 years of exploration had produced negative impressions of California. Accounts had sometimes acclaimed the area's beauty, the ripeness of its people for Christianity, and stressed the hope of finding the ever-elusive Strait of Anián, but the accounts' most vivid images of California exploration remained the toil, suffering, biting winds, and rugged and impenetrable landscapes, along with the dangers of Native hostility.

In 1606, Spain issued a royal order prohibited further exploration of California. For more than 150 years, no Spanish sailors admitted visiting the remote coast. Popular maps once again imagined California as an island. The fact that California was part of the mainland had to be rediscovered with great surprise in 1702, during Father Eusebio Kino's overland exploration of southern Arizona and the Colorado River region.

Explorers and Natives: An Assessment

Since Europeans produced all written records of exploration, it is impossible to know exactly how Native Californians perceived the strangers or what goals they pursued in interactions with the travelers. Some general observations are possible, however, based on explorers' descriptions, patterns of encounters elsewhere in the New World, and what has been since learned about California Native American cultures through archaeology, oral traditions, and testimony from descendants.

Information available shows that Californians' responses to the Europeans were hardly uniform or predictable, nor anything like popular legend. Some Indians were awestruck at first seeing the strangers, some fled at the approach of Europeans, others quavered in fear. Bewildered by the intruders' origins and their deadly weapons, many Californians could account for them only by fitting them into their own mythology, as powerful spirits or ghosts of departed ancestors, beings best avoided.

Other Indigenous groups seemed less concerned. In many places, although they were cautious, few people appeared to view the newcomers as a serious threat. Firearms, steel blades, and other European weapons appeared to furnish a decided advantage in theory, but in reality, they were surprisingly unreliable. The danger of firearms was blunted by the scarcity of ammunition and gunsmiths. Coastal tribes such as the Chumash, too, vastly outnumbered the newcomers. Often sick, weakened, and hungry after an arduous voyage, the Europeans appeared inept in comparison to the Indians, who enjoyed advantages of their own, in their vigorous health and mastery of a familiar landscape topography and resources that could be deployed as gifts, essential supplies the Europeans sorely needed, or, if necessary, as effective weapons.

Most groups, however, initially did meet the intruders with some measure of suspicion, if not outright hostility. Most were accustomed to defending their territories aggressively, and many already knew of Spanish assaults on inland peoples. Thus, Californians often perceived the Europeans as dangerous interlopers to be driven away. As Europeans landed along the coast, from Baja California to San Diego, Morro Bay, Drake's Bay, and beyond, tribes attacked immediately, with no apparent provocation beyond violation of their territory. Some groups successfully prevented landings altogether. At Morro Bay, local inhabitants drove Unamuno away and thwarted his plans. Spanish gunfire, in this case, failed to scatter the warriors, serving only to enrage them further. In many places, it was only after Natives were convinced that the seafarers intended no harm, that they set aside their weapons and interacted peacefully with the strangers.

Overall, however, local defiance did restrict European explorers. It had been so widespread that, by the 1590s, officials routinely warned explorers to expect violence everywhere. The constant threat of resistance kept Europeans on the defensive, confined them to a narrow coastal strip and forced them to expend time and energy fortifying their camps, generally making the ordeal of exploration even more arduous. The likelihood of armed conflict prompted officials to forbid exploration by Manila galleons after 1595. Additional landings might have improved European knowledge about California, perhaps even led to earlier colonization, when the Spanish empire remained strong and settlement might have been more effective than it turned out to be.

But not all Californians resisted the Europeans, even when first encountering them. From the beginning, some saw the strangers as objects of wonder, or perhaps of pity. The powerful Chumash and other tribes that came to trust the explorers approached them fearlessly, as equals. They seemed eager to learn about European tools, ornaments, language, and customs. Like Native Americans elsewhere, some Californians also seemed to view European visits as opportunities for profit. They brought food, baskets, and other trade goods to exchange for fascinating European items that surely carried status and wealth within their communities. They also provided services in exchange for trade goods. When Cabrillo's expedition landed in the Santa Barbara Channel in 1542 in dire need of supplies, many Chumash worked for three days bringing the ships wood, food, and water. Indeed, Cabrillo, Drake, Cermeño, and perhaps other explorers probably would not have survived without the services and supplies Californians provided.

The explorers themselves sometimes rose above stereotypical European racism. Despite frequent battles, most seemed more favorably inclined toward the Indigenous peoples than would later interlopers—missionaries and soldiers, for example. As was typical of Europeans of that age, the travelers condemned Native nudity, "heathenism," and thievery, and certainly assumed themselves to be superior beings, of superior culture. But the Europeans were usually as curious about the Indians as the Indians were about them. Those who remained long among the Californians found much to admire. Chroniclers of the Cabrillo, Drake, Cermeño, and Vizcaíno expeditions praised the local peoples' complex and successful cultures, trade systems, well-ordered villages, artfully constructed boats and tools, and their ingenious methods of hunting and fishing. The visitors also marveled at Native strength, agility, and robust good health, often commending them for honesty, generosity, friendliness, fearlessness, and quickness to learn European ways. While the explorers certainly regarded Californians as primitive and inferior beings, they nevertheless recognized them as a skilled, vigorous, and likable, if potentially defiant, people.

During these brief visits, these visitors seemed to have had little direct impact on local cultures. Through trade and shipwreck, European products entered into local material cultures. Some Indians acquired beads, cloth, glassware and pottery, tools, coins, cutting edges, and other metal objects. These products were relatively few in number and kind, however, and the Indians lacked the raw materials, technology, and skills needed to reproduce them.

Some biological interchange between explorers and Indians was likely. Sexual encounters undoubtedly occurred during the long stays of Drake and Cermeño, and perhaps even those of Cabrillo and Vizcaíno. Some of these interludes probably led to offspring after the ships had sailed. Given what happened elsewhere in the New World, Natives may also have contracted deadly diseases from the explorers, who were often sick when they arrived. Some Indigenous people may also have later become sick or even died from mysterious afflictions against which their medicines proved powerless. Surprisingly though, no long-lasting epidemics appeared to have followed these fleeting encounters. When Spaniards returned to colonize a century and a half later, Native California appeared populous and thriving.

All in all, first contacts between Europeans and Californians exposed a wide range of possible relations—violence, friendship, economic exchange, cultural exchange, and sexual and biological encounter. Later, in the longer and more intense period of colonization, interactions between hosts and guests would be similarly complex and contradictory.

Although these visits made little difference in the culture and everyday life of most Californians, the appearance of large birds flying swiftly on white wings over the water, bearing odd beings from unknown worlds, must have challenged the psychological and cultural certainties of many individuals. First contact with the newcomers made a profound impression on coastal peoples. They passed news of such events along to other groups, and it was remembered in tribal lore for centuries. In this sense, the soldiers and missionaries who came to California to settle in 1769 did not arrive as total strangers.

Spanish California

6

Imperial Problems and the
Founding of Spanish California

After a century and a half of neglecting its northern possession, European imperial rivalries and warfare rekindled Spanish interest in Alta California. In 1763, treaty ended the Seven Years' War and victorious Great Britain took Florida from Spain, and all of Canada and the eastern Mississippi Valley from France, Spain's ally. France compensated Spain with the gift of New Orleans and the Louisiana country, sprawling as far as the Rocky Mountains. Spain once again faced an old and powerful enemy, England, along its northeastern frontier. The Russians menaced Spanish possessions as well, as their fur-trading operations slowly spread from Alaska southward along the Pacific Coast. Worse still, mounted Native warriors on Spanish horses roamed the southern Great Plains, attacking struggling Spanish outposts in Texas, New Mexico, and Arizona. In 1765, Spain launched a counter-offensive. Visitor-General José de Gálvez arrived in New Spain to overhaul its corrupt bureaucracy and to improve its defenses against British and Native threats along its northern frontier. To check the Russians, Gálvez also carried orders to establish a colony in Alta California.

After more than two centuries as a colonial power, Spain had a well-established procedure for seizing the homelands of others: a combined military, religious, and civilian offensive. Soldiers led the assault against Native resistance and established *presidios* (forts) to maintain control. Civilians planted farms, *pueblos* (towns), and *ranchos* (livestock ranches) to feed the colony and produce tax-generating exports. Soldiers, town

65

dwellers, and ranchers would become the local ruling class. Central to Spain's plans, however, were the missions, religio-economic institutions operated by religious orders. The missionaries' objectives were complex: to pacify Native peoples, convert them to Catholicism, teach them European skills and culture, and transform them into a malleable labor force. By the mid-eighteenth century, a fragile string of presidios, pueblos, and ranchos stretched thinly across Florida, Texas, New Mexico, Arizona, and Baja California.

Spanish Missions, Presidios, and Pueblos to 1824

Adapted from *Historical Atlas of California*, by Warren A. Beck and Ynez D. Haase. Copyright © 1974 by the University of Oklahoma Press.

Through 1768 and 1769, Gálvez carefully planned the colonization of Alta California. To serve as the new colony's governor he chose Captain Gaspar de Portolá, then serving as governor of Baja California. Control over the new missions Gálvez entrusted to Father Junípero Serra and a group of Franciscan priests already managing missions in Baja. Logistically, Gálvez's plan rested on the reports of early explorers, especially Vizcaíno. Portolá and Serra were to establish two beachhead positions: a presidio and mission at San Diego and a presidio and mission at Monterey Bay, 400 miles farther north. The initial plan called for five additional missions in between and at least one more presidio in coastal areas with dense Native populations. Acknowledging the difficulties faced by early explorers, Gálvez organized a four-pronged invasion, with separate parties traveling by land and sea from the Baja peninsula to the well-charted bay of San Diego. Two ships, *San Antonio* and *San Carlos*, would set sail from La Paz in January and February 1769, carrying supplies for the new mission and settlement and additional soldiers to thwart the expected resistance by San Diego tribes that previous explorers had experienced. The overland expeditions began in March, when Captain Fernando Rivera and a company of leather-armored troops headed north, driving cattle and horses. Finally, Portolá and Serra set off in May, leading a combination of battle-hardened soldiers and Baja mission neophytes across the peninsula's rugged, arid wastes toward San Diego.

Despite Gálvez's precautions, settling Alta California proved just as difficult as earlier efforts to explore its coastline. In making their passages, all four new settlement parties endured costly delays, unimaginable hardships, and fierce Native resistance, and they straggled late into San Diego from March through June. More than half of the 300 colonists died, particularly those who traveled by sea, where scurvy and dysentery took a heavy toll. Many others deserted the floundering land expeditions along the way, especially some Baja mission Indians, who returned to Mexico. Weakened, the survivors spent weeks erecting fortifications at San Diego, burying the dead, and trying in vain to heal the sick. Now far behind schedule, the expedition quickly ran low on supplies. Only a few of the local people would trade with them, and soldiers, sailors, craftsmen, and clerics lacked the skills to forage in a wilderness, even one as bountiful as California. An additional provision ship sent from Baja was lost at sea, and starvation loomed. Desperate, Portolá sent the *San Antonio* back to Mexico for more people and supplies.

Junípero Serra

Saint . . . or Sinner?

Miguel José Serra was born November 24, 1713, to a humble family on the Spanish Mediterranean island of Majorca. Serra attended Franciscan schools and, after graduate studies in philosophy and theology, was ordained a Franciscan priest, taking the name "Junípero" after the brother of St. Francis. His fame as a preacher and professor of philosophy spread quickly, and he seemed destined for a distinguished ecclesiastical career. But Junípero also embodied Franciscan virtues of personal humility, fierce religious devotion, and militant activism on behalf of the faith. He passionately longed to spread the gospel among the unconverted, and even relished the opportunity to one day die a martyr's death. Forsaking all comforts, in 1749 Serra embarked on the rigorous life of a missionary among the Indians of New Spain.

Serra served two decades in various missions in eastern and northern Mexico, where he mastered the religious and economic techniques developed by his predecessors to minister to New World Indians. He earned a reputation as an able administrator and champion of Native welfare. In 1767, Spain charged Serra with oversight of 15 missions in Baja California.

Serra had only been on the peninsula a few months when José de Gálvez arrived and began planning the occupation of Alta California. Seized by a vision of new vineyards of souls to harvest, Serra volunteered for the expedition. Gálvez chose the friar to lead the Franciscans who would establish the new missions. On the journey north with Portolá in early 1769, Serra suffered grievously from ulcerated legs and feet, ailments that plagued him through the end of his life. For much of the journey he could not walk or reach the saddle unaided. His companions alternately hoisted him on and off his mule or carried him on a stretcher.

Junípero Serra and the California Indians

Serra, as portrayed in a nineteenth-century illustration. *The Huntington Library, San Marino, California.*

Father-President Serra took up residence at Mission San Carlos near Monterey. Nearly an invalid when he reached Alta California, his legs troubling him constantly, he spent much of the next 15 years traveling the coastal frontier, founding missions, baptizing Indians, and guiding the new communities through difficult years. Serra, in the spirit of St. Francis, loved and admired the Indians, unlike many of his contemporaries. He described them as having "fine stature, deportment, conversation, and gaiety" and rejoiced that they were "so amenable and so well fitted . . . to receive the Holy Gospel." Serra struggled to master the many complex Native languages so that he could better instruct them in his faith. He sweated alongside them in mission shops and fields, shared food, tears, and laughter in their homes, and counted Natives among his dearest friends. The otherwise meek Franciscan could be stubborn, even aggressive when he deemed it necessary for the welfare of the missions or the Indians. He berated churchmen and government officials alike for neglecting the missions, and repeatedly defended the Indigenous peoples against assault and exploitation by soldiers and civilians. However, like most of his contemporaries, Serra viewed the Indians as childlike, at best. Like all good fathers of his era, he believed that children needed strict discipline, sometimes even the lash.

When Junípero Serra died at San Carlos on August 28, 1784, he left behind a firmly established mission system of nine communities and 5,000 mission Indians. He ignored his failing health almost to his dying day, limping miles to baptize or administer last rites to isolated Natives. (*continued . . .*)

For these and other sacrifices, in 1985, Pope John Paul II declared Serra "venerable," the first step toward sainthood. A storm of controversy erupted as Californian and other Native American groups pointed to the missions' destructive impacts on Native California. When the Pope visited Mission Carmel in September 1987, 75 Costanoan Indians demonstrated nearby. In their view, Serra and his Franciscan brothers had served not as benevolent proselytizers of civilization and uplift but rather as willing agents of Spanish imperialism, slavery, and even genocide. Despite such vehement objections, John Paul advanced Serra's cause by taking the second step in the canonization process the following year when he beatified Serra and proclaimed him "blessed."

At that point, however, the controversial sainthood effort stalled. For nearly three decades the matter lay dormant until its sudden and surprising revival in 2015. In January of that year, Pope Francis announced his intention to complete Serra's canonization, setting off another round of acrimonious debate over the Franciscan achievements in California, which one Native American leader in Sacramento bitterly characterized as "slavery, murder, disease, and basically genocide." Still another, speaking in Los Angeles, angrily denounced Father Serra as "the mastermind of the brutal mission system" that carried out the "genocide of indigenous Californians."

Nevertheless, like John Paul before him, Francis forged ahead with his plans to perform the first canonization ever to take place on U.S. soil. On September 23, 2015, at a huge outdoor Mass celebrated in Washington, D.C., and attended by 25,000 people, including Vice President Joseph Biden, Pope Francis elevated Junípero Serra to sainthood.

Today, Father Serra's ambiguous and deeply contested legacy is frankly acknowledged by his leading biographers, most of whom remain quite sympathetic to the man while candidly admitting his faults. As Steven Hackel puts it, "By and large, Serra is now remembered in not one way but three: as a pioneer, as a religious icon, and as a colonial imperialist. To many, Serra is the man who brought agriculture to the Golden State and who laid the foundation for California's future greatness." To many Roman Catholics, Serra "remains a heroic and saintly embodiment of the religion's timeless virtues." To still others, however, "Serra's life embodies the evils inherent in a colonial system that promoted cultural genocide, sanctioned corporal punishment, and brought about the devastation of California's Native peoples." Given such disparate views, a broad consensus on Father Serra is not likely to emerge any time soon. Instead, over 300 years after his birth, Serra's life work will continue to "resist easy categorization, prompting debate and reinterpretation" rather than harmonious agreement.

(RJO and MFM)

With orders to also settle Monterey, Portolá and 60 emaciated soldiers left San Diego on July 14, 1769, leaving Serra behind to care for the sick and oversee construction of the San Diego mission. Suffering from exposure, hunger, and illness, Portolá's party beat a tortured overland path northward through the uncharted, broken country, hugging the rugged coast wherever possible. Like earlier explorers, Portolá was alternately harassed and aided by Natives he met along the way. The Spaniards were forced to hunt and forage for food. Although they were sometimes able to trade with friendlier tribes, ultimately just to stay alive, they had to slaughter their own mules, which made travel even more arduous. Months later, they reached the latitude given by Vizcaíno for the "port" of Monterey. Although he scoured the rugged, cold, and windy coastline, Portolá saw nothing that matched Vizcaíno's glowing description.

Puzzled, Portolá pressed northward along the coast. On November 2, he found the way blocked by a giant "arm of the sea or estuary" (the then-undiscovered and unmapped San Francisco Bay). Mistaking this for Drake's Bay, Portolá realized that he must have passed Monterey. He retraced his steps southward but, again failing to find the magnificent port described by Vizcaíno, the defeated Spaniards slogged south. In late January 1770, half a year after they had left, they finally arrived at San Diego, exhausted, disheartened, and nearly starved.

Conditions were no better at the new settlement. A log stockade had been built, along with a few stick-and-mud buildings. But help had not arrived from Mexico. The garrison was nearly out of food, some men dying. Hostile Natives not only raided their slim supplies, they also attacked the fort. On one occasion, they wounded several colonists and killed a Baja neophyte child. With only a handful of local people willing to trade with them, the Spaniards had been reduced to exchanging their clothes for food. They were saved when the *San Antonio* finally sailed in on March 19, just in the nick of time, only one day before the leaders had set to abandon the expedition and retreat to Mexico.

Refreshed by food and reinforcements, the settlers planted crops and improved their buildings. Leaving behind a small contingent to occupy the rising mission and presidio, Portolá and Serra again headed north to find Monterey, the former by sea and the latter by land. Following Vizcaíno's coordinates, they returned to the same depressing scoop of coastline they had rejected before. This time, Portola conceded that this must be the "port" of Monterey and he started building the presidio and Mission San Carlos. As ordered, he proclaimed Monterey the capital of Alta California. San Carlos became its mother mission and headquarters for Serra, as father-president of the mission system. His orders fulfilled, Portolá turned over command to Lieutenant Pedro Fages on July 9, 1770, and presumably with a prayer of thanksgiving, set sail for Mexico.

The Founding of San Francisco

The Spanish presence in Alta California grew slowly over the next five decades. Serra established three more missions between San Diego and San Carlos: San Gabriel (1771), San Antonio de Padua (1771), and San Luis Obispo (1772). He left each in the care of a small detachment of Franciscans, soldiers, and converted Natives from other missions. Many early colonists died or deserted, however, and some of the original soldiers and sailors were eventually ordered back to Mexico. Thus, as late as 1773, Spanish California counted no more than 100 *gente de razón* (literally "civilized people"), with no non-Native women and children. For decades, Spain's hold over Alta California remained weak and dependent on constant reinforcements from Mexico.

These reinforcements eventually included a handful of Spanish women and children. In 1773, for example, Maria Feliciana Arballo accompanied Captain Juan Bautista de Anza's first overland expedition from Tubac in southern Arizona to Alta California. Unlike many women of this era, Arballo managed to leave her mark on the historical record. Arballo was evidently a free spirit. A well-born *criollo* (a Spaniard born in the colonies), she defied social conventions by marrying a *mestizo* (person of mixed European and Native parentage). Her soldier husband died as she was preparing for the expedition, but Arballo convinced Anza to allow her to continue

without a male chaperone. She joined over the vehement objections of the missionary, Father Pedro Font, who found occasion to complain about her in his diary. One night, Font reported, the "very bold widow" joined the others in singing and drinking around the campfire. To the delight of her fellow travelers, she "sang some verses which were not at all nice."Arballo ignored the disapproving friar and traveled by horse as far as Mission San Gabriel, with one daughter riding in front and the other behind. At San Gabriel, she asserted her independence again, marrying another mestizo solider. The tenacious matriarch made another lasting impression on California history through two of her grandchildren, Andrés Pico and future governor, Pío Pico.

Although the Spanish population of the province remained small, Spain's enthusiasm was revived in 1775, when Juan Manuel de Ayala sailed into the large bay that had stymied Portolá. Further exploration revealed that it was not Drake's Bay, but an uncharted harbor of immense importance, which the Spaniards named San Francisco Bay, in honor of St. Francis of Assisi. Plans to occupy its shores followed immediately. In the winter of 1775, Bautista de Anza and a party of 240 colonists set off on a second overland expedition from Arizona settlements. Hot, dry, and more than 500 miles long, the trail followed the Gila River to the Colorado River, then crossed the desert to Mission San Gabriel. After a brief rest, the party continued to the fledgling San Carlos Mission at Monterey, where feeding and outfitting the large party strained the outpost's meager stores.

In June 1776, the soldiers and settlers, accompanied by Fr. Francisco Palóu, Fr. Pedro Cambón, and three neophytes, headed north. The party reached the tip of the San Francisco peninsula on June 27 and began building a presidio on a windswept bluff overlooking the mouth of the bay. Work on Mission San Francisco ("Mission Dolores," as it came to be called) began at a sunnier, better-watered site several miles to the southeast. Friendly Costanoan Indians pitched in, cutting and hauling wood, and helping with construction. Rudimentary pole and mud structures were completed by mid-September. On October 9, 1776, settlers and Indians gathered for a joyous ceremony to formalize the founding of the new mission. Father Palóu recalled that High Mass was followed by "repeated salvos of muskets, rifles, and swivel-guns that were brought from the bark [ship] for this purpose, and also with rockets." Apparently stunned by the explosions, all the Natives in the vicinity immediately vanished. Several days later, they returned, packed up their belongings, and moved down the peninsula, away from the Spaniards. Mission San

Francisco did not record its first Native baptism until nearly a year later. And then, according to Palóu, "the rest of the heathen came no more."

The Missions

The missions became the largest and most productive communities in Alta California. The tireless Father Serra established the first nine missions between 1769 and his death in 1784, locating them every 50 to 75 miles between San Diego and San Francisco. A far cry from their twentieth-century restorations, these early settlements were initially no more than crude camps, marked by stick, mud, and thatch buildings, marginal agriculture, and tiny neophyte populations. Missionaries had to relocate some missions several times to escape flood, disease, water shortages, and hostile local Natives.

After Serra's death, Fermín de Lasuén replaced him in 1785 as father-president. Tactful and capable, Lasuén founded nine additional missions through the end of his tenure in 1803, reducing the distances between missions in the attempt to solidify Spanish control. Lasuén also fostered irrigation projects, agricultural and industrial expansion, and the economic diversification needed to improve productivity and self-sufficiency in the mission system. As the missions expanded, so did their population. By the early 1800s, the missions of Spanish California included some 20,000 neophytes. Reflecting their growing maturity, wealth, and labor forces, missionaries replaced the shabby pioneer structures with more elaborate stone, abode, and tile-roofed chapels and outbuildings. By the early 1820s, 21 missions spanned the 500 miles between the first mission at San Diego and the last, San Francisco Solano, founded in 1823. Father Jose Altimira planted this northernmost mission amongst Pomo, Miwok, and other Native peoples. Hispanic settlers interpreted their name of this place as "Sonoma," the Valley of the Moon.

Franciscan missionaries played diverse and sometimes contradictory roles in Spanish, and later Mexican, California. In the early years, most of the 142 men who served the missions were deeply religious, idealistic, and devoted to saving Indian souls. Yet most padres insisted that converts also accept European customs. Missionaries viewed acculturation as synonymous with religious conversion: Native resistance to one signaled failure of the other. Thus missionaries attempted to regulate the lives of the neophytes down to minute details of waking,

Mission San Carlos, 1794

One of the oldest drawings of a California mission, this sketch was made by artist J. Sykes, who accompanied Captain George Vancouver's British naval expedition to the Pacific. This and other views illustrate the rudeness and disorder in the difficult early years of a mission's existence. At first, buildings were simple stick-and-thatch structures, and, as was the case at San Carlos, the neophytes continued to wear Native garb and live in Native dwellings for some time. When Vancouver visited, San Carlos was becoming a more mature settlement. The present stone chapel was under construction at the left of the drawing. It was completed in 1797, nearly 30 years after the mission's founding. *Courtesy of the California History Room, California State Library, Sacramento, California.*

sleeping, eating, working, worship, amusement, family, and sex. Not surprisingly, this provoked much resistance among neophytes. Treating them as unintelligent if not belligerent children, the missionaries' attitudes towards Natives ranged from bemused paternalism at best, to race-based animosity at worst.

Officially, Spanish law invested the missionaries with absolute authority over the Indians, as teachers and as custodians of their persons, labor, and properties. In theory, missionaries held the mission lands in trust for their Native charges until such time as the neophytes became *gente de razón*. Then, in theory, the missions would become secular settlements, and the fathers would release their inheritance to the Christianized, Europeanized neophytes. But missionaries' assimilationist strategies often undermined their religious goals and led to conflict with other colonial interests. Serra, Lasuén, and Narciso Durán bickered constantly with civilian and military leaders, who viewed the Natives primarily as virtual slave laborers. The Franciscans argued against secularization, which would have meant an end to missionary control over the neophytes and their patrimony. Although most missionaries were sincere in their desire to defend the Natives against exploitation by others, the fact remained that they were refusing to relinquish their own control, thus delaying the planned-for advancement of the Natives as free peoples, in charge of their own civilian settlements. This conflict over an inherently contradictory assimilation policy reduced the coordination and effectiveness that might have been possible between missionaries, civilians, and military authorities, thus hampering imperial plans for a peaceful, productive, and profitable California colony.

Presidios and Pueblos

To control Indians and discourage its imperial rivals, Spain needed a strong military presence in California. Fortified with stockades, firearms, and artillery, presidios watched over local districts and guarded the strategic approaches at San Diego, Monterey, San Francisco, and Santa Barbara. Five or ten heavily armed soldiers also were assigned to each mission to discipline neophytes and catch runaways. Like their counterparts on the Anglo-American frontier, California soldiers also surveyed land, carried mail, engaged in crafts, and constructed churches, barracks, stores, roads, and bridges. Presidios were marketplaces and government centers; scattered around the stockades were churches, farms, stores, houses, and saloons.

Officials also planned agricultural communities to support the presidios and missions, thus minimizing the need to import supplies from Mexico. In 1777, Governor Felipe de Neve founded California's first two *pueblos de gente de razón* ("towns for civilized people"). A group of 68 individuals from Anza's original expedition, and from San Francisco and Monterey, established the pueblo of San José near the foot of San Francisco Bay. Just east of the new Mission Santa Clara, San José supplied food to the northern presidios and missions. Four years later, Neve authorized a southern pueblo ten miles west of Mission San Gabriel. Eleven families were recruited to travel from northern Mexico along Bautista de Anza's trail to the banks of the Río de Porciúncula. Initially called Nuestra Señora la Reina de los Angeles de la Porciúncula, the pueblo's name was soon shortened to "Los Angeles." With fertile soil and plentiful water, it soon developed into the largest secular settlement in Spanish California.

Offering Hispanic settlers protection and more efficient production, the pueblos developed into farming villages and centers of secular life in the colony. Beginning in 1769, almost all *gente de razón* lived in, or adjacent to, the pueblos or presidios, with only a few employed at missions. Authorities provided each pueblo with a formal charter granting lands and establishing local government. To encourage migration and development, officials initially supplied residents with food, clothing, tools, and livestock, plus house lots, farming and grazing land on the outskirts, and several years' salary. In return, settlers were required to grow crops, serve in the militia, improve their lands, and work on public projects and communal lands.

Spanish officials instituted rudimentary urban planning. Rectangular plazas hosted entertainments, religious festivals, and military parades. The church, government buildings, and residences of prominent citizens fronted the plazas. On paper, street grids emanated from the plazas, but the thoroughfares that developed were usually meandering lanes haphazardly lined with tiny adobe, tar-and-stick-roofed houses. Small farms ringed village outskirts. Beyond were open ranges for cattle, horses, sheep, and goats. Public lands interspersed throughout provided room for future expansion and for raising the crops and herds needed for town revenue. Knitting the settlement together were open, publicly maintained *zanjas* (ditches) that carried water for drinking, irrigation, and drainage. Poor, disorderly, and rarely proceeding according to plan, Spanish California's first civil communities attempted to impose orderly European values upon the land.

Drawn from the diverse populations of Mexico, the settlements were heterogeneous. Only a select few—colonial governors, high-ranking military officers, and Franciscan missionaries—were *peninsulares* (Spaniards born in Spain), and others were *criollos*. Most newcomers to Spanish California were a mixture of Spanish, Mexican Indian, and African ancestry. Town records differentiated between people of light and dark skin, but most settlers were equally poor, and in this remote, thinly populated province, there were few instances of discrimination among the *gente de razón*. Because some settlers (many of whom were mixed race) intermarried with Natives, California's *gente de razón* population

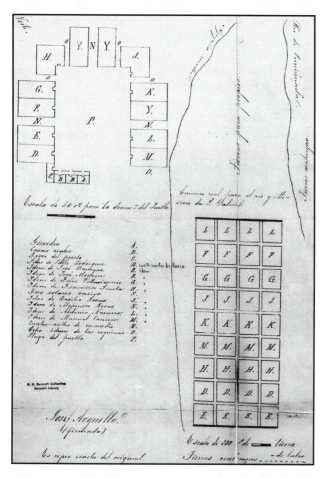

José Argüello's Plan of the Los Angeles Pueblo, 1786
This early plan of Los Angeles demonstrates the inception of urban planning in California. At the upper left is the plaza, surrounded by the pueblo's major buildings. The main irrigation ditch leaves the river at the top and threads down through the middle of the town, past the town's farm plots. *Courtesy of The Bancroft Library, University of California, Berkeley.*

became increasingly racially diverse. But, between those considered to be *gente de razón* and the pure-blood California Natives, however, distinctions were sharp and relationships strained, despite some intermarriage.

Most pueblo-dwellers, in Los Angeles for one example, lived in simple dwellings, but at least one rundown district housed lower-caste residents, usually Native gentiles. Their villages overturned by violence and disease, some Natives were conscripted as laborers or lived voluntarily in the towns, working as domestic servants and farm laborers. Within a few years of its founding in 1781, Los Angeles depended on poorly paid gentile laborers, many of whom were routinely cheated, flogged, jailed without cause, and required to toil against their will. Having brought few women from Mexico, townsmen took Native women and girls as concubines. By the end of the 1780s, Los Angeles had adopted complicated, though often-ignored, regulations governing working conditions and Native-white relationships. Intended to preserve and discipline its gentile labor force, the ordinances banned extreme cruelty toward Natives, prohibited sex between Natives and *gente de razón*, required Natives to live in specific neighborhoods, and forbade them from working or sleeping inside settlers' houses and congregating in large groups. Missionaries and leading Angelenos alike complained that availability of Native slave labor made many among the *gente de razón* idle, and spread the colonists' vices and venereal diseases to the Natives. At the same time, the harsh treatment gentiles received from the colonists kept most of them away from the missions, thus perpetuating their Native cultural practices. But the lure of cheap Indian labor was strong and the authority of missionaries weak. By 1803 Los Angeles had a population of 359 *gente de razón* and 200 gentiles. The labor system, and its abuses, continued.

The Spanish presence also disrupted the lives of Natives living outside the settlements, for example those north and west of San Francisco Bay. The life of Isidora Filomena Solano (Chiructos/Satiyomi) illustrates this impact. Born in a Wappo community around 1800, Isidora's people had lived in the Napa-Sonoma region for centuries. She and other women gathered acorns, fruits, herbs, and tubers and, on occasion, hunted small game. They joined the men in harvesting clamshells from Pomo territory, then working them into disks they traded for awls, carrying baskets, split-stick dice, and arrows. Isidora's people lived at the center point of a thriving trade network. Located between the Coast Miwok and Pomo, neighbors often came to their villages to trade and then stayed to visit." We lived our lives with joy," Isidora recalled. Food was abundant and everyone had a home of tule reeds. She also noted how clean her people were: "We loved to bathe," she said, "because bathing makes you strong . . . my people always had white teeth that we cleaned with branches of ash trees."

But the Wappo world was also fraught with conflict as missionaries extended influence over the area. Patwin peoples had occasionally encroached into Wappo land; then, in 1810, the Carquin, the last of the communities standing between the Patwin and the mission in San Francisco, converted to Catholicism. With no buffer between themselves, the Spanish missionaries, and the soldiers, the Patwin moved northeast into Wappo territory. The disaster was compounded for the Wappo when Mission San Francisco Solano was established in the early 1820s. It grew even worse when a Patwin leader, Sem Yeto (known to colonial settlers as "Chief Solano") converted to Catholicism. He and his men began hunting fugitives and gentiles with the soldiers, killing and capturing Natives for delivery to the missions. In 1835, Sem Yeto captured Isidora and took her to the priest at Mission San Francisco Solano to train as a Christian wife.

Economic Development, Labor, and Society

Spanish California was a far cry from the productive pastoral land celebrated in romantic legend. The province was a crude frontier that struggled for decades to become self-sufficient. Cut off from the outside world, hampered by unreliable rainfall, capital, labor, supplies, machinery, transportation, and markets, simple subsistence was the best most settlers could do. Fortunately, they had a useful heritage of Mediterranean- and Mexican/Native-irrigated agriculture on which to draw. Settlers dug ditches to divert water from streams onto their fields, practicing a blend of European and Native American farming techniques developed earlier in colonial Mexico. Pueblo settlers relied on Native laborers to help cultivate their small plots of corn, wheat, melons, and other fruits and vegetables; European poultry and livestock roamed freely. In Los Angeles and other large communities, improved irrigation led to larger orchards and gardens. But overall, pueblo agriculture grew slowly. With small populations and erratic water supplies, most pueblos barely succeeded in feeding themselves, much less producing a surplus.

The most successful agriculture emerged at the missions, where the Franciscans made good use of farming techniques developed in colonial Mexico, their larger populations of laborers, and existing systems of discipline and organization. Although voluntary conversions came slowly at first, missionaries and soldiers soon amassed sufficient numbers of neophytes. By 1784, the nine existing missions counted roughly 100 *gente de razón* in charge of roughly 5,800 neophytes. By the early nineteenth century, the missions' Native population numbered around 20,000.

In practice, missions were industrial schools, converting Natives to Catholicism while training them in the European handicrafts and agricultural skills needed for self-sufficiency. Accustomed to highly refined skills in their own cultures, Natives quickly learned to plow, plant, harvest, tend livestock, and construct implements from stone, wood, leather, and small supplies of imported iron. Priests taught specialized skills, designated the best-trained neophytes as overseers, instituted European labor practices, and meted out discipline. As was true in the pueblos, Native labor sustained the missions.

Expanding neophyte populations allowed construction of larger and better irrigation systems, which expanded the cultivation of crops and made missions more productive than the pueblos and other settlements. Starting with simple diversion lines, missions eventually developed elaborate waterworks with storage reservoirs, masonry aqueducts, and miles of canals. The masonry dam in the mountains behind Mission Santa Barbara was 100 feet long, 17 feet thick, and 17 feet high. Each of its main stone canals was three miles long, carrying water to crops as well as buildings, shops, and elsewhere. Mission irrigation systems supported larger, more diverse farms, with greater dependability. Missionaries sowed European crops, such as wheat, barley, oats, citrus and deciduous fruits and nuts, grapes, hemp, and flax, as well as crops originally developed over thousands of years by pre-Columbian Native groups, including corn, beans, squash, melons, cotton, and tobacco. Reaching their peak in the early 1820s, the missions cultivated some 5,000 to 10,000 acres, producing over 100,000 bushels of crops annually. Mission San Gabriel was particularly successful, boasting nearly 200 acres just of fruit trees.

Nonetheless, mission farms suffered significant disadvantages. Even at their zenith, the missions were limited by access to markets, lack of funds to buy iron and other vital materials, unreliable shipments of supplies, and high rates of death and fugitivism among neophyte laborers. Soil depletion also caused crop yields to decline (a problem that could have been reduced by penning livestock and collecting their waste for fertilizer). Moreover, large neophyte populations relied on mission gardens. The residents of presidios and pueblos also drew on the missions for food, their requisitions steadily increased through the 1820s during the unstable transition to Mexican rule. Even in good years, neophytes endured a lean and unbalanced diet. Conditions worsened in drought years, when mission Indians and *gente de razón* alike went hungry. At such times, the padres reluctantly allowed neophytes to leave the missions and forage for wild foods. Such forays weakened mission discipline and increased contact between neophytes and gentiles. But despite these problems, the missions provided Spanish California with new crops and introduced new farming techniques. Later generations would draw from the models developed by missionaries, especially their systems of irrigation.

As was true for the pueblos and later ranchos, livestock formed the core of mission commerce. Open-range grazing was ideal in coastal valleys and hills, with plentiful grasses, acorns, and shrubbery; ponds and perennially flowing streams; and a gentle climate that made sheltering animals unnecessary. Cattle-raising was especially rewarding: the animals reproduced in the wild, roamed for their own forage and water, and stored themselves until their products were needed. After being rounded up, they were butchered and processed for meat, horns, hides, and other valuable goods, including their tallow (rendered fat), which yielded soap, oils, candles, and lubricants. Other livestock included sheep for mutton and wool, hogs for lard, and horses, donkeys, mules, and oxen that provided transportation and worked the land. By 1830, the breeding stock brought north by early settlers had propagated so successfully that the missions counted two million head of cattle, sheep, goats, horses, and mules. Most of it roamed loose on vast mission lands, tended by neophyte *vaqueros*.

Officials encouraged manufacturing to make the settlements self-supporting, but only the missions had the means to diversify production. At San José and other mature missions, neophytes produced cloth, blankets, rope, pottery, bricks, tiles, leather goods, candles, soap, furniture, and iron hardware. All of the missions had grain or lumber mills driven by water, animal, or human power. Some missions had specialties: San Gabriel, for example, was famous for its wine; San Juan Capistrano for smelting and casting iron. Although essential to life on an isolated frontier, these unrefined goods were of too little value to transport and sell to the outside world.

Spanish California's sparse population and lack of commercial resources also stifled economic development. A few soldiers and townspeople worked as carpenters, masons, blacksmiths, musicians, or merchants, but necessity forced most people to focus on simple subsistence.

The colony had virtually no doctors, lawyers, teachers, or other trained professionals, other than a handful of priests and high-ranking officers. Since virtually no schools existed outside the missions, most *gente de razón*, even high-ranking persons, were illiterate. Beyond the limited music, architecture, and decorative arts of the missions, Hispanic settlers had neither time nor energy to develop folk arts.

From 1769 to 1821, the economy of Spanish California advanced little. The expansion of farming, livestock ranching, and simple industry barely compensated for the growing numbers of *gente de razón*, mission neophytes, and partially assimilated gentiles, nor could these gains compensate for declining governmental subsidies. Most people's standard of living remained low. Although settlers usually produced enough food for themselves (except in periods of drought), Spanish California exported very little before 1800. Even then, the modest, illegal exports were limited surplus grain sales to the Russian colony at Fort Ross, and a beginning, but small, hide-and-tallow trade with British and American sailing ships. Without much industry or funds of its own, the colony depended on limited trade with visiting ships for manufactured goods, and on the Spanish government for financial support. After 1800, though, these funds dried up. The colony's economic problems discouraged further immigration, sapping the settlers' initiative, further reducing revenues and souring relations among civilians, missionaries, and Natives.

Settlers were further hindered by the colony's weak authority structure. Short of arms, soldiers, courts, administrators, and funds, officials enforced the laws haphazardly. Colonial politics quickly degenerated into factionalism between rival cliques of *gente de razón*, complicated by the long-standing tensions that roiled missionaries, governors, and military commanders. Vice and violence abounded, especially in the pueblos. Epidemics, poor diet, water pollution, and barbaric medical practices ravaged colonial populations, as did the earthquakes that toppled buildings, floods that washed away settlements, droughts that seared crops, and recurring plagues of insects and rodents.

Unsurprisingly, outsiders disparaged Spanish California and few immigrants sought its shores voluntarily. The number of *gente de razón* reached 500 by 1779 but grew slowly thereafter: 1,800 in 1800, 3,300 in 1821, most of the gain through natural increase. New Mexico's population, by comparison, was ten times larger. After 50 years of effort, Spain's northern empire amounted to only a few struggling outposts spread thin along a 500-mile frontier. Spanish California was a mere vestige of European civilization, hanging on to the coastline by its fingernails.

The European Conquest of Nature

Native impact on California's land, water, plants, and animals had been relatively gentle. Spaniards, however, like most European immigrants to the New World, arrived with both the tools and the will to transform the landscape. Their limited interpretation of Judeo-Christian religious traditions led them to believe that God had devised the natural world for the sole benefit of man, thus sanctioning exploitation of the environment. Over the centuries, Europeans had denuded their own continent of forests, reduced fertile valleys and hillsides to wastelands, and eradicated whole species of plants and animals. By the eighteenth century, European settlers were poised to destroy large stretches of the New World as well. Intentionally and unintentionally, Spaniards in California introduced physical, economic, and biological changes that triggered an environmental revolution.

The colonization that began in 1769 had astounding ecological effects. Settlers stripped local forests for fuel and building materials, denuding the land and causing flooding. Spanish irrigation projects reorganized the hydrological landscape, leaving dry riverbeds in some places, drowning others under makeshift reservoirs and drainage ditches. Along with destructive plowing and soil management practices, the European system of monoculture (single-crop agriculture) eroded topsoil, exhausted nutrients, and displaced Native species. Some mission and pueblo lands had to be abandoned after only a few years, and were then reclaimed by introduced foreign weeds rather than Native grasses and trees.

Baggage and grain sacks from Mexico carried European crop seeds, along with useless weeds that quickly invaded cultivated fields and beyond. Birds, livestock, and wind bore the new seeds miles inland, threatening perennial Native grasses and plants. Local species could not compete with hardier invading annuals, particularly on land disturbed by cultivation or livestock grazing. Native plants soon faded from settled areas, and far inland onto unmissionized Natives' food-gathering areas. The Spaniards compounded these grassland problems when they forced Natives to abandon their traditional autumn controlled burns. Intending to preserve free pasturage for European livestock, instead the newcomers unwittingly spread unproductive weeds and brush onto the grasslands. With Native populations quickly declining, the colonists now had to clear the brush themselves, by hand.

Livestock ranching was easily the Spaniards' most destructive practice. Although the number of colonists was small, they owned dense herds of horses, cattle, and other livestock. The hooves of thousands of wandering livestock denuded the hillsides of vegetation, leading to erosion. Thirsty cattle collapsed the banks of rivers and streams, compounding the problems of erosion. By competing for grass seeds and acorns, Spanish livestock displaced native species, especially deer and elk, and overturned the traditional hunting-and-gathering-economies of Native peoples. The damage was so extensive that even colonial officials noticed. Beginning in the 1780s, authorities periodically ordered large-scale roundups and slaughtering of surplus cattle to protect the rangelands.

Although Spanish settlers were few and their technology limited, they drastically altered California's fragile landscapes and wildlife, particularly along the coast. By the early nineteenth century, grasses were depleted, lands were eroded, and native species had grown scarce in southern California coastal valleys and around the bays at Monterey and San Francisco. By the 1820s, new ecological patterns introduced by the Spaniards were advancing inland ahead of settlement, weakening Native peoples' resource bases, especially food supplies. Spread by winds and herds of feral cattle and horses, European weeds and grains edged out native bunch grasses and other food-producing plants deep into the interior, a process that began only 20 years from the first Spanish settlement and accelerated thereafter.

Simultaneously, a new environmental assault had begun, this one aimed at fur-bearing mammals. In the 1820s, American and British mountain men began trapping California's mink, otter, and beaver. Within two decades, these animals were nearing extinction in the central valleys. By the late 1700s, Russian and American fur companies were slaughtering seals and sea otters; their numbers, too, were soon in free-fall.

Missions and the Acculturation of Native Peoples

Interaction with Natives shaped colonial policy in California. As the colony's founders had intended, the missions became the nexus of Native-Spanish relationships. Some earlier historians like Herbert Bolton insisted that the missions were benevolent institutions that transmitted Christianity and European culture and shielded Native peoples from abusive soldiers and civilians. More recently, historians, anthropologists, and other social scientists, including many Native American scholars, have offered alternative interpretations. The missions, they charge, were built on the ethnocentric assumption that Natives and their cultures were inferior. Missionaries brutalized their charges, using compulsion to concentrate, exploit, and whip Native peoples into submission. As a result, critics conclude, the missions were instruments of destruction rather than protection. In their stark contrasts, neither view is entirely satisfactory. The missions were instead paradoxical communities, where both good and evil reigned. The behavior of individuals—missionaries, colonists, soldiers, neophytes, and gentiles—was varied, ambiguous, and frequently contradictory.

As the experiences of Estanislao's people at Mission San José suggest, a wide range of Indian-colonial relationships existed. Indians responded to colonization efforts according to their culture and prior relations with

San Buenaventura Mission Church and Figueroa Plaza

Founded in 1782, the last of the Junípero Serra missions, the building is authentically restored and is used daily as a parish church. *Photograph by William A. Bullough.*

others, including Europeans. Some Natives were initially intrigued by the newcomers' apparent magic, as well as their valuable trade goods, and the allure of possible alliances against local enemies. Such groups interacted freely with the newcomers, providing food, labor, and other services. The Yuma, for example, rescued Juan Bautista de Anza's first trailblazing expedition in 1774, when it was lost in the desert. Natives helped them ford the Gila and Colorado rivers, directed them to trails and water holes, and guarded their equipment and livestock while a small party forged ahead to the coast.

Most neophytes entered the missions willingly, at least initially. Many resisted giving up all their lifeways, however, and, given the language barriers, probably very few could be considered genuine converts at first. But the Franciscans eventually wooed many into the fold, with their colorful liturgy, music, gifts, food, and the promise of shelter and protection. Facing declining supplies of wild plants and game, the decision to accept some aspects of mission life was a rational response to a new reality. As missions absorbed growing numbers of Natives, traditional gentile village life became increasingly untenable. The missionaries compounded the pressure by focusing on village leaders, who would bring others with them to the missions. Once the padres deemed the Natives successfully converted to Catholicism, they could not legally leave. Entire Native communities did occasionally evacuate to the missions, but this was rare. Some groups continued to live in their traditional fashion, just beyond the pale of colonial settlement. Others, fearing starvation and soldiers in equal measure, fled farther into the interior. Shunning the missions, some Natives instead gravitated to the presidios, pueblos, and ranchos, where they were absorbed as low-caste servants and laborers. Many died of European diseases.

Over time, converted and unconverted Natives learned some Spanish, new agricultural methods, and European industrial arts. Those affiliated with the missions absorbed the fundamentals of Catholicism. Missionized and unmissionized Native Californians acquired metal knives, saws, arrowheads, fishhooks, plows, and kettles, along with other trade goods that modified their economies and cultures. They associated with civilians and soldiers both inside and outside the missions. Spanish culture and technology thus traveled beyond the missions' orbit, especially among southern groups, who were particularly receptive. By the 1830s, the inland Cahuilla, Cupeño, Ipai, and Tipai lived freely, herding sheep, cattle, horses, and poultry, sometimes with loose associations to the Spanish settlements. They adopted Spanish irrigation techniques along with wheat and other foreign crops. Only occasional farmers before contact, many unmissionized southern peoples slowly became agriculturalists.

Despite these influences, few Natives were completely Hispanicized. Even highly assimilated Natives took what was valuable from the new culture while retaining much of their own. Many neophytes only superficially converted to Catholicism, participating in mission activities while secretly adhering to their own traditions. Even neophytes commonly refused to accept all European practices, especially rigid sexual norms. Many Natives who spoke Spanish and practiced European crafts still, especially at some less-developed missions, lived in tule houses, dressed in Native costume, hunted and gathered, and spoke old dialects. They continued also to use traditional tools and handicrafts, remained loyal to traditional leaders, celebrated Native rites, and consulted shamans as needed. Spanish interaction with Natives did not produce a totally assimilated laboring class, as colonial leaders had expected, but rather an amalgamation of cultures.

Nevertheless, missions succeeded in altering the lives of both neophytes and gentiles. Spanish reorganization and weakening of the natural environment largely prevented reversion to traditional ways. Even after the mission system collapsed and neophytes were free to go, most huddled around the crumbling old missions and pueblos, sometimes for generations, practicing a blend of Catholicism and aboriginal rites, laboring for farmers and townspeople, and hunting and gathering whenever possible. When he visited the ruins of Mission San Carlos in the 1870s, 40 years after secularization, Scottish author Robert Louis Stevenson found a community of neophyte musicians there, still performing the music their forebears had learned from the Franciscans.

Early Indian Resistance: The San Diego and Colorado River Rebellions

As Estanislao's rebellion suggests, not all Native Californians accepted missionization. The appearance of explorers and missionaries often provoked immediate resistance. Colonial settlements, attacks on Natives and their villages, and the induction of local groups into the missions all violated tribal territories. Beyond immediate and observable declines in food and game, the arrival of Spaniards disrupted family and community life, upset the balance of power among tribelets, and challenged the authority of Native leaders. Equally alarming, the foreigners' presence coincided with outbreaks of strange and deadly diseases. Soldiers, in particular, but civilians as well, raped women and children, assaulted and enslaved Native men, and captured and held women and children as household servants and laborers. Missionaries complained bitterly about these practices, and some commanders attempted to control civilian and military populations, but abuse of Natives continued unabated. It is not surprising that many Natives not only rejected missionization but relocated as far as possible beyond the Spanish frontier.

Others retaliated with violence. San Diego tribes attacked the Portolá-Serra party several times in 1769 and 1770. The Spaniards imposed an uneasy peace by force of arms, but the Natives seethed under continued abuses. Finally, escaped neophytes and gentiles of the Ipai and Tipai forged an alliance of perhaps as many as 40 villages in November 1775. Led by the neophyte Francisco, they were determined to eject the foreigners and return to the old ways. About 800 warriors stormed the presidio and burned the mission, killing Father Luis Jayme and three colonists. The following year, soldiers drawn from several posts finally managed to regain control. At San Gabriel, La Purísima, San Luis Obispo, Santa Clara, San Francisco, San Miguel, and San Antonio missions, neophytes and gentiles engaged in conspiracies, organized revolts, and attacked travelers and priests. Native peoples, however, failed to offer more than sporadic resistance; they were as hampered by local feuds among tribelets as they were by superior Spanish firepower.

The most successful offensive took place on the Colorado River. Hoping to pacify Yuman groups along Bautista de Anza's trail, in 1780 Spaniards planted two missions, Purísima Concepción and San Pedro, near present-day Yuma. Francisco Garcés, the famed explorer-priest who had accompanied Anza, was in charge. Although locals liked Garcés and initially welcomed the settlements, relations soured when Spanish soldiers committed abuses and stole prize farmland. Yumans had already divided into pro- and anti-Hispanic factions when the last straw fell in the summer of 1781. The settlers Lieutenant Governor Fernando Rivera was bringing from Mexico to found Los Angeles turned their cattle loose to graze and trample Indian crops. On July 17 and 18, after part of the expedition had departed, the Yuma assaulted both missions, killing Rivera, Garcés, three other Franciscans, and 30-plus soldiers and settlers. Subsequent efforts by Spain, and later Mexico, utterly failed to defeat the Yuma. They remained the undisputed lords of the

Colorado River for the next 70 years. What the Spanish called the "Yuma Massacre" sealed off the trail, virtually ending overland immigration. Loss of the route stifled the growth of Spanish California, forcing New Spain to once again use expensive and unreliable sealanes to resupply the province. No other defeat at Native hands weakened the colony more.

Disease, Fugitives, and Horses

By the early nineteenth century, Native-Spanish contact had dramatically altered Native life. When Spanish abuses intensified local defiance, the colony was further weakened. Missionaries compounded resistance, inflicting harsh punishments on neophytes who maintained their traditions. For even minor breaches of work, sexual, or religious rules, missionaries and neophyte overseers lashed and jailed offenders and assigned them extra labor, short rations, and other punishments. Chronic runaways were chained to logs or boulders, which they dragged about their chores. These practices were commonplace in eighteenth-century Europe and colonial America, but Natives considered

such cruelty only suitable for enemies. They chafed under overcrowding, poor diets, and miserable lodgings.

European diseases swept throughout the New World, including California, killing many Natives. Concentrated in unsanitary mission compounds, weakened by hunger and mistreatment, neophytes also lacked immunity to Old World diseases. Mission diseases also spread quickly to local gentiles and through them to interior tribes. Epidemics of smallpox, dysentery, malaria, influenza, venereal disease, and other illnesses began with the first missions and peaked between 1800 and 1820. The 1806 measles epidemic around Mission San Francisco wiped out more than one-third of the neophytes, especially those under age ten. By 1815 the indigenous Indian population of the Bay region was virtually extinct. Demographer Sherburne F. Cook has estimated that few children born in the missions before 1820 lived to adulthood.

Between 1769 and 1846, the Native population declined from more than 300,000 to about 100,000. Due primarily to disease, large coastal and Central Valley tribes were nearly annihilated. Sickness eradicated entire tribelets, disorganized families, upset leadership

San Francisco's Presidio, 1816

This published version of Louis Choris's 1816 drawing of the San Francisco Presidio, perched above the Golden Gate, reflected a then-common view among enlightened Europeans that, in Spanish California, Indians lived in a climate of force and fear. Here, mounted soldiers watch over and drive Indians as they would beasts of burden. The fort's farm fields are at lower left. Although the treatment of Indians was often harsh at the presidios, this particular image illustrates the dangers inherent in reading historical documents superficially. Choris's original drawing, made in California, depicted no menacing soldiers. They were inserted in the drawing later by printers in Europe to conform with their expectations of how missions were supposed to look. *The Huntington Library, San Marino, California.*

systems and prompted power struggles. Demoralized, survivors lost faith in traditional religions, which had apparently lost their protective powers. In California as on other European frontiers, it was disease, rather than superior weaponry, that allowed newcomers to overwhelm local peoples.

Women bore the brunt of violence, disease, and colonization policies that threatened the survival of Native peoples and cultures. Women were most likely to die of disease, within and outside the missions, also dying younger and in higher numbers than men. Those who survived were weakened and often left infertile by venereal disease. Syphilis became virulent after Spanish occupation of California. Infected mothers often miscarried, or produced stillborn, disabled, and infected babies. The shortage of Spanish women prompted many soldiers and settlers to kidnap Native women and girls, forcing them into concubinage and prostitution. Native women captured to become colonial wives, concubines, or servants were lost to their own communities, as were the resulting offspring. Colonial armies sometimes killed or dispersed village males, capturing and delivering surviving women and children to the missions. Women and girls who entered the missions were unavailable to gentile men, further hindering tribal ability to restore lost population through natural increase.

Sharp reductions in the female population, combined with the traditionally low Native birthrate and high rates of mortality in battle, shattered family structures, further depressing reproduction. Many groups faced extinction, even those that avoided missions and settlements. These patterns only accelerated after American conquest in 1846. By the 1850s, gender balances were severely askew in many groups. Taken as a whole, only one-third of California Natives were female.

Discontent was common among neophytes. Some refused to speak Spanish, went on hunger strikes, stole livestock and other property, and assaulted mission officials. Women also protested assimilation through abortion and infanticide. Fugitivism was a potent indicator of Native resistance. Neophytes fled by the thousands, escaping to the interior to escape punishment, hunger, and disease, many hoping to regain their old lives. Officials routinely sent soldiers to retrieve runaways and they punished culprits severely, but they could not stem the tide of defection. There were too many Natives and too few soldiers. Sherburne Cook found that the missions lost an average of 10 percent of their population to fugitivism each year, sometimes more. In 1817 alone, nearly 2,500 neophytes escaped, many permanently. When the American fur trapper Jedediah Smith visited the San Joaquin Valley ten years later, he met Spanish-speaking Natives everywhere, many probably escaped neophytes. After 1800, the influx of embittered, partially assimilated runaways like Estanislao embroiled the Yokuts and other interior groups in conflicts; ironically, this probably also accelerated cultural change.

Fugitivism and the dramatic decline in Native populations drove authorities to attempt new methods of maintaining the mission population. Their strategies included capturing and delivering interior peoples to the missions, although compulsory conversion was against church and civil law. After 1800, colonial expeditions into the interior were brutal campaigns to recapture runaway neophytes, punish the tribes that sheltered them, and collect new recruits, especially women and children. Captives were often driven to the missions and held until they agreed to convert. In 1805, for example, a punitive raid on a village near the Stanislaus River, perhaps among Estanislao's people, killed ten Indians and seized 27 gentiles, including 25 women and girls. The men were sentenced to hard labor in the San Francisco presidio, the women and children imprisoned at Mission San José. After they had served their sentence, *all* "chose" to accept Christianity. It is difficult to believe that such conversions were genuine.

The introduction of Spanish horses is closely linked to the explosion in fugitivism. Already aware of the revolutionary impact of horses on Natives elsewhere, officials had initially forbidden neophytes and gentiles to own or even ride horses. Yet the law proved unenforceable, as the free-range livestock industry depended on mounted Native *vaqueros*, often required to work far beyond mission surveillance. Many neophytes thus became skilled horsemen. They rode horses into the interior during escapes and on approved visits, often trading horses and other livestock secretly to gentiles. Some runaways arrived with entire stolen herds to ingratiate themselves with gentile protectors. "Today they come," one missionary complained in 1818, "and tomorrow they leave, not on foot but on horseback, so that, with such guests, there is not a safe horse in the whole valley of the north."

As in the Southwest and on the Great Plains, horses, once introduced, wrought cultural transformations. Horse meat, much of it rustled, became a new staple for the Yokuts and other interior groups. Mounted tribes became mobile, powerful, and militaristic, better equipped to resist colonial patrols and to strike back fiercely. The horse and the growing menace of the Spanish intruders caused inland groups like the Yokuts, Cahuilla, and Cupeño to become more assertive. In some cases, tribes learned to cooperate among themselves as they never had before. Some groups decimated by disease or warfare joined others, creating new social units. Leaders with broad support—many of them former neophytes like Estanislao—emerged to unite the tribelets and direct their resistance. By the 1820s, visitors to the interior found not only stolen horses but also saddles, bridles, firearms, cattle, and other European products. Some tribes were observed hunting wild game, like Great Plains tribes, on horseback.

Once set off, cultural changes accelerated and spread at astonishing speed. Where there were only a few horses in the interior in 1800, by 1820 most San Joaquin Valley and southern desert tribes were on horseback. Horse-trading fairs became common. When the supply of local horses proved insufficient, inland tribes raided settlements and ranchos, striking quickly and then vanishing. Whole villages mounted large-scale attacks, slaughtering horses and distributing their meat. These raids soon depleted mission and ranch herds, discouraging further colonial expansion and fomenting dissension among the colonists. The Monterey and San Francisco Bay regions, including Mission San José, bore the brunt of these assaults, but all settlements southward to San Diego suffered. Officials took the attacks very seriously. In 1819, Father Durán at Mission San José warned that, unless the powerful San Joaquin Valley tribes were stripped of their horses, "California might in time become the theater of a second band of Apaches."

Vainly the colony attempted to squelch the horse revolution. Officials considered building missions in the interior to pacify the tribes, but expense, remoteness, and hostile Natives doomed this project. Instead, they resorted to punitive expeditions. Dozens of campaigns were launched by soldiers, neophytes, civilian militiamen, and allied gentile auxiliaries, assaulting and burning villages to punish horse eaters, retrieve stolen horses, and capture mission runaways. If the guilty parties could not be found, some colonists vented their rage on the Natives at hand. Predictably, such attacks only intensified the cycle of violence and attempted retribution. Greatly outnumbering the colonists, Native warriors sometimes won, but with few firearms, many were killed. Those the soldiers captured were delivered to the missions, and the cycle began anew.

Brutality abounded on both sides. Natives tortured prisoners and mutilated dead soldiers, and colonists responded in kind, routinely taking battle trophies, cutting off warriors' heads, ears, and genitalia, sometimes from living victims. As was true of Vallejo's 1829 campaign against Estanislao, not all prisoners made it back to the settlements alive; some were tortured or murdered along the way. Lofty Spanish rhetoric about carrying civilization to the "heathen" quickly evaporated in the fierce heat of frontier conflict.

For all their brutality, the punitive expeditions accomplished little beyond further inflaming Indian-colonial relations. Few neophytes or horses were recaptured. Unchastised gentiles redoubled their raids. The horse culture spread to new groups. Resistance and fugitivism at the missions increased. Emboldened, mission Indians in the 1820s mounted two of their largest insurrections—the Chumash in Santa Barbara in 1824 and Estanislao's rebellion in 1829. In both instances, the rebels attempted to ally themselves with San Joaquin Valley tribes. By the time of Estanislao's rebellion, the entire frontier was engulfed in warfare, and wise foreigners ventured abroad only with well-armed escorts.

Disease proved the greatest threat to Natives' ability to resist colonization. In the 1830s, the worst outbreaks of epidemics yet struck the interior, destroying entire tribelets and greatly weakening others. The Yokuts, a key group in the emerging new culture, were especially hard hit. One catastrophic epidemic in the summer of 1833—probably malaria or yellow fever carried by British trappers from the Pacific Northwest—killed about 20,000 Indians, perhaps 75 percent of the San Joaquin Valley's population. One trapper, J.J. Warner, reported that on his way south in 1832, "the banks of the Sacramento and San Joaquin, and numerous tributaries of these rivers, were studded with Indian villages with up to 1,200 inhabitants each." But when he returned north the following year, Warner found that "death had obtained a victory. The first struck down were buried. But the increasing dead gave no time to the living to dispose of their departed fellows. The decaying bodies compelled us nightly to pitch our tents in the open prairie." Other Central Valley tribes fought on into the 1850s, attacking settlements, stealing livestock, and frustrating the ambitions even of later American pioneers but, except for scattered remnants, Yokuts culture was shattered.

Spanish California on the Eve of Mexican Independence

Although 50 years had passed since the arrival of Serra and Portolá, Spanish California remained weak in 1820, with a subsistence economy and a tiny population that was barely growing. Disease and Native resistance crippled its major institution, the mission. Colonists had succeeded in disrupting Native life but were unable to conquer or control interior tribes. The consequences of their failure were enormous. Native resistance, within and outside of the missions, disorganized the colonial economy, made governance difficult if not impossible, and delayed further exploration and settlement.

After 1810, while the movement for independence raged in Mexico, Spanish imperial leaders ignored California. Vital supplies and military reinforcements dried up. Buildings, equipment, and firearms deteriorated to the point of uselessness. Had Gálvez been alive to see it, he might have thought that Spanish control over California was weaker after colonization than it had been before.

"Rodeo Riders"

Since California cattle ran wild over thousands of acres of range land, the rodeo, an annual roundup, was necessary for sorting out ownership and branding. It became a festive occasion in Mexican California. *Courtesy of The Bancroft Library, University of California, Berkeley.*

PART THREE

The Pastoral Era

In 1821, after more than ten years of revolutionary turmoil, Mexico won its independence from Spain, thus gaining sovereignty over California. But Mexican control of the province was relatively short-lived and in many respects seemed a mere continuation of the Spanish experience, prompting historian Charles Chapman to assert, "strictly speaking, there was no Mexican period of California history." This, however, is a simplification that ignores the fundamental economic and social changes occurring in the period: development of the hide-and-tallow trade after 1822; secularization of the missions in the mid-1830s; and the emergence of a rancho society that arose in conjunction with both these events all had enormous social and economic consequences for the province. Finally, the arrival of the American frontier movement in 1841 was the beginning of the end of Mexican rule.

Many aspects of rancho life in the Mexican era have led writers to romanticize it. After all, the great rancheros really did live in spacious homes with many Native American servants; they dressed in fine clothes and celebrated any significant occasion with feasting and dancing. Accordingly, the tendency has been to describe the Californians of this era, as Carey McWilliams put it, as "one big, happy, guitar-twanging family," dancing the fandango and living out their days basking in the sun. Mexican California, however, produced a much more complex society than this suggests.

While inheriting Spain's culture and institutions, the new nation also inherited its problems in administering California. Isolation, poverty, lax authority, military weakness, and conflict with Indigenous people characterized Mexican rule and ultimately contributed to its overthrow. Impoverished and torn by factionalism, the Mexican government failed to establish its authority in the province or to prevent the later intrusion of Americans, who played an important role in the loss of California to the United States. While early British and American settlers became naturalized Mexican citizens and made important contributions to the life of the province, these later American arrivals did not. By 1846, they constituted a growing, unassimilated population, restless and unhappy with Mexican policy. Many of them joined in what came to be known as "the Bear Flag Revolt," and participated in the subsequent American conquest.

Even though the episode took place at the end of the Mexican period, it vividly illustrates the problems Mexico faced from the very beginning in administering the isolated province. In constant financial trouble, the Mexican government rarely sent funds to pay for the government or defense of California. By the mid-1830s civil and military officials were reduced to squabbling over the revenues from the hide-and-tallow trade, echoing a growing rivalry between northern and southern *Californios* (Hispanic and Hispanic-Native settlers born in California) characterized by bombastic verbal threats and, for the most part, by bloodless military action. The conflict in 1846 between José Castro, California's military *comandante general*, based in Monterey, and Governor Pío Pico, based in Los Angeles, was simply an example of experience going back to the 1820s.

The participation of Americans in the "revolutions" by which the Californios settled their grievances against the Mexican government and with each other was an ominous sign. Throughout the period, Mexico and the Californios feared the growing presence of American mountain men, settlers such as William B. Ide, and the ubiquitous John C. Frémont, but seemed powerless to deal with the growth of an American frontier population in California. The Bear Flag action, therefore, contains many of the elements of the Mexican experience in California. A curious episode that has been both lampooned and romanticized in popular histories, it nevertheless served as the first step in the separation of California from Mexico by the United States.

The *Bear Flag Revolt*

7

The decade from 1836 to 1846 saw increasing tension between Mexico and the United States. Immigrants from the United States led the 1836 revolt that carved the Lone Star Republic out of Mexico's borderlands, and the prospect of American annexation of Texas embittered relations with Mexico for years. Meanwhile, the arrival of the American frontier movement in California, beginning in 1841, spread the fear among Mexican authorities that this isolated, weakly defended province, too, might go the way of Texas. In 1845, the United States finally annexed Texas and President James K. Polk sent troops into the borderlands in dispute between Texas and Mexico; they clashed with Mexican soldiers and war began in May 1846. However, before news of the war reached California, events there took the province along the road of "another Texas." Thus, the Bear Flag Revolt of June 14, 1846, not only revealed Mexico's problems in administering California, but it was also the prelude to the war with Mexico in California.

The spring of 1846 in California seemed like so many that had gone before—warm days, cool nights, and a sense of peace and contentment in the air. The simple frontier province, an appendage of the Federal Republic of Mexico since 1821, was dominated by Californios, with their great ranchos, huge herds of cattle, and easygoing way of life. Hospitable and proud, they enjoyed their colorful rodeos and fandangos and, like many colonial peoples, profited from the trade of hides and tallow from their cattle for finished goods from Europe and the United States.

But Don José Castro, *comandante general* of the Department of California (the chief military official of the province), had more important matters on his mind than rodeos

5

and fandangos, for beneath the seemingly serene surface of life in the province major forces were on a collision course. Since January, in fact, events had been unfolding that were soon to throw California into turmoil. Born into a modest family and raised near Monterey, José Castro had been a youthful protégé of Pablo Vicente de Solá, the last Spanish governor of California. Politically active from an early age, Castro served briefly as interim governor in the mid-1830s. Now, at age 36, he was California's *comandante general* with headquarters in Monterey. While he was not a large landholder, Castro was a man of influence and considerable power, especially among the lower classes, and some people expected him to displace the present governor of California, Pío Pico. Clever and ambitious, José Castro took his responsibility for the security of the province seriously.

That security, however, seemed threatened by an American military expedition moving boldly along the foothills of the great Central Valley. John C. Frémont of the U.S. Corps of Topographical Engineers was leading his second expedition to California. Only 33 years old, Frémont was already a well-known figure whose reports of his western explorations had excited the nation. Courageous, witty, and magnetic, yet often arrogant, he elicited a fierce loyalty from his followers. Now accompanied by 60 armed, rough-looking ex-mountain men, his presence worried many Californians, particularly General Castro, who kept a wary eye on the expedition moving through the interior.

In January, Frémont and a handful of his men, in the company of Thomas O. Larkin, the American consul, appeared in Monterey seeking supplies from the *comandante*. While marked by the cordial hospitality characteristic of the Californios, the meeting with Castro led to a misunderstanding. Frémont assumed he had been given approval to move freely about the province, while Castro believed that Frémont had assured him his expedition would not approach the coastal settlements before continuing north to Oregon. The misunderstanding had unfortunate consequences.

On leaving Monterey, Frémont gathered his men near San José and camped a few miles south, at the vacant Rancho Laguna Seca. On February 22, the Frémont expedition got underway again, but, to the dismay of the Californians, Frémont moved south over the Santa Cruz Mountains and a few days later rode along the shore of Monterey Bay. As it neared Monterey, the expedition turned south along the Salinas River and encamped at William P. Hartnell's Rancho Alisal, only 25 miles from Monterey.

José Castro

A lieutenant colonel in the Mexican army, Castro was addressed as "General" by virtue of his position as *comandante general* of California. *Courtesy of The Bancroft Library, University of California, Berkeley.*

General Castro reacted quickly to this penetration by armed Americans into the immediate vicinity of northern California's most important settlement. He saw it as an ominous move at a time of tension between the United States and Mexico, and a violation of his understanding with Frémont. He dispatched a sharp note notifying Frémont that his presence there was prohibited by law and that he must "retire beyond the limits of the department."

Frémont replied promptly and curtly that he would not obey an order he regarded as insulting to himself and the government of the United States. The next day, he moved into the Gavilan Mountains and occupied a formidable position (near present-day Frémont Peak) overlooking San Juan Bautista and the main road to Monterey. Here Frémont constructed a crude log fortification and brashly hoisted the American flag.

John C. Frémont

Few persons have provoked more controversy among historians than John C. Frémont. Self-serving and opportunistic, he also played an important role in the conquest of California in 1846–1847 and was easily elected one of the first United States senators from the state. *Courtesy of the California History Room, California State Library, Sacramento, California.*

Incensed, Castro sent a small military force to keep an eye on Frémont and issued a call to the local citizenry to join him in "repelling the invasion." He was not eager to attack Frémont's nearly impregnable position, manned by 60 sharp-shooting frontiersmen (especially when only a handful of citizens answered his call to action). So Castro's troops from time to time galloped a short way up the road toward the peak, while Frémont readied an ambush should they come nearer. For three days, the tense confrontation created great excitement in the area.

One of those most distressed by the affair was Thomas O. Larkin, the American consul. Larkin had been in California since 1832. Unlike most foreigners who had come in the early days of the hide-and-tallow

trade, Larkin had retained his American citizenship. He proved to be a shrewd businessman and became one of the most influential residents of Monterey. Recognition of his success came with his appointment as U.S. consul in 1843 and as President Polk's secret agent in 1845. Thereafter, he reported at great length on the disorder and uncertainty of government in California and on the strained relations between Californians and Mexico. Worried that the British might at any time "pluck the ripe pear," Larkin's reports dwelt on the infirmity of Mexico's hold on the province.

With considerable skill, Larkin had been working to neutralize British influence and to promote closer American relations with California. By 1846, he was convinced that many prominent Californios were willing to consider the creation of an independent California that might eventually seek the protection of the United States. Small wonder that, as Frémont lay behind his barricade in the Gavilan Mountains, Larkin worked feverishly to keep the peace. On March 6, he sent a note to Castro counseling caution and trying to explain Frémont's action as a possible misunderstanding. On March 8, he wrote to Frémont urging him to move farther away immediately or, through a "proper representation to the general and prefecto," obtain permission to stay.

Larkin's note to Frémont may have had some effect, along with Frémont's recognition that hostile action against the Mexican government in California would set off an international incident. On March 10, Frémont left his fortress and moved slowly east into the San Joaquin Valley. By March 21, he was camped on the American River near Sutter's Fort. Three days later, he headed up the Sacramento Valley toward Oregon, leaving behind a greatly relieved General Castro.

Frémont's departure, however, did not end Castro's troubles. There remained the most serious problem of all: the appearance of the vanguard of the American frontier movement in California. Ever since Jedediah Smith penetrated the eastern frontier in 1826, American beaver trappers had entered California over the Sierra or through the deserts of the Southwest. Rough, fiercely independent individuals, most came for a season and left with their packs of beaver skins. A few had remained over the years, many of them unassimilated "floaters," roaming in and out of the California settlements. Their growing numbers were a source of concern to Californios—especially when they joined in the petty political wars so characteristic of Mexican California.

But in 1841, a far more menacing movement of Americans began when the first frontier settlers, drawn by glowing reports of earlier visitors, made their way over the Sierra. Thirty-four arrived in 1841, another 38 in 1843, and 53 more in 1844. Then, in 1845, an alarming 260. One group, led by a former Massachusetts schoolteacher, William B. Ide, numbered about 150. These were land-hungry farm folk who had ignored notices published by the Mexican government in Midwestern newspapers that they could not remain in California without passports and Mexican approval. Once in California, the foreigners bought, rented, or "squatted" on Mexican land grants belonging to others. The newcomers mostly kept to themselves in the interior valleys north of San Francisco and Sacramento, posing a growing threat to Mexican control of the region.

José Castro watched the arrival of the American settlers with apprehension, conscious that these were the kind of migrants who had poured into Texas in the 1830s and led the revolt that tore that territory from Mexico. His orders from Mexico were to stop the entry of Americans into California from Oregon and the east. But lacking funds and soldiers, Castro could do little but summon newly arrived residents to meetings where he wrung from them promises to obey the laws and apply for proper permission to remain. Now, with the coming of spring, there was talk that thousands more Americans could be heading to California by May.

The *comandante's* desire to protect California against foreign intruders, however, was plagued by internal conflict, especially by a festering struggle for power with his former ally, Don Pío Pico. Together, Castro and Pico had led the 1844 revolt that forced out the incumbent Mexican governor of California. In the aftermath, Pico, as governor and Castro as *comandante*, had divided the civil and military powers between them, an arrangement eventually endorsed by the Mexican government.

This arrangement had pleased neither man. Pico moved the capital from Monterey to Los Angeles where he controlled the government through the southern-dominated provincial assembly. Castro remained in Monterey, controlling the customs house and thus the funds of the territory. Sharp conflict arose over Castro's allocation of these funds, which favored the military, and each leader began to defend his own interests and complain to Mexico City about the other.

With all these problems in mind—his rivalry with Pico, the Frémont expedition, and the American overland movement—Castro summoned a military junta in Monterey at the end of March 1846. The junta recommended that the *comandante* prepare to defend California by fortifying the northern towns, that he invite Governor Pico north to participate in the effort, and

that he establish military headquarters at Santa Clara. Castro agreed, but when he began to carry out these recommendations, his actions were seen in a considerably different light by his various antagonists. Pío Pico became convinced that Castro was amassing troops to overthrow him as governor, and began assembling his own military force. In the north, the rumor spread that Castro was preparing to throw the Americans out of California by force, and anxious settlers began to consider active resistance. Then word reached them that Frémont had returned to the Sacramento Valley.

Frémont had left the Gavilan Mountains in a surly mood. Incensed by the tone of General Castro's order to leave California, he realized he had no real choice in the matter. Certainly, the orders for his expedition did not include starting a war with Mexico. Moving east and north at a leisurely pace, Frémont entered the Sacramento Valley and, a few weeks later, reached the 22,000-acre Rancho Bosqueto of Peter Lassen, between present-day Chico and Red Bluff. He spent the first three weeks of April 1846 at Lassen's ranch, having sent men off to the San Joaquin Valley for fresh horses. Finally, on April 24, Frémont headed for Oregon, marching east of Mount Shasta through the Pit River and Tule Lake region.

By early May, Frémont was at Klamath Lake where, on the night of May 8, he received news that an American officer, Lieutenant Archibald Gillespie, was trying to overtake him with an important message from Washington. Taking a handful of men, Frémont rode back into Gillespie's camp the next night.

Just what Gillespie told Frémont that night remains a mystery, since Frémont's many versions of the meeting were contradictory. It seems clear, however, that Gillespie was convinced—by what he had seen and heard in Mexico and by his contact with American naval officers in the Pacific—that war was imminent. The two young men talked long into the night about the possibility of war and what course of action they should follow. As a consequence, Frémont, who perhaps also wanted to settle accounts with Castro, decided to return to California. The next day, accompanied by Gillespie, he cautiously retraced his route to Lassen's ranch, where he arrived on May 24. Five days later, he was encamped at a secure point on the southeastern slopes of the Sutter (Marysville) Buttes, just north of Sutter's Fort.

Frémont's reappearance marked the end of Mexican California. Frémont's camp immediately became the rallying point of worried settlers, most of them Americans who had not become Mexican citizens or legal landholders. Singly and in small groups, often

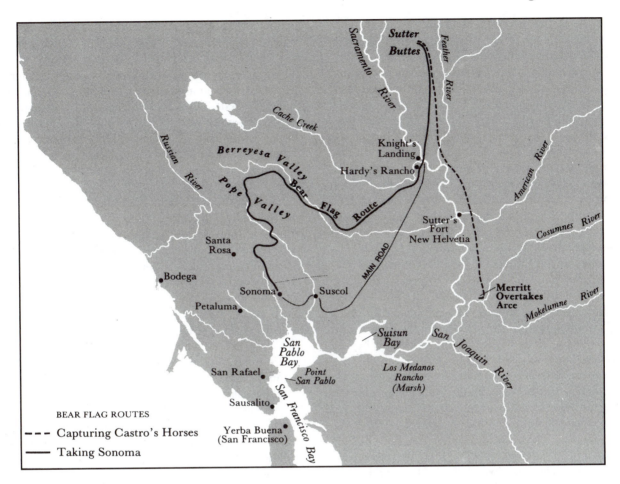

Route of the Bear Flag Party

The Bear Flag party captured Castro's horses, then took Sonoma, where the Republic of California was established. Mariano G. Vallejo, his brother, and his brother-in-law were sent to Sutter's Fort as prisoners.

led by the lanky, weathered ex-mountain man Ezekiel Merritt, Frémont's "field lieutenant" among the immigrants, they converged on Frémont to voice their concerns. It was rumored, they said, that Castro had issued a proclamation threatening to drive all unnaturalized foreign settlers out of California; they had heard that he was gathering his military forces at Santa Clara. Word had it that Castro was urging the Indians to burn the settlers' wheat fields and steal their animals. Many of them feared they would have to fight for their property or flee. More and more "floaters" like Merritt began to hang around Frémont's camp.

Reacting first to the rumored Native attacks, Frémont decided to "anticipate the Indians and strike them a blow which would make them recognize that Castro was far and I was near." Frémont's force swept down from the Buttes, crossed the Sacramento River, and rode south,

raiding the string of Maidu villages along the river. Confident that he had eliminated a real threat to the settlers by his surprise attack on the Maidu, and still smarting from his earlier encounter with the comandante, Frémont next turned his attention to General José Castro.

With military preparations made even more urgent by Frémont's return to the Central Valley, Castro visited Colonel Mariano Vallejo, commander of the northern military district, at Sonoma in early June to arrange for the transfer of a large herd of horses to his headquarters at Santa Clara. Soon news arrived at Frémont's camp that Castro's men were driving some 170 horses around the bay, stopping at Sutter's Fort on the way. Reasoning that if those horses could be prevented from reaching Santa Clara Castro would have trouble carrying out any threats against the northern settlers, Merritt and ten others rode out from the Buttes in pursuit. Meanwhile, a call went out to the settlers to meet at Frémont's camp. Thus began, on the spur of the moment, a series of events that culminated in revolution.

Merritt's men included Robert Semple, a dentist and printer whose height (6 feet, 8 inches) excited comment wherever he went; Granville Swift, noted as a crack shot, and other experienced riflemen from the Sacramento Valley. They quickly caught up with lieutenants Francisco Arce and José María Alviso at the Cosumnes River and, in a surprise attack on June 10, forced Castro's men to lay down their arms. Since the object of the raid was to capture only the horses, Arce and his men were sent on to Castro's headquarters—carrying Merritt's boast that he would take Sonoma next—while the horses were driven to Frémont's camp.

Among those at Frémont's camp was 50-year-old William B. Ide, who was determined to protect the foothold he had established in the area. In 1845, Ide had led some 150 men, women, and children, with many head of cattle, over the Sierra to California. After a hard winter tending cattle in the Sacramento Valley, he had moved his family in the spring of 1846 to Josiah Belden's Rancho La Barranca Colorado, near the present-day town of Red Bluff. There Ide had obtained a position caring for Belden's cattle for which, after three years, he would receive half the 17,700-acre rancho.

Ide and the other men who gathered at Sutter's Fort faced a critical decision following Merritt's return with Arce's horses. They anticipated that Castro would retaliate and reasoned that if Sonoma, the main military garrison north of San Francisco, could be seized, then control of the north bay area would be secured, making action by Castro extremely difficult. The decision was made to take Sonoma.

With 20 men, including Ide, Merritt set out on June 11 for Sonoma. Riding swiftly west, picking up recruits as they went, and avoiding the well-traveled main road, they ascended Cache Creek and crossed the rugged Blue Ridge to Berreyesa Valley. On June 12, they reached the upper Napa Valley, where more settlers joined them. Its numbers swelled to 34, the party pushed on and rode into the surprised, sleepy community of Sonoma at dawn on June 14.

No one expected a fight—and there was none. Colonel Vallejo had discharged most of his soldiers long ago for lack of funds to pay them, and a mere handful of men now served him. Vallejo had also taken the precaution of sending away his ally Sem Yeto (Chief Solano), the Patwin warrior who had joined Vallejo in his campaigns against the local Wappo, Miwok, and Pomo peoples. With almost complete control over local Natives, Sem Yeto also held special military status, including the right to carry arms and have a color guard. Somewhat sympathetic to Larkin's plans for a peaceful transfer of California to the United States, Mariano feared Sem Yeto would retaliate against the Americans, especially if they threatened his household. Sem Yeto went north, but left behind Isidora Filomena Solano, the Wappo bride he had kidnapped in 1835, to fend for herself and eight children, including several daughters Vallejo counted among his household servants.

Awakening to find the rough-looking, leather-clad crowd at his door, Vallejo was his usual gentlemanly self. He invited Merritt, Semple, and William Knight,

Sonoma Plaza

An early painting of General Mariano Vallejo's compound at Sonoma, which the Bear Flag party seized in June 1846.
Courtesy of The Bancroft Library, University of California, Berkeley.

The Bear Flag

The Bear Flag was raised at Sonoma by William B. Ide's men as the flag of the California Republic. Some accounts state that a green turf was painted under the bear, as in the present state flag of California. *Courtesy of The Bancroft Library, University of California, Berkeley.*

as interpreter, inside. There Vallejo entertained his "guests" with typical Californio hospitality, including plenty of brandy and polite conversation, hoping to make his "surrender" as agreeable as possible.

As time passed, the men outside waited with growing impatience. At last, they elected John Grigsby captain and sent him inside to see what was delaying the surrender. When more time had passed without a report from Grigsby, William Ide was sent in. Ide later reported what he found:

> The General's generous spirits gave proof of his usual hospitality, as the richest wines and brandies sparkled in the glasses, and those who had thus unceremoniously met soon became merry companions. . . . There sat Doct. S[emple], just modifying a long string of articles of capitulation. There sat Merritt—his head fallen; there sat Knight, no longer able to interpret; and there sat the new made captain, as mute as the seat he sat upon. The bottles had well nigh vanquished the captors.

Under Ide's sober eye, articles of capitulation and guarantees of security of life and property were quickly signed. General Vallejo, his brother, Captain Salvador Vallejo, and Lieutenant Victor Prudon were placed under arrest. General Vallejo's brother-in-law, Jacob Leese, arrived to act as an interpreter, only to be placed under arrest as well. Merritt, Semple, and a handful of men then took their illustrious captives to Frémont, who forwarded them to Sutter's Fort for detention.

The men left behind at Sonoma debated their next actions. A motley group of farmers, hunters, and floaters, they were all united in the belief that they were justifiably acting in self-defense, since General Castro would surely send an army to run them off. Ide emerged as a vigorous proponent of revolution. They could not stop now, he said, and thereafter claim that their motives were honorable. Dramatically crying, "Choose ye this day what you will be!" and "We are robbers, or we must be conquerors!" Ide urged the men to declare independence for California. Persuaded (or perhaps amused) by Ide's flamboyant rhetoric, they elected him as their commander and set about creating the trappings of government. First, a flag had to be made. A search for material produced a piece of unbleached cotton on which the flag maker painted a star and a grizzly bear in red and the words CALIFORNIA REPUBLIC in black. A strip of red flannel sewn to the bottom completed the job. Unfortunately, the grizzly bear, chosen as "an emblem of strength and unyielding resistance," bore enough resemblance to a pig to make the artist, William Todd, the target of many a jest thereafter.

Now calling themselves Osos (bears), Commander Ide set to work writing and polishing a wordy and pretentious "proclamation" declaring their determination to establish a new government. He invited "all peaceable and good citizens of California, who are friendly to the maintenance of good order and equal rights" to join them "in establishing a republican government." A second proclamation promised security of life and property to all who would not take up arms against them. Ide took care to acknowledge that the Bears were acting alone, without official American support, though he sent word of their actions to the commander of the warship *Portsmouth*, then anchored at San Francisco. An officer from the *Portsmouth* visited the garrison the next day and assured the Bears that the U.S. would remain neutral.

With these matters settled, the men fortified their defenses. Expecting General Castro to move quickly to retake Sonoma, they divided their troops into a ten-man artillery company and another ten-man rifle squad. They "requisitioned" supplies from the local citizens, although Rosalía Vallejo de Leese and others called it "stealing." George Fowler and Thomas Cowie were sent off to the rancho of Henry D. Fitch on the Russian River for a keg of gunpowder, while William Todd and another Oso rode to neighboring ranches to drum up additional manpower. Meanwhile, each day Ide's "proclamation" drew more Bears to Sonoma. Within a week, the Sonoma garrison numbered more than 90 men and was still growing, as the Bears waited nervously for Castro's expected attack.

At Santa Clara, Castro was stunned to hear of the capture of Sonoma. On June 17, he issued two proclamations that rivaled Ide's in wordiness and bombast. Exhorting Californios to "arise in mass," he urged them to rally to his banner and put down the rebellion. A second proclamation assured peaceful foreign residents of their security, and warned of dire consequences for those who joined the revolt. Organizing the men who answered his call to arms into three small companies, he sent one led by Joaquin de la Torre across the bay from San Pablo to San Rafael to quash the Sonoma insurgents.

At Sonoma, when Fowler and Cowie failed to return from their mission to obtain powder, Ide's lieutenant, Henry L. Ford, sent more men to Fitch's rancho. On their return, they reported that Fowler and Cowie had been captured and brutally murdered by a force of Californios under Juan Padilla. Concerned now for the safety of Todd and his companion, Ford sent a message to Zeke Merritt at Sacramento to bring more men to Sonoma and set out with a rescue party of some 18 men. Near the present-day town of Novato, Ford's party followed Padilla's trail to Rancho Olompali where a few men could be seen outside an adobe house. Charging the house, Ford's force was surprised as men came "pouring out of the house" and more appeared from the nearby woods. Padilla had been joined by Torre's detachment. Ford's men took cover in the woods and soon drove Torre's troops off toward San Rafael and rescued Todd, who had been captured and held prisoner in the house. One of Torre's men had been killed and several wounded, and the Bear Flag incident was beginning to take on substantial proportions.

On June 20, Captain Frémont was camped on the American River near Sutter's Fort, waiting anxiously for news of the Sonoma attack and of the activities of General Castro. What he heard that day propelled him into action. Two of the settlers returned from the south bay area to report that Castro had sent forces to attack north of the bay. Then Merritt received Ford's call for help. Frémont quickly gathered 30 settlers, in addition to his company of 60, and headed for Sonoma. On June 25, this "army" of mountain men, drifters, farmers, and Frémont's Delaware Indian bodyguard rode into the plaza of Commander Ide's capital. Dressed in buckskin, the famous Hawken long rifles across their saddles, and pistols and skinning knives at their waists, they were a formidable sight.

Frémont's intervention in the Bear Flag Revolt required some delicacy. As an American army officer, his participation in any conflict with the Californios could well cost him his appointment. Moreover, Ide clearly sensed that Frémont was a threat to his position as commander. Relations between the two cooled rapidly when Frémont disagreed with Ide's plans to extend the rebellion to San Francisco.

However, the paramount issue of the moment was the disposition of Castro's forces under Torre. With more than 200 men now at Sonoma, the Bears had emerged as a potent military force, strong enough to go in pursuit of Torre. Claiming "that he had come down, *not to take part in the matter;* only to see the sport, and *explore* about the Bay," Frémont disguised his appearance and rode south toward San Rafael with Lieutenant Ford and 125 men.

Upon reaching the mission at San Rafael the Bears were disappointed to find Torre gone, and for the next two days, scouts tried to locate the Californios. One such party under Frémont's chief scout, Kit Carson, cold-bloodedly shot José de los Reyes Berreyesa, father of Sonoma's *alcalde*, and his twin nephews, Ramón and Francisco de Haro. A message from Castro to Torre was found on one of the victims, but there was much controversy in later years over what Carson and others called retaliation for the murder of Fowler and Cowie. On the same day, another scouting party captured an Indian with a message from Torre to Castro stating that the former planned to attack Sonoma on June 29. Ford and Frémont hurried back to Sonoma to protect the Bear Flag capital, only to find they were victims of a ruse. With Frémont and Ford riding hard to Sonoma, Torre commandeered a launch at Sausalito and escaped with his soldiers back across the bay to join Castro's forces at San Pablo. Thus, by diverting Frémont from the main scene of action, Torre had averted a possible disaster for the *comandante*.

At Sonoma, Ide's forces had also heard the rumor of an impending attack and were waiting, cannons and rifles ready, when Frémont's men rode into the hamlet near dawn. Fortunately, the defenders recognized their friends' voices and held their fire. Chagrined by Torre's ruse, Frémont then led another expedition to Sausalito and, with the aid of an American trader, crossed the Golden Gate to the old ungarrisoned Castillo de San Joaquin overlooking the shores of the bay, where he spiked its ancient guns. The next day, July 2, the officials at Yerba Buena were taken prisoner, one of the captors reporting that "the Captain of the Port, couldn't go, because he had died the day before." Even so, his replacement put up a struggle because "he had a game of billiards to finish."

Frémont's "nonparticipation" ended when he returned to Sonoma. Ide's companions had loaded a launch with a single cannon and 100 muskets from the Sonoma arsenal, hoping to arm settlers on the eastern side of San Francisco Bay whom, they had heard, wished to join the revolt. Frémont opposed the idea and forced postponement until after July 4. A disappointed Ide noted:

Two hundred and seventy-two men had signed our roll. We were in quiet, and for the time, in undisturbed possession of all California north and east of the San Joaquin River. We had taken possession of Yerba Buena and spiked the cannon there. All that was necessary was to have pursued our victory, to have made it complete.

For the moment, though, all joined in a celebration of the independence of the United States and the birth of the California Republic.

On July 5, Frémont moved to assume the dominant role in the revolt. He called a meeting that was attended by the Bears, his original survey party, and even a handful of navy officers from the *Portsmouth*, whose captain had been keeping a close eye on the revolt. Frémont told the men of the serious military situation confronting them and offered his experienced leadership. In short order, the men at Sonoma enrolled in what was now called the California Battalion. Under Frémont's direction, the Battalion was organized into four companies; in the process, William B. Ide found himself demoted to private. By California standards, Frémont now had control of a major army of about 350 men. Leaving 50 men at Sonoma, Frémont headed for Sacramento.

Frémont was now in charge, but embarked on a risky course. If the United States went to war against Mexico, as most people expected would soon occur, his actions would be seen as commendable. But he had no evidence that such a state of war existed. In its absence, Frémont's actions certainly risked dishonor and even court-martial. He was in luck, however, because the United States had in fact been at war with Mexico since May 13, 1846. News of the early battles of the war soon reached the Pacific coast. On June 8, the American naval commander at Mazatlan, Commodore John D. Sloat, set sail for Monterey, under long-standing instructions to seize California if war broke out, before any other nation could do so. On July 2, Sloat sailed into Monterey, but without evidence of a clear declaration of war, he hesitated to act. When he learned of the Bear Flag Revolt and Frémont's association with it, Sloat raised the American flag on July 7 and sent orders to U.S. naval commander John B. Montgomery on the *Portsmouth* to take Yerba Buena and San Francisco Bay. Frémont's men and the Bear Flaggers, the California Battalion, were soon fighting under the American flag. The Bear Flag episode was over, and the short-lived California Republic had come to an end.

The end was also near for Mexican California and José Castro's career as *comandante general*. Despite his popularity among his own people and despite his urgent proclamations, Castro failed to collect more than 160 men at Santa Clara and was no match for the American forces now converging on him from Monterey and the north. Nor was there comfort in the knowledge that Governor Pico's armed forces in the south had been collected not to help him but to attack him. He could only retreat, importuning Pico to come to his aid, while his armed force melted away as he moved south. In mid-July, Castro and Pico met near San Luis Obispo and were reconciled, Pico having learned of the Bear Flag action and the American occupation. Together they retreated south to the Los Angeles region, but the continuing sectional, as well as personal, rivalry weakened their resistance to the Americans who landed at San Diego and San Pedro in August. As the invaders approached Los Angeles, a dejected Castro occupied a mesa south of town with barely 100 discontented men, and he and Pico both prepared to flee to Mexico. The night of August 9, having disbanded his forces, José Castro slipped away to the northern Mexico province of Sonora, where he spent the next year petitioning the beleaguered Mexican government for assistance that never came. California was firmly in American hands.

Two Mountain Men

Not all mountain men wore fringed deerskin clothing, but they were an awesome sight when they rode into Sonoma with Frémont. Mountain men and "floaters" like Ezekiel Merritt made up a large portion of the California Battalion in 1846–1847. *Courtesy of The Bancroft Library, University of California, Berkeley.*

The conquest over, William B. Ide returned to his cabin on the Sacramento River that November, eventually to become the owner of the Rancho La Barranca Colorado. His desire for prestige and influence was finally satisfied when Colusi County was formed in 1850 (including the present counties of Colusa, Tehama, and Glenn). In a brief but satisfying two years before his death from smallpox in 1852, Ide held, at various times, the following county positions: associate justice and member of the court of sessions; county judge; deputy county clerk; county treasurer; county clerk; clerk of the Ninth District Court; clerk of the county court and of the court of sessions; clerk of the probate court; county recorder; and county auditor.

Castro's departure from Los Angeles coincided with the arrival of John C. Frémont's conquering California Battalion. Frémont was eventually named military governor of California, only to act so impetuously that he was court-martialed. Nevertheless, his unique personality and opportunism enabled him not only to survive conviction but also to move forward to important political success as one of California's first U.S. senators and later as the Republican Party's first candidate for president.

As the Mexican War drew to a close in 1848, the U.S. military governor of California, Colonel Richard B. Mason, made a conciliatory gesture to José Castro, inviting him to come back to his home. Castro accepted the offer and returned to Monterey. Homecoming did not bring happiness, however, for he was often seen sitting in local restaurants, a proud and bitter figure, muttering darkly about "the reconquest of the region." Only on moving to Baja California in the 1850s did he regain his former status, serving as governor and military *comandante* there until his death in 1860.

By then, a group known as the Pioneers of California was hosting annual celebrations of the Bear Flag Revolt in Sonoma. It posted ads in Napa newspapers inviting all pioneers—but especially those who had "served on the side of the United States"—to come celebrate. Those who gathered toasted the men who stormed Sonoma, roasted an ox "in the old style," and then ran a Bear Flag up a flagpole. Reminiscences by Bears often appeared in the *Napa Recorder*, in accounts that sometimes described the Californios as "greasers." When one by one, the Osos began to die, local newspapers printed obituaries that constructed their deeds as heroic.

Naturally, the conquered saw the Osos differently. Rosalía Vallejo de Leese, for example, never forgave them. A member of one of wealthiest families in Mexican California, the Bears had taken her husband, Jacob Leese, prisoner, along with her brother, Mariano Guadalupe Vallejo. Thereafter Vallejo de Leese refused to speak with the men she termed thieves, rapists, and "rough looking desperados." When she was interviewed in 1874 by an assistant of Hubert H. Bancroft, the author and bookseller who was producing a multi-volume history of California, Vallejo de Leese spoke Spanish "through clenched teeth." The Osos, she reported, "inspired me with such a large dose of hate against their race, that though 28 years have elapsed since that time, I have not yet forgotten the insults they heaped upon me, and not being desirous of coming in contact with them I have abstained from learning their language." She recalled the dangers the men posed to Native and Hispanic women:

> During the whole time Frémont and his gang were in Sonoma, robberies were very common: ladies dared not go out for a walk unless escorted by their husbands and brothers—among my servants I had a young Indian girl about 17 years of age; and I assure you that many a time John C. Frémont sent me orders to deliver her to the officers at the barracks, but by resorting to artifices I managed to save the unhappy girl from the fate decreed to her by the lawless band.

In their *testimonios*, Californio men also accused the Osos of violence against their womenfolk. Antonio María Osio reported the attempted rape of one of the daughters of Don Angel Castro. Indigenous women fared no better: Salvador Vallejo said Frémont's men rode through the Napa Valley assaulting Native women at will. Isidora Filomena Solano did not say if her three daughters, servants in Mariano Vallejo's household at the time of the revolt, escaped molestation. But Solano agreed with Vallejo de Leese that the Americans were thieves. She lived on Mariano Vallejo's property in her old age, remembering her life before the *blancos* (whites) came. Left with only one child who had not died of disease or "sadness," Solano found refuge in alcohol. "I drink a lot of liquor," she told an interviewer, "because I no longer possess my land, teeming with live stock because the white men stole everything; nothing was left."

Another eyewitness, María Higuera Juárez, managed to defeat the Osos, at least on one occasion. She and her husband, Sergeant Cayetano Juárez, lived in Napa. Her husband on duty at the presidio, often for weeks at a time, Higuera Juárez was left to protect herself, her eleven children, and her substantial land holdings. According to her granddaughter, she was very handy with a spear:

> In August 1846, General Frémont passed by the *ranchería* with one-hundred and fifty men. Sixty of them came to the Juárez rancho and while Don

Cayetano was away, stole cattle and horses and saddles. They approached the house and attempted to take a very handsome saddle belonging to Señora María Juárez. She threatened to attack them with a heavy spear with which she was armed and which she could adeptly use and they rode off without her saddle.

The Bears were anything but heroic to the Hispanic and Native settlers who had long made their home in California. Isidora Filomena Solano probably spoke for many when she said, "I do not like the white man much because he is a liar and a thief." At the time, though, few contemporary historians paid much attention to the views of the vanquished. It was the victors' version of events that became official history. And, of course, it was their hastily crafted banner that became the official state flag of California in 1911. Preempted as it was by the outbreak of the Mexican War, the Bear Flag Revolt would have bequeathed no enduring legacy had it not been for the statutory resurrection of its provocative pennant, which had been destroyed in its museum home during the San Francisco earthquake and fire of 1906. Well aware of the crudeness of William Todd's original artistry, the state legislature prescribed in law the improved standard design and colors of the lone red star and brown grizzly that have adorned the California Bear Flag ever since.

Mexican
California
1821–1848

The California that evolved as a province of Mexico was a far cry from the colonial appendage it had been under Spain. The revolutionary fervor sweeping through the Spanish colonies broke out in New Spain in 1810. Eleven years later, on September 28, 1821, a revolutionary junta presided over by an ex-royalist, Agustín Iturbide, declared Mexican independence. Iturbide quickly proclaimed himself emperor of Mexico but just as quickly fell from power the following year. In 1824 liberal reformers established a new constitution creating the Federal Republic of Mexico, a democratic form of government inaugurated in the United States just 35 years earlier and a dramatic change from the autocratic Spanish colonial system. However, few Mexicans could read or write, or had experience with representative government, leading to an era of constant political conflict as liberal and conservative factions fought for control of the federal government. Under the new Constitution, California, like Mexico's other frontier provinces of Texas and New Mexico, became a territory theoretically governed directly by the Mexican Congress. But the Congress failed to establish any clear policies for administration or financial support of the territories, leaving them in a state of confusion and destitution.

On the other hand, the reformers of 1824 broke sharply with some of the most restrictive policies of Spain, laying the groundwork for dramatic changes over the next two decades. Native Americans were to be integrated into Mexican society with equal political and social status; the poorly enforced prohibition of trade with foreigners was ended; and foreigners who embraced Catholicism were allowed to become citizens and to own land. The new political order in Mexico also seemed to promise Californios access to political offices previously denied them, producing strong personal and sectional rivalries and a growing desire for home rule. California under Mexico thus began as a neglected and isolated province where the descendants of soldiers and early *pobladores* (settlers) struggled to build a new society of their own.

Establishment of Mexican Government in California

In 1822 Iturbide's short-lived government established a new structure of local government for California, appointing a new governor and providing for the election of a *diputación*, or provincial assembly, to advise the governor; an *ayuntamiento*, or town council, for each of the two pueblos, San José and Los Angeles; and a provincial representative to the new Mexican Congress.

Luis Antonio Argüello was the first *hijo del país* (native son) appointed to the new position of governor of California, and he enjoyed wide popular support. Argüello's chief concern as governor was reviving the economy. The revolution had all but eliminated coastal shipping between California and Mexico, causing the last Spanish governor, Pablo Vicente de Solá, to relax many of the colonial restrictions on trading with foreigners. In 1822, just before leaving office, Solá allowed William E. P. Hartnell and Hugh McCullough, who represented the British firm of John Begg & Co., to sign three-year contracts with almost all the missions for their production of hides and tallow. Argüello granted similar privileges to William Gale, who was acting on behalf of the Boston firm of Bryant & Sturgis, which eventually dominated the trade. The prospect of increased revenue from trade in hides and tallow may also have encouraged Argüello to issue several large land grants between 1823 and 1824.

Argüello's appointment ended in 1825, when the first governor appointed under the Republic arrived at San Diego. José María Echeandía, a gaunt, hypochondriacal lieutenant colonel in the Army Corps of Engineers, has probably been underestimated as governor, partly because he immediately contributed to the developing rivalry between north and south. Announcing that the foggy climate of the capital, Monterey, was bad for his health, he made San Diego his chief place of residence and the unofficial capital, a move that pleased southerners and offended northerners. But Echeandía deserves credit for dealing, as best he could under difficult circumstances, with several major problems: rebellious soldiers and Natives, the ominous appearance of American fur trappers from the east, and the Mexican government's instructions to begin the secularization of the missions.

Echeandía inherited a demoralized military establishment. Many of the soldiers sent to California were undisciplined ex-convicts, misfits, and vagabonds, the source of constant conflict with missionaries and townspeople, and the government was far in arrears in their pay. Consequently, a serious mutiny erupted at Monterey in 1829, led by a former soldier-convict, Joaquín Solís. Solís and a force of unpaid soldiers marched south against the governor, only to flee back to Monterey when Echeandía appeared on the battlefield near Santa Barbara with his own troops. The problem of the soldiers' pay remained unsolved.

A related problem was the Mexican policy of sentencing convicts to a life in California as punishment for their crimes. A substantial population of disreputable persons therefore roamed the province, foraging, stealing, fighting, and provoking consternation and resentment among the townspeople, whose protests, relayed by Echeandía, finally convinced the government to end the practice of dumping convicts in California. Echeandía, meanwhile, absorbed much of the blame for the trouble these criminals caused.

Within a year of his arrival, Echeandía was also confronted with the breakdown of the province's security on its eastern border. In 1826 an American mountain man, Jedediah Smith, led a party of fur trappers from the Rocky Mountains across the Mojave Desert to Mission San Gabriel, the first Americans to enter California from the east. Appalled by the precedent, Echeandía jailed Smith, refused him permission to hunt beaver in the province and, after weeks of indecision, ordered him to return to the United States. But, with good reason, he worried that Smith would be followed by others.

However, Echeandía devoted most of his attention to Indian affairs. He arrived in San Diego shortly after a serious Native revolt in the southern missions and only with difficulty persuaded the frightened padres to continue to clothe and feed the families of his soldiers. He also made a modest attempt to begin secularizing the missions, to the Franciscans' great dismay. Echeandía sympathized with the democratic principles of the revolution and the government's determination to integrate the Indians into Mexican society. Influenced by a report by the government's Commission for the Development of the Californias, he announced a plan in 1826 whereby certain Indigenous families might leave a few specified missions. As the mission fathers predicted, few left and Echeandía was further discouraged by accounts that those who did were incapable of an independent existence.

The fact that it took four more years for Echeandía to develop another plan for secularization reflected not only the failure of his first attempt but also his realization that the missions supported two-thirds of the Mexican population of California, and that disruption of the system would be disastrous. It was a real dilemma: secularization of the missions seemed necessary in order to integrate the Natives into Mexican society; yet secularization could ruin the existing supply system. California could not grow if the mission system remained intact but seemingly could not survive without it. Echeandía issued a new proposal in January 1831, but before it could be implemented a new government came to power in Mexico and Echeandía was replaced.

The new governor, Colonel Manuel Victoria, contrasted sharply with his predecessor. Reactionary, militaristic, and ruthless, he had little faith in republicanism and little respect for the Californios. Reflecting the conservative, pro-clerical new regime in Mexico, he halted plans for secularization, refused to call the territorial *diputación* into session, and ruled in a dictatorial fashion, all of which offended the emerging local elite.

Victoria's harsh regime came to an end with the first of many "revolutions" of the period. On November 29, 1831, several prominent southern Californios issued a *pronunciamiento* against Victoria, demanding that he be expelled and replaced by ex-Governor Echeandía. Victoria gathered a small band of soldiers and marched south to meet the rebels in combat. At Cahuenga Pass, just north of Los Angeles, the opposing forces met and exchanged harmless volleys until one of the rebels, José María Avila, dashed forth, wounded Victoria with his lance, and killed the governor's aide before he himself was killed. Victoria made his way to the nearest mission, San Gabriel, where, on December 9, he arranged to turn his authority back to Echeandía. On January 17, 1832, after less than a year in office, he sailed for Mexico.

Having deposed Victoria, the Californios quarreled among themselves. Southern Californios, particularly Juan Bandini, Pío Pico, and José Carrillo, who had led the revolt against Victoria, were unhappy with Echeandía's assumption of both military and civil authority. The territorial diputación, meeting in Los Angeles, elected Pío Pico as governor, but Echeandía managed to overturn the appointment. Meanwhile, northern Californios led by Captain Agustín Zamorano (Victoria's former secretary, better known for bringing the first printing press to California) disputed Echeandía's return to power, and opposing "armies" were again in the field. Bloodshed was averted with a truce whereby Zamorano retained military command north of San Fernando while Echeandía commanded the area to the south.

The events in California convinced Mexican officials that experience was a highly desirable quality for their next appointee, and they found it in 40-year-old General José Figueroa, who was named governor on May 9, 1832. Figueroa had been *comandante general* of Sonora and Sinaloa and a judge in the Supreme Tribunal of War and Marine. He was proud of his Indian blood and sympathized with the liberal aims of the Mexican revolution. He was, without doubt, the most capable Mexican governor of California. Despite some shortcomings, his engaging personality and political abilities soon endeared him to prominent Californios, particularly in the north, where he assumed office in January 1833. He also won the support of southern Californios by issuing a proclamation of amnesty for all participants in the revolt against Victoria.

Figueroa's instructions emphasized promoting colonization, especially in the areas threatened by Russian or American activity. Accordingly, one of his first acts was to send Ensign Mariano Guadalupe Vallejo north to reconnoiter the Russian base at Fort Ross and to select a site for a presidio north of San Francisco. Vallejo, who then commanded the San Francisco presidio, was also authorized to grant land to qualified settlers who would move into the northern frontier. Within the next few years, Vallejo established the towns of Petaluma and Santa Rosa and directed the development of a substantial rancho economy in this area, effectively cutting the Russians off from expanding inland—a major factor in their decision to abandon Fort Ross at the end of the 1830s. In the process, Vallejo became one of the largest landowners in northern California.

Secularization of the Missions

The most pressing problem for Figueroa remained Indian policy and the future of the missions. As early as 1813 the Spanish government had ordered secularization of all missions that had been in existence for ten years, but the Mexican revolution had prevented enforcement of the decree. Almost immediately after independence, contradictory pressures built up in Mexico over ending the mission system. Idealistic followers of democratic revolutionary principles worked to make Natives throughout Mexico free citizens. Others, in league with Californios, hoped to appropriate the missions' lands, herds, and wealth for themselves. Mexico City was deluged with charges that the missions failed to assimilate the Natives and treated them cruelly.

Although the mission system had many flaws, much of the criticism was sheer hypocrisy, coming as it did from California soldiers, civil officials, and a growing class of rancheros, who themselves exploited and abused Natives and were seeking even freer access to mission lands and neophyte labor. Nevertheless, because of confusion and conflict over their status and future, the missions were disintegrating by the time of Figueroa's appointment.

The Gómez Farías Plan

José Figueroa's arrival in Monterey coincided with another political change in Mexico. New elections in 1833 brought to power an unlikely coalition of military figures led by the unprincipled General Antonio López de Santa Anna and liberal democrats led by Valentín Gómez Farías. Although elected president, Santa Anna decided to spend a few months resting at his estate near Jalapa, leaving Vice President Gómez Farías as acting chief executive—the first civilian to govern Mexico since independence. For many years, Gómez Farías had favored integration of the Indians into Mexican society through secularization of the missions. He also shared the anxiety of many Mexicans about Russian encroachment on the weak California settlements. Seizing the opportunity afforded by Santa Anna's absence, he advanced a plan to combine secularization of the California missions with a colonization scheme to strengthen the settlements between San Francisco and Fort Ross.

The first step in this plan was a law, introduced in Congress in April and signed by Gómez Farías in August 1833, ordering the complete dismemberment, or secularization, of the Baja and Alta California missions. The clergy's temporal authority over the Indians was to be removed, the missions converted into ordinary churches, and the missionaries replaced by parish priests. A second bill, also introduced by the Gómez Farías government in April, provided a detailed plan for distribution of the vast properties of the missions, not only to the neophytes but also to a number of other groups, including soldiers, colonists, naturalized foreigners, and convicts. Significantly, those who already held land in the region were not included. The bill also dealt with the administration of the land and property distribution. Unfortunately, the proposed property-distribution bill was never adopted and the opportunity for an orderly secularization process coordinated with colonization was lost.

Gómez Farías not only saw colonization as an important adjunct to secularization, he also regarded it as an effective means of defense. Accordingly, he planned

Mariano Guadalupe Vallejo

Haughty and reserved, but honest and loyal, General Mariano Guadalupe Vallejo controlled vast landholdings and the military compound at Sonoma. In Thomas O. Larkin's view he was "the most independent man in California." While Vallejo was not politically inclined, his support was critical to the ambitions of Juan B. Alvarado and José Castro. *Courtesy of the California History Room, California State Library, Sacramento, California.*

and organized a major expedition under the leadership of José María Híjar aimed at occupying mission lands on the northern frontier between San Francisco Bay and Fort Ross. Híjar, a friend of Gómez Farías from Guadalajara, was also appointed director of colonization *and* governor of California, to replace Figueroa on arrival in California. José María Padrés, also a friend of Gómez Farías and a familiar figure in California, was named second-in-command of the colony and appointed military *comandante* of California. The Híjar-Padrés expedition, consisting of some 250 people, left Mexico City in April 1834. Since the law outlining land and property distribution of secularized missions had not been adopted, Gómez Farías gave Híjar a hastily drawn, but similar, set of instructions for implementing the secularization act of August 1833.

Secularization Under Figueroa

Meanwhile, Governor Figueroa, while anxious to carry out the intent of his own instructions for secularizing the missions, had doubts about the wisdom of wholesale emancipation of the Native peoples. Experience under Echeandía had been that the neophytes, when freed from the missions, soon lost their property and gravitated toward a degraded status as servants of local *gente de razón*. Father Narciso Durán, the leading Franciscan in California, persistently pointed this out to Figueroa in a campaign to prevent or delay secularization. Moreover, Figueroa, painfully aware that for 20 years the military and civil personnel and their families in California had survived only with the help of the missions, was reluctant to move precipitously. Nevertheless, under great pressure from Californios, who coveted mission lands, he referred the question to the territorial *diputación*, which with Figueroa's assistance drew up a plan that the governor issued on August 9, 1834.

This plan of secularization provided that ten missions would be converted to towns and the padres replaced by parish priests at once; six of the remaining eleven were to be secularized in 1835, and five in 1836. The plan also provided for distribution of land and property and for administration of the process. Unlike Gómez Farías's plan, Figueroa's called for distribution of mission lands and property only to neophytes in grants to each family of 33 acres of cultivable land, whether irrigated or not, along with grants "in common" of "enough land to pasture their stock," an amount that the administration could increase or decrease. Also, it called for dividing one-half of the mission herds of livestock proportionately among the Indigenous families, with all surplus livestock and property remaining in the care of an appointee of the governor. Finally, it provided that the "emancipated" Natives, at the discretion of the governor, could be forced to work on the mission's undistributed lands. Thus the way was opened for the Californios to acquire mission lands while still partially retaining the mission supply system.

Figueroa's plan had hardly gone into effect when the governor received word that Híjar and half the members of his colony had landed at San Diego, while Padrés and the rest of the colonists were expected in Monterey momentarily. At the same time an overland courier from Mexico City brought instructions from President Santa Anna, who had now taken over the government from Gómez Farías, canceling Híjar's appointment as governor and Padrés's appointment as military *comandante*. Bitterly disappointed, Híjar and Padrés finally agreed to settle the colony in the Sonoma area, north of San Francisco. Although the colony was criticized for including too many people not suited for agriculture, California desperately needed the skilled craftsmen and schoolteachers who made up the majority of the colonists. In any event, the settlement in Sonoma went badly, and rumors abounded that a revolution was brewing.

Figueroa was not one to ignore such rumors, and his relations with Híjar and Padrés worsened with reports that they were plotting against his administration. Finally, in the spring of 1835, he ordered that all colonists be free to settle wherever they might wish, in effect dispersing the colony, and instructed Vallejo to arrest Híjar and Padrés and ship them back to Mexico. By May 1835, this had been done, and Figueroa was at work on a manifesto designed to explain his actions for posterity. Figueroa eventually resigned in poor health and turned his office over to the young José Castro. The ex-governor died in September 1835, shortly after completing his manifesto.

Despite the trouble over the Híjar-Padrés colony, secularization proceeded. Though Figueroa personally sought to protect Indian rights, he lacked funds and soldiers to enforce secularization on his own. Instead, he was forced to appoint leading *gente de razón* such as Pío Pico and Mariano Vallejo to oversee the distribution of mission assets. After Figueroa's death, his successors ignored the intentions behind secularization.

Predictably, local administrators and their supporters made off in most cases with the bulk of the missions' cattle, horses, equipment, and cash—in some instances even taking altar pieces and bells. Neophytes received allotments of land and livestock that were too small to support them. Encroaching *gente de razón* quickly forced neophytes to sell out, while local officials made little attempt to protect them. Even the respected William Hartnell, appointed *visitador de misiones* in 1839 to investigate complaints about secularization, could not halt the abuses and resigned bitterly after two years as the most fertile mission lands fell into the hands of local rancheros. The Indigenous peoples themselves participated in the destruction of the missions, having no love for a system that had kept them forcibly institutionalized. Many abandoned their lands and refused to work on the "surplus" mission lands. Although a few neophytes remained in the mission Indian pueblos, most soon drifted away. Some congregated around towns and ranchos, where they were exploited as before. Others fled to the interior, resumed the Native life, and gave new impetus to the cultural revolution of gentile tribes. From the 1830s to the 1850s, many returned to the coast time and again, now heading Native cavalry attacks on the settlements and their herds.

The decline of the missions continued until the end of the Mexican period, and the failure of secularization to improve Indian-white relations stands as a stark illustration of the general failure of Hispanic Indian policy in California. Like Spain, Mexico had continued the disruption of coastal California Native societies but, despite the population decline caused by the ravages of European diseases, had failed to dominate interior groups. Thus Indian resistance and aggression effectively inhibited settlement of the interior, a critical factor in the success of the American frontier movement into California after 1840.

Political Turmoil

Figueroa's departure plunged the province into political turmoil once again. José Castro and Nicolas Gutiérrez each served a short term as acting governor until Mexico sent Colonel Mariano Chico to take the office in 1836. Chico was so impolitic—attempting to pass off his mistress as his "niece," for example—that he lasted only three months; another "revolution" sent him back to Mexico. His rejection also signified California's discontent with the new centrist government, which had suddenly discarded the liberal constitution of 1824. Gutiérrez followed Chico and was similarly ousted after a disagreement with Juan Bautista Alvarado, the dashing 27-year-old president of the *diputación*. Alvarado and José Castro collected a small "army" of 75 men, recruited Isaac Graham, an American ex-trapper running a distillery in the Pájaro Valley, and about 50 of his cohorts, and marched on Monterey. One cannon shot induced Gutiérrez to leave, whereupon the *diputación* elected Alvarado governor and Mariano Vallejo *comandante general*.

Upon assuming the governorship, Alvarado was soon involved in another conflict between forces from the north, led by José Castro, and the south, led by Alvarado's uncle, Carlos Carrillo. After one man had inadvertently been killed, Castro persuaded the southerners to accept a compromise, awarding them, in effect, a sub-governor (an arrangement authorized by Mexico's establishment of the *prefectura*, creating such an office). By 1838 the Mexican government had formally appointed Alvarado as governor and Vallejo as *comandante general*, and California enjoyed relative political peace for the next four years. Under Alvarado, secularization was essentially completed, development of the rancho economy accelerated, and the hide-and-tallow trade continued to dominate that economy.

The Hide-and-Tallow Trade

The demise of the missions fundamentally changed California's economic development. By the time of secularization, the missions had established a flourishing cattle economy, controlling 10 million acres of land and counting in their herds some 400,000 head of cattle, nearly the same number of sheep, and tens of thousands of horses. Also, over the years the Franciscans had developed a modest trade with other parts of the Spanish empire in cowhides and the tallow rendered from animal carcasses. At the same time, a limited, clandestine trade with foreign fur traders and whalers had acquainted the outside world with the province's developing cattle economy. When the Mexican revolution disrupted California's communication with the rest of New Spain, this illicit trade increased. By the time of Mexican independence, the foundation had been laid for what became the key to the economic survival of Mexican California: the production of hides and tallow for export.

The decision of the new Mexican government to open California to trade with foreigners was crucial for the development of the hide-and-tallow trade. Mexico opened the ports of Monterey and San Diego to foreign ships, levying substantial duties on the goods they carried. Local officials soon relaxed these regulations in the interest of promoting increased revenues through increased trade. Thus Governor Argüello permitted company representatives to build storehouses on shore and carry on trade at many other points along the coast.

Resident foreign company representatives such as Hartnell and Gale played an essential role in the growth of the hide-and-tallow trade by linking California with British and American companies, particularly the growing leather-goods industry in and around Boston. The foreigners soon controlled most of the business aspects of the trade; by the mid-1830s, British and American trading ships were a permanent part of the California scene, while the region's economic ties to New England were strengthened.

The classic contemporary description of the California hide-and-tallow trade is Richard Henry Dana's *Two Years Before the Mast*, published in 1840. Dana was a 19-year-old Harvard student when he signed onto the ship *Pilgrim*, which was bound for California, where he spent 16 months in the hide-and-tallow trade. *Two Years Before the Mast* grew out of this experience (and led, incidentally, to some important legal reforms concerning the treatment of sailors in the merchant marine).

Dana described in vivid detail the process whereby ships put in at Monterey, paid duties on their cargo, and then plied the coast as "floating department stores." Small schooners made frequent runs between Hawaii and California, resupplying the trading ships and bringing native Hawaiians (Kanakas) to work as sailors and "hide droghers."

Ships such as the *Pilgrim* carried a vast array of goods. Gold thread, holy pictures, musical instruments, bells, and other items useful for religious services were brought to the mission fathers. For the Californios, Dana reported, the cargo consisted of "everything under the sun:"

> We had spirits of all kinds (sold by the case), teas, coffee, sugars, spices, molasses, hardware, crockery, tinware, cutlery, clothing of all kinds, boots and shoes from Lynn, calicoes, and cotton from Lowell, crapes, silks; also shawls, scarfs, necklaces, jewelry, and combs for women; furniture; and, in fact, everything that can be imagined, from Chinese fireworks to English cart-wheels. . . .

The arrival of a company ship produced great excitement as local residents flocked to choose from its cargo and days of buying, selling, and entertainment followed. Eventually, foreign merchants such as Abel Stearns and Thomas Larkin established retail businesses that provided these goods year-round, but shipboard sales remained a fixture of the trade throughout the Mexican period. Most transactions were on credit, there being little currency available in California, and purchases were paid for in hides—"California banknotes," usually worth a dollar or two apiece—while resident "supercargoes" (company representatives) assembled hides and tallow at collection points along the coast.

Bringing the hides and tallow on board ship was a particularly difficult task, since San Francisco, San Diego, and Monterey were the only convenient harbors. Everywhere else, ships had to anchor three to four miles offshore while goods were ferried to and from the beach in small boats. Dana drew a memorable picture of hides piled on the beach and hide droghers carrying them, balanced on their heads, through the surf to the boats. The leather bags of tallow, called *botas*, were then loaded into the small boats and rowed out to the ship, exceedingly hazardous work in heavy seas.

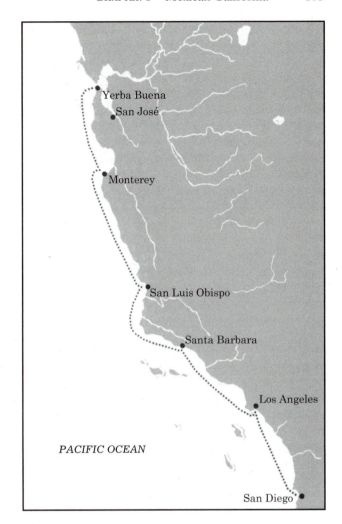

Hide and Tallow Trade Ports of Call

Once collected along the coast, hides had to be cured. Accordingly, the trading companies maintained large warehouses at the safe harbor of San Diego, where the curing process began. San Diego was considered the best place on the coast for this work because southern California had the biggest missions and ranchos, and because cured hides could be loaded without getting them wet in the surf; once cured, hides would spoil if they became wet. Each raw hide was soaked in the ocean to soften it, and then pickled in a vat of brine, cleaned of fat and other residue, spread in the sun, scraped free of grease, and dried. Dana reported that each man in his crew cured 25 hides a day and noted their long faces when they were informed that the company's storehouse held 40,000 hides.

The hide-and-tallow trade became almost the sole source of revenue for the government, a fact that accounts for the persistent efforts of southerners to get the capital and customs house moved to Los Angeles or San Diego. Unfortunately, it has been estimated that one-fourth to one-third of legitimate duties were evaded by smuggling. Nevertheless, the hide-and-tallow trade permitted the development of the rancho society that is so closely identified with the Mexican period. It provided almost all the manufactured items obtained by Californios, who had little incentive to develop domestic industry to replace mission industries, and enabled them to make raising cattle their sole means of support. With secularization of the missions, the ranchos produced most of the available goods and services, and the great rancheros became more firmly established as landed elite.

Rancho and Pueblo Society

The popular conception of life in Mexican California has probably been unduly influenced by descriptions of the almost feudal estates of the ranchero class. Contemporary accounts, biographies, memoirs, popular histories, and modern-day films and pageants have all romanticized the "pastoral era" and engendered a stereotype built on the best features of life on the ranchos. This glowing picture has some basis in fact. These proud upper-class Californios created what historian Douglas Monroy has called a "seigneurial" culture in which "a pattern of submission, hierarchy, and obligation" governed relations between the rancheros and their women, children, and Indigenous laborers. They controlled huge tracts of land with thousands of head of cattle, horses, and sheep; their adobe homes were often very large and well furnished; they were attended by great numbers of Indian servants and *vaqueros*. They dressed splendidly and were lavish in their hospitality with much music, singing, and dancing. Weddings and fiestas were regarded as opportunities to display an openhanded generosity that symbolized their social status. For them, perhaps, it *was* an idyllic time.

But the great ranchos were few and far between. Society was dominated by a small elite consisting of the mission fathers, civil and military officials, and only a handful of large landowners, most claiming direct Spanish descent. Wealth, family influence, land, and ethnicity all served to distinguish them from the vast majority of the non-Indian population—the mestizo *pobladores* who were soldiers, ex-soldiers, colonists, and their families. Most of these settlers lived in the pueblos and presidio towns, where they owned lots on which they built small adobe homes and farmed adjacent public land. Others lived on small grants of land, where they carried on subsistence farming. The men often worked as *vaqueros*, saddle makers, blacksmiths, and at other skilled pastoral trades. Families were small, with an average of three or four children, and all were expected to contribute to the needs of the family. For most Californios, it was a typically hard frontier life.

Women had much of the responsibility for the farming and livestock operations of this family-based economy, and often worked as seamstresses and cooks as well. Some women also worked at the missions, supervising kitchens and manufacturing of clothing or teaching neophytes domestic tasks. Such was the case for Victoria Bartolomea Reid, born to a prominent Tongva family (the Spaniards called the Natives who lived near the mission "Gabrieleños"). The missionaries gave her an Hispanicized name and education. Victoria met and married Hugo Reid, a Scottish merchant, who had settled in nearby Los Angeles in 1834. Four years later Mexico acknowledged Victoria's years of service to the church with a 128-acre parcel of land, in her own name. It was one of only a handful of tracts granted to a Native Californian by the Mexican government.

Secularization of the missions in the 1830s produced a significant change in the social structure of Mexican California. The process expanded the large landholding class, greatly weakening the church by stripping the missionaries of their influence. Indeed, by 1845 there were only six Catholic priests in Alta California. Thus, by the 1840s the ruling elite consisted of civil and military officials; an expanded class of great rancheros, some owning 200,000 acres of land or more; and a few leading merchants and other assimilated foreigners. Far below them in power and influence there also developed a significant class of mestizo rancheros—ex-soldiers, colonists, and others—who had received smaller grants of land for past services and who engaged in cattle ranching and subsistence farming on a significant but lesser scale. In the pueblos and presidio towns, the *pobladores* still constituted 60 to 80 percent of the non-Indian population and an important source of seasonal labor. At all times Native Americans were at the bottom of the social scale, performing almost all the manual labor on the ranchos and in the pueblos and acting as servants to the *gente de razón*.

The large ranchos were a natural outgrowth of the secularization of the missions and the government's desire to promote the hide-and-tallow trade. A few private land grants had been made in the Spanish period, some carved from mission lands for soldiers who married mission Indians. Most were sizable—such as the

Rancho Simi, a tract of more than 100,000 acres granted to an uncle of Pío Pico, and the Rancho San Pedro, a 75,000-acre area granted to Juan José Domínguez. Still, by 1820 only 20 such grants had been made, and there were probably no more than 50 by 1830. But between 1834, when secularization began, and 1846, more than 700 private land grants were made covering more than 8 million acres of land—this in itself was a measure of the fundamental economic and social change wrought by secularization. Under Mexican law, individual grants were limited in size to eleven square leagues, or nearly 50,000 acres, but since some rancheros owned more than one grant, there were some very large holdings.

The well-favored found it easy to obtain land. The applicant presented a petition to the governor, including a *diseño* (map) of the desired land, then set about marking the boundaries of the grant, a decidedly casual process. Riders, each trailing a lasso of a certain length, rode quickly from one identifiable object to another, making rough approximations of the distance between. Key points might be a creek bed, large tree, skull, or large rock, any of which might disappear or change position with time. Some grants were "floating grants," a specific number of leagues that the grantee might locate anywhere within a large, vaguely defined area. Most rancheros were equally casual about complying with other grant requirements, such as occupying the lands, making improvements, and properly recording the grant, resulting in tragic loss for many of them when called on to prove title to their holdings after the gold rush.

A significant number of these ranchos were owned and operated by women. Some 60 grants, over 335,000 acres, were made to women, including the 4,449-acre Rancho Rodeo de las Aguas, of which María Rita Valdez de Villa was a joint grantee, and the 4,439-acre Rancho Purísima Concepción near San José, granted to Juana Briones de Miranda. Moreover, under Mexican law, married women retained ownership of any separate property possessed prior to marriage and were granted community property rights. Widows also controlled large ranchos. Doña Vicente Sepúlveda, for example, managed Rancho Los Palos Verdes for 30 years after the death of her husband. In Contra Costa María Manuela Valencia de Briones managed the Rancho Boca de la Cañada del Pinole. Both ranchos were more than 13,000 acres in size.

Many rancheros moved onto their land and built large adobe homes, architectural forerunners of the California ranch-style house. One-story, tile-roofed structures, with long covered porches and often an inner courtyard, they were usually built on a hill with plenty of open

Andrés Pico

Pío Pico's brother, Andrés, dressed in the finery of the great ranchero. In the 1850s Andrés Pico served in the state legislature and authored the 1859 resolution dividing the state at the Tehachapi Mountains. The U.S. Congress, immersed in the slavery controversy, did not act on the proposal. *The History Collection / Alamy Stock Photo.*

space around as a precaution against raids by Natives from the Central Valley. Some were unusually large. The *casa* of Don Bernardo Yorba near Los Angeles, for example, reportedly consisted of 30 rooms plus another 21 for servants' quarters and workrooms. Well-to-do rancheros imported furniture and other fine articles from New England, while even the lesser rancheros managed to have such luxuries as embroidered bedspreads and pillowcases. Many of the larger landholders lived in town while their more isolated ranchos were operated by relatives or mestizo *mayordomos* (ranch foreman or manager). These rancheros constituted from 10 to 20 percent of the non-Indian pueblo population and were frequently the chief local civil and military figures, as well as the social leaders of the province.

The ranchero was the unquestioned master of his estate. Fathers locked up unmarried daughters, arranged

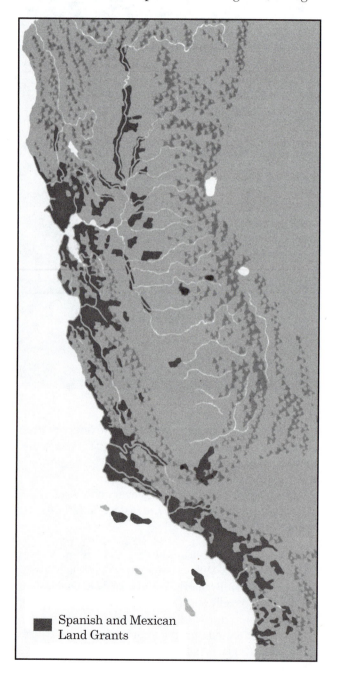

■ Spanish and Mexican
Land Grants

marriages, and often controlled the lives of children after marriage. Yet there was a reciprocal obligation to treat women and children with respect and consideration, and women were provided legal protections against abusive husbands. Children were instructed in religious values and proper conduct from an early age. Disobedience and disrespect for one's elders were regarded as grave offenses. There was little formal education for young Californios, and most were illiterate or, at best, semiliterate. The sons of the rancheros, however, might be sent abroad for schooling. Daughters of any class were seldom provided such opportunities.

The work of the rancho focused on producing hides and tallow for export and food for its own personnel. During the annual rodeo, neighboring families rounded up cattle from the open range for identification and branding. The Californios, both men and women, were widely regarded as the best riders in the world. The rodeo, a major social event, was often accompanied by a gala celebration, with days of feasting, singing, and dancing. The men of the rancho usually conducted the great *matanzas* (slaughters). Cattle were driven to areas convenient for the transport of hides and tallow to the trading ships along the coast. There they were slaughtered and skinned, and their hides stretched out to dry. Meat was dried, and tallow melted and placed in skin bags. The remaining carcasses were left for wild animals. Guadalupe Vallejo, in reminiscing about his days at Mission San José, noted that many a serenade was broken up by grizzly bears wandering through the streets on their way to and from the mission's *calavera*, or slaughter corral.

While cattle were the main product of the ranchos, sheep and horses were abundant; sheep provided wool for cloth and blankets. In addition, a few hogs were raised, mainly for lard, since both Californios and Native people regarded pork with disfavor. The missions and pueblos—and to a lesser extent, the ranchos—also produced substantial quantities of wheat, using primitive methods. Iron-tipped wooden plows broke the soil, which was smoothed out with brush or tree branches after sowing. The wheat was harvested by hand and often threshed by dumping the cut wheat into a hard-packed corral and running horses around and around over it. The wheat was then winnowed by tossing it in the wind until the chaff blew away. This process could take many weeks.

Ranch women shared the burden of administering a sometimes extensive organization, managed a large corps of household workers, and participated in cattle drives and rodeos. Their daughters usually married in their teens and spent much of their young lives bearing children, many of whom died within six months. Still, among the ranchero class, large families were not uncommon. Maria Teresa de la Guerra, daughter of José de la Guerra y Noriega, married William E. P. Hartnell and presented him with 18 children. Don José himself was survived by more than 100 descendants. Preparing food was also a major responsibility, and while all celebrations were accompanied by great feasts, Californios, as one writer noted, ate well at all times:

> A family breakfast would include eggs or *frijoles* (beans) . . . coffee with rich cream, or chocolate, or tea, honey and tortillas. Dinner came at noon and was a solid meal of beefsteak and boiled beef, stewed chickens or hash made of *carne seca* (dried beef) mixed with scrambled eggs, onions, tomatoes well seasoned and sprinkled with red chili pepper, beans prepared with plenty of gravy, tortillas, and *vino del país* (locally made wine). . . . Supper was slightly less solid . . . consisting of soup, roast duck perhaps, or richly flavored *guisado de carne* (beef stew), sweet potatoes, frijoles, and lettuce salad.

Male or female, young or old, the rancheros loved entertainment. Weddings, baptisms, feast days, rodeos, and visitors provided occasions for celebrations that sometimes lasted for days. Dancing, a special

Rancho San Pedro

A Classic Spanish Land Grant

For many modern Californians, the state's Spanish-Mexican heritage evokes images of the great land grants that became the ranchos of the pastoral era. The vast majority of such grants were actually made under Mexican rule but most Californians still think of them as "Spanish land grants." Rancho San Pedro was one of the few genuinely Spanish land grants; indeed, it was the first in Alta California. Its history is closely linked to the history of Los Angeles.

The original grantee of Rancho San Pedro was Juan José Domínguez, a foot soldier with Portolá's 1769 expedition. Two years after he retired in 1782, he successfully petitioned his former commander, Governor Pedro Fages, for permission to use the grant to raise cattle. As was the custom, the permission included no specific title to the land. No survey or map of the grant was ever recorded. Domínguez and two friends marked out the tract, which generally included the area bounded on the east by the Los Angeles River, on the west and south by the ocean, and on the north by a line running from the present-day city of Compton to a point midway between Hermosa Beach and Redondo Beach. They described the line as "commencing at a large sycamore tree [on the] road leading from San Pedro to Los Angeles . . . thence running [westerly] to a stone placed near the high road," and so on. The description included the occasional *"un poco más o menos"* (a little more or less), estimating the amount of land involved—in this case, over 75,000 acres.

As Domínguez grew older, he left the management of his grant to others, which led to the kinds of disputes common among all California rancheros. For example, Domínguez argued constantly with his old

(continued . . .)

Rancho San Pedro

The original extent of the Rancho San Pedro, outlined on a current map of Los Angeles.

friend, Manuel Nieto, who had obtained a neighboring grant, about their common boundary, the Los Angeles River. The waterway often changed its course during winter flooding, sometimes by as much as half a mile. Another conflict involved the Sepúlveda family, which had been granted permission by Domínguez's executor to pasture cattle in the western portion of Rancho San Pedro. The Sepulvedas eventually carved more than 30,000 acres out of the Domínguez ranch, creating Rancho Los Palos Verdes for themselves. Domínguez's heirs, nephew Cristobál and grandnephew Manuel, spent years petitioning the Mexican government for regranting of the original rancho and confirmation of their title. In 1846, a battle in the U.S.-Mexican War took place on the rancho. In the Battle of Domínguez Ranch, sometimes called the "Battle of the Old Woman's Gun," a group of Californios with a small cannon that had been hidden in an old woman's yard during the initial U.S. occupation of Los Angeles, beat back American troops attempting to retake the city. As was true of most for the region's large land holders, there were family squabbles over shares in the rancho and, after the American conquest, a long struggle for confirmation of title from the United States Land Commission. Shortly after war's end, part of the rancho was sold to Phineas Banning and some associates, eventually becoming San Pedro harbor. The first railroad in the area was built through Rancho San Pedro. In the 1920s the Domínguez Hills oil field, one of the richest in California, was discovered on the rancho, part of which in 1966 became the campus of today's California State University, Domínguez Hills.

Surprisingly, the Domínguez family has held on to much of Juan José's grant. Grandnephew Manuel, who served as mayor of Los Angeles and was a member of the 1849 constitutional convention, died in 1882, leaving his wife and daughters more than 24,000 acres of the Domínguez Rancho. Through judicious development, the family has retained control of a substantial portion until modern times, a rare circumstance that makes Rancho San Pedro not only one of California's oldest grants, but also one of the few to stay in the family.   (RBR)

enjoyment, included the lively *jaramba* and the sedate *contradanza*. The more formal affairs on the ranchos were called *bailes*, while the less formal events were known as *fandangos*.

This elaborate way of life depended on an abundant supply of cheap Indigenous labor; large numbers of ex-neophytes performed most household duties. Mariano Vallejo's wife, Benicia, described her household staff as follows:

> Each of my children, boy or girl, has a servant who has no other duty but to care for him or her. I have two servants for myself. Four or five grind the corn for the tortillas, for here we entertain so many guests that three grinders are not enough. Six or seven serve in the kitchen. Five or six are constantly busy washing the clothes of the children and servants, and nearly a dozen are required to attend to the sewing and spinning.

Ex-neophytes and gentile Indians performed the ranch work, while competent ex-neophytes sometimes acted as *mayordomos*, supervising the work of the Native labor force. Only a few were paid even a subsistence wage, while most worked simply for food and shelter. Many of the wage earners quickly lost their freedom to move. Because their purchases at the rancho *tienda* (store) frequently outpaced their meagre wages,

they often fell into a legal state of debt peonage, unable to leave their employer until they somehow managed to settle their accounts. Nevertheless, despite their lowly status, their importance cannot be ignored. Almost all foreign observers were quick to note the dependence of the rancho economy and way of life on the Indigenous people. The seeming indolence of the Californios, and their avoidance of all manual labor, merely reflected that dependence. On the other hand, many Indians, their culture and economy destroyed by European contact, were dependent on the ranchos for food and shelter. This mutual dependence was fundamental to the rancho economy and social system.

The expansion of trade after 1822 contributed to the growth of towns where hides and tallow were exchanged. Los Angeles and Monterey, surrounded by the most productive ranchos, became the respective centers of influence in the south and north, while San José developed as a prosperous pueblo in the San Francisco Bay region. (Yerba Buena, forerunner of the city of San Francisco, was not founded until 1835.) Santa Barbara, while relatively isolated, exported many hides.

The constitution of 1824 accorded each town, or pueblo, a representative *ayuntamiento*, or council, but the key figure remained the *alcalde*, who was not only the chief executive officer but also the chief judicial

Doña Marcelina's Grapevine

This Edward Vischer drawing shows rancho life near Santa Barbara, with guitar players, strolling señoritas, and Indian servants—a way of life that lasted well into the 1870s. Ironically, southern California boosters chopped down this grapevine and sent the pieces east to advertise California's fertile soil. *The Huntington Library, San Marino, California.*

figure for the community. Most disputes were settled by the *alcalde* through a conciliatory process, although he referred more serious matters to the governor. The lack of a court system proved difficult for Americans to adjust to, but the *alcalde* was a respected figure and regarded as a true city father.

Town life, particularly in Los Angeles and Monterey, was rather more complicated than life on the remote ranchos. Here military and civil officials, and a growing population of merchants and prominent foreigners, shared power and status with those rancheros who maintained town houses. They dressed more fashionably and their social activities were more elaborate, although they displayed the same generosity and hospitality that characterized the country people.

In the pueblos and mission towns the non-Native population lived in small adobe buildings that usually had thatched roofs and earth floors, and, in many respects, they tried to emulate the life of the upper classes, although family size was generally smaller, averaging three to four children per family. They ate simple but plentiful food and enjoyed feasting, singing, and dancing. Bull and grizzly-bear fights, cockfighting, and horse racing were common entertainments in the pueblos. With secularization, substantial numbers of Natives took up residence in squalid quarters, and pueblo life changed markedly. At one time, conditions in the Indian section of Los Angeles became so bad that the towns-people forced its removal across the river.

In spite of the stratified social structure of Mexican California there is a certain element of truth in historian Carey McWilliams's depiction of the *gente de razón*, the small non-Indian population, as "one big happy guitar-twanging family." Religious ties, especially godparent relationships between members of different classes, a common culture, common social activities, and the nature of rancho life, all made for personal loyalties binding groups together. In this sense, California society attained a remarkable cohesion that transcended class status in many ways.

Mexican California thus remained, as in the Spanish period, much like an overseas colonial possession— isolated and neglected. Left to their own resources and absorbing much of the revolutionary ideology of the day, Californios made significant changes in their own religious and economic institutions, producing the great rancho society and cattle economy with all its romantic, as well as coercive, elements. Still, it remained very much a frontier society, and one that was soon to be challenged.

Foreign Penetration

of California

9

No feature of the Mexican period in California had more far-reaching consequences than foreign penetration of the province. Prior to Mexican independence, Spain's colonial policies kept California essentially closed to foreign settlement, although contact with British, American, and Russian fur traders and whalers heightened interest in the area and, after 1810, encouraged a clandestine trade during the war for Mexican independence. A good deal was learned about California during these years, especially that it was an attractive land—and almost defenseless. Foreign observers were quick to see that Spain, and later Mexico, did not have a firm hold on the province. With independence, the bar to immigration was withdrawn and in the 1820s and '30s British and American hide-and-tallow traders made their way to California. These early immigrants were welcomed, became assimilated, and made important contributions to the region's economic development. In the same period a substantial number of beaver trappers, the "mountain men," migrated into the area, some of them remaining in various useful occupations. But the nature of foreign immigration changed dramatically when the American frontier movement reached California in 1841. Until then, neither Spain nor Mexico had successfully colonized California. Now the Americans threatened to do just that. Mexican authorities saw this threat, but were never strong enough to stop the migration.

Fort Ross, circa 1830

Cut off from expansion inland by Mexican development of the Sonoma region, the Russians sold the fort to John Sutter in 1841. *Courtesy of the California History Room, California State Library, Sacramento, California.*

The Russians in California

The establishment of the Russian colony at Fort Ross, not far from San Francisco, in 1812 was an early sign of Spain's weakness. In 1806 Count Nikolai Rezanov visited San Francisco seeking supplies for the starving and scurvy-ridden outpost of the Russian-American Fur Company at Sitka, Alaska. Trade with foreigners was illegal, but his betrothal to Concepción Argüello, the daughter of San Francisco's *comandante*, helped him to secure the provisions he sought. Unhappily, Rezanov died on the return trip to Russia. The young Concepción faithfully waited years for his return before learning of his death; their love affair provided raw material for new romantic California literature. Rezanov's visit also led to the establishment of a Russian settlement north of San Francisco as a base for shipping food to the Alaskan fur-trading posts and for hunting sea otter and seals along the California coast. In 1810 Ivan Kuskov scouted the Bodega Bay area and returned two years later to establish Fort Ross, a picturesque wooden structure on a bluff near the sea. Using Bodega Bay as their port, the Russians ultimately extended their influence several miles inland and employed several hundred Alaskan Aleut hunters along the coast and in San Francisco Bay, and more than 200 California Pomo Indian farm workers. Ignoring Spanish orders to leave, Kuskov supplied manufactured implements, utensils, furniture, and boats to Native and Hispanic traders in return for foodstuffs.

But several factors prevented the Russian foothold in California from prospering. The climate of Fort Ross was unsuited to raising wheat and the colony could never meet the needs of the Alaskan trading posts. In addition, expansion inland was blocked by Mexican enterprises, a declining sea otter population made the fur trade unprofitable, and Mexico's relaxing of trade restrictions reduced their need for the settlement. By 1839, Fort Ross had become a losing proposition. Also, by then the Russians believed that California would ultimately be absorbed by the United States. In 1841, they sold out to John A. Sutter.

A few other foreigners made their way to California before 1820, but their arrival was typically more accidental than intentional. In 1814, for example, an English ship dumped John Gilroy, an ailing Scottish sailor, in Monterey. Later baptized and naturalized, he married a daughter of Ignacio Ortega and became a ranchero; the present-day town of Gilroy bears his name. In all, probably no more than 20 foreigners took up permanent residence in California in the Spanish period, and they were soon absorbed by the local population.

The Hide-and-Tallow Traders

Mexico's opening of the ports of San Diego and Monterey to trade also opened the door to substantial additional foreign settlement. Beginning with Hartnell and Gale in 1822, the hide-and-tallow trade brought 15 to 20 new foreign settlers each year. Some, like Gilroy, became residents by force of circumstance, leaving no memorable record, but many others were essential to the successful development of California's commerce, especially since Californians lacked both the experience and the inclination to manage commercial affairs. With few exceptions, hide-and-tallow traders were assimilated into the local elite. They became Catholics and naturalized citizens, arranged marriages with ranchero families that gave them access to land,

Hispanicized their names, and adopted Californio ways and dress.

William E. P. Hartnell was typical of the resident business agent. He came to California after two years with John Begg & Co. in Peru, converted to Catholicism, married Maria Teresa de la Guerra, and acquired Rancho Patrocino del Alisal, 20 miles inland from Monterey. Naturalized in 1830, he held numerous civil posts. His most important assignment, as *visitador de misiones* of the secularized missions, proved to be a hopeless effort to stem the tide of plunder following secularization. A cultivated man who spoke French, German, and Spanish fluently, Hartnell became one of the most respected foreign residents of Mexican California. Many others followed Hartnell's example—among them William G. Dana, Henry Delano Fitch, and John R. Cooper (all Yankee sea captains of the trade), Alfred Robinson, and William Heath Davis, Jr., each of whom contributed to stronger economic ties with the United States.

Abel Stearns, another New Englander turned Californian, was naturalized in Mexico, entered California in 1829, and went into business selling hides and spirits in Los Angeles. Not a handsome man, he was known as Cara de Caballo, or "Horseface," but this did not prevent him from winning the hand of a southern California beauty, Doña Arcadia Bandini. Stearns's business flourished, he acquired huge landholdings, and he became the wealthiest man in southern California, also holding a number of important local offices. He was almost unique in being childless.

Like Stearns, Hugo Reid, a Scotsman, came to California in the early 1830s from Mexico and became prominent in southern California affairs. Reid wed a Tongva neophyte the missionaries named "Victoria." She received a sizable land grant from Mexico, and Reid obtained Rancho Santa Anita for himself. He devoted his attention to Indian customs and wrote some of the earliest criticism of the mission system, based largely on Doña Victoria's own childhood experiences at Mission San Gabriel.

Thomas Oliver Larkin was a singular exception to the pattern of assimilation of the hide-and-tallow trade immigrants in that he did not become naturalized. He came to California in 1832 and in the following year married Rachel Hobson Holmes, whom he had met on board ship. (She thus became the first American woman to reside in California.) Settling in Monterey, Larkin became perhaps the most successful merchant in the province, establishing close relations with Mexican officials, and lending money to the hard-pressed government. Yet he did not particularly sympathize

with Mexican rule and in later years worked for American acquisition of California. Larkin did not become a ranchero, although he dealt in real estate, but he built a fine house in Monterey, pioneering the "Monterey" style of architecture. So successful were his dealings in merchandise, lumber, and real estate that his sight drafts on funds he had on deposit in the United States circulated like banknotes in currency-starved California. Although remaining an American citizen, Larkin became a respected and influential figure in California affairs. In 1843 President John Tyler appointed him U.S. consul in Monterey, and, in 1845, President James K. Polk appointed him as a confidential federal agent. Larkin's lengthy dispatches and observations are an important resource for the history of the period.

Like Hartnell, Stearns, and Larkin, most foreigners connected with the hide-and-tallow trade performed a valuable function in the cattle economy. They were, in fact, encouraged to become permanent residents through such devices as the Mexican colonization laws of 1824 and 1828, which made naturalized citizens eligible for land grants. Welcome additions to the ranks of the Californios, many occupied prestigious positions in the province.

The Mountain Men

The arrival of the mountain men was viewed in a decidedly different light. Seemingly safe from American expansionism behind the wall of the Sierra Nevada and the deserts of the Southwest, Mexican residents were justifiably alarmed when Jedediah Smith breached these barriers, appearing with a large group of men at Mission San Gabriel in 1826. Smith's feat was the direct result of the rendezvous fur-trade system, whereby beaver trappers exchanged pelts for merchandise at an annual meeting in the Rocky Mountains. This extended their range some 1,500 miles, and brought Smith into California.

Jedediah Smith was a literate, observant young man, in addition to possessing the heroic qualities so often associated with his kind. His account of the 1826 expedition lay forgotten in an attic until its discovery in 1967. A fascinating story of the opening of California to the American frontier movement, it was published in 1977 as *The Southwest Expedition of Jedediah S. Smith: His Personal Account of the Journey to California, 1826–1827*. In partnership with William L. Sublette and David E. Jackson, Smith took over the Rocky Mountain Fur Company in 1826 and launched an expedition through the Great Basin (probably the least-known part of North America at the time) to the Southwest to open new beaver country. Leaving the rendezvous, Smith and 17 men traveled south to the Great Salt Lake and then southwest to the Colorado River. At the Mojave villages, near the present-day town of Needles, Smith decided to push west into California, making his way through the Mojave Desert to an outlying rancho of Mission San Gabriel in November 1826, guided by two neophytes who had fled from the mission. He announced his arrival in a note to Father José Bernardo Sanchez requesting his permission to replenish his supplies. Smith received a reply in Latin, prompting him to observe that "as I could not read his Latin nor he my english [sic] it seemed we were not likely to become general correspondents."

Nevertheless, the amiable Father Sanchez welcomed Smith's party, providing them with comfortable quarters and good food while Smith traveled on to San Diego for permission to trade and hunt beaver. Seeing Smith's arrival as a dangerous sign, Governor Echeandía detained him for six weeks then released him with instructions to leave California the way he had come. Smith departed from San Gabriel in January 1827, retracing his path until he passed through the San Gabriel Mountains at Cajon Pass. There he turned north, asserting that he had fulfilled the governor's instructions. He crossed the Tehachapi Mountains through the old Tejon Pass, picking up runaway mission Indians as guides. Trapping in the San Joaquin Valley through the end of March, Smith left most of his party on the Stanislaus River and, with two men, crossed the Sierra Nevada at present-day Ebbets Pass, claiming distinction as the first white men to do so. After a harrowing trek across the parched Great Basin, Smith reached the 1827 rendezvous at Bear Lake, in northern Utah.

Mindful of the men he had left at the Stanislaus River, Smith was off again within ten days. Following his route of the previous year, Smith, 18 men, and two Indian women traveled without incident until the Mojave villages. There, the Mojave, peaceful the year before, attacked as Smith's company as it crossed the river, killing the women and ten men and wounding several others. The survivors limped into San Gabriel, where Smith obtained horses and supplies and hurried north to join the company he had left at the Stanislaus River the year before. In need of supplies, Smith rode into Mission San José for assistance, but Father Durán seized him and packed him off to Governor Echeandía, then on one of his infrequent visits to Monterey. Echeandía clapped him in jail, but soon released him on the condition that Smith and his trappers leave California.

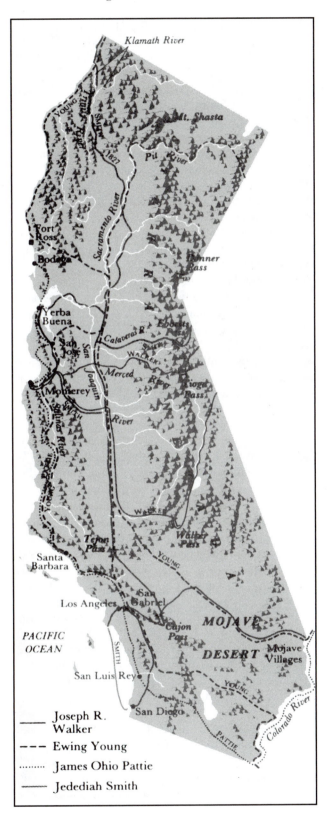

Routes of the Mountain Men

Making the first recorded overland journey up the coast of California into Oregon, Smith reached the Umpqua River in mid-July, where Indians killed all but Smith and two others in his party. The survivors fled to the Hudson's Bay Company post at Fort Vancouver. Smith returned to hunting and trapping in the Rockies. In May 1831, Comanches left him dead on the Santa Fe Trail.

Jedediah Smith was in California for only two brief periods, yet he had a major impact on the state's history. It was he who first opened California to the east, bringing it within reach of the American frontier movement. He was the first to cross the Sierra Nevada and to travel between the Sierra and Great Salt Lake, and he opened a trail between California and Oregon that was soon improved and traveled by Hudson's Bay Company trappers. A pious, thoughtful young man, his descriptions of the terrain he covered and the people he saw are a unique contribution to the history of western America.

Other mountain men soon followed. In 1827, James Ohio Pattie and his father, Sylvester, joined a party heading down the Gila River to the Colorado. Emerging in Baja California, south of San Diego, missionaries turned them over to Governor Echeandía. His worst fears now being realized, the governor threw the Patties in prison, where Sylvester Pattie died. James later claimed that he had brought with him a supply of smallpox vaccine and was freed on the condition that he distribute it to the Californios. Pattie recounted his experiences in *The Personal Narratives of James Ohio Pattie*, published in 1831. Although it blurred fact with fiction, the *Narrative* was significant for bringing California to the attention of American readers.

A less colorful, but nevertheless important, figure in the list of mountain men who threw open the doors to California was Ewing Young. Like the Patties, Young worked out of Santa Fe, New Mexico. He helped develop an overland desert trail to California known as the "Old Spanish Trail" that ran from Santa Fe to the Mission San Gabriel. In the 1830s Young brought large trapping parties into California, ranging all the way north to Oregon and the Klamath Lake region. Several of the men in Young's expeditions elected to stay in California under the liberalized Mexican colonization laws of 1828, which encouraged foreign settlement. Among them was Isaac Williams; by the end of the Mexican period, his Rancho Santa Ana del Chino gave him an income then calculated at $30,000 per year. Jonathan Trumbull Warner and William Wolfskill also became prominent, while others found new occupations in the pueblos. The newcomers merged with an unassimilated and unpredictable floating population of foreigners that was con-temptuous of Mexican authority and often participated in the region's frequent political turnovers. In 1840 Governor Alvarado sent Isaac Graham, a particularly notorious member of this group, to Mexico in chains, along with several dozen of his cohorts. The severity of this punishment indicates the level of menace Mexican officials saw in the intruders.

The opening of a central route over the Sierra was pioneered by Joseph Reddeford Walker in 1833. Leading a large force of trappers, he crossed the Great Basin to the Humboldt River, proceeded across the desert, and came to the lake and river east of the Sierra that now bear his name. Following the river, Walker's party made the first east-to-west crossing of the Sierra. His was probably the first such group to see the region's giant sequoias and the grandeur of Yosemite Valley. Thousands of migrants would later follow Walker route into California.

The importance of the mountain men to California history cannot be exaggerated. They blazed the trails that opened the region to the east, publicized its glories to a reading public, and led the first American settlers over the Sierra passes and the Old Spanish Trail. More than any others they brought the American frontier movement, with all its potential for disruption of the romantic rancho era, to the "land of promise" in the Far West.

Mavericks

Two nonconformists who came to California in the 1830s, "Dr." John Marsh and John A. Sutter, made important contributions to the penetration of the province by the American frontier movement. Marsh came from Santa Fe in 1836. A graduate of Harvard University, he convinced local residents that his bachelor of arts degree was a certificate to practice medicine, and began a career as a doctor in Los Angeles, accepting hides in payment of his fees. In 1837 he purchased a large rancho on the eastern slope of Mount Diablo, across the bay from San Francisco, where he lived a reclusive life. His primary importance was as a publicist. Convinced that California could be another Texas, the articulate Marsh wrote dozens of letters extolling the country's virtues to acquaintances in the East. Widely published in the Midwest, his letters stimulated a significant movement of settlers to California.

John Sutter, originally Johann Augustus Sutter, was a Swiss émigré who, in 1834, left bad debts, an unhappy wife, and several children behind to seek his fortune in America. After spending some time in the fur trade in the Rocky Mountains and St. Louis, he came to California by way of Hawaii, Alaska, and eventually Oregon.

Sutter's Fort

Sutter's fort dominated the interior of northern California in the 1840s. Sutter encouraged and protected American frontier settler migration from 1841 to 1846. Ironically, when John C. Frémont placed one of his men in charge of the fort at the time of the Bear Flag Revolt, Sutter became a virtual prisoner in his own house. *Courtesy of The Bancroft Library, University of California, Berkeley.*

Upon arrival he wangled a huge grant of land in the unoccupied Sacramento Valley, as well as extensive civil authority from Governor Alvarado, who appointed him local military commander and judge "to represent . . . all the laws of the country in the area." Selecting a site at the junction of the Sacramento and American rivers, Sutter in time developed a little barony that he called New Helvetia. As the Spanish had before him, Sutter relied on local Natives as laborers and trading partners. An element of compulsion sometimes marred these relationships. As Isidora Filomena Solano recalled, "Sutter forced the Jalquineros to exchange hides and dried fish for liquor."

In 1841 Sutter bought out the Russians at Fort Ross for a trifling down payment and a large promise to pay. With the cannon from Fort Ross, Sutter erected his own fort, which not only was a major defensive bulwark against Indian raids, but also made him largely independent of Mexican control. He established a large cattle and sheep business, planted a sizable wheat crop, built a grist mill and a distillery, and employed large numbers of Hawaiians, Californios, and Natives.

Sutter's importance to the development of California, however, is not merely the result of his colorful character and independent feudal domain. New Helvetia lay at the terminus of the main westward trails. Sutter encouraged American migration along these trails and frequently

sent supplies east over the Sierra to emigrant parties in trouble, receiving them with warm hospitality when they arrived. He gave them work, sold them land, leased them Indian laborers, gave them passports, and otherwise promoted the advance of the American frontier.

Frontier Settlers

By 1840 California had a permanent foreign resident population of perhaps 380, almost all of them men who came with the hide-and-tallow trade or in search of beaver. For the most part, they had been accepted and assimilated by the local society, but the growing number of former mountain men such as Isaac Graham and his friends created some anxiety among officials. Then, in 1841, a portentous change occurred as the American frontier movement began to make its way over the Sierra.

The appearance of land-hungry American farm families stemmed from the activities of the mountain men, the repeated and glowing reports of California's attractions, the pressures of the depression years of the 1830s, and British-American rivalry in the Northwest. The United States' claim to Oregon in particular attracted the attention of frontier settlers, and in the 1840s migration along the Oregon Trail increased rapidly. Until 1849 the number of pioneers moving to Oregon was eight to ten times the number coming to California, but the movement along the Oregon Trail stimulated interest in California as well.

The first organized company of frontier settlers to leave Missouri for California was the Bidwell-Bartleson party of 1841. In 1840, letters from John Marsh and speeches by trapper Antoine Robidoux excited enough interest to result in the Western Emigration Society, some 500 people who pledged to assemble the next spring at Sapling Grove, on the Missouri River, and go to California. In the spring of 1841, only one of the original members of the society, former teacher John Bidwell, appeared at the designated meeting place. Sixty-eight new members eventually joined him and then elected John Bartleson as captain of the company.

Despite warnings against overland travel to California that Mexican authorities published in U.S. newspapers, the Bidwell-Bartleson pioneers began their six-month odyssey on May 19, 1841, under the guidance of mountain man Thomas "Broken Hand" Fitzpatrick. The journey was untroubled until they reached Soda Springs, the turning point for California. Half of the group decided to go on to Oregon with Fitzpatrick, and the remaining 34 headed for California. The party included one woman, 18-year-old Nancy Roberts Kelsey and her 18-month-old daughter, Martha Ann; her infant son had died only three months earlier. When her husband Ben announced his intention to migrate to California, Nancy was determined to go too. "Where my husband goes, I go," she later said. "I can better endure the hardships of the journey than the anxieties for an absent husband."

In mid-August the company turned south to follow the Bear River. In the blazing desert west of the Great Salt Lake they were forced to abandon their wagons and pack everything on horses, mules, and even several oxen. The party stumbled upon the headwaters of the Humboldt and followed its path across Nevada. Nancy rode bareback, holding her baby. Occasionally, Paiutes blocked their path. "At one place the Indians surrounded us, armed with bows and arrows," said Nancy, "but my husband leveled his gun at the chief and made him order his Indians out of arrow range."

The company next reached the sink of the Humboldt near present-day Lovelock and began a grueling 40-mile trek across the desert. Crossing the Walker River, low on food and nearly exhausted, they began the climb into the Sierra Nevada, which Bidwell described as "naked mountains whose summits still retained the snows of perhaps a thousand years." Unable to locate either the Carson or Sonora passes, the emigrants managed to force their way over the steep eastern slopes of the Sierra, which they finally crested on October 18. Fortunate that the snows were late that year, they nevertheless found themselves facing a new challenge. Recalled Nancy:

> We had a difficult time to find a way down the mountain. At one time I was left alone for nearly a day, and as I was afraid of the Indians, I sat all the while with my baby in my lap on the back of my horse. . . . It seemed to me while I was there alone the moaning of the wind through the pines was the loneliest sound I ever heard.

When they found the path, the descent was so steep they were forced to walk. "At one place," Nancy said, "four pack animals fell over a bluff." They killed and ate the cattle when their provisions ran out. Nancy walked barefoot, her shoes worn through. They eventually found the Stanislaus River and followed it down into the San Joaquin Valley. On November 4, 1841, the Bidwell party finally arrived at the ranch of Dr. John Marsh near Mt. Diablo. Marsh sold them meat and flour at what they considered exorbitant prices and, also for a stiff fee, obtained passports for them from reluctant Mexican authorities. When the party subsequently dispersed, several, including Bidwell, went to work for Sutter, whose generous treatment of them contrasted sharply with Marsh's. Bidwell later acquired the Rancho Chico north of Sacramento and eventually became one of the state's leading citizens. Five months pregnant at the end of the trail, Nancy Kelsey became the first woman to cross overland to California from the United States. Her fortitude inspired the men. Fellow traveler Joseph Chiles said "she bore the fatigue of the journey with so much heroism, patience and kindness, that there still exists a warmth in every heart for the mother and her child."

Not long after the Bidwell party arrived, another group arrived from Santa Fe under the leadership of William Workman and John Rowland. Some 25 Americans, in company with New Mexican traders, followed the Old Spanish Trail to southern California, where they had little difficulty in obtaining permission to settle. Workman and Rowland, along with another member of the group, Benjamin D. Wilson, became prominent rancheros in the Los Angeles area. Wilson, known as Don Benito, married Ramona Yorba (whose father owned the Rancho Santa Ana) founded the town of Alhambra, and was the second mayor of the city of Los Angeles. The nearby Mount Wilson is named for him. That same year the first small group of what became a substantial movement of pioneers from Oregon made their way down from the north. The ease with which the migrants of 1841 obtained permission to settle illustrates the breakdown of Mexican authority in the province. After the Texas revolution of 1836, Mexico looked with disfavor on American migration to its territories, yet the ability and willingness of local officials to grant passports (often for profit) undermined government policy.

No organized groups of migrants arrived in 1842, but the movement resumed in 1843, when Lansford W. Hastings arrived with part of a group of settlers he had taken to Oregon the year before. In the same year, Joseph B. Chiles, who had come with Bidwell and returned east in 1842, recruited a party of about 50 that he took along the Oregon Trail to Fort Hall. From there, Chiles and some ten men proceeded to California via the Pit River, while the remaining settlers, led by the veteran Joseph Reddeford Walker, came south by way of the Owens Valley and Walker Pass. The year 1844 saw the first wagons roll across the Sierra and what was to be the main route to California, opened when the Stevens-Murphy party crossed the mountains over what is now called Donner Pass.

To this point the migration to Mexican California, while unwelcome, had been insignificant. In 1845, however, this changed as more than 250 Americans poured over the Sierra. Among them were half a dozen large groups such as the Grigsby-Ide party of 50 men and their families. Moreover, they brought with them reports that thousands more planned to make the trek the next year. In fact, some 1,500 did.

The pioneers of 1846 arrived to find California already in American hands. The most famous overland group, the Donner party, was one of these groups. A large company of some 87 men, women, and children, the Donner party suffered from inexperience, lack of leadership, dissension, and delay. Their first mistake was attempting the so-called Hastings Cut-Off, leaving the Oregon Trail to travel south of the Great Salt Lake, which proved to be a difficult and time-consuming journey. With delays occasioned by disagreements and dawdling, the party arrived too late in the year at the Truckee River, nearly 6,000 feet high in the Sierras. There they were trapped by heavy snowfall. Demoralized, short of supplies, and without effective leadership, they failed to make the crossing and remained snowbound on Alder Creek and Donner Lake, where 39 died and some of the starving members were reduced to cannibalism. Relief parties organized at San Francisco and Sutter's Fort finally managed to bring 48 survivors over the mountains. Their story became a source of morbid fascination for future generations.

Mexican authorities were alarmed by the sudden increase in American immigration. Propagandists such as Lansford Hastings, who published his fanciful *Emigrant's Guide* in 1844, were boldly promoting settlement in California, and the new immigrants were not so easily absorbed into California society as earlier ones. The farm families who settled in the interior were reluctant to become Mexican citizens or Catholics. Whether they bought or rented land, claimed rights to questionable land grants, or simply squatted on lands already granted to others, the newcomers constituted a growing threat to Mexican control of the interior. They were doing what Spain and Mexico had never been able to do: colonize California. Dismayed but helpless, Mexican authorities seemed unable to stop them.

The Breakdown of Mexican Government

Increasing evidence of Mexico's inability to control affairs in California foreshadowed the end of the Mexican period. Governor Alvarado's administration had been characterized by rapid development of the rancho economy and the hide-and-tallow trade as the mission system was dismantled, and by relative political stability. Sectional rivalry over the location of the capital and customs house continued but, for the most part, Alvarado successfully avoided conflict over these issues. He did, however, fall into disagreement with General Vallejo, his uncle (though only two years his senior), over the military capabilities of the government. Vallejo, who despaired of disciplining "an army of unpaid relatives and friends," bombarded Mexico City with reports urging the strengthening of defenses and calling for a reunited political and military authority, a plan that Alvarado opposed.

Late in 1842 Mexico responded to Vallejo's entreaties by appointing General Manuel Micheltorena as governor and *comandante general*, replacing Alvarado and Vallejo. An attractive and gracious man, Micheltorena arrived with a force of 300 men to bolster the defenses of the province. Unfortunately, this army consisted mostly of ex-convicts and, as usual, the governor could not pay them. Consequently, they took to foraging, which outraged the local population. Although Micheltorena attempted with some success to administer California, he could never overcome the rampages of his convict army or the fact that he was an outsider. In November 1844, another "revolution" broke out, engineered, as in 1836, by Alvarado and José Castro with support from southern Californians led by Pío Pico. Both sides had foreign contingents in their forces. Micheltorena was supported by Sutter and a motley group under Isaac Graham, who still smarted from his treatment by Alvarado in 1840. Castro, Pico, and Alvarado were joined by foreigners in the south, including Stearns, Workman, and Rowland. The armies confronted each other at Cahuenga Pass in February 1845 in an artillery duel that killed a horse and wounded a mule. When the foreigners on both sides held a meeting and agreed to refrain from combat, Micheltorena's support vanished, and he agreed to leave California with his soldiers. He was replaced by another regime that returned to the principle of separation of civil and military authority. Pío Pico, as senior member of the *diputación*, became interim governor, while José Castro assumed the position of *comandante general*. As the Bear Flag Revolt revealed, this arrangement merely heightened sectional rivalry and further weakened Mexican authority.

Probably no issue was more important, or better demonstrated the weakness of government in California, than the Indian problem. All through the Mexican period, the Indians of the interior periodically drove off large numbers of horses from the mission and rancho herds, as well as cattle that they slaughtered for hides. During the 1830s the Indian raids were so serious in the San Diego district that most of the ranchos there were periodically abandoned. The Californio population declined by almost 50 percent.

Efforts to control the Indians were never really successful. In the north, Vallejo spent years chasing Indians as far as the Tuolumne and Stanislaus rivers after raids on local missions and ranchos. Sutter's records recount many punitive expeditions after Indians who had stolen his horses and burned his fields.

The political turmoil and military weakness did not go unnoticed by foreigners. In April 1846, Thomas Larkin wrote his unofficial vice-consul in San Francisco, William Leidesdorff, that "the pear is near ripe for the falling." Most observers expected it to fall into American hands.

American Interest

Since the 1820s the United States had looked westward with an acquisitive eye and acted to protect its western territorial interests. The Monroe Doctrine of 1823 was in part an effort to maintain these interests against Russian encroachment, and led in 1824 to an agreement in which Russia relinquished its claims south of 54°40′ north latitude, while the United States abandoned its claims north of that line. At the same time, American fur companies such as those of William Ashley and Jedediah Smith competed with the British Hudson's Bay Company for furs and national hegemony in the Pacific Northwest. In the process they opened the Northwest, particularly Oregon, to the American frontier movement.

In the 1830s a number of developments sharpened American interest in California. Texas, for one, was very much on the minds of Americans and Mexicans. After the revolution of 1836, Texas remained independent for almost ten years, but annexation by the United States was continually under consideration. The issue muddied political waters in Mexico and the United States for many years and fueled the American expansionist impulse. In the 1830s the American government began to focus its attention more directly on California. In 1835 Andrew Jackson offered Mexico half a million dollars for San Francisco Bay and the territory north of it without success. He also tried to use Texas's revolt against Mexico as an opportunity to negotiate for the area from San Francisco north, but again failed. Interest in the region remained high, however, and the United States began to send military exploration parties to wander, sometimes uninvited, in and out of Mexican territory, specifically California. A naval expedition led by Lieutenant Charles Wilkes spent the years 1838 to 1842 on the West Coast, charting the waters and observing conditions there. While ostensibly devoted to surveys in the interest of the whaling industry, Wilkes's expedition included a sizable party that went overland from Oregon to San Francisco through the Sacramento Valley. At the same time, a great deal of concern was expressed over the Isaac Graham affair, and American naval forces in the area were strengthened.

A good deal of this activity was a reaction to the interest of other countries in the "ripening pear" on the Pacific. In 1839, Alexander Forbes, British vice-consul in Tepic, Mexico, published his *History of California*, the first English-language book on the territory, in which he proposed that Mexico's British creditors cancel Mexican bonds and take over California in return. Sir George Simpson of the Hudson's Bay Company seemed to endorse this plan when he visited San Francisco in 1841. Many other such plans were voiced freely by British representatives in the West—to the consternation of Americans such as Larkin who worked to prevent such schemes, whether British, French, or Russian. Actually, the British government never took the suggestions of its western agents seriously, and British policy did not include any suggestion of seeking control of California aggressively. Still, Anglo-American rivalry in Oregon

The Pueblo of Monterey, 1842

This lithograph portrays California's capital, Monterey, at the time of the arrival of the U.S. Squadron of the Pacific under Commodore Thomas ap Catesby Jones. Decades after its founding, Monterey, now under Mexican authority, still bore the marks of the rude frontier life in Hispanic California. The harbor lacks wharf facilities, and the pueblo's houses are scattered and virtually devoid of ornamental greenery. Walls confine household livestock—and guard against the ever-present danger of Indian attack. *Courtesy of The Bancroft Library, University of California, Berkeley.*

and the Americans' traditional Anglophobia contributed to the persistent belief that the British were maneuvering to do so.

Interest continued, therefore, in negotiating with Mexico for the cession of California, or part of it, to the United States. In fact, Daniel Webster, secretary of state under President John Tyler, worked out a complicated deal in 1842 by which the United States would pay Mexican debts to British and American creditors in return for Texas and part of California and Oregon as far north as the Columbia River. This tripartite arrangement was opposed by American expansionists who objected to giving up the territory north of the Columbia. When Commodore Thomas ap Catesby Jones seized the port of Monterey in October 1842, in the mistaken belief that war had broken out, the plan collapsed. Jones learned he was in error within hours and retired with apologies, but his action was a clear signal of American intentions.

The election of James K. Polk as president in 1844 made it even more obvious that the spirit of Manifest Destiny was reaching a climax in the United States. Polk, a protégé of Andrew Jackson, shared his predecessor's distrust of British intentions and had campaigned for the presidency on a platform of aggressive expansionism and resistance to British imperialism in America. This meant primarily the annexation of Texas and occupation of the disputed Oregon territory, but Polk, supported by a growing clamor in the American press, made it clear that he also intended to acquire California. Like presidents before him, Polk attempted to acquire the region by purchase, sending John Slidell to Mexico with an offer of up to $40 million for Upper California and New Mexico. At the same time he took another tack, probably well aware that Slidell's mission had no real chance of success. In 1845 he appointed Consul Larkin a "confidential agent" with instructions to try to persuade Californians to declare their independence from Mexico and seek the protection of the United States.

It took six months for Larkin's appointment letter to reach Monterey, but once it arrived in April 1846 Larkin energetically went to work. He enlisted the aid of important foreign residents, including General Vallejo's brother-in-law Jacob Leese in Sonoma, Abel Stearns in Los Angeles, and J.J. Warner in San Diego. Since the Californians had always resented Mexican interference in their affairs, many, including even General Vallejo, were also receptive to Larkin's proposals. However, John Charles Frémont's sudden arrival on the scene quickly triggered a series of events that made Larkin's plan superfluous.

John C. Frémont

Few Americans captured the imagination of their time as completely as did John C. Frémont. Although of illegitimate birth, he obtained a commission in the Army Corps of Topographical Engineers and won the hand of the beautiful Jessie, daughter of Thomas Hart Benton, the powerful expansionist U.S. senator from Missouri. After leading five major expeditions into the American West, Frémont wrote and published reports, with the aid of his talented and ambitious wife, which profoundly affected Americans. Containing masterful descriptions of the flora, fauna, and geology of the regions he traversed, and carefully mapped routes for future migrants, Frémont's reports particularly appealed to a generation of Americans moved by the spirit of Manifest Destiny. These accounts also made Frémont a romantic hero; he and his wife achieved a popularity enjoyed by no other couple of the age.

For two decades Frémont—a natural showman, an adventurer, and an opportunist whose ambition and ego were almost boundless—was a prominent national figure. He was one of the first two U.S. senators from California, first presidential candidate of the newly founded Republican Party, and, as a Civil War general, one of the first to attempt to free southern slaves. He was criticized as merely a follower of the trails that others blazed, court-martialed for his refusal to obey army orders, and forced by Lincoln to curtail his efforts to emancipate slaves in his Missouri command. He also resigned his commission before the Civil War was over and engaged in political maneuvers that almost cost Lincoln his reelection. Historians have tended to view him as either a hero or a scoundrel, but, in either case, his significance to the American westward movement is undeniable.

Frémont's second and third expeditions were probably even more significant than his first. In 1843 and 1844, he traveled west to the Columbia River, turned south, and crossed the Sierra by way of Carson Pass in the middle of winter. After resting at Sutter's Fort, Frémont's company traveled the length of the San Joaquin Valley, crossed Tehachapi Pass to the Mojave Desert, followed the Old Spanish Trail into southern Utah, and then struck out for St. Louis by way of the Sevier River and Bent's Fort on the Arkansas River. From November 1843 to July 1844, no word was heard in the East from Frémont, and anxiety for the "lost expedition" mounted. When he emerged from the wilderness and published his report of the journey, it became an immediate popular success and the chief source of information for would-be migrants.

In 1845, Frémont set off on his third expedition, this time to map the trail west through the Rocky Mountains. It was not in his instructions to enter California, but he did. One section of his company crossed the Sierra at Walker Pass in the south, while Frémont led another group up the Truckee River and over Donner Pass, arriving at Sutter's Fort in early December. His arrival sparked the chain of events that culminated in the Bear Flag incident, which itself can be considered the beginning of the Mexican War in California. When Frémont assumed command of the Bears, he positioned himself to play an important role in that war.

The Prize of War

In March 1845, Congress finally adopted a joint resolution to annex Texas. Along with Texas, the United States also acquired its new territory's disputes with Mexico, particularly one involving its western and southern border. Texans had themselves been expansionists, some envisioning a Texas that encompassed all of the Southwest and California. In any event, by 1845, Texans claimed a western and southern border that ran the length of the Rio Grande del Norte, from its mouth to its source. Mexico asserted that the border was on the traditional line, the Nueces River, and prepared to occupy the ground between the two rivers. Congress's resolution of annexation was silent on the matter. James K. Polk's election to the presidency in 1844 brought an unabashed expansionist to power in the United States. Polk supported the Rio Grande line and sent General Zachary Taylor to the region with instructions to regard a Mexican crossing of the Rio Grande as an act of war. When Polk signed the resolution admitting Texas to the Union as the 28th state in December 1845, both sides prepared for war.

In the spring of 1846, as José Castro and John C. Frémont moved toward their own fateful confrontations, Mexican and American soldiers jockeyed along the disputed Texas border. Finally, in May, American forces under Taylor entered the no man's land between the Nueces and Rio Grande rivers, drawing Mexican fire. The expected war had begun.

There were two distinct phases to the war in California. The first consisted of the almost uncontested seizure of the province by American forces. Reports of Taylor's activities in Texas reached Commodore John D. Sloat, who commanded the Pacific squadron at Mazatlán, in June 1846. Since Sloat's instructions were to occupy California upon a declaration of war between the United States and Mexico and he was fearful of British designs, he rushed north to Monterey Bay. But Sloat did not occupy the town, since he lacked evidence of an actual declaration of war. His hand was forced when he learned of the successes of the Bear Flaggers and that Frémont had joined them. On July 7, 1846, he raised the American flag at Monterey and issued a proclamation stating that "henceforth California will be a portion of the United States." It was a conciliatory document, promising Californians U.S. citizenship, religious freedom, and freer trade. Two days later, the American flag was raised at Sonoma, Sutter's Fort, and San Francisco.

Aged and ill, Sloat turned his command over to a much more aggressive commander, Commodore Robert F. Stockton. A prominent easterner, Stockton was flamboyant, adventurous, and ambitious. On questionable authority, he promoted Frémont to the rank of major, and later to lieutenant colonel. Stockton also enlisted the California Battalion as horse marines and sailed off with them for Los Angeles—to the discomfort of most of Frémont's seasick mountain men. On July 28 Frémont and his men landed at San Diego, while Stockton landed at San Pedro with a force of marines and sailors. Marching north, Frémont joined Stockton and on August 13 they occupied Los Angeles, as Pío Pico and José Castro fled to Mexico. In Los Angeles, Stockton issued offensive statements against California authorities and unnecessarily imposed martial law and a strict curfew. Leaving Captain Archibald Gillespie and 50 men as a garrison, Stockton and Frémont returned north.

Where courteous and diplomatic actions might have been called for, Gillespie chose to enforce Stockton's martial law and curfew harshly and rigorously. Led by José María Flores, the Angelenos rebelled, attacked Gillespie, and, after a short siege, forced his surrender on September 29. Meanwhile, warned of Gillespie's plight, Stockton recruited a force to sail to San Diego, while Frémont marched south with the 300-man California Battalion. At the same time, General Stephen W. Kearny was approaching from the east.

General Kearny had been sent to the southwest to obtain control of lands that President Polk hoped to acquire from Mexico. He took possession of New Mexico at Santa Fe without encountering any opposition and proceeded west to California with some 300 men. When he met Kit Carson returning east with the report that California had been occupied without resistance, Kearny sent most of his force back to Santa Fe and persuaded Carson to guide his remaining troops to the West Coast. In early December, Kearny reached San Pascual, an Indian village east of San Diego, his men and animals showing the effects of the long 2,000-mile march. Confronted by a large force of Californians under Andrés Pico (Pío Pico's brother), Kearny sent his exhausted men on a charge that strung the company out widely. The Californians, riding superior horses and armed with long lances, struck the disunited Americans. Sixteen or 18 Americans were killed, and an equal number, including Kearny, were wounded seriously. Pico's men came away virtually unscathed and proceeded to pin Kearny down in a desert siege. At this point, Carson and Lieutenant Edward F. Beale slipped through the lines to San Diego, where Stockton organized a relief force. With this aid, Kearny finally reached San Diego on December 12.

Re-conquest of the south, the second phase of the war in California, soon followed. It took Kearny and Stockton another month to march north to Los Angeles, which was recaptured on January 10, 1847. Flores, leaving Andrés Pico in command of the Californians, fled to Sonora. Reluctant to surrender to the harsh Stockton, Pico rode north to capitulate to Frémont at San Fernando. Learning that Frémont had already pardoned a relative, Jesús Pico, for violating his parole in the rebellion, Andrés correctly gambled on similar treatment. On January 13 the two men agreed to the Cahuenga Capitulation, ending the revolt without rancor.

With California at last securely in the hands of the United States, Commodore Stockton, again on questionable authority, appointed Frémont governor and sailed off for Mexican waters. In spite of the presence of Kearny, a brigadier general who had been sent west with specific orders to organize a government in the conquered province, Frémont issued orders establishing his government in Los Angeles. When Kearny attempted to exert his authority, Frémont, a mere lieutenant in the army a few months previously, infuriated him by arrogantly refusing to comply, asserting that his orders from Stockton came from a superior command. After dispatches from Washington confirmed Kearny's position, Frémont was forced to return to the East with Kearny under arrest, and was court-martialed. Though defended by his powerful father-in-law, Senator Benton, Frémont was convicted of mutiny, disobedience, and conduct to the prejudice of good order and military discipline, but he was recommended for clemency. President Polk confirmed his guilt on only the second two counts, granted clemency, and ordered him back to duty. Frémont, however, resigned his commission rather than admit the justice of the decision; the court-martial, oddly enough, only enhanced his attractiveness as a political figure. Meanwhile, Kearny had left the able Colonel Richard B. Mason behind as military governor.

The war with Mexico left little other imprint on California and finally ended when the Treaty of Guadalupe Hidalgo was signed on February 2, 1848, and ratified by the U.S. Senate on March 11. By its terms, as had been expected, California was ceded to the United States. The "ripe pear" had been plucked.

Culture in Spanish and Mexican California

California's isolation and its relatively primitive existence made it a cultural desert. Indeed, officials appointed to serve in California found it difficult to persuade their womenfolk to follow them into what was perceived as a social wasteland. The difficulty of life in provincial California is reflected in the exceedingly limited and short-lived attempts at education and in the near absence of arts and letters, although the more affluent rancheros imported some fine furniture, clothing and a few *objets d'art*. Perhaps the most significant cultural contribution of the period was the development of the architecture of the missions, ranchos, and Monterey-style homes.

Education was badly neglected, both inside and outside the missions. Mission schooling was limited to musical training and development of industrial arts. As many as 50 elementary schools existed at various times outside the missions, but none lasted any reasonable length of time. Some Spanish governors, notably Diego de Borica and Pablo Vicente de Solá, set up schools in old granaries or barracks, with retired soldiers who could read and write and do simple arithmetic serving as teachers. Using disciplinary methods such as a small cat-o'-nine tails, they stifled student interest as effectively as they imparted learning, as Mariano G. Vallejo vividly recalled. As late as 1845, scarcely 100 Native Californians were able to read and write.

A lucky few youngsters were given personal instruction by priests, military officers, and foreigners. As youths, Juan B. Alvarado, José Castro, and Mariano G. Vallejo were taken under the wing of Governor Solá, who taught them from his personal library, and, of course, his protégés became important figures in Mexican California. Near Monterey, with the financial assistance of Governor Figueroa, William P. Hartnell conducted classes for his own and neighbor children.

Petaluma Adobe
The double veranda of the restored main building at Mariano Vallejo's Petaluma Rancho (circa 1840)—the largest non-ecclesiastical adobe building in Hispanic California—attests to the influence of the new Monterey style. *Photograph by Richard J. Orsi.*

His Colegio de San José closed soon after Figueroa's death. The most favored were the boys whose families could afford to send them to Hawaii, Chile, or even Europe for their education. Girls were much less likely to receive any formal schooling other than training in cooking, sewing, and household management.

Given its low levels of literacy, it is not surprising that Mexican California produced little in the way of an indigenous literature. However, the writings of Francisco Palóu—including *Noticias de la Nueva California*, the first book written in California, and *Vida de Junípero Serra*—are basic works on the early history of Spanish California. With no printing press available before the 1830s, the region is distinguished more by the descriptive writings of foreign residents and visitors than by its native works. The most famous of these is Richard Henry Dana's *Two Years Before the Mast*, but many argue that Alfred Robinson's *Life in California* is superior. The mountain men also contributed to this literature, notably James Ohio Pattie's *Personal Narrative*. John C. Frémont's reports on his expeditions were also widely read. Jedediah Smith's account of his pioneering 1826 expedition to California was undiscovered until 1977.

The most pervasive cultural influence of Spanish and Mexican California has been its architecture. The "Mission" style became popular at the turn of the twentieth century. Early missions were essentially mud huts with thatched roofs, but as Indian neophytes acquired construction skills, mission fathers replaced them with adobe and stone buildings. Reflecting Roman-Moorish influences, California mission style sprouted archways, long colonnades, and thick walls and tile roofs (lessons taught by earthquake and fire). With few architectural adornments, the lines of Mission style were simple and clean. The Spanish and Mexican periods also saw the evolution of the now-ubiquitous "ranch" style house. Square or oblong, made mostly of thick adobe walls, with spacious rooms and long covered porches, rancho houses proved to be comfortably cool in summer heat but warm in the winter. A fusion of the California rancho house with New England architecture later became known as the "Monterey" style, introduced by Thomas O. Larkin for his home and customs house. The wide upper-story balcony, adobe construction, and white woodwork typical of this style can be seen in the restored buildings of modern Monterey.

Hydraulic Gold Mining

While Alfred A. Hart was documenting the construction of the Central Pacific Railway during the 1860s, he also recorded hydraulic gold miners at work. Twenty years later, their activities would precipitate the "debris wars" between the miners and valley farmers. Even when Hart made the photograph, however, environmental damage from hydraulic mining was evident. *The Huntington Library, San Marino, California.*

PART FOUR

Gold and the Americanization of California

Assessments of the California gold rush often apply a romantic gloss, suggesting that the colorful "Days of '49" were a brief, exciting interlude in an otherwise orderly narrative. The gold rush was romantic, brief, and exciting, but it was much more. For historian John W. Caughey, gold was the cornerstone of California's late-nineteenth-century history. The string of events that began at Sutter's Mill on the American River had momentous consequences for the state, for the nation, and even for the world.

A rush for gold accelerated California's development and compressed its history. Hundreds of thousands of Argonauts flooded the region, providing an instant, mostly American population imbued with both a lust for riches and that sense of entitlement known as "Manifest Destiny." In just over a year, the newcomers leap-frogged over the nation's traditional territorial period to make California the 31st state. Mining thoroughly transformed the economy: manufacturing to provide tools and other essentials; financial institutions to manage anticipated wealth; commercial and transportation facilities to distribute money and goods; agriculture to feed a hungry populace. Just as quickly, American social and cultural institutions appeared, a process epitomized by the "instant city," San Francisco.

The lure of the mines created a unique and diverse population that quickly made minorities of the earlier settlers—Indians and Californios. In the process, the gold rush exposed one of the uglier aspects of the American psyche, a sense of racial and cultural superiority that often translated into expressions of bigotry and, just as often, acts of violence. The velocity of events placed a heavy burden on the immigrants' traditions, including their institutions of law and justice. Energetic gold-seekers ruthlessly exploited the land and its resources, inflicting great ecological damage with little concern for the consequences. They magnified long-standing squabbles over land and water rights, introduced wildcat speculation in real estate, and a host of new problems that would plague the state for generations.

Within the span of a very few years, a carpenter's discovery near Sutter's Fort would transform the century-old Hispanic province of Alta California into a thoroughly American state of the Union, with all the positive and negative attributes that come with that status. The rapid "Americanization" of California, while admittedly short on excitement and romance, more than matches the gold rush in terms of short- and long-term historical significance.

Dame Shirley

A Yankee Lady in the California Mines

Men dominated the non-Indian population of gold rush California (more than 90 percent in 1852), and the male-female ratio began to approach parity only during the late 1860s. Impressions introduced by fiction such as Bret Harte's "Outcasts of Poker Flat" and "The Luck of Roaring Camp" and perpetuated by entertainment media often stereotype a substantial proportion of the female 10 percent as prostitutes. In reality, women of all sorts traveled to California, even aboard the first steamship from Panama in 1849. Although few in number, they were influential socially, culturally, and economically. One penned perhaps the most perceptive existing account of early gold rush life. "Dame Shirley," for whom the trip to the mines was principally an adventure, did not typify female gold rush Californians, but her letters provide not only information about the lives of women in the mines and the composition of mining camp populations, but also details about the miners' work and play, attempts to civilize their environment, personal characteristics, prejudices, and much more.

Late in the summer of 1851, a Yankee lady arrived at Rich Bar on the East Branch of the North Fork of the Feather River, "at almost the highest point, . . . where gold has been discovered, and indeed, within 50 miles of the summit of the Sierra Nevada itself." In the first of 23 letters to her sister Molly at home in "the States," she anticipated inevitable questions: "How did such a shivering, frail, homeloving little thistle ever float safely to that far away spot, and take root so kindly . . . in that barbarous soil? . . . And for pity's sake, how does the poor little fool expect to amuse herself there?" During the following year, she provided answers by "taking pains to describe

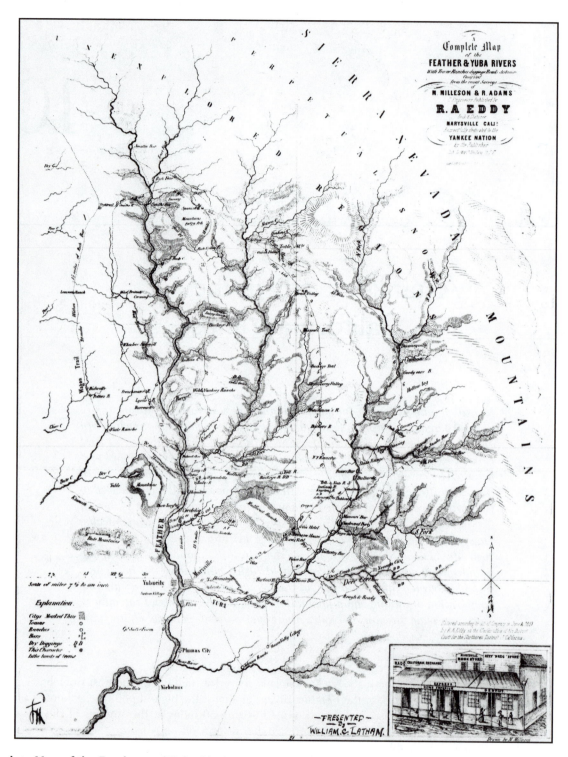

A Complete Map of the Feather and Yuba Rivers . . .

Produced in 1851, the map shows both Dame Shirley's route and her destination. She and her husband departed from relatively civilized Marysville on a two-week journey over barely marked trails. After traveling for 100 miles, they reached Rich Bar, on the very edge of California's "Unexplored Regions" and not far from an area identified only as "Perpetual Snow." *Courtesy of The Bancroft Library, University of California, Berkeley.*

things exactly as I see them, hoping thus you will obtain an idea of life in the mines as it is." She succeeded— probably far better than she expected.*

Best known by her pen name, "Dame Shirley," Louisa Amelia Knapp Smith Clapp assumed that she would be the "only petticoated astonishment" in the mines; she was not, but she was a remarkable person indeed. Born in 1819 in Elizabeth, New Jersey, she was descended from prominent New England families. When her father died in 1832 and his wife followed him to the grave in 1837, they left seven orphans. Despite the loss of their parents, however, the children were well provided for, loved, and educated. Louisa, who became the ward of a prominent attorney, attended the Female Seminary in Charlestown and Amherst Academy, where she received a contemporary young woman's standard training in writing, literature, languages, and music. Subsequently, she taught school and began a lifelong friendship-by-correspondence with career diplomat Alexander Hill Everett. Although he was 20 years older than Louisa, Everett's interest in her was more than fatherly. She did not return his affection, but she did respond to his encouragement of her literary pursuits and began to publish her work. Later in the 1840s, Louisa Smith met Fayette Clapp, five years her junior but, like her, a descendant of respected New Englanders. Although Clapp began his higher education in theology, when he received his degree from Brown University in 1848, his interest had shifted to medicine. For about a year, he studied with a cousin, Dr. Sylvanus Clapp, and attended classes at Castleton Medical College in Vermont. In 1849, he contracted gold fever, married Louisa, and sailed for California with his bride.

Little is known about the couple's voyage around the Horn or their stay in San Francisco, but they soon left the foggy city for the more wholesome climate and greater opportunity of the region around Marysville. Then, in June 1851, Dr. Clapp (who had somehow obtained his medical credentials from Castleton while living in California) departed for Rich Bar on the Feather River, hoping to establish a practice, recover his health, and perhaps strike it rich. Late in the year, he felt confident enough to return for his wife, who had spent the summer on a ranch in the vicinity of Marysville. The prospect of a winter in the mountains "perfectly enchanted" her, to the dismay of her local acquaintances:

> Some said that I ought to be put in a strait jacket. . . .
> Some said that I would never get there alive, and

if I did, would not stay a month; others simply observed . . . that even if the Indians did not kill me, I should expire of ennui or the cold before spring. One lady declared in a burst of outraged modesty, that it was absolutely indelicate, to think of living in such a large population of men; where at most there were two or three women.

Shirley decided to go, but soon after the couple began the trek to Rich Bar in September 1851, her enchantment diminished and her friends' warnings began to seem prophetic.

The 100-mile expedition over barely-marked trails commenced on muleback. On the first stage of the journey, a defective saddle dumped Shirley in the dust, "which filled eyes, nose, ears, and hair." The couple did not reach Marysville until after midnight. A few days later, the doctor and the animals set out for Bidwell's Bar, a "rag city" 30 miles upriver, and his wife followed by stagecoach. Fleas and other pests so infested Bidwell's accommodations that the Clapps decided to press on to Berry Creek House, another ten miles distant. They missed the trail, became hopelessly lost, and spent the night under the stars. When they did arrive at the way-station, after a 30-mile detour,

> every one that we met [there], congratulated us upon not having encountered any Indians for the paths which we followed were Indian trails, and it is said, that they would have killed us for our mules and our clothes. A few weeks ago, a Frenchman and his wife were murdered. . . . They generally take women captive, however, and who knows how narrowly I escaped becoming an Indian chieftainess, and feeding for the rest of my life upon roasted grasshoppers [and] flower seeds?

The experience neither extinguished Shirley's enthusiasm and sense of humor nor increased her husband's caution or skills as a pathfinder. The doctor's later errors resulted in another night in the open, this time in Indian and grizzly country. But after two weeks on the trail and more near disasters, the couple arrived safely at Rich Bar.

The journey to the diggings added several new elements to Shirley's experience, including her first encounter with "live" Indians. From the stagecoach window on the way to Bidwell's Bar, she observed Indian women collecting flower seeds to flavor their acorn bread. The sight produced an ambivalent reaction:

> Each one carried two brown baskets . . . woven with a neatness which is marvellous [sic], when one considers that they are the handiwork of such degraded wretches. . . . It is evident by the grace with which they handle them, that they are exceedingly light.

---

* The "Shirley Letters" first appeared in print in the short-lived San Francisco magazine, *The Pioneer*, in 1854 and 1855.

The gleaners, with "their regular motion, . . . dark shining skin, beautiful limbs, and lithe forms, . . . [were] by no means the least picturesque features of the landscape."

Later, at Wild Yankee's Ranch, "a *herd* of Indians . . . crowded into the room to stare at us." One, she observed, presented a remarkable contrast to the "general hideousness" of the others:

> A girl of 16, perhaps; with those large magnificently lustrous eyes . . . shyly glided, like a dark, beautiful spirit into the corner of the room. A fringe of silken jet swept heavily upward from her dusky cheek, [and from it] the richest color came and went like flashes of lightning. Her flexible lips curved slightly away from her teeth like strips of cocoa-nut meat, with a mocking grace infinitely bewitching. She wore a cotton chemise, disgustingly dirty, I must confess, girt about her slender waist with a crimson handkerchief; while over her night black hair . . . was a purple scarf of knotted silk.

Shirley was "perfectly enraptured with this wild-wood Cleopatra," but later in her letter she expressed attitudes characteristic of even the most sympathetic white nineteenth-century Americans:

> I always *did* "take" to Indians; though it must be said that those who bear that name here, have little resemblance to the glorious forest heroes that live in the Leather Stocking Tales [of James Fenimore Cooper]; and in spite of my desire to find in them something poetical and interesting, a stern regard for truth compels me to acknowledge, that the dusky beauty above described, is the only moderately *pretty* squaw that I have ever seen.

Dame Shirley arrived at Rich Bar a year after the first gold discovery there, when few of the original 500 miners remained in the camp. Reluctant to risk the hazards of winter or having squandered their accumulated gold on gambling, most had drifted away in pursuit of other *bonanzas* (rich strikes), real or rumored. In the summer of 1851, about 200 men lived there in rude log cabins, tents made of calico, *ramadas* constructed of brush, and a variety of even less permanent shelters. A fortunate few resided in one of the community's more substantial lodgings. The Clapps, for example, enjoyed the comforts of the Empire Hotel, "the only two-story building in town." About the Empire, Shirley wrote,

> you will find two or three glass windows, an unknown luxury in all other dwellings. It is built of planks of the roughest possible description; the roof, of course, is covered with canvas, which also forms the entire front. . . . You first enter a large apartment, level with the street, part of which is fitted up as a bar-room, with that eternal crimson calico, which flushes the whole social life of the "golden State," with its everlasting red. . . . A table covered with a green cloth—upon which lies a pack of monte cards, a backgammon board, and a sickening pile of "yallow-kivered" literature with several uncomfortable looking benches, complete the furniture of this most important portion of such a place as "The Empire."

The remainder of the room was a store where clothing, tools, and groceries were stocked, "cheek by jowl . . . in hopeless confusion." Four steps led up to the hotel's parlor, with its selection of well-worn furniture and a "quite decent looking-glass," and four more rose to the upper floor and four tiny bedrooms. The Empire was crude, with "floors so very uneven, that you were always ascending a hill or descending a valley" and interior walls consisting mainly of canvas. Shirley called it "just a piece of carpentering as a child two years old, gifted with the strength of a man, would produce." Nevertheless, this "impertinent apology for a house" cost its builders $8,000 at the time, since every item in it had to be freighted from Marysville at a rate of 40 cents a pound. Originally, the hotel was built as a brothel, but it failed, which Shirley attributed to "the everlasting honor of the *miners*." By the time the Clapps arrived, it was owned and operated by Curtis A. Bancroft, a brother of future California historian Hubert Howe Bancroft, and his wife.

Dame Shirley was surprised to learn that she was not the only female inhabitant of the camp. Four others lived at Rich Bar, but the Yankee lady was not at first particularly impressed by them. Mrs. Bancroft was "a gentle and amiable looking woman, about 25 years of age," but, Shirley continued,

> I will give you a key to her character which will exhibit it better than weeks of description. She took a nursing babe of eight months old, from her bosom, and left it with two other children—almost infants—to cross the plains [with her husband] in search of gold.

At the Empire, Shirley found the woman calmly cooking dinner for the hotel's half-dozen guests, while her youngest child, just two weeks old and born in the mines, "lay kicking furiously in his champagne basket cradle."

A second Rich Bar woman was Mary Stanfield, the "Indiana Girl," who assisted her father, the proprietor of the Indiana Hotel. During the previous winter, she had packed a 50-pound sack of flour through five feet of snow over the mountain to the mining camp. According to Dame Shirley, she was a

> gigantic piece of humanity [who] wears the thickest kind of miners' boots, and has the dainty habit

of wiping her dishes upon her apron. . . . The far-off roll of her mighty voice, booming through two closed doors and a long entry, added greatly to my severe attack of nervous headache.

One of Shirley's few regrets was that the Indiana Girl left the settlement before the two met in person.

The Dame did meet the other two Rich Bar women. One was the diminutive "Mrs. R—" who tended bar and otherwise assisted at the "Miners' Home," which her husband owned and where miners congregated to eat and drink. The place was

> a canvas house, containing a suite of three "apartments" . . . which, considering that they are all on the ground floor, are kept surprisingly neat. There is a bar-room, blushing all over with red calico, a dining room, kitchen and a small bed-closet. The little 68-pounder woman is queen of the establishment.

Tiny "Mrs. R—" was also a favorite of the miners, one of whom explained to the Clapps that she "earnt her *old man* . . . $900 in nine weeks, clear of all expenses, by [taking in] washing! Such women ain't common; if they were, a man might marry and make money by the operation." The man's chauvinism annoyed Dame Shirley, but she had to concede that she had "known of sacrifices, requiring, it would seem, superhuman efforts, made by women in this country, who at home were nurtured in the extreme of elegance and delicacy."

The fourth Rich Bar woman was Nancy Ann Bailey, the young wife of a miner and the mother of two children; she died of peritonitis shortly after the Clapps' arrival, and Shirley described her funeral, which began at the Baileys' cabin:

> On a board, supported by two butter-tubs, was extended the body of the dead woman, covered with a sheet; by its side stood the coffin of unstained pine, lined with white cambric. The bereaved husband held in his arms a sickly ten months old, which was moaning piteously at its mother. The other child, a handsome, bold-looking girl six years of age, was running gaily around the room, perfectly unconscious of her great bereavement. . . .

> About 20 men, with the three women of the place, had assembled at the funeral. An *extempore* prayer was made, filled with all the peculiarities usual to that style of petition. Ah! how different from the soothing verses of the glorious burial service of the church.

> As the procession started for the hill-side graveyard—a dark cloth, borrowed from a neighboring monte table, was flung over the coffin. Do not think that I mention any of these circumstances in a spirit

of mockery; far from it. Every observance . . . that was *procurable*, surrounded this funeral. All the gold on Rich Bar could do no more; should I die tomorrow, I should be marshaled to my mountain grave beneath the same monte-table pall, which surrounded the coffin of poor Mrs. B.

A sobering experience for Dame Shirley, the funeral improved her attitude toward her female companions. In an early letter, she commented sarcastically, "Splendid materials for social parties this winter, are they not?" But later observations reflect a different opinion, even admiration.

In the fall of 1851, the Clapps moved to Indian Bar, a mile or so downstream, where rumors of a rich strike produced a bustling new community. The bar was littered with miners' dwellings like those at Rich Bar, and there was a hotel, the Humbolt ("without the *d*," Shirley noted, although she insisted on restoring it in her letters). At Indian Bar, she had her own log cabin, which she described to her sister:

> The room into which you have just entered is about 20 feet square. It is lined over the top with white cotton cloth, the breadths of which been sewed together only in spots, stretch apart in many places, giving one a bird's-eye view of the shingles above. The sides are hung with a gaudy chintz . . . a perfect marvel of calico printing. . . .

> The fireplace is built of stones and mud, the chimney finished off with alternate layers of rough sticks and this same rude mortar; contrary to the usual custom, it is built inside, . . . and you can imagine the queer appearance of this unfinished pile of stone, mud and sticks. The mantelpiece . . . is formed of a beam of wood, covered with strips of tin procured from cans, upon which still remain in black hieroglyphics, the names [of their former contents]. . . . Two smooth stones—how delightfully primitive—do duty as firedogs. I suppose that it would be no more than civil to call a hole two feet square in one side of the room, a window, although it is as yet guiltless of glass. . . . I must mention that the floor is so uneven that no article of furniture gifted with four legs pretends to stand on but three at once, so that the chairs, tables, etc., remind you constantly of a dog with a sore foot.

Comments on improvised furniture and candlesticks, Dr. Clapp's pipes and tobaccos on the mantel, and the couple's meager library arranged on a candle-box bookshelf completed the guided tour.

Dame Shirley's home was elegant by mining-camp standards, but it was not the most luxurious in the district. Honors for that—and for sheer ingenuity—

belonged to five miners who apparently spent as much energy on creature comforts as they did on prospecting. Their cabin boasted an efficient fireplace for heat and cooking and windows made by mortaring empty jars into the walls. From mounds of discarded materials that cluttered the camp, they devised an array of functional candlesticks and lanterns and built bunks and other furniture. A visit inspired Shirley to comment, "Really, everybody ought to go to the mines, just to see how little it takes to make people comfortable in the world."

Miners' cabins could be innovative and even homey; but gold, not comfort, was the principal concern at Rich Bar, and finding it was an arduous, hazardous, frequently disappointing pursuit. Shirley tried panning just once and wrote, "I wet my feet, tore my dress, spoilt a pair of new gloves, nearly froze my fingers, got an awful headache, and lost a valuable breastpin, in this my labor of love." Her efforts were rewarded with $3.25 worth of gold dust, which miners assessed as a fine prospect for one panful. But the Dame was not impressed; she sent her treasure to her sister with a terse comment: "I am sorry I ever learned the trade."

For Shirley, searching for gold was a lark; for miners, it was backbreaking toil. By the 1850s, the gold pan and its successor, the rocker or cradle, were no longer the principal tools of extraction. As early as the Clapps' arrival on the Feather River in 1851, the individual prospector and the rudimentary methods of 1848 and 1849 were on their way to extinction:

> Here in the mountains, the labor of excavation is extremely difficult, on account of the immense rocks which form a large portion of the soil. Of course, no man can "work" a "claim" alone. For that reason . . . they congregate in companies of four or six, generally designating themselves by the name of the place from whence the majority have emigrated. . . . In many places, the surface soil, or in mining phrase, the "top-dirt," "pays" when worked in a "Long Tom." This machine, . . . is a trough, generally about 20 feet in length, and eight inches in depth, formed of wood, with the exception of six feet at one end, called the "riddle," . . . which is made of sheet iron, perforated with large holes about the size of a large marble. Underneath this cullender-like portion of the "long tom," is placed another trough, about ten feet long, the sides six inches perhaps in height, [with slats across its bottom], called the "riffle box." . . . [Several] spadesmen throw in large quantities of the precious dirt, which is washed down to the "riddle" by a stream of water leading into the "long-tom" through gutters or "sluices." When the soil reaches the "riddle," it is kept constantly in motion by the

man with the hoe. Of course, by this means, all the dirt and gold escapes through the perforations into the "riffle-box" below, one compartment of which is placed just beyond the "riddle." Most of the dirt washes over the sides of the "riffle-box," but the gold being so astonishingly heavy remains safely at the bottom of it [behind the slats].

Because much "top dirt" had already been thoroughly prospected, more complex methods became necessary:

> Many of the miners decline washing the "top dirt" at all, but try to reach as quickly as possible the "bed-rock," where are found the richest deposits of gold. The river is supposed to have formerly flowed over the "bed-rock," in the largest "crevices" of which, it left . . . the largest portions of the so eagerly sought for ore. . . .
>
> When a company wishes to reach the bed rock as quickly as possible, they "sink a shaft," . . . until they "strike" it. Then they commence "drifting coyote holes" . . . in search of "crevices," which . . . often pay immensely. These "coyote holes" often extend hundreds of feet into the side of a hill. . . . [The miners] generally proceed, until the air is so impure as to extinguish [their] lights.

At that point, they began again, after scraping tunnel walls with knives, searching for a crevice possibly overlooked.

Such burrows could fill with water from underground springs, making them unworkable, causing them to cave in, and even drowning the miners. But water also was essential to placer mining, and it was transported over great distances to "dry diggings" by difficult and ingenious methods:

> In most cases, it is brought from ravines in the mountains. A company . . . has dug a ditch about a foot in width and depth, and more than three miles in length, which is fed in this way. . . . When it reaches the top of the hill [at Rich Bar], the sparkling thing is divided into five or six branches, each one of which supplies [several] "long-toms." . . . This "race" . . . has already cost the company more than five thousand dollars.

To recover part of their investment, builders often formed ditch companies that sold water to other miners.

On some occasions, too, miners attempted to get at bed-rock by constructing a "flume, an immense trough, which takes up a portion of the river, and, with the aid of a dam, compels it to run in another channel, leaving the vacated bed of the stream for mining purposes. . . . Sometimes these fluming companies are eminently

Miners at Work

Dame Shirley's descriptions, as well as daguerreotypes from the early years of the gold rush, document rapid changes in mining methods. At first, a few basic tools and hard work sufficed (*top left*). By 1850 and 1851, elaborate flumes (*top right*) and water wheels to drive machinery (*bottom left*) were essentials. The physical labor required of miners, however, rarely diminished (*bottom right*). *Courtesy of The Bancroft Library, University of California, Berkeley.*

successful; at others, [they] are a dead failure." Unfortunately, failure was more frequent than success.

Most of the miners the Clapps encountered remained eager participants in "Nature's great lottery scheme," despite the ever-lengthening odds against them:

> They are always looking for "big strikes." If a "claim" is paying them a steady income, by which . . . they could lay up more in a month than they could accumulate in a year at home, still, they are dissatisfied, and, in most cases, will wander off in search of better "diggings." There are hundreds now pursuing this foolish course, who, if they had stopped where they first "camped," would now have been rich men. Sometimes a company of these wanderers will find itself upon a bar, where a few pieces of precious metal lie scattered upon the surface of the ground; of course, they immediately "prospect" it, which is accomplished by "panning out" a few basinsful of the soil. If it "pays," they "claim" the spot, and build their shanties; the news spreads that wonderful "diggings" have been discovered at such and such a place. . . .

Hordes of enthusiastic gold seekers inevitably followed the news; just as certainly, so did gamblers, "those worse than fiends, rush vulture-like upon the scene." The more industrious miners worked their claims for adequate rewards, but too many, in their quest for immediate riches, either gambled away their gains or hurried off in quest of even richer strikes.

But all was not drudgery in the diggings. At Indian Bar, Paganini Ned, the mulatto cook at the hotel, was equally skilled in culinary arts and on the violin. The meal he prepared to welcome Shirley to Indian Bar—complete with oyster soup, dessert, claret, and champagne—she called an accomplishment "the memory of which the world will not willingly let die." And she was just as impressed by Ned's musical talents when he and another man treated her to an impromptu serenade.

Isolation from creature comforts and diversions not only made most miners appreciate talents like Ned's but also forced them to organize for sociability, as well as for the task of extracting gold. In mining camps, an unwritten law forbade working claims on Sundays. On their day of rest, miners occupied themselves with such chores as washing and mending clothes and repairing shelters, tools, and equipment. They also told stories, played cards, gossiped, and hunted and fished, not only to while away time but also to vary monotonous diets. Some even captured wild animals to keep as pets.

Among residents of the mining camps, exceptional acts of kindness and solicitude often occurred. When Nancy Ann Bailey died, her husband's comrades attended the funeral, consoled the man, and helped with the care of his children. Similarly, when an accident mangled the leg of a young miner, his friends acted as nurses both before and after Dr. Clapp amputated the limb. During winter months, when supplies were scarce, miners frequently shared what they had while awaiting the first pack trains of spring.

During the same months, they were hardest pressed for amusement. Observing holidays, including those of foreigners in the mines, furnished diversion. Dame Shirley was amazed at the variety among the residents of Rich Bar:

> You will hear on the same day the lofty melody of the Spanish language, the piquant polish of the French, . . . the silver, changing clearness of the Italian, the harsh gargle of the German, the hissing precision of the English, the liquid sweetness of the Kanaka, and the sleep-inspiring languor of the East Indian.

But her own countrymen's attitude toward foreigners and their languages perplexed her. Most of them believed that when they had "learned *sabe, vamos . . . pocotiempo, si,* and *Bueno . . .* they had the whole of the glorious Castilian at their tongue's end." Others simply assumed that "by splitting the tympanum of an unhappy foreigner, in screaming forth their sentences in good, solid English," they could be understood by anyone. Yankees also joined exuberantly in foreigners' festivities. When a company of Chileans celebrated the anniversary of their country's independence, for example, Shirley observed that

> it was impossible to tell which nation was the most gloriously drunk; but I will say, even at the risk of being thought partial to my own beloved countrymen; "that though the Chilenos reeled with better grace, the Americans did it more *naturally!*"

Traditional American holidays, including the Fourth of July, provided welcome departures from routine in the mines. In 1852, Independence Day festivities at Rich Bar drew residents of camps from up and down the river. When the day's proceedings began at the Empire, politicians introduced one another and a speaker imported for the occasion "pronounced beautifully a very splendid Oration." At the dinner later, "the toasts were quite spicy and original." By nightfall, two "new ladies from the hill" appeared, "so lately arrived from the States, with everything fresh and new, they quite extinguished poor Mrs. B. and myself, trying our best to look fashionable in our antique mode of four years ago." One of the newcomers favored celebrants with "three or four beautiful songs," and substantial quantities of "the spirit" disappeared. Still, "everything passed off quite respectably at Rich Bar . . . [despite] a small fight in the bar-room . . . during which much speech and some blood were spouted."

Dame Shirley also described a rather less civilized Christmas and New Years' celebration that followed months of confinement, cold and boredom. Throughout the day, troops of miners—"an army of India-rubber coats (the rain was falling in riversful)"—descended on Indian Bar, and at night the celebration began:

> At nine o'clock in the evening, they had an oyster and champagne supper in the Humboldt, which was very gay. . . . I believe that the company danced all night; at any rate, they were dancing when I went to sleep, and they were dancing when I woke the next morning. The revel was kept up in this mad way for three days, growing wilder every hour. On the fourth day, they got past dancing, and, lying in drunken heaps about the bar-room, commenced a most unearthly howling. . . . Many were too far gone to imitate

anything but their own animalized selves. . . . Some of these bacchanals were among the most respectable and respected men upon the river . . . [who] had never been seen intoxicated before.

Toward the latter part of the week, people were compelled to be a little more quiet from sheer exhaustion; but on New Years' day, . . . at Rich Bar, the excitement broke out again, if possible, worse than ever.

Dame Shirley forgave the excesses, writing to Molly that "the miners as a class, possess many truly admirable characteristics."

No real authority existed in remote mining districts, even after California's admission to the Union in 1850. The situation forced their residents to attend to legal and political affairs, especially those pertaining to mining activities:

As there are no state laws upon the subject, each mining community is permitted to make its own. Here, they have decided that no man may "claim" an area of more than 40 feet square. This he "stakes off" and puts a notice upon it, to the effect that he "holds" it for mining purposes. If he does not choose to "work it" immediately, he is obliged to renew the notice every ten days; for without this precaution, any other person has the right to "jump it," that is, to take it from him. There are many ways of evading the above law . . . [such as hiring someone else to work a claim]. After all, the "holding of claims" by proxy is considered rather as carrying out the spirit of the law, than as an evasion of it. But there are many ways of really outwitting the rule, . . . which give rise to innumerable arbitrations, and nearly every Sunday there is a "miners' meeting" connected with this subject.

Some camps relied on general meetings to settle disputes; others elected claims officers or committees to maintain registers and resolve conflicts. Frequently, too, miners' meetings assumed authority for other matters of law, and on occasion state or county governments sent officials to the mining camps, with varied results.

On the Feather River, a man called the Squire (perhaps Thomas D. Bonner, who recorded the memoirs of black pathfinder James P. Beckwourth) was appointed justice of the peace. Shirley doubted his ability to uphold the law in the camps, and his first "opportunity to exercise (or rather to *try* to do so) his judicial power upon a criminal case" confirmed her opinion. After a Swede called "Little John" squandered unexplained money on gambling and was arrested for theft, the Squire attempted to conduct the subsequent trial:

When the . . . mighty people had assembled at the Empire, they commenced proceedings by voting in a president and jury of their own; though they kindly consented . . . that the "Squire" might *play at judge*, by sitting at the side of *their* elected magistrate! This honor, the "Squire" seemed to take as a sort of salve to his wounded dignity, and with unprecedented meekness accepted it.

At the trial, Little John maintained that the sudden wealth that was evidence against him was a gift from his father. Nevertheless, despite a vigorous defense by an appointed counsel and the Squire's opinion of innocence,

the jury brought in a verdict of guilty, and condemned [Little John] to receive 39 lashes at nine o'clock the following morning, and to leave the river, never to return to it, within 24 hours; a "claim" of which he owned a part, [was] to be made over to Mr. [Bancroft], to indemnify him for his loss.

More serious episodes, however, received almost no response from miners' tribunals. When, during "a drunken frolic," one man stabbed another with "not the slightest provocation," a puzzled Shirley wrote that "the people have not taken the slightest notice of this affair, although for some days the life of the wounded man was despaired of." As public disorders increased in frequency and changed in character during the spring and summer of 1852, her letters hinted at the nature of the transformation; like her compatriots, she began to refer to all miners of Hispanic origins as "Spaniards"—when fewer than 300 individuals from Spain were in all of California.

During April 1852, the miners' meeting at Rich Bar made the point more emphatically when it passed laws "to the effect that no foreigner shall work the mines." Immediate results were migration of most Spanish-speaking miners to Indian Bar, an increase in the number of establishments catering to them there, and a vigorous complaint from Shirley: "On Sundays, the swearing, drinking, gambling, and fighting which are carried on in some of these houses, are truly horrible." Clearly, too, earlier camaraderie among miners was evaporating. When an American stabbed a "Spaniard" because the latter requested payment of a debt, Shirley protested that "nothing was done, and very little was said about this atrocious affair." But there was more to come.

Following the July 4 celebration, several "of the *elite* of Rich Bar, drunk with whisky and patriotism," attacked and injured several "Spaniards." For this incident, Shirley concluded, "Sir Barley Corn was to blame, for many of the ringleaders are fine young men, who, when sober, are . . . friendly to the Spaniards." But she also sensed a "gradually increasing state of bad feeling exhibited by our countrymen . . . toward foreigners." She rightly feared that the episode was not the last of its kind, despite efforts by "the more intelligent foreigners, as well as the judicious Americans."

Numerous "drunken fights . . . with the usual amount of broken heads, collar bones, stabs, etc." punctuated July 1852, when almost every Sunday was "enlivened by some such merry event." In one incident, a "Spaniard" stabbed an Irishman in a dispute over a Mexican woman. The Irishman (a naturalized U.S. citizen) died, his attacker escaped, rumors of conspiracies spread, and conflict seemed imminent. The "Spaniards thought the Americans had risen against them; and our countrymen fancied the same of foreigners." When armed Americans and foreigners converged on Indian Bar, Shirley and the other women in the camp retreated to the hill to observe. Two miners—an Englishman who survived and a "Spaniard" who died— were wounded when a rifle discharged accidentally; the "frightful accident recalled the people to their senses, and they began to act a little less like madmen, than they had previously done."

Events of the "fatal Sabbath," as residents began to call it, had important results. Perhaps in imitation of San Francisco, Indian Bar organized a Vigilance Committee. In its first official act, the committee sent a posse after "Spaniards" suspected of instigating the previous Sunday's disturbance and tried "a *Mejicana*, who had been foremost in the fray. . . . She was sentenced to leave the Bar by day-light." The vigilantes next "tried five or six Spaniards who were proven to have been ringleaders in the Sabbath-day riot. Two of them were sentenced to be whipped, the remainder to leave the Bar that evening; the property of all to be confiscated to the use of the wounded persons. Oh Mary! imagine my anguish when I heard the first blow fall upon those wretched men." Punishment could have been worse, however; most in the community clamored for a hanging.

The committee's work continued during July with the conviction of a black cook (not Paganini Ned) for murder. Sentenced to hang, he cut his throat in a suicide attempt while in custody. Then, "Their majesties the mob, with that beautiful consistency which usually distinguishes those august individuals, insisted upon shooting [the prisoner]." As the self-control of committee members deteriorated, Shirley wrote, "The state of society has never been so bad as since the appointment of [the vigilantes]." She believed that committee leaders also led a group of rowdies called the "Moguls," who

parade the streets all night, howling, shouting, breaking into houses, taking wearied miners out of their beds and throwing them into the river, and in short, "murdering sleep," in a most remorseless manner.

Fall did not increase public peace, but during late September and early October the Clapps escaped from the disorders when they journeyed to the American Valley near present Quincy. The doctor was a delegate to a nominating convention being held there, and Shirley decided to accompany him. She said little about the convention, except that "horse-racing, and gambling, in all their detestable varieties" seemed to characterize frontier politics. But she was moved by the sight of pioneer women who were widowed on the trail and arrived in California "looking as haggard as so many Endorean witches; burnt to the color of a hazel-nut, with their hair cut short, and its gloss entirely destroyed by the alkali, whole plains of which they are compelled to cross on the way." Shirley was delighted to end her "dreadful pleasure tour of the American Valley" and return to her cabin.

It was a disappointing homecoming. Indian Bar had changed during her absence. Signs of impending harsh winter were visible everywhere, new mining operations undertaken to salvage the community's faltering economy were a disaster, and "nearly every person on the river received the same step-mother's treatment from Dame Nature, in this her mountain workshop." The miners dispersed almost as quickly as they had gathered: "It is said, that there are not 20 men remaining on Indian Bar, although two months ago, you could count them up in the hundreds." Those who stayed "amused themselves by prosecuting one another right and left," keeping the Squire's court busy for the first time.

Since the Clapps had no reason to remain at Indian Bar, they planned to leave in late November. Despite the hardships of her year on the Feather River, however, Dame Shirley regretted the decision. To her sister, she lamented that she had never learned to sketch from nature. Nevertheless, her letters sparkled with vivid descriptions of the spectacle surrounding her and revealed her love for the mountains, even in bitter winter when

the Storm King . . . stole silently down, and garlanded us in a wreath of shining snow-flakes, and lo! the next morning you would have thought that some great white bird had shed its glittering feathers all over rock, tree, hill and bar.

And while waiting to leave the mountains, she penned her farewell:

My heart is heavy at the thought of departing forever from this place. I like this wild and barbarous life; I leave it with regret. The solemn fir trees, "whose slender tops are close against the sky" here, the watching hills, and the calmly beautiful river, seem to gaze sorrowfully at me, as I stand in the moon-lighted midnight, to bid them farewell. . . . Yes, Molly, smile if you will at my folly; but I go from the mountains with a deep heart sorrow. I took kindly to this existence, which to you seems so sordid and mean. Here, at least, I have been contented.

She probably never again experienced such contentment. After the Clapps returned to San Francisco in November 1852, the doctor left. He sailed to Hawaii, returned to New England in 1854, and then drifted to Illinois and finally to Missouri. Dame Shirley remained in California and divorced her husband *in absentia* in 1857; he remarried and served as a Union Army surgeon during the Civil War. As Louisa Clapp (sometimes Clappe), she made numerous friends in San Francisco and taught in local public schools until 1878, when failing health forced her return to the East to live with family and friends. She died in 1906, leaving in her letters an incomparable legacy: the opportunity for later generations to share with gold rush Californians the experience that they called "seeing the elephant."

The New *El Dorado*

11

O n May 12, 1848, Sam Brannan waved a quinine bottle filled with glittering dust at San Franciscans, shouted his fabulous news, and perhaps calculated its impact on his own fortunes. "Gold!" he cried, "Gold, gold from the American River!" Reaction was immediate. Within days, half of the city's population had departed. Within weeks, settlements from Sonoma to San Diego became virtual ghost towns. And within months, reports of the discovery crossed oceans and continents to lure adventurers from all points of the globe to the new *El Dorado*.

The Great Discovery

T he sequence of events that set the world in motion began almost by chance. In 1847, John Sutter and his employee James Wilson Marshall decided to build a sawmill. Born in New Jersey in 1810, Marshall learned his father's skills as a carpenter and wheelwright, drifted into the Ohio Valley as a young man, and joined a wagon train to Oregon in 1844. He eventually wandered south to California where he worked for Sutter, joined the Bear Flag Revolt, and soldiered in the California Battalion. Shortly after the Cahuenga Capitulation, Marshall returned to Sutter's employ and convinced Sutter that the sawmill business would be profitable.

Marshall located a suitable site on the South Fork of the American River, 30 miles from New Helvetia near a Maidu village called Cullumah (Coloma). A construction crew composed of village Indians and Mormon Mexican War veterans began construction and the mill was almost done by the end of 1847. To accelerate the process, Marshall allowed the river to flow through the millrace each night, using erosion to clear debris.

139

John Sutter and James Marshall

Sutter (*left*) and Marshall (*right*) were, quite unexpectedly, among the losers in "Nature's great lottery scheme."
Courtesy of The Bancroft Library, University of California, Berkeley.

During his regular morning inspection of January 24, 1848, he made the discovery that changed the course of California history: he spotted a glint in the bottom of the ditch. Marshall scooped up a handful of gravel, examined it, and concluded that he had found gold. He took a sample to Sutter. When tests proved the substance actually was gold, the partners concluded that they must keep the discovery secret. Surprisingly, their workers obeyed, for the moment at least. The men remained at their tasks, kept reasonably mum, and prospected on their own time.

Most Californians at the time doubted the rumored strike, but a few were able to reap handsome rewards. Sutter and Marshall were not among them; both ultimately joined the ranks of gold rush casualties. When Sutter died in a Philadelphia hotel room in 1880, he was alone and destitute. Squatters and speculators had stripped him of his land and the state had terminated his

$250 monthly pension. Marshall remained at Coloma, trying unsuccessfully to collect private debts, secure confirmation of his land claims, and to convince the state and the nation that he deserved some sort of compensation. He died a drunkard in 1885, with $218 to his name. Sam Brannan, the man who announced *la bonanza* (rich vein or fair weather) and brought the world to California, fared no better.

Sources of *La Bonanza*

The lure of gold that brought fortunes to some and ruin to others was nothing new in human history. Yet in at least one sense the rush to California was unique. Most of the ore was placer gold—transported, deposited, and eventually extracted by the action of water—and located in areas of dense Indian habitation. Generations of Native Californians could not have missed its glitter

Sam Brannan

Forty-Eighter

Although he was not yet 30 when he arrived in California, Sam Brannan was an Elder of the Mormon Church, chosen in 1846 to lead East Coast Saints "out of Babylon." He chartered the ancient *Brooklyn* and loaded her with supplies (including his printing press) and 200 California-bound Mormons. Upon arrival in the Mexican village of Yerba Buena, the flock set about its mission: preparation for the coming of the Nauvoo Saints, who were already on the overland trail from Illinois. But Brigham Young, who succeeded the murdered Joseph Smith as leader of the church, chose the Valley of the Great Salt Lake, not California, to be the Mormons' New Zion.

Conflict with Young over that decision and other matters eventually led to Brannan's excommunication, but personal ambition competed with religious zeal from the time of his arrival on the West Coast. Publication of the *California Star*, speculation in Yerba Buena (San Francisco) real estate, and other ventures made him rich, and he built the finest house in the village using tithes and labor commandeered from the Brethren. Few *Brooklyn* comrades, however, attended the galas held there; nor did Brannan share his affluence with the church.

Late in 1847, he embarked on a new venture: a general store at Sutter's Fort, where in 1848 workers began to pay for purchases with gold. Brannan went to Coloma to investigate, confirmed the source of his customers' wealth, and began to stockpile goods useful to miners in his warehouse. In May 1848 he returned to San Francisco to break the news, and as prospectors spread throughout the Sierra, Brannan & Co. followed them. Profits from sales (the Sutter's Fort store then grossed up to $5,000 a day) went into new stores, into land speculation, and into investments in railroads, shipping, and waterfront development. Brannan also involved himself in local politics and in the Vigilance Committees of 1851 and '56.

Success and fame brought the final conflict with Brigham Young. When the Leader heard of Brannan's wealth, he sent emissaries to collect $40,000 of "the Lord's money." But the San Francisco Elder had an ultimatum of his own: the money in return for a receipt "signed by the Lord." This finished Brannan as

Sam Brannan
Courtesy of The Bancroft Library, University of California, Berkeley.

a Mormon, but as California's first millionaire he used his resources to promote the state and to increase his wealth. He helped to organize the Society of California Pioneers and endowed fire companies, drill teams, and other civic and social associations. He founded a bank and a mint and financed a mail service, and in 1861 he bought an immense tract of Napa Valley land where he built his estate, Calistoga. During the 1860s, however, Brannan began to suffer reverses. A dandy and a social lion, he also made enemies, including a squatter whose bullet left him partially paralyzed. Speculation in Hawaii land and Nevada silver, and plans to finance a revolution in Mexico, depleted his assets. Finally his wife, who preferred cultured Europe to raw California, sued for divorce and was granted half of his fortune in cash.

(continued . . .)

The settlement brought poverty, and the pain of paralysis and arthritis led to alcohol, which alienated friends. Still, Brannan remained ambitious. During the 1870s, he promoted settlement on Sonora land granted in recognition of his services to Mexico. Later, he sold real estate near San Diego and, in the garb of a *campesino* (peasant), raised figs at Escondido. All of the ventures failed, and Sam Brannan finished his days supported by brother Odd Fellows lodge members and relatives. When he died in 1889, only his landlady, Magdalena Moreno, was present to ease his passing.

(WAB)

as they crossed streams or followed trails where rivers once ran, but unlike their Central and South American counterparts, they considered gold of little use. Thus the wealth of the Sierra waited thousands of years to be "discovered" by people sufficiently "civilized" to appreciate it.

Natural forces formed California's mountains during the Mesozoic Era (200 to 70 million years ago) and distributed and deposited their gold. Over millennia, upheavals fragmented ore-bearing rock and erosion scattered it. Rivers carried it in their currents and dropped it in holes in their beds or pockets along their banks. During the Tertiary Period of the Cenozoic Era (70 to 3 million years ago), streams altered courses and left deposits buried under layers of rock and gravel or exposed as cliffs. The process created the fabled Mother Lode, a band more than 100 miles long and up to 20 miles wide along the Sierra's western slope, and similar deposits in the Feather-Yuba River and Trinity-Shasta-Siskiyou regions of California. Nature also trapped gold in the bowels of the earth, where magma cooled in fissures. Throughout the gold rush decades, miners scoured the Sierra for such veins, believing them to be origins of placer gold.

Potential bonanzas provided a main ingredient in the mythology of gold stretching from Jason's quest for the Golden Fleece to the search for *El Dorado* ("the golden one") to Garcí Ordoñez de Montalvo's tales of Calafía's island. Fantasies of gold inspired the legend of Cíbola and prompted explorers and visitors from Sebastian Vizcaíno to Richard Henry Dana. But until 1842 there was no tangible basis for the myth of gold in California. That year, Francisco Lopez found a *placero* (pocket of gold) in San Feliciano Canyon (now Placerita Canyon) north of Mission San Fernando. The discovery generated some enthusiasm among Mexican officials and a modest influx of miners from Mexico. The first 20 ounces of California gold were sent to the U.S. Mint. But well before the Treaty of Guadalupe Hidalgo was signed, the *placero* was exhausted.

The Gold Rush of 1848

Skepticism following the San Feliciano episode may explain doubts about the authenticity of the 1848 discovery, when word began to leak out. Sent to Monterey to register his American River claim, Sutter's emissary crowed about the discovery to men that he met along the way. Children of sawmill employees chattered about it to a teamster delivering supplies. Workers at Sutter's Mill began to offer nuggets and dust in exchange for goods at Sam Brannan's nearby store. Sutter himself could not resist telling his friends John Bidwell and Mariano Vallejo. But not even physical proof—actual gold samples—could convince the skeptics. Nor were news-hungry journalists impressed. The first report appeared as a kind of postscript on the last page of the *Californian* of March 15. Subsequently, Edward C. Kemble reported events at Coloma in the *California Star*, the province's only other newspaper, comparing the new strike to the San Feliciano episode. In April Kemble traveled to Sutter's Mill himself. Back in San Francisco, he wrote enthusiastically about the beauty of the region but said little about the mines.

Still, some took the find seriously. A mill worker, for example, found a rich deposit and conveyed his success to friends from his Mormon Battalion days. The friends visited Coloma and returned home to discover their own bonanza near Mariposa. As spring approached and the weather improved, new visitors arrived to investigate. Bidwell, noting geological similarities between the American River terrain and his own region near Chico, went home and started digging at Feather River. Pierson B. Reading visited Sutter's Mill, made observations like Bidwell's, and returned home to begin successful prospecting on the Trinity River and near Mt. Shasta. Charles M. Weber of Stockton assembled a crew of Indigenous workers and put them to work taking gold from the Stanislaus and Mokelumne rivers.

Marshall's workers managed to complete the mill, but they soon contracted gold fever. Their defection, beginning in March, marked the beginning of the end for Sutter. By early April, he had only a skeleton crew at the sawmill and little timber to cut—most of Sutter's logging crews had gone prospecting. Work at New Helvetia ground to a halt as workers abandoned the flourmill and tannery, leaving thousands of hides and bushels of grain to rot. Clerks, carpenters, and teamsters all abandoned the certainty of Sutter's high wages for the seduction of gold.

This handful of local miners and a few more from southern California monopolized the gold fields from January until May, when Brannan's announcement ended their quiet interlude. Although Kemble announced that the stunt was "a sham, got up to guzzle the gullible," the effect in San Francisco was electric. Residents departed in droves, with little thought for preparations or provisions. Some set sail aboard anything that would float; others struck out overland on horses or mules, trailed by scores more on foot. Sailors deserted ships, often led by their officers, and soldiers from local garrisons were close behind. Realtors, physicians, merchants, and lawyers boarded doors and windows and followed their clients to the mines. By mid-June, only 200 souls—a fourth of the population—remained in town. As news of gold rippled through the territory in May and June, residents of other towns repeated the San Francisco exodus. Like a magnet, news from the mill on the American attracted Californios, *gringos* (whites), and Indians. It seemed, the editor of the *Californian* wrote, that "the whole country from San Francisco to Los Angeles and from the seashore to the base of the Sierra Nevada responds to the sordid cry of . . . GOLD!"

Spreading the News

Californians did not monopolize the bonanza for long. Traders carried the news quickly to Hawaii, the Pacific Northwest, Mexico, and the Pacific coast of South America. By the end of 1848 word of the discovery had reached China, the east coast of the United States, and Europe. The population influx increased California's non-Indian population to about 20,000 in 1848. Hawaiians and Hispanic-Americans accounted for most of the growth. Through the winter of 1848, migration from "the States" remained insignificant. Although Thomas O. Larkin sent the *Californian*'s announcement to the U.S. State Department, apparently no one read it. The New York *Herald* printed a letter from California that predicted a "Peruvian harvest" of gold. In mid-September, the New Orleans *Picayune* published an interview with Lieutenant Edward F. Beale, then on his

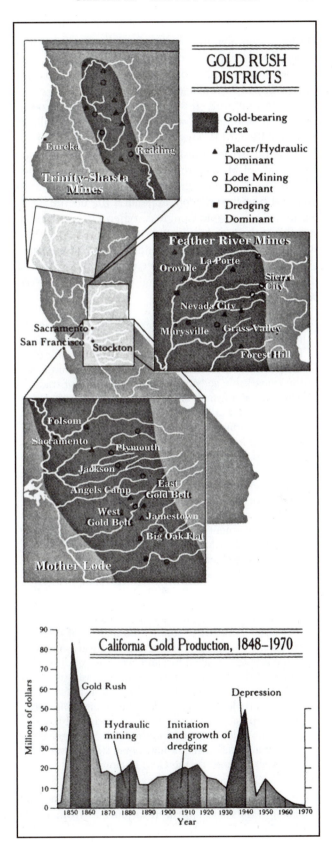

GOLD RUSH DISTRICTS

- Gold-bearing Area
- ▲ Placer/Hydraulic Dominant
- ○ Lode Mining Dominant
- ■ Dredging Dominant

Trinity-Shasta Mines

Eureka · Redding

Feather River Mines

Oroville · La Porte · Sierra City · Nevada City · Marysville · Grass Valley · Forest Hill

Sacramento · San Francisco · Stockton

Folsom · Sacramento · Plymouth · Jackson · Angels Camp · East Gold Belt · West Gold Belt · Jamestown · Big Oak Flat

Mother Lode

California Gold Production, 1848–1970

Gold Rush · Hydraulic mining · Initiation and growth of dredging · Depression

Millions of dollars

1850 1860 1870 1880 1890 1900 1910 1920 1930 1940 1950 1960 1970

Year

way to Washington with confirmation of the discovery. During subsequent months, eastern newspapers printed stories from California, often grossly exaggerated, and samples of dust appeared. Nevertheless, Americans east of the Mississippi remained skeptical.

On December 7, 1848, Lieutenant Lucien Loeser arrived in Washington with a dispatch from military governor Richard B. Mason and 230 ounces of gold. By the time he arrived, President James Knox Polk already had a copy of Mason's report, confirming the presence of gold—perhaps enough to finance the Mexican War "a hundred times over." Polk appended the document to his annual message to Congress. When Loeser's sample arrived, he had it placed on display in the War Office. Response to the president's confirmation of the discovery was instantaneous. Horace Greeley's description of the "California frenzy" appeared in the New York *Tribune* on January 30, 1849:

> A resident of New York coming back after a three month's absence, without having heard of California fever, would be almost doubtful of the identity of the place. He would find it impossible to account for the remarkable activity in certain branches of trade which are not usually subject to sudden change. He would wonder at the word "California," seen everywhere in glaring letters, and at the columns of vessels advertised in the papers as about to set sail for San Francisco. And finally, he would be puzzled at seeing a new class of men in the streets, in a peculiar costume—broad felt hats of reddish brown hue, loose rough coats reaching to the knee, and high boots. . . . Even those who have watched the gradual progress of the excitement are astonished at its extent and intensity. The ordinary course of business seems for the time to be changed. The bakers of sea-bread keep their ovens hot day and night, . . . without supplying the demand; the provision stores of all kinds are besieged by crowds of purchasers; manufacturers of India rubber goods, gutta percha, oil cloth, etc. have very large demands to supply; the makers of rifles, pistols and bowie knives can scarcely furnish as many of the articles as called for; and even the vendors of nostrums share a part in this windfall of business. . . . In fact, goods of every description sell just at present, and articles which have long been unsalable are packed up and sent away. Boxes, barrels and bales crowd the sidewalks, and hundreds of drays convey to the wharves the freight now being stored away in 70 vessels [bound] for the Gold Regions.

Greeley did not exaggerate. By the middle of the year, similar accounts had appeared in journals from Hamburg to Hong Kong. As a result, by the end of 1849, California's non-Indian population reached nearly 100,000. When the state conducted a census in 1852, the count exceeded 200,000.

By Sea to California

Residents along the East Coast felt the bite of the gold bug first. With a strong maritime tradition, departure points close at hand, ships at the ready, and the routes well known, most traveled to California by sea.

For many Argonauts, the route across the Isthmus of Panama seemed most promising. Shorter, theoretically faster and safer than the five-month, 17,000-mile Cape Horn passage, the Isthmus was open year round. Moreover, Congress had subsidized steamship service between the two coasts via the United States Mail and the Pacific Mail companies beginning in 1849. Hopes for a safe, swift journey by ship to the Isthmus, across to the Pacific, and then by sea to San Francisco seldom materialized, however. Steamships could accommodate only a few of those eager for passage, so ancient sailing vessels, often grossly overloaded, were pressed into service. Tickets covered only the ocean legs of the trip, leaving travelers to negotiate with Panamanians for transit 40 miles up the Chagres River and 20 more overland to the Pacific, where passengers usually encountered additional inconveniences. The first Pacific Mail steamer, the *California*, arrived on the western side of the Isthmus in mid-January, and found more than 700 ticket-holders clamoring for its 250 berths. Vessels dumped as many as 1,000 passengers daily at the eastern mouth of the Isthmus, but only a handful of ships were available on the Pacific side. By the end of February, several thousand Argonauts were stranded in Panama, where the delays depleted both resources and health. Conditions improved in 1850, when steamship lines began to coordinate services, and again in 1855, when a trans-isthmian railway was completed. From 1855 until completion of a mainland transcontinental railroad, the Panama passage was the gold-seeker's favored route from "the States" to California.

A greater volume of seaborne traffic to California arrived by way of the long and hazardous Cape Horn route around the tip of South America. About half of those who rounded "Cape Stiff" formed joint-stock companies, some of them well capitalized and outfitted. Members of the Northwestern Mining & Trading Company of Boston, for instance, refitted an old ship, turned her into a "floating dry goods emporium," and set sail with uniforms, a cook, and a brass band. When they reached San Francisco, the company hoped to sell

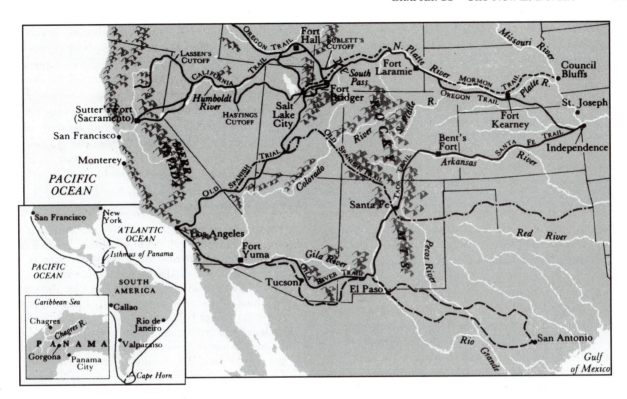

Routes to the Gold Fields

the ship and cargo to finance the voyage, but too many others had the same idea. The San Francisco waterfront quickly became a graveyard for derelict ships and a dump for surplus merchandise, and even the best-organized companies disbanded to search for gold as individuals or with a few companions.

The voyage around the Horn did little to prepare Argonauts for mining. Even seaworthy ships manned by competent crews (and they were few) took fearful beatings from the elements, and so did their passengers. Seasickness, spoiled food and stagnant water, boredom, and confinement in close quarters added to the misery. Months of inactivity and poor diet inevitably took their toll when the hard labor of mining began. But the Cape Horn passage had at least one positive result: to pass the time, many travelers kept journals, making the California gold rush one of the best-documented migrations in history.

Crossing the Plains

For those who crossed the Plains, journeys began in spring, when grasses provided food for animals and warmer weather melted some of the snow barriers in the mountains. For most, knowledge of the Donner tragedy

in 1846 inspired caution, but a few parties tempted the elements by leaving too early or too late, or by setting off alone, typically with disastrous results. In 1849, for example, the Royce family stopped to rest at Salt Lake City, instead of joining a guided party then preparing to leave. The decision put them far behind schedule. Following hand-written directions for crossing the Humboldt Sink, they lost even more time and severely fatigued their oxen. Sarah Royce walked and carried her child to conserve their animals' energy, but ultimately the family had to abandon its wagon and finish their journey on foot. They were among the last to cross the Sierra in the bitter winter of 1849, and only the timely arrival of a rescue party prevented a tragedy like the Donners'. A similar error in 1851 was more costly to Roys Oatman and his family. After they left their train and set out alone on the Gila Trail, Yavapai warriors killed most of them and sold two daughters, Olive and Mary Ann, into captivity among the Mojave.

Fortunately, most of those who crossed the Plains in 1849 and the early 1850s traveled in companies. During March and April, they transported wagons and supplies to departure points such as Independence, Missouri, where they bought animals and additional provisions, and the wisest among them hired experienced guides.

When all was ready, the trains departed many wagons abreast. Although there was safety in numbers, there were also dangers. As a member of one of the first companies to head west observed,

> Our daily task will be to get past those in advance of us, and to so travel that no trains will overtake us. In this way only can we hope to maintain our animals. The locusts of Egypt could scarcely be a greater scourge than these great caravans, as grass and whatever else is green vanish completely before them.

Very soon, kegs of nails, anvils, iron stoves, and other heavy cargo jettisoned to lighten loads littered the Plains.

Many adventurers were certain that their greatest menace would be Indians. In fact, the early gold-seekers were their own worst enemies. Some brought cholera up the Mississippi River from New Orleans, where it took a terrible toll. So did accidental wounds from guns or axes, fractures caused by animals or wagon wheels, and injuries sustained while hauling wagons up and down mountains and across rivers. Equally dangerous, perhaps, were the useless guidebooks published in 1849 and 1850, and the temptation to leave established routes for unproven "cut-offs."

Despite the hazards, between 25,000 and 30,000 crossed the Plains in 1849. They paused briefly to rest at trading posts and among the Mormons at Salt Lake City, and then joined the 40,000 souls who had already arrived in California by sea, plus a few thousand more who came by land from Mexico and the Southwest. During the 1850s, more than 200,000 sojourners arrived by overland routes, but not all remained. Records of the U.S. Customs House at San Francisco indicate that annual departures were as high as 70 percent of arrivals.

Table 11.1   San Francisco Maritime Arrivals and Departures

Year	Arrivals	Departures
1850	36,000	26,000
1852	64,000	23,000
1855	31,700	23,000
1858	40,700	28,000
1860	30,800	14,500

Although similar data do not exist for overland routes, estimates suggest that between 500 and 1,200 traversed the Plains eastward during each year of the 1850s.

Of those who remained in California, nearly one-fourth were foreign-born. They came from points in the United States and from around the globe, contributing to the Babel that Dame Shirley described. Despite vast differences between them, however, the newcomers had points in common. Whether from New England or Canton, they were young (less than 30 years old, on average) and male (more than 90 percent). In gold rush California "a gray beard was almost as rare as a petticoat." Argonauts also tended to be enthusiastic and optimistic. When he arrived in San Francisco in 1849, Stephen J. Field observed:

> There was something exhilarating and exciting in the atmosphere which made everyone cheerful and buoyant. . . . Everyone in greeting me said, "It's a glorious country," or "Isn't it a glorious country?" . . . or something to that effect. In every case the word "glorious" was sure to come out. . . . I had not been out many hours before I caught the infection, and though I had but a single dollar in my pocket and no business whatever and did not know where I should get my next meal, I found myself saying to everybody I met, "It's a glorious country."

Although just another exuberant adventurer at the time, Field would ultimately be elected to California's first legislature, write the state's first civil and criminal codes, serve as chief justice of the state supreme court, and be appointed to the U.S. Supreme Court in 1863.

Whether California was "glorious" or not, few Argonauts regarded it as fit for permanent residence. Instead, most saw California as a land to be exploited and divested of its treasure, before they returned home in style.

Searching for *La Bonanza*

In addition to being predominantly young, male, and enthusiastic, early Argonauts shared another attribute: most were professionals, semiprofessionals, skilled craftsmen, and small merchants. Because the cost of transportation and equipment was substantial—$750 to $1,000 in an era when "a dollar could do wondrous things"—a winnowing process took place before the gold-seekers ever left home. Few of the earliest arrivals belonged to the laboring classes. Ultimately, the talents they brought to California became assets to local life and society. But as miners, they began as rank amateurs—in many cases, experiencing physical labor for the first time. Having the resources to buy untested manuals or devices actually increased their disadvantages, since few of the authors or inventors had never seen a mine either.

For most Forty-Niners and those who followed them, searching for gold meant learning an unfamiliar skill by trial, error, and imitation. Fortunately, many useful techniques were outlined in translations of Georgius Agricola's sixteenth-century treatise, *De Re Metallica*. The Sierra strike also attracted teachers: the novices relied on Sonorans from Mexico, Southerners from earlier strikes in the Carolinas and Georgia, coal and iron miners from both Pennsylvania and Britain, lead miners from the Midwest, and experienced Europeans to teach them their new trade.

Equally fortunate were the early conditions in California. Amateurism mattered little in the early days. Abundant surface deposits of placer gold were easily mined with rudimentary tools and little skill. Spoons, knives, shovels, and even cooking utensils could be used to scoop pay-dirt from river banks and beds. Readily mastered washing techniques separated gold from sand and gravel without complex equipment. Mexicans and Southerners used panning to wash small amounts of pay dirt, flush away sediment, and leave only the heavier gold behind. Mexicans used a wooden *batea* with sloped sides, Southerners a metal pan designed for the purpose. As washing greater quantities of dirt became necessary, Georgians and Carolinians introduced another device—the "rocker" or "cradle." Simple enough to be constructed on the spot, the cradle was a variation on panning, but its operation required a team of at least three miners: one to shovel dirt into a hopper, one to pour in water, and one to "rock the cradle." The process carried away debris and left gold particles behind cleats that were inspected and cleaned periodically.

Mining conditions changed rapidly, however. By 1852, all the surface deposits had been discovered and claimed. It became necessary to process tons of dirt to recover ounces of gold. Ore-bearing gravels were sought deeper in the earth, and the "long toms" and other devices that Dame Shirley described became essential. No longer could an individual or a few partners work a claim. Miners organized companies to supply the labor and to attract the capital needed to construct flumes, dams, and sluices, and to dig the ditches that could transport water from distant sources. Companies also tunneled into hillsides to reach gold-bearing tertiary gravels. The work was expensive, up to $20 a foot. If pay dirt was found, hauling it out of tunnels for crushing and washing also required costly equipment. All too often, months or even years of effort and investment brought disappointment, disaster, or both.

Mechanized Mining

In 1852, while working a low-yield Nevada County claim, Anthony Chabot devised a more efficient means for moving large quantities of earth to uncover gold deposits. He attached a hose to his flume and used water pressure to erode topsoil. A year later, Edward E. Matteson refined the method by attaching a nozzle to the hose; hydraulic mining—California's principal contribution to mining technology—was born.

The technique was an immense success as early as 1854 when the Sacramento *Weekly Union* described "a claim on Iowa Hill [that] had been worked . . . by the application of hydraulic power until it was 120 feet from the top of the hill to the bed rock of the claim."

> With a perpendicular column of water 120 feet high, in a strong hose, . . . ten men who own the claim are enabled to run off hundreds of tons of dirt daily. So great is the force employed, that two men with the pipes, by directing streams of water against the base of a high bank, will cause immense slides of earth, which often bring with them large trees and heavy boulders. To carry off these immense masses of dirt, they have constructed two sluices. . . . After these immense masses of earth are undermined and brought down by the streams forced from the pipes, those same streams are turned upon the tons of fallen earth, and it melts away before them, and is carried away through the sluices with almost as much rapidity as if it were a bank of snow. No such labor-saving power has ever been introduced to assist the miner in his operations.

Decades later, valley farmers would launch attacks on hydraulic miners, whose debris choked irrigation streams and flooded towns, and still later environmentalists would condemn their devastation of the landscape. But at the time Californians accepted the damage as the inevitable price of progress.

Another form of placer mining, dredging, caused more severe environmental damage, but it became important only after an 1884 court decision restricted hydraulic mining. Dredging had been tried in 1850, when a group of New England capitalists converted a river steamer to work the Yuba River near Marysville. The efforts failed, but the Risdon Iron Works of San Francisco later developed a bucket dredge, based on a New Zealand design and first put into operation near Oroville in 1898. From then until the 1940s, the process remained an important mining method in California, and it was profitable even if each cubic yard of earth yielded less than a half-ounce of gold. Eventually these clattering monsters—often several stories high—worked around the clock to gouge tons of rock and gravel from river beds, process it to wash gold free, and dump the piles of tailings that remain visible alongside rivers from the Smith and Trinity in the north to the Stanislaus and San Joaquin in the south.

Least significant in early California was tunnel mining, also called quartz, hard-rock, or lode mining. Most early efforts to burrow into underground deposits of placer gold were bankrupt by the mid-1850s; lack of both capital and experience destroyed them. Argonauts learned from Cornishmen and others to sink reasonably safe shafts and to ventilate them at great depths, and Mexican miners introduced the *arrastra* to crush ore brought to the surface; through a circular rock-lined trough, an animal dragged stones around a central pivot to grind gold-bearing quartz. Chileans made the device somewhat more efficient by substituting an axle and stone wheel for the cumbersome grinders. Experienced Hispanics also taught neophytes to use mercury or quicksilver to extract gold from pulverized rock.

Tool-making and foundry operations like the Risdon, Union, and Vulcan works in San Francisco soon refined crude implements. They produced improved equipment for drilling and tunneling, rail cart and elevator systems to transport ore to the surface, pumps to reduce flood hazards, the California stamp mill to smash rock more efficiently, and steam engines to power them all. Mining entrepreneurs like Alvinza Hayward in Amador County and his counterparts in Trinity and Nevada counties used such locally developed advances in mining technology with substantial success during the 1860s and '70s. In the process, they helped to sustain the state's gold production after the initial boom years. The new equipment and techniques became even more significant, however, when they were applied in the Comstock silver mines in Nevada during the 1860s and as they gave impetus to California manufacturing.

Life in the Mines

Shortly after completing a voyage around Cape Horn in December 1849, Dr. J.D.B. Stillman described conditions surrounding the Sacramento hospital that he established with two partners:

> The people at home can have no conception of the amount of suffering in the vicinity. Hundreds are encamped in tents, throughout the rains and storms, scantily supplied with food and covering. Men are driven from the mines for want of food, and are begging for employment. Yesterday there were 25 deaths. The sickness does not arise from the severity

of the climate but largely from overwork, scanty and bad food, disappointment and homesickness.

Clearly life in the mines could be physically and emotionally devastating. But Stillman's presence illuminates another aspect of gold rush history: urban services arrived with the first Argonauts, the doctor and his hospital being but one example. Gold seekers dispersed rapidly from the American River region northward to the Feather River and Trinity-Shasta-Siskiyou diggings and southward to the Amador and Mariposa districts, carrying with them blueprints for the societies they had left behind.

Little can be added to Dame Shirley's eloquent descriptions of life in mining camps, except to emphasize the reluctance of most of their residents to abandon the cultural norms of communities left behind. To be sure, some easily tolerated the bedrolls, brush huts, and crude nourishment. But others quickly built sturdy cabins and acquired the furniture they deemed necessary to make life comfortable. Drinking, gambling, and carousing often characterized miners' diversions. But a book was as highly prized as a deck of cards. The arrival of a live performer, physician, or even a clergyman was cause for jubilation. Photographers (who often doubled as barbers or dentists) found eager clients for their tintypes, daguerreotypes, and other services. And a "petticoated astonishment" typically brought out the best in the miners. Mining camps were more than bastions of unfettered male hedonism. They helped to keep miners in touch with the societies they had left behind; they offered not only saloons, brothels, and gambling dens but also schools, churches, newspapers, and similar institutions.

Mining camps also introduced rudimentary political structures to California's wild interior. Because the mining districts were quite literally lawless, miners formed committees, elected officials, and carefully devised rules for mining and other necessary activities. They specified methods for making and maintaining claims, recorded titles and transfers, and settled ownership disputes. Often a rough logic prevailed. Where gold deposits were rich, claims might be limited to a ten-foot square. In another region, a miner stood at the center of his prospective "dig" and heaved his pick at the points of the compass to establish his corners. Principles originated by local committees were sound enough to eventually be incorporated into the state's mining code, its land ownership laws, and its water policies.

Other aspects of mining-camp law proved far less worthy of emulation. Initially the camps had very little serious crime. When theft, claim-jumping, or the like occurred, miners' tribunals, sometimes supervised by a locally-elected justice of the peace or an *alcalde*, convened to deal with the problem. There were no jails, so punishments were immediate: fines, banishment, or flogging. The explosion of newcomers from a variety of backgrounds and strange lands soon altered the situation. Now the newcomers included the kinds of fugitives memorialized in the contemporary ballad:

What was your name in the States?
Was it Thompson or Johnson or Bates?
Did you murder your wife and flee for your life?
O, what was your name in the States?

Early miners rarely asked such questions of their comrades. But as crime and competition for gold increased, so too did suspicion and demands for swift justice.

Unfortunately, popular tribunals degenerated all too easily into lawless mobs. The first recorded incident occurred in January 1849 at Dry Diggings (subsequently called Hangtown and now Placerville). Five miners who spoke only French and Spanish were reportedly caught stealing; they were tried and flogged. Two of them (some accounts say three) were accused of a previous theft and murder and were lynched over the protests of local citizens. An even more egregious episode occurred in Downieville, a small mining community on the North Yuba River. Residents were celebrating the nation's birthday with a drunken spree that began on the Fourth of July and lasted into the wee hours of July 5, 1851, when a Latina named Josefa ("Juanita" in some accounts) killed a popular Englishman, Fred Cannon. According to the *Alta California*, the intoxicated Cannon had broken down Josefa's door and entered her cabin during the festivities. According to Cannon's friends, he returned on the 5th to pay for the damage. But Josefa's supporters claimed that Cannon had been pursuing her sexually. Josefa herself reported that she stabbed Cannon in the heart, killing him instantly, when he called her a whore. For Josefa, Cannon's slur on her honor, more than his physical threat, justified her actions. But Cannon was popular with the miners, their nativist sentiments inflamed after a day of hard drinking and patriotic speeches. An enraged mostly American throng carried Josefa to the town plaza for a pseudo trial. A Dr. Aiken asserted that Josefa was pregnant; he pleaded for leniency for the sake of her innocent child. The angry crowd shouted him down. Another defender spoke up, but he soon abandoned Josefa for his own safety. Among the spectators was future governor John B. Weller, who was later accused of pandering to the mob for votes. Josefa was hustled to the Jersey Bridge where she climbed a scaffold and then walked a plank out over the river. The crowd cheered as the plank was cut away and Josefa fell. Her body twisted and writhed for half an hour before she was cut down.

Had she not been lynched, students of California history probably never would have heard of Josefa. Hubert H. Bancroft admitted that "no one ever thought of her" until she was hanged. Those who stood by, and even those who participated, seemed troubled by the event. Observers uniformly condemned the mob, but many condemned Josefa as well, suggesting that her status as a "foreigner" and prostitute were somehow to blame. More recently, historians have refocused attention on Josefa, viewing her as a symbol of Latina resistance in Anglo- and male-dominated gold rush California.

Bancroft exaggerated when he described the trees of mining districts as "tasseled with the carcasses of the wicked," but extra-legal punishments like these happened often enough to cast a dark shadow over the state's early history. Through the first half of the 1850s, mob justice broke out regularly in rural as well as urban areas, including San Francisco and Los Angeles. Some of the individuals punished may have been criminals, but many others were targets of local political animosities, moral prejudices, economic frustration, or nativist and racist sentiments.

Bonanza to *Borrasca*

During the first half of the gold rush decade, mining changed significantly from an individual pursuit of instant wealth to an organized corporate enterprise that required specialized skills and equipment and substantial capital. The transformation had a major impact on the development of California society, especially on the expectations of the thousands of Argonauts who crossed the isthmus, rounded the Horn, or traversed the Plains in search of fortune. For many of them, the anticipated bonanza soon became *una borrasca* (a storm or tempest). The value of gold extracted by various means during the first dozen years of the California gold rush was spectacular indeed:

Table 11.2	Value of Gold by Year		
1848	$245,000	1854	$69,433,931
1849	10,151,360	1855	55,485,395
1850	41,273,106	1856	57,509,411
1851	75,938,232	1857	43,628,172
1852	81,294,700	1858	46,591,140
1853	67,613,487	1859	45,846,599

Totals must be multiplied at least tenfold to place them in the context of present dollar values. They must also be assessed in terms of the worth of gold in the nineteenth century, $16 an ounce, and the number of miners at work: 5,000 in 1848; 40,000 in 1849; 50,000 in 1850; 100,000 in 1852. Between 1852 and 1860, the number remained fairly stable.

Gold production tended to decrease as the number of miners increased, and that had important implications. Initially, the quest for gold was fairly democratic. Deposits encompassed some 35,000 square miles, room for a multitude of prospectors. In addition, the treasure was located in the public domain, apparently there for the taking. Under the circumstances, few willingly submitted to legal, political, or economic authority or accepted work for wages. During the halcyon years of 1848–50, when each miner searched for the "big strike," a daily wage was defined as the value a person extracted from the ground. As the volume of gold diminished and miners more frequently worked for others, however, the term acquired a more conventional meaning and rewards diminished significantly.

Table 11.3	Average Daily Wage for White Miners		
1848	$20	1852	$6
1849	16	1853	5
1850	10	1854–55	5
1851	8	1856–60	3

Chinese, Indians, and other nonwhite miners received considerably less. For individuals arriving in California expecting to make their fortunes, disappointment at declining potential was severe.

Through the 1850s, Californians' compensation compared favorably with the average daily wage in "the States," $1.00 to $1.25 for a skilled eastern miner, but living costs in California were far higher. More importantly, declining wage levels and the fact that after 1855 most miners were employees, not independent prospectors, suggest that the average Argonaut did find the anticipated bonanza. Rare enough even in 1848 and '49, big strikes became rarer still in later years. Once placer deposits were depleted, mining became an increasingly complex and corporate enterprise. Individual prospectors virtually disappeared, replaced by wage-earners working for entrepreneurs who organized labor forces, supplied essential machinery, and furnished the capital. The situation was not what most participants in "nature's great lottery scheme" anticipated, and many of them vented their frustration on Californios and Indians.

Californios in the Mines

More effectively than war with Mexico, waves of Argonauts flooding the region accomplished the American conquest of California. Two-thirds were Yankees who carried with them their customs, attitudes, and prejudices—including the nativism that prevailed in "the States" at mid-century. Eventually, all people of color in California, especially the Chinese, became targets. But the first to suffer from American bigotry were the Californios and Natives, all of whom were reduced to minority status in their own homeland. For Spanish-speaking residents, loss of lands would later complete what Leonard Pitt called "the decline of the Californios."

Californios in the mines did not immediately experience the tempest. During the rush of 1848, about 1,300 Hispanic settlers found success in the gold fields. Members of the Coronel, Sepulveda, and Carrillo families of Los Angeles organized a party that headed for the Stanislaus River. They mined on their own, traded trinkets for nuggets with some Indians, and hired others to work for them. Antonio Coronel accumulated 45 ounces of gold in just one day. An associate found a 12-ounce nugget, and another gathered a "towelful of nuggets" in a few hours. He then sold his claim to another, who extracted 52 pounds of gold in a week. A third owner of the site also became rich.

When the mining season of 1848 ended, successful Californios returned to their homes to enjoy their wealth and to lay plans for 1849. By then, however, conditions were less congenial. During Coronel's return journey, a belligerent ex-Bear Flagger attacked and severely injured a companion. In the diggings, the party encountered Yankee hostility and open threats to all "foreigners." They also witnessed California's first lynching, the flogging and execution of a Frenchman and a Chilean at Hangtown. Coronel's group retreated to more isolated regions but found Americans there, who announced that the gold belonged exclusively to Yankees. Confronted by overwhelming numbers, obvious hostility, and a genuine potential for violence, these and other Californios made the logical decision: they left. Coronel later wrote: "For me, mining is finished." He probably spoke for most of his compatriots, who were rare in the mines after 1849. Occasionally a *patron* (sponsor) led a party into the southern districts, only to be intimidated by surly gringos who resented Hispanics and their competition. Hispanics remained in all mining regions, but most were neither California-born nor independent prospectors. Instead, they were Mexicans and South Americans employed by American companies. A few also were cooks, merchants, *arrieros* (muleteers) whose mules carried supplies to remote camps.

After 1848, Yankees assumed proprietary rights and asserted their sense of ethnic and moral superiority. They argued that the Treaty of Guadalupe Hidalgo made California a "white man's country," conveniently ignoring treaty provisions that protected the rights of provincial residents and offered them citizenship. Like Dame Shirley, Yankees inaccurately lumped all Hispanics together as simply "Spaniards" (although only 470 individuals from Spain lived in California as late as 1860). As competition and antagonism increased, "Spaniards"—including Californios—became "Sonorans," "greasers," *cholos* (a disparaging term for Hispanic males), or worse. Americans justified their hostility by claiming that their hosts engaged in gambling, prostitution, and other allegedly "Latin" vices.

Initial efforts to control the Hispanic presence were spontaneous and informal: threats, mob action, claim-jumping, and occasional beatings. Quickly, however, local miners' committees enacted laws excluding "noncitizens" from many districts, giving prejudice a semblance of legality. Whether formal or informal, nativist attitudes were often vicious. Miners' tribunals consistently meted out the severest punishments to Hispanics, often demanding flogging or mutilation. "Their majesties the mob" also took justice into their own hands, as the events recorded by Dame Shirley testify. Nor did impromptu anti-Hispanic legislation abate when California gained admission to the Union.

The Foreign Miners' Tax Law of 1850

Yankee miners appealed to the first state legislature to institutionalize their prejudices. Their principal advocate was Senator Thomas Jefferson Green of Sacramento, a Texan who attempted to introduce slavery into the Yuba River mines and whose hatred for Mexicans was notorious. The 1850 law that Green drafted and lawmakers approved imposed a $20 monthly fee on all noncitizen miners. Support for the measure was not universal, but California's need for revenue convinced most legislators to vote for it.

Because the tax was too high for most "foreigners" to pay, and since it was selectively enforced, the law generated little revenue. Rarely were miners of European origins asked to pay, but one serious incident did occur

when agents in Sonora attempted to collect the tax. Frenchmen and Germans allied themselves with 4,000 unarmed Mexicans to protest the tax. In the "French Revolution" that followed, dissidents encountered hundreds of armed Americans assembled to support the district tax collector. One Mexican was stabbed. The Europeans who instigated the protest were arrested, fined $5 each, and released, but Mexicans were ordered to pay the tax in full. For most of them, the point was made: they packed their belongings and departed.

In one sense, the tax law worked. It drove most Hispanics from the mines. Otherwise it was a failure. It produced neither the anticipated $2.4 million in revenue nor the expected cheap, docile labor force. What was worse, it failed to eliminate the right "undesirables:" Hispanic workers, restaurant, hotel, and store patrons left the area, much to the distress of local merchants and corporate mine owners. Tradesmen and would-be employers protested the law, citing the Treaty of Guadalupe Hidalgo, the U.S. Constitution, and traditional American ideals in appeals to the governor, legislature, and state supreme court to repeal or modify it. Late in 1850, the governor reduced the monthly fee. Early in 1851, agitation by citizens of Sonora, Stockton, and other towns forced the law's repeal. But the repeal did not lure Hispanics back to the mines, nor did it halt the "decline of the Californios."

"Diggers" in the Mines

The gold rush experience of California Indians paralleled that of the Californios, with even more devastating results. Argonauts stereotyped them as "diggers," assuming that theirs was a primitive culture based on gathering roots and trapping rodents for sustenance, but historian James J. Rawls has demonstrated that the term could have a different application. Indeed, Richard B. Mason's report to President Polk estimated that half of the 5,000 gold diggers during the summer of 1848 were Indians. Most worked for wages for individuals like Marshall, Sutter, or prominent Californios. Antonio Maria Suñol, for instance, took 20 from his Bay Area rancho to prospect on the American River. The Coronel-Sepulveda-Carrillo party included Indians as well.

Pre-1846 non-Hispanic settlers employed the greatest number of Indian miners. Charles M. Weber arrived in 1841 and established a rancho near Stockton. He had nearly 1,000 Native people working for him along Weber Creek near Placerville, and his Yokuts miners made the first major strike in the Calaveras-Stanislaus region. John M. Murphy was married to the daughter of a Miwok chief; he employed 600 Indigenous people on the North Fork of the Stanislaus. Emigrant Pierson B. Reading employed Indians to prospect along Clear Creek in Shasta County and on the Trinity River, while John Bidwell's Native American crews at Bidwell's Bar on the Feather River helped him gather the riches that paid for his purchase of Rancho Chico.

Not all Indians mined for whites, however. At first, amused by effort wasted in search of something neither edible nor wearable, they soon learned that white men prized gold and that it could be traded. Coronel recorded a typical exchange in 1848. Several Miwoks entered his camp, each carrying a bag of dust and obviously interested in trading:

> One . . . took [a saddle blanket] and pointed to the sack filled with gold; he pointed out a certain spot as the amount he was offering. . . . There was then in the area no way to replace the blanket so I refused the offer. . . . He increased it . . . lowering the place where he pressed the sack with his thumb; I refused again. He increased again and then one of my servants asked me why I did not give it to him—[saying] that he would make some saddle blankets of grass.

The Californio received seven ounces of gold ($112) for a blanket that, when it was new, cost only two *pesetas* (less than 50 cents). Other trades included exchanging glass beads ounce-for-ounce for gold. Established trading posts systematically fleeced Native people, setting "Indian" prices for goods that were often double those charged to whites, and keeping lead weights—"digger ounces"—to weigh Indian gold dust. They rationalized their policies on grounds that, as one trader put it, "no Christian man is bound to give full value to those infernal redskins; . . . they got no religion, and tharfore no conscience, so I deals with them accordin'."

Solving the "Indian Problem"

Newcomers' journals written in 1848 refer frequently not only to Native Californians but also to Walla Walla, Chinooks, and an occasional Delaware in the mines. By late 1849, however, few are mentioned, and by the 1850s, almost none. During the early gold rush, Californios and others accustomed to local Indians dominated in the diggings, but that changed with arrival of hordes of gold seekers. Contact between these later arrivals and the Native peoples quickly devolved into violence.

Free State Slavery

California's Indian Act of 1850

In his colorful memoir of early Los Angeles, Horace Bell described a grim civic ritual performed each week by municipal law enforcement officers. At sundown on Sunday evenings, the town marshal and his deputies advanced through the streets arresting Indians for vagrancy and public intoxication. Then, on Monday mornings, their Indian prisoners "would be exposed for sale, as slaves for the week" and "bought up by the vineyard men and others at prices ranging from one to three dollars." As Bell acidly observed, "Los Angeles had its slave mart, as well as New Orleans and Constantinople."

In its harsh exploitation of involuntary Indian labor, Los Angeles was not at all unique in California during the Gold Rush and Civil War years. As state geologist William Brewer discovered during a visit to Crescent City in 1863, "It has for years been a regular business to steal Indian children and bring them down to the civilized parts of the state, even to San Francisco, and sell them." According to Brewer, "it is said that some of the kidnappers would often get the consent of the parents by shooting them to prevent opposition."

Like Bell, Brewer provided one of many frank eyewitness accounts that reveal an important truth consistently overlooked in traditional narratives of antebellum America: California was not truly a free state. Despite the fact that California banned African American slavery and voted to enter the Union in 1850 as free soil, the very first state legislature nevertheless proceeded to establish a racially based system of Native American servitude. Designed to satisfy gold rush California's heavy demand for cheap and reliable farm workers and household domestic servants, the notorious and ill-named Act for the Government and Protection of Indians legalized three forms of bound servitude that, in actual practice, amounted to a thinly disguised species of slavery.

Sections 14 and 20 of the Indian Act laid the foundation for the Los Angeles slave mart later recalled by Bell. Specifically, these two provisions authorized local authorities to lease destitute Indian prisoners convicted of vagrancy and other misdemeanors to any white employer willing to pay their fines. Sentenced to terms of up to four months in private custody, Indian convicts provided a convenient supply of temporary workers during peak periods of demand, such as the harvest seasons for wheat, wine grapes, and other commercial crops.

Meanwhile, the need for more permanent year-round workers was met by various provisions of the Indian Act that, in combination, effectively perpetuated the system of debt peonage that had previously sustained the rancheros under Mexican rule. Indian laborers whose purchases at the rancho *tienda* (store) outpaced their monthly wages lost their freedom to walk off the job. Until they managed to clear their accounts at the *tienda*, indebted workers were subject to arrest as runaways if they attempted to flee or seek employment elsewhere.

Indentured servitude offered yet another means of legally binding Indian hands to white masters. Section 3 of the Indian Act allowed employers to confine Indian children to white households until they reached the age of majority (18 for males, 15 for females). Obtaining custody of an Indian child did not require parental consent, only approval by a local justice of the peace.

In 1860, the state legislature dramatically amended Section 3 to permit white employers to retain Indian children as "apprentices" well past majority. In some instances, females and males could be held until they reached the respective ages of 25 and 30. The amendment also authorized ten-year terms of indenture for adult Indians captured in war or declared vagrants by county judges.

Not surprisingly, the widespread demand for unfree Indian labor quickly spawned the brutal and illegal slave trade depicted by Brewer. Serving as both cause and effect in California's numerous frontier Indian wars, the kidnapping and trafficking of Native Americans, especially women and children, proved remarkably lucrative, with individual captives fetching prices running anywhere from $30 to $250 each ($915 to $7,622 in 2018 dollars). Denounced by federal Indian Superintendent George M. Hanson as "this unholy traffic in human blood and souls," California's Indian slave trade, centered in Humboldt and Mendocino counties, flourished until 1863, when Hanson and other anti-slavery Republicans in Sacramento finally gained enough strength to repeal Section 3 in the wake of President Abraham Lincoln's Emancipation Proclamation. By that point, it is estimated that the grand total of Native Americans reduced to involuntary servitude since 1850 approached 20,000, of whom perhaps 4,000 were kidnapped children sold into bondage throughout the ostensibly "free state" of California.   (MFM)

Among the first to appear in California's gold fields were Oregonians, fresh from the Whitman massacre at Walla Walla in 1847 and subsequent Cayuse wars. Those incidents, and the clashes Oregonians had on the trail to California, conditioned their attitudes. When they encountered Indians working productive mines, they were outraged. In March 1849, Oregon miners attacked a Maidu village on the American River. Indians retaliated by killing five Oregonians. The dead men's compatriots assembled in force, pillaged another village, slaughtered many inhabitants, and took a score prisoner. It is unlikely that the captives belonged to the tribe that killed the Oregonians, but seven were marched to Coloma and summarily executed. When James Marshall and others protested, the mob threatened their lives too. Indian-fighting subsequently degenerated into scalping, beheading, and other forms of mutilation and sadism. Californios were disgusted by Americans'

violence, like the one who asked, "What courage is displayed by such warfare as this, what honor is to be gained in it, and why have so many of your Oregon men shot down scores of Indians like wolves?"

But "Oregon men" were not the only ones involved. Gold-seekers from around the United States brought their hostilities and prejudices with them. Some antagonisms resulted from stereotypes in the minds of individuals who, like Dame Shirley, had never before seen a "real" Indian. Imagination, too, produced fantasies of incredible proportions. In 1850, for example, Governor Peter Burnett reported to the president that 100,000 armed braves were awaiting a signal to wage a war of extermination against whites. At the time, the entire Indigenous population of the new state barely equaled that number. Indian resistance only exacerbated these fears. The Pomo near Clear Lake responded to the labor exploitation, physical beatings, thievery, and sexual

A Fight with the Indians

An engraving from a Sacramento newspaper depicts a Trinity County incident in which residents reportedly avenged the murder of a local butcher by slaughtering more than 100 local Indians. It also illustrates the attitudes of most settlers in California during the gold rush era. *Collection of Peter E. Palmquist.*

violence of the Americans who had moved onto their land by killing two of the perpetrators, Andrew Kelsey and Charles Stone. In Napa, when an American named Preston shot and wounded Manuel Vera, Vera shot back.

Most such resistance was met with further violence. In response to the killing of Kelsey and Stone, the U.S. Army slaughtered over 500 Pomo men, women, and children living at Clear Lake and along the Russian River. In response to Vera's action, Americans in Napa blackened their faces, stormed the county jail, and lynched him. Determined to take revenge on real and imagined cattle thefts, white settlers rode into Wappo, Patwin, and Pomo villages and *rancherías* and, in some cases, killed entire communities of men, women, and children. Napa newspapers printed accounts of white men "hunting" Indigenous peoples.

In 1850, to solve the "Indian problem," state legislators enacted laws similar to the "black codes" adopted in the post-Civil War South. The notorious Act for the Government and Protection of Indians permitted the virtual enslavement of Indians as indentured servants, debt peons, or leased convicts. Meanwhile, Governors Peter Burnett and John McDougal encouraged outright extermination, while others leaned toward the somewhat more humane policies of removal or confinement to federal reservations.

Private forces continued their sporadic forays against the Indians until state- and nationally-funded militia forces lent legitimacy to such campaigns. Militias killed perhaps as many as 12,000 Indians by the 1860s, although many more died of disease and starvation. Some of those involved in the attacks on Natives claimed that they did so to end Indian peonage, a labor system they equated with racial slavery. Others resented Indian competition with white labor for the state's gold. Many acted on the assumption that "the only good Indian is a dead Indian," and a vicious few simply enjoyed the killing. Historian Hubert Howe Bancroft justly called the conquest of the California Natives "one of the last human hunts of civilization, and the basest and most brutal of them all."

Indeed, some more recent historians have come to portray the violent subjugation of Native California as "an American Genocide." While others strongly dispute the sweeping use of "genocide" to describe the fate of all California tribes during the Gold Rush and Civil War years, there is no denying that white miners and settlers intentionally waged genocidal campaigns of

CHAPTER 11   The New *El Dorado*   **155**

extermination against at least 18 tribal groups, including the Wiyot, Yana, and Yuki.

Federal officials considered annihilation repugnant and removal impractical. They sanctioned an alternate approach. In 1850 Congress appointed three commissioners to implement a segregation program. The trio negotiated agreements with a score of tribes that accepted relocation to reservations in areas remote from white settlement, but the solution was untenable. Californians protested that the 11,700 square miles allocated to Indians constituted 7.5 percent of the state's total area, and in 1852 the U.S. Senate rejected all of the treaties.

A year later, Congress approved a measure proposed by Edward F. Beale, U.S. Indian Superintendent for California, to establish several reservations of up to 30,000 acres each. Only Fort Tejón in the San Joaquin Valley near the Tehachapi Mountains attracted many Indians or functioned well even temporarily. By the early 1860s political manipulation and incompetence reduced California reservations to near ruin. Fort Tejón itself was abandoned in 1868.

Some California Natives resisted removal, as in the Modoc War of 1872–73. In northeastern California, 50 poorly armed warriors, led by Chief Kintpuash (Captain Jack) and accompanied by women and children, fortified themselves in the lava beds region and held off nearly 1,000 U.S. Army regulars. After months of fighting that cost the lives of 65 Americans and perhaps 30 Native men, women, and children, the Modocs were defeated and Captain Jack was executed. Other tribes, like the Mill Creeks during the 1850s and '60s, attacked whites who raided villages, raped women, stole children, and invaded territories. But most—like the Yahi described in Theodora Kroeber's *Ishi* and the Yosemite who, during the retaliatory "Mariposa Wars" of the 1850s, followed Chief Tenaya into the Sierra wilderness and ultimately joined Mono Lake Paiutes—retreated before the inevitable. Against devastating numbers and debilitating disease, however, neither resistance nor retreat was effective. By 1870, only 30,000 Indians survived anywhere in California.

Whether directly attacked or not, Native Californians could not endure the cultural conflict ushered in by the gold rush. Miners—and later loggers and farmers—rendered streams and forests of their habitat virtually useless to them. In contrast to earlier Spaniards and Mexicans, new settlers penetrated into areas that were isolated Native habitats, even in remote portions of the state. With evident satisfaction, an editor of the *Humboldt Times* in 1857 observed:

> Seven years ago, [this region] . . . was innocent of any knowledge of the Anglo-Saxon race. The Indian roamed over its wilds . . . until the bold and enterprising hand of the white came. Now the scene is changed. . . . Another cycle of years and the last vestiges of the race will be well nigh obliterated, . . . crushed out like other imbecilities, under the iron heel of progress and the steady and resistless march of civilization.

During the 1850s and '60s, most white Californians undoubtedly shared his view.

The

Thirty-First

State

12

C arey McWilliams reinforced John W. Caughey's observation that gold was the cornerstone of California's nineteenth-century experience when he described a "gold-energy equation" that telescoped history and gave events unprecedented velocity. Developments that took decades elsewhere occurred in years; those that required centuries took decades. Only months after the first Forty-Niners arrived, a convention at Monterey drafted a state constitution and applied for admission to the Union. San Francisco emerged as an "instant city" with a cosmopolitan population, mature social and economic institutions, nascent manufacturing establishment, and developing cultural life. Just as quickly, California entered the mainstream of national affairs and became embroiled in the slavery issue, the rising tide of nativism, and changes in American political and economic life.

The Military Interregnum

F rom the Cahuenga Capitulation in January 1847 until late 1849, political authority in California struck a precarious balance between American military government and Mexican-era institutions, a hybrid arrangement that satisfied no one. A series of military governors administered the province as a whole, five during the first ten months of occupation: Commodores John D. Sloat and Robert F. Stockton, General Stephen W. Kearny, and Colonels John C. Frémont and Richard B. Mason. General Persifor F. Smith replaced Mason in February 1849, followed by General Bennett Riley in April. Mason issued his *Laws for the Better Government of California* in 1848. Unsurprisingly, inconsistency, not the absence of laws, made administration ineffective.

Local government adhered to Mexican forms, in keeping with the Treaty of Guadalupe Hidalgo. An *alcalde*, whose office combined executive, legislative, and judicial authority, governed each settlement. Most *alcaldes* were Californios, but some were not. U.S. Navy Lieutenant Washington Bartlett was the first American *alcalde* in Yerba Buena (San Francisco) and John W. Geary the last. In Monterey, Walter Colton was appointed in 1846, and in Marysville, Stephen J. Field was elected in 1849. Appointed *ayuntamientos* advised the *alcaldes*.

Military government and remnants of the Mexican system contradicted Americans' political traditions and inaction in Washington magnified discontent. Late in 1846, when it was apparent that Mexican lands in the West would fall under U.S. jurisdiction, Pennsylvania Congressman David Wilmot introduced his proposal to exclude slavery from new territories in advance of acquisition, embroiling Congress in controversy. Northern representatives supported the principles of Wilmot's Proviso, Southerners demanded an extension of the Missouri Compromise line, and nativists opposed annexing "foreigners," meaning Hispanics and Indians. None would compromise, and California's status drifted without definition, even after the war ended.

The Constitution of 1849

Thousands of Americans swarming into California became impatient with chaotic political arrangements, and in February 1849, San Franciscans defied the military governor and replaced the local *alcalde* and *ayuntamiento* with a traditional town government. During succeeding months, Americans at San Jose, Monterey, and Sacramento, unhappy with both local arrangements and Congressional delays, demanded immediate action. To forestall popular agitation, military governor Bennett Riley exceeded his authority in June 1849 and—probably with support from President Zachary Taylor—ordered the election of delegates to attend a constitutional convention, scheduled for September in Monterey.

None of the 48 constitution makers who assembled were miners; only twelve arrived in California after 1847. Eight delegates were Californios, among them Pablo de la Guerra, José Carrillo, and Mariano Vallejo. The majority had settled in California before the Mexican War—men like Thomas O. Larkin, Esteban Foster, Abel Stearns, and the president of the convention, Bear Flagger Robert B. Semple. Most were young. Three-fourths were under 40 (the average age was 36) and nine were under 30. More than half had prior political experience, either in California or "the States."

Several issues might have disrupted or even dissolved the convention. One was the choice between state and territorial status, but that question was quickly resolved—with tacit approval from Washington—in favor of statehood. The volatile issue of slavery posed surprisingly few problems. Even delegates from Southern California opposed importing the institution. The convention's decision reflected neither abolitionist sentiments nor sympathy for black equality. Instead, their votes were motivated by racism and hostility toward competitive slave labor. When a Kentuckian proposed exclusion of free blacks from the state, the convention only balked because the measure violated the U.S. Constitution and thus might delay statehood.

The controversy that nearly ended the convention concerned state boundaries. Some delegates advocated a state stretching all the way to the Rocky Mountains, another faction argued for an eastern border formed by the Sierra, and compromisers proposed several intermediate state lines. Heated debates swirled around related issues: the difficulty of governing such a large area, protecting settlers, responsibility for Indigenous affairs, potential intrusion of slavery, and overlap with the proposed Mormon state of Deseret in Utah. Finally, the small-state faction prevailed and delegates adopted California's present boundaries: 42° north latitude eastward to 120° west longitude, then southward to 39° north latitude in the center of Lake Tahoe; then southeasterly to intersect with the Colorado River at 35° north latitude, then down the center of the river to Mexico.

Expediency guided another unique feature of California's first constitution when the Monterey Convention opted to incorporate Mexican laws that, unlike the English and American system, allowed married women to hold property in their own names (although subsequent legislatures and jurists limited these rights). Delegates may have been responding to the nation's first woman's rights convention, held the previous year at Seneca Falls, New York, but more probably they were trying to make the state attractive to married women like Forty-Niner Luzena Stanley Wilson. Traveling overland with two small children, Luzena and Mason Wilson arrived in Sacramento on the last day of September 1849. The day before, as she stood over a campfire, cooking her family's last supper on the trail, Luzena made a lucrative discovery:

> A hungry miner, attracted by the unusual sight of a woman, said to me, "I'll give you five dollars, ma'am, for them biscuit." It sounded like a fortune to me, and I looked at him to see if he meant it. And as I

hesitated at such, to me, a very remarkable proposition, he repeated his offer to purchase, and said he would give ten dollars [over $300 in 2018 dollars] for bread made by a woman, and laid the shining gold piece in my hand.

A few days later, the Wilsons sold their oxen and purchased an interest in a hotel. Luzena went to work in the kitchen, and two months later they sold their partial interest for $1,000 and started their own hotel. The family lost everything in a devastating flood later that year, and Luzena decided to begin again on higher ground. The Wilsons borrowed $700 for transportation to Nevada City, whereupon Mr. Wilson "hurried away up the mountain" for building materials. Luzena recalled:

> When I was left alone in the afternoon—it was noon when we arrived—I cast my thoughts about me for some plan to assist in the recuperation of the family finances. As always occurs to the mind of a woman, I thought of taking boarders. There was already a thriving establishment of the kind just down the road, under the shelter of a canvas roof, as was set forth by its sign in lamp-black on a piece of cloth: "Wamac's Hotel. Meals $1.00." I determined to set up a rival hotel. So I bought two boards. . . . With my own hands I chopped stakes, drove them into the ground, and set up my table. I bought provisions at a neighboring store, and when my husband came back at night he found . . . 20 miners eating at my table. Each man as he rose put a dollar in my hand and said I might count him as a permanent customer. I called my hotel "El Dorado."

Within six weeks Luzena had enough money to repay the family's debt. She eventually took her husband "into partnership" in her hotel.

Whatever motivated the constitutional convention's decision to protect married women's property rights, the decision was radical for its day, almost as radical as its provisions prohibiting the use of paper money, restricting the issue of securities, and imposing stringent regulations on corporations, especially banks.

The Constitution of 1849 was fairly conventional when it banned dueling, authorized the legislature to create a university and public school system, and to secure federal land grants to build colleges. From the U.S. Constitution, the delegates borrowed the bicameral legislature and the separation of powers. They also borrowed freely from other state constitutions, including those of Iowa (the most recently admitted western state) and New York (which had recently been revised). The result was an organic law that focused on the principles of government and left writing laws to the legislature.

Before it adjourned, the convention raised two issues with long-term implications. Southern Californians, who were badly outnumbered with only eleven delegates, protested revenue policies that placed the tax burden almost exclusively on owners of real property (such as grazing lands) and exempted personal property (such as profits gained from mining on public lands). Their concerns were borne out by later events, but in 1849, they were easily outvoted. The second issue was symbolic: when the convention adopted California's "Great Seal," delegate Mariano Vallejo objected to including a grizzly bear in the design. Recalling Bear Flaggers' mistreatment of the Californios, Vallejo proposed adding a *vaquero* leading the beast on a *reata* (rope). He too was overruled. Ironically, American California chose the *Ursus californicus* for its state seal (and eventually its state flag), and then immediately set to work killing them off. Within 75 years of the gold rush, the newcomers managed to track down and kill every grizzly bear in the Golden State. In 1922, a Fresno County farmer shot the last grizzly left in California.

Great Seal of the State of California

Despite Mariano Vallejo's objections, the grizzly remained on the Great Seal, without the *vaquero* and *reata*. Minerva, the Roman goddess of wisdom, invention, and the arts, surveys the scene. Over all spreads the state's motto, *Eureka* ("I have found it!").

Statehood Celebration

On October 29, 1850, San Franciscans celebrated California's admission as the 31st state. *Library of Congress.*

Statehood

The Monterey Convention completed its task in just six weeks. With a vote of 12,064 for and 811 against, voters overwhelmingly approved the constitution in November 1849, and elected their first officials on the same day. Peter H. Burnett was elected the state's first governor and John McDougal the first lieutenant governor. Thirty-six men were chosen for the assembly, 16 for the senate. The number of leaders in each body later grew, with the assembly expanding to 80 members in 1853 and the senate to 40 members in 1861. Under the state's first constitution, Californians voted annually. Assemblymen were elected each year to one-year terms. Senators served two-year terms, but with overlapping terms so that half the body was elected annually. Terms of office later doubled in both houses. After 1863, assembly members would serve for two years, senators four. Californians elected state leaders every other odd year until the state's constitution was rewritten in 1879. Thereafter general elections would be held in even years.

As decreed by the constitution, the new government began operations that December in the "Pueblo de San Jose." Leaders immediately elected two Californians to represent the state in the U.S. Senate, John C. Frémont and William M. Gwin. Despite California's self-assured beginnings, uncertainty reigned. For the next eleven months, southern representatives in the U.S. Congress blocked California's admission as a free-soil state.

Unlike the men elected to the Monterey Convention, most of those who served in the first state legislature had no previous political experience. Many were motivated by self-interest, but Senator Thomas Jefferson Green's frequent calls to adjourn to his nearby saloon were also well received. Its reputation for hard-drinking earned the first legislature its nickname: "The Legislature of a Thousand Drinks." Inebriation might explain why the legislature failed to agree on a location for the state capital. Rival towns commenced a bidding war for a legislative home, keeping state officials on the move, from San Jose (1849) to Vallejo (1852) to Benicia (1853), and finally to Sacramento in 1854.

Yet the first American administrators included many competent and serious individuals, including assembly member Stephen J. Field, who drafted the state's first civil and criminal codes, using those of his native New York as models. Legislators also formulated policies for establishing local governments and law-enforcement agencies, creating new counties, and collecting revenue to support the government.

Although these were important accomplishments, California's attention remained focused on Washington, for without approval from Congress, decisions made by California's governors meant nothing. In the nation's capital, partisan controversy, especially over slavery, delayed statehood for California. Finally, leading Whigs and Democrats brokered an agreement that settled the impasse. The Compromise of 1850 admitted California

David Broderick and William Gwin

The rivalry between Democrats David Broderick (*left*) and William Gwin (*right*) dominated California's early political life and added to its turbulence. *Courtesy of The Bancroft Library, University of California, Berkeley.*

as a free state, and divided the rest of the Mexican cession (the land gained in the U.S.–Mexican War) into the territories of Utah and New Mexico, where voters could decide the slavery question themselves. The measure also abolished the slave trade (but not slavery) in the District of Columbia, and provided southern slave owners with a tougher fugitive slave code. The statehood bill became law on September 9, 1850, but Californians learned of their victory one month later. Jubilant celebrations met the news throughout the new state.

Early Political Rumbles: Broderick and Gwin

During the 1850s, California's political affairs were influenced less by changing administrations, conflicting ideologies, party realignments, or national issues than by two individuals: David C. Broderick and

William M. Gwin. The pair had several things in common. Both were Democrats who arrived in California in 1849, ambitious men who coveted a seat in the U.S. Senate, and experienced politicians able to establish solid personal support. But there similarities ended.

Born in Washington, D.C., Broderick was the son of Irish immigrants. As a youth in New York City, he received no formal education but a thorough schooling in the rough-and-tumble city. Blunt, affable, and occasionally unscrupulous, he was a saloonkeeper, hack driver, and unsuccessful Congressional candidate before moving west. In San Francisco, he renewed acquaintances with former New Yorkers, became involved in Democratic politics, built a machine centered on local volunteer fire companies, and increased his personal wealth by speculating in waterfront lots and a private mint. Opposition to slavery and Jacksonian principles gave him local appeal, especially among wage-earners, and as a member of the first state senate, Broderick used patronage to control the San Francisco party and muster statewide support among Northern "Tammany" Democrats.

Fifteen years older than Broderick, Gwin left successful political careers in his native Tennessee and in Mississippi when he emigrated. Trained in law and medicine, he was a Jacksonian Democrat with Jeffersonian agrarian principles. His polished manner, origins, and connections made him the natural leader of the Southern "Chivalry" Democrats who settled in California, as did his position on slavery. Gwin supported the institution's exclusion from California, but he consistently rejected federal authority to regulate it. He also became an effective U.S. Senator. None of the transcontinental railway bills that he sponsored became law, but other efforts on the state's behalf—Mare Island Navy Yard near Vallejo and a branch mint in San Francisco—were successful. Gwin's status in the national Democratic Party also gave him influence over the distribution of federal patronage in California.

The political milieu in which Broderick and Gwin operated was peculiar indeed. Neither Whigs nor newly organized Republicans influenced California affairs significantly. The anti-foreign and anti-Catholic American or "Know-Nothing" party (called *los ignorantes* by Californios) held power briefly after 1855, but only because of Democratic factionalism. On the surface, local divisions resembled those in the national party, but discord among California Democrats involved mainly state issues and Broderick's ambition.

By 1855, Broderick felt sufficiently secure as leader of the "Tammany" faction to challenge Gwin for his place in the U.S. Senate, but a badly divided legislature chose neither of the rivals—nor anyone else. Instead, it left only Senator John B. Weller, elected to replace Frémont in 1852, to uphold state interests for the next two years. Broderick's premature bid and Democrats' disunity also allowed Know-Nothings to elect J. Neely Johnson governor and David S. Terry chief justice of the state supreme court in 1855. During national elections a year later, the newly organized Republican Party compounded confusion by running John C. Frémont for president. The "Pathfinder" had alienated Californians by inattention to his senatorial duties and by selling his Mariposa estate to corporate mining interests. As a result, he ran far behind Democratic and Know-Nothing candidates in the state. Despite the defeat, the Republicans—organized locally by Leland Stanford, Mark Hopkins, Charles Crocker, and Collis P. Huntington—soon became an important force in state politics.

In 1857, though, the major local issue remained the senatorial question. Broderick used his influence in the legislature and carefully distributed favors to secure a full term in the U.S. Senate. Gwin filled the vacant seat for the remaining four years of its term. President James Buchanan filled federal positions in California only with "Chivalry" Democrats, and an outraged Broderick openly denounced both his rival and the president. His actions set in motion events that brought him to an unexpected end. In the state campaign of 1859, "Chivalry" Democrats swamped disorganized "Tammany" forces. During the contest, former Broderick ally Chief Justice David S. Terry aligned with Gwin in his quest to remain a U.S. senator. Already enraged by other defections, Broderick denounced the jurist, both viciously and in public. Terry resigned his office and challenged Broderick to a duel. When the two met in San Mateo County on September 13, 1859, Broderick fired first. His shot went wild, but Terry aimed carefully, mortally wounded his antagonist, and ended one turbulent phase in California's political history. Three decades later, Terry himself met a similarly violent fate.

Building a State

Fortunately, the Broderick-Gwin feud did not absorb all of Californians' political energies. They also attended to the business of establishing state institutions, including schools. The legislature provided for a future state university, mandated the use of property taxes for local school districts, and devised a system to apportion state funds among them. During the 1850s and '60s, the government's contribution to public education rarely amounted to more than "a pittance almost beneath contempt."

Failure to support education resulted partially from a shortage of revenues, but early efforts to raise funds through taxation exacerbated sectional conflicts and even led to a separatist movement in 1859. The protests of southern Californians at the Monterey Convention seemed prophetic when an 1851 law exempted mining claims from all property taxes. This was blatantly unfair; in 1852, 6,000 residents of six "cow-counties" in the south paid $42,000 in taxes—twice as much as 120,000 residents of twelve northern mining counties. Californians from south of the Tehachapis complained that they contributed more but received less than their northern counterparts. In 1859 Los Angeles assembly member Andrés Pico introduced—and voters approved—a plan to form a distinct territory from counties from San Luis Obispo southward, but the proposal died in Washington.

Congress was in no mood to reward secessionists on a remote western frontier.

State leaders dawdled on a number of significant issues. Not until 1858, for example, would legislators create a state agency to oversee the disposition of California's public lands. By then, speculators had already snapped up most of the state's public lands. But the state legislature moved quickly in other areas. By the end of 1852, the state passed measures regulating administration and law enforcement in cities and counties. Thanks to Stephen J. Field, California adopted codes of civil and criminal law and created a judicial system.

Not surprisingly, early legislatures devoted considerable time and energy to mining questions. Between 1850 and 1852, lawmakers passed, rescinded, and reinstated foreign miners' tax laws and enacted tax exemptions favorable to miners and mining entrepreneurs, but they failed to devise a comprehensive state mining code. For the most part, miners working claims in the public domain were content to occupy rather than own the land, and they relied on local codes to protect their interests. Consequently, codified mining laws seemed unimportant until the late 1850s, when corporate mining threatened individual entrepreneurs. The federal government ultimately settled the issue. Congress passed the Mining Act of 1866, which protected open access to mineral deposits in the public domain, confirmed local codes, upheld land titles acquired under them, and gave current occupants the option of acquiring title to some public lands. The act was principally intended to prevent mineral lands from falling into the hands of corporate interests, but it also codified the region's existing mining policies and practices.

Vigilante Justice: "Their Majesties the Mob"

Codes of law did not assure the existence of enforcement agents or courts. Consequently, early Californians often resorted to extralegal methods of dispensing justice. Many early histories of the state romanticized vigilantism, defending it as the right of citizens to take the law into their own hands. Others found a macabre humor in California lynch mobs. Bret Harte, for example, wrote of a popular tribunal advised to render a "correct" verdict because the defendant had already been hanged. In reality, there was nothing romantic, justified, or amusing about vigilante justice, nor can it be reconciled with genuine Anglo-Saxon legal traditions.

Americans did not introduce popular justice to California. In 1836, a "defense committee for the public safety" in Mexican Los Angeles removed a man and woman from custody and shot both for allegedly killing the woman's husband. But after 1848, such incidents happened with greater frequency. Since law enforcement and judicial authorities were rare, mining camp residents selected their own officials to preserve law and order. But, as Dame Shirley observed, "law" frequently degenerated into lynching and "order" into mob rule.

Popular tribunals appeared in both urban and rural settings in the 1850s. In Los Angeles, 44 murders in just over a year confirmed the town's reputation for violence. In 1851, officials created a vigilance committee that hanged five alleged murderers, at least one of whom was certainly innocent. Early in 1855, Mayor Esteban Foster halted a mob bent on lynching a prisoner. Foster resigned his office, joined in the hanging, and then accepted immediate re-election. A total of 20 lynchings occurred in Los Angeles in 1854 and '55. Hangings in Southern California multiplied in 1857, as companies of "rangers" formed to pursue *bandidos*. Eleven lynchings took place in 1857, and 1863 saw seven in just one month.

Popular justice in Southern California and in the mines often involved hostility toward "foreigners." San Francisco followed a similar path. In 1849, local merchants hired a group of discharged U.S.–Mexican War soldiers to police the city. The hired guns were to return sailors to their ships and keep order on the waterfront. Instead some joined forces with recent immigrants from Australian penal colonies and, as "the Hounds," launched a reign of terror on local citizens. With headquarters in a tent called "Tammany Hall" at Pacific and Dupont streets, the Hounds attacked Hispanic settlers clustered at Clark's Point and "Little Chile," a tent colony at the foot of Telegraph Hill, raping women and making off with possessions. On July 15, 1849, after an afternoon of marching and drinking, the Hounds formed into companies and spread out across the city to "whip and drive every damned Chileno out of town." They shot men, raped women, and stole jewelry, clothing, furniture, and gold dust before retiring to their tent to celebrate with stolen wine. The following day, Sam Brannan and others gathered at Portsmouth Square to denounce these outrages. They formed a Law and Order Party, also along military lines, to capture and try the Hounds for their crimes. Punishments included fines, imprisonment, and exile from San Francisco. Several prisoners were later executed in the mining camps. Citizens took up a collection for survivors and thereafter Chileans were relatively safe in San Francisco.

That was the end of the Hounds, but not crime or vigilantism in San Francisco. In February 1851, a popular tribunal headed by William Tell Coleman tried and convicted two "Sydney Ducks" suspected of robbing and beating a merchant. The pair escaped the rope because of a divided jury—a fortunate result since one defendant was mistakenly identified and certainly innocent. Later in the year, the city experienced its fifth great fire. Residents claimed the fires were set to cover crimes and blamed the courts, politicians, lawyers, and the Ducks. In June, San Franciscans formed the Vigilance Committee of 1851, with Brannan and Coleman in the lead. With some 500 members, the Committee soon caught, tried, and hanged a Duck accused of stealing a safe. Vigilantes eventually tried and executed three more Sydney men, one for murder and the others for lesser crimes. Committee members also searched homes and businesses, deported and whipped individuals suspected of crimes, and abused citizens who seemed reluctant to cooperate with them. The Committee finally disbanded that September.

The "Revolution" of 1856

San Francisco's best-known popular tribunal was the Vigilance Committee of 1856. Two private murders precipitated the city's return to semi-official public murder. In November 1855, theater-goers William Richardson, a U.S. marshal, and his wife found themselves seated behind the well-known gambler Charles Cora and his mistress, prostitute and brothel-keeper Arabella Ryan. Richardson asked Cora and Ryan to leave, but the couple refused. A quarrelsome, possibly intoxicated Richardson confronted Cora the following evening. In the argument that followed the gambler fatally shot the marshal. Although Cora was arrested and jailed, his trial resulted in a hung jury, sending Cora back to jail. Crusading journalist James King of William seized upon the Cora affair as a symbol of "good versus evil" in San Francisco. King (who added "of William" to his name to distinguish his otherwise common name) had made a name for himself as a reformer among the city's growing population of white, middle-class businessmen. Their wives, especially, resented sharing streets, hotels, restaurants, and theaters on apparently equal footing with prostitutes and their paramours. James King quite agreed, and used the pages of the *Daily Evening Bulletin* to attack San Francisco's corrupt politicians—especially the Democratic, Tammany-style political machine of David Broderick—who winked at vice and crime. Charles Cora was still in jail, awaiting re-trial when King published evidence that city supervisor James P. Casey had served time in New York's Sing Sing prison. A distraught Casey waited on the street for King the following evening, drew a revolver, and mortally wounded the newspaperman. Casey was immediately arrested, but a crowd gathered around the police station to demand vengeance. William Tell Coleman and Brannan swung into action and before a new day dawned, San Francisco's Committee of Vigilance was reborn.

On Sunday, May 18, a Committee of 2,000 armed men marched in formation to the city jail. The Committee intimidated the sheriff into releasing Casey and Cora, and then marched the prisoners to its headquarters at 41 Sacramento Street. Committeemen built a scaffold at the entrance to the building, and surrounded it on three sides with solid walls of sandbags piled ten feet high and six feet across, guarded by cannons at either corner (earning it the affectionate name "Fort Gunny-bags"). The Committee began its murder "trial" on May 20, the day King died, resulting in a "jury" verdict of guilty. Cheering crowds gathered for the double hanging on May 23, 1856.

Some local leaders—the mayor, sheriff, and militia commander William T. Sherman—expected that the executions would end the affair. They were wrong. Vigilantes continued to root out "criminals," with the support of local newspapers. The main exception, the *Herald*, suffered dwindling subscription and advertiser lists and entire issues were burned in the streets. Some clergymen, like Presbyterian minister William Scott, dared to dissent, but pressure exerted by congregations and committee members stifled most criticism. Early in June, municipal authorities appealed for help to the governor, who called out the militia, but the few troops who reported for duty were outnumbered and poorly equipped. When officials attempted to supply them from the federal arsenal at Benicia, vigilantes intercepted the boat and commandeered the weapons. With little effective opposition, the Vigilance Committee essentially controlled San Francisco. By August, when leaders decided to dissolve the membership (but not the executive committee), two more accused murderers had been hanged, one prisoner had committed suicide, and 30 "undesirables" had been deported. Scores also were intimidated or subjected to sham trials. Among them was Chief Justice Terry, arrested for stabbing a vigilante while defending a witness to the arms-shipment theft.

On August 18, 1856, vigilantes marched through the city 6,000 strong. With this show of strength, the Committee disbanded. Leaders proclaimed their purpose served, but records document no significant decrease in crime or increase in convictions in subsequent years. Vigilante justice, moreover, carried a high price tag. Subversion of basic American legal principles—such as the presumption of innocence and rights to representation, trial by jury, and appeal—can hardly be considered as genuine reform. In another sense, vigilante leadership may have succeeded only too well. During the next decade, the committee's political successor—the People's Reform party—gained control over municipal government. Its insistence on inexpensive government left police and teachers unpaid, schools, waterfront, and other public facilities in disrepair, and civic morale at low ebb.

Contemporaries and historians alike defended the Committee of 1856, on much the same grounds as the vigilantes—that is, popular action was warranted because the populace was truly suffering, their incomes and livelihoods demolished by the financial Panic of 1855, during which elected officials imposed outrageous taxes that they spent lavishly on themselves, benefiting only machine politicians like David Broderick. What was worse, claimed apologists, courts, police, and lawyers were corrupt, permitting vice, crime, and immorality to flourish in the city. Detractors, on the other hand, argued that the 1856 Committee of Vigilance was primarily interested in gaining cultural and ethnic dominance. The election that brought James P. Casey to the board of supervisors marked the city's growing presence of Irish-Catholic immigrants and their children. The vigilantes, many of whom were native-born Protestants recently arrived from "the States," reasserted control over local politics by arresting and exiling their opponents, a disproportionate number of whom were first- or second-generation Irish Catholics. Recent scholars find little evidence to prove that San Francisco was immersed in an unusual crime wave. Costs of government were not particularly high, since the Consolidation Act of 1856 cut municipal costs and improved efficiency by merging city and county governments. Broderick, the alleged corrupt influence, had even supported this reform. Moreover, the worst effects of the Panic of 1855 seemed to have passed by 1856. Ironically, some scholars argue that, by cutting funds for streetlights, police, and firefighting, leaders of the "Revolution of 1856" may have done more than their predecessors to abet crime and vice.

A Cosmopolitan Society

Vigilantism often involved anti-foreign sentiments, and the nativism prevalent in "the States" at mid-nineteenth century periodically infected California. In the 1850s, the new state was by far more racially diverse than the rest of the nation. A quarter or more of all Californians were African American, American Indian, Asian, or Latino. The racial and ethnic diversity of the population grew through the decade, as migrants from other lands poured in. Some were propelled west by dislocations in Europe—especially the potato famine in Ireland, but the lure of gold was motivation enough for most. Newcomers represented nearly every nation on earth, creating a uniquely cosmopolitan society. By 1860, nearly 40 percent of the state's residents were foreign-born and more than half had at least one foreign-born parent.

During the 1850s, 80 percent of the foreign-born came from Mexico, Britain and Ireland, the German states, and France. Scandinavian countries and eastern and southern Europe accounted for the remainder. For European immigrants, California promised a congenial

Membership Certificate, Vigilance Committee of 1856

On the elaborate and highly symbolic membership certificate of Hiram S. Wheeler, the motto of the Vigilance Committee of 1856 reads *Fiat justicia ruat coelum:* "Let justice be done though the heavens fall." *Courtesy of The Bancroft Library, University of California, Berkeley.*

home. In eastern cities like Boston, Philadelphia, and New York, Irish Catholics encountered overwhelming hostility, bigotry, and physical attack, but in California, Irish immigrants assimilated with relative ease. Barring nativist flare-ups like that of 1855, American California seemed to welcome the Irish, valuing their contributions to local economic development.

Thousands of Jews escaping persecution in Europe and eastern U.S. cities also encountered occasional anti-Semitism in California, but it was significantly less pervasive or virulent than elsewhere. Jews settling in San Francisco and the gold regions maintained their own cultural and religious identities, but also affiliated with local associations like the Odd Fellows and Masons, becoming respected and valued members of gold rush society. Solomon Heydenfeldt, for example, achieved high office as a justice of the state supreme court. Entrepreneur Levi Strauss amassed a great fortune and was admired by San Franciscans for his liberality in donating to good causes, both private and public.

Recent arrivals to San Francisco found a community with all the problems of big cities on the East Coast—crime, disease, overcrowding, poor or non-existent sanitation—but without the municipal structures that, elsewhere, had evolved slowly over time. To meet the city's emergencies as well as its everyday needs, residents organized volunteer fire companies and militia units, charities, hospitals, and all the other service associations that were typical of nineteenth-century American communities.

Men quickly founded ethnic and fraternal societies to offer food, shelter, and medical attention to those in need. During the cholera epidemic of 1850, the Odd Fellows set up a temporary hospital; members prepared meals, nursed the sick, and buried the dead. German and Polish Jews founded two permanent charities, the Eureka Benevolent and the First Hebrew Benevolent societies. In the 1870s, Jewish men founded an orphanage, followed by an old folks' home. In the '80s, Mt. Zion Hospital was opened to serve the indigent sick; unlike the orphanage or senior facility, it was open to all, regardless of creed.

The elite white women who came in the 1850s to join their husbands formed their own woman-led charities. The first was the San Francisco Protestant Orphan Asylum, founded in 1850 by several ministers' wives. Three years later, the San Francisco Ladies' Protection and Relief Society appeared, to "render protection and assistance" to "sick and dependent women and children." In 1867, the wives of several prominent businessmen launched the San Francisco Female Hospital, which provided poor women with gynecological and obstetric services (this hospital, like most in this era, was a charity institution; those who could afford it received medical attention at home). The wives of elite Jewish businessmen also organized charities. The Hebrew Ladies' Benevolent Association and the Ladies' Society of Israelites were both founded in 1855 to care for their community's small number of destitute women and children. In the 1860s, black San Franciscans organized their own charities, including the woman-led Ladies' Benevolent and Ladies Pacific Accumulating and Benevolent societies, both of which offered medical and burial services to the city's small black community. By the 1880s, city leaders had come to rely almost exclusively on these private male- and female-led charities. For the city's poor and working classes, they provided the lion's share of social welfare services then available in San Francisco.

Anti-Chinese Prejudice

Non-Europeans found life in gold-rush California considerably less congenial, especially the Chinese whose presence initiated one of the ugliest and enduring trends in California history. Fewer than 1,000 Chinese lived in the United States in 1850, almost all to visit "gold mountain," *jinshan* in Mandarin, *gum san* in Cantonese. Although more than half were married, very few brought their wives. In San Francisco, there were 4,018 Chinese men but only seven women. Two years later, a state census counted more than 25,000 Chinese in California, about 10 percent of the population. By 1860, their numbers had reached 35,000. Consular reports indicate that, for many, the goal was to earn $400 and return home as wealthy men, but few ever achieved this aim.

Chinese miners on the gold mountain worked and reworked the least productive diggings for meager wages and lived in miserable conditions. Because their agreements included repaying contractors for the costs of their trans-Pacific voyage, as well as food and board, their debts usually became larger, not smaller. Few managed either to pay what they owed or to save enough to return home.

Chinese miners also became prime targets for white miners' hostility. Miners denounced the similarities between contract labor and racial slavery, accused the Chinese of gambling and various "Oriental" vices, and deplored conditions in the racialized villages, or "Chinatowns," in which the Chinese congregated. The real source of antagonism between white and Chinese miners was competition. The Chinese were tolerated as domestic servants or other unskilled workers, but attitudes changed when they vied for diminishing gold resources.

Lawmakers gave an official stamp to the hostility in 1852 when they revived the Foreign Miners' Tax Law. The new version imposed a $3 (later $4) monthly fee on "aliens ineligible to citizenship" (language borrowed from a federal statute that limited the naturalization process to free whites). Lawmakers in Oregon, Idaho, and Montana quickly copied the California model and imposed similar taxes on their Chinese miners. To block additional immigration, in 1855 California passed "An Act to Discourage the Immigration to this State of Persons Who Cannot Become Citizens," which imposed on ships' captains a tax of $50 for each passenger barred from naturalization. When white miners found legal methods inadequate, they resorted to violence. One California newspaper reported:

> An American yesterday attacked a Chinaman, beating him shamefully. The Chinamen in the neighborhood were afraid to intervene and the Americans, of whom there was a large crowd, stood by and saw the poor Chinaman abused. The assailant held the unfortunate Celestial by the queue [the long braid men were required to wear under Chinese law] and kicked and beat him until he was tired, and when the poor fellow got loose and was going off a policeman came up, saw by his bloody face that he had been in a fight and arrested him.

Chinese had few legal defenses. In April 1850, the legislature had limited the rights of blacks and Native Americans to testify in court against whites. Four years later in *People v. Hall*, the state supreme court ruled that Chinese could not testify against whites on the novel theory that the Chinese were technically Indians, since the ancestors of Native Americans had migrated from Asia. Stephen J. Field and others denounced attacks against the Chinese, but most Californians condoned both official and unofficial harassment. Many Chinese left the mines seeking other employment, but hostility against them only increased as white wage-earners learned to fear them as competitors for jobs. Soon Chinese provided the "indispensable enemy" that unified white California laborers behind the federal Exclusion Act of 1882.

Scholars have examined in great detail the oppression that the Chinese endured in nineteenth-century California, but research has shifted to focus on the Chinese themselves. Historian Sucheng Chan has described the surprising variety of the Chinese experience. Companies of Chinese miners were able to save sufficient capital to buy claims and valuable mining equipment. In places like Marysville and Sacramento, independent merchants, artisans, and cooks catered to the needs of compatriots and even local whites. In the San Joaquin Valley, Chinese farmers raised the crops that fed many mining camps and towns. Despite hatred and discrimination, some sojourners managed to succeed in the gold rush era. Conditions for California Chinese deteriorated in the 1870s and '80s, however, as competition increased, opportunities faded, and economic recessions prompted whites to more forceful expressions of hostility.

African American Argonauts

Anti-Chinese sentiment in gold rush California probably lessened hostility toward black people, who were relatively few despite their presence since the Spanish settled in Los Angeles. By the end of the Mexican period, identifiable black Californios numbered only a handful, but the gold rush raised their numbers to 2,000 by 1852, and 4,000 by 1860. Many early arrivals were slaves brought west to work in the mines. After the constitutional ban on slavery in 1849 and statehood in 1850, those who remained were frequently retained by their masters as indentured servants. A few free blacks, like Dame Shirley's Paganini Ned, found work in the mines, but most settled in towns like Sacramento, Stockton, San Francisco, and Marysville.

Although the constitution prohibited slavery, free blacks enjoyed few protections under California law. Like the Chinese, the state constitution denied them suffrage and, in 1850, the legislature barred black testimony against whites in court matters. That same year, a black woman undertook one of the earliest attempts to overcome the ban when Sarah Carrol of Sacramento filed a charge of grand larceny against her white common-law husband. Her case was dismissed when the defendant pointed out that there was "none but Colored testimony against him."

Coupled with a state fugitive slave law that allowed slave masters to retain ownership of their slaves while "visiting" the state, the testimony ban threatened all black Californians. In 1856, a Missourian named Brown asked Auburn authorities to arrest Lucy, a free black woman, as a fugitive slave. Local residents felt Brown knew his father had freed Lucy before she immigrated to California, and was simply hoping to profit from California's testimony ban. Lucy called for her (white) lawyer, with whom she had prudently deposited papers proving her status. The ambiguity of California law meant that blacks were neither slaves nor citizens.

Some slaves found friends in California. In 1851, Bridget "Biddy" Mason, a slave from Mississippi, arrived by way of Utah with her three children, several other slaves, and her Mormon master, Robert Smith. Mason met free blacks in Los Angeles and San Bernardino counties, including Robert Owens, a local businessman and property owner. When Smith decided to take his slaves to Texas in 1855, Mason's friends persuaded local authorities to issue a writ of habeas corpus for her. Accompanied by deputies and his own *vaqueros*, Owens removed Mason and her enslaved companions to the safety of the county jail. A sympathetic judge thwarted the testimony ban by taking Mason's testimony in chambers. In a landmark decision, the court freed Mason, her three children, and eleven others. Employed by black physician John Strother Griffin, Mason established herself as a midwife and nurse, using skills in folk medicine probably learned on the plantation and perhaps from Mexican *curanderas* in Los Angeles. She later bought property on Spring Street to provide a home for herself and her children. During the 1880s she sold part of her land for $1,500 and built a commercial building on another parcel, eventually amassing a sizeable fortune in southern California real estate. In the interim, Mason helped establish the First African Methodist Episcopal Church (sometimes paying its minister from her own funds), becoming well known and respected for her public and private philanthropy to all races.

Archy Lee, also from Mississippi, arrived in Sacramento with his owner, Charles Stovall, in October 1857. When Stovall proposed to return to Mississippi in January, Lee protested that he was free under California's constitution and found refuge in the local black community. With the sheriff's help, Stovall arrested Lee and the case came to trial later that month. A county judge ruled in Lee's favor, finding that Stovall was a resident of California and thus could not own slaves. Stovall had already arranged for a second arrest by state authorities. This time, the sympathies of the judge, former California governor Peter Burnett, lay with Stovall. In February, the state court declared Lee Stovall's property. Stovall quickly tried to spirit Lee away, but his escape was blocked by a local black civil rights organization, the California Colored Convention. Both Lee and Stovall were taken into custody and the Convention went to work on Lee's defense. The men were aided by black women's organizations in San Francisco and Sacramento, which held dances and crafts fairs to raise funds for legal fees. In March, a federal judge ruled that Lee was free. Still trying to capitalize on gaps between legal jurisdictions, Stovall claimed to a U.S. Commissioner (a Southerner) that Lee was violating the 1850 Fugitive Slave Act. This maneuver also failed and on April 14, 1858, Archy Lee was declared a free man. He quickly exercised that freedom by heading for the Fraser River mines—and a more predictable legal climate—in British Columbia.

Although the Mason and Lee cases affirmed California's ban on slavery, laws still denied black people voting and testimony rights. During the 1850s, activists organized three statewide Colored Conventions to petition the legislature for change, especially for voting rights. Lawmakers resisted until 1863, when federal authorities forced California to rescind its limits on black suffrage. California's testimony ban stood until 1870, when it was overturned by the federal Civil Rights Act, passed to enforce post–Civil War amendments to the U.S. Constitution.

In the interim, black Californians relied on their own resources. Philip Alexander Bell's *Pacific Appeal* appeared in 1862, and businesses and benevolent associations provided stability and identity. In Sacramento, black women led the fight to desegregate public schools. When successful businesswoman Mary Ellen Pleasant was ejected from a San Francisco trolley, she sued the streetcar company. By her lawsuit, Pleasant demanded more than simple transportation: she was also claiming her right to be treated like a lady in public, deserving of the same courtesies enjoyed by white women of her class. In the landmark decision, Pleasant won her suit but later lost on appeal. Although they were not immediately successful, lawsuits like Pleasant's eventually undermined the legal foundations of segregation in California.

Californios and the Land-Grant Question

When California became a state, about 14 million of its acres were included in more than 800 land grants, ranging in size from one square league (4,426 acres) to eleven square leagues. Often called "Spanish," most grants had been made by Mexico, and all were protected under the Treaty of Guadalupe Hidalgo. Large holdings had made sense in Mexican California: a small population occupied the province and vast tracts were vital to cattle-grazing. Abundant land also resulted in casual boundaries that lacked surveyors' precision and relied on natural features, crude maps called *diseños* (designs), and descriptions that often included the phrase *un poco mas o menos* (a little more or less). Mexican law stipulated residence and improvement to validate titles, but a home and a few outbuildings sufficed on cattle-raising *haciendas*. Americans, in contrast, were accustomed to quarter-section (160-acre) public grants, intensively farmed, with fences marking boundaries and improvements clearly visible. Therefore, they frequently squatted on apparently vacant rancho land. Conflict with grantees inevitably resulted.

Inconsistent opinions compounded discord. Captain Henry W. Halleck's 1849 investigation concluded that most Mexican titles were legally flawed and that many were outright fraud. Only a year later, William Carey Jones examined the matter for the U.S. Secretary of the Interior and determined that most grants were legal under Mexican or American law. (It is worth noting that Jones was married to Jessie Benton Frémont's sister, and one of the contested claims included the Mariposa estate belonging to his brother-in-law, John C. Frémont).

Following the outbreak of violence between squatters and rancho claimants during the summer of 1850, Congress moved quickly to resolve the thorny problems of property titles and boundaries. The controversial Land Act of 1851 forced Californios to prove the validity of their titles in order to receive a federal land patent confirming their rightful possession. In the interim, their titles remained uncertain and vulnerable to the competing claims of squatters, who argued that they were rightfully occupying public lands, not private property. Hoping to restore order and clarity, Congress authorized the President to appoint a three-member commission to review titles, and required claimants to present proof of their claims within two years. Claimants and other interested parties were allowed to appeal the Commission's rulings in federal court.

Eventually 813 claims were filed under the Land Act. The problems claimants encountered were substantial. Their documentation often was missing or difficult to locate. Commission meetings were held in San Francisco from 1852 to 1856 (one session met in Los Angeles), which required frequent and expensive travel. Few Californios spoke English well enough to defend themselves, adding lawyer fees to their costs. Even those whose grants were ultimately confirmed faced as many as six hearings before receiving patented titles, and the process could require two decades or more. Litigation time averaged 17 years. In the meantime, rancheros watched estates dwindle as squatters invaded and as land was sold to pay attorneys' fees, survey costs, taxes, and other obligations.

The experiences of María Amparo Ruiz de Burton demonstrate the difficulty Latinas faced in the American legal system. María was born in Baja California in 1832 to an elite, land-holding family. When the Treaty of Guadalupe Hidalgo ended the Mexican War, American soldiers like Captain Henry S. Burton began returning from Baja to the States. Burton arranged to bring over 400 Baja Californians, including María, to settle and farm near Monterey. Maria and Burton soon married and moved to San Diego, where Burton took command of the army post and purchased part of a large Mexican grant, Rancho Jamul. In 1869 he died, leaving Maria behind with two small children. In theory, California law and the Treaty of Guadalupe Hidalgo protected María's title to Rancho Jamul. Unfortunately, the Land Act required Maria to defend her title against squatters who promptly filed 160-acre claims on her land, which remained tied up in the courts until long after her death in 1895. Like many Latinas, Ruiz de Burton died in poverty.

The cumbersome legal machinery set in motion by the Land Act generated widely disparate outcomes. The Serrano family lost the San Diego-area rancho it had occupied since 1819 because it relied on a temporary permit to establish the origins of its grant. Had the Serranos not presented that document, their title would have been confirmed on the basis of longevity of occupancy. In contrast, Frémont's title to the Mariposa Estate was upheld, even though original grantee Juan B. Alvarado had utterly failed to comply with Mexican law requiring occupancy (he had never even seen the place). The land commission ultimately confirmed 512 titles. Holders of 132 denied claims appealed to the courts, more than 100 of them successfully. Government attorneys appealed more than 400 cases but won only five.

Outright frauds abounded as well. José Limantour's claim to four square leagues that included most of San Francisco was confirmed in 1853, forcing property owners to purchase quit claim deeds from him. Two years later, Limantour's documents proved to be forgeries, and he departed for Mexico considerably richer.

The Land Act accelerated the decline of the Californios, but they were not the only losers. Prolonged uncertainty deterred settlers from purchasing property for homes or farms and impeded operation of the Pre-Emption Act of 1841, the Homestead Act of 1862, and similar policies. Few would risk buying or improving land without assurance of valid titles. Finally, by the time cases were adjudicated, much of the property was in the hands of speculators, setting the stage for the state's emphasis on agribusiness rather than traditional family farming.

Pioneer Agriculture

Despite land title problems, substantial agricultural development began during the 1850s, stimulated by the demands of an exploding population. At first, imports from Oregon, Hawaii, and Latin America satisfied needs, but persistent shortages and inflated prices combined with the potential of rich soil and good climate to encourage change. Many experienced farmers among the Argonauts took a brief fling at mining and then turned to more familiar and hopefully profitable pursuits.

Cattle ranchers felt the impact of the gold rush first, as prices soared toward $500 a head. By the mid-1850s, more than three million animals grazed on the "thousand hills" of Southern California and the ranges of the San Joaquin Valley, but the golden era ended abruptly. Increased production and rising competition drove down prices, over-grazing depleted natural grasslands, and many ranchers refused to modernize their methods. Finally, a disastrous flood in the winter of 1861–62, followed by droughts lasting through 1864, wiped out thousands of cattle and permanently crippled an industry that had once seemed so promising.

During the same years, however, farmers began to diversify local agriculture. Because of the time and expense involved in shipping produce, even to local markets, they selected growing areas proximate to population and mining centers. They also chose higher rainfall locales or those with artesian wells or flowing streams to provide water. As a result, most early agricultural development clustered in the northern and central regions, especially adjacent to San Francisco Bay and in fertile valley districts such as those near Visalia. By dry farming or planting in the autumn to capitalize on winter rains, pioneer farmers grew standard frontier crops: wheat, barley, oats, and other small grains.

Another agricultural area developed in the Delta formed by the intermingling of the Sacramento and San Joaquin rivers. Before 1848, the Delta was a region of 1,000-plus square miles of meandering streams, sloughs, and tule marshes. Half the Delta was at or below sea level, protected from flooding by natural levees along the riverbanks. Heavy outflows from inland streams kept the sea at bay, and most waterways were fresh most of the time. A natural reservoir, the Delta collected half the state's freshwater runoff before discharging it into San Francisco Bay. In the gold rush era, steamers plied the rivers between San Francisco and inland ports, and pioneers settled along Delta riverbanks, cutting trees to sell as firewood to steam-powered riverboats. Others

Pacific Brewery Advertisement, *Trinity Journal*

Frederick Walter, a German immigrant, established Weaverville's Pacific Brewery in 1852. He and entrepreneurs like him brought creature comforts to remote mining districts. They also brought new economic, political, and social leadership to gold rush California. Both the *Trinity Journal* and Walter's brewery building still exist. *Collection of William A. Bullough.*

quickly recognized the Delta's agricultural potential: the soil was rich, water was close at hand, and passing riverboats offered access to urban markets. By 1851, settlers were building levees of peat and tule sod blocks to enclose artificial, below-sea-level "islands" to raise corn, wheat, cattle, vegetables, and orchard crops. Reclamation was slow and grueling, but crop yields and profits were large.

Until the mid-1860s, when California farmers began shipping surplus wheat to Great Britain, growers produced only modest harvests that were milled and sold locally. Traditional methods also permitted cultivation of small-scale vegetable plots and fruit orchards, and raising limited quantities of poultry and dairy cattle, but little more. In Southern California, renovated Mexican-era irrigation systems or new ones built by Mormons at San Bernardino and German immigrants at Anaheim allowed only limited agricultural development during the 1850s and '60s.

Conditions confounded growers of many crops but were ideal for wine and brandy production, which had several advantages. Argonauts' legendary thirst provided a market, grapes needed minimal irrigation, processing required no complex equipment, and products could be transported without fear of spoilage. Cuttings from mission vineyards provided the original basis for expanding ordinary wine production in areas near Missions San Gabriel and San Fernando during the early 1850s. By the '60s, the industry spread to San Francisco Bay area counties, where conditions were ideal. Individuals like Agoston Haraszthy—the Hungarian-born father of California viticulture who introduced European grape varieties to the state—made raising grapes for wine-making California's leading fruit industry by 1870. Quality remained inconsistent, but quantity was substantial: two million gallons of wine annually from 40,000 acres of vineyards.

By 1870, 25,000 farms then valued at $141 million operated in the state, and reports of 22-pound onions, 200-pound squash, and two-foot-long radishes suggested enormous potential. Nevertheless, agricultural progress during the 1850s and '60s was erratic. Production and profits failed to match expectations and most farmers shunned experimentation. Disputed titles to Mexican grants inhibited improvement, and labor and capital remained both scarce and expensive. Hostile interests—miners and cattlemen—influenced policies that deterred farmers: legislative apportionment that left agriculture underrepresented, heavy taxes on improved farm land, fence laws that placed burdens for compliance on farmers, and inconsistent water laws that discouraged

irrigation. Furthermore, California remained *terra incognita* to farmers from other regions, and no public agency existed to supply information about such matters as climate, rainfall, or effective irrigation practices. Finally, markets offered little incentive: the small, dispersed local population grew slowly after the early 1850s, and the state was too remote from potential alternate customers. Indeed, when the trans-continental rails met in 1869, California had only one potentially profitable farm product to offer East Coast consumers: wine.

Land Speculation on the Urban Frontier

Frequently regarded as a recent California phenomenon, speculation in urban real estate began even before American possession was confirmed. In 1846, Thomas O. Larkin and Robert Semple bought a plot on the Carquinez Strait from Mariano Vallejo, surveyed a town site, and called the place "Francisca." They advertised its fog-free deep-water port and direct access to the interior in Semple's *Californian* and began to sell lots. Meanwhile, in January 1847, Yerba Buena speculators like Sam Brannan convinced the local government to change their town's name to San Francisco and to hire surveyor Jasper O'Farrell to lay out a city plan. Contemptuous of would-be competitors, Semple gave away his San Francisco property—worth $500,000 two years later—and changed his new town's name to "Benicia."

Directly across the Bay, another "instant city" appeared. In 1849, Horace Carpentier arrived and, a year later, the young lawyer and two partners squatted on Vicente Peralta's land and somehow convinced the *don* to grant them a lease. Within weeks, they hired a surveyor to plot a town, filed a claim under the Pre-Emption Act of 1841, and began selling lots. Carpentier then appealed to his friend David Broderick, who persuaded the state legislature to incorporate it as the town of Oakland in 1852. Next, the three partners set up a government, elected themselves to office, and granted to Carpentier Oakland's entire waterfront and rights to collect use fees for 37 years.

Other prospective town-sites—some, like Vallejo, ambitious to displace San Francisco—appeared around the Bay and in Southern California during the 1850s. Speculators also were active in the interior, among them Stephen J. Field. Shortly after he arrived in 1849, he journeyed to the junction of the Yuba and Feather rivers where he found real estate promotion in full swing. He was impressed:

It was a beautiful spot, covered with oaks, and it reminded me of the parks of England. I saw at once that the place, from its position at the head of practical navigation [to the gold regions], was designed to become an important depot for the neighboring mines and that its beauty and salubrity made it a pleasant place for residence.

Field's assets totaled $20, but he subscribed for 65 parcels of land at $250 each, precipitating a rumor that "a great capitalist had arrived to invest in lots in this rising town." Because Field was an attorney, residents asked him to draw up deeds of sale and to record them. They also elected him *alcalde* and justice of the peace, and he participated in naming the town "Marysville" for the only American woman around. Profits from such ventures could be spectacular, as Field recorded: "At one time I had $14,000 in gold dust in my safe." But so could losses: "I [later] lost all that I made more quickly than I had acquired it and found myself also in debt."

Places like Marysville, Sacramento City, and other towns founded on speculation played an important role in the history of the state, as did settlements that originated as mining camps. In 1850, for example, John Weaver and two companions built cabins near a creek in remote Trinity County, and hundreds of miners congregated to make Weaverville a typically rowdy mining camp. Quickly, however, merchants, artisans, brewers, professionals, clergymen, and other permanent settlers arrived, some with their families. In 1857, the editor of the *Trinity Journal* was able to boast with pride,

> It is pleasant to note the change in the state of society in this place which a few years have effected. Formerly every other house was a gambling saloon, or something equally as bad. Fatal quarrels were of daily and nightly occurrence; drunken men paraded in the streets; blasphemy was heard on every side, and law and order were things heard of but never seen. Now gambling is abolished; a very drunk person is a curiosity; deadly assaults are of rare occurrence. Ladies now promenade our streets and the air resounds with the innocent prattle of little children.

Residents of Weaverville had created in the wilderness a microcosm of urban American society complete with churches, schools, a water system, a fire company, two hospitals, brick business buildings, and a basic town plan. Ethnic associations included the Sons of Hibernia, the German Citizens Society, and a *Turnverein* (gymnastics club), a Jewish *minyan*, and two Chinese tongs. A brass band performed at public and private functions, while the Cosmopolitan Art Association, Odd Fellows and Masonic lodges, and active partisan associations contributed to cultural, social, and political life, as did two newspapers that kept residents in touch with local, state, and national affairs.

Cultural Americanization

The transformation of California from Hispanic to American emanated from San Francisco, the "instant city." A crude village fronting a mud flat in 1848, it astounded a visitor in 1856:

> That a city of the respectability of San Francisco could be raised in the short space of five or six years, appears incredible. Possessing the appearance of an old city of a century . . . it conveys to the mind the idea of being within a day's journey of the Emporium of the nation.

San Francisco, the "Instant City," in 1852
Courtesy of The Bancroft Library, University of California, Berkeley.

The vista was no accident: promoters defied politics, logic, and geography to create it, surveying a town site and selling lots, some under water. When Argonauts reached San Francisco in 1849, derelict ships moored on the shoreline provided shelter, warehouses, offices, hotels, and even a jail. As vessels sank or burned, debris and earthen fill were used to cover them and to provide more land for sale and development.

Speculators pushed wharves hundreds of yards into the bay, and during the 1860s defeated the "Bulkhead

New England in California

Departing members of the Boston & California Joint Stock Mining and Trading Co. carried these instructions to California: "Take your Bibles in one hand and your good New England civilization in the other." Many remembered the advice, establishing a tradition that persisted through the nineteenth century. In 1895, for example, Congregationalists in Lewiston built this New England-style church overlooking the cemetery that began receiving pioneers in the 1850s. *Photograph by William A. Bullough.*

Bill" scheme to make the public waterfront a private monopoly. Wells Fargo's and Adams & Company's express and banking operations and the Merchant's Exchange established headquarters in the Montgomery Block, an office building completed in 1853, and made San Francisco the nexus of state economic activity. Three years later, the Consolidation Act merged city and county governments, provided a police force, and reorganized volunteer fire companies to protect citizens and property. Streets that were "impassable, not even jackassable" received attention, and such elite neighborhoods as Rincon Hill and South Park emerged by the mid-1850s. The Parker House and El Dorado hotels, restaurants like the Poulet d'Or (later the "Poodle Dog"), and theaters presenting renowned performers adorned the emerging urban landscape. By 1860, San Francisco's population of 57,000 ranked it 15th among American cities and first among cities west of the Mississippi River.

Physical and economic development, however, were not the city's only contributions to Americanization. In 1848, Timothy Dwight Hunt took leave of his Presbyterian congregation in Hawaii—"for three months with the privilege of continued absence . . . as Providence should dictate"—to become chaplain to San Franciscans of all Protestant denominations. Five years later, the city boasted 30 houses of worship, including six Roman Catholic churches and two synagogues. The Roman Catholic Church created the Archdiocese of San Francisco with Bishop Joseph S. Alemany in charge and, in 1860, Thomas Starr King arrived in San Francisco to assume the pastorship of the local Unitarian congregation and to become one of the city's most popular preachers. During the Civil War years, Starr King's eloquent speeches secured Californians' support for the U.S. Sanitary Commission and helped to cement loyalty to the Union. Equally eloquent descriptions of California's flora and fauna placed him among America's foremost naturalists by the time of his death in 1864 at age 40.

American journalism and literature, too, arrived in California by way of San Francisco. Two weekly newspapers, Sam Brannan's *California Star* and Robert Semple's *Californian*, merged in 1849 to become the *Daily Alta California*. Literary journals also appeared: *The Golden Era* (1852) with 2,200 subscribers in the city and 1,100 more in mining towns, *Hutching's Illustrated California Magazine* (1856), the *Californian* (1864), and *Overland Monthly* (1868). Newspapers and journals brought the work of Bret Harte, Ina Coolbrith, Joaquin Miller, Mark Twain, and others to eager local readers. And in 1854, John Rollin Ridge established a national reputation and created a historical myth with *The Life and Adventures of Joaquin Murieta.*

But San Francisco did not monopolize the process of cultural Americanization. Many mining district towns followed Weaverville's course, and familiar institutions, including common schools, soon linked residents with the rest of the nation. Although early legislatures sanctioned public education, in 1854 the state superintendent of public instruction Andrew Jackson Moulder complained that only 4,000 students attended any state-supported school, and education remained principally a local function. A dozen years later, his successor John Swett—a New Englander called the "Horace Mann of the Pacific"—influenced passage of a comprehensive "Act to Provide a System of Common Schools in California." In the interim, responsibility fell to private groups, including black churches, and communities like North San Juan, where a handful of residents in 1857 contributed $2,000 to build a schoolhouse and employ a teacher.

Thus, by the end of the gold rush era, the 31st state, its people, and its institutions were thoroughly Americanized, bound to the Union during the crisis of the Civil War and prepared to capitalize on the Comstock silver strike in Nevada and the completion of the transcontinental railway in 1869.

The Bloomer Cut on the Central Pacific Railway Line, West of Auburn, in the 1860s

In late-nineteenth-century California, new railways disrupted society as well as nature. *California State Railroad Museum.*

PART FIVE

The Railroad Era

The railroad was the most significant nineteenth-century technology. It generated new patterns of transportation, communication, time, and distance, which in turn revolutionized economies, institutions, and personal and social behavior. Railroads not only accelerated settlement of the West, but also forged much of what we call "modern" in American life. Like the rest of the nation, California experienced these transformations beginning in the 1860s and continuing into the twentieth century.

As is often true of new technologies, the railroad's influences in California were complex and contradictory. This was evident from the outset of the railway era. Like most Americans, Californians associated the railroad with individual enrichment and community progress. This was especially true after 1855, when the mines petered out, industrial development lagged, immigration slowed, and the state was rocked by frequent depressions. Many Californians saw railways as the panacea for these problems. As one writer put it in 1856, "If we shall live to see the day when the iron horse, with his impetuous speed, shall come from the Atlantic to quench his fiery thirst in the cool waters of the Pacific, then will our fondest visions have been realized and clouds of doubt will no longer obscure the bright future of California."

At least one Californian disagreed. In the 1860s, Henry George was an itinerant San Francisco-area journalist. As the first transcontinental railroad was rushing toward the Pacific Coast, George published a dour article in the *Overland Monthly* entitled "What the Railroads Will Bring Us." "The California of the new era will be greater, richer, more powerful than the California of the past," George admitted, but the railways would also aggravate social inequities and make the state more vulnerable to national economic upheavals. He also regretted that "the consequent great increase of business and population will not be a benefit to all of us but only to a portion. As a general rule . . . those who *have*, it will make wealthier; for those who *have not*, it will make it more difficult to get." "The locomotive is a great centralizer," he warned. "It kills little towns and builds up great cities, and in the same way kills little businesses and builds up great ones." George also predicted that the railway would give rise to "large corporations and other special interests," phrases that already described California's Central Pacific Railroad, with its immense capital, employee force, and widespread political influence. "Can we rely," he wondered, "upon sufficient intelligence, independence and virtue among the many to resist the political effects of the concentration of great wealth in the hands of a few?" Writing these words in 1868, before the rail line was even finished, George's dissenting voice proved prophetic.

The sweet promises of progress that accompanied railroad construction in the 1860s soured in the '70s. Ironically, as was true throughout the nation, the railway age brought great economic development, cultural maturation, and modernization, but with it came confusion and conflict. Economic and political dissent intensified, with much of citizens' ire now directed toward the Southern Pacific Railroad, the monopolistic corporation formed by the merger of the Central Pacific and most other lines serving the state. But conflict in California was much more complicated than simple opposition by the masses to the era's most powerful corporations. Although some groups focused their criticisms on corporate power, especially that of railroads, other symptoms of the dramatic changes of the late-nineteenth century became battlegrounds as well: water and agricultural development, urban growth, social inequality, interethnic tensions, resource and environmental policies, sectional and intercommunity rivalries. As a result, from the 1860s to the '80s, California reaped the profits of the new technological order, while continuing to bear the burdens of an older, equally turbulent society.

Confrontation

at Mussel Slough

13

1880

Popular folklore and many scholarly histories agree that the Central Valley land war that emerged between the railroad and settlers was a pivotal event, a battle symbolic of that era's larger conflicts between ordinary citizens and emerging corporate power. In exchange for construction of a southern transcontinental rail line through the area, Congress had granted considerable Central Valley land to the Southern Pacific Railroad, one company controlled by the near transportation monopoly assembled by the owners of the Central Pacific Railroad. Some settlers of the Mussel Slough district of the Tulare Basin, however, contended that the grant was illegal. They challenged the railroad's title and moved onto the land without permission. A decade of conflict ensued, culminating in the famous gun battle at Mussel Slough on May 11, 1880.

Into the twenty-first century, historians and popular writers have generally relied on local legend and secondhand accounts to side with the settlers against the Southern Pacific. For many students of California history, the settlers' contest with the railroad epitomized the corruption of big business in the industrial era, and the struggle between private greed and public good. On the other hand, primary evidence—original letters, railroad records, public documents, and contemporary newspapers—reveals a far more complicated story, one in which guilt and innocence are difficult to assess. The drama at Mussel Slough is more than a struggle between "good" and "evil," "the people" versus "big business." The events that unfolded around the Tragedy Oak are part of a larger saga of sweeping economic, social, and environmental change, the complex interplay between dreams of success and personal failure, and the bewildering conflicts that followed the rails into late-nineteenth-century California.

On the bright morning of May 11, 1880, U.S. Marshal Alonzo W. Poole climbed into a buggy and headed away from Hanford, a small town in what was then Tulare County. His companion was railroad land-grader William H. Clark. As the men rode north through the unpaved streets of the village and through the flat fields beyond, Poole could see that a dry spell hung over Mussel Slough. Winter rains had not come. Roadside weeds shriveled in the dust, irrigation ditches ran dry, and thin clumps of sun-burned grain baked in the fields. Poole detested his orders. After years of struggle over Southern Pacific Railroad land-grant titles, a federal court had decided that squatters were illegally occupying the company's land. Marshal Poole was charged with evicting them, while Clark was to identify the tracts. Like many Californians, Poole sided with the squatters, some of whom were old friends. But he was determined to do his duty.

Armed with light revolvers, Poole and Clark were headed five miles northwest toward the tracts of land that Mills Hartt and Walter Crow had purchased from the railroad two years earlier. Along the way, Poole and Clark met up with a wagon carrying Hartt and Crow, and the men drove on together. Hartt and Crow had packed pistols, rifles, and shotguns under their wagon seat.

As soon as Poole had left town, riders from the Settler's Grand League's "militia" had set out to alert John Storer that the marshal was on his way. Storer and Henry Brewer were squatting on Crow's land. The disputed lot was an unfenced, 320-acre wheat field that Brewer and Storer had been cultivating for several years. As was typical in Mussel Slough, the disputed parcel was adjacent to their valid claim on non-railroad land—an 80-acre homestead on which Brewer had built a house and barn. Storer intercepted Poole and Clark on the road and the men stopped and spoke quietly. Crow repeated his offer to sell the land to Storer and Brewer. Storer agreed to repeat the offer to Brewer and the men continued together.

The party reached the property around 10:30 AM, and found Brewer plowing the field. Just as Storer rode ahead to confer with Brewer, 40 or 50 men with rifles rode onto the land and halted 50 yards away. Crow and Hartt reached for their firearms, but the marshal cautioned against it. "I think I had better go and meet them," Poole muttered, and he jumped down and strode towards the riders.

As much as any other region of post-gold-rush California, residents of Mussel Slough experienced the railway era's contradictions and conflicts. The slough occupied the west side of Tulare Basin, a natural sink in the central San Joaquin Valley. Snow-fed streams like Kings River and Mussel Slough, one of its branches, meandered westward from the Sierra Nevada and finally emptied into Tulare Lake. Fertile soils, gentle slopes, and abundant surface and groundwater gave the basin unusual agricultural promise. Yet, lacking transportation, the Mussel Slough country, like most of California, was virtually undeveloped as late as 1870. During the gold rush, the eastern basin, with more rainfall and nearer mining markets, had become one of California's first thriving agricultural and cattle-raising areas. Visalia, hub of the region's economy and seat of Tulare County after 1852, quickly grew into the largest valley town south of Stockton. Twenty miles westward, however, the air was dry and the settlers few.

The country began to change in 1869, when the Southern Pacific Railroad Company started laying rails south from San José. Enticed by a Congressional land grant, the company intended to run the line south-eastward across the Coast Range, through the Mussel Slough basin, down the San Joaquin Valley to Southern California, and east across the desert to the Colorado River. A few months after it began, however, construction stopped at Tres Piños, south of Hollister, where rugged mountains blocked access to the Tulare Basin. Determined to tap valley's rich agricultural potential, the company's new owners, the famous "Big Four"—Leland Stanford, Collis P. Huntington, Charles Crocker, and Mark Hopkins—decided instead to extend a branch of their completed railway, the Central Pacific, southward into the San Joaquin Valley.

Lacking a federal land grant for their Central Pacific branch line, the Big Four asked Visalia and Tulare County to provide a cash subsidy and right-of-way through the town, which lay east of the best route down the valley. This was a common way to encourage railway construction nationwide, but the subsidy demand provoked disagreement. Residents of Visalia approved the plan, which would promote the town and improve their businesses. Stage and wagon companies objected vociferously, fearing railroad competition. Settlements left off the projected rail line also objected, as did cattlemen who feared an invasion of farmers on their open ranges. From the beginning,

Tulare County was divided between pro- and anti-railroad factions.

In 1870 anti-railroad Governor Henry H. Haight vetoed legislation that would have allowed San Joaquin Valley counties to subsidize railroad construction. The Central Pacific decided to avoid the existing settlements, bypass Visalia, and to build the cheapest, most direct route through the valley's uninhabited central lowlands. Crews completed the Central Pacific branch line to Goshen, west of Visalia, in 1872, where it joined the as-yet unbuilt Southern Pacific route through Mussel Slough country. An independent railroad linked Visalia to the Southern Pacific line at Goshen two years later, but many valley residents still resented the company. Then in 1872, the Southern Pacific Railroad, now under its own corporate name, resumed construction of its main line on its route southward from Goshen to Los Angeles (reached in 1876) and a transcontinental connection in Texas in (1881).

Racing to acquire as much of its federal land grant as possible before the 1878 deadline stipulated by Congress, the Southern Pacific in 1877 completed a spur line along its approved route west of Goshen through the Mussel Slough country. New rail towns sprang up at Hanford, Lemoore, and Huron. Construction halted at Huron in 1877, at the eastern edge of the rugged coastal mountains, however, and the gap in the line was never closed.

Even before the railroad built through it, business in Mussel Slough country had quickened. Crops could now be hauled by wagon the short distance east to Goshen and other railheads on the Central/Southern Pacific main line, creating new markets and spurring new development. Settlers poured into the district. Unoccupied and open grazing lands were subdivided and shifted to hay, grains and, where water was available, fruit and specialty crops. During the early 1870s, sloping land and abundant flowing water convinced some more well-to-do landowners to form mutual companies to dig irrigation canals from the Kings River and Mussel Slough. Ditches supplied water to more than 60,000 acres by 1879, and Mussel Slough had developed into one of California's first intensively cultivated and irrigated small-farm regions. Newly irrigated farms specialized in corn, alfalfa, and, increasingly, vegetables, deciduous fruits, and dairy cattle. Unirrigated farms were limited to less profitable dry-farming of grain, hay, and a few other crops. Tulare County's population increased nearly 150 percent in the ten years after 1870, from 4,500 to 11,300—three times the state's slow rate of growth—with most of the development around Mussel Slough.

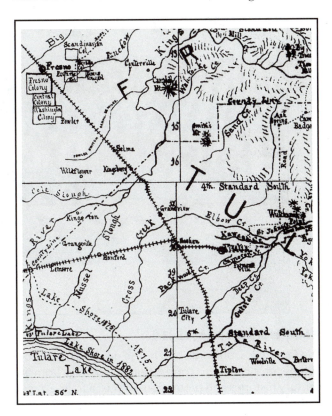

The Mussel Slough of Tulare and Fresno Counties in 1883

This contemporary map illustrates the major features of Mussel Slough geography in the late-nineteenth century, as well as the location of the Central/Southern Pacific's main north-south rail line bisecting the valley. Tulare Lake now has nearly vanished, its former bottom drained and covered with large corporate farms. *Courtesy of the California History Room, California State Library, Sacramento, California.*

Population growth and exploding agriculture transformed the countryside. At midcentury, the federal government had surveyed the San Joaquin Valley into the traditional gridiron of sections, each one square mile, or 640 acres, and offered them for purchase. Before the railroad, most public land in the Mussel Slough area was unsold. As the railroad approached in the early 1870s, hundreds of buyers and homesteaders converged on the Tulare Basin, many of them small-scale speculators who claimed the land in expectation of price increases. Competition for good locations was keen, and furious trading drove prices for unimproved farmland from $1 to $2 per acre in 1870 to $10 to $20 per acre by 1880.

The scramble for land put newcomers on a collision course with the Southern Pacific even before railroad

A Mussel Slough Farm, 1883

The farm fields, orchards, and house gardens made possible by irrigation and railway development along Mussel Slough are clear in this contemporary woodcut from an early county history. Typical of illustrations in nineteenth-century histories and promotional tracts, a train—a mechanical symbol of economic and cultural progress—chugs in the distance. *Courtesy of the California History Room, California State Library, Sacramento, California.*

tracks entered the area. To subsidize and encourage construction, the federal government had already reserved for the railroad nearly half the unclaimed public land in the Mussel Slough region, in odd-numbered, one-mile-square sections, in a checkerboard on either side of the route from Goshen to the dead end at Huron. The future railroad land grant was closed to other entries or purchase. The intervening even-numbered sections remained public land, however, open for private parties to homestead or buy. Unfortunately for settlers, the cumbersome "patenting" procedure intended to transfer deeds smoothly from the government to the railroad companies quickly broke down, producing decades of legal wrangling.

Competing county, state, and federal legal maneuvers added to the chaos. The 1866 federal land-grant law allowed the railroad to choose its own route between San Francisco Bay and the Colorado River, but the company's state incorporation charter stated that it intended to build a main line southward along the coast to San Diego. In early 1867, however, the federal Department of the Interior accepted a map by the Southern Pacific's original owners for a route revision through the San Joaquin Valley south to Los Angeles and east to the Colorado River. The Department closed the vacant

public land to other settlement along the new line in the expectation that the railroad would eventually complete the route and be awarded title to the land.

Within a year, contrary pressure on the Interior Department was building. A group of coastal counties determined to secure the coastal rail line described in the state charter objected to the railroad's route change. A national ring of speculators led by the California land baron William S. Chapman had also lobbied against the railroad's valley route, hoping to add value to their holdings there and to monopolize forfeited, former railroad land in the valley. In 1868, the Secretary of the Interior, who personally opposed grants to railroad companies, ordered the Southern Pacific's land grant revoked on the grounds that the revised route violated the company's state charter. The secretary, however, lacked the legal authority to revise a law of Congress, and never actually restored the reserved land to public entry. The Big Four, who had just purchased Southern Pacific, joined valley communities to convince the Department, now headed by a different secretary, to suspend the order.

Official maps at government land offices continued to show land in the San Joaquin Valley as reserved for the railroad and closed to other settlement. In 1870 the railroad and valley residents persuaded Congress and the state legislature to confirm the legality of the altered route. Four years later, the Department of the Interior began issuing the railroad deeds for land along the completed segments of track from San José south to Tres Piños and from Goshen south to Bakersfield. But those years of uncertainty, when the Southern Pacific's title seemed in question, had raised a possibility in some people's minds that the railroad's land titles might someday be overturned. If that happened, valuable land along the tracks would be opened to other parties. As happened often across the West, squatter-speculators rushed into take up land along Mussel Slough in hopes of valuable free land.

John J. Doyle led the charge onto the railroad's lands. In 1870, he read a San Francisco news article predicting that the route controversy would one day void the railroad's land grant. Doyle sold his farm and moved onto reserved railroad land near the hamlet of Grangeville, a few miles north of the proposed rail line through Mussel Slough country.

A squatter by his own admission and now calling himself a lawyer, Doyle spread word across the valley that the railroad company's title was flawed. The squatter movement expanded quickly along with the boom caused by the railroad's building through Goshen to the east. By 1875 hundreds of claimants were squatting on railroad land throughout the Mussel Slough district. Doyle established a land business predicated on overturning railroad titles. He secretly contracted with several hundred neighbors to defeat the railroad's title for a fee of 25 cents per acre. The lure of free, fertile lands produced a speculative mania. Some settlers sold farms on government land and moved with their buildings to unoccupied railroad sections. Others expanded their legitimate farms to include adjacent railroad lands. Still others came from across the state to establish claims.

Those who flocked to Mussel Slough wrapped themselves in the mantle of American pioneering. Like other God-fearing small-scale farmers, they claimed, they had ventured forth in good faith into the desert, carving out new homes for their families on what was vacant public land. The railroad, they charged, was a corrupt, tyrannical monopoly that was using its illegitimate power to steal their hard-won farms and homes. A few Mussel Slough settlers actually were bona fide homesteaders whose claims the Department of the Interior did approve. But the great majority established their speculative claims after 1871 on land closed for granting to the railroad, on the gamble that the company would eventually lose its title. According to local land and tax records, however, few Mussel Slough squatters qualified as legitimate

settlers. Many did not inhabit their claims, residing on nearby farms or towns. Some had more than one claim on railroad land, or legally held the adjacent even-numbered government sections. Some had aggregate claims as much as several thousand acres.

Many settlers, particularly the leaders of the squatter movement, were clearly land speculators. The absence of capital improvements was one indication. Most squatters made only the barest investment of money or labor on their railroad claims. Admittedly, these were risky ventures, and settlers used the land accordingly: some lay vacant, some was used for grazing, and some was plowed and planted in unirrigated grain fields. Many squatters located the bulk of their improvements, including houses, barns, wells, irrigation systems, and fences, on their even-numbered sections, with their railroad lands almost untouched.

Doyle and other squatters cooperated to attack Southern Pacific's title. They trooped to the federal land office in Visalia to file mass claims under the preemption and homestead laws, charging that the Department of the Interior had invalidated the railroad's claim and reopened the land to settlement. Local federal land officers rejected virtually all these claims, since the railroad's granted land was reserved and closed to other settlement. Doyle appealed dozens of cases and, in each instance, the Department of the Interior upheld local land office decisions favoring the railroad. Squatters refiled claims several times under different federal land laws, typically with the same result. Doyle and the others lobbied Congress, protested against the issuing of more deeds to the railway, and unsuccessfully introduced bills to revoke the Southern Pacific grant or to legitimize their claims retroactively.

Southern Pacific officials were certainly capable of bribery or chicanery, but in this case, the claimants' major obstacle was their shaky legal position. Few understood how railroad land-grant law had evolved through the 1870s; most of the squatters' arguments had already been rendered moot by decisions of Congress, the United States attorney general, the secretary of the interior, and the courts. The Mussel Slough squatters were bucking nearly a decade of legal precedent, and their victory would have cast doubt over titles to millions of acres within dozens of railway land grants in nearly every western state. Undaunted, the squatters redoubled their efforts.

The claimants also took steps to keep the railroad from selling the disputed tracts to others. In 1878, 500 squatters founded the Settlers' Grand League, vowing to resist "the occupation of so-called railroad lands in the

Mussel Slough district by the Southern Pacific Railroad Company." Members' dues helped finance appeals, while their leaders lobbied politicians and built public sympathy. At the same time, the League warned that they would tear up tracks, burn depots, and incinerate the crops and buildings of anyone who tried to purchase land from the company. From headquarters at Hanford, Leaguers sent anonymous letters ordering land buyers, railway agents, and local residents who criticized the squatters out of the valley. Members assumed the paraphernalia befitting a secret society, including masks, hoods, and long red robes, evoking the Ku Klux Klan and other white-supremacy groups then popular in the

Thomas Jefferson McQuiddy, 1900

A former cavalry officer and secret service agent for the Confederacy, "Major" McQuiddy had come to Mussel Slough by way of Tennessee and Missouri in 1873. He purchased large tracts of even-numbered government sections near Hanford and, like some of his neighbors, moved over to establish claims on odd-numbered railroad sections. An experienced politician and soldier, McQuiddy emerged quickly as a leader in the new community, a natural choice for the Grand League's president and militia commander. *Courtesy of the California History Room, California State Library, Sacramento, California.*

southern states from which many Mussel Slough residents had recently migrated.

Troops of armed and hooded riders roamed the countryside, making nocturnal calls on railroad sympathizers and land buyers. Perry Phillips, for example, had feuded with the squatters for years. He repeatedly ignored the League's warnings to leave the land he had purchased from the railroad. On November 21, 1878, 150 night-riding Leaguers drove out Phillips's tenant, along with his terrified wife and children, then burned their home and possessions. A few days later, Leaguers captured Phillips and two employees on another disputed tract. They held them prisoner while men with 51 teams of horses plowed up Phillips' fields and turned the tract over to squatter James B. Fretwell. Phillips and the railway protested but local authorities took no action. Leaguers insisted that "Indians" were responsible for the attacks. Although it succeeded in generating some support, the League's methods also provoked opposition in the valley, undermining its efforts to unite local people against the railroad.

Into the spring of 1879, the Southern Pacific continued to file trespass complaints against some squatters. At a mass meeting in March, the League organized a "cavalry" commanded by its president, Thomas Jefferson McQuiddy. McQuiddy periodically drilled and paraded the settler militia through the streets of Hanford and other towns. Some Californians denounced the squatters' vigilantism, but in the depressed 1870s, many had come to believe that the railroad, with its political influence, high freight rates, and virtual transportation monopoly, was the root of the state's ills. Anti-railroad politicians, newspapers, and organizations rallied to the claimants' cause and urged them on to defeat the evil "Octopus." Fueling the settlers' armed resistance, the anti-railroad San Francisco *Chronicle* likened them to the colonial patriots at the Boston Tea Party. Unless the Southern Pacific ceased its oppression, the *Chronicle* warned, these farmers would "strike the first blow against land monopoly and corporate greed."

By the end of the 1870s, the Mussel Slough struggle was engulfed in a rising tide of anti-railroad politics. Labor unions and anti-monopoly political parties jumped on the settlers' bandwagon, including the Workingmen's Party of California (WPC), a San Francisco-based group generating statewide influence with its anti-Chinese, anti-corporate rhetoric. John Doyle, who also happened to be an official in the WPC, secured its endorsement of the squatters' cause. The WPC's fiery leader Denis Kearney delivered passionate orations to crowds at Grangeville, Hanford, and Lemoore in 1879, exhorting the squatters to defeat the Southern Pacific. According to one observer, when Kearney shouted "murder the red-eyed monsters" and promised to lead an army of 40,000 San Francisco workers to defend them from the corporate tyrant, the squatters "hurrahed as if they would split their throats."

Faced with such bitter opposition, the railroad was in a quandary. The Southern Pacific viewed its land as a legitimate corporate asset, justly earned through the risk and expense of laying tracks through uninhabited country. But the company's overall objective was still to manage its land grant in a businesslike fashion, leading to population growth, economic development, freight and passenger revenues, and thus corporate profits. Thus the railway initially took a conciliatory stance toward its rival claimants.

Over its entire land grant in five states, the company generally enjoyed cordial relations with homesteaders and buyers on its lands, but conflicts inevitably arose. Faulty surveys and maps, sloppy administration, or honest errors by settlers, government land officials, and the railroad resulted in a number of overlapping claims. Most conflicts were resolved amicably, often with the railroad withdrawing its claim or selling to settlers at the government price. Some disagreements became tangled and acrimonious, leaving a residue of bitterness against the Southern Pacific.

Not all the railroad's contestants, however, were good-faith settlers. As typically happened on American frontiers, squatters and resource thieves often invaded railroad lands. These persistent interlopers used well-known frontier devices to detach land from its owners. They forged claims and dates of settlement, moved surveyor's markers, extended their fences to enclose railroad land, filed multiple homestead claims on government and railroad sections under fictitious names, transported cabins from tract to tract to establish residence in many places, planted crops, grazed livestock, cut trees, removed gravel and building stone, and diverted water from railroad land. Railway leaders had quickly learned to distinguish between legitimate and illegitimate settlers. Although the company refrained from vigorously asserting its rights against good-faith settlers, it spared no effort or expense to defeat challenges by squatters. Seemingly innocuous cases might establish dangerous precedents losing the company thousands of acres later.

Torn between a determination to defend company lands against trespassers, and a corporate policy of accommodating settlers for the sake of future profits, Southern Pacific leaders moved slowly in Mussel Slough. They were confident that their position was ethical and legal, based on previous court cases and government decisions, and that the Mussel Slough squatters' claims were illegitimate. But these claimants were unusually numerous, organized, and vociferous. Moreover, they were attacking the validity of an entire grant, jeopardizing millions of acres. Convinced that important legal issues were at stake, executives told their San

Southern Pacific Land Agent D. K. Zumwalt

In his popular 1901 novel *The Octopus*, based on the Mussel Slough land controversy, the great California writer Frank Norris fashioned one of the most loathsome characters in American fiction, S. Behrman, the Southern Pacific Railroad's corrupt land and political agent for the San Joaquin Valley. Ironically, Behrman's true-life prototype, D. K. Zumwalt, was a long-time resident and respected leader in Visalia and the valley. On many occasions, he persuaded Southern Pacific executives to soften policies toward buyers and squatters on railroad lands. *Courtesy of the California History Room, California State Library, Sacramento, California.*

Joaquin Valley agent: "Spare no pains, or any reasonable expense, to win this land for the company."

Proving title before a court was one thing, physically removing 500 to 600 squatters was another. Aware of their numbers, significant popular support, and the possibility of wider political and economic reprisals, the company tried to coax the squatters into buying or leasing claims legitimately, thus acknowledging the validity of the company's title. Ultimately, the Southern Pacific hoped to defend its title, while converting the squatters into customers.

The company began preparing Mussel Slough land for sale immediately after receiving its patents there in 1877. In early 1878, the company sent an experienced land-grader, William H. Clark, to inspect and price the land, based on comparable land prices nearby. As was customary, the railroad then reduced Clark's prices 20 percent. To quell rumors that the company would sell land out from under the squatters, Jerome Madden, head of the Land Department in San Francisco, announced that the company would first offer occupied lands to those in possession. For residents who refused to buy, the company offered leases so that they could harvest their crops and remove private property, including any improvements. Based on prior experience with squatters, officials believed the Mussel Slough people would eventually come to terms.

At the end of April 1878, Madden sent letters to hundreds of illegal occupants of railroad lands. According to the railroad's usual procedure, the letters announced the land's price per acre and gave squatters 30 days to purchase their land, at which time the land would be placed on the market for public sale. The price per acre varied from parcel to parcel, but in each case the rate was substantially higher than the official government rate for public land, $2.50 an acre. However, officials considered Mussel Slough lots the most valuable land in the entire railroad grant. Plus, it was the railroad that had brought the land transportation and market access.

Madden's letters sent a shock wave through the district. On May 10 the Settlers' Grand League denounced the railroad, claiming that it was demanding from $20 to $50 per acre, in some cases as much as $80 an acre. Squatters charged the Southern Pacific was attempting to profit from the settlers' improvements, especially their irrigation works, which were the true source of rising land values, not the railroad's construction. Leaguers still insisted that the company's title was invalid, but even if the title were valid, then the railroad was required to set prices at the government price on public land, $2.50 per acre.

Subsequent writers have taken at face value the outrageously high prices cited by the settlers. But Southern Pacific maps, price lists, and sales records for the San Joaquin Valley reveal that the squatters were exaggerating the company's prices from 100 to 400 percent. Of the hundreds of tracts the railroad offered for sale in the district, almost all were priced between $10 and $20 per acre. Virtually none sold for more than $25 an acre, except for a half-dozen tiny suburban plots adjacent to railroad towns. Most of the tracts were 40- to 160-acre parcels, and the company offered a variety of low-interest, long-term mortgage and lease terms, further reducing settlers' out-of-pocket expenses if they chose to legitimize their claims.

The railroad's actual asking prices on lands claimed by the League's leaders were typical. Doyle's farm was priced at $20 per acre, McQuiddy's several claims at $9 to $13.50, and Henry Brewer's lots at $19 per acre. These prices were indeed higher than most, but not all, Southern Pacific lands elsewhere in the valley, but a recent study of prices throughout the district confirms that rates on the railroad's Mussel Slough tracts were comparable or lower than prices prevailing on unimproved land exchanging hands on non-railroad sections in the district. Leaguers themselves used these prices throughout the 1870s, as they often bought and sold land on even-numbered sections for $11 to $25 per acre. In 1874, for example, when Henry Brewer subdivided his legal holding on the public section next to his railroad claim, he priced the land at $15.87 per acre. Mussel Slough acreage was unusually valuable and everyone—from railroad executive to indignant squatter—knew it.

Although they were surprised by the vehemence of the League's response, the Southern Pacific began selling its patented land. To avert confrontation, it periodically sent letters to those claiming the disputed tracts, renewing the railroad's offer of sale. Only a few accepted the railroad's offers. Still, the company resisted the temptation to sell disputed tracts to outsiders. Hoping that residents would finally agree to buy their land, in July 1878 Southern Pacific reduced its prices another 10 to 25 percent. They also made purchasing or renting more attractive by offering to take one-fifth crop-share leases in lieu of cash, applying rent towards future purchases. From May to October, some Mussel Slough claimants overcame their fear of League reprisals and accepted the railroad's terms.

As 1878 came to end, Southern Pacific leaders were running out of patience. In their view, they had been more than fair. They'd given the squatters free use of railroad land, in some cases for six or seven *years*. But the land was not free to the company: as soon as the company received titles from the federal government, Tulare and Fresno counties had begun levying property taxes on the land. Although they fumed over their rising overhead, executives still were reluctant to provoke direct confrontation. As company balance sheets continued to bleed red, officials decided they could wait no longer. In October 1878, the Southern Pacific put the disputed tracts on the market, after giving occupants one last chance to exercise their option to buy.

The company's decision to put the contested lots on the market provoked the ensuing tragedy. The Southern Pacific's Mussel Slough problem now came to a dramatic head, as the conflict moved into another phase, from squatter-versus-corporation, to squatter-versus-settler. Squatter pressure was reviving long-simmering disputes, between old-timers and newcomers, ranchers and would-be farmers, land owner/buyers and squatters without clear titles, haves and have-nots—in short, among many who had come to the Tulare Basin in search of opportunity.

Ingrained social conflict in the county had started in the 1860s, long before the railroad arrived. As was true throughout the West, Tulare County's transition from open-range cattle-raising to agriculture was rough and bloody. By the late 1860s, pioneer grazers occupied most available public land, especially the well-watered tracts. Connected by intermarriage and commercial ties, ranchers' families prospered modestly and became entrenched as the local elite. Their dominance weakened after 1872, when the Southern Pacific arrived at Goshen and farmers rushed in. Some were Confederates fleeing the chaos of the post-Civil War South. By the mid-1870s, these late-comers constituted the majority of the population, and clashed with the pioneer grazers over the remaining tracts of public land, local politics, land use, and, most importantly, shares in the irrigation companies, which were dominated by the old-timers who had come before 1870. Conflict degenerated into smoldering feuds, beatings and shootings, burned barns and crops, torn-down fences, ruined irrigation ditches, and slaughtered livestock. Many of those who chose to purchase railroad tracts belonged to the pre-1870 faction, fueling the animosity of recent arrivals.

Squatters later insisted that those who agreed to buy their claims from the railroad were outsiders, thugs, and hooligans hired by the company. Actually, almost all the buyers were local residents or at least from neighboring areas, including Perry Phillips, Mills Hartt, and Walter Crow. These men and others faced fierce resistance when they purchased and began cultivating railroad land, particularly after 1878. Leaguers threatened violence against railroad land purchasers, and made good with nighttime raids of masked riders, arresting and evicting buyers and burning their crops and possessions.

More threats and violence increased pressure on the railroad. After attacks on the company's land buyers, and even some of its employees, sales and rentals of railroad land declined sharply. By the summer of 1879, the company's land transactions had ceased altogether. Reluctant buyers and tenants admitted that they feared the Leaguers, who were roving throughout the basin making threats and demanding support for the squatter movement. Deteriorating conditions compounded the Southern Pacific's dilemma. The company's very chain of command, or lack thereof, made coordinated decision-making difficult. Each of its four owners had equal ownership and influence over the company's multitude of railroads and other properties, fragmenting authority and complicating leadership. Control was further divided by dual headquarters, at San Francisco (Stanford and Crocker) and New York (Huntington). Compounding the decentralized authority was the cumbersome communication of the era and deteriorating personal relationships among the surviving three who had started the company. Although they agreed that the Southern Pacific must defend its land titles, they differed sharply over how best to deal with the squatters. Stanford and Huntington considered the claimants innocent dupes of unscrupulous advisers. Rather than oust the squatters and further damage the company's public image, they favored an additional reduction in prices. If the settlers bought the land, the company would protect its titles in California and elsewhere, far outweighing any losses the company incurred by underselling Mussel Slough land. On the other hand, Charles Crocker, titular president of the Southern Pacific Railroad and legally responsible for its land grants, insisted on strict enforcement of both title and land prices, pressing for a show of force against the squatters. Unable to agree on a plan of action, Southern Pacific leaders vacillated, their actions contradictory and ineffective.

In late 1878, with violence intensifying and land sales almost dead, the company's executives finally decided to start eviction proceedings, which they thought would force the squatters to come to terms. As a bonus, the company hoped the suits would discourage more squatters from settling on railroad lands elsewhere. However, still reluctant to further antagonize opponents, company leaders instituted test cases, against only a handful of squatter leaders. The evictions were to be prosecuted slowly, giving the masses of squatters both time and incentive to negotiate for the land.

After informing squatters a final time that they would be evicted if they did not buy, lease, or abandon railroad land, officials filed the first lawsuits in December 1878. Some squatters capitulated immediately. By January 1879, dozens had contacted the railway, proposing to buy or rent, and asking that the suits be dismissed. The company halted proceedings as soon as settlers signed contracts. For some cash-strapped squatters, it even agreed to pay court costs. Late in April, the Southern Pacific was patiently waiting for the remaining eviction cases to run their course, still holding off on initiating proceedings against the remaining squatters.

The League, however, responded aggressively, organizing a militia and increasing attacks on purchasers. In April 1879, an informant alerted the company that the remaining squatters had signed a secret pact with the League to ignore the test cases, resist eviction, and force the company to sue and evict them one by one. Convinced that its moderated legal strategy would not succeed, the company immediately filed lawsuits against all remaining squatters. By mid-1880, several hundred ejectment suits were pending before the federal circuit court in San Francisco.

The first court decision, *Southern Pacific Railroad Company v. Pierpont Orton*, was announced in December 1879; *Orton* set the pattern for the rest. The judge rejected all of the settlers' arguments. The company's route change was legal; the 1867 map filed by the railroad, according to law and established procedure, transferred those land titles to the corporation; the Interior Department had no legal authority to revoke land grants made by Congress; and, finally, grants along the finished portions were valid even though the company had failed to complete the entire line by its 1878 deadline. The court further held that Orton and, by extension, everyone else who settled after 1867, had no standing to challenge the validity of railroad's title. The Southern Pacific eventually won each of its ejectment suits, usually gaining not only eviction orders but also court costs and damages. For the Mussel Slough squatters, the rulings were a stunning blow.

After *Orton*, Southern Pacific leaders were confident that their cautious strategy would now work. More and more settlers were coming to terms; many more were likely to do so to avoid the costs of losing in court. Roughly half of the 500 to 600 squatters reached agreements with the company. To woo the stragglers, early in 1880 the company again liberalized its land-sales procedures, reducing mortgage interest rates from 10 to 7 percent. The railway again offered to withdraw eviction suits if squatters signed contracts or abandoned their claims. To give holdouts enough time to buy or leave, the company announced that it would postpone enforcing the eviction orders and damage judgments until April 1, 1880.

Yet, some squatters stood firm. About 200 remained militant and inflexible, convinced that their claims would still be validated. John J. Doyle convinced the state legislature to voice support for the squatters and to call on Congress or the Supreme Court to reverse *Orton*. Meanwhile, Leaguers promised to forcefully resist evictions.

Many squatters and other residents of the region, however, admitted the squatter movement had failed. In February 1880, a delegation quietly contacted Crocker and offered a compromise proposal: they would acknowledge the railroad's title if the company would sell at the prices the company advertised in its general land sales pamphlets, "viz: from $2.50 to $5 per acre." Crocker agreed to meet with the group and negotiate prices "upon the basis of the value of the land," but he flatly rejected the offered price range, which was inaccurate and lower than stated in the railroad's pamphlets. For the first time, what had begun as a contest over titles became a squabble over prices.

Leland Stanford chose this moment to intervene personally in the conflict. Still harboring political ambitions, the former governor offered to confer with the Settlers' Grand League to reach "an amicable adjustment of all differences." Meeting in Sacramento on March 4, 1880, Doyle, McQuiddy, and Stanford reached a preliminary agreement: legal proceedings on both sides would be stayed, settlers would no longer question the railroad's title, and Stanford would inspect the disputed lands and try to arrange for lower prices. Although the visit took place and both sides expressed cautious optimism, negotiations ultimately failed, in part because the company's leaders continued to disagree among themselves. Crocker's later letters to Huntington make it clear that Stanford and Huntington still favored deep cuts in price to end the impasse, while Crocker, irritated by Stanford's intervention, refused to go along. He would agree to reduce prices by only $1, to $4 dollars per acre.

Furious League spokesmen denounced the railroad for yet more deception. Doyle, McQuiddy, James Patterson, and 25 armed and masked men descended on the company's land agent at Hanford and drove him out of town. A handful of squatters signed contracts, but Doyle managed to rally the rest for one last legal challenge before the U.S. Supreme Court. To bolster the League's unraveling alliance, leaders scheduled a mass protest meeting in Hanford for May 11. Their attorney, the famously bellicose David S. Terry, was scheduled to deliver a rousing address on the justice of the settlers' cause. Tempers in the valley were raw.

In San Francisco, Southern Pacific leaders pondered their next move. Like the settlers, they now saw the conciliation effort as a ruse: the squatters had only pretended to negotiate in order to gain time for yet another legal challenge and to grab yet another free year on the railroad's lands. Moreover, some of those who had purchased contested lots—in some cases years earlier— were threatening legal action if they were not given immediate use of the land. Most insistent were Mills Hartt and Walter Crow. An exasperated Crocker finally asked the circuit court to enforce some eviction rulings. Land agent Madden wrote Hartt alerting him that a U.S. marshal would arrive in Hanford on the morning of May 11 to drive him, Crow, Perry Phillips, and several others to take possession of their lands.

On the fateful morning of May 11, Marshal Alonzo Poole got down from his buggy and walked across Storer and Brewers' disputed claim toward the Settlers' League riders. Poole was immediately surrounded by an angry crowd, obscuring him from his own party's view. Poole informed the Leaguers of his mission and tried to read the court orders, but the men drowned him out, shouting that they could not permit the marshal to enforce eviction orders while the cases were still under appeal. Poole admitted that the settlers' cause had merits but, as a federal officer, he had a legal duty to perform.

James Patterson, who appeared to be in charge, demanded the marshal's revolver. Poole refused, but assured them that he did not intend to use it. Someone shouted, "On peril of your life, surrender your pistol!" When Poole remained steadfast, Patterson allowed the marshal to keep his gun, but he placed Poole under armed guard.

While Poole and the settlers argued, William Clark, Mills Hartt, and Walter Crow waited nervously on their wagons. Unable to see Poole amidst the shuffling men and horses, they could only make out menacing gestures and unintelligible shouts and curses. As Clark later said, all he could see was someone waving a revolver in the air and crying, "God damn you, give up your arms!" Crow again reached for his gun, but Clark stopped him, saying, "Walter, keep cool. All depends on keeping cool." The crowd broke apart, revealing the marshal and his two guards, and the militia rode forward and surrounded the wagons, revolvers drawn. One of the riders, James Harris, brandished his pistol at Clark, Hartt, and Crow and demanded their weapons. Clark refused and Hartt appeared to move towards his gun, but Crow restrained him.

With everyone tense and confused, a shouting match erupted between Crow, Hartt, and several of the riders. The stomping horses raised a cloud of choking dust. The horse under one of Poole's guards suddenly lurched, and the marshal was accidentally knocked to the ground. Believing he'd been attacked, Hartt and Crow dove for their arms and in an instant, they and Harris all fired. It was impossible to say who fired first, but Hartt fell mortally wounded; Harris and settler Iver Knutson died on the spot.

The horses hitched to the wagons bolted and Crow hit the ground running, firing both a revolver and a shotgun. Heading for the fallen marshal, he exchanged fire with Poole's guards and killed them both. Within a minute, 20 or 30 shots were fired but Poole and Clark, like most of the men, held their fire.

The shooting ended abruptly, the field a dusty chaos of gun smoke, bucking horses, bouncing wagons, and cursing men. Hartt and five others lay dead or dying; miraculously, Poole, Clark, and Crow were unharmed. More men arrived by the minute, until soon 100 were shouting and demanding answers. While the dead and wounded were being carried to the shade of an oak tree, Poole and Clark took Crow aside and warned him that he would probably be killed when the crowd knew what had happened. Crow slipped away, still carrying his shotgun and revolver. Later that afternoon a search party found Walter Crow's body a mile and a half from the battle site. He'd been shot in the back at close range.

Clark and Marshal Poole drove away toward safety in Hanford. Within a mile, they were intercepted and surrounded by yet another throng, this one led by militia-leader Thomas Jefferson McQuiddy. McQuiddy handed Poole a paper forbidding the marshal to enforce evictions. "This is a bad business, Major," Clark told him. "Yes, it's a bad business," McQuiddy returned, "but we are fighting for our homes, and we propose to fight for them." He warned Poole and Clark that they would never reach Hanford alive and detailed a guard of four armed men to escort them north to Kingsburg instead. Arriving late in the afternoon, Clark and the marshal checked into a hotel for the night, but a stagecoach driver warned them that a troop of squatters was coming to kill them. Poole and Clark caught the first northbound train for San Francisco.

"Tragedy Oak"

The dead and wounded Mussel Slough settlers were placed under a sprawling valley oak in Brewer's front yard. The last surviving witness to the battle, the tree was marked with a state historical plaque in 1948. Now blighted by pollution and excessive watering from farm irrigation, "Tragedy Oak" may not survive another generation. *Photograph by Richard J. Orsi.*

Only a few dozen individuals participated in the gunfight at Mussel Slough, yet the battle became an overnight sensation. The stunning news pulsed through telegraph wires across the state and around the nation. Within hours, Huntington and Stanford read about it in New York. Public reaction was explosive but mixed. Most Tulare County groups condemned the Southern Pacific, but the state's major newspapers—even some that had praised the squatters—now branded them as criminals and demanded that they be punished. After having encouraged squatter vigilantism, San Francisco's *Chronicle* turned about and denounced those who "by their rash course . . . in opposing armed resistance to the law, [had] placed themselves clearly in the wrong before the tribunal of public opinion and terribly prejudiced their case." Even San Francisco *Post* columnist Ambrose Bierce, a trenchant critic of the Southern Pacific, took its side against the squatters. He accused John Doyle, whom he knew well, of being "the Mephistopheles who for his own aggrandizement has led these settlers into all the trouble in which they find themselves."

Such early critical judgments, however, were soon drowned by popular sympathy for the squatters, who were transformed into martyrs murdered by the railroad. Businesses in the Mussel Slough area closed their doors in mourning and several days after the battle, long processions of weeping mourners buried the dead Leaguers. For months after the shooting, farm, labor, and civic groups around the state held mass anti-railroad meetings, many organized by leaders of the Settlers' Grand League. Fund drives raised thousands of dollars for the squatters' relief and defense. Tens of thousands of people signed petitions pleading for clemency toward

"Impending Retribution"

One of the foremost political cartoonists of his era, George Frederick Keller, who drew for San Francisco's satirical magazine *The Wasp*, viewed the growing anti-railroad movement of the early 1880s as "retribution" for the Big Four's oppression of the Mussel Slough settlers. That theme was sounded by cartoons, editorials, and political orations for decades. This cartoon was published on October 7, 1882. *The Wasp*.

the squatters and a revocation of the Southern Pacific's land grant. Eastern anti-corporate newspapers such as New York's *Sun* hailed the Mussel Slough martyrs as an advance guard in the war against monopoly.

Local officials at first refused to arrest those who had confronted Marshal Poole. Although rumors flew regarding the identity of Crow's killer, no one was ever charged. The Southern Pacific repeatedly pressed the U.S. Attorney General to prosecute and finally, in the summer of 1880, a federal grand jury in San Francisco indicted eleven settlers, including Doyle, McQuiddy, and Patterson. At the December trial, Doyle, Patterson, and three others were found guilty of obstructing the marshal in the performance of his duty. Sentenced to a bizarre eight-month sentence in unlocked cells at the San José jail, the five settlers attended church, lodge meetings, and dinners in their honor. While travelling back to Mussel Slough, they were celebrated and entertained along the way. Neighbors in Hanford gave them a hero's welcome, complete with bands, banners, parades, and anti-railroad orations.

McQuiddy vanished. Sheltered by friends and local officials, he evaded capture for years. While a fugitive, he became the hero of anti-corporate groups, and a nominee for governor by both the Anti-Monopoly League and the Greenback Party in 1882. In the election, he finished a distant fourth to Democrat George Stoneman. Federal prosecutors finally dismissed charges against him four years later.

What happened to the remaining squatters? As had been true from the beginning, the residents of Mussel Slough remained sharply divided. Discredited in the eyes of many, the Grand League limped along into the late '80s. Still under the sway of Doyle and McQuiddy, it tried to keep buyers from dealing with the Southern Pacific, collected fees from landowners, and mounted unsuccessful legal appeals. Although they resented the railroad, leading businessmen, landowners, and others urged squatters to settle with the company for the sake of community peace. Some discontented Mussel Slough residents formed an anti-League organization, the Farmers' Club, and condemned the squatter movement for producing violence, disharmony, and economic stagnation.

Though shocked by the violence, Southern Pacific leaders persisted in their policy of defending the railroad's titles in court while attempting to settle privately with individual settlers. Within a year all the squatters had been sued. The lawsuits and local disenchantment with the League finally brought many claimants to settle. In late May 1880 a delegation of community leaders from Hanford and Lemoore negotiated a compromise with Charles Crocker. The railroad president agreed to lower prices by an additional 12.5 percent, retroactive for those who had already purchased.

Some squatters complained that the price reduction still wasn't enough, but droves of them rushed to buy, most using Southern Pacific credit plans. In June, in an attempt at further conciliation, the company began crediting the amounts squatters paid in court judgments towards their purchase and lease agreements. By December 1880 most of the squatters had legalized their claims. Except for a few small disputed tracts either unoccupied or still awaiting court judgments, all disputed Southern Pacific land in the Mussel Slough region was either sold or leased by June 1881.

The settlers finally won their long-awaited legal hearing when the U.S. Supreme Court accepted three test cases on appeal. In December 1883, the court rejected the settlers' arguments and upheld earlier decisions in favor of the railroad. John J. Doyle lost his lawsuit

and paid a judgment of $1,214. A few squatters held on, refusing to bargain with the railroad, obey eviction orders, or pay judgments. Lax local sheriffs and federal marshals delayed serving papers for months, even years, allowing squatters to use the land in the interim. Most remaining squatters vanished or were evicted within a year or two, but several were still illegally occupying land as late as 1887. Sporadic violence persisted for years among settlers competed for remaining railroad land.

The Mussel Slough affair etched in bold relief the struggle between individuals and corporations in late-nineteenth-century America. At Hanford, annual public memorials kept the memory of the battle vivid, cementing the myth of pure-hearted pioneers combating an evil monopoly. The gunfight inspired songs, poetry, short stories, and novels, the most famous of which was Frank Norris's *The Octopus* (1901). Drawn from the settlers' own pamphlets and back issues of anti-railroad newspapers, the novel reflected the popular legend. Although completely misstating what had actually happened, Norris's book intensified public outrage against the Southern Pacific and railroads in general. In its popularity, his account helped pave the way for progressive, anti-corporate reformers to capture state government in 1910 and to enact tougher controls on railroads. According to a friend of the great progressive president, *The Octopus* convinced Theodore Roosevelt that "conditions were worse in California than elsewhere."

The *Coming of the Railroad*

14

Transportation Problems
in Gold Rush California

At midcentury, commerce in California labored under serious burdens. Vast distances separated the state from the outside world, and even within the state, distance and travel difficulties hampered trade. Landlocked by mountains, areas such as the southern San Joaquin Valley and the interior valleys of Southern California remained isolated, sparsely populated, and their resources untapped. Travel by water was possible on some northern rivers, though it was frequently limited by periodic drought and flooding. Goods arriving by sea often had to be transferred multiple times between ferries, riverboats, and wagons before reaching interior destinations, multiplying costs. The flow of products and information could be delayed for weeks or months. With supplies and prices unpredictable, California businesses were prone to failure, complicating the state's volatile post-gold-rush economy.

The costs and hazards of ocean and overland travel also discouraged immigration. When the frenzy and quick profits produced by the gold rush cooled in the mid-1850s, population growth in California became sluggish, and women and children remained a minority. As mining waned and Californians began exploring new enterprises, they pleaded in newspapers, pamphlets, and public meetings for improved transportation.

Early Transcontinental Railroad Schemes

While California was being settled, steam railroads were revolutionizing trade, industry, agriculture, and urban fortunes in the eastern states. Even before the Mexican War, prophets of America's "manifest destiny" envisioned a transcontinental railroad that would spread civilization across the forbidding Great Plains, secure American control of the Pacific Coast, and channel U.S. manufactured and agricultural goods to millions of coveted customers in Asia. The acquisition of Texas, Oregon, and California lent urgency to this idea, as did the discovery of gold at Sutter's Mill. In the late 1840s and '50s, eastern and western cities flooded Congress with transcontinental railway bills favorable to their regional interests. Almost all of these plans recognized that laying tracks across 2,000 miles of rough wilderness was beyond the capacity of private business. Thus most plans—including legislation proposed by California's Senator William Gwin in 1853—called for heavy government subsidies.

Little resulted from these early efforts. Although Americans agreed on building such a rail line and the need for government subsidy, they clashed over the placement of routes and the terms of construction, as well as competition between free and slave states. Californian interests, ostensibly the major beneficiaries of a railway, also deadlocked over the western terminus. San Francisco, Benicia, Vallejo, Sacramento, Stockton, Los Angeles, and San Diego all claimed to be the logical Pacific terminus. An 1853 railroad convention in San Francisco, for example, deadlocked on all major issues. According to the city's *Alta California*, the meeting turned out to be a "miserable abortion." Through the 1850s, local and national politics doomed early Pacific railway bills.

Pioneer Rail Lines

Unable to get the national government to subsidize the Pacific railway, Californians in the 1850s and early '60s focused on constructing short railways to replace existing stage, wagon, and steamboat lines. Businessmen organized elaborate railroad-building ventures and advertised their towns as the future trade centers of the West Coast. Plagued by delay, corruption, incompetent engineering, and scarce machinery and labor, most speculative railroad projects failed to progress from paper and hot air to steel and steam. One exception, the Sacramento Valley Railroad, laid tracks 23 miles from the Sacramento steamboat port, then northeast up the American River canyon to tap the lucrative mining trade. In 1856, it became California's first working railroad. It was an immediate, though limited, success. Rails now offered quicker transportation than the dusty wagon roads then in use, and the new town of Folsom sprouted at the end of the line.

Other early railways operated in the San Francisco Bay Area, the state's wealthiest and most populous region. The first regional line broke ground in 1861 and took two years to build a mile between the town of Oakland and its waterfront. The San Francisco & San Jose Railroad spanned 50 miles of western bayshore plains and marshes between those communities in 1866. The same year, the San Francisco & Alameda Railroad opened a line along the East Bay from Alameda to Hayward, an agricultural settlement 15 miles to the southeast. Although suffering from insufficient capital, heavy debt, poor construction, and opposition from rival communities and transportation companies, these early railways sparked agricultural and urban booms and strengthened the San Francisco Bay Area's hold on the state's economy.

Theodore Judah, Visionary

Above all others, Theodore D. Judah kept alive the hope of a transcontinental railroad binding California to the rest of the nation. When the Sacramento Valley Railroad hired him to construct its railway, the 28-year-old already had a reputation as a builder of eastern canals, bridges, and railroads. Judah completed the line in less than two years, a remarkable feat in an era of shaky railway ventures. But, as was typical, the company was saddled with debt, mostly the result of excessive profit-taking by its organizers and construction company. Bankrupt, the line reached no farther than Folsom and Judah left his job as chief engineer in 1856.

Ambitious and persistent, Judah was intrigued by the idea of a transcontinental railway. He was convinced that a line could be built through the Sierra Nevada and he scoured the mountains for a buildable route, all the while canvassing community leaders, addressing public meetings, and publishing pamphlets and surveys aimed at getting backing he needed to form a railroad company. To win federal subsidies, Judah took his cause to Washington, wooing federal officials and eastern capitalists. So passionately did the young engineer pursue his vision of a railroad over the central Sierra that scoffers dubbed him "Crazy Judah." Leery investors doubted his business acumen as well as the feasibility of the Sierra

The Founding of the Central Pacific Railroad

Theodore D. Judah

California State Railroad Museum.

By the time Judah returned from Washington, a lucrative trade had developed between California and the emerging Comstock Lode of western Nevada, increasing local interest in a railroad across the Sierra. A consortium of San Francisco financiers already dominated the Comstock mining trade via steamboats and the ailing Sacramento Valley Railroad. The hodge-podge delivery system funneled goods and travelers by water to Sacramento, then by rail to Folsom, finally by wagon over the Sierra south of Lake Tahoe to the Comstock Lode. The consortium now turned its sights to the north side of Lake Tahoe, formulating plans to build another rail and wagon route over the Sierra north of the lake, thus monopolizing Comstock commerce. Judah was hired to design this new line.

While working the new Sacramento Valley Railroad line, Judah discovered a route through the central Sierra. He secretly made plans to found his own company to tap the Comstock trade and build the western segment of a future transcontinental railroad. Judah finally settled on a path that started at Sacramento, rose 70 miles northeastward through the 7,000-foot-high Donner Pass, and plunged down the Truckee River canyon to the Nevada border. Although Judah's plan would require the railroad to combat huge snowfalls, bore expensive tunnels, and scale unprecedented grades, the Donner Pass route was shorter than its rivals and mounted only one summit to cross the Sierra. With a definite route now in hand, Judah and a few others formed the Central Pacific Railroad in October 1860. With limited financial resources, they could raise only a few thousand of the $115,000 in stock subscriptions the state required to incorporate the company.

Unwisely, Judah openly sought backing in San Francisco. He was rebuffed again and, what was worse, the Sacramento Valley Railroad got wind of his plan. Outraged that one of its employees had disclosed confidential information to promote a rival company, the railroad fired Judah. It publically attacked his scheme as poorly planned and impossible to construct, undermining investor confidence in the Central Pacific for years.

At this point, Theodore Judah's railroad resembled most others in California: it existed only on paper and in the mind of its promoter, and it was unlikely to be built. To salvage his plan, Judah turned to small investors in Sacramento and other towns along the Donner Pass route. He proposed that the company seek quick profits by laying tracks from Sacramento northeast to the foothill mining community of Dutch Flat, and

route; to many, Judah was an impractical pest. Still, he kept the transcontinental railway in the public eye, though he failed to win government or private funding for the project.

In 1859 Judah and other would-be railway promoters convinced the state legislature to summon another Pacific Railroad Convention to meet in San Francisco. Although local jealousies again prevented agreement on a specific route, the delegates managed to pass general resolutions favoring a route from the San Francisco Bay eastward through the central Sierra. Judah was appointed to present the plan to Congress. Arriving in Washington in late 1859, Judah pressed for a bill subsidizing transcontinental railways. His timing was terrible: the conflict between North and South and the looming presidential election absorbed national energies. Although he believed he had won some Congressional Republicans over to his plan, his route faced southern opposition as too far north. In the summer of 1860, Judah returned to California, ending four frustrating years of railway promotion in failure.

simultaneously building a wagon road along the planned rail route from Dutch Flat to Virginia City, Nevada, thereby quickly seizing the Comstock trade. When completed, the wagon road would also ease rail construction through the remotest stretches of the Sierra, as well as offer a continual outlet to the Nevada mines.

After fruitless public meetings, Judah gained the attention of Sacramento hardware merchant Collis P. Huntington. Huntington brought in his partner Mark Hopkins, along with other Sacramento businessmen, including Charles Crocker, his attorney brother Edwin (who was also a state supreme court judge), and Leland Stanford. The group agreed to buy enough stock to incorporate Judah's company. In April 1861, in the Huntington-Hopkins hardware store, the Central Pacific Railroad was reorganized to admit the new investors. A committee composed of Judah and Dutch Flat dentist David Strong later nominated Stanford president, Huntington vice president, Hopkins treasurer, Edwin Crocker as chief attorney, and Judah chief engineer; directors approved the new slate of officers. When the Central Pacific was incorporated on June 27, 1861, the struggle began to convert dream into reality.

Huntington, Stanford, Charles and Edwin Crocker, and Hopkins quickly emerged as the most powerful leaders of the new company. The "Associates," or "Big Four," as they came to be known after Edwin died, brought much-needed business strength to Judah's struggling venture. Though by no means wealthy, they were respected as successful businessmen and city leaders whose word and credit were as good as gold. Huntington was a particularly valuable addition because he knew eastern suppliers and financiers. The Associates also had important political ties. They were among the tiny, militant band of anti-slavery men who had founded California's Republican Party in 1856. As leaders of the new party, the Associates labored tirelessly in John C. Frémont's losing presidential campaign, then rode to victory with Abraham Lincoln in November 1860. Now with close ties to the Lincoln administration, as well as local and national Republican leaders and congressmen, the Associates wielded the political clout that Judah had always lacked.

The Civil War and the Transcontinental Railway

Because California settlers hailed from both the North and the South, racial and sectional issues of the 1850s and '60s deeply divided the state. When slave states seceded from the Union and Civil War erupted early in 1861, only a small minority of Californians openly favored the Confederacy. Although at first pockets of Confederate supporters held some power in Southern California and parts of the San Joaquin Valley, in most places immigrants from northern states outnumbered those from the South, and the state remained staunchly Union. When secessionist speakers, journalists, politicians, or clergymen became too outspoken, they were silenced by public opinion, shouted down by unfriendly mobs, or arrested by military authorities. Republicans, the minority party at the onset of the 1860s, rose on the tide of pro-Union votes, gaining sufficient strength to dominate state and local government in California for most of the decade. Under the leadership of famed Unionist supporter and Unitarian minister Thomas Starr King, by war's end in 1865, Californians had contributed more than $1 million to the U.S. Sanitary Commission and other Union charities. California volunteers also saw combat with the Second Massachusetts Cavalry, manned western garrisons, and patrolled southern routes into the state.

Nevertheless, the Civil War's impact on California, though significant, was far less direct or immediate than it was for Americans living closer to the battlefields. For Californians, the greatest impact of the war was its disruption of commerce by creating shortages of supplies from eastern states, especially those now diverted to Union armies. Wartime disruptions forced Californians to rely more on their own resources, accelerating economic diversification, local industries, and trade with the outside world, particularly Asia. New firms increasingly canned foods, milled grain, and manufactured iron, wagons, cigars, sugar, textiles, blasting powder, leather goods, and other products that had earlier been imported from the East. Although the state initially lost some population to the Nevada silver boom during the 1860s, it regained some new population from the arrival of easterners escaping the wartime draft, and recouped financial losses by increasing its dominance of commerce in the Comstock Lode and throughout the Pacific Rim.

The Civil War also improved the Central Pacific Railroad's prospects. In control of Congress and the White House, Republican leaders were already committed to the idea of a transcontinental railway built with federal aid. Indeed, the war made the project even more urgent. Proponents argued that such a railway was vital to the Union war effort; a through route to the Pacific would assure the allegiance of the frontier and strengthen military control of the Far West. More importantly, secession removed the southerners who had earlier blocked California railroad bills, leaving the path through Congress open for a northern route.

The Central Pacific Besieged

Even so, monumental obstacles still blocked the Central Pacific in 1861. Practically every facet of the ambitious project—engineering, building, and financing—was unprecedented. Experts smugly predicted that locomotives would never be able to haul cars over high Sierra grades. Even if they did, critics scoffed, the railroad could not operate in the heavy winter snows and arctic temperatures of Donner Pass. Adding to the difficulties, most construction and operating equipment, including rails, cars, locomotives, and heavy machinery, would have to be shipped at great expense by sea around the Horn. Wartime shortages of iron, railroad machinery, and available ships, as well as the federal government's inflationary monetary policies, would balloon prices and cause endless delays. Finally, how could the railroad hope to complete its route with so few construction workers available in California?

Even with Judah's overly optimistic estimates, the cost of building the Central Pacific, especially the Sierra segment, would far exceed federal subsidies. The private wealth of the Sacramento businessmen was no match for the costs, nor could Judah's group expect much help from the San Francisco business community. Already committed to steamship lines or potential rail competitors of the Central Pacific, most San Francisco area financiers were also unlikely to assist any venture that might benefit arch trade rival Sacramento. Nor was private investment an option: in the tight wartime investment market, large risky ventures like the Central Pacific and other would-be transcontinental railroads could raise virtually no cash by selling stocks or bonds.

Illustrating how thin the Central Pacific's resources really were, its first stock subscription in 1861 brought in only $10,000, which the railroad committed for Judah's more detailed survey of the Donner Pass route. The money ran out before the work was complete, however, and in the summer of 1861, Judah returned from the mountains with the disheartening news that his original survey had been seriously flawed. The distance through the Sierra was 140 miles, not 115, and more than three miles of tunnels would have to be bored through some of the hardest granite in North America. Building as far as Nevada would cost at least $13 million, or $88,000 per mile, costs more than 50 percent higher than Judah's original estimate, and several times the likely federal subsidy.

To make matters worse, the outbreak of Civil War and the imminent passage of Congressional assistance spawned a host of new rail companies, all vying for a share in the federal funds. Both the San Francisco & San Jose Railroad and the Sacramento Valley Railroad mounted formidable campaigns of their own to get the transcontinental subsidy. Powerful San Franciscans controlled both railways, still the state's only working lines. Other threatened vested interests, such as the giant Pacific Mail Steamship, California Steam Navigation, and Wells Fargo companies concerned with losing federal mail contracts, joined rival cities—San Francisco, Stockton, Placerville, and Marysville—to smash Sacramento and its paper railroad.

The Pacific Railway Act of 1862

With little support outside Sacramento, the leaders of the Central Pacific, their private fortunes now committed, turned to securing the crucial federal charter and subsidies. To assure that the state would favor their company, the Associates ran Stanford for governor on the Republican ticket. In September 1861 he triumphed, bringing with him a group of sympathetic Republican legislators and congressmen. With the state government more or less under control, Judah, Huntington, several investors, and Congressional Republican allies set sail for Washington in the fall of 1861. They arrived to find the nation's capital aswarm with railway promoters anxious to cash in on the proposed rail subsidies. The Central Pacific's powerful Republican friends, along with several of Huntington's business associates, secured positions on the legislative committees charged with writing a railway bill. They, in turn, had Judah appointed to a key position as clerk of both the House and Senate railway committees. Now in charge of directing committee affairs, Judah could guard Central Pacific interests as Congress shaped the railway bill.

Judah and Huntington lobbied furiously through the winter and spring of 1862. To bribe legislators and leaders of other railroads, Judah and Huntington lavishly gave away Central Pacific stock. The company's friends overcame one major obstacle when they worked out a bargain with the San Francisco & San Jose Railroad. In exchange for Central Pacific's agreement to assign it the right to build and collect the subsidy for the transcontinental segment between San Francisco and Sacramento, the SF&SJ would drop its opposition to legislation favoring Central Pacific.

Judah and Huntington achieved a stunning victory in July, when President Lincoln signed the historic Pacific Railway Act. This law empowered the Central Pacific to construct tracks from San Francisco Bay, or the navigable waters of the Sacramento River, to the eastern boundary of California. The Union Pacific Railroad would complete the connection from the Missouri River. Both lines were awarded federal charters, rights-of-way, the right to take timber and stone from the public domain for construction, and grants of ten alternate sections of public land per mile of rail line, in a checkerboard pattern within ten miles on each side of the tracks. The act also authorized a loan to the companies of 30-year government bonds at variable rates: $16,000 per mile of track across low-elevation plains at each end of the line, $48,000 per mile through mountains, and $32,000 per mile across the Great Basin. The railroads were authorized to sell the bonds and land to raise capital for construction.

Path-breaking as it was, the 1862 act by itself probably would not have resulted in a transcontinental railway. Not only was the subsidy much lower than projected construction costs, but the law itself imposed serious restrictions. Each company was obligated to complete the entire line by 1876 if the other failed to build its portion, and the U.S. government would assume the assets of a company that did not meet its responsibilities. Because the bond-loan and land-grant subsidies would be delivered gradually after railroads had completed segments of track, the funds would not be available during the critical early years. Moreover, the government's loan of bonds was secured by a first mortgage against the railroad's property, reducing the company's own bonds to less-valuable second mortgages. These provisions discouraged private investors. As late as 1864 neither the Union Pacific nor the Central Pacific had been able to sell enough of its own securities to complete the short mileage needed to qualify for the federal loans.

Local Subsidies and Mounting Opposition to the Central Pacific

For the moment, Judah and the Associates concentrated on financing construction through local and state subsidies, plus loans secured by their personal assets. In the nineteenth century, state and local governments commonly subsidized new businesses, particularly transportation ventures. During his 1862–64 term Gov. Stanford assured that this kind of support favored his company. He and his allies pushed through many laws supporting the Central Pacific, granting millions of dollars in state bonds and allowing local communities to subscribe to its stock. A number of hotly fought elections were blemished on both sides by charges of bribery and ballot-box stuffing; in the end, voters in San Francisco,

Sacramento, Placer, and elsewhere purchased more than $1 million in Central Pacific stock.

Opponents of Sacramento and the Central Pacific redoubled their efforts to destroy the infant railroad. In league with railway, steamship, and wagon competitors, communities far from the Donner Pass route tried to get the legislature to revoke Central Pacific subsidies and extend them instead to rivals. They filed lawsuits challenging the legality of state and local aid, attempted to overturn local subsidy elections, and launched a blistering propaganda war against the company. Pamphlets and editorials attacked the Donner Pass route as impractical and condemned the railroad as a speculative venture intended to seize subsidies, build the Dutch Flat wagon road, and then default on its bonds and go out of business. Opponents claimed that Central Pacific's executives had awarded themselves exorbitant construction contracts that would ruin the railroad, and that the company had won its victories only through bribery and corruption. The Central Pacific, its enemies sneered, was the "Great Dutch Flat Swindle."

These accusations were largely self-serving. The Central Pacific was indeed financially weak, its engineering untried, its leaders, particularly Judah and Stanford, guilty of conflict of interest, and its investors attracted to the enterprise by government subsidies. But these problems also characterized the company's critics, most of whom also served special interests. There is no evidence that the Central Pacific's owners did not intend to build the railway. It was popular enthusiasm for railways, not corruption that turned the tide in local subsidy elections—although it appears that Stanford's friends did indeed bribe voters to increase the margin in San Francisco. Conflict of interest, justifiably distasteful to modern sensibilities, was widespread in the nineteenth century, even among otherwise respectable people. Once again, most Central Pacific rivals were equally guilty. Likewise, early railroads and other large-scale building projects, including Judah's Sacramento Valley line, commonly employed "dummy" construction companies to overcome insufficiencies of capital and credit.

After 1862 Leland Stanford, as state governor and president of the railroad, led the fight to preserve the Central Pacific's privileged position. The company dispatched organizers to help local supporters get subsidy measures passed; partisans reached compromises with communities regarding stock purchases, and thwarted competing lobbyists in the legislature. The company successfully defended almost all of the lawsuits. By 1865 most of the opposition had been subdued, at least temporarily, and the railroad finally began to receive much-needed local funding.

But the anti-Central Pacific campaigns of the early 1860s were damaging, depleting the railroad's funds, delaying subsidies and probably completion. Also, the company's own tactics, amplified by exaggerations and untruths hurled by partisan opponents, gave the Central Pacific a reputation for corruption and ruthlessness. Many Californians were predisposed against the Central Pacific long before it had laid a single mile of track. Born in the business and community rivalries inherent in early railway building, these suspicions laid the groundwork for later anti-railroad movements.

Breaking Ground

While it battled its rivals through 1862 and into 1863, the Central Pacific began construction. The railroad still could not raise substantial funds but the public needed to see some tangible progress. Executives scraped together cash through new stock subscriptions and levies on its few stockholders, including contributions of $35,000 each from the Big Four, so that work could commence on the Dutch Flat wagon road. In December, Crocker resigned from the board of directors and, in league with other Central Pacific investors, founded Charles Crocker & Co., which received the contract to build the first segment of rail line. Finally, on January 8, 1863, ground was broken at the flood-ravaged Sacramento riverfront with prayers, speeches, parades, waving American flags, and the music of the Sacramento Brass Band. Gov. Stanford cast the first shovelful of dirt, ceremonially launching the transcontinental railway.

But after several months, work on the roadbed halted about 18 miles into the empty countryside. Grading crews had become enmired in the mucky valley earth, and the railroad again ran out of money before any tracks had even been laid. As it stood, the Central Pacific lacked rails, cars, locomotives, and enough workers to complete the rail line.

In March 1863 Huntington went east in a desperate attempt to sell $1.5 million in nearly worthless Central Pacific bonds, needed to purchase rolling stock and construction materials. The Union Pacific and other builders of the transcontinental railroad had raised virtually no capital in the stringent wartime market, yet Huntington, relying on old business friends and the excellent credit of his hardware firm, coaxed financiers into lending him several hundred thousand dollars, secured by discounted company bonds and his own personal guarantee of repayment. This was the company's first significant influx of outside funding. With it, Huntington bought rails, locomotives, and other equipment and had it shipped around the Horn, using cash and more bonds and personal promissory notes. The Central Pacific Railroad was finally in business, though carrying heavy debt.

Judah versus the Associates

Huntington returned from the East in the summer of 1863 to find the Central Pacific in shambles. Enemies still tied up local subsidies; some stockholders had defaulted on payments due on their subscriptions; and Stanford had lost his party's nomination for a second term as governor. Unless it obtained more capital, and quickly, the company could not finish the first 50 miles of track required by Congress's November 1864 deadline. In that case, the railroad would lose the federal subsidy and probably go under, taking with it the personal fortunes of its founders. Under mounting pressure, company leaders fought bitterly over control, engineering, and finances.

The Associates, who owned most Central Pacific stock and had already mortgaged their personal assets to begin construction, insisted that delinquent stockholders pay their subscriptions and that all investors be further assessed. Less wealthy minority stockholders, led by Judah, who had received his stock free and had little of his own money in the railroad, were equally determined that the company raise funds by further mortgaging its equipment and the uncompleted roadbed. The Huntington faction objected that this would saddle the shaky company with ruinous debt.

Judah also demanded absolute control over engineering and construction. Opposed to the draining of profits from the Central Pacific into a company in which he held no stock, Judah blocked the letting of additional construction contracts to Crocker & Co. The Associates countered that the outside construction firms did shoddy work, charged higher prices, and often defaulted on their contracts. Already upset with what he saw as the Associates' questionable methods, Judah was furious when Gov. Stanford persuaded the state geologist to declare that the Sierra Nevada began with the first low rises seven miles east of Sacramento, instead of the steeper grades 27 miles farther east, a move that added substantially to early construction subsidies.

For their part, the Associates had long been exasperated by Judah's unrealistic cost estimates and his damaging mistakes in designing roadbeds, bridges, and culverts. As the company was flirting with bankruptcy, he also was planning to build grandiose train stations. Judah, the Associates had concluded, was a careless engineer and an impractical obstructionist who would ruin the railway and take their personal fortunes with it.

In July the Huntington faction won control of the board of directors; it demanded that other board members pay their stock assessments or relinquish their seats. When Judah and his supporters refused, the Big Four insisted that Judah buy them out or consent to sell his stock. Eventually, an agreement was reached. Again unable to raise cash, Judah exchanged his stock for $100,000 in Central Pacific bonds and withdrew from the board. He retained his post as chief engineer at a salary of $5,000 per year, as well as an option to buy out the Big Four for $100,000 each. In early October 1863, Judah left by steamer to try to borrow the money from eastern railroad financiers. He contracted yellow fever while in Panama, however, and died in New York City

The Big Four

Villains or Heroes?

"The Big Four," as the surviving members of the Associates were known after Edwin Crocker stepped down, in many ways typified frontier success. Contrary to the popular "rags-to-riches" myth, nineteenth-century American business and political leaders came primarily from northeastern middle- and upper-class families. Leland Stanford (1824–1893), Collis P. Huntington (1821–1900), Charles Crocker (1822–1888), and Mark Hopkins (1813–1878) all fit this pattern. Each hailed from middle-class families and had either been born or resided in New York state. Each arrived in gold-rush California with business and political experience and capital or goods to invest. Each tried mining "the golden fleece" but soon turned to the more reliable trade of "fleecing" the miners. Weathering flood, fire, depression, and personal adversity, the four established successful supply businesses in Sacramento in the 1850s.

The Big Four

Left to right: Leland Stanford, Collis P. Huntington, Charles Crocker, and Mark Hopkins. *California State Railroad Museum.*

Building the Central and Southern Pacific railroads soon made the Associates wealthy and powerful. The resulting transportation monopoly, and their aggressive business and political tactics, real and imagined, earned them many enemies. They were widely charged with pocketing excessive profits from public construction subsidies, destroying their competitors unethically, inhibiting California's development by charging shippers "all the market will bear," and corrupting public officials to get their way. Collis P. Huntington gained particular infamy in 1883, when the chance publication of his private letters to David Colton, a lesser company official, revealed that the Big Four had indeed bribed Congressmen and state politicians. Particularly after he ousted the more popular Stanford as president of the Southern Pacific companies in 1890, Huntington came to symbolize the greed and corruption of late-nineteenth-century business. Business rivals and political reformers accused him of every conceivable evil, and journalists and cartoonists made their reputations by pillorying him. Later historians have cast Huntington as the state's most despicable villain.

(continued . . .)

Despite harsh public criticism, the Big Four saw themselves as honest, loyal California pioneers, and they took pride in their railroad's importance in spurring the state's growth in commerce, land values, personal incomes, and community welfare. "I am satisfied with what I have done," Huntington wrote privately near the end of his life. "No man is perfect and the man does not live who can look back and say that he has made no mistakes; but the motives back of my actions have been honest ones and the results have redounded far more to the benefit of California than they have to my own."

Like Andrew Carnegie and other giants of nineteenth-century business, the Big Four also made large donations of property and money to build parks, schools, and other community facilities. In Sacramento, Edwin Crocker founded the renowned Crocker Art Museum. Hopkins's heirs gave a good share of his money to endow the San Francisco Art Institute and the Hopkins Marine Laboratory near Monterey. Similarly, Huntington's nephew Henry and widow Arabella channeled much of Collis's wealth into San Marino's Huntington Library and Art Gallery. To honor the memory of their son, Leland and Jane Stanford donated immense land holdings and practically their entire fortune to create Stanford University.

Huntington merits reconsideration in another respect. Unlike many of his fiercest critics, Huntington, like others of the Associates, was an ardent opponent of racial prejudice and discrimination. As had the Crocker brothers, Huntington had been an abolitionist before the Civil War, and he later donated hundreds of thousands of dollars to support African American churches in California, and schools and colleges in the southern states, most prominently Booker T. Washington's Tuskegee Institute. Though it was politically unwise, Huntington ordered his companies to give equal employment and pay to black workers, and he publicly opposed the exclusions of black and other non-white children from public schools, as well as other "Jim Crow" restrictions then being enacted in the South and elsewhere. In newspaper columns and public speeches in the West, Huntington praised the Chinese for their culture and industry, and condemned state and federal discrimination against American Indians and Chinese, Filipino, and Japanese immigrants. "If we deny to the individual, no matter what his creed, his color or his nationality, the right to justice which every man possesses," he told a gathering of California civic and railway leaders in 1900, "there will be no enduring prosperity and [the nation's] decline will surely follow."

Were the Big Four "robber barons" or public benefactors? As with much else about California history, the answer is not simple.   (RJO)

the following month. The career of one of California's most colorful figures had ended tragically.

Many histories of the era cast Judah as a martyr to the Associates' greed. Relying on hindsight and the worshipful memoirs of his wife, Anna, some historians have speculated that the railroad would have been less corrupt had Judah gained control. His contributions to the Central Pacific were undeniably important. He popularized the transcontinental railway, located a feasible route, conceived the original plan for the Central Pacific, and with Huntington lobbied through the Pacific Railway Act of 1862. Judah remains a true hero of California history. But in that era, Judah was only one of many would-be railroad builders. When he left California, the Central Pacific was still a speculative venture, lacked assets, and was indistinguishable from similar projects that had failed. Judah's engineering talent was adequate for preliminary work, but he made several costly errors, and he had yet to prove that he could solve the technical problems looming

in the Sierra. Judah also shared many of the lax business ethics for which his generation was infamous, and his business skills and political influence were minimal. The company's victories had come primarily in politics, finance, and administration, areas in which the Associates' contributions were consistently more important than Judah's. It is likely that if Judah had wrested control from his partners, the Central Pacific would have failed.

The Pacific Railway Act of 1864

The Central Pacific's 1863 management crisis was the nadir in its history. With the future clouded, the Associates resumed work on the roadbed and bridges. The company set October 26 as the date for the laying of the first rails, but it avoided fanfare. "These mountains look too ugly and I see too much work ahead," Huntington complained. At this point, the Associates were eager for Judah to buy them out.

But even in the gloomy fall of 1863, the tide was beginning to turn. Crews were finally driving rails through the streets of Sacramento. On November 9, the first locomotive, *Gov. Stanford*, belched steam and began shuttling supplies, work gangs, and dignitaries back and forth between the river port and construction sites. The railroad's finances also improved dramatically. Starting in September, favorable resolutions were reached in the suits blocking state and local subsidies. County and municipal subsidy bonds started trickling into the Central Pacific's coffers, and state grants soon followed.

Huntington again headed east to secure all-important amendments to the Pacific Railway Act. Although the Central Pacific's enemies mounted another campaign to deny aid to the railway, Huntington struck an alliance with the Union Pacific, which was having even greater trouble raising capital and had yet to break ground. Six months of lobbying by Huntington and the Union Pacific's Thomas Durant produced the Pacific Railway Act of 1864, which modified most of the burdensome features of the 1862 law. The new act extended the deadline for completing the first 50-mile portion to 1865 and doubled the land grant to 20 sections per mile. More importantly, the 1864 law reduced the federal subsidy bonds to a second mortgage and allowed the railways to sell their own first-mortgage bonds in amounts equal to the government subsidy, thereby doubling potential construction capital for both companies. Two years later, hoping to induce the railroads to build faster, Congress authorized each company to construct as much of the transcontinental line as it could.

The second Pacific Railway Act was a turning point for the Central Pacific. Realizing the company's superior position, its rivals either went out of business or reoriented their lines to feed into the Central Pacific. With local and federal subsidies assured, investors grew more confident. For the first time, Huntington could sell the company's securities and government bonds. Investors, however, would purchase the bonds only at heavy discounts. The Central Pacific was lucky to receive one-half the face value of the securities, although it would be obliged to repay the entire amount, with interest. Laboring under a heavy debt and staggering interest payments, the railroad stood days or hours away from financial disaster many times over the next few years, especially as the high costs of mountain construction strained the company's finances. But with his close ties to American and European investors, his willingness to pledge his own or his Associates' businesses or to juggle funds in deceptive ways, Huntington always managed to buy supplies and cover interest payments. The Central Pacific's credit remained spotless and Huntington came to be acknowledged as one of the business geniuses of his era.

Completing the Transcontinental Railway

Fueled by new capital, construction on the Central Pacific steadily gained momentum. In April 1864, locomotives first hauled passengers and freight the 18 miles between Sacramento and Roseville. Passenger trains sped along at an astounding 22 miles per hour (15 miles per hour for freight), but traffic remained light until June, when the company completed the track to Newcastle and the Dutch Flat Toll Road to the Comstock Lode. The Central Pacific's combined rail and wagon service immediately proved faster and cheaper than anything its competitors could offer and they soon controlled most of the Comstock trade. As income began to exceed operating expenses, stocks and bonds became easier to sell. The Central Pacific looked like it might yet turn a profit.

Nevertheless, when the company tried to push its line higher into the Sierra in the winter of 1865, it again bogged down, this time with labor problems. Few men answered the company's call for 5,000 construction workers. Many of those who did quickly deserted to the Comstock mines, particularly after a taste of working in deep snows for $35 per month. Having employed Chinese construction laborers on the Dutch Flat Road, Charles Crocker ordered that Chinese workers be tried. Although some leaders objected, the experiment was an instant success. Chinese workers learned quickly, labored tirelessly, and soon excelled at skilled tasks. They eagerly accepted both the hard work and the low wages, which were only 60 to 90 percent of the rates paid Caucasians. By May 1865 the Chinese composed two-thirds of the Central Pacific's labor force. For the next four years, the company relied on the Chinese, as well as substantial numbers of Portuguese and other immigrant groups, to win its race with the Union Pacific. When labor needs exceeded the supply of local immigrants, Crocker arranged with San Francisco labor contractors to import workers directly from China. So efficient did the Chinese crews become that, after the transcontinental connection was completed, the company transferred them to extension lines it was building in California and states to the east. Before long, other western railroads also employed Chinese workers.

Chinese Laborers Filling the Secret Town Trestle

Once they had proven their skills, Chinese immigrants came to comprise a high percentage of the Central Pacific's work force, even after the completion of the first transcontinental line. In the 1870s Collis P. Huntington's friend Carleton E. Watkins, who often worked on assignment for the Big Four, took this famous photograph of Chinese laborers filling in the 1,000-foot-long Secret Town trestle, 62 miles east of Sacramento. *The Huntington Library, San Marino, California.*

Beyond Auburn, Central Pacific crews grappled with some of the most forbidding terrain in the country. The road faced a climb of more than 5,000 feet in 40 miles over the Sierra crest, before reaching the treacherous cliffs at Donner Pass. Below-zero temperatures and 40-foot snows halted work for weeks at a time. In summertime, the men were harried by insects and swarms of rattlesnakes, their dens disturbed by construction. Illness ravaged the overworked and underpaid workers. Cave-ins and misfired explosions killed and maimed scores of workers. Conditions were so unbearable by the spring of 1867 that even the normally compliant Chinese went on strike, demanding more pay and shorter working hours. After a week, the intransigent Crocker broke the strike by cutting off supplies and starving the Chinese back to work.

Somehow, the Central Pacific inched upward. The company invented new railway construction techniques and worked its force of more than 14,000 in round-the-clock shifts. The Chinese bored away at tunnels a few inches a day from both ends, and chipped out narrow ledges to carry the tracks around precipices, while the company used the Dutch Flat Road to move materials and rolling stock ahead by wagon—by sled in winter—so that work could proceed on multiple fronts. To shield its line from the crushing drifts of Donner Pass, in 1868 crews began building miles of long wooden snow sheds, to this day a distinctive feature of the Pacific railway.

The work devoured capital. Many stretches, particularly the tunnels, cost between $150,000 and $1 million per mile, and the company teetered perpetually on the brink of insolvency. Finally, after nearly three years of strenuous mountain construction, trains chugged over the summit of the Sierra in November 1867. The next May, the line finally reached Nevada, still only 140 miles from Sacramento.

Once clear of the mountains, the Central Pacific began to race across the relatively flat Great Basin towards the Union Pacific, now stalled in the mountains northeast of the Great Salt Lake. Though plagued

Snowsheds on the Central Pacific
Alfred Hart photographed the Central Pacific's famous snowsheds while they were under construction in the late 1860s. *The Huntington Library, San Marino, California.*

by extreme temperatures and scarce and alkali-tainted water, Crocker's experienced Chinese and European immigrant crews worked at an astonishing pace. During the next year they completed 550 miles.

On May 10, 1869, the Central Pacific had linked with the Union Pacific. Hundreds of jubilant laborers, executives, dignitaries, and reporters gathered at Promontory Summit, north of the Great Salt Lake, for a legendary ceremony. After the customary prayers and speeches, Leland Stanford swung his hammer at a golden spike fastening the last rail, and the transcontinental railroad was finally joined. Telegraph wires attached to the spike and hammer announced the grand moment to an eager outside world. Festivities were already in full swing in California. When word arrived at Sacramento, thousands surged through the streets celebrating the city's victory. Their wild cheers were quickly drowned in a clangor of church bells, whistles, fire bells, pistol shots, and cannon blasts. To the east, a nation still grieving

from years of civil war rejoiced in the heroic building feat, and looked forward to a new age of prosperity, westward expansion, and national unity. A four-mile-long parade danced through the streets of Chicago. In Philadelphia, the Liberty Bell pealed from the tower of Independence Hall.

The Associates and the Emerging Rail System

Dramatic though it was, the driving of the golden spike was only the beginning of California's railway age. Capitalizing on the line's potential for stimulating development, promoters organized dozens of railways in the late 1860s and '70s. Locomotives soon whistled around the flats of San Francisco Bay and up its flanking valleys. Tracks penetrated the Sacramento Valley north of Marysville and into the San Joaquin south of Stockton, for the first time entering many of the

Thomas Hill's The Last Spike

Commissioned years later by Leland Stanford, Thomas Hill's romantic depiction of the driving of the golden spike at Promontory Point portrays a cross-section of those associated with the building of the transcontinental line: leaders such as Stanford (*at center, holding the hammer*); Chinese laborers (*to Stanford's left*); Irish immigrant workers, smoking their characteristic pipes (*to the right and below Stanford*); Indians (*foreground*); and a wagon train, the transportation mode being supplanted (*background*). Also in the painting were persons not present at the spike driving, including Collis P. Huntington, who was in New York at the time. Theodore Judah, dead for nearly six years, is resurrected at the lower right. Scorned by Stanford, the painting now hangs in the California State Railroad Museum at Sacramento. *California State Railroad Museum.*

state's lightly populated interior regions. In 1869, the Los Angeles & San Pedro Railroad, the first operating southern line, connected the old pueblo of Los Angeles to its new harbor at Wilmington. Within three years, small railroads extended lines into Los Angeles's fertile hinterland. Other railways welded regions together into the first statewide transit system. Of the state's major population centers, only the isolated northwest and central coasts, the Sierra foothills, and the San Diego area still lacked direct railroad service in the 1870s. By the early twentieth century, the rail network included these areas too.

If new rail lines were not themselves built by the Central Pacific, they usually fell quickly into the Associates' grasp. Often outgrowths of real estate schemes or designed by their promoters for quick speculation

rather than long-term profitable operation, the new companies could not remain independent, weakened as they were by shoddy construction and equipment, light traffic, and ruinous debt. Their builders were all too eager to skim off profits and unload their shaky companies. The Big Four had reasons of their own for acquiring other lines. The revenues of the Central Pacific were at first disappointing. The Suez Canal, also completed in 1869, siphoned off much of the Asian trade. Traffic from eastern states in goods, tourists, and immigrants also failed to match overly optimistic predictions. In the late 1860s and early '70s the Big Four were deeply in debt and anxious to sell the Central Pacific. But due to the company's immensity, its troubled finances, and the recurrent depressions of the 1870s, the Associates could not dispose of the railroad, though they tried repeatedly.

Southern Pacific Lines

IN

CALIFORNIA AND NEVADA

11-'22   Copyright by Rand McNally & Co. Chicago.

The only way to avert disaster, Huntington convinced his partners, was to continue to build new lines, to defeat or absorb potential competitors, and to somehow make the roads profitable. Borrowing heavily and reinvesting all available profits, the Associates purchased other transportation companies. By the end of the 1870s, they had transformed themselves from railroad builders into railroad operators.

Most independent California railway companies came within the control of the Associates in the 1860s and '70s, either voluntarily or pressured by lowered Central Pacific freight and passenger fares they could not match. The first to fall was their old nemesis, the Sacramento Valley Railroad, whose owners sold out in 1865, followed three years later by the railroads around San Francisco Bay. With these lines, Central Pacific trains from the East arrived at the Bay a few months after the ceremony at Promontory. To the dismay of Sacramentans, their city's hard-won fame as the western terminus of the transcontinental ended in 1869, when the Central Pacific moved its terminal to Oakland, and in 1873 its headquarters to San Francisco.

Throughout the 1870s and into the twentieth century, the Big Four and their successors continued to expand their transportation holdings. To reduce water competition, they reached a rate and traffic agreement with the Pacific Mail Steamship Company in 1871. A few years later, in 1874, they formed their own trans-Pacific firm, the Occidental and Oriental Steamship Company, giving them a large measure of control over San Francisco's oceangoing commerce. The Big Four also absorbed inland riverboat enterprises and several San Francisco Bay ferries. Some of the newly acquired routes were integrated into the Central Pacific system. Others were reduced to branches or closed down altogether. While many communities thrived from the increased commerce, the hopes of some towns for urban greatness were dashed. Disappointed townsfolk added their voices to a growing anti-Central Pacific chorus.

Southern Pacific Rail Lines in California and Nevada, 1923

In this map of main California and Nevada railroads near their peak of expansion, Southern Pacific Company tracks appear as wide, those of rival companies as narrow, lines. *Courtesy of the California History Room, California State Library, Sacramento, California.*

The Associates' prize acquisition was the Southern Pacific Railroad. Severe winter weather and high elevations along the Central–Union Pacific route shifted national attention to building a southerly, low-elevation rail line near the Mexican border. Founded in 1865, the Southern Pacific secured a federal franchise and land grant to build that part of the line from San José to the Colorado River. Thus, when they purchased the unbuilt Southern Pacific in 1868, the Associates were assured of control of the western portion of the proposed southern transcontinental route.

Immediately upon acquiring their new road, the Big Four set off to capture the strategic crossing of the Colorado River at Yuma, Arizona Territory. Between 1869 and 1876, they extended one Southern Pacific line south of San José to Tres Piños, and another through the San Joaquin Valley. Then, in a feat rivaling the crossing of the Sierra, the company surmounted the Tehachapi Mountains to descend into Southern California. In 1872, the Southern Pacific had agreed to build through Los Angeles in exchange for a subsidy from the city. On September 5, 1876, another driving of a golden spike connected Los Angeles to the state's northern railway system and the Central Pacific's line to the East. Meanwhile, the Associates had acquired most other Los Angeles railways, including the line from the city 20 miles to its harbor. Already they had begun building the Southern Pacific eastward, across the cattle ranches of the San Gabriel and San Bernardino valleys and the parched Colorado Desert. In 1877, the Southern Pacific illegally bridged the Colorado River, before federal approval, and steamed into Yuma.

To the consternation of eastern railroad moguls who coveted the southern transcontinental route for themselves, in 1879 the Southern Pacific resumed construction east across Arizona and New Mexico without a federal subsidy. In 1881 the company's Chinese track-laying crews reached El Paso, Texas, a major rail crossroads. For several years Huntington had been quietly securing control of a string of Texas and Louisiana railroads, and in early 1883 Southern Pacific locomotives used these lines to enter Houston and New Orleans, with their Atlantic ports on the Gulf of Mexico. The Big Four had now brought the first coast-to-coast railway system under their own management. Trains between San Francisco and New Orleans, the famed Sunset Route, began operating in February 1883. Acquisition and completion in 1887 of the Oregon & California Railroad between the northern Sacramento Valley and Portland, and the subsequent absorption of additional Oregon lines, rounded out the Big Four's railroad empire.

The Southern Pacific Company

By the end of the 1870s the Big Four monopolized California transportation. Capitalized at $225 million, their California railroads in 1877 controlled 2,340 miles of track, including 85 percent of all railroad tracks in the state and all the important lines in the San Francisco Bay Area, Los Angeles, and the Sacramento and San Joaquin valleys. Their successful enterprises had brought the Associates great fortunes. From modest beginnings as Sacramento shopkeepers, they now ranked among America's richest and most powerful business leaders.

Acquiring widely separated companies, however, caused acute management problems. Linking and operating the many new companies proved unwieldy, particularly after acquisition of the Texas and Louisiana railroads. The companies varied according to different national, state, and territorial regulations they had to comply with, differences in financial solvency, and differences in the lease and ownership arrangements by which the Associates controlled them. To solve these problems and provide a better mechanism for distributing traffic, capital, equipment, and profits among their far-flung lines, Huntington convinced his partners in 1884 to set up a holding company, the Southern Pacific Company, and to transfer their holdings to the new company, which they would own in equal shares. To broaden its powers and shield it from legal and political attack in the West, the holding company was incorporated in Kentucky. In early 1885 the Associates transferred their commonly owned stock, leases, and property to the new firm. From headquarters in San Francisco and New York City, the Southern Pacific Company modernized and integrated the Associates' properties to produce more efficient, more profitable operation. By the end of the 1800s, all of the Associates' rail properties were commonly referred to as the "Southern Pacific."

Transportation competition revived somewhat for California in later years however. By constructing some tracks and deftly forcing the Southern Pacific to let it use others, the Santa Fe Railroad entered Los Angeles on its own tracks from the Midwest in the mid-1880s. There it engaged the Southern Pacific in a rate war that helped ignite a Southern California real estate boom. In the 1880s, the Santa Fe brought and extended an independent line up the San Joaquin Valley, and in the '90s built a connection to San Francisco Bay at Richmond. After 1900 both the Union Pacific and a new Western Pacific Railroad completed their own lines to the East. Nevertheless, the Southern Pacific still controlled most important tracks in the major markets, and it could often convince rivals to reduce competition. The company influenced California's economic and political life well into the age of automobiles and airplanes.

California's Railway Era

Economic Development and Social Unrest

15

"The Terrible Seventies"

In 1914 Gertrude Atherton coined the phrase "The Terrible Seventies" for a chapter in her book, *California, An Intimate History*. Certainly, it was a difficult decade for some Californians, but not for all. Many thousands of urban laborers, white-collar workers, and business, land, and farm owners benefited from the opportunities the railroads brought. Yet Henry George's gloomy prophecy at the dawn of the railway age came true for many people. Railroads aggravated some old problems and introduced new ones. In general, they offered the greatest benefits to those who already had property and influence. Railroads were a boon to industries and communities served by the new transit system, but undermined some not so fortunately placed. By improving access to California, railways also made the state more vulnerable to nationwide economic disturbances. Despite remarkable development after 1869, the next decade was also one of the most turbulent in the state's history. The '70s were more paradoxical than terrible.

Urban Growth

Railroads encouraged economic growth in California by reducing transportation costs, making remote lands and resources accessible, widening markets for producers, raising land values, and increasing many people's incomes. One of the first results was rapid urbanization. A prime example was Oakland, a steamboat port settled in the 1850s across the bay from San Francisco. In 1868, the ultimate coastal terminus of the transcontinental railway was still in doubt. Oakland's scheming founder and most powerful citizen, Horace Carpentier, assured his own fortunes by deeding large tracts of prime shoreline to the Oakland Waterfront Company, of which he and Leland Stanford were principal owners. In return, the Big Four agreed to locate the railway's western terminus at Oakland, rather than continue the line around the bay to San Francisco. At first Carpentier was hailed as a local hero, and Oakland's future seemed bright, although the city had to fight a protracted legal battle with the railroad after the 1890s to recapture its waterfront.

The arrival of Central Pacific trains had an immediate, spectacular effect on Oakland. Passengers jammed downtown shops, hotels, and restaurants. Commerce quickened and land values rose, sparking downtown building booms and new subdivisions filled with ornate Victorian homes. Industries rushed into the city, as firms vied for sites near the rail terminal. Wharves and warehouses proliferated. As employment soared, so did population. In 1868 Oakland was a bucolic village, its 2,000 residents easily outnumbered by the sprawling oaks after which the town was named. In 1870, the population exploded to 10,500 and, by 1880, with 35,000 residents, Oakland had grown into the second largest city in California and the Far West.

Oakland's rapid modernization after 1869 was typical of rail-era cities. The railroad boom increased the community's size and diversity, expanded its wealth and tax base, and brought new ideas and technologies. Schools, churches, and municipal agencies multiplied, as did social, cultural, and professional organizations. Almost all the oaks were uprooted; the streets were straightened and extended. Water, sewer, and gas utilities were expanded. In 1878, only two years after Alexander Graham Bell had invented it, the telephone arrived in Oakland, easing communication within the city and to San Francisco. Electricity followed in the early '80s. Oakland's efficient transit system of horse car lines, Central Pacific steam commuter trains, and cable cars extended into the countryside, connecting the city to Berkeley to the north and San Leandro and Hayward to the south, and igniting more suburban booms along the way. By the early '80s, Oakland was the hub of a growing East Bay metropolitan region, a thriving, attractive, comfortable city, equal or superior in modern facilities to much older eastern centers.

Railroads likewise transformed other towns, though not as spectacularly. Already the dominant southern California town, Los Angeles came alive in 1872, as soon as its citizens voted to subsidize the Southern Pacific Railroad. Even as the city awaited its outside rail link, trade expanded, downtown buildings rose, outlying property was subdivided for residences, additional farms sprouted in the countryside, and local rail lines gravitated toward the future terminus of the southern transcontinental route. Although the city had grown little in the 1860s, by completion of the Southern Pacific's southbound line in September 1876, the city had tripled its 1870 population of 5,700. Although the boom collapsed in the nationwide depression of the late 1870s, the city could still boast 33,381 residents in 1880, a 500 percent increase over the previous decade. By comparison, rival San Diego, having lost the all-important rail connection, languished with a population of about 3,000 throughout the 1870s. The railroad's arrival pushed Los Angeles along in its evolution from a colonial pueblo into a thoroughly Americanized city, a process that was completed in the '80s by another railroad-related boom.

New towns took root as tracks were laid through unpopulated areas like the Central Valley and southern San Joaquin Valley. Outside parties sometimes started settlements adjacent to the lines, but through the 1870s, the Central Pacific's construction and real estate development arm, the Contract and Finance Company (after 1879, the Pacific Improvement Company), founded numerous market towns. The company laid out streets in the familiar gridiron pattern and built shops, stations, yards, warehouses, loading docks, stock pens, and housing for its workers. A hotel and restaurant were often added to lure travelers and provide a social center. Trees were planted to shade and beautify the new community; the Associates also donated lots and cash toward the building of parks, schools, churches, and major businesses. The railroad often built and operated the first water systems necessary to lure people to arid regions. The company advertised the town sites, pairing lot auctions with festive picnics and bringing in prospective buyers on low-fare excursion trains. Instant rail towns materialized within weeks of the first sounding of a locomotive's whistle. Although

Depot at Truckee

On the east slopes of Donner Pass, the High Sierra town of Truckee resembled many communities springing up along rail lines throughout the state. Hitherto a tiny turnpike way station, Truckee became the gateway to California when the Central Pacific located yards and maintenance facilities there in 1868. Within a few years, the town's population had soared and it had become a major rail operations center as well as one of the leading manufacturers and shippers of ice and lumber in the American West. After the turn of the century, Truckee became California's first winter sports capital and the location for many early outdoor motion pictures. This photograph was taken by Alfred Hart in the late 1860s. *The Huntington Library, San Marino, California.*

some never progressed beyond way stations, others— such as Modesto, Merced, Fresno, Tulare, Hanford, Bakersfield, Niles, Livermore, and Colton—developed into prosperous trade centers.

San Francisco: From Instant City to Pacific Metropolis

Before completion of the transcontinental railway, San Francisco was "the City" for California and the Far West. San Francisco's meteoric rise as a gold rush center had resulted primarily from its early command of an incomparable deep-water harbor. In the 1860s its residents expected railroads to converge there, and real estate speculators swarmed around the few potential sites for railway operations along the city's southern waterfront. But San Francisco's grand ambitions were soon dashed. The city was on the tip of a peninsula

nearly 100 travel-miles farther from mining and farming districts than were its East Bay rivals. One of the first California cities blessed with nominal rail service, San Francisco lost the contest for important terminal facilities to cities with better rail locations: Oakland, Sacramento and, after the 1880s, Los Angeles. No wonder San Francisco soured on railroads in the 1870s. Frustrated journalists and business leaders bemoaned the rail isolation of their city, belittled and tried to undercut urban competitors, and blamed their business woes on the perfidious railroad. For the rest of the nineteenth century, San Franciscans furnished much of the energy behind anti-Southern Pacific politics.

Although disappointed that the Central Pacific invested in end-of-the-line improvements in other cities, San Francisco generally prospered during the railway era. Its head start on rivals was too long, its prestige too great, its facilities too convenient, and its banks and investors too flushed. The Central Pacific itself moved its corporate headquarters from Sacramento to San Francisco in 1873, and other major businesses opened offices there as well. Much of California's commerce with the outside world, particularly bulky goods, continued to arrive by sea. Oakland's harbor was at first too shallow, so San Francisco remained the major Pacific Coast port and city, with steam ferries chugging cargo and passengers back and forth between the city, Oakland, and other bay points. To a significant degree, San Francisco continued to dominate coastal trade, as well as riverboat traffic with interior valleys.

San Francisco was the commercial metropolis of the Pacific Coast by 1880, when the city stood ninth among the nation's cities in manufacturing and population. Its 234,000 residents came from nearly everywhere on earth. Half were foreign-born and three-fourths had at least one foreign-born parent. Within two decades of statehood, San Francisco was one of the nation's most cosmopolitan and ethnically diverse cities.

Industrialization

In 1860 San Francisco had ranked 15th in size among U.S. cities, but only 22nd in manufacturing output and 51st in industrial employment, because local conditions discouraged heavy industry in both the city and state. Coal and iron ore were scarce and expensive. Monthly interest rates as high as 15 percent meant that investment capital was expensive. Other development investments away from the city—land, transportation, and mining stocks—were thus more appealing. Because of the strong lure of inland mines, particularly the still-booming Comstock Lode, factory labor remained scarce in San Francisco and other California cities. As a result, ships departing California ports usually carried raw materials, such as logs, raw cattle hides, and unmilled grain, instead of lumber, finished leather goods, and flour.

Circumstances changed during the 1860s and early '70s. The transformation of western mining into a large-scale industry encouraged economic diversification. Hydraulic and hard-rock mining corporations replaced the prospector-owned placer companies of the early gold rush. Particularly in Nevada's Comstock silver region, shafts and tunnels plunged to unprecedented depths. Mining on such a grand scale required heavy equipment designed specifically for the Sierra and the Comstock.

San Francisco entrepreneurs responded quickly. The Irish-born Donahue brothers, for example, arrived in 1849 and began turning scrap metal into shovels for miners. Their Union Iron Works thrived, but in 1860 it remained basically a glorified blacksmith shop. The firm shifted to producing mining machinery and, a decade later, employed 600 workers molding imported iron into heavy equipment for mines and other industries. Other factories machined tools for manufacturers, and produced cable, pumps, stamp mills, steam engines, and other essentials of the new mining technology, as well as rails, cars, and locomotives for the West's growing transportation network.

Other railroad-era economic changes had similar consequences for San Francisco industry. The expansion of lumbering and new town construction required heavy milling equipment and stimulated furniture making. In the early gold rush, entire buildings had been shipped around the Horn from the East. By the 1870s, California's own mills and shops were fashioning boards, shingles, posts, windows, grilles, and a phantasmagoria of Victorian gingerbread to adorn the state's growing cities. San Francisco, like Oakland, San José, and other cities, also specialized in processing California's multiplying farm crops. Bonanza wheat farms that developed in the 1870s needed plows and harvesters designed for California's unique soil conditions and unusually large farming operations. By the 1870s, San Francisco's grain mills were beginning a flourishing trade in flour to China and Europe. Surplus cattle hides inspired a thriving tanning industry, followed by boot-making and other leather-goods enterprises. The growth of sheep ranching prompted the 1878 merger of the Pioneer and Mission mills, creating one of the nation's largest producers of high-quality woolen goods. Across the state, breweries, wineries, distilleries, grain and cloth mills, and vegetable and fruit canneries sprang up around rail sidings, yards, and waterfronts.

Financing such operations required capital, which was soon available in San Francisco and other cities. Capital accumulated from land and mining-stock speculation and grain production, while the decline of profits from the Comstock Lode forced entrepreneurs into alternative investments. San Francisco's John W. Mackay, for example, the Comstock magnate whose income of $25 a minute at one time made him the wealthiest man in the world, turned to manufacturing. Others followed suit. By the time the Bank of California temporarily closed its doors and touched off a panic in 1875, William C. Ralston had invested his own and the bank's funds—not always wisely—in lock and clock factories, food and textile plants, machine-tool shops, mining mills, and smelters. Adolph Sutro, Claus Spreckels, James Phelan, and scores of others with more modest fortunes also diversified through investment in manufacturing.

The 1870s also brought San Francisco the final ingredient essential to industrial development: a labor force. After 1869, the Central Pacific released some of its Chinese workers, most of whom migrated to San Francisco. By 1880 Chinese comprised 15 percent of the city's total work force of 100,000, and nearly 90 percent in cigar making, textile and clothing manufacture, shoe production, and other light industries. Other groups also gravitated to the city, including former railroad workers, men idled by depletion of the Comstock and Sierra mines, and thousands riding the rails to escape economic depressions and labor troubles in the East. The growing labor pool transformed the city's social character. No single enterprise dominated, but by 1880 San Francisco had become an industrial city with half its workers employed in manufacturing. Smaller cities experienced similar shifts.

Railroads and the Bonanza Wheat Era

California's climates and soils held rich agricultural potential, but progress was uneven during the 1850s and '60s. While some success was achieved in producing livestock, cereals, vegetables, and fruit, farmers suffered a lack of information about growing conditions, inexperience with agriculture in arid lands, poor transportation, and, particularly, limited markets.

Surprisingly, the start of transcontinental rail service in 1869 offered little immediate assistance to many California farmers. Shipping time along the Central Pacific route was too long, and extreme winter and summer weather delayed and spoiled cargoes. Freight charges were high—in part because traffic was low and train operation through rugged territory was expensive, but also because the Big Four hoped to make the most of its monopoly. Many California farm products could not hold their own against better and cheaper competitors grown closer to eastern markets. But the development of local rail service within the state did transform agricultural practices. As illustrated in Mussel Slough country, the shorter lines unlocked the virgin soils of fertile areas, which connected farmers with local market towns and coastal ports, encouraged settlement of new regions, and spurred the development of new crops, machinery, and techniques.

A prime example is wheat growing in the late 1860s and '70s, which evolved from a decentralized business producing food for local consumption to a large-scale, highly structured export industry. The boom in wheat cultivation followed the railroad tracks through the San Francisco Bay region, up the Sacramento Valley, and down the San Joaquin and Salinas valleys. The crop offered an apparently ideal solution to California's agricultural challenges. Wheat required little or no irrigation and actually benefited from long dry summers. Its culture was well-known and inexpensive. Although too bulky and low in value to ship east by rail, it was a nonperishable crop that could be transported profitably to distant markets in sailing ships. Growers followed the railroads onto flat valley lands and wheat acreage soared.

Essential in a poor marketing zone such as California, an elaborate structure emerged overnight to link wheat growers with consumers around the world. Relying on telegraphic communication, British and American companies bought wheat in California and sold it on exchanges in England and elsewhere. Isaac Friedlander, a German Jewish immigrant, assembled an international network of banks, warehouses, shipping companies, and grain-sack factories. From San Francisco, Friedlander could forecast wheat output, control finance and supply, and reserve ships to carry the harvest. Although they stabilized the wheat trade, brokers like Friedlander and a few others reaped bonanza profits and exercised monopolistic powers that angered some growers.

In favored regions, such as Mussel Slough, small farmers raised wheat profitably. But most grain was produced on vast tracts of leased or cheaply purchased land. These ranches employed industrial work forces and huge plows, harvesters, and steam tractors, much of the machinery developed and manufactured nearby. The largest grower, Colusa County's Hugh J. Glenn, amassed an empire of 66,000 acres and employed nearly 1,000 laborers. Investing more than $300,000 in machinery and draft animals, by 1880 Glenn produced a million bushels of wheat a year. Glenn and other bonanza growers hauled sacks of grain in wagons to railside platforms, where they were snatched up by Southern and Central Pacific wheat specials. These long trains converged on San Francisco Bay and the Carquinez Strait, particularly at Port Costa. Endless strings of boxcars crept across specially built wharves, their wheat loaded directly into the holds of sailing ships for the voyage to China, Australia, or the British Isles.

During the 1870s and '80s, California wheat growing developed into the most mechanized and structured form of agriculture in the world, becoming the state's major export industry. Production reached a peak of 41 million bushels in 1890. During the boom years, the fortunes of Friedlander, Glenn, and other "wheat kings" rivaled those of the Big Four and mining-stock speculators.

The bonanza wheat era ended abruptly in the 1890s. Other wheat farmers broke new ground on the Great Plains and in Europe, Asia, and Australia, many using techniques and machines imported from California. Overproduction of wheat glutted world markets and sent prices plummeting. At the same time, yields declined sharply on California's eroded and exhausted soils. Improved irrigation facilities and rail connections to the East encouraged growers to subdivide their fields for more profitable uses. Wheat growing dwindled into a minor endeavor in California after 1900.

Fruit and Specialty-Crop Farming

Cultivation of specialty crops—citrus fruit, deciduous fruit, winter vegetables, melons, rice, and cotton—emerged slowly after 1870. California would later become famous for these crops, although many had been grown as early as the mission era. Still, major economic, technological, institutional, and environmental changes were necessary before fruit and specialty-crop agriculture could become a reliable industry. Fragile, perishable, and unfamiliar to American farmers, the new crops needed specific climates, soils, and handling, requirements that were poorly understood at first. In particular, such crops required more water than nature provided. Because individual farmers had difficulty solving these complex problems, California agriculture became highly organized late in the nineteenth century.

From the beginning of American settlement, growers formed crop commodity groups to raise standards, sponsor innovation, combat disease and pests, disseminate information, and lobby the government for aid. Farmers first met locally and then, in 1854, launched the California State Agricultural Society. Dominated by the wealthiest growers, the society won a modest subsidy from the miner-controlled legislature. It managed the state fair and several local expositions, published useful technical papers, and persuaded the state to reward experimental growers. Growers of livestock, wine grapes, deciduous fruit, oranges, raisins, and nuts created pressure groups of their own. Small-scale farmers gravitated to the Patrons of Husbandry (The Grange), organized at local, county, and state-wide levels, and often favoring more militant policies at odds with wealthier growers.

After the 1880s, when limited markets were still causing overproduction and low prices and profits, many farmers turned to more powerful marketing cooperatives. The first successful cooperative was the California Fruit Growers' Exchange ("Sunkist"), founded in 1893. To eliminate middlemen, the Exchange and similar groups raising walnuts, almonds, deciduous fruit, raisins, dairy products, poultry, and other crops, limited production, regulated prices, adopted grading standards, and took charge of packing and marketing. Between 1900 and the '20s, the cooperatives acquired more control of production and convinced the state to erect elaborate governmental machinery to manage supplies, prices, and marketing conditions in the interests of growers and producers. By the early twentieth century, California agriculture had become dominated by complex, interlocking organizations with strong influence on their members, as well as public policy.

At the behest of farm pressure groups, all levels of government provided services to modernize agriculture. After the 1860s, federal agencies such as the Army Signal Corps (later the U.S. Weather Bureau) gathered, tabulated, and distributed statistics on climate, information that helped farmers choose crops and design operations more wisely. U.S. Department of Agriculture scientists developed, tested, and introduced crops. Most notable was the Washington navel orange, a superior seedless, winter-ripening fruit that the Department imported from Brazil in 1873 to save the struggling Riverside colony. The national and international resources of the Department also aided in discovering cures for new crop diseases brought to California as parasites on imported plants and now thriving in the genial climate.

Even more important were state agricultural agencies. Farm organizations promoted formation of the State Board of Agriculture (1863), Board of Viticulture (1880), Horticultural Commission (1883), Board of Silk Culture (1883), Dairy Bureau (1895), and State Veterinarian (1899). Although troubled by poor administration and funding, as well as opposition from rival groups, state agencies sponsored research, published reports, organized growers' conventions, advertised new farm products, and secured regulatory and quarantine legislation. By the turn of the twentieth century, growing state bureaucracies were important forces for agricultural change. In 1919 the legislature consolidated them under the State Department of Agriculture.

Private businesses engaged in agricultural development also encouraged innovation with capital and organization. While they were profiting from land speculation, developers like William S. Chapman, who built up the Fresno area in the 1870s, reorganized land for higher use, promoted compact settlement, financed farm purchases, and encouraged higher-value crops and more efficient farming methods. Before the 1880s private water companies, such as the joint-stock ventures begun by Mussel Slough settlers, built most small irrigation facilities that farmers needed to cultivate thirsty new crops. Organized colonies—among the most important of which were the Mormons at San Bernardino and the Germans at Anaheim (both founded in the 1850s), Riverside, Pasadena, and the Fresno raisin colonies (1870s), and irrigation genius George Chaffey's Ontario and Etiwanda colonies east of Los Angeles (1880s)—pooled capital, water rights, labor, expertise, and machinery. Cooperatively, they bought and improved land, developed irrigation, introduced new crops, and provided social and cultural amenities to reduce the isolation of the farm frontier.

The major business promoting agriculture was the Central/Southern Pacific. The railroad became convinced by the 1870s that the future of the state, as well as the company, depended on farm progress. Through its low-interest land-purchase loans and crop-share arrangements, the railroad advanced capital to finance many new small farms in emerging regions such as Mussel Slough. A powerful friend of scientific agriculture, the railroad compiled most of the climate, crop production, and water statistics used by early experimenters, agricultural agencies, and until the early 1900s, the U.S. Army Signal Corps and U.S. Weather Bureau. The company supported the University of California's agricultural teaching and experiments in various ways, from lobbying to protect the beleaguered institution's funds and independence, to providing monetary grants and free transportation for university staff and supplies. In cooperation with the university in 1908, the railroad began annual instructional trains through rural districts to teach farmers scientific cultivation. The company also promoted public irrigation and the preservation of forest watersheds.

The Southern Pacific's marketing services supplemented those of farm organizations and state agencies. The company's all-weather southern route to the Midwest (completed in 1883), along with the Santa Fe's line to Chicago (open in 1885), linked California farmers to the national market, and made possible the expansion of high-value specialty crops. After 1883 the Southern Pacific also instituted faster direct service to the East, ran special fruit-marketing trains, and pioneered in the development of ice manufacturing, fruit cooling plants,

The University of California and the Beginning of Higher Education

Religious denominations, concerned with educating clergy and lay people to strengthen their new churches, dominated higher education in nineteenth-century California. University of the Pacific (Methodist), Santa Clara University (Catholic), and University of San Francisco (Catholic) originated as private, sectarian schools in the early 1850s. With sporadic expansion of a public-school system also demanding more teachers, the state established a few normal schools, beginning with San Francisco in 1862.

Resistance to financing public schools, particularly colleges, ran high among most transient pioneers, however, and the legislature refused to establish a state university. To overcome this opposition in California and other states, Congress in 1862 passed the Morrill Land-Grant Act, which allocated federal lands to states to establish colleges fostering agricultural, mechanical, and military education. To qualify for the land grants, the legislature in 1868 assumed control of the College of California, a struggling Oakland institution started by Congregationalists and Presbyterians in 1855, and converted it into the state's first public university.

The new university floundered at first. When it opened at the old Oakland campus in the autumn of 1869, only 38 students showed up, despite tuition of only $20 per term. Mismanagement of the land grant also caused delays in realizing the federal subsidy and the legislature skimped on funding the university. Students also faced a bleak social life in the early years, particularly after 1873, when the university moved to an isolated rural campus on a Berkeley hillside. With little housing or other services, students were forced to commute miles from their rooms in Oakland; a few endured the two-plus hour trip by ferry and horse car from San Francisco.

But the university gradually won public approval, gaining the financial support needed to expand curriculum and services. With its improved prestige and facilities, the university attracted more students, as well as distinguished faculty. Over the next few decades, the university added graduate programs and professional schools of medicine (1873), pharmacy (1873), law (1878), dentistry (1881), and veterinary science (1894). In 1870 California's new university opened its programs to female students "on equal terms, in all respects, to young men."

(continued . . .)

The University of California, 1874

Carleton E. Watkins photographed the isolated, rural Berkeley campus of the University of California the year after it opened. The mansard roof and dormers of South (*left*) and North (*right*) halls illustrate the influence of the French Second Empire style, a popular Victorian style of the 1870s. *Courtesy of The Bancroft Library, University of California, Berkeley.*

The university helped make the late nineteenth and early twentieth century a time of great occupational gains for women. Within a few years, its female graduates were embarking on careers as physicians, lawyers, journalists, educators, and engineers. By the early twentieth century, the University of California had developed into one of the finest public institutions of higher learning in the world. It was an important cultural center for the state and a training ground for leaders in the arts, science, business, government, and the professions.

The University of California also worked to modernize farming. Like other early university programs, the College of Agriculture initially had few students and a meager curriculum. Farmers, led by the Grange, and laborers denounced the college as elitist and agitated to abolish it. Reorganized after 1874 under Dean Eugene W. Hilgard, a German-born soil chemist hired from the University of Mississippi, the College of Agriculture became more scientific, assembled a faculty of fine teachers and researchers and experimented in soil chemistry, fertilizers, climate, crop testing, irrigation methods, and pest control. Particularly significant were the program's efforts to develop grape vines resistant to *phylloxera*, a tiny root louse that devastated vineyards in the 1870s and 1880s. With federal aid starting in 1887, the university established a string of experiment stations to adapt crops and techniques to the state's diverse environments, an ambitious program that brought working farmers much practical information. By the turn of the century, the University of California was a major stimulus to state agriculture.

As railroads spread and cities grew, Californians founded other colleges, including the University of Southern California (Los Angeles, 1879), Stanford University (Palo Alto, 1891), California Institute of Technology (Pasadena, 1891), as well as distinguished smaller liberal arts colleges such as Loyola University (Los Angeles, 1869), Mills College (Oakland, 1885), Occidental College (Los Angeles, 1887), Pomona College (1887), Whittier College (1901), and Redlands College (1909). By the early twentieth century, California boasted a surprisingly elaborate framework of higher education, given its small population and remote location.   (RJO) and refrigerated cars and shipping systems. Because of competition from the Santa Fe, the company reduced freight rates on a broad range of farm products, though not enough to satisfy some shippers. The Southern Pacific also helped farmers organize marketing cooperatives and assisted them in mass advertising campaigns to urge reluctant Americans to consume California's new crops, such as oranges, prunes, apricots, raisins, and out-of-season and out-of-region produce in general. Some conflicts remained over freight rates but, ironically, most of California's highly organized growers were reconciled to "the Octopus" by the time Frank Norris published his famous novel.

Conversion to modern, higher-profit agriculture was facilitated by innovations in crops and cultivation methods introduced by immigrants with experience in regions with growing conditions similar to California's. The production of fine wines was a specialty of immigrants from southern and eastern Europe, like Hungarian-born Agoston Haraszthy, but also many from Italy, France, and Germany. European immigrant orchardists were often the first to introduce fruit culture, as they did in the 1850s and '60s, converting the Santa Clara Valley into the state's first important fruit district.

The Chinese migrated from different types of agricultural regions in the old country with experience in both arid and semitropical wetlands agricultural environments. As a result, they were especially valuable as farm innovators. Beginning with early mining districts and then spreading across the state, it was the Chinese who initiated truck gardening, raising vegetables on small rented plots and marketing them directly to town dwellers. Although most of the rural Chinese worked as laborers, clearing land and building levees and irrigation works, forward-thinking Caucasian land owners often contracted with entrepreneurial Chinese immigrants, who leased land as tenants and independently broke the soil, reclaimed wetlands, and began orchards and vineyards. In this manner, the Chinese pioneered in the production of strawberries, potatoes, wine grapes, raisins, and deciduous fruit. Although their reclamation and settlement of the Sacramento–San Joaquin Delta left a major mark, Chinese farmers were also in the forefront of agricultural change in the larger Central Valley, the Santa Clara Valley, and other San Francisco districts. After 1890, growing numbers of Japanese, Korean, and Filipino immigrants played innovative roles, as had their Chinese and European predecessors.

Between 1870 and the early 1900s, fruit and specialty-crop agriculture became the state's major industry. Problems were gradually overcome, new crops spread, and some livestock and grain ranches gave way to smaller farms. Orange groves spread through the upland valleys of Southern California, lemons along the coast. Most viticulture shifted northward to San Francisco Bay valleys, where fine dry-wine grapes flourished in the vineyards of European immigrants. Deciduous fruit and nut orchards invaded the Bay Area, the Sacramento Valley, and the northern San Joaquin Valley. Millions of raisin-grape vines and acres of drying racks basked in the hot Fresno sun. After 1900, prompted by progress in refrigeration, irrigation, and marketing, lettuce, melons, tomatoes, dates, and other new crops spread into the Salinas Valley and the fierce, below-sea-level deserts of the Imperial and Coachella valleys.

By 1900 the number of California farms had grown to 72,500, then collectively valued at $708 million. In 1925, the state's 136,400 farms were worth more than $3 billion. By the early twentieth century, California had become the nation's most diverse agricultural region and its leading producer of wine and table grapes, raisins, winter vegetables, lemons, almonds, walnuts, tomatoes, sugar beets, plums, prunes, apricots, and lesser crops. Bountiful farm harvests also sustained urban and industrial growth from 1870 to 1930.

Water Resources

Mines, farms, cities, and factories could not have expanded had pioneers not reorganized California's natural resources, particularly water. The speculative gold rush mentality prevailed even among later settlers, and most pursued short-term private gain with scant regard for the interests of others, including future generations. To support population and economic growth, California settlers transformed most waterways and inhabited low-elevation lands into artificial environments. This carefree assault on nature had drastic results that are still felt today.

In semi-arid California, water manipulation was fundamental. San Francisco, Oakland, Los Angeles, and other boom towns developed hearty thirsts. Water companies satisfied these by drilling wells, tapping local rivers, and building reservoirs to catch the runoff from surrounding highlands. By the 1870s expanding city water systems were dominated by large corporations, such as San Francisco's Spring Valley Water Company, which often intervened in local politics, encroached into the countryside, and aroused the opposition of farmers and small-town dwellers who also needed water.

Contradictory water laws at first inhibited development of agricultural as well as urban water. During early statehood, the legislature, in the traditionalism typical of frontier governments, adopted the "riparian" doctrine—an old principle in Anglo-American common law that gave landowners along watercourses the sole right to divert water, and only for use on their own land. Growing from experience in the well-watered East, the riparian doctrine restricted large-scale irrigation and discouraged agricultural and urban growth in drier lands such as California. Later in the 1850s, the legislature, mostly responding to mining pressure, confused the water issue further by also legalizing the Hispanic "prior appropriation" doctrine, which allowed miners and others to preempt water rights on public lands on a first-come, first-served basis and to transport water to areas removed from the water source for "beneficial use." Bitter disputes between riparian and appropriation claimants resulted in endless litigation that was usually, though not always, won by riparians. In 1870 only 60,000 acres—a tiny fraction of the state's cultivated lands—were being irrigated.

During the next 20 years, expanded irrigation fostered modest plantings of fruit and specialty crops. By 1889, one million acres, or 26 percent of the state's crop acreage, was being irrigated—most by small private water companies, and the rest by cooperative colonies and individual farms using wells or water from flowing streams. Throughout this time, however, water rights remained uncertain, larger irrigation projects were hampered, and water deliveries were erratic. Decades of legal confusion finally climaxed in *Lux v. Haggin* (1886). In this case, pitting rival giant land interests fighting for control of the Kern River's flow, the state supreme court determined that the riparian rights of downstream landowners (the Miller-Lux Land and Cattle Company) superseded the appropriation rights of upstream water diverters (James B. A. Haggin and Lloyd Tevis). Irrigation and agriculture suffered a serious setback.

Under pressure from agricultural interests, in 1887 the legislature passed the Wright Irrigation Act. This path-breaking law authorized the formation of local irrigation districts, bestowed on the districts the power of eminent domain—authority to condemn private water rights and irrigation facilities for public use—and empowered districts to levy taxes and sell bonds to build reservoirs and canals. Although several dozen districts immediately sprouted up, few survived. Hamstrung by insufficient funds, poor management, and lawsuits by riparian owners and some small farmers who objected to higher land taxes, most districts lapsed without delivering a drop of water. As late as 1910, the nine still-functioning districts covered only 600,000 acres and had raised only $23 million through bond issues.

Reforms passed in 1911, 1913, and 1917 strengthened the planning and state supervision of the districts and greatly expanded the scope of California irrigation. Between 1909 and 1920, 60 new districts were founded. Irrigated acreage grew from 2.6 million to 4.2 million, and capital invested in irrigation from $19 million to $195 million. Public water accounted for most of the increase. The golden age of California irrigation had dawned. After 1900, acreage, production, and the profitability of fruit and specialty crops increased sharply. Once established by the Wright Act, public management of irrigation water spread to other western states, and ultimately the federal government. The National Reclamation Act (1902) inspired the construction of still larger federal irrigation systems in twentieth-century California.

The Assault on Nature and the Beginning of Environmental Concern

Environmental alteration after the gold rush was especially rapid because of dramatic population growth, the settlers' intense profit motives, the powerful new industrial organization and technology, widespread water development, and a near absence of public planning and control. With the abandon described by Dame Shirley, miners ripped open hillsides, cut down watershed forests, disrupted streambeds, polluted water supplies, and stripped away top soils. Much of the Sierra foothills became, in Mark Twain's words, a "torn and guttered and disfigured" wasteland. Meanwhile, farmers and livestock raisers protecting their fields and herds, as well as market hunters capitalizing on early food shortages preyed ruthlessly on shore birds, waterfowl, eagles, condor, deer, elk, pronghorn, mountain lion, wolf, and other native species, seriously depleting their numbers by the 1870s. By the early 1900s some species, such as the California grizzly, which had awed Indians and Hispanic colonists, had vanished from the state. Many others, including the elk, bighorn, and condor, were driven into tiny, remote enclaves.

Overpopulated herds of cattle, sheep, and horses reduced large stretches of fragile grasslands to man-made deserts. Lumbermen using fire and other destructive methods denuded the accessible redwood slopes that had flanked San Francisco Bay and the coast from Big Sur north to Crescent City. With an eye toward maximum quick profits in a highly speculative industry, bonanza wheat ranchers farmed the soil without crop rotation or fertilizers and, within ten years of first planting, rendered the land barren. By the 1870s, erosion from hydraulic mining, disturbed riverbeds, and watershed decline unleashed devastating floods on the Central Valley and elsewhere.

In towns and some areas of dense farms, environmental alteration was nearly total. In the San Joaquin/Sacramento River Delta, for example, 1,000 miles of levees created 60 large, drained agricultural islands, supporting farm and river port towns such as Isleton, Walnut Grove, Rio Vista, and the Chinese community of Locke, some situated below water level. By the early twentieth century, virtually the entire natural structure of the Delta had been replaced by a man-made world of fields, fences, canals, boat channels, irrigation works, and flood-control projects. By the mid-twentieth century, Delta farms annually produced hundreds of millions of dollars in crops from deep soils and inexpensive water, all shielded behind an intricate earthen levee system. But even as settlers conquered the currents and tides, they were upsetting the Delta's delicate environmental balance. The natural banks and levies eroded rapidly after their trees were cut. Composed of spongy peat, the settlers' dikes soon began to cave in as well. Flood waters repeatedly poured over the hard-won islands, destroying farms, threatening towns and homes.

The same transformation was true of farm regions, such as the booming Mussel Slough country, where wild open lands were quickly subdivided, settled, fenced, and plowed in rectangular patterns. Wagon tracks and county roads marched out along the section lines, accentuating the geometric order being imposed on the land. In keeping with "efficient" land-management practices, natural watercourses and marshes were drained, filled, plowed over, or diverted to irrigation. Farmers with large plows and graders leveled the undulating land into the flat planes suitable for straight furrows, irrigation, and large farm machines. Wells were bored, and groundwater bubbled to the surface in artesian springs or was pumped by windmills and steam engines. By 1880, as in other settled areas, human culture had replaced nature as the principal determinant of landscape and life. Unable to survive, many of the remaining native species quickly vanished, their places taken by alien crops, weeds, ornamental plants, animals, and later even insects and birds. Like much of settled California in the last half of the nineteenth century, the Mussel Slough country had been transformed into a largely man-made world.

Bewitched by "progress," few Californians noticed these changes at first. Even fewer opposed them. Typically, local boosters celebrated them as the natural and inevitable by-products of civilizing the wilderness, the value of which virtually no one questioned. Only a few prophets, such as the great naturalist John Muir, raised lonely voices against the assault on nature. Only occasionally, when environmental destruction impinged on other economic interests, was wider dissent aroused. Out of the few nineteenth-century environmental clashes, however, emerged important principles of scientific resource conservation and management in California.

John Muir and Early Wilderness Preservation

In the late-nineteenth-century scramble for development and profit, most Californians were indifferent or hostile toward wilderness preservation. But a few dedicated writers, artists, and scientists attuned to the spiritual and long-range economic value of the wilderness became early defenders of the environment. The growth after 1870 of irrigated agriculture and tourism—industries with a stake in protecting mountains and forest watersheds—brought powerful allies from farm and business groups. To promote irrigation, agriculture, tourism, and hence its freight and passenger business, the Southern Pacific Company often furnished political leverage, financing, and leadership for resource-conservation and wilderness-preservation movements.

Particularly inspiring was John Muir, a Scottish-born, Wisconsin-bred naturalist. A promising young inventor, in 1867, Muir was almost blinded in an industrial accident, and the trauma convinced him to explore God's handiwork in nature. In 1868, after walking thousands of miles and making several sea voyages, Muir arrived in Yosemite Valley. Enthralled with Yosemite's beauty and scientific and spiritual significance, Muir began there to build a worldwide reputation for his discovery of the valley's glacial origins and, later, for his writings as a champion of wilderness preservation. Until his death in 1914 Muir dedicated himself to studying and protecting wilderness regions around the world. In terms of influence on human thought and action, John Muir was perhaps the greatest of all Californians.

(continued...)

One of the foremost early ecologists, Muir was a pioneer of modern environmentalism. He believed that humans erred in assuming that all nature was created solely for their benefit. With machines that tore up the earth and disordered nature, "Lord Man," Muir felt, had usurped the power of God to determine which species died or lived. Instead, Muir maintained, nature existed for its own mysterious purposes; all beings were interrelated, and the long-term welfare of humanity depended on the preservation of nature's fullness down "to the smallest transmicroscopic creature that dwells upon our conceited eyes and knowledge." Nature also provided insights into the rest of creation and divinity itself. "The clearest way into the Universe," he wrote, "is through a forest wilderness." Like Emerson and Thoreau before him, Muir maintained that contact with nature refreshed souls wearied by the conflict and superficiality of modern civilization. "Climb the mountains," he recommended. "Nature's peace will flow into you as the sunshine into trees." For Muir, preserving wilderness was as essential to human welfare as it was to maintaining natural ecological balances.

John Muir, circa 1912

This photograph of Muir was taken by W. E. Dassonville. *Courtesy of The Bancroft Library, University of California, Berkeley.*

The high, rugged, and still-pristine peaks, meadows, and forests of the Sierra Nevada were the first objects of the preservationists' concern. The monoliths, meadows, and waterfalls of Yosemite Valley, first "discovered" by militiamen chasing Indians in the early 1850s, were quickly recognized as valuable landmarks. In 1864, when the federal government closed it to further private settlement and entrusted it to the perpetual care of the state, Yosemite Valley, in effect, became the nation's first wilderness preserve. The development-fixated state, however, initially permitted poaching lumbermen, livestock herders, and farmers to swarm illegally into the valley. In the 1880s Muir and a few cohorts launched a crusade to save Yosemite. Aided by eastern conservationist friends and Southern Pacific Company leaders, Muir finally overcame powerful vested interests who wanted to keep all the Sierra open to exploitation. In 1890 he and his allies persuaded Congress to convert the territory surrounding the valley into a large national park for tougher protection.

To encourage appreciation of wilderness, Muir and San Francisco Bay Area intellectuals, scientists, and business leaders founded the Sierra Club in 1892. In 1905 and 1906 Muir and the Sierra Club, again in league with the Southern Pacific, pushed bills through the legislature and Congress returning Yosemite Valley itself to federal control for inclusion in the national park.

In the 1890s and early 1900s preservationists and irrigators in the San Joaquin Valley, aided by the railroad, also secured the establishment of Sequoia National Park, the giant Sierra Forest Reserve, and national forests around Lake Tahoe. Nearly 200 miles of the Sierra Nevada had come under federal protection. A similar coalition pressed the state in 1902 to buy one of the few remaining stands of virgin redwoods in the Santa Cruz Mountains and to found Big Basin Redwoods Park, the beginning of the modern state park system. Although much of the California natural landscape had already been despoiled or altered beyond recognition, at least a remnant would remain as a legacy for future generations.   (RJO)

Especially significant was the uproar over hydraulic-mining debris. By the 1870s, miners armed with powerful water cannons had gouged out gigantic artificial canyons in the northern Sierra foothills. Billions of cubic yards of gravel and sand clogged valley riverbeds, reducing navigability and worsening the flood problems of Sacramento, Marysville, other river towns, and surrounding farmland. When they receded, the floods deposited an infertile layer of mining debris, often several feet thick, enough to ruin many farmers. Hydraulic mining debris particularly devastated the San Joaquin/Sacramento Delta, permanently narrowing and raising channel beds by as much as 15 feet. When settlers responded by piling their levees higher, their reclaimed land fell even farther below water levels, raising the likelihood of inundation in rainy seasons.

Hydraulic-mining devastation developed into one of the most explosive issues of the 1870s and '80s. Aided by the Southern Pacific, valley people organized anti-debris associations, but the large mining companies were powerfully entrenched, with allies in the legislature and the courts. Anti-debris forces pushed a bill through the legislature in 1880 requiring hydraulic miners to catch debris behind dams built under state supervision, one of the first California laws aimed at controlling environmental destruction. Most mining companies, however, refused to comply and ignored valley court injunctions. When the state supreme court declared even this mild law unconstitutional on a technicality, farmers, financed by the Southern Pacific, sued in U.S. Circuit Court in San Francisco. In January 1884, the court issued a permanent injunction against all discharge of mining debris into streams. "Hydraulicking" was dead. Mining companies closed down overnight, thriving towns emptied, and decay spread through the hydraulic regions. Valley people had established the important principle of governmental responsibility for prohibiting severe environmental damage, even if it meant an entire industry's destruction.

In the late nineteenth century, Californians also groped toward more enlightened policies to replenish depleted fisheries, control floods, and protect forests from fire, but most people, accustomed to exploiting resources at will, resented and ignored even the most innocuous conservation measures. Systematic, modern conservation awaited the Progressive era. Meanwhile, resource waste and environmental deterioration continued unabated.

Social and Political Conflict

Society in gold rush California, although not rigid, had always been structured. As in the eastern United States, wealth, ethnicity, and family background divided Californians into sharply different classes. While the social structure was not totally closed, upward mobility for the working- and lower-middle classes—a group that included miners, laborers, and small farmers—was slow and frustrating. At first, California's quick population turnover obscured social inequities. In a society composed mostly of transients, unsuccessful people returned home or moved on, shuttling from one temporary community to the next, remaining largely invisible. In the 1870s, however, turnover rates slowed and sojourners began to be replaced by families. As glaring inequities between groups became more obvious, the potential for explosive conflict grew apace.

During the 1870s San Francisco assumed the physical characteristics of an industrial city. Disparities in wealth and transportation innovations altered the city's social landscape, producing specialized residential, commercial, industrial, and entertainment districts. After 1873 and the introduction of Andrew Halladie's cable cars, wealthy citizens colonized the city's hills, erecting palaces fit for the kings of railroads, mining, and bonanza agriculture. Streetcars allowed middle-class families to

Nob Hill Mansions

In 1878 Eadweard Muybridge photographed Charles Crocker's elegant home (*foreground*) with Collis P. Huntington's darker one behind it. The wall looming at the rear of the Crocker mansion is the famous "spite fence," built by the railroad king to isolate a stubborn neighbor who refused to sell his property. *Courtesy of the Department of Special Collections, Stanford University Libraries.*

migrate west into pleasant new residential subdivisions, escaping the bustle, noise, and pollution of industry and commerce. Unable to afford transportation, the working-class—who made up the majority of the city's population—stayed behind in densely-crowded neighborhoods, where small houses, cheap apartments, and boardinghouses intermingled with machine shops, breweries, canneries, foundries, and slaughterhouses. The once-exclusive South-of-Market Street neighborhood deteriorated, becoming, in the words of visiting writer Rudyard Kipling, "a hopeless mass of small wooden houses, dust, street refuse, and children who play with empty kerosene tins." The contrast between such wretched poverty in the hollows and the ornate mansions rising atop Nob Hill aggravated social strife in San Francisco. Oakland, Sacramento, Los Angeles, and other cities also developed into stratified communities.

Restricted by prejudice to the bottom rung of the social ladder, Chinese, Mexican, African American, and some European immigrant minorities were pushed into the least desirable urban neighborhoods. Barred from most business and employment opportunities, segregated or excluded altogether from schools, churches, and other majority-dominated institutions, politically neutralized by gerrymandered ward boundaries and stringent voting requirements, minorities were isolated from mainstream society.

Yet minority groups had strikingly different experiences. Many African Americans, for example, found unique opportunities in California. Manuscript census returns indicate that African Americans typically lived, not in homogeneous black neighborhoods, but dispersed throughout cities, while a few, including some farm owners and renters, resided in rural areas. A small black middle-class serving their small urban populations had already emerged by the 1860s, when the census counted only 4,086 blacks in the state, less than 1 percent of the population. Elite groups emerged in San Francisco, Oakland, and Los Angeles, led by railroad workers, skilled laborers, small business owners, teachers, newspaper editors, ministers, undertakers, and a few real estate developers. Beneficiaries of increasing railroad passenger travel in later decades of the century, some African American men found stable and relatively high-wage employment as Pullman car waiters and porters, headquartered in terminals such as Oakland and Los Angeles.

Although most urban blacks were relegated to low-paying service or industrial jobs, community members found a variety of social and political organizations to aid them. Black women's charities, like the Ladies

Pacific Accumulating and Benevolent Society, provided not only welfare services but also served as foot soldiers in ongoing civil rights campaigns, raising funds for the Franchise League and the California Colored Conventions. Black newspapers appeared in larger cities, such as San Francisco's *Mirror of the Times*. In San Francisco and Sacramento, teachers like Priscilla Stewart, Lucinda Blue, and Annie E. Vincent used the black press to pressure the legislature to repeal the 1852 law barring black children from public schools. The legislature finally dropped the ban in 1880, guaranteeing black school children the right to a public education, though many, if not most, still attended separate schools. Despite these early successes, African Americans in California continued to face general exclusion, especially in housing, education, and occupation. After 1910, large-scale migration of African Americans from the East and South led to the emergence of large, dense black neighborhoods like Watts in Los Angeles.

The more numerous Chinese Californians experienced harsher residential and occupational discrimination, as well as intensifying white violence. The census of 1870 counted more than 60,000 Chinese in the United States, three-quarters of them in California, almost all of them male. With completion of the transcontinental railroad in May 1869, the Central Pacific transferred most of its Chinese labor force to constructing its Southern Pacific subsidiary and other extensions. However, some released workers chose to settle down and seek other employment. The sudden influx of Chinese competing in the labor market, at the same time as railroad building was unsettling economic conditions and worsening unemployment, combined to make Chinese immigration again an explosive political issue. Also, as hostility and violence toward the Chinese mounted in rural areas, many retreated to urban "Chinatowns," the largest of which developed in San Francisco. These densely populated communities arose in part from legal housing discrimination and in part by choice, as newcomers clustered together for mutual support and self-protection. Like other immigrant groups, however, the Chinese did establish community institutions, businesses, and recreations that gave them a degree of sustenance, autonomy, and defense, particularly from the powerful Six Chinese Companies, which controlled much of the commerce with China and within the Chinatowns and could marshal some support from powerful Caucasian leaders.

Because almost no Chinese had brought their wives during the gold rush era, Chinatowns had few women, other than prostitutes, and even fewer children. In 1872, the San Francisco Board of Supervisors counted 722 school-aged children in Chinatown, although only 59 lived in what supervisors considered legitimate families (households that fit the white middle-class norm). Most Chinese inhabited a variety of living arrangements, from all-male boardinghouses to all-female households, most of them probably brothels. Their distinctive living arrangements added fuel for growing anti-Chinese violence and politics.

Ironically, government policies made it even harder for Chinese Californians to form families. In 1875, Congress passed an act sponsored by California's first-term U.S. Senator, Horace Page. The Page Act classified as criminals all women "imported for purposes of prostitution" and made importation of "any subject of China, Japan, or any Oriental country" without their consent a felony. Assuming, in essence, that all Chinese women harbored illegal or immoral intentions, the Page Act nearly ended the immigration of unmarried Asian women into the United States.

Mexican lives in California followed yet another trajectory. The pre-gold rush Mexican majority in 1848 had meant a promising start, with eight Californios among the 48 delegates to the 1849 constitutional convention. But the rapid arrival of non-Mexican gold-seekers overwhelmed nascent Mexican political power, especially at the state level. Also, the California Land Act of 1851 stripped most of their lands, reducing many to low-waged workers, sometimes on land that had once been theirs. Other displaced Mexicans drifted towards urban centers like Los Angeles and Santa Barbara. *Barrios* (Spanish-speaking neighborhoods) emerged in communities with substantial Mexican populations. The modernization and economic development brought by the railways generally bypassed the *barrios*. In the 1880s, fast-growing Los Angeles, a city that had recently been mostly populated by Californios and recent Mexican immigrants, was inundated by new industries and thousands of new people from eastern states, excluding the previous residents from jobs and neighborhoods they had once controlled. Other Southern California towns and cities, such as San Diego and Santa Barbara, were similarly transformed.

Immigration from Mexico continued through the end of the century, though in very small numbers, and some returned to Mexico, while at the same time migration by non-Mexicans soared. As discrimination increased, the *barrios* grew in size, becoming more ethnically homogeneous and increasingly economically deprived. By the turn of the century, for example, a complex Mexican neighborhood emerged in East Los Angeles, and

ethnic pride and self-defense movements began. By the early 1900s, increasingly marginalized Mexican Americans constituted a small and shrinking percentage of the city's population.

However, when immigration from Mexico increased sharply after 1910, newcomers arrived to find some ethnic businesses and community service organizations already in place in the *barrio. Mutualistas* (mutual-aid associations) thrived. They often had specific goals, but all met members' social needs with meetings, family gatherings, lectures, and commemoration of U.S. and Mexican holidays. In addition to building ethnic pride, associations also provided services, including emergency loans, legal aid, mediation of disputes, and medical, life, and burial insurance.

Rural Inequities

Social stratification also increased generally in California rural areas. Held for speculation or lease to wheat producers, fertile land, particularly that with water rights, was expensive in most desirable, easily cultivated areas. High costs for land, fencing, irrigation facilities, orchard planting, mortgage interest, and other requirements for the new delicate crops raised farm-building beyond the means of most. Praised as the salvation of the small farmer, irrigation turned out to be a mixed blessing. Expensive to install and operate, water improvements gave an edge to those with capital by allowing them to raise more valuable fruit crops. However, as they became more dependent on water systems with limited storage capacity, irrigating farmers opened themselves up to greater loss during water shortages. Severe droughts during the 1870s and early '80s pushed many farmers close to bankruptcy and forced others to abandon the land altogether, compounding tensions in areas such as Mussel Slough. As a final outrage, high railroad rates, limited markets, and falling crop prices often ate into the profits farmers managed to make in bountiful years.

To prepare land and irrigation facilities and to plant and harvest grain and fruit, growers continued the gang-labor practices inherited from missions and ranchos. When, by the 1860s, declining Indian population no longer met growing labor requirements, many farmers turned to the oppressed and easily controlled Chinese, recent European immigrants, unemployed city workers, and children. Farm laborers roamed the countryside in large groups performing seasonal tasks for subsistence wages, camping in ragtag tent villages, and rarely putting down local roots or starting farms. By exploiting the economic distress and racial prejudice of the era, farmers became accustomed to making up for high irrigation and marketing costs by paying rock-bottom wages and assuming no responsibility for stable employment. After the 1890s, farmers augmented their labor supply with Japanese and Mexican immigrants. By 1900 California's "peculiar farm labor system" was firmly entrenched.

Because of high farm costs, public land policies favoring monopoly by speculators, and the growers' power to exploit low-paid laborers, immense landholdings dominated California for the rest of the nineteenth century. In 1872, of 27,000 agricultural holdings, the 122 persons who each owned more than 20,000 acres had amassed a combined six million acres, much more than the total of all other farms. The rise of irrigation and fruit culture caused some land to be subdivided. But most new growers were fairly well-to-do persons, many migrating from other states, who were transferring capital from other farms or businesses, and some new large estates continued to be engrossed. Between 1870 and 1900 the average farm size decreased only from 500 to 400 acres. California farms remained about twice as large as the national average. Geography, climate, and economic and social conditions conspired to prevent California from developing into an agrarian democracy.

Unstable farm profits, along with glaring social, economic, and political inequality, produced bitter rural conflict after the 1860s. Protesting small-scale farmers banded into spontaneous "clubs" to elect more sympathetic officials and secure better tax, land, fence, and mortgage laws, as well as regulation of railroads, wheat-trade monopolists, and other middlemen. In the early 1870s, many local groups affiliated with the emerging national movement, the Patrons of Husbandry, or Grange; a state Grange followed in 1873. By 1874 more than 13,500 farmers had flocked into California's 231 Grange locals, rallying small-scale farmers to push for political solutions for entrenched social and economic inequities.

Early Labor Movements and the "Indispensable Enemy"

The gold rush, which attracted many skilled workers, coincided with increasing union activity among the nation's craftsmen. High labor demand in early pioneer years encouraged organizational efforts, but unions had only modest success. San Francisco typesetters, brewers, building tradesmen, musicians, and others combined to protect their interests and keep wages abreast of high living costs during the 1850s. Spontaneous strikes in the city and mining districts often succeeded temporarily, but an unstable economy and high turnover among workers constantly undermined union efforts.

Despite reversals, especially after 1855, when gold production and wages declined, craftsmen continued organizing. In the 1860s and '70s, union agitation spread from San Francisco to industrial mining districts and emerging cities such as Oakland and Los Angeles. Although laborers periodically struck for higher wages, the principal statewide goal during the 1860s was the eight-hour day. In 1868, under pressure from unions, the legislature enacted an eight-hour law over employer opposition. Although workingmen rejoiced, the victory was more apparent than real. The law could not be enforced, especially during hard times when workers would agree to almost any employment conditions.

The "Terrible Seventies" decimated the early union movement. The first westbound trains, the Comstock boom collapse, and the nationwide Panic of 1873 had devastating consequences. Cheap often better quality goods arrived from all over the nation on the new trains, driving down California prices, wages, and production. While unemployment soared, thousands of new people flooded labor markets: released railroad-construction laborers, unemployed workers from eastern states and fading Nevada mines, and more Chinese immigrants (20,000 in 1876 alone). Neither unions nor the few organized charities could relieve the situation nor meet increasing demands for aid. Some workers clung to their weakened craft unions, while a few affiliated with the national Knights of Labor, with little success. In short, the railroads' effects, which had once promised prosperity to the state, were undercutting the position of labor.

Mounting working-class frustration vented itself not only on employers but on California labor's "indispensable enemy"—the Chinese, who were, ironically, among the most exploited Californians. As in the mining era, white workers blamed the Chinese for unemployment and low wages and attacked them both politically and physically. Unions and "anti-coolie" clubs agitated for state and federal laws restricting the immigration and employment of Chinese. In 1871, a Los Angeles mob swarmed through the city's Chinatown and massacred a score of its residents.

Although violent outbursts occurred statewide, anti-Chinese sentiment climaxed in San Francisco in the summer of 1877, in what became a season of nationwide strikes and labor violence. A July 23 meeting of enraged San Francisco workers burst forth, crying "On to Chinatown!" Within hours, much of that district was in ruins. On subsequent days, mobs attacked firms that employed Chinese workers. Blaming the violence on malcontents, "communists," and youthful hoodlums, Governor William Irwin called out the militia, which, assisted by a businessmen's vigilante "Committee of Public Safety" armed with pick handles, restored "order" and preserved property. Periodically, eruptions of violence and Chinese expulsions swept the state, even small towns and rural areas, into the early 1900s.

The Workingmen's Party of California

Out of San Francisco's depression and turmoil, the rabidly anti-Chinese Workingmen's Party of California (WPC) was born in September 1877. Party leaders argued that capitalists monopolized wealth and property, used political influence to keep workers subordinate, and employed cheap Chinese labor to enrich themselves and keep other workers down. As a remedy, they recommended a workingmen's political movement to combat corporations and eject the Chinese. They preached their gospel so effectively that the WPC mustered 10,000 members to march in San Francisco's 1877 Thanksgiving Day parade.

At the head of the column strode the WPC's new president, Denis Kearney, the young, self-educated

Anti-Chinese Cartoon

This anti-Chinese cartoon by George Frederick Keller appeared in *The Wasp* on December 8, 1877. *Courtesy of the California History Room, California State Library, Sacramento, California.*

Irish immigrant owner of a small, troubled wagon company. Traditional labor leaders dismissed Kearney's demagoguery, but thousands thronged to his sandlot meetings. A natural orator, he appealed directly to working-class fears. Kearney proclaimed the dignity of labor, denounced railroad barons, landowners, bankers, and the "money power" in general, and called on workers to arm themselves against the Chinese and the corporations. Threats of violence and a concluding chant—"The Chinese must go!"—enlivened each speech.

Workingmen quickly made the WPC a force in San Francisco and California affairs. Although the state and cities passed laws limiting freedom of assembly and expression and periodically jailed Kearney and other leaders, the WPC made inroads among disenchanted laborers, lower-level white-collar workers, and small business owners in San Francisco, Oakland, Los Angeles, and other towns. By 1878 the party had elected a state senator and local officials in Alameda County, members of the legislature, a mayor, a majority of San Francisco's board of supervisors, and scattered local officials around the state. It also captured one-third of the seats in the state Constitutional Convention of 1878–79. WPC-dominated governments in San Francisco, Oakland, Los Angeles, and other centers strengthened ordinances discriminating against the Chinese in housing, employment, and public services.

Despite some notoriety and political victories, the WPC was transitory, more an emotional outlet for distress than a permanent influence. By 1880, internal dissension, the absence of a consistent reform program, and a brief economic revival had reduced its appeal. Members deserted and returned to more traditional unions and parties.

Anti-Railroad Politics

Along with the Chinese, large corporations were a target for discontented groups in the 1870s. Although Californians actually suffered from many economic, social, political, and environmental ills, most visible were the growing monopolies over land, the wheat trade, and transportation. As the state's largest business, landowner, and employer of Chinese workers, with an annual income that dwarfed the entire state budget, the Central/Southern Pacific Railroad provided a convenient scapegoat. The company was not without guilt. Its owners were using the wealth they had derived from public construction subsidies to buy out or destroy competitors and control transportation rates. To protect its privileges, the railroad fielded a force of lawyers, lobbyists, and political bosses, and was not above using bribery and power politics. Although contemporary opponents and most later historians exaggerated its power and malevolence, the Central/Southern Pacific was a formidable foe, as the Mussel Slough squatters discovered.

In particular, discontented farmers, workers, and urban shippers in the 1870s charged that monopolies controlled transportation rates, discriminated against some regions, towns, and shippers, deprived producers of just profits, and caused unemployment in many industries. Central/Southern Pacific officials countered that higher operating expenses over rugged and thinly populated terrain, not monopoly, raised tariffs higher than on eastern lines. Moreover, it was more efficient, and led to lower overall rates, for the company to charge lower rates on large shipments and long hauls and to award favorable terminal status only to some cities. In truth, the self-interested and contradictory rate demands of Californians would have been impossible for any railroad to reconcile. The furor was mostly raised by conflicting classes of shippers who sought advantage over competing business and communities, not equal or lower overall rates.

The rate issue was complex, however, and failed to align everyone against the railroad. Favored communities, farmers, and businesses, along with those who hoped to win rail service in the future, opposed railroad regulation and a general lowering of rates, while the Grange and others not favorably located agitated for state control of tariffs. In 1876, against strenuous lobbying by the railroad and its supporters, the legislature created an advisory railway commission. Ignored, the weak body was abolished within three years.

The Constitution of 1879

In 1878 continuing clamor by disaffected groups such as the WPC and the Grange pushed the legislature into calling a convention to revise the 1849 constitution to accommodate three decades of social change and to limit the power of corporations. The WPC shared the elected membership equally with Grangers and "nonpartisans" (primarily Democrats and Republicans). With such disparate groups present—including reformers and representatives of vested interests—conflict and confusion were inevitable. The delegates harangued each other for 157 days at Sacramento during late 1878 and early 1879 before finally hammering out a compromise constitution.

The question of regulating railroads and other corporations consumed the most energy. The new constitution declared railroads "subject to legislative control" and called for a railroad commission of three elected members with authority to fix maximum rates and prohibit railroads from discriminating among shippers. The document made intangible corporate assets (profits, franchises, and the like) subject to taxation, raised taxes on railroad and other corporate property, established a board of equalization to increase state revenues and stabilize tax rates among counties, transferred mortgage tax obligations from borrowers to lenders, and tightened banking regulations. The delegates also modernized the state's judicial system, reorganized and increased funding for the state's schools and university, and sanctioned the eight-hour-day principle on public works. Concerning the Chinese, the constitution authorized the legislature to act against "dangerous or detrimental" aliens, forbade Chinese employment by corporations or on public works, and legalized residential segregation of the Chinese. In other matters, the convention ran into problems. Although the delegates debated ways to redistribute land, little could be done without violating private property rights. Many representatives, particularly land-owning farmers, vigorously blocked any land reforms. Characteristically, the all-male convention squashed a proposal advanced by female and male reformers to enfranchise women.

In the end, the convention produced one of the world's longest, most complex constitutions, more closely resembling a legal code than an organic law. The overly detailed compromise document satisfied almost no one. Corporate interests condemned its regulatory and taxation provisions as confiscatory and communistic. Protesting that the constitution did not resolve their grievances, disillusioned workers also called for its defeat. Somewhat appeased by promises of railroad rate control and more equitable taxation, rural voters probably accounted for the document's narrow passage in May 1879, by only 11,000 out of 145,000 votes cast.

Whatever its shortcomings, the new constitution established important principles of state economic regulation, including supervision of public utilities such as railroads. The document also distributed the tax burden more widely, particularly by reducing the unfair share hitherto paid by farmers, and created the machinery for increasing state revenues. The state now possessed a stronger legal and fiscal framework for dealing more actively with the economic, scientific, and environmental problems of modernization.

But many of the constitution's most innovative measures had little immediate effect. Like its predecessor, the new railroad commission was usually ignored.

Legislators refused to finance it properly or enforce its edicts. When the commission frequently sympathized with railroads and approved their rate proposals, critics ridiculed the body as a tool of the Southern Pacific. Nevertheless, after 1880, because of more efficient operations, the opening of the Southern Pacific's own southern transcontinental route, and competition from the Santa Fe and other lines, overall rates on the Southern Pacific fell consistently for several decades. But many continued to denounce the railroad for charging excessive and discriminatory tariffs and exerting illegitimate political power. Lawsuits also delayed or overturned the constitution's provisions to tax corporate assets and equalize tax rates. The fundamental problem was that the principle of corporate regulation was not yet accepted in American law.

Chinese Exclusion

The new constitution did little to assuage the anti-Chinese movement. Broadly rooted in racism, suspicion of cultural differences, and economic rivalry, opposition toward the Chinese was not limited to a few radicals and labor leaders, but cut across socioeconomic, partisan, and even ethnic lines. Some other oppressed ethnics—most notably many African Americans and European immigrants—were hostile toward Chinese religion and culture and fearful of economic competition with the numerous Asian immigrants. These groups remained fervent supporters of anti-Chinese agitation. For decades, "the Chinese question" remained an explosive issue that could not be ignored in contests for local and national office. During the 1870s, the U.S. Supreme Court had repeatedly struck down discriminatory state and local laws as violations of the U.S. Constitution, the Burlingame Treaty with China, or the Civil Rights Act of 1870. Anti-Chinese provisions of the new state constitution met similar fates. Each federal action in defense of the Chinese aroused indignation in the state. Perhaps out of concern for future elections, President Rutherford B. Hayes negotiated a treaty with China in 1880 allowing the United States to regulate immigration. Under the terms of that agreement Congress, pressured by its California members, enacted a bill in 1882 suspending the immigration and naturalization of Chinese for ten years.

The Exclusion Act of 1882 did not deport Chinese immigrants already in the country and therefore failed to satisfy many Californians, especially labor leaders. They organized boycotts of Chinese-made goods and agitated for expulsion. Into the twentieth century,

whites continued to discriminate against, ridicule, beat, and occasionally lynch the Chinese with virtual impunity. Into the early 1900s rioting mobs periodically terrorized and burned their neighborhoods. Numerous rural communities rounded up and expelled local Chinese altogether. Pressure from California again influenced Congress in 1888 to strengthen the Exclusion Act to prohibit reentry by workers after visits to China and, in 1892, to extend its provisions for another ten years. By 1904 treaties and legislation had made exclusion permanent. Only during World War II, as a gesture to an ally, did the United States reopen its shores to Chinese immigrants.

Culture in the Railroad Era

For several decades after 1865, California culture remained essentially derivative. Some progress was made in founding cultural institutions, best symbolized by the persistent, if fitful, expansion of colleges and public schools. Lagging behind, however, was the development of a regional culture, with aesthetic themes reflecting the state's distinctive landscape, peoples, and history. Second-generation Californians, following the lead of the gold rush pioneers, continued to mimic the cultural styles of the ancestral homelands they so much venerated, particularly the northeastern United States.

Developments in architecture were illustrative. While the houses and business buildings of ordinary people continued to be erected in the venerable New England frame tradition, the wealthy and middle classes, anxious to demonstrate their new respectability, copied the architectural fads of eastern trend-setters. Country estates and fashionable subdivisions in railroad towns were built in a succession of increasingly elaborate (some would say gaudy) Victorian styles—Gothic Revival, Italianate, French Second Empire, Queen Anne, and Richardson Romanesque, among others—each of which evoked distant places and bygone eras. At the same time, builders catering to their customers' conservative tastes shunned native stone and redwood, or disguised them with paint, stain, and other surfaces so that they could masquerade as standard eastern construction materials. For the most part, Californians lacked the maturity and sense of place and history that, beginning in the 1890s, would give rise to a creative regional architecture.

Reflecting the general population, some "carpetbagger" authors stayed for a few years, wrote briefly about their California experience, then wandered on. Such were Mark Twain and Bret Harte, who arrived in the twilight of the mining era and produced nostalgic short stories about the humor and heroism of pioneer prospectors of the 1840s and '50s or the fading miners and camps of the 1860s. Unable to support themselves by writing fiction, both turned to journalism, Harte as the first editor of *The Overland Monthly* (founded in 1868), Twain as an itinerant lecturer and newspaper reporter. The most significant event of Twain's three-year stay was the 1865 publication of his rollicking mining-camp story "The Celebrated Jumping Frog of Calaveras County," which established Twain's reputation as a frontier humorist and launched his literary career. Anxious for the state to repress its disorderly gold rush origins, many California critics rejected the stories of Twain and Harte. Twain (in 1867) and Harte (in 1871) returned to the East, where they were more appreciated and where better opportunities existed for professional writers.

Ina Coolbrith was the bright star of an otherwise lackluster poetry. Fleeing a troubled early life in Southern California, Coolbrith resettled in San Francisco in the mid-1860s. A poet since childhood, she was immediately accepted into the city's growing literary community. Several years later, she became Harte's assistant editor at *The Overland Monthly*. As editor and later as librarian for the Oakland Public Library, one of the state's first and finest free circulation libraries, Coolbrith was for decades friend and patroness to important California writers. Her own verse, which at first inclined toward eroticism and romantic love, turned later to celebrating California's hills, birds, and flowers. Coolbrith was honored by the legislature in 1915 as California's poet laureate.

The transformation of Coolbrith's poetry suggested that, while California culture remained mostly imitative, distinctive regional themes had begun to sound before century's end. Some authors and artists discovered the spiritual and aesthetic potential in the state's magnificent landscapes. Joining John Muir in seeking beauty and meaning in unique natural surroundings, pioneer photographers such as Carleton E. Watkins and Eadweard Muybridge and painters such as Thomas Hill and the visiting Albert Bierstadt attempted to capture on film and canvas the spectacular scale and delicacy of Yosemite's cliffs, meadows, and waterfalls. The major figure of California's "nature school" of painting was William Keith, Muir's long-time friend and cohort in the wilderness-preservation crusade. For five decades before his death in 1911, Keith painted Yosemite Valley, the Sierra, and other California landscapes in a style that combined realistic attention to fine detail with the traditional romanticism of the Hudson River school he had

emulated in his early years. Late-nineteenth-century California writers and artists stressed nature's fertility, harmony, and beauty and the imperative of achieving peaceful coexistence between the people and the land. Often, the Eden-like California landscape provided a contrasting background to the conflict and corruption of human society, a theme that became a hallmark of the state's culture in the twentieth century.

At the same time, railroad-era economic inequities and political corruption gave birth to a strong social-protest theme in California arts and letters. The tradition's founder, Henry George, arrived in San Francisco as a young man in 1858. While struggling to overcome grinding poverty, George worked as printer and reporter on various San Francisco, Sacramento, and Oakland newspapers and magazines and was already a well-known journalist by the time he published his 1868 *Overland Monthly* article questioning the benefits of railroad construction. By the early 1870s, George was increasingly distressed by the inequality and poverty that appeared to be the price of industrial "progress." His first major work, *Our Land and Land Policy, National and State* (1871), condemned the monopoly in land fostered by railroad land grants, other federal and state laws, and rampant speculation. As a remedy for the land monopoly and the unemployment that were smothering opportunities for ordinary people, George recommended confiscatory taxes on large land holdings. George's California experience also inspired his classic *Progress and Poverty* (1879), which advocated the single-tax theory, a simplistic cure for industrial evils that attracted a wide following outside the state. Like many contemporary cultural figures that attained fame, George soon left for greener pastures in the East, where he became a leading reformer and one of the most widely read and influential of California authors.

Others, however, took up Henry George's crusade against privilege. Journalist and short-story writer Ambrose Bierce produced cutting satire, particularly of the Southern Pacific's power. Illustrators such as *The Wasp*'s George Frederick Keller and the San Francisco *Examiner*'s Homer Davenport and James Swinnerton honed the acid political cartoon to a fine art. At the turn of the century, Edwin Markham's poem, "The Man with the Hoe" (1899), and Frank Norris's classic of naturalism, *The Octopus* (1901), attacked monopolies and defended the oppressed farmers.

By the end of the nineteenth century, social protest had become an integral part of the California literary tradition. In the 1870s and '80s, María Amparo Ruiz de Burton wrote and produced a five-act comedy based on

Cervante's *Don Quixote*, becoming the first Mexican-American woman to publish in the English language. When she published her first work in 1876, Burton was living in San Diego with her husband, Captain Henry S. Burton. In her two novels, *Who Would Have Thought It?* (1872) and *The Squatter and the Don* (1885), Burton voiced the bitter resentment Californios felt towards their American invaders. *Who Would Have Thought It?* shows northern abolitionists coming to the Far West as xenophobic racists, and offers the Mexican perspective through the eyes of a child, Lola, whom the newcomers rescue from Indian captors, and then relegate to the kitchen and force to sleep with the servants, because of her "black skin." *The Squatter and the Don* is an historical romance that details the repercussions of the California Land Act of 1851: the Californios' loss of land to litigation and American squatters. The novel reprised Burton's own struggles as an impoverished widow trying, in vain, to retain her Rancho Jamul in San Diego County.

The first local histories of counties and cities appeared in the 1860s, as Californians began to reflect on the meaning of their own experiences. By the early twentieth century, more than 150 county histories had appeared. Typically written by amateur boosters and journalists, local histories were usually little more than simple chronologies of major events and compilations of biographies of leading residents. In keeping with the intense ethnocentrism of the period, these works rejoiced in the displacement of "inferior" Indian and Hispanic cultures and uncritically celebrated the heroism, democracy, and progressivism of the American pioneers. Despite these many shortcomings, local histories preserved much information that might otherwise have been lost and provided guides to further research and a foundation for twentieth-century restoration movements.

Franklin Tuthill, a physician and journalist, wrote the first serious state study, *History of California* (1866). In the 1870s and 1880s, more substantive works followed. Economist and journalist John H. Hittell published *A History of San Francisco and Incidentally of the State of California* (1878). Other works included a four-volume state history published in stages by Hittell's brother, attorney Theodore Hittell; Charles H. Shinn's *Mining Camps: A Study in American Frontier Government* (1884); and Josiah Royce's *California, From the Conquest in 1846 to the Second Vigilance Committee in San Francisco: A Study of American Character* (1886). Of the major nineteenth-century state historians, only Shinn and Royce had professional graduate historical training, both at Johns Hopkins University in Baltimore, Maryland. Both works offer modern readers valuable insights into the state's turbulent early history. With California's universities still immature, however, Shinn and Royce both turned to careers in fields other than history. Born and raised in California, Royce, after a brief tenure on the faculty at the University of California, moved to Harvard, where he became a leading American philosopher. Shinn became an administrator of agricultural-research agencies. The writing of early California history was left largely to boosters and talented amateurs.

By far the most important of these talented amateurs was Hubert Howe Bancroft. A San Francisco publisher and bookshop proprietor, Bancroft collected Californiana—newspapers, books, pamphlets, documents, and manuscripts. By the early 1870s, his library had more than 10,000 items and Bancroft had conceived a grandiose plan for using the information to produce a multivolume epic Pacific Coast history, which he would sell by subscription to the wealthy leaders whose exploits the books would feature. To assist in this gargantuan task, Bancroft established what amounted to an assembly line for group research. He hired scores of assistants, including talented researchers and writers such as Henry Oak and Frances Fuller Victor, who actually

H. H. Bancroft, "Boss Historian"

Hubert Howe Bancroft was widely criticized in the late nineteenth century, not only for his questionable sales techniques and the high price of his histories, but also for his use of ghost writers. George Frederick Keller elevated Bancroft to his "gallery of cranks" in this cartoon, published in *The Wasp* on April 18, 1885. *Courtesy of the California History Room, California State Library, Sacramento, California.*

wrote some of the finest volumes, but to whom Bancroft gave little or no credit. During the 1870s and '80s, Bancroft's series multiplied to 39 volumes, eleven of which dealt specifically with California. Using deceptive methods that anticipated modern subscription marketing, Bancroft eventually sold 6,000 sets, worth more than $1 million.

Although some denounced him as a charlatan, Bancroft, more than any other individual, paved the way for the modern study of California history. Whatever their authorship, Bancroft's comprehensive volumes, rich in detail and footnote references, are still the starting point for serious examination of the state through the 1880s. Although he shared the booster ethos of the period's local histories, and thus dwelt on the theme of progress during the American period, Bancroft, like Tuthill, the Hittells, Shinn, and Royce, examined the state's history critically and attempted to create generalizations from confused and contradictory events. These major nineteenth-century California historians denounced the disorganization, violence, and racial oppression of the 1840s and '50s and praised the efforts of solid citizens to impose order and community.

Bancroft's most enduring legacy proved to be his library. The histories completed, Bancroft in the late 1880s sought to sell his collection to the state. His tainted reputation and the legislature's apathy toward cultural matters, however, repeatedly thwarted the sale. Finally, in 1905 the University of California was able to acquire the library for $250,000, nearly half of which Bancroft himself donated. By then the priceless collection numbered more than 65,000 volumes and 100,000 manuscripts—including many valuable recollections by displaced Californios. The collection then moved to Berkeley, just in time to save it from annihilation in the great San Francisco earthquake and fire of 1906. Surviving decades of expansion and some controversy—including Governor Ronald Reagan's attempt in the early 1970s to have its most valuable holdings sold to pay general university expenses—the Bancroft Library has become one of the nation's major archives and an invaluable treasure for preserving America's Far Western history.

Suffragettes Marching, circa 1910, in the northern mining town of Sawyer's Bar, with Heckler in Clown Suit

Progressive Era reforms were not the sole province of big-city professionals. Reform ideas and the controversy they provoked spread into California's most remote communities. *Photographer Irving Eldridge, 1910.*

PART SIX

California and the Nation

1880–1920

Much of the written history of California reinforces the late Carey McWilliams's assertion that the state has been "the great exception." In many ways, California was—and indeed is—unique. Yet it also has been intimately involved with the nation's history, even in the gold rush decades but particularly during the years that followed the Civil War and the completion of the transcontinental railway. Throughout the Civil War, most Californians remained essentially loyal to the Union, and by the time the railroad ended their isolation the state was a microcosm of the nation firmly planted on the Pacific Slope.

During subsequent decades California came to resemble the rest of the nation even more closely. Economic transformations, including the rise of industry and the emergence of new forms of corporate organization that accompanied it, paralleled changes occurring elsewhere. Throughout the last decades of the nineteenth century, the state—like the nation—endured cyclic depressions, socioeconomic dislocations, and labor strife. The simultaneous process of urbanization accelerated the growth of San Francisco and spawned another instant city, Los Angeles. It also brought to the state problems of political tension and social adjustment similar to those experienced in longer-established cities. Indeed, by the time Chris Buckley assumed his position as the "Blind Boss" of the Democratic party in San Francisco and California in 1882, the thirty-first state was no longer a frontier province but an important element in the nation's history. It experienced the growing pains of urbanization and industrialization and episodes such as the farmers' revolt that produced the Populist movement concurrently with the nation—not a decade or more later, as some have argued. Patterns of parallel historical development continued during the first decades of the twentieth, as individuals calling themselves progressives organized and sought to implement new social and political understandings that were compatible with economic and technological transformations in both the state and the nation.

Eadweard Muybridge

Photographer of the City

In 1849, California began to attract practitioners of the novel art of photography, invented exactly a decade earlier. The first were itinerants who traveled the state making daguerreotype and tintype portraits and producing stereoscopic views, even in very remote regions. Later arrivals established studios, but they too remained wanderers; Carleton E. Watkins made some of the earliest images of Yosemite Valley, Alfred A. Hart documented the construction of the transcontinental railway, Adam Clark Vroman photographed the remains of deteriorating missions and Indian life in southern California and the Southwest, and Arnold Genthe recorded life in San Francisco's Chinatown before the earthquake of 1906. Among the most influential members of California's nineteenth-century photographic corps was "Helios," the eccentric English-born Eadweard James Muybridge.

Muybridge settled in San Francisco in 1855 when he was twenty-five years old and began his photographic career in 1867. He traveled into the field, often in his horse-drawn "Flying Studio," to make pictures of Yosemite, Alaska, Modoc War sites, and Central America. He also devised an ingenious system of cameras and trip-wires to settle Leland Stanford's wager that all four of a trotting horse's hooves leave the ground simultaneously during its stride. During the 1880s, Muybridge's technique took him to the University of Pennsylvania where he conducted and published extensive studies of human and animal locomotion. His finding not only revolutionized artists' representation of moving people and animals but also laid the foundations for motion picture technology.

Eadweard Muybridge
Library of Congress.

In 1894, poor health forced Muybridge to return to England where he died ten years later. Before he left San Francisco, however, he created a remarkable and informative historical document. In 1878 he poised his 18- by-24-inch glass-plate camera on the roof of Mark Hopkins's mansion atop Nob Hill. From his vantage point, he made a series of thirteen photographs of growing and diverse city. In Muybridge's panorama, business establishments, factories elegant houses, tenements, and hotels have replaced the ramshackle village on a mudflat that occupied the spot barely a generation before. Selections from his series provide a 180-degree view of the busiest, most densely populated half of the city. The virtual absence of people, animals, and vehicles in his images resulted from extremely long exposures required by the wet plates used in his mammoth camera; only stationary objects could be recorded.

Muybridge first pointed his camera northeastward (1) across the city and beyond Yerba Buena Island to the Contra Costa ("opposite shore"). The Appraisers Building, the Montgomery Block, and other commercial establishments dominate the center of the photograph. California Street, with cable car tracks in place and St. Mary's Church at the right center descends Nob Hill. In the lower left is Leland Stanford's stable, complete with mahogany stalls and crystal chandeliers, nestled against working-class residences. His second view (2) looks eastward across the roof of Stanford's mansion toward the busy waterfront. Grace Cathedral occupies the middle left on California Street, with the Wells Fargo building two blocks beyond. The ornate tower of

the San Francisco Merchants' Exchange is seen in the center of the photograph; beyond it to the right is the Occidental Hotel. Smoke emerging from the South-of-Market-Street districts testifies to a developing manufacturing economy.

In the next image (3), William Ralston's Palace Hotel (center) on Market Street dwarfs the adjacent Grand Hotel to the right in the scene east-southeast of Nob Hill. Built in 1875 at a cost of $5 million, the 7-story Palace provided luxurious accommodations for 2,400 guests. Beyond Market Street are the city's factory-tenement districts surrounding the once-elegant Rincon Hill neighborhood and the mouth of China Basin.

(continued . . .)

Churches furnish landmarks in Muybridge's view to the southeast (4): Temple Emanu-El on Sutter Street with its Byzantine steeples (left foreground), the rear of St. Patrick's Church on Mission Street (left center), and Trinity Episcopal Church on Powell Street (right center). Beyond the city are more of China Basin and, in the distance, Mission Bay; both have been filled to provide more space for urban expansion.

A southerly view (5) of the city records the extent of its growth and the variety of land use within its boundaries in 1878. To the left of center at Powell Street at Market is the Baldwin Hotel and Theater, built in 1872 at a cost of $2 million by Elias "Lucky" Baldwin but destroyed by fire in 1898. Just beyond the hotel are the twin chimneys of the U.S. Mint. The First Congregational Church on Mason Street occupies the center of the photograph. The foreground and background provide additional evidence of growing congestion and industrial development.

All Muybridge photos courtesy of the Department of Special Collections, Stanford University Libraries.

When Muybridge turned his camera to the southwest (6), he recorded evidence of urban maturity. Sherith Israel Synagogue stands at the center of his picture, and Market Street, making its way into still-unsettled hills, bisects it at the top. On the far side of Market, the Industrial Pavilion, an exhibition hall, nears completion with Woodward's Gardens, the city's most popular amusement park barely visible just beyond. Across Market Street from the Pavilion is the new City Hall; begun in 1872 and completed in 1897, it was destroyed by earthquake and fire in 1906. Many of the buildings seen in these selections suffered the same fate.   (WAB)

"This Was Our Place"

16

Asian Immigrants and Delta Agriculture

I n late April 1913, President Woodrow Wilson sent Secretary of State William Jennings Bryan on a cross-country mission to Sacramento, in an attempt to prevent California lawmakers passing a bill likely to injure relations between the United States and Japan. Almost immediately after the famed orator and former presidential candidate's arrival, state officials escorted Bryan to the small town of Florin, approximately ten miles south of Sacramento, in order to underscore the need for alien land laws prohibiting Japanese ownership of agricultural land. Hence Florin, dubbed the "classic instance of Japanese agrarian aggression," entered the national spotlight, its proximity to the state capitol making it a convenient showpiece for visiting politicians like the esteemed Secretary of State, "an object lesson right at the doors of the Legislature."

In spite of Japanese outcry and Bryan's in-person attempt to sway California politicians, Governor Hiram Johnson signed the bill into law on May 19, 1913. Under the California Alien Land Act, all aliens "eligible to citizenship" had the same property rights as American citizens, while all other aliens, notably Chinese and Japanese immigrants, who could not become naturalized citizens, were divested of the right to buy real estate in California. The alien land law further stipulated that individual and corporate leases were allowed for terms of three years maximum.

Since the arrival of Chinese immigrants who reclaimed and cleared Delta swamp land for farming in the late nineteenth century, to the settlement of Japanese and Asian Indian farmers, and later the seasonal migration of Filipino farm laborers, white Californians considered the significant presence of Asian immigrants in the Sacramento-San Joaquin Delta region as both an inevitable economic necessity and a looming threat to their livelihoods and racial identity. Gov. Johnson claimed the 1913 alien land law was designed to "protect our agricultural lands" from Japanese acquisition. California attorney general Ulysses S. Webb, co-author of the bill, had additional objectives in mind, stating that the law sought

235

Japanese laborers on George Shima's ranch in Stockton, c. 1910

Courtesy of The Bancroft Library, University of California, Berkeley.

to limit the presence of the Japanese "by curtailing their privileges which they enjoy here." Webb predicted that Japanese immigrants would "not come in large numbers and long abide with us if they may not acquire land."

The Sacramento–San Joaquin Delta provides a window into the paradox of California agriculture in the late nineteenth and early twentieth centuries. White growers relied heavily on nonwhite labor while professing that farming needed to be maintained as a livelihood for white American families. Lying between the present-day cities of Sacramento, Stockton, Tracy, and Antioch, extending 24 miles east to west, 48 miles north to south, comprising parts of five counties (Sacramento, San Joaquin, Contra Costa, Solano, Yolo), the Delta was (and is) a rich agricultural area formed by the confluence where the Sacramento River flowed south to meet the north-flowing San Joaquin River. Florin sat at the periphery of the Delta, but it took center stage in the debate over California's first alien land law. At this time, the Delta was an Asian American environment, a place where Californians struggled over concerns about race,

geography, and culture, as well as a place where Asian immigrants rooted their communities.

What was it about Florin that made it so much of a "problem" for anti-Japanese forces in 1913? To understand this supporters and opponents of the Japanese believed traveling to the region in question was of paramount importance. Writing for *Harper's Weekly* in 1913, Edward Hungerford implored readers interested in viewing "the Japanese situation through the eyes of California" to take a drive out to Florin as he had done. As soon as Bryan's plans to travel to California were announced, officials discussed arrangements to give him a tour of Florin. Editors of the Sacramento *Union* declared that Secretary Bryan's road trip to Florin and neighboring Walnut Grove would convince him of the Japanese menace more than "all the vials of legislative eloquence that could be uncorked." They put their trust not in the persuasive words of elected representatives, but in viewing the conditions on the ground: "Seeing is believing. The secretary of state will see, and, having seen, it will not be difficult to make him comprehend that this is an evil which threatens California everywhere." Along these lines, Gov. Johnson called Florin "California's best argument for an anti-alien law." Recognizing the delicate nature of his mission in the region from the start, Bryan declined to comment on what he had seen on the two-hour car trip, stating, "I am using my eyes and my ears, but not my tongue." He praised the surroundings and noted it was "a very pleasant ride" in which he saw "not only a Japanese settlement, but also a beautiful valley."

Anti-Japanese forces hoped the trip would plainly show Florin's demographic imbalance. They felt assured that Bryan would conclude unequivocally that he was "looking upon a section of California where the Japanese already is in the majority and the Caucasian in the minority." The most frequently cited population numbers for Florin were 1,500 Japanese and 300 to 400 white Americans. Gov. Johnson and state assembly member Hugh Bradford, who represented the district that included Florin, were fixated on providing their distinguished guest with numerical proof of Florin's majority-Asian status. They took Bryan to the public school in town, informing him that there were normally 26 Japanese and 22 white students in the primary department (another account claimed there were 22 Japanese to 20 white students, proving majority status). On that day, however, the visiting party found only 18 Japanese and 19 white children. Bryan was told that there were 42 Japanese children out of a total enrollment of 67 pupils in the Florin public schools. The men proceeded next to the Florin Basket Company, which manufactured wooden baskets for strawberries. They highlighted the disproportionate racial makeup of the white-owned factory, whose employees were all or nearly all Japanese.

Politicians, commentators, and other observers constructed the problem of Florin simultaneously as one of numbers, or too many Japanese, and moreover, as one of threat, or too many *aggressive* Japanese, meaning upwardly mobile Japanese immigrants. Compared to Chinese immigrants and African Americans, observers declared the Japanese were "different," in that they "embarked in all lines of business with eminent success," whether on the farm, or in trade and business. John Reese, town sheriff and Florin store owner known for his colorful language and rabidly anti-Japanese views, described forceful Japanese takeover tactics with a metaphor from nature:

> They try to buy in the neighborhoods where there are nothin' but white folks. Then it's just like when you throw a rock in the river. Mr. Jap is the rock and when he splashes into the midst of a section of country thickly populated by white folks he starts a wave of migration that keeps gettin' wider and wider just like the ripple in the river until all the white folks have moved out an' the Japs have moved in. . . .

Hungerford espoused a similar theory, noting a Japanese, not content to live in the "cheaper and older parts of the town," would "go into the part of a city that he likes" and pay an outrageous sum for a house, leading the value of other properties on the block to decline. At that point, he noted, the Japanese and his compatriots would purchase adjoining homes at the lower price, soon occupying the entire neighborhood.

In the late nineteenth century, the shallow, bedrock soil of Florin was planted mostly in hay and wheat. The only specialty crops found suited to the impoverished soil were strawberries and grapes, which required intensive and laborious cultivation. In the aftermath of Chinese exclusion, Japanese immigrants arrived in the 1890s as berry harvesters to replace the decreasing numbers of aging Chinese farmhands. Gradually they began to lease farmland. Conditions in Florin made it advantageous for white landowners to lease hay land to Japanese farmers for strawberry cultivation, while at the same time converting their property into vineyards. As young grape vines were maturing, Japanese tenants dug irrigation ditches and loosened the soil for their strawberry crops. White farmers who were already converting their land to grapes and strawberries shifted to Japanese tenancy as a way to ensure accessibility of labor in a period of labor scarcity. In large part, this pattern of agricultural development explained why Japanese were flocking to Florin and taking up berry cultivation, a niche that whites had ignored.

Some Florin residents disputed their town's portrayal as a degraded Japanese colony. Instead they defended Florin as a typical community of small fruit farms. Florin farmer Alice M. Brown, a Stanford-educated, ardent pro-Japanese pamphleteer and activist whose family owned a 30-acre vineyard, wrote letters to William Jennings Bryan before and after his Sacramento trip. Brown explained that the Florin Japanese were small farmers on "little five, ten, and 15 acre homes." They lived interspersed with white American homes, Brown explained, "all mixed up there; [there] is a Japanese house, and here is an American neighbor." Contrary to nativists' claims, insisted Brown, Florin was in no sense a majority-Japanese colony. Brown complained to Secretary Bryan about the Florin resident that Gov. Johnson had chosen as Secretary Bryan's local liaison. Brown did not identify the liaison by name, but called him an "ignorant, whisky soak[ed] man . . . an irresponsible fanatic," most likely referring to the afore-mentioned John Reese.

Brown and an Issei resident surnamed Suzuki, secretary of the local Japanese Association, countered by reprising Bryan's automobile tour of Florin with Sidney Gulick, a Congregationalist minister and supporter of improved U.S.–Japanese relations. After a three-hour automobile tour, Gulick concluded that "Florin is not a Japanese village either in appearance, customs, or morals. It impressed me rather as a typical prosperous community of small American farmers." To Secretary Bryan, Brown and Gulick lamented that politicians and newspaper correspondents eagerly lapped up Reese's stories, while ignoring the moderate voices of Florin's truly "representative citizens."

Passage of the 1913 alien land law did not stop Japanese immigrants from farming in Florin or elsewhere in California, but it did force California Japanese to choose between accepting the restrictions or trying to evade them. Since Nisei children were U.S. citizens under the U.S. Constitution's 14th Amendment, Japanese immigrants could purchase land in their children's names, thus circumventing alien land laws. Japanese farmers also created corporations to purchase farmland, with Nisei as the majority stockholders.

If Gov. Johnson had taken Secretary Bryan for a drive just a few miles south of Florin, to the heart of the Sacramento-San Joaquin Delta, Bryan would have observed a markedly different picture of Asian dominance. There, reclaimed swamp lands formed one of the most fertile agricultural districts in California. The Delta's geography had produced a unique type of farming that, from early on, relied on a large, mostly Asian labor force. In order to take advantage of the rich peat soil, landowners invested enormous amounts of capital and resources in building an extensive network of levees, dikes, and drainage ditches to protect the area from flooding. Before the introduction of the clamshell dredger in 1879, Chinese immigrants were the only laborers available to do this kind of reclamation work, and to farm the thick peat sod, often called "muck" soil. Not only was the muck difficult to work with, it was unhealthy. After a few years of cultivation, the broken peat sod turned into a fine black dust that caused pneumonia and other ailments for those working the land.

Delta landowners soon learned that the area could not be profitably settled by white families on small farms. Reclamation costs were so high that only large corporations with expensive modern dredging equipment could afford to perform the work. Unlike their Florin neighbors, Delta landowners believed that their holdings could only thrive with large Asian workforces. Just as alien land law advocates advised Secretary Bryan to see conditions on the ground in Florin himself, preferably via automobile, Delta farmer John P. Irish invited readers to see the Delta by ship. Speaking in 1913, Irish explained that from this vantage visitors could appreciate the bucolic landscape flanked by "graceful willows" and the processions of barges and steamers taking the "fruit of the earth" to market. Irish said bluntly that he doubted the region could ever be a place of independent small farms. Instead Delta landholdings were destined to remain large corporate concerns leased to Asian tenants. Because Delta landowners were "too satisfied with their Asiatic hordes," they were unlikely to upset the status quo. In Irish's mind, the "hordes" were not a negative presence, but a practical necessity.

In his 1913 excursion to the Sacramento-San Joaquin Delta, reporter Barton Currie used similar terms to describe the Delta's Asian farmers. Although he was transfixed by the "land of wonder crops," Currie labeled the Asian "hordes" mere pawns of big landowners, victims of the "get-rich-quick game of working the delta for all the soil would crop."

In addition to swampland reclamation, white landowners in the Sacramento-San Joaquin Delta had early hired Chinese as farm laborers and tenants to grow grain, hay, potatoes, onions, beans, and other vegetables. On the islands of the central Delta which lay below sea level, some Chinese immigrants leased land from the large corporations that were financing Delta reclamation. Chinese entrepreneurs like Big Jim, Hung Lee, and Chin Lung operated thousands of acres in the Delta and, between them, oversaw dozens of Chinese labor camps. They gained notice in the press as daring crop gamblers who netted huge profits on potatoes, in some years making "$100,000 killings on single crops." Unfortunately, after three consecutive years of potato cultivation, peat soil developed a fungus. Chinese growers then discovered that in the Delta's fine peat soil, asparagus spears grew straight, facilitating easy packing and canning. Chinese labor dominated asparagus fields and canneries in the early decades of the twentieth century. In the 1890s, as the Japanese population in the Delta began to increase, the Issei followed in the footsteps of the Chinese.

According to John Irish, the Delta's cultural diversity was a benefit to white landowners, who could draw on what he called "a museum of races" to perform their agricultural labor. Irish enumerated the various ethnicities found in the Delta, from Italians and Portuguese to Afghans and East Indians, and finally "the preponderance of the Japanese." All were adapted to work on crops requiring "a constant stooping or squat position . . . in a temperature of 100 to 110 degrees." These were the "fixed physical conditions" that Irish claimed white landowners must take into account when adapting a labor system to their locality.

Asian landowners, like their white neighbors, also learned to adapt to their locality. Undoubtedly the most successful Asian farmer in the Delta was George Shima. Born Kinji Ushijima in Japan's Fukuoka prefecture in 1864, Shima arrived in San Francisco in 1889 with about $1,000 (roughly $28,000 in 2018 dollars). Like many Japanese immigrants before him, he found work as a domestic servant, acquiring English skills and a degree of comfort interacting with white Americans. He then worked as a field hand in Stockton and soon became a labor contractor. Realizing that swamp land and islands periodically flooded by the Sacramento and San Joaquin rivers could be purchased for as little as $3 per acre (an acre of prime Delta farmland then commanded $150 or more), Shima decided to invest in 15 acres of barren Delta lowlands. He drained the land, built dikes, and planted potatoes, onions, and asparagus. Shima later recounted how for six years he had watched "the methods of the Chinese, Italian and Irish potato growers, asking them questions by the hundred, and reading the reports of the department of agriculture," determined to find a better method for growing potatoes on reclaimed Delta land.

After some trial and error and a series of financial mishaps, in 1897 Shima earned his first profits from this previously underutilized wasteland. Over time, his potato crop thrived and earned him a fortune, at which point he formed partnerships with other Japanese to purchase more land. He started the Empire Navigation Company, which maintained a fleet of steamboats, barges, tugboats, and launches to transport his crops from the Delta to San Francisco and surrounding cities. By 1910, Shima was known as the "Potato King" of California. He and his partners owned 420 acres and rented another 8,300. By 1912, he controlled 10,000 acres of potatoes valued at half a million dollars (about $13.1 million in 2018 dollars). Film footage of Shima's Delta property in 1914 featured numerous migrant laborers from India in turbans, Punjabi Sikh men (erroneously called "Hindus" by local whites). By 1920, Shima produced a stunning 85 percent of California's potato crop.

Many observers expressed awe and admiration for the Chinese and Japanese agricultural entrepreneurs who prospered in the challenging physical environment of the Delta. The Los Angeles *Times* commended George Shima as "an example of what the Jap can really accomplish . . . more than any other in California." Chester Rowell, a Progressive Party leader and newspaper editor who was also a close political advisor of Gov. Johnson, called Shima "the richest Japanese in California" and an employer of "a small army of Japanese, Chinese, and Hindus." Irish applauded Shima and others for having "given to California a Delta two-thirds as large as that of the Nile, and its equal in production." George Shima acknowledged his appreciation for Irish's support in 1923, when he served as a pallbearer at Irish's funeral.

Ironically, praise for Asian agricultural pioneers in the Sacramento-San Joaquin Delta emerged simultaneously with the vehemently nativist rhetoric that surrounded Japanese settlement in Florin, only a few miles north. Both praise and criticism of California's Asian farmers was highly racialized. Even those Anglos who espoused flagrantly anti-Japanese stances could not help but be impressed with Shima's business acumen. Writer Walter Woehlke conceded that Shima had cornered the West Coast potato market by possessing "superior knowledge, better foresight, and greater daring" than his white counterparts, which earned Shima a reputation for "honesty, ability, shrewdness, and daring among the white men with whom he came in contact." His 1910 profit of $250,000 on potatoes was just "one of many spectacular chapters in his career." Stockton landowner and commission merchant John Perry remarked in 1913 that quite simply, no white man had been as successful in the Delta region as Shima. Barton Currie likewise described Shima's exploits with wonder and approval, concluding that, as much as "the Californians dislike the Nipponese race they cannot deny the fact that Shima has taught them a few lessons in how to realize the vast possibilities of their island empire." According to Currie, the brash and cunning Shima did not "invent" or "originate," but engaged in the business of imitating and experimenting with the latest machinery and methods of seed selection and soil cultivation.

Shima's entrepreneurial success did not insulate him from the anti-Asian racism of early twentieth-century California. An uproar followed his 1909 purchase of a two-story house on Berkeley's College Avenue, when white neighbors objected to the presence of a Japanese family in their upscale residential district, whether its patriarch was a self-made millionaire or not. Local newspaper headlines announced "Yellow Peril in College Town," "Jap Invades Fashionable Quarters," and "Jap Puts On Airs."

At the time, white neighbors had no legal grounds to challenge Shima's purchase of a home in California. But with the passage of the state's 1913 alien land law, white residents could prevent Japanese immigrant families from moving into their neighborhoods. No doubt with memories of the demeaning experience in Berkeley on his mind, Shima wrote to Gov. Johnson in May 1913 on behalf of the Japanese Association of America, asking that "justice and humanity which we conceive to be the fundamental principal of the American nation . . . not [be] forgotten at this time."

There was a fine line between Anglo admiration and intimidation. Shima's agricultural achievements earned him respect and accolades, but at the same time made him the prime target of a growing anti-Japanese coalition. Nativists called Shima an "example of the range of the spectacular features of the so-called Japanese menace" whose agricultural undertakings in the Delta made "no line of business . . . 'safe' from the yellow invasion." In response, Florin's Alice Brown emphasized the singularity of Japanese immigrant prowess in agriculture: "There is only one George Shima in the state," she said; Shima stood in stark contrast to most Japanese farmers that Brown had encountered, who cultivated small plots "on the poorest of that poor soil."

Shima also defended the Issei, pointing to the insignificance of Japanese landholdings in California. He wrote several letters to the governor in 1911, expressing delight at Johnson's victory and his opinion that the "Japanese Question" was resolving itself, since the number of immigrants from Japan continued to decrease. "The lands owned by the Japanese are only 11,000 acres," wrote Shima. "What small acrage [*sic*] they have in this State. Speaking of the vast area of California, it might be well to say that no Japanese have land in California." Shima was right: given the reality of Asian exclusion, the denial of landholding, voting, and citizenship rights to Asian immigrants, and the myriad other forms of racial discrimination to which they were subjected, Asians in California, as in other parts of the West, were no threat to Anglo dominance.

Despite state and federal legislation against them, and no matter how Anglos argued over their positive or negative impacts, Asian immigrants remained a strong and vibrant presence in the Delta well into the twentieth century. This is best exemplified by the Delta town of Locke, a rural Chinatown founded in 1915. There Chinese pioneers were able to secure a foothold in Delta agriculture, one they maintained for five decades. Singular as a completely Chinese town, built by and exclusively for Chinese immigrants, designated a National Historic Landmark in 1990, Locke is the oldest remaining rural Chinatown in North America. According to the National Park Service, Locke is "the largest, most complete example of a rural, agricultural Chinese American community in the United States." Ironically, Chinese immigrant leaders established Locke just two years after state officials castigated Florin as a majority-Asian place and attempted to prohibit the formation of such spaces through law.

The history of Chinese exclusion makes Locke's existence all the more remarkable. By 1890, the number of Chinese in the Delta region had declined sharply. White growers keenly felt the effects of the 1882 Chinese Exclusion Act, which barred the Chinese laborers from entry into the United States. Rio Vista's *Sacramento River News* predicted in 1890 that all Chinese would be gone from the region within a few years, since no new immigrants could replace those who returned to China. Indeed, Chinese settlements were disappearing from rural towns throughout California, as many of the remaining Chinese relocated to urban centers. The river Chinatowns that persisted did so, in part, because Japanese agricultural laborers recruited to replace Chinese workers took up their deserted housing.

By the early twentieth century, with asparagus becoming a profitable crop almost overnight, the Chinese laborers who had worked in the Delta during the 1880s returned, along with many new arrivals from Guangdong. Together with other immigrant laborers, they made the Sacramento-San Joaquin Delta the world's premier asparagus-growing region. When the San Francisco earthquake and fire destroyed municipal records in 1906, Chinese developed the "paper-son system," claiming that they were American-born citizens whose children born in China were also eligible for citizenship. To connect these newcomers with jobs, Chinese merchants often served as labor contractors, running ads in local newspapers. For example, the *River News* in February 1915 advertised that "All kinds of Chinese help for farmwork can be secured on short notice by applying to or addressing Toy Goon, Hop Lee Jan, Front Street, Rio Vista, Calif."

Chinese immigrants from the Zhongshan district of Guangdong province built Locke after a fire destroyed Walnut Grove's Chinatown in 1914. Zhongshan immigrants had already lived alongside the Delta's Sze Yup Chinese for two generations. Both groups kept their distance as well as distinct economic niches. Zhongshan Chinese specialized in fruit growing in the natural levees of the northern Delta, while Sze Yup immigrants from the Taishan district of Guangdong cultivated potatoes in the swamps to the south. The Zhongshan dialect closely resembled the Cantonese spoken in the provincial capital of Canton (now Guangzhou), but the Sze Yup dialect was virtually incomprehensible to the Zhongshan and to those who spoke "standard" Cantonese. The Sze Yup Chinese comprised the bulk of immigrants to the continental United States. With the exception of the Delta region, the Zhongshan were a minority among Chinese immigrants in California. Ping Lee, son of Locke's co-founder, summed up the age-old differences:

Zhongshan, Taishan, all right, we're speaking of a district. Zhongshan is a half hour north of Macao. Taishan is further, over a mountain range. Now, in China, in the old days, you would never be on the other side. You wouldn't marry anybody on the other side. Stick on this side and speak a different dialect, that's the way it was. . . .

In 1914, Ping Lee's father, businessman Charlie Bing, and a delegation of fellow Zhongshan merchants decided to "secede" from the Walnut Grove Sze Yup Chinese. Ping Lee recounted that

when Walnut Grove burned down, the idea was, you got to start all over. But you can't buy land. Chinese can't buy land in those days, you've got to remember that. You've got to rent it from somebody.

Because of the alien land law, Walnut Grove farmers needed the backing of a white landowner. They approached the family of Sacramento merchant and pear grower George Locke, who agreed to lease them property for a new Chinatown, built and financed exclusively by Zhongshan Chinese.

With Locke's verbal agreement, Bing and his associates secured a town site on about nine acres. Next, they financed construction of boarding houses, restaurants, gambling halls, a slaughterhouse, and stores. They named the town for Locke, whose heirs continued to lease their property to the Chinese. In 1915, approximately 200 Chinese field hands, mostly Zhongshan who had lived in Walnut Grove, moved to the new Chinatown. They were soon joined by hundreds of other Chinese migrant laborers from other parts of the Delta. At harvest time, as many as 1,500 Zhongshan and other Chinese workers crowded into Locke. Later, during the nation's experiment with prohibition, whites visited, looking for alcohol and games of chance.

Locke was where Chinese immigrants in the Delta found leisure, community, and sustenance, as well as a refuge from racial discrimination. Bing Fai Chow described the racism Chinese encountered in towns outside Locke: "Before [World War II], in Isleton, Rio Vista, places like that, the whites wouldn't take your order in the restaurant. You wouldn't even get served in the bakery shop. Chinese couldn't go to the bars." White racism sometimes escalated into violence. "In the past, the whites would attack you with stones when you walked through some of these towns," he recalled. "We never dared to walk on the streets alone then—except in Locke. This was our place."

Wong Yow was one of the many farm workers who rented a room in Locke. He arrived in the United States in 1921 as a "paper son" to join his father in the Delta. Wong was detained two months at the Angel Island immigration station in San Francisco Bay, opened in 1910. From 1921 to 1935, he worked ten to twelve hour days in the surrounding fields and orchards, living in labor camps during the weekdays. On the weekends, ranchers shuttled the Chinese workers to Locke. For Wong, a "typical day" in Locke consisted of

some shopping, get my hair cut, maybe go to the movies. We would just sit on the benches on Main Street and visit, watching the people go by, or read the newspapers, it didn't really matter. It was just nice to have a day like that, the opportunity of going to town.

The numerous gambling halls in Locke functioned as recreational meeting places for Chinese men, where they retrieved mail, read Chinese newspapers, and played rounds of dominoes or fan-tan. These gambling joints even served as hiring halls where local farmers recruited workers. Now preserved as a museum for tourists, Dai Loy gambling house, one of Charlie Bing's establishments, was a social center for Chinese in Locke from 1916 to 1950. Jo Lung reminisced about going to Dai Loy on his day off from work:

I liked to play. And I win a little bit, too, playing dominoes. Every night, day and night, people came to the gambling houses. . . . Yeah, I liked to win, liked to win money. But oh crazy head! Charlie Bing, he get your money. You lose, you don't win.

Chinese immigrants might have had regrets about losing money, but they rarely referred to gambling as a morally objectionable vice. Former workers spoke of gambling in neutral terms, as a pastime that some engaged in and some did not. According to Wong Yow, who boarded in Locke on the weekends during the 1920s and 1930s, gamblers

never caused any problems here at all. The gambling houses were all up on Main Street, and it was up to you whether you wanted to hang around those people or not. If you didn't like gambling, you just stayed away, like I did. I never gambled.

Wong felt no pressure from his peers to reconsider his choice, nor did he attach any stigma to gambling.

Opening of Locke Chinese School, 1926

Courtesy of Sacramento River Delta Historical Society.

It was each to his own, he mused, "They didn't bother you, and you didn't bother them." Some of the most respected families in Locke were involved in the gambling business. They used their profits to contribute a new well to supply the town with water, bought equipment for the Chinese school, and made donations to the Baptist mission.

San Francisco-born Chinese American Effie Lai, wife of a prosperous Chinese tenant farmer who was foreman of a large fruit orchard on Grand Island in the Delta, relished the bustling atmosphere of Locke in its heyday. She described herself as a woman who "married into Locke." Childhood sojourns to visit relatives in Locke left positive impressions, and she had long viewed the area as "so different from San Francisco's scenery. . . . The weather there was nice, and the conditions—not the crowded conditions. Everything was so spacious." Lai's uncle, a Locke storekeeper, introduced her to her husband, and the couple married in 1922. They lived on the Grand Island ranch her husband managed, but Locke was their center of socialization and community. Lai recalled that

Every weekend we'd come into Locke. . . . That's the day, oh, that was the happiest day in our lives. I'd see my uncle, Wah Lee, and his family. And all the people from the ranches come up here and congregate; catch up on the news—who died, who married, what's happening back in the old country, what's happening around the area there, the economic situation, all those things you talk about.

In 1927, as the American economy began to falter, the white landowners they worked for went bankrupt. The Lai family moved from Grand Island and settled in Locke. They struggled to make ends meet during the Great Depression. While her husband worked as an itinerant Delta farm laborer when he could obtain employment, Effie Lai supported the family by sorting pears, picking tomatoes, canning asparagus, and even bootlegging rice wine until she became too scared of the raids and arrests to continue.

Surprisingly, a town called the "Monte Carlo of the State" by the *Sacramento Bee* because of its numerous gambling halls, brothels, speakeasies, and opium dens, was home to many Chinese American families.

In old-timers' recollections of Locke, the presence of children running in the streets was mentioned as frequently as the high concentration of gamblers. Tommy King, whose family moved to Locke from Walnut Grove in 1928, estimated that there were 30 to 40 families living in Locke during the Depression era. The Delta in fact remained one of the few places in rural California that saw Chinese American family formation during the exclusion era. The adult Chinese female population comprised a mix of immigrant women from China and second-generation women born in Delta Chinatowns and San Francisco. Most of the houses where families lived were located on Second and Key Streets, away from Main Street businesses. Many of these homes had vegetable plots that backed into the waterway for access to irrigation. Roberta Yee, who grew up in Locke the daughter of a pear sharecropper, remembered women tending their gardens together, carrying buckets to and from a common faucet for watering. Gardening was a social activity, Yee observed, "where women got together and participated in a bit of back fence gossip." Like many Chinese American children raised in Locke, she had fond memories of swimming and fishing in Delta riverways. Every evening, she would stop to listen to the whistles of the Delta King and Delta Queen steamboats "churning up the river. . . . It was nostalgic even then, though I don't know why."

Even as the numbers of Chinese were declining in every other agricultural district in California, the Chinese populations in Delta counties like San Joaquin and Contra Costa increased substantially after 1900. Exclusion laws had turned the Chinese in California into an urban population, except for those in the Delta. There, the Chinese farmed for a longer time than anywhere else in the state and maintained a continuous presence for over 150 years. Because there was ample work, the Delta drew new Chinese immigrants well into the 1940s.

Apart from measured admiration for the achievements of Asian farmers in the Delta and a general acceptance of their large numbers there, a concerted campaign to promote colonization of the Delta by white residents emerged by the early 1920s. Boosters called for settlement and building projects "worthy of the white man's attention and consideration" under the slogan "Make the Delta White." This was part of a larger agricultural colonization movement which, at its peak between 1915 and 1924, aimed to settle white families onto small farms in planned communities to blunt Japanese penetration into California. Though these schemes failed for a host of reasons, including the trend towards agricultural consolidation and irrigation policies that ultimately contributed to the rise

Main Street Locke, 1939

Courtesy of Russell Ooms.

of urban conglomerations, the vision of racial purity in rural California persisted.

In the early 1920s, the Holland Land Company hosted a series of promotional events at Clarksburg, 15 miles south of Sacramento in the northwestern edge of the Sacramento-San Joaquin Delta. Located across the river from the Asian enclave of Walnut Grove, Holland Land Company aimed to attract buyers for land that it had spent around $2.5 million to reclaim and enclose with levees. Sacramento judge C.E. McLaughlin spoke at one of these "down river picnics," which drew, among others, numerous well-to-do, educated Bay Area residents interested in purchasing a country home. McLaughlin implored young men in the audience to "get on the land" in the Delta and thereby solve the "great problem confronting the people of America," namely "the non-assimilable peoples of other lands."

But the advertisements and other promotional material generated by the Holland Land Company made practically no reference to race or the need for whites to resettle the Delta. The company's first president and treasurer J.V. Mendenhall frequently spoke on the topic of "interdependence" between backcountry and city, and seemed to target wealthy businessmen interested in investing in a second home. If Mendenhall mentioned the presence of Japanese farmers, desirable or undesirable, it was only to note that since the passage of the renewed 1920 alien land act, Delta land had become "more attractive to American farmers." Instead, Mendenhall's company leased extensive tracts of reclaimed land to Chinese and Japanese tenants. In general, Delta landowners had little interest in subdividing and selling. Rather they chose to rent, lease on shares, or assign managers to each parcel of land.

John P. Irish considered himself an expert on Delta agriculture, having "studied all the possible and impossible conditions of farming in the islands." He lambasted the slogan "Make the Delta White," not because it was racist, but because it was "impracticable" and held out "a false and impossible promise."

The islands of the Delta had to be farmed in tracts with levee frontage, making subdivided landlocked tracts of no use. For this reason, Irish observed, whites on the Holland Tract, south of his own property, had deserted farms purchased on deferred payment plans.

Despite campaigns to "Make the Delta White," for many Asian immigrant farmers and their families in the early twentieth century, the Sacramento-San Joaquin Delta was home, a region they claimed as "our place." For politicians and journalists in the alien land law era, Florin represented the epitome of the Japanese "menace" and an aggressive "peaceful penetration" of California farmland. Yet residents and those claiming insider knowledge of the region painted a more complicated picture based on geographic nuances. They offered alternative constructions of Asian dominance in the Delta, one steeped in the rhetoric of profit and economic dependence. Even after the 1913 alien land law, the all-Chinese town of Locke flourished, against all odds, as a vibrant rural Chinese American community. As Roberta Yee recalled, "It may look a bit like a ghost town now, but in her heyday—wow!" As much as the Delta was a place of rigid racial hierarchy and economic exploitation, it was also a testament to a rich history of struggle and resilience.

Beginnings of Modern California

17

Although California's population increased at a rate slower than that of the nation at large during post-gold-rush decades, its residents numbered 865,000 by 1880 and 1.5 million by 1900. The newcomers, along with the transcontinental railway, ended the state's seclusion from the rest of the nation. During the same decades, however, impressions persisted of Southern California as an alien frontier outpost, populated principally by outlaws. The opinion was uninformed, except in one sense: developments that bound the state to the nation before the 1880s occurred mainly in northern and central regions, leaving the south isolated and sparsely populated. During the turn-of-the-century decades, however, events integrated the entire state—not just a portion of it—with the nation and predicted Southern California's ultimate rank among the most important and influential regions in the United States. At the same time, California men and women joined with other Americans in demands for change and reform.

Southern California

In 1862, when San Francisco counted 56,000 inhabitants, the entire population south of the Tehachapis barely surpassed 30,000. Mountain men and traders had visited Southern California during the Hispanic periods, but few foreigners settled. Those who did, for all practical purposes, became Californios themselves, and in 1846 a meager population of 1,200 made *La Ciudad* (*El Pueblo* until 1835) *del Rio y Valle de la Reina de los Angeles de la Porciúncula* the largest settlement in the Mexican province. During the gold rush, the town was a way-station for Argonauts arriving by way of Mexico and southern overland routes; among them were a few individuals who gave Los Angeles

245

and its environs an early reputation as a haven for outlaws (real and imagined) and made its *calle de los negros* (literally, "people of darkness") one of California's most notorious districts.

Southern California's permanent residents hardly contributed to the region's notoriety. San Bernardino, settled by Mormons during the 1840s, was a stable farming community by the 1860s. Forty-Niner Elias J. ("Lucky") Baldwin invested in Los Angeles real estate and laid the foundation for one of the state's great fortunes. Along with future governor John G. Downey, Phineas Banning purchased part of the Dominguez rancho and began to develop a port and the hamlet of San Pedro. A few rancheros prospered during the 1850s by selling beef to hungry gold seekers, but the 1860s brought competitive southwestern cattle, severe droughts, declining local markets, uncertainty over land titles, and ruin to most. Not even increased demand sparked by the Civil War could save them, and their estates passed into the hands of "gringos," sheep ranchers like James Irvine in southern Los Angeles County, syndicates of wheat growers in the San Fernando Valley, vintners like J. De Barth Shorb near San Gabriel, or speculators who carved rancho lands into plots to sell to farmers. Expansion continued but relatively slowly. Los Angeles grew in population to 3,530 by 1850, 11,333 by 1860, and 15,309 by 1870. That year, only 5,491 people lived in the enormous county of San Diego.

The southern population remained heavily Hispanic, but most political and economic leaders were Americans. Many fell prey to the epidemic of railroad fever that infected the state during the 1850s. Hindsight makes the outcome of the resulting contest for rail connections and regional supremacy between Los Angeles and San Diego seem obvious, but as late as the 1860s it was not so apparent. Los Angeles remained an isolated village, located 20 miles from a mediocre port; by contrast, San Diego fronted a fine natural harbor and had superior access to the interior. Phineas Banning attempted to redress the imbalance by constructing a rail connection between Los Angeles and the coast, laying out the town of Wilmington and improving the harbor. Still, many Angelenos conceded defeat, and most probably subscribed to the opinions expressed in an 1869 Los Angeles *Star* editorial:

> We are too far inland and have no reliable harbor in our country. We must be content to be the political and social capital of south California; we must be satisfied with our genial climate, our fruitful soil, our generous wines, our golden fruit . . . [and] our cattle upon a thousand hills.

San Diego, the writer concluded, was destined to be the commercial center of the region.

San Diegans agreed. During the 1850s, when only a handful of settlers populated the place, owners of waterfront property urged Congress to adopt a southern route (favored by many in government) for a transcontinental railway and organized a local company to build a connecting link to the anticipated line. The Civil War and the Pacific Railway Act dashed their hopes, but peace revived them. Under the leadership of former Union general William S. Rosecrans, San Diegans entered into complex negotiations that eventually involved the federal government, John C. Frémont, Thomas A. Scott of the Pennsylvania Central, and the Central Pacific itself. In 1865, in collaboration with a syndicate of San Franciscans, they organized the Southern Pacific Railway Company to build a coastal route, but that firm fell under the control of the Big Four. Then, in 1871, Rosecrans and his San Diego associates formed the California Southern Coast Railway Company to link their city with the transcontinental rails. Neither their vigorous efforts nor those of less energetic Los Angeles rivals, however, determined the outcome of the competition.

During the 1870s, Los Angeles leaders like John G. Downey became more optimistic about the town's future and eager to end its isolation. In 1872, they investigated possible ties with the Texas Pacific or Central Pacific, but Collis P. Huntington and his southern California agent, William P. Hyde, actually dictated the outcome. Anxious to protect its monopoly in the state, the Central Pacific began laying track for the Southern Pacific line. Instead of following the coast, as San Diegans had planned, the route cut through the San Joaquin Valley and the Mussel Slough country toward the two major southeastern approaches to the state, Needles and Yuma. As the rails neared the Tehachapis in 1876, Los Angeles interests resumed negotiations, and ultimately conceded to the corporation a $610,000 subsidy from municipal funds, rights to Banning's Los Angeles-San Pedro railway, and land for a depot in the city. In return, the company built a 50-mile link between the valley line and Los Angeles. Its completion left San Diego isolated.

Population: The "One Great Desideratum"

Until 1876, Los Angeles remained essentially a bucolic Hispanic *pueblo*; the rail connection began its transformation into a typical American city. Between

Coronado Hotel and Balboa Park, San Diego

San Diego ultimately placed second in its rivalry with Los Angeles during the 1870s and '80s, but it, too, became an important Southern California city. Resorts such as the luxurious Coronado Hotel (*top*), built in 1887, introduced a thriving tourist industry. Economic and cultural development continued, and by the early 1900s the city was ready to build beautiful Balboa Park (*right*) to challenge San Francisco for the right to host the Panama-Pacific Exposition of 1915. *Courtesy of The Bancroft Library, University of California, Berkeley.*

1870 and 1880, the population doubled to more than 33,000, while San Diego's increased by just 337 to 2,637. Other changes also became evident. Cattlemen shifted from range-grazing to feed-lot operations and vintners expanded their wine production. Louis Prevost and others organized the California Silk Association and the California Cotton Growers and Manufacturers Association; it predicted things to come in the twentieth century when it planted 10,000 acres in cotton near Bakersfield and imported a community of black Southerners to work the fields.

More promising than ill-fated experiments with silk and cotton was citrus production. Spanish *padres* had planted citrus crops in the region, but none were commercially important until the 1870s. Then it was discovered that the local climate and dry interior valley and coastal foothill soil could, with irrigation, provide ideal growing environments. Almost simultaneously, an orange called the Bahia navel (also known as the "Washington" navel because of the U.S. Department of Agriculture's role in its introduction) arrived from Brazil. In 1873, just two Bahia trees grew near Riverside; by the end of the 1880s, more than a million were producing throughout Southern California. In 1884, the state's oranges swept most of the prizes at an exhibition in New Orleans, and in 1886, 2,000 carloads of navels were shipped from the state.

Successful citrus agriculture, however, did not provide what Southern California boosters regarded as "the one great desideratum" for their region's success—population—and during the 1870s they launched an aggressive advertising campaign to remedy the situation. Individual landowners traveled east to promote their tracts, but the Central Pacific, with its millions of acres to sell, took an early lead in the effort. Its land office commissioned numerous books and pamphlets touting Southern California, where much of its available land was located. Charles Nordhoff's *California for Health, Pleasure and Residence* (1874) and B.C. Truman's *Homes and Happiness in the Golden State of California* (1883) typified the scores of widely distributed titles. To lure prospective buyers, the railroad offered travelers low fares on Spartan "emigrant cars" and way-stations along the route, plus relocation services, credit arrangements for fares and land purchases, employment agencies, and even translators for settlers recruited by agents in Europe. In addition, Californians formed statewide associations such as the California Migrant Union and the Pacific Land Bureau to attract settlers. The Los Angeles Board of Trade founded the Southern California Immigration Association to advertise their land as a "veritable sanitarium" offering health to the infirm and unlimited opportunity to the ambitious.

Results of their vigorous propaganda campaigns disappointed Southern Californians. The population increased, but not at the dramatic rate that was both anticipated and essential. Distance and cost inhibited response. With fertile land available at similar prices closer to home, Easterners or Midwesterners were reluctant to uproot families and undertake a long, expensive trip to California. Another problem involved competition: Oregon and other regions were more familiar, promoted themselves just as aggressively, and offered equally attractive inducements. Finally, the advertising itself inhibited success: in graphic detail, booster literature depicted attributes of the life and land that Southern Californians believed made their region "the greatest country on earth." But the arid landscape and peculiar agricultural systems described in the brochures seemed alien to many prospective migrants and not very conducive to permanent settlement.

The "Boom of the '80s"

External influences ultimately accomplished what local promoters could not achieve and, as usual, the railroads were involved. During the 1880s, the Atchison, Topeka & Santa Fe extended its Arizona line to Needles, and reached San Bernardino in 1885. The company then purchased several intrastate lines and entered Los Angeles in 1887, broke the monopoly of the Central Pacific (reorganized under Kentucky laws in 1884 and renamed the Southern Pacific) and precipitated a railroad rate war. The $125 fare between Kansas City and Los Angeles fell to half that, then to a fourth, then even lower, triggering the so-called "Boom of the '80s" in Southern California.

Boosters' promotional campaigns finally paid dividends. Thousands of farmers, health-seekers, and others who had read the literature and contemplated a visit or a move to the Golden State now seized the opportunity. Once in California, many skeptics changed their attitudes and decided to remain. Although Los Angeles was a small city, it did not appear backward. Permanent buildings, telephones, electric lights, schools, and other amenities already were in place. Prosperous businesses and substantial homes lined broad streets, street railways provided transportation, and churches and civic associations functioned actively. The climate, too, lured settlers, as did apparently abundant land for towns and farms.

Potential profits also attracted a contingent of "boomers," promoters with experience on previous frontiers. Opportunists all, they acquired titles to land, planned towns, began construction of hotels and other impressive buildings, and opened sales offices. Picnics, barbecues, lavish entertainments, and extravagant publicity convinced customers to purchase lots in communities that often existed only on paper. Some were located in dry creek beds or on other worthless land, and titles frequently were shaky at best. Nevertheless, many of the boomers' communities did materialize, eventually to be absorbed into greater Los Angeles or to become cities in their own right. Before the excitement collapsed in 1889, it had produced 60 new towns covering almost 80,000 acres in Southern California and had attracted the long-desired population: more than 100,000 in Los Angeles alone in 1890, 170,000 in 1900, and 500,000 in 1910.

Migrants to Southern California created a society unlike the one that had evolved in the northern part of the state during the gold-rush decades. Foreign-born residents were relatively few. In Los Angeles, for example, Europeans accounted for 15 percent of the total population in 1890, Asians for about 2 percent,

Downtown Los Angeles, circa 1905

Although the "Boom of the '80s" was brief, it began the process that made Los Angeles a bustling city by the turn of the century. The Hollenbeck Building stands at a busy intersection, surrounded by pedestrians and trolleys, which transported residents to Hollywood, Griffith Park, and other regions of the already-sprawling metropolis. *The Huntington Library, San Marino, California.*

and Mexicans less than 1 percent. American-born ethnic minorities also were small; black Americans and descendants of the Californios and Indians each accounted for about 2 percent of the city's population. Age distribution and marital status closely resembled the national norm, as did the number of men for every 100 women: 109 in 1890 and 97 in 1900. About a third of the new arrivals came from elsewhere in California, but whatever their origins, they brought with them strains of their conservative Midwestern, Protestant, Republican traditions.

Thus, the "Boom of the '80s"—brief though it was—introduced new elements into California history. Equally significant, when the boom collapsed in 1889,

it did not disable the Southern California economy. Like profits, losses often were only on paper; in *Millionaires of a Day*, T.S. Van Dyke's 1890 satire of the episode, a character observed: "I had half a million dollars wiped out in the crash, and what's worse, $500 of it was in cash." Individuals and syndicates new to the region absorbed much of the loss, and many of them departed. The more successful remained, however, and population continued to grow. Despite nationwide economic fluctuations, prosperity returned, not only in Los Angeles but also throughout the southern counties. Established banks and businesses survived the recession that followed 1889 and development persisted on a reasonably stable course.

The First Oil Boom

While growers in the Central Valley increased operations to place California second only to Minnesota in wheat production by 1890 and San Francisco's manufacturing and commercial activity expanded, the southern California economy remained principally dependent on agriculture, real estate speculation, service industries, and retail trade. Recognition of this imbalance during the late 1870s and early '80s prompted Los Angeles interests to form the Home Industry Protection League and the Society for the Promotion of Manufactures to encourage diversification. Editorials in major local newspapers—the *Times* and the *Herald*—also expressed concern and advocated investment in industry. But Los Angeles lagged far behind San Francisco in the 1890s and behind other comparable western cities in terms of manufacturing output, investment, and employment. The few existing industrial firms in Los Angeles and Southern California in general usually were related to other economic activities: agricultural processing, meat packing, fabricating household goods, construction, and the like. Industrial development, especially production for export from the state, would await the new century.

Nevertheless, during the 1880s and '90s, Southern California experienced the beginning of a bonanza that ultimately surpassed gold in importance. Petroleum's presence was known in previous eras. Indians waterproofed boats and baskets and attached arrowheads with the tarry substance that oozed from the ground. Spaniards and Mexicans called it *brea* (tar) and used it to seal roofs. *Padres* at missions San Fernando, Santa Barbara, and San Buenaventura distilled small quantities of lamp oil from it, as did Andrés Pico near San Fernando and others near Carpinteria. But petroleum had little commercial value until E.L. Drake perfected mass-extraction technology and drilled the first well in the Oil Creek region of western Pennsylvania in 1859. During the following decade, Californians attempted to tap deposits throughout the state. R.S. Baker drilled in what is now central Los Angeles, and Phineas Banning's Pioneer Oil Company explored near Wilmington. In 1857, George S. Gilbert began a small operation refining crude oil that seeped from Sulphur Mountain on Rancho Ojai in Ventura County, and in 1865 San Francisco capitalists organized the Union Mattole Oil Company to sink the state's first well at Petrolia in Humboldt County.

Only Gilbert's modest success received recognition, but it was sufficient to persuade Thomas A. Scott of the Pennsylvania Railroad to send Benjamin Silliman, the Yale University geologist who surveyed the Pennsylvania fields, to assess California's potential in 1864. Silliman's conclusions, based principally on Gilbert's enthusiasm rather than objective investigation, predicted huge and immediate profits from petroleum in the state, and Scott responded by purchasing Rancho Ojai and several more properties—more than 250,000 acres. He also sent his young nephew Thomas R. Bard to oversee the operations and begin drilling in 1865. Local geology made drilling difficult and expensive, competition from eastern products drove prices down, wells produced only small amounts of poor quality crude, and Scott's California Petroleum Company encountered severe financial problems. In 1867 he divested himself of the project and placed his oil properties on the market as ranch lands. Scott was not the only loser: by the end of the 1860s, 70 companies capitalized at nearly $50 million had invested more than $1 million in 60 wells; they produced just 5,000 barrels of oil worth $10,000. One individual, however, did profit from the debacle. Thomas R. Bard deserted the oil business but remained in California to reap a fortune from the sale of his uncle's and his own lands.

Black Gold

Others refused to abandon the quest during the 1870s and '80s. Lloyd Tevis of Wells Fargo and state senator Charles N. Felton, for example, incorporated the Pacific Coast Oil Company in 1878 to explore in the San Francisco Bay region. Most oil seekers, however, were Pennsylvanians in partnerships and small companies who focused on Southern California. Employing their expertise, they located deposits, improved drilling and refining techniques, and built pipelines in anticipation of a bonanza. In 1883, Lyman Stewart and Wallace L. Hardison, moderately successful partners in Pennsylvania, joined the search in California.

Stewart and Hardison pooled their capital and, with crews of Pennsylvanians, began drilling at Newhall in northeastern Los Angeles County, near the Ventura County line. During the next three years, they bought and leased additional land for exploration and moved into refining and marketing. The partners experienced modest success, but numerous dry holes and increased expenses kept them constantly overextended and deeply in debt, without the capital necessary to expand in the way that Stewart thought essential. To remedy the situation, they turned to the wealthiest man in Ventura County, Thomas R. Bard, who had returned to the oil business near Santa Paula and who, like Hardison, also had extensive interests in local citrus agriculture and real estate. In 1886, Bard, Stewart, and Hardison founded the Sespe Oil Company, which a year later produced 50,000 barrels of oil, about 15 percent of the state's total output. By 1890, when they formed Union Oil Company of California headquartered in Santa Paula, they were producing a fourth of the state's petroleum products. During the 1890s, Union continued to expand, established refineries at San Pedro and at Oleum on the Carquinez Strait, built tankers and pipelines to combat ruinous railroad rates, survived Standard Oil's takeover attempt, and developed oil resources in

San Luis Obispo, Santa Barbara, Kern, and Los Angeles counties, as well as in the Ventura region. When Bard left the firm in 1900, Union ranked among the nation's major petroleum operations.

Union was the largest and most successful petroleum company in California by the 1890s, but it was not alone in the field. Pacific Coast Oil Company continued its operations in the Bay Area, and in 1892 Edward L. Doheny triggered a "backyard" oil boom in Los Angeles. He laid the foundation for his Pan American Oil Company empire when he and a partner hand-dug a producing well near the La Brea Tar Pits. In 1900, Standard acquired control of Pacific Coast Oil and in 1906 renamed it Standard Oil of California, and one year into the new century, San Joaquin Valley operators organized Associated Oil Company. In addition, both the Southern Pacific and Santa Fe railway companies became involved in California petroleum production as leasers of land and major shareholders in oil corporations.

Like gold mining, oil production rapidly became a corporate rather than an individual enterprise in California, partially due to conditions. Local operators were in constant combat with Standard Oil's campaign to expand its national monopoly by flooding the West with cheaper eastern products. California's geological formations demanded more difficult and deeper drilling, greater expense, and unique equipment, much of it fabricated under Lyman Stewart's supervision in Union Oil Company shops. Making the state's asphaltum-based crude usable for lubricants and fuels also required more extensive refining than Pennsylvania's paraffin-based product, and many customers had to be convinced to use it at all. Even in the coal-starved West, railroads and industries were reluctant customers until oil companies themselves devised methods to convert locomotives and steam engines to burn oil. On the other hand, the asphalt residue of California refining, considered waste until the mid-1890s, proved to be an ideal base for paving material and was marketable nationwide. By 1900, the nation also stood on the threshold of the automobile age that would make gasoline—formerly a minor by-product of refining—the most profitable product of the petroleum industry.

Early Oil Well

In 1877, Carleton E. Watkins photographed one of California's earliest oil-drilling rigs, Pico No. 4, near Newhall. The petroleum industry was then in its infancy and still something of a curiosity. *The Huntington Library, San Marino, California.*

Fighting Against Monopoly

California's politics, like its economic development, closely paralleled the national experience. From the 1870s onward, the people and government of the United States experienced a period of adjustment to rapidly changing conditions that included the emergence of huge, monopolistic corporations to replace more traditional economic units. Defining relationships of those entities to the governments under which they existed proved to be a singular problem. In "Granger case" decisions such as *Munn v. Illinois* (1877), the U.S. Supreme Court upheld the principle of state regulation of corporate activity. But in subsequent decisions, perhaps influenced by social and economic Darwinism (more properly "Spencerianism"), the court reversed its interpretation. Despite the Interstate Commerce Commission, created in 1887, and the Sherman Antitrust Act of 1890, the issue remained unresolved. In some parts of the nation, battles over corporate control involved farmers' demands for fair freight rates. Elsewhere they focused on practices of such industrial giants as Standard Oil Company or the American Sugar Trust. In California, the conflict centered on the Southern Pacific and its transportation monopoly, its land policies, its evasion of taxes, and its influence in politics. Californians had expected great things of the railroad, but after the "Terrible Seventies" and the Mussel Slough affair they were disenchanted. For many, the railroad that was to save them became the "Octopus" that would strangle them, and they turned to government for help. Provisions of the state constitution of 1879 that created a Railroad Commission with regulatory authority and permitted the assessment of intangible assets for taxation were sufficiently unique to inspire imitation and even attract the attention of Karl Marx. They also had a significant impact on political alignments within the state. Most Republicans were conservatives who opposed regulation, but a minority faction included individuals such as future U.S. Senator Thomas R. Bard and former U.S. Senator Cornelius Cole. Among Democrats, a small group of opponents to regulation included John P. Irish, editor of the Oakland *Times* and San Francisco *Alta California*, and Stephen J. Field, elevated to the U.S. Supreme Court in 1863 but still considered a California Democrat by himself and others. Party leaders throughout the state comprised the antimonopoly majority led by Reginaldo Del Valle and Stephen Mallory White of Los Angeles County, Barclay Henley of Sonoma, and George Hearst and Chris Buckley of San Francisco.

During the early 1880s, the conflict involved taxation of the railroad more than its regulation by an impotent state Railroad Commission. The company contested assessments made under the provisions of the constitution of 1879, and its attorney, Creed Haymond, brought suit against several counties, including San Mateo and Santa Clara. When the cases reached federal courts in 1882 and 1883, Stephen J. Field upheld the railroad's position. The decisions he wrote also set far-reaching precedents by defining a corporation as a legal "person" with 14th Amendment rights under the U.S. Constitution that were identical to those of "the humblest citizen." Subsequently, Haymond proposed a compromise that, in effect, permitted the railroad to set its own tax rates. To Governor George Stoneman, the proposition was "humiliating," and in 1884 he called the legislature into special session. Every effort to enact stringent, enforceable measures to collect unpaid taxes failed miserably. Pro-railroad Democratic senators voted with Republicans to defeat each proposed change.

Majority Democrats reacted at the party's 1884 state convention at Stockton, where delegates adopted a strict antimonopoly platform, nominated only antimonopoly candidates for the impending election, read pro-railroad members out of the state party, and refused to support their bids for office. Finally, they denounced Field for his decisions and repudiated his aspirations for their party's presidential nomination. The action split the Democracy and produced very mixed election results: Grover Cleveland won the presidency, but he lost in California—which sent only one Democrat, Barclay Henley, to Congress. Democrats elected Washington Bartlett to the governor's office but could not provide the legislative majority needed to prevent Leland Stanford's selection as U.S. Senator in 1885. In San Francisco, party "boss" Chris Buckley's machine barely held its own. Despite their losses, anti-monopolists in the party continued to pin their hopes on the fight against the "Octopus." Henley wrote to White, "The fact is, that if we take no backward step—and stick to principles we will win."

Political Change in the 1890s

Henley was wrong. Democrats attributed their defeats to railroad manipulations, but other forces were involved. During the 1880s Californians became increasingly concerned with national issues that were divisive rather than unifying. Some in the state, for example, favored Grover Cleveland's tariff reduction policies, but commercial interests and many agrarians, regardless of party, feared the potential for increased foreign competition. As the monetary issue gained importance late in the decade, most Californians favored a return to silver coinage, but many others remained suspicious of possible inflationary consequences.

Also during the 1880s, the Santa Fe broke the Southern Pacific monopoly, mitigating Californians' most pressing grievances over rates and fares and prompting many Democrats—including Hearst and Buckley—to reject rigidly anti-monopolist positions and make peace with ousted party members. Penetration by the Santa Fe had added consequences, not the least of them the arrival of the "tenderfoot vote." Migrants flocking to the state included thousands steeped in the orthodoxy of Midwestern Republicanism. Moreover, they settled in Southern California, where antagonism toward the railroad was less entrenched, and began to alter state's political balance.

Most importantly, however, states could not regulate the practices of nationally organized corporations like the Southern Pacific until policies changed at the federal level. This did not occur until the twentieth century, but during the 1890s, reform-minded Californians scored several significant victories. Although efforts to secure direct election of U.S. Senators failed, in 1891 a bipartisan effort passed an Australian secret-ballot law. Two years later, the legislature sent Stephen M. White to the U.S. Senate to replace the deceased Stanford, enacted a Purity of Elections Law, and took steps to reduce corruption in franchise-granting and other municipal government functions. They also succeeded modestly in local battles with the railroad. The legislature overcame vigorous lobbying to pass the Railroad Reassessment Act of 1893, making it possible to collect $2.2 million in overdue taxes from the Southern Pacific. When the new century opened, state and federal governments had won two more important struggles: the fights for a publicly-controlled port at Los Angeles, and against a "Funding Bill" intended to refinance the railroad's debt to the nation.

The Free Harbor Fight and the Funding Bill

Phineas Banning, who began port development at Wilmington–San Pedro, was also responsible for securing federal appropriations for inner-harbor improvements between 1870 and 1890. Without a breakwater, however, the port could not accommodate ocean-going vessels, and the Los Angeles Chamber of Commerce and other groups began a campaign for more federal assistance to complete one. In 1890, the Corps of Engineers studied several potential harbor sites in the area, reported in favor of San Pedro, and recommended a federal expenditure of $4 million to build a breakwater. Angelenos rejoiced, but in 1892 Collis P. Huntington became involved. He had purchased most of the Santa Monica waterfront for the Southern

Pacific Company, and he pressured Congress and the administration for a second survey, which again favored San Pedro. Members of the Los Angeles Free Harbor League, formed to oppose spending public funds for a harbor controlled by Huntington, were therefore astonished to learn that an 1896 Rivers and Harbors Bill included a $2.9 million appropriation for a breakwater at Santa Monica. Los Angeles *Times* publisher Harrison Gray Otis led the campaign against the measure in California, and Senator Stephen M. White (known in the state as "Our Steve") brought his considerable oratorical skills to bear in Washington. Following a third study, which reiterated the results of the first two, Congress passed an amended bill and appropriated funds for San Pedro. Despite Huntington's delaying tactics, construction began in 1899 on the breakwater that made the Los Angeles-San Pedro Harbor one of the coast's major ports. Ultimately, it would accommodate two-thirds of California's maritime commerce and rank second among the nation's harbors and among the most important on the Pacific Rim.

For Huntington and the Southern Pacific, defeat in the Free Harbor fight was significant, but simultaneous controversies over the Funding Bill were potentially more important. Government loans of $28 million, secured by 6 percent bonds and payable in 1899, had financed the Big Four's construction of the Central Pacific. An 1878 federal law required that the Central Pacific set aside funds to retire the debt, but the company refused to comply. As the due date approached, Huntington sought means to have the payment delayed, perhaps permanently, and in 1896 used his influence to bring before Congress a measure that extended the term of the loan to 100 years and reduced the interest to 1 percent.

Even Californians accustomed to Huntington's audacity were outraged. Adolph Sutro, elected mayor of San Francisco on the Populist ticket in 1894, mustered the city's resources against the measure. William Randolph Hearst collected 200,000 signatures opposing the bill and sent them to Washington, followed by *Examiner* satirist Ambrose Bierce and cartoonist Homer Davenport. Chris Buckley denounced the proposal, and legislators petitioned Congress against it. Huntington argued that paying the debt would bankrupt the Southern Pacific, but California lawmakers were unsympathetic; indeed, they urged the national government to foreclose and assume operation of the railroad. When Congress rejected the Funding Bill in January 1897, it did not precipitate the company's collapse. But the action was a blow against its unbridled corporate power and Californians rejoiced in it.

Agrarian Revolt

Californians' conflicts with the Southern Pacific were local manifestations of a national mood that spawned the Populist revolt of the 1890s. To protect themselves against the implications of an increasingly corporate economy, discontented members of the wage-earning classes formed a variety of associations: the reformist Noble Order of the Knights of Labor, the craft-oriented American Federation of Labor, and a few radical unions led by individuals such as Marxist Daniel DeLeon and Socialist Eugene Debs. Even more emphatic expressions of dissatisfaction emanated from farmers, who seemed to be losing their time-honored place in American society.

Some agrarian problems resulted from overextension and overproduction, but other conditions were beyond farmers' control. Railroads charged exorbitant rates and often controlled brokerages and warehouses to which farmers sold. The federal government seemed antagonistic; reciprocity treaties allowed cheap foreign produce into the country while tariffs increased the prices of manufactured goods. Deflationary policies resulted in the demonetization of silver—the "Crime of 1873"—and the scarcity of silver in circulation forced payment of debts in "dear" money.

The nationwide Patrons of Husbandry, or Grange, was formed in the 1870s and influenced several states to pass laws controlling railroad practices. During the 1880s, however, federal courts consistently struck down regulatory legislation. Subsequently, the National Farmers' Alliance and numerous state and regional Alliances attempted to improve the situation through political action. They advocated nationalization of the means of transportation and communication, a monetary system based on paper currency and silver, and political changes including the Australian secret ballot, direct election of senators, and similar measures to give the public greater voice in government. In some states, usually in concert with local Democratic parties, Alliance programs were moderately successful, but many goals required action at the national level, a necessity that produced the People's (Populist) Party.

At their first national convention in 1892, Populists drafted their Omaha Platform calling for a host of radical reforms, including nationalization of the railroads, government ownership of telegraph and telephone systems, unlimited coinage of silver, the eight-hour day, federally owned savings banks, and such political reforms as the initiative and referendum, secret ballot, and the direct election of U.S. Senators. During the 1892 elections, Populist presidential candidate James B. Weaver polled over one million votes while the party captured several state governments and sent a substantial delegation to Congress. Four years later, the People's Party supported Democratic presidential candidate William Jennings Bryan against Republican William McKinley and suffered a resounding defeat that ended the agrarian revolt.

Populism in California

Californians participated in each phase of the agrarian revolt. Hard times returned after the harsh winter of 1889–90 decimated many state crops. Commercial and other economic activity declined, and by 1890 nearly 25,000 unemployed people sought work in San Francisco alone. At the same time, hostility toward the railroad revived with a vengeance, but the only consequence of efforts to regulate the "Octopus" was that, according to Hearst's San Francisco *Examiner*, "legislators and [Railroad] Commissioners have gone on the [Southern Pacific] pay-roll." Indeed, suspicious lawmakers attempted to abolish the commission in 1892 and '93.

By then, many Californians had concluded that traditional politics could not represent their interests. Some were prepared to consider alternative economic systems and welcomed the 1888 publication of Edward Bellamy's *Looking Backward*, a utopian novel that described the peaceful evolution of a nationalized economy and democratic society of equals. Nationalist clubs sprang up across the nation and around the world, but nowhere with greater speed than in California. The first appeared in Oakland in 1889; a year later, the state's 62 clubs represented a third of the total in the nation. Strongest in Southern California, the movement attracted 4,000 men and women from a spectrum of society representing everything from businessmen to socialists.

Despite members' enthusiasm, Nationalism's life was all but over in California by 1891, when many of its adherents joined the Farmers' Alliance organized at Santa Barbara. In California, the Alliance attracted not only Nationalists, Grangers, disaffected farmers, anti-monopolists, and currency reformers, but also former Republican U.S. Senator Cornelius Cole and other major-party leaders. At their first state convention at San Jose in 1890, leaders organized the California Farmers' Alliance and Industrial Union, elected Ventura County rancher Marion Cannon as president, and adopted a platform that denounced monopoly and Wall Street and condemned politicians' subservience to the "money power." A year later, delegates representing

30,000 members from 34 counties met at Los Angeles, discarded previous policies of avoiding direct political action, and formed the People's Party of California.

The new party absorbed some Democrats like Cannon and Thomas V. Cator, but it gained more followers from Republicans, especially Southern Californians like Stephen Bowers, editor of the Ventura *Observer*. In 1892, the party sent Cator and Cannon to the national Populist convention, adopted the Omaha platform, pledged support to presidential candidate James B. Weaver, and named candidates for statewide offices and Congress. Populist nominees often ran with Democratic Party endorsements, and when the votes were counted in 1892, Democrats gained a majority in the state legislature, where they were joined by eight Populists who captured seats in the assembly. Most impressively, Marion Cannon won election to Congress, albeit with Democratic Party backing.

In 1893, Populists in the legislature participated in enacting political reforms and in sending Democrat Stephen M. White to Washington. The 1894 election was the party's high point in California. Populists gained strength in depressed rural counties in the north and in the Central Valley, and gubernatorial candidate J.V. Webster received 18 percent of the vote in a three-way contest won by anti-monopolist Democrat James H. Budd. In San Francisco, the Populists elected Adolph Sutro as mayor. These victories, however, resulted less from wide acceptance of the party's principles than from reaction to specific events, especially a continuing economic depression and repressive government reaction to the Pullman Strike that spread to the state earlier in the year. By 1896, the year that pitted Bryan against McKinley and silver against gold, the California People's Party was sundered by internal conflicts. Two years later, radicals in the party were defecting to socialism, while many moderates returned to the Democratic or Republican folds.

The People's Party failed to implement sweeping reforms or to attain central goals such as limiting corporate power in politics. Indeed, through its active Political Bureau, headed by William F. Herrin after 1893, the Southern Pacific continued to influence election of legislators and a succession of sympathetic governors: Henry T. Gage (1898), George C. Pardee (1902), and James N. Gillett (1906). Nevertheless, Populism in California and the nation served an important purpose. It publicized a variety of social, political, and economic reform principles and set the stage for future change. Many measures considered radical when introduced by Populists became acceptable when embraced by progressives early in the twentieth century.

The Urban Scene: Prelude to Progressivism

One inspiration for utopian schemes like Nationalism—and perhaps for the Populist revolt as well—was dramatic change in American cities. Urban centers of the 1890s differed radically from familiar mid-century "walking cities" (compact communities of about two and a half miles in radius and limited by topography), by the amount of energy residents could spend in the conduct of their activities, and by transportation dependent on muscle power. Walking-city neighborhoods were heterogeneous and included people of various socioeconomic and ethnic groups, as well as most social and economic groupings. Political life also focused on neighborhoods (wards), where residents conducted elections to choose city officials and send representatives to city councils, school boards, and other governing bodies. In short, the walking city was simply "the village writ large," and most of its activities were conducted on a face-to-face basis.

San Francisco was a walking city of 35,000 when it adopted the Consolidation Act of 1856, but during the 1870s, it underwent significant change. Real estate and transportation interests influenced the shift of urban activity southward toward Market Street, and industrial development altered not only physical configurations but also social and economic relationships. By the end of the decade, when San Francisco's population had reached 250,000 and pioneer photographer Eadweard Muybridge made his panorama of the city, the transformation was virtually complete: San Francisco was an industrial city. But some things had not changed—among them fundamental assumptions about municipal government. The Consolidation Act remained in force, but it was a patchwork of often-contradictory amendments that produced political anarchy and fostered widespread corruption in municipal government.

In that unhappy regard, San Francisco resembled many other American cities, where obsolete charters contributed to municipal chaos and to the rise of political bosses and machines. Efforts toward change in San Francisco also followed national patterns. In 1873, Mayor William Alvord proposed a revised city charter to modernize the city's government, eliminate political corruption, and minimize state intervention in municipal affairs. His attempt failed, as did four more recharter campaigns before 1898. They did, however, establish the principles upon which later reforms would be based: home rule, increased mayoral authority over personnel and fiscal matters, control of partisan activities, public ownership of utilities, and specific procedures for granting municipal contracts and franchises. Subsequent charter reformers added professionalism, efficiency, and non-partisanship to the agenda, in keeping with the dictum, "The management of cities is not politics, it is business."

During the 1890s, inspired by reports of success elsewhere, the San Francisco recharter movement gained new momentum. In 1893, members of the city business elite formed the Merchants' Association and called for election of a Board of Freeholders to draft a new organic law. The document that the Freeholders produced in 1895, however, seemed to please no one but themselves and members of the Merchants' Association. The local Labor Council, teachers, and small businessmen objected to their exclusion from the board's deliberations. The Catholic Church denounced the influence of the American Protestant Association on sections related to public schools. Traditional politicians condemned the elimination of voting by wards, and one critic objected to making the mayor "a grand municipal mogul." In 1896, voters rejected the charter, but they did put wealthy businessman and recharter advocate James D. Phelan in the mayor's office. Soon after his inauguration, he appointed another committee, larger and more representative of the population, to draft yet another new organic law.

The committee's document embodied the standard "good government" principles, and, like its predecessor, it encountered resistance. But by 1898 reformers had learned the rules of the political game. They appealed to the legislature for a law to allow charter issues to be decided at special elections, and they closed the polls two hours before sunset, in defiance of state law. A minority of San Franciscans voted and approved the new charter by a slim margin.

Municipal reform took a different tack in Los Angeles, but it was an equally important prelude to progressivism. Despite the Free Harbor Fight, the city government remained subservient to special interests like the railroads. In 1898, respected physician John Randolph Haynes organized a Direct Legislation League to campaign for reform. The league's proposed new charter failed in 1900, but during the following year civic leaders formed the Good Government League to continue the effort. The driving force behind reform, however, remained Haynes, an exponent of direct public legislation and an advocate of "Christian socialism" blended with traditional political ideology. Haynes assembled a coalition of businessmen, labor leaders, socialists, Bellamyites, and other reformers to draft and support a charter based on the National Municipal League model. Opponents like publisher Harrison Gray Otis of the Los Angeles *Times* ridiculed members of the Good Government League as "goo-goos," but in 1903 voters approved a new city charter.

In its principles of efficiency, expertise, and corporate management, the Los Angeles charter resembled those adopted in San Francisco and other cities during the same period. But it was also the first in any American city to include provisions (adopted from the Populists) for the initiative, referendum, and recall. Very quickly, Angelenos took advantage of their new authority. In 1904 they recalled a city councilman whose voting record identified him with railroad interests and with Harrison Gray Otis. Simultaneously, Los Angeles *Express* publisher Edwin T. Earl employed Edward A. Dickson to write an exposé of remaining railroad influence in city government, and Dickson joined with other citizens in 1906 to form the Non-Partisan Committee of 100 to nominate a full slate of candidates for municipal office. All won, except the nominee for mayor. Three years later, however, a determined campaign very nearly made the winner, Arthur C. Harper, the first American mayor to be recalled from office; only timely resignation denied him the dubious honor.

Pre-Progressive Women

After the 1860s, families more frequently accompanied male migrants westward, and the gender imbalance that typified American California began to diminish throughout the state. Demographic patterns, however, made change most apparent in the cities, where social and economic potential attracted young women from the rural countryside. Urban life also exposed legal and traditional constraints on opportunity for women. In American cities, including Los Angeles and San Francisco, women began to find the cohesiveness and collective voice they needed to mount an assault on restrictive laws and policies. Although initial efforts did not always succeed, they marked important preludes to reform.

Fundamental to women enjoying greater economic opportunity was access to higher education. By the 1880s, state normal schools at San Jose, Los Angeles, and Chico, and programs at Claremont and Pomona colleges and the University of Southern California, were preparing women as teachers. By 1900 female educators staffed almost all elementary classes in San Francisco and Los Angeles, but at salaries substantially lower than male teachers, a discrepancy that had irritated

California women for decades. In 1874, Irish-born Kate Kennedy led San Francisco teachers in an "equal pay for equal work" campaign. The campaign prompted legislation requiring that teachers be compensated solely on the basis of qualifications and performance. In practice, however, few nineteenth-century women possessed the same educational advantages as their male counterparts, thus male teachers were consistently better paid than females.

California women next turned their eyes to traditionally male-dominated occupations. Lucy Maria Field Wanzer applied to medical school in 1873 but her application was rejected due to her sex. Wanzer successfully appealed, leading Regents of the brand new University of California to issue a new precedent: "women offering themselves for admission and passing the required examination must be received to all the privileges of the Medical Department." Wanzer graduated in 1876, becoming the state's first professionally trained woman doctor. The University of Southern California School of Medicine granted its first degree to a woman in 1888. By 1890, 10 percent of Los Angeles physicians were women, as were 10 percent of the students at Cooper Medical College in San Francisco. Growing numbers of women were also preparing for

Lucy Maria Field Wanzer

Wanzer was the first female graduate of a medical school west of the Mississippi. *Master Hands in the Affairs of the Pacific Coast: A Resume of the Builders of Our Material Progress* (1892).

careers in nursing at the San Francisco Hospital for Children and Training School for Nurses, founded in 1873 as the Pacific Dispensary for Women and Children by Dr. Charlotte Amanda Brown and a consortium of elite San Francisco women.

Contemporary gender conventions supported women desiring to enter medicine, who insisted that medicine was a natural extension of women's traditional caregiver roles. No such argument existed to support women as lawyers. San Jose's Clara Shortridge Foltz became the state's first woman to break that gendered barrier. Following her divorce in 1869, Foltz needed an occupation to support her five children. She asked a lawyer friend of the family if she could study law in his office, then the common means of preparing for the legal profession. He declined, saying that "A woman's place is at home, unless it is as a teacher." Furious, Foltz recalled that she "silently went about preparing to do battle against all comers who would deny to women any right or privilege that men enjoyed" and found another lawyer to oversee her studies. Foltz then wrote an amendment to California's legal codes that deleted "any white male citizen" from the qualifications of those eligible to practice law, and substituted "any citizen or person." Foltz convinced a state senator to present the measure to the legislature in 1876. Senate Bill 66, popularly known as the "Woman Lawyer's Bill," provoked a fierce outcry. Foltz recalled:

> The bill met with a storm of opposition such as had never been witnessed upon the floor of a California Senate. Narrow-gauge statesmen grew as red as turkey gobblers mouthing their ignorance against the bill, and staid old grangers who had never seen the inside of a courthouse seemed to have been given the gift of tongues and they delivered themselves of maiden speeches pregnant with eloquent nonsense.

The bill passed by a narrow margin and the governor signed it in the last hour of his last day as governor, with Foltz standing over him, "hat awry and hair disheveled." In essence, the statute granted California women the right to practice whatever profession they chose. In September 1878, Foltz was sworn in as the first woman admitted to the practice of law in California, entering under the code that she herself had written. The following year Foltz joined Stockton newspaper woman and suffragist leader Laura deForce Gordon in suing Hastings College of the Law to admit women. Foltz argued the case and won.

Additional gains for women followed adoption of the new state constitution in 1879, which forbade state universities from excluding applicants on the basis of sex.

The number of female college graduates climbed steadily thereafter. In 1891, UC Berkeley graduated only eight women. Twenty years later, the number rose to 195.

At the turn of the century, more women than ever entered the urban work force as clerks, stenographers, and librarians. Both nationally and in California, these were occupations that, like teaching, men had abandoned. Significant numbers of women also entered male-dominated trades such as photography and typography, but those who lacked skills or education took jobs where they could find them. In anti-union Los Angeles, women workers usually accepted whatever wages they were offered, but in San Francisco many became labor activists. They established the Ladies Assembly of the Knights of Labor in 1885 and, in the 1890s, joined such unions as the Co-operative Shirtmakers of the Pacific Coast, Steam Laundry Workers, Glove Makers, and Bottle Caners. In addition, women joined previously all-male unions to advocate for higher wages, shorter hours, and improved working conditions. Women unionists also joined their fellows in maligning their competitors for unskilled jobs, the Chinese.

Despite women's growing access to education and the professions, opposition to woman suffrage proved insurmountable in the nineteenth century. On February 18, 1868, Laura deForce Gordon gave the state's first public speech on woman suffrage in San Francisco's Platt's Hall. The following year she campaigned for a seat in the state legislature. Though she lost, Gordon used her campaign as a platform to argue for women's rights.

Also in 1869, Gordon and others formed the California Woman Suffrage Association, which unsuccessfully petitioned the legislature for an amendment to the state constitution giving votes to women. In 1870, suffragists presented a petition with over 3,000 signatures, but this too failed. The women returned to the legislature with a new petition in 1872, with the same result. Suffragists lobbied the 1879 constitutional convention and failed again. The next organized push came with the surge of reformist politics in the 1890s. Buoyed by support in the agrarian, populist, and currency movements of that era, suffragists succeeded in pushing an amendment to the state constitution through the legislature but, in November 1896, California voters rejected it.

Voluntary work through woman-led charities and reform organizations continued to appeal to elite, white, urban women. Chapters of the Woman's Christian Temperance Union (WCTU) in Los Angeles, San Francisco, Sacramento, and other cities campaigned against saloons and vice. Women's social and literary clubs took up various reforms. In 1891, Caroline

Clara Shortridge Foltz

In 1878, Foltz became the first woman admitted to the practice of law in California. *I.W. Taber, circa 1900.*

Severance and ten friends founded the Friday Morning Club to "consider and discuss objects of general interest," whether literary, social, or educational. The club quickly grew to 200 members. Although Severance was herself a suffragist, the club downplayed politics per se. Instead members worked to expand private kindergarten programs (before kindergartens became part of state public education), to improve education, improve treatment of juvenile criminal offenders, and provide affordable housing for working women. The Woman's Parliament of Southern California, formed in 1892, initially focused on civic improvements. Within the year, however, members decided that the vote was vital to achieving their goals.

In 1900, clubwomen formed the California Federation of Women's Clubs, which connected California women to a national federation of organized woman-led associations. An umbrella organization for hundreds of California women's clubs, overnight the Federation became the state's largest women's association. It organized many small clubs into a cohesive structure with state officers and committees, annual conventions, and regular publications. Some clubs retained their focus on literary and civic improvements, while others took up the crusade for woman suffrage.

The career of Katherine Philips Edson illustrates how some California women gained and used political power in the years before they could vote. Edson had campaigned for women's vote in 1896, but she switched tactics when she moved to Los Angeles in 1900. Edson joined the prestigious Friday Morning Club and devoted herself to studying municipal problems. In 1908 she and her Committee on Public Health were able to link the city's rising infant mortality rates with bovine tuberculosis. State laws prohibited the sale of milk from unhealthy animals, but inspections were haphazard. Edson and her committee began inspecting local dairies themselves, publishing their findings—including the names of dairies producing tuberculin-infected milk—in a monthly publication. In 1910, the Los Angeles *Herald* showered Edson with praise for her thorough investigation of "the milk peril." Edson thereafter gained a seat on the Los Angeles County Medical Milk Commission, its only non-doctor member and, two years later, was elected to the Los Angeles City Charter Revision Committee. By working for various civic causes, Edson secured a place for herself in the political life of Los Angeles, even before she could cast a vote.

In 1890, journalists, writers, and publishers founded the Pacific Coast Women's Press Association (PCWPA), an organization that not only advocated professional goals for women but also encouraged them to join social and political causes. Indeed, Charlotte Perkins Gilman recalled that membership in San Francisco's PCWPA, WCTU, and other women's associations contributed to her development as a feminist economist and activist.

Other San Francisco women made important contributions as individuals. Phoebe Apperson Hearst, wife of U. S. Senator George and mother of newspaperman William Randolph, was a civic dynamo. Founder of the National Congress of Mothers and the first woman regent of the University of California, Hearst used her great personal wealth to fund kindergartens, teacher training programs, and university scholarships for, in Hearst's words, "worthy young women" of "high character and noble aims." In this way, a woman who had always regretted her own lack of formal education was able to carve for herself a unique role in state and even national politics.

Reformers exercised another brand of political power. In 1878, Kate Douglas Wiggin moved from Southern California to San Francisco where, with her German-born teacher Emma Marwedel, she established the state's first free kindergarten among working-class neighbors in the South-of-Market district. In the 1890s, New Zealand-born Donaldina Cameron began her 40-year career "rescuing" Chinese women from prostitution. In San Francisco, women joined in the national settlement house movement. Following an 1893 visit to San Francisco by Hull House's Jane Addams, elite Jewish women founded the Emanu-El Sisterhood for Personal Service, a South-of-Market settlement house intended to find jobs and homes for recent Russian Jewish immigrants, and to teach them the rudiments of English language and American citizenship. Faculty from the University across the Bay organized the South Park settlement that same year, catering mostly to newcomers from Ireland. In Los Angeles, Mary Julia Workman began a career that would energize similar social service activities among that city's Roman Catholic women.

California women of color were active as well, although they lacked the same access to higher education and to powerful men that white women enjoyed. Chinese women met with varying degrees of success in their efforts to protect their own and their communities' interests. In 1884, Mary Tape, a westernized Chinese woman who arrived in San Francisco 20 years earlier, sued the city when it refused to allow her daughter to attend an all-white public school. The suit was successful but the city escaped integration by establishing a separate school for Chinese children. The Chinese Exclusion Act of 1882 also severely limited options available to immigrant Chinese, although some women used the legal system to resist exclusion. With unequal positions in the United States and in their own communities, women who could afford it hired attorneys, filed affidavits, testified on their own behalf, and resisted labeling as prostitutes. Some succeeded in fighting deportation and gaining admission to the country.

Indigenous women in California found it difficult to protect their lives and cultures, much less assert autonomy, yet it was not impossible. In the winter of 1871–72, the revivalistic *Bole Maru* (dream dance) cult spread through Kashaya Pomo, Wappo, Coast and Lake Miwok tribes. Like Ghost Dancers of the Great Plains, California Indians found in Bole Maru a way to resist the influence of European and American cultures. Dreamers were predominantly women: Annie

Jarvis, head Dreamer for the Kashaya Pomo from 1912 to 1943, stressed the doctrines of Indian nationalism and isolationism, outlawed intermarriage with non-Indians, forbade gambling and drinking, and halted attempts by government officials to take Indian children to boarding schools.

African American women likewise found strength in numbers. Founded in Oakland in 1899, the Fanny Jackson Coppin Club provided members with social and educational events as well as badly needed social services, including building and operating their Home for Aged and Infirm Colored People. Black women used their clubs to assert their claims to respectability, something that middle-class white women took for granted. When, for example, the all-white National Federation of Women's Clubs proposed to hold its biennial convention in Los Angeles in 1902, the National Association of Colored Women's Clubs spent all of 1901 urging the organization to let black women's clubs attend. The controversy played out in the local newspapers, exposing "large deposits of race hatred in California, much of it expressed by 'southern' women who sounded like crusaders for the Jim Crow ideal." The spurned clubwomen promptly organized the California Association of Colored Women's Clubs, which then devoted itself to defending the interests of members and all black Californians.

Through the second half of the nineteenth century, women of various backgrounds in urban California engaged in activities that paralleled the settlement house movements, labor organization, civil rights, and political, educational, and social reform campaigns then underway in the East and Midwest. Women's experiences introduced them to increased opportunities but also exposed the legal and traditional barriers that hampered American women's ambitions. Their responses echoed the cries of Susan B. Anthony, Elizabeth Cady Stanton, Jane Addams, and others, and predicted the efforts of twentieth-century Californians to confirm women's place as equal members of the polity.

18

Progressive California

S panning the first two decades of the twentieth century, the so-called "Progressive Era" was one of the most dynamic periods of social and political reform in
American history. Drawn mostly from the ranks of white middle-class property
owners, businessmen, and educated professionals, progressive reformers rose to prominence in both major parties and comprised the core constituencies of Republican president Theodore Roosevelt and his Democratic counterpart Woodrow Wilson. Though
firmly committed to capitalism and free enterprise, the Progressives rejected laissez-
faire and called for dramatic expansions of governmental powers in order to solve the
many problems that accompanied America's industrial revolution: the ascent of corporate monopolies, the deplorable working conditions in factories and mines, the spread of
rural poverty, the growth of crowded and filthy urban slums, and the rise of ethnic and
racial tensions caused by massive immigration from foreign nations.

Fearing the threats of corporate plutocracy from above and radical unrest from below,
middle-class progressives sought sweeping yet moderate reforms designed to strengthen
democratic government, and to meet the legitimate demands of angry agrarian Populists
and militant urban socialists and trade unionists. In California, the powerful currents of
progressive reform would lead in 1910 to the electoral triumph of Hiram W. Johnson, the
most successful and influential governor in the Golden State's history. As fate would have
it, Johnson's meteoric rise to power was launched, in part, by one of California's greatest
natural disasters.

Abraham Ruef and the Union Labor Party

On the morning of April 18, 1906, an earthquake of magnitude 7.8 on the Richter scale rocked San Francisco as the earth ruptured along a 290-mile stretch of the San Andreas Fault. The initial shock toppled hundreds of buildings and instantly ignited over 50 separate fires triggered by broken gas lines, fallen chimneys, and upended stoves and furnaces. The flames quickly raged out of control, as firefighters stood by helplessly, unable to draw water from the city's severed and sundered mains. For three days and two nights, San Francisco burned. An estimated 3,000 people perished in the catastrophe, and when the flames finally subsided, some 500 city blocks lay in utter ruin.

The streets and buildings of San Francisco were not the only things left in shambles in April 1906. Despite a reform charter adopted in 1898, municipal government also was in disarray; at the center of the chaos was local political boss Abraham Ruef. Born in San Francisco in San Francisco in 1864 to middle-class French Jewish parents, Ruef was ambitious and intelligent. He graduated from the University of California (1882) and Hastings College of Law (l883), passed the state bar examination (1886), and began a successful legal practice. Early political activities predicted a career as a reformer, but he fell under the wing of Chris Buckley's first mentor, Bill Higgins. When the old boss died, Ruef completed his apprenticeship under Martin Kelly and Phil Crimmins, and added an element of integrity to their machine. Then, in the Republican primaries of 1901, he attempted to strike out on his own, but the two professionals gave their protégé a sound thrashing at the polls.

Circumstances, however, gave Ruef a second chance. In the spring of 1901 the San Francisco Employers' Association, formed earlier to oppose unionism in the city, was embroiled in a bitter dispute with local labor organizations, including the Teamsters, the City Front Federation of waterfront workers, and the Labor Council. A strike all but paralyzed the port. The Association responded by locking out union workers, hiring strikebreakers, and convincing Mayor James Duval Phelan to assign city police to protect them. Before Governor Henry T. Gage intervened to end the strike in October, five were dead and wage-earners were disenchanted with Phelan and his Democratic party. Despite opposition by labor leaders, others organized the Union Labor Party (ULP) to champion working-class interests.

General Frederick Funston sent troops from the Presidio to dynamite a fire break, but their lack of experience contributed to the spread of flames.

Families throughout the city, like this Japanese woman on Geary Street, cooked meals outdoors because of ruptured gas pipes in buildings.

Ruef had shown no previous interest in labor causes, but he used tested political skills to move swiftly into the leadership of the ULP. He engineered the nomination of his close friend and client Eugene Schmitz, president of the musicians' union, to run for mayor. During the

Destruction of the recently completed new city hall revealed shoddy conduction with inferior materials.

Refugee camps such as this one in Golden Gate Park were home to many San Franciscans for months.

1901 campaign, the debonair Irish-German Catholic used his popularity in both society and labor circles to win. Schmitz triumphed again in 1903 and in 1905 when ULP nominees captured all 18 seats on the Board of Supervisors. Then triumph turned to disaster.

From the time that Schmitz first took office, he and Ruef conducted a variety of highly profitable illicit activities: selling favors to utility companies and other interests, protecting the city's "French restaurants" (code for eateries with brothels upstairs), and even using public funds to build a brothel known as the "Municipal Crib." The ULP supervisors elected in 1905 were political novices, but they were astute enough to know what was going on and demand a share of the profits. Despite Ruef's protests that he only accepted "fees" as a private attorney, he needed supervisors' votes and was forced to divide the substantial spoils received from Pacific Gas and Electric, United Street Railway Company, Spring Valley Water Company, and other firms. Worse yet, greedy supervisors began to freelance for individual opportunities (bribes), employing tactics that embarrassed even Ruef and Schmitz.

Indictment and Trial

Shortly after Schmitz's first inauguration, editor Fremont Older of the San Francisco *Bulletin* published a series of articles revealing conditions at City Hall, but response to his exposés was minimal. After the mayor's reelection in 1905, Older sought and received financial backing for an investigation from sugar heir Rudolph Spreckels and other businessmen, and a promise of cooperation from the local district attorney. Next, he solicited help from President Theodore Roosevelt who provided the services of two of the government's finest investigators: Secret Service Chief William J. Burns and special prosecutor Francis J. Heney. After delays resulting from the earthquake and fire, Older and his allies struck.

In November 1906 a grand jury indicted Ruef and Schmitz for protecting vice operations in the city, but Heney and his fellow prosecutors were not satisfied. They wanted to convict givers of bribes as well as takers, corporate law breakers as well as corrupt politicians. Early in 1907 Burns trapped two supervisors by bribing them to vote for a phony city ordinance. He then convinced them to confess what they knew in return for immunity. By the end of March 1907, the remaining supervisors had seized similar opportunities and the grand jury returned 65 more indictments against Ruef, Schmitz, and officers of several utility companies.

Within a month Ruef himself had confessed in exchange for immunity, resulting in 20 more indictments against the mayor, United Railway Company's president Patrick Calhoun, the firm's chief counsel Tirey L. Ford, and others. The trial took place in the temple of Sherith Israel, offered by Rabbi Jacob Nieto to take the place of the ruined courthouse. During the subsequent prosecution, the longest of its kind in American history, hundreds of potential jurors were called and dismissed. When one juror's shady past was revealed during questioning, he returned to the courtroom and nearly killed chief prosecutor Heney with a pistol shot to the head. Hiram W. Johnson took over as prosecutor and the juror later committed suicide in jail. In equally bizarre incidents, dynamite destroyed the front of a supervisor's home, and newly appointed police chief William J. Biggy disappeared from a police launch while on a night trip across the Bay.

Despite such sensations, nationwide publicity, and the expenditure of substantial time and money, the prosecution failed. By the end of 1908, only Ruef and Schmitz had been convicted of anything. The verdict against the mayor required two trials and was eventually reversed on a technicality. Angered by Ruef's refusal to tailor testimony to their purposes, Heney and Johnson reneged on promises of immunity and prosecuted him. Ruef was found guilty of bribery and sentenced to 14 years in San Quentin. None of the accused bribe-givers was convicted, and in 1910 the case against the last defendant, Calhoun, was dropped.

By then, San Franciscans had tired of the entire affair. Business leaders who initially supported the investigation defected when the prosecution turned against members of their own class. In 1909 the voters elected a city administration committed to ending the trials. More surprising was the crusaders' change of heart: by 1912 Older was publishing Ruef's memoirs in the *Bulletin* and campaigning for his early release. In 1915 Ruef was paroled and returned to San Francisco to manage his real-estate interests. He was pardoned in 1920 and died in 1936, bankrupt and obscure. Schmitz turned to investments in oil and mines, but in 1915 he ran again for mayor and polled 35,000 votes. Even more incredibly, in 1917 he was elected to the first of several consecutive terms on the Board of Supervisors! When he died in 1928, Schmitz was buried with full civic honors and with Abe Ruef among his mourners.

The Lincoln-Roosevelt League

Democrats might have brought organized progressivism to California early in the twentieth century, except for the ambition of William Randolph Hearst. For personal and political reasons, the publisher twice sabotaged Democratic gubernatorial candidates running on reform platforms. In 1902, Franklin K. Lane lost by a few thousand votes, as did Theodore Bell in 1906. With the backing of the publisher, a nominal Democrat, either could have won. Instead, with support from railroad interests, victory went to George C. Pardee and, later, to his successor, James N. Gillett. At the same time, the Southern Pacific became increasingly active in state politics, financing sympathetic candidates while continuing to charge "whatever the traffic will bear" for its services. Public indignation found expression in newspapers throughout the state, including all of San Francisco's major journals, Charles and James McClatchy's Sacramento *Bee*, Chester H. Rowell's Fresno *Republican*, Harrison Gray Otis's Los Angeles *Times*, Edwin T. Earl's Los Angeles *Express*, and many others. Their outspoken criticism and the publication of

"Atonement"

William Randolph Hearst made his opinion of both Abe Ruef and the methods of the graft investigation abundantly clear in the pages of the San Francisco *Examiner. Collection of William A. Bullough.*

Votes for Women

A postcard published to promote votes for women included a poem:

> They said to him "We'll get your goat;"
> He said "It is the *System*;"
> With weapon of the *Woman's Vote*
> They shot; and never missed 'im.

National Museum of American History, Kenneth E. Behring Center, Smithsonian, Washington, DC.

Frank Norris's *The Octopus* in 1901 added support to demands for reform.

By 1907, an insurgent movement had emerged within the Republican Party. Earl sent Edward A. Dickson to Sacramento to cover the legislature for the *Express*. There Dickson met Rowell, and the pair discovered that the Southern Pacific's manipulations and their own Republican party's subservience were more endemic than either had suspected. When Dickson returned to Los Angeles, he and other progressives organized as "Lincoln Republicans." Rowell likewise found substantial sympathy and support among associates in northern California and valley districts. Urged on by Dickson and Rowell, delegates from throughout the state convened in Oakland in August 1907 to form

the League of Lincoln-Roosevelt Clubs, or Lincoln-Roosevelt League. These maverick Republicans were determined to recover their party from railroad control, to support progressive candidates in the 1908 elections, to send pro-Theodore Roosevelt delegates to the party's national convention, and to campaign for such reforms as direct primary elections, the direct election of U.S. Senators, and woman suffrage.

This last was music to the ears of California suffragists. As had happened during the agrarian revolt, in the early twentieth century insurgent political factions again courted female support, promising women the franchise in return for their help in securing desired reforms. The rising progressive tide breathed new life into the California Woman Suffrage Association, founded in 1869.

Leaders dropped "Woman" from the group's name in 1904 to gain male support, becoming the California Equal Suffrage Association (CESA). That year CESA affiliated with the National American Woman Suffrage Association and hired one of its workers as a full-time organizer. By 1905, CESA counted 52 new suffrage societies formed and 20 dormant societies revived. Over the next four years, CESA gained endorsement by the State Federation of Labor, California Teachers' Association, and the California State Farmers' Institute.

Another important ally was the College Equal Suffrage League, founded on the East Coast and exported to California in 1906. Chapters formed at state universities and Stanford and membership soon exceeded 1,000. Teachers, students, and professional women toured the state, polling legislators, engaging speakers, and staging lively debates and plays on behalf of the cause. The Wage Earners' Equal Suffrage League, founded in 1908, brought new converts as well, with labor leaders arguing that the vote would improve the lot of working women.

Leaders of the revitalized crusade showed their grasp of American political forms through shrewd use of the media. Past failures had taught leaders the importance of controlling the suffrage narrative. Newspaper woman Mabel Craft (Mrs. Frank) Deering produced short pro-suffrage pieces and distributed them to journals around the state. By 1907, 203 newspapers were regularly publishing Deering's essays.

Clubwomen supplied crucial support as well. By 1910, Katherine Philips Edson of the prestigious Friday Morning Club was calling for suffrage. When the Lincoln-Roosevelt League endorsed woman suffrage, Edson campaigned for League candidates, arguing that, together, clubwomen and progressive men would "clean up" politics in California.

With 40 clubs and 6,000 members, the California Federation of Women's Clubs provided the movement with both troops and leaders, including Lillian Harris (Mrs. Horace) Coffin. Rejecting the California Club for its failure to endorse suffrage, in 1906 Coffin formed the San Francisco Equal Suffrage League. That year she took command of CESA's executive committee and guided state suffrage efforts for the next five years.

Coffin first moved to gain political allies in the Democratic and Republican parties. As she told CESA women, "it takes a politician to catch a politician." The Democrats' endorsement came in the fall of 1906. When Republican Party leaders rejected Coffin's request, she began a long-game strategy to win over the party's progressive wing. At CESA's annual convention in October 1907, leaders vowed to work for the reforms most important to Lincoln-Roosevelt Republicans. Coffin pledged that CESA members would only campaign for politicians committed to "progress" and "good government." In November 1907, organized San Francisco women worked for Democrat E.R. Taylor's mayoral bid and, according to observers, helped to secure his victory.

Despite the women's efforts, legislative success remained elusive. In 1907, 1908, and 1909, friends in the state legislature presented constitutional amendment bills granting women the vote. To suffrage leaders' dismay, each went down to defeat.

Meanwhile, progressive Republicans were busy fanning the flames of popular contempt for the railroads and their policies, from revelations emanating from the Ruef trials, and from increasing public identification with the progressive policies of President Theodore Roosevelt. Lincoln-Roosevelt clubs sprang up throughout the state. A small number of progressive Republicans won assembly seats in the 1908 elections, aided by the energetic campaigning of California women. "Regular" Republicans outnumbered "progressives" in the legislature seated in 1909, yet progressives managed to secure key victories, including amendments to several railroad reform bills and a preferential (but not binding) popular vote on U.S. senators. Most important to reformers was passing the direct primary law. Progressives believed that by eliminating party-controlled nominating conventions, direct primaries would reduce the influence of special interests in the selection of candidates. Indeed, passage of the 1909 direct primary law set the stage for subsequent progressive achievements.

Hiram Johnson and the Election of 1910

Progressive Republicans realized that the new primary election law afforded an opportunity to gain control not only of their party but also of the state government, if they placed electable candidates before the voters in 1910. The recognition that he received as graft-trial prosecutor made Francis J. Heney a logical choice for governor. But his outspoken attacks had alienated much of the business community, his recovery from the wound received in 1908 remained in doubt, and he was a registered Democrat. Progressive Republicans, therefore, turned to Heney's replacement in the graft trials, Hiram Johnson.

Like many, if not most, progressive leaders in the state, Johnson was a native Californian and a successful professional. Born in Sacramento in 1866, he was the son of Grove L. Johnson, a conservative Republican and former assemblyman who counted the railroads among his law firm's clients. Hiram Johnson studied law in his father's office and joined him in practice in 1888. Gradually, however, father and son became politically and philosophically alienated, and in 1902 the younger man moved to San Francisco to establish his own practice, with clients ranging from business interests (but not the railroads) to organized labor. He subsequently gained statewide recognition through participation in the graft trials and from his vociferous denunciations of corporate influence in politics and government. Indeed, because of his aggressive demands for reform, some Californians were calling him a "western Theodore Roosevelt."

Still, Johnson was not eager to seek the gubernatorial nomination. His practice prospered and San Francisco suited him better than Sacramento. Only substantial pressure from associates—and perhaps recognition that the governorship might lead to a seat in the U.S. Senate—persuaded him. Once convinced, Johnson proved to be a formidable campaigner. To symbolize both his modernity and his independence of the

Hiram Johnson
Courtesy of the California History Room, California State Library, Sacramento, California.

railroad, he toured the state in a bright red Locomobile roadster, announcing his arrival in isolated communities with a cow bell, and speaking from the car's rumble seat. Johnson armed himself with facts and used his data to document his condemnation of the railroads, their business practices, and their political influence. In the August primaries, he won the Republican nomination, as did progressive candidates for most state offices. He continued his vigorous campaign and, in November, captured the governor's office.

But Johnson's was neither an easy victory nor a landslide. Two other candidates campaigned on progressive issues and platforms. Democrat Theodore Bell won more than 150,000 votes and Socialist J. Stitt Wilson of Berkeley nearly 50,000. Only overwhelming strength in Southern California raised Johnson's total to more than 177,000. No matter for whom they voted in 1910, however, nearly 380,000 Californians cast their ballots for progressivism and political change.

Hiram Johnson and other victorious progressives had formulated few specific programs before they were elected. They were agreed in their determination to end corruption and exploitation of public resources—including human resources—in California, but means to that end were not clearly defined. Therefore, in the interlude between his election and inauguration, Johnson sought advice from Theodore Roosevelt, from Wisconsin governor Robert M. LaFollette, and from leaders of the Lincoln-Roosevelt League throughout the state. When the new governor and his allies took office in 1911, they were prepared to act.

Economic Regulation

Progressives in the 1911 legislature took swift action on the issues of railroad and utility regulation and unethical business practices in general. Early in the session, lawmakers received a measure drafted by Railroad Commissioner John M. Eshelman and introduced by Senator John W. Stetson of Alameda. The Stetson-Eshelman Act, which received unanimous legislative approval, increased the authority of the Railroad Commission and empowered it to fix both passenger and freight rates. Constitutional amendments designed to extend and reinforce the legislature's regulatory powers received popular approval at a special election in October. During the following month, the senate and assembly passed a Public Utilities Act without one dissenting vote. The law created a five-member Public Utilities Commission (PUC), empowered the governor to appoint commissioners, and gave the agency authority over all public utilities, not just the railroads.

These and other measures enhanced previous legislation that supported the principle of economic regulation in the state. The Bank Act of 1909 had created a state superintendent of banks to review and assess the soundness of financial institutions and to oversee savings and loan operations. A year later another law clarified revenue policies that had been embroiled in controversy since 1879. It authorized a state assessment on corporate incomes and turned property-tax collection over to the counties, under the supervision of a state board of equalization.

Thus progressives accomplished in a few years what a generation of reformers had failed to achieve since the 1870s. But theirs was not an anti-business program, as some opponents claimed. Many progressives were businessmen and -women themselves, whose financial and corporate interests favored new banking and taxation legislation. Indeed, support for progressive policies was both statewide and universal, and representatives of even the largest businesses understood not only that regulation was inevitable, but that it could be profitable. Regulation freed the railroads from rebate arrangements with oil and agricultural interests and from ruinous price wars with each other. Other enterprises benefited similarly. Indeed, during the early years of the PUC, utility companies brought competitors before the courts, and the commission more often than customers sued them. In 1913, William F. Herrin—by then a Southern Pacific vice president—expressed the new attitude:

> There could be no more insidious or vicious practice than to favor one shipper or class of shippers at the expense of others. . . . Yet these vicious discriminations were frequent before they were abolished by the force of government regulation.

Except for a few reactionaries who denounced all forms of control as socialism or worse, business interests found regulation at state expense congenial, many realizing that they could live more comfortably with regulation than cutthroat competition among themselves.

California's program was not particularly unique in the early twentieth century. Populists and other nineteenth-century reformers had suggested much of it, and Hiram Johnson solicited advice from progressive leaders elsewhere in the nation. Success in the state also depended on actions by the national government. Investigations conducted under authority of the federal Hepburn Act of 1906, for example, provided the information required to draft and pass the Stetson-Eshelman Act, and the U.S. Supreme Court finally dissolved the troublesome

corporate connection between the Southern Pacific and Union Pacific in 1913.

Still, the principle of public regulation established during Gov. Johnson's first term was an important turning point in California history, and he contributed significantly to the transition. He participated in drafting bills, encouraged their passage, rallied popular support for progressive programs, and signed laws that most of his predecessors would have vetoed.

Political Reform

Hiram Johnson and his allies believed that powerful party organizations, not California's form of government, were the principal causes of corruption in the state. They were not the first, however, to reach this conclusion: in 1891 the legislature attempted to curb partisan influence by adopting the Australian secret ballot and followed in 1893 with a law to regulate campaign practices. An amendment in 1901 also regulated primary elections, but progressives were not content.

Johnson's platform proposed to draw "the people" more directly into public affairs and prescribed specific mechanisms for doing so: the initiative, referendum, and recall. The initiative allowed voters to propose and approve laws and constitutional amendments, the referendum permitted a popular veto of pending legislation, and the recall provided for removal of elected officials prior to the expiration of their terms. To place measures on the ballot, citizens would circulate petitions to gather a specified number of signatures, between 5 percent and 8 percent of the vote in the previous election. Amendments providing for the "direct democracy" policies, as progressives liked to call them, met with stubborn opposition from professional politicians and other vested interests. But in 1911 they received nearly unanimous legislative approval and, following Johnson's vigorous campaign on their behalf, overwhelming voter support.

Progressives attempted to reduce party influence even further with two additional policies: nonpartisanship and cross-filing. Legislation in 1911 and 1913 forbade party endorsement of candidates in primary elections, and forbade partisan identification on ballots for judicial, county, and municipal offices, as well as the state superintendent of public instruction. The 1913 legislature also created a California anomaly: the cross-filing system. Cross-filing allowed candidates for state office to place their names without stating their party affiliation on primary election ballots of all parties. The practice extended the principal of nonpartisanship but struck at legitimate purposes of party organizations.

It also had some unusual, perhaps unanticipated results. By winning the primaries of both major parties, candidates could—and did—win office without facing any serious challengers in a general election. Cross-filing greatly increased the potency of name recognition and, from 1913 to 1959, gave incumbents a very powerful advantage.

Progressives regarded their efforts to "take the politics out of politics" with some satisfaction, but they neither increased popular participation nor curbed the influence of special interests. Californians did not hasten to implement the "direct democracy" offered by the initiative, referendum, or recall. As the number of voters increased, moreover, so did the number of signatures needed to qualify ballot measures, until they reached prohibitive levels. Later in the century, a multitude of highly-organized and well-financed special interest groups, often directed by skilled lobbyists in the guise of trade or professional associations, adopted direct democracy measures for their own purposes.

The Sixth Star: California Women Gain the Vote

The electoral successes of progressive candidates in the August 1910 primaries convinced suffragists that California could, at last, become the "sixth star" in the suffragist banner, joining Wyoming (1869), Colorado (1893), Utah (1895), Idaho (1896), and Washington (1910). That November a committee of Republican legislators led by Senator Charles W. Bell met to draft an amendment to the section of the California constitution that governed voter eligibility. Bell's measure, favored by CESA, eliminated all references to gender. The 39th Legislature heard testimony for and against the Bell amendment from mid-January into early February. Delegations of women from CESA, the Federation of Women's Clubs, and other groups attended the hearings to observe and testify. Elisabeth S. Gerberding, recently elected CESA president, opined that woman suffrage would bring more families to California. Speaking for the Wage Earners' League, Maud Younger argued that working women would benefit from voting. Past CESA president Lillian Coffin warned legislators that they must honor past campaign promises.

They got the message. On January 26, 1911, the state senate overwhelmingly approved the Bell amendment with a 33–5 vote. One week later, on February 3, the bill easily cleared the assembly, with 66 in favor and 12 opposed. After years of failure, the suffragists were on the verge of final victory. The measure permitting California women to vote would appear as a ballot proposition in the next statewide election.

Now suffrage leaders faced a new hurdle: convincing California voters—all of them male—that woman suffrage was in their best interests. They succeeded: slightly over half of those casting votes on October 10, 1911, agreed to share the franchise with women.

No sooner were the votes counted than national suffrage leader Dr. Anna Howard Shaw lauded the milestone victory. Women voters would "be a great power" in presidential politics, claimed Shaw, as California cast as many electoral college votes as all previous woman suffrage states combined. Women leaders immediately took "the California Plan" nationwide, urging suffragists elsewhere to do as California did: organize across class lines; collaborate with progressive men; and focus narrowly on amending state constitutions.

California women rushed to exercise their newfound prerogative. In Los Angeles, the non-partisan Women's Progressive League registered over 70,000 women in time to vote in the hotly contested December 1911 municipal elections. Surprisingly, 65,000 women cast ballots, only slightly fewer than male voters.

Women of color celebrated their new privileges as well. The vote had long been important to California's women of color, who typically sought it as a means to fight white racism. Black women leaders had been calling for suffrage since the 1890s. When the California movement revived at the turn of the century, black women joined in. A statewide umbrella group, the Woman's Suffrage Advocate, coordinated the efforts of white- and black-led suffrage clubs, especially in Los Angeles, home to the state's largest black community. For once, success was so important to white suffragists that they agreed to collaborate with black women, in a rare show of gender solidarity that crossed racial lines.

The Republican Party benefited from woman suffrage as well. In California and elsewhere, black men tended to support the party of Lincoln. After the 1911 victory, black women also rallied for Republican candidates. *California Eagle* editor Charlotta Spears Bass urged all eligible blacks, male and female, to register and to vote "in every city, county, and state election," but only for candidates sympathetic to their needs. In 1918, black women actively campaigned for Frederick M. Roberts, the first black man elected to California's assembly.

Women of Asian descent also exercised their new rights. California denied citizenship to foreign-born Chinese, but second-generation Chinese American women held birthright citizenship. In 1911, Clara Lee and Emma Tom Leong of Oakland and Tye Leung of San

Francisco were among the state's first Chinese-American women to register and cast ballots. San Francisco's Chinese-American daughters put their status as citizens to good use, writing letters to state and local officials protesting racist legislation, petitioning federal leaders for an end to the 1882 Chinese Exclusion Act, and registering American-born Chinese to vote.

The vast majority of California women who entered political life after 1911 did so as "municipal housekeepers," women determined to improve conditions in their communities. Armed with the vote at the high point of the progressive era, California's new voters set their sights on influencing the 1913 state legislature. The Federation of Women's Clubs held strategy sessions in Los Angeles, Sacramento, and San Francisco, and formed a special lobbying body, the Women's Legislative Council of California, to press their concerns. The Council's platform included 17 items, including a health certificate for marriage; joint guardianship of children; community property; mothers' pensions (later known as Aid to Dependent Families); maternity homes; parole and treatment for mentally-ill criminals; state registration of nurses; a state training school for girls; raising the age of majority to 21 for women; ethical, vocational, and hygienic training in the public schools; compelling fathers to support illegitimate children; civil service reform; an anti-prostitution measure; conservation of the environment; and a minimum wage for women. The Council took a room at the Sacramento Hotel for the duration of the 1913 legislative session, enabling them to attend hearings and pressure legislators. When the legislative year ended, the majority of the Council's proposed bills had been written into law.

Although it was a bold step, many California women also ran for public office. The first women to run for state and national office did so as early as 1912. The Republican Party put forward no female candidates that year, but Democrats threw their weight behind assembly candidate Mary Ellen Ridle. The Socialists supported seven female candidates for the assembly, as well as California's first female candidate for the state senate, Mina Dominguez of Santa Barbara and Ventura counties. The Prohibition Party favored Helen Stoddard as California's first woman in Congress. None of 1912's female candidates succeeded. Not until 1918, three full election cycles after gaining the vote, did Californians elect a woman to state office.

California's first women politicians faced unique challenges as political candidates. Name recognition, so vital to the successful politician, could be problematic. In 1918, one assembly contestant ensured that voters knew her both as "Mrs. Elizabeth Hughes" and as "Mrs. J. B. Hughes," the conventional style of address for white, middle-class women. Ironically, the tradition implied that a woman's most important identity was that of wife. At the same time, wives and mothers faced challenges that seldom troubled male candidates. Although her children were grown, for example, reporters asked Gertrude V. Clark who would look after her five grandchildren if she were elected lieutenant governor. Clark acidly observed that voters had yet to reject a grandfather on those grounds.

Clubwomen presented female politicians with an unexpected obstacle. Woman-led groups had lobbied tirelessly for woman suffrage, arguing that women needed the vote to secure important social reforms, to aid women, children, the sick and the poor. Women who sought political power for themselves flew in the face of this tradition of female activism for altruistic causes. Katherine Philips Edson feared that female office-seekers could jeopardize the influence exercised by clubwomen such as Edson herself. Thus women's clubs, including the all-powerful Federation of Women's Clubs, insisted that they were strictly non-partisan and refused to endorse female candidates.

In the end, the greatest challenge faced by California's first female politicians was a widespread, fundamental belief in gender difference. For many, ambition and the desire to lead were natural only in men. It would require feats of intellectual gymnastics to convince voters that women, too, could be political leaders.

While female office-seekers struggled for traction in state politics, Anna Howard Shaw was quickly vindicated in her prediction that California woman suffrage would reshape national politics. By the end of 1911, California women had organized clubs for each of the three major presidential candidates: Democrat Woodrow Wilson, Progressive third-party candidate and former president Theodore Roosevelt, and the incumbent, Republican William Howard Taft. In 1912, Roosevelt finally, begrudgingly, spoke in support of woman suffrage, turning the tide in his favor in California, where more women than men registered and voted in the May presidential primaries. As a result, newspapers reported, women secured California for Roosevelt and his vice-presidential running mate, Governor Hiram Johnson (the nation ultimately sent Wilson to the White House).

The impact of California suffrage was more pronounced in the 1916 presidential race. According to the New York Times, Wilson's slogan "He Kept Us Out of War" captured the "woman's vote," allowing Wilson to take both California and the White House. Wilson failed to keep the nation out of World War I but, soon after the Armistice, he reversed his long-standing opposition to woman suffrage. Some credited women's war work, but a more plausible explanation was the looming 1920 presidential race. Unfortunately for Wilson, by then Californians wanted nothing to do with his style of idealism; they voted instead for Republican Warren G. Harding.

Momentous as the woman suffrage victory felt in 1911 California, within a few years Americans knew that they had little to fear from female voters. The "woman's vote," with its potential for upheaval in public and private life, had failed to materialize. To the surprise of many, women did not vote as a bloc. Instead, women tended to vote as same-race, same-class men did. Nor did women voters consistently promote feminist causes. More importantly, rates of political participation among both men and women declined. Just as American women finally secured the franchise, voting seemed unimportant. In San Francisco, 1920 census records revealed that approximately two-thirds of eligible men registered to vote, but no more than one-third of eligible women did so. Compared to the national high-water mark of 79.3 percent voter turnout in 1896, an abysmal 49.3 percent of voters, male or female, bothered to vote in 1920.

Just like the "direct democracy" policies that reformers had promoted with such enthusiasm, woman suffrage had less of an immediate impact than expected. However, within two generations, California men and women would learn how to use both weapons to great effect.

California's "First Four"

Anna Saylor, Elizabeth Hughes, Grace Dorris, and Esto Broughton

In 1911, Californians voted by the slimmest of margins—only 4,000 votes—to enfranchise women. The ink was barely dry on the state's newly amended constitution when women began running for political office. Eleven women staged primary campaigns in 1912, setting their sights on the state assembly, state senate, and U.S. Congress.

Twenty-two women ran for state and national office in 1914, including the posts of lieutenant governor and California secretary of state. Yet no female candidate succeeded until 1918, when four women finally won election to the state assembly: Anna Saylor (R-Alameda), Elizabeth Hughes (R-Butte), Grace Dorris (R-Kern), and Esto Broughton (D-Stanislaus). As the Sacramento *Union* observed, Californians had shown that they were "willing that daughters vote but dubious about putting them in office."

A confluence of circumstances supported election of California's first female legislators. The first was reunification of the Republican

L to R: Grace Dorris, Elizabeth Hughes, Anna Saylor, Esto Broughton

In 2018, WICP 100 celebrated the 100th anniversary of the first four women elected to the California legislature. More at http://www.wicp100.org/. *1921 photograph courtesy of Sunny Mojonnier, CEO, Women in California Politics Foundation.*

Party, which reunited progressives and conservatives and helped to rally support for women candidates. Also important was the 19th Amendment, which extended the franchise nationally. Approved by Congress in 1918, states were then in the process of ratification. U.S. entry into World War I in 1917 was another factor. Many

(continued...)

elective offices were left open, meaning that female candidates were less likely to run against incumbents. In fact, from 1916 to 1918, the number of male candidates dropped 21 percent, while the number of women running for office doubled. California's unique political structure helped as well: the First Four utilized the 1909 primary law, by which voters chose candidates before the general election, and the 1913 cross-filing provision, by which candidates could capture nominations by multiple parties.

The First Four had much in common. Each began her quest for office with a college education. Saylor, Hughes, and Dorris had been school teachers, while Broughton was a practicing lawyer. Indeed, the women were better educated than many of their male counterparts: only half of the men elected to serve with them in 1918 had attended college.

Another commonality was deft use of California's political system. Through cross-filing, Berkeley clubwoman Anna Saylor won the nominations of the Democratic, Progressive, and Prohibition parties, as well as her own Republican party. She advanced to the general election with only one (Socialist) challenger. As was true of her female colleagues, Saylor campaigned with the support of prominent men. In Saylor's case, it was Republican progressive and former assembly speaker, C.C. Young, who stepped down to run for lieutenant governor. He recommended Saylor as his replacement and, when Young won, he became an important ally in Sacramento. Likewise, Saylor could count on the support of prominent women. Although women's clubs initially refused to endorse candidates, individual members were free to do so. Members of Berkeley's Twentieth Century Club actively campaigned for Saylor, their former president, as did the president of the California Federation of Women's Clubs.

Another commonality: the First Four faced similar difficulties. In her campaign, Saylor walked a careful line between male and female political styles. She attended private tea parties arranged by women's political clubs, but emphasized the "good government" themes common to male Lincoln-Roosevelt Republicans. Indeed, so successful were Saylor's speeches to groups of women that male candidates began holding tea parties of their own. When male candidates staged teas to woo women voters, they were revealing women's success in re-gendering California's political landscape.

Although men could campaign as women did, the First Four knew that the reverse was not true. A woman who too-openly attacked opponents risked striking voters as "unladylike." A Sacramento newspaper acknowledged this truth when it attributed the following quote to Saylor: "Vice, the liquor interests, unscrupulous business influences and indifferent citizenship [were] the greatest enemies of good government." In the next sentence, editors assured readers that Saylor was "a quiet, earnest little woman, with a long record of club activities" directed towards "civic and social betterment." California's First Four presented themselves as tough enough to lead while, simultaneously, "womanly" enough to maintain voters' approval.

Oroville resident Elizabeth Hughes ran as a Republican to represent Butte County, successfully cross-filing on the Democratic, Prohibition, and Socialist party tickets. Like Saylor, Hughes ran with the support of powerful men. She impressed local businessmen in 1914 when she helped Oroville retain the Butte County seat; in turn, they backed her run for the assembly. Hughes rallied prominent women to her cause, promising that she would support legislation aiding "the home, the school, the community, [and] orphaned or fatherless children." Hughes nonetheless struggled against her era's tendency to view leadership skills as masculine. With World War I raging overseas, her male opponent in the Republican primary race insisted that 1918 was "no time for experiments." The legislature, he insisted, was "no pink tea job." Butte County needed "a virile man who can come back with a punch." Hughes deftly turned her opponent's sexism to her advantage. In the next day's newspaper, she asked "Are the women who, at their country's call, have gone out upon the farms, into the orchards and munitions factories" or the "brave Red Cross nurses, working day and night at the front" serving in "pink tea jobs"? With most of the state's women actively engaged in war work, Hughes silenced her opponent and won the GOP nomination with 53 percent of Republican votes. She also captured the nominations of the Democratic, Prohibition, and Socialist parties, thereby running unopposed in the general election.

Grace McMillan Dorris ran and won her assembly seat for Kern County. Like the others, Dorris benefited from the support of prominent men: her lawyer husband had campaigned for the assembly before deciding to enlist in the U.S. Navy. He symbolically passed the baton to his wife, who then capitalized on her husband's patriotism. Dorris campaigned on progressive issues, including prohibition, an end to war, and "full equality of man and woman before the law." Five years' work in her husband's law firm had convinced Dorris of the need to reform community property laws for widowed women, a topic that probably resonated with recent war widows. Dorris ultimately bested two Republican opponents, taking 49 percent of the vote.

Esto B. Broughton of Modesto in Stanislaus County was the fourth woman elected to the assembly in 1918. Broughton differed from her colleagues in that she was unmarried, a Democrat, and an attorney. Two years before her race, Broughton graduated from Hastings College of Law. Her specialty was irrigation law, a critical arena in her rural agricultural district. Broughton similarly benefited from the backing of powerful men; one was her banker father, the other a former state senator with eleven years' service as district attorney for Stanislaus County. Broughton won all party nominations in her primary and ran unopposed in the general election.

The First Four's electoral victories revealed the ways that notions of gender continued to shape opportunities for women, even after woman suffrage. Their careers as politicians, on the other hand, illustrated how resistant to change California's political culture would be.

The 43rd Legislature was sworn in on January 6, 1919. From this moment, assembly leaders treated the First Four differently. First the body debated how to address them. Anna Saylor insisted that they be called "Assemblymen," just like everyone else. Then officials chose to seat the women together, in "preferred seats" flanking the assembly hall's center aisle. Again Saylor insisted that the women had no desire for special treatment: they preferred the seats assigned to their predecessors.

In another courtesy, Esto Broughton was privileged to read her party's appeal to the assembly's 14 Democrats, asking them to elect Republican Henry W. Wright speaker of the house; Broughton and Elizabeth Hughes seconded the nomination. Yet the gesture was meaningless: speaker Wright's victory had already been decided, in a compromise between the assembly's "wet" and "dry" factions. Later, as the 43rd Legislature drew to a close, members passed a resolution praising the women, noting that the First Four had served "with distinction to themselves and credit to their constituents." The legislators concluded by congratulating "the womanhood of California" for choosing "such representative members of their sex to serve in the Legislature," suggesting the First Four were elected by women, for women. Leaders' gallantry towards the First Four simply served to emphasize their status as political outsiders.

What did the First Four do with their newfound power? They hurled themselves into the decidedly unglamorous business of government. Hughes served on six committees, Broughton and Dorris on five, and Saylor on three. Hughes was chair of the Education Committee, on which Saylor and Dorris also served. Over 77 days, that committee considered 113 measures. Altogether, the First Four introduced 79 of the 1,118 assembly bills tendered that term, a creditable performance. In April 1919, the Sacramento *Union* acknowledged that the state "had no more earnest and tireless workers than the four women members of the assembly." The women were "nearly always present at roll call, whether it was at midnight, or in the early morning hours."

Californians had expected the First Four to promote "Women's Special Bills," as one newspaper put it, and to some extent they did. Dorris proposed limiting the hours of domestic servants to ten per day (the measure failed). Saylor asked for and received the legislature's and governor's support for a child hygiene bureau managed by the state Board of Health, a measure long favored by California clubwomen. Dorris, Saylor, and Broughton presented a total of seven measures to aid wives and widows, proposing amendments to laws affecting community property and inheritance rights. Defeat of the latter measures owed in part to Gov. William D. Stephens. Despite the promise to support "equality in property and other rights for women" Stephens made in his opening address to the legislature, he pocket vetoed two of the community property measures that reached his desk. Ultimately only one of the seven measures became law.

In addition to championing laws for women and children, the First Four also sponsored legislation unrelated to gender. Dorris (unsuccessfully) urged California to create a county public defender's office, arguing that

(*continued . . .*)

"it was obviously wrong that the state should place all its influence behind the prosecution in criminal cases, providing no really competent legal counsel for the defense." Saylor pressed (unsuccessfully) for a psychiatric clinic at San Quentin Prison to aid convicts with mental health problems. Broughton proposed a court of small claims, an idea launched five years earlier in Ohio. The legislature withheld approval in 1919 but adopted a comparable measure in 1921.

Like their male counterparts, Hughes, Saylor, and Broughton also proposed "pork barrel" projects, or appropriations that specifically benefited their constituents. Hughes secured $32,000 (over $462,000 in 2017 dollars) to expand Chico Normal School, later known as CSU Chico, thereby expanding the pool of trained rural schoolteachers. Hughes also bid, unsuccessfully, for state and federal funds to build a Feather River highway. Broughton pushed through a bill that authorized irrigation districts to develop and sell hydroelectric power. This proved a boon to her constituents, as it provided water for agriculture as well as jobs and electric power. Two additional Broughton irrigation bond measures failed, as did Broughton's bill for a reclamation project that would also employ World War I veterans. Like their male counterparts, the First Four experienced both loss and success.

They resembled male legislators in another way: they did not always agree. The First Four split evenly over maximum hours for industrial laundry workers, and three-to-one on limiting the hours of domestic servants. Dorris and Saylor divided over the latter's bill to separate the Berkeley School for the Deaf and Dumb into two separate institutions. However, as many Californians had feared, all four voted for prohibition.

Despite the women's strong legislative records, their tenure in state government was brief. Although they enjoyed an electoral advantage as incumbents in California's cross-filing nomination process, each found herself in the political crosshairs in the hard-fought campaigns of 1920, 1922, and 1924. Hughes chose to retire after serving two terms in office, deciding not to seek re-election in 1922. Dorris went on to campaign for and serve three terms in the assembly. Saylor and Broughton served four terms each but, by 1926, their time in state politics was over. Saylor and Broughton declined to seek re-election in 1926. That year Dorris, attempting a comeback, went down to defeat.

The story of the First Four underscores the difficulty women have encountered in reaching equal representation in California politics. Just as winning the vote was a bitter struggle, women have also battled to gain political office. Far more California women have competed for state and national offices than have gained them. From 1912 to 1970, more than 500 California women campaigned for state and national elective office, but only 18 women won their races. The words of the Sacramento *Union* in 1919 still rang true 50 years later: Californians agreed that women should vote, but not that women should lead.

(MAI)

Labor in Progressive California

Before 1900 active labor organization in California had centered in San Francisco. Workers there had lost some ground since the 1880s, but they still earned more than the current national annual average wage. To preserve their position, local unions formed the Representative Assembly of Trade and Labor Unions, the Coast Seamen's Association, the Federated Iron Trades Council, and other regional associations. In addition, increasing numbers of women in the workforce, especially in the garment and service industries, joined unions to protect their interests. Simultaneously, employers banded together to combat unionism, and the erratic economy of the late nineteenth century gave them an advantage. Prosperity after the Panic of 1893, however, brought with it renewed worker activism and organization of the Building Trades Council and the City Front Federation.

The new century also revived employer resistance, led by the well-funded Employers' Association of San Francisco. Conflict and strikes kept the city in turmoil for much of 1901, but no clear winners emerged. Mayor Phelan and Democrats lost labor support and many workers joined the Union Labor Party. The Employers' Association failed to discredit unionism, but for wage-earners results were mixed. They received no tangible benefits from their prolonged strikes, but they did preserve their right to organize, which they used effectively for the next decade.

In Southern California, unionism before 1900 mainly involved conflict between Harrison Gray Otis and employees of his Los Angeles *Times*. A union activist as a youth, by 1880 Otis was a determined foe of organized labor. He fought his battle alone until late in the nineteenth century, when the population, the number of employers, and union activity all increased in Los Angeles. In the 1880s, the Merchants' and Manufacturers' Association (M&M) formed to promote commerce. Simultaneously, the American Federation of Labor (AFL) and other national unions sent their organizers to the city and, during the early 1900s, strikes and lockouts became more frequent. With backing from Otis, publicity in the *Times*, and a municipal anti-picketing law passed in 1910, M&M members resisted unionism with substantial success.

Where trade unionism was viable, even California's diluted brand of radicalism attracted few wage-earners. Jack London failed miserably as the Socialist candidate for mayor of Oakland in 1901 and 1905. In Berkeley, hardly a working-class community, voters in 1911 chose a Socialist mayor, Methodist minister J. Stitt Wilson. A few Californians also supported Socialist Eugene Debs' presidential candidacies, and they sent an occasional Socialist to the state legislature. In Los Angeles, however, where employers defied unions and wages were 30 percent less than elsewhere in the state, socialism had greater appeal. Organization began during the 1880s under the leadership of millionaire real-estate developer H. Gaylord Wilshire and continued during the 1890s under labor-lawyer Job Harriman.

Harriman ran unsuccessfully for governor in 1898 and for vice-president on the Eugene Debs ticket in 1900. In May 1910, members of several unions went out on strike with support from the citywide Labor Council,

Jack London

Sometimes Socialist

Born in San Francisco in 1876, Jack London was the illegitimate child of spiritualist Flora Wellman and astrologer William Chaney. When Chaney denied his son and departed, Jack's mother married John London, a widower with five children, and joined a family that lived constantly on the brink of disaster. After the failure of an Oakland grocery store and a succession of farms in Alameda, San Mateo, and the Livermore Valley, the Londons returned to Oakland where Flora ran a boarding house and John did odd jobs. Jack contributed his meager income from a paper route and work in local canneries to the family's support. He attended school when he could and read voraciously, but by his 15th birthday, he was well on his way to becoming a delinquent on the Oakland waterfront. To escape, in 1893 he signed on for a gruesome seal-hunting voyage to the Bering Sea and a year later he joined Jacob Coxey's army of protesting unemployed workers marching to Washington, D.C. He made it as far as Chicago, drifted to Buffalo where he was jailed for vagrancy, and returned home to try his hand at writing. Then in 1897, he departed again—this time for the Klondike in search of gold.

London's early experiences provided raw material for much of his writing: *The Call of the Wild* (1903), *The People of the Abyss* (1903), *The Sea Wolf* (1904), *White Fang* (1906), *The Road* (1907), *Martin Eden* (1909), *John Barleycorn* (1913), and more. They also influenced a philosophy that owed as much to Herbert Spencer and Friedrich Nietzsche as it did to Karl Marx.

Jack London and his dog Rollo, circa 1885

Courtesy of The Bancroft Library, University of California, Berkeley.

(continued . . .)

His ideas were confused and often contradictory. As a self-proclaimed socialist, London advocated the brotherhood and equality of man in lectures and writings, yet he was personally committed to notions of Anglo-Saxon superiority. He promoted the ideals of social responsibility and justice, but he understood life as a tooth-and-claw struggle that allowed only the fittest—those like himself—to survive. London championed the cause of the working classes, yet his associates were "The Crowd"—artists and intellectuals who populated the elite artists' colony at Carmel. London defined success in materialistic rather than ideal terms, but when he achieved it as an author and journalist, he used its rewards for personal gratification, especially building his 45-foot yacht, the *Snark*, for an ill-fated around-the-world voyage, and his Beauty Ranch and Wolf House near Glen Ellen. He squandered his money, often unwisely and rarely to benefit wage earners.

London's life, like his socialism, was a contradiction. Physical and mental fitness obsessed him, but he abused his body and his mind by gorging on blood-rare meat and consuming prodigious quantities of alcohol and drugs to combat insomnia and ease pain. Indeed, his death at Beauty Ranch in 1916 resulted from an overdose of morphine; whether it was accidental or intentional remains uncertain.   (WAB)

the AFL, Socialists, and organized labor throughout the state. The strike spread, city officials enforced the anti-picketing ordinance, and workers joined Socialists to form the Union Labor Political Club and nominate Harriman for mayor. On October 1, at the height of the strike, an explosion killed 20 employees in the Los Angeles *Times* building.

Investigations led to union activists John J. and James B. McNamara, who denied both their guilt and union involvement in the bombing. Labor organizations across the nation raised funds and employed Clarence Darrow to defend the brothers against a suspected frame-up. At their trial in 1911, however, the McNamaras admitted guilt; John received life in prison and James 15 years. Public support for organized labor evaporated, union members quit in disgust, and anti-picketing ordinances were passed throughout the state. At first, apparent persecution of the McNamaras increased Harriman's chances for election, but their confession doomed his candidacy and the Socialist party in Los Angeles. The episode also resulted in victory for Otis and opponents of organized labor, where the "open-shop" principle prevailed until the 1930s.

Six years later, similar events had similar consequences in San Francisco. In 1916, the local Merchants' and Manufacturers' Association renewed its resistance to unionism. During the same year, the Chamber of Commerce formed a "Law and Order Committee" with a million-dollar budget to break a longshoremen's strike for higher wages. Within a week strikers returned to work without pay increases. Almost simultaneously, San Franciscans held a "Preparedness Day" parade in response to the nation's potential involvement in World War I in Europe. As the procession moved along Market Street

on July 22, a bomb blast killed ten people and maimed 40 more. Days later, police arrested several union activists, including Tom Mooney and Warren K. Billings. Unlike the McNamaras, however, the accused San Franciscans maintained their innocence through a long and hysterical trial that bore little resemblance to a judicial proceeding. In January 1917 both were found guilty and sentenced, Mooney to death and Billings to life in prison.

Although Mooney's sentence was commuted, he remained behind bars despite appeals from around the world, evidence that contradicted much of the testimony against him, and proof that District Attorney Charles M. Fickert had encouraged perjury. Governor Culbert Olson finally pardoned Mooney in 1939, but as an immediate result of the affair, public and official hostility toward unionism reached unprecedented heights in California.

Fears of Radicalism

As an attorney, Hiram Johnson had defended organized labor and, as governor, he appointed union leaders to positions in state government. But most progressives in California and elsewhere did not support the principles of labor organization. They could not, however, ignore either their working-class constituencies or their own commitment to the ideals of social justice. Associations like the San Francisco Labor Council and the State Labor Federation had enthusiastically endorsed progressives' candidacies and proposed policies that the state government adopted. Among these were an Employer Liability Act to define responsibility for on-the-job injuries, an Industrial Accident Board to review cases, eight-hour and minimum-wage laws for women, an Industrial

Welfare Commission to regulate working conditions for women and children, and a state workers' insurance program. These and similar measures were long overdue departures from established tradition and demonstrated progressives' concern for the welfare of wage-earning Californians.

Many progressives nonetheless remained suspicious of organized labor. In 1911, the legislature nearly approved a compulsory arbitration bill that was a step toward abolishing the right to strike. It also defeated a bill introduced by Senator Anthony Caminetti and supported by other progressive Democrats that would have limited the use of judicial injunctions against strikes, forbade employers' "black lists" and "yellow-dog" contracts, and legalized boycotts and peaceful picketing. Some progressives, in fact, exhibited no sympathy at all for striking workers and agreed with a remark attributed to James D. Phelan: "If they don't want to be clubbed, let them return to work." Several things influenced their attitudes. Some identified with employer interests; others rejected the notion of "class" in American society. More general was repulsion at events like the *Times* building bombing. The fear of "radicalism" and its equation with working-class militancy was most significant in shaping their attitudes.

This aspect of the progressive disposition manifested itself quite early. When anarchist Emma Goldman appeared in San Francisco in 1908 and '09, city and state authorities resorted to harassment and arrest to deny her a forum. Even more significant was the arrival of the radical Industrial Workers of the World (IWW or "Wobblies"). Founded in Chicago in 1905, the IWW began to make some progress among workers in the mines, forests, and fields of the West. In 1910 California it had only 1,000 members in eleven locals, but that was enough to prompt Fresno, San Diego, and several other cities to pass laws outlawing the Wobblies' primary organizing tactic: making speeches and singing anti-capitalist songs in public places. When IWW members tested the law in Fresno in 1910, they were jailed, doused with fire hoses, and threatened with lynching. Two years later in San Diego, Wobblies were denounced by a hostile press, confronted by a vigilance committee of armed businessmen, beaten brutally, and arrested. Two were killed while in jail, one of them kicked to death.

As governor, Hiram Johnson could not ignore such episodes. He ordered an investigation and appointed Sacramento merchant Harris Weinstock to direct it. No friend of labor, Weinstock nevertheless joined Fremont Older and Chester Rowell in challenging the legality of local anti-IWW laws (all were declared unconstitutional by state and federal courts) and condemning the actions of citizens and authorities in Fresno and San Diego. Still, the Free Speech Fights, as they came to be known, neither reduced hostility toward radicalism nor ended IWW activity in progressive California.

The peak of IWW activity in California came in the summer of 1913, when 2,800 adults and children responded to recruiting literature from the Durst hop ranch near Wheatland, south of Marysville. When workers arrived, they found that only 800 harvesters actually were needed, that housing and campsites (rented from Durst) were grossly inadequate, that sanitary facilities consisted of eight crude privies, that the only thing to drink in the scorching fields was "lemonade" (citric acid and water) purchased from Durst's cousin, and that a "bonus" promised for working through the harvest was actually a holdback from wages, to be paid at season's end. Among the workers were Wobblies who organized a meeting to protest conditions. Sheriff's deputies confronted the assembled workers, shots were fired, and five people were killed: two deputies, two workers, and the district attorney of Yuba County.

In the aftermath of the Wheatland incident, IWW members Blackie Ford and Herman Suhr were tracked down, convicted of second-degree murder because they organized the protest, and imprisoned. Meanwhile, the Commission on Immigration and Housing, established earlier in 1913, investigated living and working conditions of California farm laborers—nomads who existed almost invisibly on the fringes of society—and documented their universally appalling situation. The committee's report resulted in passage of the Labor Camp Act of 1915, but concern was not sufficiently sustained to overcome growers' resistance or to end the state's perennial farm-labor problem. Nor did it lessen the progressive generation's suspicion of radicalism.

The Criminal Syndicalism Act, 1919

Events in California—including Goldman's visit, the Free Speech Fights, Wobblies' presence at Wheatland, bombings in Los Angeles and San Francisco, and active Socialist Party agitation—increased fears of radicalism, however defined. Local attitudes also mirrored a national mood reinforced by involvement in World War I, by the Bolshevik revolution in Russia in 1917, and by hysteria generated by U.S. Attorney General A. Mitchell Palmer's "red raids" during the summer of

1919. During the early twentieth century, more than 20 states enacted antiradical laws, but none was more energetically enforced than California's 1919 Criminal Syndicalism Act.

The vague statute made it illegal to promote "any doctrine or precept advocating . . . unlawful acts of violence . . . as a means of accomplishing a change in industrial ownership or control, or effecting any political change." Neither action nor encouragement of action was required for prosecution; mere advocacy of an ideology that accepted violence was sufficient. During the next five years, more than 500 individuals faced trial under the act, beginning with 52-year-old Oakland philanthropist and social worker Charlotte Anita Whitney, a descendant of prominent New England and California families. She was a pacifist who became a Socialist in 1914, joined the Communist Labor Party in 1919, and was arrested for her activities shortly after the Criminal Syndicalism Act became law. Her trial in 1920 resulted in conviction and a sentence to 14 years in the state penitentiary. While Whitney remained free on bail, Fremont Older and others supported a series of appeals and attorney John F. Neylan fought her case all the way to the U.S. Supreme Court, which in 1927 upheld both her conviction and the constitutionality of the California law. A month later, Governor Clement C. Young pardoned her, not because an injustice had been done but because sending a 60-year-old woman to prison would create a martyr in the cause of radicalism. The law continued to function until 1968, when federal courts invalidated it.

Race in Progressive California

Given the diversity of its population, race relations were more complicated in California than elsewhere in the nation. In the 1850s, a quarter or more of all Californians were African American, Native American, Asian, or Latino. People of color represented just 5 percent of the population by 1900, yet even then, California remained ethnically and religiously diverse. Before 1920, half or more of all white Californians were immigrants or the children of immigrants. Irish, German, and British predominated, followed by Scandinavians, Italians, Portuguese, Greeks, and Armenians. After 1910, growing numbers of Mexicans joined existing Latina/o communities, many of which preceded American conquest. California was also home to African Americans, significant numbers of Chinese and Japanese, plus immigrants from Korea, the Philippines, and India.

Meanwhile, the population of Native Californians continued to decline, reaching 20,000 in 1900. Some whites were sympathetic. Charles Fletcher Lummis, for example, founded the Sequoia League in 1901 to lobby on their behalf. The League took up the cause of the Cupeño of San Diego County, when former California governor John G. Downey won title to a Mexican land grant that included their villages at Agua Caliente. When Downey began eviction proceedings against them, the League tried to interest President Theodore Roosevelt in their case. The government offered them new land, but the Cupeño refused. Said Cecilio Blacktooth: "If you give us the best place in the world, it is not as good as this. This is our home. We cannot live anywhere else; we were born here, and our fathers are buried here." Nonetheless, in May 1903, the 200 Cupeño were removed to Pala, California, 75 miles away.

Native Californians organized on their own behalf in the fall of 1919, when 75 leaders representing every tribe in Southern California met at the Riverside home of Jonathan Tibbets to organize the Mission Indian Federation. Also present were state senator Samuel Carey Evans and Stella Atwood of the California Federation of Women's Clubs. A close friend and colleague of John Collier, future Commissioner of Indian Affairs, Atwood helped shape the "Indian New Deal" of the 1930s. Such influential whites were useful advocates for the Federation, whose slogan was "Human Rights and Home Rule."

California's black population remained relatively small before World War I—about 2 percent of the population. Blacks experienced discrimination in housing and employment, and responded by forming chapters of the National Association for the Advancement of Colored People (NAACP) and the Urban League. These groups hosted NAACP cofounder W.E.B. DuBois during his 1913 national tour. Black Californians were politically active. In Los Angeles they helped to elect the state's first black legislator, assembly member Frederick M. Roberts, who served from 1919 to 1934.

During the first decades of the twentieth century, Spanish-speaking descendants of the Californios were rapidly outnumbered by tens of thousands fleeing political and economic dislocations in Mexico, so that Mexicans in California increased from 8 percent in 1910 to 25 percent in 1930. During the 1920s, the Mexican-born population in California doubled. Although some were members of the white-collar and professional classes, most found work as menials and laborers. They established *barrios* in Los Angeles, Santa Barbara, San Diego, and other cities, or *colonias* in agricultural regions, where Mexican Californians became the mainstay of farm labor.

World War I stimulated additional immigration from Mexico. When the United States entered the conflict, California growers worried about labor shortages convinced federal officials to exempt Mexicans from the 1917 Immigration Act and allow Mexicans to enter the country as temporary workers. To ensure an adequate labor force, some citrus growers offered housing. In Corona in 1918 Riverside County, the Chase Plantation built 36 adobe houses for workers and their families. On the Sespe ranch in Ventura, Mexican workers were provided with land, but they had to build their own houses.

Unlike Chinese and Japanese farm workers, Mexican laborers sometimes traveled and worked as family units. In many citrus villages, wives operated small businesses, selling lunches to workers in their homes, or preparing foods sold from a cart or booths at *jamaicas* (Sunday street fairs). Occasionally women ran boarding houses for traveling pickers and packers. Small family-operated stores were an accepted occupation for Mexican wives and children. The *Placentina Comercial Mexicana*, founded in the late 1920s by José Aguirre and operated by Doña Marina Aguirre and her daughter, sold staples to citrus workers. Villagers had no objection to Mexican wives and mothers as business owners, as long as they fulfilled their traditional domestic responsibilities (which they usually did while tending store). These woman-run businesses meant a higher standard of living for their families. As future labor leader Dolores Huerta recalled, her mother, a "very ambitious woman," started with a little lunch counter in 1930s Stockton. "Then she got a bigger restaurant, and when the war came she got a hotel. That's how I was able to go to school and how I got a more affluent background than the other kids."

By 1920, Mexicans formed the largest single ethnic group among farm workers in California, becoming the mainstay of large-scale, specialty-crop agriculture. Mexican immigration continued after World War I ended. Less concerned about labor shortages, grower interest in providing workers with housing declined. In the 1920s Imperial Valley, most Mexican farm workers lived in lean-to shacks or tents. Workers formed squatter camps on the banks of irrigation canals, set up during harvest season and abandoned when the season ended. Growers allowed free camping during the harvest, but charged $2.50 per family per month once the season was over.

Continued immigration may have undermined opportunities for some Mexican Californians, yet successive waves of newcomers also helped to preserve and reinforce elements of Mexican culture. Churches and *mutualistas* helped as well, providing a focus for community social life and helping immigrants adapt to life in the United States. Acknowledging the need for Mexicans as laborers, Anglo Californians generally ignored them, tolerating rather than actively persecuting Mexican communities.

Such was not the case for the Asian migrants arriving at the turn of the century. With the restrictions imposed by the Chinese Exclusion Act, farmers and growers had again turned to Asia. From 6,000 to 7,000 East Indian immigrants entered the country between 1907 and 1917, when Congress prohibited their entrance. Many came from India's Punjab province and labored as seasonal farm workers in the Central and Imperial valleys. Not more than 30 East Indian women immigrated to the West Coast in all the years before World War I. Despite the small numbers of Indian women, Californians viewed their arrival with alarm. When one arrived in 1910, bringing the total number of Indian women in the state to four, a newspaper headline screeched: "Hindu women next swarm to California."

Substantial immigration of Japanese, Korean, and Filipino workers from Hawaii began in 1900, when the U.S. annexed the islands. From 1905 to 1910, around 1,000 Koreans traveled by way of Hawaii to California. The 45 Korean women who arrived in that era worked as domestics or joined men in the fields. Many Koreans joined the circuit of seasonal farm workers but some became tenant farmers and fruit growers. The best known were Charles Kim (Kim Ho) and Harry Kim (Kim Hyung-soon). In 1921 they established the Kim Brothers in the San Joaquin Valley, where they managed six farms and 500 acres. They developed several species of hybrid fruit, including a nectarine, with saplings they imported from Korea.

Japanese migrants likewise came to California by way of Hawaii. Recruiters actively sought married men, unlike earlier Chinese recruiters, expecting wives to work in the fields and as cooks, laundresses, and seamstresses. Japanese numbers grew quickly: the 1880 census counted only 86 Japanese in California, but 10,000 ten years later. Most were male: census takers counted only 410 Japanese women in the entire United States.

Like white Californians, Japanese pioneers met community needs through voluntary societies. The country's first was the *Fukuin Kai* (Gospel Society), established in San Francisco in 1877. Japanese churches—Christian, Buddhist, and Shinto—soon followed. Japanese women founded separate organizations that offered social activities and instruction in English and Japanese languages. In 1900 Sacramento, members of the Buddhist

Women's Associations raised funds for the temple and provided their small community with social services. By the 1930s, virtually every Japanese community had its own *nihon gakko* (Japanese-language school) operated by a church or Japanese association.

Although they started in the fields, the *Issei* (first-generation Japanese immigrants) were not content to remain laborers. Some obtained land—often marginal tracts bought or leased from large growers—and became successful truck farmers, raising tomatoes, vegetables, and a variety of fresh produce. Their success inflamed Californians already predisposed against Asians. Founded in May 1905, the labor-sponsored Asiatic Exclusion League mounted a campaign to exclude Japanese and Koreans from the United States. The following year, the League convinced the San Francisco Board of Education to segregate the city's 93 Japanese schoolchildren. The incident resulted in a diplomatic crisis. President Theodore Roosevelt intervened and secured the "Gentlemen's Agreement" of 1907: San Francisco rescinded the segregation order and Japan limited immigration by laborers, though parents, wives, and children could join laborers already in the United States.

For many Californians, this solution fell short. Labor leaders agitated for additional restrictions against Asians. James D. Phelan, Harrison Gray Otis, Chester Rowell, and Katherine Philips Edson joined the chorus, as did the political parties (including Socialists), small farm operators, and citizens of nearly every national origin. Beginning in January 1909, Anthony Caminetti and other legislators introduced anti-Japanese bills every year. The proposed bills restricted Japanese land ownership and required segregation in schools and housing. Only continued resistance from the White House and pressure from San Francisco's business community—then laying plans for a post-earthquake world's fair—scuttled these efforts.

Perhaps as Californians had feared, the Gentleman's Agreement increased immigration by Japanese women. Thousands of "picture brides" joined their husbands in California, although many met for the first time after passing through the Angel Island immigration facility in San Francisco Bay. In 1910, census-takers counted 41,000 Japanese in California, with more women and growing numbers of *Nisei* (American-born children). Issei farmers owned about 17,000 acres, leased about 80,000 more, and sharecropped another 60,000 acres. From 1910 to 1920, Japanese farmers became important producers and growers of crops: truck farming along the coast, in the Central Valley, and in Southern California; grapes and tree fruit in the Central Valley and Southern

California; strawberries in a number of locations; and rice in Northern California. Their numbers and success exacerbated white hostility.

Exclusionists despaired early in 1913, when Democrat Woodrow Wilson entered the White House. Wilson opposed anti-Japanese legislation and even sent Secretary of State William Jennings Bryan to California to present his views, quite ineffectively. The state's Republicans felt little loyalty to the new president and even Democrats were unenthusiastic. With only token Democratic opposition, and with the backing of Gov. Johnson, in 1913 the legislature passed the Alien Land Act by 35 to two in the senate and 72 to three in the assembly. Under the law, "aliens ineligible to citizenship" could not purchase California land or lease it for more than three years. Although it also applied to Korean, Filipino, Sikhs, and other Asian immigrant farmers, the 1913 law was aimed primarily at the Japanese. As Gov. Johnson declared, the law had "laid [to rest] the ghost of the Japanese question."

Johnson, however, spoke prematurely. The Alien Land Act contained loopholes. Many Japanese evaded its constraints by buying or leasing land in the names of their American-born children or in partnerships with whites. Consequently, anti-Japanese agitation quickly resumed and culminated in 1920 when California voters, by a three to one margin, approved an initiative that further tightened the Alien Land law.

Water for Cities: Hetch Hetchy and Owens Valley

Progressives at the state and national levels introduced important conservation policies but differed on just what conservation meant. Utilitarians, represented by U.S. Chief Forester Gifford Pinchot, advocated resource conservation for economic use, while preservationists, like the naturalist John Muir, sought to protect special wilderness areas for their aesthetic and spiritual values. In California, San Francisco's drive to obtain water from the Hetch Hetchy Valley on the Tuolumne River and Los Angeles's effort to tap the Owens River sharply exposed these divisions within progressive ranks regarding early environmental policies.

With no reliable source of water for a growing population, San Francisco relied on private contractors, especially the Spring Valley Water Company, to supply its needs. The charter of 1898 provided means to end the dependency through municipal ownership of the local water system, but the expanding city still needed to acquire additional sources of water outside the Bay Area. After considering several possibilities,

Mayor James D. Phelan and city officials committed themselves in 1900 to tapping the Tuolumne River as it flowed through Hetch Hetchy Valley, located high in the Sierra Nevada range. Because the site lay within Yosemite National Park, San Francisco required congressional approval, but the city's application touched off a 13-year conflict between opposing factions of conservationists. The state's congressional delegation lobbied their House and Senate colleagues in favor of the project, but opposition was just as vigorous, especially from John Muir and the Sierra Club, which Muir founded in 1892. Preservationists denounced damming the valley, which they a called "miniature Yosemite," and argued that destroying it would deprive Californians of its natural benefits. Utilitarians argued that a reservoir would be just as beneficial and that San Francisco's dependence on private contractors placed the city in physical and political jeopardy.

Until 1913, however, neither side prevailed. Then Woodrow Wilson appointed Franklin K. Lane, former San Francisco city attorney, as Secretary of the Interior. With Lane's backing, a measure introduced by John E. Raker of Alturas provided the necessary Congressional approval. Passage of the Raker Act in 1913 gave utilitarians a victory, and construction began immediately on a dam and 200-mile aqueduct to deliver water to San Francisco. When it was completed in 1934, the Hetch Hetchy system supplied both water and hydroelectric power to residents of the city and other Bay Area communities.

If San Francisco was dry, Los Angeles was parched, and water wars there pitted preservationists against utilitarians—and utilitarians against one another. By the early twentieth century, population growth had created a water crisis in the city. In 1904 former mayor and city engineer Fred Eaton suggested tapping the Owens River, 240 miles away on the eastern watershed of the Sierra. Eaton began buying land around Long Valley at the head of the Owens Valley, as part of his private scheme to sell water to local farmers and distant city dwellers. When a drought depleted Los Angeles reservoirs, Eaton enlisted the help of his friend, city engineer William Mulholland. Simultaneously, federal reclamation activities in the valley negated his original idea and, with Mulholland's support, Eaton arranged to sell his holdings to Los Angeles. He also acted as the city's agent, buying additional land and water rights in the name of the municipality.

Both Eaton's activities and the city's involvement remained secret until July 1905, when the Los Angeles *Times* and its rival, the *Examiner*, published dramatically different treatments of the project. Harrison

Gray Otis's *Times* enthusiastically detailed Eaton's plan and cataloged its benefits to the city. According to the *Examiner*'s version, though, a syndicate of speculators—including Otis and Henry E. Huntington of the Pacific Electric Railway—had bought property in the dry San Fernando Valley and intended to use the Owens River to increase its value at public expense. Allegations did not deter local voters: in September 1905 they approved a bond issue and work on the project began. Mulholland supervised construction of the aqueduct system, which he designed to operate by siphoning action, virtually without pumping. Federal officials cooperated by including Owens Valley lands in the Sierra National Forest, thereby preventing homestead and other claims from interfering with the aqueduct's right-of-way. In November 1913, the great project was completed and commenced delivering water to Los Angeles and the recently annexed San Fernando Valley.

The Owens River project encountered opposition from preservationists, but the most vocal critics were utilitarians: residents of the valley who feared loss of their own water resources. They fought the aqueduct from the beginning, even resorting to sabotage and dynamite during the 1920s. Their fears, if not their tactics, were justified. Eaton's $1 million asking price for his Long Valley property prevented municipal construction of a permanent dam and storage reservoir on the Owens River. As a consequence, until 1941 the city simply drew off the annual flow of the river, magnifying the adverse impacts of the project on Owens Valley's devastated towns and farms. Subsequent enlargement of the project also threatened the Mono Lake Basin after 1941, as the Owens Valley system constantly expanded to meet Los Angeles's constantly increasing need for water.

The End of an Era

Two events in 1906 marked the opening of the progressive era in California: the San Francisco earthquake and fire, and the beginning of the graft trials. Two more in 1917 delineated the beginning of its demise: U.S. entry into World War I and Hiram Johnson's departure for the U.S. Senate.

The outbreak of war in Europe in August 1914 nudged a sluggish economy, as demands for food and war materiel stimulated the state's industries and accelerated the pace of corporate organization. After the war ended in 1918, economic expansion continued into the 1920s. In the meantime, more than 150,000 Californians served in the military, the state's universities provided officer-training programs, and the public bought Liberty Bonds. But war disrupted the progressive movement.

Progressives rarely achieved consensus on the issue of foreign affairs, even before 1914, and before U.S. entry into World War I they clashed over American relations with European belligerents. Many Californians saw no connection between British or French interests and their own, and supported a League of Neutrals to maintain commerce with all warring powers. Progressives also were at odds over proposals to keep Americans from traveling into submarine zones on belligerent ships, and over the preparedness policy advocated by the Wilson administration. Like Hiram Johnson, who called preparedness "bunk" as late as 1917, they saw the heavy hands of munitions makers and international bankers behind it. After an armistice was signed in 1918, progressives were equally unable to agree on the treaties negotiated in Paris and plans for a League of Nations. Thus the war and related issues fragmented the progressive movement and hastened its decline in both California and the nation.

Hiram Johnson contributed to the same end, not only by his departure for the Senate in 1917 but also by his personality. He was self-centered, self-righteous, abrasive, ambitious, and, some say, messianic. By the end of his first term, he was regarded by many—perhaps including himself—as the embodiment of California progressivism. He was intolerant of disagreement and alienated former allies, including founders of the Lincoln-Roosevelt League, and his insistence on the formation of a California Progressive Party in 1913 added to the discord. When Francis J. Heney won the 1914 Progressive nomination for the U.S. Senate over Johnson's preferred choice, the governor felt betrayed. Heney, in turn, accused Johnson of engineering his defeat when Heney lost to Democrat James D. Phelan. Nor did Johnson's 1914 re-election reduce problems or diminish his ambition for a U.S. Senate seat. By cross-filing in the Republican and Progressive primaries, Johnson won the office in 1916, but his tactics deepened divisions in reformers' ranks.

Earlier events also predicted strife. In the 1914 Republican primary, Helen K. Williams, publisher of *The Woman Citizen* magazine, became a candidate for state lieutenant governor on a slate with gubernatorial candidate John M. Frederick of Los Angeles. Two years later, Williams formed the Women's Republican Central Committee, an alternative to the party-sanctioned Women's Auxiliary of the Republican State Central Committee. In addition, when John M. Eshelman,

Johnson's hand-picked lieutenant governor, died early in 1916, it forced Johnson to placate progressives in Southern California by filling the vacancy with William D. Stephens, whom he distrusted. The governor then refused to step down for two weeks after taking the oath as U.S. Senator. Only the president's call to an emergency session of Congress forced Johnson's resignation. In the interim, the fragile unity of California progressives eroded.

As governor, Stephens compiled a modestly progressive record, but by 1917 cohesion was gone. Even Johnson was soon back in Republican ranks. The war distracted attention from issues of reform and produced bellicose patriotism and aggressive racism in California. The war was disillusioning, too, especially its failure to "make the world safe for democracy." In its aftermath, Hiram Johnson and many other progressives became rigid isolationists and irreconcilable foes of the League of Nations.

But even earlier, most Californians had turned their energies to the economic development that characterized the 1920s. By then, most of those who had spearheaded the great reform crusades of the late nineteenth and early twentieth centuries—mostly white, educated urban men and women—had lost their taste for crusading.

California progressives' record was a mixed one. Their political reforms did not achieve all that they expected and, in some cases, had negative consequences. Despite their advocacy of social justice, they presented few programs to assist workers, or to address the discrimination faced by state minorities, including blacks, Native Americans, Mexicans, and Asians. Indeed, many progressives—including newly enfranchised women like Katherine Philips Edson—were bigots. Clubwomen did leave their mark on the political sphere: Berkeley's Twentieth Century Club, for example, was able to send a member, Anna Saylor, to the state assembly. One of the first four women to serve in that body, Saylor led successful campaigns to abolish the death penalty for minors, secure protective child labor legislation, and aid the elderly. But other equally well-intended moral reforms fell short. Efforts to eliminate gambling, alcoholism, and prostitution typically focused on the symptoms of problems rather than their causes. After the Red Light Abatement Act passed in 1913, for example, 200 prostitutes gathered in the chapel of the San Francisco evangelist who had led the attack and asked him how they should earn a living.

Nonetheless, progressives made drastic changes in the defined role of government and its relationship with citizens. They agreed with Abraham Lincoln, who reportedly said that governments exist to do for the people what they cannot do for themselves. Progressives recognized that increasingly complex urban-industrial societies multiplied governments' responsibilities and, to their credit, they acted on that recognition.

Turn-of-the-Century California Culture

Because the state's cultural development remained more imitative than innovative, Californians self-consciously sought something to call their own. In the process they discovered, reinvented, and romanticized the region's Spanish heritage. Myths and misnomers abounded in popular art, architecture, and promotional literature. Nostalgia for an imagined past prompted mission restoration programs and marking the old mission trail with little mission bells; the route was renamed "El Camino Real," a name popularly, though mistakenly translated as "the King's Highway." (In the Spanish era, the phrase was applied to any public, as opposed to private, road.) Boosters organized annual celebrations including the Ramona Pageant at Hemet, the Old Spanish Days Fiesta in Santa Barbara, and the ride of *los rancheros visitadores* through Ventura and Santa Barbara counties.

The most immediate and emphatic manifestation of the pastoral California appeared in the arts and architecture. Residents responded enthusiastically to New Yorker Helen Hunt Jackson's romance of early California, *Ramona* (1884). Within a year they had their own proponent of the Spanish-Indian heritage. Late in 1885, New England-born and Harvard-educated Charles Fletcher Lummis arrived at San Fernando after walking from Ohio to recover his health. He found employment with the Los Angeles *Times*, and a decade later became editor of *Land of Sunshine* magazine, subsequently called *Out West*. In the interim, Lummis wrote for the *Times*, published *A Tramp across the Continent* (1892) and the *Spanish Pioneers* (1893), steeped himself in the lore of Spanish California, adopted the *charro* (Mexican cowboy) costume, and called himself "Don Carlos." In his role as editor, Lummis published his own work and that of like-minded writers of scholarly studies and fiction. He became a cult figure and guru to a colony of artists and academics living along the Arroyo Seco near Pasadena in villas built of native stone and adobe, decorated with Indian artifacts (usually Hopi or Navajo), and filled with rough-hewn "mission" furniture.

Despite his overt flamboyance, Lummis's commitment to the West and its history ran deep, and he influenced the careers of numerous talented westerners. He published Mary Austin's first work and praised her *The Land of Little Rain* (1903), romances like *Isidro* (1905) and *Santa Lucia* (1908), feminist novels including *Woman of Genius* (1912), and extended essays such as *California, Land of Sun* (1914). He printed Jack London's early short stories, applauded Frank Norris's *McTeague* and *The Octopus*, and encouraged Robinson Jeffers, soon to be California's premier twentieth-century poet. Fresno-born painter Maynard Dixon likewise received Lummis's support before he focused his talent on the Southwest. To preserve California's past, Lummis worked to establish The Southwest Museum, but when it opened in 1914 his health had begun to falter, as had his influence. To a generation maturing in a complex industrial society and about to become involved in a world war, his romantic vision of a simpler age no longer seemed appropriate. From his home on the Arroyo Seco, where he died in 1928, Don Carlos lamented the fading of his dream.

Turn-of-the-century California architects also responded to the rediscovered Spanish heritage and expressed it in Mission Revival designs for public buildings and in tile-roofed imitations of adobe villas. During the early 1900s, Charles and Henry Greene of Pasadena introduced a more unique structure and style: the bungalow, combining beauty and utility in open patios, uncluttered interiors, and broad verandas with construction in native materials. Although the Greenes built for wealthy clients, imitators made the bungalow a favored residential style among all Californians. A different approach, however, resulted from the work of New Yorker Arthur Page Brown, who arrived in San Francisco in 1889. Before he died seven years later at age 36, Brown charted new directions by assimilating styles ranging from Classical to Mission Revival and integrating native materials with modern glass and steel. Brown's firm also provided employment and experience for individuals who continued to develop a local architectural tradition, including New York-born Bernard Maybeck.

Maybeck served temporarily as Professor of Geometry and informally as Professor of Architecture at the University of California, but he lost the position in 1901 to another New Yorker, John Galen Howard. Subsequently, Maybeck designed Bay Area residences and evolved a personal approach that integrated traditional styles with natural materials, unpainted shingle exteriors with lightly-tinted accents, and integrating living space with landscape in the Asian manner. He also harmonized industrial products—steel, asbestos,

The Ultimate Bungalow

Greene and Greene's Gamble House, completed in Pasadena in 1908. *Photograph by Richard J. Orsi.*

and cast concrete—with past architectural traditions and natural elements, exemplified in his 1910 design for Berkeley's Christian Science Church. His major contribution to public architecture is the sole survivor of the 1915 Panama-Pacific Exposition, the San Francisco Palace of Fine Arts, permanently rebuilt after the original structure deteriorated. In addition, Maybeck taught and encouraged such students as Julia Morgan, the first woman to receive an engineering degree from the University of California (1894), the first to graduate in architecture from the Ecole des Beaux Arts in Paris (1902), and the first woman licensed to practice architecture in California (1904).

When Morgan established her own firm in San Francisco, she was a competent civil engineer who undertook and supervised projects such as rebuilding the Fairmont Hotel, gutted in the disaster of 1906. But

Morgan was more. A master of architectural traditions, she expressed them in her Spanish treatment of buildings on the Mills College campus, in her application of Tudor Revival, Moorish, and Mediterranean elements to Piedmont residences, in the Renaissance design of the Oakland YMCA building, in the Neo-Classical facade of a gymnasium on the UC Berkeley campus, and in William Randolph Hearst's eclectic mélange at San Simeon, *La Cuesta Encantada*, more popularly known as "Hearst's Castle." To each style she added her own sense of line, form, mass, and proportion. Until she retired in 1950, Morgan continued to evolve new principles that produced unobtrusive exteriors blended with landscape and open, functional interiors bathed in light. Along with her teacher and friend Maybeck, Morgan was a major influence on the development of a recognizable California architectural aesthetic.

"The Migrant Mother"

In her famous work, "The Migrant Mother," photographer Dorothea Lange captured the suffering endured by many newcomers seeking California's "promised land" during the Great Depression. *From "Migrant Mother Collection" by Dorothea Lange, Library of Congress, #LC-USF34-9058-C.*

PART SEVEN

California Between the Wars

1920–1940

As modern California emerged from the progressive era and World War I, important economic transformations and dramatic population changes were under way. New thriving industries in oil and motion pictures turned Los Angeles into a booming manufacturing city just as a new migration brought hundreds of thousands of residents to the region. To keep the boom going, southern California boosters successfully reached out for distant water and hydroelectric power supplies. The decade after World War I was one of rapid economic development, marked by the evolution of modern, large-scale business organizations and the pervasive influence of the automobile. Many of the new migrants were conservative Midwestern Protestant Republicans who strengthened the political base for the fundamentalist, nativist, and prohibition movements that characterized the 1920s. They flocked to hear the evangelist Aimee Semple McPherson, who, in spite of her own tumultuous personal life, understood and comforted them.

When the boom of the 1920s went bust, few were more devastated than the migrants, whose dreams were shattered by the Great Depression. Sister Aimee led them in fending for themselves and in helping others when state and local assistance proved inadequate. And although Towsendites, the Technocracy movement, the Utopians, and Upton Sinclair all had ready answers to the economic disaster, it was the New Deal that had the greatest impact on the state, as the administration of President Franklin D. Roosevelt attempted to pull the nation out of the worst depression it had ever known. The New Deal's programs were designed to provide relief for the unemployed and stimulate the economy. They involved the state in huge public construction projects and a myriad of smaller works involving actors, writers, artists, and musicians. At the same time, the New Deal threw the weight of the federal government behind labor's long-time demand for the right to organize and bargain collectively with employers, making the decade one of the most important in California labor history. The 1930s ended with the state's businesses and agriculture struggling out of the depression as a new world war began.

Super Sister

Aimee Semple McPherson in Los Angeles

In the late 1920s Carl Sandburg made the laconic observation that "God once took the country by Maine as the handle, gave it a good shake, and all the loose nuts and bolts rolled down to Southern California." Many Americans probably shared this view, regarding Los Angeles in particular as a haven for faddists, fanatics, and fakes. The scene of sometimes scandalous Hollywood goings-on and a refuge for countless religious cults, the city had more than its fair share of flamboyant personalities, but few can compare with Aimee Semple McPherson, evangelist supreme. From her arrival in Los Angeles in 1918 to her death in 1944, "Sister Aimee" preached her novel brand of religious revivalism to literally millions and had a remarkable impact on the city. McPherson made the front pages of the major Los Angeles newspapers an average of three times a week for nearly ten years, and appeared almost as frequently in the rest of the nation's press. One columnist called her "the most original, exciting, and newsworthy space-getter in the land." Aimee's experiences in Los Angeles also tell us a great deal about Angelenos and their times.

After years of traveling the country as an itinerant revivalist preacher, Aimee Semple McPherson arrived in Los Angeles in December 1918 with her mother and two children and, she enjoyed saying later, "one hundred dollars and a tambourine." From these humble beginnings, she managed, in the next five years, to build a 5,300-seat temple, organize her own Church of the Foursquare Gospel, and found the first religious radio station in the United States. She attracted a congregation of 10,000, estimated to be the largest in the world, and established branch churches, called "Lighthouses," all over the country and overseas. Her congregation was organized into departments that provided music, players for dramatizations of her sermons, community services of all kinds, and missionaries who spread the Foursquare Gospel throughout the world.

"Sister," as she was known to her followers, became a major influence in the life of the city. She had a shrewd instinct for publicity and adopted attention-getting methods, such as scattering leaflets announcing her services from an airplane. Her sermons were vaudeville-style theatrical productions, sneered at by her critics as "supernatural whoopee." But even her detractors had to agree that she put on "the best show in town." An honorary member of the police department, honorary battalion chief of the fire department, and member of the Chamber of Commerce, she was constantly in the news. Then, one day in May 1926, Aimee Semple McPherson disappeared.

During that spring the 35-year-old McPherson had begun regular excursions to swim at Ocean Park beach. On May 18, accompanied by her secretary, Emma Schaffer, she drove to the shore and spent the afternoon alternately swimming in the ocean and writing a new sermon on the beach. At about 3:30, Schaffer could not find McPherson and waited nearly an hour for her friend to return from the sea. At last, thoroughly frightened, Schaffer called McPherson's mother to report her daughter's disappearance. By nightfall the news had flashed through the city. Newspaper "extras" blanketed the area, Aimee's mother publicly announced her daughter had drowned, and thousands crowded Angelus Temple and Ocean Park beach in a state of shock. For the next three days McPherson's faithful followers, joined by droves of curious onlookers, watched and prayed while police, lifeguards, airplanes and divers sought the evangelist's body.

Who was this person who could create such a commotion? One of Aimee Semple McPherson's favorite sermons was "The Story of My Life," and she told it with a riveting eloquence that always held her audiences spellbound. Born on October 9, 1890, on a farm in Ontario, Canada, she was the daughter of Mildred and James Kennedy. Her mother, eventually known to millions as Minnie or "Ma Kennedy," had long been active in the Salvation Army and dedicated Aimee to that cause. The child demonstrated a strong will, a flair for the dramatic, and unusual leadership qualities. When teased at school one day about her Salvation Army background, she quickly took charge of the situation. Soon she had

the children following her around the schoolyard in a Salvation Army parade. A natural actress, she loved to be the center of attention and delighted in starring roles in school plays.

As a teenager, Aimee's interest in dancing, movies, and ragtime music brought her into conflict with her mother. Minnie's world had no place for such frivolities, and many a stormy scene resulted. James Kennedy, some 30 years older than his wife, was more tolerant, but the domineering Minnie usually prevailed. When a new Pentecostal mission came to town and the 17-year-old Aimee asked to attend its meetings, her mother would not allow it. Minnie frowned on speaking in tongues and other physical manifestations of the power of the Spirit, the hallmark of the Pentecostalists. "Shouters" and "Holy Rollers," she called them. But Aimee persuaded her father to take her to the mission, and on her first visit she was captivated by the handsome preacher.

Robert Semple, a tall, dark-haired young man with intense blue eyes, had a dramatic style that held enormous attraction for Aimee. She began sneaking away from school to attend his meetings and one day "fell under the Power" in an exciting conversion experience. Before long she realized that she was in love with Robert, and he with her. After a brief courtship, they were married in the summer of 1908 and lived for a short time in Stratford, Ontario. Although they were poor, Aimee was supremely happy. She adored Robert, reveled in her position as the preacher's wife, and perhaps for the only time in her life willingly submitted to the will of another. Robert spoke often of going to China as an evangelist and Aimee shared his enthusiasm. In 1910, after several months of work as evangelists in Chicago missions, they financed their voyage to Hong Kong through collections taken at farewell meetings with Robert's parishioners. But the excitement and novelty of missionary work among the Chinese soon turned to disaster. Within months of arriving in China, Robert contracted malaria and died. One month after Robert's death, Aimee gave birth to a daughter, Roberta, and six weeks later, in January 1911, the two were on their way back to America.

Lonely and dispirited, she drifted aimlessly among east coast missions until she married Harold McPherson, a middle-class businessman. This marriage, which she later admitted had been an effort to provide a home for Roberta, was not a happy one, and Aimee became seriously depressed. Even the birth of a son, Rolf Kennedy McPherson, failed to revive her spirits. Her condition worsened until she found herself near death following an operation. At this point, she was fond of telling her audiences, she heard a nurse say, "She's going," and then God called her to go out and "preach the Word":

> Just before losing consciousness, as I hovered between life and death, came the voice of my Lord, so loud that it startled me: "Now-will-you-go?" And I knew it was "Go," one way or the other. . . . And with my little remaining strength, I managed to gasp: "Yes—Lord—I'll—go."

Then, Aimee recalled, "the Lord poured such strength into me that within a few days I was able to be up and go home." Within a short time, she was on her way to Canada, leaving Harold McPherson behind. Aimee joined her parents in Canada in the summer of 1915 and spent the next few months attending a Pentecostal camp meeting nearby. One day, when asked to preach at Mount Forest, a small local town, she set out to conduct the first revival meeting of her new career.

Despite the eagerness with which Aimee prepared her first sermon she found herself facing only a handful of people and a great many empty chairs. When the next night brought the same scant audience, she set out to fill the hall. Picking up a chair, she strode down the main street to the center of town, put her chair down, and stood on it. Arms outstretched, eyes closed, and standing motionless, she began to pray. Curious passersby stopped and stared at her, and soon a crowd gathered. All at once Aimee snapped open her eyes, jumped down, and shouted, "Quick! Follow me!" Snatching up her chair, she raced back to the meeting hall and through the doors with the crowd at her heels. "Shut the doors; don't let anyone out," she ordered the ushers and launched into her sermon. The crowd loved it. "From that day to this," she would later tell her congregations, "I've always preached to crowds."

With her first "offering," as she called the money collected at her meetings, she bought a tent and went from town to town holding revival meetings. As her career progressed she bought bigger tents to hold hundreds of people, and a touring car on which she painted, "Jesus Is Coming Soon—Get Ready" and "Where Will You Spend Eternity?" Traveling from New York to Florida and back, she preached to whites and blacks, often together. She became an expert at pitching tents in the wind, driving stakes with a heavy maul. She founded a small religious magazine, *The Bridal Call*, and sold subscriptions at her meetings, forming a network of helpers wherever she went. In the face of frequent harassment, she preached a message of love and joy, and she always preached to crowds.

Harold McPherson joined Aimee for a time as her business manager, but detested the itinerant life. They separated again in 1917 and were divorced in 1921. Aimee turned to her mother for help, forming a stormy partnership that took them both to the pinnacle of success. Minnie Kennedy joined the caravan in Florida in the winter of 1917 and, blessed with a fine instinct for business, soon had their financial affairs in order.

In 1918 the caravan traveled north again. In New York, little Roberta was stricken with the deadly influenza then sweeping the country. Frightened by the near loss of her daughter, McPherson decided to take her family west to a more healthful climate. She headed for Los Angeles in a large touring car with her mother, the two children, and a woman companion. McPherson, who did the driving, was probably the first woman to drive across the United States, a considerable accomplishment in an era when roads were almost non-existent and tires in constant need of repair. Towns were few and far between; at times they crossed vast empty stretches with the aid of a compass. Often they had to clear boulders and fallen trees from the road in order to pass. Sometimes in mud to the hub caps, sometimes in snow, the three women and two children made their lonely way from New York through the Southwest to California, holding revival meetings in the towns and camping out between settlements. Through it all McPherson remained cheerfully undaunted, a pillar of strength to her family. It was an experience many of her followers could identify with, and they never tired of hearing her tell it in her dramatic way.

McPherson and her family arrived in Los Angeles shortly before Christmas, 1918. Already famous, she was immediately invited to preach to a local congregation. She recognized that people were tired of the Calvinist style of preaching and of being told they were damned and destined for hell, so instead adopted an affectionate, anecdotal style, preaching an emotional, charismatic revivalism that emphasized love and hope. Aware that her followers longed for a cheerful, positive religion she would say, "Who cares about old Hell, friends? Let's forget about Hell. Lift up your hearts. What we are interested in, yes Lord, is *Heaven* and how to get *there*." As one writer later commented, "Calvin must have turned over in his grave."

Aimee Semple McPherson achieved instantaneous success in Los Angeles. She shrewdly observed that a steady stream of God-fearing Midwesterners flowing into Southern California promised a constantly growing audience, and decided to put down roots. By 1921 she had such a large and devoted Los Angeles following that when she mentioned wistfully in her sermons her family's need for a home, they quickly volunteered to build her one. "The house that God built," as McPherson called it, was her first piece of property.

From 1916 to 1921 Sister Aimee became famous for her successful faith-healing. Always a secondary part of her service, healing nevertheless stole the show when she held a revival in San Diego in the summer of 1921. For years the sick had congregated in the seaside city, hoping to return to health in its balmy climate (and giving it an astonishingly high death and suicide rate). When McPherson appeared, they swarmed around her in such numbers that she finally consented to hold a special meeting in Balboa Park devoted to healing only. Nearly 15,000 people jammed the place, requiring special squads of police to manage the crowd, while the sick and disabled "fell over one another in their rush to the platform—in chairs, in litters, in wheelbarrows, or staggering on foot." For two days McPherson administered to them, "laying on hands" and praying fervently, as countless miraculous "cures" amazed onlookers. Overnight she became a sensation, and the local press dubbed her the "Miracle Woman." For several years, much of McPherson's ministry was devoted to faith-healing until 1923, when her emphasis shifted. Never comfortable with what she could not control, McPherson insisted that the cures were really the work of God and that she was merely His instrument.

At about this time McPherson had begun to enunciate the basic tenets of her religious beliefs more clearly. She called her theology the Foursquare Gospel—belief in the literal infallibility of the Bible, conversion, physical healing through faith, and the return of Christ to earth. Yet she remained essentially an itinerant preacher: she had no real church of her own, just thousands of passionately devoted followers held together by her little magazine, now called *The Foursquare Monthly*, and by the power of her personality. She began to dream of building her own tabernacle, where her people could be organized into a more permanent denomination, and where they might become a permanent source of income, enabling her at last to give up the itinerant life. They had built her a house, so why shouldn't they build her a church? The design for a great temple began forming in her mind.

With $5,000 her mother had managed to save through tight-fisted management, McPherson bought a pie-shaped piece of property across from Echo Park, where the trolley lines met in the fastest-growing section of Los Angeles, and ordered the foundations begun for her tabernacle. Then she set out on another of her frequent whirlwind tours of the country to raise a building fund. Using every enticement at her command, McPherson accumulated the funds that kept construction going. When not out raising funds, she was on the site leading volunteer workers in prayer and directing the design and construction of what she now called Angelus Temple.

Almost unnoticed by Angelenos in the building boom of the times, the structure rose through 1922 at Echo Park. On January 1, 1923, McPherson formally dedicated the temple to the cause of worldwide evangelism. To architects the structure was a monstrosity, but to Sister Aimee and her followers it was glorious: a huge white building shaped like a wedge of cake, with a large stage at the point and several sections (including two spacious balconies) fanning out from the stage. Along the sides of the temple were stained-glass windows designed by McPherson. The ceiling was a large shallow dome painted sky blue and speckled with glass stars. The stage lighting rivaled that of the most modern theaters. Adjoining the temple was a large, luxurious home, known as the "parsonage," that housed Aimee and her family. The entire project cost more than $1 million (roughly $14.5 million in 2018 dollars).

Construction of Angelus Temple was a turning point for McPherson. Her prodigious energies could now be concentrated in one location. The results were remarkable. She organized her followers into the Church of the Foursquare Gospel with 24 departments. Temple workers answered telephones around the clock, to minister to the troubled and lonely; the City Sisters provided childcare, distributed food to the needy, and tended the sick; the Brotherhood helped ex-convicts find jobs. The Children's Church, the Bible School, and an evening school for working-class men reached other members of the congregation, while teams of the faithful prayed 24 hours a day, year after year, in a Tower of Prayer. Everyone who joined the Foursquare Gospel Association had something to do, even if only typing for the *Monthly* or ushering at services. In return, Sister Aimee gave her people the sense of purpose and personal importance they craved in the complex, impersonal society of Los Angeles in the 1920s. And she gave them a good time as well.

With the assistance of Thompson Eade, a former vaudeville performer, McPherson wrote, produced, and starred in lavishly staged illustrated sermons. Each one featured a large choir and orchestra, dozens of actors costumed by the Western Costume Corporation (which also supplied all the major movie studios), and McPherson, engulfed in flowers. Writing for *Harper's* magazine, Sarah Comstock described a visit to the temple:

Aimee Semple McPherson and Converts

A regular feature of Sister Aimee's services included individuals possessed with "the spirit" clapping, shouting, and flopping on the floor. Many, overcome with emotion, had to be assisted by her helpers. *Courtesy of The Bancroft Library, University of California, Berkeley.*

. . . in this unique house of worship called Angelus Temple in the city of Los Angeles the Almighty occupies a secondary position. He plays an important part in the drama to be sure but the center stage is taken and held by Mrs. McPherson. It is in her praise that the band blares, that flowers are piled high, that applause splits the air. It is to see her and hear her that throngs travel, crushed in the aisles of electric cars, thrust, elbow, and bruise one another as they shove at the doors of her Temple. . . . Over the great lower floor and two balconies attendants are hurrying to seat the mob, a full hour before the entrance of the star. Men and women stand against the wall, they sit upon the steps of the aisles, and still, when the final whistle blows, there are thousands turned away, thousands who stand for two, three, four hours on the street in the nearby park, to listen to the concert and the inspired utterances as they scream themselves forth from the loud-speaker outside the building. . . . Aimee Semple McPherson is staging, month after month and even year after year, the most perennially successful show in the United States.

In 1924 Temple members raised $75,000 to build a powerful radio station (over $1,000,000 in 2018 dollars), and thereafter McPherson's services were broadcast each night to thousands of listeners over station KFSG (Kall-Four-Square-Gospel), only the third radio station founded in Los Angeles. McPherson became the first woman to hold an FCC broadcaster's license.

By the end of 1925 McPherson was at the peak of her success. She had the largest Christian congregation in the world; its contributions made her a millionaire. She was a national figure and often called the "world's greatest evangelist." In the three years since the dedication of Angelus Temple, McPherson had made it the center of a network that spanned the globe. She had survived the animosity of rival preachers who saw their parishioners drifting to Angelus Temple, and the sneers of detractors who called her services "a sensuous debauch served up in the name of religion." McPherson had also survived petty politics and factionalism within her organization resulting from her success and Minnie's heavy-handed control of church funds. But beneath her ebullient, vivacious surface Sister Aimee was not altogether happy.

Day after day McPherson made the monotonous walk from house to temple and back again. At the height of her success she was experiencing a star's loneliness. She had no close friends and her dream-come-true, Angelus Temple, was beginning to seem like a prison. It was then that the voice of Kenneth Ormiston, her radio engineer, took on new meaning for her. Each night when she broadcast her sermons, she talked to Ormiston by telephone from the stage while the choir sang or some other group performed. He would advise her how the program was going over the radio and would give her encouragement and support. "You have done splendidly tonight," he would say, or "Your voice sounds as if you are tired tonight, Mrs. McPherson." More and more she began to feel that he was the only one in the world who cared about her as a person, and their conversations became more personal. Soon they were spending time alone together in the broadcasting studio of the temple.

Minnie Kennedy was frightened by this turn of events. A shrewd bargainer, domineering, undiplomatic, and sharp-tongued, she had relentlessly fought her way to economic security. The Echo Park Association had been incorporated to hold all she had managed to retain of the prodigious sums McPherson raised at her meetings. The temple, the parsonage, and all other church properties were mortgage-free and belonged to Kennedy and McPherson. Thousands of dollars were collected weekly, and Kennedy reveled in this financial success. ("Only quiet money tonight, folks," McPherson would sometimes say during a collection. "Sister has a headache.") Now this security was threatened. The acoustics in the temple were so fine that, even with the choir singing, some of McPherson's giggling telephone conversations with Ormiston (a married man) had been overheard in the balcony. People were beginning to ask questions. Worried about a possible scandal, Kennedy scolded and nagged her daughter.

Then one day in January 1926, Kenneth Ormiston quit his job at Angelus Temple and dropped from sight. At about the same time, McPherson left Los Angeles to tour the Holy Land. A few weeks later Kennedy heard a rumor that Ormiston had joined McPherson in Europe. Terrified, she cabled this news to her daughter. Soon afterward, Ormiston casually appeared at the temple "to advise on the radio operation" and then drifted off again. When McPherson returned she settled into her old routine and Minnie heaved a sigh of relief. All seemed well—except that McPherson took to staying in a hotel at the beach in order, she said, to avoid the noise and dust from construction of the new five-story Bible College next door. And she began to demand more money. Under strong pressure from her daughter, Kennedy finally agreed that the collection taken on the first Sunday of each month, usually several thousand dollars, would go directly to McPherson, without being counted and with no questions asked. McPherson pocketed the money, and, as the weather warmed, began to go for a regular swim at the beach—until she disappeared that day in May.

For five weeks Minnie Kennedy tried to carry on the work of the temple, but she was tormented by secret suspicions as to why Sister Aimee had vanished, and by a press openly suspicious about the absence of her body. Swarms of journalists investigated McPherson's disappearance as the two great rival Los Angeles newspapers, the *Times* and Hearst's *Examiner*, competed for scoops. Reporters dug out Ormiston's name and spread rumors that McPherson had run off with him or that her disappearance was a publicity stunt. Hoping to offset these allegations, Kennedy offered a $25,000 reward for her daughter's safe return.

On June 23, 1926, five weeks after her disappearance, Aimee Semple McPherson suddenly surfaced in the small Mexican border town of Agua Prieta near Tucson, Arizona, with a dramatic story of having escaped from kidnappers. She was immediately taken to a hospital across the border, where Los Angeles police interviewed her and reporters mobbed her. McPherson told them that two men and a woman had seized her on May 18 through a ruse—asking her to administer to a sick

Aimee Outside Preaching
Evangelist Aimee Semple McPherson (far right, standing with raised arms), c. 1930. *Everett Collection / Alamy Stock Photo.*

baby—and that two of them had held her in a shack in the desert until her escape. She estimated she had wandered 15 or 20 miles in the scorching heat before finding help in Agua Prieta. The next day Minnie Kennedy and McPherson's two children arrived for a tearful reunion while the world hummed with the news.

On June 26 McPherson returned by train to Los Angeles, where her reception surpassed any before seen in that city. No foreign monarch, no president, no national hero had ever evoked such an outpouring of emotion. Airplanes rained rose petals from the air, city police carried her regally from the train station to her automobile in a sedan chair, and youngsters flung down a carpet of flowers in her path. Perhaps 100,000 people lined the streets for McPherson's triumphal cavalcade home. Within minutes of her arrival at Angelus Temple,

she was on stage, recounting the story of her kidnapping to her nearly hysterical followers.

Exciting and dramatic, the story lacked but one thing—credibility. From the moment Sister Aimee met police investigators and the press in Arizona, they began asking questions that made their skepticism clear. They demanded to know why she had not immediately asked for water after wandering miles across the hot desert, why her clothes showed no signs of perspiration, why her shoes were not scuffed. They wanted explanations for reports that she had been seen in a car resembling that of Kenneth Ormiston, who had also seemingly dropped out of sight. Further doubt was cast on her story by failure to locate the shack she claimed had been her prison for weeks. To her dismay, McPherson found the attention of the investigation focused more on the veracity of her statements than on the apprehension of the kidnappers. By the time she met her followers at Angelus Temple following her return to Los Angeles, McPherson was heaping scorn on her doubters and demanding that authorities redouble their efforts to find the criminals.

Had Aimee Semple McPherson left the matter where it was and turned away the reporters who hounded her every step, the affair might have eventually died from lack of interest. But, staking everything on the credibility of her story, she embarked on another tour of the country, demanding vindication from an increasingly skeptical public. In the process she set into motion a chain of events that resulted in sensational court hearings that tarnished her image. When it was all over, Sister Aimee was no longer Mrs. McPherson the great evangelist. To the world she was just "Aimee."

Her demand for vindication and pressure from competing clergy as well as the Chamber of Commerce finally goaded the district attorney, Asa Keyes, to action. A Los Angeles grand jury was called to look into the case and McPherson made a dramatic appearance before it. It found "insufficient evidence to warrant an indictment," meaning her story was unconvincing. McPherson, however, claimed she had been vindicated and seemed to want the matter laid to rest. But aggressive reporters, not willing to let a good story die, continued to dig into the case until at last they unearthed evidence that Kenneth Ormiston had spent ten days at the little resort town of Carmel-by-the-Sea, near Monterey, with a woman whom residents identified as McPherson. Experts identified the handwriting on grocery slips as hers, and the case became a sensation again. The sleepy village of Carmel, with its sand streets, artsy atmosphere, and reclusive citizenry, was immediately overrun by newspapermen asking questions and sightseers looking for the "love cottage," while McPherson's rival evangelists demanded a new inquiry. The grand jury was again called into session and strange things began to happen. A female grand juror took the damaging grocery slips into the restroom and they disappeared; secret files of the police vanished; the prosecuting attorney and chief investigator were removed from the case; and when members of the grand jury tried to cover up their destruction of evidence, they were dismissed in disgrace.

Meanwhile the case went on. In September, McPherson, Kennedy, and Ormiston were indicted for corruption of public morals, obstruction of justice, and conspiracy to manufacture evidence, and the grand jury hearings became a spectacle and the talk of the town. On November 3, after six exhausting weeks, the presiding judge wearily ordered McPherson and her co-defendants to stand trial in January 1927. City editors gleefully contemplated a long one. During November and December, however, the prosecutor's case crumbled and the case was dismissed. Through it all McPherson's story was the only one that did not change.

It was not surprising, as Carey McWilliams later wrote, that the controversial story of McPherson's disappearance became "one of the great news stories of the decade":

> It contained . . . all the right ingredients: sex, mystery, underworld characters, kidnappers, the ocean, hot desert sands, an escape, and a thrilling finale. It was a story made for the period, a period that invested the trivial with a special halo, that magnified the insipid, that pursued cheap sensationalism with avidity and passion. While admittedly quite a story, the "kidnapping" of Sister Aimee became invested with the proportions of a myth and the dimensions of a saga in the great vacuum of the age.

The end of the kidnap case did not take Aimee Semple McPherson out of the headlines however. For the next ten years major Los Angeles newspapers assigned reporters to cover McPherson, her family, and temple activities full-time. Kennedy and McPherson were, each in her own way, masters at using the press for publicity, while the press had learned how to use the Angelus Temple to sell newspapers. It was a convenient relationship, and one that lasted into the mid-1930s as McPherson weathered one crisis after another.

In 1927 McPherson set out to break free once and for all from Kennedy's domination, bluntly informing her mother that she was going to take over control of all temple affairs. Kennedy resisted but her daughter won by threatening to resign as pastor if she did not have her way. Reluctantly, Kennedy retired with a settlement that assured her an income of $10,000 a year, after a church reorganization that gave McPherson absolute control of its religious and business affairs.

Unfortunately, Kennedy had been right. McPherson lacked business sense and her managers involved her in one fiasco after another. One was a proposal to sell burial plots in a "Blessed Hope Memorial Park" cemetery, the closer the plot to Sister Aimee's, the higher the price. "Buy a Grave and Go Up with Aimee," was reportedly the slogan. One after another of these schemes collapsed, leaving McPherson with a myriad of lawsuits for breach of contract and a steady stream of court appearances.

McPherson's effort to upgrade her appearance under the glare of the public spotlight also became an issue. In her early years in Los Angeles, she had adopted as her normal public attire a blue cape over a white dress that resembled a nurse's uniform, prompting one reporter to describe her as "robust and motherly." Gradually, however, McPherson shed the motherly image and developed into a glamorous figure, slim and elegantly dressed. This and other changes brought her into conflict with her mother when Kennedy returned to the Temple to try to salvage the business organization.

A number of Lighthouses seceded, producing more negative publicity. In 1930 McPherson's iron constitution finally gave way and she suffered a nervous breakdown. By 1931 she had recovered sufficiently to elope with David Hutton, who sang in the choir and had been giving her singing lessons. But two years later they separated and, in 1934, they quietly obtained a divorce.

Despite her personal problems, McPherson began to throw her great energy into alleviating the distress of the Great Depression. Los Angeles teemed with retired farmers and trades people who had been ruined by the economy's collapse after 1929. State, county, and city relief funds were pitifully inadequate to deal with the suffering as the crisis deepened. By 1931 there were 200,000 unemployed in Los Angeles alone. For most of the early 1930s, McPherson's Los Angeles followers were everywhere, giving Depression victims aid and sustenance. In November 1931 she opened her first soup kitchen, serving meals to all who came. Soon she opened another, which served 5,000 persons a day. When the school system could no longer serve pupils hot lunches, Sister Aimee took over. Her City Sisters cared for people all over the Los Angeles basin. McPherson enlisted the police and fire departments to distribute clothing to the destitute, established a free medical and dental clinic, staffed by dozens of volunteer doctors and dentists, and a school to train practical nurses, especially in the care of the malnourished young and elderly. She cajoled and pressured ranchers, meatpackers, business groups, and grocers into donating supplies, then talked truckers into delivering goods free of charge. McPherson even persuaded the federal government to open an unused army camp east of Los Angeles to 25,000 unemployed, providing them a place to live and grow their own food.

The huge relief effort, and her own personal troubles, took a toll. McPherson was frequently ill and periodically went on a tour or a cruise to regain her health, only to become embroiled in another crisis on her return. All the while, she continued to design, organize, and

The Glamorous Aimee

By the 1930s the "glamorous" Aimee had appeared. She loved fine clothes and rarely appeared without a corsage pinned to her dress. Her followers took great pride in her chic appearance. *Everett Collection / Alamy Stock Photo.*

produce sermons that surpassed the spectacles offered in local theaters. But by the mid-1930s McPherson was becoming obsessed with a fear that others were conspiring to take control of Angelus Temple away from her, a fear that drove her into her last great conflict—this time with her daughter, Roberta, and another evangelist, Rheba Crawford. The conflict eventually led McPherson to dismiss both women, in a messy disagreement that, as usual, landed in court. In 1937 Roberta Semple won a libel suit against her mother's attorney, and McPherson, who had no heart for further legal maneuvering, settled with Crawford out of court. This left the disheartened Sister Aimee with only her son, Rolf, to support her in temple affairs.

After this episode Aimee Semple McPherson faded from the headlines. By then both she and the press seemed to agree that the public had become satiated with her antics. Besides, world affairs were pushing frivolous matters from the front page. The vacuum filled by McPherson and those like her was now occupied by concerns such as the Spanish Civil War, Japan's attack on China, and mounting fears of Hitler. McPherson quietly rebuilt her church, expanding the number of Lighthouses nationwide, while her son took over her business affairs. When World War II came, McPherson made numerous appearances to conduct revival meetings for servicemen and to sell war bonds. In late September 1944, she traveled with Rolf to hold a revival meeting in Oakland, where she filled the auditorium with 10,000 enthusiastic people. The next morning Rolf found her near death in her bed, sleeping pills spilled around her. By midmorning she was dead. Doctors reported that the barbiturates she had taken had probably led to loss of memory, confusion, and an accidental overdose. Sister Aimee's last front-page headline, "Aimee Is Dead," appeared in the newspapers on September 27, as Rolf hurried to Los Angeles to arrange her funeral. The temple overflowed with grief-stricken followers praying and wailing in disbelief, while newspapers printed long obituaries inadequate to explain her life.

Fifty thousand mourners filed past the bronze casket where McPherson lay dressed in her temple uniform, with a Bible bound in white satin clasped in her hands. The temple was so filled with flowers that five carloads were turned away unloaded, and, when Rolf cried out for a rededication to carry on McPherson's work, congregants surged to their feet, hands upraised in the gesture of joy she had taught them. Aimee Semple McPherson was buried on Sunrise Slope at Forest Lawn Memorial Park on her 54th birthday, October 9, 1944.

Through her long, sensational career, many of McPherson's contemporaries shrugged her off as one of the "loose nuts" that had rolled down to Southern California. To them, she symbolized the frivolous and trivial aspects of the times, while to her devoted followers, and those who benefited from her depression-era relief work, McPherson represented hope and a cheerful, active religious faith.

From the vantage point of history, the story of Aimee Semple McPherson's life can be viewed not only as the story of a colorful, dynamic personality, but of a colorful, dynamic age propelled, like McPherson, by a restless and capricious energy. Sister Aimee's venturesome coast-to-coast drive across primitive roads in 1918 was the precursor of an historic, and equally speculative, automobile migration that brought hundreds of thousands of new residents to California in the 1920s and '30s. Her lavish productions in the extravagant Angelus Temple paralleled increasingly lavish productions in Hollywood, as the movie industry prospered and expanded. Her establishment of the first religious radio station marked the dawn of the radio era and a turning point in American popular culture. The ease with which McPherson attracted huge crowds and dominated newspaper headlines testified to the cultural vacuity of the period. Yet, when times turned suddenly dark and challenging McPherson, like most of Californians, turned her energies to coping with the depression and, later, supporting the war effort. McPherson's death near the end of World War II coincided closely with the end of one age and the start of another. When the war was over, the California Sister Aimee had known would be no more.

Prosperity and the Rise of Southern California

20

W hen Aimee Semple McPherson drove her battered Oldsmobile into Los Angeles, enormous changes were underway in California. In the next decade, nearly two million Americans followed her west, two-thirds of them settling south of the Tehachapis. By 1930 the state's population center had shifted to Southern California, Los Angeles had emerged as the dominant city of the west, and the region symbolized California as an Eden—an image that persists.

From 1880 to 1920 there developed in the south what Kevin Starr calls a kind of "Southern California Raj—an orchestration of business, financial, political and governmental power, all of it controlled by one oligarchy." It was this private elite that had the vision and power to acquire for Southern California, especially Los Angeles, the resources permitting the region's spectacular growth. In the 1920s this meant the development of water, oil, gas, and hydroelectric power, supporting a new manufacturing economy with transportation and labor policies agreeable to the business community. The huge real estate boom that followed built the "decentralized" city and underwrote the industries that made Los Angeles a major manufacturing center. Meanwhile, urban competition for federal military facilities helped put California at the center of the nation's post–World War II military-industrial complex.

Water and Power for Growth

Migration to the arid south at a rate not yet seen in the state revived the search for water, and two new projects emerged: extension of the Owens Valley aqueduct to the Mono Lake watershed (completed in 1941), and the Boulder Canyon Project on the Colorado River, which was linked to development of the Imperial Valley.

The Salton Sink, 150 miles southeast of Los Angeles, was part of a large arid basin, much of it below sea level, with a thick layer of fertile soil and a great potential for agriculture that required only water. In 1896 Charles R. Rockwood and George Chaffey incorporated as the California Development Company (CDC), intending to cut into the Colorado River north of the border and, by agreement with the Mexican government, turn water from the river into the Alamo, an ancient flood channel running south of the border, then north into California. In June 1901 the first water arrived, and over the next eight months 400 miles of canals and laterals were built, 100,000 acres were prepared for cultivation, and the area gained the more attractive name "Imperial Valley."

Unfortunately, the CDC cut into the wily Colorado without adequate protections against high flood levels. In 1905 an extremely heavy runoff broke through the company's flimsy wooden head gates, turning the entire flow of the Colorado into the Alamo. For 16 months the river emptied directly into the Salton Sink, creating the Salton Sea at the north end of the Imperial Valley, submerging the tracks of the Southern Pacific's New Orleans line, and flooding towns and hundreds of farms. The CDC went bankrupt trying to control the river, and its assets were eventually taken over by the Southern Pacific.

The railroad finally stopped the flow in February 1907 by dumping millions of tons of rock into the half-mile-wide break, and the development of the valley resumed. After 1917, with the financial assistance of the Southern Pacific, a newly formed Imperial Irrigation District took over CDC facilities. By 1920 425,000 acres were under cultivation in the valley. But the directors of the Imperial Irrigation District were never entirely happy with the Alamo facilities, which led to demands for an "all-American" canal on the California side of the border. Phil Swing, the water district's energetic lawyer, became the foremost advocate of this campaign.

At the same time, Arthur Powell Davis, director of the U.S. Reclamation Service, was lobbying vigorously for structures that could control the Colorado River, prevent future flooding, and impound water for irrigation. In 1919 Davis and Swing joined forces to urge Congressional approval of a high dam at Boulder Canyon, plus an all-American canal to the Imperial Valley. Representatives of states along the upper reaches of the Colorado immediately opposed the measure, afraid that the project would inhibit irrigation projects in their own states. Under a little-used section of the Constitution, Congress acknowledged the legitimacy of these fears by establishing a commission to negotiate a treaty between the involved states. Consisting of one representative from each interested state, and under the chairmanship of Secretary of Commerce Herbert Hoover, the commission met in 1921 and 1922. Together they hammered out the Colorado River Compact, an extraordinary agreement whereby the watershed of the river was divided into an upper basin (Wyoming, Colorado, Utah, and New Mexico) and a lower basin (Arizona, California, and Nevada), and the estimated average annual flow of the river, some 15 million acre-feet of water, was divided between them.

Meanwhile, Phil Swing, now a congressman, and Hiram Johnson, now a U.S. Senator, introduced legislation calling for construction of the All-American Canal with a dam at Boulder Canyon. When Arizona refused to ratify the Colorado River Compact, the Swing-Johnson bill was amended to allow Congressional approval when ratified by only six states, as long as California was one of them. The amendment further limited California's share of lower-basin water to 4.4 million acre-feet per year. The state legislature adopted this self-limiting legislation and on December 21, 1928, President Calvin Coolidge signed the Boulder Canyon Project Act into law.

Much of the support for the Swing-Johnson Act came from officials in Los Angeles, who hoped to alleviate a threatening power shortage and were also concerned by the city's perennially expanding demand for water. Studies had shown that a large storage reservoir at Boulder Canyon would allow water to be economically delivered to the greater Los Angeles area. The Metropolitan Water District (MWD), embracing Los Angeles and many surrounding communities, was created for this purpose. The district began planning for construction of Parker Dam, halfway between Needles and Blythe on the Colorado River, and for a great aqueduct to bring water 242 miles to Lake Mathews, for distribution to the cities and irrigation districts. In 1931, despite the Depression's adverse effects, MWD voters approved a $220 million bond issue for construction of the dam and aqueduct. Construction finally began in 1933, after the Reconstruction Finance Corporation, established by Congress to stimulate business activity, agreed to buy the bonds. The completed system delivered its first water in 1941. The

80-mile-long All-American Canal to the Imperial Valley was completed that same year, and a 125-mile extension to the Coachella Valley was finished in 1948.

The Boulder Canyon (Hoover) Dam and Colorado River Aqueduct were not built without a major battle over whether the new system's electric power would be dispensed by public or private hands. In the years leading up to the Boulder Canyon Project the development of hydroelectric power made major advances. In 1893 there were only four hydroelectric plants, two of them in Southern California, producing power for commercial purposes in the United States. Thirty years later California far outdistanced any other state in the production of hydroelectric energy. Yet major problems remained to be solved: huge dams and power plants had to be built, often in remote mountain areas, to store sufficient water to run turbines year-round, and means had to be found to transmit the electricity to end users. At the time, there was little thought given to potential environmental consequences.

Development of electrical utilities required large amounts of capital. A few well-financed corporations merged with or absorbed smaller companies and came to dominate the field. The 1905 merger of San Francisco Gas and Electric with California Central Gas and Electric, for example, created Pacific Gas and Electric (PG&E), eventually the state's largest utility. With additional acquisitions it continued to grow; by 1930 it served 38 northern and central California counties. By then, the second-largest consolidated utility, Southern California Edison, was serving two million people in Southern California. A few municipally owned systems were also formed in the progressive era. The largest was Los Angeles's Bureau of Power and Light, which distributed electricity throughout the city from facilities linked to the Owens Valley project.

Municipal generation, distribution, and marketing of hydroelectric power led to serious conflict between advocates of publicly owned facilities and privately held, highly profitable enterprises. In Los Angeles, that bastion of free enterprise and the open shop, ideology succumbed to the need for cheap power. Ironically, the city joined the fight to include hydroelectric power production and distribution in the Boulder Canyon project. At the same time, the major private utilities fought to restrict competition from public entities. Los Angeles obtained the power it needed for continued growth in 1930, when the Secretary of the Interior approved a contract allocating 36 percent of the Boulder Canyon dam power to the Metropolitan Water District, and gave the district first call on unused power to pump water through the Colorado Aqueduct. In addition, MWD claimed two of the four generating units at Parker Dam. An important consequence of these developments was that Los Angeles gained control over enough water and power to coerce surrounding communities into annexation with the city, ensuring them access to the resources they needed to grow.

California and the Automobile

One of the largest migrations in the history of the United States, the movement to California in the 1920s, also uniquely demonstrated the impact of the automobile on American life. The motor car was generally regarded as a rich man's toy until the 1920s, when Henry Ford's assembly-line methods brought the price of his Model T down to $280. As a result, from 1919 to 1929, automobile ownership in the U.S. increased from seven million to 23 million. Well suited to the automobile, Californians registered two million vehicles in 1929, more cars per person than any other state.

The impact of widespread automobile use on California cities was enormous. Automobiles stimulated suburban home development, dispersed business areas, and overwhelmed local rail transit systems. In Southern California, Los Angeles emerged as the first modern decentralized American city. The 1930 census revealed that the population of Los Angeles County had grown from 936,455 in 1920 to 2,208,492, the fruit of three decades of boosterism. As one observer commented: "Los Angeles has not grown; it has been conjured into existence."

Drawn by the promise of a better life, midwestern farmers, bankers, and merchants abandoned declining rural midwestern towns for Southern California, where the explosive growth in the oil, movie, and manufacturing industries—and the migration itself—stimulated property values and created new job opportunities. Legions of real estate sellers greeted the thousands of new arrivals with open arms, producing a boom reminiscent of the 1880s, as city planners approved 30 to 40 new subdivisions each week, the emphasis always on the separate single-family home rather than the row houses popular in the East. No longer bound to electric car lines, automobile owners gravitated toward the subdivisions spreading over the region like spilled milk. From one March to the next in 1923 and 1924, over 125,000 homes were built just in Los Angeles County.

Heavy speculation fueled the boom. In 1924, excursion buses lined Los Angeles streets to take sightseers out to new subdivisions for "a free ride and a free lunch." High-powered salespeople made their deals with hard-to-crack prospects in special "closing booths." To promote sales developers organized country clubs, golf clubs, swimming clubs, hunting clubs, lake clubs, trout clubs, and beach clubs. They also hired Hollywood stars to attract customers. The speculative bubble collapsed in 1925, but the steady stream of newcomers and continued home construction softened the blow. Indeed, the level of real estate activity remained high until the end of the decade, as countless acres of the famous "California bungalow" spread across the landscape.

The results surprised observers. Thousands of suburban residents driving their cars to work and shop in the downtown business district of Los Angeles snarled traffic, hurting local businesses and ruining rail transit schedules. By the mid-1920s both the Pacific Electric and the Los Angeles Railway were losing money, but neither had the capital required to establish separate rights of way, or to expand service to new suburbs. The city chose to deal with the problem by easing automobile congestion, approving traffic controls and wider streets. At the same time, the motor truck made possible the dispersal of business and manufacturing industries to suburban areas. In the long run, this decision to depend on the automobile for transportation doomed the rail transit systems and established the pattern that would one day typify modern urban/suburban development: by 1930 over half the residents of Los Angeles lived in detached single-family homes—three times the number of any other major American city—yet the city was one of the major manufacturing areas of the country.

The automobile had a similar effect on metropolitan development in Northern California, particularly in Alameda and Contra Costa counties and south of the San Francisco peninsula. As the population of cars and people grew, so too did traffic congestion. In the new suburban areas, congestion prompted freeway construction, especially after World War II. Ironically, in the 1980s, when congestion overwhelmed the freeways as well, Californians clamored for railroads, ballyhooing the superiority of mass transit systems over private automobiles.

Downtown Los Angeles, circa 1929

Downtown 7th Street in Los Angeles, in about 1929, decorated for a Shriner's convention. Note the automobile traffic and Pacific Electric cars. Auto congestion contributed to the financial decline of the Pacific Electric and its eventual replacement with bus lines. *The Huntington Library, San Marino, California.*

The increase in automobile ownership also prompted highway construction by the state. The construction industry joined the California State Automobile Association and Southern California's Automobile Club, with many wealthy and influential members, in promoting a statewide highway system. With politicians acutely aware of the new "highway lobby," the state embarked

Henry E. Huntington and the "Big Red Cars"

Southern California captivated Henry Edwards Huntington during a visit in 1892. The nephew of Southern Pacific president Collis P. Huntington had learned the intricacies of railroading and was traveling from the East to San Francisco and a new position as watchdog over the company's Pacific Coast operations. His uncle hoped that the appointment, and Henry's arranged marriage to a distant relative, would perpetuate family control over the transportation empire. It was not to be, however. Collis died in 1900, and Edward H. Harriman of the

Union Pacific bought controlling interest in the Southern Pacific.

Henry divested himself of his Southern Pacific stock and San Francisco property, bought Rancho San Marino and moved his personal and business activities south in 1901. Long intrigued by the investment potential of electric streetcars, Huntington quickly purchased scores of street-railway companies in the region. Within a few years, in partnership with the Southern Pacific, he consolidated them into the Pacific Electric Railway, the largest interurban system in the nation, serving the entire Los Angeles basin. Converting the company's entire track to standard railroad gauge allowed his "Big Red Cars" to move both people and goods efficiently among 40 cities in a radius of nearly as many miles. It was an impressive achievement that made Huntington wealthy, but not exclusively on the basis of fares and freights. He made shrewd land investments in regions soon to be penetrated by his lines, subdivided the property into housing tracts, and subsidized the company's often red-ink operation with real estate profits.

In 1910, Henry Huntington sold his share of the railway to the Southern Pacific and devoted himself to managing the rare books, manuscripts, and paintings that he was collecting at his San Marino ranch. Before he died in 1927, he had donated the estate, his magnificent collection, and much of his personal wealth to endow the Huntington Library and Art Gallery. "The Huntington" became immediately renowned as one of the state's outstanding art museums and a Mecca for the world's literary and historical scholars.

For decades after the Pacific Electric's sale and Huntington's death, the railway provided dependable, inexpensive transportation throughout the Los Angeles area. With routes that predicted freeway rights of way of later years, the Pacific Electric facilitated the region's phenomenal growth between 1910 and 1930. As late as 1945, despite increasing competition from buses and private automobiles, the "Big Red Cars" still carried more than 100 million passengers annually.

Henry Huntington at the Doors of His Library, 1920s

The Huntington Library, San Marino, California Library.

In the next decade, however, California's love affair with the automobile made the Pacific Electric obsolete. Rubber, auto, bus, petroleum, and other interests allegedly conspired to buy out and shut down the railway, but its days were numbered in any case. As automobile registrations soared, the number of streetcar passengers decreased. One by one, Pacific Electric routes ceased operation. In 1961, the last "Big Red Car" made its run on the Los Angeles-Long Beach line. Since then, neither Los Angeles nor any other California city has managed to devise a mass-transit system approaching Huntington's in reliability and economy.   (WAB) on a program of extensive road construction, financed by a large bond issue and a gasoline tax. Gas stations, hotels, motor courts, orange juice stands, and other auto-related businesses sprouted along each new road. Towns mushroomed where thoroughfares crossed, and new highways soon snaked to remote peaks and hollows.

Widespread auto ownership also stimulated tourism and recreation. As a new federal highway program tied the country together in the 1920s, touring became a popular national pastime. The lure of California's climate, natural beauty, and burgeoning cities attracted many to the Golden State, some visitors contemplating future settlement. Vacation centers such as Lake Tahoe in the north and Big Bear and Lake Arrowhead in the south led the way in resort development, and an extensive system of beaches and parks emerged, now within reach of the average car-owning family.

The automobile contributed in fascinating ways to the revolution in morals then underway. In 1919 hardly 10 percent of American automobiles were enclosed; by 1927 more than 80 percent were, prompting Pasadena's police chief to proclaim that "the greatest menace now facing the morals of Pasadena youth is the coupe and the sedan."

How Do You Say M-O-T-E-L?

A California Original

A modern motorist can scarcely imagine highways without glitzy façades and neon signs beckoning *VACANCY*; mispronouncing M-O-T-E-L is unthinkable. Yet before December 1925, when the Milestone Motel, designed by Pasadena architect Arthur S. Heineman, opened on Pacific Coast Highway near San Luis Obispo, neither circumstance was impossible. To early customers, operators—and even newspapers like the Los Angeles *Times*—had to explain the facilities and note that "motel" rhymed with "hotel."

During the 1920s, when Californians began their passionate love affair with Henry Ford's "Tin Lizzies" and more exotic machines, any excursion more ambitious than a one-day outing could become an unpredictable adventure. Overnight accommodations consisted of traditional hotels in downtown districts, occasional "auto camps," or whatever travelers might improvise by the roadside. Hotels could be inconvenient, auto camps rustic, and tent camping downright primitive. Heineman's innovation responded to the immediate needs of an increasingly mobile populace.

But it did more. Original plans projected a series of motels situated, like the Spanish missions, "a day's journey apart" along the coastal highway. That enterprise never materialized, but the Milestone Motel prospered and also introduced a word, copyrighted by Heineman, to Americans' vocabulary and an institution to the national landscape.

The Milestone Mo-Tel (later the "Motel Inn," circa 1930

Courtesy of the History Center of San Luis Obispo County.

The Milestone Motel, circa 1994

Photograph by William A. Bullough.

Motels had distinct advantages over traditional hotels. They were less formal and roadside locations eliminated searches through unfamiliar city streets. Cars waited at the traveler's door, ready to resume journeys without bothersome treks from hotels to parking garages. Laundry and eating facilities on the premises added convenience, and the Milestone, like many of its successors, provided the oil changes and other ministrations that early vehicles often demanded.

Heineman's fusion of architecture and advertising also established a permanent standard. To attract customers, the Milestone Motel's highly visible facade emulated the bell tower of Mission Santa Barbara 60 miles to the south; a less pretentious version of mission design guided hungry sojourners to the restaurant. Behind the Spanish Revival veneer, adequate guest bungalows were far less spacious or elegant than the highway vista suggested.

Over decades, motel design responded to changing architectural vogues, but Heineman's pioneer pattern—elaborate façades fronting modest accommodations—not only persisted but became ubiquitous phenomena flanking the highways of California, the nation, and the world. Despite their proliferation, lexicographers did not deem them sufficiently significant to warrant including the word "motel" in dictionaries until 1950.   (WAB)

Oil

New developments in the oil industry contributed to the popularity of the automobile and to a stronger economy, especially in Southern California. The industry also illustrated a phenomenon typical of the period: integration and consolidation of business structures. By 1911, when John D. Rockefeller's Standard Oil trust was dissolved by the U.S. Supreme Court, the newly independent Standard Oil Company of California had already become, with Union Oil, one of the state's major producers and refiners. To a lesser degree, Shell and General Petroleum were also emerging as leading companies.

Several new oil fields opened at this time, among them the highly productive Coyote Hills and Baldwin Hills fields near Los Angeles. In the San Joaquin Valley, the Kern River, Sunset, and Midway fields expanded rapidly, stimulated by western railroads' switch from coal to oil as a fuel and U.S. entry into World War I. Wartime conditions also increased emphasis on gasoline refining, for which California's crude oil, with its naturally high content of isooctane hydrocarbons, was particularly suited.

The wartime stimulus proved to be but a prelude to the golden years of the 1920s, when phenomenal fields of high-gravity oil were discovered in the Los Angeles basin. Standard Oil discovered the first field at Huntington Beach in 1920. The next year Union Oil opened the Santa Fe Springs field, and Shell tapped the fantastically rich Signal Hill site. Within three years, California crude

oil production rose from 105 million to 264 million barrels annually. Additional fields at Dominguez Hills, Torrance, Whittier, and Wilmington, along with coastline

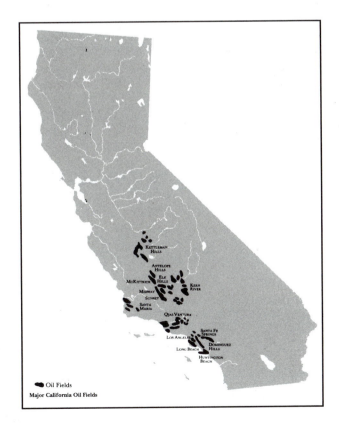

Oil Fields
Major California Oil Fields

drilling from Huntington Beach to Santa Barbara kept California the first-ranked state in oil production until the 1930s.

A frenzy of speculation in oil stocks accompanied this oil boom and led to the "Julian scandal." Chauncey C. Julian was an oil-field worker who bought oil leases, adopted a polished appearance, and mounted an advertising campaign aimed at small investors that, within a few months, produced $11 million from 40,000 subscribers, presumably to develop Julian's holdings. In 1924 the high-living speculator sold out to a couple of smooth-talking operators, S.C. Lewis and Jack Bennett, who proceeded to issue nearly five million shares of unauthorized stock in the Julian Petroleum Company and to organize stock pools attracting some of the most prominent businessmen in the region. In 1927 the overcapitalization became known, the bubble collapsed, and thousands of small investors were ruined.

The oil boom of the 1920s promoted restructuring of the industry. At first, hundreds of large and small companies produced a tidal wave of oil, overwhelming refineries and storage facilities. By 1925, however, 57 refineries processed some 186 million barrels of oil per year; by 1928 the larger companies had tank farms capable of storing more than 340 million barrels of oil, nearly a two-year supply. The flood of oil also depressed world prices, accelerating the trend toward consolidation through mergers and purchase. By 1930 an oligopolistic industry had emerged, dominated by a handful of integrated companies—Standard, Union, Shell, Tidewater-Associated, General Petroleum, Richfield, and the Texas Company—that could stabilize prices well above those of the newly opened Texas and Oklahoma fields.

The use of natural gas (a by-product of the search for oil) for heat and power evolved slowly in the 1920s. The huge expansion of oil production in the decade meant a similar increase of natural gas, but consumption was only a tiny fraction of modern-day use. Further developments would reveal natural gas as an important energy source.

The Movies

No other enterprise had as great an impact on the world's view of California as the motion picture industry. From 1896 to 1946 movies were America's most popular form of mass entertainment, and between 1916 and 1946 movie-making was the biggest industry in Southern California. With tens of thousands of employees and payrolls in the hundreds of millions of dollars, movie-making had an enormous impact on the state.

For several years after 1900 companies such as Biograph, Vitagraph, and Edison produced a multitude of one-reel movies, each 12 to 15 minutes in length. They were used primarily by storefront theaters in working-class neighborhoods that charged a nickel for admission. Nickelodeons provided a brief, cheap, and convenient form of entertainment that was popular with American workers, most of whom worked an 11- or 12-hour day, six days a week. As nickelodeons grew in number, enterprising individuals established distribution exchanges to provide them with new films, while others began to build strings of movie houses.

In 1908, Thomas A. Edison and other moviemakers organized the Motion Picture Patents Company, known as the "movie trust." Then, by pooling camera and projector patents, Edison attempted to monopolize all phases of the industry. But the Edison trust instead drove independent distributors and theater owners into movie production. A group of companies in the hands of new movie "moguls" emerged to dominate the industry. Many of the movie moguls were Jewish immigrants who had started life in America dealing in clothing, furs, rags, or jewelry. Adolph Zukor, Samuel Goldwyn, Louis B. Mayer, Marcus Loew, Jesse L. Lasky, and others built an integrated industry around a few major studios—Paramount, Fox (later 20th-Century Fox), Metro-Goldwyn-Mayer, Universal, Columbia, Warner Brothers, and RKO—and the filmmaking trade coalesced around them.

Most of the state's first movies, however, were produced by movie-trust companies. One such firm was Essanay, which made 375 Bronco Billy westerns between 1910 and 1916. Essanay had joined Charlie Chaplin's company and others at Niles, near San Francisco, before moving south to take advantage of Southern California's ideal climate. Los Angeles's open shop labor policy yielded a ready supply of cheap labor, as well as easy access to a variety of terrains that could pass for almost anywhere else in the world: deserts, snowy mountains, ocean, and islands. By 1914 more than 70 firms were producing films nearby. Most operated studios in and around the community of Hollywood, on the western outskirts of Los Angeles, which soon became the motion-picture capital of the world.

Major advances in moviemaking accompanied the move west. The short one-reel films of the early 1900s gave way to the "feature" film several reels long. Production techniques changed dramatically too. Probably the foremost filmmaker of the era was Edwin S. Porter, who in 1903 produced the classic *The Great Train Robbery*. Porter explored a wide range of now-familiar techniques, including the use of dissolves to move from one image to another, multiple shots of the same scene, side lighting, and close-ups. Twelve years later Hollywood director D.W. Griffith, in a cinematically brilliant display of the possibilities of the new medium, used all of the techniques pioneered by Porter in *The Birth of a Nation*, the nascent film industry's first blockbuster. A popular success, the three-hour feature film glorified the Ku Klux Klan as the savior of the South from the chaos of Reconstruction and depicted African Americans as a vicious, inferior race. Selling racist propaganda as a historically accurate account, Griffith's film showcased the power and influence of Hollywood to shape mainstream American values. It also promoted white supremacy. Immediately after the film's release, membership in the Klan surged, reaching 5 million nationwide by 1924. The Klan used the film as a recruiting tool for decades.

With development of the feature film, moviemakers reached out to a whole new audience, the growing American middle class. Simultaneously, the "star" system developed, as moviegoers chose favorites among heretofore anonymous actors and actresses. By 1916, star-struck youngsters and gawking tourists flocked to Hollywood, where one of their favorites, Charlie Chaplin, could successfully demand $10,000 a week from Mack Sennett's Keystone Company.

In addition to would-be stars, Hollywood also attracted talented writers, directors, and artists, many of them women. Anita Loos, June Mathis, and Frances Marion were leading scriptwriters; Lois Weber was a well-known director and independent producer. Many other women, including Elinor Glynn and Dorothy Arzner, were successful film directors. In addition, the studios employed thousands of women and men as camera operators and film editors, as well as carpenters, electricians, and painters who built and maintained movie sets in scores of locations.

Complete integration of the movie industry was achieved in the 1920s when the major studios developed their own theater chains. Loew's Theaters (with its MGM production subsidiary), Zukor's Paramount studio, Fox, and RKO all built lavish movie palaces to exhibit their films. These lush structures lured a growing number of middle- and upper-class Americans to the movies, some theaters so richly appointed it seemed worth the price of admission just to use the restroom.

Yet older Hollywood residents were apprehensive about the arrival of the movie colony. The scandalous conduct of some of the stars and a series of risqué movies prompted many to demand censorship. In 1922 industry representatives persuaded Postmaster General

Will H. Hays to leave President Harding's cabinet for a $150,000 per year position as "movie czar." Thereafter the Hays Office issued a code of ethics and self-regulation that helped the studios regain public approval.

In 1927, Warner Brothers, one of the smaller studios, revolutionized the industry with its production of *The Jazz Singer*, the first talking picture. As with the early silent films, the new talking pictures benefited from free-ranging ideas and experimentation. The Marx Brothers movie *Duck Soup* (1933), for example, has been called "as thorough a satire on politics and patriotism as any film before *Dr. Strangelove*." Similarly, Mae West's *She Done Him Wrong* (1933) represented a daring departure from accepted feminine stereotypes.

Sex continued to be portrayed openly in some films, leading the Roman Catholic Church to organize the Legion of Decency, which threatened to boycott films it considered indecent. In 1934, hemorrhaging millions of dollars to the Great Depression, Hollywood agreed to stronger self-regulation. The resulting Breen Office oversaw a new code of ethics and for the rest of the 1930s, with few exceptions, Hollywood produced glamorous, appealing, and noncontroversial fare. Comedies, mysteries, westerns, lavish musicals, pictures based on classic literary works, and films featuring child stars reinforced traditional values and allowed audiences to temporarily escape their cares. Big moneymakers for the studios, a new "golden age" buoyed Hollywood through the 1940s.

Hollywood attracted many well-known American writers, as well as a large number of well-known European refugees from Hitler's Germany. Their contributions to Southern California's cultural awakening were impressive. Some were critical of Hollywood culture, despite their place in it. Nathanael West's *Day of the Locust* and F. Scott Fitzgerald's *The Last Tycoon* are examples of this disillusionment. California's premier writer of the era, poet Robinson Jeffers, rejected the Hollywood scene and abandoned Southern California for the central coast region, where he wrote lyrical poetry that situated human history within the epic history of the natural world.

Agribusiness

The new business structure of the 1920s was especially apparent in agriculture, where California became the nation's foremost example of industrialized farming. By 1930 "factories in the fields" had replaced the traditional family farm. Industrialized and corporate farms, processors, shippers, and bankers dominated the state's agriculture. Closely allied with the scientific community through the University of California's College of Agriculture at Davis, they exerted their political strength through the powerful California Farm Bureau Federation, formed in 1919. Land ownership was increasingly concentrated so that by the 1930s only 4 percent of the state's farms controlled 62 percent of all farmland. Farming in California had become agribusiness.

The development of the Tejón Ranch Company provides one example. Like so many other large holdings, the Tejón operation was based on several large Mexican land grants—in this case, those of Edward F. Beale. As a young officer with Commodore Stockton, Beale had entered California in 1846, where he came to the aid of General Kearny at San Pascual. Beale served as the state's first Superintendent of Indian Affairs in the 1850s. His 221,838 acres, acquired mostly in the 1860s, included the Liebra, Alamos y Agua Caliente, Castaic, and Tejón grants. By his death in 1893 Beale had purchased an additional 100,000 acres. In 1912 his son, Truxton, sold these holdings for $3 million to a group of Los Angeles capitalists headed by Harry Chandler. Thereafter the Tejón Ranch Company, a modern corporate farm, became one of the state's largest producers of livestock, alfalfa, fruit, and potatoes.

Another agricultural giant grew out of the 1903 incorporation of the Kern County Land Company, which assumed control of 350,000 acres of Kern County land from James Ben Ali Haggin and his associates. This company developed into one of the largest and most successful corporate farming operations in the world. By the 1920s, Miller and Lux, the Newhall Land and Farming Company, the Irvine Company, and Standard Oil Company of California, among many others, also ran corporate farms.

Concentration of land ownership, or horizontal integration, encouraged vertical integration, in which a company operated not only vast farm acreage but also food-processing, distribution, and marketing enterprises. In 1916, Mark J. Fontana organized four large packing companies into the California Packing Company, making it the largest canning company in the world. The company bought and farmed thousands of acres of land and contracted with hundreds of independent growers for their fruits and vegetables. CalPack then processed and shipped these crops to its nationwide network of warehouses for marketing under its Del Monte label, establishing a relationship between food processors and growers that characterizes California agriculture to this day. Joseph DiGiorgio, an Italian immigrant, achieved similar success with the organization of a vertically

integrated company, the DiGiorgio Corporation, dealing primarily in fruit and wines, and marketing canned goods under the S&W label.

For decades the citrus industry dominated California agriculture, but an expanding market for fruits and vegetables after World War I made California agriculture more diversified. By the end of the 1920s, the state was producing such a variety of crops that it was in a class by itself. With some 200 commercial crops, compared to 12 or 15 in most farming states, California dominated national production in such products as vegetables, fruits, nuts, and poultry. Patterning the marketing of their specialty crops after the pioneering California Fruit Grower's Exchange ("Sunkist"), growers of walnuts, almonds, dates, figs, and raisins, among many other crops, all organized cooperatives designed to assure orderly, profitable distribution.

The University of California's College of Agriculture also made important contributions to specialty crop and business farming. University scientists made increased yields, scientific business methods, and farm mechanization their first priority. Seeing the business farms as their primary clientele, institutional research became oriented to the agribusiness community. With offices at the College of Agriculture, the California Farm Bureau Federation exerted exceptional political influence on behalf of corporate farmers.

The spectacular growth of specialty crops tended to overshadow other important changes in the state's agriculture, including the rapid development of two major staple crops, rice and cotton. Introduced by Japanese immigrant farmers, rice was an important Sacramento Valley farm crop by the 1920s. Rice growers achieved the highest yields in the nation, and California soon ranked third in national production. At the same time, scientific farming and irrigation combined to transform the San Joaquin Valley into a new cotton kingdom. In that decade, growers achieved yields three times those of the country's traditional cotton-growing areas, making California one of the top cotton states in the nation.

Despite the value of their contribution to agriculture, white nativists continued to rail against the Japanese in California. By 1920, there were approximately 72,000 Japanese residents in California. The emigration of Japanese women as "picture brides" peaked during the 1910s, and the Japanese immigrant community transformed from a predominantly male society to one that increasingly consisted of young families. By 1920, women constituted over one-third of the Japanese population in California. With almost 8,500 Japanese, Los Angeles County had the largest concentration, with many Japanese immigrants drawn by the city's rapid expansion during the boom years; others abandoned San Francisco after the earthquake of 1906. By World War II, two-thirds of the country's Japanese residents were American-born citizens.

Whether urban or rural, the Japanese community remained firmly tied to agriculture and its offshoots—wholesaling, retailing, distributing. Like their white counterparts, Japanese growers organized their produce and flower industries vertically, from raising the plants to retail sales, though many remained dependent on white landowners for access to land, particularly after the passage of the 1913 Alien Land Law that denied landownership to Asian immigrants.

Alarmed by the growing presence of Japanese farm families and jealous of their hard-won achievements in agriculture, white farmers maintained a steady anti-Japanese drumbeat. After World War I, with crop prices falling, they joined with V. S. McClatchy, editor of the Sacramento *Bee*, and leaders of the American Legion, Native Sons of the Golden West, and other nativist groups to press for further restrictions against the Japanese. In 1920 voters overwhelmingly approved an initiative strengthening the 1913 law. The revised 1920 alien land law barred "aliens ineligible to citizenship" from leasing land, even temporarily, or investing in companies that owned real property. The following year legislators amended the state codes to allow the establishment of segregated schools for children of "Chinese, Japanese, or Mongolian parentage." Once separate schools were established, those children could not attend other public schools. School districts in Sacramento County maintained segregated schools for Chinese, Japanese, and Filipino children in the communities of Florin, Walnut Grove, Isleton, and Courtland until World War II.

California's efforts to bar Japanese immigration completely succeeded with the Immigration Act of 1924. Intended by Congress to cut off immigration from southern and eastern Europe, California representatives successfully pushed for a provision barring Asian immigration entirely. Despite Japan's protests, the law remained and exacerbated existing tensions between the two nations.

Farm Labor

Political influence helped farmers manage another fundamental element of successful large-scale specialty agriculture in California: a ready supply of cheap harvest labor. Large-scale farm operations had always depended on a supply of migrant labor that could be hired at the lowest cost for the shortest possible time. Corporate farmers demanded an oversupply that guaranteed their crops would be harvested on time and wages would remain low. Also, fewer and fewer growers employed more and more of the migratory labor force. By 1935, one-tenth of California's growers hired three-fourths of the harvest labor. Incidentally, the same growers controlled half of the state's specialty crops.

To ensure the labor supply they needed, in the 1920s California growers organized labor bureaus or exchanges. Growers in each agricultural district banded together to estimate their harvest labor needs, set wage rates, and establish an organization to provide the workers. The growers and processors who supplied funds for these exchanges enforced the agreed-on rates. In effect, farm workers were hired by the local industry, not by individual growers; as a result, laborers found it almost impossible to bargain for higher wages. The system reduced labor costs by as much as 30 percent in some areas.

In the fields, working conditions remained poor. Growers took little responsibility for decent treatment of harvest workers and used their political influence to prevent government action on the laborers' behalf. Their goals were shared by processors, canners, teamsters, railroads, utilities, and all others who depended on the profitability of corporate agriculture. Thousands of workers continued to live in unsanitary conditions in tent villages or automobiles and to work exceedingly long hours for low pay. It was a situation ripe for trouble when the depression of the 1930s revived the spirit of unionism.

The main sources of farm labor also changed drastically, as growers turned increasingly to Filipino and Mexican workers. As residents of an American protectorate, Filipinos were entitled to freedom of movement within the jurisdiction of the United States and thus could legally enter the country at a time when other Asian migrants were barred. California growers actively recruited in the Philippines, and the Filipino population on the U.S. mainland grew from over 2,600 in 1920 to over 20,000 by 1930. As farm workers, Filipinos would have a profound impact on labor relations, providing union leadership through the 1920s and 1930s.

Growers depended on Mexican and Mexican American workers as well. The first farm labor force to rely on the automobile for their mobility, thousands of Mexican immigrants entered California after 1920, drawn by the needs of agribusiness but also by the boom in Southern California's manufacturing, food-processing, garment, and construction industries. This led some Californians to demand, unsuccessfully, that Mexico be added to the 1924 Immigration Act's quota system. The decade ended with Mexicans comprising nearly 80 percent of the California farm labor force.

Meanwhile, a growing community of Mexican Americans and Mexican immigrants settled in East Los Angeles. With Anglos clearly in the majority, Latina/os experienced discrimination in employment, pay, and housing. Nonetheless, they established a stable community rooted in work, religion, and family. Women led the way in creating associations among Mexican Americans, such as *El Club Anachuac* and *La Sociedad Montezuma* for young women and men, and *La Sociedad Mutualista Mexicana*, an inter-barrio, inter-organizational coordinating agency. By 1930, the Mexican population of Los Angeles had tripled to over 97,000 and was one of the largest urban concentrations of Mexican residents outside of Mexico City.

Other Industries

The impact of population growth and the trend toward consolidation, efficiency, and order affected other industries as well. Amadeo P. Giannini, who founded the Bank of Italy in San Francisco in 1904 as a bank "for the little fella," salvaged the bank's assets from the San Francisco fire in 1906. Within days he had reopened for business. In the next two decades, Giannini acquired additional banking interests in New York and Italy and pioneered the concept of branch banking—particularly in California's booming agricultural regions where, by 1927, the Bank of Italy held mortgages on one of every eleven farms. In 1930 the Giannini bank holdings were merged to form the Bank of America, which in 1945 became the largest bank in the world. In Los Angeles, Joseph Sartori formed another giant, the Security Pacific Bank, by merging the First National Bank of Los Angeles with Security National Bank.

Population growth, the aggressive development of water and electricity, and cheap labor attracted a number of major national industries to Southern California. In 1919 Goodyear Tire and Rubber Company established the West's first branch plant in Los Angeles, where its huge water needs could be met. Firestone, B. F. Goodrich, and U.S. Rubber Company soon followed, making Los Angeles the nation's second-largest tire manufacturer. In 1927 the first automobile assembly plants in California were opened in Los Angeles by Ford and Willys-Overland Motor Company. In the same decade Owens-Illinois Glass Company, Swift & Company, Procter and Gamble, Bethlehem Steel, U.S. Steel, and many other firms located branch plants in Los Angeles. The city moved from 28th among U.S. manufacturing centers in 1919 to ninth place by 1930, surpassing San Francisco, while California was ranked eighth among the states in the value of its manufactured products.

The Decline of Organized Labor

A marked decline in the power and influence of organized labor accompanied economic expansion in the years after World War I. As the nation entered a period of "red-baiting," many Americans found it relatively easy to apply the "radical" label to unions and, seizing this opportunity, California employer associations mounted aggressive campaigns to establish the open shop throughout the state. In Southern California, the Merchants and Manufacturers Association redoubled efforts to prevent unions from gaining a foothold in the area. By 1929 the Los Angeles *Times* proudly ran a month-long series of articles titled "The 40-Year War for a Free City," which attributed the "phenomenal" growth of Southern California industry to employer success in maintaining the open shop.

In the north, the battle between organized labor and employers quickly resumed when the war ended. By 1921 the longshoremen's and seafarers' unions had been demolished, the former replaced by new company unions under company-controlled foremen, and the Building Trades Council had been overpowered by San Francisco employers. San Francisco's Industrial Association successfully instituted an area-wide open shop in the following years. It set up a system for hiring and training nonunion labor, denied employers of union labor access to building materials, and pressured banks to deny credit to union employers. Union membership and influence declined in California, as it did in the rest of the country.

California's criminal syndicalism law, enacted in 1919, was the chief weapon of antiunion forces. It was successfully used to eliminate the IWW (Industrial Workers of the World) as a factor in agricultural labor and effectively intimidated all labor organizations in the postwar decade. As the 1920s ended, the state's labor organizations were at their lowest ebb since the 1870s.

Urban Rivalry and the Military

While business and labor clashed over unionization, they generally cooperated to promote urban growth and development. The dramatic expansion of Southern California sparked an intense rivalry between cities for urbanization. Local businesses, labor, and government came together to promote growth, and many of the public projects of the 1920s and '30s such as the great municipal water projects, bridges, transit systems, and international expositions of the era were a part of this competition.

This community of interest also applied to efforts to obtain a steady flow of federal funds into cities through the favorable location of military facilities. Accordingly, throughout the 1920s and '30s, San Diego, Los Angeles, San Francisco, Vallejo, and Alameda vied with each other to attract military bases. In 1919, the United States Navy created the Pacific Fleet and began the search for its home base, kicking off a bidding war eventually won by San Diego, despite the general agreement that San Francisco was the "strategic center" of the West Coast. San Diego simply outbid and politically outmaneuvered all others. The strategy paid off: the Navy was soon pouring millions of dollars each year into the San Diego economy.

Similarly, Southern California successfully attracted Army Air Force bases, particularly March Field, developing close economic and personal ties with the Army. Air Force and Navy installations and the research and experimentation they stimulated were important considerations in the decisions of such aircraft manufacturing companies as Douglas, Lockheed, and Consolidated to locate in Southern California—laying the foundation for the area's domination of the aerospace industry after World War II. By 1941, California cities had developed a civil-military partnership of enormous and continuing significance.

A Changing Society

Commenting on American society in the 1920s, historian Lawrence Levine once noted, "The central paradox of American history . . . has been a belief in progress coupled with a dread of change; an urge toward the inevitable future combined with a longing for the irretrievable past." The diversified, explosive, paradoxical society emerging in California in the 1920s bears this out. Like most Americans, Californians embraced the automobile, the movies, the radio, and other products of the new technology. Many were fascinated by the new moral standards, "flappers," and "modernist" religious teachings. Yet a great many white residents rejected any form of radicalism or labor organization, and many feared the growing presence of ethnic minorities. Such traditionalists supported prohibition, religious fundamentalism, and the nativism of the Ku Klux Klan as they struggled to retain what they perceived to be an eroding sense of community and morality.

For many Californians, the 1920s were a time of change. This was true for California's African American population. Their numbers remained small after World War I. In San Francisco and Los Angeles, for example, blacks were no more than two to three percent of the population. Two-wage-earner families were typical. Most black men found work with the railroads or as laborers. Over half of working-age women earned salaries, although generally their opportunities were restricted to domestic service. By 1930, as the population approached 40,000, distinctive African American communities had emerged. Blacks were concentrated into segregated communities such as Watts in Los Angeles and, to a lesser extent, West Oakland in northern California.

African American women continued to serve as community leaders. In 1919, pioneer Oakland newspaperwoman and essayist Delilah Leontium Beasley published the first history of African Americans in California. The name she chose for her volume, *The Negro Trailblazers of California*, claimed black Californians' significance as "Old Pioneers in the State of California," and the credit she felt they were due. Frances Albrier, educated at Howard University and the University of California, galvanized Berkeley's and Oakland's black middle-class to protest discrimination in jobs and housing. In Los Angeles, Charlotta Bass edited the *California Eagle* and spent many years in a variety of African American organizations formed to protect the community.

Despite the black community's efforts, white hostility towards them increased. This is amply demonstrated by the growth of the Ku Klux Klan, whose membership grew after World War I. "Klaverns" appeared in San Francisco, Oakland, Sacramento, Fresno, and other San Joaquin Valley towns, but its real strength was in Los Angeles and the surrounding communities, where, for a time, the Klan controlled the city of Anaheim. Since many Americans associated the use of alcohol with foreign Catholic immigrants, Klan members were often active in efforts to enforce prohibition.

For white middle-class women, the 1920s ushered in new freedoms. They entered colleges in great numbers and went to work in the business world. The typical American woman discarded at least half the volume of clothing worn by her mother, and many smoked cigarettes, drank alcohol, drove automobiles, and demanded the same social freedoms enjoyed by men. California women's prominence in sports and aviation, in the new sportswear industry, and in public service bespoke their new status. By 1930 almost 30 percent of female American airplane pilots were Californians. Louise Thaden, who moved to California in 1926, set records for altitude, speed, and endurance; in 1928, she won the first National Women's Air Derby.

Women also made modest progress in control of reproduction. State law made performing an abortion a felony, but by 1930 it was seldom enforced and illegal abortions were generally available, though often with terrible consequences for the patient. Although public discussion of birth control was almost nonexistent, thousands of California women received advice on contraception from personal physicians, or in clinics established by the American Birth Control League. Moreover, many women insisted on greater autonomy and equality in marriage, or what was known as "companionate" marriage.

No cause as grand as suffrage united California women in the 1920s, yet women remained active in innumerable clubs and organizations and continued to promote various causes. Few women were elected to public office—San Francisco's Florence Prag Kahn, who replaced her husband after his death, was California's lone female representative in Congress—but those with money got results. Backed by chocolate heiress Myra Hershey and others, Arti Mason Carter inaugurated the "Symphonies Under the Stars" series in a location that would become the Hollywood Bowl (Mrs. Carter personally halted the earth-moving equipment brought in to develop the site for another purpose). Other Southern California women philanthropists, including Estelle Doheny, Mabel Beckman, and Ellen Browning Scripps, contributed significant sums to education and the arts.

Despite the state's obsession with combating "the yellow peril," Asian women also found new opportunities in California. Early in the twentieth century, for example, Korean immigrant women in San Francisco organized mutual assistance associations that raised funds for social welfare services. Unlike white women's clubs, however, their goals were nationalistic: they sent money to leaders of the Korean independence movement. The *Taeban Yoja Aikuk-dan* (Korean Women's Patriotic Society) had branches in every Korean California community. For decades, virtually every Korean in America gave the equivalent of one month's wages each year to end the Japanese occupation of Korea. Chinese American women were also active. In 1911, a San Francisco group organized the Chinese Women's *Jeleab* (Self-Reliance) Association. Borrowing the language of white women's clubs, leaders described their goals as "social intercourse, benevolent work, educational advantages, and mutual assistance and benefit." Like their Korean counterparts, they also espoused political aims and forwarded most of the funds they raised to Dr. Sun Yat-Sen's revolutionary cause. Revealing another American influence, members urged their Chinese American sisters to take advantage of their opportunities in the United States to improve women's status at home and in China. In 1924 a group of young Chinese American women formed San Francisco's Square and Circle Club after reading about the floods and famine then raging in China. They responded with a jazz dance to raise funds for the victims. Members registered voters among American-born Chinese, wrote letters to federal officials demanding more favorable immigration legislation for the Chinese, and protested racism at the state and municipal levels.

Robinson Jeffers

Poet of the Coast

When asked what characterized great poetry, Robinson Jeffers observed that "permanent things, or things forever renewed, like the grass and human passions, are the materials for poetry." From an early age Jeffers had learned to love and respect the natural environment, but as he matured he became deeply disillusioned with humanity. In powerful, violent, and often controversial poems he extolled nature while portraying the dark side of human passions. His long narrative poems—such as *Tamar, Roan Stallion, The Women of Big Sur, Cawdor,* and *Thurso's Landing*—described rape, incest, murder, and insanity against the ruggedly majestic background of the central California coast.

Jeffers was a transplanted Pennsylvanian who emerged as California's master poet in the 1920s. He had come to California in 1903 at the age of 16, when his father, an austere Presbyterian college professor and Old Testament scholar, moved his family to Highland Park in Southern California in hopes of improving his health.

Young Robinson spent much of his youth studying the classics under his father's stern eye, and later enrolled at Occidental College, a Presbyterian school in Highland Park. There Jeffers enjoyed the usual student activities and wrote poetry for the student magazine, which he edited in his senior year.

An important element in Jeffers's emergence as a major poet was his 1913 marriage to Una Kuster. They met in 1905, when Robin (as he was known to friends and family) attended the University of Southern California. At 20, Una was two years his senior and had been married to Theodore Kuster for three years. For the next seven years, their love affair dominated Robinson's life as he studied medicine at USC, forestry at the University of Washington, and led a bohemian life at Hermosa Beach, where he wrote poetry and roamed the coast and mountains. Una's husband filed for divorce in 1912, and the next year Robin and Una married, moved to Carmel, and began a new life together.

Living on the Big Sur's dramatic coast, Jeffers absorbed the environment around him. Long walks with Una, and later their twin sons, along the beach or through the mountains that plunged to the shore, filled Jeffers with the images he used in his poetry. He built their home, Tor House, and a retreat for Una called Hawk Tower on a point near Carmel, overlooking the ocean. He hauled stones up from the beach and set them in mortar himself, while he mentally framed his day's writing. His disciplined routine was jealously guarded by Una, whose wide-ranging intellect complemented his own.

Robinson Jeffers

Photograph by Edward Weston. Courtesy of The Bancroft Library, University of California, Berkeley.

Jeffers's first two books of poems had been in the traditional mode, but after moving to Carmel he began to experiment with unconventional styles, producing the long narrative poems whose rhythms have been likened to those of the sea. But the controversial subject matter of these poems was unacceptable to publishers, leading Jeffers to use his own funds to publish *Tamar* in 1924. Favorable reviews of the book marked him as a major literary figure, and the next year Jeffers began publishing important new work almost annually for the next 15 years. At the height of his popularity in the 1930s, he was featured on the cover of *Time* magazine and regarded as the nation's leading, path-breaking poet. During and after World War II, in poems such as *The Double Axe*, Jeffers spoke out against war and the threat of atomic weapons, warning of the very extinction of humankind. In 1946 he demonstrated another facet of his talent, writing a new stage version of *Medea* for his friend Judith Anderson. It was a major Broadway success and remains a mainstay of performing groups.

The fire that Una kindled in Robinson Jeffers died with her death from cancer in 1950. In the next dozen years, he produced only one major work, living what he regarded a "rudderless" existence until his own death in 1962. Jeffers then faded from view, but new admiration for his work has revived his reputation, so much so that, in 2010, the California Historical Society devoted an entire issue of its quarterly, *California History*, to his life and work.   (RBR)

Religion

Aimee Semple McPherson was the most famous of many faith healers, spiritualists, health faddists, and cult leaders who played to the emotional needs of Southern Californians and gave Los Angeles a reputation for being peculiarly hospitable to the unorthodox. The population of the south differed markedly from that of the older, more cosmopolitan north. Probably no more than one-fourth of the residents of Los Angeles in the 1920s had been born there—newcomers were always in the majority. Many, like earlier migrants, were health-seekers, but the majority were rural Southerners and Midwesterners fleeing the cold winters, stifling summers, and drudgery of farm life. Seeking a sense of community, they organized State Societies and attended annual state picnics to hobnob with folks from "back home." A land of paradoxes, at the same time H.L. Mencken was calling the city "Double Dubuque"—a hundred Midwestern towns laid end to end—others were decrying the 1920s as the "Golden Age of Crackpotism" in Los Angeles.

Religion had always been a large part of Midwestern migrants' lives. Although they had left the stern life of the Old Testament behind, in Los Angeles Aimee Semple McPherson offered an upbeat religion in a form that competed with the best Hollywood had to offer. McPherson understood the Midwesterner's loneliness, bewilderment, and love of fantasy. Substituting a gospel of love for the gospel of fear, she preached salvation in the here-and-now, stressing God's grace rather than the pessimistic doctrines of original sin. Filling her sermons with humor, she entertained while offering hope. In Kevin Starr's words, she helped thousands of "nobodies become somebodies in Los Angeles." When McPherson held services in the Mexican American community, a young Anthony Quinn interpreted. Enraptured, he spent years playing the saxophone in her orchestra. Through her radio station, KFSG, her melodious voice became the most recognizable in the West. Throughout the 1920s, McPherson symbolized the hopes of thousands of Californians. At the time of her death in 1944, her Church of the Foursquare Gospel counted 410 churches in North America, 200 missions, 29,000 members, and assets of $2.8 million. By 1992, under her son Rolfe's leadership, it had grown to over 25,000 churches worldwide, with 1.7 million members.

Sister Aimee was not the first woman evangelist to attract Southern California's attention. The Theosophical Society, which followed various Buddhist and Brahman theories, produced two earlier evangelists. In 1900, Katherine Tingley moved the international headquarters of the society to Point Loma near San Diego. There, she established an upper-class utopian community according to ideas that combined humanitarianism and a universal call to brotherhood with the occult. At its peak, Point Loma had 500 members, many of whom were highly educated. Another theosophist, Annie Besant, established a colony on a large tract of land in the Ojai Valley, where she brought the spiritualist Krishnamurti as the "new messiah." World-renowned for her advocacy of women's rights, birth control, Socialism, Marxism, and an independent India, Besant made Ojai an important center of the theosophic movement from her arrival in the 1920s until her death in 1933.

Prohibition

Many of the same people who supported nativism in the 1920s also supported prohibition. California ratified the 18th Amendment in 1919 after a bitter campaign between "wets" and "drys." Once prohibition was the law of the land, California, like every other state, found it a nightmare to enforce. The Volstead Act, which went into effect on January 17, 1920, prohibited the manufacture or sale of any beverage containing more than one-half of 1 percent alcohol. The Act required federal enforcement of prohibition but left open state and local enforcement options.

In 1920 California's Anti-Saloon League pushed for the Harris Act, which would have provided for state enforcement. A legislature dominated by rural and southern representatives passed it, but the wets defeated the bill in a referendum. Since no major city in the state had a dry majority, two more years passed before legislation was adopted to put state officers nominally behind the enforcement of prohibition. Even then the state effort was not overwhelming. In 1929 California spent only $1,767 to thwart alcohol consumption. At the local level, 26 counties and 56 cities and towns passed "little Volstead" ordinances, motivated mainly by the revenue produced by fines levied on violators. By then, though, it was obvious that some cities, especially San Francisco and Sacramento, were going to stay, as one witness said, "hilariously wet." San Francisco's Board of Supervisors refused to permit assignment of city and county officers to prohibition enforcement. In the south, with many thousands of rural midwestern newcomers, prohibition had much greater support. Even so, Los Angeles did not adopt prohibition under local option before the Volstead Act took effect, and the wets there were a large majority.

California, with its 1,200-mile coastline, was a rum-runner's paradise. The chief sources of illegal alcohol were ships that sailed down the coast from Vancouver, British Columbia, where exporters enjoyed a thriving trade with thirsting Americans. By 1926 smuggling liquor from Canada had become a major industry. Southern California alone illegally imported an estimated 150,000 cases of Scotch whiskey valued at $10 million per year. Canadian exporters took orders and arranged for deliveries to a variety of bootleggers. Some big operators owned ships carrying up to 10,000 cases, speedboats to run liquor ashore, and a fleet of trucks and converted passenger cars for distribution on land. Smaller operators simply bought "over the rail" from Canadian supply ships 30 miles or more offshore and ran the goods ashore in speedboats. Hijackers, meanwhile, raced with police to intercept the speedboats as they came ashore at places such as Oxnard, Summerland, Seal Beach, Santa Barbara, and coastal inlets around San Francisco.

Although many groups publicly defended prohibition as a return to traditional, sober morality, large numbers of individuals defied the law. There is no way of knowing how many illicit stills existed in California, but clearly there were many. In 1927 alone, prohibition agents seized 185 distilleries and 572 stills from basements, garages, canyons, stables, dairies, and tents. But the government simply lacked the resources to enforce the law effectively. For California's drys, prohibition was a long, sorry tale of failure.

It was also a difficult period for local wine makers. California wine production fell drastically in the 1920s. At the same time, however, sales of table grapes to eastern buyers rose phenomenally. The sale of grapes for home wine-making and illegal wine production enabled growers to survive. They were able to recapture their dominant position in the American wine industry in 1933, when prohibition was repealed.

One-Party Government

Politics in the 1920s reflected California's paradoxical society. The influx of midwestern Republicans to Southern California, the increased power of large-scale business, the peculiarities of cross-filing, and the emotional issue of prohibition all combined to make California solidly Republican. The Democratic Party, already diminished by the progressive crusade, split so badly on the issue of prohibition that it nearly disappeared. Between 1920 and 1930 Democrats won only 25 of the 555 contests for partisan office in the state,

and not one Democrat won a statewide executive office. The Democratic decline led essentially to one-party government throughout the 1920s, with most important political contests taking place between the conservative and progressive wings of the Republican Party or along sectional lines. Regardless of which faction controlled state government, its policies and actions reflected the decade's prevailing business ideology, with its emphasis on corporate organization, efficiency, and order.

When Hiram Johnson left California in 1917, the breakup of the Progressive Party followed and most of its members drifted back into the Republican fold. Moreover, Johnson's successor, William D. Stephens, represented much of the conservatism of the southern counties. He was an ardent prohibitionist, expressed antiunion sentiments, supported the anti-Japanese initiative of 1920, and played an active role in passage of the Criminal Syndicalism Act of 1919.

On the other hand, Stephens did manage to hold the progressive coalition together well enough to be elected governor in 1918 and to attain a number of pragmatic progressive goals. State regulation of business was expanded, and he supported conservation, public development of water and power resources, and a $40 million bond issue to build a modern highway system. Perhaps his most important contribution was in the area of fiscal policy and management. To meet the growing role of government in public affairs, Stephens successfully sought a 50 percent increase in the biennial state budget in 1921 and a 35 percent increase in corporation taxes to pay for it. At the same time, he consolidated dozens of independent state agencies into five major departments and installed a modern budgeting and accounting system.

In 1922 Stephens sought reelection on his record as a pragmatic business-manager politician, but he fell victim to the emotional, conservative appeal of Friend W. Richardson, publisher of the Berkeley *Gazette* and incumbent state treasurer. Richardson aggressively attacked the Stephens budget increases and called for a massive reduction in state expenditures, decisively defeating the incumbent governor in the Republican primary, which was tantamount to election.

Friend Richardson proved to be all he said he would be. The old-guard Republicans swept back into power with his election. In 1923 he submitted—and the conservative legislature adopted—a budget that slashed expenditures for education, social welfare, and a host of state services. In addition, Richardson vetoed a large number of spending bills and supported the antiunion proposals of employer organizations.

Whittier Boulevard, 1928

California highway development in the 1920s was the envy of the nation. This 1928 photo of Whittier Boulevard as it cuts through Los Angeles County orange groves shows the concrete roadway, with curbs, typical of highway construction of the period. *California Department of Transportation.*

The conservatism of Richardson's administration led to the formation of the Progressive Voters League, which orchestrated the election of many progressives in 1924 and produced a standoff between the two Republican factions in the legislature. Richardson gave no ground, even when the League attempted to force substantial increases in the 1925 budget. The governor, in fact, vetoed more than half the bills passed by the legislature in 1925, a record that still stands.

The Progressive Voters League challenged Richardson in the gubernatorial primary of 1926 with Lieutenant Governor C.C. Young, former state assembly member, teacher, and businessman. Young's progressive platform called for continued government reorganization, highway development, conservation, forest preservation, tax reform, and development of water and hydroelectric resources. Successfully defusing Richardson's campaign rhetoric on economy in government, Young narrowly defeated the governor in the primary and was easily elected in the general election.

With Young as governor, progressives made important gains, including support for conservation and parks, the first state old-age pension law in the country, and aid to the blind, physically handicapped, and needy. Although his personality was rather bland, Young has been regarded as one of the ablest of California's governors, and his administration's record supports the contention of some historians that progressivism remained quite alive in California despite the conservatism of the times.

Reapportionment was an important factor in the election of 1926. The census of 1920 indicated that Southern California deserved increased representation, but the legislature failed to pass reapportionment bills in 1921, 1923, and 1925. Southerners attempted to force the issue with an initiative creating a reapportionment commission, but northern and rural interests countered with another initiative that proposed what they called the "federal plan." Under this plan, the assembly remained apportioned on a basis of population, but the state senate was apportioned by counties, with no county having more than one senator and no senator representing more than three counties. The federal plan initiative carried, while the commission initiative was defeated. The result was nearly 40 years of underrepresentation for urban counties, especially in Southern California, where by 1965 the Los Angeles County state senator represented 450 times as many people as the senator representing Mono, Inyo, and Alpine counties. A peculiar alliance of urban business and agribusiness interests successfully defeated efforts to return the state senate to population-based apportionment until the 1964 U.S. Supreme Court "one man, one vote" ruling in *Reynolds v. Simms* forced the change.

C.C. Young probably would have been reelected in 1930, had the prohibition issue not caused confusion in the Republican primary campaign. Whereas Young supported prohibition, his chief opponent appeared to be "soaking wet" James ("Sunny Jim") Rolph Jr., long-time mayor of San Francisco. But former governor Richardson then persuaded Los Angeles district attorney Buron Fitts, a crusading dry, to enter the race. Between them, Young and Fitts split the dry vote. Rolph won the nomination and was elected governor in November. This was Richardson's revenge for his own defeat by Young in 1926.

In Governor James Rolph Jr., California elected one of its least competent governors for one of its most critical eras. With the misery of the Great Depression descending upon the state, Gov. Rolph suggested that the best way to deal with it was for everyone to take a vacation to stimulate the economy through spending—advice he followed by going fishing. The Rolph administration, however, belongs to the story of the Great Depression in California.

The
Depression
Decade

21

The Great Depression was a terrifying worldwide economic collapse that shook the faith of millions of Americans in their government. In 1932 the nation reacted by turning to new political leadership, electing Democrat Franklin Delano Roosevelt as president. Faced with the example of authoritarian states emerging elsewhere in the world, Roosevelt proposed instead a program aimed at preservation of the American system. In an astonishing record of legislation enacted in the first 100 days of his administration, Roosevelt's New Deal changed the role of the federal government in American society. It restructured federal-state relationships, bringing the federal government into the lives of citizens through relief, social security, and federal tax programs. It pumped huge quantities of money into the economy through public works projects, adopted legislation strengthening organized labor, and enacted a program of federal oversight and business regulation designed to prevent another such collapse. The New Deal had such a profound effect on the nation and California that, 75 years later, when an economic collapse rivaling the Depression (and called the "Great Recession") struck, many looked to the New Deal for solutions. The political framework had changed, however, and supermajority vote requirements allowed Republican minorities to prevent Democratic majorities in both Congress and the state legislature from enacting a New Deal-like response to the Great Recession.

Impacts of the Depression

The good times of the 1920s came to an end with the great stock market crash of October 1929. That blinding flash of disaster started a long, grinding decline of the American economy, the worst business contraction and deflation the world had known. By 1932 national income had declined by 50 percent; per capita production of goods and commodities fell to the rate of 1889; housing construction barely reached 15 percent of the 1929 rate; and nearly 15 million workers, almost a third of the nation's work force, were unemployed. Millions of Americans roamed the country, frightened and perplexed by the calamity.

One of the myths of the Great Depression pictured California as a balmy paradise of orange groves and Hollywood fantasy somehow shielded from the disaster. In reality, modern business and agriculture, the automobile, radio, and hundreds of other connections had so closely tied the state to the rest of the nation that there could be no escape. Moreover, some of California's chief products—specialty crops, tourism, and movies—made the state particularly vulnerable to shrinking incomes.

California therefore felt the full impact of the depression. Its agricultural revenues, $750 million in 1929, fell to $327 million in 1932. Its rural areas were suddenly poverty-stricken. The oil industry produced more oil than it could sell, leading to thousands of layoffs. Developers and real estate firms, construction companies, and savings and loan associations—the high flyers of the 1920s—crumbled, revealing a sad picture of fraud, embezzlement, and other forms of financial chicanery that spelled ruin for thousands. Even the movies, propped up temporarily by the introduction of the "talkies," eventually went down with the other industries, losing millions.

Southern California—with an unusually high percentage of the work force in service occupations, a large number of lower-middle-class white-collar workers, and the highest proportion of elderly people in the nation—was devastated. Southern and Midwestern migrants living on savings and investments were wiped out by the financial crash. Older persons were the first to be unemployed as the region's new manufacturing industries laid off workers. With one-fifth of its population on relief (at $16.20 per month per family) Los Angeles County's public welfare costs increased tenfold. No

Sacramento "Hooverville"

Unemployed workers who had lost their homes lived in shantytowns made of salvaged boxes, boards, tin, and tar paper. Usually called "Hoovervilles" to mock President Hoover's failure to ease the depression, they appeared on the outskirts of most sizable towns. *Courtesy of The Bancroft Library, University of California, Berkeley.*

wonder city officials welcomed the aid of Aimee Semple McPherson's commissary and her Foursquare Brothers and Sisters. In San Francisco, home of the state's largest corporations, the unemployment rate approached 25 percent in 1932 and remained there for several years. State and local leaders faced huge increases in delinquent taxes and drastic reductions in revenues.

The human toll of the depression was incalculable. Thousands of formerly secure people were reduced to selling apples or pencils on street corners. Some rushed out at street intersections to clean auto windshields, hoping for a tip from the driver. Others just sat in whatever shelter they could find, lived off pitiful relief payments of a few cents a day, and waited, giving a strange kind of stillness to their communities. Those with jobs often worked only two or three days each week at reduced wages, yet frequently supported relatives who had lost jobs and homes. For African Americans, Latina/os, and Asian Americans, massive unemployment meant increased discrimination. Activists like Frances Albrier used local organizations to fight discrimination in hiring, often in alliance with white women's groups. Unions, however, seldom admitted blacks or other minorities. Others, particularly Mexican American women, built self-help organizations to meet the crisis in their own communities.

Under a barrage of front-page newspaper stories covering the nation's economic collapse and the shady dealings of prominent Californians, the people's faith in the business community, Herbert Hoover's business-oriented presidency, and, for some, the whole economic system, was shattered. In the process, a large segment of the voting public was radicalized, ready to consider the most unorthodox proposals for their betterment.

The New Deal in California

The New Deal as it evolved consisted of a mind-boggling array of federal agencies designed to provide relief of the unemployed, recovery of the American economy, and reform of the system that had failed so miserably. Relief was the most urgent problem of the early 1930s. Until the end of his presidency, Herbert Hoover clung to the Republican's belief that the federal government had no responsibility to help individual citizens; the burden of relief, he felt, belonged to state and local agencies. At the local level, California had long provided some forms of aid to the poor. In times of economic crisis the unemployed received aid or were employed by the state in public works projects. As always, private charities and church groups like Sister Aimee's provided relief to the poor.

The depression, however, simply overwhelmed this system, and the number of homeless and unemployed skyrocketed. The state diverted funds to counties and municipalities for relief and to a greatly expanded public works program. In 1931 the state Unemployment Commission was established to coordinate unemployment relief.

Transient and homeless men and women were a major problem in California, far more serious, a 1931 Census Bureau report noted, than in eastern states. Wandering families and unattached men, women, boys, and girls entered the state at a rate approaching 1,000 a day. To aid them, the Unemployment Commission recommended state labor camps, and in 1931–1932 28 forestry camps and two highway camps were established to house and feed transient and homeless men while they cleared firebreaks and built campground facilities and roads in state parks and national forests. But state expenditures for relief and public works soon exhausted the $30 million surplus Governor James Rolph Jr. had inherited. By 1933 he was faced with a $9.5 million deficit. With the nation's financial system foundering and almost all banks shuttered, Californians, like most Americans, looked to their new president for help when he took office in March 1933.

Help came quickly. Roosevelt had none of Hoover's reservations about the role of the federal government in relief; within 100 days of Roosevelt's inauguration, Congress had adopted a wide range of legislation attacking the problems of relief for the unemployed and economic recovery and reform. The Federal Emergency Relief Administration (FERA) provided matching funds to the states for relief, administered in California by a quickly established State Emergency Relief Administration. Opposed to simple handouts, New Dealers instituted a program of work relief through the Civil Works Administration (CWA), which in 1933–1934 employed more than 150,000 Californians building airports, bridges, roads, schools, and other public structures. At the same time, the Civilian Conservation Corps (CCC) took thousands of unmarried, unemployed young men between the ages of 18 and 25 out of cities and put them to work in forest and soil conservation programs, not unlike the state's 1931 forestry camps. By 1935 federal expenditures for relief in California amounted to $285 million.

A new phase of federal relief activity in California began in 1935, when Congress established the Works Progress Administration (WPA) to supersede the FERA and CWA and to concentrate relief in public works projects. For the rest of the decade, hardly a school, post office, city hall, bridge, or road was built without

WPA funds. Through the Federal Writers Project, the WPA engaged unemployed writers and historians in research projects such as producing county histories. The Farm Security Administration put photographers such as Dorothea Lange to work recording the impact of the depression on farm families, creating a priceless heritage of documentary photographs. Working through the Federal Theatre Project, unemployed actors and musicians presented plays and musicals throughout the country, paying special attention to rural communities unused to such fare. And more than 200 Federal Arts Project muralists covered California public buildings with art, a unique style of painting heavily influenced by the Mexican muralist Diego Rivera. Ironically, California's New Deal art expressed a kind of cultural nationalism stressing the strengths of American society and the middle-class values promoted by Roosevelt's New Deal. It was, as one analyst observed, an art form that "affirmed traditional American values in the visual style of a Mexican Marxist."

Large-Scale Public Works

New Dealers saw public works not only as a way to provide unemployment relief but also as a means to promote economic recovery through stimulation of the construction industry. Accordingly, they allocated vast sums of money to large-scale construction projects, often contracted to private industry through a variety of federal agencies. Many important municipal improvement projects, such as Orange County's development of Newport Harbor, were financed by the Public Works Administration (PWA), set up to manage major undertakings. Meanwhile, the Reconstruction Finance Corporation (RFC) provided loans for construction of such large projects as the Oakland-San Francisco Bay Bridge. Even these ventures were surpassed by the Bureau of Reclamation's Colorado River and Central Valley projects.

The works comprising the Colorado River Project made it a stupendous enterprise: the world's largest and highest dam at Black Canyon; the world's largest

Dorothea Lange and Florence Thompson

The Photographer and the Migrant Mother

On a rainy March day in 1936, in a farmworkers' camp near Nipomo, Dorothea Lange focused her camera on a woman and several children in their canvas shelter. The images that she produced were among the scores taken for the California Rural Rehabilitation Administration and the hundreds still to come under the federal Farm Security Administration (FSA) program that documented rural America in the 1930s. An established San Francisco photographer recently married to University of California economist and political activist Paul S. Taylor, Lange joined the FSA and, with her husband, toured California taking photographs and writing descriptions, especially of Dust Bowl migrants from the drought-ravaged South and Midwest. At Nipomo, Lange's subject was Florence Thompson, a 32-year-old widow and mother of six, who had just sold her automobile tires in order to feed her children. Frost had destroyed the local pea crop and there was no work for her or hundreds of other pickers.

To the public, Thompson became known as the "Migrant Mother," a symbol of the trials of the Great Depression. The title of Lange's photograph could not have been more fitting. For most of the 1930s,

Dorothea Lange: The Photographer

Dorothea Lange atop automobile in 1936 California. *Farm Security Administration photo by Rondale Partridge. Library of Congress.*

Thompson worked as an itinerant farm laborer in California, picking whatever was in season. Years later, she described putting her babies in bags during cotton harvests and carrying them along with her as she picked her way down the rows. She recalled averaging "around 450, 500 [pounds of cotton a day]" and earning 50 cents for every 100 pounds she picked.

After the women's brief encounter, the photographer's reputation soared. Lange earned a Guggenheim fellowship and exhibitions of her work were featured at the New York Museum of Modern Art and elsewhere. But the Migrant Mother herself remained obscure and anonymous, even to Lange. Thompson followed the crops until the 1940s, when she settled in Modesto and gave birth to four more children. To keep her family afloat, Thompson often worked 16 hours a day, seven days a week. "I worked in the hospitals, I tended bar, I worked in the field," she told reporters in 1979, "I done a little bit of everything to make a living for my kids." For a time, the proud woman objected to appearances of the photograph depicting her early poverty, but during the 1970s, widowed again and in poor health, she publicly associated herself with the famous image. She hoped that she might receive some compensation for its repeated use, but as property of the federal government, the photograph was in the public domain and she received no royalties for its use. In 1983, after Thompson had a stroke, her children capitalized on her identity as the iconic Migrant Mother and raised $15,000 to defray her medical bills. Thompson died soon thereafter.

Despite vast differences in their lives, both women made contributions to California. Lange's is tangible: a photographic record, housed in the Library of Congress and the Oakland Museum, documented and influenced a crucial period in state and national history. Thompson's contributions are less immediately apparent: it was her toil, and that of thousands like her, that allowed California agriculture to flourish even in the depths of the Great Depression.

(CMT, WAB)

and longest aqueduct, carrying Colorado River water to the Los Angeles basin; and the All-American Canal to the Imperial Valley. The RFC bought more than $200 million worth of Metropolitan Water District (MWD) bonds to finance the aqueduct, and the Bureau of Reclamation financed the rest. The most spectacular of these spectacular works proved to be the great dam on the Colorado. Begun during the presidency of Herbert Hoover, it was initially called Boulder Dam then renamed Hoover Dam in 1947.

Approval of a 1930 contract to sell electricity generated by the dam led Congress to appropriate initial construction funds. In April 1931 the contract for construction was awarded to a syndicate of firms incorporated as the Six Companies, with Henry J. Kaiser as chairman of the board. Frank Crowe, as superintendent of construction, was the driving force of dam construction. The job required enormous facilities: a complete air-conditioned community (Boulder City, Nevada) built near the site to house workers, and four by-pass tunnels, each a mile long and 50 feet in diameter, carved into the canyon walls before the riverbed could be cleared. The dam itself stood 660 feet thick at the bottom, 45 feet thick and 726 feet high at the top. When

completed, it created Lake Mead, holding 32 million acre-feet of water. With profits of more than $10 million from building Hoover Dam, the Six Companies moved on to sink the towers for the Golden Gate Bridge, build the Oakland-San Francisco Bay Bridge, and complete the Grand Coulee and Bonneville dams on the Columbia River, before taking on major defense contracts in World War II.

The building of the Golden Gate Bridge was another of the magnificent technological achievements in this age of public works. Financed by Marin and San Francisco county bond issues, the bridge was begun in 1933 and completed in 1937. It was an engineering challenge, given the difficulties of construction in the narrow opening to the Bay, with its swift currents and tides. It was, for a time, the longest suspension bridge in the world. Construction of the Oakland-San Francisco Bay Bridge, built at the same time within the calm confines of the inner Bay, proceeded more quickly and was finished in 1936. San Francisco civic leaders hoped that the two great bridges would revive the city's position as the business and population center of the Bay Area, but ironically they accelerated population dispersal and contributed to San Francisco's relative decline in following years.

Golden Gate Bridge

The Golden Gate Bridge was one of the engineering marvels of the 1930s. Construction of the span claimed the lives of ten workers, despite elaborate safety nets strung beneath. In 1939–40, completion of the Golden Gate Bridge and the San Francisco–Oakland Bay Bridge was celebrated with the Golden Gate International Exposition on Treasure Island. *Courtesy of The Bancroft Library, University of California, Berkeley.*

The Central Valley Project

New Deal financing finally broke down opposition to another gigantic California undertaking, the Central Valley Project (CVP). As temporary Californian Mark Twain once quipped, "whiskey is for drinking—water is for fighting over." That certainly was true of the San Joaquin/Sacramento River Delta. The region faced serious environmental problems almost immediately, the result of converting tens of thousands of acres of tule marshes into farms, greatly reducing the Delta's capacity to store fresh water and to withstand saltwater intrusion from the San Francisco Bay. Salt water is a greater hazard to the Delta than to other regions. Lying below water level and lacking natural drainage, its soils cannot be easily drained or leached of accumulated salts that stunt or destroy crops.

By the early twentieth century, irrigation, cities, and sugar and petroleum refineries taxed the Delta's freshwater supply. Even more significant were declining flows from upstream. As the San Joaquin and Sacramento valleys boomed, irrigation projects and cities sucked up ever more water, leaving less to find its way to the Delta. San Francisco and Oakland dammed major tributaries of the San Joaquin River and imported their water directly by aqueduct, bypassing the river and the Delta altogether. By 1920, the volume and velocity of Delta rivers declined dramatically, especially during dry summer months, and the mean saltwater line moved steadily eastward. At first it polluted the industrial and municipal supplies of the western Delta, then it threatened Delta irrigation works. Wells began to draw salt water into underground basins. When droughts struck in the 1920s, freshwater slowed to a trickle, and the Delta teetered on the brink of ecological disaster.

Delta water users struck back to defend their water supply in 1915. They joined the city of Antioch in suing to prevent upstream irrigation districts, private land and water companies, and individual irrigators from diverting Sacramento River water further, but upstream interests ignored them. The state supreme court ruled in 1922 that upstream interests had vested rights to river water, that Delta users had no right to the preservation of water quality, and that there was no legal requirement that valuable water be "wasted" to flush the Delta.

During the 1920s, recurrent drought, the likelihood of future water shortages, and Delta water wars finally forced California to adopt comprehensive water planning, but different interests disagreed over solutions. Different regions and economic groups usually pursued narrow interests with little regard for the overall welfare of the environment. To escape litigation and regulation of their water use, Sacramento Valley diverters campaigned for a barrier or dam across the western Delta to keep saltwater out. Some western Delta industries and Bay Area cities supported this plan because it might assure their own water supply, but inner Delta interests strenuously objected that such a barrier would raise water levels and flood their farms and towns. Some scientists predicted that the entire Delta region would become hopelessly polluted if the barrier were built. Delta agricultural interests demanded that California confirm their legal right to enough freshwater flow to hold back saltwater intrusion, and were vigorously opposed by upstream users. Inland shipping and coastal fishing interests joined to fight the saltwater barrier, as it would impede ships and spawning fish bound for the interior. State and federal water experts favored large upstream dams in the northern Sacramento Valley. These dams could store excess winter water, channel it into canals to irrigate the interior, and release it in summer to flush salt from the Delta. This plan was supported most forcefully by the San Joaquin Valley, already facing water shortages and hoping to import water from northern streams and the Delta. Southern California strongly opposed all these schemes. Geographically isolated and developing its own water supply from the Owens Valley and Colorado River, southerners objected to spending state general funds to benefit those living north of the Tehachapis. From the 1920s on, decisions about water provoked bitter controversy.

Years of intensive arguing and study finally led to a water transfer plan in 1931, compiled by state engineer Edward

The Delta

In this Delta cabbage field, salt encrusts the surface and stunts the plants. *California Department of Water Resources.*

Hyatt. The plan proposed: (1) to build Shasta Dam on the northern Sacramento River to store water for irrigation, flood control, navigation, and Delta flushing; (2) to modify natural channels to carry purer and more abundant Sacramento River water into the San Joaquin portion of the Delta; (3) to install giant pumps to raise water from the southern Delta into gravity canals down the west side of the San Joaquin Valley; and (4) to construct the Contra Costa Conduit to supply the salt-plagued western Delta with fresh water. To placate the inner Delta and Southern California and to improve chances for passage, the costly saltwater barrier was dropped.

After acrimonious debate, the legislature passed the Central Valley Project bill in 1933. Enemies, particularly Southern California and private power companies that objected to the inexpensive public electricity the project would generate, forced the bill into a referendum later that year. It narrowly passed by a margin of only 35,000 votes. San Franciscans endorsed the measure two to one, while Angelenos rejected it by about the same proportion. By then, however, the deepening depression made state financing unlikely. Luckily for CVP advocates, the most pressing political issue in 1933 was taxation. Lobbyists for the major corporate taxpayers—particularly oil, railroad, and utility interests—were so involved in the taxation issue that they paid scant attention to the Central Valley Project bill, ably promoted by state senator John B. McColl of Redding. Much to their surprise, McColl's bill was adopted that year and signed by the governor. The act authorized a $170 million revenue bond issue to finance the CVP and included provision for public distribution of publicly generated power—an obvious bid to draw New Deal money. To state leaders' relief, in 1935 President Roosevelt and Secretary of the Interior Harold Ickes decided to make the CVP a Bureau of Reclamation project. Federal funds were allocated to the Bureau to start work, and two years later Congress assigned the CVP to the Bureau of Reclamation. Construction began in February 1937 and continued into the 1950s. As it stands today, the CVP is one of the most complex and massive water transfer systems ever built.

The chief components of the initial system were Shasta and Keswick dams on the Sacramento River, Friant Dam on the San Joaquin River, and the Delta-Mendota, Friant-Kern, and Madera canals. Shasta Dam at the time of construction was second only to Hoover Dam in size. It impounds the waters of the Sacramento, Pit, and McCloud rivers just north of Redding, creating the four and one-half million acre-foot Lake Shasta. Water from the lake flows south to the Sacramento-San Joaquin Delta and then is lifted to the huge Delta-Mendota Canal, which carries it 117 miles south into the San Joaquin Valley. Friant Dam impounds the waters of the San Joaquin River east of Fresno for distribution south to the Bakersfield area via the Friant-Kern Canal, and north by the Madera Canal. Well over 700,000 acres of San Joaquin Valley land came under irrigation with construction of this project. Since completion of the initial plan, the waters of other rivers were integrated into the system, bringing many thousands of additional acres into production. For example, the Trinity River, which normally flows to the coast, is impounded by Trinity and Lewiston dams, and most of its waters diverted through tunnels to the Sacramento Valley via the Whiskeytown Dam and Reservoir. Construction of Folsom and Nimbus dams added the American River to the system; construction of the New Melones Dam added the Stanislaus River. Completion of the two and one-half million acre-foot San Luis Reservoir west of Los Banos, which stores winter runoff for release to the west side of the San Joaquin Valley, increased the capacity of the CVP even further.

Although the original state plan had listed saltwater control as a responsibility of the CVP, federal authorization laws failed to mention it. When appealing for support in the late 1930s and early '40s, the federal Bureau of Reclamation promised to release water from Shasta Dam to maintain the Delta's water purity. Once the project was operating, however, the Bureau insisted it had no legal obligation to use Shasta water to maintain Delta water quality beyond what was needed to assure the quality of water exported south. Increasingly, federal and state experts viewed releasing fresh water to flush the Delta and Bay as a waste of valuable resources that could be used to stimulate development elsewhere. The Bureau of Reclamation's position—that as a federal agency it was not bound by state laws, including water standards—was generally upheld by federal courts. In drought years, the CVP refused to cooperate with California to maintain Delta water quality. By the 1950s Delta water rights had eroded still further.

Other controversies accompanied the burst of large-scale New Deal public works. Especially acrimonious was conflict over the distribution of electric power produced by the CVP, and over Bureau of Reclamation policies limiting to 160 acres the amount of land that could be irrigated with federally subsidized water. Nevertheless, the state and federal governments spent hundreds of millions of dollars creating thousands of jobs, relieving the impact of the depression and endearing the New Deal to many Californians.

The Revival of Labor

The Depression and New Deal ushered in a whole new era for organized labor in California, one characterized by a new militancy and radical leadership that eventually overturned the open-shop policies of the 1920s. In 1932 one of four workers in San Francisco and one of three in Los Angeles was out of work. In some fields, such as the building trades, unemployment ran as high as 50 percent. Workers scavenged at restaurants and produce markets, assisted charitable organizations in return for food, or sought public relief. Employers, in contrast, saw layoffs, reduced wages, longer hours, and the "speed-up" as ways to maintain profits and stay in business.

On the waterfront, particularly in San Francisco, these conditions were most troublesome. There employer-controlled "blue-book" unions operated their own closed shops. Hiring was accomplished by the degrading "shape-up," whereby longshoremen assembled each morning on the dock and company-controlled foremen selected men for a day's work, generally picking those who would kick back part of their wages or who were compliant participants in the speed-up. Others might get "casual" work for a day or two per week, in a system that fostered inequality in work distribution and discrimination against pro-union workers.

The adoption of the National Industrial Recovery Act (NIRA) as the New Deal's program for business recovery inspired organized labor to challenge this system. Section 7(a) of the NIRA for the first time guaranteed by law workers' right to organize and to bargain collectively with employers. An unprecedented era of union formation and strikes followed. When the U.S. Supreme Court declared the NIRA unconstitutional in 1935, Congress quickly passed the Wagner Act, which maintained labor's guarantees and established the National Labor Relations Board (NLRB) to oversee their implementation. Employers, however, refused to comply until court decisions upheld it; they sometimes encouraged defiance of the law even then.

Confrontation in the maritime industry came in 1934. That spring, membership in the International Longshoremen's Association (ILA) rose dramatically all along the Pacific Coast from Seattle to San Diego, and its members, in a test of strength, successfully challenged the "blue-book" union on Matson Company docks in San Francisco. Then, joining forces with other maritime unions, the longshoremen demanded shorter hours, higher pay, and an end to the shape-up. They also called for a union-controlled hiring hall and coastwide bargaining. Led by San Francisco's Industrial Association, the shipping companies refused to deal with the union, which they said was in communist hands. Nor would they consider coastwide bargaining or what they called the "un-American" closed shop.

On May 9, 1934, the longshoremen went out on strike. They were joined by unions representing stewards, sailors, masters and mates, marine engineers and firemen. A total of 3,500 men quit work, paralyzing the entire Pacific Coast. In June the Industrial Association negotiated an agreement ending the strike with conservative eastern leaders of the ILA, only to have it voted down by the union rank and file. The strikers then established a Joint Maritime Strike Committee and elected Harry Bridges, the longshoreman who had emerged as the militants' leader, as chairman.

Waterfront employers in San Francisco, determined to reopen the port, forced the issue on July 3, by sending a fleet of trucks from Pier 38 under police escort. A two-day battle ensued, ending on July 5, a day that became known as "Bloody Thursday," with scores injured and two longshoremen dead. That night Governor Frank Merriam sent the National Guard to patrol San Francisco's docks.

Bloody Thursday evoked massive sympathy for the strikers. San Francisco unions voted overwhelmingly for a general strike to protest that day's violence. On July 16 tens of thousands of workers left their jobs, and the city fell silent in a display of labor solidarity that shocked and frightened the rest of California. Four days later the general strike ended when strikers and employers agreed to arbitration of the longshoremen's dispute, and

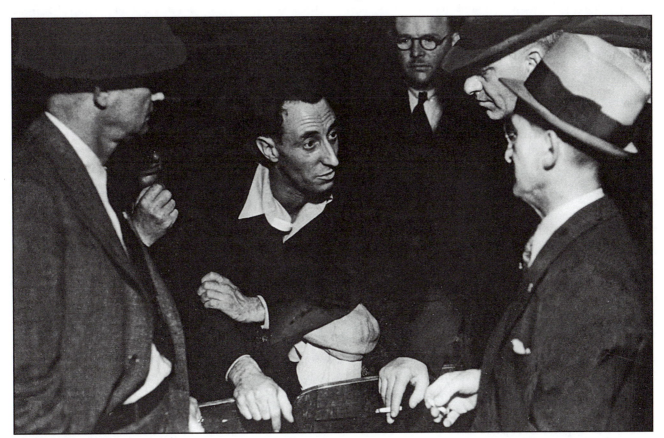

Harry Bridges

The longshoremen's and general strike of 1934 produced, in Harry Bridges (*leaning forward, center of photo*), one of California's most imaginative and innovative labor leaders. Born in Australia, Bridges migrated to California as a seafarer and became a key figure in the strikes of 1934, expanding the union inland, developing an areawide contract, eliminating racism in union membership, and adapting, in later years, to containerization. Accused of being a Communist Party member, he was harassed for 20 years with efforts to deport him. *Courtesy of The Bancroft Library, University of California, Berkeley.*

employers agreed to recognize and bargain with maritime unions. On July 31 the maritime strike ended, and on October 12 the National Longshoremen's Board's arbitration decision was handed down.

The decision was a substantial victory for Harry Bridges's longshoremen. It provided for recognition of the ILA as bargaining agent for the workers, and called for coastwide bargaining, jointly operated hiring halls with union-selected dispatchers to guarantee fair work distribution, a six-hour work day, and a substantial wage increase. It did away with the hated shape-up and established the basic structure of a longshoremen hiring system that is still used. By early 1935 the other maritime unions had negotiated their own settlements with employers.

The success of the young militants under Harry Bridges next led them to protect their flanks by organizing the poorly paid, local warehousemen. In what has been called "the march inland" that led to a major strike in 1936–37, Bridges's group brought almost all Bay Area warehousemen into a union affiliated with the ILA. In 1937, they were brought together in the International Longshoremen's and Warehousemen's Union (ILWU) when the ILA broke away from the American Federation of Labor (AFL).

The great maritime and general strikes of 1934 were symbolic of labor's rush to organize. They were also an inspiration to others. Older unions were rejuvenated and new unions sprang up among a host of previously unorganized workers. Union membership in California tripled between 1933 and 1938. But labor on the march was not always invincible and the open shop gave way slowly. In San Francisco the Employers Council, formed in 1938, ultimately replaced the Industrial Association and reasserted the right of employers to bargain collectively. In 1938 the Council negotiated a landmark contract with the ILWU, in which Bridges accepted a multiemployer agreement covering an expanded geographical area. Other unions and employers adopted this concept, and within a short time most Bay Area workers were covered by such contracts. The regional, multiemployer union contract is standard in California today.

The Open Shop in Los Angeles

As might be expected, Los Angeles put up an even stiffer defense of the open shop. When workers flocked to join unions after passage of the NIRA, the Merchants and Manufacturers Association (M&M) and the Los Angeles *Times* swung into action, pressuring employers to resist both unionization and Section 7(a). The M&M mounted a vast propaganda campaign,

pouring hundreds of thousands of dollars contributed by local businesses into the effort. It organized Southern Californians, Inc., as a steering committee and formed numerous front organizations such as The Neutral Thousands (note the acronym) and Women of the Pacific as strikebreakers. Its tactics—use of spies, blacklists, tear gas, and toughs—earned it the condemnation of the La Follette Committee, a subcommittee of the U.S. Senate Committee on Education and Labor, for its violations of basic civil rights. The M&M's campaign effectively slowed labor's drive to organize the unorganized, but could not stop it. From 1934 to 1939 unions increased their economic power and successfully eroded the open shop in Southern California until they claimed more than half the Los Angeles work force. In that period the auto, tire, movie, oil refining, and airplane industries were organized, and union membership shot from 33,000 to over 200,000. In July 1939 Los Angeles mayor Fletcher Bowron noted that "even the most conservative manufacturers have come to realize that . . . the effort to maintain the open shop is a lost cause."

Several factors explain the stubbornness of the open shop in Los Angeles. Only one-fifth of the city's total employment was in manufacturing in the 1930s. Also, nearly 68 percent of its work force was in service occupations or unorganized trade industries. Furthermore, Los Angeles was a regional market, with few industries dominated by any one employer. Plus the nature of the state and city economy—dependent on extractive industries such as oil and agriculture and on the businesses associated with them—made organization of those workers especially difficult. Only the stimulus of the New Deal, the development of branch plants in Los Angeles by national corporations accustomed to dealing with unions, and the industrialization of the area when World War II began, finally broke down the city's barriers to unionism.

Conflict within the union movement produced some of the 1930s' agitation and violence. Militant labor leaders such as Harry Bridges fervently believed in organization along industrial lines, while older AFL leaders clung to organization by craft or job task. In 1935 the AFL reluctantly set up the Committee for Industrial Organization (CIO) under the aggressive John L. Lewis, head of the United Mine Workers, to undertake industrial organization. Lewis successfully organized the auto, steel, and rubber industries in bitter campaigns, attracting others to the principle of industry-wide organization. In 1937 the ILWU and several maritime unions affiliated with the CIO. But AFL leaders became increasingly unhappy with CIO political activities and with radical influences in the CIO, several of whose unions had been infiltrated by communists. Attempts to discipline CIO unions finally led to their expulsion and the establishment of an independent Congress of Industrial Organizations in 1938. Consequently, work stoppages in the later 1930s often stemmed from disputes between rival AFL and CIO unions. Nevertheless, as the period closed, employer-employee relations in California had been irrevocably transformed.

Agricultural Labor

No such transformation took place in agriculture, due to the nature of California farming, the composition of its labor force, and successful organization of growers to resist unionization. The NIRA explicitly denied agricultural workers the right to organize and bargain collectively. To appease powerful Southern Democrats who balked at the prospect of unionized tenant farmers, sharecroppers, and maids, New Dealers deliberately excluded farmworkers and domestic workers from the protections of Section 7(a). The fact that California's agricultural workforce in the Depression era was approximately three-fourths Mexican and one-fourth Filipino generated far less public support for farm labor unionization, in contrast to the sympathy Californians showed white industrial workers.

In the 1930s, fear and anxiety about foreigners allegedly taking jobs and welfare benefits from native-born white Americans drove the deportation of over one million Mexican nationals and American citizens of Mexican descent. In California, the program of so-called "voluntary" repatriation saw federal and local officials rounding up Mexican immigrants and their families at parks, hospitals, markets, and other public places, and herding them into vans and trains bound for Mexico. An estimated 400,000 Californians of Mexican ancestry were deported in these raids. During the Depression, the annual rate of Mexican immigration to the United States fell from more than 50,000 to under 8,000.

Forced repatriation of Mexican Americans in the 1930s was supported by agricultural interests due to Mexican participation in efforts to organize farm worker unions and to a number of spontaneous strikes for higher wages. Such activities attracted the attention of the Communist Party, which formed the Trade Union Unity League (TUUL) and entered the agricultural field with the TUUL-affiliated Cannery and Agricultural Workers Industrial Union (CAWIU). In 1933–34 CAWIU-led strikes in California accounted for more than half the farm strikes in the nation, and three-fourths of them won wage increases for farm workers. Nearly 15,000 workers were involved in the 1933 San Joaquin Valley cotton strike, making it the largest in the history of American agriculture. Two years later John Steinbeck used the strike as the basis for a short but powerful novel entitled *In Dubious Battle*. Communist leadership provided a convenient excuse for growers to use intimidation and violence in dealing with farm workers, and grower political pressure eventually resulted in the arrest and conviction of CAWIU leaders under the state's criminal syndicalism law. This, along with a shift in Communist Party strategy away from organizing their own unions to infiltrating mainstream unions, destroyed the CAWIU.

Mexican Americans and Mexican immigrants dominated most of the successors to CAWIU, sometimes under female leadership. In Southern California, the *Confederación de Uniones de Campesinos y Obreros Mexicanos* (CUCOM) led several successful mid-1930s strikes for higher wages and better working conditions. By 1938 attempts to organize agricultural labor centered on the United Cannery, Agricultural, Packing and Allied Workers of America (UCAPAWA) of the reorganized Congress of Industrial Organizations (CIO). Initially successful in California, the Dust Bowl migration, grower resistance, and harassment of alleged Communist organizers weakened it after World War II. UCAPAWA, however, was exceptional in successfully organizing both urban and rural Mexican workers, and in its reliance on women leaders, including the dynamic Luisa Moreno, one of its chief organizers. With Josephine Fierro de Bright and others, Moreno cofounded *El Congreso de Pueblos de Habla Española* (Congress of Spanish-Speaking Peoples), a civil rights organization that grew out of the labor movement. Fierro de Bright, another charismatic Latina, brought significant financial support to the Congress through her husband, screenwriter John Bright.

The most important grower organization developed to respond to the strikes of 1933–34 was the Associated Farmers of California (AF). Ostensibly representing growers and processors, but actually a front for a cross-section of California business interests, the AF was financed by contributions from San Francisco's Industrial Association, Southern Californians, Inc., PG&E, Southern Pacific, Holly Sugar Corporation, and the Spreckels Investment Company, among others. From its inception, the AF played a dominant role in suppressing farm labor organization. It formed what amounted to a private vigilante army of men (often deputized by local sheriffs) who protected strikebreakers, disrupted workers' meetings, and attacked pickets. The AF successfully pushed for anti-picketing ordinances in agricultural areas and generally made a deliberate policy of violent resistance to unionization. It was responsible, said the La Follette Committee, for "the most flagrant and

John Steinbeck

Bard of the Long Valley

Signs in Salinas, in the surrounding 100-mile Long Valley, and around Monterey proclaim that "This Is John Steinbeck Country," but it was not always so. Indeed, the author once observed that residents of Salinas, where he was born in 1902, "want no part of me except in a pine box." Time, recognition, and awards—including the 1962 Nobel Prize—altered public opinion before Steinbeck died in 1968.

His youth in the Long Valley profoundly affected Steinbeck's life and career. Work in its fields, packing sheds, and processing plants provided the settings, characters, and sympathies that appeared in some of his finest novels. His parents introduced him to literature and music and, on his ninth birthday, gave him Thomas Malory's *Morte d'Arthur*. The book engendered a lifelong fascination with the ideas of knighthood, chivalry, and the heroic quest and perhaps confirmed his decision to write. Steinbeck pursued that ambition during his high school and Stanford University years, but without success. He supported himself with odd jobs while he embarked on his own quest, completion of his first book, *Cup of Gold* (1928). Not until the 1935 publication of *Tortilla Flat*, a novel based on *paisano* (country) life on the Monterey Peninsula, did Steinbeck achieve recognition: the annual Commonwealth Club Award for the best book on a California subject. A year later, *In Dubious Battle* captured the same prize.

John Steinbeck
Courtesy of The Bancroft Library, University of California, Berkeley.

Despite its social commentary and overtones of the Arthurian legend, *Tortilla Flat* could be read as humor; *In Dubious Battle* could not. It related the bitter, violent, and tragic Depression-era conflict between growers and communist-led farm workers, with little sympathy for growers or their tactics. In the Salinas Valley, it branded Steinbeck as subversive, an opinion apparently confirmed by the Pulitzer Prize-winning narrative of dust-bowl migrants, *The Grapes of Wrath* (1939). Steinbeck's neighbors condemned his work as "trash" full of "lust, sex, and vile words!" and saw it as a political, moral, and economic threat. Local libraries would not stock his books; his mother could not even give them away.

Passing years and fame apparently heal even the deepest wounds. In 1968 the author's ashes were welcomed back and interred—not in a pine box—in his beloved Long Valley. In the Salinas Victorian home where he spent his boyhood, tourists buy gourmet delicacies, books, and souvenirs, and profits from sales are distributed among local charities serving farmworkers and their families. The Galahad in John Steinbeck would have certainly understood and probably enjoyed the irony.   (WAB and PJB) violent infringement of civil liberties." Others labeled AF actions "farm fascism."

Whatever their methods, California growers effectively thwarted organization of farm labor. Even in the late 1930s, when UCAPAWA organizers entered the fields with the support of Governor Culbert Olson, they could not overcome the antiunion climate engendered by the AF and its allies. In this atmosphere, the AFL abandoned efforts to organize California farmworkers.

Depression Politics

The liberal deficit-spending policies of the New Deal were offset by the tight-fisted conservatism of California's Republican governors. While Gov. James Rolph supported the expenditure for relief payments of the $30 million surplus he inherited from Gov. Young, and approved forestry and highway work-relief camps recommended by the State Unemployment Commission, his 1933–35 budget of $258 million was $24 million less than the 1931–33 budget, which did little to relieve depression suffering. Having cultivated a glad-handing "smile with Sunny Jim" political image, Rolph found it difficult to deal seriously with the depression. He offended even his friends by condoning violence against striking farmworkers and, remarkably, by publicly approving the 1933 lynching of two kidnap-murder suspects in San José.

Gov. Rolph died suddenly in June 1934, after embarking on a strenuous reelection campaign against the advice of his doctors. His successor, Lieutenant Governor Frank E. Merriam, seemed to be cut from the same conservative cloth. Merriam would very likely have been replaced by a Democrat that year, had Upton Sinclair not appeared on the political scene.

The Democrats had every reason to expect a return to power in 1934. The Depression had discredited Republican policies; Democratic voter registration had rebounded from a three-to-one disadvantage to equality with Republican voters; and the party itself had come into the hands of leaders with close ties to the immensely popular Roosevelt administration. Instrumental in the Democratic revival was William Gibbs McAdoo, a major figure in national Democratic affairs, who relocated to Southern California in 1922. In 1932, he won the party's nomination for the U.S. Senate and helped switch the California Congressional delegation's allegiance to Roosevelt, assuring the latter's nomination. In the ensuing election Roosevelt won the presidency and McAdoo was elected to the U.S. Senate. Thus the time seemed ripe for the Democrats to win the governorship in 1934.

The party, however, was split north-south. Northerners backed Justus Wardell, a San Francisco magazine publisher, while southerners backed McAdoo's old friend George Creel, a federal relief administrator in California. Both were moderate to conservative Democrats; in supporting them, party leaders ignored the depression's radicalizing of hundreds of thousands of normally moderate middle-class voters. Failure to reckon with this churning, dissident force proved disastrous when Upton Sinclair took up the cause of the desperate with his End Poverty in California (EPIC) program.

Sinclair was a progressive-era muckraker who wrote *The Jungle* and dozens of other controversial books; he was the Socialist party candidate for governor in 1926 and 1930. Far more attuned to the misery caused by the depression than Democratic Party leaders, Sinclair published a pamphlet in 1933 outlining a program of action to end poverty in California, from which the EPIC movement sprang. That fall he changed his registration to Democrat and announced his candidacy for the party's nomination for governor by publishing a book entitled *I, Governor of California and How I Ended Poverty: A True Story of the Future*, in which he set forth his ideas in detail.

Desperate victims of the Depression eagerly embraced EPIC. More than 2,000 California EPIC clubs were formed, and Sinclair's supporters registered over 330,000 new Democrats, among them one former Republican, Edmund G. (Pat) Brown of San Francisco. An almost fanatical fervor imbued their campaign—not surprisingly, since Sinclair's proposals were a radical departure from Democrats' past platforms.

The EPIC program contained many attractive features, including repeal of the sales tax, shifting the burden of taxation to the wealthy and corporations, and a monthly pension of $50 for aged, blind, and needy people aged 60 and over. The most controversial, however, was Sinclair's plan for unemployment relief through a program he called "production-for-use." This scheme called for California to acquire idle factories and agricultural land where the unemployed would be employed in a system of cooperative self-help, with the exchange of goods facilitated by state-issued scrip. A $300 million bond issue would enable California to purchase the necessary properties. The production-for-use proposal appealed to a huge middle class experiencing real poverty for the first time. Their support turned Sinclair's campaign into a crusade that won him the Democratic gubernatorial nomination with more than 52 percent of the vote in a large field of candidates. EPIC-backed Sheridan Downey, a Sacramento lawyer and a spellbinding orator, won the nomination for lieutenant governor, becoming the other half of a team that newspapers dubbed "Uppie and Downey."

Party leaders deserted Sinclair in the general election campaign, influencing President Roosevelt's decision not to endorse Sinclair—a fatal blow to his chances. The campaign itself has been called the most bizarre in California history, its central issue becoming Sinclair himself. For 30 years Sinclair had attacked established social institutions in his writings and, as a socialist, he had consistently denounced the capitalist system. Fearing potential socialist control over California's economy, state business leaders poured millions of dollars into a vicious anti-Sinclair campaign. Political consultants and advertising executives took excerpts from Sinclair's writings out of context to depict him as an atheist, an advocate of free love, and a communist. Cartoonists pictured him as a wild-eyed fanatic. EPIC was renamed "Easy Pickings in California." The movie industry ground out fake "newsreels" showing thousands of the unemployed migrating to California, accusing Sinclair of deliberately attracting hoboes and relief chiselers to the state. Newspaper stories, often fabricated, and editorial cartoons ridiculed the new society envisioned by EPIC. The campaign against Sinclair has been called the first modern "media" campaign, a precursor of politics in the age of television.

In contrast to Sinclair, Gov. Merriam, who had easily won the Republican nomination, projected an image of reason and moderation. Although he had called out the National Guard to deal with the 1934 waterfront strike, he now came out in favor of collective bargaining and a shorter work week; he also let it be known that he would cooperate with Roosevelt's New Deal programs. Leaving the vituperative personal attacks on Sinclair to others, Merriam presented himself as a moderate, pragmatic reformer. These tactics were effective and former Lieutenant Governor Merriam easily won election in his own name. Sinclair retired from politics to write the story of the EPIC campaign in a book titled *I, Candidate for Governor and How I Got Licked*. The EPIC organization disintegrated rapidly, and the Democratic Party began another long struggle to rebuild cohesion and unity.

In retrospect, popular support for Upton Sinclair was a measure of the seriousness of the depression and the structural weakness of the state's post-progressive political system. Merriam's election denied Democrats the state house at a time when Democrats were winning offices nationwide. When California Democrats finally regained power in 1938, the reform impulse had passed.

Merriam's "Pragmatic Conservatism"

Gov. Merriam has long been regarded by historians as a do-nothing conservative who held his state still as the New Deal marched by. But Merriam's conservative rhetoric must be contrasted with his moderate-to-liberal actions. Merriam led California as far into the New Deal as his party would let him, using political skills he had developed in 16 years as assemblyman, assembly speaker, state senator, lieutenant governor, and as chairman of the Republican state central committee.

Calling for "social justice without socialism," Merriam promoted establishment of the State Emergency Relief Administration (which qualified the state for federal relief funds), approved federal takeover of the Central Valley Project, and backed a pension law that brought the state additional federal funds under the Social Security Act of 1935. To finance other social legislation, Merriam unabashedly secured a state income tax, higher taxes on inheritance, banks, and corporations, and a liberalized sales tax that exempted groceries, fuel, and prescription drugs. But opening the state to the grant-in-aid programs of the New Deal was as far as he could go, and after 1937 he generally resisted liberal social legislation.

While Merriam was governor, Democrats sought to recover from the debacle of 1934. Party regulars were in disarray but the "radical" wing coalesced around Culbert Olson, who had been elected as Los Angeles County's state senator in 1934 with EPIC backing and had emerged as the leading proponent of Democratic reform proposals in the legislature. Olson announced his candidacy for governor in September 1937, running on a liberal platform that included a modified production-for-use program, increased welfare and pension payments, progressive taxation, slum clearance, low-cost housing, public ownership of public utilities, and support for organized labor. In a deal of questionable legality, Olson secured the support of labor leaders with a commitment to pardon Tom Mooney as his first act in office. Mooney had spent nearly 22 years in prison, convicted on perjured testimony for San Francisco's 1916 Preparedness Day parade bombing. Labor's support proved decisive and Olson won the Democratic nomination in the 1938 primaries.

Democratic prospects for the general election were excellent. The New Deal was still popular and President Roosevelt endorsed Olson. Democrats were at last united and Olson's "New Deal for California" slogan attracted wide support in both parties. Gov. Merriam, on the other hand, was in deep trouble. His cooperation with the Roosevelt administration had offended

Republican conservatives, and his 1935 proposal to impose liquor, oil, and mineral severance taxes had offended the powerful state business interests whose wholehearted support he required. As expected, Californians elected Olson in November 1938, bringing the twentieth century its first Democratic administration. It was not a Democratic sweep, however, as Republicans regained control of the rural-dominated state senate and reduced the Democratic majority in the assembly.

Utopian Schemes and the Pension Movement

Hard times produced a wide variety of self-help organizations that received financial aid from New Deal agencies. In addition, radical and sometimes utopian schemes to provide for the elderly and unemployed proliferated in Depression-era California. One popular movement was Technocracy, which proposed to replace the existing monetary system with an energy system whose basic units were called "ergs." It attracted wide support in 1932, but collapsed within months. Similarly, the Utopian Society, which offered a vague "new economic order," found favor in 1933 and by 1934 claimed a membership of 500,000. The society's heavy emphasis on social activities led one observer to call it a "colossal Lonesome Club."

In many respects, the social movements of the 1930s substituted economic cults for the religious cults popular in the 1920s; indeed, Upton Sinclair had successfully directed those energies into his political movement. The old-age pension phenomenon was quite different. Of all the movements of the decade, pension plans attracted the widest support and caused the biggest headaches for politicians. By the mid-1930s, observed Jackson Putnam, "it was virtually raining pension plans." While California's 1929 Old Age Security Act was the nation's first mandatory state pension plan, the depth of the depression made it sadly inadequate. Pension requirements (essentially one had to be a propertyless indigent with no support from relatives) seemed degrading, yet a growing number of older people were faced with the prospect of permanent unemployment. Sinclair was one of the first to appeal to this group when he proposed a monthly pension of $50 and a ten-year reduction in the age of eligibility. His primary victory in 1934 was partly the result of older Californians' support, but he probably lost much of that support in the fall election by rejecting the Townsend plan, which by then had become surprisingly popular.

Borrowed from various sources, the Townsend plan was the product of an unsuccessful Long Beach physician and sometime real estate promoter, Francis E. Townsend. In 1934 Townsend, with a realtor named R. Earl Clements, launched the Old Age Revolving Pensions plan. The proposal called for Congress to adopt a national sales tax in order to provide all persons over 60 years of age with a monthly annuity of $200, on the condition that it be spent within the following month. The organization's newspaper, *The Townsend Weekly*, soon had a circulation of more than 100,000. Older Americans flocked to join Townsend clubs across the state and nation, and the Townsend Plan became a factor in national politics from 1934 on. However, when the Townsend Party was formed in 1936 and became involved in right-wing opposition to Roosevelt, the organization went into decline. At the same time, Congressional adoption of the 1935 Social Security Act blunted the plan's appeal.

The most sensational of the pension plans came to be called "Ham and Eggs" when someone at a rally shouted, "We want our ham and eggs!" It began in 1936 as the brainchild of an unscrupulous radio personality and promoter, Robert Noble, who was ousted and replaced in 1937 by the even shadier Allen brothers, Willis and Lawrence. The plan called for the state to issue 30 $1 pieces of scrip every Thursday to all unemployed persons over age 50; the scrip would then circulate like money. Every Thursday a holder of scrip was to put a 2-cent stamp on the back of the scrip dollar. At the end of fifty-two weeks, the state would redeem the scrip for a dollar, thus collecting four cents per scrip dollar to cover the program's administrative expenses. Picking up where Sinclair and Townsend had left off, the Allens by 1938 had gathered more than a million supporters. That year, "Thirty Dollars Every Thursday" qualified as a ballot initiative, becoming an important issue in the general election. Merriam endorsed the plan; Olson equivocated. Narrowly defeated in 1938, a new ballot measure qualified again in 1939. Now Gov. Olson came out against it and helped organize opposition to the measure as economically unsound, causing the measure to lose decisively. The Allens faded from public view, but not before hiring George McLain, an organizational genius who would dominate old-age pension politics for years thereafter.

The Townsend and "Ham and Eggs" movements had much in common: attractive plans, leaders who were skilled propagandists, and autocratic organizations that nevertheless offered supporters important psychological and emotional returns. They played an important role in forging California's elderly into a potent, highly vocal political interest group that put the state in the forefront in programs for senior citizens.

Olson's "New Deal for California"

Democratic expectations were unduly high when Olson took office in January 1939, and his administration proved to be a study in frustration. He failed to achieve passage of almost all of his principal reform proposals and so offended the legislature that it stripped the lieutenant governor of his committee-appointing powers, replaced a pro-Olson assembly speaker with a conservative Democrat, and forced Olson to seek relief funds in driblets from special sessions.

Nevertheless, Gov. Olson had his successes. His pardon of Tom Mooney momentarily made him the most famous governor in the United States. He achieved significant humanitarian reforms in the state's mental-health and parole systems. He vigorously protected civil liberties and minority groups, raised the standards of living conditions for migrant labor, and took satisfaction in the appointment of liberals to numerous judgeships. Ironically, the outbreak of World War II made Olson's reform program essentially irrelevant, and American entry into the war led him to cooperate, against his better judgment, in one of the most tragic events of the period—the 1942 removal and incarceration of Japanese Americans.

The "Okies"

A dramatic change in makeup of California's harvest labor force further undermined efforts to organize farm labor in the 1930s. Between 1935 and 1939 nearly 300,000 Southerners and Midwesterners migrated to California. Most came from the lower Plains states, notably Oklahoma, Arkansas, Missouri, and Texas, but they were generally dubbed "Okies." A variety of factors accounted for this migration. Years of drought had made their small farms unprofitable, especially when the depression hit. The New Deal Agricultural Adjustment Act (AAA) that paid farmers not to plant grain or cotton allowed landowners to evict tenant farmers. Mechanization made larger holdings more efficient, eliminating other tenant farmers. The great dust storms of the mid-1930s ruined large areas for farming. Poverty-stricken, "blowed out," and "tractored out," the Okies moved their families west.

California was a logical destination, given the image of the state created by years of boosterism. Moreover, favorable reports from friends and relatives of good wages picking cotton and fruit encouraged the move west and transportation was easy by automobile on Route 66. Like migrants of the 1920s, nearly half settled in metropolitan areas, primarily Los Angeles. The rest, however, turned north to the San Joaquin Valley where they sought work in California's complex, industrialized agricultural system. Ineligible for relief for one year because they were new to the state, they accepted the low wages that Mexican workers would not. In a short time Okies almost completely displaced Mexicans in California fields. When the Okies became eligible for unemployment relief, the state relief administration under Gov. Merriam cut off relief payments if farm work was available, forcing Okies into the relief-harvest labor-relief cycle that had historically subsidized California growers' low wages.

Important distinctions divided the Okies and traditional harvest laborers. As white Anglo-Saxon Protestants who settled in Central Valley towns, sent their children to local schools, and—importantly—registered to vote, their poverty could not be ignored. Living in shocking conditions in tent camps along irrigation ditches, they exposed the exploitation of farm labor in California's peculiar agricultural system and became a highly visible burden in local communities, particularly in the San Joaquin Valley. In 1939 their plight entered the national consciousness with the publication of John Steinbeck's *The Grapes of Wrath* and Carey McWilliams's *Factories in the Field*. Unfortunately, the focus on white Dust Bowl migrants rendered invisible the Mexican and Filipino farm laborers who had endured those conditions for years and continued to struggle for survival.

Grower satisfaction with the Okies was short-lived. The flood of migrants in 1937 created an embarrassing oversupply of labor, and the squalor of their camps reflected poorly on the industry. In 1938 it became apparent that the Okies were politically embarrassing as well. They were Democrats, supported Culbert Olson, and displayed firm loyalty to the New Deal. They also disrupted the strong Republican hold on rural communities, a fact that led to the formation of the California Citizen's Association (CCA), which, like the Associated Farmers, fronted for banking, oil, railroad, real estate, and insurance interests allied with agribusiness. The CCA, determined to attack the New Deal and Olson through the migrants, launched a publicity campaign that, as Walter Stein observed, went a long way toward creating a popular view of the Okie in California as a "degenerate, degraded loser in the American struggle for survival." By 1939 the CCA campaign had engendered widespread antagonism toward the migrants and their sympathizers, justifying harassment and discrimination against them. Olson's appointment of Carey McWilliams to head the Division of Immigration and Housing indicated his concern for farmworkers, but it also angered the conservative bloc in the legislature, which began a running battle with the blunt McWilliams. Nonetheless, McWilliams effectively used his position to publicize the shameful conditions of California's migrant farmworkers.

Organized labor might well have expected to capitalize on Okies' disappointment and anger at their treatment. But Okies brought with them such a strong individualism and antiradical patriotism that proletarian rhetoric about collectivism and class struggle was lost on them. When the CIO established UCAPAWA in 1937, it got nowhere with the newcomers. Ironically, the ideologies of the Okies led them to sympathize with farm owners, and they frequently served as strikebreakers. Their arrival impeded the unionization of farmworkers and lowered further an already insufferable standard of living.

In the long run, the inhospitality of Californians contributed to the creation of an "Okie subculture," defined by notions of personal toughness, economic justice, nativism, and Americanism—a group identity reinforced through the lyrics of country music. It was a subculture with considerable political and cultural impact on California, including a militant racism. When World War II nearly quadrupled California's African American population, blacks met resistance everywhere, but it was Okies who found the newest migrants most difficult to accept, leading to tension and violence. Moreover, while nominal Democrats, Okies moved away from California's more liberal Democratic Party, developing the kind of populist conservatism expressed by George Wallace 30 years later.

World War II dramatically ended the poverty of the Depression and altered the Okie experience in California. After 1939 the migrants, joined by 600,000 more Southerners and Midwesterners, drifted rapidly into war industries in urban areas, while an army of Mexicans, the *braceros*, replaced Okies in the fields. Those who remained were better paid and experienced greater acceptance. While the war ended the Depression era in California, the influence of the Okie subculture remained, as the continued popularity of religious radio stations and country music attest.

The Cultural Scene between the Wars

The good times and expanding economy of the 1920s brought increased support for the arts, while the automobile age promoted an orientation toward the outdoors that was reflected in architecture and leisure activities. San Francisco maintained its role as the state's cultural leader in this period. Construction of the de Young Museum in Golden Gate Park and the Palace of the Legion of Honor provided the city with two outstanding art galleries by the mid-1920s. At the same time, plans proceeded for construction of the War Memorial Opera House, completed in 1932 as the nation's first municipal opera house. City taxes supported not only opera but also the excellent San Francisco Symphony, established in 1911. Attracting outstanding conductors such as Alfred Hertz and Pierre Monteux, the symphony earned a reputation as one of the nation's best.

Los Angeles, meanwhile, developed its cultural institutions, despite the fact that many migrants of the 1920s preferred Aimee Semple McPherson to the opera. In 1919 William Andrews Clark Jr. endowed the Los Angeles Philharmonic Orchestra, which in 1921 began its famous series of summer "Concerts Under the Stars" in the Hollywood Bowl. The Huntington Library and Art Gallery rapidly became a world-renowned institution, especially with its acquisition of Thomas Gainsborough's painting *Blue Boy*. Establishment of the Otis Art Institute in the home of Harrison Gray Otis and the Chouinard Art Institute gave Los Angeles an important place in the visual arts.

Also significant was the arrival in the 1930s of thousands of European intellectuals fleeing the spread of Hitler's Nazi regime. Bringing "high culture" primarily to Southern California, where many worked in the movie industry, their homes became cultural "salons" for lively discussion. The famous novelist Thomas Mann, playwright Bertold Brecht, composer Arnold Schoenberg, conductors Otto Klemperer and Bruno Walter, as well as numerous well-known artists and actors, were a part of this migration which continued through the war years and contributed immensely to the subsequent "cultural explosion" of that region.

Architecture between the wars reflected and encouraged a trend toward outdoor living, notably in Southern California, where Richard Neutra—like Frank Lloyd Wright a student of Chicago's Louis Sullivan—introduced "functionalism." An Austrian immigrant, Neutra pioneered the "art moderne" style that opened houses to light. Wright and Neutra both subscribed to the concept that "form follows function," and their homes, with extensive use of glass, rock, and split-level design, contributed significantly to the evolution of the modern California ranch-style house.

In northern California "form follows function" was also the creed of Irving F. Morrow, consulting architect on San Francisco's Golden Gate Bridge in the mid-1930s. A modernist, considered by many to be radically ahead of his day, Morrow combined beauty with simplicity. For the bridge, he designed functionally graceful arching lamps over the roadway, insisted on a rail with open balusters so motorists and pedestrians could see through to the magnificent view, emphasized the height of the portals by having them diminish in width as they rose upward, and designed a vertical facet motif that he used subtly on piers and braces. Most daring of his innovations was painting the bridge "international orange." Noting that fog made San Francisco gray and colorless much of the year, Morrow criticized local architecture for adding more gray and no color. By choosing a full polychrome beginning with red-orange and culminating in a pure metallic gold on the monumental towers, he created a true "Golden Gate."

Another bright addition to the 1930s was the exuberantly cheerful musical style known as "swing," which Californians helped to launch. When Benny Goodman brought his first "big band" to Los Angeles at the end of an unsuccessful 1935 cross-country tour, Southern California youth gave him such an enthusiastic reception at the Palomar Ballroom that, as one observer noted, "the swing era was born." Goodman became known as the "King of Swing" and in 1936 organized the first integrated big band when he hired black pianist Teddy Wilson and vibraphone player Lionel Hampton. For the next two decades, California hotels and ballrooms were especially popular bookings for the swing bands of Goodman, Glenn Miller, the Dorsey Brothers, Duke Ellington, and others.

Musicians, artists, writers, historians, and actors and actresses were frequently found on the rolls of varied New Deal programs. WPA artists covered the walls of public buildings with murals that are only now attracting the attention they deserve. Dorothea Lange did some of her most powerful work as a photographer for the Farm Security Administration; her photographic documentations of the depression's effect on farm workers became classic works in the world of photography. Popular fiction often reflected the anxieties of the depression years, producing a number of bleak

novels such as James M. Cain's *Double Indemnity* and Raymond Chandler's *The Big Sleep*.

Compassion for California's agricultural workers produced equally powerful literature, such as John Steinbeck's *The Grapes of Wrath*, which was quickly made into a successful movie starring Henry Fonda. Carey McWilliams joined Steinbeck in exposing the plight of migrant farmworkers with publication of *Factories in the Field* (1939), a well-researched study of California agriculture. The Colorado-born McWilliams migrated to California and worked for the Los Angeles *Times* in the 1920s, attended law school in his spare hours, and joined a prestigious law firm. But he devoted much of his time to researching and writing on California themes, and most of his works on these topics were published in the 1940s. *North from Mexico* (1949) was a sympathetic account of the difficulties endured by Mexican migrants. *California: The Great Exception* (1946) developed the theme of the uniqueness of the state, while his *Southern California Country* (1949), republished as *Southern California: An Island on the Land* (1973) remains one of the best surveys of that region. McWilliams left the state in 1953 to become editor of *The Nation*. Another side to California's agriculture, ranching and the huge cattle-feeding business, is delightfully captured in Robert Easton's *The Happy Man*, published during the war and reissued in 1993.

Other fine writers made California and the West their themes. University of California professor George R. Stewart published *Ordeal by Hunger* (1936), a gripping account of the Donner party disaster, while at San Francisco State, Walter Van Tilburg Clark was writing *The Ox-Bow Incident*, published in 1940. The San Joaquin Valley was the locale for much of the writing of William Saroyan, whose heartwarming accounts of his boyhood in Fresno's Armenian community appeared in *My Name Is Aram* (1940). Two of Saroyan's best works, *The Time of Your Life* (1939) and *The Human Comedy* (1943), were made into movies. Saroyan's work, especially *The Time of Your Life*, which deals with the foibles of some down-and-out San Francisco waterfront characters, revealed a refreshingly positive view of human nature. In contrast to Saroyan, the era also produced Robinson Jeffers, who took a gloomy view of his fellow man.

Thus the "Roaring '20s" and the Great Depression, two strikingly different decades, produced some of the most moving and contradictory literature in California history. The essential innocence and optimism of Saroyan's view of life generally pervaded the era despite the hardships of the Depression, while the somber view of

Jeffers played a disturbing subdominant theme, warning of the dark destructive side of human nature.

San Francisco's Golden Gate International Exposition of 1939–1940, held on a large man-made island attached to Yerba Buena Island, embodied the optimistic view. Commemorating completion of the Golden Gate and Bay bridges, the "Treasure Island" world's fair dazzled visitors with exhibits of the latest technological developments, including television, and entertained guests with everything from "swing" to opera. Ironically the fair opened under the darkening shadow of war. Upon its closing, Treasure Island became a major facility of the U.S. Navy during World War II.

Woman in Vegetable Garden

The internees produced a good deal of their own food in vegetable gardens such as this one at Manzanar.
Courtesy of The Bancroft Library, University of California, Berkeley.

PART EIGHT

World War II and Postwar Expansion

World War II proved to be an important watershed for California, setting the stage for extraordinary growth and prosperity in the postwar years. At the same time, the war brought the culmination of 100 years of anti-Asian racism in the state, with the forced removal of Japanese Americans, two-thirds of whom were U.S. citizens, and their detention in America's version of concentration camps. The experiences of the Uchida and Wakatsuki families described in Chapter 22 illustrate the consequences of unjustified questioning of loyalty, as well as the power of racial bias. The narrative of the Wakatsuki family's experiences is based on the book *Farewell to Manzanar* (1973) by Jeanne Wakatsuki Houston and James D. Houston. The Uchida family's story is based on the book *Desert Exile: The Uprooting of a Japanese-American Family* (1982) by Yoshiko Uchida. Their stories have important ramifications for other people of color, particularly for Hispanic and African American populations, which grew rapidly in the postwar period, and for the history of racial relations in the state.

The war also lifted the state out of the depression and set in motion the development of what came to be called "high-technology" industries. California dominated this field, particularly the aerospace industry, and soaked up a huge proportion of the federal government's expenditures for research, development, and production of sophisticated military hardware and space vehicles. Wartime economic development also began a new migration to California that rivaled the state's growth rate of past decades, while total population leaped from 6,900,000 in 1940 to 15,650,000 in 1960. The strains of such expansion were apparent everywhere, but especially in education, housing, transportation, and recreation.

The postwar years also saw the development of an often vicious anticommunist movement when American relations with the Soviet Union deteriorated into the Cold War. California had its own version of anticommunist "witch hunting" in this period, which affected state politics for years to come. Meanwhile, the state's economic and social growth attracted national attention, its politicians became national figures, and its affluent society set the pace for the rest of the nation.

A Question of Loyalty

22

Japan's attack on Pearl Harbor, December 7, 1941, played directly into California's long history of hostility toward minorities, especially Asians, and created a war hysteria that brought down on Japanese Americans the full force of that legacy. Organizations such as the California Joint Immigration Committee, successor to the old Asiatic Exclusion League, and the Native Sons of the Golden West loudly questioned the loyalty of all persons of Japanese ancestry and demanded their removal from the state, a proposal endorsed by politicians and public alike. The resulting incarceration of Japanese Americans such as the Wakatsuki and Uchida families marked a turning point in the relations of Caucasians and Asians in California.

Tall and lean, Ko Wakatsuki stood proudly at the helm of his trawler, the *Nereid*, while his two older sons, William and Woodrow, readied it to join the fishing fleet heading out of the Los Angeles area's San Pedro harbor. It was a beautiful December day, and on shore his wife, Riku, and two of his daughters joined a handful of other women to watch the familiar procession of white boats gather, turn seaward, and begin to sail into the distance.

Wakatsuki had reason to be satisfied. A good wife and ten children, some of them married and starting families of their own, looked to him as the head of the family, a classic Japanese patriarch. At 54 he had been in the United States for 35 years, and was the proud owner of two fishing boats, one a $25,000 trawler. In spite of the fact that, as an

Issei, he could not become a citizen or own land, he was pleased that his Nisei children were citizens and possessed more opportunities than his generation.

On shore, the women lingered, watching the boats even after they could no longer see the men on board. Then, strangely, the white specks on the horizon began to grow larger, and the women realized that the boats were returning. But why? they asked. The sky was cloudless. Had there been an accident? Suddenly a man ran down from the nearby cannery, waving his arms and shouting, "The Japanese have bombed Pearl Harbor!" The women looked at each other in puzzlement, calling to him as he rushed by, "What is Pearl Harbor?" But he passed before they got an answer.

Until this time Ko and Riku Wakatsuki had lived with their younger children at Ocean Park near Los Angeles, but now they moved to Terminal Island in San Pedro harbor to be with their older children and the Japanese community there. Fear and confusion reigned, especially for the Issei, as their country of residence plunged into war with their homeland. They were now enemy aliens, and the anti-Japanese hysteria on the west coast filled them with anxiety. Two weeks later the FBI came for Ko Wakatsuki, as they came for most Japanese with commercial fishing licenses, and took him away. His family did not see him again for almost a year, and two months passed before they even learned where he had been taken—Fort Lincoln, North Dakota, an all-male internment camp for enemy aliens. Meanwhile, the family had moved again. The U.S. Navy, with a major base on Terminal Island and reacting to rumors of sabotage and espionage, gave the Japanese American families on the island 48 hours to leave. Drawn together by the two older boys, Bill and Woody, the Wakatsukis were soon huddled in rented housing in Los Angeles, wondering what would happen next.

On the same December day that Ko Wakatsuki's boat strangely returned to shore, the gentlemanly Dwight Takasai Uchida took his wife and two grown daughters to the Japanese Independent Congregational Church in Oakland, as he did every Sunday. Uchida, too, could take pride in his life in America. After working his way through Doshisha University in Kyoto, where he was converted to Christianity and given the name Dwight, he had come to America in 1906 at age 22. Precise, punctual, and efficient, he became successful in business and in 1917 obtained a position in the San Francisco branch of Mitsui & Co., one of Japan's largest export-import firms. That same year he married Iku Umegaki, a fellow graduate of Doshisha University, in a union arranged by faculty members who had known

them both. Now, at age 57, he had retired from his position as assistant manager at Mitsui. One daughter, Keiko (Kay), had graduated from Mills College, and the other, Yoshiko (Yo), was a senior at the UC Berkeley. Ordinarily, church services were followed by the entertainment of friends for dinner at the Uchidas' Berkeley home, but this Sunday was an exception. The family had just sat down to a simple lunch when suddenly the radio blared forth the terrible news. Pearl Harbor had been bombed by Japan! Distressed and frightened, the family nevertheless dismissed the bombing as the work of fanatics, and Yo went off to the campus to study for finals. There, her friends all agreed it was incredible that Japan would attack the United States.

That very afternoon, however, the FBI came for Dwight Uchida—as they had come for Ko Wakatsuki and many other Japanese American community leaders—and took him away for questioning. It was a week before his wife and daughters knew where he had been taken, and nearly six months before he was allowed to rejoin them. The three women were left to assume duties and responsibilities they had never dreamed they could or should have, at a time when rumors and war hysteria filled them with apprehension.

Probably no group in America watched the deterioration of relations between the United States and Japan with more apprehension than Japanese Americans, who were hardly more than 1 percent of California's population. When war came, they were powerless and vulnerable. Since their arrival in California in the 1890s, they had been subjected to the same hostility and discrimination that the Chinese had suffered before them. They were denied the right to become naturalized citizens, to own land, or to control property through corporations. Social indignities were heaped upon them. Attempts were made to force their children into segregated schools, and restrictive covenants denied them housing of their choice. They were denied service in commercial establishments, forced into segregated facilities in public places, and had to endure harassment and physical abuse. All the while they were the focus of a persistent campaign in the California press warning of the "yellow peril," an irrational fantasy of Oriental conquest of western America.

Like most other immigrant groups, the Issei developed their own economic niches and subculture. Applying the labor-intensive methods of their homeland, they eventually dominated important segments of California agriculture and played an important role in the state's advance in specialty crops. Perhaps half were employed in farming by 1920, while the rest organized small businesses that catered largely to the "little Tokyos" emerging in urban centers. Thrifty and hard-working, they retained what ties they could with family in Japan and with Japanese tradition, through Japanese-language newspapers and social clubs. In America, the Issei created a social order in which age, sex, and generation determined status, in which relationships and conduct were governed by precise rules, and in which group solidarity took precedence over the individual.

Most of their children, the Nisei, came of age in the 1920s and '30s and, like most children of immigrants, developed a measure of social distance from their parents. Born and raised in the United States, they considered themselves American but faced discrimination and barriers to full citizenship and acceptance. For example, after Kay Uchida graduated from Mills College with a major in child development, she could find work only as a glorified nursemaid and had to take her meals in her employers' kitchen. The Nisei struggled to find a place in mainstream American social and economic life, creating a unique bicultural identity that, at least in the prewar years, did not equate loyalty to the U.S. with severing ties to Japan.

Life in America proved even more difficult for a subgroup of the Nisei, the Kibei, who, while born in the United States and thus American citizens, had been sent to Japan as children to be educated. On returning to the United States, they had much less in common with their Americanized brothers and sisters, found the English language a barrier, and were more oriented to the customs and social arrangements of their parents.

The Wakatsukis joined a close-knit Japanese American community in Los Angeles when they moved from Terminal Island and watched panic grip the state as rumors of a Japanese invasion spread, fed by the amazing successes of Japan's military and naval forces in the Pacific. Within six months Japan overran French Indochina, Singapore, the Dutch East Indies, the Philippines, the major Pacific island chains, and American bases at Wake and Guam. By the middle of 1942, its forces threatened India and Australia. In California, cities were blacked out at night, civil-defense forces were organized, and plans to repel an invasion were hastily prepared.

Attention quickly turned to Japanese Americans concentrated on the West Coast. Anti-Asian views of the Japanese as sly, devious, unassimilable, and dangerous were again aired in the press and radio. Charges were made that Japanese-American fishermen such as Ko Wakatsuki were fueling Japanese submarines at sea. Public opinion was further inflamed by newspaper columnists and radio commentators who proposed that Japanese

Americans be removed from California and even that Nisei be stripped of their citizenship. Japanese Americans kept to themselves as word spread that they might be forced to leave their homes and even their state.

As the weeks passed, the situation worsened. Important political figures, including Los Angeles mayor Fletcher Bowron and state attorney general Earl Warren, began to join the anti-Asian forces in calling for removal of all persons of Japanese ancestry from the "war zone." It was impossible to tell the loyal from the disloyal, they said, so all should go. Then in February 1942 came the news that President Roosevelt had signed Executive Order 9066 authorizing the army to remove any person, alien or citizen, from military areas if required by military necessity. Some sort of removal appeared imminent, and how to react to it became a matter of serious debate among the Japanese Americans. Most concluded that only a cooperative attitude would prove their loyalty.

With their father gone, the elder Wakatsuki children devoted their efforts to holding the family together and finding housing in the same district so they would not be separated. Other than that, they could only say to one another *shikata ga nai* ("it cannot be helped," "it must be done"), a Japanese phrase of resignation to enduring something difficult but unavoidable.

In Berkeley, the Uchida women tried to go on living normally like other Americans, while letters from Dwight, now imprisoned in an army internment camp in Missoula, Montana, begged for news and grew more and more anxious about reports of a mass evacuation. They could not give him information they did not have, but they began to prepare for a forced move, packing up books and household goods. Already, an 8:00 PM to 6:00 AM curfew and a five-mile travel limit had been imposed on all Japanese Americans, while their radios, binoculars, cameras, and firearms had been designated contraband to be turned in to local police. The Uchida daughters' box cameras remained in the Berkeley police station for the rest of the war.

Early in March, General John L. DeWitt, commander of the Western Defense Command, began to exercise the authority delegated to him under Executive Order 9066 with a proclamation establishing Military Area No. 1 as all of California, the western half of Oregon and Washington, and southern Arizona. This area was prohibited to enemy aliens and any person of Japanese ancestry. DeWitt's proclamation actually encouraged the Japanese to move out of Military Area No. 1 voluntarily,

Copy of WCCA Exclusion Order, 1942.

WESTERN DEFENSE COMMAND AND FOURTH ARMY
WARTIME CIVIL CONTROL ADMINISTRATION
Presidio of San Francisco, California
May 3, 1942

INSTRUCTIONS
TO ALL PERSONS OF
JAPANESE
ANCESTRY
Living in the Following Area:

All of the County of San Mateo, State of California.

Pursuant to the provisions of Civilian Exclusion Order No. 35, this Headquarters, dated May 3, 1942, all persons of Japanese ancestry, both alien and non-alien, will be evacuated from the above area by 12 o'clock noon, P. W. T., Saturday, May 9, 1942.

No Japanese person living in the above area will be permitted to change residence after 12 o'clock noon, P. W. T., Sunday, May 3, 1942, without obtaining special permission from the representative of the Commanding General, Northern California Sector, at the Civil Control Station located at:

> Masonic Temple Building,
> 100 North Ellsworth Street,
> San Mateo, California.

Such permits will only be granted for the purpose of uniting members of a family, or in cases of grave emergency.

The Civil Control Station is equipped to assist the Japanese population affected by this evacuation in the following ways:

1. Give advice and instructions on the evacuation.
2. Provide services with respect to the management, leasing, sale, storage or other disposition of most kinds of property, such as real estate, business and professional equipment, household goods, boats, automobiles and livestock.
3. Provide temporary residence elsewhere for all Japanese in family groups.
4. Transport persons and a limited amount of clothing and equipment to their new residence.

The Following Instructions Must Be Observed:

1. A responsible member of each family, preferably the head of the family, or the person in whose name most of the property is held, and each individual living alone, will report to the Civil Control Station to receive further instructions. This must be done between 8:00 A. M. and 5:00 P. M. on Monday, May 4, 1942, or between 8:00 A. M. and 5:00 P. M. on Tuesday, May 5, 1942.
2. Evacuees must carry with them on departure for the Assembly Center, the following property:
  (a) Bedding and linens (no mattress) for each member of the family;
  (b) Toilet articles for each member of the family;
  (c) Extra clothing for each member of the family;
  (d) Sufficient knives, forks, spoons, plates, bowls and cups for each member of the family;
  (e) Essential personal effects for each member of the family.
All items carried will be securely packaged, tied and plainly marked with the name of the owner and numbered in accordance with instructions obtained at the Civil Control Station. The size and number of packages is limited to that which can be carried by the individual or family group.
3. No pets of any kind will be permitted.
4. No personal items and no household goods will be shipped to the Assembly Center.
5. The United States Government through its agencies will provide for the storage, at the sole risk of the owner, of the more substantial household items, such as iceboxes, washing machines, pianos and other heavy furniture. Cooking utensils and other small items will be accepted for storage if crated, packed and plainly marked with the name and address of the owner. Only one name and address will be used by a given family.
6. Each family, and individual living alone, will be furnished transportation to the Assembly Center or will be authorized to travel by private automobile in a supervised group. All instructions pertaining to the movement will be obtained at the Civil Control Station.

Go to the Civil Control Station between the hours of 8:00 A. M. and 5:00 P. M., Monday, May 4, 1942, or between the hours of 8:00 A. M. and 5:00 P. M., Tuesday, May 5, 1942, to receive further instructions.

> J. L. DeWITT
> Lieutenant General, U. S. Army
> Commanding

SEE CIVILIAN EXCLUSION ORDER NO. 35.

but few did so. Reports from those who attempted to move voluntarily told of migrants being clapped into jail and harassed by vigilante groups. Finally, effective March 29, DeWitt issued another proclamation prohibiting all Japanese Americans from leaving Military Area No. 1. Evacuation had been put in the hands of Colonel Karl Bendetsen, one of the early and most insistent advocates of removal, who was now appointed to head the Wartime Civilian Control Administration (WCCA) under DeWitt's command.

Bendetsen's plan was relatively simple. He divided the west coast into 108 "exclusion areas," each containing approximately 1,000 persons of Japanese ancestry, and established a civil control station for each area. The plan included a program to remove these persons, first to assembly centers and then to inland camps for detention. The assembly centers were racetracks, exhibition centers, and fairgrounds; some 20,000 persons were moved directly to two of the inland camps, euphemistically called "relocation centers," and administered by a new civilian agency, the War Relocation Authority (WRA). On March 30, 1942, three and a half months after the attack on Pearl Harbor, the WCCA issued the first civilian exclusion order and the uprooting of Japanese Americans from their homes began.

For weeks the Uchidas had watched pressures mount for their forced removal, anxious over the hysteria and racism in the statements of the press, public officials, and the military. Now they helplessly packed their belongings and awaited the exclusion order for their area. Even then they were shocked when it came. On April 21 the newspapers announced: "Japs Given Evacuation Orders Here." Numbly, they read that Berkeley's 1,319 Japanese aliens and citizens would be evacuated to Tanforan racetrack, south of San Francisco, by May 1. Ten days' notice! Kay, as the oldest citizen, assumed the position of head of the family, reported to the local Civil Control Station for registration and returned with identification tags for all of their belongings. From then on the Uchidas were just family No. 13453. Frantically, they tried to pack and dispose of possessions accumulated over 15 years. Many years later Yo remembered their plight:

> We surveyed with desperation the vast array of dishes, lacquerware, silverware, pots and pans, books, paintings, porcelain and pottery, furniture, linens, rugs, records, curtains, garden tools, cleaning equipment, and clothing that filled our house. . . . We sold things we should have kept and packed away foolish trifles we should have discarded . . . desperate as the deadline approached. Our only thought was to get the house emptied in time, for we knew the Army would not wait.*

The piano, a few pieces of furniture, boxes of books, and some other possessions were stored with friends and neighbors, while larger pieces such as beds, mattresses, and rugs were put in commercial storage. The Uchidas had been told to bring only what they could carry, but also bedding, dishes, and eating utensils, so these were bundled into a large canvas bag into which they stuffed what would not fit into the two suitcases apiece they planned to carry. Then, after one last night in their now-barren house, the Uchidas reported with suitcases and an enormous, bulging bag to the Civil Control Station, where they were unnerved by the armed soldiers who guarded it. Depressed and angry, they boarded buses and were driven across the bay to the Tanforan racetrack, which had been hastily converted into an assembly center for Bay Area Japanese Americans. There, behind barbed-wire fences punctuated by tall guard towers, they were assigned to Barracks 18, Apartment 40, a hastily renovated horse stall in a long stable. Linoleum had been laid over the manure-soaked floorboards, but the smell remained. The partition between the stalls had been whitewashed, but it ended a foot or more below the roof, providing little privacy for the various families housed in the stable's 25 stalls. This 20-by-18-foot "apartment" became the Uchidas' new home for the next five months. As she stood in the long line for meals, Yoshiko Uchida was overwhelmed by feelings of degradation, humiliation, and longing for her Berkeley home.

Life in an army-run assembly center—there were 13 in California—was truly traumatic for the internees. The women found the lack of privacy in latrines and showers especially humiliating, and some took to covering their faces with newspapers when using the open facilities. The army, unequipped to provide living quarters for women and children, made little attempt to meet their needs. Laundry had to be done by hand, and hot water was gone by early morning. Some women arose at 3:00 or 4:00 AM to do their washing. Food was generally bad and skimpy (on the day of their arrival, the Uchidas were greeted with two sausages, a baked potato, and some unbuttered bread for dinner), leading to constant illness and physical complaints.

Above all, it was communal living, with only semiprivate sleeping quarters. There was no way or place to be

---

* All quotations concerning the Uchida family are taken from Yoshiko Uchida, *Desert Exile: The Uprooting of a Japanese-American Family* (Seattle: University of Washington Press, 1982).

alone, no way to avoid others or escape the constant noise. For those with young children and teenagers, the close quarters, mess-hall eating, and lack of activity put severe strains on family ties. The barracks and stalls carried every conversation two or three families away. Discipline broke down under such conditions. Yet, for many, the family unit was crucial to survival. More than one resident remarked that only the stabilizing influence of the family enabled them to cope with life in the center.

For the Uchidas, living at Tanforan was at least brightened by the return of Dwight as head of the family; after five months in the army's Missoula, Montana, camp for "dangerous enemy aliens," Dwight was released on parole. After all, he had been retired from Mitsui & Co. for two years, had an impressive record of public service and was well recommended by many prominent Bay Area friends. With his return, the Uchida "home" once again became a social center for their many friends. Dwight spent long evenings recounting to them (and neighbors listening over the partition) his experiences in Missoula.

The internees had to create a whole new community behind the barbed wire at Tanforan, an experience being repeated at other centers in Washington, Oregon, and California. Food, medical, and postal services were established, an educational system organized, and recreation provided for. Within a few weeks local mess halls serving sections of the camp replaced the huge grandstand mess hall, evacuee chefs took over the cooking, and meals improved. Kay and Yo Uchida helped build a school system, Kay heading up a nursery-school program, where, for the first time, she could practice the profession she had trained for in college. Yo was soon teaching second grade (at a salary of $16 a month). By the end of June, 40 percent of the internees were either teaching or attending school.

The need for recreation was obvious. The internees organized 110 softball teams, musical theater, art classes, music lessons, hobby-shop programs, Saturday night dances, and talent shows that attracted hundreds of participants. Many turned to gardening and transformed the center's appearance with vegetable and flower gardens and a small parklike area. Within the barracks, scrap lumber and materials obtained from catalogue sales converted the horse stalls into modest living quarters with window curtains, shelves, tables, and chairs.

The great effort the evacuees at Tanforan put into making their incarceration bearable, turning horse stalls and barracks into "homes," was tinged with irony; they all knew that they would eventually have to move again.

Finally, in late August the word came: they would be moved between September 15 and 20.

As September progressed the Uchidas began packing again. Dwight dismantled the scrap-lumber tables and chairs to make packing boxes and suitcases. Then, on September 16, the Uchidas and the other residents of their mess-hall unit were registered, counted, and marched between two rows of armed soldiers to a train pulled up at a racetrack siding. That night, with curtains drawn, their train left Tanforan—destination: the Topaz Relocation Center in Utah.

In Los Angeles, in the meantime, the Wakatsukis watched the initial sympathy of whites for their difficult situation erode, as FBI raids picked up more and more Issei men and rumors of Japanese American sabotage and espionage flared in the press. By March the evacuation was a certainty and the Wakatsukis were resigned to it. At least, the older children said, they would be under government protection and away from the growing hatred in the war zone. When the order came, the Wakatsukis met at the Los Angeles Buddhist Church designated as their pick-up point.

It was a scene they would long remember. Old people leaned in confusion on the young. Small children hung wide-eyed on their mothers' skirts, while their older brothers and sisters struggled with the mass of suitcases, duffel bags, and bulging bundles. Confused, bewildered, and frightened, they clung together in little family groups. For many besides the Wakatsukis, "Papa," the family head, had already departed, snatched from their midst for "questioning" only to disappear without notice. Here and there, lonely individuals appeared with no family to absorb and comfort them.

Behind them lay the shattered remains of their lives as free people. Furniture worth hundreds of dollars had been sold to second-hand dealers for five or ten dollars. Homes, farms, and businesses acquired through years of hard work and frugality had been sold for pennies on the dollar, or left in the care of friends. For the youngsters, there was the puzzling, unanswered question of why they had suddenly been pulled out of school—in many cases, just as they were about to graduate.

Under the watchful eyes of armed soldiers, the Wakatsukis registered, received identification tags to attach to their clothing, and were herded to trucks and buses where they heaped their belongings in great piles with matching numbered tags. When they boarded the bus the order was given to close the window curtains. As the buses rolled through the city and into the countryside late in the day, the curtains were drawn to reveal a harsh desert-like terrain, where windblown dust and sand yellowed the sky and turned the sun red. The passengers found themselves approaching the camp that, for many, was to be their home for more than three years. At last the buses drove through a large gate in a high barbed-wire fence where soldiers watched from towers spaced at intervals around the compound. Rows of black tar-paper barracks came into view, and a number of waiting people gathered around looking for friends and relatives among the new arrivals. The passengers sat frozen in apprehensive silence as their vehicle eased to a stop. Finally, Jeanne, the youngest Wakatsuki, threw open a window, leaned out, and cried, "Hey, this whole bus is full of Wakatsukis!" and suddenly tension-relieving laughter rocked the bus.

They had arrived at Manzanar, in the high-desert Owens Valley east of the Sierra, one of the two camps that served as assembly centers before conversion to relocation centers. Here, in this isolated area subject to extreme temperatures of near 0°F in winter and more than 100°F in summer, the army was constructing row upon row of flimsy barracks—single-thickness pine plank walls covered with tar paper, with gaping cracks and knotholes in walls and floors through which the wind carried clouds of dust. Each building was divided into six units measuring 16 by 20 feet, with one bare light bulb hanging from above and one oil-stove for heat. Open ceilings were an invitation to lively young boys to climb into the rafters and spy on neighbors.

The Wakatsukis were assigned two of these units for the twelve in their immediate family. Woody and Bill and their wives, with Woody's baby, took one unit, which they partitioned with a blanket. Riku, her mother, and the five youngest children were crammed into the other. Eleanor, the recently married oldest daughter, and her husband were assigned another one-room unit with six strangers—another couple, like themselves recently married, and a third couple with two teenage boys.

With the camp still under construction, problems abounded. Lack of refrigeration spoiled food so frequently that the "Manzanar runs" became a condition of life. The latrines were shocking to a people whose cultural traditions placed so much emphasis on personal privacy. The wash basin was a long metal trough on a concrete slab, with hot and cold water spigots at intervals. In the same room, twelve toilets were arranged in two rows of six, back-to-back without partitions. At one end of the room was a bank of open showers. The women, in particular, were appalled at these facilities and devised countless schemes to affect a bit of privacy. One woman had a huge cardboard carton she set up around one of the toilet bowls when her turn came.

Even standing, her head barely appeared over the top. She was kind enough to lend it to Riku.

The cold wind off the Sierra rolled up clouds of sand and dust, which poured through the gaping cracks and knotholes in the barracks walls. The new arrivals woke up after their first night with hair and eyebrows covered with a fine powder as though dirty flour had been sifted over them while they slept. Woody's first priority was to set the younger boys to work nailing tin-can lids over the knotholes and stuffing the cracks with paper. Few were prepared for the cold. Riku had lived in eastern Washington and knew how cold the April winds could be, so the Wakatsukis had all arrived with warm overcoats but, like the other residents, they lacked sufficient cold-weather clothing. The army issued surplus World War I woolen clothing, almost all of it too big, and the evacuees shuffled about in their loose trousers, as Jeanne remembered, like "a band of Charlie Chaplins marooned in the California desert."

Even when the food improved, the mess-hall eating was resented, especially by the Issei. They saw the rapid disintegration of their families as children chose to eat with friends, often hopping from one mess hall to another in search of the best food. Family living was replaced by communal living and the barracks became mere sleeping quarters. In the daytime the camp population circulated in the open, seeming to Jeanne like "10,000 people on an endless promenade inside the square mile of barbed wire."

In September 1942, Ko Wakatsuki was paroled from Fort Lincoln and sent to Manzanar. His return was a shock to his family. Limping because his feet had been frostbitten in the −30°F weather of North Dakota, he seemed to have aged ten years. Morose and humiliated by his imprisonment and the imputation of disloyalty, he moved in with Riku and six others in her cubicle. He refused to leave the room and took to drink, making a kind of brandy in a little homemade still. Frequently in a rage, he was a man without a home, a job, or any control over his life—a powerlessness that all shared.

For months, anger and humiliation festered in the camp, dividing friends, families, and age groups. Because Japanese-language newspapers were prohibited, rumors filled the communications vacuum, particularly for the Issei. Yet the mess-hall bells rang day after day, calling meetings to demand better food or higher wages (the top pay for evacuee professionals was $19 a month, while Caucasian personnel received $150 to $200 a month), to look into charges of corruption, to plan revolt, to urge common sense, to seek repatriation to Japan, or to prove their loyalty.

Manzanar Relocation Center was located east of the Sierra Nevada in the high desert region of the Owens Valley.
Courtesy of The Bancroft Library, University of California, Berkeley.

Above all, the meetings focused on those Nisei in the Japanese American Citizens League (JACL) who had been early arrivals and had obtained the best jobs in the camp's administration, or who had most loudly advocated the policy of cooperating with the evacuation as a way of "proving our loyalty," or who looked on the Issei as a declining class that should relinquish its leadership position to the next generation. Rumors flew through the camp that those who were most cooperative with the administration were *inu*, the Japanese word for "dog"—that is, informers or even traitors. Many Issei willingly believed this, as did many of the Kibei. The JACL, they believed, was destroying the group solidarity that had enabled the Japanese to survive so long in America, a view that even many Nisei came to accept as their detention continued. That fall the Issei and Kibei gradually regained power in the community, and the most prominent members of the JACL were isolated as *inu*. Passions boiled over on December 5, when Fred Tayama, Manzanar's representative to a JACL convention in Salt Lake City, was severely beaten. When a popular Kibei named Harry Ueno was jailed as a suspected assailant, the community rose to demand his release in what came to be called the "Manzanar Revolt." Thousands of evacuees marched to the administration area, while others attacked the hospital looking for Tayama and other *inu* to "finish the job" the assailant had started. In the ensuing melee, some guards opened fire on the crowd. One young man was killed, and several were wounded; one died the next day. But order was finally restored.

The next great issue to strain the community was the loyalty oath controversy. In February 1943 the WRA sent around a questionnaire designed to speed up the clearance process for relocation of evacuees to eastern communities; everyone over the age of 17 was required to complete it. At the same time, the army was organizing an all-Nisei infantry group, the 442nd, and was seeking volunteers from the camps. It was thought that the questionnaire could serve both purposes, so it included two questions originally intended only for Nisei of draft age:

27.n Are you willing to serve in the armed forces of the United States on combat duty, wherever ordered?

28.n Will you swear unqualified allegiance to the United States of America and faithfully defend the United States from any or all attack by foreign or domestic forces, and forswear any form of allegiance or obedience to the Japanese emperor, or to any other foreign government, power or organization?

Naively, administrators thought this would provide the means to weed out "disloyals," who would be sent to one center—Tule Lake, California.

Crowded Barracks at Manzanar

At Manzanar and other relocation centers, evacuees had to put up with a minimum of space and privacy. *Courtesy of The Bancroft Library, University of California, Berkeley.*

Family in Mess Hall, Manzanar

Mess-hall meals made it difficult to maintain traditional family life. *Everett Collection Inc / Alamy Stock Photo.*

The camp was again thrown into an uproar. Question 28 was absurd for the Issei, who were prohibited by law from becoming American citizens. Renouncing their only citizenship would leave them stateless. For the Nisei, a "yes" answer could be said to imply that some form of allegiance to Japan had in fact existed. The question was eventually rewritten to read:

> 28.n Will you swear to abide by the laws of the United States and to take no action which would in any way interfere with the war effort of the United States?

Issei could more easily respond affirmatively to this revised question, but the two questions increased tensions between Issei and Nisei, as did the call for volunteers for the all-Nisei army unit. Ko and Woody Wakatsuki carried on a running argument for weeks, then reached a compromise—Woody would answer "yes, yes" but would not volunteer. Meanwhile, embittered elements in the community organized a movement to promote "no, no" answers and exerted pressure for a mass refusal to cooperate. This debate finally forced Ko Wakatsuki out of his self-imposed isolation. There had never been any doubt that he would answer "yes, yes" on the questionnaire. He was infuriated at the attempt to bully the whole block into a "no, no" vote. Cleaned up and sober, he attended the mess-hall meeting called by the protest organizers and spoke his mind. Murmurs of *inu* passed through the audience until one man actually spoke it aloud. Ko attacked and the two scuffled until they were finally pulled apart. That night Ko sat up late drinking tea and tearfully singing

songs in Japanese, but he no longer remained shut up in the barracks. He had taken his stand.

For all the conflict and pain it caused, by the spring of 1943 the loyalty questionnaire succeeded in speeding up the relocation process. Riku, who had taken a job as a camp dietician, got the family moved to new quarters that doubled their space. There, a new pattern of life evolved that lasted until the end of the war. Woody and Bill sheetrocked the walls and ceilings, laid linoleum on the floors and built furniture from scrap lumber, and the barracks became livable. Ko drank much less and puttered outside; he pruned and cared for the trees in an abandoned apple and pear orchard next to the camp, built and maintained a rock garden around the barracks entrance, painted watercolor landscapes, and hiked to the streams at the foot of the nearby mountains for wood to carve. His resigned manner (*shikata ga nai*) seemed to typify the dominant mood of camp life.

Manzanar essentially became another small American town in this period—the largest, in fact, between Reno and Los Angeles—with schools, churches, police and fire departments, Boy Scouts, softball leagues, and other usual community activities. The younger children were engrossed in schoolwork and recreational activities, while the older ones took jobs. That fall Woody was finally drafted, and the next spring Bill, his wife, and five more Wakatsuki children relocated to New Jersey, where they had found jobs in a frozen-food plant.

Ko and Riku, Riku's mother, and the three youngest children were the only Wakatsukis remaining at Manzanar in 1945. By then the Supreme Court had ruled that the government could not detain an "admittedly loyal citizen" indefinitely, and the WRA announced that it would close all camps except Tule Lake by the end of the year. Still the Wakatsukis, like so many others, remained. Where would they go? What would they do on the "outside"? Rumor had it that those returning to their former homes had been received with hostility. Even when the war ended in August 1945, a fearful paralysis still gripped thousands in the camp. Ko decided to wait until the government forced him out. With no home, no job, and no word of his boats, he had nothing to look forward to.

That summer the schools at Manzanar closed for good and farm operations shut down. The government announced that those who did not leave the camp voluntarily would be assigned dates and taken by bus to the destination of their choice. In October the Wakatsukis learned they were at last scheduled to leave. Ko, in one last gesture of defiance, went to the nearby town of Lone Pine and bought a car, determined to leave Manzanar in style. When the day to leave arrived, the Wakatsukis were able to drive away with dignity from what had been their prison home. Later that afternoon they arrived in Long Beach where they began the long road back in vacated defense-worker housing.

No record was left of Ko's boats. Moreover, the silver, furniture, and other possessions for which Riku had paid storage fees while the family was held at Manzanar

had "unaccountably" been stolen from the warehouse. Riku went back to work in the local cannery, while Ko went from one occupation to another, trying to make his own way independently. Finally, some six years after leaving Manzanar, he took up farming in the Santa Clara Valley near San José. For the rest of his life, he was the proud producer of premium strawberries.

While the Wakatsukis were struggling to survive at Manzanar, the old, crowded, and heavily guarded train carrying the Uchidas and 500 others from Tanforan to Topaz sped eastward. As the train departed they stole one last look out of the sides of the drawn curtains, "unutterably saddened" by this furtive peek at all that had meant home to them.

At Delta, Utah, they were transferred to buses for the final leg of their journey into the heart of the barren Sevier Desert, south of the Great Salt Lake. There the vegetation disappeared and "dry skeletal greasewood" replaced trees and grass. Finally Topaz appeared—"rows and rows of squat, tar-papered barracks sitting sullenly in the white chalky sand." The one-mile-square camp contained 42 blocks of twelve barracks, each block with a mess hall, latrine, washroom, and laundry. Overnight the army had created a city of 8,000, the fifth-largest in Utah, in a desolate wasteland. Army bulldozers had turned the old lake bed into a mass of loose sand; each step sent up swirls

Topaz Relocation Center
The dust begins to roll across Topaz Relocation Center, located in one of the most isolated sections of the West. As in almost all War Relocation Authority photographs, the barbed-wire fences and guard towers do not appear. *Courtesy of The Bancroft Library, University of California, Berkeley.*

of dust. The Uchidas were greeted by friends who "looked like pieces of flour-dusted pastry" and escorted to their new home. Like the Wakatsukis at Manzanar, they were appalled by their new home: a room of 20 by 18 feet, with four metal army cots, no ceiling, a bare light bulb hanging from the rafters, and a stove not yet installed. Ribbons of powdery dust streamed in through knotholes in walls and floors. A quick inspection by Yo and Kay revealed toilets without seats, no hot water, and no electricity in the latrine or laundry room. In despair they unpacked, sickened by the realization that this was a prison camp.

The next morning there was ice in the tea kettle they kept in their room, a reminder that at 4,600 feet in the desert of central Utah, extremes of weather were common. Severe dust storms periodically engulfed the camp, churning the sands and blasting it through every opening. Visibility might be no more than five to ten feet. When Yo was caught in a sudden storm after their arrival, her hair, eyebrows, and eyelashes were turned a chalky white. As winter deepened, temperatures approached 0°F, there were coal shortages, and hot water was available only from 7:00 to 9:00 PM daily. Yo and Kay caught a succession of colds, and upset stomachs and diarrhea afflicted the whole camp for weeks at a time. Not until mid-November were ceilings installed and sheetrock applied to barracks walls, at last making them habitable.

One day Yo Uchida visited the barracks of a Caucasian teacher who, with her husband and child, lived in the administration compound. They occupied one-half of a barracks (three evacuee families were assigned to an equal amount of space), and had carpeted floors, a fully equipped kitchen, separate bedrooms, and a living room. Yo returned to the cubicle she shared with the rest of her family "filled with envy, longing, and resentment."

Despite their despondency, the Uchidas, following Dwight's example, devoted themselves to public service. Kay became involved in planning a nursery-school system for the camp, while Yo got a job teaching in one of the two elementary schools. Classes at first were held in unfinished, completely bare barracks: no supplies, no equipment, no blackboards, no heat. The teachers noted angrily that work went ahead on the barbed wire fence and guard towers around the camp. Because of the cold, class time was shifted to the afternoon, when the sun provided some warmth, but dust storms were more frequent later in the day and disrupted classes. When the head of the elementary schools reprimanded Yo and the other teachers for dismissing classes during one particularly bad storm, he touched off a near mass resignation. Because of his arrogant and insensitive attitude toward the internees,

he was replaced. Finally, a succession of dust storms, rain squalls, and snow, with temperatures under 10°F, forced a closing of the schools in mid-November. They reopened only after sheetrock walls, ceilings, stoves, and a minimum of basic equipment had been installed.

Meanwhile, Dwight and Iku once again made their home a gathering place for their friends and spent countless hours befriending and counseling old and young alike, in an effort to counteract the deterioration of family ties that camp life engendered. Because of his background, Dwight soon became involved in the camp's business affairs. From the beginning, he was chairman of the board of directors of the Consumers Cooperative and president of the Cooperative Congress, which operated such services as the canteen, barber shop, radio repair shop, movie houses, and dry-goods store. Within a few months he was also on the camp's judicial commission and arbitration committee, and had been asked to run for city manager.

At Christmas, many evacuees were touched to receive gifts from strangers all over the United States in response to an appeal from the American Friends (Quaker) Service Committee. Still, Yo and Kay were miserable in the bleak camp and by the end of December were determined to relocate. Many of their friends had relocated or gone to schools somewhere in the East. Yo eagerly followed the efforts of educators to get colleges and universities across the country to accept students from the camps, despite the army and navy's frequent refusal to continue training or research programs at institutions enrolling Japanese Americans.

Growing controversy within the camp created additional anxiety in the Uchida family. Malcontents began to harass Dwight about the operation of the cooperative. In addition, he often attended meetings of Issei and Nisei until late at night, trying to conciliate and arbitrate the differences of contending factions. In February 1943 the loyalty questionnaire triggered even greater anger and bitterness. A pro-Japan faction arose, made up primarily of tough, arrogant Kibei and Issei who began to intimidate those trying to be cooperative. The head of the art school was beaten one night, and on another occasion a church minister was assaulted by masked men wielding lead pipes. Dwight was accosted by two men from the pro-Japan faction and denounced as "obsequious" to the white administrative staff. The anger in the camp was kept boiling when a soldier shot and killed a 63-year-old man near the fence surrounding the camp. The guard claimed the old man had tried to crawl under the fence and get away, but the evidence indicated otherwise.

Relief for the Uchidas came in the summer of 1943. In May, Kay got word that she had been appointed as

Internees at Fence

Over 700,000 Californians served in the armed forces in World War II and made the difficult adjustment to peacetime after 1945. Among them were thousands of young Japanese Americans whose families spent the war in American concentration camps. Here internees watch Nisei volunteers depart from Topaz Relocation Center for Army service. Army personnel seldom acknowledged the contradiction of soliciting volunteers and drafting Japanese Americans for military service from behind barbed wire. *Courtesy of The Bancroft Library, University of California, Berkeley.*

an assistant in a nursery school run by Mount Holyoke College and could spend the summer at a Quaker study center in Pennsylvania. Shortly thereafter, Yo received a full graduate scholarship to Smith College and an opportunity to spend the summer with friends in Connecticut before school began. By the end of May, both daughters were on their way east.

Not long after Yo and Kay departed, a stink bomb was thrown into the Uchidas' room, and the threat led the camp administration to arrange the relocation of Dwight and Iku to Salt Lake City. By the summer of 1943, the Uchidas were once again on the "outside." They eventually joined their daughters in New York where Dwight, having lost all his Mitsui retirement benefits,

began working as a packer in the shipping department of a church organization. When he returned to California after the war, Dwight found work in a dry-cleaning business owned by a friend. Once a prominent business executive, he remained there until his second retirement, still the generous, community-spirited person he had always been.

Like the great majority of Japanese Americans incarcerated during World War II in the most desolate regions of the country, the Wakatsukis and Uchidas lived through their ordeal of personal loss and the humiliation of having their loyalty questioned with determination and dignity. This was their contribution to the war effort, and to all Americans.

World War II

The Beginning
of an Era

23

For many Americans, World War II was the defining event of the twentieth century. Lasting six years, this was "total war" in which whole populations were mobilized for war, and it killed millions upon millions of soldiers and civilians alike. In the process, it covered much of the earth and changed the world in countless ways for the rest of the century and beyond. For the 15 million men and women who served in the armed forces of the United States, and the rest of the American people, mobilized into the world's most powerful war machine, this was a matchless moment of their lives. It began in the summer of 1939 when Adolf Hitler invaded Poland, provoking declarations of war from its allies, France and England. In 1940, introducing a new form of mechanized warfare, *blitzkrieg* ("lightening war"), and running roughshod over neutral nations, the Germans conquered western Europe within months, isolating England. While the United States declared its neutrality in the conflict, public opinion was generally sympathetic to the British and their allies, allowing substantial American aid short of war. In the summer of 1941, Hitler launched a surprise attack on the Soviet Union in an enormous expansion of the war. The United States extended its aid to the Russians and the war in Europe settled into a grinding struggle to push the Nazis back to Germany.

Meanwhile the attention of many Americans, especially Californians, turned to Japan. In the 1930s the Japanese embarked on a plan to dominate Southeast Asia and the Pacific, eventually calling this their "Greater East Asia Co-Prosperity Sphere." Japan's aggression began with the seizure of Manchuria in 1932, followed by war with China in 1937, then expansion into French Indochina in 1940–41. The United States resisted each step along the way by denying Japan war materials and other critical supplies. In the fall of 1941, the new military government of Japan, now a part of the Berlin-Rome-Tokyo

Axis, finally concluded that war with the United States was preferable to what it regarded as a slow economic death. Japan's senior admiral, Isoroku Yamamoto, was assigned the task of designing a surprise attack on the Pacific Fleet in Pearl Harbor, Hawaii. In late November a Japanese fleet of aircraft carriers crept across the North Pacific and, by surprise, struck Pearl Harbor at dawn on Sunday, December 7, 1941. Yamamoto's plan was wildly successful, sinking or disabling all but one of the American battleships in the harbor and many other warships. Although the three American fleet aircraft carriers were not in the harbor, the attack was devastating. It was followed by Japan's seizure of the Dutch East Indies, Britain's Southeast Asia possessions, the Philippines, and all the United States' Pacific island possessions west of Wake Island. Japan had become the master of the Pacific. Yamamoto, who had lived and studied in the United States, lost his life in the ensuing war, but not before he made the prophetic comment "all we have done is awaken a sleeping giant."

California in World War II

The Wakatsukis and the Uchidas returned to a California far different from the one they left in 1942. The outbreak of World War II in 1939 brought the economic recovery Franklin D. Roosevelt's New Dealers had struggled unsuccessfully to achieve since 1933, as war work finally ended the Great Depression. Then, America's entry into the war following Japan's attack on Pearl Harbor turned the nation's economy to war production on a scale that profoundly affected California's economy. By 1945, the war had sped up the development of the west and ushered in the post-industrial era, in the process changing California from a resource-based, dependent section into the "pace-setter for the nation." The need of war industries for workers also triggered another wave of migration that soon made California the most populous state in the Union, faced with the serious consequences of such rapid growth.

When Hitler's troops marched into Poland in September 1939, Californians on the whole were engaged in the production of goods unrelated to war. Agriculture, mining, fishing, textiles, metalworking, and making furniture and movies still comprised much of their economy, along with tourism and real estate development. On the other hand, the state had a significant potential for war work. Its oil, aircraft, shipbuilding, auto, and tire industries—as well as its amazingly productive agricultural system—were capable of rapid expansion and conversion to military use. In addition, California's wide

variety of terrain was well adapted to training troops for battle almost anywhere in the world, and major bases at San Diego and Mare Island in San Francisco Bay facilitated a rapid naval expansion.

The European war brought a flood of war orders and military spending to California. With institution of a military draft in 1940, the Army expanded its already substantial training facilities, such as Fort Ord near Monterey and Camp Roberts near Paso Robles. The Marine Corps began to construct a major west coast base at Camp Pendleton near Oceanside, which proved to be ideal for training in amphibious warfare. As relations with Japan deteriorated, the Navy expanded its California facilities as well.

One of the first California industries to feel the impact of the war was shipbuilding, a result of Germany's frighteningly successful submarine war on British shipping. Hunting in "wolf packs," German U-boats sank hundreds of thousands of tons of Allied shipping early in the war, threatening Britain's survival. By 1941 orders for transports had revived private shipbuilding in Los Angeles and the San Francisco Bay Area. Similarly, steel, chemicals, textiles, machine tools, and agricultural products all began to respond to the war's stimulus, while the state's young aircraft industry nearly quintupled in size. Tremendous change was therefore well under way by the end of 1941, as employment expanded, wages rose, and thousands of workers made the shift from service-related jobs to production work. The Great Depression was over.

The Impact of Pearl Harbor

With so many historical ties to Hawaii, the reaction of Californians to the shocking attack on Pearl Harbor was highly emotional. The fear of invasion was quickly spread by alarming press and radio accounts of the destruction of the Pacific Fleet, as well as the bombardment of Santa Barbara by a Japanese submarine. Cities were immediately blacked out and coastal defenses strengthened. The call to remove the state's Japanese Americans began, as unfounded rumors of Japanese sabotage, espionage, and planned attacks circulated widely in California.

California assumed a key role in turning the United States into an awesome war production machine. World War II was far-flung, with major battlefields in western Europe, the Soviet Union, Africa, and the western Pacific. In the Pacific, island-hopping tactics made amphibious warfare essential, and the attack on Pearl Harbor and the battles of the Coral Sea and Midway in

1942 demonstrated that the naval war would be dominated by aircraft carriers. Moreover, highly technical communications and electronic equipment became essential. California possessed the industries necessary to meet these needs and enjoyed close, long-standing relations with both the Army and Navy. Consequently, the federal government poured some $40 billion into California—more than 10 percent of the nation's wartime expenditures.

The state's geography and location also affected its contribution to the war effort. Its deserts proved ideal for training tank corps that went into action in North Africa in 1942. Its beaches provided the training ground for thousands of soldiers and marines sent ashore on Pacific islands. Its climate permitted year-round training of Air Force personnel. A huge expansion of military training facilities followed Pearl Harbor. In 1942, General George Patton established the Desert Training Center in the Mohave Desert near Needles, where his famous armored divisions were first created. Almost overnight Fort Ord became a city of 50,000. The Navy took over Treasure Island in San Francisco Bay and vastly expanded its other facilities in the Bay Area, San Diego, and on Terminal Island in Los Angeles. Air Force bases up and down the state were expanded, and many new ones were established. March Field, McClellan, Mather, Travis, and George Air Force bases became major establishments. Naturally, California became the staging area and depot for the war against Japan. Ships, planes, tanks, trucks, personnel, and incredible amounts of food and matériel funneled through California to Pacific battlegrounds. Almost all Army troops sent to the Pacific were processed through huge staging facilities such as Camp Stoneman near Pittsburg and Antioch; likewise Navy and Marine Corps personnel made their way to Pacific through California bases.

Meanwhile the state's chief ports, San Francisco, Los Angeles, and Oakland, hummed with activity. Strikes were a thing of the past as longshoremen and military personnel worked night and day. It could be dangerous work and led to one of the state's worst wartime tragedies, at Port Chicago on Suisun Bay east of San Francisco. There, on the night of July 17, 1944, a ship that had been fully loaded with ammunition from the nearby Naval Ordnance Depot exploded with a tremendous blast, killing 323 people, demolishing 350 nearby homes, and breaking windows 35 miles away.

Among the dead were 200 black seamen from segregated units commanded by white officers, standard policy in the armed forces at the time. When surviving seamen were ordered to resume loading munitions, most refused, citing the dangerous conditions and sheer terror. Fifty eventually faced court martial, charged with mutiny. During their trial, defendants' testimony revealed that their officers condoned hazardous conditions and exhibited blatant racism. Nevertheless, the verdict was guilty and each of the 50 defendants was sentenced to 15 years in prison and a dishonorable discharge. Subsequent appeals from Thurgood Marshall, Navy Secretary James Forrestal, and First Lady Eleanor Roosevelt led to reduced penalties. In January 1946, the sentences were set aside and the men returned to duty, eventually to be discharged "under less than honorable conditions" and denied veterans benefits. In the 1990s, California Congressmen Pete Stark and Ron Dellums sponsored legislation authorizing the Navy to reexamine these cases. In 1994 the Navy upheld the original decision.

The Port Chicago trial focused attention on Jim Crowism in the Navy. The Navy began eliminating segregation policies in 1942, but in 1946 Secretary Forrestal ordered a complete end to the policy, two years before President Truman's order desegregating all branches of the military.

The Rise of the Aircraft Industry

One of the most spectacular effects of the war was to turn aircraft construction in California into a giant industry that became a critical part of the state's postwar economy. Until the war, several factors made the state's fledgling aircraft industry weak and unstable. Initially, airplane manufacturers were dependent for their survival on wildly fluctuating government demand for military aircraft. Moreover, rapidly changing technology made for a high rate of obsolescence and high engineering costs, compounding the problems caused by the long design-manufacturing cycle. Consequently, the industry's progress was episodic.

California's airframe industry (motors were built in the East and Midwest and shipped to California assembly plants) began in 1912 when Glenn Martin formed a company in Southern California, followed soon after by the Loghead and Christofferson companies near San Francisco. Their production was negligible, however, and even World War I, during which Martin moved to the East, did not stimulate much growth. In fact, most California aircraft companies failed in the postwar depression, when the government dumped wartime planes on the market.

A turning point came in 1920, when Martin's chief engineer, Donald Douglas, formed his own company and located in Southern California. The region had several attractions: the climate permitted year-round testing and minimal building maintenance, investment capital was available, it was a nonunion area with low wages and nearby military airfields. Douglas was soon building planes for the Army and Navy and, in 1924, scored a major success when he built the single-engine biplanes that made the first round-the-world flight. In 1926 he organized the Douglas Aircraft Company, the first to succeed in California. That same year Allan and Malcolm Loghead (whose original company had gone out of business in 1921) joined with John K. Northrup to form the Lockheed Aircraft Company, a phonetic spelling of their name deemed necessary to eliminate mispronunciations. A year later, the firm Claude Ryan had organized in San Diego achieved fame by building Charles Lindbergh's *Spirit of St. Louis*, the first airplane to fly nonstop from New York to Paris.

Douglas, Ryan, and Lockheed all designed passenger planes, since government mail contracts promoted the development of commercial air travel, but military construction remained basic to their survival. In 1935, though, the company introduced the DC-3, one of the most successful commercial aircraft ever built. Valued for its economy of operation and stability in flight, the DC-3 captured 95 percent of the rapidly expanding passenger airline business by 1939. Favorable conditions attracted other aircraft manufacturers to California. In 1935 Consolidated Aircraft Corporation moved to San Diego, and in 1936 North American Aviation moved to Los Angeles. By 1939 more than half the aircraft workers in the nation were employed by southern California firms.

The expansion of the state's aircraft industry after Pearl Harbor was one of the extraordinary events of the war years. A massive infusion of federal funds, some $10 billion, increased employment from 20,000 in 1939 to 280,000 by 1944. When President Roosevelt called for production of 50,000 planes per year at the start of the war, people scoffed, but the industry built nearly 100,000 planes in 1943 alone. This record was made possible by the huge numbers of women moving into industry jobs. Concentrated in Los Angeles, Orange, and San Diego counties, the giant new industry became the base of the aerospace industry that developed after the war.

Shipbuilding

California's shipbuilding industry, traditionally centered in the San Francisco Bay Area, underwent a similar expansion. Employment in state shipyards soared from 4,000 to 260,000 as the federal government poured more than $5 billion into California for ships of all kinds. Private and Navy yards in Sausalito, Vallejo, Alameda, Oakland, and San Francisco built hundreds of transport, cargo, amphibious, and naval craft in a huge burst of activity. Most impressive was the creation of a great new facility at Richmond by the ubiquitous Henry J. Kaiser. This shipyard relied on all the techniques of management, engineering, design, and construction technology that Kaiser had developed in his years of directing the construction of such massive projects as Hoover Dam, and the venture brought assembly-line methods to the shipbuilding industry. Amazing production records were achieved at Richmond. The yard built one-fourth of all the Liberty ships produced in the United States during the war and, by prefabricating huge sections, ships were built in record time. When the war began, these rugged, dependable freighters took nearly 250 days to construct. Kaiser brought the time down to 25 days and set a record of eight days with construction of the *Robert E. Perry*. Here, again, the movement of thousands of women from low-paying jobs to war industries played a major role in setting such impressive records.

In addition, Kaiser established the state's first integrated blast furnace and steel-rolling mill at Fontana, 50 miles east of Los Angeles. When completed in 1942, the Fontana plant increased the state's steel production by 70 percent, and the dependence of the state's war industries on steel shipped from distant eastern plants was significantly reduced.

The Kaiser shipyard was responsible for a soaring increase in Richmond's population, from 20,000 to more than 100,000, including a very large number of "Rosie the Riveters." Kaiser took the lead in constructing low-cost housing to relieve the strains that came with such rapid growth. He also pioneered the concept of prepaid health care by organizing the Kaiser Foundation Health Plan for his workers, probably reflecting the large numbers of women among them.

Other War Industries and Agriculture

Conversion of California industry to war production was thoroughgoing. Oil production increased by 50 percent between 1941 and 1945, as the state produced most of the high-test aviation fuel and fuel oils necessary for the war against Japan. The state's rubber industry developed plants to produce synthetic rubber when Japan overran Southeast Asia and shut off America's supplies of natural rubber. Surprisingly, synthetic rubber proved to have qualities superior to natural rubber for many important uses and became

Richmond Shipyard at Night

At Henry J. Kaiser's Richmond shipyard, whole sections of ships that had been prefabricated on shore were lifted onto the spillways by huge cranes, which worked around the clock like great mechanical spiders. The production of Liberty ships at Richmond was an important factor in winning the fight against Hitler's submarine "wolfpacks" during World War II. *Courtesy of The Bancroft Library, University of California, Berkeley.*

a permanent industry in California. Many other state industries were converted to war production—from radios to electronic devices such as radar and sonar; from furniture to plywood subchasers and torpedo boats; from automobiles to tanks. Thousands of new plants produced amphibious craft, airplane parts, munitions, and electrical equipment. Heavy industry became a major part of the California economy and tripled its industrial labor force.

Increased prosperity and population growth, plus government purchases for troops being trained in California and for shipment overseas gave most types of agriculture a mighty boost. Dairy products, fruits, nuts, vegetables, cotton, and livestock all increased two to three times in value, and the overall value of agricultural products rose from $623 million in 1939 to $1.75 billion in 1945. California's position as the leading agricultural state in the Union was solidified in the process.

The chief wartime problem in agriculture was a shortage of harvest labor. The entry of more than 700,000 Californians into military service, the booming war industries soaking up the Okie population, and the internment of the state's Japanese Americans meant that California growers faced a sudden, drastic labor shortage. Grower complaints finally persuaded the federal government in 1942 to arrange a guest worker program with Mexico. Under this program, the United States agreed to provide transportation, health care, decent housing, and prevailing wages to Mexican workers under six to twelve-month contracts. This was the origin of the *bracero* program, its name derived from the Spanish term for a manual laborer. The United States admitted the first *braceros* in September 1942 in time for the sugar beet harvest in Stockton. The *bracero* program employed 26,000 workers in California at its peak in 1944. Although the program began as a temporary wartime measure, growers continued to take advantage of it after the war, as the oversupply of labor benefited farm owners and contributed to their record profits in the postwar years.

Science

When the war came, California had developed one of the nation's foremost scientific communities in its institutions of higher education. The California Institute of Technology, Stanford University, and the University of California, especially at Berkeley and Los Angeles, had faculties and laboratories that constituted a significant scientific resource. Turned to military work, they made important contributions to the war effort, developing rocket-assist systems for aircraft and new torpedoes that followed sounds emanating from their targets. In addition, most campuses of the state's universities carried on sizable officer- and specialist-training programs for the various branches of the armed forces.

Most important, however, was the role of UC Berkeley in developing the atomic bomb. During the 1930s professor of physics Ernest O. Lawrence developed the cyclotron, or atom smasher, and synthesized new elements and isotopes, such as neptunium, uranium 235, and plutonium, that were important in nuclear research. His achievements attracted bright young scientists to Berkeley—among them J. Robert Oppenheimer—whose work put the university in the forefront of atomic science. In 1942, fearful that German scientists might be developing an atomic bomb, the U.S. government embarked on an urgent, top-secret program for the same purpose: the Manhattan Project. The government recruited the free world's best minds for the project and—at a laboratory in Los Alamos, New Mexico, managed by the university—teams of scientists under Oppenheimer's leadership developed the first atomic bomb. Use of the bomb on the Japanese cities of Hiroshima and Nagasaki in August 1945 ended World War II and ushered in a whole new age for the world.

Women in the War

The bombing of Pearl Harbor created a unity and commitment to war lacking before 1941. After the initial shock, fear, and chagrin of the attack, many Californians turned to the task of winning the war. In the next four years, thousands of California women joined the expanded Army and Navy Nurses Corps (ANC/NNC), women's branches of the Army (WACs), Navy (WAVES), and Coast Guard (SPARS). For the most part, they were seen as replacements for men who could be sent to combat areas. Many also saw service abroad, some in dangerous conditions.

Nationally, thousands more left low-paying jobs for work in shipyards, airplane assembly plants, and hundreds of other war-related industries, taking over production jobs previously dominated by men. Where a female employee in heavy industry would have been a rarity before 1941, thereafter roughly two million women found work in war industries, half in aerospace alone. Many flocked to California, attracted by the pay and nature of the work. Soon women accounted for 40 percent or more of aircraft employees.

The war proved to be an important turning point for California women. As men entered the armed forces, employment opportunities for women were greatly expanded. Women moved into other types of employment that had rarely accepted them before. Many took jobs as chemists, engineers, railroad workers, lawyers, and journalists, and in such rapidly expanding service industries as banking, retail sales, and education. Barriers that had always denied women access to a wide range of employment were lowered. For the first time, women enjoyed true occupational mobility.

Women's reasons for taking civilian or defense industry jobs were varied and complex. A combination of patriotism and high wages motivated Jade Snow Wong. Born in San Francisco's Chinatown, Wong found work as a clerk with the War Production Board downtown. She found the job mind-numbingly tedious, but took comfort in the thought that in a small way she was contributing to the war effort and saving for her graduate education. Maya Angelou's reasons were less tangible. The 15-year-old African American noticed that women had taken over as conductors on San Francisco's streetcars. She was captivated by the image of "sailing up and down the hills . . . in a dark-blue uniform, with a money changer at my belt." Angelou was also determined to break the streetcars' color barrier. On her first visit to the Market Street Railway Company, the startled receptionist told her no jobs were available. When Angelou asked why the company was advertising for "motorettes," the receptionist said the personnel manager was away. Angelou returned again and again, slowly wearing down her adversary's resistance. After three weeks, she was hired as the first African American on the San Francisco streetcars.

African American women, in particular, benefited from the opportunity to leave low-paid jobs, and the number in domestic service declined from 55 percent to 40 percent. Early in the war employers often refused to employ blacks in war work and unions would not admit them to membership. But by organizing to get help from the federal Fair Employment Practices Committee, African American men and women forced significant changes. By 1944 blacks were over 7 percent

Women Aircraft Workers

Women workers assemble aircraft fuselage sections in a Los Angeles area plant. World War II produced a major shift of women into industrial jobs. Although men returning from war service typically displaced them, their war work earned many women workers a new self-confidence that profoundly affected postwar society. *Glasshouse Images / Alamy Stock Photo.*

of war industries' work forces. In the process, African American women workers led the way in securing state funds for child-care services and the adoption of the state's first Fair Employment Practices Commission.

War industries suffered both a severe labor shortage as well as a high turnover rate. Lack of access to housing, food, and transportation placed unique pressures on women workers, many of whom needed somehow to balance paid labor with motherhood and homemaking. In some plants, these problems contributed to turnover

rates of 100 percent and higher per year. When the war ended, to the disappointment of many women workers, they were displaced by returning veterans.

Incarceration of Japanese Americans

The forced removal of Japanese Americans such as the Wakatsukis and Uchidas from the West Coast and their detention in prison camps has been called "our worst wartime mistake," the result of fear, falsehoods, and racial prejudice. Following the bombing of Pearl Harbor, the FBI arrested over 2,000 Issei men who were already under surveillance. Most were businessmen, clergy, Japanese language teachers, and community leaders. Nearly 1,400 German nationals and over 250 Italians were detained as well. But whereas the Justice Department eventually released most of German and Italian "enemy aliens," it continued to imprison the Japanese, ostensibly until they underwent hearings to determine their potential risk to national security.

Lieutenant General John L. DeWitt, in charge of the Fourth Army and Western Defense Command in San Francisco, believed that Japanese Americans constituted a major national security threat and questioned the allegiance of Japanese born and raised in the United States. "The Japanese race is an enemy race," he declared, predicting that Japanese Americans would "turn against this nation when the final test of loyalty" came. In February of 1942, DeWitt requested military action to remove the entire Japanese population from the West Coast, and secured approval from California attorney general Earl Warren. Soon after DeWitt's certification that mass removal was a military necessity, on February 19, 1942, President Franklin D. Roosevelt signed Executive Order 9066, which authorized the secretary of war to prescribe military areas from which any and all persons could be excluded. The secretary delegated this authority to DeWitt, who ordered all individuals of Japanese ancestry residing in Military Area No. 1 (all of California, western Oregon and Washington, and Arizona) into assembly centers by June 1942. This included approximately 93,000 Japanese American residents of California. With less than a week's notice, they were forced to sell their property at great losses, give up their homes, and leave jobs and schools. In the next few months, the incarcerees were transferred to ten internment camps spread from eastern California to Arkansas. The federal government euphemistically called the camps "relocation centers" and referred to the mass removal as an "evacuation." The Nisei, who were American citizens, became "non-aliens" in Army communications. In reality, President Roosevelt authorized the forced removal and incarceration of over 110,000 people, two-thirds of whom were U.S. citizens, based on race, without due process or evidence of wrongdoing.

A few Japanese Americans mounted legal challenges contesting the constitutionality of internment. In *Hirabayashi* (1943), *Korematsu* (1944), and *Endo* (1944), the U.S. Supreme Court handed down decisions upholding mass removal on the basis of military necessity.

In *Hirabayashi* and *Korematsu*, the Court refused to question the judgment of military officials on the existence of a military necessity, despite the evidence that DeWitt's orders were based on prejudiced racial views. In a famous dissent, Justice Frank Murphy stated that the exclusion orders had gone "over the very brink of constitutional power . . . into the ugly abyss of racism." Although the Court decided in the *Endo* case that detention of citizens in the relocation centers was unconstitutional, it evaded the question of whether the government had exceeded its war powers in the evacuation.

Forty years later Fred Korematsu's conviction for violating the evacuation order was vacated in the U.S. District Court of San Francisco, Judge Marilyn Hall Patel stating that the evacuation and internment had been "based upon unsubstantiated facts, distortions and misrepresentations of at least one military commander whose views were affected by racism." Using the Freedom of Information Act, Korematsu's attorneys demonstrated that the government had suppressed evidence that a "military necessity" no longer existed when the evacuation took place. Gordon Hirabayashi's conviction was reversed on similar grounds in 1987. "I didn't feel guilty because I didn't do anything wrong," Korematsu said of his decision to sue the U.S. government over the constitutionality of its actions: "Every day in school, we said the pledge of the flag, 'with liberty and justice for all,' and I believed all that. I was an American citizen, and I had as many rights as anyone else."

The economic cost of the removal was never resolved. Forced from their homes and businesses, Japanese Americans disposed of property at fire-sale rates, left possessions and property in the hands of sometimes unreliable friends or acquaintances, and frequently, like the Wakatsukis, were robbed of everything while locked up in WRA camps. In 1942 the San Francisco Federal Reserve Bank estimated the incarcerees' losses at $400 million, yet Congress denied aid for their economic rehabilitation. Not until 1948 was the Japanese American Evacuation Claims Act adopted by Congress; even then claims were limited to $2,500 each. After reviewing extensive testimonies and documents, the Commission on Wartime Relocation and Internment of Civilians reported in 1983 that the wartime imprisonment of Japanese Americans had been a "grave injustice" motivated by "racial prejudice, war hysteria and the failure of political leadership." Acting on the recommendations of the commission, Congress passed the Civil Liberties Act of 1988, and President Ronald Reagan signed it into law. The act brought a formal apology and reparations payments of $20,000 to each surviving internee.

Finally, there is probably no measure of the human costs of internment. Who can measure its effect on Ko Wakatsuki and his family? The great majority of Japanese Americans accepted it and cooperated, like the Wakatsukis and Uchidas, in the spirit of *shikata ga nai* and in the hope that it would prove their loyalty to the United States. Their primary interest was to keep their families intact and make the best of the situation. Still, there was widespread bitterness over the injustice of incarceration, though the deep sense of loss, invasion of privacy, and humiliation was often suppressed, not to surface until many years later. Only when their children and grandchildren, influenced by the civil rights movement of the 1960s, began to question why mass resistance to incarceration failed to emerge did Nisei begin to express themselves. Jeanne Wakatsuki Huston wrote *Farewell to Manzanar* nearly 30 years after the fact, and Yoshiko Uchida wrote *Desert Exile* 20 years after her removal to Tanforan and Topaz.

Wartime Community Dynamics

Two million new residents arrived in California from 1941 to 1945, and for the first time a significant percentage of them were African Americans. Shipyard work, especially in Los Angeles, Oakland, and Richmond, attracted southern blacks in large numbers, as did new military installations. In 1940 African Americans were 1.8 percent of the California population, a figure that nearly quadrupled during the war. But their increased numbers generated increased hostility. Until World War II other racial groups, most notably Asians, had been the chief targets of discrimination in California. Housing discrimination, in particular, led to the formation of small ghettos in Los Angeles, San Francisco, Oakland, and Richmond, beginning a cycle of rising black population coupled with rising white racism.

Discrimination in housing and employment, in turn, produced impoverished inner-city neighborhoods. From 1945 on, as war production wound down, whites moved out of war industries to peacetime jobs, leaving African Americans in soon-to-be-closed war plants. When the war ended and plants shut down, blacks found themselves out in the cold. Good peacetime jobs were filled and African Americans were at the bottom of hiring lists. Unemployment and welfare benefits became the chief refuge for a great many. The foundation for the explosive Watts riots of the 1960s may well have been laid during World War II.

Racial conflict was pronounced in Los Angeles, where war work, educational opportunity, and other benefits attracted a sizable Mexican migration. Mexicans, like African Americans, were subjected to discrimination in housing and employment, and limited to residence in the *barrios* of East Los Angeles. In the early 1940s, many Mexican American youths adopted a distinctive style of dress, the "zoot-suits" that local law enforcement associated with criminalism and juvenile delinquency. White military personnel demanded proper "respect" and often harassed young Mexican Americans. In the summer of 1943, about 50 U.S. seamen dragged Mexican American, black, and Filipino youths from bars, movie theaters, and restaurants and beat them in the streets. For ten straight nights, white sailors cruised Mexican American neighborhoods in search of zoot suiters, who responded with like violence. Articles in Los Angeles newspapers and the national press referred to "marauding Latin gangs" and "roving wolf-packs" of Mexican Americans engaging in criminal behavior. No one was killed during the riots, but scores of Mexican Americans were beaten by mobs and later arrested for disturbing the peace.

Nevertheless, the war enabled large numbers of Mexican American workers to move from unskilled to semi-skilled and skilled labor jobs. In 1930 8 percent of males were in semi-skilled positions; in 1950 it was 21.6 percent. Similarly, in 1930, 13.6 percent of Latina workers held clerical positions; in 1950, almost 24 percent were so employed. A growing Mexican American middle class developed new community organizations and set the stage for participation in the civil rights movements of the 1960s.

While Japanese Americans were forcibly removed from their homes and detained, conditions improved for other Asian populations in California improved after Pearl Harbor. Chinese, Filipinos, and Asian Indians, whose native lands were now allies of the United States, experienced greater acceptance and found new job opportunities in fields previously closed to them. Resident aliens were allowed to enlist in the military, with promises of U.S. citizenship in exchange for their service. Over 13,000 Chinese Americans served in the armed forces, including 22 percent of all Chinese adult males in the United States. In California, 16,000 Filipinos, comprising 40 percent of their numbers in the state, registered for the first draft, viewing military service as a chance to become "soldiers of democracy" instead of farmworkers and domestic servants. In Los Angeles, 300 Chinese American laundry workers closed their shops to work on the construction of the ship *China Victory*. In 1943, Chinese workers constituted 15 percent of the San Francisco Bay Area's shipyard workforce.

Most surprisingly, over 30,000 Nisei served in the U.S. military during WWII. The War Department formed the 100th Battalion in Hawaii on January 19, 1942, as a segregated unit composed of Nisei volunteers. In 1943, the War Department created the segregated 442nd Regimental Combat Team, made up solely of internment-camp volunteers. The 442nd and 100th fought valiantly in the European theater, ultimately earning seven Presidential Unit Citations, 21 Medals of Honor, 29 Distinguished Service Crosses, 560 Silver Stars, 4,000 Bronze Stars, and more than 4,500 Purple Hearts. This impressive war record, combined with the civil rights movements of the 1950s and '60s, called public attention to the injustices of 1942. Reacting to the new national mood, in 1952 Congress removed the prohibition against naturalization that had made enemy aliens of Ko Wakatsuki and Dwight Uchida.

Wartime migration produced a shortage of housing that plagued the state's cities during the war years, particularly in communities near military installations and defense industry plants. San Diego's aircraft and naval facilities produced a population increase from 203,000 in 1940 to 362,000 by the end of the war. Shipbuilding nearly quadrupled the populations of both Vallejo and Richmond. Towns near Air Force bases, Army training camps, and major processing centers experienced similar growth.

Material and labor shortages caused by the war substantially reduced new construction. Some companies built low-cost, dormitory-style, barracks-like buildings near new war plants to provide minimal housing for their workers. Thousands of low-cost units were built by the National Housing Authority (NHA) and many large tracts of single-family homes were constructed by private builders under Federal Housing Authority (FHA) programs. The government, however, made little effort to prevent racial segregation in local officials' allocation of public housing. Supply never caught up with demand, and the war years were characterized by the crowding of two and three families into single-family homes and apartments. The wartime migration also stretched related municipal services such as sewers, water, gas, electricity, and telephones to the limit, while almost all highway construction was essentially suspended and street repairs indefinitely delayed.

California's reputation for a superior public school system suffered due to wartime population growth. In 1940 Richmond's schools had 3,000 students. In 1943 they had 35,000. Unable to adapt immediately to such rapidly swelling student populations, schools were forced onto double-session schedules with half their students attending a morning session and half in the afternoon. Although parents expressed concern that the quality of education would suffer, the practice seemed permanent in some metropolitan areas, as the educational system faced even greater population growth after the war.

Waiting in lines to board crowded buses and streetcars, or at the local meat counter, became a part of daily life in wartime California. Grocery store shelves were quickly depleted of scarce items and most Californians had their first experience of rationing. A variety of necessities, such as meat, dairy products, sugar, and gasoline, were rationed, and the ration-coupon book became an important household item. Thousands of families planted backyard vegetable gardens at the government's urging to "grow your own for victory." For the highly mobile Californians, the rationing of gasoline involved the greatest sacrifice and curtailed travel sharply. Although a black market in gasoline ration stamps arose, the vast majority of Californians saw adherence to the rules as a part of the war effort and, through carpooling and careful planning, managed transportation on their allotted share.

Californians not directly employed in war work found other ways to contribute to the war effort. Hollywood actors and actresses, including a future politician named Ronald Reagan, made training and propaganda films for the government, while others worked for the Red Cross and the United Services Organization (USO). The USO was perhaps most fondly remembered by World War II veterans for its canteens, which offered refreshments and dancing with local girls. At the Hollywood canteen, a volunteer dance partner might turn out to be a famous movie star!

Civil defense was another field in which Californians showed their support for the war. Volunteer "block wardens" inspected their territories for blackout violators, while other citizens joined aircraft-spotting units. Long after any real threat of a Japanese attack had passed, if one ever existed, such activities continued to give thousands the sense of contributing to the war effort.

Preparing for Peace

The year 1944 marked the beginning of the end of World War II. Soviet armies, which had stopped Hitler's invasion of Russia at Stalingrad in 1943, began their relentless march from the east on the Third Reich. Americans and the British, under General Dwight D. Eisenhower, crossed the English Channel on "D-Day" in June to begin the march on Germany from the west and, in October, American troops landed in the Philippines.

By then there was little doubt about the outcome of the war, and thoughts turned to preparations for peace.

In San Francisco a momentous meeting took place in April 1945, when representatives of 46 nations met to establish the United Nations. Meanwhile, planning began for winding down the tremendous war production machine of the United States. In California, orders for tanks, ships, aircraft, and other war matériel were gradually reduced, with a similar decline in related industries. Shipyard and aircraft workers were laid off, and there developed a growing concern that the war would be followed by another serious economic downturn, as World War I had been.

Those who feared a recession, however, overlooked some important facts. In a very real sense, the war years had returned the nation to prosperity. During this period in California, personal income rose from $3 billion to $13 billion. Although individual spending increased with rising incomes, increases in savings were also considerable: Californians' liquid assets rose from $4.5 billion to $15.25 billion during the war. Thus the war ended with a huge, pent-up buying power. Moreover, the state's population grew nearly 30 percent during the war, creating an enormous demand for consumer goods, housing, and services. Finally, the Servicemen's Readjustment Act of 1944 (the "GI Bill of Rights") proved to be not only an effective buffer to unemployment for millions of men and women returning to civilian life, but also an important stimulus to the economy. The act provided veterans with low-interest loans for farm and home purchases, and paid the full educational costs of veterans returning to school. Millions of veterans thus enrolled in colleges all over the nation to complete baccalaureate and graduate degrees. The impact on state university systems was enormous, more than tripling wartime enrollments.

Careful analysis revealed that, under the hothouse stimulus of the war, California had developed a complex, modern, technological economy with enormous potential for the future. The war years, then, provided the economic base that was to make the state the pacesetter in the development of the high-technology society of the late twentieth century.

The Warren Administrations

Suspension of partisan politics generally accompanied the war. To no one's surprise, the popular Republican attorney general Earl Warren easily defeated Gov. Culbert Olson in 1942. Governor Warren went on to establish one of the state's most notable records in

that office. Warren has often been compared to Hiram Johnson because he dominated the political arena of his era in the same fashion. Like Johnson, he had an uncanny ability to appeal to a broad range of voters, and he never lost a bid for state office.

Born in Los Angeles in 1891, Warren earned a law degree from UC's Boalt School of Law in 1914, and, after a short stint of private law practice, was elected district attorney for Alameda County in 1926, where he emerged as an important Republican Party figure. As chairman of the Republican State Central Committee, Warren played a key role in establishing the California Republican Assembly (CRA). The CRA was formed in 1934 as an informal organization representing local Republican voters' groups. It could perform such regular political party functions as pre-primary endorsements, which were prohibited under state election codes. It became a vital mechanism that helped Republicans remain in power in California for 25 years after the New Deal, when Democrats became the state's majority party.

Earl Warren
Courtesy of the California History Room, California State Library, Sacramento, California.

In 1938 Warren won election as state attorney general, the only Republican elected to statewide office that year. With the attack on Pearl Harbor, he became one of the leading politicians calling for the mass removal of Japanese from the state, whether citizens or not. His election as governor in 1942 signified Warren's emergence as the preeminent practitioner of California's unique style of politics, a product of progressive reforms. Distrustful of political parties and fearful of bossism, California progressives, through nonpartisanship, cross-filing, and a stringent elections code, had succeeded in weakening parties to the point of impotence. Candidates campaigned independently of their party, playing down party affiliation and emphasizing the individual over party and platform. Incumbency was a huge advantage under cross-filing, since the incumbent led the list of candidates on primary ballots without mention of party affiliation.

Earl Warren also pioneered the practice of hiring public relations firms to manage his political campaigns. In his 1942 campaign for governor, he had the help of Clem Whitaker and Leone Baxter, whose firm, Campaigns, Inc., used modern advertising techniques to manage political campaigns. Warren's campaign became the prototype of present-day campaigning. By 1946 Warren had so mastered progressive-style politics that, by cross-filing, he captured the nomination of the Democrats as well as the Republicans, the only person ever to win both major party nominations for governor. In 1950 Warren became the first California governor to be elected to a third term; he remains the only one ever elected to three consecutive terms.

In national politics, Warren accepted the Republican's nomination for the vice presidency as Thomas E. Dewey's running mate in 1948. When President Harry Truman's famous "Give 'Em Hell Harry" whistle-stop campaign produced the political upset of the century, Earl Warren suffered his one and only election defeat. He remained prominent in national Republican Party affairs, however, and in 1952 was instrumental in Dwight D. Eisenhower's nomination. After the latter's election as president, Eisenhower promised Warren appointment to the next opening on the Supreme Court, a position the Californian had long coveted. It was only by chance that the first vacancy turned out to be the position of chief justice, from which Warren led the Court into epoch-making decisions in the fields of civil and individual rights.

As governor of California from 1943 to 1953, Warren proposed, and obtained, significant reductions in taxes, yet managed to build a substantial surplus in the state treasury as a "rainy-day fund." As the war came to a close, he promoted planning for demobilization and reconversion to a peacetime economy, persuading the legislature to authorize special state construction projects to provide jobs for returning veterans.

Throughout his career, Warren was a typical progressive. Non-ideological on the issues, he preferred a scientific approach. He regularly appointed boards and commissions to study specific problems and based his legislative proposals on those recommendations. He was unusually effective in securing bipartisan support for his legislative proposals, 90 percent of which were adopted in one form or another.

Warren took great pride in the modernization and upgrading of the state's departments of public health, mental health, and corrections; in the expansion of workers' compensation and unemployment benefits; and in a program of aid to families with dependent children (AFDC). He strongly supported the state's systems of higher education and expanded state expenditures on highways, housing, and public schools.

Detractors of Earl Warren often criticized him, claiming his budgets were too high, he sponsored unnecessary taxes, and meddled too much in social issues. It was in the last field, actually, that Warren's record was mixed. For several years he sought legislation for a social-security type of medical health insurance plan, only to lose to the California Medical Association lobby, which employed Whitaker and Baxter against him. He unsuccessfully called for the establishment of a commission on political and economic equality to protect the rights of California's ethnic minorities. Not until he wrote his memoirs, published after his death, did he express regret for the role he played in the detention of the state's Japanese in 1942. In the economic field, Warren's long battle with utility interests, especially PG&E, over public distribution of Central Valley Project power from Shasta Dam, ended in a compromise generally regarded as favorable to the utility.

Warren served California as governor through a period of booming growth and prosperity and enjoyed nearly universal press support. These advantages, along with his ability to cover the political middle of the road and his mastery of progressive-style politics, made him the state's most successful politician since Hiram Johnson.

Amazing Growth

24

California after World War II

D ancing in the streets with an elation, fervor, and relief that Americans of today may never experience, Californians celebrated V-E (victory in Europe) Day in May 1945, when Germany surrendered to Allied forces in Berlin. The following August they celebrated V-J Day, when Japan surrendered after the atomic bombing of Hiroshima and Nagasaki, bringing World War II to an end. In their joy, few gauged the meaning of the use of atomic weapons, or anticipated that relations between the United States and the Soviet Union would soon deteriorate.

Like the Gold Rush, World War II stands as a major turning point in California history. It began another era of migration and population increase that made California the most populous state in the Union and ushered in a period of amazing growth and development. By 1970 California had become such an economic force that, if regarded as an independent nation (as many Californians are inclined to do), it ranked seventh in the world. Only the United States itself, the Soviet Union, Great Britain, France, West Germany, and Japan had a higher gross national product. With this great growth, Californians established a way of life that became the envy of the world. To many, the state seemed on the cutting edge of American civilization, with an economy pushed by World War II to the forefront of the post-industrial society of the future.

The Great Migration

When World War II ended, California was in the early stages of a population explosion that rivaled its rate of growth in the 1920s. Between 1940 and 1970 the state grew by 13 million persons. The increase in the state's population alone exceeded the total population of any other state except New York, and in 1962, California surpassed New York as the nation's most populous state. Nearly two-thirds of the growth of the 1940s and '50s represented migration from other states. The pattern of settlement again mirrored that of the 1920s, with the great majority of migrants headed for Southern California. The population of the counties south of the Tehachapis, 3.5 million in 1940, grew to 5.5 million by 1950 and to 9 million in 1960. Moreover, 90 percent of residents lived in what were officially classified as metropolitan areas, making California not only the nation's most populous state but also its most urbanized.

Most of the state's new residents came for the same old reasons: climate and economic opportunity. Among the first arrivals were veterans who had trained in California or those who liked what they saw when passing through on their way to military action. More than 300,000 servicemen and -women from other states took their discharges in California. They were followed by a huge number who took advantage of the loan and educational benefits of the GI Bill of Rights to leave colder climates in the East for a new start in the Golden State. Young, productive, highly skilled, and eager for success, they gave the state an infusion of new blood and great energy.

Gay men and lesbians were an important element in the new migration. Many had come during the war years and discovered a more liberal social climate than they had known elsewhere. In Los Angeles, Harry Hay found veterans discharged in an Army purge of homosexuals. In 1950 they formed the Mattachine Society, the nation's first public gay rights organization. Five years later in San Francisco, Phyllis Lyon and Del Martin quietly organized a lesbian social group, the Daughters of Bilitis. Police persecution prompted early activism, as when the San Francisco Police Department repeatedly raided the Black Cat Café, a popular gathering spot for the city's gay community. The state suspended the bar's liquor license on the grounds that it was a "hangout for homosexuals." In the resulting lawsuit, the state supreme court sided with the bar's owner, holding in 1951 that absent "illegal or immoral conduct," gays had the same rights as others to congregate in public places.

Through the 1950s and '60s, gays and lesbians pressed assembly member Philip Burton and other sympathetic politicians to introduce legislation legalizing sex between consenting adults, but they met with little success. Politicians became more sympathetic as signs of a gay voting bloc emerged. In the 1959 San Francisco mayor's race, tax assessor Russ Wolden charged that incumbent Mayor George Christopher had allowed San Francisco to become the "headquarters of organized homosexuals in the United States." His smear tactics pushed homosexuality into mainstream city politics for the first time in California history, and galvanized the gay and lesbian community into political action. The Mattachine Society sued Wolden for slander and received substantial public support. Christopher won reelection by a substantial margin and the campaign stimulated a gay and lesbian political consciousness. "The important issue here for homosexuals," wrote Del Martin in 1960, was "to register—and vote."

Postwar Economic Growth

A short period of economic decline followed the end of the war in 1945, though it was not as serious as expected, since population growth served to lessen the impact of conversion to a peacetime economy. Of all the Sun Belt states, California enjoyed the greatest expansion of defense-related industries and the accompanying population growth. In the 1950s and '60s, California was America's first-choice destination.

Nationwide, GI Bill loans to veterans took up much of the slack and the unmet demand for consumer goods of the war years provided a quick stimulus to business. In California, the surge in population created a whole new range of jobs in home and highway construction, real estate and financial services, retail sales, and automobile-related industries. It quickly became evident that the war had promoted substantial diversification in the state's economy, which had previously been centered on agriculture, oil, movies, and tourism. After the war, these remained important industries, but now the state also produced electronics, footwear, clothing, frozen foods, and other goods. Moreover, this growth encouraged national companies to open branch plants in California, producing such items as technical instruments, automobiles, tires and tubes, chemicals, and cosmetics in smaller cities like San José, Stockton, and Sacramento.

Women workers were critical to this postwar surge in productivity. After World War II, the female workforce increased dramatically. Nationally, before the war only one out of four women over the age of 16 worked. By 1960, two out of five held jobs; by the end of the decade, almost half of all adult women earned wages. The new woman worker was likely to be middle-class and married. In 1940, only 15 percent of wives worked. In 1950, 21 percent did; by 1970, over 40 percent of married women earned wages. New postwar wage-earners in an expanding pool of low-paid white- and pink-collar jobs joined working-class Latinas and African American women who had balanced work and motherhood for decades.

Despite the paeans to domesticity that filled women's magazines and advice books, working women made the affluent 1950s possible. Working-class families entered the middle class via GI Bill home loans and added wives' wages to make mortgage payments. For many middle-class families, married women's wages paid for household appliances, cars, and college tuition. Paid labor had other long-term consequences as working women felt empowered by their financial contributions to the family. Their entry into the labor force in the 1950s and '60s planted the seeds of resurgent feminism in the 1970s.

The Defense and Aerospace Industries

Ironically, California's peacetime economy was dominated by industries that grew out of war and international tension. The spirit of common interest and cooperation that had characterized Soviet-American relations during the war was quickly replaced by mutual distrust and confrontation, culminating in the Soviet blockade of Berlin in 1948. The American government adopted a policy of containment of Soviet expansionism and entered the Cold War, a long period of military spending that lasted until the breakup of the Soviet Union in the 1990s. In 1950 the Cold War intensified as the United States moved to defend South Korea against invasion from North Korea.

In the meantime, technology had changed the nature of military equipment drastically. Development of jet engines and rockets put emphasis on supersonic aircraft, missiles, and sophisticated electronic devices. In 1957, when the Soviet Union successfully launched Sputnik, the first artificial satellite to orbit around the earth in space, Americans reacted with another great technological effort: in 1961 President John F. Kennedy set the national goal of sending a man to the moon.

Mind-boggling sums were involved in the nation's defense and space programs. The wartime development of giant aircraft manufacturing firms provided a superb manufacturing base for the production of modern weapons. Companies such as Douglas, Lockheed, and North American easily converted in the missile era. The state's scientific establishment was without parallel in the country. The California Institute of Technology,

Stanford University, and UC Berkeley possessed faculty and research laboratories that offered the greatest collection of scientific talent in the world. California continued to attract the specialists and technicians necessary to the modern defense industry, and the defense and scientific establishment easily adjusted to the needs of the new era.

Thus federal funds poured into California's defense and space industries, turning California's prewar "metropolitan-military complex" into the foremost "military-industrial complex" in the country. It was the political and economic power of this combination that Dwight D. Eisenhower warned of in his famous speech as he left the presidency.

Southern California became the nation's foremost center of planning, research, and manufacturing in the new aerospace industry of the 1950s. The region's economy soon centered on the production of intercontinental ballistic missiles (ICBMs) and other missiles, supersonic and jet aircraft (military and commercial), and space equipment. New companies such as Rocketdyne, Aerospace Corporation, and Litton Industries joined the field of defense and aerospace contractors. By 1960 the industry employed 70 percent of San Diego's manufacturing workers and 60 percent of those in Los Angeles and Orange counties. Twenty-five percent of the nation's defense expenditures and 42 percent of Defense Department research contracts went to California firms. In the 1960s, after the National Aeronautics and Space Administration (NASA) was organized, that agency spent 50 percent of its funds in California. Most of the components of the Apollo space craft that landed men on the moon were made in California.

The state's dominance over the aerospace industry meant that the industry likewise dominated the state's economy through the 1950s and '60s. This made California especially vulnerable to political decisions regarding the federal defense budget. Significant cuts in defense spending in the late 1950s, and again in 1968 and 1973, led to hard times in Southern California and some south San Francisco Bay communities dependent on defense employment. Unlike the victims of other recessions, the unemployed this time were relatively highly paid technicians and engineers, white-collar professionals to whom unemployment was a new and terrifying experience. Numerous bankruptcies accompanied these recessions, and even Douglas and North American were forced into mergers to survive. Lockheed eventually needed a government loan to stay in business.

By the 1970s the aerospace industry no longer dominated the state economy to the same extent. Cutbacks in defense spending, conclusion of the moon-landing program, population growth, and continued economic diversification all contributed to a more balanced, stable economy. A major aspect of this diversification was the emergence of yet another high-technology industry, pioneered and dominated by Californians and centered on the research, development, and manufacture of computers, semiconductors, communications equipment, and related materials such as computer software. Because the companies involved in this new industry were concentrated in the Santa Clara Valley near San José, that region came to be called "Silicon Valley."

The Housing Boom

The enormous growth of the California economy after World War II was fueled by a phenomenal growth in population. Between 1940 and 1970 California's population nearly tripled, increasing by 50 percent in the 1940s and again in the 1950s. The state grew at the rate of 1,500 persons a day for most of the period. A spectacular rise in marriage and birth rates also fueled this growth. From 1947 to 1964, American couples reversed the trends of earlier decades to marry and procreate in record numbers. At the peak of the baby boom in 1957, the fertility rate was 122.9 per thousand women, compared to only 79.9 per thousand in 1940. As California's population grew, an insatiable demand for single-family dwellings arose with it.

Homebuilders had developed mass production techniques during the war that soon covered the landscape with "tract" homes. These were homes of almost identical plan built by crews moving from one site to the next, one laying foundations and basic plumbing, another framing, the next roofing, another finishing interiors, and a final crew painting and cleaning up. Prefabrication speeded the process even more. An amazing record of construction emerged, along with handsome profits for homebuilders and tract developers.

The uniformity and boxy style of postwar housing elicited a good deal of humor, since it was frequently difficult to tell one home from another, but these houses were home to two-thirds of California's new residents, many of whom had never owned property before. For most, the opportunity was simply too good to pass up. Veterans' loans often made it possible to purchase a home for no money down and monthly payments that, as one said, "made any kind of rent seem like extortion."

Fueled by wartime migration, the housing boom pushed into agricultural areas surrounding urban centers. Rural communities suddenly swelled to the size of major cities. In the south, Los Angeles and Orange counties and portions of Ventura, Riverside, and San Bernardino counties rapidly changed from agricultural to residential. In the north, the peninsula counties south of San Francisco, along with San José and the East Bay counties of Alameda and Contra Costa, grew nearly as rapidly.

As sprawling tract-housing suburbs multiplied, counties and cities struggled to gain control over the process, imposing stricter standards on real estate developers, larger lots, better streets and drainage systems, sidewalks, and even parks and schools. The California ranch-style house that was popularized by the architect Cliff May and others evolved at this time and became almost universal in the subdivisions of the 1950s and '60s. Larger than earlier tract homes, usually one-story, shake-roofed, and more expensive, the ranch-style homes were built by mass production, with modest variations in design to avoid the regimented look of earlier neighborhoods. Developers now sold what they called "California living," the concept of a leisurely, self-indulgent lifestyle that emphasized the outdoor patio, barbecue, and swimming pool as integral parts of the home.

The rise of suburban California brought a new set of problems. Developers of subdivisions and shopping centers gobbled up some 3 million acres of the best agricultural land in the state. Farmland in the path of residential development skyrocketed in value. Property taxes followed suit, forcing growers to sell out to developers. Southern California saw a substantial shift of the citrus industry to the San Joaquin Valley as a result. Mass-produced housing far outstripped the ability of most communities to provide residents with essential services, leading to insufficient water, gas, electric, and sewage-treatment facilities. A year's wait for telephone service was not uncommon. Special districts, financed from a portion of the county property tax, usually provided most other services such as flood control, air-pollution control, and even mosquito abatement. Today there are approximately 5,000 special districts in the state, ranging from tiny zones allocated for cemeteries, some 1,000 school districts, to the large Bay Area Rapid Transit and South Coast Air Quality Management districts.

Perhaps the most serious consequence of the suburban housing boom was the decline of the inner city, as a substantial number of white residents from city cores migrated to new, so-called "bedroom communities." Racism and inadequate finances combined to leave ethnic minorities and the poor behind. Adding to this pattern of postwar housing development were the efforts of realtors and financial institutions to limit new housing to whites through restrictive covenants and other forms of discrimination. Continued heavy migration of African Americans to Northern California led to their concentration in San Francisco's Bayview and Hunters Point, and, across the Bay, in portions of Oakland and Richmond. In Los Angeles, African American newcomers settled in Watts and the district vacated by Japanese Americans during the war. In San Diego and Los Angeles, the swelling Mexican population was confined to inner-city *barrios*. Inferior housing, high unemployment, dependence on welfare, de facto segregation of schools, and high crime rates produced mounting frustration among residents of these districts.

The postwar construction boom was not confined to housing. Population growth generated a major expansion of state and federal government services that required enlarged public building programs. New state and federal office buildings, courthouses, and correctional facilities met pressing needs throughout the state. In Sacramento, the new Capitol Mall and the expansion of the Capitol Office Building reflected this development. In metropolitan areas, height restrictions were removed or relaxed, and high-rise commercial buildings and office towers rapidly changed skylines. The most dramatic change took place in downtown San Francisco, where a soaring new skyline dwarfed such famous landmarks like the Ferry Building. However, it was the great postwar housing boom that created the most serious problems in other areas.

Transportation

One such field was transportation. "California living" meant mobility, among other things, and mobility meant automobiles. Since the 1920s it had become clear that Californians were determined to solve their transportation problems with personal vehicles. The postwar years saw no change, even though the housing boom and suburban development put a severe strain on existing highways. Very soon after the end of the war, pressure mounted for the construction of limited-access highways to facilitate the commute from suburban bedroom communities to downtown workplaces, resulting eventually in the legislature's enactment of the Collier-Burns Act of 1947.

An extraordinary piece of legislation, the Collier-Burns Act committed the state to a huge construction program of some 12,500 miles of freeways and expressways. It established a state gasoline tax of seven cents per gallon, which would be deposited not in the state's general fund, but in a special gas-tax fund available only for construction and maintenance of the highway system. In the 1950s federal highway programs provided another important source of funding for the state's ambitious plan, including 90 percent of the funds for interstate freeways and half the funds for other federal highways in the state. By the end of the 1950s, California spent $1 million *per day* on freeway construction. Freeways encircled and plunged through the heart of all the great metropolitan centers of the state, promoting continued suburbanization. Los Angeles in particular became identified with the freeway age; one famous four-level interchange was known as "the mixmaster." Registration figures reflected this dependence on the automobile: by 1970 there were nearly 12 million autos registered in California, twice the number in any other state.

Reliance on the automobile spawned a culture particularly associated with California. Satellite shopping centers surrounded by oceans of asphalt, easily accessible by car, became the norm. Drive-through fast-food restaurants, movies, banks, and services of all kinds blossomed. Motel construction became a major industry, even in the downtown areas, formerly the city's hotel section. Trucking became a major industry, moving 90 percent of the goods distributed in the state in 1970 and boasting an $8 billion payroll.

An ominous associated development was the appearance by the mid-1940s of smog in the Los Angeles basin. Scientists tracked its cause to the introduction of chemicals into the air by a variety of sources, most importantly the automobile. A new environmental movement developed to deal with the problem, and California moved to the forefront of efforts to improve air quality.

What some have called California's love affair with the car also meant the demise of the fine electric-rail transit systems that had been so important to the state's early growth. The Pacific Electric in Los Angeles and the Key System in the San Francisco Bay Area were allowed to die, their routes eventually converted to bus service. On the lower deck of the Bay Bridge, the Key System's two rail lines became auto lanes. Elimination of the Pacific

The Coming of the Freeways

The Hollywood Freeway, looking east to Los Angeles Civic Center, 1956 (*upper left*). The Bayshore Freeway entering San Francisco from the south, 1955 (*upper right*). Looking southeast along the Santa Ana Freeway, as subdivisions encroach on orange groves, 1955 (*lower left*). The Nimitz Freeway, which opened southern Alameda County agricultural lands to subdivisions, 1959 (*lower right*). *California Department of Transportation.*

Electric and Key System made a return to electric rail transit more difficult and expensive in later years, even in the 1970s, when Californians first experienced oil and gasoline shortages.

In the north, business and construction interests successfully led a drive to recreate public transportation with the Bay Area Rapid Transit District (BART). Completion of the system in 1974 marked the first electric rail transit system to be built in the United States in 25 years. But critics assailed BART's self-supporting financial model, arguing that passengers would not be able to afford its fares, and pointed out that the skeletal track design only linked East Bay suburbs to downtown San Francisco and Oakland. Without a considerable expansion of track and subsidized fares, they claimed, BART would never become a true mass-transit system. But no politician came forward to champion their cause, an important reason a European-style public transportation system never developed in the state. Meanwhile, the vast majority of Bay Area commuters continued to travel to work by auto.

Freeway construction also produced criticism. Bureaucratic planners rarely took account of the social cost of building freeways through communities, as they wiped out large sections of housing, razed historic landmarks, and destroyed neighborhood cohesion. Thus on occasion builders encountered groups of irate citizens who successfully blocked their plans. San Franciscans forced a halt to construction of the half-completed Embarcadero Freeway and stopped a proposed freeway through Golden Gate Park. Citizens of Laguna Beach and Pasadena likewise rose up to stop freeways that would have destroyed the attractive qualities of their communities. Similarly, conservationists blocked plans for a freeway through the heart of north coast redwoods. On the whole, however, these were minor obstacles to the juggernaut set in motion by the Collier-Burns Act.

Education

The postwar baby boom, coupled with the great influx of population, put immense pressure on school facilities in California. Schools in suburban areas continued double and even triple sessions, which created a serious shortage of teachers. School construction proceeded at a feverish pace, with local tax and bond issues for expansion of facilities constantly before the voters. But by the 1970s, it became apparent that state leaders had not accurately calculated future needs, as graduating baby-boom students left school districts with expensive, vacant facilities on their hands.

In the field of higher education, the number of veterans attending California colleges and universities on the GI Bill forced a similar expansion in the 1950s, which continued as the baby-boom students reached college age in the '60s, and the proportion of high school graduates going to college jumped to 50 percent. College enrollments only began to level off in the mid-1970s. By then California led the nation in access to essentially free public higher education. The state established more than 100 two-year junior or community colleges, financed largely through local property taxes, by 1975.

In the same period, public state colleges expanded their role from primarily teacher training institutions to become four-year liberal arts colleges granting baccalaureate and master's degrees in all major fields. At the same time, new state colleges were established to meet rising student demand, while older state colleges built feverishly to relieve overcrowded facilities.

The University of California system grew rapidly as well. It poured funds into the development of UC Los Angeles, making that campus an institution rivaling Berkeley. It also acquired the old Santa Barbara State College, made "general" campuses out of its specialized agricultural units at Davis and Riverside, and established new campuses at San Diego, Irvine, and Santa Cruz. By 1960 the student population of these public systems numbered in the hundreds of thousands.

Rivalry for state budgetary support between the new community colleges, state colleges, and the university system led to a new study in the 1950s, which resulted in the Higher Education Act of 1960, also known as "the Master Plan for Higher Education." The Act resolved budget conflicts by differentiating the functions of each component. The UCs became the state's primary research and professional training institution, with only the top 12.5 percent of high school graduates eligible for direct admission. California State Universities, or CSUs, were organized into one system with a governing board of trustees similar to the UC Board of Regents. These institutions offered undergraduate, liberal arts, and baccalaureate degree, and generally limited graduate training to the master's degree. The top one-third of graduating high school students would be eligible for direct admission to any CSU. Finally, the Act confirmed the functions of community colleges: students might complete two-year certificated vocational programs or, in a two-year academic track, transfer to either a CSU or UC campus.

The Master Plan of 1960 made California a model for other states with similarly competing segments of public higher education. The act also marshaled strong popular support for free public higher education, as hundreds of thousands of California college graduates helped to make the state a leader in the modern industrial world. The state continued its support for free public education through generous budget allocations. Many superb private institutions, such as Stanford University and the California Institute of Technology, contributed to this admirable record. The state's high per-capita income and its advanced industrial society were closely related to the broad availability and high quality of its system of public higher education.

Recreation

Migrants to California, as well as tourists, have always been attracted by the state's magnificent landscape and excellent system of beaches and parks, as well as by the Yosemite, Sequoia, Kings Canyon, and Lassen national parks, various national monuments, and extensive national forests. It is not surprising, then, that postwar population growth put tremendous pressure on those resources. Forest Service records revealed a jump from 14 million visitor days in 1940 to 60 million in 1970. At the same time, local communities struggled to develop urban park sites in the face of escalating land prices. As might be expected, the increased number of trailers, campers, backpackers, sightseers, and off-road vehicles brought increased litter, water pollution, and noise to California's scenic areas, providing another stimulus to a renewed environmental movement.

The great demand for recreational outlets also attracted profit-oriented businesses. The creation and fantastic success of Disneyland near Anaheim, opened to the public in July 1955, prompted construction of similar amusement parks and entertainment facilities in other metropolitan areas. The popularity of travel trailers, motor homes, and other recreational vehicles (RVs) spawned the development of private summer camps. Boise-Cascade, Fibreboard, and other corporations actively promoted RV and summer home developments in mountain areas, with mixed results. The giant entertainment conglomerate Music Corporation of America (MCA) entered the field when it took over Yosemite Park and Curry Company in 1977.

Unfortunately, interest in making money often took precedence over such considerations as preservation of the environment, as seemed to be the case in early proposals by MCA to build high-rise visitor facilities at Yosemite and a tram from the floor of Yosemite Valley to Glacier Point. In later years, the crush of public park users, plus a concern for personal security, produced for-profit organizations such as American Trails and Thousand Trails, which catered to RV owners and campers demanding guaranteed, secure campsites in park-like settings.

The New Hollywood

For many reasons, the motion-picture industry, Southern California's leading prewar business, had the hardest adjustment to make after the war. The federal government immediately pressed antitrust suits that in 1948 forced the major studios to divest themselves of their profitable theater chains. At the same time, costs of production increased due to higher taxes and the rise of independent producers, directors, and stars. Unlike the arrangement under the old contract system, independents demanded, and got, a percentage of the studio's gross profits on their films. Some produced their own films, renting studio space and facilities for this purpose. Meanwhile, talented foreign producers and directors from Sweden, Japan, France, and Italy challenged Hollywood's domination of the moviemaking field, producing films of exceptional quality that sold well in the United States. The studios themselves joined the trend toward producing movies "on location" all over the world, and some even sold off their old Hollywood studio lots where they had once constructed elaborate sets. The prewar studio system had become uneconomical.

Likewise the introduction of television after the war challenged Hollywood's dominance in the entertainment field. Television shows not only siphoned off movie patrons but changed public tastes, as viewers demanded greater realism than Hollywood's formulaic films could provide. It took several years for the Los Angeles-based movie industry to adapt to the challenge of television. One of the first film directors to do so was Walt Disney. In time others joined him in producing shows for television along with traditional movies. By the end of the 1950s, Hollywood had developed a television production and transmission industry rivaling that of New York, the early leader of the field. With a growing recording industry as well, Los Angeles was once again a leading center of mass entertainment, transformed from a regional cultural center to one of national and international importance.

Postwar Politics and the Anticommunist Crusade

The Cold War and the Korean War affected politics as well as the economy, touching off a new wave of red scares and intolerance. The search for "un-American" attitudes and activities became a surefire formula

Walt Disney

Last of the Movie Moguls

It is a tribute to a particular quality of perseverance that, when Walt Disney died in 1966 at age 65, he was called "the last of the movie moguls." There is also a certain irony in the fact that, of all the Hollywood studios, Walt Disney Productions was the strongest and most profitable of the postwar era, and that it reached such status by embracing television.

Walt Disney

Walt Disney (*on the right*) with television variety show host Ed Sullivan and Disney characters. *Moviestore collection Ltd / Alamy Stock Photo.*

Oddly enough, Walt Disney had no great ability as an artist, but he had a sure feel for the cinematic tastes of the average American. He also had an eye for technological innovation and great organizational ability. Disney came to Hollywood from Kansas in 1923. With some experience in making animated short films in Kansas City, and lacking any other work, Disney began producing cartoons. His golden touch became evident when he won all but two Academy Awards for animated shorts from 1932 to 1942. An able editor, Disney attracted the best animators available, gave them the finest equipment and professional training, and adopted technological advances as they came. In 1927 Disney introduced Mickey Mouse, drawn from his experiences as a Kansas farm boy and his observations of the field mice he kept as pets in his Kansas City studio.

With production of *Steamboat Willie* in 1928, Disney introduced sound to cartoons. In 1931, he produced his first animated short in color. Two years later his *Three Little Pigs* was a sensational hit, making Disney a significant figure in Hollywood. By then, he had begun work on his first full-length animated feature, *Snow White*, which consumed most of his annual profits, required him to expand his staff from 150 to 750, and took five years to complete. *Snow White* was released in 1937 and became another box-office sensation, encouraging Disney to embark on a series of expensive animated cartoon features that included *Pinocchio* (1940), *Fantasia* (1940), and *Bambi* (1942). The outbreak of World War II, however, cut off his foreign sales and reduced his profits by nearly 45 percent. Only government contracts for propaganda and military training films enabled Disney's studio to survive the war years.

In the late 1940s, Disney pointed the company in new directions. He reduced emphasis on expensive animated films, increased production of live-action, family-oriented movies, a series of nature films, and construction of an amusement park, an idea he had cherished since 1930. It proved to be the formula for a stable prosperity that he had always sought. His live-action feature films dominated the family movie market just when the old major studios deserted the field for more adult fare or left it to television.

Disney was unafraid of television; indeed, in 1954 he entered the field himself, hosting programs first on ABC and later on NBC. *The Wonderful World of Disney* and *The Mickey Mouse Club*, which premiered in 1954 and 1955, respectively, were essentially designed to promote Disneyland, the revolutionary amusement park Disney opened in Anaheim in 1955. Its phenomenal success made the Disney organization Hollywood's most profitable studio, and the only one that did not sell its library of films to television or rely on independent producers for content. By 1965, Walt Disney, who had been more or less tolerated by movie moguls of the prewar era, sat at the top of the heap. He left behind a business organization that would survive, adapting to changing times and new technology without him—a classic example of modern entrepreneurial success. (RBR)

for political success. In California and elsewhere Republicans rushed to label Democratic incumbents "soft on communism." In the early 1950s Senator Joseph McCarthy of Wisconsin gained political power by wielding this weapon. Flamboyant and reckless, McCarthy claimed that communists had infiltrated the government. In the process, he fanned a near-hysterical fear of communism nationwide and gave the name "McCarthyism" to unsubstantiated accusations based on guilt by association.

Richard M. Nixon emerged as California's foremost practitioner of the latest red scare tactics. He first came to public attention in 1948, when he ran successfully for Congress against the incumbent Democrat Jerry Voorhis by questioning Voorhis's loyalty and implying his association with subversive forces. In 1949 Congressman Nixon achieved national prominence through service on the House Un-American Activities Committee (HUAC), especially with his dogged questioning of New Dealer Alger Hiss, a former official of the U.S.

State Department. Hiss's conviction for perjury following his testimony before the committee established Nixon's anticommunist credentials. The following year he defeated Congresswoman Helen Gahagan Douglas for election to the U.S. Senate. Again his campaign relied heavily on red scare tactics, associating Douglas with subversive groups by innuendo and by constant references to his opponent as "the Pink Lady." In 1952 Nixon parlayed his anticommunist reputation into the vice president's spot on Dwight D. Eisenhower's presidential ticket, when the more liberal Eisenhower wing of the party sought unity with the conservative faction.

HUAC had its counterpart in California. In 1947 the state senate established its own Un-American Activities Committee, chaired by state senator Jack B. Tenney, whose only other claim to fame was composing the song "Mexicali Rose." Tenney became a heavy-handed anticommunist who used the committee to bully witnesses, make unsubstantiated charges of disloyalty, and ruin the reputations and careers of those called before him.

Fearing a conspiracy to inject films with communist propaganda, HUAC held hearings in Hollywood and subpoenaed over 40 well-known screenwriters, directors, and producers. Most of them cooperated with the committee as "friendly witnesses," including actor Ronald Reagan, who testified that a "small clique" of communists had "a disruptive influence" within the Screen Actors Guild. Walt Disney also alleged that communists were responsible for a strike at his studio. Nevertheless, ten of those subpoenaed refused to give the names of colleagues with supposedly communist sympathies. They also refused to answer the question "Are you now or have you ever been a member of the Communist Party?" on the grounds that it violated their First Amendment rights. HUAC found the so-called "Hollywood Ten" in contempt of Congress and sentenced each to a year in federal prison.

Red-baiting provoked intense conflict in the film industry and led to the blacklisting of hundreds of writers, actors and actresses, directors, and producers. Left without the means to earn a living, some of the blacklisted found other lines of work. Where they could, a few writers went into the black market and worked for cut rates. After being imprisoned in a federal penitentiary for 11 months, screenwriter Dalton Trumbo wrote some 30 movies under various pseudonyms.

Tenney's activities also tarnished the state's illustrious university system. In 1949 UC officials, fearful of a threatened Tenney committee investigation, recommended adoption of a loyalty oath for all its employees, which the Board of Regents approved. The oath sparked an immediate controversy, since most faculty members regarded it as both unconstitutional and a violation of academic freedom. Governor Earl Warren attempted to get the Regents to rescind the oath, but he was opposed by John Francis Neylan, the erstwhile defender of Charlotte Anita Whitney in the 1920s, and by Regent Amadeo P. Giannini, who claimed that "flags would fly in the Kremlin" if Warren succeeded. In 1950, badly split, the Regents fired 46 non-signing faculty members for insubordination, bringing on the university the condemnation of the prestigious American Association of University Professors (AAUP).

The dispute then moved to the courts where, in April 1951, the district court ruled in *Tolman v. Underhill* that the oath was a violation of tenure and unconstitutional. Led by Neylan, and over Gov. Warren's objections, the Regents appealed the decision. More than a year and a half later, the state supreme court invalidated the oath and ordered the dismissed faculty reinstated. The court, however, based its decision on the narrow grounds that

the state legislature had preempted the field when it passed the Levering Act in 1950, which required an anticommunist oath of all state employees. Ironically, later Earl Warren, as Chief Justice of the U.S. Supreme Court, issued a series of rulings that eventually prompted the state supreme court to declare the Levering Act unconstitutional. It was a measure of revenge for the former governor's treatment by the Board of Regents.

Meanwhile, the Tenney committee had become an embarrassment. It was abolished in 1949, when Tenney injudiciously alleged that some members of the legislature were "tainted with communism." It was soon replaced with a state senate Committee on Un-American Activities under the chairmanship of Hugh Burns, who kept the committee's activities low-key. The committee was abolished in 1971, when members discovered that committee staff had been compiling files of personal information on other state senators. By this time the near-hysterical anticommunism that had earlier fueled these activities had subsided. It left in its wake a trail of shattered friendships, careers, and reputations, ruined by innuendo and unproved accusations. Like the internment of the Japanese Americans in 1942, the red scare proved again the power of mass hysteria.

Goodwin Knight Moves Left

Earl Warren left the governorship in 1953 for the U.S. Supreme Court, having established a remarkable record for holding the state in the political middle of the road in wartime and through a time of extreme pressure from right-wing elements within the Republican Party after the war. The effectiveness of Warren's moderate political stance was not lost on his successor, Lieutenant Governor Goodwin J. ("Goody") Knight.

A lawyer, businessman, radio commentator, and popular after-dinner speaker, Knight had been elected lieutenant governor in 1946 with the rare personal endorsement of Gov. Warren. Once elected, however, Knight lined up with the conservative wing of the Republican Party and opposed Warren on the oath controversy, medical insurance, fair employment legislation, and other issues. He even toyed with the idea of running against Warren in 1950, but thought better of it and instead ran for reelection as lieutenant governor. Knight cross-filed and won the nomination of both Democrats and Republicans. His patience was rewarded when Warren went to Washington, leaving the governor's seat to him.

As governor, Knight shrewdly moved left to the political center to pick up Gov. Warren's following. He backed

Warren-like programs in mental health, higher unemployment benefits, workers' compensation, old-age pensions, and child-care centers. Most importantly, he vigorously opposed so-called "right-to-work" legislation, which organized labor considered simple union busting. As a result, labor backed Knight for reelection in 1954. In fact, Knight had so successfully adopted Warren's political style that, after cross-filing in the primaries, he almost won both Republican and Democratic nominations for governor.

Though an effective successor to Warren, after 1954 Knight found himself in a bitter political power struggle, fighting with Richard Nixon and U.S. Senate majority leader William Knowland for control of California's Republican Party. In 1957, Knowland announced that he planned to challenge Knight in the gubernatorial primary. As a moderate sympathetic to organized labor, Knight faced a serious threat, as the Republican Party grew more conservative. Knowland, Nixon, and Eisenhower convinced Knight to abandon Sacramento to run for a seat in the U.S. Senate. Instead, in 1958 Knowland lost the governor's seat by a wide margin to Edmund G. "Pat" Brown, while Knight was defeated by U.S. Senator Clair Engle. This left Nixon in control of California's Republican Party, with hopes for his party's presidential nomination. Knight contended that he had been "sandbagged." The campaigns of 1958 led to disaster for the state's Republican Party and to a Democratic revival in California politics.

California Culture in Transition

California had been a promised land for Americans since the time of the gold rush, as periodic migrations to the state have attested. After World War II people began to regard the Golden State as the symbol of a new culture and a harbinger of the nation's future. California lifestyles were the subject of countless magazine articles, Hollywood movies, and television shows, inspiring a national interest in leisure living and informality. Swing, jazz, and the upbeat big-band music of the 1930s carried into the 1950s. San Francisco's new black neighborhood, the Fillmore, was "jumping," noted photographer and filmmaker Elizabeth Peppin:

> Locals shaking off the working week drudgery could walk past Billie Holiday as she opened the door into the New Orleans Swing Club. . . . Walk down the street and they might find John Coltrane, Chet Baker, or Dexter Gordon hanging out at Bop City, occasionally taking the stage to jam with the regulars.

The sophisticated jazz quartet of Dave Brubeck, who was born and raised in Concord, topped popular music charts of the era, while the Monterey Jazz Festival became one of the national events in the world of popular music. At the same time, the new sound of rock 'n' roll had emerged, absorbing elements of country and western styles.

Just as they had in the 1920s and '30s, a new generation of artists and social critics rebelled against urban and suburban culture in the film noir of the mid-1940s and '50s. Based on earlier popular fiction, films such as *Double Indemnity*, *The Blue Dahlia*, and *The Postman Always Rings Twice* offered tales of violent crime and powerless protagonists trapped in threatening urban settings. Shot on location in Los Angeles, the dark and existential mood of film noir belied the sunny dreams of southern California boosters.

Despite such dissent, California culture also reflected the postwar emphasis on rebuilding lives dislocated by the war, family formation, and on the avid pursuit of material well-being. Hollywood's wholesome, noncontroversial movies of the 1930s carried into the 1950s and '60s, particularly through such popular Disney vehicles as *The Shaggy Dog* (1959), *The Absent-Minded Professor* (1961) and *Mary Poppins* (1964). Los Angeles also produced family-oriented television, including such profoundly popular comedies as *I Love Lucy*, which premiered in 1951, and shows built around well-known radio personalities Jack Benny, Bob Hope, and others.

As was true in the 1920s, California's postwar years were a prosperous time for a rapidly growing middle class with increased leisure time. The state's array of parks, peaks, and beaches fueled a recreation industry devoted to skiing, surfing, boating, hiking, and camping, activities that also required investment in recreational paraphernalia from tents to wet suits. Spectator sports attracted large crowds, and students created huge cheering sections at college games.

In architecture, the housing boom of the postwar years brought the California ranch-style house to the zenith of its popularity. With its low profile, gently sloping roof, wide overhang, and split-level design, the modern ranch house had much in common with its antecedent, the Mexican rancho. The ground-hugging silhouette of the rancho resulted from the difficulty of building multilevel structures of adobe brick. The low-pitched roof reflected the region's mild climate, while wide roof overhangs protected the vulnerable adobe walls from weather. The low profile of the postwar ranch house, on the other hand, conformed to modern principles popularized by Frank Lloyd Wright, Cliff May, and other architects who demanded that the design flow organically from the site.

Low eaves and wide overhangs now protected large glass walls, while ground-level floors promoted the unity of indoor and outdoor space. Like its Mexican forebear, the modern ranch house concentrated family life in an outdoor patio. The California ranch house, with innumerable variations, has dominated western residential architecture since World War II.

The postwar years also spurred an explosion of cultural activities in Southern California. Many new arrivals were well educated, sophisticated, and affluent, including a large proportion of professionals. With strong interests in scientific and intellectual pursuits, and heavily influenced by the large contingent of European writers, artists, and musicians who fled Hitler's Germany for California, they demanded broader cultural offerings. Their influence was reflected in the 1960s and '70s with the energetic development of museums, art institutes, and facilities for the performing arts, especially in Los Angeles.

Jack Kerouac

King of the Beats

The Beat Generation, whom San Francisco *Chronicle* columnist Herb Caen dubbed "beatnicks," represented the "lost generation" of World War II and, for some, pioneers of a new romantic movement in postwar literature. Reacting to parents' seeming obsession with security, beatniks dismissed the adult world as a kind of modern Hell. They rejected atomic warfare, wars of containment, and the Cold War. To them, their fathers were "organization men," enduring a stultifying nine-to-five work day for the sake of accumulating material goods, retreating at day's end to suburban sameness, where boredom, divorce, and stifled creativity and self-dependence awaited them. The Beats rejected it all.

Jack Kerouac

Courtesy of The Bancroft Library, University of California, Berkeley.

The heroes that Beat Generation writers created refused to enter the "phony" competitive world with its middle-class institutions. Instead, they projected idealized visions of childhood innocence, and looked inward to the self, placing their faith in their own emotions and sensations. For some Beats, this meant disparaging regular employment, material goods, and the usual forms of communication, and possibly experimenting with mind-altering drugs, all in an effort to heighten the sensations of mind and body.

Jack Kerouac, "King of the Beats," produced a series of novels that included *On the Road* (1957), *The Subterraneans* (1958), *Dharma Bums* (1958), *Big Sur* (1962), and *Visions of Cody* (1972), Kerouac described his generation's desperate search for alternatives to the traditions of white, middle-class America. *On the Road* is Kerouac's best-known book. With its focus on the migrant hero and the lure of California, it can be considered a work in the tradition of Jack London's *The Road* and John Steinbeck's *The Grapes of Wrath*, yet for Kerouac life on the road was a form of rebellion against the empty values of an older generation.

Kerouac called his writing style "spontaneous prose," an attempt to imitate both the spontaneous creativity of jazz musicians as well as the conversational style of Neal Cassady, perhaps the most zealous of the Beats.

Kerouac's style was picked up, in modified form, by such Beat successors as Ken Kesey, who published *One Flew Over the Cuckoo's Nest* in 1962.

Kerouac's books are essentially a chronicle of the Beat scene, especially the doings of poets and writers such as Allen Ginsberg, Michael McClure, John Clellan Holmes, and Lawrence Ferlinghetti, who made San Francisco's North Beach district an artist's Mecca in the 1940s and '50s. Kerouac's works provide a running commentary on the anxiety of those who came of age during and after World War II. Although critics complained that Kerouac made no effort to analyze and really understand the experiences he narrated, he succeeded in projecting a vivid sense of a world that was "vibrating apart." Kerouac spoke for many who found themselves unable to communicate with their parents or community. But Kerouac never reconciled himself with the realities of American life in the postwar era, nor did the central characters of his novels. Kerouac's anti-heroes followed a path prophetic of Kerouac's own: he died in 1969 at the age of 47 from the effects of drugs and alcohol.   (RBR)

Meanwhile, California universities produced a number of talented writers. Stanford's Wallace Stegner published *Mormon Country* (1942) and *Big Rock Candy Mountain* (1943). At Berkeley, George R. Stewart turned natural phenomena into vivid novels with *Storm* (1941) and *Fire* (1948). At the same time William Everson, who taught periodically at UC Santa Cruz, emerged as California's best poet since Robinson Jeffers.

The uniformity and conformity of the war years and postwar culture provoked the rebellion of a small but vocal group of poets and writers in the 1940s and 1950s who called themselves "the Beat Generation." Rejecting traditional forms they protested in writing and lifestyle what they regarded as the numbing effect of suburban culture. Led by poet Allen Ginsberg and writer Jack Kerouac, the Beats paved the way for a harsher, more cynical California literature in the late 1950s. But most Californians chose to ignore the warnings of the disenchanted and the specter of nuclear war by immersing themselves in comfort and a sense of well-being that characterized the 1950s but failed to survive the '60s.

Police and Student Protesters, University of California, Berkeley, 1964

Police removing students from Sproul Hall. The 1960s, which began in optimism, ended in pessimism and upheaval. Local, national, and international issues increasingly divided Californians into hostile camps. *Courtesy of The Bancroft Library, University of California, Berkeley.*

PART NINE

The 1960s and After

The election of President John Fitzgerald Kennedy in 1960 brought a note of cautious optimism to California and the nation. Kennedy's victory was a narrow one, and a majority of Californians gave their votes to native (if not always favorite) son, Republican Richard Milhous Nixon. Still, there was something appealing and reassuring about the young, energetic president-elect, his "New Frontier," and his inaugural challenge: "Ask not what your country can do for you; ask what you can do for your country."

The hopeful mood gradually evaporated as recurrent international crises punctured the calm: the Bay of Pigs incident, the Cuban missile crisis, and escalating U.S. involvement in Vietnam. Domestically, an erratic economy continued to sputter, racial tensions persisted, and the assassinations of John Kennedy in 1963 and of Robert Kennedy and Martin Luther King Jr. in 1968 shocked the nation. That year, when President Lyndon B. Johnson refused to seek reelection, Americans sent Richard Nixon to the White House, hoping for better things. To some degree, they were rewarded. Nixon reestablished diplomatic relations with mainland China and détente replaced previously aggressive relations with the Soviet Union. U.S. involvement in Vietnam also came to an end. But domestic affairs were less promising. Persistent controversy derailed Nixon's promise to "bring us together again," and the economy faltered. Racial tensions remained high, and the protracted Watergate scandal—lasting from the spring of 1972 until the summer of 1974—resulted in the first presidential resignation in U.S. history, further undermining Americans' confidence in their elected officials.

Californians' reactions to these events made the state a virtual microcosm of the nation. They began in 1958 by electing Democrat Edmund G. ("Pat") Brown to the governor's office, then replaced him with Republican Ronald Reagan in 1966, went Democrat again in 1974, with Edmund G. "Jerry" Brown Jr., followed by another Republican, George Deukmejian, in 1982. Voters' choices mirrored changing national moods, shifting from optimistic liberalism to hesitant conservatism to something that defied definition and sundered the state's neo-progressive political tradition, perhaps permanently.

379

Prologues to Violence

25

Genesis of a Ghetto

Before an audience seeking relief from stuffy homes on the warm evening of August 11, 1965, a piece of street theater unfolded as a California Highway Patrol officer made an arrest in the Watts district of preponderantly African American south-central Los Angeles. Principal players were Officer Lee Minikus, who was white, and 21-year-old Marquette Frye, who was black. The drama tilted toward tragedy as Frye's mood shifted from jocular to belligerent. His family and friends appeared on the scene, officers reinforced Minikus, and rumors of police brutality flew through the neighborhood. More people spilled into the streets, igniting a tragic six days of violence, destruction, and looting.

The episode stunned white Californians. They were well aware of the violence that accompanied the struggle for civil rights in the American South, but seemed oblivious to the discrimination that constrained black lives at home. After all, thought many, California had no "Jim Crow" laws. State laws mandated equal opportunity in housing and employment, and African American neighborhoods, mostly single-family residences on tree-lined streets, looked nothing like the ghettos of New York or Chicago. Blacks held elective office in California: in the state assembly sat W. Byron Rumford (elected in 1948), F. Douglass Ferrell and Mervyn Dymally (elected in 1962), and Willie F. Brown Jr. (1964). They would be joined in 1966 by Yvonne Brathwaite Burke, the first black woman elected to California's legislature. In 1962 white and black Californians elected Augustus Hawkins, an assembly member since 1940, to the U.S. House of Representatives. Consequently, many white Californians persisted in the comfortable assumption that their state's racial climate was uniquely benign. Indeed, even after the riots began, Police Chief William H.

Parker claimed—and probably believed—that "Los Angeles is quiet as far as race problems are concerned." In charge of the department since 1950, Parker knew first-hand how often local communities of color complained of police brutality. Yet, like many white Angelenos, Parker had a blind spot where race was concerned, one that color-coordinated with the city's history as "the white spot of America," as newspaperman and real estate developer Harry Chandler once put it. Part of a history Angelenos should have known, but did not, the forces that produced the Watts Riots stretched back to the 1880s and continued through the 1960s. Unfortunately, those same forces also reached forward, into the present day.

The word "ghetto" immigrated to the United States from Europe, where residence typically involved some element of coercion, based more often on religion than on race. As immigration to the United States surged in the nineteenth and early twentieth centuries, distinctive ethnic communities appeared as newcomers clustered together, producing recognizable neighborhoods with such names as "Little Italy" or "Over the Rhine." Typically these clusters were voluntary. Italians in San Francisco, Chicago, and other U.S. cities, for example, brought with them the old-world tradition of *campanilismo*, or residing within sight of one's church steeple. Jews clustered together on New York's Lower East Side, where they could be close to synagogues, kosher butchers, and other Yiddish-speakers. Yet residents of the same religion or language rarely composed more than half of a district's population. One-third might constitute the dominant element giving the neighborhood its character, while the majority belonged to diverse groups that shared socioeconomic status rather than ethnic origins. The exception to this rule was 1870s San Francisco, where local ordinances confined Chinese settlers to one ten-block district.

The boundaries of the first U.S. ghettos were remarkably permeable. Immigrants typically left behind the crowded, squalid tenements they first called home as soon as economic circumstances permitted. For most, learning English and acquiring citizenship were the keys to escape. The pattern was different for African Americans, who possessed both English language and birthright citizenship. Although they flocked to the same U.S. cities, and usually for the same reasons—opportunity and freedom from persecution—African Americans found it almost impossible to escape their ghettos.

This was true for the pueblo that became Los Angeles, founded in 1781. More than half of the original *pobladores* were of mixed Native, African, and European ancestry, including Maria Feliciana Arballo, "the very bold widow" who accompanied Captain Juan Bautista de Anza to become the matriarch of the prominent Pico family. During the Spanish and Mexican eras, black Californios assimilated, intermarried, and all but disappeared as an identifiable group. The Mexican-American War and gold discovery brought a handful of African Americans to the pueblo, but few remained. At mid-century the most notorious street in Los Angeles was known as *calle de los negros*, but the name referred to criminals, or "people of darkness." Later-arriving Americans would translate the name as "Nigger Alley." The *calle's* name proved apt in 1871, when a mob of 500 Anglos and Hispanics staged the town's first full-blown race riot and murdered as many as 20 Chinese Angelenos.

Among Los Angeles's earliest permanent black settlers was former slave Biddy Mason, who won her freedom in 1856. Robert Owens, the freedman who helped Mason, her three children, and eleven others escape slavery, arrived from Texas in 1850. Owens established a thriving livestock business and employed a dozen *vaqueros*. Like Mason, Owens invested profitably in downtown and suburban real estate. Another successful black Angeleno, Dr. John Strother Griffin, formed a water company with several partners. In 1868, the company provided water to the city; it later sold its assets at a handsome price to the Los Angeles municipal water system.

Table 25.1   Population Growth, Los Angeles County, 1850–1960

Census Year	Total Population	White	Black	Census Year	Total Population	White	Black
1850	3,530	3,518	12	1910	504,131	483,478	9,424
1860	11,333	11,246	87	1920	936,455	894,507	18,738
1870	15,309	14,720	134	1930	2,208,492	1,949,882	46,425
1880	33,381	31,707	188	1940	2,785,643	2,660,042	75,209
1890	101,454	95,033	1,817	1950	4,151,687	3,877,944	217,881
1900	170,298	163,975	6,323	1960	6,039,834	5,453,866	461,546

LA Almanac, "Historical Census Records: Ethnic Groups in Los Angeles County, 1850 to 1960" (2018). http://www.laalmanac.com/population/po20.php, accessed 4-7-18.

Mason, Owens, Griffin, and other black pioneers formed the nucleus of a stable African American middle-class in nineteenth-century Los Angeles. Most settled in and around the Central Avenue area, where they lived in individual homes, apartments, or boarding houses, often buying or renting from black property owners. Another African American enclave emerged seven miles south of downtown Los Angeles on a segment of *El Rancho Tajuato*. The original Mexican land grant survived the 1851 Land Commission but, as so often happened, slowly shrank in size, reduced by squatters, lawyers, and tax assessors. When the original grant holder died in the 1870s, his will distributed the remainder among numerous heirs. The lots were further subdivided and sold to railroad workers, including African American Pullman car porters and *traqueros* (Mexican and Mexican American track workers). In 1902, the family of Charles H. Watts donated the land that became the Pacific Electric Railway's Watts Station.

The black population of Los Angeles exploded during the 1880s and '90s, as African Americans responded to the same boosterism and railroad rate wars that more than tripled the city's Anglo population. The city's black population grew almost tenfold, but—because the total population also grew exponentially—blacks remained a tiny minority, fewer than 2 percent in 1890. Indeed, that year census-takers counted twice as many Chinese as black Angelenos. The town's Mexican population also grew, recruited by the Santa Fe and Southern Pacific railways. In 1900, Mexicans constituted 15 percent of the city's population. From 1900 to 1930, Mexican Angelenos grew tenfold, from 5,000 to 50,000.

In the early decades of the twentieth century, black Angelenos could feel optimistic about the future. Laborers, skilled craftsmen, and service workers found reasonably steady work, although at lower wages than whites. The lure of travel and relatively good wages attracted African Americans to work as "red caps" and Pullman car porters in the burgeoning railroad business. Professionals, including black attorneys, dentists, and physicians, served their own community as well as white clients. Black Los Angeles also supported four newspapers, including *The New Age*, whose publisher, Frederick M. Roberts, white and black Angelenos elected to the state assembly in 1918, and the *California Eagle*, California's oldest continuously published black newspaper.

The main limitation on black residence throughout the city was the financial ability to rent or buy property. In 1910s Watts, black home ownership increased when black realtor Charles C. Leake began selling lots for as little as $25 (about $620 in 2017 dollars), with one dollar down and one dollar per week. During the San Fernando Valley's early-twentieth-century "bungalow boom," Black Angelenos also found whites eager to sell them their homes. Indeed, in 1930, approximately one-third of all black families in Los Angeles owned their homes, about the same proportion as whites.

For black Angelenos, early community life revolved around their churches. In 1872, Biddy Mason paid taxes and other expenses for the First African Methodist Episcopal, the city's first autonomous black church. Along with the Second Baptist, founded in 1885, local churches provided sites for social and political meetings, education, and social welfare services. Women formed their own church auxiliaries to raise funds and address community needs, but also to deal with issues of gender, including improved work, political, and educational opportunities for black women.

Civil rights organizations were community focal points as well. Black leaders and a smattering of white intellectuals formed a chapter of the National Association for the Advancement of Colored People (NAACP) soon after W.E.B. DuBois visited in 1913. DuBois later rhapsodized that black Angelenos were "without doubt the most beautifully housed group of colored people in the United States." The businesses he described included "a splendid merchant tailor shop with a large stock of goods," "a contractor who was putting up some of the best buildings in the city," and "physicians, lawyers and dentists with offices in first-class buildings."

Racism was present, of course, as the founding of an NAACP chapter attested. Its initial cause was challenging Hollywood filmmaker D.W. Griffith's 1915 release of *Birth of a Nation*. Community leaders first pressed the city to censor the film. When that failed, they demanded, unsuccessfully, that the city ban the film.

As the title of Griffith's film suggested, the experiences of black Angelenos were part of a larger, national story. Consequential as the Civil War was, for African Americans World War I marked the division between "past" and "future." U.S. entry into WWI in 1917 sparked the Great Migration, leading an estimated 500,000 African Americans to northern and midwestern cities. They were responding both to the pull of war work and the push of oppression, segregation, and racial violence in the rural American South.

What is often overlooked in the Great Migration was its dual nature: whites also deserted the South in large

Red Caps Employed by the Southern Pacific, circa 1920–1930, Los Angeles
"Red caps" carried passengers' baggage at railroad stations. This photo was taken at Central Station, located on Central Avenue in downtown Los Angeles and a major railroad depot in the 1920s and 1930s. From left to right: First row, Percy Bradshaw, George W. Jones, Edward Ringgold, Arthur Henderson, Frank S. Pierce, James Armstrong and Walter Hughes. Second row, Lafayette Rogers, Columbus B. Fulghum, Arnold Bankston, Sam W. Thompson, John Wilson, Fountain A. Brown (Head Red Cap), William H. Young, Robert Lindsey, Oliver Artis and Virgil Williams. Third row, Herbert Galloway, Charles Holmes, Octie C. Jones, Robert Lee Harrison, Thomas Long and Charles Benford. Fourth row, Alvin Spivey, Ernest S. Dixon, James Carothers, Clifford Palmer, James Boutte, Robert L. Beverly and William L. Downs. *Charlotta Bass / California Eagle Photograph Collection, Southern California Library, Los Angeles, California.*

Baptist Ministers Meeting, Pleasant Hill Baptist Church, Los Angeles, 1930

Black Angelenos founded the Pleasant Hill Baptist Church in 1912. From the 1860s forward, churches were at the heart of community life, providing spiritual instruction, community service, and leadership in crucial civil rights campaigns. Today's Pleasant Hill Baptist Church is a symbol of both change and continuity: in 1983 the name of its street was changed from "Santa Barbara" to "Martin Luther King Jr. Boulevard." *Shades of L.A. Photo Collection, Los Angeles Public Library.*

numbers. When black Southerners established their much-noticed northern and midwestern communities, white Southerners were barely noticeable among them, yet they outnumbered black newcomers roughly two to one.

This great exodus of white and black Southerners underlay the dramatic episodes of white-on-black violence that occurred in sites of new black settlement. In July 1917, for example, whites swarmed East St. Louis, Illinois, indiscriminately attacking African Americans. The official death toll in "the East St. Louis Race War" was 39 blacks and nine whites, though some suggest that the African American death toll was much higher. Twenty-six race riots occurred nationwide over the "Red Summer" of 1919, as white violence met returning African American servicemen. Observers alternately attributed the carnage to labor disputes, white fear of armed black servicemen, and the stereotype of black men as sexual predators, but fear and loathing were the common denominators.

California escaped the Red Summer, perhaps because it was barely affected by the first Great Migration. Between 1910 and '20, the black population of Los Angeles doubled which, although significant, paled in comparison to increases in other cities.

The period 1920–30 held far greater import for black Angelenos. The city's black and white population totals increased (147% and 118%, respectively), but the greatest significance was the source of white migration: the majority came from just four states: Texas, Louisiana, Arkansas, and Oklahoma. Residents were well aware of the Midwesterners and Southerners in their midst, yet white and black Angelenos saw the newcomers differently. To novelist Irvin S. Cobb, in Hollywood through the 1920s and '30s, they were harmless hicks, "at heart . . . a vast cross-section of the Corn Belt set down incongruously in a Maxfield Parrish setting." Black Angelenos saw them in far less positive terms. The *Eagle* sounded an alarm, calling on the community "to prevent and eradicate the growth of southern prejudice in our state." Indeed, editors linked the transplants to the explosion of Ku Klux Klan activity in Los Angeles.

Unlike its rural southern ancestor, the new KKK was an urban phenomenon. Members targeted blacks, of course, but also Asians, Mexicans, Jews, Catholics, communists, union organizers, immigrants, and—because they associated immigrants with alcohol use—bootleggers. Klansmen in one April 1922 episode, for example, claimed that they were after an illegal bootlegging operation in then-rural Inglewood, eight miles from downtown Los Angeles. More than 100 armed and hooded Klansmen broke into the home of two Basque immigrants, hauled them outside, and beat them savagely. An Inglewood traffic officer who happened upon the scene ordered the attackers to drop their weapons. The resulting gunfight left two Klansmen wounded and one dead. The fatality, it was later revealed, was a Los Angeles County constable. A search of the KKK's downtown headquarters produced white robes, crosses, and 4,000 membership cards. Prominent local Klansmen included the sheriff and chief of police, a member of the district attorney's office (who later insisted he had

joined in error), and a city council member (who never denied membership).

The local KKK had little to fear from white Angelenos: the city councilor won five subsequent reelections. The grand jury convened in the bootlegging case indicted 35 Klansmen for assault with intent to commit murder, but none were convicted.

In the 1920s, the Klan staged numerous marches in the town of Watts, then contemplating election of an African American mayor. When the *Eagle* reported in 1925 that the KKK planned to prevent that outcome by pressuring Los Angeles to annex Watts, the Klan sued the paper for libel. The KKK lost in court, proving that the *Eagle*'s reports were true. All the same, the city annexed Watts the following year. Many residents approved annexation, despite the loss of autonomy, because it linked them to Los Angeles's water supply.

Ku Klux Klan Gathering, Downtown Los Angeles, 1924
Members of the Ku Klux Klan gather at 5th and Olive streets in downtown Los Angeles for church service at Temple Baptist Church, June 29, 1924. Copyright © 1924 *Los Angeles Times.*

Another impact of the Great Migration was a shift in community policing tactics. The white and black southern exodus that accompanied WWI introduced southern law enforcement practices to northern and midwestern communities. By WWI, admitted one Chicagoan, that city's black community viewed the police "as the armed representative of white hostility." The posting of northern black servicemen to southern communities also provided a brutal introduction to southern policing. In August 1917, Houston police officers removed an African-American woman from her home, publicly beat and then arrested her. The crowd that gathered to watch included a soldier attached to the all-black Third Battalion. When the soldier questioned the officers, they beat and arrested him. A second member of the Battalion visited the police station, resulting in another beating and arrest. That night, 156 armed black soldiers marched on Houston. In the riot that followed, four black soldiers and 15 whites—including four policemen—died.

Black complaints of police violence were so pervasive through WWI that the national NAACP carried on simultaneous campaigns against lynching and police brutality. The Los Angeles chapter, however, did not publicize problems with local police, for fear of linking blackness with criminality in the public mind.

With sometimes overlapping membership, the Los Angeles police and KKK enforced the color line in an increasingly segregated city. When newspaperman and real estate developer Harry Chandler promoted Los Angeles as "the white spot of America," he meant to describe a city untainted by municipal corruption or labor unrest. But for others, Chandler's slogan was interchangeable with "white supremacy." During the 1920s, as some northern Californians agitated to "Make the Delta White," some white Angelenos chanted "Keep the White Spot White," hoping to block Japanese from their neighborhoods. Local governments and businesses also adopted "Jim Crow." Restaurants, hotels, theaters, clothing stores, and other businesses increasingly refused to serve black customers. Law or intimidation barred blacks from public facilities such as swimming pools, parks, and playgrounds. Discrimination in employment—as often the product of union policies as employers' practices—restricted the occupations available to people of color. African Americans secured jobs as menials: porters, laborers, janitors, waiters, maids, and servants. By the 1930s, even in those occupations, black Angelenos were clustered at the bottom: hotels employed numerous black bell "boys," for example, but rarely a black bell captain. Whites monopolized

Dr. Ralph Johnson Bunche at the 1963 March on Washington

In many ways, the life of Ralph Bunche illustrated the promise that early Los Angeles held out to African Americans. A Midwesterner, Bunche migrated as a child with his family to Los Angeles. He graduated from UCLA in 1927, continued to Harvard University, and earned a doctorate. A professor of government at Washington, D.C.'s Howard University, in 1941 Bunche began a long, distinguished career as a diplomat for the United States and United Nations. For his service as leader of the U.N.'s Palestine Commission, he was awarded the Nobel Peace Prize in 1950, the first African American to be so honored. Bunche was one of an estimated 250,000 demonstrators who joined Martin Luther King Jr's "March on Washington for Jobs and Freedom," one of the largest political rallies for human rights in United States history. On August 28, 1963, King delivered his historic "I Have a Dream" speech. *Science History Images / Alamy Stock Photo.*

most forms of industrial employment in Los Angeles. Sales and clerical opportunities were limited: in 1930, the city's retail sales force exceeded 11,000, but fewer than 30 were African American.

Residential segregation grew more rigid through the 1920s. All Los Angeles minorities—blacks, Japanese, Mexicans, Jews, and Chinese—faced restrictive covenants that prohibited the sale, lease, or rental of real estate to non-whites. These, too, were products of the Great Migration, developed by northern and midwestern property owners to preserve white neighborhoods. Restrictive covenants reached Los Angeles during the "Boom of the '80s" and, by the 1920s, were ubiquitous. Excluded Angelenos filed dozens of lawsuits between 1917 and 1945, but none succeeded.

In 1919, the case of *Los Angeles Investment Co. v. Albert Gary* set a new precedent. The state supreme court decided that it was illegal to restrict sale, rental, or lease of property on the basis of race, but race-based restrictions on occupancy were legal. *Gary* meant that people of color could buy, rent, or lease property, but they could not live in it. Restrictive covenants remained in force until 1948, when the state supreme court declared them unconstitutional. By then, however, the Los Angeles ghetto was an established fact. Despite their illegality, "private

African Americans at Organizational Meeting, circa 1930–1940, Los Angeles

African American women gathered for what appears to be an organizational meeting. The tall woman in the black jacket, standing fifth from the left, is Pauline Slater, one of the first African American elementary school teachers in Los Angeles. The woman on the far right is Jennie Bruington, who moved to Los Angeles from Kansas with her husband, James, in 1887. Their daughter, Bessie Bruington Brooks, was a Los Angeles teacher who in 1939 became the city's first African American principal. *Charlotta Bass / California Eagle Photograph Collection, Southern California Library, Los Angeles, California.*

understandings" between property owners continued to circumvent the court's decision. Later fair housing laws were also routinely violated. As a result, with each passing decade, living conditions deteriorated in the areas open to people of color.

At the same time, white transplants flocked to the city's whites-only districts. In 1922, a billboard outside Ingleside proclaimed it an all-white community. One year later, advertisements for Eagle Rock, located seven miles from downtown, promoted that suburb as open only to the "Caucasian race." A 1924 ad encouraged Angelenos to protect their families by moving to the all-white Hills of Hollywoodland. Home Gardens, 43 miles from downtown, declared itself "a town of,

Angelenos outside the Alabam Club, 4015 Central Avenue, Los Angeles, ca. 1954

The relatively open environment of early-twentieth-century Los Angeles produced numerous black-owned businesses, including popular nightclubs that appealed to both white and black patrons. Hollywood stars such as Fatty Arbuckle, Tom Mix, and Hoot Gibson went "slumming," as they called it, at hot spots like the Alabam Club, opened in 1931. Although patrons were racially mixed, performers were African American. The Cotton Club opened in 1927 on Washington Boulevard near La Cienega in Culver City. Trumpeter Louis Armstrong guest starred there with the Les Hite Band for months at a time. The city's movie, radio, and recording industries nurtured the talents of Armstrong and other black artists and entertainers, who often recorded soundtracks for Hollywood movies. Lionel Hampton (standing at left in photo) played often at the Alabam Club. Hampton migrated with his family from Alabama to Los Angeles in 1927, and attended the University of Southern California. After playing with the Benny Goodman Quartet, Hampton started his own orchestra, moved to New York, and won international acclaim as one of the country's greatest jazz artists. *Shades of L.A. Photo Collection, Los Angeles Public Library.*

by, and for workingmen" but only those of the "white race." South Gate maintained its whites-only policy through World War II.

Communities also imposed whites-only restrictions retroactively. In the 1920s, KKK pressure convinced Manhattan Beach to condemn waterfront property owned by black families since the 1910s and to close its beach to African Americans. The state supreme court in 1928 confirmed this practice, ruling that even when blacks lived in neighborhoods before restrictions were established, they must vacate newly covenanted properties. Resistance sometimes succeeded, as when realtor Booker T. Washington Jr. went to court to keep his San Gabriel Valley home.

Where legal mechanisms failed, extra-legal forms succeeded. In 1925, a black attorney launched a real estate development in Huntington Beach, but it mysteriously burned to the ground. Patrons and investors in a country club in Corona were so intimidated that the business failed.

The Great Depression slowed the city's population growth in the 1930s, but World War II led to a Second Great Migration. During the 1940s, almost five million African Americans moved north and west. This Great Migration reached California, bringing the state its first significant influx of African Americans, approximately 400,000.

The black population of Los Angeles tripled between 1940 and '50, while the number of white Angelenos grew by only 45 percent. Yet these newcomers faced vastly different residential options. The city's black population had grown by 115,000 percent since 1880, but in 1950 most of the city's 218,000 African Americans lived in the same four areas settled by the first black pioneers.

Ironically, internment of Japanese Angelenos somewhat ameliorated conditions, as African Americans took over the area known as "Little Tokyo." Temporarily renamed "Bronzeville," for three years the district was a black neighborhood with jumping jazz clubs and night spots. When internment ended, many of Little Tokyo's former residents returned, bringing Bronzeville to an end.

As the city's minority population grew, relations with the Los Angeles Police Department (LAPD) worsened. In the early 1920s, before annexation, an alliance of African American and Mexican Watts residents petitioned Los Angeles County to remove their police chief "due to his ceaseless harassment of their communities," without success. Local law enforcement focused instead on suppressing communism. Through the 1930s, LAPD's notorious "Red Squad" scrutinized labor unions, leftist political clubs, and—because officials believed them to be communist fronts—black civil rights organizations. In 1938, a reform mayor abolished the Red Squad and promised to "professionalize" the LAPD. Unfortunately, professionalization only increased complaints of police brutality. As the department began collecting crime and arrest statistics, leaders came to see crime in racial terms, as a problem specific to communities of color.

Professionalization of the force continued into the 1960s, but outlines of the "preventive patrol" model of policing were clear long before. Commanders elected to maximize their relatively small police force (118 officers per 1,000 residents in 1959, about half the ratio of New York City) by deploying them in areas with high crime rates—that is, neighborhoods of color. In the 1950s, 34 officers per square mile patrolled Newton division, a 4.8 square mile tract that was home to 101,000 mostly African American residents. The concentration in Hollenbeck, the Mexican-American district of East Los Angeles, was 14 officers per square mile. In contrast, the LAPD assigned fewer than two officers per square mile to the 259 square miles of the Hollywood, Wilshire, and Foothill divisions. This deployment pattern meant that, through the 1950s and beyond, African American and Hispanic residents were far more likely than white residents to interact with the LAPD.

Citizens of color could not help but notice the distinctions the LAPD drew between them and white citizens. In June 1943, for example, uniformed police officers stood by passively during the city's second full-blown race riot, when mobs of U.S. servicemen, off-duty police officers, and civilians roamed the streets attacking young Latinos, blacks, and Filipinos sporting "zoot suits."

Although LAPD officers did little to defend citizens of color, officers insisted that minorities demonstrate both prompt obedience and respect for the badge. Citizens police deemed disrespectful were likely to experience a sharp dose of "street justice," with punishments ranging from arrest to assault. Some LAPD officers seemed unable to distinguish between hoodlums and ordinary citizens going about their business. The *Eagle* regularly reported the indignities the LAPD meted out to black men and women, as did the more conservative *Sentinel*. For example, Don Whitman and his wife reported involvement in a minor traffic accident in 1959; when officers arrived they handcuffed Whitman, placed him in a squad car, beat him repeatedly in transit to the station, then continued to punch and kick the still-handcuffed Whitman. A well-respected black physician, Dr. Joseph Ayes, who had served three years in the army medical corps during World War II, was pulled over because, officers reported, he "looked suspicious." According to Ayes, they beat him in the head with gun butts until he passed out.

Despite the frequency of community complaints, politicians and community leaders enthusiastically supported the LAPD, even when their community interactions proved fatal. In August 1948, officers encountered three brothers outside the La Veda Ballroom. The contact ended with Herman Burns dead, John Burns hospitalized, and Julius Burns jailed for possession of a rusty pocketknife. Authorities maintained that Herman, a father, army veteran, and member of a well-respected local family, was "troublesome" and possessed of a "bad character," and identified the cause of death as heart attack. A coroner's jury likewise found no evidence of police misbehavior.

Burns's death followed a series of fatal interactions between police and minorities, including the March 1948 death of Augustino Salcido, which the local Congress of Industrial Organizations Council reported as "Police Terrorism against Mexican-Americans." A delegation of African Americans confronted Mayor Fletcher Bowron, demanding that he curb police violence. He dismissed their complaints as "communistic." Lamented the *Eagle*,

Mayor Bowron steadfastly defended the police in every reported incident of brutality. The cold-blooded killing of August Salcido and the fatal beating of Herman Burns climaxed the uninhibited "legal lynching" campaign of terror that the police department has been carrying on against Negroes and Mexicans for some time.

White Angelenos seldom heard of such incidents. When mainstream media did report allegations of police misbehavior, they dismissed charges of police brutality, repeating LAPD assurances that complainers were criminals, communists, or both.

The exception came in 1951's "Bloody Christmas," when black and Hispanic Angelenos accused drunken off-duty police officers of savagely beating seven young men, five Latino and two Anglo. New police chief William H. Parker issued a televised defense of his department in which he too defined complaints against the police as communistic attempts to undermine democracy. At the same time, Parker quietly launched investigations that ultimately led to the suspension of 39 officers and transfer of 54 others, including two deputy chiefs. For the first time in LAPD history, a grand jury indicted eight officers on criminal charges. Separate trials later produced the department's first convictions for use of excessive force. Despite confirmation that

members of the LAPD engaged in criminal violence, LAPD seemed impervious; complaints continued that it used excessive force in communities of color.

Meanwhile, the terrible social and physical conditions of Watts drew federal censure. A WWII-era study commented on the lack of quality and integration in area schools; the inability of black youth to take advantage of the city's community colleges; the lack of leadership and employment opportunities; and conflict between the community and the police. In 1947, a city planning commission investigation called Watts "an obsolescent area in which all of the social and physical weaknesses of urban living are to be found." It identified deficient recreational facilities; deteriorating streets; decaying private and public buildings; inefficient public transportation; limited shopping facilities; and high disease, death, and delinquency rates. Another study two years later echoed its predecessors, but no change followed.

Overcrowding in Los Angeles's black neighborhoods intensified between 1950 and '60, when the city's black population doubled again, piling almost 250,000 newcomers into the same overcrowded and dilapidated housing. Congestion worsened through the '60s, when "urban renewal" programs demolished whole neighborhoods, displacing residents and relocating them to already-congested areas. The city's sprawling freeway system Balkanized black districts, creating new difficulties. For people with automobiles, freeways increased mobility and opportunity, but for those without cars or reliable public transit, freeways were Berlin Walls that precluded both. By 1960, Los Angeles was as racially segregated as almost any city in the South. Only two northern cities, Cleveland and Chicago, were more segregated.

To resolve the state's black housing crisis, in 1963 lawmakers passed the Rumford Fair Housing Act. Unfortunately, a referendum on the 1964 ballot repealed the law by a two-to-one margin. Governor Pat Brown appropriately called the referendum "a vote for bigotry." The state supreme court reinstated the Rumford Act in 1965, and the U.S. Supreme Court upheld that decision two years later. By then, decades of pent-up rage had already boiled over in Watts.

Watts was a powder keg of accumulated frustration when motorcycle officer Lee Minikus stopped Marquette Frye for reckless driving on Avalon Boulevard near 116th Street around 7:00 PM on Wednesday, August 11, 1965. In the vehicle were Marquette and his brother Ronald, whom he had picked up from work. The Frye brothers admitted that they had stopped for a few beers on their way home. The traffic stop took place before some 50 witnesses, outside to escape the heat of a hot summer day. They watched as Officer Minikus administered and Frye failed several sobriety tests. "I told him he was under arrest," Minikus recalled, "but he was real nice about it. He was joking around, putting on a show for the crowd."

Marquette's mood changed when his mother, Rena, arrived and began to scold him. Marquette began cursing and shouting. Minikus' partner, Bob Lewis, arrived and, because the crowd had grown, radioed "officer needs help." Minikus attempted to handcuff Marquette but Marquette resisted. According to the state-led investigation, Lewis swung his baton at Marquette Frye's shoulder, but the blow struck Frye's head. With Frye bleeding, Rena launched herself at the officer, which resulted in her arrest. Angry citizens milled about, shouting at the police, as Marquette, Ronald, and Rena Frye were placed in squad cars and taken away.

Rumors spread quickly through the angry crowd, now estimated at 1,000. One held that the police had assaulted Rena (she later denied it). The officers arrested a man and woman for inciting violence, leading to another rumor that the woman was pregnant and the officers had assaulted her. Later reports also discredited this rumor, but the clarification came too late. That night, the citizens of Watts were furious.

The crowd broke into smaller groups that began moving through the streets. On Avalon Boulevard and Imperial Highway, roving bands of mostly African American youth stoned police cars. Some attacked passing automobiles, pulling out and assaulting white drivers. Others smashed store windows. Television camera crews arriving to report on the unfolding drama became targets for violence. Some residents rescued stranded whites, providing them with shelter and protection in their homes.

At police headquarters on Wednesday evening, Chief William Parker told reporters that the problems in Watts were isolated and the work of a few "outside agitators." Black Angelenos knew better on both counts. Community leaders scheduled a meeting at Athens Park for the afternoon of Thursday, August 13, hoping to avert another night of violence. But circumstances conspired against them. All night, Southern California's notorious Santa Ana winds blew hot desert air over the city. By 8:00 AM Thursday morning, thermometers registered 80 degrees. By 1:30 PM, temperatures hovered near 90.

Authorities and community leaders met at Athens Park to discuss strategies for diffusing the anger. Present were Congressman Augustus Hawkins, County Supervisor Kenneth Hahn, representatives from the NAACP, clergymen of several denominations, delegates from the police, sheriff, fire departments, and district attorney's office,

Marquette Frye
Everett Collection / Alamy Stock Photo

and several social service agencies. They agreed to enlist the help of neighborhood gangs in maintaining calm. A local minister agreed to make a televised appeal for peace. Leaders planned to ask the LAPD to restrict police presence in Watts to African American officers in plainclothes.

The Athens Park meeting took an unexpected turn when television news reporters arrived, accompanied by dozens of citizens determined to voice their grievances. Most recited litanies of accumulated frustrations. Rena Frye, free on bail, begged officials "to help me and to help others in this community to calm the situation down so that we will not have a riot tonight." Only one incendiary speaker advocated violence, warning whites that rioters would be attacking their neighborhoods next.

Peacekeeping efforts foundered. CBS affiliate KNXT-TV recorded the faith leader's appeal for calm, but aired it at 5:45 PM, before the evening news, when audiences were small. The evening news broadcast that followed, when audiences were substantial, included only the comments of the one incendiary speaker. Deputy Police Chief Roger Murdock agreed to limit police presence on Thursday evening to routine patrols, but refused the request for black officers in plainclothes. Appeals to gang-leaders fell mostly on deaf ears. By nightfall, members of the Businessmen, Slausons, Gladiators, and other gangs had joined the mayhem.

Only a few random incidents occurred on the afternoon on Thursday, but by 7:00 PM crowds had assembled at numerous points along Avalon Boulevard. Residents futilely appealed to authorities to block the street. When some attempted to divert traffic themselves, they were arrested. By 8:00 PM, roving crowds were attacking passing automobiles. Looters descended on liquor stores and pawnshops. Rioters torched cars and businesses, then attacked fire trucks responding to alarms. Shortly before midnight, the California National Guard contacted the LAPD to offer assistance, but LAPD declined.

In the early morning hours of Friday, August 13, city officials advised Lieutenant Governor Glenn Anderson (Gov. Pat Brown was in Greece) that the situation was under control and that the LAPD would not need National Guard backup. By then at least twelve cars had been burned and 76 buildings looted or torched. Assured that all was well, Lt. Gov. Anderson left Sacramento for an event in Berkeley. A confident Mayor Sam Yorty likewise left for a speaking engagement in San Francisco. By noon, however, Chief Parker knew that the LAPD had lost control. He appealed to Sacramento for National Guard support, but help was delayed as Anderson's office attempted to reach him. When Anderson received the request, he vacillated, unsure of procedures for activating the National Guard.

Meanwhile, conditions on the ground were changing. Rioting spread beyond its central Watts origins, moving northwest to the University of Southern California (USC) and Coliseum. The number of participants also increased dramatically. People of all ages and both sexes joined in, looting, setting fires, and assaulting passersby, civilians, police, and firefighters. Crowds gathered to applaud the mayhem and cheer on the destruction.

The first National Guard units, some trained in crowd control, arrived on Friday afternoon. They stood by for hours as authorities disagreed over how to deploy them. At 11:00 PM, National Guard troops were finally authorized to move; they set up road blocks and began moving through the streets, searching for lawbreakers. Meanwhile, new violence broke out at Oak Park Hospital, four miles south of USC, as gunfire struck medical personnel attempting to treat the injured.

At dawn on Saturday, August 14, smoke hung over much of the Los Angeles basin. Dozens of buildings flamed and smoldered. Scorched hulks that had once been cars lined the streets. After several hours of quiet,

rioting flared up again. Near Imperial Highway, a minister who had attended the Athens Park meeting fell asleep over his shotgun, having spent the night guarding his church. When he awoke around 9:00 AM, he saw the shopping center and Safeway store across the highway in flames. By noon, another 50 structures had been torched, looted, or both.

More National Guard reinforcements arrived, some flown from Northern California or diverted from annual training duty at Camp Roberts near Paso Robles. Because they lacked adequate maps and information, some convoys got lost, unable to find their assigned sectors. One convoy spent several hours lost in the maze of Los Angeles freeways but, by Saturday night, about 13,000 guardsmen were on duty.

Faulty intelligence and an overloaded Emergency Control Center (ECC) continued to hamper operations, allowing unfounded rumors to circulate and adding to the toll of violence. Roadblocks and curfew orders proved contentious, as citizens who were unaware of curfew orders approached barricades, where they encountered armed, extremely nervous young men. Mistakes and misunderstandings on both sides resulted in additional deaths and injuries.

The soldiers' show of force in Watts succeeded in deterring additional violence there. North of Watts, however, conditions were deteriorating. Along Central Avenue new fires flared on Saturday, as aged, flimsy buildings defied attempts to douse the flames. At the perimeter of the riot zone, on Washington Boulevard near Central Avenue, just blocks from downtown Los Angeles, waves of looters systematically stripped a major department store, despite 200 LAPD arrests there. New fires broke out along Broadway, the last area to be torched. Snipers on rooftops kept firefighters away until the National Guard assigned teams of riflemen to accompany the firetrucks.

By Sunday, August 15, authorities considered the riot zone stable enough to permit Gov. Pat Brown to tour the area. The ECC continued to receive sporadic reports of vandalism and gunfire through Monday morning. By then, however, businesses that had not burned to the ground began to reopen. On Tuesday morning, authorities ended the curfew. The last of the National Guard troops pulled out one week later, on August 23.

Similar flare-ups occurred in other southern California communities but none approached the level of destruction seen in Watts. The uprising involved at least 10,000 participants, and suppression required the efforts of the California Highway Patrol, law-enforcement officers on loan from other jurisdictions, and approximately 13,000

National Guard troops. The official toll was 34 dead, 31 of them African American, and over 4,000 arrests. Estimates of the numbers seriously injured ranged from 849 to 1309. Property damage costs (principally to white-owned businesses) approached $40 million (over $316 million in 2017 dollars).

Despite the large swath of devastation, destruction was not universal. Many structures stood unscathed in the middle of what some called "a war zone." In some cases, residents saved their homes from flames by dousing them with garden hoses. Many maintained a constant vigil, sometimes armed, over homes and businesses. The tide of violence simply flowed around some neighborhoods, bypassing them entirely. Some businesses survived, not only those owned by African Americans but also a few whose white owners had earned the community's respect; in several cases, black neighbors turned to protect white neighbors.

Following the riot, the state-sponsored McCone Commission report, *Violence in a City—An End or a Beginning?*, identified numerous causes for the explosion, including repeal of the Rumford Act. Later studies reiterated inequities and conditions that had been documented 20 years earlier but allowed to worsen: overcrowded, decayed neighborhoods, police brutality, severe under-employment, discriminatory hiring practices, substandard educational facilities, functional illiteracy, increased poverty and dependency, and the generalized, pervasive racism that characterized the experiences of most black Californians. Unfortunately, reporting problems was not the same as solving them.

In California and elsewhere, African Americans continued to protest police lawlessness. Police violence was the trigger for many of the 159 riots that rocked the United States in 1967, including the Newark, New Jersey, and Detroit, Michigan, upheavals that left 69 dead and thousands injured. In February 1968, the federal government acknowledged the problems of inner-city residents in the Kerner Commission report. The Commission berated federal and state governments for failed housing, education, and social-service policies. It aimed some of its sharpest criticism at the mainstream media for persisting in viewing the world "with white men's eyes." Among other things, the report called on leaders to create new jobs and housing, to end de facto segregation, and to hire more diverse and sensitive police forces. Civil rights leader Martin Luther King Jr. pronounced the report a "physician's warning of approaching death, with a prescription for life." Yet many of the same conditions persisted; indeed, most worsened.

Positive proof that LAPD policing techniques had not improved came in March 1991. An amateur filmmaker stepped out onto his Los Angeles balcony and recorded four LAPD officers—three white and one Hispanic—beating a black motorist, later identified as Rodney King. Over 20 officers stood by as officers struck King more than 50 times. The filmmaker delivered the video to a local news station, and it quickly reached an audience of millions in the United States and around the world, confirming the truth of decades of complaints by Americans of color.

A grand jury indicted four of the involved officers but declined to press charges against 17 others. When a Simi Valley jury acquitted four of the officers in April 1992, Los Angeles again exploded in violence. The 1992 riots lasted five days, cost 55 persons their lives, and damaged property valued at $750 million ($1.33 billion in 2017 dollars).

LAPD Police Chief William Parker's successor, Daryl Gates, resigned in the wake of the King beating. The Christopher Commission, which investigated the incident, recommended and the city agreed to a two-term limit for LAPD police chiefs, so that no one could rule the department for 10-plus years, as both Parker and Gates had done. In 1991, Gates' successor, Willie L. Williams, became Los Angeles's first African American police chief. Yet the LAPD's reputation did not immediately improve. In 1995, a Los Angeles jury heard evidence that former football player-turned actor O.J. Simpson had murdered his ex-wife Nicole Brown and her friend Ron Goldman. Simpson's defense team gained his acquittal, in part, by conclusively demonstrating the racism of investigating LAPD officers. The King video and the exoneration of involved officers in 1992 explained why so many African Americans believed that the LAPD had framed Simpson, a viewpoint that baffled many white observers.

The '90s ended with a two-year investigation of the LAPD's Rampart Division that implicated over 70 officers in a dizzying range of criminal behavior, including beatings and shootings, planting and covering up evidence, stealing and selling drugs confiscated as evidence, and even bank robbery. Three of the Rampart officers were accused of involvement in the as-yet unsolved murder of Christopher "Notorious B.I.G." Wallace.

The King video launched a national debate about race and policing that continues in the present day. In recent years, cellphones with cameras have allowed ordinary citizens to capture police interactions that resulted in the deaths of African American men, such as Eric Garner (Staten Island, 2014), Ezell Ford (Los Angeles, 2014), Brendon Glenn (Venice Beach, 2015), Alton Sterling (Baton Rouge, 2016), and Philando Castile (St. Paul, 2016). Incidents in which police shot and killed unarmed black men have sparked national outcry, particularly when juries returned not guilty verdicts against officers (for example, Cleveland, Ohio, 2012; Hummelstown, Pennsylvania, 2015; and Tulsa, Oklahoma, 2017). For their part, police officers have argued that the public does not understand the pressures police face. Following Eric Garner's death in 2014, New York City placed the officer filmed choking him on modified assignment. The officer's union representative promptly labeled the reassignment "a completely unwarranted, knee-jerk reaction" that denied the officer the "benefit of a doubt that has long been part of the social contract that allows police officers to face the risks of this difficult and complex job." In Los Angeles, the LAPD officers' union chastised the city for settling the wrongful death claim of Ezell Ford's family for $8 million. "This fiscally irresponsible pattern of settling civil claims, in spite of legal and investigative findings supporting police officers' actions," said the union, "is sending the wrong message to trial lawyers that the city's treasury is nothing more than an ATM."

The LAPD has seen a number of reform campaigns since the scandals of the 1990s. In 2014, the department reported that 37 percent of its officers were white, compared to 59 percent white in 1992. Following the Rampart scandal, anti-gang and narcotics officers were required to disclose their finances. Civil rights lawyer Connie Rice instigated many of these changes through a series of lawsuits against LAPD. She filed the suits, recalled Rice, at a time when the police were "still at war with the black community." LAPD abuses had prompted Rice to call the department "a militaristic and cruel force: abusive, hostile, openly racist and uninterested in change."

Despite Rice's criticisms, or perhaps because of them, when Bill Bratton became LAPD police chief in 2002, he enlisted Rice's help as a consultant. She continued in that role with Charlie Beck, who became chief in November 2009. According to Rice, the LAPD has made "enormous changes." Top leadership no longer openly indulges in racist jokes and epithets, or displays hostility towards minority officers. The majority of the force is no longer white and male. Commanders require officers "to view the poor minority community as human and deserving of protection. That's a sea change," Rice remarked. While she admitted that the LAPD is not yet "an interracial nirvana," its "culture no longer flagrantly celebrates racism."

Dreams Deferred

The Long 1960s

26

When Californians elected Edmund G. ("Pat") Brown to the governor's office in 1958, they expressed their optimism about their future and, at the same time, broke with a long-standing tradition. Voters not only elected the second Democratic governor since the 1890s, but they gave Democrats control of both houses of the California legislature for the first time in 80 years. It was more than simple partisanship: Brown was heir to the ebullient, expansive strain of California progressivism that dated back to Hiram Johnson. A disciple of Franklin Delano Roosevelt and the New Deal, as California's attorney general, Brown was the only Democrat holding statewide elected office in 1958. Thus he was the Democrats' logical choice to run for governor.

Democrats had been preparing for this moment since 1953, when 20 years after the founding of the California Republican Assembly (CRA), they belatedly founded their own California Democratic Council (CDC). An outgrowth of the informal Adlai Stevenson Clubs of 1952, the CDC was designed to coordinate political activities statewide. The organization became increasingly effective when Palo Alto journalist Alan Cranston took over in 1954. Another assist came with a voter referendum that modified the state's cross-filing law, requiring candidates to designate party affiliation on primary ballots. Since its introduction by progressive Republicans, cross-filing had favored incumbents (usually Republicans) by listing them first on the ballot without party identification. The new 1952 requirement gave Democrats at least an equal chance in their own primary elections. Thereafter, Democrats won often enough through the 1950s to reduce Republican majorities in the legislature.

The acrimonious infighting between Gov. Goodwin Knight and his Republican rivals Senator William Knowland and Vice President Richard Nixon benefited California Democrats. Both Knowland and Nixon hoped to succeed Dwight D. Eisenhower in the White House in 1960, and both considered winning the California governorship an important step in that direction. They worked to garner the support of the state Republican party's right wing to rally behind Knowland's bid for governor in 1958, thereby ousting Knight, who knew he would be denied campaign funds if he chose to wage a primary fight. As a result, California voters faced a stark choice for governor in 1958, a fight between two experienced politicians with dramatically different philosophies.

The First Governor Brown

While California Republicans faced divisive intraparty disputes in the 1958 gubernatorial race, Democrats demonstrated unified support for one candidate, Edmund G. ("Pat") Brown, a second generation Californian whose Irish and German ancestors arrived in the state during the 1850s. Born in San Francisco in 1905, Edmund Gerald Brown acquired his nickname at Fremont Grammar School when he closed a World War I Liberty Bond speech with Patrick Henry's stirring "Give me liberty or give me death!" For the rest of his life, he would be "Pat." Gregarious, bright, ambitious, and athletic, Brown stood out at Lowell High School as a solid basketball player and accomplished debater who held twelve student government offices. After graduation, he worked at his father's cigar store and then a law firm while he studied law at night. In 1927 Brown graduated first in his class from the San Francisco College of Law, passed the state bar exam, and took over his former employer's law practice. Brown married his high school sweetheart, Bernice Layne, the daughter of a San Francisco police captain, in 1930.

Pat Brown's political career began when he entered the 1928 state assembly race as a Republican. With a campaign staff composed principally of friends and family members, he waged a creditable effort but failed. Brown's political ambitions persisted, but the Great Depression shook his faith in the GOP.

In 1934, as conditions in California worsened and Republican officeholders seemed disinclined to help, Brown jumped ship. Now a confirmed New Dealer, Brown joined the Democratic county committee and became active in the party. Although he shared President Franklin D. Roosevelt's commitment to the poor, unemployed, and aged, Brown also hoped to reform local government, clean up law enforcement, and curb the influence of lobbyists in Sacramento.

Brown embarked on a second quest for office in 1939, this time challenging Matthew Brady, the 22-year incumbent San Francisco district attorney. Brown was demolished at the polls. Undeterred, he campaigned for Brady's office four years later, using the slogan "Crack down on crime, elect Brown this time." With the support of major local newspapers, he won a decisive victory over Brady that astonished the professional politicians and gamblers who had given five-to-one odds against him. Brown won again in 1947 and three years later, with Gov. Earl Warren's support, Brown claimed the state attorney general's office. The otherwise clean Republican sweep left Brown in position to run as the Democratic candidate for governor.

Warren gave Brown more than his political backing. He taught by example while serving as district attorney for Alameda County in the 1930s, making the office honest, efficient, and vigorous in its pursuit of lawbreakers. Ten years later Brown used Warren's methods to transform the outmoded, historically corrupt San Francisco district attorney's office into a body that aggressively attacked corruption, vice, gambling, and juvenile delinquency. Brown defied popular opinion when he opposed efforts to deport labor leader Harry Bridges, denounced Japanese American incarceration during World War II on moral and constitutional grounds, and supported efforts to provide decent housing for the thousands of African Americans lured to San Francisco by jobs in the defense industry.

In a vigorous campaign, Brown stressed confidence in the future, articulated his philosophy of "responsible liberalism," condemned his opponent's negative conservatism, and stressed labor issues. As attorney general, Brown had already established himself as a friend of labor when he forced a change in the title of Proposition 18 on the 1958 ballot from "Right-to-Work" to "Employer and Employee Relations." Knowland, on the other hand, had earned labor's enmity with his support of the "open shop," "right-to-work" laws, and other antiunion policies that he reiterated in 1958.

When Californians elected Brown, they also resoundingly rejected the anti-labor Proposition 18. Voters chose a broad slate of Democrats for almost every state-wide office, gave Democrats a majority in both houses of the legislature, and sent a strongly Democratic delegation to Congress for good measure.

The California Water Plan

Brown's inauguration in 1959 began four years of governmental activism unmatched since the regime of Hiram Johnson. Among the first Brown administration's accomplishments, adoption of the California Water Plan (CWP) stands high. The CWP represented the first comprehensive effort to cope with the state's perennial water problems. The fierce postwar population boom taxed available water resources, especially in Southern California. About half of the state's people now inhabited a region with less than 1 percent of the state's natural water supplies. At the same time, the long-simmering feud with Arizona over the Colorado River Compact imperiled California's share of the water. In *Arizona v. California* (1963) the U.S. Supreme Court ordered California to relinquish half of its Colorado entitlement when the Central Arizona Project was completed.

Facing soaring demand and shrinking resources, the state found it had little control over water storage and distribution. Major facilities were in the hands of local districts or, in the case of the Central Valley and Colorado River projects, the federal government. The Bureau of Reclamation ignored state policies and many feared it would start enforcing the so-called "160-acre principle," the provision in the 1902 National Reclamation Act that limited subsidized water deliveries to 160 acre (homestead-size) parcels. If the provision was applied to the Central Valley Project, the Imperial Irrigation District, or other federally aided water projects, California's most valuable land would have to be sold or subdivided. Naturally, agribusiness opposed the 160-acre rule and delayed its enforcement in California. Many landowners simply refused to accept federal water and urged the state to provide cheap, state-subsidized water instead.

Pressed on all sides, state leaders embarked on a daring water program to satisfy demand through the mid-twenty-first century. The California Water Plan envisioned a network of dozens of reservoirs, pumping stations, and electrical generating plants, linked by thousands of miles of aqueducts and pipelines. The CWP's central objective was to impound the runoff of Sacramento River tributaries, to transport the water through a north-south artery to irrigate the dry western and southern San Joaquin Valley, and then to pump it over the Tehachapi Mountains into Southern California. Along

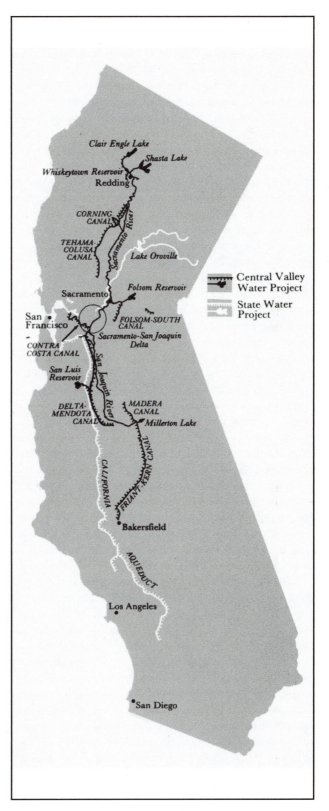

"Re-plumbing" California

the way, shorter aqueducts would carry water over the Coast Range to quench the future thirsts of growing seaside cities from San Francisco Bay to San Diego. The plan, known collectively as the "State Water Project," would require six decades and cost more than $13 billion (over $134 billion in 2018 dollars) to complete.

As with the CVP, the San Joaquin/Sacramento River Delta stood at the heart of the CWP. Water from the Sacramento River, particularly from the proposed Oroville Dam on the Feather River, had to be transferred into the San Joaquin basin. State engineers planned to rebuild additional channels so that the pure water could be moved across the Delta without adulteration by salt and pollutants. A large pumping plant west of Stockton would lift the water into the California Aqueduct for its journey south. The CWP made it clear that state water planners, like federal water planners, saw the Delta primarily as a conduit to transport surplus water from the northern part of the state to the central and southern parts. The freshwater needs of the Delta and San Francisco Bay ranked low.

Predictably, the CWP sparked immediate controversy. Especially troubling was the plan's failure to guarantee Delta water quality. Repeatedly stung by saltwater intrusion, invasion of its water supply by rival regions, and broken government promises, Delta water users adamantly opposed additional exports. Allegiances began to shift. The Bay Area had once favored large water developments and had favored the CVP, and some Bay Area communities stood to gain supplies of state-funded water, but many were beginning to appreciate that the Bay's health was closely related to Delta water purity. Even though some Bay Area communities stood to gain supplies of state-funded water, many saw the CWP as simply a southern raid on northern resources. Residents of northern and central districts asked, once the pipeline to the south was opened, what was to keep southerners from tapping more northern streams?

Projected recipients—agribusiness in the San Joaquin Valley and communities south of the Tehachapis—strongly supported the CWP. Southern California, once the principal opponent of large-scale state water projects, did a complete about-face. Southern residents now favored using state funds to import water to meet their future needs and to compensate for possible losses of Colorado River water to Arizona. The only major reservation was raised by the Metropolitan Water District, the mammoth agency that supplied water to most southern communities, which protested that the CWP did not permanently guarantee southern rights to northern water. So vehement were its

California's Longest "River"

The California Aqueduct follows the foothill contours of the Antelope Valley near Palmdale, carrying northern water on its 500-mile journey to Southern California. *California Department of Water Resources.*

objections that it threatened to move independently to seize the Eel River, much as the city of Los Angeles had once acquired the Owens River. Cowed, the legislature amended the CWP to prohibit the state from reneging on its promises to the south. Now the Metropolitan and most other southern districts favored the plan. The state's few environmentalists raised lonely warnings of dangers arising from large water-transfer systems, but they were largely ignored.

Gov. Brown responded to critics with characteristic energy. First, he appealed to Congress (unsuccessfully) for an exemption from the 160-acre limit. In response to regional conflicts, Brown practiced diplomacy and emphasized the mutual benefits of jobs, progress, and an end to historic sectional controversy. Brown identified himself as a conservationist and stressed the environmental controls that would be part of his proposal. Finally, he reduced his request for an initial bond issue from $11 billion to $1.75 billion and embarked on an extensive television campaign to win support.

At the governor's insistence, the legislature passed the Burns-Porter Act in 1959, calling for a referendum to approve $1.75 billion in bonds for the central transfer system from Oroville Dam to Southern California. The 1960 referendum was a classic north-south struggle over water. Reflecting its growing population and political power, Southern California won, though narrowly. Every northern county except for Butte County, proposed site of the Oroville Dam, voted against it.

Polarized along a north-south axis, California embarked on the construction of the most elaborate plumbing system in history. Oroville Dam, then the world's tallest, first trapped Feather River water in 1967. Delta channels were reconstructed and pumping plants were in place the next year. In 1973 the first northern water heaved over the Tehachapis into southern reservoirs. By 1975 the project exported two million acre-feet from the Delta each year. Existing contracts bound it to deliver nearly 4.25 million acre-feet in the year 2016. By then, additional dams, aqueducts, and pumps were to be operating.

By the end of the 1970s, some benefits of the CWP were apparent. New water transformed thousands of acres of unfarmed, grazing, or oil land—especially in the western and southern San Joaquin Valley—into large-scale, modern, irrigated vineyards, orchards, cotton fields, and rice bogs. The land, largely owned by the Southern Pacific Company, multinational oil firms, and industrial agriculture, was completely transformed. Urban users benefited as well. Towns east of San Francisco Bay and in the Santa Clara Valley used the water to reduce overdependence on groundwater and to purge underground aquifers of intruding salt water. In Southern California, although all the water was not yet needed, new supplies promised to make up for future losses of Colorado River entitlements. In fact, by the mid-1970s, the CWP was producing a surplus, particularly below the Tehachapis. Most unneeded supplies were resold to large San Joaquin irrigators, at below-market-value prices subsidized by urban water users. One later component of the CWP, however, remained highly controversial: the often-proposed peripheral canal around the Sacramento-San Joaquin Delta.

Yet the CWP compounded the problems begun by the federal Central Valley Project. The state's pumps removed more fresh water, while rebuilt channels failed to coax enough additional Sacramento water into the southern Delta to compensate. Salt water struck deeper and more often into the Delta. In dry seasons even the water pumped southward became heavily polluted. By the 1970s, freshwater flows from the interior had declined and exports increased, to the point that the Delta could no longer relinquish water without adulterating it. Moreover, pollution decimated fish populations in Delta, San Francisco Bay, and offshore waters.

Civil Rights

Veterans returning to post-World War II California found a society transformed. Service in the military and civilian mobilization for the war effort had raised new expectations and brought heightened awareness of inequality. Working independently while sharing ideas with one another, women and minority groups began pushing for equal rights even before the war in the Pacific had ended.

Latina/os in California, for example, numbered around 1.5 million by the end of World War II. The state's Hispanic population included descendants of the Californios as well as more recent arrivals from the Southwest, Mexico, and elsewhere. Most were residents of urban *barrios*, poorly housed and underemployed. Latinos only occasionally gained notoriety, as in the 1943 "zoot suit" riots in Los Angeles, but World War II stimulated civic organization and activism.

In 1945, a group of Mexican-American parents tackled discrimination head-on when they sued Orange County school districts for segregating their children in Mexican schools. In *Mendez v. Westminster* (1946), a federal court agreed. Eight years before the landmark Supreme Court ruling in *Brown v. Board of Education*, a California court ruled that school segregation was unconstitutional. One year later the state legislature repealed the last remnants of school segregation *de jure* (by law).

That year journalist Ignacio Lutero López, a veteran of the Office of War Information, organized the Civic Unity League. Designed to mobilize political participation in the *barrio*, the League protested discrimination in housing, public accommodations, police services, schools, and the courts. In 1949, it helped elect Chino's first Mexican-American city council member, Andres Morales. In the 1950s, the Community Service Organization (CSO) picked up where the League left off. Mexican immigrants and Mexican Americans dominated CSO branches, with membership equally divided between women and men.

Despite historians' emphasis on female domesticity in the 1950s, Latinas were extremely active in the CSO and other civic and trade associations throughout the decade. For some, the war had raised their expectations. Hope Mendoza left a low-paid garment industry job for a defense job at Lockheed. At war's end, she returned as an organizer for the International Ladies' Garment Workers Union. Mendoza later joined the CSO and chaired its labor relations committee.

African Americans made slow progress in California during the 1960s. In 1960, they numbered 600,000, or 6 percent of the state's total population. Most had settled in cities to take advantage of opportunity for industrial employment, but there they encountered social, legal, and economic discrimination. Responding both to local conditions and an emerging national civil rights movement, the 1959 legislature enacted a law forbidding discrimination in the workplace and created the Division of Fair Employment Practices to enforce the new provisions. Legislators also passed the Unruh Civil Rights Act, which banned discrimination in business dealings (including real estate transactions), and promised unrestricted access to restaurants, public accommodations, and subsidized public housing.

Though ambitious, such legislation could not enforce equal opportunity, especially when so many employers, unions, businesses, and real estate interests actively resisted the new laws. Still, the actions of the 1959 legislature, and the Rumford Fair Housing Law of 1963, named for Assemblyman William Byron Rumford, placed California in the vanguard of the national civil rights movement.

Asian Americans found somewhat less hostility in postwar California, but progress was also slow. Japanese Americans worked to rebuild their lives and communities in the aftermath of their wartime incarceration. In 1948, Congress authorized compensation for property lost during internment, as well as the return of confiscated bank accounts. But collecting proved painfully difficult, and neither state nor federal governments pressed for expedition. On the positive side, the state supreme court overturned the 1913 Alien Land Act in 1952, making it possible for Asian immigrants to again legally own and lease land in California. In the same year Congress passed the McCarran-Walter Act, which eliminated the racial basis for naturalization entailed in the "aliens ineligible for citizenship" prohibition. For the first time, Japanese and other foreign-born Asians were eligible to become U.S. citizens. For the most part, however, Japanese, Chinese, Filipinos, and other Asians in California were left to fend for themselves.

Native American population numbers in the postwar era had slowly begun to rebound from their nadir at the turn of the century, climbing from just 20,000 in 1900 to 75,000 in 1965. Most were not the descendants of local Natives but newcomers from other states. The

Governor Pat Brown with Assemblyman William Byron Rumford (*left*)

Courtesy of The Bancroft Library, University of California, Berkeley.

vast majority (about 90 percent) lived in cities, interspersed among the general population. This important shift in the demography of Native California began in the 1950s, when the U.S. Bureau of Indian Affairs (BIA) accelerated its policy of "terminating" federal supervision and support of reservations. Congress responded with Public Law 280, which gave the states jurisdiction over their Indian residents. Until then, Californians had considered Indian affairs a BIA function. Many resented the new responsibility and its potential cost. State leaders had already removed legal and civil distinctions between Indians and other citizens, which gave Native Californians equal access to public education and other services. But changes in federal law presented California with novel problems. Beginning in 1953, the state senate's Interim Committee on Indian Affairs revealed that most California Indians opposed termination. They likewise deplored the inadequate compensation that the federal government offered as a substitute for reservations. The committee responded with a series of new policies.

The Brown administration acted on these recommendations in 1961 with the Advisory Committee on Indian Affairs (ACIA). The ACIA conducted additional studies and documented the limited educational opportunities available to California Indians, along with the abject poverty in which most lived. But the ACIA produced few tangible improvements.

Private initiatives were more effective. On the Morongo Reservation near Palm Springs, Jane K. Penn (Wanikik Cahuilla) collaborated with a young anthropology student, Lowell Bean, and others to found the Malki Museum, intended to preserve Native California culture and crafts. The first museum on a California reservation, it opened in 1965, along with the Malki Museum Press, an outlet for Native American research. In the same decade, Native and white Californians organized the American Indian Historical Association and the California Indian Education Association, both of which promoted college-level Native American studies. In the following decade, the Cupeño established the Cupa Cultural Center at the Pala reservation near San Diego, where they offered classes in language, history, and culture.

Reforms in Politics and Government

Legislators grappled with other long-standing problems during the first Brown administration. Jesse M. Unruh was instrumental, first as chairman of the assembly ways and means committee, and later as speaker of the assembly. Cross-filing, modified earlier in the 1950s, was abolished entirely in 1959. So too was the 1927 "federal plan" of allocating state senators one-per-county. The federal plan had consistently resulted in gross overrepresentation for residents of rural regions and underrepresentation for those in cities. In 1964, in its "one man, one vote" ruling (*Reynolds v. Sims*), the U.S. Supreme Court declared the plan unconstitutional. The results were dramatic. Los Angeles County, which historically had sent just one senator to Sacramento, suddenly had 13. The seven counties south of the Tehachapis saw their representation in the state senate increase from seven to a far more equitable 21. Brown and Unruh seized this long overdue opportunity to substantially alter governing procedures.

For more than a century, California government had functioned (critics say mal-functioned) under the Constitution of 1879. Over the years, the document was amended nearly 350 times and increased more than fourfold in volume. By 1960 the organic laws of only two states (Alabama and Louisiana) and one nation (India) were longer, and few were as complex. The amendment process was difficult and time-consuming, requiring approval by two-thirds of each house of the legislature and the voters. In addition, efforts to make even minor changes usually encountered determined opposition from vested interests. Governors William D. Stephens (1917–1923), C.C. Young (1927–1931), and

legislative commissions during the 1940s and '50s had all attempted revision without success. Confusion and obsolescence remained the state constitution's principal distinctions. Finally, in 1962 the legislature appointed a 60-member constitutional revision commission to operate until 1974.

The commission's efforts produced significant results, including a 50 percent reduction in length. Over ten years, the body proposed changes to the voters a few at a time; 75 percent passed. Among the additions were sections guaranteeing that the rights of Californians would not be diminished as a result of interpretations of the U.S. Bill of Rights; another protected the property rights of aliens. In addition, the commission reduced the percentages of voters needed to qualify ballot initiatives, increased requirements for appointments to the judiciary, and expanded city and county authority over local affairs. Other changes were designed to improve efficiency: measures abolished the 120-day limit on legislative sessions, the separate budgetary session, and the $500 ceiling on legislators' salaries; and the governor, with legislative consent, was authorized to reorganize and streamline the executive bureaucracy.

With Brown's backing, Unruh guided through the legislature additional reforms that eliminated some obsolete executive agencies, consolidated others, and created new bodies to deal with current issues and problems. The legislature itself underwent thorough reorganization, with year-round sessions, increased compensation to make service in the legislature more attractive, and streamlined procedures for the legislature and its staff. Critics denounced the creation of a "super-government" in Sacramento, but the reforms of the 1960s made California's government more professional and efficient, prompting national recognition for Jesse Unruh.

Schools and Society

As it did in the rest of the nation, the Soviet Union's successful Sputnik launch in 1957 precipitated a sweeping assessment of public education in California. Responses included the 1960 adoption of the Master Plan for Higher Education. To upgrade the quality of instruction in public schools, the legislature approved the Fisher Act of 1971, requiring students to major in academic subjects, rather than "education," as before, to qualify for California teaching credentials. In addition, the state increased its level of funding for public schools at all levels and funding for programs ranging from teaching basic skills to advanced scientific and technical training.

Like the drives for efficiency in government and educational improvement, other actions of the first Brown administration recalled elements of progressivism, especially the commitment to social and economic justice, concerns for the environment, and use of public authority to attain desired ends. By the end of 1962, the legislature had raised payments of unemployment, disability, and workers' compensation, and set up the Office of Consumer Affairs and the State Economic Development Agency. Within the next few years, it enacted the most stringent air quality laws in the nation and established an Air Quality Control Board to oversee their implementation.

Such policies were expensive, as were paying interest on CWP bonds, raising legislators' salaries, funding schools and mental health programs, and improving the highway system. Brown had inherited a treasury deficit, produced when the Knight administration depleted Earl Warren's "rainy-day fund." Eliminating the red ink and, at the same time, financing both new and established programs meant higher taxes and larger budgets ($2.2 billion in 1959 and more in each successive year). But few Californians protested. Tax increases had not been levied for several years, and the new rates generally conformed to population growth, inflation, and expanded levels of government service. Californians felt confident in the future of their state, in its economy, and in its leadership.

The Election of 1962

Although Pat Brown was an eminently successful first-term governor, he suffered setbacks for both his programs and his political reputation. Throughout much of his career, for example, he had been an energetic advocate of minimum-wage laws. Despite his vigorous efforts as governor to establish $1.25 as the minimum for the state, agricultural and other interests squelched the measure. Brown had been an equally staunch opponent of capital punishment, but his attempts to eliminate the practice in California fell short. He granted a stay in the celebrated Caryl Chessman case, but Chessman ultimately went to the gas chamber in 1960, one of 32 prisoners executed during Brown's two-term tenure. During the same year, events at the Democratic National Convention tarnished Brown's image as a master politician. A badly splintered California delegation refused to follow the governor in supporting the candidacy of John F. Kennedy. The defection cost Kennedy the 36,000 votes by which he lost California and very nearly lost the White House.

Yet Brown's record and his popularity made him a strong candidate for re-election in 1962. This position was made stronger by his opponent, Richard Nixon. Still smarting from defeat in the 1960 presidential race, Nixon had little real interest in being governor of California; it was simply part of his bid for the White House. Nixon was unfamiliar with state issues and resorted to accusing Brown of being "soft" on communism and radicalism. These tactics did not impress voters, who returned Brown to office by another wide margin. Nixon responded by blaming the press for his defeat and promising journalists that they would not have him "to kick around any more."

But the 1962 Democratic victory was not as complete as it had been in 1958. The party's legislative majority diminished, the delegation to Washington had more Republicans, including Senator Thomas Kuchel and the ultraconservative Max Rafferty, state superintendent of public instruction. Nevertheless, prospects for a successful second term seemed auspicious for Pat Brown and Californians generally.

Shortly after the election, an event heavy with symbolism confirmed popular confidence in Brown. On November 24, 1962, a huge counter straddling the Oakland-San Francisco Bay Bridge ticked over to 17,393,134, marking the state's emergence as the most populous in the nation. The count was based solely on estimates and projections and was not official. Indeed, both New York and the U.S. Census Bureau disputed the figure, but the 1970 federal census ultimately confirmed California's number-one ranking. Later generations would be less enthusiastic about the benefits of numbers, but at the moment residents of the state remained disciples of the nineteenth-century booster who asserted that "population is the one great desideratum."

Among the newcomers were professionals and highly-skilled technicians attracted to California's burgeoning aerospace and other industries, as well as the apparent economic potential these industries offered. In 1962, it did not seem to matter to Californians that the influx included even larger numbers of African Americans from the rural South, Mexican-Americans from the Southwest, or displaced blue-collar workers from around the nation. The future seemed to have space in it for any number of people, of all kinds. If bigger was better, then biggest must be best. An elated Gov. Brown gave state employees a holiday on December 31 and set aside four "California First Days" for popular celebrations.

Early in Brown's second term, the legislature confirmed its own optimism by enacting the Rumford Fair

Housing Law to forbid racial discrimination in real estate transactions. It was not long before events made clear that the public mood was changing. Property owners contested the Rumford Law in the courts and, in November 1964, Californians by a two-to-one margin approved Proposition 14 to repeal the law. An outraged Brown called it "a vote for bigotry." Even though the state supreme court subsequently overturned the repeal, the white backlash that it represented was a portent of difficult times to come.

The Politics of Confrontation

In the aftermath of the 1965 Watts Riots, militant and radical political action groups rapidly emerged. Most notable was the Black Panther Party for Self-Defense. The organization was founded in Oakland in 1966 in reaction to local conditions and to Stokely Carmichael's nationwide "Black Power" movement, which stressed pride in black culture and black control of community institutions. Articulate leaders like Huey P. Newton, Bobby Seale, and *Soul on Ice* author Eldridge Cleaver attracted young African American men and women, calling upon a mixture of Marxist-Maoist rhetoric and advocacy of resistance to the police and other symbols of white authority.

The Panthers soon became synonymous with armed resistance. During a 1967 debate on a gun control measure aimed principally at radical groups, a contingent of Black Panther members, some armed, entered the Capitol in Sacramento to observe the proceedings. No violence ensued at the Capitol, but later clashes with the police in 1967 and '68 resulted in death and injury for several officers. Both Newton and Cleaver were wounded and arrested in these confrontations. Newton's protracted trials for manslaughter ended without conviction, and he subsequently assumed leadership of a party more dedicated to social programs and prison reform than to armed resistance. In 1968, while Cleaver was the Peace and Freedom Party candidate for president of the United States, California revoked his 1966 parole on a previous assault conviction. Cleaver chose exile in Algeria rather than return to prison; there he continued to preach armed insurrection. The following decade, Seale lost his bid to become the first black mayor of Oakland.

By the end of the 1960s, the Black Panther Party was splintered and the radical faction was embroiled in power struggles with militant groups like Ron Karenga's cultural nationalist organization "Us." Conflict arose over control of the UC Los Angeles Afro-American

Studies Center in 1969 and led to the shooting of two Black Panthers, plus retaliatory shootings on both sides. The result, however, was a devastating blow to support for Us, the Panthers, and black militant groups in general. An episode in August 1970 had equally negative effects, when an abortive attempt to free African American inmate George Jackson and the "Soledad Brothers" at San Rafael's Marin county courthouse ended in four deaths, including a judge, and the wounding of a convict and two hostages. While imprisoned, Jackson authored a series of letters, published in 1970 as *Soledad Brother*, which became a classic of black literature and political philosophy.

Yet the turmoil of the 1960s produced at least two positive results for black Californians. It made whites more sensitive, if not more sympathetic, to questions of civil rights. It also stimulated increased mainstream black political participation. In 1966, 50 years after the state assembly greeted the first four female legislators, voters elected the first African American woman to that body, Yvonne Braithwaite Burke. In 1970, voters sent Ronald Dellums to Congress and Wilson Riles to the office of Superintendent of Public Instruction. Two years later, Yvonne Burke became the first African American woman California sent to the U.S. House (one of only three women ever elected to that body), Mervyn Dymally became state lieutenant governor, and more black legislators appeared in Sacramento. In 1978, Los Angelenos elected Diane Watson, another African American woman, to the state senate, making Watson the senate's first woman of color. Thereafter Watson won four reelection campaigns. Through the 1960s and beyond, black officials became more numerous in state, county, and municipal governments. Although impressive, these political gains did not immediately result in improved conditions for most black Californians.

Native Americans also benefited from the political turmoil of the 1960s, especially political action groups like Indians of All Tribes (IAT). The IAT flowed directly from the federal termination program of the 1950s, which brought so many Native Americans to California. In November 1969, a group of approximately one hundred men, women, and children converged on Alcatraz Island, an abandoned federal penitentiary in San Francisco Bay. The group included members of the IAT, around 80 students from UCLA's Indian Studies program, and a number of Bay Area Native Americans. The IAT descended on the deserted island and demanded that the site be turned over to them as an Indian cultural and medical research center. Although they did not achieve that objective, they

Indians Invade Alcatraz

San Francisco History Center, San Francisco Public Library.

managed to hold "the Rock" under an 1882 provision which held that abandoned federal facilities could be used as Indian schools. In the interests of fairness, the IAT offered to buy the island $24 "in glass beads and red cloth, a precedent set by the white man's purchase of a similar island [Manhattan] about 300 years ago." The IAT's occupation of Alcatraz through June 1971 brought national attention to the demands of Native Americans, and increased the political participation of Indigenous peoples in California.

By the 1960s, Latina/os were a significant part of the state's population, but their numbers had not conferred political power. They were seriously under-represented as leaders of state agencies. Few of their children benefited from the 1965 federal Elementary and Secondary Education Act, or the state's 1965 Miller-Unruh Reading Act, designed to improve public K-12 education.

Middle-class citizens found their political voice in organizations such as the Mexican American Political Association (MAPA), established in Fresno in 1960. That year MAPA supported John F. Kennedy's presidential campaign. Two years later, MAPA helped send

Los Angeles city councilman Edward R. Roybal to Congress. MALDEF, the Mexican American Legal Defense and Education Fund, was founded in 1968, to litigate for social change. Yet despite substantial effort, commitment, and a large voting population that included many new citizens of Mexican ancestry, political power proved elusive.

Internal divisions went deeper than most Anglo Californians realized. The state's Hispanic community included longtime residents as well as new arrivals from Mexico and Central and Latin America. A community that, to Anglos, appeared unified and cohesive was in fact deeply divided. The generation gap yielded another divisive force, as Latina/o youth found inspiration in the Cuban Revolution, civil rights and Black Power movements, anti-Vietnam War protests, and on-going efforts to unionize farm workers. Younger activists formed the militant Brown Berets and the culturally oriented *La Raza* (the people), identifying themselves as *Chicanos*, a name probably derived from *chico* (child), which Anglos in California once employed much as Southern whites used "boy" to refer to black men. Although "Chicano" had decidedly derogatory overtones before the 1960s, activists claimed it as a way to express ethnic solidarity and, at the same time, to distance themselves from older generations of Mexican American hyphenates, whom they sometimes derided as *Tio Tacos* (an accommodating Uncle Tom) or *pochos* (people who had lost or rejected their cultural identities). Usage of "Chicano" spread among different factions of ethnic Mexicans, popularized by *corridos* (folk ballads) such as *"Yo Soy Chicano,"* until eventually the label became a generally positive expression of cultural and political unity.

Student organizations were the backbone of the Chicano *movimiento* (movement). In March 1967, Moctesuma Esparza and other students at California State College, Los Angeles (later CSU Los Angeles) organized the first chapter of United Mexican American Students (UMAS). Its constitution demanded greater voice for Latina/o students in shaping college programs; improved education in predominantly Mexican American neighborhoods; and election of Chicano candidates to political office. UMAS members also took steps to increase Chicano college enrollments, encouraging students at East Los Angeles high schools to graduate and enroll in college.

Roosevelt High graduate Victoria M. Castro experienced culture shock when she entered college. "I grew up in a world where everybody was Chicano," she remembered. But when she got to CSULA, she wondered "Where'd all the Mexicans go?" In 1967, Castro, Esparza, and other East Los Angelenos founded Young Chicanos for Community Action (YCCA), a neighborhood service club. YCCA members' quasi-military style of dress prompted the Los Angeles Police Department to mockingly refer to them as "Brown Berets." YCCA seized upon the label, as well as the LAPD slogan "to serve, observe, and protect." Uniformed members, both male and female, patrolled their Mexican-majority neighborhoods as a community policing force. Simultaneously, the Brown Berets were a blatant challenge to the older generation's insistence on assimilation and accommodation.

Students even younger than Vicky Castro organized the era's most dramatic demonstration of the politics of confrontation. In March 1968, 10,000 to 20,000 high school students stared down school personnel, the city's board of education, and even the LAPD in a week-long protest against educational inequality. Guidance came from Lincoln High School teacher Sal Castro and members of UMAS and the Brown Berets, who helped the students formulate a list of demands designed to improve facilities and instruction in their schools. When school administrators dismissed their demands, the youngsters began planning the largest demonstration of student power ever seen in the United States, before or since. Beginning March 1, students from seven Mexican-majority high schools walked out of their classrooms, some chanting "Walk Out!" Students spilled out onto the sidewalks waving placards proclaiming "Viva La Raza!" and "Student Power!" while Brown Berets stood by as security guards.

Walkout!

The civil rights boycotts, marches, and demonstrations that originated in the American South attracted more attention than the 1968 East Los Angeles student walkouts. Yet the brief but dramatic uprising of the city's Chicana/o youth demanding better schools was no less a part of that historical moment in U.S. history.

The frustrations that prompted the walkouts had been brewing in Los Angeles for decades. Eastside parents and community leaders had long complained about their aging, dilapidated schools. Wilson High, for example, had seen few improvements since it opened in 1937 on the site of a former mule farm. By comparison, it seemed that no expense was spared on the Westside schools that served Anglo children. Fairfax High, established in West Hollywood in 1927, was almost completely rebuilt from the ground up from 1965 to 1968. The Fairfax High campus "was amazing," Paula Crisostomo recalled many years later, "like a luxury hotel." Crisostomo was one of a small group of Lincoln High School students who accompanied teacher Sal Castro on a tour of the nearly completed campus in 1968.

Subpar education was another sore point for Eastside parents and community leaders. Their high schools had the city's highest drop-out rates and the lowest rates of college attendance. Eastside educators and administrators pursued a dual-track system for their mostly Mexican American students. A handful of students that teachers considered their best and brightest took college preparatory courses, but the majority they funneled into classes that, at best, prepared them for menial, low-waged occupations. Crisostomo was on

(continued . . .)

Lincoln High's college track, although she did not know it at the time. "No one ever told me that I could go to college," she said. When she graduated from Lincoln High, she "didn't even know what an SAT test was."

More damaging than poor education and crumbling buildings were the racist attitudes of many Eastside teachers and administrators. Crisostomo recalled one memorable exchange with her eleventh-grade geometry teacher. As her classmates worked quietly at their desks, she went to his desk with a question about the assignment. He responded, "loud enough for other students to hear, 'Now Paula, we all know that you're not going to college. You and your little girlfriends will all be pregnant by the end of summer. Just go back to your seat and sit down.'" Because Crisostomo was "used to being talked down to" by her teachers, she accepted the rebuke, assuming that "all schools were this way."

By 1968, though, Crisostomo had learned that all schools were not the same. The 17-year-old was writing articles reporting substandard conditions in her school for *La Raza Newspaper and Magazine*, *Inside Eastside*, and *Chicano Student News* (later *Chicano Student Movement*). With the help of Sal Castro and local college students, especially Moctesuma Esparza and Vicky M. Castro, she and other Lincoln High students developed a survey to query Eastside students about their school experiences. Drawing on the surveys, they developed a list of 39 demands, which included improved school facilities; bilingual, bicultural education; dismissal of blatantly racist educators; more teachers, counselors, and administrators of Mexican descent; and elimination of the tracking system that funneled Mexican Americans into vocational programs rather than academic courses that prepared them for college.

Predictably, school administrators refused to act on students' demands. Crisostomo and students from the other Eastside schools turned to Sal Castro and members of UMAS and the Brown Berets to help them organize a protest. From March 1 to 9, 1968, as many as 20,000 students walked out of their classrooms in a well-coordinated protest against inadequate educational facilities and instruction in East Los Angeles Schools.

Most terrifying for educators and civic leaders was the presence of uniformed Brown Berets at the walkouts. Fearing a repeat of the 1965 Watts riots, the Los Angeles Police Department massed police officers outside Eastside high schools with orders to keep the youngsters inside. School and law enforcement leaders controlled the public's access to information about the walkouts. Print and television news outlets either ignored the protests or mischaracterized them as isolated incidents involving one or two disaffected youth or as the work of Communists and outside agitators. In particular, the media misrepresented encounters between students and police. On March 7, 1968, the Los Angeles *Times* reported that "violence erupted at Roosevelt High" but insinuated, incorrectly, that students had attacked the police. Subsequent reports followed this tack, eliciting sympathy for injured police officers without mentioning students' injuries.

Three days after the Los Angeles School Board met with parents and community leaders to discuss the students' demands, authorities arrested and jailed 13

Brown Beret Security Guard

Brown Beret David Cruz providing security for demonstrators in downtown Los Angeles, 1968. *From the La Raza Photograph Collection, UCLA Chicano Studies Research Center.*

Roosevelt High School Student Climbing School Fence to Walk Out

School administrators at Belmont, Garfield, Lincoln, and Roosevelt high schools chained campus gates to keep protesters off the streets. Students at Roosevelt and Lincoln broke through the chains, the latter by attaching them to future Belmont Junior High School principal Vicky Castro's car. *Copyright Devra Weber. From the La Raza Photograph Collection. Courtesy of the UCLA Chicano Studies Research Center.*

"Viva La Raza!"

Conchita Mares Thornton (holding "Viva La Raza" sign) demonstrating at Roosevelt High. Conchita was on the staff of the Chicano student newspaper and a member of a *teatro* (theater) group. *Copyright Devra Weber. From the La Raza Photograph Collection. Courtesy of the UCLA Chicano Studies Research Center.*

walkout leaders, including teacher Sal Castro. Each faced felony charges of "conspiracy to disturb the peace," which carried 30-year jail sentences. Within hours, adults and students were protesting outside the Hall of Justice in downtown Los Angeles. Authorities eventually dropped all charges against "the L.A. 13," but Lincoln High had meanwhile fired Castro. The community again swung into action: a crowd of 2,000 protestors swirled outside Central Police Station demanding that Castro be reinstated. In time, Lincoln rehired Castro and he returned to the classroom.

Although Eastside students were among the fiercest proponents of freeing the L.A. 13 and for reinstating Castro, these legal battles deflected community focus away from the students' list of demands. Eastsiders poured their energies into demands for legal justice and away from pressing the school board to improve schools and the education their young people received.

(continued . . .)

Lincoln High Students Running from Police on Soto Avenue

From the La Raza Photograph Collection, UCLA Chicano Studies Research Center.

Garfield High School Students Walking Out

Signs read "Oppressed Students Strike for Education," "What About Me?" and "We Want Freedom or Else!" *From the La Raza Photograph Collection, UCLA Chicano Studies Research Center.*

In time, many of the 1968 student demands would be met, including instruction in Chicano history, textbooks that acknowledged the contributions of Mexican Americans, and an end to the infamous tracking system. Many 1968 student leaders went on to become community leaders. Mario T. García earned a bachelor's degree from University of Texas, El Paso, and a Ph.D. from UC San Diego. In 2018, 50 years after the student walkouts, he served as professor of Chicana/o Studies at UC Santa Barbara. Victoria M. Castro earned a bachelor's degree from CSU-LA, a teaching credential from UC Santa Cruz, and, from Pepperdine University, a Master of Science degree in Urban Education and Administration. Over the next 25 years, Castro was an educator in the Los Angeles Unified School District. In a wonderful touch of irony, Castro--whose job in 1968 was to distract the principal for as long as possible while Lincoln High School students walked out--herself became principal of Belvedere Junior High School. Castro served from 1986 to 1993, when she won election to the Los Angeles City Board of Education, only the second Mexican American to hold that position (after Julian Nava).

Paula Crisostomo graduated from Lincoln High and earned her college degree at CSU Sonoma but remained a community activist. Speaking in 2018, Crisostomo encouraged students to know that they are powerful. "Youth has so much power." "The Occupy Wall Street movement," which brought sustained attention to the problem of income inequality in America, "was a youth movement." Most of the Zuccoti Park occupiers were in their teens and 20s. Same for the Black Lives Matter movement: "that began with a youth group." "Believe in yourself," said Crisostomo. "And organize."   (MAI)

The walkouts stunned Angelenos. As demonstrator Mario T. García later explained, until that moment "few had thought of Chicanos as part of the civil rights struggles in the country, outside of César Chávez and the farmworkers movement." Eastside parents and community leaders were equally stunned, not only by the demonstrations but by the vehemence and even violence that met their children's protests. Teachers and school officials attempted to lock students inside classrooms and school buildings. Some police officers shoved and struck students with their batons.

Eastside parents and community leaders then coalesced behind their youngsters. On March 11, 1968, they organized the Educational Issues Coordinating Committee (EICC) to push civic leaders to resolve the underlying inequities that prompted the walkouts. On March 28, 1968, over 1,200 people—students, parents, and Eastside community leaders—crowded into the EICC's meeting with the Los Angeles Board of Education. Although change came slowly to Eastside schools, the city's young people, most aged 12 to 17 years old, had helped to launch a powerful urban Chicano movement.

Inspired by the walkouts, Latina/o high school and college students joined La Raza Unida Party (LRUP), a political party organized to increase Mexican-American representation in California politics and government. The northern California communities of Oakland and Berkeley produced LRUP's first chapter in November 1970. By the end of 1971, active LRUP chapters existed throughout California, focusing on voter registration, electing Mexican Americans to political office, and securing a place for LRUP on statewide ballots as an official political party.

Once again, despite substantial effort, commitment, and a large pool of Mexican-American voters, Chicanas and Chicanos found success elusive. La Raza Unida Party was in decline by 1973, the victim of internal divisions as well as failure to achieve ballot status. The Brown Berets crumbled too, facing constant scrutiny by city, state, and national law enforcement bodies. The original group disbanded in 1972.

The uprising of Chicana/o youth, the growth of groups such as UMAS, the Brown Berets, La Raza Unida Party, and EICC marked the emergence of a full blown, urban-based Chicano movement. Yet each of these groups drew strength and inspiration from the great unionizing movement then taking place in the fields. In the 1960s, California agricultural workers finally succeeded in capturing public attention and even political support. Although agricultural workers accounted for only 20 percent of the state's Latina/o population, few endured worse experiences.

Since the late nineteenth century, Mexican and Mexican American farm workers had provided the labor needed for the state's industrialized agriculture. They lived in floating subcultures with minimal access to the benefits of society, even education for their children. Farm workers had periodically made their presence known through strikes and incidents such as the Wheatland Riot of 1913 and the violence of the 1930s, but most Californians remained comfortably oblivious to their presence.

That began to change in the late 1950s, when Maria Moreno was driven by the hunger of her twelve children to speak for migrant farmworkers. Like an earlier, more famous "Migrant Mother," Moreno came to California with the Dustbowl Migration of the 1930s. A woman of multiple identities, Moreno was born in Texas, her father was orphaned in the Mexican Revolution, and her mother was Mescalero Apache, making Moreno simultaneously a U.S. citizen, Mexican American, American Indian, and migrant farmworker. Moreno found her political voice in 1958, when a flood in Tulare

County left more than 300 farmworkers unemployed and starving, but the county declared them ineligible for food aid. Fresno *Bee* reporter Ron Taylor published Moreno's appeal for justice, which created such a stir that welfare authorities reversed their policies and provided food for the farmworkers.

When the AFL-CIO sent Norman Smith to California to launch the Agricultural Workers Organizing Committee (AWOC) in 1959, he hired Moreno as an organizer. Moreno became a labor organizer decades before second-wave feminism took hold, at a time when farmworkers lived in segregated camps and worked on segregated crews, and when growers consciously pitted workers of different ethnic groups against each other to break strikes and to keep wages low. An impassioned speaker, Moreno "could move a group" recalled journalist/photographer George Ballis, which explained why blacks, Filipinos, white migrants from Oklahoma and Arkansas, and Mexican-American members of AWOC elected her to represent them. Moreno's AWOC work ended in 1961, when she and several others the AFL-CIO considered too independent were fired. Many original AWOC members drifted away, but Filipino members remained and took control of their AWOC chapters.

The farmworkers' movement gained momentum in 1964, when Congress refused to renew Public Law 78 authorizing World War II's bracero program. For two decades it had extended the law, importing Mexican farmworkers and depressing domestic farm laborers' wages. In September 1965 AWOC leader Larry Itilong led farmworkers in a walkout against grape growers in the southern San Joaquin Valley town of Delano. Workers demanded that DiGiorgio Corporation and 30 other growers agree to higher pay, improved working conditions, and recognition of workers' right to organize. Itilong then convinced the National Farm Workers Association (NFWA), headed by Dolores Huerta and César Chávez, to join the strike.

Chávez spent his youth and his early adult life as a migrant farm worker, and he experienced the handicaps of that life, including a formal education that consisted of about eight years in 40 different schools. He was, however, a devout Catholic concerned with the plight of his fellow workers. During the 1950s he committed his energies to community and social service work, especially through NFWA. Unlike AWOC, neither NFWA nor Chávez espoused the traditional goals of organized labor. Chávez himself remained unconvinced of the effectiveness of agricultural strikes. Nevertheless, he threw his own and his association's support behind

César Chávez, Dolores Huerta, and "La Causa"

The Union as Social Movement

A new era in farm labor relations began in California in 1962 when César Chávez and Dolores Fernández Huerta organized the National Farm Workers Association. For decades farm employers had successfully beaten down attempts to organize their workers. In Chávez and Huerta they encountered charismatic leaders who turned the organization of a farm labor union into a social movement that spoke to ethnic minorities, church leaders of many faiths, student activists, and the whole spectrum of 1960s and '70s civil-rights and antipoverty forces.

Born and raised on an Arizona farm, Chávez came to California in 1938, where his family joined the ranks of migrant farm laborers and endured that era's discrimination, disgraceful working conditions, and low pay. In 1952, after wartime service in the Navy, Chávez became an organizer for the Community Service Organization (CSO), a Mexican American civil rights organization, and later its executive director.

Huerta's father was a migrant worker, traveling a circuit from New Mexico to Wyoming while the family stayed behind. When her parents divorced, she and her mother relocated to California, like Chávez's family, during the Great Depression. Huerta was a 25-year-old wife and mother in 1955 when she joined Stockton's CSO, and began registering voters to help elect Spanish-speaking representatives. "After a big voter registration drive in 1960 where we registered 150,000 people," Huerta recalled, "Cesar got this bright idea to send me to Sacramento" to lobby for farm workers' rights. As head of the CSO's legislative program for 1961, Huerta's central concern was that farm workers were excluded from New Deal benefits such as social security, disability insurance, and retirement pensions. She fought for these benefits and others, including keeping the police from "searching and harassing people arbitrarily," ensuring that farm workers had equitable access to county hospitals, for "the right to register voters door to door, and the right for people to take their driver's license exams in Spanish."

Dolores Huerta and César Chávez
Walter Oleksy / Alamy Stock Photo.

After almost a decade working together in the Stockton CSO, Chávez and Huerta co-founded the National Farm Workers Association to focus on farmworkers' rights. Chávez relocated to Delano and, with his wife Helen working ten hours a day in the fields to support the family, launched a new kind of union organization. Building on the duo's CSO experiences, and Chávez's commitment to Gandhian nonviolent tactics and religious beliefs, the Association supplied members with a wide range of social services, including credit unions, co-ops, death benefit programs, and assistance in dealing with government agencies from schools to welfare offices. Chávez's emphasis on Mexican cultural and religious values made union meetings a religious experience that incorporated Catholic ritual and prayer. Additionally, Chávez recruited support from students, clergy, civil rights leaders, and liberal Democrats, turning the union movement into a broadly based social movement with the motto "La Causa" (the Cause).

In September 1965 the NFWA joined the Agricultural Workers Organizing Committee (AWOC), an AFL-CIO affiliate, in the famous Delano grape strike. A year later the two groups merged to form a new union, now known as the United Farm Workers of America. As second-in-command to Chávez, Huerta assumed leading roles in the organization, challenging not only the social and economic order but also her community's traditional gender roles. In 1965, Huerta was strategic planner for the grape strike, leading workers on picket lines and enduring the first of her 20 arrests. In 1968 and 1969, Huerta directed the table grape boycott in New York City and then the entire East Coast.

During the 1965 Delano grape strike, Chávez and Huerta mobilized supporters for a dramatic, highly publicized, 300-mile march to Sacramento that placed enormous pressure on growers. Chávez used fasting as a protest, a tactic that reinforced his emphasis on nonviolence and gained national publicity and support (Robert Kennedy attended the Mass at which Chávez ended his first fast in 1968).

In the 1970s, when growers refused to renew contracts and shielded themselves from the UFW with "sweetheart" contracts with the Teamsters, the UFW launched new boycotts of lettuce, Gallo wine, and table grapes. Chávez took the boycott international, even obtaining an audience with Pope Paul VI, which strengthened church support for La Causa. Eventually the UFW succeeded in driving the Teamsters from the fields. These successes had much to do with passage of the historic Agricultural Labor Relations Act of 1975, the first law to recognize the right of California field workers to collective bargaining.

After 1982, however, Republican governors filled the ALRB with grower-friendly appointees, and union membership among farm workers began to decline. The organization lost its two most visible leaders when Chávez died in April 1993 and, in 2000, Huerta, a 70-year-old great-grandmother, stepped down from the executive board.

Chávez's successor was his son-in-law, Arturo Rodriguez. Rodriguez returned to the union's founding tactics and philosophy by bringing farmworkers back into the public eye. In June 2010, in the face of virulent anti-immigrant rhetoric, the UFW launched a new campaign, "Take Our Jobs." The organization's website invited "citizens and legal residents" to replace farm workers in the field. Applications were posted online and, by the end of the month, reported Rodriguez, at least 4,000 people had responded. "Only a few dozen," he noted, "actually followed through with the process." Despite a dismal 2010 job market, a national unemployment rate of 9.5 percent, and 14.6 million people out of work, few Americans were willing to accept "back-breaking jobs in triple digit temperatures that pay minimum wage."   (RBR)

AWOC's Delano strike. It was at first an uneasy alliance between the mainly Filipino, AFL-CIO-oriented AWOC and the principally Mexican-American NFWA. Still, the coalition led to creation of the United Farm Workers Organizing Committee (UFWOC) and ultimately to the AFL-CIO-chartered United Farm Workers of America (UFW).

Unity won the strike at Delano. Through the winter of 1965, growers hired strikebreakers and armed guards to combat the union. Strikers received support from the AFL-CIO, but they also encountered vigorous and often violent opposition from Teamsters determined to control the fields. Finally, following a 24-day march of nearly 300 miles from Delano to Sacramento, Chávez and his allies won their first concessions. In June 1966, Schenley Industries announced it would negotiate. Soon after, DiGiorgio authorized elections at its Delano site. Field workers chose UFW to represent them, and shed workers and drivers selected the Teamsters.

Although further arbitration was required, an important precedent had been set. The organizational effort spread southward to the Imperial Valley, leading to a nationwide boycott of table grapes, and finally the negotiation of additional UFW contracts with growers in the Coachella Valley and elsewhere.

During the early 1970s, the UFW campaign expanded to other regions of California, especially the Salinas Valley, where field workers faced vigorous opposition. Teamsters attacked picket lines with baseball bats and tire irons, killing two UFW members. In 1970 growers' associations secured injunctions to limit union activity, and in 1972 they spent millions on Proposition 22, which curtailed farm workers' rights to organize and negotiate. By then, however, the UFW had gained substantial public support. The measure lost by 1.3 million votes and, shortly thereafter, the state supreme court invalidated previously granted anti-union injunctions, another farmworker victory.

More Students in Revolt

The energy generated by farm protests, the Chicano movement, anti-war protests, campaigns for civil rights in the South, and for Black Power in U.S. cities stirred up youth on college campuses. Events of the 1960s revealed that the "silent generation" of college students—those who barely reacted to the Tenney Committee or the McCarthy witch-hunts—had left the building. When the House Un-American Activities Committee met in San Francisco City Hall in 1960, hundreds of students protested, prompting police to disperse them with clubs and fire hoses. Brief and isolated as it was, the incident predicted more serious confrontations to come.

UC Berkeley soon became a volatile flash point for student dissent. During the 1960s, civil rights activism increased on campus, a vocal "ban-the-bomb" movement emerged, protests against U.S. involvement in Southeast Asia grew louder, and representatives of various unconventional and radical political philosophies took to the streets. As Berkeley students became more outspoken, the university administration and Board of Regents restricted on-campus political activity, despite a 1963 U.S. Supreme Court decision declaring such policies unconstitutional. In response, Berkeley students united behind philosophy major Mario Savio in the Free Speech Movement (FSM) of 1964. When the university disciplined several students for violating its no-politics policy, the FSM occupied Sproul Hall. Although members considered it a legitimate gesture of civil disobedience, the occupation provoked a confrontation with Gov. Pat Brown and Berkeley police. More than 700 students were arrested and nearly 600 tried and found guilty of trespass, resisting arrest, or both. The disturbance shocked California parents, taxpayers, and especially students. Philosopher Savio had failed to explain that civil disobedience had a price. Henry David Thoreau, after all, went to jail for the principle; Socrates paid with his life.

Within a month, the university rescinded its ban on political activities, but this did not bring calm. Instead, five more years of campus-related disruptions ensued. As was the case throughout the nation, various kinds

Mario Savio (speaking, center of photo) **Giving Interview**
Courtesy of The Bancroft Library, University of California, Berkeley.

of unrest were blooming. By the end of 1965, destructive violence and systematic "trashing" of property were integral elements of campus protest, especially when Students for a Democratic Society (SDS), the Youth International movement ("Yippies"), drug-oriented "hippies" or "flower children," and politically radical organizations became involved. Official responses simultaneously increased in aggressiveness and violence, often including armed riot police equipped with Mace, tear gas, and attack dogs. Such campus disruptions brought other negative consequences, both immediately and long-term. Student unrest reduced public confidence and support for state institutions of higher learning, and they tarnished the national reputation of one of its finest universities.

Similar incidents spread outward from Berkeley. Late in 1967, an anti-draft protest that attempted to close the induction center at Oakland ended in a riot. A year later, a strike supporting ethnic studies programs and other causes degenerated into weeks of disruption, destruction, and violence at San Francisco State College. Stanford University experienced a major dislocation in 1969, and the same year brought the "People's Park" incident, with mobilization of the National Guard, helicopters spraying tear gas over Berkeley, and one student fatality. A second student died in February 1970 during a demonstration at UC Santa Barbara.

These fatalities, along with the killing of four students by National Guardsmen at Kent State University in Ohio in May 1970, dampened enthusiasm for demonstrating on college campuses. So, too, did the "get-tough policies" of new Gov. Ronald Reagan, who dismissed Clark Kerr from the presidency of the University of California and appointed S.I. Hayakawa to restore order at San Francisco State. Equally important was the loss of many of the students' causes. Opposition to the war in Vietnam had made its point and by the early 1970s, the United States was drawing down troops. The movement for racial equality was also making slow but observable progress. In 1971 the 26th Amendment gave 18-year-olds the right to vote, making conventional politics more attractive.

Tom Hayden, a founder of Students for a Democratic Society in 1962 and one of the "Chicago Seven" convicted of conspiring to disrupt the 1968 Democratic Convention, demonstrated this shift. Hayden campaigned for California's Democratic nomination for U.S. Senator (1976), espoused consumer rights through his Campaign for Economic Democracy, and received appointments to serve on various state commissions. In 1982 Hayden won a seat in the state assembly, ultimately serving a total of 18 years there and in the state senate.

For Hayden and others like him, the radicalism of the 1960s had become the common sense of the 1970s.

The 1960s: An Assessment

Neither California nor the nation would be quite the same after the 1960s. On the one hand, activism persisted as a fact of political life, not only for the young and radical but for citizens of all ages and persuasions. Teach-ins and the like focused on contemporary issues, heightening political awareness among a generation of students and even their parents. Many Californians became increasingly vocal in expressing discontent with their quality of life and about an array of concerns that ranged from environmental pollution and exploitation to suburban sprawl and urban blight to ineffective public education and hazardous thermonuclear power plants.

California women exemplified both the new political vigor and its limitations. By the 1960s, California women could see that the state had compiled a fairly positive record on feminist issues. Yet some saw the state's modest progress as a double-edged sword, one that bred complacency while allowing serious inequities to continue. After the National Council on the Status of Women was formed in 1961, California took three years to found its own, making it the 44th state to do so. Similarly, when a 1964 federal law required equal pay for equal work, Californians presumed that it would make little difference, since similar legislation had been on state books since 1949. In reality, however, women in California still earned nearly 40 percent less than their male counterparts.

Armed with statistics from the Women's Bureau of the U.S. Labor Department and energized by the spirit of the decade, in 1964 leaders of moderate women's groups convinced a reluctant legislature to form a state Commission on the Status of Women. After conducting systematic research, in 1967 the commission presented its findings and recommendations. The report extended far beyond evidence of inequitable compensation to include more controversial issues such as child care, abortion, divorce and property law reform, and access to education, as well as a score of proposals for legislation. By then, however, Ronald Reagan was governor, and he received the report with significantly less sympathy for feminist causes than even his lukewarm predecessor. Yet California women had laid a promising foundation for subsequent achievements.

Conflict in the cities and the fields shattered the optimistic mood that put Pat Brown into the governor's office in 1958 and 1962. Changes in federal spending priorities, inflation, and rising taxes likewise resulted in a faltering economy, reducing confidence still further.

Extremism remained a force to be reckoned with. On the right was the John Birch Society, still active, vocal, and politically influential. On the left, frustrated militants resorted to terrorism. In 1975, the Symbionese Liberation Army assassinated Oakland superintendent of schools Marcus Foster and kidnapped heiress Patricia Hearst. The Army committed a series of bank robberies and other crimes; only a fiery Los Angeles shootout brought it to an end in 1975.

The controversies of the 1960s also undermined unity among Democrats. Members of the party remained generally in support of civil rights legislation and social programs, but the war in Vietnam split the party during the 1964 elections and allowed Republican song-and-dance man George Murphy to capture a seat in the U.S. Senate. It sundered the California Democratic Council, precipitated the dismissal of its president Simon Cassady, rendering the organization virtually useless in Pat Brown's 1966 bid for a third term. Brown lost additional backing because his responses to campus disturbances were too lenient for some, too harsh for others.

In sharp contrast to Democrats' disarray in 1966, Republicans were united. During the 1966 primary campaigns, most abided by the party's "Eleventh Commandment:" speak no ill of fellow Republicans. After moderate Republican Mayor George Christopher of San Francisco lost his bid for the gubernatorial nomination, the party rallied behind a single candidate: actor-turned-politician Ronald Reagan.

Eras of Limits

Reagan, Brown, and Deukmejian

Governor Jerry Brown summarized his view of government's role in society with the phrase "era of limits." That concept could justly be applied to the public mood that elected his predecessor. By the mid-1960s the expansive optimism that made Pat Brown appealing had evaporated. The fabric of California's society was unraveling, and the state's economy, which had promised an improved quality of life for all, staggered erratically. Universities and colleges, the pride of many Californians, were plagued by discord, and the cost of maintaining the ship of state was escalating. Reaction to these developments was the cautious conservatism that made Reagan governor in 1966. Eight years later, public attitudes had changed little, and Californians opted not for a return to the enthusiastic progressive-style leadership of the first governor Brown, but for the unique mixture of philosophies espoused by the second.

The Rise of Ronald Reagan

Born in Illinois in 1911, Ronald Reagan matured in the midwestern heartland. After college, he worked as a radio announcer in Iowa before leaving for Hollywood in 1937, beginning a 20-year career as a movie actor, principally in Westerns. A politically active college student, he later served as president of the Screen Actors' Guild (SAG). As a young adult, Reagan was a Democrat with liberal tendencies, but his conversion to conservatism followed a World War II stint in the military. He was a militant supporter of SAG's effort to purge suspected communists from its ranks during the later 1940s and a Democratic adherent of Dwight Eisenhower in the 1950s. Reagan became a public relations executive for General Electric Company and in 1960 he backed Richard Nixon's campaign for the presidency, still as a Democrat. Finally, he registered Republican to campaign for Barry Goldwater in 1964.

Thus Ronald Reagan was hardly a political neophyte when he decided to run for governor in 1966. During years of making speeches and hosting television shows for General Electric, he honed his version of conservatism and distilled it to a few adaptable points: free enterprise, lower taxes, and small government. Earlier campaign experiences also made it as clear to him that "money is the mother's milk of politics." In 1965, wealthy backers known as the "Friends of Ronald Reagan" provided the nourishment essential to a quest for the governor's mansion and even the White House. Reagan understood, too, that chance did not produce election victories. He hired political consultants to make his 1966 bid for office a polished and professional performance.

For Democrats, the 1966 campaign was anything but polished or professional. Pat Brown ran on his record, but his progressivism no longer appealed to the electorate. Indeed, conservative Mayor Sam Yorty of Los Angeles took nearly a million votes from Brown in the primary. Brown had no backing from the CDC, the liberal wing of his party refused its support, and organized labor defected, alienated by the incumbent's housing and jobs policies for African Americans.

Reagan successfully used his media skills to attack Brown's record. He held the governor accountable for "the mess at Berkeley" and for urban disturbances, assailed his stance on the Rumford Fair Housing Act and Proposition 14, and blamed Brown for increased budgets and taxes. Reagan defused charges of extremism by insisting that support for Reagan meant acceptance of Reagan's ideas, not those of right-wing Reagan supporters such as the John Birch Society. Throughout the campaign, Reagan recycled versions of his set speech: defending free enterprise and political morality, attacking liberals as extremists, and promising reductions in taxes, budgets, and the scope of government.

Reagan's message was congenial to Californians in 1966, who elected him governor by a margin of almost a million votes. They also elected Republicans to nearly every statewide office, substantially reducing Democratic majorities in the legislature.

The First Reagan Term

Like politicians before and after him, Governor Reagan quickly learned that it is easier to articulate ideologies than it is to implement them. His "creative

Ronald Reagan, Governor of California, March 1974
Terry Fincher, Fincher Files / Alamy Stock Photo.

society" program faced hostile majorities in the state senate and assembly, but Reagan counted on support from conservative Democrats. He then discovered that many programs requiring state expenditures were mandated by law or tied to federal policies. Reagan also found that Californians, his own constituents among them, had vested interests in perpetuating and even expanding costly programs. Finally, inflation and an economy weakened by periodic recession made it impossible to "squeeze and cut and trim" spending across the board. Instead, just six months after his inauguration, Reagan "bit the bullet" and approved the largest budget (more than $5 billion) and the greatest tax increase (almost $1 billion) in state history.

There were, however, areas in which cuts might be made with substantial popular support: welfare, higher education, and mental-health services. Reagan acted on his promise to "clean up the mess at Berkeley" by pushing out UC President Kerr in 1967. Despite increased enrollments and inflated costs, the governor cut funding for state universities and colleges by 30 percent. Reagan advocated an end to tuition-free higher education, arguing that paying tuition would make students more responsible, more likely to attend classes, and less likely to attend demonstrations. Although most Californians approved his "crackdowns," students still rebelled and both legislature and Regents rejected tuition hikes as rank anti-intellectualism.

Reorganizing state mental-health care had significant long-term consequences. In the 1950s, California's mental-health program was regarded as the most progressive in the nation. Only the seriously ill were institutionalized; others received outpatient care, a transition begun when John F. Kennedy signed the 1963 Community Mental Health Act. Although it never received adequate funding, the program was to provide federal dollars to build community-based mental healthcare and treatment facilities. A 1965 act, Medicaid, extended the trend towards deinstitutionalization. Congress approved Medicaid as a state and federally funded health insurance program for low-income children, elderly, blind, and disabled people. In response, California and other states transferred mental hospital patients to nursing homes or released them to community outpatient programs because, as the Act explained, funding did not extend to people in "institutions for mental diseases." Two years later, the state legislature passed the Lanterman-Petris-Short Act, which made involuntary hospitalization of the mentally ill difficult.

Acting with state, federal, and popular support, Gov. Reagan closed state mental hospitals, abolished many outpatient clinics, and eliminated more than 2,500 public healthcare employees. The number of patients in California mental hospitals fell from their 1959 Brown-era peak of 37,500 to 22,000 in 1967. Pharmaceutical innovations encouraged hospital administrators to return patients to their communities, where local mental health centers could oversee their care. The long-term success of this strategy depended on patients' continued medical care, along with proper housing, and the support of friends and family. Unfortunately, these support services failed to materialize. By 1984, medical professionals and state and federal leaders agreed that releasing the majority of the nation's mentally ill from hospitals to communities was a major failure. Even former governor Pat Brown admitted that he and others had "gone far, too far, in letting people out."

Cutting state spending on welfare programs proved less controversial, but more difficult than Gov. Reagan expected. To strike "welfare cheaters" from assistance rolls, Reagan reduced MediCal payments to low-income Californians (an action later reversed by the courts) and vetoed legislation pegging welfare payments to cost-of-living increases in Social Security benefits. Only legislative opposition and fear of conflict with the federal Department of Health, Education, and Welfare (HEW) prevented additional cuts.

Reagan succeeded in his campaign promises to "get tough" on crime, resulting in legislation mandating tougher sentencing on violent crime. However, he could not keep his promise to repeal the Rumford Act. Reagan blocked plans to dam the Feather and Eel rivers, which won him grudging approval from conservationists. Despite all his efforts to "squeeze and cut and trim," at the end of his first term, the state budget approached a record $7 billion.

Reagan lost his 1968 bid for the Republican presidential nomination to Richard M. Nixon, but the contest had positive results for the governor. The election put a Republican in the White House and gave Reagan a valuable national forum. California saw modest Republican majorities in the legislature, but this was a mixed blessing for Reagan, who could no longer blame "a few willful Democrats" for his inability to fulfill campaign promises. Democrats managed to send Alan Cranston to the U.S. Senate, replacing Thomas Kuchel.

The Election of 1970

Gov. Reagan's first term disappointed many, particularly fiscal conservatives, but his potential for reelection in 1970 was excellent. Reagan could remind voters that despite increasing budgets, their rate of growth diminished during his first term. Failure to achieve fiscal reform goals could also be blamed on the legislature and his opponent, former assembly speaker Jesse Unruh. But the Republican majority elected in 1968 was so disorganized that it could not even nominate a speaker, let alone overcome Democratic opposition. Unruh stressed Reagan's failure to keep the promises of 1966, but his was an uphill battle against a well-financed campaigner with superb media skills. Furthermore, Unruh's reputation as "boss" of California's Democratic machinery proved impossible to overcome.

Reagan won by a margin of 500,000 votes, yet the 1970 victory was personal rather than partisan. He campaigned actively for Republican candidates for statewide office, the legislature, and Congress, and they won all but two statewide offices: Democrat Wilson Riles, the state's first African American judge, became superintendent of public instruction, and Edmund G. "Jerry" Brown Jr. became the new secretary of state. The governor was less help in legislative contests: Republicans held a majority by two seats in the senate and by six in the assembly. Democrats increased their majority in the Congressional delegation, and Democrat John Tunney took the formerly Republican U.S. Senate seat. In 1970, Reagan and the Republicans lost more than they gained.

The Second Reagan Administration

Reagan began his second term by vetoing a reapportionment bill then leaving the matter to the courts. This further antagonized Democratic lawmakers, reducing their willingness to cooperate with Reagan on tax and welfare reform. To Reagan, welfare reform meant drastically cutting the number of recipients, but the number of Californians on public assistance increased during the 1960s and early '70s. The governor proposed more stringent standards for eligibility and a "work-fare" program to further pare relief rolls, but these policies produced no significant savings. Nearly 90 percent of assistance recipients were aged, disabled, or children. Many state programs were tied to federally mandated payment levels, and the private sector economy remained too weak to support a work-fare system.

The stalemate was broken when Reagan allied with the new assembly speaker, Democrat Robert Moretti. Their compromise bill, the California Welfare Reform Act of 1971, tightened requirements for participation in Aid to Families with Dependent Children (AFDC), included work-fare policies, and attempted to reduce MediCal costs through a prepaid insurance scheme. But the law did not include the governor's principal objectives: reduced benefit levels and an absolute ceiling on welfare spending.

Rising welfare costs contributed to California's problem of rising taxes, but inflation also contributed. With the budget close to $7 billion in 1971 and few alternatives, Reagan signed a bill instituting payroll deductions for state taxes, a move that increased annual tax revenues by about $100 million.

The governor again turned to Moretti for help with school financing. In *Serrano v. Priest* (1971), the state supreme court held it unconstitutional to use property taxes to finance schools, shifting the burden for school funding to the state. The solution was a 1972 tax bill that raised the sales tax to 6 percent and hiked corporate tax rates. This created sufficient revenues to offset homeowners' exemptions and other tax-relief measures, and even produced a treasury surplus. But the bill did not permanently alleviate the problem of financing schools, nor did it deal with Californians' major complaint: property taxes.

Efforts to limit property taxes had a long history in California but, during the 1960s, inflation increased both property values and assessments, making the problem particularly acute. In 1968, Los Angeles County tax assessor Philip Watson proposed a 1 percent property-tax limitation that qualified as a ballot initiative. Although the measure failed, it prompted the legislature to enact both a general reduction and special reductions for senior citizens. Voters defeated a second Watson initiative in 1972, prompting Reagan to introduce his own measure, Proposition 1, the following year. The measure amended the constitution to prohibit legislatures from raising tax rates above a stipulated percentage of Californians' cumulative income. Opponents convinced voters that the measure would transfer fiscal responsibility to local agencies and ultimately result in higher property taxes. The measure's length and complexity forced Reagan to admit that he did not fully understand the proposition, which contributed to its defeat.

After two terms as governor, Ronald Reagan's record was mixed. Reductions in taxes and budgets had proven impossible and, beginning in 1967, both increased faster than the population or the cost of living. The rate of increase in government spending declined somewhat, but Reagan's last budget in 1974 exceeded $10 billion. Nor had he managed to implement "creative society" principles that shifted the cost of social programs to communities and the private sector. Democratic legislators had been uncooperative, but the governor himself lacked the skills or experience required to deal effectively with lawmakers, even Republican ones. Most Reagan policies were negative, requiring reduction or elimination of existing programs, without providing alternatives. On the other hand, although Reagan's environmental attitudes angered conservationists, he signed measures establishing the nation's most stringent standards for air and water quality, and requiring environmental-impact studies for public works projects.

Despite his failures, Regan retained a positive public image when he stepped down in 1974. Indeed, although he announced that he would not seek a third term as governor, he might have been re-elected. But the decision was sound, given revelations of wrongdoing in the Watergate scandal, which discredited politicians in general and Republicans in particular. Even Reagan could not escape its tarnish.

Jerry Brown, Governor of California, 1971

Governor Brown speaking at final session of Operation PUSH (People United to Serve Humanity). At right is Reverend Jesse Jackson, who founded Operation PUSH in December 1971. *Everett Collection Historical / Alamy Stock Photo.*

The Second Governor Brown

In contrast, Edmund G. ("Jerry") Brown Jr. projected the image needed to counter popular mistrust of politicians. Born in San Francisco in 1938, he attended Catholic schools—institutions famous for their tough discipline. Intelligent, energetic, and inquisitive, Brown led chums into mischief, impressed them with four-letter words learned from Pat's cohorts, and allegedly lit a fire under a playmate's feet to discover how Indians burned their captives. Indeed, many doubted that Brown the Younger would last one term in a Catholic school.

By the time Brown graduated from St. Ignatius High School in 1955, he had decided to study for the priesthood at Sacred Heart Novitiate in Los Gatos. Brown entered the seminary and began the required 15 years of study. The rigor, discipline, and periods of silent meditation appealed to him. Uncertainty overwhelmed conviction in Brown's third year. After securing release from his vows, Brown left the seminary in 1960. He considered medicine but, at the University of California, demonstrated little aptitude for science. His years observing the workings of politics left him with distaste for public service. Still unsure, Brown graduated from UC Berkeley in 1961 with a classics degree.

Jerry Brown's seminary training taught him humility and the dignity of physical labor. When he arrived in Berkeley, waves of student dissent had not yet crested, but undercurrents were apparent. Brown discussed the lunch counter sit-ins in the South, segregation in California, the menace of a nuclear arms race, and the morality of capital punishment. He joined Dorothy Day's Catholic Workers' Group to experience farm laborers' problems in the Sacramento Valley, and went to San Francisco's Hunter's Point to learn about life in an urban ghetto. Pat Brown eventually sent his son to Judge Matt Tobriner, who persuaded Jerry to study law at Yale University. When Brown arrived in New Haven in the fall of 1961, he embraced his studies as well as political activism. Brown traveled to Mississippi in the spring of 1962 to join in the desegregation movement. He began to doubt the wisdom of this choice when he discovered that locals did indeed use dogs, clubs, and water hoses to intimidate "agitators." After several marches and covert conferences with civil-rights activists, Brown returned to Yale with Mississippi on his mind.

While he was at Yale, the country endured the Bay of Pigs crisis and the John Kennedy assassination. The civil rights movement expanded, conflict in Vietnam escalated, and student protests against racism and war rocked the nation's campuses. An outspoken opponent of U.S. involvement in Vietnam, in 1968 Brown organized for antiwar candidate Eugene McCarthy during his California campaign for the Democratic presidential nomination, and was a delegate to the Chicago Democratic convention. At Chicago Brown's distaste for traditional politics returned, as party leaders subverted every peace plank proposed for the national platform, and Chicago police attacked demonstrators outside the convention hall.

In 1969 Brown won a seat on the Los Angeles Community College Board. As the board's only liberal member, Brown accomplished little during his tenure, but he did enliven meetings with suggestions that a campus be named for Martin Luther King Jr., that the board protest the deaths of four students at Kent State University in Ohio, and that it spend money on academic programs rather than physical education facilities. In 1970 he set his sights on the California secretary of state's office. In November, Brown conducted a vigorous and well-financed campaign; capitalizing on popular mistrust of politicians, he promised to reform California campaign practices.

As secretary of state, Brown opposed Proposition 22 in 1972, a measure restricting union organizing activity among agricultural workers, and revealed that some signatures were fraudulent. Gov. Reagan refused to act, allowing Proposition 22 to remain on the ballot, but Brown's revelations contributed to its defeat. In 1974 Brown sponsored an initiative to create a Fair Campaign Practices Commission, control campaign funding, and require full disclosure of candidates' assets and spending. Having achieved these successes, Brown was ready to make a bid for governor.

The Election of 1974

Brown entered the gubernatorial race as a champion of organized labor and political integrity, and on the strength of his record as secretary of state. Although he had held himself aloof from traditional partisan politics and its practitioners, Brown had an enormous asset in his familiar name. He understood the importance of media exposure as well, particularly television's influence as a molder of opinion. Throughout the campaign, Brown appeared often on television and in print, stressing his record and his unique approach to politics. Brown gained his party's nomination over a pair of seasoned, familiar Democrats: speaker of the assembly Robert Moretti and San Francisco mayor Joseph Alioto.

The most likely Republican candidate was Lieutenant Governor Ed Reinecke, who suddenly found himself under investigation for perjury. Instead the party chose state controller Houston Flournoy. Brown initially underestimated his opponent, relying on the Watergate scandal, Gerald Ford's controversial pardon of Richard Nixon, and his own reputation as a political reformer and champion of labor. Brown conducted a dull, low-keyed campaign that was short on specifics and long on abstractions, but narrowly won a second term.

Democrats generally did well, winning most state offices in 1974. It was a year of firsts: state senator Mervyn Dymally became the state's first African American lieutenant governor. Wilson Riles, the first African American elected to statewide office, won his second term as state superintendent of public instruction. March Fong Eu won election as secretary of state, the first woman to hold that office and the first Chinese American ever to win state office. The party claimed solid majorities in the legislature and increased its control over the U.S. Congressional delegation. Thus, the new governor had every reason to expect his party's full-throated support.

New Blood

The postwar civil-rights movement profoundly changed American attitudes toward minorities. No longer tied to numbers, the concept of "minority" came to be associated with any group subjected to discrimination and denied its share of political, social, and economic power. These shifting attitudes were especially clear in California, as the new governor abandoned long-standing tradition in political appointments. Instead of drawing primarily from the ranks of middle-aged white businessmen and professionals, Gov. Brown appointed members of minority groups to the higher echelons of state government. These included Wiley Manuel, the first African American justice of the state supreme court, Mario Obledo, the first Latino secretary of Health, Education and Welfare, and Vilma Socorro Martinez, first Latina regent of the University of California.

The civil rights movement of the 1960s brought new attention to different forms of gender inequality. In 1911, California became the sixth state to permit woman suffrage, but gaining equal representation in office proved more difficult. The first four women won election to the state assembly in 1918, but it was not until 1967 that Californians elected a woman to statewide office: state treasurer Ivy Baker Priest. Nine years later, voters sent the first woman, Rose Vuich, to the state senate. California women also won national office. Political widow Mae Ella Nolan finished her husband's term in the U.S. House in 1921, then won one term in her own right. Likewise Florence Prag Kahn finished her husband's term in 1925, then won election five times in her own name. In 1945, Helen Gahagan Douglas (D-Los Angeles) campaigned for and won the first of three terms in the U.S. House. These were impressive achievements, but women lost far more often than they won. From 1912 to 1970, more than 500 California women campaigned for state and national elective office, but only 18 women won election.

Gov. Jerry Brown used his appointment powers to put more California women in government. During his two terms, Brown appointed women to over 1,500 positions in state government and supported creation of the 17-member state Commission on the Status of Women. Brown's choices sometimes sparked opposition, as when he nominated actress Jane Fonda to the California Arts Council (controversial for her opposition to U.S. involvement in Viet Nam). The legislature rejected his nominee. Equally controversial was Brown's nomination of Berkeley classmate Rose Elizabeth Bird to head the Department of Agriculture and later as the state supreme court's first female justice. She later became the court's first female chief justice.

Women's equality was a matter of economics as well as political power. World War II stimulated major changes for women in the workplace, and that trend continued afterwards. From 1960 to 1980, the numbers of women wage-earners increased by 95 percent. A 1983 federal study reported that women comprised a majority in six categories of jobs that were once the province of men: insurance adjusters, examiners, and investigators; real-estate agents and brokers; photographic process workers; bill collectors; checkers, examiners, and inspectors;

and production-line workers. The percentage of women in other job categories, including lawyers, physicians, bus drivers, and bartenders, had also increased substantially. Much of women's economic progress owed to increased access to colleges and universities, and to professional and graduate programs. A 1986 poll reported that most California men and women favored equality for women, government-supported child care, and equal pay for comparable work. Yet most respondents noted that, despite changing attitudes, working women still performed 70 percent or more of housework.

Feminist groups lobbied the state legislature to ensure women the same pay as men for "comparable work," defined by a 1983 federal court decision as "the provision of similar salaries for positions that require or impose similar responsibilities, judgments, knowledge, skills, and working conditions." In 1981 San José municipal workers went on strike to give women the same pay as men for comparable work. The strikers failed in their specific demands, but the city accepted the concept and began a process of funding pay raises designed to eliminate such wage discrepancies. Other cities and counties moved in a similar direction.

Politically, the focus of attention in the 1970s was the Equal Rights Amendment (ERA), an amendment to the U.S. Constitution stating that "equality of rights under the law shall not be denied or abridged by the United States or by any state on account of sex." Californians joined the fight with the National Organization for Women, its chief proponent. Congress passed the amendment in 1972 and California quickly ratified it, but the amendment failed.

Another legacy of the civil rights movement was the post-WWII emergence of a lesbian, gay, bisexual, transgender, and queer (LGBTQ) voting bloc in San Francisco and Los Angeles. Openly homosexual communities emerged in those cities, assisted in part by social and political organizations such as the Mattachine Society in Los Angeles and the Daughters of Bilitis in San Francisco. By 1977, San Francisco's LGBTQ community had developed enough political strength to elect the first openly gay politician, Harvey Milk, to the Board of Supervisors.

No issue affected California's LGBTQ citizens more than the AIDS (Acquired Immunodeficiency Syndrome) crisis that emerged in the 1980s. Initially, AIDS was seen as strictly a disease related to homosexual activity. More than 80 percent of AIDS victims were homosexuals and intravenous drug users. Shocked by the soaring death rates, LGBTQ leaders urged lifestyle changes. By the end of the 1980s, when the disease had spread to heterosexual men and women, it finally gained recognition as a national health crisis. By then, researchers had identified the human immunodeficiency virus (HIV) that caused AIDS and had begun to develop drugs to fight the onset of AIDS in those infected with the virus.

Farm Labor

Governor Brown's unusual political selections caused a major disruption in California tradition, but his actions on behalf of farm labor were unprecedented. His union sympathies already well known, one of Brown's first acts as governor was drafting the Agricultural Labor Relations Act of 1975, in collaboration with Rose Bird. The law recognized the right of farm workers to organize unions, an unprecedented step for the state and the nation, given that the National Labor Relations Act had specifically excluded farm workers (largely at the insistence of California agribusiness interests). The 1975 Act assured farm workers the right to organize, bargain collectively, and select their bargaining agents by secret ballot. It allowed them to use labor's traditional weapons—picketing, strikes, and boycotts—in disputes with employers, but protected growers' interests by specifying conditions under which such tactics could be employed. It also set up a five-member Agricultural Labor Relations Board (ALRB) to supervise elections, decide cases of alleged unfairness, and oversee enforcement.

Many growers resisted the policy and objected to individuals appointed to the Board. Funding the ALRB also proved a problem. During its first few months in operation, the ALRB supervised nearly 200 elections in California's fields, and the unexpected level of activity depleted its original $1.3 million budget. When the agency appealed for additional funds, the legislature refused and the ALRB ceased its work in April 1976. Later that year, to defuse the threat of the United Farm Worker-sponsored Proposition 14 "Farm Labor Initiative," an initiative to reconstitute the board with additional authority, lawmakers approved funds to continue the ALRB. Unfortunately, César Chávez chose to proceed with Prop 14, which lost by a two-to-one margin. Defeat at the polls critically weakened the UFW with growers, farmworkers, and the legislature, which again cut ALRB operating funds.

"Small is Beautiful"

Appointing women and members of minority groups to office and using government authority to uphold the interest of farmworkers placed Jerry Brown in the vanguard of California's liberal-progressive political tradition. It is more difficult to categorize other Brown actions and policies, many derived from British economist E.F. Schumacher's *Small Is Beautiful*. Schumacher argued that contraction of production and consumption, not expansion, provided the soundest foundation for a humane society, and Brown adopted this philosophy as his own. It formed the basis for his "era of limits" concept, and he applied it to issues ranging from environmental conservation to fiscal policy.

Brown was committed to preserving California's natural setting and its resources. Of particular concern was an ever-increasing demand for energy. Borrowing from Schumacher, Brown founded the Office of Appropriate Technology (OAT) to explore natural gas and non-fossil fuel energy sources, and environmentally friendly economic development. Brown appointed conservationists to head state agencies such as OAT, the Air Resources Board, and the Energy Development and Conservation Commission. Recalling the New Deal, Brown created the California Conservation Corps to alleviate the problem of youth unemployment while providing a work force for wilderness and urban improvement projects.

For personal, political, and ideological reasons, Brown advocated stringent controls on nuclear-power development, supported a ballot initiative to create the California Coastal Commission, proposed increases in the state's protected parklands, and joined the movement to save Pacific whales. Brown opposed construction of the New Melones Dam and fought efforts to rescind the 160-acre limitation on farm water developed using federal funds.

Naturalists and others concerned about the quality of life in California applauded Brown's policies. Their admiration diminished, however, when he made it clear that "small is beautiful" and "era of limits" ideologies applied to them as well as to industry and government. Brown reversed himself on the 160-acre irrigation issue, recommended construction of a peripheral canal around the Sacramento-San Joaquin Delta, opened negotiations for an Alaskan pipeline oil terminal at Long Beach, and limited funding to agencies charged with implementing environmental programs.

Brown lost support in other quarters as well. In 1974, he had repeatedly denounced government policies that sent "dollars chasing a problem." But numerous issues involving Californians' quality of life demanded additional expenditures. Reagan-era economic policies and persistent inflation had left colleges and universities underfinanced. The economy slowed, unemployment increased and, along with it, the number of public assistance recipients. Scandals and fraud discredited the MediCal insurance program. Numerous state agencies and departments were understaffed and their employees demoralized, their workloads increasing even as salaries fell further and further behind the cost of living.

It was soon apparent that these and other problems would need to be chased by dollars, but Brown adhered to campaign promises not to raise taxes, and to his vow that budget increases would not overtake the rate of inflation. The 1975–76 budget of $11.3 billion was just 5 percent higher than the previous year's. Each subsequent budget was equally austere.

The governor's refusal to approve appropriations to deal with pressing problems sparked confrontation with legislators, especially Leo McCarthy and Willie Brown Jr. Indeed, Brown's conflicts with Democratic lawmakers were even more persistent than those with his Republican predecessor. Brown exacerbated the conflict by resorting to "small-is-beautiful" rhetoric, as when he admonished public school teachers to live on their "psychic income."

However, public criticism could spur the governor to action. After the Los Angeles *Times* denounced his inattention to unemployment, Brown launched a major public works program: a sewer project that would produce more than 30,000 jobs and improve water quality and waste disposal. The measure had broad appeal, especially since it would cost state taxpayers nothing: federal funds that were allocated for the project but illegally impounded during Richard Nixon's presidency became available in 1975.

Brown nonetheless retained his image as a humane fiscal conservative able to effectively "squeeze and cut and trim." As he confided to aides, he did so by appearing to "move left and right at the same time," producing "a flurry of activity" when the occasion demanded. Gov. Brown's mercurial political style was noted by Sacramento insiders. As another of his aides phrased it, the governor had "a whim of iron."

The Era of Possibilities

It seemed to some that California's government was hostile to business and economic growth. Gov. Brown's support for farmworkers alienated agribusiness interests, as did his appointments of pro-farmworker individuals to the ALRB. Naming liberals and conservationists to state regulatory and licensing agencies likewise drew fire from utility, timber, and other industries. Brown's environmental policies, such as opposition to the New Melones Dam and to

nuclear plants, made enemies in both business and labor circles.

Brown's critics found support in a Dun & Bradstreet report that gave California low marks for its business climate, and when Dow Chemical decided against building a plant near Sacramento. Although they tarnished Brown's reputation, the examples were unfair. The Dun & Bradstreet survey was based on 1974 data, gathered when Ronald Reagan was governor, and the Dow withdrawal involved failure to obtain local, not state, permits.

Nevertheless, the governor reacted to mounting criticism by switching gears, abandoning his "era of limits" rhetoric in favor of an "era of possibilities." In 1977, Brown launched another "flurry of activity" that included a well-publicized "California Means Business" campaign. Brown journeyed to Japan, Canada, Mexico, and England, and toured several states to tout the state's advantages. He also capitalized on the impending flight of the space-shuttle *Enterprise*, scheduled for that August. In July, Brown attended a symposium at NASA-Ames Laboratory in Sunnyvale in Santa Clara County, where he stressed the state's leadership in aerospace and electronics. His comments about Gerald O'Neill's ideas of space colonization prompted Chicago columnist Mike Royko to dub him "Governor Moonbeam." Brown installed astronaut Russell Schweikart, on leave from NASA, as science and technology adviser, suggested California launch its own satellite, and proposed a $6 million space institute at the University of California.

To improve relations with industry, Brown appointed growers to the ALRB, named figures prominent in business to important state agencies, and made it clear that henceforth, when the environment and jobs came into conflict in California, jobs would receive priority.

By the 1978 governor's race, Brown had mended his political fences. He handily defeated his Republican opponent, state attorney general Evelle Younger, but voters dealt him a blow with an initiative reinstating the death penalty. Democrats lost their advantage in the legislature, and saw two Republican white males replace two path-breaking African American Democrats: Mike Curb replaced Mervyn Dymally as lieutenant governor and George Deukmejian thwarted Yvonne Braithwaite Burke's bid for state attorney general.

African Americans otherwise did well in 1970s elections. In 1977 Lionel Wilson won the Oakland mayor's race, becoming the city's first black mayor. He kept the post through two subsequent elections, and Wilson Riles won reelection as superintendent of public instruction. In 1973, former police officer Tom Bradley became Los Angeles's first African American mayor. Bradley thereafter won four reelections, ultimately serving a record 21 years.

But a political tragedy soon followed. On November 28, 1978, law-and-order advocate and former San Francisco supervisor Dan White assassinated mayor George Moscone and supervisor Harvey Milk. Apparently angered by the mayor's opposition to his return to the board and by Milk's advocacy of gay rights, White smuggled a pistol into City Hall to kill both. The San Francisco Board of Supervisors chose Dianne Feinstein to complete Moscone's term, making her the first female to fill that office. Feinstein ran and won the mayor's office in 1979 and 1983.

The Tax Revolt of 1978

The major political issue in 1978 was property taxes. The conditions that prompted Philip Watson's tax initiatives in 1968 and 1972 and Ronald Reagan's Proposition 1 in 1973 had only worsened during the first administration of Jerry Brown. Inflation pushed prices and incomes upward and wage-earners into higher tax brackets, creating a treasury surplus. Property values increased dramatically, and property assessments and tax bills inevitably followed. Republicans proposed tying income tax brackets to cost-of-living increases, but the governor resisted. New initiatives to limit taxation levels, especially on property, appeared on ballots but failed. By the mid-'70s Californians were more adamant than ever about tax reform. They demonstrated this most clearly in the 1978 primaries.

Prop 13 was by no means a grassroots movement. One of its nominal leaders, Utah-born Howard Jarvis, migrated to California during the l930s, formed a manufacturing firm, lost it during World War II, became director of the Los Angeles Association of Apartment Owners, and in 1977 joined Arkansas native Paul Gann, another depression-era migrant, to form the United Organization of Taxpayers (UOT). A year later they introduced their Jarvis-Gann initiative, which limited property taxes to 1 percent of assessed value, and applied to both residential and business property. It used 1975 values as the assessment basis; restricted assessment increases to 2 percent a year; forbid reassessment except in cases of sale or improvement; and required a two-thirds popular vote for the state and local governments to institute new taxes. The measure had tremendous appeal and a sizeable bankroll. UOT hired the Butcher-Forde Consulting Agency to manage the $2.5 million campaign, which easily gathered the signatures needed to place Prop 13 on the ballot.

Tom Bradley, Mayor of Los Angeles
Before he was elected the first black mayor of Los Angeles in 1973, Tom Bradley served on the city's police force and city council. He subsequently won reelection, serving a record five terms. In 1982, Bradley ran and lost a campaign for governor of California. *Courtesy of The Bancroft Library, University of California, Berkeley.*

Gov. Brown and most office-holders opposed it. They argued, correctly, that Prop 13 would benefit owners of rental and business properties more than homeowners. It would also severely limit funds available for public services, lead to dismissal of many public employees, and damage an already under-funded educational system. Democrats offered an alternative, the Behr Bill, which would provide tax relief to residential property only, a measure Brown supported. Instead Californians voted almost two-to-one for Prop 13.

Predictions of disaster soon followed. In an editorial published in *Harper's* in November 1978, California supreme court chief justice Ronald M. George warned,

The initiative has not proved to be a very sound means of enacting legislation. Initiatives are typically emotional reactions to an issue, poor substitutes for the hearings, debates, compromises, and deliberations that distinguish the legislative process. And so with

Howard Jarvis Holding News Conference on East Steps of State Capitol, Sacramento

According to Jarvis (*speaking, center of photo*), the boxes were filled with letters Californians had written in support of Proposition 13. *Center for Sacramento History, Sacramento Bee Collection, 1983/00/SBPBP04054.*

Prop. 13. . . . As houses are built and change hands, they will receive far higher assessments than voters were led to believe. And because families move more often than corporations, the heaviest property tax burden will shift from them to individuals. If corporations and property owners are the winners, the losers are the middle class, the working class and the poor.

Immediately following the June primaries, Gov. Brown began to implement Prop 13 in what he called "a humane way." He opened negotiations with legislators to distribute the state's $35 million treasury surplus—termed "obscene" by Jarvis—to local and county governments as "bail-out" funds. Brown used his executive authority to halt state hiring and to freeze state employees' salaries. He created a special commission headed by retired legislative analyst Alan Post to study Prop 13's fiscal implications and to recommend appropriate responses.

But the tax revolt did not end in 1978. One year later Paul Gann sponsored another initiative, Proposition 4, or "The Spirit of 13." The measure tied all government spending to rates of inflation and population growth.

Voters approved the measure by a 3–1 margin. Yet in 1980, Jarvis's Proposition 9—called "Jaws II" by its opponents—failed. Although the initiative would have cut state tax rates by 50 percent, its extremity plus Jarvis's own intemperate speeches, were too much even for California's tax warriors.

Energy Crisis and Response

Like their nineteenth-century predecessors, twentieth-century Californians often assumed that their resources were infinite. Unfortunately, events of the 1970s proved them wrong. During and after World War II, demands for energy increased annually, while sources of petroleum, natural gas, and hydroelectric power remained constant or diminished. Consequences became all too apparent in 1973 when the Organization of Oil Exporting Countries (OPEC) declared an embargo on oil shipments to the United States, raising the cost of imported crude oil more than tenfold by 1980. Gasoline prices escalated while impatient drivers waited in long lines at pumps. OPEC policies had devastating effects on plastic, chemical, fertilizer, power, and other petroleum-dependent industries in the state and on the economy in general.

Residents and California businesses considered the situation critical: they relied on petroleum to fill over half of their energy needs. About one-third was met by natural gas, and hydroelectric power and other sources supplied the remainder. California oil companies reopened abandoned fields and explored for additional sources, especially beneath coastal waters. Environmentalists opposed offshore drilling, but federal support allowed the industry to sink new offshore wells.

Controversy also surrounded proposals for terminals at Point Conception to import and store liquid natural gas, and at Long Beach to receive oil from the Alaska Pipeline. Although both projects won approval, expense and danger prevented construction and operation. None of the expedients, in any case, would have eliminated California's dependence on foreign products. Developing alternate sources of energy was essential. Individuals, public agencies like OAT and the University of California, and private interests such as Pacific Gas & Electric (PG&E) searched for substitutes to fossil fuel. Proposals ranged from tapping solar and geothermal sources, to harnessing the wind and tides, to generating electricity by burning the refuse and methane gas found in garbage dumps. The greatest expenditure of money and research, however, focused on the most controversial possibility of all: nuclear fission.

In 1957, the experimental Vallecitos generating plant began operation near Livermore, but its construction on an earthquake fault forced its closure. PG&E opened its problem-ridden Humboldt Bay facility in 1963, but was denied approval for another at Bodega Bay the following year. Southern California Edison Company's huge station at San Onofre near San Diego went on-line in 1968. One year later, PG&E began construction at Diablo Canyon near San Luis Obispo. Except for environmentalists, these early nuclear generation plants encountered little sustained opposition.

But by the 1970s, however, reports about potential hazards published by the federal Atomic Energy Commission (AEC), the Nuclear Regulatory Commission (NRC), and the California Energy Commission (CEC) (founded in 1975), increased public concern. Nevertheless, the Rancho Seco plant near Sacramento began operation in 1975. Californians defeated by a wide margin a 1976 initiative to halt nuclear power plant operation and construction and, that same year, the CEC rejected a San Diego Gas & Electric Company proposal for a nuclear plant in Riverside County.

The real catalyst for popular resistance to nuclear power came with the 1979 partial-core meltdown at Pennsylvania's Three Mile Island plant. Californians mobilized to stop PG&E's planned facility then under construction at Diablo Canyon. Organizations like the Abalone Alliance fought PG&E in the courts, and the NRC and CEC demanded major design changes and reinforcement against possible earthquake damage. PG&E claimed that the plant would save millions of barrels of oil annually and provide cheap power, yet when it began operation in 1985 its cost had surpassed $2 billion, resulting in higher costs to customers, further undermining popular support for nuclear power.

Other energy alternatives began to show promise, including cogeneration, which used wasted industrial heat and energy to generate electricity. Regulatory agencies and industry, including power and construction companies, took steps to increase energy efficiency and reduce waste. The energy crises of the 1970s prompted consumers to demand more energy-efficient homes, automobiles, and other products, even as rising energy costs forced many households to reduce energy consumption.

In 1982, for the first time in California history, two Southern Californians dominated the governor's race: Democrat Tom Bradley, mayor of Los Angeles, and Republican George Deukmejian, then state attorney general and formerly state senator for Long Beach. Intriguingly, both candidates also represented "law and order."

Deukmejian carefully avoided the issue of race in his campaign against the African American former police captain, but his race probably contributed to Bradley's narrow loss at the polls. Running on a "back-to-basics" platform, William Honig captured the nonpartisan superintendency of public instruction, replacing Wilson Riles. Democrats increased their majorities in the assembly and senate, to the dismay of Republican leaders. Through the end of the decade, Republicans blamed their failure to gain control of the legislature on what they regarded as a "badly gerrymandered" apportionment of the legislature by Democrats after the census of 1980.

After Thirteen

Governor Deukmejian and legislators who took office in 1983 were the first to confront the long-term effects of Prop 13. As critics had feared, the measure reduced tax liabilities for corporations and large landholders, and shifted a disproportionate share of the state's revenue burden to homeowners.

Alternative Energy Sources

The energy crisis of the 1970s prompted an intensified search for alternatives to petroleum, especially in renewable resources. Pacific Gas & Electric Company built geothermal generating plants near Geyserville in Sonoma County (*top left*) and constructed windmill "farms" on Altamont Pass in Alameda County (*top right*). PG&E's most controversial effort was and remains the Diablo Canyon nuclear power plant on the coast near San Luis Obispo (*bottom*). *Courtesy of Pacific Gas & Electric Company.*

Public facilities showed the result of long-deferred maintenance, while inflation meant higher costs for repairs or replacements. The direst predictions offered by the measure's opponents—massive layoffs in the public sector, drastically reduced or eliminated services, and rapidly-deteriorating roads, parks, and buildings—did not immediately materialize, but the state's treasury surplus quickly disappeared. As agencies at all levels struggled for survival, Deukmejian and the legislature deadlocked over the state's first unbalanced budget. After years of budget surpluses, in 1983 the treasury faced a $1.5 billion deficit, more than any other state.

The implications of the budget shortfall were nowhere clearer than in California's once-envied educational system. After World War II California boasted one of the finest public K–12 systems in the country, ranking high in the percentage of state funds spent on education. California's system of public higher education stood as a national model. Prop 13, however, made public schools and community colleges almost entirely dependent on state instead of local funds. In the spring of 1983, the San José School District declared bankruptcy. Trustees of the state college and university systems substantially increased students' costs and community colleges imposed tradition-shattering "fees" (so called because the state constitution prohibited charging "tuition").

Federal and state reports in the 1980s put California almost last among states in per-pupil funding, and gave it equally low marks for student-teacher ratios. As funding fell, schools deferred much-needed maintenance. Buildings crumbled, as did the quality of education. On national achievement tests, the scores of California students fell steadily, which prompted the reform campaign of former schoolteacher William Honig, elected in 1982 as state superintendent of public instruction on a hard-hitting "back-to-basics" campaign. Honig called for a new curriculum, better assessment, improved teacher training, modernized texts, and increased parent involvement in the schools. Additionally, in 1983 the legislature adopted a sweeping educational reform bill. Senate Bill 813 lengthened the school day and year; tightened graduation requirements; and created a "mentor teacher" program.

In 1988 Honig sponsored Proposition 98, a measure intended to change the state's constitution and introduce a complex formula that forced the state to spend at least 40 percent of its general fund each year on K–14 education (that is, K–12 plus community college). Suspension of Prop 98 would require the vote of two-thirds of legislators. Voters narrowly approved the measure, which quickly proved difficult to implement. The legislature

has temporarily suspended it twice, both times during deep economic recessions. Writing in 2010, the New York *Times* blamed Prop 98 for making it "extremely difficult" for California to balance its budget.

California's economy lurched through Gov. Deukmejian's first term. The General Motors plant in Fremont closed its doors, as did technology industries in northern California's Santa Clara Valley, soon to be known as "Silicon Valley." Smaller businesses failed with alarming frequency. But the economy began to stabilize during Gov. Deukmejian's second year. Inflation slowed, resulting in increases in the state's treasury balance and decreases in unemployment. In 1984, with federal approval, the idle General Motors facility reopened in Fremont as New United Motors Manufacturing, Inc. (NUMMI), a joint venture with Toyota of Japan.

Despite Gov. Deukmejian's opposition, in 1984 voters approved a ballot initiative creating a school-funding lottery that promised 34 percent of all proceeds to public education. In addition to increasing funding for schools from primary grades through the universities, Deukmejian approved funds for new highway construction and renovation of old ones. He earned the approval of state employees when he approved long-deferred salary increases.

Gov. Deukmejian could not entirely avoid controversy. Environmentalists applauded his toxic-waste elimination program, but they were alarmed by his support for a peripheral canal and offshore drilling, and his opposition to the California Coastal Commission. His vetoes of welfare legislation likewise prompted criticism.

Another "Boom of the '80s"

Former governor Ronald Reagan gained the White House in 1980 with an agenda that included reducing federal income tax rates; cutbacks in social welfare spending; sharp reduction of government regulation; and a massive increase in military spending. A Congress dominated by conservative Democrats and Republicans acquiesced, resulting in booming prosperity for business. Critics, however, labeled the period an "era of greed." The rich got richer as the American middle class seemed to shrink, threatening to create a "two-tiered" society of rich and poor.

Given the state's dominance in federal defense and aerospace programs, it is not surprising that California's economy boomed during the Reagan presidency. By the mid-1980s, 20 percent of Defense Department expenditures went to California, while the state absorbed one-third of both Department of Energy and NASA expenditures. Vast sums poured into the Los Angeles area, which had become the nation's largest manufacturing center and a world leader in aerospace.

Los Angeles developed as a magnet for other businesses. A majority of the state's largest companies were centered in and around the city, where cumulative income surpassed incomes in all but three states. The region accounted for one-eighth of the nation's total gross domestic product (GDP) and a majority of the state's population growth. Simultaneously, Los Angeles had a growing impact on American popular culture, as it dominated U.S. film and television production.

Gov. Deukmejian capitalized on the booming economy to win reelection in 1986. In his campaign, he promised to fight crime, keep a lid on government spending, and improve the state's business climate. However, Deukmejian's second term revealed deepening divisions in the state's government, as the conservative Republican squared off against a legislature controlled by Democrats. The legislature refused to approve several Deukmejian appointments. In retaliation, the governor used his line-item veto to slash programs approved by the legislature, especially social and environmental programs. Republicans in the legislature united to prevent the two-thirds vote necessary to override the governor's vetoes. Each year brought both sides into bitter conflict over the budget.

Deukmejian kept his pledge never to approve a new tax. For the most part, he approved only limited increases in existing levies. His resistance to new spending of any kind led critics to call him a "caretaker" governor who put the state "on hold" for eight years. By the mid-1980s, however, state revenues had risen to such levels that Deukmejian was able to approve increases in state spending on existing programs, including education and prison construction. Indeed, in 1987, the governor approved a $1 billion "rebate" to taxpayers.

Deukmejian's greatest impact was in the area of criminal justice. He was convinced that punishment, not rehabilitation, was the fundamental purpose of criminal justice. As a state senator, Deukmejian had authored a bill that restored the death penalty in California as well as laws mandating tougher sentencing for crimes involving guns. State attorney general Deukmejian reduced funding to the department's environmental protection unit while increasing spending in its criminal division. He also conducted a very public feud with the liberal Rose Bird, chief justice of the state supreme court. Capitalizing on public concern about crime, Governor Deukmejian pushed the legislature to adopt a 250-percent increase in state prison capacity and a 310-percent

increase in the budget of the Department of Corrections. As a result, between 1984 and 1994 California's prison population tripled.

On the other hand, the governor refused to allocate funds for infrastructure repairs. He opposed implementation of the Department of Transportation (DOT) freeway "retrofit" program, adopted after the 1971 San Fernando Valley earthquake. Neither Ronald Reagan nor Jerry Brown had supported roadwork projects, with predictable results. Indeed, when Oakland's Cypress Freeway collapsed in the 1989 Loma Prieta earthquake, killing dozens of motorists, critics claimed that the fatalities might have been avoided had the governors released DOT funds earmarked for earthquake reinforcement. Southern California's freeway system was tottering as well, as the 1994 Northridge quake revealed.

In 1986, Rose Bird and two other Jerry Brown supreme court appointees lost their reconfirmation bids, giving Gov. Deukmejian the opportunity to reshape the state's judiciary. By the time he left office, Deukmejian appointees dominated the court and three-fourths of the state judiciary overall. The state supreme court took a decidedly conservative turn. Even so, while the overall crime rate in the state declined, rates of violent crime increased.

A Technology Revolution

The "high-tech revolution" that created Silicon Valley and ultimately affected all of California occurred in two phases. First, in the 1920s Stanford University professor Frederick Terman encouraged formation of local electronics enterprises to rival those of Harvard and the Massachusetts Institute of Technology. Development progressed slowly until World War II, when former Stanford students William Hewlett and David Packard entered the field. The area's nascent electronics revolution came to fruition after the war. In 1956, Stanford's William Shockley described the principle of the transistor, a tiny device that reduced the size of electronic systems by replacing tubes and wired circuits. The idea had potential applications ranging from personal radios to missile guidance.

The next great breakthrough came three years later: the silicon microchip. Individuals working independently at different companies solved problems that hindered the integration of electronic circuitry. In 1959 Jack Kilby of Texas Instruments created the first prototype integrated chip and patented the principle of integration, setting off a patent war that would not be resolved until a 1966 cross-licensing agreement.

Bay Bridge Collapse, October 17, 1989
Following the Loma Prieta earthquake, a California Highway Patrol officer views the damage from the upper deck of the San Francisco–Oakland Bay Bridge collapsing onto the lower deck. *AP Photo/George Nikitin.*

The microchip's potential applications seemed limitless. A single chip incorporating thousands of circuits could store an incredible volume of information; execute multitudes of commands; and perform tasks as sophisticated as space navigation or as mundane as telling time. So tiny were the chips and so universal their applications that, once production consistency was achieved, the microchip made transistor-based systems obsolete.

New firms proliferated, joining the established giants: INTEL, Fairchild, National Semiconductor, and IBM. The chip's diminutive size, the presumed environmental friendliness of chip-manufacturing, and the ease of conducting research, development, marketing, and manufacturing at widely separated sites all contributed to high technology's unprecedented geographic mobility. By the early 1970s production facilities spread throughout the state.

The revolution's second phase flowed from continued technological development, which produced the personal computer (PC) and the software to guide it.

In 1976, Steve Jobs and Steve Wozniak formed Apple Computer Company and began to market their Apple II. One year later, Bill Gates and Paul Allen founded Microsoft in Seattle; when IBM introduced its PC in 1981, it was powered by Microsoft's disk-operating system. Microsoft's enormously successful Windows program came in 1985.

Subsequent developments were nothing short of explosive. Dozens of IBM clones appeared almost immediately, and Apple's Macintosh competed with the IBM version. Continuing research produced increasingly sophisticated software and made hardware cheaper and more efficient. Demand for PCs, components—microprocessors, motherboards, disk drives, and so forth—and the software programs required to run them seemed nearly insatiable. In 1985 just over 13 percent of U.S. households had PCs. Within five years, the number of households with PCs had doubled, and PCs were commonplace in the nation's businesses, libraries, and classrooms.

IBM Plant Development, San José, 1954–1984

During the post–World War II era, California became a Mecca for high-tech industries, with International Business Machines (IBM) among the leaders. In 1954, IBM purchased farmland for a plant site (*top*) adjacent to Highway 101 south of San José. A decade later (*center*) other industries had joined IBM in the Santa Clara Valley's fields and orchards. By 1984, agriculture had virtually disappeared, replaced by industrial, commercial, and residential development (*bottom*). *Courtesy of International Business Machines Corporation.*

The Internet was a related innovation. It emerged during the Cold War when military and scientific researchers sought a way to maintain communications during a nuclear war by global computer network. In 1983 the modern Internet was created when protocols for transmitting, routing, and receiving information were promulgated internationally. Known as Hyper Text Markup Language (HTML), this standardized language provided the world with an enormous source of information. Ten years later, this resource was available via "the World Wide Web" to anyone with a computer and a modem. These revolutionary changes in computer and communications technology placed California at the forefront of world technological innovation.

The social and cultural ramifications of the PC were so vast as to defy description. Words, for example, were no longer written or typed—they were "processed." Implications of the new technology ranged far beyond anything that early developers could have envisioned. To most observers, it promised unlimited benefits. High technology would expand employment and economic opportunities, accelerate advancements in telecommunications and medicine, create new consumer conveniences, and transform education.

By the mid-1980s, however, less sanguine commentators—Ian Rienecke and Theodore Roszak among them—expressed reservations. As acids and other toxins used in high-tech manufacturing seeped into water tables and wells, the potential for accidental release of deadly gases became apparent. Environmentalists denounced as illusion the industry's "clean" reputation. Law enforcement agencies likewise found the new technology a mixed blessing that could facilitate identification and the collection of data, but also spawn crimes, including counterfeiting, industrial espionage, and theft of the highly portable, easily disposable chips and components.

Most importantly, perhaps, were critics' warnings about job obsolescence and the absence of an internal promotion ladder within technology manufacturing. At the top were a handful of highly paid, upwardly mobile individuals in management, research and development, and marketing. Their remuneration contrasted sharply with the thousands of semi-skilled production and assembly workers at the bottom of the pyramid, workers toiling in a sanitized version of the nineteenth-century sweatshop.

The Arts

The 1960s, '70s, and '80s brought maturity, diversity, and national recognition to California culture. California artists participated in such movements as pop art, op art, and the geometric hard-edge school that reduced painting to the essentials of color and design. Pop art printmaker Ed Ruscha focused on the commonplace to produce works reminiscent of the earlier "Ashcan" school of painting. Cristo discarded tradition entirely to build his nylon "Running Fence" which from 1972 to 1976 stretched from the Marin hills to the Pacific Ocean.

Musicians contributed to California's vibrant arts scene. The influence of Dave Brubeck (1920–2012) on jazz continued, while Southern California's Beach Boys and their "surfin' sound" set trends in popular music. Joan Baez added a political dimension to the folk-music revival that began with the Works Progress Administration 1930s' efforts to preserve that genre. Classical music likewise achieved new vigor and popularity. From 1962 to 1978, the Los Angeles Philharmonic Orchestra attained great prominence under the baton of maestro Zubin Mehta. San Francisco's Symphony Orchestra advanced under the music director Seiji Ozawa (1970 to 1977) and Edo de Waart, who débuted there in 1975 and was music director from 1977 to 1985. A series of conductors—notably innovative African American Calvin Simmons, whose death in 1982 ended a brilliant career at age 32—breathed new life into the Oakland Symphony.

California cities also invested in sophisticated performance centers. In 1967, Los Angeles earned a place among the cultural centers of the West with the opening of its Music Center complex and Dorothy Chandler Pavilion. San José completed its Community Center in 1972, Oakland refurbished the Art Deco Paramount Theater in 1973, and performances began in San Francisco's Louise M. Davies Symphony Hall in 1980.

At the same time, Californians provided facilities to house art, historical documents, and scientific exhibits. During the 1960s, the Los Angeles County Museum modernized its facilities and added the Page Museum, devoted to prehistoric animal life. In 1986 the Los Angeles County Museum of Art opened the Robert O. Anderson Building. Almost simultaneously Los Angeles's Museum of Contemporary Art presented its first exhibit of work by practicing artists. In 1969, the new Oakland Museum launched its reputation as a leading collector and exhibitor of California art and historical artifacts. Five years later, the public gained access to Pasadena's Norton Simon Museum, housing the private art collection of industrialist Norton Simon (1907–1993), with European masterworks from the Renaissance to the twentieth century, and South and Southeast Asian art spanning 2,000 years. In 1981 Sacramento opened its California Railroad Museum, built collaboratively by

The Walt Disney Concert Hall, Home to the Los Angeles Philharmonic
Photo by John O'Neill.

the state and the Railroad and Locomotive Historical Society. Three years later, the Monterey Bay Aquarium opened on Cannery Row, endowed by the family of electronics magnate David Packard.

Some Californians believed the state's culture to be alive and well, but there were dissenters, including young writers who followed in the traditions of William Saroyan, John Steinbeck, and Nathanael West, whose works expressed pessimism about the so-called "California Dream." Ken Kesey's disturbing *One Flew Over the Cuckoo's Nest* (1962) reflected disenchantment with society's enforcement of arbitrary norms and a deep critique of treatment of the mentally ill. With wit and biting irony, Richard Brautigan's *Trout Fishing in America* (1967) denounced the demise of the environment and the values of rural-agrarian society. Joan Didion's essays in *Slouching Towards Bethlehem* (1968) and novels such as *A Book of Common Prayer* (1977) expressed nostalgia for a California-that-might-have-been. Simultaneously, established writers produced fine literature such as Wallace Stegner's Pulitzer-Prize winning *Angle of Repose* (1971). Gerald Haslam based his essays and short stories on the "other California" of the Central Valley and on "Okie" culture, later collected as *Snapshots* (1985), *Voices of a Place* (1987), and *Coming of Age in California* (1990).

Jefe Rojas

The Vaqueros' Homer

In 1987, writer Gerald Haslam introduced his readers to a unique Californio. Born in Pasadena in 1896, Arnold R. "*Jefe*" (Chief) Rojas was descended from the Sephardic Jews who fled Spain and the Inquisition during the sixteenth century, and from Yaqui and Mayo Indians who migrated from Mexico to California during the Spanish era. Following the untimely deaths of his parents, Rojas lived in an orphanage until he was twelve. His ambition to become a *vaquero* (and to avoid a life picking fruit) led to a stint as a novice rider on a ranch east of Paso Robles. Rojas later made his way to the San Joaquin Valley, where Miller and Lux, Inc., the Tejón Ranch Company, and others ran immense herds on thousand-plus acre spreads. In the valley, Rojas recalled, he "found the miracle of his youth, great ranches, horses to ride, and matchless story-tellers turning

(*continued . . .*)

back in retrospect the pages of their adventurous lives." For a quarter-century, Rojas learned the skills that had made his mentors expert at riding horses and managing cattle, and absorbed the lore and legend of an already-vanishing breed. In 1935, Rojas settled near Bakersfield where he established his own stable, the BAR-O, "because I had to borrow everything."

Despite only two or three years of formal education, Rojas' keen mind and curiosity led him through the literary canon, introducing him to the works of Alexander Dumas, Miguel de Cervantes, Rudyard Kipling, Robert Louis Stevenson, O. Henry, and Jack London. Also intriguing to him were the *chismes* (literally "bits of gossip") handed down from one generation of *vaqueros* to the next, which Rojas collected and published. His first volume, *California Vaqueros*, appeared in 1953. *The Lore of the California Vaquero* followed in 1958 and *The Last of the Vaqueros* in 1960, prompting a reviewer to declare "the *vaquero* has found his Homer!"

Rojas' work collected fading fragments of California's past: the experiences of *paisano*, *gringo*, Indian, and occasional black *vaqueros*, the alternating drudgery and excitement of their lives, the idiosyncrasies of the animals they handled, and the recollections of contemporaries and los *viejos* (old-timers). Vignettes recounted episodes involving California characters such as cattle baron Henry Miller and cattlewoman Mae Arnold, and preserved scraps of *el español que no está escrito* (the unwritten idiom peculiar to time and place). In the process, Rojas's lively pen demolished Hollywood's romanticized versions of cowboy history, with their low slung pistols, flashy outfits, and swaggering manners.

Jefe **Rojas, the** *Vaqueros'* **Homer**
Courtesy of Chuck Hitchcock, Shafter, California.

From his first book in 1953 to his last in 1979, *Vaqueros and Buckaroos*, *Jefe* Rojas demonstrated pride in his Mexican heritage, years before that expression became fashionable or politicized. When he died in September 1988, he left a singular legacy to the history of California culture: vivid sketches of a past that might otherwise have been lost and forgotten.

(WAB)

Writers drew upon personal history to describe the experiences of minorities in a white-dominated, frequently hostile society. In 1965, Luis Valdez's *El Teatro Campesino* dramatized both the cultural pride and bitter experiences of California farmworkers. His audience expanded with *El Teatro*'s 1976 European tour and, two years later, with his play *Zoot Suit*, based on Los Angeles's 1942 Sleepy Lagoon murders. In 1959, José Villareal published *Pocho*, a novel illuminating the cultural conflicts confronting Mexican migrants and their children. Maxine Hong Kingman pursued analo-

gous themes in *The Woman Warrior* (1976) and *China Men* (1980). In *Yellow Back Radio Broke Down* (1969) and *The Last Days of Louisiana Red* (1974), novelist Ishmael Reed challenged established African American literary canons.

Many younger Californians felt alienated by a repressive, materialistic, and militaristic society, as demonstrated by the war in Vietnam. By the mid-1960s, colonies of dissenters—called "hippies," "flower children," or the "love generation"—appeared throughout the nation. The largest concentration was in San Francisco's

Haight-Ashbury district, where young people claimed they were establishing a community based on love, peace, and individualism. In a sense, they followed in the state's utopian traditions. However, unlike their predecessors, the flower children lacked a cohesive philosophy on which to found their "Age of Aquarius." Instead, they vacillated among ideologies that ranged from astrology to Zen Buddhism, to the advice of Harvard professor Timothy Leary, whose mantra was "tune in, turn on, and drop out." Active use of mind-altering substances such as marijuana and LSD transformed the counterculture into a drug culture, often with tragic consequences. Health problems, antisocial behavior, psychosis, and drug-induced suicide were far too common.

Theodore Roszak assessed young dissenters' efforts to create a new society in *The Making of a Counterculture* (1969), but the hippies' greatest impact may have been on popular music. The laid-back "surfin' sound" of the Beach Boys gave way to the hard-driven, amplified, strobe-lit "acid rock" of groups like Jefferson Airplane and the Grateful Dead. Indeed, music marked both the apogee and perigee of hippie culture. Following San Francisco's 1967 "be-ins" and "summer of love," an estimated 300,000 gathered for a free Rolling Stones concert at Altamont Speedway east of Livermore late in 1969. During the performance, several people were severely beaten and one was killed. The "love generation" never quite recovered: by the mid-1970s, "yuppies" (young urban professionals) not hippies, occupied the gentrified Haight-Ashbury, which simply became a stop on the itineraries of curious tourists.

Cultural Diversity

Elusive or not, California's historic image as a western Eden gave the state its dynamic and shifting population. This trend continued through the 1970s and '80s, as the state and the nation experienced massive immigration. Unlike earlier eras, which experienced migration from other regions of the United States, national population increases after 1980 came primarily from overseas.

The U.S. Immigration Act of 1965 abandoned the national-origins-based policy of the 1920s. With new admission criteria based on education and occupation, the nation would accept 170,000 persons from the Eastern Hemisphere and 120,000 from the Western Hemisphere. Also, after withdrawing from Vietnam in 1975, the United States created a special category for refugees from Southeast Asia. As a result, the sources of immigration shifted dramatically: before 1965, 60 percent of

immigrants to the United States came from Europe. By the 1980s, more than 80 percent came from Asia and Latin America.

The Immigration Act of 1990 further raised the 1965 ceilings, providing greater encouragement to skilled workers, and setting aside a substantial number of visas for large investors. New immigration policies also permitted U.S. citizens to sponsor immigration by family members. Earlier immigrants became citizens and took advantage of this provision. By 2000 Immigration and Naturalization Service (INS) figures revealed that two-thirds of all legal immigrants had been family-sponsored.

National immigration policy changes opened California to an immigration surge from Asia and Latin America. At the end of the 1980s, over one-quarter of the state's population identified as Hispanic. Primarily of Mexican origin, California's 7.6 million Hispanics were concentrated in Southern California, especially East Los Angeles, the focal point of Mexican American life in California since the progressive era. Its residents had provided essential labor for the growth of manufacturing and industry in the city through the 1920s and again after World War II. Traditionally the distribution point for California's Mexican farm-labor force, East Los Angeles was alternately described as a "metropolis within a megalopolis" and one of the "ethnic marvels of urban America."

A number of factors spurred the growth of the state's Mexican American population and the development of East Los Angeles after World War II. The *bracero* program and postwar industrial and manufacturing development in Southern California attracted a large number of migrants, both legal and illegal. Mexican farm labor continued to look to César Chávez for leadership in the uphill struggle against California growers. After 1975 the organization of farm field labor was virtually stagnant, with Chávez's United Farm Workers struggling through a new grape boycott to maintain the small gains it had made in the 1970s, while "illegals" continued as a reliable source of inexpensive farm labor.

By the 1980s the changing nature of the state's economy, as it shifted to service and light-industrial-assembly occupations, reflected the availability of a large pool of low-wage, unskilled labor which, ironically, attracted additional Mexican immigration. In Mexico, declining economic conditions and a soaring birth rate provided the push for thousands to come to the United States. In East Los Angeles newcomers found a Spanish-speaking community, inexpensive housing, restaurants, and businesses catering to Mexican tastes, plus Spanish-language radio, television, and theater.

Mural on the Wall of a Neighborhood Food Market, Decoto District of Union City, California

California *barrios* experienced cultural revivals after 1960, made possible by renewed immigration and surging ethnic pride. A flowering of traditional Mexican mural art was one manifestation. This mural in the East Bay community of Union City celebrates Hispanic contributions to agriculture, achievements in education, and the political activism that in the early 1970s prevented the state from replacing the Decoto barrio with a new freeway. *Photograph by Richard J. Orsi.*

As the Mexican population of East Los Angeles expanded, residents expressed concerns about their quality of life. Postwar freeway construction had torn through the heart of the *barrio*, choking the district with traffic congestion and smog. Housing was scarce and of low quality. Schools were overcrowded, poorly attended, and understaffed, and the dropout rate of Mexican Americans was nearly twice that of non-Latina/o white students. The Chicano cultural and political movement of the 1960s and 1970s, along with that era's renaissance of Mexican art and literature, renewed interest in social, economic, and political change.

Meanwhile, the structure of California's Hispanic population became more complex in the 1980s, with increased legal and illegal immigration from Central America. The surge was due, in part, to American involvement in the civil wars of El Salvador and Nicaragua during the presidencies of Ronald Reagan. California's Hispanic population became more diverse in terms of nationality and culture, complicating Latina/o efforts to achieve a sense of community and to enhance their political power.

Community leaders shifted their focus of attention from farm workers to the urban residents of East Los Angeles and the San Francisco Bay region, which contained the third-largest concentration of Hispanics in the country, after Los Angeles and San Antonio, Texas. For many years Mexican Americans lacked political representation, especially in the city and county of Los Angeles. Unlike African Americans, Mexican Americans had not established effective national political organizations, and, in part because of language barriers, their political participation was minimal. In the 1970s more than half the eligible Hispanic voters in California were not even registered to vote.

This began to change in 1974, with the founding of grassroots Southwest Voter Registration Education

Project, the first and largest non-partisan Latina/o voter participation organization in the United States. Also important was William C. "Willie" Velasquez's Southwest Voter Registration Education Project (SVREP), founded the same year in San Antonio, Texas. Velasquez had been a co-founder of the Mexican American Youth Organization in 1965 and, in 1968, the independent third party La Raza Unida, prompting years of surveillance by the FBI. SVREP opened regional offices in Los Angeles in 1984. Over the next four decades, SVREP would register 2.5 million voters.

An early Latina standard-bearer was Los Angeles-born Gloria Molina, one of ten children born to a Mexican-American father and Mexican mother. Molina attended public schools, Rio Hondo Community College, and CSU Los Angeles. She supported herself as a legal secretary while attending college, earned an adult education certificate, and taught clerical skills at the East L.A. Skills Center. In 1982, Molina won election to the state assembly. Five years later, Molina won election to the Los Angeles City Council, where she served until 1991. She then won a seat on the County Board of Supervisors. Each election marked a first in the history of California Latinas.

By the end of the 1980s, 2.7 million Asians—primarily from China, Hong Kong, Taiwan, Korea, and the Philippines—lived in California, and 40 percent of all Asians in the United States were California residents. Asians accounted for almost 30 percent of San Francisco's total population. Fifteen years after the fall of Saigon, California counted more than 280,000 Vietnamese, with more than 63,000 just in Los Angeles.

To some extent, California's rapidly growing Filipino population reflected the repressive administration of Philippines president Ferdinand Marcos, whose regime collapsed in 1986. Filipino newcomers tended to be professionals. Nevertheless, like the Filipino agricultural workers who preceded them, the new arrivals

Vietnamese Refugees

American withdrawal from South Vietnam in 1975 was followed by the flight of thousands of refugees fleeing the North Vietnamese takeover. Many were processed at hastily constructed camps such as this one at California's Camp Pendleton Marine Corps base near San Diego. *Universal Images Group North America LLC / Alamy Stock Photo.*

faced discrimination in job placement. Many were forced to take positions for which they were overqualified. A growing influx from South Korea also boosted California's Asian population. Locating primarily in Los Angeles, Koreans gave the city the largest Korean population outside of Seoul, South Korea.

After decades of mistreatment, Japanese Californians scored a number of moral victories. In 1980 Congress established the Commission on Wartime Relocation and Internment of Civilians to investigate the circumstances of the mass removal of Japanese Americans. The commission later concluded that the evacuation resulted from "race prejudice, war hysteria, and a failure of political leadership," not "military necessity" as claimed at the time, an action that was "greatly unjust and deeply injurious."

The commission's investigation and passage of the federal Freedom of Information Act resulted in the release of previously suppressed documents that revealed that the government had withheld vital information relating to alleged "military necessity" in related Supreme Court cases. In 1984, U.S. District Court Judge Marilyn Hall Patel vacated the conviction of Oakland native Fred Korematsu, arrested for violating the 1942 evacuation order. In 1986 U.S. District Court Judge Donald

Voorhees invalidated the conviction of Seattle's Gordon Hirabayashi for his refusal to report for evacuation. Judge Voorhees ruled the government had engaged in "misconduct of the most fundamental character" in suppressing vital information to justify removal.

The commission's work prompted President Ronald Reagan to issue a formal apology to Japanese Americans for their treatment during World War II. Congress in 1988 appropriated $20,000 per person for reparations for all camp survivors (although payments were delayed for three more years). The negative popular response that followed the commission's reports and opposition to the financial reparations revealed that many Californians remained colossally ignorant of how Japanese Americans' civil rights had been violated.

Despite the civil rights successes of the 1960s and '70s, many black Californians continued to face severe economic problems. Civil-rights and fair-employment laws, antipoverty programs, and the end of legal school segregation brought only modest improvements in economic opportunity. Although subtle, barriers to racial justice remained and seldom attracted media attention. Unemployment, underemployment, and the complex problems of low-income, female-led households did not evoke the sense of moral indignation that fueled earlier

Japanese American National Museum, Los Angeles

Little Tokyo businessmen and veterans of WWII's famous 442nd Regimental Combat Unit first proposed the 85,000 square foot, $22 million Japanese American National Museum in 1982. State Senator Art Torres secured a funding bill to honor the "social, cultural, and economic" contributions made by California's Japanese. The complex was completed in 1992 and continues to bring the Japanese American experience to visitors. *Wikimedia Commons.*

civil-rights crusades. Opportunities had expanded for educated middle-class African Americans, but the lot of those without skills or education worsened, due in part to the loss of well-paid blue-collar jobs. African-American unemployment in the mid-1980s hovered at twice the general unemployment rate, and unemployment among black youth held at almost 40 percent. The black family's average annual income was only 60 percent of its white counterpart. For historian John Hope Franklin the civil rights movement of the 1950s and '60s remained "unfinished" in the '80s, which were characterized more by apathy than action.

Native Americans in California, on the other hand, could point to modest gains. In the 1980s, many groups still existed as more or less viable indigenous California tribes, distinct from the non-Indian population as well as from the Native Americans who had migrated to California. In 1986, for example, the tiny group of Tolowa of Del Norte County successfully applied to the federal government for tribal recognition. Decimated by disease and nineteenth-century campaigns of genocide, the Tolowa numbered about 150 in 1900, but by 1986 their numbers had grown to about 450, living in a remote section of northwestern California.

The most promising Native gain of the era, tribal gambling, began inauspiciously when the Cabazon Band of Mission Indians began running bingo and card games in a single-wide trailer on their Coachella Valley reservation. The games were open to the public and attracted both Indians and non-Indians. In 1983, the city of Indio, located seven miles away, raided the operation, shutting it down as a violation of Indio gambling ordinances. A protracted legal battle ensued. The Cabazon Band argued that theirs was a sovereign nation, therefore Indio had no legal authority to prohibit reservation bingo and card games. The suit ended in February 1983, when the 9th Circuit Court of Appeals ruled for the Cabazon.

Within days, the County of Riverside raided the Cabazon games, this time for violating county gambling ordinances. The tribe sued and ultimately won in 1986. Lawyers for the state of California appealed Riverside's loss, and the Morongo Band of Mission Indians of Riverside County allied themselves with the Cabazon in defending the Natives' victory. State attorneys argued that Indian gaming violated state law, even though California had legalized both high stakes poker and, in 1984, a statewide lottery. When the state lost in 1986, California appealed to the U.S. Supreme Court.

State attorneys argued that, in regulating tribal gaming, California was simply trying to prevent organized crime from infiltrating the reservations. Cabazon attorney Glenn Feldman countered that "California was trying to use a penal sanction to shut [the Cabazon] down and put them out of business permanently." Feldman argued that Washington could not push the concept of Indian self-determination and, at the same time, deny tribes opportunities to engage in economic development, and especially not in California, where gambling was legal. Indian cards and bingo funded reservation services that the state had never provided, without costing the federal government a penny. This, argued Feldman, was exactly what Washington had been telling Indians to do for centuries: "Don't rely on the federal government. Go out and raise the money yourselves and then provide services to your members, just like any government."

One year later, in the landmark *California v. Cabazon Band of Mission Indians* (1987), the U.S. Supreme Court sided 6–3 with the Cabazon. It held that, if state law prohibited a form of gambling, the tribes could not engage in that form. However, tribes could engage in any form of legal gambling, without state control.

California and other states next turned to Congress for the power to regulate Indian gaming. One year later, over tribal objections, Congress passed the 1988 Indian Gaming Regulatory Act (IGRA). Congress formally recognized the right of Native Americans to conduct gaming operations, but required tribes to negotiate gaming compacts with state governments. The IGRA gave state leaders leverage in their compact negotiations, approving or denying permission to play certain games and demanding other conditions. The IGRA permitted tribal gaming, but it set the stage for future conflicts between California Natives and state leaders.

Carmel Highlands, South of Point Lobos State Park
Preserving the beauty of such sublime stretches of coast proved to be one of the most ambitious, as well as frustrating, of California's environmental efforts. *Photograph by William A. Bullough.*

PART TEN

Environment and Society

Crisis in the Most Populous State

For Californians, the millennium waned and the twenty-first century dawned amid clouds of doubt. Theirs was the most materially successful of American states. Despite periodic setbacks, population had grown more consistently than in other states, often doubling about every 20 years. In 1968, California passed the 20-million mark, by 1990 the 30-million mark, by 2000, the state was home to 35 million people. In slightly more than one and a half centuries, California had developed from a remote, thinly settled colonial frontier into one of the nation's most productive and heterogeneous regions. Its varied economy was led by an agricultural system unrivaled in technology, organization, yield, and diversity. Its cities were large, complex, and affluent; its advanced high-technology industries set global standards for modern development. Only a handful of the world's nations, including the United States itself, could match California's total output of agriculture, industry, and services.

But after decades of soaring growth, complex new problems had slowed California's momentum for the first time after the 1960s. Rising foreign competition, inflation, and higher operating costs caused manufacturers of computers, automobiles, tires, steel, computer equipment, and other products to cut production, close factories, and shift operations to other states or countries. Birth and immigration rates declined beginning in the 1970s, threatening industries that relied on population growth: building, road, and utility construction; processing of lumber and building materials; education and other services. Southern and southwestern states increasingly outbid California for new migrants and industries. Immigration, especially from other countries, revived by the mid-1980s, and soared after the 1990s, but some worried that the Golden State had lost its luster.

441

California also showed the strains of overdevelopment, as resources supporting many industries became depleted. When the post–World War II boom ended, most of California's remaining resources—forests, petroleum and natural gas, farmland, scenery, open space, electricity, water, and even the air itself—seemed to teeter near exhaustion. Like overused older states to the east, much of California was congested, littered, polluted, and disfigured. Residents were destroying the unique natural heritage that provided their success. Even the state's human-built infrastructure, once the envy of the nation, gave signs of aging. Smog, traffic jams, urban sprawl, overcrowded parks, polluted water, crumbling bridges and dams, and crowded, outmoded classrooms were the most obvious manifestations of profound natural and built-environmental transformations. Each new thrust of economic development or population growth further upset the balance between humans and nature. Moreover, ever more rapid global climate change, especially warming and disruption of centuries-old precipitation patterns, intensified concern and complicated public policy. Nature was proving too intricate and unpredictable, and human knowledge too limited.

Non-environmental issues also perplexed Californians in the late twentieth- and early twenty-first centuries. Dramatic social and cultural changes swept the state in the post-war era, aggravating old problems and raising new ones. Declines in internal migration from other states and sharp increases in foreign immigration (legal and illegal) threatened to transform the state's racial and ethnic composition. The growing assertiveness of the historically voiceless—women, Native Americans, blacks, Hispanics, Asians, and others—complicated readjustment of the state's existing social, economic, and racial hierarchies. The newly politicized Californians vied against each other as well, demanding access to jobs, housing, and education, and striving for cultural and political influence. Increasingly troubling after the 1970s were high crime and drug abuse rates, shifts in moral and cultural values, crises in public education, rapid deterioration of public roads, buildings, parks, libraries, and water systems, problems compounded by natural disasters born of drought, fire, flood, and earthquake.

In the face of these challenges, state and local governments were increasingly drained of experienced leadership and financially strapped, hamstrung by rising prices, partisan bickering, and term-limits, and apparently no longer capable of dealing effectively with difficult problems. When economic recessions struck the state, bringing unemployment, poverty, and falling tax revenues, the state's difficulties reached crisis proportions. Post-millennial Californians seemed to have fragmented into competing special interest groups, sharply divided by regional, economic, party, and cultural differences, unable or unwilling to reach consensus on proposed solutions.

Along with the challenges of building a better balance between people and nature, such social, economic, cultural, and political issues cast shadows over the state's future, muting the carefree optimism that, for decades, characterized the typical Californian. More than any other part of the United States, California has long been acclaimed a paradise on earth, but it remains an elusive Eden.

California: Eden or Wasteland?

28

The "Not So Golden State"

By the 1960s, many of California's natural systems were already troubled. The state's population had tripled since World War II, with newcomers spread unevenly across the land. Affluent, skilled, and searching for a gentle climate, most flocked to coastal cities or moved to suburbs—where land and houses were cheaper—and commuted to work in private automobiles. By the mid-1960s, 80 percent of Californians inhabited its largest metropolitan areas, and more than half lived in southern counties.

While most Californians still rejoiced in their state's growth, a few lamented the destruction of its unique natural heritage. One of the earliest indictments of environmental decay was *California, Going, Going . . .* (1962). The booklet was published by California Tomorrow, a nonprofit educational group of writers and business and governmental leaders dedicated to "greater public awareness of the problems we face in maintaining a beautiful and productive California." A rare dissent to the state's worship of growth, the pamphlet was widely discussed and helped ignite California's subsequent environmental crusade. The group warned that environmental changes had accelerated since the 1940s. Rampant, unplanned population growth had consumed alarming amounts of land. Fast running out of open space, California had become congested and was overtaxing its air, water, forests, and wilderness. In the 1940s, smoke from orchard smudge pots clouded the Los Angeles air on a few winter days. Twenty years later, homes, factories, automobiles, and power stations belched 12,500 tons of contaminants per day into the air—80 percent from petroleum products—making Los Angeles notorious for its smog. By then, air pollution suffocated all California cities, at least sometimes, impairing the health of two of every five persons.

443

Two Views of Downtown Los Angeles

Two views of the same portion of downtown Los Angeles in the mid-1950s—on a clear day and on a smoggy day—illustrate the blanket of air pollution that has blighted the city, and other California urban areas, since World War II.
Courtesy of California Air Resources Control Board.

California was also destroying its waterways, as demonstrated by the Central Valley Water Project's undermining of the San Joaquin-Sacramento Delta's water quality by increasing salt content, reversing natural water channels, and threatening the survival of fresh- and saltwater-dependent species. The San Joaquin-Sacramento River Delta's crisis was symptomatic of broader statewide water problems. Sewage contaminated most inland waterways and the bays and harbors at San Francisco, Los Angeles, and San Diego, as well as offshore ocean water in many areas. One hundred industries, several cities, and countless ships were dumping pollutants into Los Angeles harbor alone, which had little freshwater flushing. By the 1960s virtually all of its marine life had vanished. According to California Tomorrow, some inland streams were so polluted that in summer they were essentially rivers of "sewage effluent." Particularly ominous were the thousands of chemicals, new just since the 1940s, that were making their way into the water and food chain, with unknown and perhaps permanently toxic results. The growing population was also "swallowing in huge gulps" the dwindling supply of the remaining pure water. With most rivers already impounded by the Central Valley Project and other systems, by the 1960s the gap between supply and demand was already greater than it had been before the projects began.

California Tomorrow writers also regretted that a "friendly invasion" of urbanites had ignited a "recreation explosion" that threatened wilderness with "general desecration." Beaches were crowded, cluttered, and closed to the public by landowners and developers. Offshore oil-drilling platforms loomed on the horizon of the Santa Barbara Channel. Off-road vehicles ravaged the deserts, leaving ruts and litter. Lumber companies clear-cut trees to feed the booming construction market, while forests disappeared, soil eroded, and watersheds weakened. No area was safe, no matter how remote. Samples of Sierra snows at 14,000 feet yielded traces of lead and other air pollutants.

California Tomorrow found that little was being done to control growth or reduce the harmful effects of environmental mayhem. Despite the efforts of well-meaning individuals and local governments, funds were short and regulations weak, and powerful development groups blocked more effective measures. As a result, natural conditions deteriorated more rapidly than solutions could be applied. In most areas, the worst was yet to come.

In the 1960s, scientists, scholars, writers, artists, journalists, and government officials joined California Tomorrow in warning of an environmental Armageddon. In contrast to California Tomorrow, which emphasized the economic problems caused by natural destruction, the angrier environmental critics rejected the materialistic, pro-development values that for so long had ruled the state. In *The Destruction of California* (1965), biologist Raymond F. Dasmann reserved special scorn for those Californians who were intent on building a world no one would want to inhabit. Greed and ignorance, Dasmann lamented, had turned California into the "not so golden state."

Twentieth-Century Conservation

Modern California environmentalism evolved from a vigorous tradition of conservation. Absorbed in commerce, most nineteenth- and early-twentieth-century Californians were apathetic if not hostile toward conservation. But by the turn of the century, an important minority dissented, and an American conservation movement was born. California's beauty attracted writers, artists, photographers, and scientists who were captivated by nature and concerned about its degradation. The University of California and Stanford acted as important organizing forces, providing funds, facilities, and experts for conservation efforts. San Francisco Bay Area citizens were particularly receptive to conservation ideas, furnishing leaders like John Muir. After his death in 1914, the Sierra Club helped keep alive this strong minority tradition of resource conservation and wilderness preservation. Smaller groups emerged, hoping to prevent the desecration of state landmarks and watersheds; they sometimes succeeded. Sequoia National Park (1890) and Big Basin Redwoods State Park (1902) grew from local preservationist movements. Particularly significant was the Save the Redwoods League, founded in 1918 by San Franciscans determined to buy surviving redwood groves and donate them to the state as parks.

At first, environmental organizations embraced two somewhat contradictory philosophies: utilitarianism and preservationism. On the one hand, they supported movements to reduce waste and exploit resources efficiently for long-range development. On the other, they worked to preserve some wilderness for present and future generations. In days when population was small, the parks were remote, and an optimistic faith in human progress prevailed, such contradictory goals seemed attainable. Only occasionally, as in the Hetch Hetchy case, did conservationists seriously differ among themselves or with dominant economic values.

Thus, railroads, lumber companies, and other California businesses with an interest in orderly growth or in promoting tourism often supported conservationism. Alliances with powerful groups brought conservationists notable victories. By the 1950s such coalitions had worked with government and private interests to create state agencies to manage resources, including the Board of Forestry (1905), Conservation Commission (1911), and Water Commission (1913). They had also set aside federal and state recreation and wilderness areas, administered by the National Park Service (1916) and the State Division of Beaches and Parks (1927). The state park system encompassed more than one hundred units, including more than 75,000 acres of redwood forest. Other federal lands were under various levels of protection by the U.S. Forest Service and the Bureau of Land Management. Large urban parks, such as Golden Gate Park in San Francisco, the East Bay Regional Parks system across the bay, Griffith Park in Los Angeles, and Balboa Park in San Diego, attempted to preserve natural settings in the midst of modern cities.

From Conservation to Environmentalism: The 1960s

The growing postwar environmental crisis forced a reassessment of traditional conservationism. The old strategy of exploiting resources more efficiently, while shielding small fragments of wilderness, failed to cope with rampant growth, and traditional conservation and wilderness preservation suffered from conflicting goals and interests. Resource exploitation and recreation, no matter how well planned, often clashed with wilderness preservation. In and around wilderness parks, the proliferating roads, campgrounds, and visitor businesses—along with continued mining, grazing, and logging—jeopardized precisely the natural ecosystems that were being saved. In resource and harvesting programs, extractive industries often dominated policy, environmental standards were lax, and public lands deteriorated. Even well-run conservation programs broke down under increased postwar use. Saving only bits of pristine nature had not worked, and the remaining wilderness appeared about to be lost forever. A new urgency gripped the conservation movement. "What we save in the next few years," David Brower, executive director of the Sierra Club, warned in 1960, "is all that will ever be saved."

By the 1960s changing scientific views were leading conservationists in new directions. The new science emphasized the interrelationships of nature's parts,

the importance of protecting all species to maintain genetic diversity, and the capacity for human-induced environmental changes to spread in dangerous and unexpected directions. Civilization, it was now thought, could survive only if it reestablished a harmony between people and environment. To accomplish this, the totality of nature, and the interrelations among species on which it relied, had to be preserved, not just isolated species or habitats, and further tampering must cease. This reassessment of humankind's dependence on the rest of nature called into question conventional forms of technological progress, as well as the practices in water development, land use, and wildlife management that conservationists had once condoned.

Conservationism thus evolved into modern environmentalism, noted for its emphasis on preservation of

Oil-Drilling Island

California's first offshore oil operation was hardly off shore at all. In 1957, Richfield Oil Company constructed an island connected by a quarter-mile causeway to the Ventura County shoreline. Decades later, with original palm plants grown to maturity, the island continues to function and to provide a backdrop for one of the state's favorite pastimes, surfing. Since the 1950s, however, drilling platforms have proliferated in the Santa Barbara Channel behind it. *Photograph by William A. Bullough.*

the environment as a whole; criticism of unrestrained economic and technological growth; apocalyptic concern for the future if environmental harmony is not restored; and refusal to compromise. The "ecology movement" appealed particularly to an expanding group of young, affluent, idealistic, and highly educated professionals who read widely, traveled, and appreciated wilderness. Ecology proved perhaps the most popular and enduring of the idealistic crusades of the 1960s. Concern for a common natural world cut across class, regional, gender, ethnic, and political lines.

Sensational incidents such as the 1969 Santa Barbara oil spill dramatized the grave ecological crisis and popularized environmentalism. Ignoring the objections of Santa Barbara Channel communities, the federal government in 1968 sold offshore drilling rights in the fragile area to a consortium of petroleum companies headed by Union Oil. Officials also waived existing safety regulations to allow drilling without the installation of casings to protect wells from breaks. On January 28, 1969, a Union well sprang underwater gas and oil leaks, and within days, a giant oil slick covered 600 square miles of ocean. Black, sticky, reeking oil sloshed across dozens of miles of treasured beaches and tidal pools. In subsequent months, thousands of oil-soaked shore birds and sea mammals died. Damage to boats and beachfront property ran to untold millions of dollars. By the time the spill was controlled more than a year later, it had developed into one of the worst human-caused ecological disasters in American history.

Public outrage at such tragedies curtailed oil drilling in sensitive coastal areas, tightened broader federal and state environmental regulations, and increased the membership and treasuries of ecology groups. By the early 1970s, public opinion polls disclosed that a majority of the state's people supported environmental preservation ideas and programs. Hitherto largely restricted to a social and intellectual elite, environmentalism had become popular. The movement flourished particularly around San Francisco Bay. By 1970 that region was home to one hundred environmental organizations. During the 1960s and '70s, the ecology movement went state- and nationwide.

California's growing environmental organizations also devised new tactics. Taking advantage of the movement's popularity, they modernized operations, organized broad membership drives, and undertook action on new fronts. The Sierra Club's membership, for example, swelled from 15,000 in 1960 to 30,000 in 1965 and, after the Santa Barbara oil spill, to 150,000 by 1974. Although still devoted to wilderness preservation, environmental

organizations moved into new policy areas, such as land use, water and air quality, population control, agriculture, chemical pollution, nuclear energy, and urban planning, often as opponents of business and governmental projects. A few paid professionals led a growing army of volunteers, often women, in projects that took on the intensity of crusades. The organizations raised large sums of money, employed modern media advertising, hired skilled attorneys to plead class-action cases, and became master gadflies and lobbyists.

Significantly, environmentalists entered electoral politics. They backed or opposed candidates for office based on their stands on environmental issues. Some militant ecologists themselves captured elective and appointed offices at the local, state, and national levels, dramatically changing the composition of officialdom. Whereas past political leaders had generally aligned with pro-development groups, the newcomers enacted new environmental laws and enforced old ones with new vigor. When entrenched interests blocked them, environmentalists turned to Progressive-era direct democracy measures— the referendum, initiative, and recall—to achieve some of their most notable victories. The decades from the 1960s into the early twenty-first century were a creative period in resource and environmental policy.

Building a Regulatory Framework

Initially most concerned about deteriorating air quality standards, California and other states pressed Congress to enact air-pollution legislation, since auto and oil companies, as well as many other industrial polluters, were national and international concerns and thus difficult to control locally. Congress responded with important environmental-policy acts in 1969 and 1970, and created the Environmental Protection Agency (EPA). The EPA has jurisdiction over federal environmental programs and requires an environmental-impact statement (EIS) and public hearings for federal actions with potential environmental influences.

At first, government agencies and private businesses ignored or subverted these laws. In the mid-1970s, however, environmentalists began suing under their provisions, with federal and state courts applying the acts broadly. Environmental lawsuits delayed or modified many large projects that otherwise would have sped to completion without challenge. Fearful of litigation, state agencies began enforcing the laws. By exposing environmental hazards, impact reports often caused projects to be altered or abandoned. Private and governmental developers began modifying proposals in advance to avoid environmental challenges. Although the EIS process has sometimes proved cumbersome and has delayed innocuous projects, the EPA and state agencies have generally used their new muscle to limit harm to natural systems.

The state created its own environmental protection agencies, especially after the Santa Barbara oil spill. In 1970, the legislature passed the California Environmental Quality Act (CEQA) in order to supplement federal legislation. Enacted over the objections of California business and labor groups who claimed it would stifle growth, the law required that an environmental impact report (EIR) be submitted for each major construction project or government proposal with potential environmental impact, and it empowered agencies to reject projects on environmental grounds.

Protecting Air Quality

Developing systems to control air pollution has also been a slow and arduous process. In the 1950s, California possessed only rudimentary environmental regulatory machinery, made up of a few agencies and largely relying on voluntary compliance by companies, individuals, and local governments. New regulatory structures were essential to combat the postwar environmental crisis. Although the outcry against smog grew intense in the late 1940s and early 1950s, authorities responded slowly. At first the cause of smog was unknown, and responsibility for solving the new problem fell to local governments. Los Angeles County, the first area to suffer severe smog, created an air-pollution-control district as early as 1947, but the agency made painfully little progress. The district identified the basic causes of smog, but it lacked the authority and technical knowledge to clean up the air. The district recommended methods for reducing pollution but its recommendations were generally ignored. Also, like most environmental problems, smog did not respect political boundaries. The origin of much pollution lay beyond the county's jurisdiction, and other local governments refused to cooperate in adopting remedies.

Obviously, broader agencies were needed. The San Francisco Bay Area led the way in 1955, founding a nine-county air-pollution-control district with authority to set air-quality standards and to regulate stationary sources of pollution. Los Angeles and other areas soon followed suit. Regional agencies banned backyard incinerators, regulated or eliminated agricultural burning, and forced reluctant industries to install smokestack emissions devices. While some progress was made toward muzzling stationary polluters, the automobile, responsible for 90 percent of urban smog, remained unregulated.

By 1960, public discontent over worsening smog compelled the legislature to pass the nation's first law forcing reduction of automobile-exhaust pollution. The act established the country's first air-quality standards and required automobile manufacturers to equip cars sold in California with emissions-reduction devices by 1966. California next established the Air Resources Board to sponsor research, set standards, and enforce the state's clean-air acts. In the 1970s the state further tightened air-quality regulations and fined automakers for selling cars that violated standards. In later years, the state mandated the sale of less-polluting gasoline blends.

The federal government offered additional support with the Clean Air acts of 1967 and 1970, both influenced by California's two decades of experience in smog control. Under the new laws, the federal government adopted air-quality standards even tougher than California's, eventually banning lead in gasolines used by new cars, establishing timetables by which automobiles and oil companies were to produce cleaner cars and fuels, and requiring states to formulate plans to meet federal clean air standards. The 1970 act and later amendments authorized the federal government to prohibit new construction and to withhold federal highway and sewer funds in states failing to meet air-quality standards.

By the 1970s, state and federal laws had somewhat cleared the air. Lead levels declined dramatically. In seriously blighted regions, smog alerts occurred less often. In some communities, expanded bus service, carpooling programs, and new mass-transit systems—such as the Bay Area Rapid Transit's electric trains, which started operating in 1971, and rail systems that opened in San Diego, Los Angeles, San José, and Sacramento in the 1980s and 1990s—wooed some commuters out of their cars. Of the state's major metropolitan areas, only the San Francisco Bay region, with naturally fresher air to begin with, quickly developed a plan that met federal air quality standards. Other areas followed, under increasing federal pressure.

Then and now, environmental regulations often provoke the ire of motor clubs, auto and petroleum companies, and other corporate polluters, which lobby constantly against controls. Some regulations have been weakened, as when the energy shortages of the 1970s provided a convenient excuse for doing so. The number of cars and industries has also soared with California's affluence and population growth. While the air freshened slightly in downtown Los Angeles and other smog centers, eyes smarted in areas never troubled before, particularly southern California suburbs, the inland southern desert, and Central Valley districts. Federal–state conflicts erupted repeatedly over the most effective and economical methods to attain air-quality standards. The state adopted a watered-down vehicle smog inspection system in 1984, later making it stricter and, eventually, mandatory.

New conflicts erupted between the state and federal government over gasoline additives in the mid-1990s, when, to satisfy federal clean-air regulations, California ordered MTBE blended into the reformulated gasoline required by the state. Refineries made this expensive change, prompting oil companies to abruptly raise gasoline prices (and profits) to the highest in the nation. When studies showed MTBE to be a dangerous carcinogen, particularly susceptible to leaking from underground storage tanks and destroying water supplies, California banned the additive. In 2001, newly inaugurated President George W. Bush responded to pressures from corn-growing, ethanol-producing, and heavily Republican midwestern states to mandate that California use that corn by-product. At a time when out-of-state monopolies also enforced high prices for the state's electricity and natural gas, Californians worried that importing huge amounts of ethanol—and again reformulating gasoline sold in-state—would further raise the price of gasoline and drain capital from the state.

State-federal conflict has not been the only hindrance to environmental protection: sometimes Californians resist as well. Since new regional air quality plans are likely to require drastic changes in business, employment, residence, and lifestyle patterns, some citizens and business groups have attacked air pollution plans, causing delays and enactment of weak plans that failed to meet EPA or court mandates. Moreover, relying as they often do on "market-based incentives" (i.e., higher auto and fuel prices and vehicle-use fees) to reduce driving, state and local plans provoke widespread resentment and opposition. As California's air grew cleaner, some complained that only the wealthy would be allowed to pollute it.

After nearly a decade of federal and state inaction under the administrations of Ronald Reagan and George Deukmejian, zeal for cleaning up the air returned in the late 1980s and early 1990s. A pioneer once more, California again tightened auto tailpipe emissions standards, required much cleaner fuels, and mandated that 10 percent of new vehicles sold in-state must meet zero-emissions standards by 2003. The state was well on its way to ridding its roads of combustion engines in 2017,

by which time Californians accounted for nearly half of all zero-emission vehicles (+250,000) in the nation.

With the nation's largest population and automobile market both in California, state standards have tended to become de facto national standards. Carmakers and petroleum companies must either meet California's standards or forego a very lucrative market, hence many now follow those standards. Other states have likewise raised their auto and fuel standards to meet California's. As a result, by the early twenty-first century growing numbers of U.S. cars met California's emission standards.

Water Pollution

Similar in operation to clean-air laws, state and federal water acts in the 1960s and '70s established minimum water-quality standards, required regions to develop implementation plans, set up enforcement agencies, and allocated funds for local water purification. Legislation established minimum water-quality standards and required regions to develop implementation plans and enforcement procedures. The laws also gave environmentalists new tools, especially the right to file lawsuits to compel enforcement of federal and state water-quality plans. Heading California's water-quality program, the Water Resources Control Board supplements the work of the federal agency. It has sponsored research, set higher water standards, and inspected water projects and sewage plants for compliance. Nine regional boards supplement the work of the state body.

Nevertheless, California's record of cleaning its waters has been spotty. Modern sewage treatment, highly effective against traditional organic contaminants, has recovered waterways and beaches for public use. Yet new synthetic chemicals continue to invade soils and surface and groundwater. Farmers, businesses, and homeowners casually release pesticides, herbicides, fertilizers, solvents, coolants, fuels, and industrial chemicals into California refuse dumps, soils, and waters. A 1979 Congressional study turned up 177 dangerous toxic dumps in California, leaking an estimated 60,000 to 70,000 different chemical compounds into its water systems. The long-range effects of most new chemicals are unknown, but initial tests suggest that many cause cancer, birth defects, neurological damage, and genetic mutations. Since most toxic wastes do not decompose and generally resist ordinary sewage processing, they lodge permanently in rivers, bays, groundwater, and the food chain.

In the 1970s and early 1980s growing public alarm prompted passage of state and federal regulations banning some chemicals, restricting their use and storage, regulating their disposal, and establishing procedures and liability for cleaning up spills. Worried Californians in November 1986 passed a stringent antitoxics initiative over the strong opposition of oil, chemical, and high-tech companies that contributed $3.7 million to defeat the measure. In the tradition of the state's trend-setting environmental regulation, the new law placed the burden on would-be toxic dischargers to prove that the chemicals are safe. The measure made it illegal to discharge chemicals causing cancer or birth defects into water supplies, held public officials criminally liable if they failed to act against illegal dumping of toxins, and allowed anyone to file suit to enforce toxics laws if the government failed to do so.

Since the 1980s, however, full enforcement of the law has been hampered by some governors, whose administrations have delayed identification of regulated toxins. Although helpful, environmental regulations are only effective when they are enforced. Federal and state rules often suffer from spotty enforcement, stingy budgets kept low by legislative opponents, and, occasionally, by collusion of public officials and corporate polluters. California's powerful petrochemicals industry and agricultural interests have also sometimes cooperated to hinder enactment and enforcement of higher standards.

"Save the Bay"

With its dramatic postwar growth and pro-ecology interests, California pioneered many new regulatory methods. The state also has invented new techniques of balancing economic need with environmental protection. The first and most important example was the "Save the Bay" movement. In 1846, San Francisco Bay was one of the largest and most beautiful inland estuaries, 50 miles long and encompassing 680 square miles. Eager to gain access to deep water and more level land for speculation, settlers began diking and filling the bay's shallow edges. After World War II, population growth and more powerful earth-moving machines increased pressure on the bay. Most of the shoreline was in the hands of private concerns plus dozens of independent, competitive local governments bent on making more room for industries, airports, warehouses, and garbage dumps. By 1960, filling had cut the Bay's area to 400 square miles. The public had access to only ten miles of the Bay's 276-mile shoreline. Each year earth-movers and paving crews gobbled up

another 2,300 acres of tidal flats and marshes, and more was fenced off, denying public access. By 2000, scientists predicted, the Bay would amount to only a few polluted channels. Although some environmental groups and newspapers denounced the abuse of a valuable regional resource, the Bay continued to shrink.

In 1961 several outraged Berkeley women started a citizen's revolution. Writers, naturalists, and civic leaders such as Kay Kerr, wife of the president of the University of California, founded the Save San Francisco Bay Association. They quickly attracted support from influential legislators, including Nicholas Petris (Oakland), Eugene McAteer (San Francisco), and Edwin Z'berg (Sacramento). For several years, Bay Area pro-development industries and local governments defeated Save-the-Bay bills in Sacramento, but by 1965 the association had the backing of 18,000 members and 18 of the region's 19 legislators. That year Petris and McAteer pushed through a bill that temporarily halted filling the Bay and created the San Francisco Bay Conservation and Development Commission (BCDC) to develop a protection plan.

Following hearings and studies, the BCDC recommended a tough "Bay Plan" to control filling and a regional agency to enforce its regulations. Fearing a precedent that could thwart development of their own coastlines, southern California businesses and governments joined Bay Area counterparts in opposing the Bay Plan. Environmental and civic groups fought back with a sophisticated media blitz. When Governor Reagan seemed poised to kill the plan, environmentalists presented him with 200,000 signatures on petitions that stretched three and one-half miles around the capitol. Buoyed by public concern in the wake of the Santa Barbara oil spill, the bill became law in 1969.

The BCDC was the first regional government imposed on an urban area by legislative fiat. Composed of representatives from concerned federal, state, and local agencies, the commission held independent jurisdiction over the Bay, tidal lands, marshes, salt ponds, and 100 feet of dry land beyond the shore. All projects affecting the water, bottom, shore, or shoreline and its structures required BCDC approval. Significantly, the act declared the estuary to be a regional rather than a private and local resource, and required a maximum of public access. The law permitted filling "only when public benefits from fill clearly exceed public detriment from the loss of water areas."

The BCDC developed the important principle of "tradeoff," or mitigation. To avoid blocking all development, the commission approved projects consistent with "public benefits" if government agencies or private

Restored San Francisco Bay Marshland

The San Francisco Bay National Wildlife Refuge was established by Congress in 1972 to protect marshes, tidal flats, and wildlife in the Bay and Delta, the Farralon Islands, Humboldt Bay, Salinas River, and elsewhere. The refuge also operates an environmental education program in Fremont for adults and elementary-school classes. At various points around San Francisco Bay, the refuge has experimented with restoring disturbed former marshland, such as this one, to its original condition. *USFWS.*

builders opened up land or improved public access elsewhere on the Bay. Such procedures made the BCDC one of the most effective environmental agencies in the nation. Despite criticism from both extreme environmentalists and developers, the BCDC's decisions have been widely supported and rarely challenged in court. Knowing requirements in advance, developers build tradeoff features into their proposals, and regional, state, and federal environmental programs have adopted the tradeoff and other BCDC innovations.

Under the BCDC's guidance, the estuary began to recover. The commission not only arrested the Bay's shrinkage, it opened hundreds of acres of formerly filled or diked land to the tides. Although the BCDC approved an annual average of $100 million worth of developments, the Bay is larger today than in 1965. Because of

the commission's actions and sewage cleanup under other state and federal laws, water purity generally improved into the 1980s. Beaches reopened and fishing revived. The area of public access increased to 90 miles of shoreline, encompassing more than 30 parks and nature preserves. As one of its former chairmen put it, the BCDC has struck "a balance between conservation and development" that is a model for environmental action.

The decommissioning of San Francisco's Presidio offered the BCDC a unique opportunity in 1994, when the former military base and Crissy Field were turned over to the National Park Service. Public and private donors raised $34.5 million to transform a dump and asphalt parking lot into a 100-acre national park, with an 18-acre tidal marsh linked to San Francisco Bay, 16 acres of dune habitat, and 105 different species of shrubs, wildflowers, and marsh plants. More than 230,000 cubic yards of dirt, sand, and mud were excavated and a channel opened to the tides in November 1999, allowing fresh and saltwater to merge along San Francisco's Marina for the first time in 100 years.

Yet despite decades of struggle to save it, San Francisco Bay remains endangered. Raw sewage outflow declined in the 1970s, but in the 1980s toxic chemical discharges increased sharply, making portions of the Bay among the most dangerously polluted waters in the world. At the same time, inland water projects further diminished the outflows of fresh water through the estuary to 40 percent of natural levels, enough to threaten the Bay's ability to support animal and plant life. Outflow from sewer systems and agricultural drains, increased diversion by existing and new water facilities, as well as recurrent pressure to ship yet more northern water south, bypassing the Delta and Bay, would compound an already serious problem.

The Delta and the Peripheral Canal

The clash between traditional growth interests and Californians favoring environmental preservation is particularly clear in the spectacular battle over the Peripheral Canal. By the 1960s, federal and state water experts were seeking ways to export additional northern river water to Southern California before the purer water mixed with the increasingly salt-polluted Delta. They decided a canal was the answer. An addition to the U.S. Bureau of Reclamation's 1930s Central Valley Project (CVP), the canal proposed in 1963 called for a new concrete trough 43 miles long and more than 100 yards wide to carry freshwater from the upstream Sacramento River system, around the eastern and southern edges of the Delta, and directly into the existing canal that carried water south. As designed, it would be able to divert as much as 700,000 acre-feet of water—more than half of the Sacramento's flow in

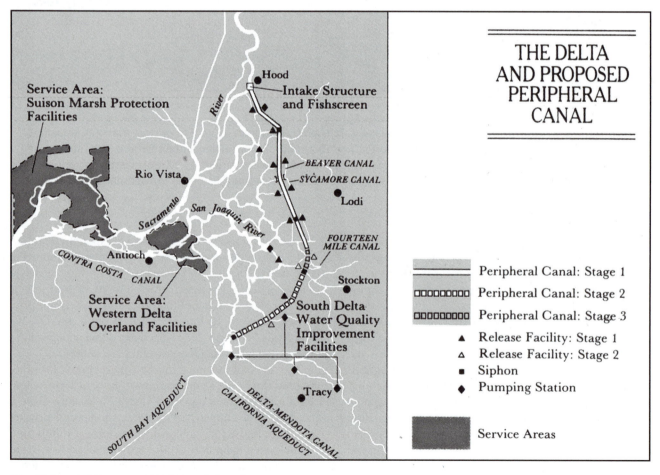

The Delta and Proposed Peripheral Canal

wet years, all of it in dry seasons—directly into export pumps and thence to Southern California.

When the federal government decided not to build the canal, California water agencies adopted it to solve the state's water problems. The limits on California Water Plan (CWP) water sent to the south state could be greatly increased without endangering the purity of the export water, by what the state now called the "Peripheral Canal," which would bypass the salt-plagued Delta. To partially compensate for the additional water diversion, the state proposed that the canal, as it made the eastern circuit, would release 10 percent of the water back into Delta channels to reduce saltwater intrusion and maintain a healthier environment for fish, birds, boaters, hunters, farmers, and town dwellers. By the mid-1960s, state construction of the Peripheral Canal quickly gained the support of state and federal water agencies, southern water users, the California Department of Fish and Game, and even, initially, some environmentalists. In 1965 the California Department of Water Resources approved the building of the canal, which was scheduled for completion in 1975.

However, as details about the project surfaced and were analyzed, opposition mounted. In 1969, local Delta water agencies condemned the Peripheral Canal because its even greater water diversions threatened local water rights and quality. Regional representatives assailed the plan in public hearings, Congress, and the legislature. Yet despite increasing opposition, planning continued. State leaders favored a joint federal-state facility to serve both the CVP and the CWP, hoping to secure federal funding without relinquishing state control. When he was elected, Gov. Ronald Reagan pushed the project forward and, in 1971, when talks with federal agencies proved unsatisfactory, he announced that California would build the canal alone.

Although construction now seemed inevitable, opposition intensified, especially in the San Francisco Bay Area. By the early 1970s, regional newspapers, local governments, business and farm groups, and political leaders became united against the canal and for protecting the Delta. As always, competing economic and regional interests dominated the debate, but environmentalists voiced objections as well. They charged that the project would reduce the Delta, which already had too little fresh-water flushing, to a reeking cesspool, injuring waters, habitats, and species in the Central Valley, San Francisco Bay, and the ocean beyond the Golden Gate. The canal, they warned, would accelerate destruction of northern California's rivers and wilderness areas, and encourage yet more unchecked sprawl

down south, where air, space, land, and the broader natural environment were already strained to the breaking point. Many Californians agreed. Agitated by the recent Santa Barbara oil spill, membership in anti-canal and ecology-oriented organizations rose swiftly.

At first canal opposition was a mostly northern movement. Soon an anti-canal alliance cut across political parties and economic ideologies. Turning to the courts, canal opponents used the 1970 federal act requiring detailed environmental-impact studies to sue and delay construction of the canal and other water projects. When court-ordered environmental studies concluded that the canal would indeed aggravate water problems, respected scientists joined a growing number of governmental agencies in criticizing the plan.

Late in 1974, only one year before construction was scheduled to begin, the state senate's Natural Resources Committee reported that the environmental effects of the canal were uncertain, federal cooperation was unlikely, and that the entire project was "premature." New governor Jerry Brown ordered additional studies and, in contrast to his predecessors, opposed the canal as incompatible with his "era of limits" philosophy. By 1975, the canal seemed doomed. For the first time, environmentalists had successfully intervened in state water policy and politics.

Opposition to the canal lost steam, however, when California fell into one of its most severe droughts from 1975 to 1977. Dire water shortages immediately bolstered support for the Peripheral Canal. Southern California cities and San Joaquin Valley agribusiness demanded the canal to greatly increase water imports from the north to compensate for the drought, as well as to irrigate additional farm acreage and to provide for the continued population growth. Southern canal supporters opposed all restrictions on water exports from the north and environmental protection measures for the Delta, San Francisco Bay, and northern rivers. Further conflicts erupted in 1976, when the Bureau of Reclamation refused to furnish water to flush the Delta, declaring that, as a federal agency, it was not bound by state water rules. To prevent serious saltwater intrusion into the Delta during the drought, state water agencies were forced to cut deliveries to some California Water Plan users, prompting them to file (unsuccessful) court motions to prevent the state from "wasting" water to preserve the Delta. Canal critics became convinced that southerners were indifferent—if not hostile—to northern water rights.

Despite state water releases, saltwater invaded the Delta as never before, polluting the region's supplies and threatening to flow directly into export pumps. The 1975–77 drought left state water experts even more convinced that a bypass canal was necessary. Pressured by agribusiness, southern Californians, and his own advisers, the previously dubious Gov. Brown switched sides and threw his support behind construction of a modified Peripheral Canal. Building the canal was to be contingent on federal agreement finally to follow state water quality standards for the Delta and federal commitment to protecting northern rivers and streams. Northern opposition forces prevailed, however, and the legislature defeated Brown's bill in February 1978.

Undaunted, Brown reintroduced the package in 1979 as SB200. Now united in support were state water departments, southern water agencies, agribusiness, and land-development firms, as well as the state Chamber of Commerce. This time the legislature approved the plan, along with a compromise to northern interests, a constitutional amendment protecting the Delta and north-coast rivers, to be put before voters for approval. In a dramatic televised ceremony, Gov. Brown signed the bill on July 18, 1980. He reassured voters that California's future hinged on shipping more water south, that the Peripheral Canal was the best method, and that the proposed constitutional amendment would protect northern waterways. "California's water wars," Gov. Brown declared, "are at an end."

But state leaders had not reckoned on the intensity of public feeling. Passage of the 1980 canal bill galvanized northern and environmentalist opponents as never before, resulting in the quick collection of 840,000 signatures—more than double the required number—to make Proposition 9, the Peripheral Canal Referendum, the first voter referendum on a legislative act in 30 years. Placed on the June 1982 ballot, the referendum set the stage for a colossal north-south confrontation, with southern counties strongly in favor and northern counties just as strongly opposed. The Proposition 9 campaign grew increasingly bitter as election day approached. Northerners vowed to allow no more water to flow south. When asked in a televised interview how far water development should go, one Kern County spokesman said, "We won't rest until not a drop of California water flows down to the sea." Shocked by the popular vehemence, Gov. Brown, now running for a U.S. Senate seat, quickly disassociated himself from the project, saying he was too busy fighting crime.

On June 8, 1982, primary election voters overwhelmingly rejected the canal and, in the later general election, Brown's Senate bid. Voter turnout was high throughout the north, where "no" votes were nearly unanimous, delivering one of the most lopsided elections in U.S. history. It was a stunning expression of California voter opposition to environmental manipulation, and the first defeat at the polls for a major state water project.

The Limits of Regional Planning: The Coast and Lake Tahoe

From the 1960s to the 1980s California attempted to solve environmental dilemmas with regional planning and regulatory agencies, many patterned after the Bay Conservation and Development Commission. But duplicating these successes proved difficult in areas where the traditions of regional consciousness and environmentalism were weaker, as suggested by the ambitious, yet conflict-ridden Coastal and Lake Tahoe commissions.

By the 1970s, helter-skelter development had blighted scenery and natural ecologies. California's coast was lined with refineries, power plants, and a jumble of commercial and residential subdivisions. Public access to the beaches remained unenforced, though required by the state constitution. Inspired by the Save-the-Bay movement and the Santa Barbara oil spill, environmental activists were determined to wrest control over coastal planning from private developers and compliant local governments. Already stung by establishment of the BCDC, oil and utility companies, real estate developers, building-trades unions, and local officials squashed several attempts to get coastal conservation bills through the legislature.

In 1971, coastal conservationists changed tactics and appealed directly to the electorate through the nonpartisan Coastal Alliance, which had the backing of 700 state organizations, including conservationists, women, laborers, sports enthusiasts, university students, senior citizens, and civic leaders. In 1972, when the legislature again rejected a coastal plan, the coalition easily collected 418,000 signatures in less than a month to place Proposition 20 on the November ballot. Opponents hired a public relations firm experienced in pro-business ballot measures and mounted a lavish television ad campaign aimed at fooling voters into thinking that a "no" vote was a vote to "Save the Coast." Lacking a large fund, the alliance mustered hundreds of affiliated groups and thousands of volunteers, and used the news media to gain free publicity with events like the "Great Coast Bike Ride" from San Francisco to San Diego. Prop 20 passed with 55 percent of the vote, a showing that astonished political experts.

The 1972 initiative created a temporary Coastal Commission to control development projects and draw up a permanent protection plan to be submitted to the legislature by 1976. Opponents regrouped to block the plan in the legislature, but environmental groups once again demonstrated their mastery of practical politics by electing pro-conservation representatives to the legislature and several key committees. Threatening opponents with another initiative, coastal protectionists and opponents worked out a compromise bill. When the new bill still fell short by one senate vote, Gov. Jerry Brown saved the day. A latecomer to the movement, Brown secured a reluctant endorsement by the California AFL-CIO, and the California Coastal Act of 1976 narrowly passed. The Act established a state Coastal Commission and six temporary regional commissions, charged overall with reducing congestion, minimizing earth slides and air and water pollution, improving public access to the shore, and protecting the coast's natural beauty. The Commission claimed development jurisdiction over the shoreline between 1,000 yards inland and three miles out to sea. The act had an immediate impact, stopping or modifying thousands of projects. One report concluded that, collectively, the coastal commission was "the most powerful state land-use regulatory body and the most powerful state coastal management agency in the United States."

Unlike the Bay Plan, however, coastal conservation provoked controversy. Regional commissions often challenged the state body, especially when the regional commissions favored development and the state did not, prompting localities to accuse the state agency of radical and elitist values. Relentlessly attacking the commission and the Coastal Act itself, opponents to coastal management introduced bills in the late 1970s and early '80s to cut the commission's budgets, exempt certain areas from its jurisdiction, reduce its general authority, and repeal the coastal program entirely. Many of these weakening measures passed. When the regional bodies were phased out in 1981, pro-development local governments strengthened their influence over coastal management under their own regional conservation plans.

The state commission itself became less environmentally protective after 1981, when half its members were replaced by officials from coastal counties. In 1982 pro-development forces gained an ally in the new governor, George Deukmejian, who had campaigned on the promise to cut back environmental programs, particularly coastal conservation, in the interest of jobs, energy, the economy, and business growth. In 1983, Gov. Deukmejian cut the commission's budget by 19 percent and its staff of experts by 25 percent. Although he had vowed

to one day abolish the Coastal Commission, he failed to inflict further damage. Working with later governors, successive attorneys general, the state departments of Parks and Recreation and Fish and Game, the Coastal Commission used the mitigation techniques pioneered by the BCDC to achieve some of its original goals, including convincing Indian tribes to build planned casinos away from the coast. Nevertheless, coastal protection remains tenuous, as opponents to coastal protection create ways to weaken the commission, especially its budget and ability to litigate. Particularly troubling was a cost-saving measure in the 2010–11 state budget that limited the commission's access to state legal services.

Regional planning for the Lake Tahoe basin took a somewhat different path. Straddling the California-Nevada border 6,200 feet high in the Sierra, Tahoe is one of the world's highest, deepest, and clearest large lakes. In the 1860s Mark Twain described it as "the fairest picture the whole earth affords." But recreation and population development after 1950 strained the environmentally sensitive lake basin. Unsightly buildings crowded the shore, tree-cutting and land-disturbance aggravated erosion, and silt, sewage, and chemical runoff contaminated the lake. Water clarity was declining, and algae scum blighted the shore during drought periods. Long lines of automobiles creeping along the mountain roads generated smog. Despite clear signs of environmental overload, ever more land continued to be subdivided for hotels, casinos, shopping centers, and vacation homes.

With jurisdiction over the area divided among two states, half a dozen counties, and numerous local, state, and national agencies, an interstate approach was needed to protect the lake. In 1969, California, Nevada, and the federal government established the Tahoe Regional Planning Agency (TRPA), with local and statewide representatives from both states empowered to manage growth and halt environmental decay. Since its inception, however, TRPA has been unable, or unwilling, to slow development. The agency's charter made it prone to dominance by local members, who usually represented local businesses and landowners. Moreover, although California's delegates generally favored conservation, Nevada's favored east-shore development. Since a majority of each state's delegates had to approve environmental standards, Nevada could veto most protective proposals.

After 1969 TRPA permitted building with minimal changes. Despite California's independent efforts to reduce sewage discharge, erosion, and subdivision of fragile lots along its shore, the basin continued to deteriorate. In 1979, frustrated by years of friction with TRPA,

California cut off its funding of the agency. Threatened with federal intervention, Nevada agreed to a revised contract with California requiring TRPA to devise a stricter environmental plan by 1983. Local and Nevada delegates still resisted, however, and TRPA issued permits as liberally as before. After the body neared agreement on a moderately conservationist plan, early in 1983 Governor Deukmejian, not a friend of environmental protection, replaced California's most outspoken environmentalists with pro-development representatives. Finally, after years of internal wrangling and explosive meetings, TRPA adopted a 20-year plan in April 1984. A substantial victory for developers, the document established only mild conservation standards. It also returned control over zoning and permits to local governments, in effect granting builders free rein.

Minutes after TRPA adopted its plan, California Attorney General John Van de Kamp and the League to Save Lake Tahoe sued the agency in federal court. In a ruling upheld by the federal Court of Appeals in July 1985, a federal judge found that the proposed TRPA plan "clearly violates the requirements" of the law and could lead to "the deterioration of the unique environmental and ecological qualities of the region." The court suspended the plan and halted all new construction in the region. Furious Nevada legislators threatened to withdraw their state from the TRPA compact, but other parties worked to find a compromise. In 1992, TRPA's long-delayed regional plan was finally announced. Although its measures went further to limit building permits, traffic, and air pollution, critics believed the plan failed to address the environmentally sensitive region's central problem: overdevelopment. TRPA continued to draw fire from local development interests that wanted the agency abolished, as well as environmental supporters opposed to the agency's continued approval of large developments.

In early 1994, the League to Save Lake Tahoe again sued TRPA, alleging it had failed to meet its obligations.

In the summer of 1996, at a well-publicized meeting of Lake Tahoe regulation agencies and specialists on the lake and region, President Bill Clinton promised federal cooperation and funds for new initiatives in a massive cleanup of the lake's waters and reversal of regional forest and land development problems. Building on the new optimism, UC Davis led an interdisciplinary and interagency project to establish a research institute at the lake to recommend solutions to the region's complex environmental problems. In the late 1990s, agreement was reached on programs to clear excessive forest growth and drought-killed trees to reduce the severe fire danger in the basin. Limited mass transit was also introduced in hopes of reducing automobile use and air pollution.

Nevertheless, the natural qualities of Lake Tahoe and its basin continued to deteriorate and agreement among involved interests remained elusive. For one example, in the 1990s, high levels of MTBE from new gasoline blends began to appear in the lake and the region's groundwater, shutting down wells and producing water shortage emergencies in South Shore resort towns. When TRPA attempted to ban the use of single-stroke boat engines, which dump up to 40 percent of their gasoline directly into the lake, boat owners and manufacturers counterattacked with lawsuits. Similarly, when TRPA approved developers' plans to tear down a mobile home park and replace it with the luxury Tahoe Beach Club, with 143 residences, 270 feet of private beach, and a private restaurant, a Sacramento federal judge in 2010 threw out a TRPA plan to add 2,000-plus buoys, piers, ramps and boat slips along the shoreline. In later years, more controversy has surrounded a new TRPA plan to accommodate continued growth in the area, while saving some remaining less-developed shoreline, by encouraging more concentrated, high-rise construction, in effect urbanizing the lake. To the casual eye, Lake Tahoe looks clear and blue, but whether or not it stays that way remains to be seen.

Ansel Adams

Californian

Photographer Ted Orland observed, quite accurately, that when visitors to California's best-known national park snap their camera shutters, many "hope that . . . the result will not simply look like Yosemite . . . [but] like an Ansel Adams photograph of Yosemite." Adams' name became familiar to the public and synonymous with the park only in the 1960s, but the association began much earlier. In 1916, when he was a 14-year-old San Francisco music student, he used a box camera to take his first photograph in the valley. A decade later he gave up classical piano to begin his life's work: promoting photography as an art form distinct from painting, and advancing the cause of wilderness preservation.

As a young man, Adams supported himself through commercial photography and operating Best's Studio in Yosemite. At the same time, he promoted his art by joining with Imogen Cunningham, Edward Weston, and other Californians in Group f/64, exhibiting his work at the De Young Museum in San Francisco (1932) and at Alfred Stieglitz's *An American Place in New York City* (1936). In 1940, he cofounded the Department of Photography at the New York Museum of Modern Art (MOMA). Through the 1940s Adams taught at art schools in Los Angeles and San Francisco while perfecting his Zone System technique. When he worked for the Office of War Information during WWII, he experienced his first political controversy. Adams photographed Japanese–American internees at Manzanar, but when MOMA exhibited the images, entitled "Born Free and Equal" in 1944, both his pictures and his commentaries encountered heavy censorship. During the 1950s and '60s, however, Adams's photographs began to receive public attention and critical approval. In 1967, he cofounded The Friends of Photography and he remained an active leader of the organization until his death in 1984.

While promoting photography, Adams advocated environmental preservation with equal energy and dedication. He joined the Sierra Club in 1919 and served the organization in capacities ranging from curator, guide, and photographer, to board member. In 1978, the club made Adams an honorary vice president. He drew public attention to the conservationist cause through numerous articles, books, and portfolios of prints; advised presidents Gerald Ford and Jimmy Carter on environmental issues; and openly and vigorously denounced the policies of the Reagan administration.

For his efforts on behalf of the environment, Adams received the Sierra Club's John Muir Award (1963), the Interior Department's Conservation Service Award (1968), and the Wilderness Society's first Ansel Adams Award for Conservation (1980). In 1980, Adams received the Presidential Medal of Freedom, his most treasured recognition. Other tributes to his work included three Guggenheim Fellowships, commendation by the state senate (1963) and assembly (1983), awards from photographic societies around the world, and honorary degrees from several universities. The most appropriate honor, however, came posthumously in 1985, when a peak in Yosemite National Park was named Mount Ansel Adams.   (WAB)

Ansel Adams with Light Meter and Camera on Tripod

J. Malcolm Greany, circa 1950.

Parks and Wilderness Areas

To preserve a vestige of California's vanishing natural lands, after 1960 federal, state, and local governments expanded wilderness, recreation, and open-space preserves. Since much undeveloped land in the mountains, forests, and southern deserts remained under federal ownership, U.S. government actions were crucial. As they had for a century, federal land policies became battlegrounds between those who advocated reservations for wilderness or public use and those eager to exploit them for private gain.

In the 1960s, the Sierra Club and other national environmental groups worked for a large Redwood National

Park along the northwest coast, a last-ditch effort to save a few remaining virgin redwoods, including a grove of the world's tallest trees that had recently been discovered east of Orick. The bill was vigorously opposed by the Save the Redwoods League, a traditional conservation group that protested that the state had already preserved enough representative groves. It also faced opposition by north-coast lumber companies, workers, and local governments. Gov. Reagan was apathetic, reportedly quipping, "When you've seen one redwood tree, you've seen them all."

Under strong pressure from preservation-oriented President Lyndon Johnson, Congress passed a compromise bill in 1968 creating a small park of separate groves. As nearby logging threatened to destroy the protected groves, a worldwide cry went out to "save the redwoods" by adding the entire ecological zone around the groves to the national park. On the chance that the park might be expanded, lumber companies quickly clear-cut the forests right up to the old park border. By the time Congress finally enlarged the park in 1978, much of the newly protected land had already been stripped.

Federal protection also began to be extended over remaining open space within or near cities. In 1972 the Golden Gate National Recreation Area and the San Francisco Bay Wildlife Refuge were formed to preserve hills, beaches, marshes, tidelands, and islands interspersed along the region's urbanized coasts. The proposed Santa Monica Mountains National Recreation Area, created by Congress in 1978 to protect one of the only remaining large tracts of open land near congested Los Angeles, was stalled in the early 1980s by land developers and President Reagan's administration, which refused to spend money already appropriated to buy lands. The Los Angeles *Times* condemned the inaction as an "outrage against the millions of people . . . who are being robbed of a park." By the time the lands were purchased, shortages of national parks' operating funds prevented their proper development as parks. Later, under subsequent presidents, the Santa Monica Mountains Area was elevated to park status.

Important decisions still loomed regarding the fate of millions of acres of remote federally managed public lands in the state, lands belonging to all Americans. Environmental groups, supported by most California congressional representatives and state officials, urged that a maximum area of public land be designated as wilderness and closed to economic development. Pro-development groups, championed by the administrations of Reagan and George H.W. Bush (and, after 2016, by Donald Trump), pressed to have much of the land sold or leased at very low prices for grazing, mining, lumbering, oil drilling, and subdividing. However, California's U.S. senators Alan Cranston, a Democrat, and Pete Wilson, a Republican, were finally able to push a compromise through Congress in 1984, designating 1.8 million acres of federal lands in California as protected wilderness or scenic areas, and opening up another 1.2 million acres to development.

The most ambitious proposal to preserve federal lands was the attempt to create new and expand existing national park and wilderness areas in the public land remaining in southern and eastern California deserts. These were sites of stunning landscapes, endangered species, and early Native peoples' historic resources, but they were declining rapidly under pressure from developers. Written by the Sierra Club and introduced by Senator Cranston in 1986, the California Desert Protection Act became one of the most controversial land-use proposals in U.S. history. Opponents included local development interests, mining companies, livestock grazers, hunters, and off-road vehicle users, this time along with Sen. Pete Wilson, Cranston's successor after 1990, John Seymour, and officials of the Reagan and Bush administrations. Reintroduced each congressional session, the desert act, though widely supported by the public and in the House of Representatives, was repeatedly defeated by opponents in the Senate. The prospects for California desert protection brightened in 1992 with the simultaneous election of two new Democratic senators from California, Dianne Feinstein and Barbara Boxer, and President Bill Clinton, all of whom favored the park. Nevertheless, as the 1994 Congressional session drew to a close, the bill was again blocked by filibusters. Senator Feinstein amended the bill to satisfy most opponents and deftly maneuvered around the filibuster. In early October 1994, the desert bill, the most extensive land preservation measure in national history, cleared Congress, designating 7.5 million acres as protected wilderness, elevating Death Valley and Joshua Tree national monuments to national park status, and creating the 1.4 million-acre East Mojave National Preserve.

National, state, local, and regional park systems continued to expand. California voters passed several large bond issues to improve existing parks and acquire new ones. By the mid-1990s the state park system had increased to nearly 300 units, encompassing more than one million acres. This included the decommissioned San Francisco Presidio military installation, founded by Spanish colonists in 1776 and still filled with historic structures. Although converted into one of the nation's largest urban national parks, it was established without ongoing federal funding. The legislation creating it required the Presidio to become self-supporting by developing or renting its lands and facilities, for profit.

Even while expanding as never before, wilderness areas and recreational parks face serious problems into the twenty-first century. State budget cuts in the wake of Proposition 13 and lowered allocations for federal parks under Republican presidents Ronald Reagan, George H.W. Bush, George W. Bush, and Donald Trump reduced public services and raised user fees; among other consequences, higher fees limited the access of low-income visitors. Nevertheless, recreational and other uses of public lands increased more rapidly than the population, causing congestion, erosion, pollution, and crumbling facilities, even in protected wilderness areas. Proposals to relieve pressure by reducing access, raising entrance fees even higher, and requiring reservation systems have provoked clashes among user groups. Opposed by local interests dependent on tourism, few were ultimately enacted.

In the early and mid-1990s, after 2001, and from 2007 to '09, when severe recessions reduced state revenues, governors and legislators responded by deeply cutting state parks' already slim budgets. The state drastically reduced park services and even considered shuttering some parks or selling them to private businesses and local agencies. The state also began to convert parks into profit-making ventures, adding hotels, concessionaire leases, and revenue-generating recreational facilities, further jeopardizing wilderness preservation values.

Farmland Preservation

Thousands of years ago, when hunting-gathering peoples first arrived in California, they congregated in low-elevation, resource-rich ecosystems, where sufficient water, plants, and animal life thrived. When subsequent farm-dependent immigrants, including Spaniards, Mexicans, and Americans, took over the land, they likewise settled farms and towns in those rich landscapes, blessed by mild climate, water, and soil fertility. As a result, the waves of immigrants who came in the nineteenth and twentieth centuries packed into some of the best agricultural land in the world. Ironically, today, when world food production lags behind population growth, California, once a leader in food and fiber production, now leads in loss of farmland and open space in general. To compensate for retired acreage, agriculture in the state has moved onto

remote, drier areas where cultivation depends on more irrigation and application of chemicals, both of which increase environmental damage. In recent decades, many groups have sounded the alarm, warning of a looming agricultural crisis.

Among methods to slow paving over valuable farms, none raised higher hopes than the 1965 California Agricultural Land Conservation Act, better known as the Williamson Act. This law permitted farmland in the path of expanding cities to be declared "agricultural preserves." Landowners could sign ten-year contracts with counties, in which they agreed to use the land for agriculture in exchange for property tax breaks. The state reimbursed the cities and counties for the property tax income they lost when farmers kept farming their property. Beginning in 1965, the state paid out approximately $40 million per year to counties for protecting about 16 million acres of California agricultural acreage. But since the 1970s, land prices soared and the real estate market boomed. Desperate for tax revenues after Prop. 13, landowners and local governments shunned land withdrawal, selling and transferring even more land to urban developers, hundreds of thousands of acres just in the last few decades.

Threats to farmland intensified after 2005, as leaders found it increasingly difficult to balance the state budget. In 2009 and 2010, Governor Schwarzenegger and the legislature drastically reduced and then abolished state tax reimbursements to counties under the Williamson Act. As a result, some counties have reduced or cancelled Williamson Act contracts, freeing more land for development.

California farmers near cities have taken some comfort, however, in the rising popularity of organic and locally grown foods. Now a national trend, the movement was inspired by the development of "California cuisine," a mix of fresh, seasonal, and locally produced foods introduced by Alice Waters at Chez Panisse restaurant, which opened in Berkeley in 1971. Local, organic foods somewhat reduce human impact on the environment by requiring fewer chemicals and less hydrocarbon-burning transportation. Especially since the 1990s, the idea has spread to consumers via diet books, television food networks, and especially outdoor farmers' markets. Featuring sales direct from growers to consumers, the markets help to keep small-scale growers in business by bypassing middlemen and increasing farm profit margins. With its mild weather, year-round production, and diverse agriculture, California leads the nation in the number of farmers' markets, particularly those that operate all year.

Mono Lake and the Public-Trust Doctrine

The crusade to save Mono Lake, a spectacular high desert body of saline water east of Yosemite National Park, proved long and frustrating. Yet it resulted in establishing one of the most important legal principles available to strengthen environmental protections. Brine shrimp thrive in the lake's salty waters, making it the breeding ground for most of California's gull population as well as a stopover for migratory birds. Los Angeles acquired the rights to streams feeding Mono Lake and, in 1941, began diverting portions of their water into the city's Owens Valley project. In 1970 the city enlarged its aqueduct and started importing the entire flow of four of Mono Lake's five tributaries, along with much of the basin's groundwater. By the end of the decade, lake water had become much saltier; brine shrimp were dying off; and the rapidly receding water exposed offshore rookeries and allowed predators to devour entire hatches of birds. Fierce winds swept billowy clouds of alkali dust from the dry, exposed lake bottom, endangering nearby animals and humans.

The decimation prompted a campaign to save Mono Lake. Local preservationists, the Audubon Society, and Friends of the Earth appealed to water agencies to reduce water diversions, but were thwarted by those agencies, along with the city of Los Angeles and the California Farm Bureau. In 1979, they sued Los Angeles, challenging the city's water rights. The state supreme court's unanimous ruling in favor of preservationists stunned water developers. In overturning more than a century of precedent, the court in 1983 agreed with the environmentalists' contention that the common-law principle of "public trust" allows water rights to be modified when water diversion causes major environmental harm. The court reasoned that "the human and environmental uses of Mono Lake—protected by the public trust doctrine—deserve to be taken into account."

Subsequent litigation relied on the public trust doctrine to further undercut Los Angeles's water rights. Particularly significant was a 1989 injunction prohibiting the city from diverting water until the lake regained a healthy depth. That same year, the state court of appeals voided the city's license to tap Mono's tributaries, in light of the public trust doctrine. With Los Angeles increasingly isolated, in 1993 even state leaders joined in opposing the city. After a year of hearings, the State Water Resources Control Board suspended Los Angeles's water rights in order to allow the lake's surface to reach 6,391 feet above sea level, and ordered the city to reduce its diversions thereafter to maintain the lake at that level. Although Los Angeles stood to lose at least two-thirds of its water from the Mono Basin, or about 15 percent of its total supply, the city surprisingly agreed not to challenge the ruling. Instead, leaders would look for ways to replace the water through conservation, reclamation, and purchases from San Joaquin Valley farmers and the Metropolitan Water District. "It's partly facing the inevitable, partly common sense," explained former Los Angeles Councilwoman Ruth Galanter, "and partly that the environmental movement is universal, even in darkest Los Angeles." In April 2019, a citizens' group, the Mono Lake Committee, reported that the lake was only 8.9 feet short of the goal.

The Mono Lake case marks the first time California water authorities rescinded water rights to protect the environment, establishing a precedent for future controversies. Like the defeat of the Peripheral Canal initiative in 1982, the rescue of Mono Lake illustrates the revolutionary impact of environmentalism on California policy. What had seemed like an unavoidable ecological disaster in the early 1980s became, by the early 1990s, an example of how a degraded resource might be rehabilitated by the application of science, grassroots agitation, and litigation to water development policy.

The Wicked Ditch, Redux

Northern Californians breathed a sigh of relief in 1982, when voters killed the Peripheral Canal Referendum. The tiny Delta town of Locke held a gleeful canal wake, at the end of which one man staggered home singing a tune adapted from The Wizard of Oz: "Ding dong, the ditch is dead, the wicked ditch is dead." As it turned out, however, the ditch was only sleeping.

In 1994, a new spirit of state-federal cooperation resulted in the creation of CalFed, a consortium of 25 state and national water agencies to examine and report on California's water situation. Over the next six months, CalFed hammered out an agreement known as the Bay-Delta Accord, designed, as the agency's website put it, "to formulate water quality standards, coordinate operations of the State Water Project and the federal Central Valley Project and work toward long-term solutions to problems in the [Delta] estuary." CalFed was to study and deliver a comprehensive water plan in ten years. Building a peripheral canal around the Delta remained essential to planners in the state Department of Water Resources and to most southern water agencies. CalFed, however, was careful to avoid those toxic words. The agency instead substituted the euphemism "cross-Delta transfer facility."

Predictably, state legislators soon became frustrated with the agency's ponderous deliberations. In 1999, before CalFed could complete its plan, the legislature created another water oversight agency, the Delta Stewardship Council. Like CalFed, it was formed to overhaul the state's water infrastructure and policies. Unlike CalFed, with its two-dozen agency members, the new Council was small: only seven individuals. Another key difference: the Council's final plan, delivered in 2012, would become state law. Hand-picked by Gov. Arnold Schwarzenegger, the majority of Council members were charged with the "co-equal goals" of restoring the Delta's ecosystem and ensuring state water supplies, an age-old problem that had never been effectively resolved before. With its hopes now invested in the Stewardship Council, the legislature proposed an $11 billion water bond to implement its findings. The bond measure was placed on the November 2010 general election ballot, withdrawn, lowered to $6 billion by Gov. Jerry Brown, and finally, in 2014 the bond passed. Environmental organizations and some water agencies remain divided in their estimation of yet another complicated state water plan.

All along, diverting more fresh Sacramento River water around the Delta to the south state remained central to state water planners. This time, however, officials changed the type of diversion facility from a surface canal to two buried tunnels. Thought to be cheaper and less disruptive to construct, after completion the Twin Tunnels' functions would be hidden from sight and, hopefully, from mind. Southern agricultural and urban users, not state taxpayers, would pay the tunnels' cost by issuing their own bonds, potentially reducing opposition elsewhere. The facility's new title, proponents hoped, would be less inflammatory. In reality, however, the facility would function as "Peripheral Tunnels," bypassing the Delta with effects similar to previous versions.

After 2010, the tunnels provoked a predictable uproar over their huge size: 40 feet in diameter with an estimated yield of 4.9 million acre-feet, capable of moving unprecedented transfers of water south. Competition also developed between water agencies to determine which agencies would pay and how much. Some asked whether saving a few fish species was worth the great expense: $15 billion, plus $8 billion for Delta habitat restoration. More radical opponents questioned the wisdom of sending any more water south. Some large southern irrigation agencies later reneged on paying their shares, such as the giant Westlands Water District

in 2016. Gov. Jerry Brown, who promoted the tunnel concept as avidly as he had once promoted the Peripheral Canal, suggested saving money by building only a single tunnel. This compromise failed to calm debate. Indeed, some southern supporters of the larger project attacked Brown's new idea for not diverting enough water south.

Missing all along in the debate was the state's central water question: with less than half the historic pre-diversion fresh water now flushing the Delta, and saltwater increasingly invading from the west, how could the estuary relinquish any more water without making unusable much of the state's developed water supply? And what would the future hold, with predicted global climate change raising ocean waters and the level of San Francisco Bay by many feet, and making ocean tides into the Delta yet more powerful? As late as 2018, the fate of the Peripheral Tunnels, as well as Delta restoration and the future security of the state's water supply itself, remained unknown.

Reaction against Environmental Reform

Resistance to the environmental movement remains strong. Antagonists include groups with financial interests at stake—real estate developers, oil, utility, and construction companies, and workers in those industries—along with those who cling to a traditional faith in economic and population growth, technological progress, and unregulated business. Also, the state and national Republican Party was the principal political supporter of both resource conservation and broader wilderness preservation in the nineteenth and early twentieth centuries. After the 1960s, party leaders switched their support to privatization, rapid development of public lands and resources, and to the corporate interests that might gain thereby. Strengthened and emboldened by such powerful supporters, opponents of environmental protection have successfully limited or abolished some environmental protections, as the fight for Lake Tahoe and the Peripheral Canal and Tunnels demonstrate. Inflation and falling government revenues after Prop. 13 and recurrent recessions (especially after 2007), have also made the public receptive to arguments that environmental regulations inhibit economic development. The 1978–1981 energy crisis, when Middle Eastern oil exporters raised the price of crude oil, undermined environmental safeguards. To increase energy supplies, the federal government periodically weakened clean-air standards and other environmental regulations, encouraged use of dirtier but more abundant fuels such as coal, and promoted fuel extraction on western public lands. Eras of drought and recession have also undermined support for environmentalism. From 1986 to 1995, membership and financial support to environmental organizations such as the Sierra Club fell precipitously.

Anti-environmentalists worked effectively to discredit environmentalism in the state and nationally. Plans to build a Dow Chemical plant in the Delta (1977) and a Standard Oil of Ohio (SOHIO) terminal for Alaskan oil at Long Beach harbor (1979) collapsed due to what critics called "trivial" environmental regulations. Similar criticisms arose in the late 1980s and early '90s, when federal and state laws protecting endangered species such as the northern spotted owl interfered with timber harvests. Criticisms resurfaced when agencies moved to protect fish populations or general water quality, threatening water projects. Answering those criticisms, protectionists pointed to studies showing that environmental management did not actually stunt business growth, but rather channeled it in new directions.

Anti-environmentalist books, speeches, newspapers, magazines, and advertisements criticized environmental regulation as anti-business, elitist, and unpatriotic. To be sure, some environmental regulations raised real issues of equity, in that they could limit new construction, increase housing costs, and make it more difficult to build in sensitive areas. The charge that environmentalists were elitists, however, was disingenuous rhetoric, used by those with little interest in the general public welfare. In one of many examples, one of the first provisions pro-development groups repealed in the 1976 Coastal Act was its requirement for low- and middle-income housing in coastal subdivisions.

Political shifts, such as the Republican Party's reversal of its historic support for environmental protection, have also undermined environmental policies, with great potential effect on California. Conservative Republican leaders have championed the free market, opposed restraints on business, especially environmental regulations, and advocated lower taxes. Even Democrat Jerry Brown, who campaigned for his first governorship as an environmentalist, was stung by the loss of the Dow and other plants, and by criticism that he was hostile to business. As a result, Brown embarked on crusades to bring more business to the state.

At the state level, agribusiness and pro-development groups supported George Deukmejian's gubernatorial election in 1982. As a southern California legislator, Deukmejian had made a name for himself by opposing

crime and favoring the export of northern water to the south. Convinced that environmentalism was threatening economic growth, when Deukmejian became attorney general in 1978, he broke up the unit of state attorneys that enforced environmental laws and reduced the legal support his office gave to state environmental agencies. When he entered the governor's office in January 1983, Deukmejian pressed the legislature to build the peripheral canal, abolish the Coastal Commission, and weaken the California Environmental Quality Act by reducing the period of review for many types of environmental impact reports to a few days. Deukmejian also supported President Reagan's 1980s efforts to open up environmentally sensitive offshore waters to oil drilling. Although the Democratic-controlled legislature rejected the governor's revived peripheral canal project and most of his environmental measures, Deukmejian achieved the same ends by trimming budgets and appointing avowed anti-environmentalists to key positions. The administrations of Pete Wilson (1991–1998) and Gray Davis (1999–2003) were lukewarm at best toward environmental protection; both supported the shipment of additional water to the south state. One of Gov. Davis's principal responses to the energy crisis was to press for reduced environmental standards to speed construction of refineries, power plants, and transmission lines.

Departing significantly from the anti-environmental tendencies of most of his Republican predecessors, Gov. Arnold Schwarzenegger (2003–2010) proved to be one of the most environmentally supportive of recent California governors, supporting aggressive restrictions on air polluting industries, particularly those contributing to global climate change. Because of his pressure, the legislature in 2006 passed pathbreaking legislation requiring the state to regulate "greenhouse gases," which experts held inhibited the radiation of heat from the Earth, thereby raising temperatures worldwide.

At the federal level, anti-environmentalist interests gained influence in the inauguration of former governor Ronald Reagan as president in January 1981. Generally unfriendly as governor toward environmental protection, President Reagan vowed to harness government and to free business from regulations. His administration brought in leaders from resource-exploiting businesses and individuals involved in anti-environmental agitation and litigation. Reagan and his appointees revoked or diluted environmental regulations adopted under presidents Johnson, Nixon, Ford, and Carter. He hamstrung environmental agencies by cutting their staffs and budgets and by appointing overseers with anti-environmentalist backgrounds. James Watt, for example, became Reagan's secretary of the interior, in charge of most environmental programs. Fond of comparing environmentalists to Nazis secretly trying to "bring America down," Watt halted acquisition of new parklands in California, tried to remove the wilderness classification from federal lands within the state, removed some northern streams from protection as wild rivers, and sidetracked plans to control habitat decline in Yosemite National Park and southern deserts. Watt expanded the selling or leasing of previously protected land to oil, lumber, and mining companies, at bargain prices. Successive Congresses, however, refused to repeal the most important protection laws. Some initially successful efforts by President Reagan and later administrations to reverse environmental legislation were later overturned.

Although George H. W. Bush campaigned for office with the promise that he would be the "Environmental President," during his term (1989–1993) he continued the Reagan administration's anti-environmentalist policies and appointments, including (unsuccessful) efforts to remove federal protection from California wetlands and wilderness. Bush's successor, Democrat Bill Clinton, entered office in early 1993 with a plan to strengthen environmental regulation. However, his most important efforts—increased protection for federal lands, higher use fees for miners, grazers, and lumber companies on public land—were blocked by special interests and congressional leaders.

George W. Bush assumed the presidency in 2001, bringing with him a revival of Reaganesque policies and tactics. Indeed, Bush brought back many Reagan-era appointees. Within its first few months, the new Bush administration delayed or reversed many Clinton-era policies, notably those tightening water pollution standards and regulations in the national parks and forests. Bush cut the budgets of federal agencies, including funds earmarked for Yosemite and other California national parks to rebuild facilities and improve environmental conditions. Other Bush-led efforts included preventing designation of new wilderness areas and national monuments; weakening environmental standards for the sake of energy exploration and development; and appointing anti-environmentalists to key posts in the Department of the Interior and elsewhere.

The curtailment of federal environmental protections gained even more momentum under Republican Donald Trump, who was elected president in 2016 partly by blaming environmental restrictions for slow economic growth. Even more openly than his predecessors, President Trump entrusted administration of government agencies to business leaders and to local and state officials who enjoyed long careers as opponents of environmental regulation. Just in his first year in office, the new president and his appointees moved to reduce the size of national monuments, weakened or abolished clean air and water regulations adopted by his predecessors, opened up offshore ocean preserves to oil drilling, sped up the transfer of federal lands at low cost to states and resource-harvesting businesses, terminated much federally sponsored research into environmental problems, prohibited federally employed scientists from speaking and writing publically about environmental issues, and quashed numerous scientific environmental reports ordered by previous administrations or Congresses.

"There Is No Plan B": California and World Climate Change

By the early twenty-first century, Californians' nearly two-century-long engagement with environmental challenges and controversies paled in the face of likely long-term climate change. Worldwide, scientists of many cultures and disciplines, applying varied empirical research and computer models over several decades, agreed that global climates are undergoing unprecedented change. The primary reason has been human burning of fossil fuels such as coal and petroleum, particularly after the late 1800s. When burned, these fuels release vast amounts of greenhouse (mostly carbon) gases, causing the atmosphere to heat up. Global changes are already evident: higher earth, air, and ocean temperatures; erratic, severe wind and storm patterns; much less rainfall over western North America; melting mountain snowpacks, polar icecaps, and permafrost; rising sea levels; and die-offs or radical life alterations of species. Long-term studies testify that the pace of change is dramatically accelerating, especially since the 1990s.

For two centuries, California's patterns of human population distribution, social and political organization, economy, and infrastructure have evolved within, and are dependent on, massive rearrangements of natural resources. All have been based on long-term climate assumptions that might no longer be reliable. By the early 1990s changes were evident in the state: temperature increase averages of several degrees, particularly at night; less rain and snow; earlier melting of mountain snow packs; longer, hotter, and more destructive wildfire seasons; higher ocean levels along the coast, predicted to be as much as two to six feet higher by the end of the twenty-first century; saltwater penetration deeper into interior rivers and underground aquifers; stronger and higher ocean waves and tides, accelerating beach sand erosion, and the flooding and undercutting of inhabited shore plains and cliffs; substantial increases in ocean temperatures off the coast, which shifts storm tracks north of the state; declining native sea species; and arrival of new, tropical species previously unknown to these shores.

California's water supply is particularly likely to be disrupted. Overall, less precipitation has fallen on the state in the last two decades. Even less is likely to fall in the future, with more of it coming in violent rainstorms rather than storable snow. For the last half-century, snowpack over the entire West has declined dramatically and ever-faster. One study based on nearly 2,000 snow-measurement stations released in early 2018 by Oregon and California scientists found "declining trends in all months, states, and climates" since 1955, with overall declines of 30 percent in the region, but 70 to 90 percent in some locales. Moreover, the snowpack was shrinking so rapidly, the study concluded, that "new reservoirs could not be built fast enough to offset the loss of snow storage." In other words, western rivers will carry much less run-off in the long term. Another study released in early 2018 by federal and university scientists predicted that runoff from the already overused Colorado River system will be reduced, perhaps to only one-third, by the end of the century.

Just to stay even—in itself problematical—California would need much larger reservoir capacity to store rainwater from storms. Almost all viable reservoir sites, however, are already occupied. Moreover, even existing dams and canals are nearing or beyond their lifespans, some in danger of crumbling under pressure. Such a tragedy almost occurred in 2017 at the State Water Project's key Oroville Dam, when storms followed by rapidly heating mountain temperatures unleashed flood torrents that nearly collapsed the dam and spillway protecting millions of downstream residents. Yet no reasonable revenue sources exist specifically to repair these older dams, much less to build new ones, even if sites were found. As had happened to early Native peoples more than a thousand years ago, radical climate change appears poised to disrupt California ways of life.

California agriculture would be hard hit. In early 2018, for example, a team of University of California scientists reviewing nearly 100 recent studies reported that "the increased rate and scale of climate change is beyond the realm of experience of the agricultural community." The state's farmers grow more than 400 different crops, including two-thirds of the nation's vegetables and one-third of its fruit. Hundreds of crops, many only grown in California or in a few other micro-climates, will be difficult or impossible to grow, including corn, table grapes, rice, tomatoes, many fruits, and all nut crops. Higher average temperatures, fewer nighttime chills and freezes, overall drought and less irrigation water, altered times of flowering, falling land values, new weeds, crop diseases, and pests may reduce harvests or drive out farming in as much as 90 percent of the San Joaquin Valley, now the most productive agricultural area in the world. State- and nationwide, the economic chaos and loss would be incalculable.

The massive, complex responses necessary to avert worldwide human disaster would require unprecedented state, national, and international coordination and funding. Yet Californians, and even more so Americans as a group, disagree about what should be done, or even if anything needs to be done. At the national level, the administrations of George W. Bush (2001–08) and Barack Obama (2009–16) accepted the scientific consensus and took increasingly aggressive steps to study and promote energy conservation and to reduce fossil-fuel burning. The federal government reversed course when Republican Donald Trump, heavily supported and funded by industries and states dependent on production of fossil fuels, assumed the White House in January 2017. While campaigning and since taking office, Trump ridiculed climate change as a "hoax perpetrated by the Chinese and Democrats to hurt the American economy," even asserting that the world was actually "getting too cold all over the place." Since taking office, the Trump administration delayed or ceased enforcing previous laws and presidential orders aimed at reducing carbon-producing energies and encouraging cleaner, renewable energies.

Many presidential moves aimed directly at California's existing environmental programs. The Trump administration abolished or delayed federal climate-change regulations; reduced or eliminated funding for long-running experiments or grants by federal agencies to study climate change and remedies for it; required that all future federal science grants pass "political review"; opened up previously closed coastal waters to oil and gas pumping, including those off California's coast; eliminated scientists from many decision-making agencies; prohibited government scientists from writing or speaking to outside groups about climate change; and even prohibited the use of the term "climate change" or discussion of its validity in federal documents. Some Trump orders specifically target California: the

Yosemite Valley in the 1980s

After World War II, Yosemite Valley, like many other popular wilderness areas, began to show the ill effects of overuse. Mobbed by millions of visitors, by the 1980s the tiny valley was thoroughly urbanized, with snarled traffic, overflowing parking lots, smog that obscured views of the waterfalls, a supermarket and numerous stores, crowded restaurants and hotels, over 1,000 campsites, and a federal court to deal with in-park crime, violence, and narcotics trafficking. Plans developed by the National Park Service to reverse overdevelopment in the valley were delayed or vetoed by users, concessionaires, and the Reagan administration. *Photograph by Richard J. Orsi.*

administration revoked California's exemption from federal air pollution standards, which for decades allowed California to require much cleaner auto emissions and higher auto fuel mileage than federal rules. The EPA suspended, then moved to weaken or end, federal Clean Water Act protections to millions of miles of wetlands and streams in California and the West, in part to promote greater coal and petroleum production. Many changes target the environmental directives of the Interior Department, principal manager of huge public lands in California. Significantly, the new president announced his intention to withdraw from the 2015 Paris Climate Agreement that required nations to reduce carbon releases. Trump's revocation made the

United States the only nation in the world to reject the agreement. Federal courts have reversed many of the administration's rulings as illegal, but the Republican majority-controlled Congress passed several new bills promoting fossil fuel production and opening up public lands to more resource harvesting.

With the president and much of Congress in denial, climate change leadership has shifted to state, local, and private levels. Although most Californians have supported aggressive measures to protect the state from effects of climate change, those who reject climate science have opposed new measures. These include the dwindling state Republican Party, some carbon-emitting businesses, some but not all workers in those industries, and a number of business organizations, particularly the California Chamber of Commerce. Nevertheless, with wide popular approval, California has for many decades been, and is likely to remain, an environmental policy leader. In fact, some state innovations—such as legislation reducing auto and industry air pollution and requiring increasingly better auto gas-mileage—have been combatting global warming for more than 50 years. By the early 2000s, when other states and the federal government adopted California's legislative strategy, much cleaner car motors were releasing ever smaller percentages of greenhouse gases.

Since the early 2000s, California governors and legislatures have expanded the scope of regulations cutting back other forms of carbon emissions, such as requiring auto makers to sell more low- or zero-emission vehicles in the state, requiring manufacturers to produce appliances that use less energy, and, importantly, pushing public and private electric utilities to rely more on such renewable resources, such as solar and wind power. By 2018, large and small utilities reported that they were ahead of deadline and on track to achieve 50 to 100 percent of their electricity from renewable sources by mid-century. The production of electricity has begun to decentralize, as many state and local agencies, private individuals, and businesses voluntarily shift to renewable power, some produced at their own facilities. Businesses and private citizens are buying more hybrid and completely electric vehicles. Local governments have joined the fight as well, adopting their own carbon reduction and energy conservation programs.

Since climate change inherently transcends local environments, efforts to stop it have spread geographically beyond state and local lines. To pool climate change ideas and programs across their region, as northeastern states had done, California, Arizona, New Mexico, Oregon, and Washington joined together in 2007 to create the Western States Climate Initiative. By 2008, two more western states, fossil-fuel producing Montana and Utah, as well as four Canadian provinces, had joined the initiative, committing an immense international area—representing 20 percent of the American and 76 percent of Canadian economies—to fighting climate change. Other western states, including several with Republican governors, and six Mexican states have participated as "visiting" members.

Since the 1990s, giant wind and solar farms have spread across California, especially in southern deserts. The transformation has been exported, as other states encouraged renewable electrical generation, often shared across state lines. As demand has soared, the efficiency of solar and wind technology has improved, reducing the price of renewable electricity enough to outprice older fossil fuels, thereby harnessing the market to reward utilities and users for switching to renewable energy.

In 2018, California moved in yet another direction to expand renewable energy: offshore electrical generation. That year the state requested approval from federal agencies to build floating windmill platforms far out to sea. Optimism was high that the projects would eventually be approved, although the Department of the Navy expressed concerns about its access to offshore operations. One spin-off would be substantial on-shore infrastructure required by the projects, creating much needed jobs and economic development in low-population counties, especially along the north coast.

After 2000, an ambitious, though controversial, "cap and trade" system became central to California's plans to regulate and reduce carbon emissions. A strong supporter of environmental reform, in 2006 Republican Gov. Schwartzenegger defied his own party and oil and other industries to push a bill through the Democratic legislature instituting a mandatory market system for reducing carbon emissions. Taking effect in 2013, the program aimed to reduce greenhouse gas emissions by 16 percent by 2020, and 40 percent by 2030. Larger electrical power plants and natural gas and petroleum distributors representing 85 percent of total greenhouse emissions were issued permits ("offsets") allowing carbon emissions at their current levels. To increase their emissions, they were required to buy more offsets sold by the state or other producers who had successfully reduced their emissions, and only through an open auction supervised by the state. The state would periodically increase the price and reduce the number of auctioned offsets allowed. Over time, as the carbon volume of offsets declined, industries would be forced to continually reduce emissions in order to operate and expand.

California's cap and trade program is now the fourth largest carbon market in the world, though it is still opposed by some businesses and politicians. The program has been successful in reducing the state's greenhouse gas emissions by several percentage points per year since 2013. If the trend continues, California will exceed program targets. The state's billions of dollars' income from selling additional offsets is committed to financing other greenhouse gas reduction programs, and to issuing rebates to citizens to compensate for any higher energy costs to them because of the program. Moreover, the program has encouraged private businesses to invest more in carbon emissions reduction projects, several hundred millions dollars' worth just by 2015. Those businesses are already factoring carbon emissions costs into future planning.

With the cap and trade program set to expire in 2020, Gov. Jerry Brown (2011–18) convinced the legislature to extend the program to 2030; to extend it to additional large industries, such as food processing plants; and to require an overall 40 percent reduction from 2017 carbon emissions levels by 2030. Importantly, the program has become more widely accepted. Former Gov. Schwarzeneger praised Brown for winning support for the bill from Democrats, some Republicans, environmentalists, businesses, even some utility companies and the oil industry's Western States Petroleum Association. "You had eight Republicans voting for this," Schwarzeneger said. "I had one. This is how times have changed." Broader approval, extension to 2030, continued annual emissions reductions, and healthy state profits from recent offset auctions have all strengthened the program. Also significant, in 2017 two Canadian provinces, Quebec and Ontario, became partners and began selling their own carbon permits on California's now-international, pooled greenhouse gas reduction market. In important ways, California is replacing the federal government in providing carbon reduction models and programs to the international community.

In late 2017, Gov. Brown was asked why California has taken such an aggressive approach to climate change. In light of its threat to quality of life, Brown responded, "There is no Plan B."

The Legacy of Environmental Reform

Despite the inroads made by pro-development forces, support for environmental protection remains strong in California. Opinion polls into the early 2000s showed that a large majority of Californians favor tough environmental laws, even if it means higher prices. Many business leaders share these beliefs and support environmental regulation. Some major California firms, including the Southern Pacific Railroad, Standard Oil of California, and the Bank of America, developed corporate environmental plans and appear to have abided by them.

Attacks by powerful individuals such as Ronald Reagan, James Watt, and George Deukmejian eroded environmental support in some quarters, but strengthened it in other ways. In the early 1980s, for example,

Watt's bombast and anti-environmental policies swelled contributions and membership in environmental organizations. In the nine months after Watt's appointment, the Sierra Club gained several hundred thousand new members and collected one million signatures calling for Watts's ouster. Overwhelming disapproval of his actions contributed to his early forced resignation. Popular rejection of President George H.W. Bush's environmental policies undermined his public approval and political support, and contributed to his reelection defeat in 1992. Similar problems weakened Gov. Deukmejian's administration in the 1980s, George W. Bush after he gained the White House in 2001, and Donald Trump after 2016. On the other hand, in millennial California, divisions remained deep over major environmental questions, especially concerning water.

Conflicts and contradictions notwithstanding, the ecology movement of the 19th century has evolved into a structure of law and regulatory machinery that has survived fierce opposition and unceasing attack. Local and private control over environmental policy has in many cases given way to centralized planning at the state and federal level. Though few serious problems have been overcome entirely, on many at least a beginning has been made. The shorelines of San Francisco Bay and Mono Lake stand as shining examples.

Yet the ecology movement has failed to resolve most historic resource issues, just as the defeat of the 1982 Peripheral Canal referendum failed to end conflict over water, or end plans to transfer Delta water. Present and future generations still face vital questions. How can the protection of nature, the public interest, and private property rights be reconciled? With soaring demand and diminishing supply, who should allocate resources? establish environmental policy? mediate among contending interests? What should be the limits of public control over environmental policy, and should local, regional, state, or federal officers wield it? What constitutes "beneficial use" of resources—immediate economic development, sustainable resource use, or preservation of natural conditions and species?

Meanwhile, the stakes have been raised by the onset of human-caused climate change and its potential for severe disruption in California. Nearly everyone admits that the answers to these questions must strike a balance between conflicting extremes, but few agree on what that compromise should be. Whether Californians can resolve these critical issues remains to be seen.

Fin de Siècle California

29

As was true of the preceding *fin de siècle* (end of the century) decade, the 1990s were a time of dramatic change for California. Global shifts elsewhere again pushed and pulled newcomers to its golden shores, though this time most came from Asia, Central America, and Mexico. The reactions of some Californians were likewise reminiscent of an earlier era, as residents worried about the impact of these changes for themselves and their families. Not surprisingly, turn-of-the-century politics in California reflected these new-but-old concerns. Battles over services for immigrants and affirmative action were major issues of the decade. The often acrimonious debate pushed Latinos, Asians, and others to mobilize politically, ultimately reversing Republican electoral fortunes.

Demographic Shifts

Census data for the two decades ending in 1990 revealed significant trends for California. Between the 1970 census—when California became the most populous state in the union—and 1980, a total of 3.7 million newcomers made their way to California, raising its total population to 23.67 million. The 1980 census brought California two new seats in Congress. A decade later, California's population climbed to 29.96 million, retaining its rank as the nation's most populous state. The 1990 census again entitled California to new seats in Congress, raising its total from 45 to 52.

The two decades ending in 1990 also revealed that California had become the state with the highest percentage of immigrants. California's share of the nation's foreign-born population rose from 8.8 percent in 1970 to 15.1 percent in 1980. That year, California edged out former first-place holder New York as the state with the largest share of foreign born by one and one-half percentage points. That gap widened in 1990, when a new census showed that California was home to 21.7 percent of all U.S. foreign-born. Put another way, in 1990 nearly one-third of all U.S. foreign-born lived in California.

The main reason for California's new ranking was its proximity to Mexico. In 1970, Mexico was in fourth place as point of origin for all U.S. immigrants. By 1980, it had leapt to first place. By the time of the 1990 census, one in five of all foreign-born in the United States hailed from Mexico. Officials had anticipated these shifts in 1980, when census questionnaires, for the first time in 210 years, asked if respondents claimed "Spanish origin or descent." Ten years later, census questionnaires further refined that category to ask if respondents hailed from Mexico, Puerto Rico, Cuba, or elsewhere in the Caribbean. Public anxiety about California's growing immigrant population intensified as the state's economy began to slide.

Recession in the 1990s

The economy was already pointed downward when Governor Deukmejian left office in 1991. The nation experienced a deep but brief recession that began in approximately July 1990. The global stock market crash of October 1987 had been an early warning of instability. The collapse of the U.S. savings and loan industry contributed to the downturn, liquidating the assets of many households and necessitating a huge, taxpayer-footed bailout. National economic conditions began improving in March 1991 but recovery was slow and uneven. Americans were still feeling the pain in June 1992, when the national unemployment rate peaked at almost 8 percent.

International events added to the suffering in California. The world watched spellbound in 1989 as defiant East and West Germans demolished the Berlin Wall, that classic symbol of the Cold War. Over the next two years, East and West Germany were reunited, the economy of the Soviet Union collapsed, and the Soviet Union disintegrated. The United States responded by ending its 40-year program of containing Soviet expansion through military expenditures, a policy that had escalated through the Reagan presidency. From $303 billion in 1980 to a peak of $428 billion seven years later, in 1998 U.S. military budgets fell to $296 billion, their lowest since the 1970s.

Ironically, the outbreak of peace was disastrous for California. The end of the Cold War hit the state especially hard, given its dominance in national defense and aerospace industries. Hundreds of thousands of high-paying jobs disappeared, most permanently, as the state's major defense companies "downsized." The federal government urged California's major defense companies such as General Dynamics, Northrup, Rockwell International, and Lockheed to convert to peacetime production. Instead, they abandoned the field, moving their facilities out of state, or slashing work forces to meet much lower levels of production. Most "conversion" replacement jobs required lengthy retraining, substantial cuts in pay, or both. By 1994 the state had lost over 550,000 jobs in defense, aerospace, and electronics, making the 1990s California's most painful decade since the Great Depression.

Cutbacks in federal spending in California precipitated top-to-bottom lay-offs in the private sector. Faced also with increased foreign and domestic competition, high-tech firms responded by slashing costs, sometimes by shifting assembly operations to other states or even to other countries, keeping only "cutting edge" research and production facilities in-state. From the mid-1980s to the mid-1990s, the number of high-tech jobs in California fell by 15 percent. The recession of the 1990s affected even upper-middle-class workers, as highly paid Silicon Valley engineers and staff found themselves unemployed.

Not surprisingly, the recession brought a sharp decline in state tax revenues, compounding the fiscal problems caused by 1978's Proposition 13. Public schools and institutions of higher education faced disaster. Cities and counties were so starved for funds that some contemplated bankruptcy.

Base Closures

Adding to California's economic troubles, in 1989 the federal government began closing military bases. By the mid-'90s some 40 California installations were scheduled for closure or for major personnel reductions, including the El Toro Marine Corps Air Station, San Diego's Naval Training Station, George Air Force Base in the Mojave Desert, San Bernardino's Norton Air Force Base, Sacramento's Mather Air Force Base, and Monterey's huge Fort Ord. The San Francisco Bay Area was particularly hard hit by the closure of San Francisco's Presidio (the city's fifth-largest employer) and six naval facilities, including the Alameda Naval Air Station, Treasure Island Naval Air Station, and Vallejo's Mare Island Naval Base, the last with the loss of 30,000 direct jobs and another 30,000 indirect jobs. Base-closure in California cost 82,000 of the 119,000 (68.9%) jobs lost nationwide.

Decommissioning bases was a complicated process. A hierarchy of federal agencies had first claim on land and buildings, followed by selected local groups empowered to negotiate with the government to purchase properties at below-market prices. Absent such selected buyers, the government could sell the property to private buyers at market rates. Environmental contamination slowed conversion at several bases, with Congress requiring complete cleanup of toxic materials before sale. Eventually, California Congressman Leon Panetta (1977–1993) persuaded Congress to amend the law to allow bases to be "parcelized," allowing development and cleanup to proceed in tandem.

In some cases, predictions of disaster were premature. At several bases, local communities actually experienced growth in population, retail sales, housing markets, and employment, as retired military personnel moved from PXs to local markets and as developers created new jobs converting military property to commercial uses. Designation of San Diego as the Pacific Fleet's home base compensated for loss of its Training Station. Creation of CSU Monterey Bay and various research facilities connected to UC Santa Cruz made good use of Fort Ord's facilities. Treasure Island in San Francisco Bay proved useful for film production.

In a 1996 effort led by Speaker of the U.S. House Nancy Pelosi, Congress passed the Presidio Trust Act, which made national parks of the Presidio's Main Post and Fort Baker, military installations that bookended San Francisco's Golden Gate Bridge. Congress charged the Presidio Trust with managing the former bases in partnership with the National Park Service and the Golden Gate National Parks Conservancy, giving the Trust until 2013 to make the Presidio financially self-sufficient.

Public protest met plans to privatize large swaths of the Presidio, as did composition of the Trust's board of directors, some with ties to powerful real estate interests. Homeless advocates wanted the Main Post's former barracks for low-cost housing. Others worried that commercial development on federal parklands would strain municipal services without increasing city revenues. Lawsuits soon followed. In 2004, the city of Sausalito blocked National Park Service plans to build a 350-room hotel and conference center at Fort Baker. Sausalito ultimately agreed to a smaller 142-room luxury hotel, which opened in 2008.

The Presidio's Main Post secured high-paying commercial tenants, including Lucasfilm at Letterman Digital Arts Center (formerly Letterman Army Hospital)

and media conglomerate The Walt Disney Company. The Trust rented some 1,200 residential units with rents ranging from $1,700 to $15,000/month. In April 2012, the Trust opened a 22-bed luxury hotel in Pershing Hall, formerly officer housing. A lawsuit blocked Trust plans for 70,000 sq. ft. of new hotel construction, but in 2016 the courts approved renovation of the Montgomery Street Barracks as "adaptive reuse" of an historic housing facility. The result was a luxurious Main Base lodge with 42 guest rooms and spectacular views. The Trust met Congress's 2013 self-support deadline, generating "small millions," as one watchdog group put it, over its annual expenses (although, technically, all profits must be spent at the Presidio).

Transportation

By 1990 California's transportation system was in crisis. Years of opposition to infrastructure repair under governors Reagan, Brown, and Deukmejian meant that highway building had ground to a halt. California ranked dead last in terms of state per capita spending on public roads, while the number of automobiles had doubled. What was worse, high inflation pushed the cost of construction to astronomical heights. Freeway gridlock became a daily feature of commuting in the state's large cities. Public exasperation peaked in 1990, leading to the adoption of bond initiatives to restructure and rebuild state roads. The gas tax was doubled to provide funds for an $18 billion highway and railroad construction program, along with specific highway, mass transit, and railroad projects. The emphasis on rail transportation, ironically, was critical in securing approval of the bond issues, since public opinion had taken a decided turn in favor of rail mass transit. If there was a sense of *déjà vu* to these proposals, it was confirmed in 1990, when the Los Angeles–Long Beach light rail transit line opened on a course almost identical to that of the Pacific Electric (Red Car) system.

The prominence of rail transit proposals in the 1990 bond issues led some observers to wonder if the end of California's freeway era was at hand. The shocking cost of completing Los Angeles's Century Freeway in 1993—$100 million-plus per a mile—should have hastened that demise. Yet Californians clung stubbornly to their cars. Destruction of segments of the southern California freeway system in the 1994 Northridge earthquake temporarily increased rail and bus ridership, but numbers dropped once roadways were repaired.

Still, the '90s saw California embark on an ambitious program of highway construction and repair and rail transit extension. The Bay Area Rapid Transit District extended service to Pittsburg/Bay Point in 1996, and opened its San Francisco Airport extension in 2003. New light rail systems were approved for both Sacramento and San José. Trains were added to the Sacramento–San José CalTrain commuter line, along with new ferry services. Los Angeles built a downtown subway line and light rail transit systems connecting the city with Orange County in the south and Riverside and San Bernardino counties to the east. Still, freeway construction barely kept pace with the state's growth through the 1990s, and transportation remained a top concern in opinion polls.

Recession-Era Politics

For Republicans, the election of 1990 was crucial. Determined to prevent Democratic control of reapportionment after the 1990 census, party leaders sought an attractive candidate for governor when Deukmejian declined to seek a third term. With the support of both Ronald Reagan and President George Bush, Republicans turned to Pete Wilson. Popular and moderate, in 1982 the ex-mayor of San Diego had gained election to the U.S. Senate, where he won reelection in 1988. Although he seemed content to remain in the Senate, White House and California Republicans pressed Wilson to run for governor. Wilson won the Republican nomination in the June 1990 primary.

Meanwhile, Democrats nominated former San Francisco mayor Dianne Feinstein, who emerged as a formidable opponent. Wilson and Feinstein were surprisingly close in their views on important issues. Wilson's triumph at the polls may have owed to his extensive media campaign, financed by a deep Republican war-chest. As expected, however, Democrats retained control of the legislature and a majority of California's congressional delegation. Another Brown—this time Kathleen, daughter of former governor Pat Brown and sister of former governor Jerry Brown—became State Treasurer.

The 1990 election also brought voter approval of term limits with Proposition 140, one of the most far-reaching political reforms enacted since the progressive era. The initiative signaled a pervasive public distrust of politicians, establishing limits of three terms (six years) for state assembly members and two terms (eight years) for state senators and for certain state offices. It also reduced the legislature's budget by 40 percent and curtailed legislative pension benefits. Legislative leaders challenged Proposition 140 in the courts, which upheld its constitutionality. (This may account for the 40 percent reduction in court funding in the legislature's next budget.) Other states quickly followed California's lead.

The issue of reapportionment took center stage after the 1990 elections, not only because it would affect the political power of the parties for the next decade, but also because the census of 1990 indicated that California would gain several seats in the next Congress. The Democratic-controlled legislature submitted three different reapportionment plans to Gov. Wilson, who vetoed all three. This threw the matter to the state supreme court, the majority of whose justices had been appointed by Republican Gov. George Deukmejian. The court referred the matter to three "special masters," two Republicans and one Democrat. Their plan "corrected" the Democratic advantages of 1980's reapportionment plan. The ruling anticipated significant Republican gains in upcoming legislative and Congressional elections.

When he assumed office in 1991, Gov. Wilson faced a daunting $14.3 billion budget deficit (it is worth noting that only two other states had total budgets as large as California's *deficit*). To meet the crisis, Wilson proposed drastic cuts in spending, particularly in welfare benefits, but Democrats rejected his proposals. After months of wrangling, the governor and legislature agreed on a budget that included an increase of $7 billion in state income and sales taxes—the largest tax increase in California history. Taxes on business were unaffected, reflecting Wilson's determination to improve the state's business climate. The budget included a 4 percent cut in payments to recipients of Aid to Families with Dependent Children, and pay cuts and layoffs for state employees. Even so, leaders had to carry forward the remaining deficit to the next fiscal year.

Few were pleased by the 1991 budget, especially since revenues continued to fall short of expenses. In 1992 the conflict between state leaders was so severe that California missed its constitutional budget deadline, forcing the state to pay its employees with I.O.U.s.

Natural disasters compounded the state's fiscal woes through the 1990s. The Loma Prieta earthquake in the mountains east of Santa Cruz, a major temblor of 7.1 magnitude on the Richter scale, caused extensive damage in the San Francisco Bay region. Nearly a thousand homes were destroyed. Sections of the San Francisco–Oakland Bay Bridge and the double-decked Cypress Freeway in Oakland collapsed, killing 63 people. In 1991 five years of drought contributed to a devastating fire that raged through the hills on the eastern border of Berkeley and Oakland, killing 25 and destroying over 3,000 homes. A year later forest

Northridge Earthquake Damage, 1994
Widespread damage to Southern California freeways in the Northridge earthquake finally spurred action on the state's neglected freeway "retrofit" program. *Joseph Sohm / Shutterstock.com*

fires destroyed over 100,000 acres of northern California timberland. In 1993, fire destroyed more than 1,000 homes in the Santa Monica–Malibu area. Finally, in January 1994, a 6.6 magnitude earthquake struck northwest of Los Angeles. Northridge apartment buildings, homes, and 9 major freeway bridges collapsed, killing 55 people and creating a transportation nightmare. Damage estimates ran into the tens of billions of dollars. In his first three years in office, Gov. Wilson issued 27 declarations of emergency, covering 56 of the state's 58 counties.

Halfway through his first term, Gov. Wilson was immune to the voter wrath of 1992, but others were not so lucky. Republicans lost ground in the state legislature and in California's congressional delegation, which included Democrat Dianne Feinstein, the first woman California ever elected to the U.S. Senate. California also voted to place a Democrat, Bill Clinton, in the White House. One year later, California sent Barbara

Boxer, a ten-year veteran of the U.S. House of Representatives, to the U.S. Senate.

When Barbara Boxer and Dianne Feinstein were elected to the U.S. Senate, California became the first state in the nation's history to be simultaneously represented by two female senators. Another seven women represented California in the House of Representatives, six served in the state senate, and 22 in the state assembly. For good measure, March Fong Eu served as California's Secretary of State and Kathleen Brown was State Treasurer.

The women's successes owed much to events in 1991. That year Anita Hill, an Oklahoma law professor, accused her former boss, Clarence Thomas, of sexual harassment. Her allegations emerged during Thomas's U.S. Supreme Court confirmation hearings. The nationally televised hearings by the all-male Senate Judiciary Committee raised public awareness of women's unequal representation in government and increased discussion

Senators Dianne Feinstein and Barbara Boxer, 1992

The election of two women from the same state to the United States Senate accentuated the growing presence of California women in politics. *Paul Sakuma/AP.*

of the pervasive problem of sexual harassment in the workplace. One result was a dramatic increase in political action by women and an increase in the number of female office-seekers.

The Election of 1994

The 1994 governor's race returned a familiar name to California politics: Brown. State Treasurer Kathleen Brown attacked Gov. Pete Wilson's economic policies, the loss of jobs in defense and aerospace, and for the state's 8.6 percent unemployment rate, which was above the national average of 6.1 percent.

Wilson's approval ratings fell through his first term, but his handling of the Northridge disaster and his aggressive stance on crime and immigration helped to restore his popularity. Crime rose to the top of voter concerns in October 1993 with the kidnap and murder of twelve-year-old Polly Klass. A recently paroled felon

with a long history of sexual crime was arrested, prompting demands for mandatory sentencing. A "three strikes and you're out" initiative qualified for the 1994 ballot. The legislature passed several "three strikes" bills and in March 1994 Gov. Wilson signed the most severe.

Wilson gained politically but at great financial cost: "three-strikes" committed California to a massive increase in prisoners, jailers, and correctional administrative costs. The research group California Common Sense (CCS) found that, over a 30-year period, "the number of people California incarcerated grew more than eight times faster than the general population." As a result, a growing share of the state's tax revenues went to prisons and corrections. From 1980 to 2012, CCS traced 55 percent of the increase in state prison system costs (after adjusting for inflation) to the growth in the numbers incarcerated. The increase in state spending on prisons and corrections came at the expense of other programs. From 1981 to 2011, the proportion of the state budget that went to corrections "increased steadily," while "higher education's share declined consistently." Especially galling to California educators, while prison guards saw annual salary increases over that period, faculty salaries remained stagnant.

Along with crime, Gov. Wilson aligned himself with white discontent over the state's growing Latina/o population. He campaigned for Proposition 187, a 1994 ballot initiative that denied all but emergency services to illegal aliens, and required teachers, health-care providers, and other state officials to report suspected illegal aliens to federal authorities. Wilson favored denying citizenship to the U.S.-born children of illegal aliens. On the theory that immigration was a federal responsibility, Wilson also urged California to sue the federal government for the cost of providing services to illegal immigrants.

Wilson earned additional popularity points by pushing through a timely state budget. Mindful of the approaching elections, as well as public fury over the I.O.U. debacle, Democrats essentially caved in to the governor's demands. The 1994-95 budget included cuts to welfare payments and aid to the aged, blind, and disabled; a 10 percent increase in fees for University of California and California State University students; no increase in per pupil spending for K–12 schools (for the third year in a row); and a rollover of a $3 billion deficit from previous budgets. Democrats agreed to abandon a proposed income surcharge on the rich and approved $120 million to expand California's prison system.

Candidate Kathleen Brown distanced herself from Wilson by taking a more compassionate position on immigration. She opposed Prop 187, calling it "a cheap political trick," and attempted to focus her campaign on plans to improve the state's economy and end unemployment. But Brown proved vulnerable on the crime issue, as she opposed the death penalty (though she promised to uphold it if elected).

The war of words over Prop. 187 seeped into the U.S. Senate race. One-term congressman and Texas transplant Michael Huffington (R–Santa Barbara) spent nearly $30 million of his own (oil) money to unseat Senator Dianne Feinstein. Huffington embraced Prop. 187 and financed a relentlessly negative media campaign against Feinstein, who opposed the measure. Feinstein's ratings plummeted, but Huffington's campaign was wrecked by revelations that he had employed an undocumented alien. (Huffington blamed his defeat on fraudulent voting by illegal aliens.)

Wilson, on the other hand, defeated Brown by more than 14 percentage points. Prop. 187 succeeded as well, with 60 percent voter approval. An injunction filed soon

thereafter prevented enactment of Prop. 187, and the law was overturned in 1999.

Republicans made other gains in 1994. Republican majorities emerged in the U.S. House of Representatives and Senate for the first time in 40 years. Republicans attained an even split in California's congressional delegation and won control of the assembly by a margin of 41 to 39. Democrats retained control of the state senate with a 21 to 17 margin, with two independents.

One year later, Gov. Wilson again aligned himself with the "angry white male" movement. Wilson led the UC Board of Regents' 1995 campaign to eliminate affirmative action in university admissions, hiring, and contracts, programs intended to mitigate past racial and ethnic discrimination. In 1996, Wilson threw his support to Proposition 209, a constitutional amendment drive designed to prohibit state institutions from considering race, sex, or ethnicity, especially in hiring decisions. The bill passed in November 1996 with 55 percent voter approval. Numerous unsuccessful attempts have since been made to invalidate it.

Indian Gaming

A long-simmering battle with Native Californians boiled over during Wilson's second term. The U.S. Supreme Court had validated tribal gaming in the landmark *California v. Cabazon Band* (1987), but the Indian Gaming and Regulatory Act of 1988 compelled tribes to negotiate gaming compacts with state leaders. This gave states leverage over tribal gaming, including which types of games tribes might operate. Forty-one California tribes were soon operating casinos, many with popular "Vegas-style" slot machines. By 1998, California tribal gaming was a $1.4 billion dollar industry.

However, California tribes had proceeded without securing IGRA-required tribal-state compacts. For years, gaming tribes had tried to negotiate compacts approving their desired games, without success. In 1997, Gov. Wilson and attorney general Dan Lungren declared tribal slot machines an illegal form of "Nevada style" gambling prohibited by California's constitution and ordered tribes to remove them or face closure.

California tribes did neither. Instead they mounted an epic political battle against the state, securing enough voter signatures to qualify Proposition 5 for the November 1998 ballot. The initiative significantly expanded gaming rights for California Natives, permitting gambling devices at tribal casinos; amending state law to permit slot machines at tribal casinos; establishing trust funds to benefit non-gaming tribes; and even

Agua Caliente Hotel, Resort, Spa & Casino—Rancho Mirage, California
Indian gambling has had a huge impact on California's tribal communities and on their role in state politics. *Melvin Surdin / Alamy Stock Photo.*

offering to reimburse California for its costs in regulating tribal casinos. Some observers saw it as a battle between Indian casino money and the Nevada casino operators who provided the bulk of funds for the anti-Prop. 5 campaign. Contemporary estimates put the total spent on Prop. 5 at over $88 million, with $63 million coming from California tribes. Prop. 5 groups also made large contributions to candidates for state office. In the end, the initiative passed with a 63 percent margin.

Native celebrations were short-lived. In August 1999 the state supreme court declared Prop. 5 unconstitutional. The tribes immediately launched an initiative to write Indian gaming into California's constitution. Campaigning under the slogan "Californians for Indian Self-Reliance," Native groups won again. Voters overwhelmingly passed the amendment in March 2000. By then, a governor more sympathetic to Native interests had taken office.

The gaming battles of the 1990s revealed a newly prosperous Native California community. Along with

political power, casino money brought economic independence, even affluence, for many. In San Diego County, the Viejas Band of the Kumeyaay launched its own bank, the Borrego Springs National Bank, as well as an RV park, large factory-outlet mall, and commercial TV station. Many casino operators agreed to share their profits with non-casino tribes. Yet many non-Native Californians remained opposed to tribal gaming.

Another Energy Crisis

In 1996 California launched a pioneering effort to deregulate its power industry. The initial impetus lay in President Ronald Reagan's free-market philosophy, which held that markets freed from government regulation would increase competition and reduce prices. Through the 1980s, the federal government deregulated airlines, communications, and other industries. In California, where utility rates were as much as 40 percent higher than the rest of the country, the California Manufacturer's and Technology Association and other business groups pressed Gov. Wilson and the California Public Utilities Commission (PUC) to deregulate the state's electric utilities. The state's three major private utilities—San Diego Gas and Electric, Southern California Edison, and Pacific Gas and Electric (PG&E)—also lobbied for deregulation, claiming that increased competition would reduce consumer utility rates by as much as half. According to contemporary Los Angeles *Times* estimates, the three utilities spent almost $1.5 million on the campaign. Through 1994 and '95, the PUC drafted various deregulation plans, and in 1996, at Wilson's urging, the state legislature took up a PUC-sponsored deregulation act.

The legislature's consideration of deregulation exposed the consequences of term limits. Wilson was essentially a lame-duck official, forced out by term limits in 1998. In the assembly, crucial deregulation decisions rested in the hands of inexperienced legislators. The assembly ignored the bill for weeks, shuttling it back and forth between committees, whose members admitted that they did not understand it. Nonetheless, the legislature voted unanimously to pass it and Wilson signed it into law on September 23, 1996. It went into effect—some say appropriately—on April Fool's Day, 1998. Energy deregulation soon proved disastrous.

The New Economy

California's economy began to bounce back in the mid-90s. Growth in foreign trade, entertainment, and tourism led the state's recovery. As the rest of the nation began pulling out of recession in the early '90s, Los Angeles and Orange County bounced back quickly, benefiting from revived demand for their manufactured and agricultural products. In a remarkable turnaround, that region replaced lost defense and aerospace jobs with jobs in the high-tech industry, entertainment, and tourism. Hollywood could take much of the credit, producing 90 percent of all prime-time television programs and three-fourths of all feature film and video productions in the nation. By 1995 wages in California's entertainment industry rivaled those of the defense sector and employed even more workers. Even the defense sector revived: by the end of the year, all previously lost defense-related jobs had been replaced.

Meanwhile, with port facilities at Long Beach and San Pedro, Los Angeles became the largest port on the Pacific Coast. At the end of 1995, Los Angeles surpassed New York as the nation's largest gateway for foreign trade. State legislators worked to create a friendlier

business climate, slashing worker's compensation costs and streamlining permit processes, ending talk of a business exodus from the state.

Yet the decade's most extraordinary economic growth remained centered in Silicon Valley. Where defense spending led the boom of the '80s, it was computers, telecommunications, and the Internet that fueled the boom of the '90s. A dazzling array of new products appeared, including e-books, web tablets, personal digital assistants (PDAs), ever smaller, faster, and more powerful personal computers (PCs), multimedia components, compact disc read-only memory media (CD-ROMs), and new software programs in the hundreds of thousands. At the same time, the cellphone, an innovation in wireless communication, gave a similar boost to the communications industry. In 1992, IBM produced the Simon Personal Communicator, a hand-held device that combined cellphone, computer, and Internet, soon dubbed "the smartphone."

With innovation came new, often well-paid jobs. In 1991, Silicon Valley boasted three times the number of jobs and twice the number of electronics firms with sales of $5 million or more. In 1993, the Internet sparked another explosion in growth with the creation of the World Wide Web, which provided access to seemingly limitless sources of information to anyone with a computer. Access to the Web, however, required a software program called a "browser." In the fall of 1993 Marc Andreessen, a young programmer working for a federal agency in Illinois, wrote the instantly successful Mosaic program and made it available on the Internet. The following year Andreessen moved to California and teamed up with Jim Clark, a Silicon Valley veteran, to produce the Netscape browser. In a matter of weeks, Netscape captured 80 percent of the market. Still, users needed some sort of indexing system to marshal the Internet's overwhelming supply of information. "Search engines" evolved, including Yahoo!, created in 1994 by Stanford University students Jerry Yang and David Filo. Browsers and search engines made the Internet, as one observer noted, "a resource whose breadth, depth, and value are almost beyond comprehension." These innovations would make the Internet the biggest business and commercial phenomenon of California's twenty-first century.

Companies large and small scrambled to get "online." Thousands of new companies appeared, offering consumers goods and services or producing new Internet hardware and software. A seemingly endless supply of capital fueled the growth. In 1999 over $6 billion was invested in San José alone, creating a flood of "instant millionaires" and an average wage that was almost 60 percent above the national average.

California's high-tech companies remained key players in the state and national economy. Initial stock offerings in new e-businesses attracted eager buyers, even though most of the new companies earned no profits. Stock prices for Internet search engine Yahoo! opened at $2.62/share in 1997 and rose to $118.75 by January 2000. An online auction service, eBay, appeared in 1995. Its shares, first offered at $7.48, climbed to $53.50 on the first day of trading in 1998, and passed $120/share in early 2000. In only ten years, computer component manufacturer Cisco Systems became one of the nation's largest corporations. Hewlett-Packard, Intel, Sun Microsystems, Netscape, and Oracle dominated the high-tech field, making Silicon Valley the technology center of the nation. At decade's end, the American Electronics Association reported that San José led all U.S. cities in high-tech employment, home computer use, Internet access, and concentration of technology workers. It also noted that Southern California accounted for more than 40 percent of the state's high-tech jobs, with Los Angeles coming in second to San José in technology employment. Despite the dominance of Silicon Valley, Los Angeles emerged as the state's largest employer in consumer and defense electronics and in information services. Orange County and San Diego also had growing high-tech establishments. Sacramento and Fresno were the fastest-growing high-tech cities in northern California. Exports of high-tech products gave a huge boost to California's foreign trade. Resulting increases in sales and other taxes produced state budget surpluses in the billions of dollars.

California's "New Economy" was riding high as the century waned. State budget analysts declared 1999 "the best year of the decade." The 1990–91 recession was decisively over, with Californians enjoying healthy employment growth, higher wages, strong consumer spending, and record home sales (each piling higher tax revenues into state coffers). California was riding high on what economists termed the "wealth effect" of a rising stock market, of which California's high-tech firms were an essential part. Tech workers, especially, benefited as tech stocks grew in value, since many firms offered stock to lure and retain the best workers. In 1999, many Californians cashed stocks to purchase new homes and automobiles; others renegotiated mortgages to afford such lifestyle upgrades as vacations and second homes. The nation recovered along with the state, buoyed by high consumer spending, especially in computers and software. Indeed, state economists partially credited California's New Economy for the national economic recovery.

Yet Californians did not share equally in "the wealth effect." A digital divide marked the tech industry, with a small number of workers earning high salaries while the majority worked for low pay. Meanwhile, the cost of living in new cyber-cities soared. Housing costs in the San Francisco Bay Area were among the nation's highest. The percentage of Bay Area workers able to purchase homes declined, forcing larger numbers to seek housing as far away as the Central Valley. The result was longer and longer commutes, with more and more cars clogging freeways. The state's transportation problems were worse than ever as the '90s ended. California's educational system also lagged behind the new affluence, with Silicon Valley companies complaining that they could not find employees with the basic skills they needed.

Change and Resistance

The 1990s saw new groups embarking on civil rights campaigns similar to those of earlier eras. At century's end, many gay and lesbian leaders concluded that political power was the key to equality. Political figures such as Roberta Achtenberg led the way. Achtenberg won election to the San Francisco Board of Supervisors in 1990. Three years later, she became the first openly homosexual appointee to high federal office, serving as assistant secretary of Health and Human Services in the Clinton administration. Others advanced to higher office via the same Board of Supervisors: Carole Migden joined in 1991 and remained until her 1996 election to the state assembly, where she served the maximum term of six years. Tom Ammiano served the Board from 1994 to 2008, when he too left for the state assembly. Tony Miller became the first openly gay politician to seek statewide office in 1994, winning election as secretary of state. Around the state, openly gay and lesbian politicians waged successful local elections, despite opposition by conservative groups such as Christian fundamentalist Rev. Louis Sheldon's True Values Coalition.

California's population was visibly changing in the 1990s, changes that began with the U.S. Immigration Acts of 1965 and 1986. By then, nearly 40 percent of the nation's Asian population lived in California. Los Angeles had developed such a broad ethnic mix that it would have required more than 100 languages to teach the city's children in their native tongues. California, always at the national forefront, had become a truly multicultural society. At least some Californians celebrated that change: in 1993, partners in 20 percent of all married couples belonged to different races.

Yet the 1991 Rodney King case revealed that racism was rampant in California. King was badly beaten by officers of the Los Angeles Police Department following a high-speed automobile chase. The beating was videotaped by a witness, revealing several officers beating the prostrate King with nightsticks while other officers looked on. The videotape soon gained national and international audiences. Many were shocked in April 1992 when a San Fernando Valley jury acquitted four of the officers. The verdict touched off five days of rioting in Los Angeles and elsewhere. The unrest brought 50-plus fatalities and property losses then calculated at $750 million—a toll that far exceeded the 1965 Watts riot. Outraged African Americans demanded federal action against the offending policemen. Late in 1993 two officers were convicted in federal court of violating King' civil rights, and a Los Angeles civil jury ordered the city of Los Angeles to pay King nearly $4 million in damages.

The King riots also revealed demographic shifts among black Californians. In 1965, the Watts neighborhood of south-central Los Angeles was predominantly African American. In 1992, Watts was predominantly Hispanic and Asian. Rising incomes had allowed many black Angelenos to move into middle-class neighborhoods in the Central Valley and the high-desert towns of the south's "Inland Empire," the state's fastest-growing regions. Thousands more fled the black enclaves of Oakland and San Francisco for suburbia, participating in what was once termed "white flight."

Despite signs of rising affluence, the 1990s revealed a decline in black political power. For years black Californians had exerted an influence almost incommensurate with their numbers. Organization and commitment to black issues had resulted in a powerful political presence, capped by Tom Bradley's unprecedented five terms as mayor of Los Angeles and Willie L. Brown's historic 31 years in the state assembly. Brown served alongside five African-American assembly members, two California state senators, and three members of Congress. Yet this advantage seeped away through the 1990s. Driven from office by term limits, Brown campaigned for and won election in 1995 as mayor of San Francisco. Brown appointed many African Americans to city boards and commissions, but these gains could not offset declining membership in black civil-rights organizations or slippage in black office holding overall.

It was a slightly different story in Los Angeles, where in 1997 the percentage of Latina/os in the electorate was greater than that of African Americans. In a sense, the rising tide of Latino and Asian immigration had submerged black California. Growing political consciousness among Hispanic Californians combined with Congressional reapportionment after the 1990 census. The result was strong Latina/o voting districts in Los Angeles and elsewhere, producing what some called the "dawn of Latino power." Over 1.15 million Latino/as voted in 1990, a presidential election year. State assembly member Gloria Molina won election to the powerful Los Angeles County Board of Supervisors in 1991, a position she held for the next 23 years. The following year, Californians elected six Latinos and four Latinas to the state legislature.

Education

In the 1990s, Californians struggled to resurrect their once-proud system of public education. Sliding student achievement scores suggested that the state's schools were failing its children. Using Scholastic Achievement Testing (SAT) scores as a rough measure of school success, in 1990 California test-takers scored 484 in Math and 419 in Verbal skills (later renamed "Critical Reading,"), five points below the national average, although they scored eight points above national Math scores.

California's SAT scores were disappointing, but they reflected national trends. In 1990, the national average Verbal score was 424, the lowest in two decades: in 1969, the national average Verbal score was 463. Math scores were falling too: the 1990 national average Math score was 476, 17 points lower than 1969.

Some held it unfair to compare California to other states. For the decade beginning 1991, California saw a 25 percent surge in its school-aged population, compared to the national average of 16 percent. Indeed, Californians aged five to 17 had grown at a faster rate than the state population overall. Another difference: California test-takers were far more diverse than in other states. Nationally, SAT administrators identified 27 percent of 1990 test-takers as "non-white." In California, that percentage was 49 percent, up from 1984's 35 percent. If anything, Superintendent of Public Instruction Bill Honig found California's 1990 SAT scores encouraging, saying: "When you take in account the demographic shift, we are outpacing the nation."

Language skills proved another drag on test scores. By 1994 the state's public schools enrolled over five million students, one million of whom were English learners. Put in national context, that year nearly half of U.S. school children with limited English skills lived in California.

The state's largest and most diverse class ever took the SATs in 1994. More than 55 percent were minority students; 25 percent (compared to 8 percent nationally) had grown up with English as a second language.

Success rates among Mexican-American students stagnated through the decade. In 1990, 45 percent of California Latina/os over age 25 held high school diplomas. Ten years later, that percentage was only two points higher. Prop. 227, which ended bilingual education in public schools in 1998, could not be blamed, though it probably did not help.

Despite the growing challenge of educating California's school children, state spending on K–12 remained well below the national average. In 1995-96, California placed 39th among 54 states and U.S. territories, spending just over $5,000 per student. State K–12 funding continued to lag behind other states through the end of the decade. Embarrassingly, California—home of the computer revolution—ranked last in schools with computers.

Frustrated Californians attempted to take matters into their own hands in 1993. Proposition 174, sponsored by private schools and religious leaders, asked the state to give each school-age child a voucher for half of the state's annual per-pupil expenditure, which voucher could be used at any public or private school. Teachers, administrators, and school board associations united with public employees to defeat the measure.

California's colleges and universities also staggered under the effects of the early '90s recession. Enormous and costly, California's system of higher education included over 100 community colleges enrolling more than 1.5 million students. Nineteen campuses of the California State University (CSU) enrolled 360,000 students and granted nearly 55,000 degrees annually, making CSU the largest system of its kind in the nation, with a budget of more than $1.6 billion a year. The state's nine University of California (UC) campuses enrolled 160,000 students at an annual cost to the state of roughly $2 billion. Even this prestigious system suffered in the 1990s, as budget cuts in all three segments of public higher education led to faculty layoffs, salary cuts, elimination of thousands of classes, and a dramatic increase in student fees. In 1994, UC Regents raised fees in a multiyear plan that would result in 1996 fees that were three times those of 1990. Students found it increasingly difficult to obtain the necessary courses to finish a bachelor's degree in four years. Thousands more found that higher fees meant they could not attend college at all.

The rising cost of attending college was the direct result of declining state investment in higher education. The percentage of the state budget that went to CSU and UC declined from 13 to 9 percent in the early 1990s. Indeed, after 1994, California spent significantly more on prisons than it did on higher education.

Fee increases contributed to lower college enrollments among minority students, particularly African American and Latina/o students, whose numbers had been steadily increasing since WWII. In 1995 alone, fee increases, program cuts, and reduced financial aid drove approximately 58,000 students out of California colleges and universities.

California's gradual economic recovery brought new funding to K–12 education mid-decade. Calling himself California's "education governor," in May 1996 Gov. Wilson pushed legislators to fund an ambitious class-size reduction program, capping classes at 20 students in first and second grade, eventually extending to third grade. Results were outstanding. Teachers reported faster student progress, fewer discipline problems, and greater parent participation. At decade's end, a watchdog group reported that the program was almost fully implemented, with more than 92 percent of all California school children in kindergarten through third grade in classes of 20 or fewer.

Class-size reduction was not easily accomplished. It required an increase in the number of classes, putting pressure on schools to find more classrooms and teachers. Increasing teaching staff (by as much as a third, in some cases) put a strain on districts: 18,000 additional teachers were hired in 1996–97 alone. In some districts, an estimated 20 percent of staff worked under emergency credentials. The CSUs, which train nearly 60 percent of California teachers, increased its crop of teacher candidates by 25 percent and recruited trainees to reflect the racial and ethnic diversity of California K–12 students.

In 1998, California schools still faced daunting challenges. K–12 schools enrolled over six million students; 65 percent were minorities, many immigrants with limited English proficiency, and many poor. That year, California faced an average high school dropout rate of 35 percent. Public pressure resulted in a $9.2 billion bond issue, Proposition 1A, which promised smaller class size, new schools, and completion of long-deferred school maintenance. The bond measure passed with 63 percent voter approval. Superintendent of Public Instruction Tom Torlakson later touted the results. "Schools are making great progress with the extra resources from Prop 98," Torlakson claimed in 2016, with reduced class sizes, new programs, and improved teaching of math, science, and English.

Awakening "the Sleeping Giant"

As the '90s progressed, it became clear that Republicans would pay dearly for immigrant bashing. The political rhetoric of the 1990s had served, as some observed, to "awaken the sleeping giant" of Latina/o political power in California. Prop. 187 mobilized Mexican Americans, encouraging them to apply for citizenship and then to vote (typically Democratic). Reaction to "angry white male" politics was especially strong in East Los Angeles where, at decade's end, 97 percent of residents identified as Latina/o.

Frustration with anti-immigrant politics climbed again in 1996, when California voters approved the anti-affirmative action Proposition 209. Outrage boiled over two years later, with passage of Proposition 227, which effectively ended bilingual education in California public schools, assigning "limited-English-proficiency" students to language remediation courses taught primarily in English. Latina/o applications for citizenship and voter registration again soared. By 1999, there were half again as many Hispanic voters as in 1990. Where a total of seven Latinos served in the state legislature in 1990, 23 served nine years later. In 1996 Cruz Bustamante, a Central Valley Democrat, became the first Latino speaker of the assembly. That same year, Democrat Loretta Sanchez became the first Latina elected to Congress from Orange County, defeating Republican Robert "B-1 Bob" Dornan. Sanchez proved her victory was no fluke in 1998, when she won reelection.

If further proof were needed, 1998 saw Cruz Bustamante elected lieutenant governor of California, and the state assembly chose Antonio Villaraigosa as its next speaker. Born Antonio Villar in 1953 in East L.A. to Mexican and Mexican-American parents, Villaraigosa volunteered with César Chávez's grape boycott at age 15. Villaraigosa then earned a bachelor's degree at UCLA and, in 1985, a law degree. In 1994, he won election to the state assembly as a Democrat. Term limits decreed Villaraigosa's departure in 2000, following stints as whip, majority leader, and speaker. Either in praise or horror, the *California Journal* proclaimed the year 2000 as the first of "The Latino Century."

Mexican Americans found less success in California's fields and orchards. César Chávez and Dolores Fernández Huerta's United Farm Workers (UFW) struggled to maintain the gains of the 1970s. Unions faced hostile Republican leaders following the 1980 election of President Ronald Reagan and, in California, the 1982 election of Gov. George Deukmejian. Deukmejian, who received large campaign contributions from corporate

Antonio Villaraigosa

Born Antonio Villar, in 1987 Villar married Montebello school teacher Corina Raigosa. He and his new wife combined their names, producing the surname "Villaraigosa." In 1990, Villaraigosa gained appointment to the Los Angeles Metropolitan Transportation Board, where he served until 1994, when he won election to the state assembly. Villaraigosa was mayor of Los Angeles from 2005 to 2013. Five years later, Villaraigosa announced his candidacy for governor of California. *Photo by Angela George.*

agricultural interests, sharply cut the budget of the Agricultural Labor Relations Board. That body enforced provisions of the 1975 Agricultural Labor Relations Act, which assured farm workers' rights to organize, bargain collectively, and select bargaining agents by secret ballot, and protected labor's traditional weapons: picketing, strikes, and boycotts. One result of the cuts, complained UFW leaders, was a huge backlog of unresolved worker complaints. In 1983, Deukmejian appointed a conservative Republican to the ALRB, a move UFW called "the fox guarding the hen house."

UFW membership declined through the 1980s, dwindling to about 10,000 by the early 1990s. New leadership followed César Chávez's death in 1993. His successor was son-in-law Arturo S. Rodriguez, who graduated from San Antonio's St. Mary's University in 1971 and, two years later, earned a master's in social work from the University of Michigan. Rodriguez soon proved an effective leader. He ignored large growers and focused instead on unionizing smaller industries like mushrooms and roses. Over the next three years, the UFW won 13 consecutive elections in California and Washington state, and added about 4,000 new members. In 1996, Rodriguez helped end a nearly 18-year strike and supermarket boycott against Red Coach lettuce, gaining a five-year contract.

UFW then launched a concerted effort to unionize California strawberry workers, especially at Coastal Berry, the nation's largest grower. At the time, reported the *Independent*, "many workers were living in shacks or caves with no access to clean water, toilets or medical care. Women complained of being forced to perform sexual favours in exchange for employment." Without long-term contracts, "anybody who tried to complain was simply fired and replaced." Growers blunted UFW efforts by forming "worker committees," which the UFW contended were illegal company unions. In 1999 the UFW secured an agreement with 18 growers to end the worker committees, but a new "worker committee" won the next labor contract at Coastal Berry. It was a bitter setback for UFW, which had slowly regrown its membership to 27,000.

Republican "Wipeout" and the 1998 Governor's Race

Gov. Wilson sparked new controversy with his 1996 bid for the Republican presidential nomination. Even Republicans denounced him, since Wilson had pledged to complete his governorship if reelected. Despite the popularity of anti-immigration politics in California and elsewhere, Wilson's presidential bid was a bust. With low ratings and limited funding, he withdrew from the race.

Wilson's stillborn 1996 presidential campaign was a harbinger of the Republican future in California. That fall, Democrats regained control of the state assembly, elected Cruz Bustamante as speaker, voted heavily for incumbent President Bill Clinton, and Democrat Loretta Sanchez won Republican Robert Dornan's seat in the U.S. House of Representatives.

The 1998 governor's contest was a race between two millionaires. Democrats chose Lt. Governor Joseph Graham "Gray" Davis, who took as his campaign slogan "Experience Money Can't Buy." Davis had served as Gov. Jerry Brown's chief of staff (1975–81); assembly

member (1983–87); state controller (1987–95); and lieutenant governor (1995–99), prompting supporters to call him "the best-trained governor-in-waiting California has produced." Republicans nominated their own "governor-in-waiting," state attorney general Dan Lungren. Lungren focused his campaign on "wedge issues:" crime, taxes, abortion, and immigration.

Davis commanded the political center on issues that California voters cared about—women's reproductive rights, gun control, health care reform, and environmental protections—to focus his campaign on voters' number one issue: education. Soundly thumping Lungren in the polls, Davis's skillful campaign and huge political war chest produced one of the most convincing victories in California history.

Along with electing the first Democratic governor in 16 years, Californians re-elected Barbara Boxer to the U.S. Senate. Democrats claimed six of eight statewide offices, including Lt. Governor (Cruz Bustamante), Attorney General (Bill Lockyer), Treasurer (Phil Angelides), Controller (Kathleen Connell), and State Superintendent of Public Instruction (Delaine Eastin). Democrats also

Governor Gray Davis

Governor Davis giving his "state of the state" speech to the assembly, January 8, 2003, Sacramento, Calif. *ZUMA Press, Inc. / Alamy Stock Photo.*

increased their majority from 43 to 48 in the assembly and, in the state senate, rose from 23 to 25.

For Republicans, November 1998 was what one analyst termed "a wipeout." The wedge issues that had worked in 1994 failed utterly in 1998. Decisive Democratic victories revealed the depth of frustration and rage that Wilson had provoked among Hispanic and Asian voters. Republicans emerged with only one major statewide office, Secretary of State.

Gov. Davis immediately made good on his promise to make education his "first, second, and third priorities." Calling a special session of the legislature to enact school reform, the result was the 1999 Public Schools Accountability Act (PSAA). PSAA gave schools money to spend more time on reading; required every high school senior to pass a written examination to graduate; and put in place a complicated school reform plan of incentives and accountability. It provided an Academic Performance Index (API) that set improvement goals for each school, and established award programs for schools that met or exceeded API requirements. Over the next two years, state K–12 funding increased by 20 percent ($7.1 billion) and per-pupil spending rose 18 percent to $6,801. By the end of the decade, 70 percent of all schools met their targets of 5 percent or higher scores on standardized tests. Nearly 40 percent achieved improvements of 10 per cent or better.

Davis also moved quickly to solidify Latina/o support. He refused to appeal a court decision overturning Prop. 187 as unconstitutional (leading to an unsuccessful campaign to recall him). In February 1999, Davis traveled to Mexico and Monterrey on a highly publicized state trade mission. That May Davis entertained Mexican president Ernesto Zedillo, the first Mexican president to visit California. Two years later, Davis issued an invitation to Vicente Fox, Mexico's charismatic new president. These state visits appealed to California's Mexican American electorate but also reflected the close economic ties between the state and Mexico. Fox and Davis vowed to promote continued good relations between Mexico and California and to work together in solving illegal immigration and drug trafficking. Fox addressed the California legislature and was greeted across the state, as one reporter wrote, "like a rock star." Unfortunately for Davis, his own days as a popular public figure were numbered.

California in the
New Millennium

30

For California, the year 2000 could not come soon enough. The 1990s had been a ten-year roller-coaster ride. The state's economy rose from the depths of a severe recession, reached giddy heights in a technology-led boom, and then free-fell into a new, even deeper recession. As the new millennium began, the state faced another crisis: the failure of its deeply flawed plan to deregulate the electric utility industry. Politicians were hard pressed to find solutions or even to respond intelligently to the dilemmas they faced. National politics assumed primary importance following the 2016 presidential election, when Democrat Hillary Clinton suffered a surprising defeat to Republican Donald Trump. With often diametrically opposed views and values, California soon found itself in Trump Administration crosshairs . . . and vice versa.

Demographic Shifts

Census data in 2000 again confirmed California's place as the most populous state in the union. The state was home to 33,871,648 persons, a gain of 4.1 million persons (13.8%) over 1990. That gain just barely entitled California to one more seat in Congress: had only 33,942 newcomers gone elsewhere, California would not have gained a new seat.

National immigration trends showed clearly in California. From 1990 to 2000, the population of U.S. immigrants increased by more than half, with Mexico again providing the lion's share (30%). California led the other states in receiving the foreign-born; more than one in four Californians hailed from other countries.

Evolving census questionnaires further clarified trends. From the simple 1980 question regarding "Spanish origin or descent," the 2000 census questionnaire offered "Mexican, Mexican Am., Chicano," plus a blank for further details. Moreover, for the first time, the 2000 census allowed respondents to claim multiple racial/ethnic identities. Census data revealed that, as predicted, California had become a "majority minority" state. In 2000, racial and ethnic groups previously termed "minorities" outnumbered whites, who fell from 61 percent of the total in 1990 to 47 percent in 2000. African Americans held steady at around 6 percent. Asians dropped one point to 11 percent. Surprisingly, California's Native population grew by 50,000. California led the nation in its Indian population, and almost 3 percent of Californians claimed Native American descent in whole or part. Undoubtedly the most dramatic change was in the state's Latina/o population. Primarily of Mexican origin, they rose from 26 to 32 percent of state totals.

H-1B visas accounted for some of California's population growth. In the late 1990s, Silicon Valley executives bemoaned the dearth of trained U.S.-born workers. Congress responded with the H-1B visa, which allowed annual entry to an estimated 115,000 college-trained foreigners. As a result, in 2000 Chinese immigrants accounted for over one third of Silicon Valley scientific and engineering personnel. That year, federal officials increased the number of H-1B visas to 195,000 annually, resulting in a surge of tech workers from India.

Unfortunately, increased Asian in-migration and growing economic competition with Japan spurred a revival of anti-Asian attitudes in the U.S. and California. In January 2001, the National Asian Pacific Legal Consortium reported a substantial increase in incidents of violence and vandalism against Asians.

A decade later, the 2010 census again ranked California the nation's most populous state, with over 37 million residents. However, this growth rate was a paltry 10 percent, the lowest since the Great Depression. As a result, for the first time since statehood, the census brought California no new seats in Congress. States with greater rates of growth gained seats: four went to Texas, two to Florida. Nevada, Arizona, Georgia, South Carolina, Utah, and Washington each picked up one seat. New York and Ohio each lost two seats. Pundits reckoned that Democrats would pay a political price for these national population shifts.

The 2010 census again identified Mexico as the primary point of origin for U.S. foreign-born (29.3%), with Asia close behind (28.2%). Over half of all U.S. foreign-born lived in just four states: California, New York, Texas, and Florida. The impact was most dramatic in California, once again revealed as home to one in four U.S. foreign-born.

The 2010 census confirmed other continuing trends. The percentages of individuals identified as "single-race Asian" rose by two percentage points, those identifying as "white" fell by the same margin, while the percentage of Hispanic Californians rose another five points.

Chinatown San Francisco, May 2015
Food market shopping in San Francisco's Chinatown, the oldest in North America and the largest Chinese community outside Asia. *Rafael Ben-Ari / Alamy Stock Photo*

Indeed, by 2014 Latinos had overtaken and surpassed the non-Hispanic white population for the first time in the state's history. With 38.55 percent of the state's total numbers, Latina/os became the state's largest ethnic group, outnumbering non-Hispanic whites by approximately 70,000.

New Century, Old Politics

In the 2000 presidential election, California voted resoundingly for Democrat Al Gore, vice president under Bill Clinton, giving Gore a twelve-point margin over the ultimately successful Republican, oilman and former Texas governor George W. Bush. Californians returned Democrats Dianne Feinstein and Barbara Boxer to the U.S. Senate, and elected Democrats over Republicans by a wide margin to the House. At home, Democrats again outnumbered Republicans in the state senate and assembly.

Senator Feinstein's 2000 reelection, along with Sen. Barbara Boxer's in 1998, demonstrated the slowly growing political clout of California women. In addition to its two female U.S. senators, women held 13 of California's 52 seats in the U.S. House of Representatives. In the state legislature, they accounted for 11 of 40 senate seats and 20 of 80 assembly seats. In October 2001, San Francisco Democrat Nancy Pelosi became the first woman ever elected U.S. House party whip. Five years later, Pelosi became the first woman elected Speaker of the House. Although California women were gaining ground in politics, they remained a minority among lawmakers, far below their share (50.2%) of the state's population.

California's Congressional delegation in 2000 remained unrepresentative in another way. Of the 52 Californians serving in the 2000 U.S. House of Representatives, 34 (65.4%) were white males, far exceeding that group's share of the state's population (9.4%). They served with a diverse group of Californians: seven white women; four African Americans (one male, three female); three Latinos; three Latinas; and one Asian American. Notably, the latter was Robert Takeo Matsui, interned at Tule Lake with his parents during World War II.

The fight for equal representation extended to California's LGBTQ community, as election of more openly gay and lesbian leaders moved the quest for equality into new arenas. Early in his term, Governor Gray Davis signed a law recognizing same-sex "domestic partnerships," giving registered partners hospital visitation rights and, in some cases, health insurance. In 2001 and 2003, the legislature further expanded those rights. But many Californians objected on moral and religious grounds to lawmakers' acceptance of homosexuality. The clearest demonstration came in March 2000, when 61 percent of voters approved Proposition 22, which held that "only marriage between a man and a woman" was valid in California. Gay rights activists had also criticized the domestic partner concept. Paraphrasing *Brown vs. Board of Education* (1954), they denounced as "separate but unequal" statutes that denied marriage to homosexual couples. In October 2003, a court in Massachusetts agreed, giving legislators there 180 days to revise state law. While Massachusetts argued, newly elected San Francisco Mayor Gavin Newsom acted. On February 4, 2004, he authorized city officials to issue marriage licenses to same-sex partners. Over the next four weeks, almost 4,000 couples obtained licenses and, on one day, almost 100 couples exchanged vows in City Hall's marble rotunda. The first ceremony joined Daughters of Bilitis founders Del Martin (83) and Phyllis Lyon (80), who had been partners for 50-plus years.

On the day that Martin and Lyon wed, the Campaign for California Families challenged Newsom in court. In March 2004 the California supreme court ordered San Francisco to stop issuing marriage licenses. Five months later, it unanimously ruled that the mayor had overstepped his authority and voided the City Hall marriages. At the same time, a same-sex marriage bill proposed by Assemblyman Mark Leno passed the state senate and assembly. Gov. Davis vetoed Leno's bill because it reversed Prop. 22, and vetoed a second gay marriage law passed by the legislature in 2007.

The next phase of the battle pitted voters against the judiciary. In May 2008, the state supreme court ruled that California's constitution protected a fundamental "right to marry." Just six months later, however, California voters responded by narrowly approving Proposition 8, a bitterly contested initiative that again banned gay marriage. Gay rights activists sued, setting off another found of legal challenges that culminated in 2013, when the U.S. federal courts finally dismissed the Prop. 8 suit, making gay marriage legal in California again.

High-Tech Boom

Economically, California entered the new century riding high, courtesy of explosive growth in high-tech. Californians breathed a sigh of relief in 2000, when economy watchers declared the painful '90s recession over. That July a gleeful *California Journal* reported: "Silicon Valley is California's rescuer. With the emergence of its New Economy, the Valley reached down and lifted California from the dank crevices of

Wedding Celebration at San Francisco's Palace of Fine Arts, May 2015

Rafael Ben-Ari / Alamy Stock Photo

recession." Prospects for continued growth looked good. California was home to 14 percent of the companies in Standard & Poor's 500 Index, including Apple, Google, and Cisco Systems. In 2000, computer manufacturers produced products used in virtually every industry: computers, printers, semiconductors, software, and more. That year, California provided a fifth of the nation's high-tech exports.

Innovations in computers, wireless communications, and software came at dizzying speed. By 2001, PDAs, PCs, laptops, tablets, and e-book readers were commonplace. In 2007, Apple Computer introduced the iPhone, improving on IBM's earlier Simon phone. Apple sold an estimated 17 million iPhones in its first three months. Competitors (and lawsuits) soon followed, along with an explosion in smartphone ownership. By 2012, an estimated 40 percent of Americans owned or used smartphones. Four years later, one in four persons on earth owned or used one. Smartphone sales were integral to the state's economy, generating $84 billion from 2013 to 2017.

Tech innovations naturally brought new jobs. In 2001, AeA named San Jose California's largest tech center with 281,000 employees. Los Angeles and Orange County followed with 175,000 and 105,000 workers, respectively. San Jose led in tech employment per capita: nearly one of three private-sector employees worked in tech. More than 90 out of 1,000 workers in San Jose, San Francisco, and Oakland worked in the industry, making the San Francisco Bay Area California's densest technology cluster, with a combined payroll over $61 billion. The work was well-paid, with Bay Area tech workers earning substantially more than those in other industries. Internet access was widespread throughout California: San Jose led with 72 percent home access; Oakland took third place with 65 percent; and San Francisco ranked sixth.

California's surging New Economy generated record tax revenues. In fiscal year 1999–00, state leaders enjoyed an $8 billion budget surplus, their fourth consecutive surplus year. In 2000–01, California collected $75.5 billion in tax revenues, with $17.6 billion just in state income taxes.

Then the bubble burst. The computer market reached saturation in late 2000, leading to slumping sales. Job cuts followed. By the second quarter of 2001, Silicon Valley had lost approximately 202,000 jobs, over half of all jobs gained from 1998 to 2000. In July 2001,

Hewlett-Packard laid off 6,000 employees; another 15,000 layoffs came in September.

E-commerce stock values fell sharply. Yahoo! stock that sold for $200/share in 1990 went unsold at $10/share in late 2002. Too late venture capitalists realized that they had staked fortunes on businesses that were only ideas, unsupported by solid business plans. Wall Street watchers estimated stock market losses from March 2000 to October 2002 at $5 trillion.

California's economy was further shaken on September 11, 2001, when terrorists attacked New York City and Washington DC. Hijackers boarded four planes bound for California—three to Los Angeles and one to San Francisco—causing the deaths of 246 passengers, another 2,606 in or near New York's World Trade Center, and 125 at the Pentagon. Officials quickly identified Osama bin Laden as leader of the assault, which was carried out by 19 individuals with ties to Saudi Arabia, United Arab Emirates, Lebanon, and Egypt.

September 11 hit California and the nation hard. Frustrated and fearful, some Californians lashed out against those who appeared Middle Eastern, including individuals wearing turbans or *hijab* (head scarves). Swaran Kaur Bhullar, a Sikh mother of three, was attacked at a traffic light near San Diego; her attackers stabbed her in the head and shouted, "This is what you get for what you've done to us." In 2004, a group of white men shouting racial slurs attacked a Portuguese man, telling him to "Go back to Iraq." According to the Council on American Islamic Relations (CAIR), Muslim hate crimes increased nationally by more than 50 percent between 2003 and 2004, with 20 percent of attacks occurring in California.

September 11 hurt travel and tourism, California's third largest industry. In the eight months after 9/11, air traffic volume at Los Angeles and San Francisco airports fell by 30 to 35 percent; hotel occupancy rates 18 to 31 percent. California's airline industry canceled new aircraft purchases, scheduled fewer flights, and laid off thousands of workers, further exacerbating the effects of the dot-com crash.

Not surprisingly, the economic downturn added to state leaders' difficulty in balancing the budget. In May 2002, Gov. Davis announced a $23.6 billion budget gap, which state analysts blamed on $19 billion in lost dot-com revenues. Davis called for drastic budget cuts and for higher cigarette taxes and vehicle license fees. Even so, the state would be obliged to borrow $4.5 billion.

Protesters Demanding State Take-Over of Private Utilities, May 2001, Ronald Dellums Federal Building, Hayward
During the energy crisis of 2001 many Californians believed that energy suppliers had taken advantage of deregulation to manipulate the energy market and rob California consumers. *ZUMA Press, Inc. / Alamy Stock Photo.*

The Price of Energy Deregulation

Californians faced a different sort of crisis in the winter of 2001. Consumer energy bills suddenly spiked, a result of the deregulation that began on April 1, 1998. The new law required utilities to transfer control and operation of transmission systems to a third party, the Independent System Operator (ISO). Legislators and free-market enthusiasts had assumed that deregulation would lead to competition, which would increase energy supplies and lower consumer energy costs. The state created the California Power Exchange, a private, non-profit agency that would set prices at auction. In the interim, ISO set temporary rate caps. Unfortunately for California, energy suppliers chose not to expand or build new facilities. Indeed, some utilities chose to sell their power generation plants. Through the end of the 1990s, demand rose 15 percent, with no corresponding increase in power generation.

San Diego Gas & Electric was first to complete deregulation. The ISO lifted its retail price caps in the summer of 1999 and, by the summer of 2000, San Diego energy bills had tripled. All told, Californians spent $10.9 billion more for "deregulated" electricity in 2000 than they had in 1999.

The worst was yet to come. On an extremely hot day in May 2000, ISO announced that heavy usage threatened power reserves; it urged consumers to conserve energy. On June 14, several generation plants shut down for maintenance—fraudulently, as it later turned out—prompting ISO to implement a series of hour-long "rolling blackouts," turning off power to one grid of homes and businesses after another. Blackouts and high heat continued through the summer, interrupting commerce and enraging consumers.

That August, Gov. Davis called for an investigation into "possible price manipulation in the wholesale electricity marketplace." The inquiry was timely: in January and February, California utilities paid Duke Energy, a North Carolina firm, as much as $3,880 per megawatt hour; the year before, the average price was $45 per megawatt hour. California attorney general Bill Lockyer launched a probe into San Diego's price spikes. Private utility companies teetered on the edge of bankruptcy. That December, Southern California Edison sued the Federal Energy Regulatory Commission (FERC) for its failure to regulate the energy market. Gov. Davis asked the FERC for a wholesale megawatt rate cap but its chief, free-market ideologue Curt Hebert, refused to "interfere."

By the time Gov. Davis called a state of emergency on January 19, 2001, the state had already spent more than $100 million for electricity on the spot market, which still had not been enough to prevent the ISO from shutting down the power grid. After two consecutive days of rolling blackouts, Davis instituted emergency procedures to expedite construction of new in-state power plants. By June, more than a dozen were in the works. At year's end, the legislature voted to sell $5 billion in revenue bonds to buy, build, and operate additional plants.

State leaders worked to cap energy prices. In February 2001, the legislature approved a $10 billion bond fund to allow Davis to negotiate long-term contracts with energy producers, and California began purchasing power directly from producers rather than the open market. Davis proposed a state takeover of transmission lines in return for bailing out utility companies. In Northern California, PG&E avoided takeover by filing for bankruptcy.

When Democrats regained control of the U.S. Senate in 2001, they launched a probe into the FERC. It promptly placed a cap on energy prices in the western states, as those states had long demanded, and launched an investigation into energy price gouging. A coalition of governmental agencies, Southern California Edison, PG&E, and state attorney general Bill Lockyear were able to prove, in Lockyer's words, "just how egregiously and extensively California was plundered, defrauded, and ripped off by the energy pirates." The state signed 39 settlements with energy suppliers for about $3.2 billion in credits and refunds. In April 2010, Sempra Energy, parent company of San Diego Gas and Electric, paid $410 million to settle claims that it had manipulated the energy market.

With soaring energy prices and a tanking economy, the only bright spot seemed to be California's exuberant real estate market. In San Diego, the price of a typical single-family home climbed 74 percent from 1996 to 2001. Over the next four years, as San Diego's population and housing supply grew by 4.8 percent, average home prices doubled. Eyeing their climbing home values, Californians spent more freely, in some cases by borrowing against their homes' equity. They felt safe in doing so: in 2004 *The Economist* reported that Los Angeles homebuyers expected their home values to increase 22% per year over the next decade.

Yet some worried that personal incomes were not rising fast enough to justify such optimism. In November 2005, the California Association of Realtors estimated that only the top 9 percent of San Diegans could afford a median-priced home with 20 percent down and a fixed-rate 30-year mortgage. Banks, however, willingly offered less qualified buyers less exacting financing. In a method of amortizing that came to be known as "subprime," many new loans required no income verification, little or no down payment, and adjustable rate mortgages. Many first-time buyers rushed to purchase homes. As demand rose, so did home prices, raising investors' and home buyers' expectations of still greater gains.

By 2002, Federal Reserve Chairman Alan Greenspan was worried enough to warn that "our extraordinary housing boom . . . cannot continue indefinitely." In Los Angeles, the *Times'* David Freedman agreed. Housing had become "part of the bubble economy," with "sky-rocketing home prices and sales" pulling the U.S. economy out of the dot-com recession. As their home values rose, consumers refinanced frequently, sometimes spending the proceeds on lifestyle upgrades. Although "mortgage refinancing pumped more than $1 trillion into consumers' pockets," Freedman declared, it was not genuine prosperity. When the bubble burst, as all bubbles must, he predicted "devastating consequences" for middle- and working-class consumers.

Recalling a Governor

In November 2002, Gov. Davis won an expensive reelection campaign against Republican contender Bill Simon. Negative campaigning on both sides kept voters away in an election with record low turnout. Only one month later, Gov. Davis announced a $38 billion budget deficit. California's days of multi-billion dollar budget surpluses were gone, vaporized by soaring energy costs, the dot-com collapse, and declining consumer consumption. To close the gap, Davis proposed increasing the sales tax by one-half percent and tripling car licensing fees. Legislators refused to hike sales taxes but agreed to hike vehicle fees; to cut 16,000 state jobs, along with payments for health care services to the poor; and to borrow $10.7 billion.

Californians were quick to blame Gov. Davis for the state's predicament. As Davis's approval rating plummeted to 35 percent, angry opponents not only filed lawsuits to prevent higher car registration fees but, for good measure, launched a recall petition drive. Fueled by the public furor that greeted the tripling of registration fees, the petition drive made history by forcing the first gubernatorial recall election ever held in California. The ensuing campaign was a wild affair that drew more than one hundred candidates into the field to replace Davis, including Democratic Lt. Governor Cruz Bustamante, Republican state senator Tom McClintock, and bodybuilder-turned-movie-star Arnold Schwarzenegger.

Born in Austria, Schwarzenegger admitted that he had emigrated to the United States to "become a star and get rich." He settled in California in the 1960s and won a series of muscle-man competitions. Schwarzenegger achieved his first Hollywood success in the 1982 film "Conan the Barbarian," followed by the blockbuster "Terminator" series. The following year Schwarzenegger became a naturalized citizen and, in 1988, he campaigned for future president George H. W. Bush, who called him "Conan the Republican." Bush later appointed Schwarzenegger to his first political office, chairman of the President's Council on Physical Fitness and Sports.

In August 2003, Schwarzenegger announced his candidacy on the *Tonight Show.* "The politicians are fiddling, fumbling and failing, and this is why I am going to run for governor." And run he did, spending $10 million of his own fortune on the race. In the special election held October 7, 2003, Californians voted overwhelmingly to remove Davis and to replace him with Schwarzenegger.

When he took office that November, Schwarzenegger inherited the growing gap between the state's income and its mandated expenses. His first step, however, widened that gap. As promised, "the Governator" promptly repealed Davis's automobile registration increases, automatically adding $4 billion to the deficit. To offset that loss, Schwarzenegger implemented a hiring freeze. Other cuts included canceling state highway and transit projects; shifting property tax revenues from local governments to the state; and borrowing $15 billion.

Schwarzenegger called for an amendment to the state constitution creating a "rainy day" fund. It came before voters as Proposition 58, the Budget Stabilization Account, and passed with 71 percent voter approval. Unfortunately, this success did nothing to resolve the state's painful budget shortfalls. By 2009, Schwarzenegger's inherited $17 billion deficit had ballooned to $42 billion.

As so many had before him, Schwarzenegger looked for gold on Indian land. During his recall campaign, Schwarzenegger attacked Davis for the 57 compacts negotiated by Gov. Pete Wilson and casino-operating tribes in 1999, which did not require Native Californians to pay "a fair share" of casino revenues to the state. In January 2004, Schwarzenegger asked California tribes for $1 billion in casino revenue in exchange for the exclusive right to operate casinos in California. That summer he announced a revenue-sharing deal with five casino-operating tribes: in exchange for 15 percent of profits, the tribes could install an unlimited number of slot machines. Speaking for the Viejas Band of Kumeyaay Indians, Nikki Symington applauded the new compacts, describing them as "something we can do" to help California.

Running for election to a full four-year term in 2006, Schwarzenegger easily defeated his Democratic opponent, the decidedly unflashy state treasurer Phil Angelides. Though he had easily won reelection, Schwarzenegger still faced daunting challenges. The governor's political agenda included prison reform, improved health care, and closing the state's ballooning budget deficit. Unfortunately, a faltering economy jeopardized these ambitious goals, as a slump in real estate values left California teetering at the edge of a fiscal abyss.

The Housing "Bubble" and Great Recession

The U.S. housing bubble dated to the 1990s end of the Cold War when, according to economist Alan Greenspan, "geo-political events ultimately led to a fall in long-term mortgage interest rates." A boom in global housing values followed, which prompted financial institutions to relax mortgage underwriting standards. The boom in subprime financial instruments, in turn, attracted investors. At the end of 2003, financial firms began to package subprime home mortgages and sell them as securities. Seeing little risk and enormous profits, foreign and domestic investors snapped up mortgage-backed securities. Even the U.S. government, through its Fannie Mae and Freddie Mac mortgage programs, invested in subprime securities. In 2003 and 2004 alone, Fannie and Freddie purchased roughly 45 percent of all subprime mortgage securities, almost all at adjustable interest rates.

Financial institutions that purchased subprime loans and mortgage-backed securities faced no requirement that they maintain cash reserves sufficient to absorb loan defaults or drops in the value of mortgage-backed securities. U.S. economic regulations passed in the Great Depression did not extend to investment banks or hedge funds, which assumed larger and larger debt burdens. By 2006 subprime loans accounted for over 20 percent of all new home mortgages. That year, a *Business Week* report credited adjustable rate mortgages (ARMs) with bringing "a whole new group of buyers into the housing market." ARMs were great for lenders, "extending the [housing] boom longer than it could have otherwise lasted." They benefited brokers too, as lenders offered them cash incentives to push ARM loans over conventional mortgages. Unfortunately, ARM mortgages were probably "the riskiest and most complicated home loan product ever created." Most began with a discounted fixed interest rate for a set number of years then adjusted to a higher rate. A homeowner with an ARM could find the monthly payments doubling as interest rates adjusted. When ARMs reset in 2005 and 2006, the rate of national mortgage foreclosures climbed. Banks could have prevented foreclosures by modifying loans, but bank executives found it more profitable to foreclose. Foreclosures continued to rise as ARMS adjusted. In 2009 alone, 2.9 million U.S. homes entered foreclosure.

The first signs of what came to be known as "the Great Recession" came in 2006, when housing prices began to slide. Many consumers found that they owed more on their mortgages than their homes were worth. In 2010, 28 percent of San Diego homeowners were "upside down," meaning they owed banks more than the assessed value of their homes.

As homes lost value, so did mortgage-backed securities. Investors and financial institutions holding large numbers of both faced huge losses. In 2007, three of the largest U.S. investment banks either went bankrupt (Lehman Brothers) or were sold to other banks (Bear Stearns and Merrill Lynch). The two remaining investment banks, Morgan Stanley and Goldman Sachs, opted to become commercial banks. World stock markets crashed. From its October 9, 2007, pre-recession all-time high of 14,164.43, on March 5, 2009, Dow Jones fell to 6,594, a dizzying drop of 46.56 percent.

When commercial banks stopped lending, the housing market crisis spilled into all sectors of the national economy. An estimated 170,000 small businesses shuttered their doors between 2008 and 2010. As consumer spending and business investment dried up, massive job losses followed. The U.S. labor market lost 8.7 million jobs, or 6.3 percent of payroll, the most dramatic loss since the 1930s. From its peak in late 2007 to its mid-2009 trough, gross domestic product (GDP) fell 4.3 percent, the largest decline of the post-World War II era. The national unemployment rate rose from 5 percent in December 2007 to 9.5 percent in June 2009, peaking four months later at 10 percent.

The Great Recession hit California especially hard. Property values plummeted in 2009, the first drop since California began keeping records in the 1930s, falling an estimated 30 to 40 percent. County tax assessors lowered the values of residential, commercial, and industrial properties. By June 2009, the reassessed value of all taxable property in California had fallen by $107.2 billion, leaving less money and more misery for state and local governments.

From late 2007 to late 2011, more than 785,000 California households lost their homes. Foreclosure rates were disproportionately high among people of color. For mortgages taken between 2004 and 2008, Latina/o and African-American homeowners experienced foreclosure rates 2.1 and 1.7 times higher than non-Hispanic whites. In that same period, Latina/os accounted for 22 percent of all loans, but 37 percent of all foreclosures.

California job losses reached 1.3 million, or 15 percent of all lost U.S. jobs. All sectors of California's economy—trade, transportation, utilities, manufacturing, finance, business services, leisure, and the service sector—fell. California's construction industry tanked as construction companies cut 37 percent of their workers. Unemployment in California was in double-digits for an unprecedented 43 consecutive months, from February 2009 to August 2012.

Even highly-paid Silicon Valley workers lost their jobs. In June 2010, Hewlett-Packard—California's largest employer and the world's largest PC manufacturer—announced that it was cutting 9,000 jobs and restructuring. That year the state's unemployment rate stood at 12.4 percent, far higher than the new national rate (9.6%).

Unemployment rates in California reached their disastrous peak early in 2010. But averaging hides significant differences between groups. In 2007, before the recession, unemployment in California was lowest for Asians (4.0%) followed by whites (4.3%), then Latina/os (6.4%,). Unemployment was highest (9.9%) for African Americans. Great Recession jobless rates also peaked in different years for different groups. Latina/os hit their peak (14.7%) in 2009. Whites' (10%) and Asians' (9.6%) highest levels of unemployment came in 2010. Unemployment peaked highest and latest for African Americans (19.7%) in 2011.

When total unemployment in California fell to 5 percent in May 2017, that average still hid significant disparities. Asian unemployment was lowest (3.3%), followed by whites (4.1%), Latina/os (6.3%), and blacks (7.5%), whose jobless rates remained the state's highest.

Joblessness also differed dramatically from one California county to the next. For the two years ending 2010, unemployment in affluent Marin County was negligible compared to agricultural Imperial County. By 2017, Imperial was still suffering, but it ran second to 18.5 percent unemployment in rural Colusa County.

With the nation's economy in freefall, Congress passed the Emergency Economic Stabilization Act in January 2008. The Act allocated $700 billion to prevent the failure of "too big to fail" financial institutions. That October Congress passed and President Bush signed

Table 30.1   The Decline and Fall of the California Job Market

Average California Unemployment Rates, 2008–2017 (%)			
	Statewide	Marin Co.	Imperial Co.
Jan. 2008	6.4	4.0	17.7
Sept. 2008	7.6	4.7	27.1
Jan. 2009	10.3	6.6	24.8
Sept. 2009	11.8	8.3	30.9
Jan. 2010	13.2	9.0	28.2
Sept. 2010	12.2	8.4	30.4
Jan. 2018 *	4.4	2.5	17.0

*Preliminary; not seasonally adjusted.

Source: California Employment Development Department.

the Troubled Asset Relief Program (TARP), allocating another $700 million in taxpayer dollars to purchase "toxic" subprime mortgage-based securities. As 2008 came to a close, the U.S. government took over subprime lenders Countrywide Financial, Fannie Mae, and Freddie Mac, and pumped taxpayer dollars into insurance company AIG, Bank of America, Citigroup, Chrysler, and General Motors (the last still filed for bankruptcy in 2009).

The Great Recession provided the backdrop for the 2008 presidential race. For Democrats it was an historic campaign, potentially resulting in either America's first African American president or its first woman president. The former was first-term Illinois Senator Barack Obama, the latter Hillary Clinton, former first lady and two-term Senator for New York. After Obama defeated Clinton in the primaries, he faced Arizona Senator and veteran Republican politician John McCain. With promises of a robust economic stimulus program, Obama won with almost 53 percent of the popular vote.

Not surprisingly, the housing meltdown intensified political wrangling between California's legislature and Gov. Schwarzenegger. Revenues from the state's three major sources of income—personal income tax, sales tax, and corporate taxes—were sharply lower. Lawmakers had expected to collect $300 million from tribal casinos in 2004, but subsequent lawsuits reduced that revenue. California also faced a series of unexpected costs, including court-ordered contributions to the state teachers' pension plan and to state prison health care programs. A gap of $17 billion in the 2008 budget prompted leaders to withhold billions of dollars from schools, hospitals, and day care centers. Vendors, legislative staffers, and state workers waited months for paychecks. Only six weeks after approving the state's budget, officials were forced to admit that the deficit was actually $68 billion.

Former governor Gray Davis appreciated the irony of Schwarzenegger's situation. "It's *déjà vu*," he told reporters in 2009. Schwarzenegger faced an enormous deficit and an ideologically divided legislature, just as Davis had. Davis did not blame Schwarzenegger alone. He divided blame between legislators, who spent rather than saved budget surpluses, and California voters, who passed ballot initiatives for costly programs without dedicated funding. More irony: when Schwarzenegger left office, his approval rating was 32 percent, half that of Gov. Davis before the recall.

Yet Schwarzenegger and the legislature should be credited for slowing California's foreclosure crisis. In 2008, almost one year before Congress enacted the Home Affordable Modification Program (HAMP), California passed laws that forced lenders to wait 30 days before issuing notices of default, contingent upon lenders' efforts to contact borrowers with options to prevent foreclosure. The law levied $1,000/day fines on lenders who failed to maintain vacant properties acquired through foreclosure, a measure that prevented further slippage in value and cooled lenders' enthusiasm for foreclose. A 2009 law increased the wait to 90 days unless borrowers and lenders agreed to loan modification. California's foreclosure prevention program was more effective than HAMP, which left loan modification to lenders' discretion. From 2008 to 2011, California's laws prevented 380,000 foreclosures at no cost to state taxpayers. HAMP, on the other hand, cost U.S. taxpayers $12.9 billion in TARP funds and helped only 1.6 million borrowers— well below its target of seven to nine million borrowers. Indeed, HAMP turned down four million applications.

Newly-elected President Barack Obama took office in January 2009. Within the month, Congress passed and he signed a new $787 billion stimulus package. The plans included $288 billion in tax cuts, $224 billion in unemployment benefits, $275 billion for "shovel ready" public works, and $54 billion in tax write-offs for small businesses.

Taxpayer bailouts of U.S. banks and corporations proved unpopular, boiling over into protests on American streets. In 2011, an activist magazine issued a declaration of war on "Corporatocracy," or rule by corporations. With complaints that echoed those raised by farmers and populists in the 1890s, the activists urged protesters to descend on Manhattan in New York City, set up tents and kitchens, "and occupy Wall Street for a few months," to force attention on "the influence money has over our representatives in Washington." An "Occupy Wall Street" rally and march took place on September 17. Protesters carried signs proclaiming themselves "the 99 percent," as opposed to the wealthy, powerful 1 percent they believed controlled the U.S. government. On October 15, an estimated 950 OWS-inspired demonstrations took place around the nation and the world. OWS protests were contemplated or held in at least 60 California communities, the largest in Los Angeles, Sacramento, Oakland, and San Francisco.

Transportation

As the twenty-first century unfolded, California's troubled economy leached into all aspects of public life. Pressure on state transportation systems grew exponentially, while a chronic lack of funds stalled infrastructure investments. When Governor Jerry

Protester at Occupy San Francisco, October 2011
Photo by Victor Grigas.

Brown first took office in 1975, California counted 14 million cars, trucks, and motorcycles. When Schwarzenegger took office in 2003, that number had doubled, though road construction and upkeep had not kept pace. A 2003 Congressional study ranked California roads among the ten worst in the nation, with Los Angeles in first place. In 2008, state transportation officials declared more than one-quarter of California's 49,477 miles of highway in disrepair.

As was their habit, Californians took matters in their own hands. In November 2006, almost three-quarters of voters approved Proposition 1A, which restricted use of gasoline sales tax revenues to improving roads, most of which had been built in the 1950s and '60s. Another solid majority voted for Proposition 1B, which earmarked almost $20 billion in bonds for transportation improvements. Angelenos approved another transportation bond setting aside $3 billion for roadwork.

Unfortunately, these funds did not ease traffic congestion in Southern California, where pocked and clogged thoroughfares connected the economically crucial ports of Los Angeles and Long Beach to the state and the rest of the nation. In 2014, federal highway analysts estimated that Los Angeles ports accounted for 44 percent of all goods imported by cargo container into the United States. Between 1994 and 2014, the volume of offloaded cargo tripled. Officials expect it to triple again by 2034.

Crucial to the economy or not, Angelenos blamed container cargo for the city's legendary traffic snarls. In 2007, the equivalent of 7.85 million 40-foot shipping containers blocked Los Angeles roads and fouled the air as they moved from port to rail yard to warehouse. Federal highway administrators agreed that the worst delays were on Los Angeles' primary truck routes. Most of that traffic—as much as 80 percent—was headed out of state. "It is not California's job to deliver cheap televisions to Omaha," complained Lee Harrington, formerly of the Los Angeles County Economic Development Corp. "That is the job of the federal government and the transportation industry." Harrington and others called on Washington to foot the $18–20 billion cost of repairing the city's container-truck-damaged roads.

The Legacy of Progressivism

The direct democracy measures Californians enacted in the 1910s cast a long shadow. Progressives believed that the referendum, initiative, and recall gave ordinary citizens the means to offset the power of entrenched corporate interests such as the Southern Pacific. Unfortunately, some initiatives have had disastrous consequences. In the 30 years since voters approved Proposition 13, for example, California's population grew by 15,000,000, with corresponding increases in demand for public services. But year after year, Californians refused to tax themselves to pay for those services. Tax-payers instead insisted that the same levels of service could be maintained without new taxes, if only leaders cut waste and improved efficiency.

Ironically, well-financed special interests—today's versions of the Southern Pacific—sponsor the majority of California initiatives, which require the signatures of at least 5 percent of California's roughly 30 million voters. Success requires hiring very expensive petition-drive management companies. As a consequence, it usually is the well bankrolled special interest that sponsors California ballot initiatives, not the ordinary citizen.

Term limits are another legacy of "government by initiative." Approved by voters in 1990, Proposition 140 resulted in the loss of much of the legislature's institutional memory and policy expertise, as each year term limits force veteran legislators out of office. The result, as the *Atlantic* described it, has been the "systematic amateurization of the California political scene." In 2004, a stressful year for California, the then-speaker of the state assembly was a freshman, who was serving under a governor (Arnold Schwarzenegger) with no direct experience in state government. In 2012 voters passed Proposition 28, modifying term limits for legislators, extending their terms to a total of twelve years in the assembly or senate, either all in one or split between the houses.

Ironically, term limits have also increased the power of special interests permanently based in Sacramento, since newcomers often turn to lobbyists for information and advice. Thus the direct democracy measures designed to limit special interests have ultimately empowered them and, at the same time, hobbled elective government. Mark Paul, former California deputy treasurer, and Joe Matthew, a close student of the Schwarzenegger years, put it this way: "Over 30 years voters slowly squeezed the life out of their legislature but never stopped complaining that it didn't work."

Education

Since Prop. 13 passed in 1978, deciding how the state's education dollars should be spent has become highly politicized. The state's boom-then-bust economic cycles further complicate matters, as have ballot initiatives and court decisions. The challenges of K–12 education in California are exacerbated by shifting demographics, growing numbers of foreign-born English learners, and an economy that has shifted away from manufacturing and towards technology and services.

Californians attempted to resolve these problems themselves via the ballot box. In November 2000, voters considered Prop. 38, a measure funded by Timothy Draper, described by *Washington Post* as "a Type A Silicon Valley venture capitalist worth millions." Draper's initiative asked California to provide parents with an annual $4,000 per-child voucher to cover the cost of tuition at private schools, including religious schools. Sponsors promoted it as a means for parents to escape low-performing public schools. Opponents called Prop. 38 a risky experiment that would drain resources from public schools. Like the 1993 voucher initiative, Prop. 38 failed by a healthy 71 percent. According to UC Berkeley's Bruce Fuller, Prop. 38 failed because it applied to all students, including those already in private schools, convincing some voters that "it was a form of tax relief for wealthy suburbanites." The *Orange County Register*'s Sal Rodriguez disagreed. California voters rejected vouchers because the California Teachers Association and other unions "aggressively campaigned against them." Teachers and unions opposed vouchers, said Rodriguez, because "the idea of schools operating without the input of the teachers unions is anathema to groups like CTA, whose idea of innovation and reform in education is to throw even more money at failed government schools and to regulate competition out of existence."

The voucher idea remains popular among many Californians. In 2017, said the Public Policy Institute of California, 60 percent of adults and 66 percent of California K–12 parents favored tax-funded vouchers for the parents' choice of public, private, or parochial school. This preference was most pronounced among African Americans (73%), Latina/os (69%), and low-income households earning $40,000 or less (68%).

Many parents dissatisfied with public schools have transferred their children to charter schools, or publicly funded schools operated by parents and community groups. Yet those schools also get mixed reviews, using such measures as academic achievement, graduation rates, and parental satisfaction. As proved true in state-operated schools, negative, neutral, and positive results varied between charter students of different races and income levels.

In November 2000, Californians also approved Prop. 39, the first significant amendment to Prop 13. Prop. 39 reduced the threshold required to pass school district bond issues from a two-thirds (66.67%) supermajority

vote to 55 percent. Silicon Valley leaders backed Prop. 39, worried that public schools were not producing the workers they needed. Prior to its passage, 60 percent of local school bond measures succeeded. Afterwards, 75 percent passed. In February 2008, for example, 39 school districts proposed bonds and 30 succeeded, 18 of which would have previously failed. The bonds pumped $21.8 billion into school construction and modernization.

Prop. 55, passed in 2004, and Prop. 1D, approved in 2006, gave K–12 schools another $16.8 billion. Most of the funds went to new construction, modernization, and reductions in overcrowding. Unfortunately, most state bond funding was exhausted by 2012, a victim of the Great Recession. Since then, local funding has outpaced state investment in school facilities. From 2004 to 2016, local school districts proposed 1,018 bond initiatives and voters passed 83 percent of them, generating $91.1 billion in locally-based school funding.

In the new century, state leaders struggled to measure the value that California received for its educational dollar. Standardized testing promised one means of doing so. Beginning in 1999, the Academic Performance Index (API) provided K–12 educators with a benchmark for measuring school success. API allowed the California Department of Education (CDE) and State Board of Education (SBE) to rank school performance and to identify high- and low-performing schools. From 2003 to 2013, administrators calculated API by combining the basic-skills portion of California's standardized tests into a single index number between 200 and 1,000. The target API for all schools was 800. Each year, under-performing schools were assigned a growth target of 5 percent of the gap between their scores and the 800 target. The first scores, reported in January 2000, ranged from 302 to 966.

Results fell short of teachers' and legislators' expectations. Organizations of classroom educators such as the California Teachers Association criticized the API as overly simplistic. They argued that the system held educators solely responsible for student learning, without taking into account such factors as poverty or low English proficiency. Even CDE gave the API low grades. In a 2003 report, CDE claimed that API had "focused attention" on student test scores, but it admitted that the program's reward and intervention system had little impact on improving scores at under-performing schools.

California added a new system for measuring school performance in 2010, when it adopted the Common Core State Standards (CCSS), part of a national effort to standardize elementary and secondary education across states. CCSS identified what students should know in each subject, grade by grade. Unfortunately, new tests gave parents new cause for dissatisfaction. In 2016, fewer than half of California 8th graders (49%) met or exceeded CCSS standards in English and even fewer (37%) in Math. Outcomes were even lower when race and income were considered. In 2016, 68 percent of all middle- and higher-income 8th graders met CCSS English standards, but only 36 percent of low-income students did so. Low-income African American and Latina/o student scores were lower than those of low-income Asian and white students.

By 2013, API was an acknowledged failure. In ten years, slightly over half of all K–12 schools met their assigned API targets. What was worse, in 2013 the numbers changed direction, with the number of schools hitting API targets dropping from 53 to 51 percent. Legislators scrapped the API and gave administrators until October 2015 to devise a new grading system. The new system was to be geared to the legislature's new performance-based school funding law, approved in June 2015. It was also to incorporate Common Core State Standards, plus such nuanced measures as absenteeism, high school and middle school graduation rates, and improvement for English learners.

SBE and CBE launched the new accountability system, the California Schools Dashboard, on March 15, 2017. They invited the public to monitor the system via its webpage (https://www.caschooldashboard.org/). State leaders called the new system an obvious improvement, but others were skeptical. Bellwether Education Partners was harshly critical, as was the Thomas B. Fordham Institute. Both preferred accountability systems that ranked schools with an A–F letter grade or easily understood numerical rankings. Instead, California offered color-coded data, where each measure of performance received a different color. Critics like Education Trust-West president Ryan Smith grumbled that the dashboard system was "more confusing than practical," especially since it lacked "clear goals and targets."

California's 114 community colleges (CCs) likewise experienced pressure to quantify student success. Four foundations, including that of Microsoft founder Bill Gates, provided funding for Guided Pathways, touted as a fundamental overhaul of CC goals and operations. Under the 1960 Master Plan, the CCs' purposes were to provide future auto mechanics, dental and medical assistants, and others with Associate of Arts degrees and the training they needed to enter the workplace. The bulk of CC students would transfer to four-year CSUs and UCs. Still others would attend CCs simply to learn more about subjects of personal interest. In the five

decades that followed, CCs evolved into open-access institutions that provided a broad array of courses, not all of which were required for AA degrees or transfer. If Guided Pathways goes as promoters intend, it will move CCs away from the "access agenda" to a "completion agenda." "The cafeteria plan," as reformers termed the original CC model, left students foundering, wasting time and money taking classes that fulfilled neither transfer nor graduation requirements.

As the costs of higher education spiraled, and as employers and leaders worried that state schools were not producing the workforce required for California's service- and technology-based economy, reformers pressed CCs to improve graduation and transfer rates. Their criticisms were well founded: in recent years only 40 percent of CC students transferred or graduated within six years. The statistics were even more dire for minority and low-income students, many of whom were the first in their families to attend college.

The Guided Pathways completion agenda called for counselors to help beginning CC students select a major program or "pathway." The undecided would enter a tapering "meta-major pathway." Each path would include suites of courses designed to culminate in transfer or a terminal degree. In this model, student mastery of specific course content mattered less than student development of "competencies" suitable for a technology- and service-based economy. For underprepared students, Guided Pathways planned to weave remedial instruction into assigned courses. Instructors' role would shift from transmitting knowledge to students, to serving students as "guides" as they "learn how to learn." Similar to K–12's API-program, Guided Pathways offered financial incentives to CC administrators, faculty, and staff that adopted and implemented the new model. Twenty CCs began implementing the Guided Pathways approach in a two-year pilot program launched in 2017.

Despite innovative new approaches, gauging the dollar-for-dollar value provided by California schools proved difficult in the new century. Finding those dollars was another challenge. When state coffers were flush with dot-com earnings, California increased education spending. In 2001–02, K–12 spending rose by 27 percent. When the tech bubble burst, state revenue plummeted and, with it, K–12 spending. The collapse of the housing bubble and the Great Recession cut further into K–12 funding, pushing California's per-pupil spending far below the national average. From 2001 to 2006, the national average of per-pupil spending rose, but California's fell year after year. In 2001–02, the gap between California per-pupil spending and the national average was −$820. By 2013–14, California's per-pupil spending fell $1,480 below the national average.

California's high cost of living further complicates direct comparison between states. The California Budget and Policy Center used a cost-of-living adjusted formula to place California 41st in K–12 spending in 2015–16. That year California's per-pupil spending was about $1,900 below the national average. This was actually an improvement over 2012–13, when CBPC ranked California dead last in per-pupil spending.

It was a similar story for California colleges and universities. Operating budgets were fully funded while the New Economy boomed. But California's public higher education spending fell as the numbers of students rose. Enrollment in public colleges and universities jumped from 4 million in 1980 to 6.2 million in 2003. State investment in higher education could not keep up, especially in lean years. Between 2007–08 and 2012–13, state appropriations to UC and CSU fell by $2 billion, a drop of more than 30 percent, even as enrollments increased.

UC and CSU responded to lower state appropriations by restricting enrollment and by raising tuition. In-state tuition at UC and CSU more than tripled over 1990s tuition, simply shifting the costs of public higher education from the state to students.

As a direct consequence, U.S. student loan debt rose to $1.4 trillion in 2016. That year, the national average student loan debt was $27,975 per borrower. California students fared a little better than the national average, with UC and CSU students racking up an average of $22,488 per borrower. Still, a little over half of all California college students graduated with debt.

University of Colorado, Boulder, law professor Paul F. Campos offered one explanation for skyrocketing college tuition costs. In a careful analysis of government spending on higher education from 1960 to the present, in inflation-adjusted dollars, Campos found that "a major factor driving increasing costs is the constant expansion of university administration." Administrative positions at U.S. colleges and universities grew by 60 percent between 1993 and 2009, ten times the rate of growth of tenured faculty positions. Between 1975 and 2008, the total number of full-time CSU faculty members rose from 11,614 to 12,019 (+3.49%), while the total number of administrators jumped from 3,800 to 12,183 (+220.61%). "The explosion in administrative personnel is, at least in theory, defensible," Campos theorized, but he could find no valid argument to support the "seven-figure salaries" schools paid top administrators.

Is a college degree still worth the time and cost? Experts believe so. From 1979 to 2006, after adjustment for inflation, California workers with bachelor's degrees saw 19.8 percent gains in real wages. Earnings for those with master's degrees or higher jumped 34.4 percent. At the same time, wages for high school graduates fell by 4.4 percent and, for those without high school diplomas, dropped a whopping 23.7 percent.

How long does it take college graduates to recoup their investment? A 2016 study found that, on average, it took twelve years. By age 34 a college graduate could earn enough to repay the cost of the degree and to recover the wages they did not earn while in school. Naturally, recouping costs was easier for college grads with full-time jobs; in 2016, they earned 67 percent more than those with only high school diplomas. College grads also fared better in the job market. That year the unemployment rate for 25–35 year olds with bachelor degrees was 2.6%, five percentage points below high school diplomates.

Unfortunately, the benefits of college were not shared equally. According to the U.S. Department of Education, African Americans who started college in 2003–04 typically owed 113 percent of their student loans twelve years later. By contrast, white borrowers paid down their debt, owing 65 percent of the original amount; the paydown for Hispanic borrowers was 83 percent of the initial loan. For black students, a college degree was likely to mean long-term debt, as 80 percent of black students took out federal loans, compared to 60 percent of students overall. Black students took a greater financial risk in going to college, in that they usually began with a smaller economic cushion, were more likely to borrow, and typically earned less than other groups upon graduation.

These cost-benefit analyses might explain why black enrollments at all four-year state colleges fell by 13 percent between 2011 and 2014. At CSU, black enrollments dropped from 7.4 percent in 2007 to 4.4 percent in 2017. At UC, black students have held at 4 percent since 2010, a function of both higher costs and tougher admission criteria. Latina/o students' share of seats in college classrooms also remains disproportionate. In 2016 Latina/os were 39 percent of all Californians, but only 27 percent (312,000 out of 1.2 million) of all students enrolled in California's four-year institutions. In 2015, Latina/os were only 24 percent of all students enrolled in the prestigious UC system, but 47 percent of all CSU and 43 percent of all community college enrollments. Said UC Davis professor Michal Kurlaender, "We are seeing more

Left to Right: **Meg Whitman, Arnold Schwarzenegger, and Jerry Brown, October 26, 2010, at 2010 Women's Conference in Long Beach**

ZUMA Press, Inc. / Alamy Stock Photo.

students of every background enroll in college," but less equality in "where they enroll."

Enrollment is one thing; graduation is another. Allen Smith agreed. In 2017 the African American CSU Sacramento graphic arts major observed: "Getting in, that's the easy part. It's staying in and getting through to graduation, that's where it gets difficult." In 2017, blacks and Latina/os were underrepresented among California college graduates. That year about one-third of all working-age Californians had a bachelor's degree; of those, 53 percent were Asian, 42 percent white, 23 percent African American, and 12 percent Latina/o. Difficult or not, Kurlaender believes that college degrees are especially critical today, "for students of all backgrounds," as a means of "ensuring access to a middle class lifestyle."

Jerry Brown, Again

Californians returned to the polls to elect a governor in 2010. The race pitted Republican and former eBay CEO Meg Whitman against Democrat Jerry Brown, state attorney general since 2007, former Oakland mayor (1999–2007), and former California governor (1975–1983). During her two-year campaign, Whitman blanketed television and radio airwaves with advertisements targeting women voters, Latina/os, and undecided Democrats and independents. Although she spent $140 million of her own money to defeat Brown, in the end Whitman failed, bruised by allegations that she had employed an undocumented worker and had a spotty voting record. Elected with 54% of the vote, Jerry Brown's inaugural address warned Californians that they faced "tough choices ahead." "The year ahead," promised Brown, "will demand courage and sacrifice."

Early in 2011, Gov. Brown began efforts to order California's financial house, proposing a budget that combined spending cuts with new taxes. When negotiations with Republicans collapsed, Brown turned to the initiative. Proposition 30 called for a quarter-cent increase in sales tax, to end in four years. Prop. 30 would create three new personal income tax brackets. The lowest was for low earners; the next was for single filers earning $250,000 or more, and for married taxpayers earning at least $500,000; and the highest rate was 12.3 percent, for single filers earning $500,000 or more, $1 million for couples. The new tax rates would begin in 2012 and "sunset" in 2019. According to Prop. 30 supporter California Budget Project, the wealthiest 1 percent of Californians—those with annual incomes of $533,000 or more—would shoulder nearly 79 percent of the tax burden. Their income taxes would rise by 1.1 percent, while taxes for the bottom four-fifths would increase 0.1 to 0.2 percent. Appealing to voters' frustrated with the "1 percent," Prop 30 passed with 54% of the vote.

By 2013, higher tax revenues, a slowly reviving economy, and sharp cuts in spending produced a balanced budget. In 2014, two years after Gov. Schwarzenegger left the state with a $27 billion deficit, the state controller made the astonishing announcement that California had $1.9 billion surplus in its general fund, for the first time since the Great Recession began. More good news, economists projected a $4.2 billion surplus for the following year. This economic turnaround helped Brown sweep the 2014 governor's race, winning a second consecutive term and an unprecedented fourth term overall.

Is the Great Recession Over?

According to economists the Great Recession ended nationally in July 2009, because GDP had risen for two consecutive quarters. A variety of indicators suggested that it ended in California then as well. Since June of that year, noted economist Sylvia A. Allegretto, "Wall Street has been booming, corporate profits have rebounded, and the wealthy are doing well." California's economy again surged ahead of other states and some nations. In 2011, California was the world's eighth largest economy, falling between Italy and Brazil. Four years later, its GDP was $2.4 trillion, prompting the International Monetary Fund to rank California's economy sixth largest in the world, behind the United States, China, Japan, Germany, and the United Kingdom. In 2016, California's $2.60 trillion GDP again placed California sixth in global economies although, when adjusted for cost of living, state economists ranked California eleventh.

Yet as late as 2016, Allegretto and others saw that many indices had not returned to their pre-recession peak. Job growth, for example, had yet to catch up to job loss. From June 2009 to February 2016, California employers added 838,000 new jobs (+ 5.4%). Although encouraging, this still fell short of the 1.3 million jobs (–8.3%) California lost over the same period. Nor had household incomes reached their pre-recession highs. Incomes from 2006 to 2011 slid 13.5 percent, pushing the average Californian's income back to mid-1990s levels. In 2014, median income for California households was 6.9

percent below 2006 levels. This was because, for most California workers, wages were stagnant. Adjusted for inflation, average hourly wages for the bottom-third and middle-third of wage-earners had risen only slightly—3 percent and 1 percent, respectively—leaving both below pre-recession levels. By comparison, average wages for the top 10 percent of California wage-earners—those who were already well off—were up 28 percent.

Home ownership provides another indicator of economic recovery. According to the Census Bureau, California home ownership peaked in 2006 at 60.2 percent, then fell to 53.8 percent in 2016, its lowest rate since World War II. The drop put California at third from the bottom in home ownership nationally. One reason for the state's lower home ownership was the fast recovery of its home prices, which rebounded to nearly pre-2007 levels by 2015. That year the typical California home cost $437,000, making California home prices 2.5 times higher than the national median. Of 50 states, only one—Hawaii—had higher median home prices.

As a consequence, most Californians rent. Unfortunately, rents in California climbed steadily through the Great Recession. The median rental price for a two-bedroom apartment in 2017 was about $2,400/month, the third highest in the country. Of course, averaging disguises the higher costs of renting in urban markets, where most Californians live. In 2017, median rent for a two-bedroom apartment in San Francisco was over $4,000/month.

Although California wages were higher in 2017 than other states, wages have not kept up with rents. In San José, where the median annual income was around $100,000, renters still expected to spend 40 percent of it on rent. Naturally, the percentage of income spent on rent is greater for low earners, some of whom spend as much as 70 percent of their paychecks on rent. Such extremes extend statewide. Consulting firm McKinsey Global Institute found that in every California metropolitan area, local rents were beyond the means of at least 30 percent of residents. High housing costs, argues McKinsey Global, damage the state's economy. It estimates that $143 billion and $233 billion are lost each year to rent and mortgage, respectively, leaving households less to spend on consumer goods. Workers unable to pay California's high housing costs leave metropolitan hubs or leave the state altogether. In a recent University of Southern California survey, nearly 60 percent of Los Angeles companies complained that the high cost of housing was hurting employee retention. High tech firms in Silicon Valley complained that the high rents and mortgages leached away skilled workers. According

Table 30.2   Income Inequality in California, 2016

	10th Percentile	20th Percentile	50th Percentile (median)	80th Percentile	90th Percentile
2007 (pre-recession peak)	$20,000	$33,000	$78,000	$152,000	$208,000
2011 (recession low point)	$15,000	$27,000	$66,000	$141,000	$195,000
Change during recession (2007–2011)	−23.8%	−17.6%	−13.1%	−7.2%	−6.2%
2014 (most recent)	$15,000	$27,000	$69,000	$145,000	$198,000
Change during recovery (2011–2014)	2.2%	2.7%	4.2%	2.6%	1.7%
Net change since 2007	−22.1%	−15.5%	−9.4%	−4.9%	−4.6%

SOURCE: Sarah Bohn and Caroline Danielson, *Income Inequality and the Safety Net in California* (2016), Public Policy Institute of California (PPIC). https://www.ppic.org/content/pubs/report/R_516SBR.pdf. PPIC authors' calculations from American Community Survey (ACS) for California.

NOTES: Dollar amounts are rounded to the nearest $1,000. Table shows pre-tax cash income. This includes income received from earnings, business, investment, retirement, unemployment insurance, cash welfare programs (SSI, CalWORKs, General Assistance) and other sources and does not account for taxes paid or tax credits received. These amounts are calculated at the family level, adjusted for inflation to 2014 dollars, and normalized for a family of four.

to the real estate website Zillow, Reno, Nevada; Austin, Texas; Boise, Idaho; Denver, Colorado; Phoenix, Arizona; Portland, Oregon; and Seattle, Washington have all seen an influx of California homebuyers driven out by the high cost of housing.

California has lost population from the bottom rungs of its economic ladder as well. From 2000 to 2015, nearly 800,000 residents with incomes near or below the poverty line left the state. Nearly three-quarters of those who left California since 2007 earned less than $50,000/year. The leading destination for California's poor: Texas. Population losses like these affect California's economy but also its political power. If the trend continues, population losses are likely to cost California seats in Congress.

The Great Recession had another seldom-discussed consequence. According to the National Alliance on Mental Illness (NAMI), deep cuts in state funding have reduced or ended hospital and community-based services for individuals with serious mental illness. From 2009 to 2012, California cut its mental healthcare budget by 21.2 percent. As a result, individuals needing mental healthcare found themselves in "emergency rooms, homeless shelters, and jails." Others simply moved to the streets, adding to the state's large and growing homeless population.

Studies of income equality help to identify which California households have not recovered from the Great Recession. According to the non-partisan Public Policy Institute of California (PPIC), state income inequality grew from 2007 to 2014. The problem was not simply that the rich became richer. Incomes at the top 10

percent also fell, though by a smaller margin. Income inequality grew because the poor grew poorer. Residents in the tenth percentile of earnings dropped farthest and recovered least. No group had recovered completely by 2017, but losses were greatest (−22.1%) for those at the bottom rung. "If incomes fell across the board at the same rate, then income inequality wouldn't change that much," explained PPIC's Sarah Bohn. "But because top incomes recover quicker and lower incomes don't, that's where the growth in inequality is coming from."

Can full employment in California eliminate income inequality and give the poor entry into the middle class? In 2010, California's Employment Development Department (EDD) identified the state's ten fastest growing occupations. Only three (biomedical engineer, market research analyst, and medical scientist) brought incomes above $49,445, then California's median income. Earnings for three of 2010's top ten jobs netted earnings below California's poverty line, which economists calculated at $30,000 for a family of four.

In 2014, when EDD recalibrated its findings, biomedical engineers fell from first to 13th place. Six of the top 13 jobs showed that California's construction industry had rebounded, but none met California's new median income of $63,538. The ninth-place job, Solar Photovoltaic Installer, revealed a surge in "green" energy jobs, but its wages too fell below the median. One bright note though: each of 2014's fast-track jobs offered an income above the poverty line.

Globalization also affects California's ability to lessen income inequality. According to a 2007 study by the California Budget Project (CBP), globalization means

Table 30.3   Fastest Growing California Occupations, 2010

Rank	Occupation	Projected Growth	Median Annual Wage
1	Biomedical Engineers	68%	$81,540
2	Home Health Aides	52%	$21,830
3	Carpenter's Helpers	52%	$27,230
4	Market Research Analysts	45.8%	$60,570
5	Masons	45.7%	$46,930
6	Personal Care Aides	43%	$20,830
7	Emergency Medical Technicians and Paramedics	42%	$30,360
8	Medical Scientists	41%	$76,700
9	Museum Curators	40%	$48,450
10	Marriage and Family Therapists	39%	$49,270

John Amis, "2010 Ten Fastest Growing Jobs in California," Associated Press, using California Employment Development Department data and U.S. Department of Labor, Bureau of Labor Statistics California median wage data for 2010.

that California's job market grows most at the high and low ends. From 1990 to 2006, CBP counted 464,700 lost manufacturing jobs in California, many of which had offered middle-class incomes. Many such jobs had moved overseas, especially to China. From 2001 to 2011, China absorbed 2.1 million U.S. manufacturing jobs, over 1 million of them in computer and electronic products. Of those lost jobs, 77,490 (2.87%) were California's. With the nation's third highest jobless rate in

2011, these were jobs that California could ill afford to lose. Lost manufacturing necessarily hurt state GDP, which fell $20.75 billion from 2008 to 2011, a larger loss than any other state.

As manufacturing jobs left California, service sector jobs remained, ranging from low-paid retail sales positions to high-income professional occupations such as doctor and lawyer. Unfortunately, even well-paid service sector jobs were vulnerable. In 2016, UC San Francisco

Table 30.4   Fastest Growing California Occupations, 2014–2024, with Median Wages*

Rank	Occupation	Projected Growth	Median Annual Wage[†]
1	Reinforcing Iron and Rebar Workers	57.90%	$53,220
2	Brick- and Block-Masons	56.40%	$60,530
3	Stonemasons	52.60%	$39,630
4	Roofers	48.80%	$51,050
5	Helpers, Brick- and Block-Masons, Stonemasons, Tile and Marble Setters	48.40%	$36,780
6	Web Developers	48.30%	$82,930
7	Insulation Workers, Mechanical	46.20%	$54,640
8	Statisticians	45%	$88,350
9	Solar Photovoltaic Installers	44.80%	$45,380
10	Cartographers and Photogrammetrists	44.40%	$80,750
11	Software Developers, Applications	42.50%	$120,710
12	Operations Research Analysts	42.40%	$91,800
13	Biomedical Engineers	41.10%	$97,990

* Califoria Employment Development Department projections, 2014–2024.

[†] U.S. Department of Labor, Bureau of Labor Statistics California median wage data for 2016.

sent approximately 100 information technology (IT) jobs to India. Adding insult to injury, administrators asked laid-off workers to train their replacements. The story was similar at utility company Pacific Gas & Electric, which in 2017 sent 70 IT jobs to India, first asking workers to train their replacements. Ron Hira, a professor of public policy at Howard University, explained that the kinds of IT work offshored by PG&E and UCSF represented the vast majority of U.S. computer jobs. By 2016, estimated Hira, American companies were paying as many as 1.5 million foreign employees for work formerly performed at home. Hira called it the "silent destruction" of high-waged American jobs.

Homelessness

Rising housing costs and disappearing labor markets have added to the state's growing homeless crisis. Homelessness has risen nationally, according to U.S. Department of Housing and Urban Development (HUD). In 2017, national homeless counts increased for the first time in seven years. Nearly all of the increase was in the country's 50 largest cities, and nearly all was among unsheltered homeless (meaning people living on streets).

California leads the nation in many categories, but none more unfortunate than homelessness. With 314,278 homeless in 2017 (second only to New York), HUD estimated that nearly half of all unsheltered persons in the nation (49% or 91,642 people) were in California. That year the state also saw the nation's greatest one-year increase (13.7%), a jump of 16,136 unhoused persons. The state with the next highest rate of increase (3.6%) was New York, with an increase of 3,151 homeless. The states with the largest homeless populations, California and New York, also had highest per capita rates of homelessness (35 per 10,000 and 45 per 10,000) compared to the national average (17 per 10,000).

Not surprisingly, experts link rising housing costs to the rise in the number of Californians living in cars, shelters, and on the streets. In the greater Los Angeles area, homeless counts rose 30 percent between 2015 and 2017. Homelessness increased in the San Francisco Bay Area despite the area's booming economy, and despite the presence of some of the world's wealthiest corporations, including Apple, Facebook, Google, Wells Fargo, and Chevron.

Homeless encampments grew in vacant lots and along freeways in many California cities, including San Francisco, Sacramento, Fresno, Los Angeles, and San Diego. The camps have attracted international attention. In an unofficial January 2018 fact-finding tour, United Nations Special Rapporteur on Adequate Housing Leilani Farha inspected Oakland encampments and compared them to camps she saw in Jakarta, Manila, and Mexico City. "Here," said Farha, "I find there to be a real cruelty in how people are being dealt with." Farha criticized Oakland leaders for the absence of clean water and toilets, for rodent infestations, fire dangers, and other hazards. Oakland city workers periodically move homeless camps so that the areas can be cleaned and garbage removed, hoping to prevent outbreaks of hepatitis and other diseases. But Farha called repeated forced movement, coupled with the absence of a realistic pathway to stable housing, "systemically cruel."

Homeless Encampment, April 16, 2018

Photograph taken from West Grand Avenue freeway overpass in an industrial area of Oakland, California. On this date, the camp included approximately 50 tents and improvised structures on Wood Street between West Grand Avenue, 24th, and 26th streets. The onramp connecting Highway 880 to Highway 80 is at photo left. The city of Oakland provided a portable toilet and hand-washing station (photo center). Just beyond the camp is Oakland's wastewater treatment plant. Encampments like these may be found near many Bay Area freeway overpasses. Operation Dignity, a veterans' assistance group, estimated in 2017 that Oakland had roughly 200 camps, ranging in size from one or two tents to sprawling, blocks-long settlements with floating populations of 50 or more persons. *Mary Ann Irwin.*

New housing might ease Oakland's problem, but only 6 percent of the housing under construction in 2018 was slated for low earners. When completed, the rest will be market-rate housing. While these new units might eventually lower Oakland housing costs, only middle- and upper-income earners will directly benefit.

The 2016 Elections

The 2016 presidential race was deeply divisive for American voters. In the Democratic primaries, a large number of Californians favored New York Senator and former Secretary of State Hillary Clinton (53.4%) over Vermont Senator Bernie Sanders (45.7%). Sanders campaigned against the power of corporate money over the U.S. political system which, argued Sanders, Clinton exemplified. Clinton insisted that Sanders' proposals promised more than he could deliver, while her plans built upon progress begun by President Obama.

When Sanders conceded the top of the ballot to Clinton, attention shifted to the Republican candidate, New York real estate developer and reality television personality Donald J. Trump. With no previous government or military experience, Trump campaigned as a political outsider whose business acumen could "make America great again." After trouncing Republican opponents in the primaries, Trump focused his campaign on the shortcoming of Obama-era policies on immigration, trade, taxes, and foreign affairs. Trump's rhetoric resonated with Americans worried about immigration and challenges to traditional mores. In California, rural, agricultural districts favored Trump over Clinton, whose support was strongest in the state's metropolitan areas.

Overall, Californians voted overwhelmingly for Clinton, giving her 61.73 percent of the popular vote, the highest margin of victory since California chose Franklin D. Roosevelt in 1936. Alternatively, Trump's share of California's vote (31.62%) was the lowest of any major-party candidate since 1924. Nationwide, however, Trump prevailed, outpolling Clinton 304 to 227 in the Electoral College, despite trailing her in popular balloting by nearly three million votes.

Californians voted Democratic in their Congressional choices too, electing Kamala D. Harris to fill the U.S. Senate seat left open when Barbara Boxer retired. The election made Harris the first African American sent by California to the U.S. Senate. California's delegation to the House of Representatives also heavily favored Democrats, but the delegation was more diverse than previously. White males were still the largest group, 25 out of 53, but their share of the delegation (47%) had fallen.

Seventeen (32%) were female. Women of color held a larger share (18%) and made up the majority (59%) of California's female representatives. They included Japanese American Doris Matsui, born in the Poston Arizona internment camp during WWII. Matsui won a special election to fill her late husband Bob Matsui's seat in 2005. She won a full term of her own in 2006 and four subsequent elections thereafter. Another was Judy Chu, elected in 2008, the first Chinese American as well as the first female Chinese American that Californians sent to the House.

Yet female politicians lost ground in California's legislature. In 2016 they were 31 of 120 members (25.8%), down from the historical peak of 30.8 percent ten years earlier. In 2018, female legislators fell to 27 (22.5%), the lowest since 1998. California exceeded the national average (25.3%) of female legislators, but ranked behind states like Arizona, where 40 percent of legislators were women. Representation by women of color improved, but still fell short of parity. In 2015, 3 percent of all Californians were African American women; 7 percent were Asian Pacific Islander women; and 19 percent were Latinas. Together, women of color made up 29 percent of all Californians and 58 percent of all California women. Yet in 2016, only 13 of California's 120 legislators (11%) were women of color (although a high percentage of female legislators, 13 of 31 (42%) were women of color).

Many Californians remained ambivalent about women in elective office. In 2016, Gov. Jerry Brown told reporters that the declining percentage of female legislators was not worrisome. "Not everything is defined by gender," observed Brown. "It's a very important category, but there's a lot of life that transcends gender."

Yet many women find it difficult to transcend gender. Workforce participation, for example, has proven resistant to change. State law opened all occupations to women in 1876. State law (1949) and federal law (1963) forbade paying women less than men for the same work. Yet workplace segregation and pay discrimination still occur. In September 2017, employees filed a class-action lawsuit against California-based Google, that year ranked sixth among the nation's 25 highest-paying employers. The suit alleged that Google systematically paid women less than men doing similar work; denied qualified women promotions and career opportunities; and segregated women in lower-paid jobs. Another employee later joined the class-action lawsuit, alleging that Google paid female teachers in its childcare center lower salaries than male teachers with fewer qualifications doing the same work. A pioneer in software programming and development confirmed the career-tracking that held down women's wages, explaining that the tech industry began to stratify early. Thereafter a distinct gender hierarchy emerged, with women generally relegated to "front-end" development, and men in the higher-paid "back-end." In January 2017, the U.S. Department of Labor accused Google of "extreme" pay discrimination and launched an extensive investigation. As of June 2019, the investigation was still underway.

The California Legislative Women's Caucus believes that pay inequality continues. In 2015 it reported that women lose $33 billion in income each year because of unequal pay; that two-thirds of California's low-wage earners are women; and that single mothers spend 44% of their income on child care. Unsurprisingly, the Caucus favors electing more women to political office. A 2012 study found that women had different political priorities than male elected officials. Women were more likely than men to express concern for education, health care, birth control, abortion, the environment, and Medicare. Another study observed that, compared to male leaders, "women in elected office make the concerns of women, children, and families integral to their policy agendas." Solutions to the persistent problem of unequal pay may lie in increasing the numbers of female office-holders.

Workplace sexual harassment is another arena where gender is stubbornly un-transcendent. Following the 1991 testimony of Professor Anita F. Hill against U.S. Supreme Court nominee Clarence Thomas, state and federal leaders outlawed workplace sexual harassment. Yet the problem persists. In October 2017, actor Ashley Judd published allegations of sexual misconduct against Hollywood movie-maker Harvey Weinstein. The shockwaves spread among activists like Tarana Burke, who had coined the phrase "Me Too" a decade earlier in her work with survivors of sexual violence. Burke's phrase reached actor Alyssa Milano, who posted it to her social media network, sparking a renewed national conversation about sexually predatory behavior in the workplace. "If you've been sexually harassed or assaulted," prompted Milano, "write 'me too' as a reply to this tweet." By the next morning, more than 30,000 people had responded "#MeToo." The message was repeated millions of times, often with accompanying revelations of unwanted sexual attention. In December *Time Magazine* chose "The Silence Breakers" as "Person of the Year" for starting what it called "a revolution of refusal."

A firestorm swept through Silicon Valley, already infamous for what *New York Magazine* called its "culture problem" of sexual harassment and discrimination. Through 2017 and into 2018, allegations of misconduct led to the departures of executives at Uber, Binary Capital, 500 Startups, Google, and other high-profile California firms.

The outcry also prompted a string of revelations about lawmakers and their staff. In Washington DC, Congresswoman Jackie Speier (D–California) penned a measure revamping Capitol Hill sexual harassment policies, including streamlining the reporting process, providing assistance to complainants, and mandating disclosure when accusers settle out of court in taxpayer-funded settlements. The bill passed in the House in February 2018, prompting the Senate to pass its own, less punitive measure.

"Me Too" shook Sacramento as well. In 2017, Raul Bocanegra left the assembly amid complaints by seven women that he had harassed or assaulted them. Around the same time, Matt Dababneh resigned from the state assembly when two women accused him of sexual assault. State senator Tony Mendoza took a leave of absence while senators investigated complaints made by female employees. When Visa lobbyist Adama Iwu was groped in front of male co-workers in October 2017, she was incensed that none intervened. One week later Iwu and 300 equally fed up women—including two retired legislators, officials from the state Democratic and Republican parties, and six of the 26 women then serving in the legislature—published an open letter saying "We Said Enough." Letter-signer Christine Pelosi, chairwoman of the California Democratic Party Women's Caucus and daughter of House Minority Leader Nancy Pelosi (D–San Francisco), underscored the fundamental disconnect in California's supposedly liberal political culture, asking "How can California be a sanctuary state for immigrants, but not when it comes to women being sexually harassed at the Capitol?"

In February 2018, one of the California's women legislators, state senator Janet Nguyen, co-authored a bill prohibiting legislators or their staff attempting to prevent reporting of sexual harassment, assault, or any other illegal activity. The measure became law on February 5, 2018. Nguyen next introduced a bill requiring lawmakers to track sexual harassment claims and to release all records pertaining to complaints, investigations, and settlement records since 1989.

Political activists hoped that "Me Too" would prompt women to run for political office, just as Anita Hill's hearings did in 1992. It worked for Rio Hondo College board member Vicky Santana, who announced her bid for Tony Mendoza's senate seat during his forced leave of absence. Santana was angry about allegations that Roy Moore, a 2017 candidate for Alabama's U.S.

Senate seat, had pursued teenage girls, and vexed by an audio recording of Donald Trump chuckling about groping women. There was nothing she could do about Alabama, said Santana, nothing about Trump, but if she were elected, she could do something in her own community. "When women are in office," said Santana, "the conversation changes a little bit."

California in the Age of Trump

In the months that followed presidential election of Donald J. Trump, he and California squared off over a variety of issues, including immigration, taxes, guns, healthcare, climate change, and the election itself. California led the charge against a number of key Trump Administration policies, sometimes successfully. In March 2018, a court ordered the Environmental Protection Agency (EPA) to identify regions of the country still exceeding federal smog levels. Working alone and with other states, California filed lawsuits on environmental issues such as coal mining on federal land; "fracking" on Native American land; vehicle fuel economy standards; and conflict of interest within the EPA, whose then-chief, Scott Pruitt, had filed 14 lawsuits against the EPA while attorney general for the oil-drilling state of Oklahoma.

California joined in a multi-state lawsuit over the Trump Administration's refusal to reimburse health insurance companies' costs for providing low-cost plans to low earners. State attorneys sued when the administration made it easier for employers to deny their employees insurance coverage for contraception on religious grounds. State attorneys argued that the policy discriminated against women and violated the First Amendment's separation of church and state.

Immigration was another site of contention. Alone and with other states, California sued to block travel bans against Muslim-majority nations; for full disclosure of details regarding Immigration Control and Enforcement (ICE) operations within state borders; and to protect the Deferred Action for Childhood Arrivals (DACA) program. On its own, California sued the Trump administration over threats to cut federal funding to "sanctuary" states unless they cooperated with ICE agents, and to prevent construction of a wall at the U.S.–Mexican border. Immigration and tariff policies have also driven wedges between President Trump and California farmers, who fear loss of cheap labor and Chinese and other export markets for California agricultural products.

Inaugurated as California's 40th governor in January 2019, Democrat Gavin Newsom has since waged what the Atlantic called "total war" against the White House. Responding via President Trump's favorite platform for public pronouncements, social media platform Twitter, Governor Newsom accused Trump of "manufacturing a crisis" at the U.S.–Mexico border and "declaring a made up 'national emergency' in order to seize power." Newsom added: "Our message to the White House is simple: CA will see you in court."

The battle has been joined between the Trump Administration and the State of California. Only time will tell which is David and which is Goliath.

The trends observed at the beginning of the century continued as the second decade neared its end. In 2018, California was still the most populous state in the union. It still led other states in the numbers and percentage of foreign-born, and as (almost) home to the nation's largest population of unsheltered homeless. The state remained difficult to govern, subject to the whims of its voting populace as well as the deep war-chests of special interests and powerful corporations. Many still considered California a western Eden, though others wondered if the state could ever live up to that image. "I don't think the California dream, per se, is over," said Gregory Rodriguez, senior fellow of the New America Foundation, maybe it is just a little "grittier." "Now, perhaps, we have to reassess the California of our imagination."

Suggested Readings

Part One: Prologue

California History, General

Hubert Howe Bancroft, *History of California* (7 vols., 1884–1890).

Robert Glass Cleland and Glenn S. Dumke, *From Wilderness to Empire: A History of California* (1962).

Earl Pomeroy, *The Pacific Slope* (1968).

W. Caughey and Norris Hundley Jr., *California: History of a Remarkable State* (1982).

Bibliographies, General

Francis J. Weber, "A Bibliography of California Bibliographies," *Southern California Quarterly* (1968).

Margaret M. Rocq, *California Local History: A Bibliography and Union List of Library Holdings* (2 vols., 1970, 1976).

Rodman W. Paul and Richard W. Etulain, *The Frontier and the American West* (1977).

Oscar O. Winther and Richard A. Van Orman, *The Trans-Mississippi West: A Guide to Its Periodical Literature, 1811–1967* (1972).

Doyce B. Nunis Jr. and Gloria Ricci Lothrop, *A Guide to the History of California* (1989).

Richard J. Orsi et al., eds., California History Sesquicentennial Series, 4 vols., 1998–2002, special issues of *California History* (Quarterly Journal of the California Historical Society).

Bibliographies, Specific

Adelaide R. Haase, *Index to the Economic Material in the Documents of the States of the United States: California, 1849–1904* (1908).

Francis Farquhar, *Yosemite, the Big Trees, and the High Sierra: A Selective Bibliography* (1948).

Pamela Bleich, "A Study of Graduate Research in California History in California Colleges and Universities," *California Historical Society Quarterly* (various issues, 1964–1966).

Richard Yates and Mary Marshall, *The Lower Colorado: A Bibliography* (1974).

Richard J. Orsi, *A List of References for the History of Agriculture in California* (1974).

Robert F. Heizer, *The Indians of California: A Critical Bibliography* (1976).

Newton D. Lowell, John Bean, and Sylvia Brakke Vane, *California Indians: Primary Resources* (1977).

Lawrence B. Lee, *Reclaiming the American West: An Historiography and Guide* (1979).

J. Carlyle Parker, *An Index to the Biographies in Nineteenth Century California County Histories* (1980).

Interpreting California History

Carey McWilliams, *California: The Great Exception* (1949).

James J. Parsons, "The Uniqueness of California," *American Quarterly* (1955).

Doyce B. Nunis Jr., "California, Why We Come: Myth or Reality," *California Historical Society Quarterly* (1965).

Dennis Hale and Jonathan Eisen, *The California Dream* (1968).

George H. Knoles, ed., *Essays and Assays: California History Reconsidered* (1973).

Kevin Starr, *Americans and the California Dream, 1850–1915* (1973), *Inventing the Dream: California through the Progressive Era* (1985), *Material Dreams: Southern California through the 1920s* (1990), and *Golden Dreams: California in an Age of Abundance, 1950–1963* (2009).

Peter W. Williams, "Reflections in/on/of a Golden State," *American Quarterly* (1976).

James J. Rawls, "The Rise and Fall of the California Dream," *California Historical Courier* (1979).

Robert V. Hine, *California Utopianism: Contemplations of Eden* (1981).

Joel Kotkin and Paul Grabowicz, *California, Inc.* (1982).

Heritage Task Force, *California's Historical and Cultural Resources* (1984).

James D. Houston, *Californians: Searching for the Golden State* (1985).

Dan Walters, *The New California: Facing the 21st Century* (1986).

David Wyatt, *The Fall into Eden: Landscape and Imagination in California* (1986).

"Envisioning California," special issue of *California History* (Winter 1989–90).

Ramón A. Gutiérrez and Richard J. Orsi, eds., *Contested Eden: California Before the Gold Rush* (1997–98).

Claire Perry, *Pacific Arcadia: Images of California, 1600–1915* (1999).

Albert Hurtado, *Herbert Eugene Bolton: Historian of the American Borderlands* (2012).

Atlases and Maps

Warren A. Beck and Ynez D. Haase, *Historical Atlas of California* (1974).

Robert W. Durrenberger and Robert B. Johnson, *California: Patterns on the Land* (1976).

Michael W. Donley et al., *Atlas of California* (1979).

David Hornbeck and David L. Fuller, *California Patterns: A Geographical and Historical Atlas* (1983).

Richard A. Walker and Suresh K. Lodha, *The Atlas of California* (2013).

Geographies

David Hartman, *California and Man* (1968).

David W. Lantis et al., *California: Land of Contrast* (1977).

Crane Miller and Richard Hyslop, *California: The Geography of Diversity* (1983).

Environment and Ecology

John Muir, *The Mountains of California* (1894).

Mary Austin, *Land of Little Rain* (1903).

Edmund C. Jaeger, *The California Desert* (1965).

Alan A. Schoenherr, *A Natural History of California* (1992).

John W. Caughey, "The Californian and His Environment," *California Historical Quarterly* (1972).

Raymond F. Dasmann, *California's Changing Environment* (1981).

Elna Bakker, *An Island Called California: An Ecological Introduction to Its Natural Communities* (1982).

William Deverell and Greg Hise, *Land of Sunshine: An Environmental History of Metropolitan Los Angeles* (2005).

Christopher J. Castañeda and Lee A Simpson, *River City and Valley Life: An Environmental History of the Sacramento Region* (2013).

Robert McLeman, *Climate Change and Human Migration: Past Experiences, Future Challenges* (2014).

Craig H. Jones, *The Mountains that Remade America: How Sierra Nevada Geography Affects Modern Life* (2017).

Alan A. Schoenherr, *A Natural History of California* (rev. ed., 2017).

William F. Deverell and Tom Sitton, *Water and Los Angeles: A Tale of Three Rivers, 1900–1941* (2017).

Flora and Fauna

Tracy I. Storer and Lloyd P. Tevis Jr., *California Grizzly* (1955).

Arthur C. Smith, *Introduction to the Natural History of the San Francisco Bay Region* (1959).

Joel W. Hedgepeth, *Introduction to the Seashore Life of the San Francisco Bay Region* (1962).

Edmund C. Jaeger and Arthur C. Smith, *Introduction to the Natural History of Southern California* (1966).

John Williams and Howard C. Monroe, *Natural History of Northern California* (1976).

Jared Farmer, *Trees in Paradise: A California History* (2013).

Geological History

N. E. A. Hinds, *Evolution of the California Landscape* (1952).

Arthur D. Howard, *Evolution of the Landscape of the San Francisco Bay Region* (1962), and *Geologic History of Middle California* (1979).

Robert Iacopi, *Earthquake Country* (1964).

Mary Hill, *Geology of the Sierra Nevada* (1975).

John McPhee, *Assembling California* (1993).

Bill Guyton, *Glaciers of California* (1998).

Michael Collier, *A Land in Motion: California's San Andreas Fault* (1999).

Joanna L. Dyl, *Seismic City: An Environmental History of San Francisco's 1906 Earthquake* (2017).

Climate

Ernest L. Felton, *California's Many Climates* (1965).

Harold Gilliam, *The Weather of the San Francisco Bay Region* (1966).

Harry P. Bailey, *The Climate of Southern California* (1966).

Prehistoric and Historic Megadroughts

Scott Stine, "Extreme and Persistent Drought in California and Patagonia during Mediaeval Times," *Nature* (June 1994).

William K. Stevens, "Severe Ancient Droughts: A Warning to California," *New York Times* (July 19, 1994).

Connie A. Woodhouse et al., "A 1200-year Perspective of 21st-Century Drought in Southwestern North America," *Proceedings of the National Academy of Sciences*, 107(50): 21283–8 (Dec. 2010).

Paul Rogers, "California Drought: Past Dry Periods Have Lasted More Than 200 Years, Scientists Say," *San Jose Mercury News* (Jan. 25, 2014).

William J. Cowan, "When California Was Waterlogged: The 1862 Floods that Ravaged the West . . . ," *Zocalo Public Square: California Humanities Community Stories* (May 19, 2014).

Jon Wilkman, *Floodpath: The Deadliest Man-Made Disaster in 20th-Century America and the Making of Modern Los Angeles* (2016).

Water

S. Bain et al., *Northern California's Water Industry* (1967).

Erwin Cooper, *Aqueduct Empire: A Guide to Water in California* (1968).

David Seckler, *California Water: A Study in Resource Management* (1971).

Merrill R. Goodall et al., *California Water: A New Political Economy* (1978).

Donald Worster, "Hydraulic Society in California: An Ecological Interpretation," *Agricultural History* (1982), and *Rivers of Empire: Water, Aridity, and the Growth of the American West* (1985).

Joe William Kahrl, *The California Water Atlas* (1979).

Donald J. Pisani, *From Family Farm to Agribusiness: The Irrigation Crusade in California, 1850–1931* (1984).

Marc Reisner, *Cadillac Desert: The American West and Its Disappearing Water* (1993).

Norris Hundley Jr., *The Great Thirst: Californians and Water, 1770s to 1990s* (2001).

Regional Divisiveness

Rockwell D. Hunt, "History of the California State Division Controversy," *Historical Society of Southern California*, Annual Publications (1924).

Roberta McDow, "To Divide or Not to Divide," *Pacific Historian* (1966), and "State Separation Schemes, 1907–1921," *California Historical Society Quarterly* (1970).

Bruce Robeck, "Urban-Rural and Regional Voting Patterns in California Before and After Reapportionment," *Western Political Quarterly* (1970).

Michael P. Rogin and John L. Shover, *Political Change in California: Critical Elections and Social Movements, 1890–1966* (1970).

Michael DiLeo and Eleanor Smith, *Two Californias: The Truth About the Split-State Movement* (1983).

Geography and Agricultural History

Varden Fuller, "The Supply of Agricultural Labor as a Factor in the Evolution of Farm Organization in California" (Ph.D. dissertation, University of California, Berkeley, 1939).

Paul S. Taylor, "The Foundations of California Rural Society," *California Historical Society Quarterly* (1945).

Howard F. Gregor, "The Industrial Farm as a Western Institution," *Journal of the West* (1970).

Lawrence J. Jelinek, *Harvest Empire: A History of California Agriculture* (1982).

Ellen Liebman, *California Farmland: A History of Large Agricultural Landholdings* (1983).

Native California, General

Alfred L. Kroeber, *Handbook of the Indians of California* (1925).

Robert F. Heizer and Mary Ann Whipple, *The California Indians: A Source Book* (1971).

Sherburne F. Cook, *The Population of the California Indians, 1769–1970* (1976).

Lowell J. Bean and Thomas C. Blackburn, *Native Californians: A Theoretical Retrospective* (1976).

Robert Heizer, *Handbook of North American Indians,* Volume 8: California (1978).

George H. Phillips, *The Enduring Struggle: Indians in California History* (1981).

Joseph L. Chartkoff and Kerry Kona Chartkoff, *The Archaeology of California* (1984).

James J. Rawls, *Indians of California: The Changing Image* (1984).

Michael Moratto, *California Archaeology* (1984).

Thomas C. Blackburn and Travis Hudson, *Time's Flotsam: Overseas Collections of California Indian Material Culture* (1990).

Sylvia Brakke Vane and Lowell John Bean, *California Indians: Primary Resources, A Guide to Manuscripts, Artifacts, Documents, Serials, Music, and Illustrations* (1990).

Lowell J. Bean, "California Indians: Diverse and Complex Peoples," *California History* (Fall 1992).

"Indians of California," special issue of *California History* (Fall 1992).

M. Kat Anderson, Michael G. Barbour, and Valerie Whitworth, "A World of Balance and Plenty: Land, Plants, Animals, and Humans in a Pre-European California," William S. Simmons, "Indian Peoples of California," and William Preston, "Serpent in the Garden: Environmental Change in Colonial California," all in Ramón A. Gutiérrez and Richard J. Orsi, eds., *Contested Eden: California Before the Gold Rush* (1997–98).

Brian Fagan, *Before California: An Archaeologist Looks at Our Earliest Inhabitants* (2003).

Victor Golla, *California Indian Languages* (2011).

Tribes, Specific

Frank Forest Latta, *Handbook of Yokuts Indians* (1949).

Bernice Eastman Johnston, *California's Gabrielino Indians* (1962).

Leif C. W. Landberg, *The Chumash Indians of Southern California* (1965).

James F. Downs, *The Two Worlds of the Washo: An Indian Tribe of California and Nevada* (1966).

Lowell J. Bean, *Mukat's People: The Cahuilla Indians of Southern California* (1972).

Malcolm Margolin, *The Ohlone Way: Indian Life in the San Francisco-Monterey Bay Area* (1978).

William McCawley, *The First Angelinos: The Gabrielino Indians of Los Angeles* (1996).

Matthew S. Makley, *The Small Shall be Strong: A History of Lake Tahoe's Washoe Indians* (2018).

Economy

James T. Davis, "Trade Routes and Economic Exchange Among the Indians of California," in Robert F. Heizer, ed., *Aboriginal California: Three Studies in Cultural History* (1963).

Chester King, "Chumash Inter-Village Economic Exchange," *The Indian Historian* (1971).

William Wallace, "Indian Use of California's Rocks and Minerals," *Journal of the West* (1971).

Douglas J. Kennett and James P. Kennett, "Competitive and Cooperative Responses to Climatic Instability in Coastal Southern California," in L. Mark Raab and Terry L. Jones, *Prehistoric California: Archaeology and the Myth of Paradise* (2004).

Science, Ecology, and Agriculture

E. F. Castetter et al., *Yuman Indian Agriculture* (1951).

Jack D. Forbes, "Indian Horticulture West and Northwest of the Colorado River," *Journal of the West* (1963).

Lowell John Bean and Katherine S. Saubel, *Temalpakh: Cahuilla Indian Knowledge and Usage of Plants* (1972).

Lowell J. Bean and Harry W. Lawton, "Some Explanations for the Rise of Cultural Complexity in Native California with Comments on Proto-Agriculture and Agriculture," in Henry T. Lewis, ed., *Patterns of Indian Burning in California* (1973).

E. K. Balls, *Early Uses of California Plants* (1975).

Harry Lawton et al., "Agriculture Among the Paiute of Owens Valley," *Journal of California Anthropology* (1976).

Travis Hudson and Ernest Underhay, *Crystals in the Sky: An Intellectual Odyssey Involving the Chumash Astronomy, Cosmology, and Rock Art* (1978).

Robert F. Heizer and Albert B. Elsasser, *The Natural World of the California Indians* (1980).

Malcolm Margolin, ed., "California Indians and the Environment," special issue of *News from Native California* (Spring 1992).

Thomas C. Blackburn and Kat Anderson, eds., *Before the Wilderness: Environmental Management by Native Californians* (1993).

Terry L. Jones and L. Mark Raab, "The Rediscovery of California Prehistory," Terry L. Jones et al., "Demographic Crises in Western North America During the Medieval Climatic Anomaly," Jack M. Broughton, "Declines in Mammalian Foraging Efficiency During the Late Holocene, San Francisco Bay," Mark E. Basgall, "Resource Intensification Among Hunter-Gatherers: Acorn Economies in Prehistoric California," Patricia M. Lambert, "Health in Prehistoric Populations of the Santa Barbara Channel Islands," Kelly R. McGuire and William R. Hildebrandt, "The Possibilities of Men and Women: Gender and the California Milling Stone Horizon," all in L. Mark Raab and Terry L. Jones, *Prehistoric California: Archaeology and the Myth of Paradise* (2004).

Kent Lightfoot and Otis Parrish, *California Indians and Their Environment* (2009).

M. Kat Anderson, *Tending the Wild: Native American Knowledge and the Management of California's Natural Resources* (2013).

Culture, Religion, and Arts

Theodora Kroeber, *The Inland Whale: Nine Stories Retold from California Indian Legends* (1959).

Cambell Grant, *The Rock Paintings of the Chumash: A Study of California Indian Culture* (1965).

James R. Moriarty, "A Reconstruction of the Development of Primitive Religion in California," *Southern California Quarterly* (1970).

Thomas C. Blackburn, *December's Child: A Book of Chumash Oral Narratives* (1975).

Lowell J. Bean, ed., *California Indian Shamanism* (1992).

Malcolm Margolin, ed., *The Way We Lived: California Indian Stories, Songs, and Reminiscences* (1993).

Social and Political Structure

Tom King, "New Views of California Indian Societies," *The Indian Historian* (1972).

Lowell J. Bean and Thomas F. King, *Antap: California Indian Political and Economic Organization* (1974).

Edith Wallace, "Sexual Status and Role Differences," in Robert Heizer, *Handbook of North American Indians, Volume 8: California* (1978).

Robert L. Bettinger, *Orderly Anarchy: Sociopolitical Evolution in Aboriginal California* (2015).

Part Two: Europeans and Indians

Estanislao's Rebellion

José María Amador, "*Memorias sobre la Historia de California*," and Joaquin Piña, "*Diario de la expedición al valle de San José*," June 13, 1829 (Bancroft Library, University of California, Berkeley).

George Tays, "Mariano Guadalupe Vallejo and Sonoma—A Biography and a History," *California Historical Society Quarterly* (1937–1938).

Francis F. McCarthy, *The History of Mission San Jose, California, 1797–1835* (1958).

Sherburne F. Cook, "Colonial Expeditions to the Interior of California: Central Valley, 1820–1840," *University of California Anthropological Records* (1962).

Jack Holterman, "The Revolt of Estanislao," *The Indian Historian* (1970).

Alan Rosenus, *General M.G. Vallejo and the Advent of the Americans: A Biography* (1995).

Background, Discovery, and Naming

Robert Ryal Miller, *Mexico: A History* (1985), and "Cortés and the First Attempt to Colonize California," *California Historical Quarterly* (1974).

Donald C. Cutter, "Sources of the Name 'California,'" *Arizona and the West* (1961).

Spanish Colonization, General

Hubert H. Bancroft, *California Pastoral, 1769–1848* (1888).

Charles E. Chapman, *A History of California: The Spanish Period* (1925).

David J. Weber, ed., *New Spain's Far Northern Frontier: Essays on Spain in the American West* (1979).

John A. Schutz, *Spain's Colonial Outpost* (1985).

David J. Weber, *The Spanish Frontier in North America* (1992).

Ramón A. Gutiérrez and Richard J. Orsi, eds., *Contested Eden: California before the Gold Rush* (1997–98).

Spanish Exploration

Henry R. Wagner, *Spanish Voyages to the Northwest Coast of America in the Sixteenth Century* (1929), and *Juan Rodríguez Cabrillo: Discoverer of the Coast of California* (1941).

Maurice G. Holmes, *From New Spain by Sea to the Californias, 1519–1668* (1963).

W. Michael Mathes, *Vizcaíno and Spanish Exploration in the Pacific Ocean, 1580–1630* (1968).

Donald C. Cutter, *The California Coast: A Bilingual Edition of Documents from the Sutro Collection* (1969).

Harry Kelsey, "The California Armada of Juan Rodríguez Cabrillo," *Southern California Quarterly* (1979), and *Juan Rodríguez Cabrillo* (1986).

Harlan Hague, "'Here Is the Road': The Indian as Guide," *The Californians* (1985).

Drake in California

Henry R. Wagner, *Drake on the Pacific Coast* (1970).

Robert F. Heizer, *Francis Drake and the California Indians, 1579* (1974), and *Elizabethan California* (1974).

James D. Hart, *The Plate of Brass Reexamined* (1977).

Warren L. Hanna, *Lost Harbor: The Controversy over Drake's California Anchorage* (1979).

Harry Kelsey, "Did Francis Drake Really Visit California?" *Western Historical Quarterly* (1990).

Edward VonderPorten et al., "Who Made Drake's Plate of Brass? Hint: It Wasn't Francis Drake," *California History* (2002).

Robert Chandler et al., "A Hoax Gone Awry: E Clampus Vitus and Sir Francis Drake's 1579 Plate of Brasse," *California Territorial Quarterly* (2016).

Founding the California Colony

Herbert I. Priestly, *José de Gálvez, Visitador-General of New Spain* (1916).

Charles E. Chapman, *The Founding of Spanish California: The Northwestward Expansion of New Spain* (1916).

Theodore E. Treutlein, "The Portolá Expedition of 1769–1770," *California Historical Society Quarterly* (1968), and *San Francisco Bay: Discovery and Colonization* (1968).

Antonia Castañeda, "Engendering the History of Alta California, 1769–1848," in *Contested Eden: California Before the Gold Rush* (1998), "Gender, Race, and Culture: Spanish Mexican Women in the Historiography of Frontier California," in *Unequal Sisters: A Multicultural Reader in U.S. Women's History* (2004).

Missions and Missionaries

Herbert E. Bolton, "The Mission as a Frontier Institution in the Spanish American Colonies," *American Historical Review* (1917).

Maynard J. Geiger, *The Life and Times of Fray Junípero Serra* (1959), and "Fray Junípero Serra: Organizer and Administrator of the Upper California Missions, 1769–1784," *California Historical Society Quarterly* (1963).

Maynard Geiger, *Franciscan Missionaries in Hispanic California, 1769–1848: A Biographical Dictionary* (1969), and *Mission Santa Barbara, 1782–1965* (1965).

Francis F. Guest, *Fermín Francisco de Lasuén: A Biography* (1973).

Robert Archibald, "Indian Labor at the California Missions: Slavery or Salvation," *Journal of San Diego History* (1978).

John Francis Bannon, "The Mission as a Frontier Institution: Sixty Years of Interest and Research," *Western Historical Quarterly* (1979).

"Serra and His California," *The Californians* (1984).

James A. Sandos, "Junípero Serra's Canonization and the Historical Record," *American Historical Review* (1988).

James J. Rawls, "The California Mission as Symbol and Myth," *California History* (Fall 1992).

Richard Steven Street, "First Farmworkers, First *Braceros*: Baja California Field Hands and the Origins of Farm Labor Importation in California Agriculture, 1769–1790," *California History* (Winter 1996–97).

Kent Lightfoot, *The Legacy of Colonial Encounters on the California Frontier* (2006).

Lisbeth Haas, *Saints and Citizens: Indigenous Histories of Colonial Missions and Mexican California* (2013).

Steven W. Hackel, *Junípero Serra: California's Founding Father* (2013).

Rose Marie Beebe and Robert M. Senkewicz, *Junípero Serra: California, Indians, and the Transformation of a Missionary* (2015).

Presidios and Pueblos

Oscar O. Winther, "The Story of San José, 1777–1868: California's First Pueblo," *California Historical Society Quarterly* (1934).

Francis F. Guest, "Municipal Institutions in Spanish California, 1769–1821" (Ph.D. dissertation, University of Southern California, 1961), and "Municipal Government in Spanish California," *California Historical Society Quarterly* (1967).

Leon G. Campbell, "The Spanish Presidio in Alta California During the Mission Period, 1769–1784," *Journal of the West* (1977).

John W. Reps, "Expansion of the Spanish Borderlands: Urban Settlement of Arizona and California in the Hispanic Era," in his *Cities of the American West* (1979).

Richard S. Whitehead, "Alta California's Four Fortresses," *Southern California Quarterly* (1983).

Diane Spencer-Hancock and William E. Pritchard, "El Castillo de Monterey, Frontline of Defense," *California History* (1984).

Joseph P. Sánchez, *Spanish Bluecoats: The Catalonian Volunteers in Northwestern New Spain, 1767–1810* (1990).

Politics and Government

Theodore Grivas, "Alcalde Rule: The Nature of Local Government in Spanish and Mexican California," *California Historical Society Quarterly* (1961).

Edwin A. Beilharz, *Felipe de Neve, First Governor of California* (1972).

Donald A. Nuttall, "The Gobernantes of Spanish Upper California," *California Historical Society Quarterly* (1972).

Daniel S. Garr, "Power and Priorities: Church-State Boundary Disputes in Spanish California," *California History* (1978).

Social, Economic, and Cultural Development

Leon G. Campbell, "The First Californios: Presidial Society in Spanish California," *Journal of the West* (1972).

Manuel P. Servín, "California's Hispanic Heritage: A View of the Spanish Myth," *San Diego History* (1973).

Marie E. Northrup, *Spanish-Mexican Families of Early California, 1769–1850* (1976).

Oakah L. Jones, *Los Paisanos: Spanish Settlers on the Northern Frontier of New Spain* (1978).

David Hornbeck, "Land Tenure and Rancho Expansion in Alta California," *Journal of Historical Geography* (1978).

Albert Camarillo, *Chicanos in a Changing Society: From Mexican Pueblos to American Barrios in Santa Barbara and Southern California, 1848–1930* (1979) and *Chicanos in California: A History of Mexican Americans in California* (1984).

Robert R. Alvarez Jr., *Familia: Migration and Adaptation in Baja and Alta California, 1800–1975* (1987).

Douglas Monroy, *Thrown Among Strangers: The Making of Mexican Culture in Frontier California* (1990).

European Conquest of Nature

Alfred W. Crosby Jr., *The Columbian Exchange: Biological and Cultural Consequences of 1492* (1972), and *Ecological Imperialism: The Biological Expansion of Europe, 900–1900* (1986).

Burton L. Gordon, *Monterey Bay Area: Natural History and Cultural Imprints* (1977).

Michael Barbour and Valerie Whitworth, "California's Grassroots: Native or European?" *Pacific Discovery* (Winter 1992).

John Ryan Fischer, *Cattle Colonization: An Environmental History of California and Hawaii* (2015).

Native Acculturation and Indian-Colonial Conflict

Edward H. Spicer, *Cycles of Conquest: The Impact of Spain, Mexico, and the United States on the Indians of the Southwest, 1533–1960* (1962).

Jack D. Forbes, *Warriors of the Colorado* (1965).

C. Alan Hutchinson, "The Mexican Government and the Mission Indians of Upper California, 1821–1835," *The Americas* (1965).

Martha Voght, "Shamans and Padres: The Religion of Southern California Mission Indians," *Pacific Historical Review* (1967).

Delfina Cuero, *The Autobiography of Delfina Cuero, A Diegueño* (1970).

Sylvia M. Broadbent, "Conflict at Monterey: Indian Horse Raiding, 1820–1850," *Journal of California Anthropology* (1974).

George H. Phillips, "Indians and the Breakdown of the Spanish Mission System in California," *Ethnohistory* (1974), *Chiefs and Challengers: Indian Resistance and Cooperation in Southern California, 1769–1906* (1975, 2014), "Indians in Los Angeles, 1781–1875: Economic Integration, Social Disintegration," *Pacific Historical Review* (1980), and *Indians and Intruders in Central California, 1769–1849* (1993).

Thomas Blackburn, "The Chumash Revolt of 1824: A Native Account," *The Journal of California Anthropology* (1975).

Sherburne F. Cook, *The Conflict Between the California Indian and White Civilization* (1976).

Robert F. Heizer, "The Impact of Colonization on the Native California Societies," *Journal of San Diego History* (1978).

Francis F. Guest, "An Examination of the Thesis of S. F. Cook on the Forced Conversion of Indians in the California Missions," *Southern California Quarterly* (1979), and "Cultural Perspectives of California Mission Life," *Southern California Quarterly* (1983).

Victoria Brady, Sarah Crowe, and Lyn Reese, "Resist! Survival Tactics of Indian Women," *California History* (Spring 1984).

Wilbur R. Jacobs, "Sherburne Friend Cook: Rebel-Revisionist (1896–1974)," *Pacific Historical Review* (1985).

Albert L. Hurtado, *Indian Survival on the California Frontier* (1988), "Sexuality in California's Franciscan Missions: Cultural Perceptions and Sad Realities," *California History* (Fall 1992), and *Intimate Frontiers: Sex, Gender, and Culture in Old California* (1999).

David H. Thomas, ed., *Columbian Consequences: Archaeological and Historical Perspectives on the Spanish Borderlands West* (1989).

Robert H. Jackson, "Patterns of Demographic Change in the Alta California Missions: The Case of Santa Ines," *California History* (Fall 1992), "Patterns of Demographic Change in the Missions of Central Alta California," *Journal of California and Great Basin Anthropology* (1987).

Daniel Reff, *Disease, Depopulation, and Culture Change in Northwestern New Spain, 1518–1764* (1991).

Edward D. Castillo, "Gender Status and Decline, Resistance, and Accommodation among Female Neophytes in the Missions of California: A San Gabriel Case Study," *American Indian Culture and Research Journal* (1994).

Robert H. Jackson, *Indian Population Decline: The Missions of Northwestern New Spain, 1687–1840* (1994).

Robert H. Jackson and Edward Castillo, *Indians, Franciscans, and Spanish Colonization: The Impact of the Mission System on California Indians* (1995).

Randall Milliken, *A Time of Little Choice: The Disintegration of Tribal Culture in the San Francisco Bay Area, 1769–1810* (1995).

Lisbeth Haas, *Conquests and Historical Identities in California, 1769–1936* (1995).

Virginia M. Bouvier, *Women and the Conquest of California, 1542–1840: Codes of Silence* (2001).

Linda Heidenreich, *This Land was Mexican Once: Histories of Resistance from Northern California* (2007).

James A. Sandos, *Converting California: Indians and Franciscans in the Missions* (2008).

Kathleen L. Hull, *Pestilence and Persistence: Yosemite Indian Demography in Colonial California* (2004).

Steven W. Hackel, *Children of Coyote, Missionaries of St. Francis: Indian-Spanish Relations in Colonial California, 1769–1850* (2005).

Quincy Newell, *Constructing Lives at Mission San Francisco: Native Californians and Hispanic Colonists, 1776–1821* (2009).

Part Three: The Pastoral Era

José Castro and the Bear Flag Revolt

Simeon Ide, *A Biographical Sketch of the Life of William B. Ide* (1880, 1967).

Neal H. H. Bancroft, *History of California*, vol. 5 (1886).

John C. Frémont, *Memoirs of My Life* (1887).

Rosalía Vallejo de Leese, "History of the Bear Party" (1887).

John A. Hussey, "Bear Flag Revolt," *American Heritage* (1950).

John A. Hawgood, "John C. Frémont and the Bear Flag Revolution: A Reappraisal," *Southern California Quarterly* (1962).

Fred B. Rogers, *William B. Ide: Bear Flagger* (1962).

Ferol Egan, *Frémont, Explorer for a Restless Nation* (1977).

Harlan Hague and David J. Langum, *Thomas O. Larkin: A Life of Patriotism and Profit in Old California* (1990).

Andrew Rolle, *John Charles Frémont: Character As Destiny* (1991).

Linda Heidenreich, *This Land was Mexican Once: Histories of Resistance from Northern California* (2007).

Politics and Secularization

George Tays, "Revolutionary California: The Political History of California During the Mexican Period, 1822–1846" (Ph.D. dissertation, University of California, Berkeley, 1932).

Gerald J. Geary, *The Secularization of the California Missions, 1810–1846* (1934).

Manuel P. Servín, "The Secularization of the California Missions: A Reappraisal," *Southern California Quarterly* (1952).

Woodrow James Hansen, *The Search for Authority in California* (1960).

C. Alan Hutchinson, *Frontier Settlement in Mexican California: The Híjar-Padrés Colony and Its Origins, 1769–1835* (1965), and "The Mexican Government and the California Indians," *The Americas* (1965).

David J. Weber, *The Mexican Frontier, 1821–1846: The American Southwest Under Mexico* (1982).

David J. Langum, *Law and Community on the Mexican California Frontier* (1987).

Alan Rosenus, *General M.G. Vallejo and the Advent of the Americans: A Biography* (1995).

Robert Ryal Miller, *Juan Alvarado, Governor of California, 1836–1842* (1998).

Robert Phelps, "On Comic Opera Revolutions: Maneuver Theory and the Art of War in Mexican California, 1821–1845," *California History* (2006).

Carlos Manuel Salomon, *Pio Pico: The Last Governor of Mexican California* (2010).

Rancho Society

Richard Henry Dana, *Two Years Before the Mast* (1840).

Alfred Robinson, *Life in California* (1846, 1970).

W. W. Robinson, *Ranchos Become Cities* (1939) and *Land in California* (1948).

George Tays, "Mariano Guadalupe Vallejo and Sonoma—A Biography and a History," *California Historical Society Quarterly* (1937–1938).

Myrtle M. McKittrick, *Vallejo, Son of California* (1944).

Robert G. Cleland, *The Cattle on a Thousand Hills: Southern California, 1850–1880* (1941, 1951).

Robert Cameron Gillingham, *The Rancho San Pedro* (1961).

Doyce B. Nunis, Jr., ed., *The California Diary of Faxon Dean Atherton* (1964).

Madie Brown Emparan, *The Vallejos of California* (1968).

Albert Camarillo, *Chicanos in a Changing Society: From Mexican Pueblos to American Barrios* (1979).

Gloria A. Miranda, "Hispano-Mexican Childrearing Practices in Pre-American Santa Barbara," *Southern California Quarterly* (Winter, 1983) and "Racial and Cultural Dimensions of *Gente de Razón* Status in Spanish and Mexican California," *Southern California Quarterly* (1988).

Federico A. Sanchez, "Rancho Life in Alta California," *Masterkey* (1986).

Robert A. Alvarez, *Familia: Migration and Adaptation in Baja and Alta California, 1800–1975* (1987).

Albert L. Hurtado, "California Indians and the Workaday West: Labor, Assimilation, and Survival," *California History* (Spring, 1990).

Douglas Monroy, *Thrown Among Strangers: The Making of Mexican Culture in Frontier California* (1990).

Antonia Castañeda, "Gender, Race, and Culture: Spanish-Mexican Women in the Historiography of Frontier California," *Frontiers* (1990), and Castañeda, "Engendering the History of Alta California, 1769–1848," in Gutiérrez et al., *Contested Eden* (1998).

Stephen W. Silliman, *Lost Laborers in Colonial California: Native Americans and the Archaeology of Rancho Petaluma* (2004).

Michael Gonzalez, *This Small City Will Be a Mexican Paradise: Exploring the Origins of Mexican Culture in Los Angeles, 1821–1846* (2005).

Maria Raquel Casas, "Victoria Reid and the Politics of Identity," in *Latina Legacies: Identity, Biography, and Community* (2005).

Rose Marie Beebe and Robert M. Senkewicz, eds., *Testimonios: Early California through the Eyes of Women, 1815–1848* (2007).

Linda Heidenreich, *This Land Was Mexican Once: Histories of Resistance from Northern California* (2007).

Jeanne McDonnell, *Juana Briones of Nineteenth-Century California* (2008).

Louise Pubols, *The Father of All: The de la Guerra Family, Power, and Patriarchy in Mexican California* (2009).

George H. Phillips, *Vineyards and Vaqueros: Indian Labor and the Economic Expansion of Southern California, 1771–1877* (2010).

Foreigners in California

Harrison C. Dale, *The Ashley-Smith Explorations and the Discovery of a Central Route to the Pacific* (1918, 1941).

Adele Ogden, "Hide and Tallow: McCullough, Hartnell and Company, 1822–1828," *California Historical Society Quarterly* (1927), "Boston Hide Droughers Along the California Shores," *California Historical Society Quarterly* (1929), and "Alfred Robinson, New England Merchant in Mexican California," *California Historical Society Quarterly* (1944).

Susanna Bryant Dakin, *The Lives of William Hartnell* (1949).

Robert G. Cleland, *This Reckless Breed of Men: The Trappers and Fur Traders of the Southwest* (1950).

Andrew Rolle, "Jedediah Strong Smith: New Documentation," *Mississippi Valley Historical Review* (1953).

Dale L. Morgan, *Jedediah Smith and the Opening of the West* (1953).

Irving Stone, *Men to Match My Mountains: The Opening of the Far West, 1840–1900* (1956).

Andrew F. Rolle, *An American in California: The Biography of William Heath Davis* (1956).

John A. Hawgood, "The Pattern of Yankee Infiltration in Mexican Alta California, 1821–1846," *Pacific Historical Review* (1958).

George R. Stewart, *Ordeal by Hunger: The Story of the Donner Party* (1960).

David J. Weber, "Mexico and the Mountain Men," *Journal of the West* (1969).

James R. Gibson, *Imperial Russia in Frontier America* (1976).

George R. Brooks, ed., *The Southwest Expedition of Jedediah Smith: His Personal Account of the Journey to California, 1826–27* (1977 and 1989).

John D. Unruh Jr., *The Plains Across: The Overland Emigrants and the Trans-Mississippi West, 1848–1860* (1979).

Harlan Hague and David J. Langum, *Thomas O. Larkin: A Life of Patriotism and Profit in Old California* (1990).

George Harwood Phillips, *Indians and Intruders in Central California, 1769–1849* (1993) and *Indians and Indian Agents: The Origins of the Reservation System in California, 1849–1852* (1997).

Kenneth N. Owen, ed., *John Sutter and a Wider West* (1994).

Robert Ryal Miller, *Captain Richardson: Mariner, Ranchero, and Founder of San Francisco* (1995).

Charles B. Churchill, *Adventurers and Prophets: American Autobiographers in Mexican California, 1828–1847* (1995).

Thomas Frederick Howard, *Sierra Crossing: First Roads to California* (1998).

Michael J. Gillis and Michael F. Magliari, *John Bidwell and California: The Life and Writings of a Pioneer, 1841–1900* (2003).

Albert L. Hurtado, *John Sutter: A Life on the North American Frontier* (2006).

Will S. Bagley, *So Rugged and Mountainous: Blazing the Trails to Oregon and California, 1812–1848* (2010).

American Takeover

Ernest A. Wiltsee, "The British Vice-Consul in California and the Events of 1846," *California Historical Society Quarterly* (1931).

Werner H. Marti, *Messenger of Destiny: The California Adventures, 1846–1847, of Archibald H. Gillespie* (1960).

Dwight L. Clarke, *Stephen Watts Kearny, Soldier of the West* (1961).

Charles G. Sellers, *James K. Polk, Continentalist* (1966).

Neal Harlow, *California Conquered: War and Peace on the Pacific, 1846–1850* (1982).

Ramón Gutiérrez and Richard J. Orsi, eds., *Contested Eden: California Before the Gold Rush* (1998), Stephen G. Hyslop, *Contest for California: From Spanish Colonization to the American Conquest* (2012).

Tamara Venit Shelton, *A Squatter's Republic: Land and the Politics of Monopoly in California, 1850–1900*.

See also suggested readings for Bear Flag Revolt, above.

Part Four: Gold and the Americanization of California

Gold Rush Women

Jessie Benton Frémont, *A Year of American Travel* (1878).

Luzena S. Wilson, *Luzena Stanley Wilson, '49er* (1937).

Elisabeth Margo, *Taming the Forty-Niner* (1955).

J. N. Bowman, "Prominent Women in Provincial California," *Southern California Historical Society Quarterly* (1957).

Rodman W. Paul, "In Search of 'Dame Shirley'," *Pacific Historical Review* (1964).

Carl I. Wheat, ed., *The Shirley Letters from the California Mines, 1851–1852* (1965).

Christiane Fischer, *Let Them Speak for Themselves: Women in the American West, 1849–1900* (1977).

Andrew J. Rotter, "'Matilda, for God's Sake Write': Women and Families on the Argonaut Mind," *California Historical Quarterly* (1979).

Robert L. Griswold, "Apart but Not Adrift: Wives, Divorce, and Independence in California, 1850–1890," *Pacific Historical Review* (1980).

Marsha M. Allen, *Traveling West: Nineteenth Century Women on the Overland Routes* (1987).

Joan Levy, *They Saw the Elephant: Women in the California Gold Rush* (1989).

Marlene Smith-Baranzini, "Out of the Shadows: Louisa Clappe's Life and Early California Writing," *California History* (1999).

Nancy J. Taniguchi, "Weaving a Different World: Women and the California Gold Rush," in *Rooted in Barbarous Soil: People, Culture, and Community in Gold Rush California* (2000).

Miners and Mining

Valeska Bari, *The Course of Empire: First Hand Accounts of California in the Days of the Gold Rush of '49* (1931).

John H. Kemble, *The Panama Route, 1848–1869* (1943).

John Walton Caughey, *The California Gold Rush* (1948).

Oscar Lewis, *Sea Routes to the Gold Fields* (1949).

Ralph H. Bieber, "California Gold Mania," *Mississippi Valley Historical Review* (1948).

Rodman W. Paul, *California Gold* (1947), *Mining Frontiers of the Far West, 1848–1880* (1963), and *The California Gold Discovery* (1966).

George R. Stewart, *The California Trail* (1962).

Robert L. Kelley, *Gold vs. Grain* (1959).

John D. Unruh, *The Plains Across: The Overland Emigrants and the Trans-Mississippi West, 1840–1860* (1979).

James S. Holliday, *The World Rushed In: The California Gold Rush Experience* (1981).

Douglas R. Littlefield, "Water Rights during the California Gold Rush: Conflicts over Economic Points of View," *Western Historical Quarterly* (1983).

Malcolm J. Rohrbough, *Days of Gold: The California Gold Rush and the American Nation* (1997).

J. S. Holliday and others, "National Gold Rush Symposium," *California History* (1998).

J. S. Holliday, *Rush for Riches: Gold Fever and the Making of California* (1999).

James E. Davis, ed., *Dreams to Dust: A Diary of the California Gold Rush, 1849–1850* (1989).

Mary Hill, *Gold: The California Story* (2000).

Will S. Bagley, *With Golden Visions Bright before Them: Trails to the Mining West, 1849–1852* (2012).

Land, Politics, and Statehood

William H. Ellison, *A Self-Governing Dominion: California, 1849–1860* (1950).

Earl Pomeroy, "California, 1846–1860: Politics in a Representative Frontier State," *California Historical Society Quarterly* (1953).

Paul W. Gates, "The Adjudication of Spanish-Mexican Land Claims in California," *Huntington Library Quarterly* (1958), "The California Land Act of 1851," *California Historical Quarterly* (1971), and *Land and Law in California: Essays on Land Policies* (1991).

Theodore Grivas, *Military Governments in California, 1846–1850* (1963).

Robert H. Becker, *Diseños of the California Land Grants* (1964) and *Designs on the Land* (1969).

Michael P. Rogin and John L. Shover, *Political Change in California, 1800–1960* (1970).

Royce Delmatier et al., *The Rumble of California Politics, 1847–1970* (1970).

Robert J. Chandler, "The Velvet Glove: The Army during the Secession Crisis in California, 1860–1861," *Journal of the West* (1981).

Spencer C. Olin Jr., *California Politics, 1846–1920* (1981).

Richard Griswold del Castillo, *The Treaty of Guadalupe Hidalgo: A Legacy of Conflict* (1990).

Gordon M. Bakken, *Practicing Law in Frontier California* (1991).

Christian Fritz, *Federal Justice in California: The Court of Ogden Hoffman, 1851–1891* (1991).

David A. Johnson, *Founding the Far West: California, Oregon, and Nevada, 1840–1890* (1992).

Beverly E. Bastian, "'I Heartily Regret That I Ever Touched a Title in California': Henry Wager Halleck, the Californios, and the Clash of Legal Cultures," *California History* (Winter 1993/94).

Donald J. Pisani, "Squatter Law in California, 1850–1858," *Western Historical Quarterly* (1994).

Arthur Quinn, *The Rivals: William Gwin, David Broderick, and the Birth of California* (1994).

Rosaura Sanchez and Beatrice Pita, "Maria Amparo Ruiz de Burton and the Power of Her Pen," in Vicki L. Ruiz et al., *Latina Legacies: Identity, Biography, and Community* (2005).

Leonard L. Richards, *The California Gold Rush and the Coming of the Civil War* (2007).

Race, Nationality, and Ethnic Conflict: General

Rosalía Vallejo de Leese, "History of the Bear Party" (1887).

Allyn C. Loosely, "Foreign Born Population in California" (M.A. thesis, University of California, Berkeley, 1927).

Peyton Hurt, "The Rise and Fall of the 'Know-Nothings' in California," *California Historical Society Quarterly* (1930).

Rodman W. Paul, "The Origin of the Chinese Issue in California," *Mississippi Valley Historical Review* (1938).

Doris M. Wright, "The Making of Cosmopolitan California: An Analysis of Immigration, 1848–1870," *California Historical Society Quarterly* (1940).

Bradford F. Luckingham, "Immigrant Life in Emergent San Francisco," *Journal of the West* (1973).

Gerald Stanley, "Racism and the Early Republican Party: The 1856 Presidential Election in California," *Pacific Historical Review* (1974).

Robert E. Levinson, *Jews in the California Gold Rush* (1978).

R. A. Burchell, *The San Francisco Irish, 1848–1880* (1980).

Tomas Almaguer, *Racial Fault Lines: The Historical Origins of White Supremacy in California* (1994).

Lisbeth Haas, *Conquests and Historical Identities in California, 1769–1936* (1995).

Susan L. Johnson, *Roaring Camp: The Social World of the California Gold Rush* (2000).

Miroslava Chávez-García, *Negotiating Conquest: Gender and Power in California, 1770s to 1880s* (2004).

Stacey L. Smith, *Freedom's Frontier: California and the Struggle over Unfree Labor, Emancipation, and Reconstruction* (2013).

D. Michael Bottoms, *An Aristocracy of Color: Race and Reconstruction in California and the West, 1850–1890* (2013).

David Torres-Rouff, *Before L.A.: Race, Space, and Municipal Power in Los Angeles, 1781–1894* (2013).

African Americans

Rudolph M. Lapp, *Blacks in Gold Rush California* (1977), and *Afro-American Californians* (1987).

James A. Fisher, "A History of the Political and Social Development of the Black Community in California, 1850–1950" (Ph.D. dissertation, SUNY, 1971).

James A. Fisher, "The Political Development of the Black Community in California, 1850–1950," *California Historical Quarterly* (1971).

Douglas H. Daniels, *Pioneer Urbanites: A Social and Cultural History of Black San Francisco* (1980).

Glenda Riley, "American Daughters: Black Women in the West," *Montana* (1988).

Dolores Hayden, "Biddy Mason's Los Angeles, 1856–1891" *California History 68* (1989).

Delores Nason McBroome, *Parallel Communities: African Americans in California's East Bay, 1850–1963* (1994).

Susan Bragg, "'Anxious Foot Soldiers': Sacramento's Black Women and Education in Nineteenth-Century California," in *In Search of the Racial Frontier: African Americans in the American West, 1528–1990* (1998).

Willi Coleman, "African American Women and Community Development in California, 1848–1900" in Lawrence B. DeGraaf et al., *Seeking El Dorado: African Americans in California* (2001).

Lynn M. Hudson, *The Making of "Mammy Pleasant": A Black Entrepreneur in Nineteenth-century San Francisco* (2003).

Barbara Y. Welke, "Rights of Passage: Gendered-Rights Consciousness and the Quest for Freedom, San Francisco, California, 1850–1870," in Quintard Taylor et al., *African American Women Confront the West, 1600–2000* (2003).

Shirley Ann Wilson Moore, "'We Feel the Want of Protection:' The Politics of Law and Race in California, 1848–1878," in *Taming the Elephant: Politics, Government, and Law in Pioneer California* (2003).

Stacey L. Smith, "Remaking Slavery in a Free State: Masters and Slaves in Gold Rush California," *Pacific Historical Review* (2011).

Californios, Mexicans, and Latin Americans

Carey McWilliams, *North from Mexico* (1948).

Leonard Pitt, *The Decline of the Californios* (1966).

Vivien Juárez Rose, *The Past is Father of the Present: Spanish California History and Family Legends, 1737–1973* (1974).

Abraham P. Nasatir, "Chileans in California during the Gold Rush Period and the Establishment of the Chilean Consulate," *California Historical Quarterly* (Spring, 1974).

Genaro Padilla, *My History, Not Yours: The Formation of Mexican American Autobiography* (Madison: University of Wisconsin Press, 1993).

Rosaura Sánchez, Beatrice Pita and Bárbara Reyes, *Nineteenth Century Californio Testimonial* (1994).

Rosaura Sánchez, *Telling Identities: The Californio Testimonios* (1995).

Rosaura Sanchez and Beatrice Pita, "Maria Amparo Ruiz de Burton and the Power of Her Pen," in *Latina Legacies: Identity, Biography, and Community* (2005).

Linda Heidenreich, *This Land Was Mexican Once: Histories of Resistance from Northern California* (2007).

John Boessenecker, *Bandido: The Life and Times of Tiburcio Vasquez* (2010).

Edward D. Melillo, *Strangers on Familiar Soil: Rediscovering the Chile-California Connection* (2015).

Native Americans

Theodora Kroeber, *Ishi in Two Worlds: A Biography of the Last Wild Indian in North America* (1961).

James J. Rawls, "Gold Diggers: Indian Miners in the California Gold Rush," *California Historical Quarterly* (1976), and *Indians of California: The Changing Image* (1984).

Lynwood Carranco and Estle Beard, *Genocide and Vendetta: The Round Valley Wars of Northern California* (1981).

Albert L. Hurtado, *Indian Survival on the California Frontier* (1988).

William Strobridge, *Regulars in the Redwoods: The U.S. Army in Northern California, 1852–1861* (1994).

Karl Kroeber and Clifton Kroeber, eds., *Ishi in Three Centuries* (2003).

Michael F. Magliari, "Free Soil, Unfree Labor: Cave Johnson Couts and the Binding of Indian Workers in California, 1850–1867," *Pacific Historical Review* (2004).

Michael F. Magliari, "Free State Slavery: Bound Indian Labor and Slave Trafficking in California's Sacramento Valley, 1850–1864," *Pacific Historical Review* (2012).

Michael F. Magliari, "Naming the Crime: Genocide, Extermination, or Ethnic Cleansing?" *H-AmIndian* (2016).

Brendan C. Lindsay, *Murder State: California's Native American Genocide, 1846–1873* (2012).

Benjamin L. Madley, *An American Genocide: The United States and the California Indian Catastrophe, 1846–1873* (2016).

William J. Bauer Jr., *California Through Native Eyes: Reclaiming History* (2016).

Vigilantes

James A. B. Scherer, *"The Lion of the Vigilantes": William T. Coleman and the Life of Old San Francisco* (1939).

John W. Caughey, *Their Majesties the Mob* (1960).

Mary F. Williams, *The History of the San Francisco Vigilance Committee of 1851* (1964).

Roger Olmsted, "San Francisco and the Vigilante Style," *American West* (1970).

Robert W. Blew, "Vigilantism in Los Angeles, 1835–1874," *Southern California Quarterly* (1972).

Richard Maxwell Brown, *Strain of Violence: Historical Studies of American Violence and Vigilantism* (1975).

Roger W. Lotchin, *San Francisco, 1846–1856: From Hamlet to City* (1974).

Roger McGrath, *Gunfighters, Highwaymen, and Vigilantes: Violence on the Frontier* (1984).

Robert M. Senkewicz, S.J., *Vigilantes in Gold Rush San Francisco* (1985).

Kevin J. Mullin, *Let Justice Be Done: Crime and Politics in Early San Francisco* (1989).

Nancy Taniguchi, *Dirty Deeds: Land, Violence, and the 1856 San Francisco Vigilance Committee* (2016).

John Mack Faragher, *Eternity Street: Violence and Justice in Frontier Los Angeles* (2016).

Kelly Lytle Hernandez, *City of Inmates: Conquest, Rebellion, and the Rise of Human Caging in Los Angeles, 1771–1965* (2017).

Pioneer Agriculture

Paul W. Gates, *California Ranchos and Farms, 1846–1862* (1947) and "Public Land Disposal in California," *Agricultural History* (1975).

W. W. Robinson, *Land in California* (1948).

Vincent P. Carosso, *The California Wine Industry, 1830–1895: A Study of the Formative Years* (1951).

Gilbert C. Fite, *The Farmers' Frontier, 1865–1900* (1966).

Rodman W. Paul, "The Beginnings of Agriculture in California: Innovation vs. Continuity," *California Historical Quarterly* (1973).

Ellen Liebman, *California Farmland: A History of Large Agricultural Landholdings* (1983).

David Vaught, *After the Gold Rush: Tarnished Dreams in the Sacramento Valley* (2007).

Social and Economic Development

Ella S. Mighels, *The Story of the Files* (1893).

George R. Stewart, *Bret Harte: Argonaut and Exile* (1931).

Martin S. Peterson, *Joaquin Miller* (1937).

Franklin Walker, *San Francisco's Literary Frontier* (1939).

Lois F. Rodecape, "Tom Maguire, Napoleon of the Stage," *California Historical Society Quarterly* (1941, 1942).

William B. Rice, *The Los Angeles Star, 1851–1864* (1947).

Edmund M. Gagey, *The San Francisco Stage* (1950).

Edward C. Kemble, *A History of California Newspapers* (1962).

Bruno Fritzche, "San Francisco, 1846–1848: The Coming of the Land Speculator," *California Historical Quarterly* (1972).

Josephine D. Rhodehamel and Raymund F. Wood, *Ina Coolbrith* (1973).

Gunther Barth, *Instant Cities* (1975).

Peter R. Decker, *Fortunes and Failures* (1978).

Eric Niderost, "Pacific Emporium: State versus Local Control of San Francisco Harbor, 1835–1863" (M.A. thesis, California State University, Hayward, 1980).

Nigey Lennon, *Mark Twain in California* (1982).

Irving G. Hendrick, *California Education* (1980).

Ralph Mann, *After the Gold Rush: Grass Valley and Nevada City* (1982).

Misha Berson, *The San Francisco Stage: From Gold Rush to Golden Spike, 1849–1869* (1989).

Richard Peterson, "Thomas Starr King in California, 1860–64: Forgotten Naturalist of the Civil War," *California History* (1990).

Harlan Hogue and David J. Langum, *Thomas O. Larkin: A Life of Patriotism and Profit in Old California* (1990).

William A. Bullough, "Entrepreneurs and Urbanism on the California Mining Frontier: Frederick Walter and Weaverville, 1852–1868," *California History* (1991).

Gerald McKevitt, "Hispanic Californians and Catholic Higher Education: The Diary of Jesús María Estudillo, 1857–1864," *California History* (1991).

George Martin, *Verde at the Golden Gate: Opera and San Francisco in the Gold Rush Years* (1993).

James F. Varley, *Lola Montez: The California Adventures of Europe's Notorious Courtesan* (1996).

James J. Rawls and Richard J. Orsi, eds., *A Golden State: Mining and Economic Development in California* (1999).

Mary Ann Irwin, "'Going About and Doing Good': The Politics of Benevolence, Welfare, and Gender in San Francisco, 1850–1880," *Pacific Historical Review* (1999), and "'The Air is Becoming Full of War:' Jewish San Francisco and World War I," *Pacific Historical Review* (2005).

Brian Roberts, *American Alchemy: The California Gold Rush and Middle Class Culture* (2000).

Shirley Ann Wilson Moore, "'We Feel the Want of Protection:' The Politics of Law and Race in California, 1848–1878," in *Taming the Elephant: Politics, Government, and Law in Pioneer California* (2003).

Barbara Y. Welke, "Rights of Passage: Gendered-Rights Consciousness and the Quest for Freedom, San Francisco, California, 1850–1870," in *African American Women Confront the West, 1600–2000* (2003).

Rosaura Sanchez and Beatrice Pita, "Maria Amparo Ruiz de Burton and the Power of Her Pen," in *Latina Legacies: Identity, Biography, and Community* (2005).

Brian Roberts, *American Alchemy: The California Gold Rush and Middle Class Culture* (2000).

Lynn Downey, *Levi Strauss: The Man Who Gave Blue Jeans to the World* (2016).

Part Five: The Railroad Era

Confrontation at Mussel Slough

Southern Pacific Company Land Records (California State Railroad Museum, Sacramento).

Daniel K. Zumwalt Correspondence (Southern Pacific Land Company, San Francisco).

Collis P. Huntington Papers (Syracuse University, Syracuse, New York).

Collis P. Huntington Correspondence (Henry E. Huntington Biographical File, Huntington Library, San Marino, California).

Settlers Grand League, *The Struggle of the Mussel Slough Settlers for Their Homes!* (1880), and *An Appeal to the People* (1880).

Frank Norris, *The Octopus* (1901).

Wallace Smith, *Garden of the Sun: A History of the San Joaquin Valley, 1772–1939* (1939).

William Clyde McKinney, "The Mussel Slough Episode: A Chapter in the Settlement of the San Joaquin Valley" (M.A. thesis, University of California, Berkeley, 1948).

James L. Brown, *The Mussel Slough Tragedy* (1958).

Barbara M. Bristow, "Mussel Slough Tragedy: Railroad Struggle or Land Gamble" (M.A. thesis, Fresno State College, 1971).

John A. Larimore, "Legal Questions Arising from the Mussel Slough Land Dispute," *Southern California Quarterly* (1976).

Morton Rothstein, "Frank Norris and Popular Perceptions of the Market," *Agricultural History* (1982).

Richard L. Rollins, "The Mussel Slough Dispute: An Inquiry Based on the Census and Real Property Evidence" (M.A. thesis, California State University, Hayward, 1990).

Richard Maxwell Brown, "California Conflict and the American Dream," in Brown, *No Duty to Retreat: Violence and Values in American History and Society* (1991).

Terry Beers, *Gunfight at Mussel Slough: Evolution of a Western Myth* (2004).

Nineteenth-Century Transportation and Communication

LeRoy R. Hafen, *The Overland Mail, 1849–1869* (1926).

Rockwell D. Hunt, *Oxcart to Airplane* (1929).

Jerry MacMullen, *Paddlewheel Days in California* (1944).

Robert L. Thompson, *Wiring a Continent* (1947).

W. Turrentine Jackson, *Wagon Roads West: A Study of Federal Surveys and Construction in the Trans-Mississippi West, 1846–1869* (1952).

Richard E. Lingenfelter, *Steamboats on the Colorado River, 1852–1916* (1978).

Thomas Frederick Howard, *Sierra Crossing: First Roads to California* (1998).

A.C.W. Bethel, "The Golden Skein: California's Gold-Rush Network," in James J. Rawls and Richard J. Orsi, eds., *A Golden State: Mining and Economic Development in Gold Rush California* (1999).

The Civil War in California

Benjamin F. Gilbert, "The Confederate Minority in California," *California Historical Society Quarterly* (1941), and "California and the Civil War: A Bibliography," *California Historical Society Quarterly* (1961).

Milton H. Shutes, *Lincoln and California* (1943).

Aurora Hunt, *The Army of the Pacific, 1860–1866* (1951).

Eugene W. Berwanger, *The Frontier Against Slavery* (1967).

Gerald Stanley, "Slavery and the Origins of the Republican Party in California," *Southern California Quarterly* (1978), and "The Slavery Issue and Election in California, 1860," *Mid-America* (1980).

Robert Chandler, "The Press and Civil Liberties in California During the Civil War, 1861–1865" (Ph.D. dissertation, University of California, Riverside, 1978), "Friends in Time of Need: Republicans and Black Civil Rights in California During the Civil War Era," *Arizona and the West* (1982), and "Crushing Dissent: The Pacific Tests Lincoln's Policy of Suppression, 1862," *Civil War History* (1984).

Judson A. Grenier, *California Legacy: The James Alexander Watson-María Dolores Domínguez de Watson Family, 1820–1980* (1987).

Ronald C. Woolsey, "The Politics of a Lost Cause: 'Seceshers' and Democrats in Southern California During the Civil War," *California History* (1990).

James McLean, *California Sabers: The 2nd Massachusetts Cavalry in the Civil War* (2000).

Andrew Masich, *The Civil War in Arizona: The Story of the California Volunteers, 1861–1865* (2008).

Glenna Matthews, *The Golden State in the Civil War: Thomas Starr King, the Republican Party, and the Birth of Modern California* (2012).

Tom Prezelski, *Californio Lancers: The 1st Battalion of Native Cavalry in the Far West, 1863–1866* (2015).

Railway History, General

Robert E. Riegel, *The Story of the Western Railroads: From 1852 Through the Reign of the Giants* (1926).

Lewis B. Leslie, "The Entrance of the Santa Fe Railroad into California," *Pacific Historical Review* (1939).

Franklyn Hoyt, "Railroad Development in Southern California, 1868–1900" (Ph.D. dissertation, University of Southern California, 1951).

John F. Stover, *American Railroads* (1961).

Julius Grodinsky, *Transcontinental Railway Strategy, 1869–1893: A Study of Businessmen* (1962).

Leslie E. Decker, *Railroads, Lands, and Politics: The Taxation of the Railroad Land Grants, 1864–1897* (1964).

Ward McAfee, *California's Railroad Era, 1850–1911* (1973).

Keith L. Bryant Jr., *History of the Atchison, Topeka & Santa Fe Railroad* (1976).

Lloyd J. Mercer, *Railroads and Land Grant Policy: A Study of Government Intervention* (1982).

Richard J. Orsi, "Railroads in the History of California and the Far West: An Introduction," *California History* (Spring 1991).

Carlos A. Schwantes, *Railroad Signatures Across the Pacific Northwest* (1993).

William Deverell, *Railroad Crossings: Californians and the Railroad, 1850–1910* (1994).

Richard J. Orsi, *Sunset Limited: The Southern Pacific Railroad and the Development of the American West, 1850–1930* (2005).

Richard White, *Railroaded: The Transcontinentals and the Making of Modern America* (2011).

The First Transcontinental Railway

Theodore D. Judah, *A Practical Plan for Building the Pacific Railroad* (1857).

Harry J. Carman and Charles H. Mueller, "The Contract and Finance Company and the Central Pacific Railroad," *Mississippi Valley Historical Review* (1927).

George Galloway, *The First Transcontinental Railroad* (1950).

Wesley S. Griswold, *A Work of Giants: Building the First Transcontinental Railroad* (1963).

Robert West Howard, *The Great Iron Trail: The Story of the First Transcontinental Railroad* (1963).

Ping Chiu, *Chinese Labor in California, 1850–1880: An Economic Study* (1963).

Gunther Barth, *Bitter Strength: A History of the Chinese in the United States, 1850–1870* (1964).

Alexander P. Saxton, "The Army of Canton in the High Sierra," *Pacific Historical Review* (1966).

George Kraus, *High Road to Promontory: Building the Central Pacific Across the High Sierra* (1969).

Robert G. Athearn, *Union Pacific Country* (1971).

John Hoyt Williams, *A Great and Shining Road: The Epic Story of the Transcontinental Railroad* (1988).

David Haward Bain, *Empire Express: Building the First Transcontinental Railroad* (1999).

Richard J. Orsi, *Sunset Limited: The Southern Pacific Railroad and the Development of the American West, 1850–1930* (2005).

Richard White, *Railroaded: The Transcontinentals and the Making of Modern America* (2011).

"Railroaded: A Special Issue," *California History: The Journal of the California Historical Society* (89: no. 1, 2013).

Glenn Willumson, *Iron Muse: Photographing the Transcontinental Railroad* (2013).

Ryan Dearinger, *The Filth of Progress: Immigrants, Americans, and the Building of Canals and Railroads in the West* (2016).

Railway Leaders

Carl I. Wheat, "A Sketch of the Life of Theodore D. Judah," *California Historical Society Quarterly* (1925).

Oscar Lewis, *The Big Four* (1938).

Helen Hinckley Jones, *Rails from the West: A Biography of Theodore D. Judah* (1969).

David Lavender, *The Great Persuader* [Collis P. Huntington] (1970).

Norman E. Tutorow, *Leland Stanford: Man of Many Careers* (1971).

Salvador A. Ramirez, ed., *The Octopus Speaks: The Colton Letters* (1992).

Norman E. Tutorow, *The Governor: The Life and Legacy of Leland Stanford* (2004).

Salvador A. Ramirez, *Inside Man: The Life and Times of Mark Hopkins of New York, Michigan, and California* (2007).

The Southern Pacific Company

Henry George, "What the Railroads Will Bring Us," *Overland Monthly* (1868).

Stuart Daggett, *Chapters on the History of the Southern Pacific Company* (1922).

Lewis B. Leslie, "A Transcontinental Railroad into California: Texas and Pacific Versus Southern Pacific, 1865–1885," *Pacific Historical Review* (1936).

John H. Kemble, "The Big Four at Sea: The History of the Oriental and Occidental Steamship Company," *Huntington Library Quarterly* (1940).

W. H. Hutchinson, "Southern Pacific: Myth and Reality," *California Historical Society Quarterly* (1969).

Bill Yenne, *The History of the Southern Pacific* (1985).

Don L. Hofsommer, *The Southern Pacific, 1901–1985* (1986).

Richard J. Orsi, *Sunset Limited: The Southern Pacific Railroad and the Development of the American West, 1850–1930* (2005).

Cities

Mel Scott, *The San Francisco Bay Area* (1959 and 1985).

James E. Vance Jr., *Geography and Urban Evolution in the San Francisco Bay Area* (1964).

Remi A. Nadeau, *City-Makers: The Story of Southern California's First Boom, 1868–1876* (1965).

Robert M. Fogelson, *Fragmented Metropolis: Los Angeles, 1850–1930* (1967).

Richard Harold Smith, "Towns Along the Tracks: Railroad Strategy and Town Promotion in the San Joaquin Valley, California" (Ph.D. dissertation, University of California, Los Angeles, 1976).

John W. Reps, *Cities of the American West: A History of Frontier Urban Planning* (1979).

William A. Bullough, *The Blind Boss and His City: Christopher Augustine Buckley and Nineteenth-Century San Francisco* (1979).

Douglas H. Daniels, *Pioneer Urbanites: A Social and Cultural History of Black San Francisco* (1980).

Robert A. Burchell, *The San Francisco Irish: 1848–1880* (1980).

Beth Bagwell, *Oakland: The Story of a City* (1982).

Andrew F. Rolle, *Los Angeles: From Pueblo to City of the Future* (1981).

Robert W. Cherny and William Issel, *San Francisco: Presidio, Port and Pacific Metropolis* (1981) and *San Francisco, 1865–1932* (1986).

Rodman W. Paul, "After the Gold Rush: San Francisco and Portland," *Pacific Historical Review* (1982).

Charles Wollenberg, *Golden Gate Metropolis: Perspectives on Bay Area History* (1985).

William E. Mahan, "The Political Response to Urban Growth: Sacramento and Mayor Marshall R. Beard," *California History* (1990).

Gray Brechin, *Imperial San Francisco: Urban Power, Earthly Ruin* (1999).

Barbara Berglund, *Making San Francisco American: Cultural Frontiers in the Urban West, 1846–1906* (2007).

Kelly Lytle Hernández, *City of Inmates: Conquest, Rebellion, and the Rise of Human Caging in Los Angeles, 1771–1965* (2017).

Business and Industry

Robert Glass Cleland and Osgood Hardy, *March of Industry* (1929).

Ira B. Cross, *Financing an Empire: History of Banking in California* (4 vols., 1927).

H. Brett Melendy, "One Hundred Years of the Redwood Lumber Industry, 1850–1950" (Ph.D. dissertation, Stanford University, 1952).

Mary F. Stewart, *Adolph Sutro: A Biography* (1962).

James David Lavender, *Nothing Seemed Impossible: William C. Ralston and Early San Francisco* (1975).

Daniel Meissner, "Bridging the Pacific: California and the China Flour Trade," *California History* (Winter 1997–98).

J. Rawls and Richard J. Orsi, eds., *A Golden State: Mining and Economic Development in Gold Rush California* (1999).

Anthony Kirk, *Founded by the Bay: The History of the Macaulay Foundry, 1896–1996* (1996), and *A Flier in Oil: Adolph B. Spreckels and the Rise of the California Petroleum Industry* (2000).

Agriculture

Robert Glass Cleland, *The Cattle on a Thousand Hills: Southern California, 1850–1880* (1941, 1951).

Herbert J. Webber and Leon D. Batchelor, eds., *The Citrus Industry* (3 vols., 1943–1948).

Claude B. Hutchison, ed., *California Agriculture* (1946).

W. W. Robinson, *Land in California* (1963).

Vincent P. Carosso, *The California Wine Industry, 1830–1895: A Study of the Formative Years* (1951).

Harry M. Butterfield, *A History of Subtropical Fruits and Nuts in California* (1963).

Gilbert C. Fite, "The Farmers' Frontier in California, 1850–1900," in Fite, ed., *The Farmers' Frontier, 1865–1900* (1966).

Paul W. Gates, *California Ranchos and Farms, 1846–1862* (1967), and *Land and Law in California: Essays on Land Policies* (1991).

Cletus E. Daniel, *Bitter Harvest: A History of California Farmworkers, 1870–1941* (1981).

Lawrence J. Jelinek, *Harvest Empire: A History of California Agriculture* (1982).

Ellen Liebman, *California Farmland: A History of Large Agricultural Landholdings* (1983).

Ann F. Scheuring, ed., *A Guidebook to California Agriculture* (1984).

Steven Stoll, *The Fruits of Natural Advantage: Making the Industrial Countryside in California* (1998).

David Vaught, *Cultivating California: Growers, Specialty Crops, and Labor, 1875–1920* (1999).

David Igler, *Industrial Cowboys: Miller & Lux and the Transformation of the Far West, 1850–1920* (2001).

Richard Steven Street, *Beasts of the Field: A Narrative History of California Farmworkers, 1769–1913* (2004).

Douglas Sackman, *Orange Empire: California and the Fruits of Eden* (2005).

Mark Wyman, *Hoboes: Bindlestiffs, Fruit Tramps, and the Harvesting of the West* (2011).

Cecilia M. Tsu, *Garden of the World: Asian Immigrants and the Making of Agriculture in California's Santa Clara Valley* (2013).

Agricultural Institutions

Rahno MacCurdy, *A History of the California Fruit Growers' Exchange* (1925).

Clarke Chambers, *California Farm Organizations: A Historical Study of the Grange, the Farm Bureau, and the Associated Farmers, 1929–1941* (1952).

Oscar O. Winther, "The Colony System of Southern California," *Agricultural History* (1953).

H. E. Erdman, "The Development and Significance of California Cooperatives, 1900–1915," *Agricultural History* (1958).

R. Louis Gentilcore, "Ontario, California, and the Agricultural Boom of the 1880s," *Agricultural History* (1960).

Gerald D. Nash, *State Government and Economic Development: A History of Administrative Policies in California, 1849–1933* (1964).

Richard J. Orsi, "'The Octopus' Reconsidered: The Southern Pacific and Agricultural Modernization in California, 1865–1915," *California Historical Quarterly* (1975).

Mansel G. Blackford, *The Politics of Business in California, 1890–1920* (1977).

Ann Foley Scheuring, *Science and Service: A History of the Land Grant University and Agriculture in California* (1995).

Colleges and Universities

Rockwell D. Hunt, *History of the University of the Pacific, 1851–1951* (1951).

Andrew F. Rolle, *Occidental College: The First Seventy-Five Years, 1887–1962* (1962) and *Occidental College: A Centennial History* (1986).

Verne A. Stadtman, *The University of California, 1868–1968* (1970).

Gerald McKevitt, S.J., *The University of Santa Clara: A History, 1851–1977* (1979).

John McGloin, S.J., *Jesuits by the Golden Gate* (1972).

Gunther Barth, *California's Practical Period: A Cultural Context for the Emerging University, 1850s–1870s* (1994).

Social Structure

Paul S. Taylor, "Foundations of California Rural Society," *California Historical Society Quarterly* (1945).

Warren Thompson, *Growth and Changes in California's Population* (1955).

Barbara Laslett, "Social Change and the Family: Los Angeles California, 1850–1870," *American Sociological Review* (1977).

Gregory Holmes, *Religion in the City of the Angels* (1978).

Peter R. Decker, *Fortunes and Failures: White-Collar Mobility in Nineteenth-Century San Francisco* (1978).

Richard H. Peterson, *The Bonanza Kings: The Social Origins and Business Behavior of Western Mining Entrepreneurs* (1979).

Ralph Mann, *After the Gold Rush: Society in Grass Valley and Nevada City, California, 1849–1870* (1982), and "Frontier Opportunity and the New Social History," *Pacific Historical Review* (1984).

Robert L. Griswold, *Family and Divorce in California, 1850–1890: Victorian Illusions and Everyday Realities* (1982).

Chinese Immigration and Exclusion

Elmer C. Sandmeyer, *The Anti-Chinese Movement in California* (1938).

Alexander P. Saxton, *The Indispensable Enemy: Labor and the Anti-Chinese Movement in California* (1971).

Sucheng Chan, *This Bittersweet Soil: The Chinese in California Agriculture, 1860–1910* (1986).

Jeff Gillenkirk and James Motlow, *Bitter Melon: Stories from the Last Rural Chinese Town in America* (1987).

Roger Daniels, *Asian America: Chinese and Japanese in the United States Since 1850* (1988).

Charles J. McClain, *In Search of Equality: The Chinese Struggle Against Discrimination in Nineteenth-Century America* (1994).

Lucy Salyer, *Laws Harsh as Tigers: Chinese Immigration and the Shaping of Modern Immigration Law* (1995).

Judy Yung, *Unbound Feet: A Social History of Chinese Women in San Francisco* (1995).

Lisa Lowe, *Immigrant Acts: On Asian American Cultural Politics* (1996).

George Anthony Peffer, *If They Don't Bring Their Women Here: Chinese Female Immigration Before Exclusion* (1999).

Sucheng Chan, "A People of Exceptional Character: Ethnic Diversity, Nativism, and Racism in the California Gold Rush," in *Rooted in Barbarous Soil: People, Culture, and Community in Gold Rush California*, Kevin Starr and Richard J. Orsi, eds., (2000).

Yong Chen, *Chinese San Francisco, 1850–1943: A Trans-Pacific Community* (2000).

Madeline Y. Hsu, *Dreaming of Gold, Dreaming of Home: Transnationalism and Migration Between the United States and South China, 1882–1943* (2000).

Nayan Shah, *Contagious Divides: Epidemics and Race in San Francisco's Chinatown* (2001).

Erika Lee, *At America's Gates: Chinese Immigration During the Exclusion Era, 1882–1943* (2003).

Wendy Rouse Jorae, *The Children of Chinatown: Growing Up Chinese American in San Francisco, 1850–1920* (2009).

Joshua Paddison, *American Heathens: Religion, Race, and Reconstruction in California* (2012).

Beth Lew-Williams, *The Chinese Must Go: Violence, Exclusion, and the Making of the Alien in America* (2018).

Water, Resources, and Conservation

Frederick D. Kershner, "George Chaffey and the Irrigation Frontier," *Agricultural History* (1953).

Robert D. Kelley, *Gold vs. Grain: The Hydraulic Mining Controversy in California's Sacramento Valley* (1959), and "Taming the Sacramento: Hamiltonianism in Action," *Pacific Historical Review* (1965).

John A. Shaw, "Railroads, Irrigation, and Economic Growth: The San Joaquin Valley of California," *Explorations in Economic History* (1974).

Burton Gordon, *The Monterey Bay Area: Natural History and Cultural Imprints* (1977).

William Kahrl, *The California Water Atlas* (1979).

William L. Preston, *Vanishing Landscapes: Land and Life in the Tulare Lake Basin* (1981).

Donald J. Pisani, *From Family Farm to Agribusiness: The Irrigation Crusade in California, 1850–1931* (1984).

Arthur F. McEvoy, *The Fisherman's Problem: Ecology and Law in the California Fisheries, 1850–1980* (1986).

Duane A. Smith, *Mining America: The Industry and the Environment, 1800–1980* (1987).

Robert Kelley, *Battling the Inland Sea: American Political Culture, Public Policy, and the Sacramento Valley, 1850–1986* (1989).

Michael Black, "Tragic Remedies: A Century of Failed Fishery Policy on California's Sacramento River," *Pacific Historical Review* (1995).

Ian Tyrrell, *True Gardens of the Gods: Californian-Australian Environmental Reform, 1860–1930* (1999).

Andrew Isenberg, *Mining California: An Ecological History* (2005).

Connie Y. Chiang, *Shaping the Shoreline, Fisheries and Tourism on the Monterey Coast* (2009).

John Muir and Wilderness Preservation

Linnie Marsh Wolfe, *Son of the Wilderness: The Life of John Muir* (1945).

Holway R. Jones, *John Muir and the Sierra Club: The Battle for Yosemite* (1965).

Douglas H. Strong, "The History of Sequoia National Park, 1876–1926," *Southern California Quarterly* (1966).

Raymond H. Clary, *The Making of Golden Gate Park: The Early Years, 1865–1906* (1980).

Michael P. Cohen, *The Pathless Way: John Muir and the American Wilderness* (1984), and *The History of the Sierra Club, 1892–1970* (1988).

Richard J. Orsi, "Wilderness Saint and Robber Baron: The Anomalous Partnership of John Muir and the Southern Pacific Company for the Preservation of Yosemite National Park," *The Pacific Historian* (1985).

Frederick Turner, *Rediscovering America: John Muir in His Time and Ours* (1985).

Michael L. Smith, *Pacific Visions: California Scientists and the Environment, 1850–1915* (1987).

Sally M. Miller, ed., *John Muir: Life and Work* (1993), and *John Muir in Historical Perspective* (1999).

Thurman Wilkins, *John Muir: Apostle of Nature* (1995).

Mark Spence, "Dispossessing the Wilderness: Yosemite Indians and the National Park Ideal, 1864–1930," *Pacific Historical Review* (1996).

Donald Worster, *A Passion for Nature: The Life of John Muir* (2008).

Workingmen's Party, Grange, and Political Protest

Henry George, *Our Land and Land Policy: National and State* (1871).

Ezra S. Carr, *The Patrons of Husbandry on the Pacific Coast* (1875).

Jack W. Bates, "The Southern Pacific Railroad in California Politics" (M.A. thesis, University of the Pacific, 1942).

Ralph Kauer, "The Workingmen's Party of California," *Pacific Historical Review* (1944).

Rodman W. Paul, "The Great California Grain War: The Grangers Challenge the Wheat King," *Pacific Historical Review* (1958).

Gerald D. Nash, "The California Railroad Commission, 1876–1911," *Southern California Quarterly* (1962).

Ward M. McAfee, "Local Interests and Railroad Regulation in California During the Granger Decade," *Pacific Historical Review* (1968).

David B. Griffiths, "Anti-Monopoly Movements in California, 1873–1898," *Southern California Quarterly* (1970).

R. Hal Williams, *The Democratic Party and California Politics, 1880–1896* (1973).

Gerald L. Prescott, "Farm Gentry vs. the Grangers: Conflict in Rural America," *California Historical Quarterly* (1978).

Ed Salzman and Ann Leigh Brown, *The Cartoon History of California Politics* (1978).

John Ludeke, "No Fence Law of 1874: Victory for San Joaquin Valley Farmers," *California History* (1980).

Spencer C. Olin Jr., *California Politics, 1846–1920: The Emerging Corporate State* (1981).

Daniel Cornford, *Workers and Dissent in the Redwood Empire* (1987).

Neil Larry Shumsky, *Evolution of Political Protest and the Workingmen's Party of California* (1992).

Culture in the Railway Era

Eugen Neuhaus, *William Keith, The Man and the Artist* (1938).

Ivan Benson, *Mark Twain's Western Years* (1938).

Franklin Walker, *San Francisco's Literary Frontier* (1939).

John W. Caughey, *Hubert Howe Bancroft* (1946).

Charles A. Barker, *Henry George* (1955).

Claude R. Petty, "John S. Hittell and the Gospel of California," *Pacific Historical Review* (1955).

Harold Kirker, *California's Architectural Frontier: Style and Tradition in the Nineteenth Century* (1960).

Robert W. Righter, "Theodore Henry Hittell: California Historian," *Southern California Quarterly* (1966), and "Theodore H. Hittell and Hubert H. Bancroft," *California Historical Quarterly* (1971).

Earl Pomeroy, "Josiah Royce, Historian in Quest of Community," *Pacific Historical Review* (1971).

Kevin Starr, *Americans and the California Dream, 1850–1915* (1973).

Nigey Lennon, *Mark Twain in California* (1982).

Gary Scharnhorst, ed., *Bret Harte's California* (1990).

David Wyatt, *The Fall to Eden: Landscapes and Imagination in California* (1986).

Anthony Kirk, "In a Golden Land So Far: The Rise of Art in Early California," special issue of *California History* (Spring 1992).

Robert V. Hine, *Josiah Royce: From Grass Valley to Harvard* (1992).

Part Six: California and the Nation

Social and Political Feminism

Norris C. Hundley, Jr., "Katherine Philips Edson and the Fight for the California Minimum Wage, 1912–1923," *Pacific Historical Review* (1960).

Donald Waller Rodes, "The California Woman Suffrage Campaign of 1911," (M.A. Thesis, California State University, Hayward, 1974).

Ethel L. Bornefeld, "Research Material for Book on California's First Women Legislators," California State Library, Manuscript 1858–1877 (1978–1981).

Mary A. Hill, *Charlotte Perkins Gilman: The Making of a Radical Feminist* (1980).

Jacqueline R. Braitman, "A California Stateswoman: The Public Career of Katherine Philips Edson," *California History* (1986).

Joan M. Jensen and Gloria Ricci Lothrop, *California Women: A History* (1987).

Gayle Gullett, "Women Progressives and the Politics of Americanization in California, 1915–1920," *Pacific Historical Review* (1995).

Linda Witt, Karen M. Paget, Glenna Matthews, *Running as a Woman: Gender and Power in American Politics* (1995).

Rosalyn Terborg-Penn, *African American Women in the Struggle for the Vote, 1850–1920* (1998).

Mary Ann Irwin, "'Going About and Doing Good': The Politics of Benevolence, Welfare, and Gender in San Francisco, 1850–1880," *Pacific Historical Review* (Aug. 1999).

Gayle Gullett, *Becoming Citizens: The Emergence and Development of the California Women's Movement, 1880–1911* (2000).

Edith Sparks, *Capital Intentions: Female Proprietors in San Francisco, 1850–1920* (2006).

Virginia Elwood-Akers, *Caroline Severance* (2010).

Susan Englander, "'We Want the Ballot for Very Different Reasons': Clubwomen, Union Women, and the Internal Politics of the Suffrage Movement, 1896–1911," Teresa Hurley and Jarrod Harrison, "'Awed by the Women's Clubs': Women Voters and Moral Reform, 1913–1914," Rebecca Mead, "'We Are Not Keen about a Minimum Wage': Union Women, Clubwomen, and the Legislated Minimum Wage, 1913–1931," and Sandra L. Henderson, "The *Civitas* of Women's Political Culture: The Twentieth Century Club of Berkeley, 1904–1929," all in Robert W. Cherny, Mary Ann Irwin, and Ann Marie Wilson, *California Women and Politics: From the Gold Rush to the Great Depression* (2011).

Linda Van Ingen, *Gendered Politics: Campaign Strategies of California Women Candidates, 1912–1970* (2017).

Progressives and Political Reform

George E. Mowry, *California Progressives* (1951).

Walton Bean, *Boss Ruef's San Francisco* (1952).

Richard B. Rice, "The California Press and American Neutrality, 1914–1917" (Ph.D. thesis, University of California, Berkeley, 1957).

Spencer C. Olin Jr., *California's Prodigal Sons: Hiram Johnson and the Progressives, 1911–1917* (1963).

James P. Walsh, "Abe Ruef Was No Boss: Machine Politics, Reform, and San Francisco," *California Historical Quarterly* (1972).

R. Hal Williams, *The Democratic Party and California Politics, 1880–1896* (1973).

Martin J. Schiesl, "Progressive Reform in Los Angeles under Mayor Alexander, 1909–1913," *California Historical Quarterly* (1975).

William A. Bullough, "The Steam Beer Handicap: Chris Buckley and the San Francisco Municipal Election of 1896," *California Historical Quarterly* (1975), "Hannibal versus the Blind Boss: The Junta, Chris Buckley, and Democratic Reform Politics in San Francisco," *Pacific Historical Review* (1977), and *The Blind Boss and His City: Christopher Augustine Buckley and Nineteenth-Century San Francisco* (1979).

Michael Kazin, *Barons of Labor: The San Francisco Building Trades and Union Power in the Progressive Era* (1989).

Tom Sitton, *John Randolph Haynes: California Progressive* (1992).

Richard Coke Lower, *A Bloc of One: The Political Career of Hiram W. Johnson* (1993).

William Deverell and Tom Sitton, *California Progressivism Revisited* (1994).

Andrea Rees Davies, *Saving San Francisco: Relief and Recovery after the 1906 Disaster* (2011).

Diane M. T. North, *California at War: The State and the People during World War I* (2018).

Race and Ethnicity in the Progressive Era

Richard Griswold del Castillo, *The Los Angeles Barrio, 1850–1890: A Social History* (1979).

"Dolores Huerta: Un Soldado del Movimiento," in Joan M. Jensen, *With These Hands: Women Working on the Land* (1981).

Mary Paik Lee, *Quiet Odyssey: A Pioneer Korean Woman in America* (1990).

Herbert P. LePore, "Prelude to Prejudice: Hiram Johnson, Woodrow Wilson, and the California Alien Land Controversy of 1913," *Southern California Quarterly* (1979).

Greg Sarris, *Keeping Slug Woman Alive: A Holistic Approach to American Indian Texts* (1993).

George J. Sánchez, *Becoming Mexican American: Ethnicity, Culture and Identity in Chicano Los Angeles, 1900–1945* (1993).

Valerie J. Matsumoto, *Farming the Home Place: A Japanese American Community in California, 1919–1982* (1994).

Gilbert G. González, *Labor and Community: Mexican Citrus Worker Villages in a Southern California County, 1900–1950* (1994).

Tomás Almaguer, *Racial Fault Lines: The Historical Origins of White Supremacy in California* (1994).

David Yoo, *Growing Up Nisei: Race, Generation, and Culture Among Japanese Americans of California, 1924–1949* (1999).

Camille Guerin-Gonzales, *Mexican Workers & American Dreams: Immigration, Repatriation, and California Farm Labor, 1900–1939* (1996).

Albert S. Broussard, *Black San Francisco: The Struggle for Black Equality in the West, 1900–1924* (1993).

Rosalyn Terborg-Penn, *African American Women in the Struggle for the Vote, 1850–1920* (1998).

Manuel G. Gonzales, *Mexicanos: A History of Mexicans in the United States* (1999).

Brian Niiya, *Japanese American History: An A-to-Z Reference from 1868 to the Present* (2000).

Manuel G. Gonzales, Cynthia M. Gonzales, *En Aquel Entonces (In Years Gone By): Readings in Mexican-American History* (2000).

Matt Garcia, *A World of Its Own: Race, Labor, and Citrus in the Making of Greater Los Angeles, 1900–1970* (2002).

Shirley Ann Wilson Moore and Quintard Taylor, *African American Women Confront the West, 1600–2000* (2003).

Douglas Flamming, *Bound for Freedom: Black Los Angeles in Jim Crow America* (2005).

Marne Campbell, *Making Black Los Angeles: Gender, Class, and Community, 1850–1917* (2016).

Mary Ann Irwin, "'The Air is Becoming Full of War:' Jewish San Francisco and World War I," *Pacific Historical Review* (2005).

Karin L. Huebner, "An Unexpected Alliance: Stella Atwood, the California Clubwomen, John Collier, and the Indians of the Southwest, 1917–1934," *Pacific Historical Review* (Aug. 2009).

Tomás Almaguer, *Racial Fault Lines: The Historical Origins of White Supremacy in California* (2009).

California Research Bureau, "Women of Color in California's Legislature: Increasing, But Still Not Representative" (Aug. 2015).

William J. Bauer Jr., *We Were All Like Migrant Workers Here: Work, Community, and Memory on California's Round Valley Reservation, 1850–1941* (2009).

Valerie Sherer Mathes, *Divinely Guided: The California Work of the Women's National Indian Association* (2012).

Populism, Labor, and Radicalism

William Carey Jones, "The Kaweah Experiment in Co-operation," *Quarterly Journal of Economics* (Oct. 1891).

Burnette G. Haskell, "How Kaweah Fell," San Francisco *Examiner* (Nov. 1891) and "Kaweah: How and Why the Colony Died," *Out West* (Sept. 1902).

Carleton H. Parker, "The Wheatland Riot and What Lay Back of It," *The Survey* (1914).

Ira B. Cross, *A History of the Labor Movement in California* (1935).

Carey McWilliams, *Factories in the Fields* (1939).

Woodrow C. Whitten, "The Trial of Charlotte Anita Whitney," *Pacific Historical Review* (1946).

Robert V. Hine, *California's Utopian Colonies* (1953) and *California Utopianism: Contemplations of Eden* (1981).

Grace H. Stimson, *Rise of the Labor Movement in Los Angeles* (1955).

Howard Quint, "Gaylord Wilshire and Socialism's First Congressional Campaign," *Pacific Historical Review* (1957).

Robert E. L. Knight, *Industrial Relations in the San Francisco Bay Area 1900–1918* (1960).

Louis B. and Richard S. Perry, *A History of the Los Angeles Labor Movement* (1963).

Alexander Saxton, "San Francisco Labor and the Populist and Progressive Insurgencies," *Pacific Historical Review* (1965).

Richard H. Frost, *The Mooney Case* (1968).

W. W. Robinson, *Bombs and Bribery: Story of the McNamara and Darrow Trials* (1969).

Woodrow C. Whitten, *Criminal Syndicalism and the Law in California, 1919–1927* (1969).

Ronald Genini, "Industrial Workers of the World and Their Fresno Free-Speech Fight, 1910–1911," *California Historical Quarterly* (1974).

David F. Selvin, *A Place in the Sun: A History of California Labor* (1981).

Donald J. Pisani, *From the Family Farm to Agribusiness* (1984).

Joyce M. Dicks, "Repression in the Progressive Era: Emma Goldman in San Francisco, 1908–1909" (M.A. thesis, California State University, Hayward, 1984).

Lisa Rubens, "The Patrician Radical: Charlotte Anita Whitney," *California History* (1986).

John McGreevy, "Farmers, Nationalists, and the Origins of California Populism," *Pacific Historical Review* (1989).

Michael F. Magliari, "Populism, Steamboats, and the Octopus: Transportation Rates and Monopoly in California's Wheat Regions, 1890–1896," *Pacific Historical Review* (1989) and "What Happened to the Populist Vote? A California Case Study," *Pacific Historical Review* (1995).

William B. Friedricks, "Capital and Labor in Los Angeles: Henry E. Huntington vs. Organized Labor, 1900–1920," *Pacific Historical Review* (1990).

Daniel Cornford, *Working People of California* (1995).

Charles Postel, *The Populist Vision* (2009).

Southern California

John E. Baur, *Health Seekers of Southern California* (1944).

Glenn S. Dumke, *The Boom of the 'Eighties in Southern California* (1944).

Clarence H. Matson, *Building a World Gateway: The Story of the Los Angeles Harbor* (1945).

Carey McWilliams, *Southern California Country* (1946).

W. H. Hutchinson, *Oil, Land and Politics: The California Career of Thomas R. Bard* (1965).

Robert R. Fogelson, *The Fragmented Metropolis: Los Angeles, 1850–1930* (1967).

Gerald T. White, *Scientists in Conflict: The Beginning of the Oil Industry in California* (1968).

Andrew Rolle, *Los Angeles: From Pueblo to City of the Future* (1981).

Kevin Starr, *Material Dreams: Southern California Through the 1920s* (1990).

Michael E. Engh, S.J., "Mary Julia Workman, the Catholic Conscience of Los Angeles," *California History* (1993).

Gilbert G. González, *Labor and Community: Mexican Citrus Worker Villages in a Southern California County, 1900–1950* (1994).

Robert Phelps, "The Search for a Modern Industrial City: Urban Planning, the Open Shop, and the Founding of Torrance, California," *Pacific Historical Review* (1995).

Phoebe S. Kropp, *California Vieja: Culture and Memory in a Modern American Place* (2008).

Glen Gendzel, "Not Just a Golden State," *Southern California Quarterly* (2008/2009).

Arts and Letters

Arnold Genthe and Will Irwin, *Pictures of Old Chinatown* (1909).

Joan London, *Jack London and His Times: An Unconventional Biography* (1939).

Franklin Walker, *A Literary History of Southern California* (1950).

Harold S. Kirker, *California's Architectural Frontier* (1960) and *Old Forms on a New Land: California Architecture in Perspective* (1991).

W. A. Swanberg, *Citizen Hearst* (1961).

Robert B. Haas, *Muybridge: Man in Motion* (1976).

Andrew Sinclair, *Jack: A Biography of Jack London* (1977).

Robert Winter, *The California Bungalow* (1980).

Peter E. Palmquist, *Carleton E. Watkins: Photographer of the American West* (1983) and *Shadowcatchers: Women in California Photography Before 1901* (1990).

Ted Orland, *Man and Yosemite: A Photographer's View of the Early Years* (1985).

Sandra Sizer Frankiel, *California's Spiritual Frontiers: Religious Alternatives to Anglo-Protestantism, 1850–1910* (1988).

Michael L. Smith, *Pacific Visions: California Scientists and the Environment: 1850–1915* (1988).

Sara Holmes Boutelle, *Julia Morgan, Architect* (1988).

William A. Bullough, "Eadweard Muybridge and the Old San Francisco Mint: Archival Photographs as Historical Documents" *California History* (1989) and "History through the

Lens: The Photographs of John Calvin Brewster, 1874–1909," *Ventura County Historical Society Quarterly* (1995).

Karen S. Langlois, "A Fresh Voice from the West: Mary Austin, California, and American Literary Magazines, 1892–1910," *California History* (1990).

Robert V. Hine, *Josiah Royce: From Grass Valley to Harvard* (1992).

Roger Lotchin, *Fortress California, 1910–1961: From Warfare to Welfare* (1992).

Gerald D. Nash, *A. P. Giannini and the Bank of America* (1992).

Robert C. Pavlic, "'Something a Little Different': La Cuesta Encantada's Architectural Precedents and Cultural Prototypes," *California History* (1992/93).

Albert Shumate, *A San Francisco Scandal: The California of George Gordon* (1994).

Robert W. Cherny, "City Commercial, City Beautiful, City Practical—The San Francisco Visions of William C. Ralston, James D. Phelan, and Michael O'Shaughnessy," *California History* (1994).

James P. Walsh and Timothy O'Keefe, *Legacy of a Native Son: James Duval Phelan and Villa Montalvo* (1994).

Felice A. Bonadio, *A. P. Giannini: Banker of America* (1994).

Part Seven: California Between the Wars

Aimee Semple McPherson

Sarah Comstock, "Aimee Semple McPherson: Prima Donna of Revivalism," *Harper's* (1927).

Nancy Barr Mavity, *Sister Aimee* (1931).

William McLoughlin, "Aimee Semple McPherson: Your Sister in the King's Glad Service," *Journal of Popular Culture* (1968).

Lately Thomas, *Storming Heaven: The Lives and Turmoils of Minnie Kennedy and Aimee Semple McPherson* (1970).

Aimee Semple McPherson, *In the Service of the King: The Story of My Life* (1972).

David L. Clark, "Miracles for a Dime: From Chautauqua Tent to Radio Station with Sister Aimee," *California History* (1978–1979).

Robert Bahr, *Least of All the Saints: The Story of Aimee Semple McPherson* (1979).

Gloria Ricci Lothrop, "West of Eden: Pioneer Media Evangelist Aimee Semple McPherson in Los Angeles," *Journal of the West* (1988).

Daniel M. Epstein, *Sister Aimee: The Life of Aimee Semple McPherson* (1993).

Matthew Avery Sutton, *Aimee Semple McPherson and the Resurrection of Christian America* (2007).

Making of Hollywood

Robert Sklar, *Movie-Made America: A Cultural History of American Movies* (1975).

Neal Gabler, *An Empire of Their Own: How the Jews Invented Hollywood* (1989).

Gregory D. Black, *Hollywood Censored: Morality Codes, Catholics, and the Movies* (1994).

Tina Balio, *Grand Design: Hollywood as a Modern Business Enterprise, 1930–1939* (1995).

Frank Walsh, *Sin and Censorship: The Catholic Church and the Motion Picture Industry* (1996).

Carl Beauchamp, *Without Lying Down: Frances Marion and the Powerful Women of Early Hollywood* (1997).

Thomas Schatz, *The Genius of the System: Hollywood and Filmmaking in the Studio Era* (2010).

J. E. Smyth, *Nobody's Girl Friday: The Women Who Ran Hollywood* (2018).

Water and Power

Norris Hundley, *Water and the West: The Colorado River Compact and the Politics of Water in the American West* (1975).

Nelson S. Van Valen, "A Neglected Aspect of the Owens River Aqueduct Story: The Inception of the Los Angeles Municipal Electric System," *Southern California Quarterly* (1977).

Kendrick A. Clements, "Politics and the Park: San Francisco's Fight for Hetch Hetchy, 1908–1913," *Pacific Historical Review* (1979).

Abraham Hoffman, *Vision or Villainy: Origins of the Los Angeles-Owens Valley Water Controversy* (1981).

Philip L. Fradkin, *A River No More: The Colorado River and the West* (1981).

Donald J. Pisani, *From the Family Farm to Agribusiness: The Irrigation Crusade in California and the West, 1850–1931* (1984).

Marc Reisner, *Cadillac Desert: The American West and Its Disappearing Water* (1986).

Joseph E. Stevens, *Hoover Dam: An American Adventure* (1988).

John Walton, *Western Times and Water Wars: State, Culture, and Rebellion in California* (1992).

Robert Sauder, *The Lost Frontier: Water Diversion in the Growth and Destruction of Owens Valley Agriculture* (1994).

Norris Hundley, Jr. and Donald C. Jackson, *Heavy Ground: William Mulholland and the St. Francis Dam Disaster* (2016).

Politics and Maturing Economy

Los Angeles Times, *The 47-Years War for a Free City: A History of the Open Shop in Los Angeles* (1929).

Russell M. Posner, "The Progressive Voters' League, 1923–1926," *California Historical Society Quarterly* (1957).

Edwin Layton, "The Better America Federation: A Case Study of Superpatriots," *Pacific Historical Review* (1961).

Louis B. and Richard S. Perry, *A History of the Los Angeles Labor Movement, 1911–1941* (1963).

Jackson K. Putnam, *Modern California Politics* (1984).

Gerald D. Nash, *A. P. Giannini and the Bank of America* (1992).

Felice A. Bonadio, *A. P. Giannini: Banker of America* (1994).

Jules Tygiel, *The Great Los Angeles Swindle* (1994).

The Great Depression and Public Works

Mary Montgomery and Marion Clawson, *History of Legislation and Policy Formation of the Central Valley Project* (1946).

Frank L. Kidner, *California Business Cycles* (1946).

Paul S. Taylor, "Excess Land Law: Pressure versus Principle," *California Law Review* (1959).

Robert L. Pritchard, "Orange County During the Depressed Thirties: A Study in Twentieth Century California Local History," *Southern California Quarterly* (1968).

James T. Patterson, "The New Deal in the West," *Pacific Historical Review* (1969).

Jerre Mangione, *The Dream and the Deal: The Federal Writers Project, 1935–1943* (1971).

Irving G. Hendrick, "The Impact of the Great Depression on Public School Support in California," *Southern California Quarterly* (1972).

James Leiby, "State Welfare Administration in California, 1930–1945," *Southern California Quarterly* (1973).

Stephen M. Gelber, "Working to Prosperity: California's New Deal Murals," *California History* (1979).

Loren B. Chan, "California During the Early 1930s—The Administration of Governor James Rolph Jr., 1931–1934," *Southern California Quarterly* (1981).

Marlene Park and Gerald E. Markowitz, *Democratic Vistas: Post Offices and Public Art in the New Deal* (1984).

Leonard Leader, *Los Angeles and the Great Depression* (1991).

William H. Mullins, *The Depression and the Urban West Coast, 1929–1933* (1991).

Kevin Starr, *Endangered Dreams: The Great Depression in California* (1996).

Anthony W. Lee, *Painting on the Left: Diego Rivera, Radical Politics, and San Francisco's Public Murals* (1999).

Stephen D. Mikesell, *A Tale of Two Bridges: The San Francisco-Oakland Bay Bridges of 1936 and 2013* (2017).

1930s Panaceas, Labor, and Politics

Paul Taylor and Dorothea Lange, *American Exodus* (1939, 1969).

Carey McWilliams, *Factories in the Field* (1939).

Mike Quinn, *The Big Strike* (1949).

Robert E. Burke, *Olson's New Deal for California* (1953).

Abraham Holtzman, *The Townsend Movement: A Political Study* (1963).

David Selvin, *Sky Full of Storm* (1966).

Jackson K. Putnam, *Old Age Politics in California* (1970).

Charles P. Larrowe, *Harry Bridges: The Rise and Fall of Radical Labor in the United States* (1972).

Walter J. Stein, *California and the Dust Bowl Migration* (1973).

Harvey Schwartz, *The March Inland: Origins of the ILWU Warehouse Division* (1978).

Francisco E. Balderrama, *In Defense of La Raza: The Los Angeles Mexican Consulate and the Mexican Community, 1929 to 1936* (1982).

Vicki L. Ruiz, *Cannery Women, Cannery Lives: Mexican Women, Unionization, and the California Food Processing Industry, 1930–1950* (1987).

Bruce Nelson, *Workers on the Waterfront* (1988).

Mario T. Garcia, *Mexican Americans: Leadership, Ideology, and Identity, 1930–1960* (1989).

James N. Gregory, *American Exodus: The Dust Bowl Migration and Okie Culture in California* (1989).

Greg Mitchell, *The Campaign of the Century: Upton Sinclair's Race for Governor of California and the Birth of Media Politics* (1992).

Camille Guerin Gonzales, *Mexican Workers and American Dreams: Immigration Repatriation, and California Farm Labor, 1900–1939* (1994).

Gilbert Gonzalez, *Labor and Community: Mexican Citrus Worker Villages in a Southern California County, 1900–1950* (1994).

Devra Weber, *Dark Sweat, White Gold: California Farm Workers, Cotton and the New Deal* (1994).

Francisco Balderrama and Raymond Rodriguez, *Decade of Betrayal: Mexican Repatriation in the 1930s* (1995).

David Vaught, "Factories in the Field Revisited," *Pacific Historical Review* (1997).

Kathryn Olmsted, *Right Out of California: The 1930s and the Big Business Roots of Modern Conservatism* (2015).

Fernando Saúl Alanís Enciso, *They Should Stay There: The Story of Mexican Migration and Repatriation during the Great Depression* (2017).

A Changing Society

Gilman M. Ostrander, *The Prohibition Movement in California, 1848–1933* (1957).

John R. Meers, "The California Wine and Grape Industry and Prohibition," *California Historical Society Quarterly* (1967).

Carey McWilliams, *Southern California: An Island on the Land* (1973).

Richard Melching, "The Activities of the Ku Klux Klan in Anaheim, California, 1923–1925," *Southern California Quarterly* (1974).

Mark S. Foster, "The Model T, the Hard Sell, and Los Angeles' Urban Growth: The Decentralization of Los Angeles During the 1920s," *Pacific Historical Review* (1975).

John D. Weaver, *Los Angeles: The Enormous Village, 1781–1981* (1980).

Ricardo Romo, *East Los Angeles: History of a Barrio* (1983).

Bruce Henstell, *Sunshine and Wealth: Los Angeles in the Twenties and Thirties* (1984).

Kenneth D. Rose, "'Dry' Los Angeles and Its Liquor Problems in 1924," *Southern California Quarterly* (1987).

Joan M. Jensen and Gloria Ricci Lothrop, *California Women: A History* (1987).

Scott Bottles, *Los Angeles and the Automobile* (1987).

Norman M. Klein and Martin J. Scheisl, *Los Angeles and the Memory of Many Hopes: 20th Century Los Angeles, Power, Promotion, and Social Conflict* (1990).

Mary Paik Lee, *Quiet Odyssey: A Pioneer Korean Woman in America* (1990).

Kevin Starr, *Material Dreams: Southern California Through the 1920s* (1990) and *Endangered Dreams: The Great Depression in California* (1995).

Christopher Cocoltchos, "The Invisible Empire and the Search for the Orderly Community: The Ku Klux Klan in Anaheim, California," in *The Invisible Empire in the West: Towards a New Historical Appraisal of the Ku Klux Klan of the 1920s* (1992).

David G. Gutiérrez, *Wall and Mirrors: Mexican Americans, Mexican Immigrants and the Politics of Ethnicity* (1995).

Judy Yung, *Unbound Feet: A Social History of Chinese Women in San Francisco* (1995).

Douglas Monroy, *Rebirth: Mexican Los Angeles from the Great Migration to the Great Depression* (1999).

David Yoo, *Growing Up Nisei: Race, Generation, and Culture Among Japanese Americans of California, 1924–1949* (1999).

Lon Kurashige, *Japanese American Celebration and Conflict: A History of Ethnic Identity and Festival in Los Angeles, 1934–1990* (2002).

Stephen J. Pitti, *The Devil in Silicon Valley: Northern California, Race, and Mexican Americans* (2004).

Linda Espana-Maram, *Creating Masculinity in Los Angeles's Little Manila: Working-Class Filipinos and Popular Culture, 1920s–1950s* (2006).

Allison Varzally, *Making a Non-White America: Californians Coloring Outside Ethnic Lines, 1925–1955* (2008).

Mark Wild, *Street Meeting: Multiethnic Neighborhoods in Early Twentieth-Century Los Angeles* (2008).

Erika Lee and Judy Yung, *Angel Island: Immigrant Gateway to America* (2010).

Shana Bernstein, *Bridges of Reform: Interracial Civil Rights Activism in Twentieth-Century Los Angeles* (2011).

Dawn Bohulano Mabalon, *Little Manila Is in the Heart: The Making of the Filipina/o American Community in Stockton, California* (2013).

Valerie J. Matsumoto, *City Girls: The Nisei Social World in Los Angeles, 1920–1950* (2014).

Arts and Letters Between the Wars

Lawrence Clark Powell, *Robinson Jeffers: The Man and His Work* (1940).

Melba Berry Bennett, *The Stonemason of Tor House: The Life and Work of Robinson Jeffers* (1966).

David Wyatt, *The Fall into Eden: Landscape and Imagination in California* (1986).

Gerald Haslam, *Voices of a Place: Social and Literary Essays from the Other California* (1987), "Literary California," *California History* (Winter, 1989), and *Many Californias: Literature from the Golden State* (1992).

James Karman, *Robinson Jeffers: Poet of California* (1987, 1995), and *Robinson Jeffers: Poet and Prophet* (2015).

Patricia Carpenter and Paul Totah, *San Francisco Fair: Treasure Island, 1939–1940* (1989).

Michael Davidson, *San Francisco Renaissance: Poetics and Community at Mid-Century* (1989).

Harold Kirker, *Old Forms on a New Land: California Architecture in Perspective* (1991).

David Fine, "Down and Out in Los Angeles: John Fante's Ask the Dust," *The Californians* (Sept/Oct, 1991).

Lawrence Lee and Barry Gifford, *Saroyan: A Biography* (1998).

K. D. Kurutz and Gary F. Kurutz, *California Calls You: The Art of Promoting the Golden State, 1870–1940* (2000).

Dorothea Lange and John Steinbeck

John Steinbeck, *The Grapes of Wrath* (1939).

Nelson Valjean, *John Steinbeck, The Errant Knight* (1975).

John Steinbeck, *The Acts of King Arthur and His Noble Knights* (1976).

Milton Meltzer, *Dorothea Lange: A Photographer's Life* (1978).

Therese T. Hayman, *Celebrating a Collection: The Work of Dorothea Lange* (1978).

John Steinbeck, *Working Days: The Journals of the Grapes of Wrath, 1938–1941*, ed. Robert DeMott (1990).

Jackson J. Benson, *John Steinbeck, Writer: A Biography* (1990).

Jay Parini, *John Steinbeck* (1995).

Linda Gordon, *Dorothea Lange: A Life Beyond Limits* (2009).

Jan Goggans, *California on the Breadlines: Dorothea Lange, Paul Taylor, and the Making of a New Deal Narrative* (2010).

Part Eight: World War II and Postwar Expansion

World War II and Race

Ansel Adams, *Born Free and Equal: The Story of Manzanar* (1944).

Jacobus Ten Broek, Edward N. Barnhard, and Floyd W. Matson, *Prejudice, War and the Constitution* (1954).

Leonard Broom and John I. Kitsuse, *The Managed Casualty: The Japanese American Family in World War II* (1956).

Audrie Gardner and Anne Loftis, *The Great Betrayal: The Evacuation of the Japanese Americans During World War II* (1969).

Harry H. L. Kitano, *Japanese Americans: Evolution of a Subculture* (1969).

Bill Hosokawa, *Nisei: The Quiet Americans* (1969).

Dillon S. Myer, *Uprooted Americans* (1971).

Roger Daniels, *Concentration Camps USA: Japanese Americans and World War II* (1971).

Jeanne Wakatsuki Houston and James D. Houston, *Farewell to Manzanar* (1973).

John Moddell, ed., *The Kikuchi Diary* (1973).

Michi Weglyn, *Years of Infamy: The Untold Story of America's Concentration Camps* (1976).

Yoshiko Uchida, *Desert Exile: The Uprooting of a Japanese-American Family* (1982).

U.S. Commission on Wartime Relocation and Internment of Civilians, *Personal Justice Denied* (1983).

Peter Irons, *Justice at War: The Story of the Japanese American Internment* (1983) and *Justice Delayed: The Record of the Japanese American Internment Cases* (1989).

Robert L. Allen, *The Port Chicago Mutiny: The Story of the Largest Mass Mutiny Trial in U.S. Naval History* (1989).

John Tateishi, *And Justice for All: An Oral History of the Japanese American Detention Camps* (1984).

Stephen Fox, *The Unknown Internment: An Oral History of Italian American Relocation During World War II* (1990).

Sandra C. Taylor, *Jewel of the Desert: Japanese American Internment at Topaz* (1993).

Richard Nishimoto, *Inside an American Concentration Camp* (1995).

Page Smith, *Democracy on Trial: The Japanese American Evacuation and Relocation in World War II* (1995).

Kevin A. Leonard, "'Is This What We Fought For': Japanese Americans and Racism in California, The Impact of World War II," *Western Historical Quarterly* (November, 1990).

Marilyn S. Johnson, "Urban Arsenals: War Housing and Social Change in Richmond and Oakland," *Pacific Historical Review* (August, 1991).

Kim Kodami Hill, *Topaz Moon: Chiura Obata's Art of the Internment* (2000).

Lawson Fusao Inada, ed., *Only What We Could Carry: The Japanese American Internment Experience* (2000).

Shirley Ann Wilson Moore, *To Place Our Deeds: The African American Community in Richmond, California, 1910–1963* (2000).

Eduardo Pagan, *Murder at the Sleepy Lagoon: Zoot Suits, Race, and Riot in Wartime L.A.* (2003).

Alice Yang Murray, *Historical Memories of the Japanese American Internment and the Struggle for Redress* (2007).

Luis Alvarez, *The Power of the Zoot: Youth Culture and Resistance During World War II* (2008).

Linda Gordon and Gary Y. Okihiro, ed., *Impounded: Dorothea Lange and the Censored Images of Japanese American Internment* (2008).

Catherine Ramirez, *The Women in the Zoot Suit: Gender, Nationalism, and the Cultural Politics of Memory* (2009).

Greg Robinson, *A Tragedy of Democracy: Japanese Confinement in North America* (2009).

Scott Kurashige, *The Shifting Grounds of Race: Black and Japanese Americans in the Making of Multiethnic Los Angeles* (2010).

Ana Elizabeth Rosas, *Abrazando el Espíritu: Bracero Families Confront the US–Mexico Border* (2014).

Lorraine K. Bannai, *Enduring Conviction: Fred Korematsu and His Quest for Justice* (2015).

Economic Impact of the War

Katherine Archibald, *Wartime Shipyard: A Study in Social Disunity* (1947).

Wytze Gorter and George H. Hildebrand, *The Pacific Coast Maritime Shipping Industry, 1930–1948* (1952, 1954).

Arlene Elliott, "The Rise of Aeronautics in California, 1849–1940," *Southern California Quarterly* (1970).

David L. Clark, *The Aerospace Industry as the Primary Factor in the Industrial Development of Southern California* (1976).

Clayton R. Koppes, *JPL and the American Space Program: A History of the Jet Propulsion Laboratory* (1982).

Gerald D. Nash, *The American West Transformed: The Impact of the Second World War* (1985) and *World War II and the West* (1990).

William A. Schoneberger and Paul Sonnenburg, *California Wings* (1987).

Mark S. Foster, *Henry J. Kaiser: Builder in the Modern American West* (1989).

Charles Wollenberg, *Marinship at War: Shipbuilding and Social Change in Wartime Sausalito* (1990).

Roger W. Lotchin, *The Way We Really Were: The Golden State in the Second Great War* (2000) and *The Bad City in the Good War: San Francisco, Los Angeles, Oakland, and San Diego* (2003).

Marilyn S. Johnson, *The Second Gold Rush: Oakland and the East Bay in World War II* (1993).

Arthur C. Verge, *Paradise Transformed: Los Angeles During the Second World War* (1993).

Paul Rhode, "The Nash Thesis Revisited: An Economic Historian's View," *Pacific Historical Review* (August, 1994).

Shirley Ann Wilson Moore, *To Place Our Deeds: The African American Community in Richmond, California, 1910–1963* (2000).

Postwar California

Warren S. Thompson, *Growth and Changes in California's Population* (1955).

Mel Scott, *The San Francisco Bay Area: A Metropolis in Perspective* (1959).

John Anson Ford, *Thirty Explosive Years in Los Angeles* (1961).

Winston W. Crouch and Beatrice Dinerman, *Southern California Metropolis: A Study in Development of Government for a Metropolitan Area* (1964).

Scott L. Bottles, *Los Angeles and the Automobile: The Making of a Modern City* (1987).

Rebecca C. Lowen, *Creating the Cold War University: The Transformation of Stanford* (1997).

Becky Nicolaides, *My Blue Heaven: Life and Politics in the Working-Class Suburbs of Los Angeles, 1920–1965* (2002).

Robert O. Self, *American Babylon: Race and the Struggle for Postwar Oakland* (2003).

Margaret Pugh O'Mara, *Cities of Knowledge: Cold War Science and the Search for the Next Silicon Valley* (2005).

Charlotte Brooks, *Alien Neighbors, Foreign Friends: Asian Americans, Housing, and the Transformation of Urban California* (2009).

Daniel Martinez HoSang, *Racial Propositions: Ballot Initiatives and the Making of Postwar California* (2010).

Mark Brilliant, *The Color of America Has Changed: How Racial Diversity Shaped Civil Rights Reform in California, 1941–1978* (2012).

Deborah Cohen, *Braceros: Migrant Citizens and Transnational Subjects in the Postwar United States and Mexico* (2013).

Politics and Politicians

Gordon Kahn, *Hollywood on Trial* (1948).

Edward L. Barrett Jr., *The Tenney Committee* (1961).

David P. Gardner, *The California Oath Controversy* (1967).

Robert L. Pritchard, "California Un-American Activities Investigation: Subversion on the Right?" *California Historical Society Quarterly* (1970).

Arthur H. Samish and Bob Thomas, *The Secret Boss of California* (1971).

James A. Fisher, "The Political Development of the Black Community in California, 1850–1950," *California Historical Society Quarterly* (1971).

Paul Bullock, "Richard Nixon's 1946 Campaign Against Jerry Voorhis," *Southern California Quarterly* (1973).

Paul Bullock, *Jerry Voorhis: The Idealist as Politician* (1978).

Edward G. White, *Earl Warren: A Public Life* (1982).

Ingrid W. Scobie, *Center Stage: Helen Gahagan Douglas, A Life* (1992).

Gayle B. Montgomery and James W. Johnson, *One Step from the White House: The Rise and Fall of Senator William F. Knowland* (1998).

Irwin Gellman, *The Contender: Richard Nixon, the Congress Years, 1946–1952* (1999).

Theodore Hamm, *Rebel and a Cause: Caryl Chessman and the Politics of the Death Penalty in Postwar California, 1948–1974*.

Jim Newton, *Justice For All: Earl Warren and the Nation He Made* (2006).

Culture and Society

Thomas Parkinson, ed., *A Casebook on the Beats* (1961).

A. Russell Buchanan, *Black Americans in World War II* (1972).

David Gebhard et al., *A Guide to Architecture in San Francisco and Northern California* (1973).

Robert A. Hipkiss, *Jack Kerouac: Prophet of the New Romanticism* (1976).

David Gebhard and Robert Winter, *A Guide to Architecture in Los Angeles and Southern California* (1977).

Dennis McNally, *Desolate Angel: Jack Kerouac, the Beat Generation, and America* (1980).

Irving Hendrick, *California Education: A Brief History* (1980).

John Margolies, *The End of the Road: Vanishing Highway Architecture in America* (1981).

John Russell Taylor, *Strangers in Paradise: The Hollywood Emigrés, 1933–1950* (1983).

Gerald Haslam, *The Other California: The Great Central Valley in Life and Letters* (1990).

Robert and Jane Easton, *Love and War: Pearl Harbor Through V-J Day* (1991).

John A. Maynard, *Venice West: The Beat Generation in Southern California* (1991).

Ted Gioia, *West Coast Jazz: Modern Jazz in California, 1945–1960* (1992).

Gregory Black, *The Catholic Crusade Against the Movies, 1940–1975* (1998).

Gary Giddins, *Bing Crosby: A Pocket Full of Dreams—The Early Years, 1903–1940* (2001).

Part Nine: The 1960s and After

Los Angeles and the Watts Riots

John A. McCone et al., *Violence in the City—An End or a Beginning?* (1965).

Jerry Cohen and William S. Murphy, *Burn, Baby, Burn! The Los Angeles Race Riot, August 1965* (1966).

Robert Conot, *Rivers of Blood, Years of Darkness* (1967).

Nathan Cohen, ed., *The Los Angeles Riots: A Socio-Psychological Study* (1970).

Lawrence B. DeGraaf, "The City of the Black Angels: Emergence of the Los Angeles Ghetto, 1890–1930," and Joseph Boskin and Victor Pilson, M.D., "The Los Angeles Riot of 1965: A Medical Profile of an Urban Crisis," both in *Pacific Historical Review* (1970).

Paul Bullock, *Watts: The Aftermath* (1970).

Mike Davis, *City of Quartz* (1991).

Bruce M. Tyler, *From Harlem to Hollywood: The Struggle for Racial and Cultural Democracy, 1920–1943* (1992).

Cecilia Rasmussen, "The 'Bloody Christmas' of 1951" (*Los Angeles Times*, Dec. 21, 1997).

Josh Sides, *L.A. City Limits: African American Los Angeles from the Great Depression to the Present* (2003).

James N. Gregory, *The Southern Diaspora: How the Great Migrations of Black and White Southerners Transformed America* (2005).

Douglas Flamming, *Bound for Freedom: Black Los Angeles in Jim Crow America* (2005).

Charles R. Epp, *Making Rights Real: Activists, Bureaucrats, and the Creation of the Legalistic State* (2009).

John Buntin, *L.A. Noir: The Struggle for the Soul of America's Most Seductive City* (2009).

Donna Jean Murch, *Living for the City: Migration, Education, and the Rise of the Black Panther Party in Oakland California* (2010).

Jerome H. Skolnick, *Justice Without Trial: Law Enforcement in a Democratic Society* (2011).

Jeffrey Marcos Garcilazo, *Traqueros: Mexican Railroad Workers In The United States, 1870–1930* (2012).

James Queally, "Watts Riots: Traffic Stop Was the Spark that Ignited Days of Destruction in L.A.," *Los Angeles Times* (July 29, 2015).

Barbara Reynolds, "I Was a Civil Rights Activist in the 1960s But It's Hard for Me to Get Behind Black Lives Matter," *Washington Post* (Aug. 24, 2015).

Angel Jennings, "Longtime L.A. Civil Rights Leaders Dismayed By In-Your-Face Tactics of New Crop of Activists," *Los Angeles Times* (Oct. 30, 2015).

Michael Newton, *Unsolved Civil Rights Murder Cases, 1934–1970* (2016).

Laura Hooton, "Black Angelenos with the 'Courage to Do and Dare': African American Community Organizers in Lower California," *California History* (Spring 2017).

Julia Bricklin, "Georgia Ann Hill Robinson: The LAPD's First African American Policewoman," *California History* (Spring 2018).

Politics and Politicians

Totton J. Anderson and Eugene C. Lee, "The 1962 Election in California," *Western Political Quarterly* (1963).

H. Brett Melendy, B. F. Gilbert, *The Governors of California: From Peter H. Burnett to Edmund G. Brown* (1965).

Lou Cannon, *Ronnie and Jessie: A Political Odyssey* (1969).

T. J. Anderson, Charles G. Bell, "The 1970 Election in California," *Western Political Quarterly* (1971).

Lou Cannon, "The Reagan Years: An Evaluation of the Governor Californians Won't Soon Forget," *California Journal* (1974).

James W. Guthrie, "Proposition 13 and the Future of California's Schools," *Phi Delta Kappan* (1975).

Edmund G. Brown, Bill Brown, *Ronald Reagan: The Political Chameleon* (1976).

Ed Salzman, *Jerry Brown: High Priest and Low Politician* (1976).

J. D. Lorenz, *Jerry Brown: The Man on the White Horse* (1978).

John C. Bollens, G. Robert Williams, *Jerry Brown in a Plain Brown Wrapper* (1978).

John H. Culver, John C. Syer, *Power and Politics in California* (1980).

Maureen S. Fitzgerald, "California's Future under Proposition 13," *California Journal* (1980).

"Dolores Huerta: *Un Soldado del Movimiento*," in Joan M. Jensen, *With These Hands: Women Working on the Land* (1981).

Bill Boyarsky, *Ronald Reagan: His Life and Rise to the Presidency* (1981).

Roger Rapoport, *California Dreaming: The Odyssey of Pat and Jerry Brown* (1982).

Jackson K. Putnam, *Modern California Politics* (1984), and "The Pattern of California Politics," *Pacific Historical Review* (Feb. 1992).

Garin Burbank, "Speaker Moretti, Governor Reagan, and the Search for Tax Reform In California, 1970–1972," *Pacific Historical Review* (1992).

John Jacobs, *A Rage for Justice: The Passion and Politics of Phillip Burton* (1995).

James Richardson, *Willie Brown: A Biography* (1996).

Lisa McGirr, *Suburban Warriors: The Origins of the New American Right* (2001).

Martin Schiesl, ed., *Responsible Liberalism: Edmund G. "Pat" Brown and Reform Government in California, 1958–1967* (2003).

Jules Tygiel, *Ronald Reagan and the Triumph of American Conservatism* (2004).

Vicki Ruíz, Virginia Sánchez Korrol, *Latina Legacies: Identity, Biography, and Community* (2005).

Ethan Rarick, *California Rising: The Life and Times of Pat Brown* (2005).

Bill Boyarsky, *Big Daddy: Jesse Unruh and the Art of Power Politics* (2008).

Bill Berkowitz, "Meet Maria Moreno: The First Farm Worker Woman in America To Be Hired As A Union Organizer," *Colorlines* (Feb. 28, 2018).

Race and Radicalism

Seymour M. Lipset, Sheldon S. Wolin, *The Berkley Student Revolt* (1965).

Raymond E. Wolfinger, Fred E. Greenstein, "The Repeal of Fair Housing in California: An Analysis of Referendum Voting," *American Political Science Review* (1968).

Philip S. Foner, *The Black Panthers* (1970).

Bobby Seale, *Seize the Time: The Story of the Black Panther Party and Huey P. Newton* (1970).

William Barlow, Peter Shapiro, *An End to Silence: The San Francisco State Student Movement in the 60s* (1971).

Roger Daniels, Spencer C. Olin Jr., *Racism in California: A Reader on the History of Oppression* (1972).

Steve Talbot, "Free Alcatraz: The Culture of Native American Liberation," *Journal of Ethnic Studies* (1975).

Peter Matthiessen, *Sal Si Puedes: Cesar Chavez and the Farm Workers* (1975).

Ralph Guzman, *The Political Socialization of Mexican American People* (1976).

Charles Wollenberg, *All Deliberate Speed: Segregation and Exclusion in California Schools, 1855–1975* (1977).

William M. Rorabaugh, *Berkeley at War: the 1960s* (1989).

David L. Goines, *The Free Speech Movement: Coming of Age in the 1960s* (1993).

Raphael J. Sonenshein, *Politics in Black and White: Race and Power in Los Angeles* (1993).

Gerard J. De Groot, "The Limits of Moral Protest and Participatory Democracy: The Vietnam Day Committee," *Pacific Historical Review* (1995).

George Ramos, "Reflecting on Ironies of an Activist's Life: Victoria Castro Recalls Her Role in 1968 Chicano 'Blowouts' at Eastside Campuses," *Los Angeles Times*, Apr. 17, 1996.

Sara Davidson, *Loose Change: Three Women of the Sixties* (1997).

Delores N. McBroome, *Parallel Communities: African Americans in California's East Bay, 1850–1963* (1997).

F. Arturo Rosales, *Testimonio: A Documentary History of the Mexican-American Struggle for Civil Rights* (2000).

Lorena Oropeza, *¡Raza Sí! ¡Guerra No!: Chicano Protest and Patriotism during the Viet Nam War Era* (2005).

Laura Pulido, *Black, Brown, Yellow, and Left: Radical Activism in Los Angeles* (2006).

Daryl J. Maeda, *Chains of Babylon: The Rise of Asian America* (2009).

Mario T. García and Sal Castro, *Blowout! Sal Castro & The Chicano Struggle for Educational Justice*, (2011).

Margaret E. Rose, "Dolores Huerta: Passionate Defender of *La Causa*" (Jan. 26, 2002).

David Montejano, *Sancho's Journal: Exploring the Political Edge with the Brown Berets* (2012).

Matt Garcia, *From the Jaws of Victory: The Triumph and Tragedy of Cesar Chavez and the Farm Worker Movement* (2012).

Joshua Bloom and Waldo Martin, *Black Against Empire: The History and Politics of the Black Panther Party* (2013).

Miriam Pawel, *The Crusades of Cesar Chavez: A Biography* (2014).

Brenda Stevenson, *The Contested Murder of Latasha Harlins: Justice, Gender, and the Origins of the LA Riots* (2015).

Lori Flores, *Grounds for Dreaming: Mexican Americans, Mexican Immigrants, and the California Farmworker Movement* (2016).

Karen L. Ishizuka, *Serve the People: Making Asian America in the Long Sixties* (2016).

Colleen Moore, Connie Tan, and Nancy Shulock, "Average Won't Do: Performance Trends in California Education as Foundation for Action," Institute for Higher Education Leadership Policy [undated], at higher-education-in-california-average-wont-do/, accessed Dec. 11, 2017.

G. Lerner, "The Walkouts of 1968 and the Press: How L.A. Opinion Met the Los Angeles *Times*" (2013).

Campaign for College Opportunity, "The State of Higher Education in California: Latino Report" (Apr. 2015).

Luis D. León, *The Political Spirituality of Cesar Chavez: Crossing Religious Borders* (2015).

Mario T. García, "An Important Day in U.S. History: The Chicano Moratorium," *National Catholic Reporter* (Aug. 27, 2015).

Water, Energy Crises, and the Environment

Stephen Anderson et al., *California Energy: The Economic Factors* (1976).

Joseph Castrovinci, "Nuclear Power: Arguments for the Defense," *San Francisco Business* (1979).

Hal Rubin, "Guide to Nuclear Power in California," *California Journal* (1979).

California Energy Commission, *Energy for Tomorrow: Challenges and Opportunities for California* (1981).

E. A. Engelbert, A. F. Scheuring, *Competition for California Water* (1982).

William L. Kahrl, *Water and Power* (1982).

Douglas Strong, *Tahoe: An Environmental History* (1984).

David R. Brower, *For the Earth's Sake: the Life and Times of David Brower* (1990).

Gray Brechin, *Imperial San Francisco: The Environmental Costs of City-Building on the Pacific Basin* (1991).

James C. Williams, *Energy and the Making of Modern California* (1997).

The High-Tech Revolution

Moira Johnson, "Silicon Valley," *National Geographic* (October, 1982).

Dirk Hanson, *The New Alchemists: Silicon Valley and the Microelectronics Revolution* (1982).

Ian Rienecke, *Electronic Illusions: A Skeptic's View of Our Electronic Future* (1984).

Everett M. Rogers, Judith K. Larsen, *Silicon Valley Fever: Growth of High-Technology Culture* (1984).

T. R. Reid, *The Chip: How Two Americans Invented the Microchip and Launched a Revolution* (Rev. ed.) (2001).

Charles Wollenberg, "The Godfather of Silicon Valley," in *Golden Gate Metropolis: Perspectives on Bay Area History* (1985).

Paul Frieberger and Michael Swayne, *Fire in the Valley: The Making of the Personal Computer* (1984).

Theodore Roszak, *The Cult of Information: The Folklore of Computers and the True Art of Thinking* (1986).

Gene Smarte, Andrew Reinhart, "15 Years of Bits, Bytes, and Other Great Moments," *Byte* (Sept. 1990).

Fred Guterl, "Reinventing the PC," *Discover* (Sept. 1995).

Christophe Lécuyer and David C. Brock, *Makers of the Microchip: A Documentary History of Fairchild Semiconductor* (2010).

Margaret O'Mara, "Silicon Valleys: Here, There, and Everywhere," *Boom: A Journal of California 1* (Summer 2011), 75–81.

Leslie Berlin, *Troublemakers: Silicon Valley's Coming of Age* (2017).

Culture and Society

Nancy Newhall, *Ansel Adams: The Eloquent Light* (1963).

Raymond F. Dasmann, *The Destruction of California* (1965).

Barbara Rose, "Los Angeles: The Second City," *Art in America* (1966).

Christopher Rand, *Los Angeles: The Ultimate City* (1967).

Joan Didion, *Slouching Toward Bethlehem* (1968).

Theodore Roszak, *The Making of a Counterculture* (1969), and *The Voice of the Earth* (1992).

Richard F. Pourade, *City of the Dream: The History of San Diego* (1977).

Landon Y. Jones, *Great Expectations: America and the Baby Boom Generation* (1980).

Mark R. Winchell, *Joan Didion* (1980).

Gene Anthony, *The Summer of Love* (1980).

James J. Rawls, "Vision and Revisions," *Wilson Quarterly* (1980).

Irving G. Hendrick, *California Education: A Brief History* (1980).

Wallace Stegner, Richard W. Etulain, *Conversations with Wallace Stegner on Western History and Literature* (1983).

Norman Giller, *The 1981 Olympics Handbook* (1984).

Richard D. Lyons, "How Release of Mental Patients Began," *New York Times* (Oct. 30, 1984).

Ansel Adams, Mary Street Alinder, *Ansel Adams: An Autobiography* (1985).

Los Angeles Times Co., *The Los Angeles Times Book of the 1984 Olympics* (1985).

Jonathan Spaulding, *Snapshots: Glimpses of the Other California* (1985) and "The National Scene and the Social Good: The Artistic Education of Ansel Adams," *Pacific Historical Review* (1991).

Gerald Haslam, *Voices of a Place: Social and Literary Essays from the Other California* (1987).

Tom Gioia, *West Coast Jazz: Modern Jazz in California, 1945–1960* (1994).

John Aubrey Douglass, *The California Idea and American Higher Education: 1850 to the 1960 Master Plan* (2000).

Part Ten: Environment and Society

Water, the Delta, and the Peripheral Canal

Roger Minick, *Delta West: The Land and People of the Sacramento-San Joaquin Delta* (1969).

Paul S. Taylor, "California Water Project: Law and Politics," *Ecology Law Quarterly* (1975).

Frank Stead and Walt Anderson, "The California Water Plan: Onward and Upward," *Cry California* (1976).

W. Turrentine Jackson and Alan M. Paterson, *The Sacramento–San Joaquin Delta and the Evolution and Implementation of Water Policy: An Historical Perspective* (1977).

John Hart, "The Delta: The Living (or Dying?) Heart of California," *Cry California* (1977).

Dan Walters, "The Evaporation of Consensus on Brown's $7 Billion Water Plan," *California Journal* (1979).

Janet Lokke, "'Like a Bright Tree of Life': Farmland Settlement of the Sacramento River Delta," *California History* (1980).

Harry Dennis, *Water and Power: The Peripheral Canal and Its Alternatives* (1981).

Daniel J. Blackburn, "The Farm Bureau's Big Switch on the Big Ditch," *California Journal* (1981).

Michael Storper and Richard A. Walker, *The Price of Water: Surplus and Subsidy in the California State Water Project* (1984).

Cheryl Clark, "Breaking the Faith—Southern California Dissidents: We Don't Need Northern Water Now," *California Journal* (1985).

Robert Kelley, *Battling the Inland Sea: American Political Culture, Public Policy, and the Sacramento Valley, 1950–1986* (1989).

Tom Harris, *Death in the Marsh* (1991).

Ted Williams, "Death in a Black Desert," *Audubon* (Jan.–Feb. 1994).

John Walton, *Western Times and Water Wars: State, Culture, and Rebellion in California* (1992).

Robert Gottlieb and Margaret FitzSimmons, *Thirst for Growth: Water Agencies as Hidden Government in California* (1991).

Norris Hundley Jr., *The Great Thirst: Californians and Water, 1770s–1990s* (2001).

U.S. Bureau of Reclamation, "Central Valley Project Improvement Act, Program Activity Review Report" (Dec. 22, 2008).

Lisa Lien-Mager, "Final Draft Interim Delta Plan Released," Association of California Water Agencies (Aug. 20, 2010).

Philip Garone, *The Fall and Rise of the Wetlands of California's Great Central Valley* (2011).

Dale Kasner, "Agencies Hesitate to Pay More for Delta Tunnels," *Sacramento Bee* (Aug. 18, 2017), and "State May Scale Back Twin-Tunnel Project," *Sacramento Bee* (Nov. 7, 2017).

William Deverell and Tom Sitton, *Water and Los Angeles: A Tale of Three Rivers, 1900–1941* (2017).

Environmental History, General

Raymond F. Dasmann, *The Destruction of California* (1965), and *California's Changing Environment* (1981).

Roderick Nash, *Wilderness and the American Mind* (1973).

Joseph M. Petulla, *American Environmental History: The Exploitation and Conservation of Natural Resources* (1977).

Ed Salzman, ed., *California Environment and Energy: Text and Readings on Contemporary Issues* (1980).

John Hart, ed., *The New Book of California Tomorrow: Reflections and Projections from the Golden State* (1984).

Richard White, "American Environmental History: The Development of a New Historical Field," *Pacific Historical Review* (1985).

Carolie Sly, coord., *The California State Environmental Education Guide: A Curriculum Guide for Kindergarten Through Sixth Grade* (1988).

Peter Steinhart, *California's Wild Heritage: Threatened and Endangered Animals in the Golden State* (1990).

Lois J. Roberts, *San Miguel Island: Santa Barbara's Fourth Island West* (1991).

Joseph B. Knox and Ann Foley Scheuring, eds., *Global Climate Change and California: Potential Impacts and Responses* (1991).

Michael Barbour et al., *California's Changing Landscapes: Diversity and Conservation of California Vegetation* (1993).

Tim Palmer, ed., *California's Threatened Environment: Restoring the Dream* (1993).

Biosystems Books, *Life on the Edge: A Guide to California's Endangered Natural Resources: Wildlife* (1994).

Burton L. Gordon, *The Monterey Bay Area: Natural History and Cultural Imprints* (1996).

James C. Williams, *Energy and the Making of Modern California* (1997).

Carolyn Merchant, ed., *Green Versus Gold: Sources in California's Environmental History* (1998).

Char Miller, *Not So Golden State: Sustainability and the California Dream* (2016).

Philip Garone, *The Fall and Rise of the Wetlands of California's Great Central Valley* (2011).

The Rise of Environmental Ideas and Groups

Samuel E. Wood and Alfred E. Heller, *California, Going, Going . . .* (1962).

Richard G. Lillard, *Eden in Jeopardy: Man's Prodigal Meddling with His Environment: The Southern California Experience* (1966).

William Bronson, *How to Kill a Golden State* (1968).

Barry Commoner, *The Closing Circle* (1971).

Robert Easton, *Black Tide: The Santa Barbara Oil Spill and Its Consequences* (1972).

A. E. Keir Nash, Dean E. Mann, and Phil G. Olson, *Oil Pollution and the Public Interest: A Study of the Santa Barbara Oil Spill* (1972).

Holway R. Jones, "John Muir, The Sierra Club, and the Formulation of the Wilderness Concept," *The Pacific Historian* (1981).

Ansel Adams, *Ansel Adams: An Autobiography* (1985).

Douglas H. Strong, *Dreamers and Defenders: American Conservationists* (1988).

Samuel P. Hays, *Beauty, Health, and Permanence: Environmental Politics in the United States, 1955–1985* (1987).

Michael P. Cohen, *The History of the Sierra Club, 1892–1970* (1988).

David R. Brower, *For Earth's Sake: The Life and Times of David Brower* (1990).

"A Century of Environmental Action: The Sierra Club, 1892–1992," special issue of *California History* (Summer 1992).

David Vogel, *California Greenin': How the Golden State Became an Environmental Leader* (2018).

Clean Air and Water

James E. Krier and Edmund Ursin, *Pollution and Policy: A Case Essay on California and Federal Experience with Motor Vehicles Air Pollution, 1940–1975* (1977).

Douglas Foster, "The Growing Battle over Pesticides in Drinking Water," *California Journal* (1983).

Jennifer F. Sugar, "Hazardous Waste Disposal in Southern California," *California Journal* (1984).

Stephen Green, "Glitches, Gremlins, and Soap: Staggering along the Road to Toxic Waste Reform in California," *California Journal* (1985).

Mary Ellen Leary, "The Water Resources Control Board: Overwhelmed with Work, It Struggles to Correct Past Failures," *California Journal* (1985).

Michael Grunwald, "The New Action Heroes," *Time* (June 14, 2007).

Peter Henderson, "California Approves Vehicle Pollution Rules in Rebuke to Trump," *Reuters* (Mar. 24, 2017).

Stephen Edelstein, "California Reaffirms State Emission, Electric-Car Rules for 2025," *Green Car Reports* (Mar. 27, 2017).

Saving San Francisco Bay

Mel Scott, *The Future of San Francisco Bay* (1963).

Harold Gilliam, *Between the Devil and the Deep Blue Bay: The Struggle to Save San Francisco Bay* (1969), and *For Better or for Worse* (1972).

Janine M. Dolezel and Bruce N. Warren, "Saving San Francisco Bay: A Case Study in Environmental Legislation," *Stanford Law Review* (1971).

Charles A. Gulick, *The Fight for San Francisco Bay: The First Ten Years* (1971).

Robert Fernbaum, "The Growing Use of Tradeoffs to Solve Development Problems," *California Journal* (1978).

T. J. Conomos, ed., *San Francisco Bay—The Urbanized Estuary* (1979).

The Coast

Stanley Scott, *Governing California's Coast* (1975).

Robert G. Healy, ed., *Protecting the Golden Shore: Lessons from the California Coastal Commission* (1978).

Drew Liebert, "Another Crisis Ahead for Coastal Commission," *California Journal* (1980).

California Coastal Commission, *California Coastal Access Guide* (1981).

Stanley Scott, ed., *Coastal Conservation: Essays on Experiments in Governance* (1981).

Stephen Green, "'Death of a Thousand Cuts': The Governor's Campaign against the California Coastal Commission," *California Journal* (1985).

Joseph E. Petrillo and Peter Grenell, eds., *The Urban Edge: Where City Meets the Sea* (1985).

Jared Orsi, "Restoring the Common to the Goose: Citizen Activism and the Protection of the California Coastline, 1969–1982," *Southern California Quarterly* (1996).

Peter Douglas, "Coastal Commission's Casino Wager," *San Francisco Chronicle* (Apr. 08, 2007).

New York Times, "The Man Behind the Coastal Commission" (May 9, 2010).

Lake Tahoe

"Lake Tahoe: The Future of a National Asset—Land Use, Water, and Pollution," *California Law Review* (1964).

Ron Roach, "Jerry's Suit for Divorce from Pat's Tahoe Marriage," *California Journal* (1978).

Hal Rubin, "Lake Tahoe: A Tale of Two States," *Sierra* (1981).

Douglas H. Strong, *Tahoe: An Environmental History* (1984).

Urban Land Institute, *Lake Tahoe: An Evaluation of Governmental, Planning, Environmental, and Infrastructure Financial Issues in the Tahoe Basin* (1985).

Peter Goin et al., *Stopping Time: A Photographic Survey of Lake Tahoe* (1992).

Kathryn Reed, "Luxury Community Planned for Lake Tahoe Shore," *San Francisco Chronicle* (May 24, 2009).

Peter Fimrite, "Judge Rejects Lake Tahoe Shoreline Plan," *San Francisco Chronicle* (Sept. 18, 2010).

Michael J. Makley, *A Short History of Lake Tahoe* (2011).

Makley, *Saving Lake Tahoe: An Environmental History of a National Treasure* (2014).

Mono Lake

Ron Bass, "The Troubled Waters of Mono Lake: Unique Ecological Resource or Wasteful Brine Sink?" *California Journal* (1979).

D. J. Chasan, "Mono Lake vs. LA: A Tug of War for Precious Water," *Smithsonian Magazine* (1981).

G. Young, "Troubled Waters of Mono Lake," *National Geographic* (1981).

H. Dunning, "The Meaning of the Mono Lake Decision," *California Journal* (1983).

Scott Stine, "Geomorphic, Geographic, and Hydrographic Basis for Resolving the Mono Lake Controversy," *Environmental Geology and Water Science*, Vol. 17 (1991).

Mono Lake Committee, *Mono Lake: Endangered Oasis* (1993).

John Hart, *Storm over Mono Lake: The Mono Lake Battle and the California Water Future* (1996).

Abraham Hoffman, *Mono Lake: From Dead Sea to Environmental Treasure* (2014).

Controlling Growth and Preserving Land

California Land-Use Task Force, *The California Land: Planning for People* (1975).

John Hart, "Petaluma: The Little City that Could," *Cry California* (1976).

Valerie C. Kircher, "The Legislative Battle over Preserving Agricultural Land," *California Journal* (1976).

John H. Dresslar, "Agricultural Land Preservation in California: Time for a New View," *Ecology Law Quarterly* (1979).

People for Open Space, *Endangered Harvest: The Future of Bay Area Farmland* (1980).

Dan Walters, "Punching Holes in the Williamson Act," *California Journal* (1983).

Jim Churchill, "Mapping the Present and Future of California's Farmland Resources," *California Journal* (1983).

Yvonne Olson Jacobson, *Passing Farms, Enduring Values: California's Santa Clara Valley* (1985).

David E. Dowall, *The Suburban Squeeze: Land Conversion and Regulation in the San Francisco Bay Area* (1984).

Rob Kling, Spencer Olin, and Mark Foster, eds., *Postsuburban California: The Transformation of Orange County Since World War II* (1991).

Stephanie Pincetl, *Transforming California: A Political History of Land Use and Development* (1999).

Julie Guthman, *Agrarian Dreams: The Paradox of Organic Farming in California* (2004).

Michael Pollan, *The Omnivore's Dilemma: A Natural History of Four Meals* (2006).

Forestry

Lee T. Burcham, *California Range Land* (1957).

Gerald D. Nash, "The California State Board of Forestry, 1883–1960," *Southern California Quarterly* (1965).

William G. Robbins, *American Forestry: A History of National, State, and Private Cooperation* (1985).

Timothy P. Duane, *Shaping the Sierra: Nature, Culture, and Conflict in the Changing West* (1999).

Alfred Runte, *Public Lands, Public Heritage: The National Forest Idea* (1991).

Reed F. Noss, ed., *The Redwood Forest: History, Ecology, and Conservation of the Coast Redwoods* (2000).

Jared Farmer, *Trees in Paradise: A California History* (2013).

Darren Speece, *Defending Giants: The Redwood Wars and the Transformation of American Environmental Politics* (2016).

Parks and Wilderness

John Muir, *Our National Parks* (1901).

Joseph H. Engbeck, *State Parks of California from 1864 to the Present* (1980).

Jennifer Jennings, "Why the State Parks Face a Troubled Future," *California Journal* (1981).

John L. Harper, *Mineral King: Public Concern with Government Policy* (1982).

Susan R. Schrepfer, *The Fight to Save the Redwoods: A History of Environmental Reform, 1917–1978* (1983).

Mimi Stein, *A Vision Achieved: Fifty Years of East Bay Regional Park District* (1984).

Alfred Runte, *National Parks: The American Experience* (1987) and *Yosemite: The Embattled Wilderness* (1990).

Lary M. Dilsaver and William C. Tweed, *Challenge of the Big Trees: A Resource History of Sequoia and Kings Canyon National Parks* (1990).

"Yosemite and Sequoia," special issue of *California History* (Summer 1990).

Richard J. Orsi, Alfred Runte, and Marlene Smith-Baranzini, eds., *Yosemite and Sequoia: A Century of California National Parks* (1993).

Mary Beth Barber, "Base Closures," *California Journal* (1994).

Richard West Sellars, *Preserving Nature in the National Parks: A History* (1997).

Lisa M. Benton, *The Presidio: From Army Base to National Park* (1998).

Frank Wheat, *California Desert Miracle: The Fight for Desert Parks and Wilderness* (1999).

Amy Myer, *New Guardians for the Golden Gate: How America Got a Great National Park* (2006).

Joaquin Jay Gonzalez III and Roger L. Kemp, *Privatization in Practice: Reports on Trends, Cases, and Debates in Public Service by Businesses and Nonprofits* (2016).

Reaction Against Environmentalism

Charles Zurhorst, *The Conservation Fraud* (1970).

"Our Faltering Conservation Crusade," special issue of *Cry California* (1979).

Bernard J. Frieden, *The Environmental Protection Hustle* (1979).

Tony Quinn, "Pacific Legal Foundation: Nemesis of the Environmentalists," *California Journal* (1979), and "Deukmejian and the Environmentalists," *California Journal* (1980).

Rush Shay, "The Sagebrush Rebellion," *Sierra* (1980).

Joseph Gughemetti and Eugene D. Wheeler, *The Taking* (1981).

Donald H. Harrison, "The Deukmejian Dilemma: Promises Meet Reality," *California Journal* (1982).

David Brodsly, *LA Freeway: An Appreciative Essay* (1983).

Wesley Marx, "Offshore Oil: A California Battleground," *California Journal* (1983).

C. Brant Short, *Ronald Reagan and the Public Lands: America's Conservation Debate, 1979–1984* (1989).

Katherine A. Kohm, *Balancing on the Brink of Extinction: The Endangered Species Act and Lessons for the Future* (1991).

Michael J. Makely, *Open Spaces, Open Rebellions: The War over America's Public Lands* (2017).

Daniel Nelson, *Nature's Burdens: Conservation and American Politics, The Reagan Era to the Present* (2017).

"Trump Administration Erodes Environmental Protections," *High Country News* (Oct. 2, 2017).

Climate Change and California

Robert W. Righter, *Wind Energy in America Today* (2011).

Katherine Hsia-Kiung et al., *Carbon Market California: A Comprehensive History of the Golden State's Cap-and-Trade Program, Year One 2012–2013* (Environmental Defense Fund, 2014).

Debra Kahn, "Court Upholds California's Cap-and-Trade Program," *Scientific American* (Apr. 7, 2017).

"Trump Will Withdraw U.S. from Paris Climate Agreement," *New York Times* (June 1, 2017).

Kurtis Alexander, "State Orders Safety Checks at 93 Dams," *San Francisco Chronicle* (July 28, 2017).

Carolyn Lochhead, "Alarming Climate Report: Extreme Weather Conditions Likely to Accelerate in State, Federal Assessment Warns," *San Francisco Chronicle* (Aug. 9, 2017).

"No Hoax: How the West is Confronting the Reality of Climate Change," *High Country News* (Special Issue, Sept. 18, 2017).

Bruce Lieberman, "California Cap-and-Trade Moving Forward," *Yale Climate Connections* (Oct. 9, 2017).

Lisa Friedman, "U.S. Report Claims Humans Change the Climate," *Sacramento Bee* (Nov. 4, 2017).

Pat Mulroy, ed., *The Water Problem: Climate Change and Water Policy in the West* (2017).

Gary Griggs, *Coasts in Crisis: A Global Challenge* (2017).

Edward Struzik, *Firestorm: How Wildfire Will Shape Our Future* (2017).

Joshua P. Howe, *Making Climate Change History: Documents From Global Warming's Past* (2017).

"Western Climate Initiative" (Wikipedia, Feb. 21, 2018).

"Declining Snowpack in the West," *Denver Post* (Mar. 4, 2018).

Recession in the 1990s

Richard Zeiger, "A Bittersweet Farewell: George Deukmejian Kept His Word, but Was It Enough?" *California Journal* (1991).

"California: The Endangered Dream," Special Issue, *Time* (Nov. 18, 1991).

James W. Sweeney, "The Joads Go Home: Has the Golden State Lost Its Luster?" *California Journal* (1992).

Dan Walters, *The New California: Facing the 21st Century* (1992).

Jackson K. Putnam, "The Pattern of Modern California Politics," *Pacific Historical Review* (1992).

Danielle Starkey, "Pete to Immigrants: 'Don't Huddle Here': Governor Says Breathing Here Ain't Free," *California Journal* (1992) and "Immigrant Bashing: Good Policy or Good Politics?" *California Journal* (1993).

Bénédicte Raybaud and Danielle Starkey, "California's Film Industry Beats the Recession," *California Journal* (1993).

Mark Nollinger, "The New Crusaders: The Christian Right Storms California's Political Bastions," *California Journal* (1993).

Mary Beth Barber, "Transportation in California," *California Journal* (1993), and "Base Closures," *California Journal* (1994).

Danielle Starkey and Vic Pollard, "The Prison Dilemma," *California Journal* (1994).

Lisa M. Benton, *The Presidio: From Army Base to National Park* (1998).

"Los Angeles—A Special Report," *California Journal* (1997).

A. G.Block, "The Republican Bust of 1998," *California Journal* (1998).

William Booth, "California Recasts Itself to Play the Lead," *Washington Post Weekly* (July 5, 1999).

Steve Scott, "The No-Party System," *California Journal* (1999).

Eric Leve, "California Budget Crisis," Global Fixed Income/ Bailard, Biehl, and Kaiser, Topic Paper (Feb. 2003).

The New Economy

Ward Winslow, ed., *The Making of Silicon Valley: One Hundred Year Renaissance* (1995).

Allen J. Scott and Edward W. Soja, eds., *The City: Los Angeles and Urban Theory at the End of the Twentieth Century* (1997).

Hal K. Rothman, "Stumbling toward the Millennium: Tourism, the Postindustrial World, and the Transformation of the American West," *California History* (1998).

Peter Schrag, *Paradise Lost: California's Experience, America's Future* (1998).

Gray Brechin and Robert Dawson, *Farewell Promised Land: Waking from the California Dream* (1999).

Wade Rowland, *Spirit of the Web: The Age of Information from Telegraph to Internet* (1999).

Larry McCarthy, "Budget Surplus and the Economy," *Cal-Tax Digest* (June 1999).

"Silicon Valley: A Special Issue," *California Journal* (2000).

Emelyn Rodriguez, "The New Economy Comes of Age in the Capitol," *California Journal* (2001).

"Tech Jobs Decline in San Jose, San Francisco, Increase in Oakland," *Valley Business Journal* (Sept. 17, 2002).

Kimberly D. Elsbach et al., "The Building of Employee Distrust: A Case Study of Hewlett-Packard from 1995–2010" (Nov. 16, 2011).

Tara Clarke, "The Dot-Com Crash of 2000–2002," *Wall Street Examiner* (Jun. 12, 2015).

Andrew Beattie, "Why Did Dot-Com Companies Crash So Drastically?" *Investopedia* (Dec. 26, 2017).

Newswise, "CENIC Recognizes Technology Projects to Combat California Wildfires" (Feb. 20, 2018).

Income Inequality and the Housing Crisis

Jesus Hernandez, "Race, Market Constraints, and the Housing Crisis: A Problem of Embeddedness," *Kalfou* (Vol.1, No.2, 2014).

Darwin BondGraham, "The Rise of the New Land Lords," *East Bay Express* (Feb. 12, 2014).

Matt Levin, "California's Rich-Poor Gap: The Reality May Surprise You," *CalMatters* (Aug. 11, 2016).

Sarah Bohn and Caroline Danielson, "Income Inequality and the Safety Net in California," Public Policy Institute of California (May, 2016).

Los Angeles Daily News, "California's Housing Crisis—It's Even Worse Than You Think" (Aug. 28, 2017).

Jonathan Lansner, "Does California Really Have a Housing Crisis?" *Mercury News* (May 15, 2017).

Sarah Bohn and Caroline Danielson, "Poverty in California," Public Policy Institute of California (Oct. 2017).

Darwin BondGraham, "United Nations Expert Describes Oakland and California's Homeless Crisis as 'Cruel'," *East Bay Express* (Jan. 21, 2018).

"California Housing Problems Are Spilling Across its Borders," *Business Times* (Mar. 20, 2018).

The Housing Bubble and the Great Recession

Ronald W. Kaiser, "The Long Cycle of Real Estate," *Journal of Real Estate Research* (1997).

David Freedman, "Housing Bubble Economy," *Los Angeles Times* (May 19, 2002).

"Option ARMS at the Center of Rate Shock Fears," *Mortgage News Daily* (Sept. 11, 2006).

Rich Toscano, "Risks of a Serious Home Price Decline," *San Diego Housing Market News and Analysis* (Nov. 27, 2005).

Danielle DiMartino and John V. Duca, "The Rise and Fall of Subprime Mortgages," Federal Reserve Bank of Dallas Economic Letter 2 (Nov. 2007).

Jesus Hernandez, "Redlining Revisited: Mortgage Lending Patterns in Sacramento, 1930–2004," *International Journal of Urban and Regional Research* (Jul. 2, 2009).

Alan Greenspan, "The Crisis," Brookings Institution (Spring 2010).

Ron Honberg et al., "State Mental Health Cuts: The Continuing Crisis," National Alliance on Mental Illness (Nov. 2011).

Bonnie Kavoussi, "Recession Killed 170,000 Small Businesses Between 2008 and 2010," *Huffington Post* (Jul. 25, 2012).

Michael Lewis, *The Big Short: Inside the Doomsday Machine* (2011).

Center for Responsible Lending, "California Foreclosure Statistics: The Crisis is Not Over" (Apr. 2012).

Robert Rich, "The Great Recession," Federal Reserve Bank of Richmond (Nov. 22, 2013).

Gary Dymski et al., "Race, Gender, Power, and the US Subprime Mortgage and Foreclosure Crisis: A Meso Analysis," *Feminist Economics* (May 3, 2013).

Peter J. Wallison, *Hidden in Plain Sight: What Really Caused the World's Worst Financial Crisis and Why It Could Happen Again* (2015).

Dan Immergluck, *Foreclosed : High-Risk Lending, Deregulation, and the Undermining of America's Mortgage Market* (2016).

Kimberly Amadeo, "The Great Recession of 2008: Explanation with Dates," *The Balance* (Apr. 27, 2017).

Benjamin Somogyi, "To Solve the Next Foreclosure Crisis, Look to Sacramento," *The Regulatory Review* (Oct. 31, 2017).

Stuart Gabriel et al., "A Crisis of Missed Opportunities? Foreclosure Costs and Mortgage Modification During the Great Recession" (Feb. 27, 2017).

Kelsey Ramirez, "CoreLogic: Housing Market Nearly Recovered from Recession," *Housing Wire* (Mar. 1, 2018).

Lydia de Pillis, "10 Years After the Financial Crisis, Have We Learned Anything?" *CNNMoney* (Mar. 16, 2018).

Jobs

U.S. Dept. of Labor, "Fastest Growing Jobs, 2000–2010" (Dec. 4, 2001).

Glenna Matthews, *Silicon Valley, Women, and the California Dream: Gender, Class, and the California Dream: Gender, Class, and Opportunity in the Twentieth Century* (2003).

"Golden State Losing its Luster as Economy Flops," *San Francisco Chronicle* (Jan. 9, 2009).

Carolyn Said, "Building Slump Blamed for State Jobless Rate," *San Francisco Chronicle* (Sept. 22, 2010).

Don Lee, "U.S. Jobs Continue to Flow Overseas," *Los Angeles Times* (Oct. 6, 2010).

"Decline and Fall of the California Job Market," *Sacramento Bee* (Mar. 19, 2010).

Douglas A. McIntyre and Samuel Weigley, "States that Have Lost the Most Jobs to China," *NBCNews* (Sept. 16, 2015).

Jake Grovum, "Which States Have the Most Job Growth Since the Recession?" Pew Charitable Trust (May 13, 2015).

Sylvia A. Allegretto, "California's Labor Market: Eight Years Post-Great Recession," Center on Wage and Employment Dynamics, Institute for Research on Labor and Employment, University of California, Berkeley (May 2016).

Sam Harnett, "Outsourced: In A Twist, Some San Francisco IT Jobs Are Moving To India," National Public Radio (Dec. 27, 2016).

Rachel Gillett, "The 25 Highest-Paying Companies in the U.S. in 2017," *Business Insider* (Apr. 12, 2017).

EDD, "News Release 18–58" (Mar. 7, 2018).

Megan Elliott, "American Companies Keep Sending Thousands of Jobs Overseas," *CheatSheet* (Jan. 12, 2018).

Education

Lynne G. Zucker, *California's Proposition 13: Early Impact on Education and Health Services* (1982).

Charles Wollenberg, *Golden Gate Metropolis: Perspectives on Bay Area History* (1985).

"Education in California: Facing the Future," *California Journal* (1986).

Larry Gordon, "Verbal SAT Scores Slip Again in 1990," *Los Angeles Times* (Aug 28, 1990).

Laura A. Locke and Steve Scott, "Education in California: The Age of Turmoil and Hope," C*alifornia Journal (June 1993).*

Laura A. Locke, "The Voucher Initiative: Breakthrough or Breakup for California Schools?" *California Journal* (Oct. 1993).

Steve Scott, "Pay as You Go: Privatizing California's 'Public' Higher Education System," *California Journal* (1994).

Steve Scott, "Doing More with Less," *California Journal* (1997).

Mark Walsh, "Voucher Initiatives Defeated in California, Michigan," *Education Week* (Nov. 15, 2000).

William Booth, "School Voucher Initiative Roils Race," *Washington Post* (Jul 19, 2000).

EdSource, "One Year Later: California's Public School Accountability Act" (May 2000).

Emelyn Rodriguez, "The State's Schools Gamble," *California Journal* (2001).

Aaron Sankin, "California Spending More on Prisons than Colleges," *Huffington Post* (Sept. 6, 2012).

Prerna Anand, "Winners and Losers: Corrections and Higher Education in California" (Sept. 5, 2012).

Hans Johnson et al., *Higher Education in California: Institutional Costs*, Public Policy Institute of California (Nov. 2014).

Paul F. Campos, "The Real Reason College Tuition Costs So Much," *New York Times* (Apr. 4, 2015).

Kimberly P. Moore and Lisa M. Blumerman, *Public Education Finances: 2013*, Census Bureau (June 2015).

Sarah Tully, "Proceed with Caution when Comparing California Test Scores," *EdSource* (Sept. 10, 2015).

Alexei Koseff, "Gov. Jerry Brown's Proposed Budget," *Sacramento Bee* (Jan. 7, 2016).

John Fensterwald, "California at Bottom in Nationwide Ranking of Accountability Systems: State Board President Disagrees," *EdSource* (Nov. 14, 2017).

Dan Walters, "California's New School Ratings: Are They Better or Just Confusing?" *Sacramento Bee* (Mar. 17, 2017).

Sal Rodriguez, "Despite Public Support, Little Chance of School Vouchers in California," *Orange County Register* (May 7, 2017).

Chris Nichols, "Do Only a Fraction of California's Latino and Black Students Go to Four-Year Colleges?" *Politifact California* (Dec. 29, 2017).

John Fensterwald, "How Does California Rank in Per-Pupil Spending: It All Depends," *EdSource* (Feb. 28, 2017).

LendEDU, "Student Loan Debt by School by State Report" (2017).

Katie Lobosco, "Average College Degree Pays off by Age 34," *CNNMoney* (Jan. 9, 2017).

Deirdre Fernandez, "For Black Students, a College Degree Means Long Term Debt," *Boston Globe* (Nov. 26, 2017).

Chris Nichols, "Mostly True: California Ranks 41st on Per Student Spending but No. 1 Per Prisoner," *PolitiFact* (Jan. 17, 2018).

Politics in the New Millenium

"Rating Gray Davis," *California Journal* (2000).

Kalle Lasn, *Culture Jam: How to Reverse America's Suicidal Consumer Binge—and Why We Must* (2000).

Richard Nemec, "Electricity in California: A Political and Economic Crossroads," *California Journal* (2001).

Peter Asmus, "California's New Energy Legacy," *California Journal* (2001).

Lou Cannon and A.G. Block, "Surviving the Republican Train Wreck," *California Journal* (2001).

Carl M. Cannon, "D.C. Eyes Gray Davis," *California Journal* (2001).

Public Policy Institute, "California's 2004 Election" (Nov. 2004).

Lynda Gledhill, "Tax Revenue Boosts Governor's Budget," *San Francisco Chronicle* (Jan. 11, 2006).

Lynda Gledhill, "State's Budget Called a Victory for All Sides," *San Francisco Chronicle* (June 28, 2006).

CNN, "America Votes 2006," (Nov. 9, 2006).

Tom Chorneau, "California Faces Potential $11 Billion Deficit in Budget Next Year," *San Francisco Chronicle* (Nov. 7, 2007).

Joseph Cummins, *Anything for a Vote: Dirty Tricks, Cheap Shots and October Surprises in U.S. Presidential Campaigns* (2007).

Matthew Yi, "Legislature Approves Record-Late Budget," *San Francisco Chronicle* (Sept. 20, 2008).

John Wildermuth and Wyatt Buchanan, "Schwarzenegger Declares Fiscal Emergency," *San Francisco Chronicle* (Dec. 2, 2008).

San Francisco Chronicle, "Why California Can't Function" (Nov. 1, 2009).

Council on American Islamic Relations, *The Status of Muslim Civil Rights in the United States* (2005).

Jeff Bliss and James Rowley, "Florida Pastor Still Seeks Meeting on New York Islamic Center," *Bloomberg Business Week* (2010).

Joe Matthews and Mark Paul, *California Crackup: How Reform Broke the Golden State and How We Can Fix It* (2010).

Bill Chappell, "Occupy Wall Street: From a Blog Post to a Movement," National Public Radio (Oct. 20, 2011).

Bryan Thomas, "A Weary State is Left Facing Hefty Price Tag," *The Daily Californian* (Nov. 10, 2005).

James Fallows, "Jerry Brown's Political Reboot," *The Atlantic* (June 2013).

John Myers, "Remember When California's Budget Was Always Late? Here's Why Fiscal Gridlock is a Thing of the Past," *Los Angeles Times*, June 18, 2016.

Bob Dreyfuss, "Can Congress Unravel the Trump-Russia Tangle?" *The Nation* (Sept. 15, 2017).

Bethany McLean, "The True Story of the Comey Letter Debacle," *Vanity Fair* (Sept. 15, 2017).

John Kruzel, "The Russia Investigation and Donald Trump: A Timeline From On-the-Record Sources," *PolitiFact* (Feb. 15, 2018).

Emily Cadei, "California Now Has A One-Two Punch on the Russia Inquiry," *Sacramento Bee* (Jan. 9, 2018).

Philip Bump, "A (So Far) Complete Timeline of the Investigation into Trump and Russia," *Washington Post* (Mar. 16, 2018).

"Resistance State: California in the Age of Trump," *CalMatters* (Apr. 12, 2018).

Ben Christopher, "Becerra v. Trump: How California is Using the Courts to Fight the Administration," *CalMatters* (Mar. 7, 2018).

Demography

Claudette E. Bennett, *We the Americans: Blacks*, Census Bureau (Sept. 1993).

Susan J. Lapham, *We the American . . . Foreign Born*, Census Bureau (Sept. 1993).

Kristin A. Hansen and Amara Bachu, *The Foreign-Born Population: 1994*, Census Bureau (Aug. 1995).

Hans P. Johnson, "How Many Californians? A Review of Population Projections for the State," *California Counts* (Oct. 1999).

Jessica S. Barnes and Claudette E. Bennett, *The Asian Population: 2000* (Feb. 2002).

Elizabeth M. Grieco et al., *The Foreign-Born Population in the United States: 2010* (May 2012).

Sonya M. Tafoya, "Check One or More: Mixed Race and Ethnicity in California," *California Counts* (2000).

Marc J. Perry and Paul J. Mackun, *Population Change and Distribution: Census 2000 Brief*, Census Bureau (Apr. 2001).

William H. Frey, "Did the 2010 Census Tell Us Anything New?" Brookings Institute (Dec. 22, 2010).

U.S. Department of Census, "Population Distribution and Change: 2000 to 2010" (Mar. 2011).

Elizabeth M. Grieco et al., *The Size, Place of Birth, and Geographic Distribution of the Foreign-Born Population in the United States, 1960 to 2010*, Census Bureau (Oct. 2012).

Pew Research Center, *From Ireland to Germany to Italy to Mexico: How America's Source of Immigrants Has Changed in the States, 1850–2013* (Sept. 28, 2015).

Pew Research Center, *Share of Foreign-Born Population, By State: 1960–2015* (Apr. 11, 2017).

Carolyn Said, "Building Slump Blamed for State Jobless Rate," *San Francisco Chronicle* (Sept. 22, 2010).

"Decline and Fall of the California Job Market," *Sacramento Bee* (Oct. 22, 2010).

Joe Matthews and Mark Paul, *California Crackup: How Reform Broke the Golden State and How We Can Fix It* (2010).

Joaquin Jay Gonzalez III and Roger L. Kemp, *Privatization in Practice: Reports on Trends, Cases, and Debates in Public Service by Businesses and Nonprofits* (2016).

Social Transformations

Albert S. Herrera, "The Mexican American in Two Cultures," in Ed Ludwig and James Santibañez, eds., *The Chicanos: Mexican American Voices* (1971).

Matt S. Meier and Feliciano Rivera, *The Chicanos: A History of Mexican Americans* (1972).

Rodolfo Acuña, *Occupied America: A History of Chicanos* (1981).

Ricardo Romo, *East Los Angeles: History of a Barrio* (1983).

Mario T. García, *Mexican Americans* (1991).

"The Latino Century," *California Journal* (2000).

Richard A. García, "César Chávez: A Personal and Historical Testimony," *Pacific Historical Review* (May 1994).

David G. Gutiérrez, *Wall and Mirrors: Mexican Americans, Mexican Immigrants and the Politics of Ethnicity* (1995).

R. Michael Alvarez and Tara L. Butterfield, "Latino Citizenship and Participation in California Politics: A Los Angeles County Case Study," *Pacific Historical Review* (1999).

Women

California Commission on the Status of Women, "Comparability: An Issue for the 80s" (1981), and *California Women* (monthly bulletin).

Ricardo Romo, *East Los Angeles: History of a Barrio* (1983).

John D'Emilio, *Sexual Politics, Sexual Communities: The Making of a Homosexual Minority in the United States* (1983).

Mildred Nichols Hamilton, "Pay Equity—Most Explosive Job Issue of the 80s," *San Francisco Examiner* (Apr. 22, 1984).

Melvin I. Urofsky, *Affirmative Action on Trial: Sex Discrimination in Johnson v. Santa Clara* (1997).

Glenna Matthews, *Silicon Valley, Women, and the California Dream: Gender, Class, and the California Dream: Gender, Class, and Opportunity in the Twentieth Century* (2003).

Marie Waldron (75th Assembly District), "Women in California Legislature," *Valley Roadrunner* (Sept. 8, 2016).

Phil Willon, "Female Politicians are Losing Ground in California," *Los Angeles Times* (Apr. 13, 2016).

Sam Levin, "Google 'Segregates' Women into Lower-Paying Jobs, Stifling Careers, Lawsuit Says," *The Guardian* (Sept. 14, 2017).

Miriam Posner, "We Can Teach Women to Code, But That Just Creates Another Problem," *The Guardian* (Mar. 14, 2017).

Sara O'Brien and Laurie Segall, "Sexual Harassment in Tech: Women Tell Their Stories," CNN Tech (2017), at http://money.cnn.com/technology/sexual-harassment-tech/, accessed 3–13–18.

Madison Malone Kircher, "Two Women Have Accused Tech Pundit Robert Scoble of Sexual Harassment and Assault," *New York Magazine* (Oct. 20, 2017).

Patrick May, "Silicon Valley Figures Get Swept Up in the Unfolding Sexual-Harassment Crisis," *Mercury News* (Dec. 6, 2017).

Chris Megerian et al., "In Her Own Words: Women of California Politics Tell Their Stories of Sexual Harrassment and Unwanted Touching," *Los Angeles Times* (Oct. 29, 2017).

Alexei Koseff, "Assemblyman Raul Bocanegra Resigns Amid Sexual Misconduct Allegations," *Sacramento Bee* (Nov. 27, 2017).

Alexei Koseff, "Matt Dababneh Will Resign From California Assembly After Sex Assault Allegation," *Sacramento Bee* (Dec. 8, 2017).

John Myers and Melanie Mason, "California Legislature Releases a Decade's Worth of Records on Sexual Harassment Investigations," *Los Angeles Times* (Feb. 2, 2018).

Katy Murphy, "Lawmakers Named in Secret Sacramento Sexual Harassment Probes," *Mercury News* (Feb. 2, 2018).

Office of Senator Janet Nguyen, "Senator Janet Nguyen Introduces Bill to Track and Release Sexual Harassment Complaint Records," *Orange County Breeze* (Mar. 14, 2018).

Institute for Women's Policy Research, "Status of Women in the States" (2018), at https://statusofwomendata.org/explore-the-data/political-participation/political-participation-full-section/, accessed 3–28–18.

Cristina Marcos, "House Passes Landmark Bill to Overhaul Sexual Harassment Policy on Capitol Hill," *The Hill* (Feb. 6, 2018).

Alexei Koseff, "Women Target Seats Held by California Lawmakers Accused of Sexual Harassment," *Sacramento Bee* (Feb. 15, 2018).

Sam Levin, "Google Faces New Discrimination Charge: Paying Female Teachers Less than Men," *The Guardian* (Jan 3, 2018).

California Native Americans

Russell Thornton, "History, Structure, and Survival: A Comparison of the Yuki (Ukomno'm) and Tolowa (Hush) Indians of Northern California," *Ethnology* (1986).

Steve Wiegand, "The Canvas Casino: California Indian Tribes Battle over Gaming," *California Journal* (1993).

Bill Ainsworth, "Betting on Politics," *California Journal* (1997).

Claudia Buck, "A Gamble That Paid Off," *California Journal* (1998).

Joana Partringenaru, "Tribes Come of Age," *California Journal* (1999).

Steve Scott, "Proposition 5's Legacy," *California Journal* (1999).

Santa Ynez Bank of Chumash Indians, "History of Native American Gaming" (2009).

Social Transformations

Randy Shilts, *And the Band Played On: Politics, People and the AIDS Epidemic* (1987).

Brian J. Godfrey, *Neighborhoods in Transition: The Making of San Francisco's Ethnic and Nonconformist Communities* (1988).

Mario T. García, *Mexican Americans* (1991).

David Rieff, *Los Angeles: Capital of the Third World* (1991).

Sucheng Chan, *Asian Californians* (1991).

Joan Walsh, "You Can See the World in Their Faces," *Image* (Feb. 9, 1992).

J. S. Taub, "Gay Politics," *California Journal* (1993).

Steve Wiegand, "The Canvas Casino: California Indian Tribes Battle over Gaming," *California Journal* (1993).

Richard A. García, "César Chávez: A Personal and Historical Testimony," *Pacific Historical Review* (May 1994).

David G. Gutiérrez, *Wall and Mirrors: Mexican Americans, Mexican Immigrants and the Politics of Ethnicity* (1995).

Bill Ainsworth, "Betting on Politics," *California Journal* (1997).

Melvin I. Urofsky, *Affirmative Action on Trial: Sex Discrimination in Johnson v. Santa Clara* (1997).

Lydia Chávez, *Color Bind: California's Struggle to End Affirmative Action* (1998).

Claudia Buck, "A Gamble That Paid Off," *California Journal* (1998).

Hans P. Johnson, "How Many Californians? A Review of Population Projections for the State," *California Counts* (1999).

Ioana Partringenaru, "Tribes Come of Age," *California Journal* (1999).

Steve Scott, "Proposition 5's Legacy," *California Journal* (1999).

R. Michael Alvarez and Tara L. Butterfield, "Latino Citizenship and Participation in California Politics: A Los Angeles County Case Study," *Pacific Historical Review* (1999).

Leland Saito, *Race and Politics: Asian Americans, Latinos and Whites in a Los Angeles Suburb* (1999).

Sonya M. Tafoya, "Check One or More: Mixed Race and Ethnicity in California," *California Counts* (2000).

Council on American Islamic Relations, *The Status of Muslim Civil Rights in the United States* (2005).

Josh Sides, *Erotic City: Sexual Revolutions and the Making of Modern San Francisco* (2009).

Nicolas Rosenthal, *Reimagining Indian Country: Native American Migration and Identity in Twentieth-Century Los Angeles* (2012).

Politics at the Turn of the Century

A.G. Block, "The Republican Bust of 1998," *California Journal* (1998).

William Booth, "California Recasts Itself to Play the Lead," *Washington Post Weekly* (July 5, 1999).

Steve Scott, "Rating Gray Davis," *California Journal* (2000).

Lou Cannon and A.G. Block, "Surviving the Republican Train Wreck," *California Journal* (2001).

Carl M. Cannon, "D.C. Eyes Gray Davis," *California Journal* (2001).

Marie Waldron (75th Assembly District), "Women in California Legislature" *Valley Roadrunner* (Sept. 8, 2016).

Energy

Richard Nemec, "Electricity in California: A Political and Economic Crossroads," *California Journal* (2001)

Peter Asmus, "California's New Energy Legacy," *California Journal* (2001), and Asmus, *Introduction to Energy in California* (2009).

Index

Note: Page numbers followed by (*m*) refer to maps.

Piña, Joaquin, 49–50
Pinchot, Gifford, 280
"Pink Lady," 373
Pinocchio (film), 373
Pioneer, The (magazine), 373
Pitt, Leonard, 150
placer gold, 16, 140, 142, 147–148
placer mining, 132, 147
placero (pocket of gold), 142
plant life, 12–14
plates, tectonic, 10
Pleasant, Mary Ellen, 167
Pleasant Hill Baptist Church, 384
pobladores (settlers), 98, 104, 381
Pocho (Villareal), 434
pochos (people who had lost or rejected their
    cultural identities), 405
poetry, 190, 226, 307, 312–313
Point Conception, 12, 56, 61, 426
Poland, invasion of, 352–353
politics
    after World War II, 371–374
    among Native Americans, 33–35
    of confrontation, 403–411
    early state, 160–161
    environmentalism and, 446–447
    in Great Depression, 331–332
    homosexuals in, 421
    in Mexican California, 102
    progressivism and, 255–260, 261–284
    radicalism and, 276–277
    in railroad era, 219–221, 223–224
    reform of, in early 20th century, 268–269
    in 1890s, 252–253
    1990s recession and, 471–473
Polk, James Knox, 85–87, 112, 119–121, 144, 151
pollution. *See also* environmentalism
    air, 368, 444, 448–449
    water, 449–450
Pomona College, 214, 256
Pomos, 33, 36, 70, 72, 90, 111, 153–154,
    259–260
Poole, Alonzo W., 178, 187, 189
pop art, 432
Pope John Paul II, 68
popular history, 5
popular justice, 162
population
    in 1900, 245
    African American, influx of, 360–361
    "boom of the '80s" and, 248–249
    California as highest, 365
    Gold Rush, influx from, 143–144
    housing boom and, 367–368
    Native American, 26–27
    Southern California, influx, 300–301
    at start of millennium, 483–485
Populist Party, 254–255
Populist-Progressive framework, 5–7
Port Chicago explosion, 354
Porter, Edwin S., 306–307
Portolá, Gaspar de, 62, 66–69
Postman Always Rings Twice, The (film), 375
Powers, Stephen, 26, 34, 36, 37
PPIC. *See* Public Policy Institute of California
    (PPIC)
"pragmatic conservatism," 322–323
prairie, 13(*m*)

precipitation, 12, 15, 19, 20, 442, 464
Pre-Emption Act of 1841, 168, 170
prefabricated homes, 367
prefectura (prefecture), 102
"Preparedness Day," 276, 332
preservationism, 445
President's Commission on the Status of Women
    (PCSW), 413, 421
President's Council on Physical Fitness and
    Sports, 489
Presidio Trust Act, 470
presidios (forts), 42, 49, 65–66, 71–73, 76, 78
Prevost, Louis, 247
Priest, Ivy Baker, 421
primary election law, 265, 266, 268, 271, 272,
    273
Principall Navigation (Hakluyt), 58
prisons, 473, 479
private schools, 479, 494
Progress and Poverty (George), 226
Progressive Era, 219, 230, 261, 270, 281, 287,
    301, 331, 435, 447, 471
Progressive Voters League, 316
progressivism, 7, 227, 255–256, 261, 264, 267,
    282, 316, 395, 402, 416, 493
Prohibition, 97, 241, 270, 272–274, 287, 311,
    314–315, 317, 361, 400
pronunciamiento (military uprising), 99
property alienation, 387
property rights, of women, 157–158
property taxes, 418
Proposition 1, 418, 424, 479, 493
Proposition 1A, 479, 493
Proposition 1B, 493
Proposition 1D, 494
Proposition 4, 425
Proposition 5, 474, 475
Proposition 8, 485
Proposition 9, 425, 454
Proposition 13, 424, 425, 426, 428, 459, 461, 469,
    493, 494
Proposition 14, 403, 416, 422
Proposition 18, 396
Proposition 20, 454
Proposition 22, 411, 420, 485
Proposition 28, 493
Proposition 30, 497–498
Proposition 38, 494
Proposition 39, 494
Proposition 55, 494
Proposition 58, 489
Proposition 98, 428, 479
Proposition 140, 471, 493
Proposition 174, 479
Proposition 187, 474, 480, 482
Proposition 209, 474, 480
Proposition 227, 479, 480
protests, 378, 404–408, 412, 420, 492
Prudon, Victor, 91
PSAA. *See* Public Schools Accountability Act
    (PSAA)
public assistance, 418
public education, 161, 173, 220, 258, 371, 400–
    401, 413, 428, 442, 478
Public Law, 400, 409
Public Policy Institute of California (PPIC),
    494, 499
Public Schools Accountability Act (PSAA), 482

Public Utilities Act, 267
Public Utilities Commission (PUC), 267–268,
    476
Public Works Administration (PWA), 322
public-trust doctrine, 460
PUC. *See* Public Utilities Commission (PUC)
pueblos de gente de razón (towns for civilized
    people), 71
pueblos (towns), 42, 65, 71–73
    in Mexican California, 104–109
Pullman car porters, 220, 382
Pullman Strike, 255
Purísima Concepción Mission, 77
Purity of Elections Law, 253
Putnam, Jackson K., 333
PWA. *See* Public Works Administration (PWA)

Q

quartz mining, 148

R

race, in progressive California, 278–280
racial segregation, 361
racism
    Chinese immigrants and, 165–166
    housing discrimination and, 278, 360, 361,
        387–389
    Japanese immigrants and, 279
    perseverance of, 478
radicalism, 276–277
radicalism, 276–277
Rafferty, Max, 402
Railroad Reassessment Act, 253
railroads. *See also* Central Pacific Railway Line;
    Southern Pacific Railroad
    bonanza wheat era and, 211–212
    Chinese immigrants and, 200–202
    Civil War and, 194
    culture and, 225–228
    early transcontinental schemes, 192
    at end of century, 471–473
    impact of, 175–176
    industrialization and, 210–211
    Los Angeles and, 209, 246–248
    Mussel Slough and, 177–190
    Pacific Railway Act of 1862 and, 195–196
    Pacific Railway Act of 1864 and, 199–200
    pioneer lines, 192
    political conflict and, 219–221, 223–224
    rate issue with, 223–224
    renewed interest in, 493
    rise of automobile and, 368–370
    San Diego and, 208
    San Francisco and, 209–210
    social conflicts and, 219–221
    taxation of, 251–252
    "Terrible Seventies" and, 207
    Theodore Judah and, 192–193
    urban growth and, 208–209
rain, 12
rain shadows, 12, 17
Raker, John E., 281
Raker Act of 1913, 281
Ralston, William C., 210, 233
ramadas (brush structures), 130
Ramona (Jackson), 283
Rampart scandal, 393, 394
ranch houses, 375–376
rancheros visitadores (visiting ranchers), 283